Secession in International Law with a Special Reference to the Post-Soviet Space

Theory and Practice of Public International Law

Series Editor

Vincent Chetail

VOLUME 8

The titles published in this series are listed at *brill.com/tppi*

Secession in International Law with a Special Reference to the Post-Soviet Space

By

Júlia Miklasová
University of Cologne

BRILL | NIJHOFF

LEIDEN | BOSTON

Cover illustration: "Rhythm" by Robert Delaney, c. 1932, gouache paint on paper. Public domain image from Wikipedia Commons

The open access publication of this book has been published with the support of the Swiss National Science Foundation.

The Library of Congress Cataloging-in-Publication Data is available online at https://catalog.loc.gov
LC record available at https://lccn.loc.gov/2024019856

Typeface for the Latin, Greek, and Cyrillic scripts: "Brill". See and download: brill.com/brill-typeface.

ISSN 2405-6847
ISBN 978-90-04-70263-9 (hardback)
ISBN 978-90-04-70264-6 (e-book)
DOI 10.1163/9789004702646

This book is printed on acid-free paper and produced in a sustainable manner.

To Lars

Contents

PART 2
Practice in the Post-Soviet Space

SECTION 3
Legal Analysis of the Status of Post-Soviet Secessionist Entities

SECTION 4
Legal Consequences Applicable to Post-Soviet Illegal Secessionist Entities

Acknowledgments

The interests underlying this book date back a long time ago – to the times of my studies at the gymnasium in Bratislava, Slovakia – when I decided to take up studying the Russian language alongside French and English. Initially attracted by the different Cyrillic alphabet, I soon found myself fascinated more by Eastern Europe's history, culture and politics, devouring book after book on these subjects. This motivated me to pursue a bachelor degree in Russian and Eastern European studies alongside law in Bratislava. Since then, I have striven to combine these two research passions.

When I later started my Master in International Law at the Graduate Institute in Geneva, there was not much hesitation regarding the topic selection of my Master thesis – the understudied case of secession of Transnistria. This was the first step, which opened many questions and ultimately led to the research question of my PhD thesis – now this book. Little did I know at the time of the selection of my PhD topic that, several years later, tragically, there would be an all-out war of aggression waged on the European continent, and the rhetoric and the tools of secession would be so tightly linked with it.

What has driven me to study the post-Soviet secessionist entities is the underlying tension at their core – it is here where the grand narratives meet the ambivalence of day-to-day life, and the appearances are seemingly more consequential than reality. The book examines the role of public international law in governing these complex processes.

I would like to express my special and sincere gratitude to my PhD thesis supervisor (and previously Master thesis supervisor) at the Graduate Institute in Geneva, Professor Marcelo Gustavo Kohen, who always encouraged me and provided me with thorough comments, answered my many questions and offered invaluable guidance. I am also grateful to Professor Zachary Douglas and Professor Angelika Nußberger – the members of my PhD jury – and to the anonymous reviewers of this book for their insightful comments and suggestions. My thank you also goes to Dr Danae Azaria for her mentorship.

I would not be able to pursue my PhD studies in Geneva without financial support, namely the Yves Mirabaud and Anoush Khoshkish scholarships. I am also thankful for a three-month Graduate Institute-IWM fellowship at the Institute for Human Sciences (IWM) in Vienna. My position as a Research Assistant at the Global Migration Centre also allowed me to stay and study in Geneva, for which I am grateful.

As a postdoctoral researcher, I have been privileged to work at the Academy for European Human Rights Protection, University of Cologne. Here, I have transformed and updated my PhD thesis into this book and further developed my research at the intersection of public international law and specialisation in area studies. I want to thank Professor Angelika Nußberger, the director of the Academy, for all her encouragement, the opportunity for academic growth and kindness.

My gratitude also goes to my cousin, Lucia, who has always supported me in my academic plans; to my aunt, Margita, who is a great enthusiast of my book; to my mother, Jana, who has taught me that life is a marathon, not a sprint; and to my family and friends, who have brought so much joy to my life. A special thank you goes to my husband, Lars, who has cheered for me and supported me while I worked on transforming my PhD thesis into this book.

Abbreviations

AA	Association Agreement
AREAC	Articles on the Effects of Armed Conflicts on Treaties
ARSIWA	Articles on the Responsibility of States for Internationally Wrongful Acts
Belarusian SSR	Belarusian Soviet Socialist Republic
CEPA	Comprehensive and Enhanced Partnership Agreement
CJEU	Court of Justice of the European Union
CoE	Council of Europe
DCFTA	Deep and Comprehensive Free Trade Agreement
DPR	Donetsk People's Republic
DoI	Declaration of Independence
EEAS	European External Action Service
ECHR	European Convention on Human Rights
ECtHR	European Court of Human Rights
EU	European Union
EUISS	European Union Institute for Security Studies
FPA	Fisheries Partnership Agreement
FRY	Federal Republic of Yugoslavia
IAC	International Armed Conflict
ICC	International Criminal Court
ICCPR	International Covenant on Civil and Political Rights
ICESCR	International Covenant on Economic, Social and Cultural Rights
ICJ	International Court of Justice
ICTY	International Criminal Tribunal for the Former Yugoslavia
IHL	International Humanitarian Law
IHRL	International Human Rights Law
ILC	International Law Commission
IO	International Organization
LPR	Luhansk People's Republic
MFA	Ministry of Foreign Affairs
MPEPIL	Max Planck Encyclopaedia of Public International Law
MSSR	Moldovan Soviet Socialist Republic
NIAC	Non-International Armed Conflict
NGO	Non-Governmental Organization
NREP	Policy of Non-Recognition and Engagement
OAU	Organization of African Unity
OHCHR	Office of the United Nations High Commissioner for Human Rights

OPT	Occupied Palestinian Territory
OSCE	Organization for Security and Co-operation in Europe
OTP	Office of the Prosecutor of the International Criminal Court
PA	Parliamentary Assembly
PACE	Parliamentary Assembly of the Council of Europe
PCA	Partnership and Cooperation Agreement
RSFSR	Russian Soviet Federative Socialist Republic
SFRY	Socialist Federal Republic of Yugoslavia
TRNC	Turkish Republic of Northern Cyprus
TSFSR	Transcaucasian Socialist Federative Soviet Republic
UK	United Kingdom
Ukrainian SSR	Ukrainian Soviet Socialist Republic
UN	United Nations
UNFICYP	United Nations Peacekeeping Force in Cyprus
UNGA	United Nations General Assembly
UNGP	United Nations Guiding Principles on Business and Human Rights
UNHCR	United Nations High Commissioner for Refugees
UNHRC	United Nations Human Rights Council
UNSC	United Nations Security Council
USA	United States of America
USSR	Union of Soviet Socialist Republics
VCLT	Vienna Convention on the Law of Treaties
VCST	Vienna Convention on Succession of States in Respect of Treaties

General Introduction

1 Hypothesis, Relevance and Objectives

What is it like to live in entities such as Transnistria or Abkhazia[1] that claim to have seceded and become States, but lack generalised recognition? How does one operate a business there or import products from abroad? To what extent is it risky for foreign economic operators to invest there? Would a divorce decree issued by the authorities in these entities be recognised in foreign jurisdictions? Who would bear international responsibility for human rights violations committed in these entities? And most importantly, what does international law have to say about these issues?

These questions have motivated the selection of the topic of this book. However, while they appear concrete, straightforward and grounded in everyday reality, the answers to them require a comprehensive two-step analysis. Such an analysis needs firstly to settle the issues of statehood and the status of these entities, and secondly to determine the legal consequences stemming from such status determination. Fundamentally, such an analysis requires situating these questions within a broad theoretical and normative evolution of international law. In fact, the answer to these questions presupposes determining the extent in which international law is relevant to the phenomenon of secession.

This is not a minor step because according to a classical view, international law is said to be neutral vis-à-vis secession, neither prohibiting nor authorising it.[2] International law merely defers to the facts on the ground.[3] Secession is held as a-legal, a purely factual phenomenon not regulated by international law.[4] This book challenges this view. It is built on the premise that international law is relevant to secession. The key objective of this book is to delimit

1 This book employs the most frequently used English names of the secessionist entities in the post-Soviet space. For the purposes of simplicity, it does not qualify them or their purported acts as 'the so-called' and does not refer to them by using quotation marks. All the titles, names and references to these entities and their acts are given without prejudice to their status and the status of their acts under international law. To establish such a status is indeed one of the objectives of this book. Translations of sources in foreign languages are mine and are unofficial. Except for source material in French, the reference always includes a note on the original language of the source. The book covers developments until 31 October 2023.

2 See Part 1, Chapter 1 in detail.

3 ibid.

4 ibid.

© KONINKLIJKE BRILL BV, LEIDEN, 2024 | DOI:10.1163/9789004702646_002

and establish the extent of such relevance. It seeks to outline a general legal framework applicable to secession.

A central, albeit not exclusive tension underpinning the issues explored in this book is one between effectiveness and legality. As such, the book demonstrates the various ways in which the principle of *ex iniuria ius non oritur* is prevalent in a contemporary regulation of secession. It shows that this principle determines the issue of the emergence of statehood via secession and also orders the relations of effective secessionist entities subsequent to the denial of such status.

Admittedly, the doctrine has analysed the topic of secession before. The issue of secession was dealt with as *part* of Professor Crawford's monograph *The Creation of States in International Law*,[5] and it was the subject of Professor Kohen's edited volume *Secession: International Law Perspectives*.[6] In French-speaking scholarship, Professor Christakis' monograph *Le droit à l'autodétermination en dehors des situations de décolonisation* also analysed the issue of secession.[7] David Raič's monograph *Statehood and the Law of Self-Determination* examined this topic too.[8] Nevertheless, a starting point of these two monographs was the issue of the right of self-determination instead.

Apart from these examples, secession has mostly been examined in a restricted or case-specific fashion. As already mentioned, classical scholarship sees secession as an a-legal phenomenon and therefore has not given it much attention.[9] Otherwise, the topic has been raised in the context of other legal questions, most notably in edited volumes primarily concerning the right of self-determination and remedial secession,[10] and partly in recent monographs on *uti possidetis iuris*,[11] the principle of

5 J Crawford, *The Creation of States in International Law* (2nd edn, Clarendon Press 2006) 374–448.

6 MG Kohen (ed), *Secession: International Law Perspectives* (CUP 2006). See also MG Kohen, 'Création d'Etats en droit international contemporain' (2002) VI Cours euro-méditerranéens Bancaja de droit international.

7 T Christakis, *Le droit à l'autodétermination en dehors des situations de décolonisation* (La documentation française 1999).

8 D Raič, *Statehood and the Law of Self-Determination* (Kluwer Law International 2002).

9 For the same assessment of this doctrine see MG Kohen, 'Introduction' in MG Kohen (ed), *Secession: International Law Perspectives* (CUP 2006) 8. Part 1, Chapter 1 provides an overview of this scholarship.

10 D French (ed), *Statehood and Self-Determination: Reconciling Tradition and Modernity in International Law* (CUP 2013); C Walter, A Von Ungern-Sternberg and K Abushov (eds), *Self-determination and Secession in International Law* (OUP 2014). See also E Milano, M Nicolini and F Palermo (eds), *Law, Territory and Conflict Resolution: Law as a Problem and Law as a Solution* (Brill Nijhoff 2016).

11 A Beaudouin, *Uti possidetis et sécession* (Éditions Dalloz 2011).

effectiveness,[12] and recognition of States.[13] The doctrine also examined this topic through the prism of analysis of the *Kosovo* Advisory Opinion.[14]

However, since secession is a multifaceted phenomenon, it requires a comprehensive analysis. Drawing on the developments of practice and examination of *opinio iuris*, the book seeks to provide a systematic and thorough analysis of the general legal framework applicable to secession. It thereby seeks to complement and add to the existing scholarship.

In this context, previous doctrinal works have already claimed that international law increasingly regulates secession, especially where it is connected to violations of peremptory norms of international law.[15] However, these works are only focused on the violation of peremptory norms related to the emergence of statehood. While this book also examines the technical aspects of this argument, it pushes this claim further by moving beyond the issue of status *per se*. It seeks to outline relevant legal framework applicable to an effective secessionist entity subsequent to the denial of statehood.

---

12 F Couveinhes-Matsumoto, *L'effectivité en droit international* (Bruylant 2014).

13 M Fabry, *Recognizing States: International Society and the Establishment of New States since 1776* (OUP 2010). It needs to be added that Fabry's monograph is not a legal analysis. Nevertheless, the book draws from its conclusions concerning the evolution of practice.

14 *Accordance with International Law of the Unilateral Declaration of Independence in Respect of Kosovo* (Advisory Opinion) [2010] ICJ Rep 403 ("*Kosovo*"). From the vast number of scholarly commentaries, the following can be mentioned here, as the book draws on them. MG Kohen and K Del Mar, 'The Kosovo Advisory Opinion and UNSCR 1244 (1999): A Declaration of "Independence from International Law"?' (2011) 24 Leiden Journal of International Law 109; M Pertile, 'Self-Determination Reduced to Silence: Some Critical Remarks on the ICJ's Advisory Opinion on Kosovo' in M Arcari and L Balmond (eds), *Questions de droit international autour de l'avis consultatif de la Cour internationale de Justice sur le Kosovo* (Giuffrè 2011); E Milano, 'Declarations of Independence and Territorial Integrity in General International Law: Some Reflections in Light of the Court's Advisory Opinion' in M Arcari and L Balmond (eds), *Questions de droit international autour de l'avis consultatif de la Cour internationale de Justice sur le Kosovo* (Giuffrè 2011); A Tancredi, 'Some Remarks on the Relationship between Secession and General International Law in the Light of the ICJ's Kosovo Advisory Opinion' in P Hilpold, *Kosovo and International Law: The ICJ Advisory Opinion of 22 July 2010* (Brill 2012); A Peters, 'Does Kosovo Lie in the Lotus-Land of Freedom?' (2011) 24 Leiden Journal of International Law 95.

15 Part 1, Chapter 2 traces the evolution of this doctrine in detail. Here only two examples are mentioned, Crawford *The Creation of States in International Law* (n 5) 96–173; Kohen, 'Introduction' (n 9). Similarly, Part 1, Chapter 4 mentions authors who claim an increased relevance of international law to secession outside of violation of peremptory norms. See for example, O Corten, 'Are There Gaps?' in MG Kohen (ed), Secession: International Law Perspectives (CUP 2006) and Kohen, 'Introduction' (n 9).

As such, the book coins the descriptive term 'illegal secessionist entity' – an effective entity denied statehood and created in violation of peremptory norms.[16] On the one hand, the applicable framework includes the consequences of peremptory territorial illegality concerning the effective relations of an entity. On the other hand, it includes the legal consequences of a change of effective territorial control. The book also outlines the interaction of these two groups of consequences.

The scholarship on the issue of the consequences of peremptory territorial illegality is fragmented. The book mostly draws from few works that examine the duty of non-recognition generally,[17] monographs on peremptory norms,[18] complicity in the law of State responsibility,[19] Ronen's and Milano's monographs that partially analyse the operation of the duty of non-recognition in the context of territorial illegality[20] and on the analyses of analogical cases involving peremptory territorial illegality.[21] Concerning the consequences of a change of effective territorial control, this book builds on the existing scholarship on the factual tests applicable in the context of IHL and jurisdiction, attribution and responsibility in IHRL.[22]

16 This notion is delimited in detail in Part 1, Chapter 6.

17 T Christakis, 'L'obligation de non-reconnaissance des situations créées par le recours illicite à la force ou d'autres actes enfreignant des règles fondamentales' in Tomuschat C and Thouvenin JM (eds), *The Fundamental Rules of the International Legal Order. Jus Cogens and Obligations Erga Omnes* (M Nijhoff Publishers 2006); S Talmon, 'The Duty Not "To Recognize as Lawful" a Situation Created by the Illegal Use of Force or Other Serious Breaches of a Jus Cogens Obligation: An Obligation without Real Substance?' in C Tomuschat and JM Thouvenin (eds), *The Fundamental Rules of the International Legal Order. Jus Cogens and Obligations Erga Omnes* (M Nijjhof Publishers 2006).

18 A Orakhelashvili, *Peremptory Norms in International Law* (OUP 2006); D Costelloe, *Legal Consequences of Peremptory Norms in International Law* (CUP 2017).

19 HP Aust, *Complicity and the Law of State Responsibility* (CUP 2011); V Lanovoy, *Complicity and Its Limits in the Law of International Responsibility* (Bloomsbury Publishing 2016).

20 Y Ronen, *Transition from Illegal Regimes under International Law* (CUP 2011); E Milano, *Unlawful Territorial Situations in International Law: Reconciling Effectiveness, Legality and Legitimacy* (Martinus Nijhoff 2006).

21 Regarding the duties of non-recognition and non-assistance in the area of economic dealings, Part 1, Chapter 7 builds on cases involving illegal settlements in the OPT, Western Sahara and the TRNC. The key text in this context is J Crawford, 'Third Party Obligations with Respect to Israeli Settlements in the Occupied Palestinian Territories' <https://www.tuc.org.uk/sites/default/files/tucfiles/LegalOpinionIsraeliSettlements.pdf> accessed 18 March 2020.

22 This includes, for example, M Milanović, *Extraterritorial Application of Human Rights Treaties: Law, Principles and Policy* (OUP 2011); Talmon S, 'The Responsibility of Outside Powers for Acts of Secessionist Entities' (2009) 58 ICLQ 493; Milanović M and Papić T,

Thus, the research and argument in this context aspire to bring added value to the scholarship in two ways. First, the book draws the link between the effects of violation of peremptory norms on the issue of statehood of the entity and its effective relations. The tension between the effectiveness and legality is not limited to the emergence of statehood via secession, but continues to be relevant once such status is denied. Second, the notion of an 'illegal secessionist entity' allows outlining legal consequences that flow both from the violation of peremptory norms and from a change of effective territorial control, which can apply *simultaneously*. All these normative layers together offer a comprehensive legal framework applicable to these entities. This is a unique view that has not been carried out in this context yet.[23]

This book is not limited to establishing a general international legal framework, but also uses it to examine cases of secession in the post-Soviet space. While post-Soviet secessionism represents a significant bulk of contemporary secessionist practice, the English-language legal scholarship[24] has mostly analysed it in an uneven fashion. A purported secession of Crimea in 2014 has received extensive doctrinal attention.[25] The purported declarations

---

'The Applicability of the ECHR in Contested Territories' (2018) 67 ICLQ 779. See Part 1, Chapter 8.

23 The book builds on a few works that deal with the question of interaction of consequences of peremptory illegality and other legal regimes, in particular V Azarova, 'Illegal Territoriality in International Law: The Interaction and Enforcement of the Law of Belligerent Occupation Through Other Territorial Regimes' (PhD Thesis, National University of Ireland, Galway 2015); V Azarova, 'Towards a Counter-Hegemonic Law of Occupation: On the Regulation of Predatory Interstate Acts in Contemporary International Law' (2017) 20 Yearbook of International Humanitarian Law 113; A Orakhelashvili, 'Overlap and Convergence: The Interaction Between *Jus Ad Bellum* and *Jus in Bello*' 12 (2007) Journal of Conflict and Security Law 157; Y Ronen, 'Illegal Occupation and Its Consequences' (2008) 41 Israel Law Review 201; P Wrange, 'Self-Determination, Occupation and the Authority to Exploit Natural Resources: Trajectories from Four European Judgments on Western Sahara' (2019) 52 Israel Law Review 3. The most recent addition to the scholarship is the following edited volume: A Duval and E Kassoti (eds), *Legality of Economic Activities, Occupied Territories: International, EU Law and Business and Human Rights Perspectives* (Taylor & Francis Group, 2020).

24 Apart from legal scholarship, the book used the following in order to establish factual developments: X Follebouckt, *Les conflits gelés de l'espace postoviétique: genèse et enjeux* (Presses universitaires de Louvain 2011); A Saparov, *From Conflict to Autonomy in the Caucasus: The Soviet Union and the Making of Abkhazia, South Ossetia and Nagorno Karabakh* (Routledge 2015).

25 For example, TD Grant, *Aggression Against Ukraine: Territory, Responsibility, and International Law* (Palgrave Macmillan 2015); S Sayapin and E Tsybulenko (eds), *The Use of Force Against Ukraine and International Law: Jus Ad Bellum, Jus in Bello, Jus Post Bellum* (Springer 2018). See Part 2, Chapter 11 for more.

of independence and Russia's recognition of the DPR, LPR, Kherson and Zaporizhzhia Regions have been marginally analysed in the context of the escalation of the Russia-Ukraine War since 2022.[26] The purported statehood of Abkhazia and South Ossetia was examined mainly in connection with the Russia-Georgia War of 2008.[27] Other purported secessions in the post-Soviet space have received comparatively less scholarly attention.[28] Importantly, the post-Soviet secessionist claims to statehood have not been examined in a single comprehensive survey. In addition, apart from journal articles analysing concrete arbitral and judicial proceedings involving these post-Soviet secessionist entities,[29] there is almost no English-language literature that would examine the relations of these effective entities beyond their claim to statehood *per se*.[30] This is a notable lacuna in international legal scholarship.

26 See, for example, J Miklasová, 'Russia's Recognition of the DPR and LPR as Illegal Acts under International Law' (*Völkerrechtsblog*, 24 February 2022) <https://voelkerrechtsblog.org/russias-recognition-of-the-dpr-and-lpr-as-illegal-acts-under-international-law/> accessed 26 July 2023. L Mälksoo, 'Illegality of Russia's Annexations in Ukraine' (*Articles of War*, 3 October 2022) <https://lieber.westpoint.edu/illegality-russias-annexation-ukraine/> accessed 28 July 2023.

27 A Nussberger, 'The War between Russia and Georgia – Consequences and Unresolved Questions' (2009) 1 GoJIL 34.

28 Purported secessions of Crimea, Abkhazia, South Ossetia, Nagorno-Karabakh and Transnistria are analysed in contributions to C Walter, A Von Ungern-Sternberg and K Abushov (eds), *Self-determination and Secession in International Law* (OUP 2014). For Nagorno-Karabkah see also H Krüger, *The Nagorno-Karabakh Conflict: A Legal Analysis* (Springer 2010). For Transnistria see CJ Borgen, 'Thawing a Frozen Conflict: Legal Aspects of the Separatist Crisis in Moldova: A Report from the Association of the Bar of the City of New York' (*Legal Paper Research Paper Series No 06–0045*, 2006) 1–98; J Miklasová, 'Secession in Contemporary International Law: The Case of Transnistria' (Master Thesis, Graduate Institute of International and Development Studies 2014).

29 See, for example, P Dumberry, 'Requiem for Crimea: Why Tribunals Should Have Declined Jurisdiction over the Claims of Ukrainian Investors against Russian under the Ukraine–Russia BIT' (2018) 9 Journal of International Dispute Settlement 506; R Happ and S Wuschka, 'Horror Vacui: Or Why Investment Treaties Should Apply to Illegally Annexed Territories' (2016) 33 Journal of International Arbitration 245; A Berkes, 'The Nagorno-Karabakh Conflict Before the European Court of Human Rights: Pending Cases and Certain Forecasts on Jurisdiction and State Responsibility' (2013) 52 Military Law and the Law of War Review 379; S Wallace and Mallory C, 'Applying the European Convention on Human Rights to the Conflict in Ukraine' (2018) 6 Russian Law Journal 8.

30 Two exceptions include N Martsenko, 'Peculiarities of Recognition of Judgments and other Acts Issued by Unrecognized Authorities – The Example of the Autonomous Republic of Crimea, and Luhansk and Donetsk Oblasts ("LPR" and "DPR")' 65 (2019) OER Osteuropa Recht 223; I Kolisnyk, 'Ukrainian Courts in Dialogue on International Law' in A Wyrozumska (ed), *Transnational Judicial Dialogue on International Law in Central and Eastern Europe* (Lodz University Press 2017).

Thus, this book seeks to fill the gap in the scholarship with respect to post-Soviet secessionist practice in two ways. First, it provides a comprehensive analysis of claims to statehood of *all* the post-Soviet secessionist entities, including the most recent developments. It is believed that a collective analysis of these situations may shed light on certain patterns that would otherwise have been missed. This can contribute to a better understanding of the legal aspects of the post-Soviet secessionism. Second, this book analyses the relations of these effective entities beyond their claim to statehood, which so far have been unexplored in English-speaking legal scholarship.

Importantly, the post-Soviet secessionist practice is not presumed to form a *special* legal category. Secession and State-creation are the phenomena of *general* international law. By analysing the under-explored instances of post-Soviet secessionism in light of the general legal framework and assessing the book's conclusions on these case studies against the practice and positions of the States vis-à-vis post-Soviet secessionism, the book seeks to contribute to a better understanding of secession in contemporary *general* international law.

Undeniably, the scope of this book is broad, cutting across different themes of public international law and requiring an in-depth, factual investigation of selected case studies. However, this structure is purposeful. It aims at demonstrating the inter-linkage between various facets of the same phenomenon of secession, which might not be immediately recognisable. Fundamentally, it seeks to highlight how concrete and seemingly technical legal issues cannot be analysed in isolation. They are dependent on the larger and more general theoretical paradigm of secession in which they are situated.

Ultimately, the examination of international law's relevance to secession goes to the heart of the origins of the original subjects of international law – States. Therefore, as a microcosm of international law at large, the legal framework of this issue captures the prevailing values in the evolution of international law. An examination of this question is not only important for purely normative reasons, but it can also inform us about the character of contemporary international law.

2 Definition of Terms

This book examines the phenomenon of secession. For the purposes of this book, the term 'secession' is understood as the creation of a new independent State through the separation of part of the territory and population of an existing State, without the consent of the latter.[31] Thus, it is a completion of the emergence of a new State; it is the mode of succession of States. For the purposes of this book, a process leading to such a final outcome is understood as a 'secessionist attempt', which by definition occurs in a pre-State context.[32] As already mentioned, this book also uses the term 'illegal secessionist entity' – an effective entity denied statehood and created in violation of peremptory norms. Part 1, Chapter 6 provides an in-depth delimitation of this notion. Throughout the following chapters, the book uses the term 'peremptory territorial illegality,' which is understood as a territorial situation in breach of a peremptory norm of international law.

It follows from the definition of secession that its defining feature is the lack of the parent State's consent.[33] This element distinguishes *unilateral* secession, which is explored in this book, from devolution as the creation of a new State through the separation of a part of the territory from another State, *with the consent* of the latter.[34] Moreover, secession, which involves the element of unilateral separation of territory from the predecessor State that *continues* to exist must also be distinguished from the dissolution of State, which involves the emergence of two or more new States on the territory of the predecessor State, which *ceases* to exist.[35] Secession must also be differentiated from decolonisation, since colonial territories enjoyed status "separate and distinct" from that of metropolitan States.[36] These other modes of State-creation fall outside the research scope of this book. Nevertheless, where appropriate to better clarify the unilateral secession, the book will also refer to these modes.

The book explores secession in contemporary international law. Therefore, it seeks to establish the state of international law, drawing primarily on the analysis of practice and *opinio iuris* dating back to 1945. Nevertheless, where necessary to explain the evolution of certain legal concepts, rules or principles, it may also refer to and build on practice and doctrine from before 1945.

---

31 This definition is built on the definition provided in Kohen, 'Introduction' (n 9) 3.

32 "Secession is not an instant fact. It always implies a complex series of claims and decisions, negotiations and/or struggle, which may – or may not – lead to the creation of a new State." MG Kohen, 'Introduction' (n 9) 14.

33 ibid 3.

34 ibid.

35 See MG Kohen, 'Création d'Etats en droit international contemporain' (n 6) 571–574.

36 See Declaration on Principles of International Law concerning Friendly Relations and Co-operation among States in accordance with the Charter of the United Nations, UNGA Res 2625 (XXV) (24 October 1970) UN Doc A/RES/2625(XXV), Annex, principle 5, para 6. See also MG Kohen, 'Création d'Etats en droit international contemporain' (n 6) 572.

The book also examines case studies from the post-Soviet space. Despite the fact that the term 'post-Soviet' may imply a temporal limit to situations after the USSR's termination, its primary function is to delimit the scope, from a geographical perspective, to territories of the former Soviet Union. The term is not meant to exclude practice that took place prior to the USSR's break-up, since in many cases secessionist attempts were initiated before the Soviet Union's end and in parallel with its gradual disintegration. Its use in this book is justified given that the Soviet legal and historical heritage is an important feature of the secessionist attempts in this geographical space. Even though the book maps all the post-Soviet secessionist cases, it only provides an in-depth investigation of secessionist attempts by entities that have remained outside their parent State's control until today – whether continuing claiming to be States or previously claiming to be States and now purportedly incorporated into another State, namely Transnistria, Abkhazia, South Ossetia, Crimea, DPR, LPR, Kherson and Zaporizhzhia Regions. Given the long-term *prima facie* effectiveness of Nagorno-Karabakh before its recent recapture by Azerbaijan, the book also examines this case extensively.

3 Structure

This book is divided into two major parts. The first part offers a comprehensive general international legal framework of secession. The second part analyses the case studies from the post-Soviet space. In line with the above observations, each of these major parts is further divided into two sections focusing firstly on the issue of the status and secondly on the consequences flowing from a status-determination.

Part 1, Section 1, Chapters 1–5 seek to establish a general international legal framework relevant to the question of the status of a secessionist entity. In short, this section seeks to establish the extent of international law relevant to the question of whether a particular entity is a State. In doing so, it challenges classical premises that secession is an a-legal and purely factual phenomenon not regulated by international law. Importantly, this section explores in detail the effects of violation of peremptory norms of international law on the claim to statehood of effective entities. Moreover, it also examines the existence of the right to secession outside decolonisation, flowing from the right of self-determination, remedial secession or unilateral referenda. Based on the mapping of the post-1945 developments, this section also determines the actual relevance of the constitutive criteria of statehood for the contemporary emergence of States through unilateral secession.

Part 1, Section 2, Chapters 6–9 then establish a general international legal framework applicable to an 'illegal secessionist entity'. On the one hand, this framework includes the consequences of peremptory territorial illegality such as in the sphere of rules of State succession, validity of acts and aggravated regime of international responsibility. The section focuses in detail on the scope and content of the duty of non-recognition in the area of purported inter-State relations, economic and other dealings, and acts and laws of illegal secessionist entity, including the scope of the *Namibia* exception. In essence, this section traces the extent of the operation of the principle of legality in the context of relations of effective entity subsequent to the violation of peremptory norms.

On the other hand, the relevant framework also includes legal consequences flowing from a change of effective territorial control in the area of human rights law, the law of occupation and State responsibility. Based on an analysis of the relevant case law, the section examines various factual tests required in these contexts. This section also outlines how these two sets of consequences, i.e. the consequences of peremptory territorial illegality on the one hand and consequences of a change of effective territorial control in the area of human rights and the law of occupation on the other hand, interact *in abstracto*.

Part 2, Section 3, Chapters 10–15 provide an in-depth legal examination of the legal status of secessionist entities in the post-Soviet space, in particular the DPR, LPR, Kherson and Zporizhzhia Regions, Crimea, Abkhazia and South Ossetia, Nagorno-Karabakh and Transnistria. This legal analysis is preceded by an overview of the fundamental tenets of the Soviet federalism and the dissolution of the Soviet Union.

Part 2, Section 4, Chapters 16–19 then outline a legal framework applicable to these post-Soviet entities, including the effects of peremptory territorial illegality and those triggered upon a change of effective territorial control. It traces the operation of the duty of non-recognition in the under-explored instances of practice concerning the post-Soviet entities in the area of purported inter-State relations, economic and other dealings and official acts and laws including the extent of the *Namibia* exception.

PART 1

Secession in Contemporary International Law

SECTION 1

Legal Analysis of the Status of the Secessionist Entity

Introduction to Section 1

A classical doctrinal narrative that has accompanied a fundamental question of connection between secession as the mode of State-creation and international law is as follows. First, secession is an a-legal, meta-legal phenomenon not regulated by the rules of international law.[1] Second, international law is neutral vis-à-vis secession, neither prohibiting it nor authorising it. Third, international law defers to the facts on the ground, with the effectiveness of the factual situation being an overriding criterion. Once the secessionists achieve the so-called constitutive or Montevideo criteria of statehood, the new State emerges. Only then does the international law register this new reality and attribute corresponding legal consequences to it.

These views are usually presented as a unified and inter-linked whole, but this book takes the position that by dissecting this standard narrative into three separate claims, a more nuanced picture emerges that allows for a more revealing analysis. Section 1 seeks to challenge each of these claims in turn.

Chapter 1 questions the classical view of the role of facts in secession and the claim that international law *does not regulate secession*. It builds its argument on three grounds. First, drawing on the elements of the history of ideas, the chapter traces the role of the factual element in secession over time. Second, it revisits Georg Jellinek's and Hans Kelsen's works to highlight their frequently overlooked positions on the role of facts in secession. Third, Chapter 1 offers criticism drawn from legal philosophy and theory. Ultimately, this chapter establishes that secession is still a matter of fact, but it is a *legal* fact predetermined by a customary international law rule – the principle of effectiveness. *Thus, the claim that international law does not regulate secession cannot be taken as correct.*

Chapters 2, 3 and 4 examine the claim regarding the *neutrality* of international law concerning secession. Chapter 2 examines in detail an increasingly accepted argument that the violation of peremptory norms precludes the emergence of a new State.[2] The book addresses this issue extensively for two reasons. First, this claim is the most consequential normative element for the

1 "Si les formules varient selon les auteurs – qui y voient tour à tour un fait historique, sociologique, anté-juridique, méta-juridique, etc. –, l'idée générale qu'expriment ces formules reste la même": "la naissance de l'État est un pur fait échappant aux règles ordinaires du droit." C Rousseau, *Droit international public* (*Tome III, Les compétences*) (Sirey 1977) 514. See Part 1, Chapter 1 for more scholarship of this classical group.

2 Part 1, Chapter 2 offers an in-depth overview of the doctrine on this issue.

outcome of contemporary secessionist struggles. Second, technical details of the operation of this claim have rarely been studied in-depth.

Chapter 2 takes two factors as the starting point of its investigation. First, it highlights the differences in the operation of the principle of *ex iniuria ius non oritur* in the context of territorial acquisitions by force occurring only *inter vivos* between existing States and in the context of secessions, which usually involve the multiplicity of actors including the parent State, non-State secessionists and potentially also the third State interfering in the secessionist process. Second, Chapter 2 examines the position of the International Court of Justice (ICJ) in the *Kosovo* Advisory Opinion according to which an international peremptory illegality can be attached to unilateral declarations of independence.[3]

Chapter 2 establishes that the act of declaring independence, frequently formalised in the declaration of independence (DoI), is a necessary voluntary element implicit in the constitutive criteria of statehood. Secession is also characterised as a subjective legal fact, which is the sum of factual and voluntary elements attributive of the status of statehood and title of territorial sovereignty. Chapter 2 conceptualises the period before the acquisition of independence as a secessionist attempt during which peremptory norms already apply both to the third States and secessionist group. Thus, to the extent of the applicability of peremptory norms, the idea of perceiving the secessionist attempt as the parent State's internal matter no longer holds. Chapter 2 also examines the scope of applicable peremptory norms, mode of their violation and legal consequences flowing from such violation.

Ultimately, when a secessionist attempt is connected with the violation of peremptory norms, the emergence of the new State is precluded for two reasons. First, the violation of peremptory norms invalidates the declarations of independence and based on the conclusions of the chapter, an apparent meeting of the constitutive criteria without a valid claim to statehood does not produce legal effects of attributing the status of statehood to the entity in question. Second, it builds on the conclusions of Chapter 1 that the criteria of statehood are *legal* criteria predetermined by a customary rule. Chapter 2 demonstrates that in line with the developments of practice and *opinio iuris* and the principle of *ex iniuria ius non oritur* more specifically, these *legal* criteria presuppose their compliance with peremptory norms of international law. The principle of legality is already assumed in constitutive criteria. However,

3 *Accordance with International Law of the Unilateral Declaration of Independence in Respect of Kosovo* (Advisory Opinion) [2010] ICJ Rep 403, para 81 ("*Kosovo*").

the non-emergence of a State does not entail that the effective entity would be detached from an international legal order. Section 2 of this book analyses the international legal framework that applies to an illegal secessionist entity.

Chapter 3 continues to investigate the claim regarding the *neutrality* of international law concerning secession by focusing on the arguments based on the existence of the right to secede under international law. It is shown that the arguments concerning the right to secede are the least consequential for the outcome of contemporary secessionist struggles. Thus, Chapter 3 only outlines the key elements of the debate that are critical for the analysis of the secessionist claims. It ultimately concludes that international law does not provide for the right to independence for a fraction of the population of the existing States. Such a right can be derived neither from the right of peoples to self-determination nor from remedial secession or successful unilateral independence referenda. However, various constitutional and conventional arrangements can give rise to the right to independence. These are connected to the parent State's consent and are analysed as the practice of devolution in Chapter 5.

Chapter 4 assesses the claim regarding the *neutrality* of secession even further. Building on the ICJ's position that "general international law contains no applicable prohibition of declarations of independence"[4] and "the scope of the principle of territorial integrity is confined to the sphere of relations between States",[5] Chapter 4 outlines the key dynamics between the territorial integrity of the parent State and the effectiveness of the secessionist entity. By reviewing the relevant practice and *opinio iuris*, especially the resolutions of the United Nations Security Council (UNSC), chapter 4 concludes that contemporary international law favours the territorial integrity of the parent State, but stops short from an outright prohibition of unilateral secession.[6] *Ultimately, based on Chapters 2, 3 and 4, it is impossible to maintain the claim regarding the neutrality of international law concerning secession.* International law not only establishes a specific prohibition of secessions in connection with the violation of peremptory norms, but also outside of such violation favours the parent State through a variety of legal tools. The neutrality of international law cannot be maintained simply based on the mere lack of a general prohibition of secession.

Chapter 5 investigates limits to an underlying fundamental assumption that *effectiveness*, as outlined in Chapter 1, is an overriding criterion concerning

4 ibid para 84 in connection with para 81.
5 ibid para 80.
6 Part 1, Chapter 4 provides an overview of authors who take the same position.

contemporary secession. It first acknowledges a theoretical limitation of a factualist vision of statehood and a declaratory theory that derives from the absence of a centralised organ authorised to ascertain meeting of the factual criteria. However, it argues that this limitation is not unique to the State-creation or international law because it reflects a deeper tension in philosophy between the realist and anti-realist vision of facts. This limitation is also neutralised on a normative level by the emergence of new rules and trends of State practice that narrow down the situations where effectiveness is the only applicable criterion. Chapter 5 maps the relevant post-1945 practice and demonstrates that since 1945 this practice has undeniably favoured a consensual State-creation. *It follows that the possibility of a classical unilateral secession based on effectiveness is severely limited, almost virtual, but not entirely excluded.*

CHAPTER 1

Legal Understanding of Statehood: Role of the Factual Element in Secession

1 Introduction

Secession seeks a total and irreversible rupture of an existing *status quo*. In many instances, it is accompanied by the use of the most radical tools and occurs in the most extreme factual scenarios.[1] Secessionists seek to bring about fundamental changes on an internal as well as international plane. Regarding a municipal law, they strive to introduce a completely new legal order by replacing or changing the constitution of a valid parent State in a manner not prescribed by it.[2] On an international plane, they seek separation from the parent State to create a new State, a new original subject of international law with its own international legal personality. As follows from a *unilateral* character of secession, the parent State usually resists any such demands. What may follow is civil unrest, revolutionary upheavals, violent clashes or even civil conflicts.

From the perspective of *legal* analysis, secession raises radical questions. First, it solicits answers concerning the normativity of facts in international law. The specificity of secession lies in the way that the factual developments, which at first occur in the sphere of the municipal law of the parent State, are linked with the ensuing legal consequences on an international plane. The factual phenomena, which originally occur within the *domain reservé* of the parent State, might be of critical importance for the success of the secession on an international plane.[3] However, questions may be raised as to the mechanism

1 The Commission of Jurists in the *Aaland Islands* case defined the situation of secession as "obscure and uncertain." See *Report of the International Committee of Jurists Entrusted by the Council of the League of Nations with the Task of Giving an Advisory Opinion upon the Legal Aspects of the Aaland Islands Question*, LNOJ, Spec Supp No 3 (1920) 6 ("*Aaland Islands* case").

2 H Kelsen, *Pure Theory of Law* (Lawbook Exchange 2009) 209. "[O]ne could say that the reason why sovereignty is a liminal concept is because it points to the paradoxical possibility that, when illegality becomes extreme, it can convert itself into a new standard of legality. One sovereignty is replaced by another so that what was before a punishable act of resistance becomes the founding act of a new state." H Kalmo, 'A Matter of Fact? The Many Faces of Sovereignty' in H Kalmo and Q Skinner (eds), *Sovereignty in Fragments: The Past, Present and Future of a Contested Concept* (CUP 2010) 114.

3 As a result of a successful secession, these facts may even later become the source of the new State's international responsibility. See the Draft Articles on the Responsibility of States

© KONINKLIJKE BRILL BV, LEIDEN, 2024 | DOI:10.1163/9789004702646_004

of this transformation.[4] Undoubtedly, this inter-linkage between facts and law and the way that factual developments drive the change of legal qualification of concrete situations are one of the key perplexities of secession from an international law point of view.

Second, secession requires reflection about the role of the international law regarding the *origins* of *original* subjects of international law – States. If at all, secession takes place somewhere on the outer limits of the sphere of international legal regulation.[5] The key issue relates to the question of how to reconcile the assumption of the relevance of a potential international law to secession with the view that "because the law emerges from the State, it would be illogical to think of the emergence of States as a legally regulated process."[6] "[I]f sovereignty is an original power that is owed to no one, how could its emergence be subjected to a rule that belongs to another legal system?"[7]

Classical international legal doctrine is deferential to the factual situation. Indeed, secession is traditionally seen as an a-legal, meta-legal phenomenon. The main message is that the emergence of a State via secession is not and cannot be a legally regulated process. Essentially, State precedes the law. States emerge *ipso facto*; the basic criterion in this regard is the *principle of effectiveness* according to which a new State emerges when the constitutive factual or Montevideo criteria of statehood are effectively met.

However, this seemingly straightforward factualist picture does not answer all the questions. Broadly, unease is provoked by the fact that "[s]omewhat paradoxically, lawyers have attempted to solve one the most fundamental problems of law, the birth and demise of legal orders, by affirming that these events are not a matter of law at all."[8] More specifically, Crawford stated that "a State is not a fact in the sense that a chair is a fact; it is a fact in the sense in which it may be said a treaty is a fact: that is, a legal status attaching to a certain state of affairs by virtue of certain rules or practices."[9] Crawford highlights, "[t]he point

---

for Internationally Wrongful Acts, with Commentaries, in 'Report of the International Law Commission on the Work of its Fifty-Third Session (23 April–1 June and 2 July–10 August 2001)' UN Doc A/56/10, art 10(2) ("ARSIWA").

4 The Commission of Jurists declared that "this transition from a de facto to a normal situation de jure cannot be considered as one confined entirely within the domestic jurisdiction of a State." See *Aaland Island* case (n 1) 6.

5 It is the objective of this book to situate secession in or beyond these outer limits of international legal regulation.

6 M Koskenniemi, *From Apology to Utopia: The Structure of International Legal Argument* (CUP 2005) 272, footnote 170.

7 Kalmo (n 2) 115.

8 ibid.

9 J Crawford, *The Creation of States in International Law* (Clarendon Press 2006) 5.

is that if the State owes its existence to a system of law, then that existence is not, or not only, a 'fact'."[10] Thus, one may wonder, what is the true nature of the principle of effectiveness? If it is a *legal* principle, how is it then possible to reconcile its legal nature with a classical view that secession is not and cannot be a legally regulated process? Does law ultimately precede the emergence or rather the creation of States?

This chapter seeks to challenge the classical view of the role of facts in secession and the understanding of secession as an a-legal factual phenomenon that is not regulated by international law. The critique is built on the following grounds. First, drawing on the elements of the methodology of the history of ideas,[11] the chapter shifts from a traditional debate concerning recognition's role in the creation of States to a historical evolution of the factual element's function in secession.[12] The understanding of the one-time prevalence of earlier doctrines helps perceive contemporary doctrinal views more critically.[13] In particular, the question is asked whether 'the factual element', ie the effective control of seceding territories and their independence from the parent States, entailed the status of the State as a legal subject of international law or whether other elements were decisive to that end. In chronological order, the chapter also presents a classical factualist view of secession.

Next, the chapter revisits Georg Jellinek's and Hans Kelsen's writings to demonstrate that, despite these works, especially Jellinek's, influenced a classical factualist doctrine of statehood, at a closer look they are more nuanced and can help better understand the role of facts in secession. Moreover, the chapter offers criticism of a classical factualist doctrine of secession drawn from legal philosophy and theory. Lastly, it synthesises previous partial conclusions and presents its argument that the criteria of statehood are laid down by international law. Law precedes the State.

---

10 ibid footnote 10.

11 "In order to escape from this hermeneutic trap, consisting of the preconditioned nature of our thinking and our expectations, a text should be firmly placed within its historic and intellectual context." JE Nijman, *The Concept of International Legal Personality: An Inquiry Into the History and Theory of International Law* (TMC Asser Press 2004) 22.

12 "Scholarship in the history of ideas aims to create understanding of past human philosophies by imaginatively analysing the available or retrievable knowledge and uncovering the historic meaning of ideas. Law is a more or less coherent set of ideas." ibid 16. See also M Clark, 'A Conceptual History of Recognition in British International Legal Thought' (2018) BYBIL 21–26.

13 Similarly, see TD Grant, 'Defining Statehood: The Montevideo Convention and Its Discontents' (1998) 37 Columbia Journal of Transnational Law 403, 418.

2 Evolution of the Factual Element in Secession during Earlier Periods

At least four inter-related factors are important when tracing the evolution of the normative and doctrinal understanding of secession and the role of facts. First, the Westphalian nation-State; second, State sovereignty as separate from the person of a monarch; third, a classical voluntarist paradigm of positivism and fourth, a doctrinal reaction to this voluntarism in the context of sociology's growing importance.

Any phenomena that occurred in the pre-Westphalian system must be understood in the context of a "theocentric meta-system, which stood behind the political system"[14] at that time and was characterised by the existence of weak government structures and dominant paradigms of feudalism, Christendom and the Holy Roman Empire.[15] The liberty of the monarch at that time "did not have any independent normative status."[16] The monarch was bound by the pre-existing normative code, which endowed him with certain powers and duties.[17] Essentially, Crawford stated, "in the pre-Vattelian period the link between the law of nations and natural law was associated with a lack of a developed distinction between States and non-state entities."[18]

However, with the Westphalian system[19] and the emergence of a "secular, national and territorial state",[20] this prevailing paradigm changed and a

14 Although the author refers only to the 16th century, this description seems appropriate for the whole pre-Westphalian period. M Keens-Soper, 'The Practice of a State-System' in MD Donelan (ed), *The Reason of States: A Study in International Political Theory* (G Allen & Unwin, 1978) 31.

15 Indeed, "to speak of 'feudal state' at that time is almost misuse of terms." A Clapham, *Brierly's Law of Nations: An Introduction to the Role of International Law in International Relations* (7th edn, OUP 2012) 3 and see also 3–7.

16 Koskenniemi, *From Apology to Utopia* (n 6) 224.

17 ibid 76–77 and 224. Some authors underline the role of papal recognition in this period, which also implicitly underscores this point. H Blix, 'Contemporary Aspects of Recognition' (1970) 130 RCADI 587, 604 and WG Grewe, *The Epochs of International Law* (Walter de Gruyter 2000) 74–82. See also Clark (n 12) 10.

18 Crawford, *The Creation of States in International Law* (n 9) 46, footnote 40.

19 For debunking the traditional international-law myth that the Treaties of Westphalia of 1648 themselves constituted a paradigm shift in the development of a State-oriented system, see S Beaulac, 'The Westphalian Legal Orthodoxy – Myth or Reality?' (2000) 2 Journal of the History of International Law 148. See also S Bhuta, 'State Theory, State Order, State System – Jus Gentium and the Constitution of Public Power' in S Kadelbach, T Kleinein and D Roth-Isigkeit (eds), *System, Order and International Law: The Early History of International Legal Thought from Machiavelli to Hegel* (OUP 2017) 408–417.

20 Clapham, *Brierly's Law of Nations* (n 15) 6. See also A Cassese, 'States: Rise and Decline of the Primary Subjects of the International Community' in B Fassbender and A Peters, *The Oxford Handbook of the History of International Law* (OUP 2012) 49–50.

sovereign State, as distinct from the person of a monarch, gradually took centre stage.[21] Against this background, it is possible to detect four broad trends; four lines of doctrinal thought and practice concerning the role of facts in secession.[22] Their outline seeks to illustrate general trends. As any classification, the boundaries are not clear-cut and might overlap. Importantly, even though the following overview places the factual elements and their link to the theoretical framework of international law centre stage, recognition's role and especially its connection to facts is also be examined.[23] This section presents three trends during earlier periods and the following section will focus on the classical view of factualist statehood.

2.1 *Dynastic Legitimism*

The issue of the legal status of rebellious entities first arose when the Netherlands and Portugal broke away from Spain.[24] Specifically, the question

21 In this context, it is important to stress the influence of Jean Bodin's work. In his *Les six livres de la république*, he offers "the first coherent theory of State sovereignty" understanding it as a concept separate from the person of the monarch – "sovereignty has become a real function which can be attributed to any person or institution." S Besson, 'Sovereignty' in MPEPIL (online edn, OUP 2011) paras 15–16. Moreover, for Bodin, sovereign authority was not absolute. Natural and divine law bound the monarch. Essentially, in Bodin's work, "it was law that made the ruler, and not, as later theories of sovereignty taught us to believe, the will of rulers that made the law." ibid 9. See for a more critical view Koskenniemi, *From Apology to Utopia* (n 6) 78, footnote 24. See also M Scattola, 'Jean Bodin on International Law' in S Kadelbach, T Kleinein and D Roth-Isigkeit (eds), *System, Order and International Law: The Early History of International Legal Thought from Machiavelli to Hegel* (OUP 2017) 89–91.

22 In order to detect the historical origins of secessionism, Coggins also refers to the Westphalian Treaties as the beginning of the inter-State system, but sees the principles therein fully developed around the middle of the 19th century. "Consequently, it is fair to say that secessionism, the modern phenomenon, only occurred from that point forward." BL Coggins, 'The History of Secession: An Overview' in A Pavkovic A and P Radan, *The Ashgate Research Companion to Secession* (Routledge 2011) 23, ftn 1.

23 D'Aspremont argues that a universalist doctrine of statehood is a product of the 20th century that has evolved as a reaction to decolonisation. Despite recognition's long being the object of doctrinal studies, international lawyers did not refer to a specific set of rules determining criteria of statehood until the post-colonial period. See J D'Aspremont, 'The International Law of Statehood and Recognition: A Post-Colonial Invention' in T Garcia (ed), *La reconnaissance du status d'Etat à des entités contestées* (Pedone 2018) 15–16.

24 The Netherlands declared independence from Spain in 1581; the King of Spain and House of Austria recognised the Netherland's independence in the Armistice Treaty of 1609; this was confirmed in Article 2 of the Peace Treaty of Münster, between Spain and the

arose whether regardless of their effective control and independence on the ground, recognition by the parent State was necessary for them to be treated as fully sovereign States.[25] Crawford underlines that this question should be in no way linked to the constitutive theory of recognition, which became dominant later, but was related to "the obligation of loyalty to a superior, which, it was thought, might require release."[26] Similarly, Fabry links the question of recognition by the parent State during this early period with the doctrine of legitimate, dynastic rights.[27] "Dynastic rights were taken to imply that the dominion of a legitimate monarchy was in principle inalienable. The only valid change of title to sovereignty or territory was through freely given consent of the affected monarch."[28]

Based on the analysis of practice, Frowein concluded that the parent State's consent was necessary before the Netherlands and Portugal were treated as fully sovereign States.[29] In the same vein, particularly with regard to the DoI of the USA,[30] Fabry concluded that prior to 1815 "there was a general consensus

---

United Netherlands of 30 January 1648. See CH Alexandrowicz, 'Theory of Recognition *In Fieri*' (1958) 34 BYBIL 176, 182. Portugal declared independence from Spain in 1641, which was recognised by Spain in 1668. See J Frowein, 'Transfer or Recognition of Sovereignty – Some Early Problems in Connection with Dependent Territories' (1971) 65 AJIL 568, 570.

25 Crawford, *The Creation of States in International Law* (n 9) 10–11.

26 ibid 12.

27 See M Fabry, *Recognizing States: International Society and the Establishment of New States since 1776* (OUP 2010) 41–42. On dynastic legitimism, see also Grant, 'Defining Statehood' (n 13) 418–420.

28 M Fabry, 'International Involvement in Secessionist Conflict: From the 16th Century to the Present' in A Pavković and P Radan, *The Ashgate Research Companion to Secession* (Routledge 2011) 255.

29 Frowein formulates the problem as the distinction between, on the one hand, recognition of sovereignty acquired by itself and, on the other hand, transfer of or exemption from the sovereignty of the parent State. Frowein mentions refusal to Portugal to send her own ambassadors to the Westphalian Peace Conference and refusal to treat the ambassador of the Netherlands on equal footing with other States before the parent State's recognition. For example, despite that Switzerland's being seen as the subject of international law even before Westphalian conference, Frowein writes, "if it is correct that the Swiss Confederacy had acquired sovereignty by itself, it might have been possible for third states to recognise that sovereignty before the mother country had done so. But even around and after 1648, state practice did not go so far." See Frowein (n 24) 568–571. See also Grewe (n 17) 183–186.

30 The United States declared independence in 1776. Only France (in February 1778) and the Netherlands (in April 1782) recognised the US before Great Britain did (in November 1782). See Fabry, *Recognizing States* (n 27) 29–33. Other authors see independence of the US more in terms of a pre-existing natural right. "Independence was not just reward for victory (although, of course, without victory there would have been no independence), but a natural right that – although with some restrictions – had belonged to the insurgents even before the War of Independence." See J Fisch, 'Peoples and Nations' in B Fassbender

that new states could be formed only with the free consent of their legitimate parent sovereign, regardless of how a new state might actually justify its own establishment."[31] Nevertheless, the lack of recognition did not appear to have precluded prior contact of the third States with such territories, including the conclusion of treaties.[32]

Regarding the then doctrine, for Pufendorf, consent by the parent State was seen as necessary for the seceding territories to obtain release "from the bond to which they were tied to him."[33] Later on, for example in von Steck's views, the parent State's release was essential, even if "the rebelling people disclaimed their obedience, separated themselves and asserted their freedom with arms."[34] Von Steck considered any recognition prior to the parent State's recognition premature and an unfriendly intervention into the affairs of the mother State[35] and, therefore, considered France's recognition of the USA as

---

and A Peters (eds), *The Oxford Handbook of the History of International Law* (OUP 2012) 33. Similarly, "from the text of the Declaration, these rights apparently were viewed by the drafters as prior to statehood – and altogether independent of whether the Colonies were internationally recognized as states." TD Grant, *The Recognition of States: Law and Practice in Debate and Evolution* (Praeger 1999) 21.

31 Fabry, *Recognizing States* (n 27) 41.

32 Frowein refers to treaties concluded with the Netherlands and Portugal before their recognition by parent States. Frowein (n 24) 568 and 570. However, Lauterpacht, for example, completely denied the relevance of dynastic legitimism in this regard, stating, "the formal renunciation of sovereignty by the parent State has never been regarded as a condition of the lawfulness of recognition." H Lauterpacht, *Recognition in International Law* (University Press 1947) 9–10. Nevertheless, with regard to the above observations, it seems Frowein's approach is more nuanced.

33 Von Pufendorf, S., *De jure Naturae et Gentium*, (1688), book VII, chapter 3, § 9, para 690 cited in Crawford, *The Creation of States in International Law* (n 9) 11, footnote 38. Vattel was in principle opposed to secession. "If those who are menaced or attacked might separate themselves from the others in order to avoid a present danger, every state would soon be dismembered and destroyed. It is then essentially necessary for the safety of society, and even for the welfare of all its members, that each part should with all its might resist a common enemy, rather than separate from the others' and this is consequently one of the necessary conditions of the political association." E de Vattel, *The Law of Nations, or: Principles of the Law of Nature, Applied to the Conduct and Affairs of Nations and Sovereigns, with Three Early Essays on the Origin and Nature of Natural Law and on Luxury* (1797 edn, Liberty Fund 2008) 211, § 200. The only exception seems to have been situation when the sovereign did not come to help territories in danger. According to Vattel, this applied to Switzerland's leaving the Holy Roman Empire. ibid, 211–212, § 201–202.

34 Von Steck's views are presented in Alexandrowicz, 'Theory of Recognition *In Fieri*' (n 24) 183. See also Crawford, *The Creation of States in International Law* (n 9) 376.

35 Von Steck's views are presented in Alexandrowicz, 'Theory of Recognition *In Fieri*' (n 24) 183–184. See also I Van Hulle, 'Britain's Recognition of the Spanish American Republics' 82 (2014) The Legal History Review 284, 299–300.

an illegal act.[36] However, once the parent State granted its recognition, there was nothing the third States could add to the already existing new State's sovereignty; their recognition was in fact unnecessary.[37] A new State's sovereignty was derived from within, in particular from the assumption of independence and the parent State's recognition.[38] Conversely, for example Moser claimed that the third States could "grant recognition before the mother country extended it."[39]

Overall, despite a gradual evolution of the concept of sovereignty as distinct from the person of a sovereign characterising this period, the acquisition of sovereignty and independence by rebellious entities remained linked with the release from the duty of loyalty to the person of a monarch and his legitimate rights. The doctrine did not specifically discuss, but simply assumed the factual control and independence of the seceding territories.

2.2 *Transitory Factualist Period*

Later, the doctrinal opinion shifted the focus more decisively towards the factual element. The new State's legitimation was seen as occurring from within and therefore recognition, whether by the parent State or the third States, was in fact unnecessary.[40] For example, German writer Martens claimed that in the context of secession, two considerations were important – DoI and the maintenance of a *de facto* independence by rebels.[41] "[A] foreign nation ... does not appear to violate its perfect obligations nor to deviate from the principles of neutrality, if, ... it treats ... as an independent nation, people who have declared, and still maintain themselves independent."[42] The parent State could either dissemble or retaliate.[43] In any case, "recognition as a constructive

---

36 Frowein (n 24) 570.

37 Alexandrowicz, 'Theory of Recognition *In Fieri*' (n 24) 183–184.

38 ibid 183.

39 Frowein (n 24) 570.

40 Alexandrowicz, 'Theory of Recognition *In Fieri*' (n 24) 187. In the same vein, Frowein writes that by the 1820s, doctrine had accepted Moser's earlier view based on effective independence. See Frowein (n 24) 570. See also Grewe (n 17) 348 and 499–500.

41 GF Von Martens, *A Compendium of the Law of Nations, Founded on the Treaties and Customs of the Modern Nations of Europe. To Which is Added a Complete List of All the Treaties, Conventions, Compacts, Declarations, &c. from the Year 1731–1789, Inclusive, Indicating the Verbal Works in Which They Are to Be Found* (Cobbet and Morgan, Pall-Mall 1802) 81. See also Alexandrowicz, 'Theory of Recognition *In Fieri*' (n 24) 185–186.

42 Martens (n 41) 81.

43 ibid; Alexandrowicz, 'Theory of Recognition *In Fieri*' (n 24) 186.

act is not conceded and as a declaratory act it is in principle superfluous."[44] Other authors such as Klüber[45] and Saalfeld[46] presented recognition as declaratory of sovereignty and independence and referred to the elements that the seceding territory needed to possess for the recognition not to be premature, and thus confirmed the alienation from the legitimism.[47] Moreover, later on Lauterpacht in particular referred to this *de facto* independence in terms of giving rise to the *right* to recognition.[48]

---

44 Alexandrowicz, 'Theory of Recognition *In Fieri*' (n 24) 186–187. Martens (n 41) 82. "According to the declaratory theory, which was dominant until at least the late eighteenth century, the legal status of a ruler was understood to be determined internally." A Orford, 'Constituting Order' in J Crawford and M Koskenniemi (eds), *The Cambridge Companion to International Law* (CUP 2012) 277. When Orford discusses the constitutive theory of recognition, she points out that "*de facto* control over territory was no longer sufficient to ground a claim to statehood." ibid 278. "No such constitutive theory of recognition existed in the pre-positivist world. In fact, the classic writers never formulated any coherent theory of recognition. If acts of recognition of States or Governments (Sovereigns) occurred in State practice, they were considered as declaratory of the existence of the recognised entity. All they meant was that the recognising entity was ready to open diplomatic, commercial and other relations with the recognised or admitted entity." CH Alexandrowicz, 'New and Original States: the Issue of Reversion to Sovereignty (1969)' in D Armitage and J Pitts, *The Law of Nations in Global History* (OUP 2017) 392.

45 The recognition was seen as intervention into the parent State's affairs unless the latter renounced her rights or was *presumed* to have done so. See for Klüber's views Alexandrowicz, 'Theory of Recognition *In Fieri*' (n 24) 187–189 (*emphasis added*). See also Van Hulle (n 35) 292 and 300.

46 Alexandrowicz cites Saalfeld as saying that "in order to consider the sovereignty of a State as complete in the Law of Nations, there is no need for its recognition by foreign powers; though the latter may appear useful, the de facto existence of sovereignty is sufficient." ibid 189. The recognition was premature when parent State still possessed fortified positions and had army in the field. Alexandrowicz, 'Theory of Recognition *In Fieri*' (n 24) 190.

47 See *infra* also for Phillimore's deviation from legitimism.

48 See Lauterpacht, *Recognition in International Law* (n 32) 12–24 (*emphasis added*). Additionally, it is also worth noting that in the late 19th century, Lorimer, a Scottish jurist in the natural law tradition, claimed that to be *entitled* to a plenary political recognition, a State must possess two elements – will and power "to reciprocate the recognition which it demands." Once these conditions are fulfilled, "State exists" and recognition cannot be withheld from it "without a repudiation of the principles of jurisprudence." It was up to the States from which the recognition is demanded, and their jurists, to examine the fulfilment these two conditions. Lorimer also devised presumptions about which creeds, races and communities are not eligible for the fulfilment of these conditions. According to Lorimer, the plenary political recognition only extended to "civilized humanity." He also foresaw a partial political recognition extended to "barbarous civilisations" and "natural or mere human recognition" extended to the "residue of mankind." J Lorimer, *The Institutes of the Law of Nations; A Treatise of the Jural Relations of Separate Political Communities* (W Blackwood and sons 1883) 108–109 and broadly 101 et seq. See also Clark (n 12) 26–38.

The question may be raised as to the theoretical foundations of this doctrinal approach, which saw the origins of sovereignty coming from within and third States' recognition only as declaratory of the existing reality. Alexandrowicz refers to a natural law tradition.[49] "Even if the law of nations was conceived as based on the consent of States, this anti-naturalist trend was not-yet allowed to extend to the field of recognition."[50] The "declaratorism in respect of recognition" was one of the "functional qualities peculiar to the 'natural law' system within the classic law of nations."[51]

The evolution of practice, particularly with respect to the USA and Great Britain recognising the independence and sovereignty of the Spanish colonies in Latin America before Spain renounced her rights, was particularly relevant.[52] On the one hand, this approach signalled the end of dynastic legitimism. Ultimately, out of all the major powers of that time, only Austria and Russia waited for the Spanish recognition before they granted one too.[53] Crawford showed that it is reasonable to summarise that, with respect to doctrine and practice, the theory of legitimacy was "rejected in terms of its influence on statehood by the 1820s."[54] On the other hand, in their position on recognitions, both the USA and Great Britain specifically referred to a *de facto* principle and a corresponding entitlement to recognition.[55] Crawford underlined that

---

49 Alexandrowicz, 'Theory of Recognition *In Fieri*' (n 24) 191. See also Grewe (n 17) 500–501 and, more broadly, 506–512 and M Vec, 'Sources of International Law in the Nineteenth-Century European Tradition: The Myth of Positivism' in S Besson and J D'Aspremont, *The Oxford Handbook of the Sources of International Law* (OUP 2017) 121–144.

50 Alexandrowicz, 'Theory of Recognition *In Fieri*' (n 24) 191. For more on the co-existence of natural law tradition with positivist doctrine, see Koskenniemi, *From Apology to Utopia* (n 6) 131–132. In particular, the State "is the professional *a priori*, the transcendental condition from which discourse proceeds and which is not itself subject to discussion ... Standard textbooks appear to construct the international order as an aggregate of the rights and duties which 'follow from' the possession of statehood *ipso facto* ... However, usually the assumptions behind this organization remain hidden." ibid 132 and 132, footnote 262.

51 Alexandrowicz, 'New and Original States' (n 44) 394.

52 See Fabry, *Recognizing States* (n 27) 49–70.

53 ibid 69.

54 Crawford, *The Creation of States in International Law* (n 9) 46, footnote 40.

55 It is interesting to see the official opinion given by Secretary of State Adams to President Monroe, in which he stated that "there is a stage in such contests when the parties struggling for independence have, as I conceive, a right to demand its acknowledgment by neutral parties and when the acknowledgment may be granted without departure from the obligations of neutrality. It is the stage when independence is established as a matter of fact so as to leave the chance of the opposite party to recover their dominion utterly desperate ... The fact and the right combined can alone authorize a neutral to acknowledge a new and disputed sovereignty. The neutral may, indeed, infer the right from the fact,

"[w]hatever view of recognition may have been entertained, in practice recognition of the South American republics was substantially declaratory of an existing situation."[56] In addition, according to Fabry, a *de facto* principle guided the creation of Belgium and Greece,[57] although these cases represented more the examples of the involvement by the Great Powers.[58]

2.3 *Constitutive Theory of Recognition*

The third line of thought – constitutive theory of recognition – gained weight in the second half of the 19th century. A strict separation between the State's factual existence and its legal existence as a member of the Family of Nations defined this position. In this connection, it is instructive to trace its evolution in Wheaton's writings.[59] The first edition of his *Elements of International Law* contains certain doubts regarding the acquisition of sovereignty by seceding territories.[60] However, in the third edition, the matter is not the object of doubt

---

but not the fact from the right." Adams to Monroe, 24 August 1818, F Worthington (ed), *Writings of John Quincy Adams*, vol 6 (Macmillan 1916) 442–3 cited in Fabry, *Recognizing States* (n 27) 55, and see also, in respect to the British position, ibid 60. Britain's recognition of the Latin American States, however, was transitory and rather contradictory in nature. Britain differentiated between three different types of recognition – *de facto*, diplomatic and *de iure*, thereby seeking to justify her diplomatic recognition by adopting a middle way between dynastic legitimism (by claiming that their recognition was only political and declaratory in nature of a *de facto* independence and therefore did not represent intervention into Spain's affairs) and a full-fledged reliance on effective separation of colonies (arguing in favour of recognition by pointing to the lack of international responsibility of unrecognised of colonies, and even by defining conditions for diplomatic recognition including ending the struggle, power, will of independence and government). Van Hulle (n 35) 292–308. It is interesting to note that this certainly evidenced a shift in Great Britain's position, since it never acknowledged that the US achieved full sovereignty before she renounced her rights. See Frowein (n 24) 571.

56 Crawford, *The Creation of States in International Law* (n 9) 379.

57 Fabry, *Recognizing States* (n 27) 80–85 and 96–98. According to the Germano-Polish Mixed Tribunal, Belgium's creation was an example of a State's creation deriving from its effectiveness, without the consent of the parent State. *Deutsche Continental Gas-Gesellschaft v Polish State*, (Germano-Polish Mixed Arbitral Tribunal) (1929) 5 ILR 11, 14.

58 Crawford, *The Creation of States in International Law* (n 9) 375.

59 For an outline of the evolution of Wheaton's position, see Alexandrowicz, 'Theory of Recognition *In Fieri*' (n 24) 192–195.

60 See ibid 192–193. "If revolution in a State be effected by a province or colony shaking off its sovereignty, so long as the independence of the new State is not acknowledged by other powers, it may seem doubtful, in an international point of view, whether its sovereignty can be considered as complete however it may be regarded by its own government and citizens." H Wheaton, *Elements of International Law: with a Sketch of the History of the Science* (1st edn, Carrey, Lea & Blanchard 1836) 73, § 19.

any more.[61] External sovereignty is not derived from within; it is recognition that renders it perfect and complete.[62] The change of Wheaton's thinking is associated with the influence of Bentham, Savigny, and above all with Hegel's philosophy.[63] Despite Wheaton's views not yet representing a fully formed constitutive theory, they can be taken as an "intermediate point."[64] Indeed, the

---

61 Alexandrowicz, 'Theory of Recognition *In Fieri*' (n 24) 195. Distinguishing between internal and external sovereignty, Wheaton writes that while internal sovereignty is entirely independent of recognition by other States and depends only on *a de facto* existence of State, "the external sovereignty of any State, on the other hand, may require recognition of other States in order to render it perfect and complete." H Wheaton, *Elements of International Law* (3rd edn, Lea and Blanchard 1846) 56–57, § 6.

62 Alexandrowicz, 'Theory of Recognition *In Fieri*' (n 24) 195.

63 ibid. Hegel in his *Philosophy of Right* (1820) states that "each state is consequently a sovereign and independent entity in relations to others. The state has a primary and absolute entitlement to be a sovereign and independent power *in the eyes of others*, i.e. *to be recognized* by them." Moreover, the legitimacy of a state in its external relations is "a purely *internal* matter," but "it is equally essential that this legitimacy should be supplemented by recognition on the part of other states." GWF Hegel, *Elements of the Philosophy of Right* (CUP 1991) 366–357 (§ 331). Earlier in his Encyclopaedia of Philosophical Sciences, Hegel even thought about recognition as the universal principle of international law. "Le droit politique extérieur repose ... sur ce que l'on appelle le droit des gens, dont le principe universel est l'être-reconnu présupposé des États." See GWF Hegel, *Encyclopédie des sciences philosophiques en abrégé* (Librairie philosophique J Vrin 2012) 560–561 (§ 547).

64 Crawford, *The Creation of States in International Law* (n 9) 13, footnote 49. For example, in earlier editions of his Commentaries Phillimore described when a formal recognition of a new State would not represent an offense to the parent State, highlighting the move away from legitimism. According to Phillimore, distinguishing between virtual and formal recognition, the third States could have proceeded to formal recognition if two conditions were met: the end of hostilities with the parent State and the consolidation of a new State. If these conditions were present, even the parent State's refusal was no "legitimate bar to the complete and Formal Recognition of the new State by other communities of the world." R Phillimore, *Commentaries upon International Law* (1st edn, T and JW Johnson, Law Booksellers 1855) 34 and see 31–39. In later editions of his work, Phillimore moved closer to the constitutive theory, adding that before recognition, the third States should investigate the capacity of a new State to discharge international obligations. R Phillimore, *Commentaries upon International Law* (2nd edn, Butterworths 1871) 16 cited in Clark (n 12) 21. However, in any case, for Phillimore the question of the origins of a State was not a matter of international concern. Phillimore said, "the question as to the origin of States belongs rather to the province of Political Philosophy than of International Jurisprudence." See R Phillimore, *Commentaries upon International Law* (1st edn, T and JW Johnson, Law Booksellers 1854) 93; R Phillimore R, *Commentaries upon International Law*, (2nd edn, Butterworths 1871) 78. Phillimore even defined 'State' as "a people permanently occupying a fixed territory (*certam sedem*), bound together by common laws, habits, and customs into one body politic, exercising, through the medium of and organized Government, independent sovereignty and control over all persons and things within its boundaries, capable of making war and peace, and of entering into all International

shift in his views may be considered a microcosm of a broader transformation in an international law doctrine.[65]

The turn towards the constitutive theory of recognition was inextricably linked with the establishment of positivism in its voluntarist paradigm as a prevailing theory of international law in the second half of the 19th century. For positivists, the consent of States was the source of the basis of obligation in international law.[66] As summarised by Crawford, since the emergence of a new State subject to international law created obligation for other States, "the positivist premiss seemed to require consent either to the creation of the State or to its being subjected to international law so far as other States were concerned."[67]

Against this background, recognition, whether understood as a treaty[68] or a unilateral act,[69] functioned as "the agency of admission into 'civilized society.'"[70] The assessment of an inherently imperialistic criterion of the "standard of civilization" by the existing States thereby became a central feature of

relations with the other communities of the globe." R Phillimore, *Commentaries upon International Law* (1st edn, T and JW Johnson, Law Booksellers 1854) 94; R Phillimore, *Commentaries upon International Law* (2nd edn, Butterworths 1871) 80. See further Van Hulle (n 35) 311–313 and Clark (n 12) 17–23. See Grant, 'Defining Statehood' (n 13) 416–418. In this context, Hall's position could be also seen as intermediate. "The marks of an independent state are, that the community constituting it is permanently established for a political end, that it possesses a defined territory, and that is independent of territorial control … So soon, therefore, as a society can point to the necessary marks, and indicates its intention of conforming to law, it enters of right into the family of states, and must be treated with law … The commencement of state dates nevertheless from its recognition by other powers … Thus, although the right to be treated as a state is independent of recognition, recognition is necessary evidence that the right has been acquired." WE Hall, *A Treatise on International Law* (Clarendon Press 1890) 18, 21 and 87. See Grant, 'Defining Statehood' (n 13) 417.

65 Crawford, *The Creation of States in International Law* (n 9) 13.

66 See for a critical view Clapham, *Brierly's Law of Nations* (n 15) 49–53.

67 Crawford, *The Creation of States in International Law* (n 9) 13.

68 "Les normes juridiques internationales se constituent par le moyens d'accords; les sujets de l'ordre juridique international commencent donc à exister au moment ou intervient un premier accord … cet accord … on appelle *reconnaissance*." D Anzilotti, *Cours de droit international* (Sirey 1929) 161. Anzilotti's view was criticised by Lauterpacht, especially the logical inconsistency of regarding an entity as able to conclude international treaties as a State, subject to international law, before *becoming* a State, subject of international law. See Lauterpacht, *Recognition in International Law* (n 32) 39–40. See also H Kelsen, 'La naissance de l'État et la formation de sa nationalité: les principes; leur application au cas de la Tchécoslovaquie' (1929) 4 Revue de droit international 613, 620.

69 A Cavaglieri, 'Règles générales du droit de la paix' (1929) 26 RCADI 311, 352–353.

70 Crawford, *The Creation of States in International Law* (n 9) 16.

the accession to the legal status of the State.[71] Summed up by Oppenheim, "through recognition only and exclusively a State becomes an International Person and a subject of International Law."[72]

Therefore, this theory created a distinction between "(natural) statehood, which is independent of recognition and membership of the international community (or full international personality), which alone is a source of rights and which is dependent on recognition."[73] In this context, authors often used the term 'State' to denote, on the one hand, an unrecognised entity in terms of its physical or sociological existence and, on the other hand, a juridical person of international law constituted through recognition.[74] Only the latter one was seen as the subject of international law.

Thus, from this perspective, the question of a physical formation or existence of States or not-yet recognised entities or States *in statu nascendi* was seen as a mere fact outside of the scope of international law.[75] "La notion de l'État précède nécessairement celle du droit international."[76] "Au point de vue positif, on ne peut pas dire simplement que les États sont sujets du droit international en vertu de la raison ou de la nature."[77] On the contrary, the consent of States expressed via recognition was at the origin of the legal existence of States. Some authors even claimed the existence of a customary rule of international law according to which international legal personality was assigned to a new State via recognition.[78] In any case, there was no right to recognition and, in line with a voluntarist paradigm, recognising States could have opted for recognition at their will.[79]

---

71 Van Hulle (n 35) 286.

72 LFL Oppenheim, *International Law: A Treatise* (2nd edn, Longmans/Green 1912) 117. See also Clark (n 12) 56.

73 Lauterpacht, *Recognition in International Law* (n 32) 38. Lauterpacht refers to Jellinek, who distinguished between States as parts of organized humanity entering *ipso facto* into a general community of States and States entering a juridical community of States through recognition. See ibid. See also J-D Mouton, 'La notion d'Etat et le droit international public' (1992) 16 *Droits, Revue française de théorie juridique* 45, 47. In addition, "Oppenheim never provides an example of a state that does exist but nevertheless still falls entirely outside of the membership of the Family of Nations." Clark (n 12) 58.

74 See Cavaglieri (n 69) 352–354.

75 Crawford, *The Creation of States in International Law* (n 9) 13. See also Cavaglieri (n 69) 340.

76 Cavaglieri (n 69) 341. International law "ne peut donc pas donner *a posteriori* une définition juridique de l'État et de sa formation, qu'il doit au contraire supposer, puisque de cette formation dépend l'application de ses règles. " ibid.

77 Cavaglieri (n 69) 340.

78 ibid 345–346.

79 ibid 349–350.

As a consequence, international law could not have been relevant to questions such as how these non-recognised entities "acquired territory, what rights and duties they had or owed to others as a result of events before they were recognized."[80] In short, "an unrecognised community has neither rights, nor duties under international law."[81] Moreover, it was not clear whether recognised States could act towards not-yet recognised States in a way international law would bar towards recognised States.[82] The issue of a *de facto* existence of a not-yet recognised State was considered to avoid a premature recognition, which would constitute an illegal intervention into the internal affairs of the parent State.[83]

As regards the practice at the time, especially the European continent was dominated by the system of the balance of powers, which determined any territorial or sovereignty changes. The separation of Serbia, Romania and Montenegro from the Ottoman Empire, which was formally recognised by the Great Powers in the Treaty of Berlin of 1878, is an example of constitutive recognition.[84] This treaty also conditioned Serbia's and Romania's recognitions by their commitment to religious liberty and equality.[85]

---

80 ibid.

81 TD Grant, *The Recognition of States* (n 30) 20.

82 See ibid. In this context, Cavaglieri held that "les actes des États anciens contre l'État non reconnu, et vice-versa, quelque regrettables et fâcheux qu'ils soient au point du vue politique et humanitaire, sont indifférents au point de vue du droit international." Cavaglieri (n 69) 348.

83 Cavaglieri (n 69) 350. See also *infra*.

84 Treaty Between Great Britain, Austria-Hungary, France, Germany, Italy, Russia and Turkey, for the Settlement of the Affairs of the East (signed 13 July 1878) arts 26, 34 and 18.

85 ibid arts 35 and 44. Indeed, there have been examples of recognition preceded by conditions. For example, Great Britain preceded its recognition of Brazil by appealing to Brazil to terminate and renounce the slave trade. See Fabry, *Recognizing States* (n 27) 66. Greece's recognition by the Great Powers was also conditioned on the respect of religious liberty. See ibid 98. When discussing Serbia's recognition during the Berlin congress, the French delegate stated, "Serbia, which demands to enter into the European family upon the same footing as the other states, should in the first place acknowledge the principles which form the basis of social organization in all the states of Europe, and accept them as necessary condition of the favour she solicits." Protocol No 10 of the Congress of Berlin (1 July 1878) cited in ibid 106. In this context, it seems impossible not to draw parallels to the context of the dissolution of the SFRY more than 100 years later. Indeed, the recognition of new republics by the Member States of the European Community was also preceded by a number of conditions. But while recognition via the Treaty of Berlin was seen as constitutive of statehood, recognition of the Member States of the European Community was only declaratory of an already existing statehood. See Declaration of the European Community and its Member States on the Guidelines on the Recognition of New States in Eastern Europe and Soviet Union (16 December 1991) reprinted in French in H Hamant, *Succession de l'URSS: Receuil des documents* (Bruylant 2010) 58–59 and Declaration of the

Moreover, based on the analysis of the 19th century practice in Europe, Fabry concluded that "whether for normative reasons or reasons of pragmatic necessity, members of the society of states moved towards recognizing indigenously established *de facto* states."[86] Crawford offered a rather nuanced view regarding State practice and showed that the evolution that would support the constitutive theory of recognition was only gradual and that the problem was largely doctrinal.[87] "Thus unrecognized States and native peoples with some form of regular government were given the benefit of, and treated as obliged by, the whole body of international law."[88]

On balance, the constitutive theory played an important role in the discussion on the creation of States up through the 20th century. Today, disfavoured by the majority of doctrines,[89] many scholars criticised this theory on a number of justified grounds.[90] It offers solutions to those who consider cognition as an important element of the acquisition of statehood.[91] However, it makes it impossible to conceive of the objective international legal personality of the State. It is inherently bilateralist and relativist. Indeed, "community recognized by one state but not another would simultaneously be state and a nonstate."[92] Such a situation has been described as "a legal curiosity",[93] as "grotesque spectacle"[94] and as provoking an embarrassing confusion.[95]

European Community and its Member States on Yugoslavia (16 December 1991) reprinted in (1992) 31 ILM 1485.

86 Fabry, *Recognizing States* (n 27) 79. It is important to take this conclusion with some degree of caution. Fabry's analysis did not acknowledge or take into account the existence of the constitutive theory of recognition; nor did it derive any conclusions from the number of treaties dealing with the issue of recognition at that time. On the other hand, Fabry's conclusion may be taken as support of the above-mentioned view that recognition before the complete independence of secessionist entities was seen as an illegal intervention in a parent State's affairs.

87 Crawford, *The Creation of States in International Law* (n 9) 13.

88 ibid.

89 But see for example J Vidmar, 'Territorial Integrity and the Law of Statehood' (2012) 44 George Washington International Law Review 101, 145–146; C Hillgruber, 'The Admission of New States to the International Community' (1998) 9 EJIL 491.

90 See Crawford, *The Creation of States in International Law* (n 9) 19–22; TD Grant, *The Recognition of States* (n 30) 2–4 and 19–22; E Wyler, *Théorie et pratique de la reconnaissance d'Etat: une approche épistémologique du droit international* (Bruylant 2013) 151–154.

91 See Lauterpacht, *Recognition in International Law* (n 32) 55. See *infra* more on Lauterpacht's duty of recognition and Kelsen's eventual inclination towards the constitutive theory.

92 TD Grant, *The Recognition of States* (n 30) 20.

93 Clapham, *Brierly's Law of Nations* (n 15) 151.

94 Lauterpacht, *Recognition in International Law* (n 32) 78.

95 T-C Chen, *The International Law of Recognition: With Special Reference to Practice in Great Britain and the United States* (Stevens 1951) 39–40.

However, most importantly, "the constitutive act creative of statehood is an act of unfettered political will divorced from binding considerations of legal principle."[96] From today's perspective, the constitutive theory is mostly seen as "a tool of *Realpolitik*, available to forge states out of communities at the will of the recognizing state."[97] Indeed, imbedded arbitrariness, subjectivism and patriarchy in relations to non-recognised entities[98] intrinsically underline the constitutive theory in its voluntarist form.

2.4 *Summary*

A *de facto* principle's role concerning secession varied depending on the period in question. At first, notwithstanding the effectiveness of the seceding territories, the parent State's recognition was an overriding criterion. Based on the doctrine of legitimate rights, this recognition was seen as release from loyalty to a previous sovereign. The doctrine did not analyse the criteria of effective independence; they were simply assumed. According to the second period's opinion, relying on natural law, sovereignty was understood as being achieved from within, based on the attainment of factual independence. Accordingly, the recognition was declaratory in nature. The scope of a required factual independence was discussed to avoid a premature interference in the parent State's affairs.

Third, the constitutive theory of recognition saw an actual formation and existence of a non-recognised entity as a mere fact, outside of the scope of international law. This theory linked the creation of the State as an international person, subject of international law, with its recognition by the existing States. The criteria of a *de facto* existence were mostly discussed to avoid a premature recognition. In summary, the major takeaway from this overview is that in neither of the outlined periods did the factual element operate on its own, but rather was linked with the parent State's recognition, natural law tradition or third States' recognition and, more broadly, with an intellectual evolution of international law.

96 Lauterpacht, *Recognition in International Law* (n 32) 41.

97 TD Grant, *The Recognition of States* (n 30) 3.

98 "A structure of power and decision-making is implicit in the doctrine because the power to 'recognise' new states is vested in the states that are already sovereign. The doctrine is premised on the existence of a sovereign state whose will establishes law and whose actions may be subject to lawyers' inquiry … Simple acceptance of this framework precludes an inquiry into how this distinction was made and why one set of states becomes sovereign while the other does not, even though anthropological and historical research subversively suggests various disconcerting parallels between these apparently disparate societies." A Anghie, *Imperialism, Sovereignty and the Making of International Law* (CUP 2004) 99–100.

3 Factualist Statehood and Declaratory Theory

3.1 *Main Point of Reference: Montevideo Criteria*

Today, a standard reference to the creation of States usually starts from the premise of the so-called Montevideo or constitutive criteria of statehood.[99] The Montevideo criteria include a permanent population, defined territory, government and the capacity to enter into relations with other States.[100] Crawford persuasively claims that the fourth criterion is not a criterion, but simply the consequence of statehood.[101] Moreover, the criterion of government is usually understood as requiring independence – "the central criterion for statehood."[102]

---

99 "The state as a person of international law should possess the following qualifications: a) a permanent population; b) a defined territory; c) government; and d) capacity to enter into relations with the other states." Convention on Rights and Duties of States (signed 26 December 1933, entered into force 26 December 1934) 165 LNTS 19, art 1 ("Montevideo Convention").

100 See for the analysis of these criteria Crawford, *The Creation of States in International Law* (n 9) 46–62; D Wong, 'Sovereignty Sunk? The Position of "Sinking States" at International Law' (2013) 14 Melbourne Journal of International Law 1, 7–10; G Kreijen, *State, Failure, Sovereignty and Effectiveness: Legal Lessons from the Decolonization of Sub-Saharan Africa* (M Nijhoff 2004) 18–25; G Anderson, 'Secession in International Law and Relations: What Are We Talking About?' (2013) 35 Loyola of Los Angeles International and Comparative Law Review 343, 356–360.

101 See J Crawford, 'State' in MPEPIL (online edn, OUP 2011) para 25. Grant, 'Defining Statehood' (n 13) 434–435.

102 Crawford, *The Creation of States in International Law* (n 9) 55 and 62. Famously, judge Huber in the Island of Palmas case stated, "sovereignty in the relations between states signifies independence. Independence in regard to a portion of the globe is the right to exercise therein, to the exclusion of any other State, the functions of a State" See *Island of Palmas case (Netherlands, United States)* (1928) II RIAA, 829, 838. According to Lauterpacht, "the meaning of independence, however, is not confined to the achievement of actual independence of the mother country. It includes also independence of any state other than the mother country." Lauterpacht, *Recognition in International Law* (n 32) 27. Judge Anzilotti formulated probably the most famous definition of independence in his separate opinion in the *Customs Regime between Germany and Austria* case, when he held that "the independence of Austria within the meaning of Article 88 [of the Treaty of Saint-Germain] is nothing else but the existence of Austria, within the frontiers laid down by the Treaty of Saint-Germain, as a separate State and not subject to the authority of any other State or group of States. Independence as thus understood is really no more than the normal condition of States according to international law; it may also be described as sovereignty (suprema potestas), or external sovereignty, by which is meant that the State has over it no other authority than that of international law." Anzilotti then highlights the difference between independent and dependent states. "The idea of dependence therefore necessarily implies … the relation between the State which can legally impose its will and the State which is legally compelled to submit to that will. Where there is no such relation of superiority and subordination, it is impossible to speak of dependence within the meaning of international law." *Customs Regime between Germany and Austria* (Advisory Opinion) [1931] PCIJ Series A/B No 41, 57–58. This case related to the independence of an existing State and not to the criterion of the creation of States. A number of

Essentially, the Montevideo criteria "are based on the principle of effectiveness among territorial units."[103]

These criteria are frequently referred to in connection with Georg Jellinek's three-elements doctrine.[104] However, despite this cross-reference, there is no evidence of a direct influence of Jellinek's theory on a drafting process of Article 1 of the 1933 Montevideo Convention itself.[105] In fact, from *travaux préparatoires* follows that the selection of the criteria did not provoke any debate and that the drafters primarily focused on the exclusion of the "standard of civilization"[106] and the codification of the declaratory theory of recognition.[107]

---

authors distinguish between formal and actual independence. While the former relates to formal arrangements relating to an entity's independence, for example under its constitution, the latter has been defined as the "minimum degree of real governmental power at the disposal of the authorities of the putative State that is necessary for it to qualify as 'independent.'" Crawford, *The Creation of States in International Law* (n 9) 72 and generally on this distinction 66–89. See also R Cohen, 'The Concept of Statehood in United Nations Practice' (1961) 109 University of Pennsylvania Law Review 1127, 1139–1140.

103 Crawford, *The Creation of States in International Law* (n 9) 46. See *infra* for more on the meaning of the term "principle of effectiveness" in the context of secession.

104 The three elements in Jellinek's theory are territory, population and power. See *infra* in detail.

105 D'Aspremont, 'The International Law of Statehood and Recognition' (n 23) 22–23. According to the argument of Becker Lorca, "[t]he writings of semi-peripheral scholars arguing for the dissolution of the standard of civilization appropriated the language of modern international law. This intellectual work paid off in the concrete rules enacted by the Montevideo Convention. In this regard, the Convention should be considered as a unique offspring of the modern semi-peripheral sensibility." A Becker Lorca, *Mestizo International Law: A Global Intellectual History 1842–1933* (CUP 2014) 308.

106 "A formal conception of statehood marked a radical departure from classical international law's substantive standard of civilization. More significant for what it excluded than for it required, a formal definition of statehood struck a potent blow to the doctrine of the standard of civilization." Becker Lorca (n 105) 306.

107 "It is not deemed necessary to comment on the stipulations regarding conditions which the State must meet as a party of International Law, its rights of equality, sovereignty and defense or matters relative to the effects of the recognition of new States." 'Report of the Second Sub-Committee: Rights and Duties of States' (1933) 1 International American Conference: Minutes and Antecedents 165, 165. The 1912 Pessôa codification project prepared for the meeting of the Rio Committee of Jurists already included the definition of statehood in the following terms: "For the purpose of this Code, a State is a permanent grouping of individuals that inhabit a defined territory and obey the same government that is in charge of the administration of justice and the preservation of order." The 1912 Pessôa codification project cited in Becker Lorca (n 105) 335, ftn 91. Alvarez's Project Number 2 submitted to the 1927 meeting of the Committee of Jurists defined the State as "a people in a territory with a constituted government, capacity to enter in relations with other states and a degree of civilization that enables it to observe the principles of international law." A Alvarez, *Considérations générales sur la codification du droit international américain (code de droit international des états américans). Mémorial présentée à la deuxième Commission de juristes réunie à Rio de Janeiro le 18 avril 1927* (Imprensa Nacional 1927) cited in ibid 338, ftn 103. For the discussion about "standard of civilization" during

According to Grant, the fact that the question of the origins of the Montevideo criteria has not received much attention in the scholarship "may reflect the fact that its content was a restatement of ideas prevalent at the time of the framing."[108] "By the 1930s, the three elements were widely assumed to be a mainstay of statehood."[109]

The practice,[110] international[111] and domestic case law[112] and literature[113] have accepted the factualist criteria of statehood. In fact, the doctrinal consensus on the matter is so overwhelming that one author pointed out that

the 1927 meeting, see ibid 338–340. Following the failure of the 1928 Pan-American conference in Habana, "in the draft prepared by the American Institute to be submitted to the next Conference in Montevideo the reference to civilization disappeared." ibid 339, ftn 107, see also 350, ftn 150. Moreover, a provision declaring the political existence of the State to be independent from recognition was included in Alvarez's project submitted to the 1927 meeting of the Committee of Jurists as Article 5 – "[t]his provision was approved without changes in 1927 and was then adopted as Article 3 of the Montevideo Convention." ibid 339. For the discussion about recognition during the 1927 meeting, see ibid 340–341. See also D'Aspremont, 'The International Law of Statehood and Recognition' (n 23) 23–24.

108 Grant, 'Defining Statehood' (n 13) 416, 414–418 and 447–448.

109 ibid 416.

110 See Resolution of Institut de droit international of 23 April 1936, which says "la reconnaissance d'un Etat nouveau est l'acte libre par lequel un ou plusieurs Etats constatent l'existence sur un territoire déterminé d'une société humaine politiquement organisée, indépendante de tout autre Etat existant, capable d'observer les prescriptions du droit international et manifestent en conséquence leur volonté de la considérer comme membre de la Communauté internationale. La reconnaissance a un effet déclaratif. L'existence de l'Etat nouveau avec tous les effets juridiques qui s'attachent à cette existence n'est pas affectée par le refus de reconnaissance d'un ou plusieurs Etats." Institut de droit international, Resolution (23 April 1936) (Session of Brussels), art 1. Two later and unsuccessful attempts at a definition of 'State' in international instruments included the Draft Declaration on Rights and Duties of States adopted by the ILC in 1949, which ultimately did not include the definition of 'State'; the ILC instead maintained that the term 'State' "is used in the sense commonly accepted by international practice." ILC, Yearbook of International Law Commission (1949) 259, para 21. Moreover, Fitzmaurice, as a Special Rapporteur on the law of treaties, suggested the following definition of state: "an entity consisting of a people inhabiting a defined territory, under an organized system of government, and having the capacity to enter into international relations binding the entity as such, either directly or through some other State." ILC, 'Report on the Law of Treaties by GG Fitzmaurice, Special Rapporteur' (14 March 1956) UN Doc A/CN.4/101, 107.

111 For example, it was held in the *Aaland Island* case "[t]he situation was such that, for a considerable time, the conditions required for the formation of a sovereign State did not exist. In the midst of revolution and anarchy, certain elements essential to the existence of a State, even some elements of fact, were lacking for a fairly considerable period … It is, therefore, difficult to say at what exact date the Finnish Republic, the legal sense of the term, actually became constituted sovereign State. This certainly did not take place until a stable political organisation had been created, and until public authorities had become strong enough to assert themselves throughout the territories of the State without the assistance of foreign troops." *Aaland Islands* case (n 1) 8–9. Moreover, in *Deutsche Continental Gas-Gesellschaft v Polish State*, it was held that "according to the opinion rightly admitted by the great majority of writers on international law, the recognition of

a State is not constitutive but merely declaratory. The State exists by itself (*par lui même*) and the recognition is nothing else than a declaration of this existence, recognised by the States from which it emanates … It was true that a State does not exist unless it fulfils the conditions of possessing a territory, a people inhabiting that territory, and a public power which is exercised over the people and the territory." *Deutsche Continental Gas-Gesellschaft v Polish State* (n 57) 13. In addition, the Badinter Commission held that "(a) the answer to the question should be based on the principles of public international law which serve to define the conditions on which an entity constitutes a state; that in this respect, the existence or disappearance of the state is a question of fact; that the effects of recognition by other states are purely declaratory; (b) that the state is commonly defined as a community which consists of a territory and a population subject to an organized political authority; that such a state is characterized by sovereignty." 'Opinion No 1 of the Arbitration Commission of Peace Conference for Yugoslavia' reprinted in (1992) 31 ILM 1494, 1495 and 'Opinion No 8 of the Arbitration Commission of Peace Conference for Yugoslavia' reprinted in (1992) 31 ILM 1494, 1522, para 1. For the ICTY's determination of whether Croatia fulfilled the Montevideo criteria of statehood on 8 October 1991 or at a later date, see *Prosecutor v Milošević* (Decision on Motion for Judgment of Acquittal) ICTY Trial Chamber Case No IT-02-54-T (16 June 2004), paras 85–115.

112 "Consequently, if the Czechoslovak nation has assumed on the ground of its sovereignty the *effective exercise of its sovereign rights* in the commune of Bratislava as a component part of its territory, in the same way as on its other territory, it is not possible to speak of a situation as existing merely in fact and requiring legal sanction by an international treaty or a treaty of peace. By this State-creating act the town of Bratislava ceased to form a part of the territory of the former Austro-Hungarian Monarchy." *Rights of Citizenship (Establishment of Czechoslovak State) Case* (Czechoslovakia, Supreme Administrative Court) (1921) 1 ILR 15, 16 (*emphasis added*). The domestic courts have also explicitly referred to the three elements doctrine or the four criteria included in Article 1 of the Montevideo Convention as the criteria of statehood. See for example, *Paul Clerget v Banque commercial pour l'Europe du nord et Banque du commerece extérieur du Vietnam* (Cour d'Appel de Paris) (1969) reprinted in (1970) RGDIP 522, 523; *In re Duchy of Sealand* (Federal Republic of Germany, Administrative Court of Cologne) (1979) 80 ILR 683, 685; *Democratic Republic of East Timor, Fretilin and Others v State of the Netherlands* (The Netherlands, District Court of the Hague) (1980) 87 ILR 73, 74–75, paras 3–7; *Morgan Guaranty Trust Company of New York and Others v Republic of Palau* (United States Court of Appeals, Second Circuit) (1991) 87 ILR 590, 653; *Klinghoffer and Others v SNC Achille Lauro and Others* (United States Court of Appeals, Second Circuit) (1991) 96 ILR 68, 73; *Kadic v Karadzic* (United States Court of Appeals, Second Circuit) (1995) 104 ILR 135, 157–158; *Caglar v Billingham (Inspector of Taxes) and Related Appeals* (England, Special Commission) (1996) 108 ILR 510, 542–545; *Parent and Others v Singapore Airlines Limited and the Civil Aeronautics Administration* (Canada, Quebec Supreme Court) (2003) 133 ILR 264, 280, para 54; *Civil Aeronautics Administration v Singapore Airlines Limited* (Singapore, Court of Appeal) (2004) 133 ILR 371, 382, para 30.

113 See, for example, F Pasquale, *International Law Codified and Its Legal Sanction: or, the Legal Organization of the Society of States* (Baker, Voorhis and company 1918) 106; R Erich, 'La naissance et la reconnaissance des Etats' (1926) 13 RCADI 427, 442 et seq.; G Morelli, 'Cours général de droit international public' (1956) 89 RCADI 437, 517–518; M Virally, 'Panorama du droit international contemporain: cours général de droit international public' (1983) 183 RCADI 9, 50–51. See also the references to the Montevideo criteria in international law textbooks including C Rousseau, *Droit international public* (Editions Sirey 1974), 15–17; I Brownlie, *Principles of Public International Law* (7th edn, OUP 2008) 70–72; S Besson, *Droit international public: abrégé de cours et résumés de jurisprudence* (2nd edn, Stämpfli Editions 2013) 33; M Dixon, R McCorquodale and S Williams, *Cases & Materials*

> même si elle est moins récurrente ou moins appuyée ces dernières années, l'affirmation apparemment corrélative qui veut que la naissance de l'État soit une question de fait reste l'un des principaux points d'accord des internationalistes.[114]

A declaratory theory of recognition, according to which recognition by other States is not constitutive, but merely declaratory of an already existing statehood,[115] complements this perception of statehood.[116] Other States are not legally obliged to recognise a new State;[117] the recognition is understood as a political act. Its legal relevance is mainly seen in terms of establishing formal bilateral relations between recognising and a new State.[118] The declaratory nature of recognition "is accepted as generally correct."[119] According to Crawford, "[a]mong writers the declaratory doctrine, with differences in

---

on International Law (6th edn, OUP 2016) 137 and 143. See also Restatement (Third) of the Foreign Relations Law of the United States (1987) paras 201 and 202. See also *infra* for the proponents of declaratory theory of recognition.

114 F Couveinhes-Matsumoto, *L'effectivité en droit international* (Bruylant 2014) 54.

115 See Clapham, *Brierly's Law of Nations* (n 15) 150–151.

116 A Peters, 'Statehood after 1989: "Effectivités" between Legality and Virtuality' (2010) 3 Proceedings of the European Society of International Law 171, 172.

117 But Grant defines the current understanding of declaratory theory more in terms of the duty to recognise. See TD Grant, *The Recognition of States* (n 30) 4.

118 Koskenniemi, *From Apology to Utopia* (n 6) 273.

119 Anderson (n 100) 368. In terms of practice supporting the declaratory theory, the following instances could be included: "The political existence of the state is independent of recognition by the other states. Even before recognition the state has the right to defend its integrity and independence, to provide for its conservation and prosperity, and consequently to organize itself as it sees fit, to legislate upon its interests, administer its services, and to define the jurisdiction and competence of its courts. The exercise of these rights has no other limitation than the exercise of the rights of other states according to international law." Montevideo Convention (n 99) art 3. "[T]he effects of recognition by other states are purely declaratory." 'Opinion No 1' (n 111) 1495. The same conclusion on the declaratory nature of recognition is in 'Opinion No 8' (n 111) 1523, para 2 and 'Opinion No 10 of the Arbitration Commission of Peace Conference for Yugoslavia' reprinted in (1992) 31 ILM, 1494, 1526, para 4. "Although recognition by other states is not, at least as a matter of theory, necessary to achieve statehood, the viability of a would-be state in the international community depends, as a practical matter, upon recognition by other states." *Re Reference By the Governor in Council Concerning Certain Questions Relating to the Secession of Quebec from Canada* (Canada, Supreme Court) (1998) 115 ILR 536, 589, para 142; UNGA Res 3314 (XXIX) (14 December 1974) UN Doc A/RES/3314(XXIX), Annex, Explanatory Note to Article 1: "In this Definition the term 'State': (a) Is used without prejudice to questions of recognition or to whether a State is a member of the United Nations." The ICJ in the Bosnian Genocide Case implicitly supported the declaratory theory of recognition when it treated a mutual non-recognition of Bosnia and Yugoslavia at the time

emphasis, predominates."[120] However, the declaratory theory does not automatically entail a pure factualist vision of statehood.[121]

3.2 *Underlying Rationales behind the Montevideo Criteria*

This factualist vision of statehood evolved as a response to voluntarist positivism.[122] Wildeman pointed out, "in a way the old difference between natural law doctrines and voluntarist doctrine became 'effectiveness' versus 'voluntarism'."[123] This evolution may be seen in the context of the influence of positivism with its reliance on a scientific objectivity of empirical facts.[124] From a practical perspective, the effectiveness "guarantees that the law is equipped with the means to meet its ends."[125] Indeed, "la légalité exige un minimum d'effectivité afin de pouvoir parler d'un Etat."[126]

> L'existence d'une autorité politique effective … capable de maintenir un certain degré d'ordre et de prémunir le nouvel Etat de l'anarchie, offre une garantie de respect des règles fondamentales du droit international

---

of the institution of proceedings on the basis of the Genocide Convention as "a defect in a procedural act which the applicant could easily remedy," while noting that the parties indeed mutually recognised each other later on in the 1995 Dayton Agreement. *Case Concerning Application of the Convention on the Prevention and Punishment of the Crime of Genocide (Bosnia and Herzegovina v Yugoslavia)* (Preliminary Objections) [1996] ICJ Rep 595, para 26. Domestic courts also explicitly supported the declaratory theory of recognition. See for example *Democratic Republic of East Timor, Fretilin and Others* (n 112) 74, para 3; *Kadic v Karadzic* (n 112) 158; *Parent and Others v Singapore Airlines* (n 112) 280, para 55; *Civil Aeronautics Administation v Singapore Airlines* (n 112) 382, para 31.

120 Crawford, *The Creation of States in International Law* (n 9) 25, and see ftn 109 for references therein. See also Restatement (Third) of the Foreign Relations Law of the United States (1987), para 202. For a modern constitutivist position, see (n 89).

121 For example, Crawford is an advocate of a declaratory theory of recognition, but also backs a legal perception of statehood. Crawford, *The Creation of States in International Law* (n 9) 96 et seq.

122 See Lauterpacht, *Recognition in International Law* (n 32) 32–38 and 61.

123 J Wildeman, 'The Philosophical Background of Effectiveness' (1977) 24 Netherlands International Law Review 335, 350.

124 "Positivism itself (the philosophical foundation of 'effectiveness'), as belief in the science of progress, physical achievement, on analogy with the natural sciences, will favour effectiveness." A Carty, *Philosophy of International Law* (Edinburgh University Press 2007) 85 (*footnotes omitted*).

125 Kreijen (n 100) 199.

126 MG Kohen, 'Création d'Etats en droit international contemporain' (2002) VI Cours euro-méditerranéens Bancaja de droit international 630.

> ou au moins, en cas de violation de ces règles, un destinataire pour la présentation des réclamations.[127]

In a way, this approach seeks to find equilibrium between both sides of the spectrum. On the one hand, it functions as the assurance against a virtual State, unable to fulfil its international legal obligations.[128] On the other hand, it ensures that where effective power exists, it is not left outside, but rather is subjected to rules and principles of international law of the highest standard – those applicable to States. Thus, ultimately, this approach limits a potential negative impact of both alternatives, which may result in the destabilisation of international legal order.[129]

3.3 *Classical Doctrinal View of Secession*

Deriving from the Montevideo criteria and a declaratory theory of recognition, the classical doctrinal view of secession is that it is merely the issue of fact, a meta-legal and a-legal phenomenon.[130] The fact of secession, the fact of the birth of a new State is seen in purely sociological and historical terms; Jellinek's normative power of factual has served as an intellectual explanation behind

---

127 T Christakis, 'The State as "Primary Fact": Some Thoughts on the Principle of Effectiveness' in MG Kohen (ed), *Secession: International Law Perspectives* (CUP 2006) 144. See also Hillgruber (n 89) 499–500.

128 Peters, 'Statehood after 1989' (n 116) 173–174.

129 For the former, see ibid 173.

130 On this point, see Christakis, 'The State as "Primary Fact"' (n 127) 141–145. A Tancredi, 'A Normative "Due Process" in the Creation of States through Secession' in MG Kohen (ed), *Secession: International Law Perspectives* (CUP 2006) 171–172. "Il s'agit là d'un processus historique dépendant des circonstances propres à chaque Etat, et qui ne répond à aucune loi, aucune norme, si ce n'est celles de l'histoire, dans la mesure où elles se distinguent de ses hasards." Virally, 'Panorama du droit international contemporain' (n 113) 50–51. "Once secession has succeeded, the effective exercise of State powers by the new authorities is sufficient to establish the existence of the new State." TM Franck and others, 'The Territorial Integrity of Québec in the Event of the Attainment of Sovereignty' in AF Bayefsky (ed), *Self-determination in International Law: Quebec and Lessons Learned: Legal Opinions* (Kluwer Law International 2000) 284; VD Degan, 'Création et disparition de l'Etat à la lumière du démembrement de trois fédérations multiethniques en Europe' (1999) 279 RCADI 199, 227 and 232; "[L]a sécession n'est pas prise en compte en elle-même par le droit international." "La sécession est un fait politique au regard du droit international, qui se contente d'en tirer les conséquences lorsqu'elle aboutit à la mise en place d'autorités étatiques effectives et stables." P Daillier and others, *Droit international public: formation du droit, sujets, relations diplomatiques et consulaires, responsabilité, règlement des différends, maintien de la paix, espaces internationaux, relations économiques, environnement* (8th edn, LGDJ 2009) 585.

a classical view that the statehood is simply a matter of pure fact outside of a legal regulation.[131] State is above all "un fait primaire dont prend acte le droit. Fait primaire veut dire un fait qui précède le droit."[132] Thus, essentially, international law is said to simply recognise the result of the power dynamics between the parent State and seceding territories, with the effectiveness of constitutive criteria being an overriding threshold in this regard. "The yardstick for measuring whether an entity has reached the status of statehood, is – from that facticist perspective – 'success or failure'."[133] This factual emergence precedes international law, which has nothing to say until the formation of a new State is complete. The status of an international legal person arises automatically from the fact of the physical formation of the State. "That an entity starts to behave and becomes treated like a State is a political process and not something created or controlled by the law".[134]

> Il n'y a pas de critère de droit … aspiration politique, elle se réalise politiquement par cette 'organisation de la puissance' qui dans l'esprit des hommes est traditionnellement associée au concept de l'Etat. L'ordre juridique international ne fonde pas l'Etat; il présuppose son existence.[135]

---

131 And for other areas of international law. Wildeman comes to the conclusion that *normative Kraft des Faktischen* plays a similar role to that of a contemporary understanding of effectiveness. See Wildeman (n 123) 345–346. See *infra* for details.

132 G Abi-Saab, 'Cours général de droit international public' (1987) 207 RCADI 9, 68. However, even according to Abi-Saab, the State is a legal fact, but nevertheless accentuates that State as a primary fact precedes the law. See G Abi-Saab, 'Conclusion' in MG Kohen (ed), *Secession: International Law Perspectives* (CUP 2006) 470–471.

133 Peters, 'Statehood after 1989' (n 116) 172. In this context it is important to mention a rather high threshold required by the so-called 'ultimate success theory,' which was developed in the US and UK case law and required that the parent State would actually give up its efforts at re-establishing its control over seceding territories or that there was certainty that the parent State would not have been successful at establishing such control. See Christakis, 'The State as "Primary Fact"' (n 127) 147–148. The theory dates back to *Williams v Bruffy* (1877) 96 US 176. See also *Autocephalous Greek-Orthodox Church of Cyprus and the Republic of Cyprus v. Goldberg and Feldman Fine Arts, Inc* (United States Court of Appeals, Seventh Circuit) 108 ILR 489, 505.

134 Koskenniemi, *From Apology to Utopia* (n 6) 272–273.

135 C De Visscher, *Théories et réalités en droit international public* (3rd edn, A Pedone 1960) 184–185 (*footnotes omitted*). This citation seems to echo Jellinek's theory of the normative force of the factual. "Les faits historiques qui engendrent la formation d'états nouveaux constituent des données pré-juridiques … L'ordre juridique international ne fonde pas l'Etat." ibid 212–213.

> L'identification d'Etat échappe à tout critère préétabli et n'obéit à aucune règle: elle est opérée de manière purement empirique, au gré des intérêts et des idéologies des membres de la "communauté" internationale.[136]

This understanding of the creation of the State and secession "acknowledges that not all situations are suited for being resolved by law".[137]

Several authors refer to the principle of effectiveness based on which factual situation or reality causes "hard facts to prevail over existing legal positions, or to effect by their own force changes in the existing law."[138] According to these writers, due to the structural characteristics of international law this principle "has a stronger and more widespread effect on a legal norm in international law than it does in municipal law."[139] Moreover, this principle has a privileged position concerning the creation of States. "Les effectivités tiennent une place de premier plan dans la théorie de la personnalité des Etats et, par conséquent, dans les conditions d'établissement et de disparition de l'ordre étatique".[140] "[L]'existence de l'Etat repose en principe exclusivement sur une effectivité, quelles que puissant être les circonstances – de droit ou de fait – qui ont permis qu'elle se réalise".[141]

4 Critical Re-assessment of the Classical Doctrinal View of Secession

Deriving from the Montevideo criteria and a declaratory theory of recognition, the following account challenges the classical doctrinal conceptualisation of secession as a mere question of fact, not regulated by international law. To do so, it revisits Georg Jellinek's and Hans Kelsen's works as their ideas are seen as influencing a factualist vision of statehood[142] and builds on the conclusions

136 J Verhoeven, 'L'Etat et l'ordre juridique international – remarques' (1978) 82 RGDIP 749, 753.

137 Peters, 'Statehood after 1989' (n 116) 172.

138 Summary of this reading of the principle by JHV Verzijl, *International Law in Historical Perspective*, vol I (AW Sijthoff-Leyden 1968) 293.

139 H Taki, 'Effectiveness' in MPEPIL (online edn, OUP 2013), para. 1.

140 C De Visscher, *Les effectivités du droit international public* (Pedone 1967) 36.

141 J Verhoeven, 'La reconnaissance internationale, déclin ou renouveau?' 39 (1993) AFDI 7, 38.

142 This may seem paradoxical, as both Jellinek and Kelsen are ranged among the authors of the constitutive theory of recognition. See *infra* on Jellinek's approach to the constitutive theory. See also Lauterpacht, *Recognition in International Law* (n 32) 38, footnote 2. For Kelsen, see Crawford, *The Creation of States in International Law* (n 9) 19, footnote 75 referring to Kelsen's later article H Kelsen, 'Recognition in International Law: Theoretical Observations' AJIL 35 (1941) 605. In his later work, Kelsen explicitly declared that he

of the above-mentioned historical analysis and insights from legal theory and philosophy.

4.1 *Revisiting Jellinek and Kelsen*

4.1.1 Common Background

It is no coincidence that the key texts on the issue of statehood and the origins of the State came from the German-speaking world of the late 19th and early 20th centuries. With respect to the legal perplexities of the German unification and under a strong influence of Hegel's philosophy,[143] a distinct school of German public law with its specific focus on the theory of the State (*Staatslehre*) developed there. Under Hegel's influence, historic and organic theories of the State were preferred to social contract theories.[144] By the turn of the century, the German-speaking world also witnessed the evolution of more extreme theories, including those that saw the State reduced to a mere expression of power or violence.[145]

Against this background, both Jellinek and Kelsen sought to reject an omnipotent, unbound and legally unchecked State and opposed monarchism, patrimonialism and absolutism.[146] Both jurists designed their theories based on a historical development that found its ultimate form in a modern, constitutional State (*Rechtsstaat*).[147] Accordingly, while Jellinek developed his vision of *Rechtsstaat* especially in his theory of auto-limitation,[148] Kelsen formulated

---

abandoned the declaratory theory. H Kelsen, *Principles of International Law* (2nd edn, Holt Rinehart and Winston 1966), 390, footnote 89.

143 For a short but poignant overview of the political situation and ensuing legal consequences, see R Portmann, *Legal Personality in International Law* (CUP 2010) 48–57; and particularly for the end of the 19th century, see M Koskenniemi, *The Gentle Civilizer of Nations: The Rise and Fall of International Law 1870–1960* (CUP 2001) 194–198.

144 Portmann (n 143) 55.

145 "Such theories were without illusion about the State. They were also politically dangerous. Either they made the legitimacy of State power suspect as ideological façade, or they dismissed public policy as altogether irrelevant in the determination of social order." Koskenniemi, *The Gentle Civilizer of Nations* (n 143) 196 and see 194–198. On the impact of Darwinism, see Wildeman (n 123) 342–343. See also JE Nijman (n 11) 112–113.

146 In respect of Jellinek, see O Jouanjan, 'Préface' in G Jellinek, *L'État moderne et son droit* (Éd Panthéon-Assas 2005) 64.

147 See H Kelsen, 'God and the State' in *Essays in Legal and Moral Philosophy* (D Reidel Publishing Company 1973) 75 and 81. See also G Jellinek, *L'État moderne et son droit* (Éd Panthéon-Assas 2005) 554.

148 Jellinek (n 147) 549–558. This draws on Kantian moral philosophy, according to which its "subject could bound himself or herself to rules." A Spadafora, 'Georg Jellinek on Values and Objectivity in the Legal and Political Sciences' (2015) 1 Modern Intellectual History 1, 19.

his theory of unity of the State and law. Kelsen sought to demonstrate that the State is "a human artefact, made by men and for men, and hence that nothing can be deduced *against* man from the nature of the state".[149] Briefly, his theory aimed at removing obstacles "in the path of *reforming* the state in the interest of the ruled".[150]

They were positivists writing under the influence of neo-Kantian philosophy. Two aspects were particularly relevant to their work. First, is a neo-Kantian premise on the issue of conceptualisation, ie that the science's object is determined by its method.[151] Second, is a Kantian premise on a clear separation

149 Kelsen, 'God and the State' (n 147) 81 (*emphasis in original*).

150 ibid (*emphasis in original*). "...Kelsen paradoxically did not embark on his project to liberate law and legal science from politics without ethical-political intentions. His rejection of the old conceptions of state, sovereignty and law was equally sustained by an ethical-political choice in favour of democracy or rather a defence of the individual against collective (post-Hegelian) freedom." JE Nijman (n 11) 179. *Contra*: J Kammerhofer, 'Book Review: JE Nijman, An Inquiry Into the History and Theory of International Law (2004)' (2008) 4 Netherlands International Law Review 304, 306–307.

151 See C Colliot-Thélène, 'Kelsen Reading Weber: Is a Sociological Concept of the State Possible?' in I Bryan and others (eds), *The Reconstruction of the Juridico-Political: Affinity and Divergence in Hans Kelsen and Max Weber* (Routledge 2016) 104. In particular, a neo-Kantian premise was that "l'*objet* de la connaissance n'est pas purement et simplement *donné*, il doit être *construit*." Jouanjan (n 146) 44 and for a neo-Kantian philosophy in Jellinek's work, see 43–54. For Jellinek, an empirical basis is indispensable, without it real knowledge is not possible. However, being aware of the limits of such knowledge, in particular the impossibility of reaching the object as it is, "jusqu'à ce point où la « chose en soi » repose...il est ramené, pour se faire un concept de l'objet et donc construire véritablement cet objet, à des fondations purement subjectives, des « hypothèses » qui lui viennent d'une prestation propre. Son *idéalisme* tient précisément en cela, en cette intimate d'un lien constitutif (et réciproque) entre l'objectif et le subjectif." ibid 49 (*emphasis in original*). According to Spadafora, Jellinek's writings suggest that he was neo-Kantian and empiricist at different times. Spadafora (n 148) 9. "In neo-Kantian theory, it is the research method chosen by the researchers following their subjective knowledge interest that constitutes the object of research. Jellinek, on the other hand, holds on to the objective existence of the object which gives way to a manifold of perspectives that has to be taken into account by the researcher." B Van Klink and OW Lembcke, 'Exploring the Boundaries of Law: On the Is–Ought Distinction in Jellinek and Kelsen' in S Taekema, B Van Klink and W de Been (eds), *Facts and Norms in Law: Interdisciplinary Reflections on Legal Method* (Edward Elgar Publishing 2016) 204–205 (*footnotes omitted*). Kelsen was undoubtedly influenced by neo-Kantism – "cognition cannot be passive in relation to its objects, it cannot be confined to reflecting things that are somehow given in themselves ... Cognition itself creates objects." H Kelsen, *General Theory of Law and State* (Harvard University Press 1945) 434–435 cited in Koskenniemi, *From Apology to Utopia* (n 6) 221, footnote 18. See for more S Hammer, 'A Neo-Kantian Theory of Legal Knowledge in Kelsen's Pure Theory of Law' in SL Paulson (ed), *Normativity and Norms: Critical Perspectives on Kelsenian Themes* (OUP 1999) 181–186. "I seek to apply the transcendental method to a theory of positive law

between 'is' and 'ought'.[152] These elements, however, were articulated rather divergently in their individual works.

4.1.2 Jellinek: Three-Elements Doctrine and the Normative Force of the Factual

An apparent underlying tension between Jellinek's subscription to positivism and a neo-Kantian separation of *Sein* and *Sollen* and his growing interest in sociology shaped his theory of the State.[153] To build this theory, Jellinek adopted different perspectives depending on different functions of the State, namely "the creation and maintenance of both the social order and the legal order".[154] Accordingly, in his General Theory of the State (*Allgemeine Staatslehre*) Jellinek designed a famous two-sided theory of the State, which regarded "the State from two aspects, or as two functions, which are characteristic of the State as a political and legal entity".[155] For Jellinek, the State from a social perspective was a "unitary association"[156] and from a legal perspective was a "corporation."[157]

... just as Kant's transcendental philosophy energetically opposes all metaphysics, so the Pure Theory of Law takes aim at the natural law, which in the field of social reality generally and in the field of positive law in particular, corresponds exactly to metaphysics." Letter from Hans Kelsen to Renato Treves dated 3 August 1933 published in H Kelsen, 'The Pure Theory of Law, "Labandism", and Neo-Kantianism. A Letter to Renato Treves' in SL Paulson (ed), *Normativity and Norms: Critical Perspectives on Kelsenian Themes* (OUP 1999) 171–172.

152 For Kant, this division was important as a tool for protecting free will and morals from the pervasive effects of physical science. See Wildeman (n 123) 341 and 344. For Jellinek's subscription to the distinction between *Sein* and *Sollen* see Spadafora (n 148) 9 and *infra*.

153 Spadafora (n 148) 6–7.

154 B Van Klink and OW Lembcke (n 151) 205. See *supra* on how this methodology does not corresponds to a pure neo-Kantianism.

155 G Donhauser, 'The State under the Rule of Law? The Relationship of State and Law in the Work of Hans Kelsen and Georg Jellinek' in I Bryan and others (eds), *The Reconstruction of the Juridico-Political: Affinity and Divergence in Hans Kelsen and Max Weber* (Routledge 2016) 129.

156 "The State is the unitary association of resident persons with original sovereign power." B Van Klink and OW Lembcke (n 151) 206. "L'Etat est l'unité d'association, composé d'hommes sédentaires et dotée originairement de la puissance de domination." Jellinek (n 147) 292.

157 "As a legal conception, the state is ... the corporation of a resident people with original sovereign power." B Van Klink and OW Lembcke (n 151) 206. "Comme concept juridique l'Etat est donc *la corporation d'une nation sédentaire dotée originairement d'une puissance dominatrice*." Jellinek (n 147) 296 (*emphasis in original*). See also Donhauser (n 155) 129.

> There is no immediate access to the thing called state … The point is to grasp 'the internal connection between the disciplines that both represent the general theory of the state' and to avoid 'the subsequent error' that you could capture the complexity of state with only one side of theory without taking account of the other side.[158]

Importantly, in Jellinek's theory "law is preceded by State".[159] "L'État, en réalité, est avant tout une formation historique et sociale, à laquelle s'ajoute ensuite le droit, qu'elle ne saurait créer, mais dont elle est au contraire la condition d'existence".[160] In particular, the secondary formation of States, ie the transformation of already existing States, results from the facts, which are completely outside of the domain of law.[161] "La formation d'un État nouveau est donc accomplie lorsque, en fait, se trouvent indubitablement réunis, dans le cas donné, tous les éléments essentiels d'un État et que l'association ainsi formée est capable d'exercer les fonctions d'un État."[162] Law does not regulate the formation of a State;[163] it is formed upon the reunion of its essential elements. In both the above-mentioned definitions, three elements stand out – people, territory and power. Thereby, Jellinek formulated his three-elements doctrine of the State. While it is true that scholars formulated the definitions of States similar to this doctrine even prior to Jellinek, they mostly depended on the above-mentioned historical contexts.[164]

---

158 B Van Klink and OW Lembcke (n 151) 205–206 (*footnote omitted*). The authors refer to Jellinek's Allgemeine Staatshlehre.

159 Donhauser (n 155) 129. "Jellinek argued for the claim that the birth of a new state is an extra-legal fact by relying on a proof by contradiction." Kalmo (n 2) 115 and see 115–118.

160 Jellinek (n 147) 424.

161 ibid 418.

162 ibid 430.

163 ibid 423. "L'existence d'un État ne peut dériver que de sa propre volonté." ibid 424.

164 It should be noted that a spatial element was not really present in the post-Westphalian 17th and 18th century doctrine focusing on statehood, which "laid emphasis rather on population, collective will, and government than on territory." D-E Khan, 'Territory and Boundaries' in B Fassbender and A Peters, *The Oxford Handbook of the History of International Law* (OUP 2012) 234. Prior to Jellinek other authors, including Phillimore, Hall and Lorimer, referred to similar criteria. However, these criteria were formulated in a theoretical context different from Jellinek's, making their conceptualization of facts different. See *supra*. Grant refers to other, similar definitions of statehood, but without distinguishing to which school of thought these authors belonged. Grant, 'Defining Statehood' (n 13) 416–418. In addition, similar criteria were also only used in the context of the definition of existing States; see for example Antoine Pillet, referred to in Becker Lorca (n 105) 307.

Jellinek's theory of the State introduced the so-called normative power of the factual (*normative Kraft des Faktischen*) linking the spheres of *Sein* and *Sollen*.[165] In this theory, "Jellinek called attention to the tendency of habitually performed actions to generate a psychological sense of normative force."[166] "Might becomes right by the psychological mechanism in the minds of the ruled."[167] Jellinek linked this theory in particular with events such as the formation of States, revolutions and coups.[168]

> La transformation de la puissance de l'État, qui partout n'est qu'un pur fait, en une puissance juridique, a toujours lieu sous l'influence de l'idée que cette donnée réelle est d'ordre normative, et qu'il faut que les choses soient telles qu'elles sont. Il y a donc là un processus d'ordre purement interne; c'est dans le cerveau des hommes qu'il s'accomplit.[169]

However, the above account of Jellinek's vision must be nuanced on two grounds. First, Jellinek was in fact a constitutivist. "L'État est tel par son organisation intérieure; mais il n'entre dans la communauté du droit international que si les membres de cette communauté l'ont reconnu expressément ou tacitement."[170] In fact, Lauterpacht criticised Jellinek's formulation of the constitutive doctrine, which differentiated between a natural statehood independent of recognition and membership in the international community as a legal person occurring via recognition.[171] Notwithstanding, according to Jellinek, the State as an international legal person did not simply grow out of the facts on the ground, but became as such by the virtue of recognition.

Second, even though *normative Kraft des Faktischen* appears to offer a seemingly simple and appealing explanation behind the transformation of the might into right, Jellinek's writings offer a more delicate perspective.

165 Jellinek insisted "there was a difference between separating 'is' and 'ought' to avoid confusing indicative and imperative propositions, and disallowing any connection between the two." Spadafora (n 148) 17.

166 ibid 21.

167 Wildeman (n 123) 345. See also Jellinek (n 147) 516–517.

168 Jellinek (n 147) 516–517.

169 ibid 517.

170 ibid 423.

171 "It seems irrelevant to predicate that a community exists as a State unless such existence is treated as implying legal consequences." Lauterpacht, *Recognition in International Law* (n 32) 39. See also J Von Bernstorff, 'Georg Jellinek and the Origins of Liberal Constitutionalism in International Law' (2012) 4 Goettingen Journal of International Law 659, 672, ftn 50.

According to Jellinek, a psychological element behind such a transformation is not sufficient. "[I]l faut, pour compléter le concept de droit, qu'il s'y ajoute des garanties de ce droit, ainsi dérivé de rapports de forces … À ces garanties s'ajoutent celles qui résultent de la forme des institutions politiques."[172] "Thus, to assert that Jellinek based his concept of law solely on the notion of power is to obscure the fact that this writer deemed the concept of legitimacy as a necessary component or criterion of the validity of law."[173]

4.1.3 Kelsen: Statehood and the Principle of Effectiveness

To understand Kelsen's theory of the State, it is important to highlight his critique of Jellinek and a traditional *Staatslehre*. Adhering to a neo-Kantian premise that the science's object is determined by its method, Kelsen believed that there could not be different methods for a single object.[174] Accordingly, by maintaining a dualistic character of the State – a sociological and legal one – previous doctrine and Jellinek were incorrect from a methodological point of view; therefore, values and power relations unduly interfered into what should have been only a legal analysis.[175]

Thus, since for Kelsen there was only one object of cognition, he formulated his theory of unity of law and the State – "stateless theory of the State."[176] For Kelsen, "the state is a relatively centralized legal order."[177] From the premise that legal order and the State were the same followed that the State's emergence could be identified with the beginning of the temporal sphere of validity of the legal order. Thus, the State's emergence was intrinsically linked with the issue of validity of legal order as understood in Kelsen's theory.

---

172 Jellinek (n 147) 517–518.

173 S Turmanidze, 'Status of the De Facto State in Public International Law: A Legal Appraisal of the Principle of Effectiveness' (LLD Disseration, University of Hamburg 2010) 28 and, for other views on this issue in German, see 24–29. See also Von Bernstorff (n 171) 669–670; M Stolleis, *Public Law in Germany, 1800–1914* (Berghahn 2000) 442.

174 See Colliot-Thélène (n 151) 104.

175 See J Feichtinger, 'Intellectual Affinities: Ernst Mach, Sigmund Freud, Hans Kelsen and the Austrian Anti-Essentialist Approach to Science And Scholarship' in I Bryan and others (eds), *The foundation of the Juridico-political: Concept Formation in Hans Kelsen and Max Weber* (Routledge 2016) 121–122. SL Paulson, 'The Purity Thesis' (2018) 31 Ratio Juris 276, 283 and 291–296. Similarly, Kelsen was also critical of Max Weber's sociological concept of the State and initially even completely rejected the possibility of any other than a legal conception of State. Kelsen's views however evolved in this regard. See Colliot-Thélène (n 151) 106–107.

176 Kelsen, 'God and the State' (n 147) 81–82; Feichtinger (n 175) 121.

177 Kelsen, *Pure Theory of Law* (n 2) 286.

It is truism to say that for Kelsen the reason for the validity of legal order was a presupposed basic norm, *Grundnorm*.[178] In this basic norm, the fact of creation and effectiveness were made condition of the validity of the legal order.[179] According to Kelsen, the legal order was valid *because* the basic norm was presupposed to be valid, but it was valid only *as long as* this legal order was *by and large* effective.[180] Thus, according to Kelsen, "effectiveness is a condition for the validity – but it is not validity"[181] because "a condition cannot be identical with that which it conditions."[182]

For Kelsen, the reason for the validity of national legal order varied depending on the perspective one took vis-à-vis the relationship between international and national legal orders.[183] If one took a monist theory with the primacy of national legal order, then the reason for the validity of national legal order was a presupposed basic norm of this national legal order, which was at the same time also the reason for the validity of international law.[184] However, if one adopted monism with the primacy of international law, the reason for the validity of individual national legal order was not a presupposed basic norm, but a norm of positive international law.[185] Then, the reason for the validity of international law was a presupposed basic norm, which was also at the same time an indirect reason for validity of individual national legal orders.[186]

In all his works, Kelsen started from the premise that positive international law determined what a State was. "Seul un ordre supérieur de l'État peut contenir les règles qui fixent le critère de la formation de l'Etat."[187] More specifically,

> si l'on envisage la question du passage d'un simple état de fait à un état de droit, c'est-a-dire de la justification d'un fait par le droit, de sa légitimation, il est évidemment impossible de trouver cette justification dans

178 ibid 212.
179 ibid.
180 ibid.
181 ibid 213.
182 ibid 212.
183 See also in detail, H Kelsen, 'Les rapports de système entre le droit interne et le droit international public' (1926) 14 RCADI 227, 263–326.
184 Kelsen, *Pure Theory of Law* (n 2) 214.
185 ibid 214–215.
186 ibid 215. However, it should be noted that for Kelsen, both monist conceptions were "equally correct and equally justified." ibid 346. The decision for either of them cannot be made within the science of law; "it can be made only on the basis of nonscientific, political considerations." ibid.
187 Kelsen, 'La naissance de l'État' (n 68) 613.

> le fait même à justifier. Le recours à un ordre supérieur, donc au droit international apparaît nécessaire.[188]

"If states are subjects of international law, this law must determine what a state is ... if international law did not determine what a state is, then its norms would not be applicable."[189] According to Kelsen, based upon the observation of practice,[190] positive international law contained the rule of a customary nature "principe juridique de l'effectivité"[191] that determined the birth of a new State.[192] This was in agreement with Kelsen's monist conception with the primacy of international law based on which the reason for the validity of national legal order was a positive norm of international law.[193]

The establishment of a new effective legal order required constitution, which was not only elaborated, but also applied on the ground in accordance with its provisions; equally, the will of the population was not relevant, but what mattered was the fact that this new legal order was regularly obeyed. Moreover, the way that this new legal order's effectiveness was reached was not decisive, "ce qui est décisif, et seul décisif, c'est l'effectivité de l'autorité nouvelle, c'est l'efficacité de l'ordre nouveau."[194]

In his earlier works, Kelsen completely rejected the constitutive theory of recognition and its distinction between a *de facto* State formed upon the

---

188 ibid 615.

189 Kelsen, *Principles of International Law* (n 142) 387.

190 Kelsen in his article 'La naissace de l'État et la formation de sa nationalité: les principes; leur application au cas de la Tchécoslovaquie' does not provide an extensive overview of practice that would support his view, but mostly provides logical arguments and applications of his thesis to the case of inter-war Czechoslovakia. Kelsen, 'La naissance de l'État' (n 68) 613 et seq.

191 Kelsen, 'La naissance de l'État' (n 68) 618.

192 "[U]n Etat est formé lorsqu'un ordre de contrainte relativement souverain, c'est-à-dire dépendant exclusivement du droit des gens, se crée et devient efficace sur un territoire donné et vis-à-vis d'une population donnée." ibid 614. In Pure Theory of Law, Kelsen describes this norm as follows: "A government which, independent of other governments, exerts effective control over the population of a certain territory, is the legitimate government; and that the population that lives under such a government in this territory constitutes a 'state' in the meaning of international law, regardless of whether this government exerts this effective control on the basis of a previously existing constitution or one established by revolution." Kelsen, *Pure Theory of Law* (n 2) 212.

193 "The time when a state begins to exist, that is, the moment when a national legal order begins to be valid ... is determined by positive international law according to the principle of effectiveness." Kelsen, *Principles of International Law* (n 142) 382.

194 Kelsen, 'La naissance de l'État' (n 68) 620 and see 615–616.

fulfilment of three criteria[195] and a *de jure* State created upon the recognition by other States because from the point of view of legal science "si … on affirme l'existence d'un Etat … ce ne peut être que l'affirmation d'un fait d'ordre juridique: il s'agit donc nécessairement d'un Etat … *de jure*."[196]

Nevertheless, in his later work, Kelsen, although still maintaining that general international law provided under what criteria "a community has to be considered a state", also added that recognition functioned as the procedure "to decide whether or not in a concrete case a community fulfils these conditions and therefore is, or is not, a state in the sense of international law."[197] This need for recognition was seen as "a consequence of the far-reaching decentralization of international law."[198] Ultimately, for Kelsen, the legal existence of a State under international law was only a relative one, "a state legally exists only in relation to other subjects of international law."[199] "There is no such a thing as absolute existence."[200]

4.1.4 Jellinek and Kelsen: Synthesis, Divergence and Impact on Future Debate

For both Jellinek and Kelsen, opening up to the factual realm was motivated by an attempt at finding balance. They[201] rejected both an idealist view of a

195 Kelsen rejected Jellinek's three-elements doctrine as tautological, as each of the three elements – people, territory and power – "can be determined only juridically, that is, they can be comprehended only as validity and the spheres of validity of legal order." Kelsen, *Pure Theory of Law* (n 2) 287 and see 287–290; M Troper, 'Kelsen, Weber and the Problem of the Emergence of the State' in I Bryan and others (eds), *The Reconstruction of the Juridico-Political: Affinity and Divergence in Hans Kelsen and Max Weber* (Routledge 2016) 111–112. "Thus, these three elements cannot define the State because they are themselves defined by the State." ibid 112. Moreover, Kelsen also rejected Jellinek's theory of the normative force of the factual on the grounds that "l'inclination naturelle consistant à s'attacher à ce qui se répète et à organiser sa répétition ne constitue pas la justification juridique d'un *Sollen*, dans la mesure où il s'agit d'un *Sein*. La théorie de Jellinek n'est donc qu'une explication « historico-psychologique »." H Kelsen, *Hauptprobleme der Staatsrechtslehre. Entwickelt aus der Lehre vom Rechtssatze* (Scientia Verlag Aalen 1984) (reprinted 2nd edn of 1923) 9–10 cited in Couveinhes-Matsumoto (n 114) 20, footnote 73.

196 Kelsen, 'La naissance de l'État' (n 68) 617.

197 Kelsen, *Principles of International Law* (n 142) 391.

198 ibid.

199 ibid 393.

200 Kelsen, 'Recognition in International Law' (n 142) 609.

201 Jellinek believed that those who promoted a purely legal order excluding values, purposes and politics, "simply introduced political and other values unconsciously into their construction of legal doctrine, often from natural law, and thus *could not* guarantee objectivity or legal certainty by excluding all values." Spadafora (n 148) 10. For Jellinek, "without a way of rationally determining which basic values should be reflected in the legal order,

complete lack of connection between law's validity and effectiveness[202] and a realist position of a complete equation between law's validity and effectiveness.[203] In Kelsen's words, it was an attempt to find a "middle road" between the two.[204] Yet, they approached this end differently.

The question arises as to what extent this balancing act was successful and what the conceptualisation of the factual element in their works entailed for the connection between statehood and international law later on. Indeed, as pointed out by Tucker, "the more extensive the application of the rule of effectiveness the nearer does this system of international law approach an identification with power."[205]

The factual element might be viewed as posing a risk for the legal order. With respect to Jellinek's theory, Kelsen believed Jellinek's dualistic conception of the State and law was in fact "nothing but power."[206] Moreover, according to Kelsen, it "continually displaces the origin of the State beyond a hierarchy of legal norms"[207] and enables "the conjuring trick of construing law out of non-law, and a legal act out of a naked act of power."[208]

Kelsen's incorporation of effectiveness is even more shocking as his pure theory of law proclaimed a blunt separation of *Sein* and *Sollen* and explicitly rejected any influence of power or values. Yet, in Kelsen's presupposed basic norm, the effectiveness of legal order is made a condition of its validity. According to some authors, Kelsen succeeded in his balancing act because effectiveness as the condition for validity remains 'outside' of the normative system.[209] However, other scholars doubted the actual value of Kelsen's

---

and without being able in turn to exclude all consideration of values and purposes from law … it might appear that law was so shot through with arbitrariness that it was a mere function of will or power, lacking both legitimacy and any objective certainty in its application." ibid 14–15.

202 Jellinek openly deviated from hardline positivists, acknowledging that the "use of the legal method alone would lead to a fruitless scholasticism detached from the realities that produced and altered the law over time." Spadafora (n 148) 17.

203 Kelsen, *Pure Theory of Law* (n 2) 211.

204 ibid 211. See for Jellinek's approach Spadafora (n 148) 15.

205 R Tucker, 'The Principle of Effectiveness in International Law' in GA Lipsky (ed.), *Law and Politics in the World Community: Essays on Hans Kelsen's Pure Theory and Related Problems in International Law* (University of California Press 1953) 33.

206 Troper (n 195) 112.

207 I Bryan and others, 'Introduction: Affinity and Divergence' in I Bryan and others (eds), *The Reconstruction of the Juridico-Political: Affinity and Divergence in Hans Kelsen and Max Weber* (Routledge 2016) 10.

208 Kelsen, 'God and the State' (n 147) 77.

209 Wildeman (n 123) 347. See also E Pasquier, *De Genève À Nuremberg: Carl Schmitt, Hans Kelsen et le droit international* (Classiques Garnier 2012) 244.

insistence on the fact that effectiveness is merely a condition of the validity of legal order and not the validity itself. In fact, several scholars saw this interlinkage between the validity and effectiveness as a denial of Kelsen's main premise resulting in a complete mix of *Sein* and *Sollen*.[210] Some authors called it "le paradoxe de Kelsen."[211] "Il est patent que, sur la question de la validité de l'ordre juridique, le *Sein* et le *Sollen* sont complètement confondus."[212] Thus, ultimately, the existence of a real difference between Jellinek's theory and Kelsen's approach has been put into question.[213]

However, despite the undoubted importance of the factual element in the theory of the creation of States for both jurists, facts never stand on their own. Mere power or facts never *ipso facto* created the State as a legal person, but conceptually the facts were always intrinsically linked to some other legal tool or law.

As far as Jellinek's theory is concerned, it is true that the State's sociological formation always preceded the law.[214] However, as already mentioned above, this factual existence of the State did not equate with the creation of the State as a legal person – this only happened by virtue of recognition.[215] Thus, as far as international law was concerned, recognition in Jellinek's theory can be seen as the expression of his adherence to voluntarist positivism. Moreover, as also mentioned above, even *normative Kraft des Faktischen* was not conceived as operating only through a psychological element of repetition, but required complementarity with legal guarantees and legitimacy of the legal order itself.

---

210 See in this regard N Bobbio, 'Kelsen et le problème du pouvoir' in *Essai de théorie du droit* (LGDJ 1981) 562–569 cited in Pasquier (n 209) 115, footnote 1. See also, in a similar critical sense, M Virally, *La pensée juridique* (LGDJ 1960) xiii, footnote 12, xiv and xviii.

211 See JF Karvégan, 'Le paradoxe de Kelsen' <http://www.ekouter.net/le-paradoxe-de-kelsen-avec-jean-francois-kervegan-a-l-universite-de-belgrade-5615> accessed 30 November 2016.

212 Couveinhes-Matsumoto (n 114) 23.

213 Friedman finds Kelsen's approach comparable with Jellinek's normative force of the factual. "How can the minimum of effectiveness be proved except by an inquiry into political and social facts?" WG Friedmann, *Legal Theory* (4th edn, Stevens & Sons 1960) 238–239; Kreijen (n 100) 224. See also C Bezemek, 'The "Normative Force of the Factual": A Positivist's Panegyric' in N Bersier Ladavac, C Bezemek and F Schauer (eds), *The Normative Force of the Factual: Legal Philosophy Between Is and Ought* (Springer 2019) 75.

214 Nevertheless, it is interesting that in passing Jellinek acknowledged the possibility of a purely legal formation of the State. "Seul celui qui croit pouvoir considérer l'Etat comme une institution exclusivement juridique, peut poser la question du fondement juridique de l'Etat concret." Jellinek (n 147) 424.

215 The same point is emphasized by F Münch, 'La force normative des faits' in *Estudios de Derecho Internacional: Homenaje al profesor Miaja de la Muela* (Editorial Tecnos 1979) 252.

Kelsen's theory represented an opposition to arbitrariness and subjectivism of theory of recognition of the voluntarist positivism. Kelsen grounded the legal existence of the State not in an arbitrary will of other States, but in their factual existence. In this respect, Kelsen's theory may be seen as an attempt at finding objectiveness in the facts, in the social reality itself.[216] However, these facts did not operate on their own. It was international law that established which factual criteria would bring about the State's legal emergence. For Kelsen, the principle of effectiveness was a positive rule of customary international law. Thus, ultimately, international law preceded the State both as a factual entity and international legal person. Nevertheless, this view was dependent on Kelsen's theory of validity of international law, which was itself conditioned by its effectiveness. Lastly, Kelsen ultimately subscribed to the constitutive theory of recognition, not as a voluntarist, but because of his conclusion that some sort of cognition and procedure independent of facts themselves was needed. In his view, "in the realm of law, there is no fact 'in itself,' no immediately evident fact."[217]

4.2 *Theoretical Weaknesses of a Classical Doctrinal View of Secession*

According to a classical view, secession is merely the issue of fact, a meta-legal and a-legal phenomenon.[218] This factual formation precedes international law, which has nothing to say until a new State's birth is complete. However, such a perception of the role of facts in the State-creation outside of any external point of reference was neither present nor intended in Jellinek's and Kelsen's writings. More subtle elements of their work were overlooked by a subsequent doctrine.

Moreover, as shown, the role of facts independent of any theoretical framework does not have any historical parallel. Even though over the centuries a *de facto* independence from the parent State has been an important, presupposed factor, in broad terms its reception in law was always linked to natural law, legitimism and voluntarist positivism. The latter two operated only via the act of recognition. Thus, in a clean break from previous tradition, which always linked the facts with a larger theoretical framework, the 'effectiveness' of the

216 "Il y a une objectivité du droit qui n'est pas une objectivité ontologique (ou "naturelle"), ni complètement subjective … L'objectivité du droit est donc fondée dans la société. Elle dépend d'une "effectivité" suffisante, liée à une intersubjectivité, qui définit un espace stable de croyance, plus fort qu'une simple subjectivité isolée, sans avoir toutefois la force de l'être-même." Pasquier (n 209) 114.

217 Kelsen, *Principles of International Law* (n 142) 388.

218 See (n 130).

Montevideo criteria as conceptualised by a classical doctrine was devoid of any such an external point of reference. The facts have been simply considered to be self-evident and self-explanatory.

Moreover, this understanding does not stand on a sound theoretical and logical basis. Indeed, as is further explained below, the facts do not simply occur outside of an external point of reference, but require construction based on some pre-existing framework.[219] Relatedly, this theory also lacks an explanatory force as to why only three specific criteria should be taken into account and not others; indeed, the very idea of constitutive criteria requires that these criteria be singled out from some external viewpoint.[220]

Furthermore, a factualist vision of statehood evolved as a reaction to voluntarist positivism. The turn to facts occurred as a reaction to the arbitrariness of the constitutive theory. The underlying assumption was that only the empiricism of pure facts seen as endowed with an inherent objectivity would function as a barrier against the deep-rooted flaws of the constitutive theory. However, declaring that the creation of the State was simply a historical and political event, the factualist theory achieves the complete opposite of the original motives behind the turn to effectiveness. While the original aim was to remove the arbitrariness of the constitutive theory, the principle of effectiveness in this version allowed for the arbitrariness to come through the back door, as it was inherent to any situation supposedly outside of the realm of legal regulation.

In addition, this view of the State as 'a primary fact' is frequently supported by reference to the anthropomorphic views of the State. It is often argued that in the same way as a person's birth is purely a factual event that cannot be regulated by municipal law, the State's emergence also escapes the purview of international law. "States, like natural persons in municipal law, attain legal personality at birth; that is, they are 'born' subjects of international law."[221]

However, this argument is flawed on two levels. First, the analogy between the State and natural person is anachronistic as a matter of general principle.[222]

---

219 See *infra*.

220 See *infra*.

221 S Talmon, 'The Constitutive Versus the Declaratory Theory of Recognition: Tertium Non Datur?' (2005) 75 BYBIL 101, 106. "Il y a là des faits qui se suffisent à eux-mêmes, même s'ils sont dus à des conduites criminelles dont les responsables peuvent ou doivent être amenés à rendre compte. De la même manière qu'un enfant né d'un viol ou d'une relation adultérine est tout autant un sujet de droit que celui-ci qui est né de la relation consentante entre deux époux légitimes." J Verhoeven, 'Sur les "bons" et les "mauvais" emplois du jus cogens' (2008) 5 Annuario brasileiro de direito internacional 133, 152.

222 S Wheatley, 'The Emergence of New States in International Law: The Insights from Complexity Theory' (2016) 15 Chinese Journal of International Law 579, 586. J

As early as 1917, Dickinson pointed to the numerous defects of this analogy and its unhealthy effect on the methodology and content of international law.[223] In particular, he highlighted that while "[h]uman beings are physical entities created by the natural processes of reproduction", "[i]nternational persons are corporate entities" created via the accepted methods of State succession.[224] These divergences require caution when applying ready-to-use analogies.

Second, on a more concrete level, the objective of the approximation between a natural person's birth and the State is to reject the role of the law in these processes. This argument, however, does not work either. Although a human being's birth is undoubtedly a factual event, the translation of this physical reality into the legal status of a physical person endowed with a legal personality operates through the prism of municipal law.[225] Indeed, for example, the history of slavery shows the birth of a human being did not always automatically entail the legal personality.[226] "Legal personality is a creature of law, not of nature."[227]

4.3 *Principle of Effectiveness Is a Legal Rule*

When one follows Kelsen's reasoning, the idea of a rule of customary international law – the principle of effectiveness – determining the criteria of statehood and their effective fulfilment, comes into play. The idea that positive international law as an anterior code predetermines the criteria of statehood is in line with the basic elements of legal theory and philosophy. "Facts alone are powerless to create law. For facts to have significance an anterior legal system

---

D'Aspremont, 'The International Law of Statehood: Craftsmanship for the Elucidation and Regulation of Births and Deaths in the International Society' (2013) 29 Connecticut Journal of International Law 201, 212–213.

223 ED Dickinson, 'The Analogy Between Natural Persons and International Persons in the Law of Nations' (1917) 26 Yale Law Journal 564, 581–591.

224 ibid 588. Skinner determines the origins of the view of the State as a legal person in Hobbes' theory. For the reception of Hobbes' theory in continental Europe and the subsequent evolution of thought in Q Skinner, see 'A Genealogy of the Modern State' (2009) 162 Proceedings of the British Academy 325, 346–360.

225 "These legal orders [national legal systems] define the moment that a physical individual comes into being as well as the moment it disappears as a subject of the law. It registers the individual administratively and defines his legal capacities at various ages and conditions and positions. The internal law, likewise, defines various kinds of juridical persons, the manner in which they come into being, the extent of their capacity, how they are registered and their dissolution." Blix (n 17) 596.

226 The same argument as Lauterpacht, *Recognition in International Law* (n 32) 45.

227 ibid.

must be assumed to exist which invests facts with normative sense."[228] In this context, Salmon stated that "une grande partie de ce qu'il est convenu d'appeler "le réel" ne s'intéresse pas le droit. Le droit n'est pas concerné par ce qu'il ne régit pas. Il ne s'embarrasse que des faits qu'il a prédéterminé."[229]

It is a mistake to consider legal consequences flowing from certain conditions as questions of law and the presence of these conditions as questions of fact; they are both questions of law.[230] Similarly, "not facts, but norms are the source of legal right; hence only the validation of facts – through a principle of law which in effect considers these facts as law creating facts – can give rise to new legal rights and duties."[231] To capture a fact entails its reconstruction in legal terms, which presupposes the existence of legal categories.[232]

Apart from Kelsen, other writers have also reasoned about the existence of a rule of international law.[233] In addition, international

---

228 Koskenniemi, *From Apology to Utopia* (n 6) 274. See also A Beaudouin, *Uti possidetis et sécession* (Éditions Dalloz 2011) 614–623.

229 J Salmon, 'La construction juridique du fait en droit international' (1987) 32 Archives de philosophie du droit 136, 140. See also Taki (n 139) para 4.

230 Tucker (n 205) 41.

231 ibid 37.

232 D'Aspremont (n 222) 206. D'Aspremont divides the doctrine "between the *facticists* and the *legalists*, that is, between those arguing that statehood is a fact and those arguing that statehood is a legal construction" and "between the *objectivists* and the *subjectivitsts*, that is, between those contending that statehood is objectively ascertained by international law and those arguing that international law accommodates inter-subjectivity in the determination of statehood." Ibid 204 (*emphasis in original*). According to D'Aspremont, a consensus emerged between the factisists and legalists according to which "state creation is a factual process but the state itself is a legal construct." ibid 205. However, as outlined in the present book, this general consensus in the doctrine is yet to be reached. See also Wheatley (n 222) 583–584. On the question of subjectivity and objectivity, see *infra* Chapter 5.

233 For example, Lauterpacht maintained that "when we assert that a State exists as a normal subject of international law by virtue of the fact of its existence, we must necessarily have in mind a State fulfilling the conditions of statehood as laid down by international law." Lauterpacht, *Recognition in International Law* (n 32) 45. According to Morelli, "[i]l appartient évidemment à l'ordre international lui-même de fixer les caractères que l'entité existante de fait doit posséder pour qu'elle devienne destinataire des normes générales du même ordre international. Ces caractères sont fixés par la coutume internationale." Morelli (n 113) 517. "Although Kelsen may not have gauged all the implications of his own reasoning, he was right when he declared that, from a legal point of view, the birth of a new sovereign state is, properly speaking never a question de facto but always *de jure*." Kalmo (n 2) 131. Similarly, Tucker claimed the fact "state" and the legal consequences attached to it, were determined by the rule of general international law, the principle of effectiveness. Tucker (n 205) 40–41. Cassese claimed, "*it is possible to infer* from the body of customary rules granting basic rights and duties to States that these rules presuppose certain general

judiciary[234] and domestic courts[235] have supported the existence of a customary rule determining the criteria of statehood.

characteristics in the entities to which they address themselves." A Cassese, *International Law* (OUP 2001) 47. "The constitutive criteria of statehood reflect a customary rule." D Harris, *Cases and Materials on International Law* (7th edn, Thomson Reuters 2010) 92. Peters also pointed out that "effectiveness is itself a legal principle which performs normative functions." Peters, 'Statehood after 1989' (n 116) 182. "From a constitutionalist perspective ... states – as international legal subjects – are *constituted by* international law." A Peters, 'Membership in the Global Constitutional Community' in J Klabbers, A Peters and G Ulfstein, *The Constitutionalization of International Law* (OUP 2009) 179. "The criteria of statehood are laid down by the law." Otherwise, "a state would be able by its own unfettered discretion to contract out of duties owed to another state simply by refusing to characterize the obligee as a state." Brownlie (n 113) 70. "For, accepting that effectiveness is the dominant principle in this area, it must none the less be a *legal* principle." J Crawford, 'The Criteria for Statehood in International Law' (1977) 48 BYBIL 93, 95. "Even if effectiveness was conceded to be a legal requirement – and not simply a self-evident fact." Crawford, *The Creation of States in International Law* (n 9) 96. Blix also refers to "legal criteria of statehood." Blix (n 17) 609. In the same vein, see D Raič, *Statehood and the Law of Self-Determination* (Kluwer Law International 2002) 51. The US Restatement of Law stipulates that "[*u*]*nder international law*, a state is an entity that has a defined territory and a permanent population, under the control of its own government, and that engages in, or has the capacity to engage in, formal relations with other such entities." Restatement (Third) of the Foreign Relations Law of the United States (1987), para 201; See reference to this definition in *Kadic v Karadzic* (n 112) 157; *Morgan Guaranty Trust Company of New York and Others v Republic of Palau* (United States Court of Appeals, Second Circuit) (1991) 87 ILR 590, 653. "L'effectivité constitue, dans cette optique, un élément de dénition du 'fait juridique étatique.'" Beaudouin (n 228) 36; AT Müller, 'The Effectiveness-Legitimacy Conundrum in the International Law of State Formation' in N Bersier Ladavac, C Bezemek and F Schauer (eds), *The Normative Force of the Factual: Legal Philosophy Between Is and Ought* (Springer 2019) 81.

234 The Badinter Arbitration Commission held that the answer to the legal qualification of the situation in the then Socialist Federal Republic of Yugoslavia ("SFRY") "should be based on *the principles of public international law* which serve to define the conditions on which an entity constitutes a state; that in this respect, the existence or disappearance of the state is a question of fact." See 'Opinion No 1' (n 111) 1495. Similarly, it also held that "state's existence or non-existence had to be established on the basis of *universally acknowledged principles of international law* concerning the constituent elements of a state." 'Opinion No 8' (n 111) 1522, para 1 (*emphasis added*). According to the ICTY Trial Chamber, "the formation of states is a matter that is regulated by law, that is, the criteria of statehood are laid down by law ... [t]hat law ... is reflected in the four criteria set out in the Montevideo Convention." *Prosecutor v Milošević* (n 111) para 87. Similarly, according to the Eritrea-Ethiopia Claims Commission an entity "reflected the characteristics of a State *in international law*" when "it exercised effective and independent control over a defined territory and a permanent population and carried on effective and substantial relations with the external world." *Eritrea-Ethiopia Claims Commission – Partial Award: Civilian Claims – Eritrea Claims 15, 16, 23 and 27–32* (2004) XXVI RIAA 195, para 48 (*emphasis added*).

235 "International law lays down three essential attributes for Statehood. The State must have a territory, that territory must be inhabited by a people and that people must be subject

Then, naturally the question arises as to the origins of this rule. Obviously, customary law emerges from the States and, therefore, States need to have existed first for a customary rule on criteria of statehood to emerge. In this regard, Koskenniemi suggested that it might be possible to argue "that any present criteria have emerged through a political, legislative act by the existing States while the creation of the first State(s) remains a matter of fact, only."[236] Moreover, to answer the same question, Kelsen differentiated between the "historical relation of facts", which means that States historically preceded the creation of a general international law and the "logical relations of norms", which means that "if we start from international law as a valid legal order, then the concept of 'state' cannot be defined without reference to international law."[237]

Thus, overall, it is clear that the principle of effectiveness is the *rule* of customary international law predetermining the so-called constitutive criteria of statehood and their effective fulfilment. Law precedes the State. However, as Verzijl highlighted, "it would be a fallacy to found on such isolated cases in which the rule of law makes its operation dependent upon the existence of certain factual elements the recognition of a supposed basic 'principle of effectiveness' in international law."[238] To understand the principle of effectiveness

---

to the authority of a Government." *In re Duchy of Sealand* (n 112) 685. "The decision must be made on the basis of the factual criteria for statehood laid down by international law." *Democratic Republic of East Timor, Fretilin and Others* (n 112) para 3. "[U]nder customary international law, four conditions must exist for there to be a State." *Civil Aeronautics Administration v Singapore Airlines* (n 112) para 30; *The Attorney-General of the Republic v Mustafa Ibrahim and Others* (Cyprus, Supreme Court) (1964) 48 ILR 6, 8.

236 Koskenniemi, *From Apology to Utopia* (n 6) 274. In line with Koskenniemi's general argument, this would in turn lead to the first sociological scenario. "As the post-medieval territorial states, which as independent empirical entities predated the emergence of international law, began to conduct their relations on the basis of law, it was necessary to identify which entities qualified as 'states' for that purpose. This in turn led the collectivity of 'states' to evolve 'not as an aggregate of separate communities but itself a community: a community of communities tied together by its constitutive practices, including those defining the attributes of statehood.' In this community of communities, sovereign statehood developed into a status 'defined by international law, not independent of it.'" M Fabry, 'The Contemporary Practice of State Recognition: Kosovo, South Ossetia, Abkhazia, and their Aftermath' (2012) 40 Nationalities Papers 661, 662 (*footnotes omitted*).

237 Kelsen, *Pure Theory of Law* (n 2) 338–339. According to Verhoeven "dans la logique du droit des gens, il y a antériorité nécessaire de l'Etat par rapport au droit dans la mesure où, comme système de relations, celui-ci ne saurait exister sans sujets préexistants; dans l'histoire du droit des gens en revanche, il y a postériorité de l'Etat dans la mesure où seule l'idée de droit progressivement forgée a configuré l'Etat et l'a imposé comme régulateur premier des rapports internationaux." Verhoeven, 'L'Etat et l'ordre juridique international – remarques' (n 136) 756.

238 Verzijl (n 138) 297.

in the latter sense would "be to apply a hatchet to the very roots of the law of nations."[239] According to Sur, the effectiveness does not constitute the fundamental principle, but

> simplement une condition posée par la règle elle-même pour son application. Bien loin ici que l'effectivité fonde le droit, c'est le droit qui aura prévu quelles conditions de fait entraîneront sont application et prévu les éléments de leur qualification.[240]

5 Conclusion

The effective independence of a seceding territory has been an important albeit sometimes only assumed factor to be considered when assessing the attainment of statehood. The chapter demonstrated that in neither of the earlier periods did a factual element create a new State; new State emerged only when establishment of effectiveness on the ground was linked with the parent State's recognition in the context of a dynastic legitimism, natural law tradition or other States' recognition in the context of voluntarist positivism. Thus, a classical doctrinal view according to which secession is a meta-legal factual phenomenon represents a clean break from the previous tradition.

The chapter highlighted that for Jellinek and Kelsen, mere facts did not create a State as an international legal person. Despite his influential three-elements doctrine, Jellinek was a constitutivist. His theory of normative force of the factual required complementarity with legal guarantees and legitimacy of the legal order itself. Although Kelsen equated a State's factual emergence and legal existence, he maintained that a rule of international law – the principle of effectiveness – dictated such an approach. The chapter also showed several theoretical weaknesses of the classical doctrinal view that secession is a 'pure fact' outside of international legal regulation.

Thus, building on the historical analysis of the role of factual element in secession, the works of Georg Jellinek and Hans Kelsen and observations drawn from legal theory, this chapter concluded that the criteria of statehood are determined by international law and, more specifically, by a customary rule of international law. While secession is still a matter of fact, it is a *legal fact* predetermined by the rule of international law. Therefore, even if this view

---

239 ibid 293.

240 S Sur, *L'interprétation en droit international public* (LGDJ 1974) 57 and 59.

is still factualist in nature, it does not entail that secession is *unregulated* by international law. Essentially, there is no international law lacuna concerning secession because international law predetermines these factual constitutive criteria.[241] In sum, it follows that even from a factualist perspective on secession, international law is not completely left out. Secession is not a question of *brutum factum*,[242] but a legal fact predetermined by international law. Law precedes the State. Indeed, "le droit peut mettre la force à son service, il en a toujours besoin, et il en trouvera."[243]

Although the practical implications of this conclusion may not be immediately discernible, because both understandings of effectiveness essentially require the investigation of factual or sociological elements,[244] the ultimate consequences are far-reaching. First, on a conceptual level, secession's understanding as a legally regulated process allows for the potential interference of other international law rules without the need to re-define the concept of secession as such. Second, it is difficult to accept that a *legal* rule would require the fulfilment of the factual conditions of statehood and that the very same rule would allow for such criteria to be attained in violation of international law.[245] Thus, the following chapters will analyse the way in which such a *legal* understanding of the factualist statehood has further implications regarding the contemporary understanding of secession.

241 On the question of lacuna in this context, see also O Corten, 'Are There Gaps?' in MG Kohen (ed), *Secession: International Law Perspectives* (CUP 2006) 231–254.

242 Müller (n 233) 81.

243 Münch (n 215) 273.

244 "Reconnaître l'existence d'une norme qui définit l'État ne revient pas à nier la nature factuelle et sociale du phénomène de l'accession à l'indépedence." Beaudouin (n 228) 30.

245 See the following Chapters, especially Chapter 2. For the same argument, see Beaudouin (n 228) 36 and 614–620.

CHAPTER 2

Prohibition of Secession in Case of Violation of Peremptory Norms

1 Introduction

Chapter 1 established that a classical factualist view of secession entailed the fulfilment of the so-called constitutive criteria. It also demonstrated that secession was not merely a fact, but a *legal* fact predetermined by a customary international law rule. The question then arises whether subsequent normative developments modified this rule. The doctrine, practice and *opinio iuris* have signalled a fundamental shift; the emergence and acceptance of peremptory norms in the international legal order is of a crucial importance.[1]

There are systemic arguments that support the proposition of relevance of peremptory norms to the emergence of statehood. For example, some scholars argue that any other approach would allow for an inherent paradox at the heart of an international legal order.[2] An underlying rationale is the principle of *ex iniuria ius non oritur*, the basic contours of which were summarised by Lauterpacht.

> [T]o admit that … an unlawful act, or its immediate consequences, may become *suo vigoure* a source of legal right for the wrongdoer is to introduce into the legal system a contradiction which cannot be solved except by a denial of its legal character.[3]

Furthermore, a wider position of peremptory norms in international law must also be considered. Indeed, "[t]he purpose behind these norms is to protect certain fundamental principles of international legal system."[4] Numerous

1 J Crawford, *The Creation of States in International Law* (2nd edn, Clarendon Press 2006) 99.

2 "Or, il serait selon nous singulièrement fallacieux d'accepter que l'annexion d'une partie du territoire d'un autre État soit nulle et sans effet, tandis que la création d'un État indépendant à la suite d'une agression doive, elle, être accueillie par le droit sur la base de la doctrine traditionnelle des 'trois éléments.'" T Christakis, *Le droit à l'autodétermination en dehors des situations de decolonization* (La documentation française 1999) 279.

3 H Lauterpacht, *Recognition in International Law* (University Press 1947) 421.

4 D Costelloe, *Legal Consequences of Peremptory Norms in International Law* (CUP 2017) 1.

scholars consider their assertion on the international scene as the expression of "communitarianism"[5] and "multilateralism in general international law."[6] The international community is frequently envisioned as a normative community via the operation of *ius cogens*.[7]

Even though the doctrine does not provide a unified stance on the effects of violation of peremptory norms on secession, a leading view is that such a violation precludes the emergence of statehood notwithstanding the effectiveness of an entity. In brief, international law is said to prohibit secession in case it is linked to the violation of peremptory norms. Such a prohibition would further undermine the view that secession is not *regulated* by international law[8] and challenge the claim on the *neutrality* of international law, at least to the extent of this special prohibition. The chapter adopts this doctrinal stance as a central theme of its investigation.

However, admittedly, the doctrine has not elaborated the precise technical implications of how this stance fits within the theoretical framework of the secessionist process and the theory of effects of peremptory norms in international law. Generally, scholars frequently classify the situations of secession in the context of peremptory violations together with the unlawful territorial acquisitions;[9] however, this analogy is not as straightforward. Thus,

---

5 See *e.g.* B Simma, 'From Bilateralism to Community Interest in International Law' (1994) 250 RCADI 217, 217–384; A Gattini, 'A Return Ticket to "Communitarisme", Please' (2002) 13 European Journal of International Law 1181; SM Villalpando, *L'émergence de la communauté internationale dans la responsabilité des etats* (PUF 2005); CJ Tams, *Enforcing Obligations Erga Omnes in International Law* (CUP 2010); See also ED Wet, 'The International Constitutional Order' (2006) 55 International and Comparative Law Quarterly 51; ED Wet, 'The Constitutionalization of Public International Law' in M Rosenfeld and A Sajó (eds), *The Oxford Handbook of Comparative Constitutional Law* (OUP 2012).

6 Costelloe (n 4) 23.

7 See R-J Dupuy, *La communauté internationale entre le mythe et l'histoire* (Economica 1986) 151.

8 "While originally the test of legality was applied to territorial acquisitions by existing states, practice indicates that the *creation* of states, previously perceived as a matter of fact only, is also regulated by the prohibition on the use of force." Y Ronen, *Transition from Illegal Regimes under International Law* (CUP 2011) 3. See also J Crawford, *The Creation of States in International Law* (n 1) 97.

9 "If the general prohibition on the use of force implies the illegality of the annexation of territory, it is very hard to see how one might legitimate the establishment of a State on the territory of another by that means (*ex inuria ius non oritur*)." M Craven, 'Statehood, Self-Determination, and Recognition' in MD Evans (ed), *International law* (4th edn, OUP 2014) 223. "The international community has with considerable consistency refused to accept the legal validity of acts done or situations achieved by the illegal use of force." J Crawford, *The Creation of States in International Law* (n 1) 132. "The presumption against the use or threat of force is fundamental and thus naturally has a corollary in the rules concerning acquisition of territory and the creation of new States." TD Grant, 'Doctrines

international law unequivocally rejects forcible territorial transfers. However, this does not pose major conceptual problems as it involves the standard application *inter vivos* to existing subjects. A similar proposition concerning secession involving the use of force or violation of other peremptory norms requires surmounting the conceptual obstacles concerning the applicability of international law to a very specific transitory process occurring on the borderline between municipal and international laws, defined by the multiplicity of the involved actors ie the parent State, a non-State secessionist entity and frequently also the third State interfering into the process on the secessionist side.

In addition, the ICJ in *Kosovo* referred in passing to the illegality attached to the declarations of independence stemming from their connection to the violations of peremptory norms,[10] but was silent on other issues, including how such illegality influences the secessionist claim to statehood.

The chapter first surveys practice and *opinio iuris*, which offer the basis for a general claim of relevance of peremptory norms to secession. It also outlines various doctrinal approaches on this matter. It argues that a stance that secession, which is connected with the violation of peremptory norms, results in statehood's denial captures the outlined practice and *opinio iuris* best.

Next, the chapter examines the technical aspects of this claim. To do so, it builds on the outlined practice, *opinio iuris* and mainly on the ICJ's pronouncement in *Kosovo*. The Advisory Opinion dealt with the DoI rather than with secession as such; therefore, the chapter settles the understudied issue of the role of the DoI in secession. Then, it examines the key elements of the proposition that the DoI and secessionist attempt fall within the purview of the peremptory norms. Based on *Kosovo*, it examines the scope of applicable law, its addressees, mode of its violation and legal consequences. This analysis

---

(Monroe, Hallstein, Brezhnev, Stimson)' in MPEPIL (online edn, OUP 2014) para 9. "[I]l resort de la pratique des États et des organisations internationales ainsi que de la jurisprudence internationale que les règles postulant l'invalidité d'un titre de souveraineté relative à un territoire acquis ou occupé illégalement, ou encore revendiqué par une entité créée illégalement revêtent un caractère coutumier." A Lagerwall, *Le principe ex injuria jus non oritur en droit international* (Bruylant 2016) 46.

10 "The illegality attached to the declarations of independence thus stemmed not from the unilateral character of these declarations as such, but from the fact that they were, or would have been, connected with the unlawful use of force or other egregious violations of norms of general international law, in particular those of a peremptory character (*jus cogens*)." *Accordance with International Law of the Unilateral Declaration of Independence in Respect of Kosovo* (Advisory Opinion) [2010] ICJ Rep 403, para 81 ("*Kosovo*").

not only provides for new insights into the law of secession, but also for the legal effects of peremptory norms.

A central question today is not "to know that a norm is peremptory; what is ultimately decisive is to know what special it brings about."[11] Thus, demonstrating that the effects of peremptory norms interfere into a pre-State order and even prevent the State-creation would bolster the claims regarding the centralising effects of peremptory norms. Ultimately, the exploration of this matter may be relevant for the understanding of the character of the current international legal order and a stage in the development of the law on secession.[12]

2 General Outline of Peremptory Norms' Relevance to Secession

2.1 *State Practice and* Opinio Iuris

2.1.1 Pre-1945 Practice and *Opinio Iuris*

Chapter 1 outlined the evolution and establishment of the effectiveness criteria regarding the creation of statehood in the early 20th century. Around the same time, normative developments including the restriction of the right to wage war in the Covenant of the League of Nations[13] and the renouncement of war as "an instrument of national policy" in the Kellogg-Briand Pact[14] brought to the forefront the corollary proposition that the acquisitions of territory obtained in breach of these treaty provisions were also "illegal and invalid"[15]

11 C Focarelli, 'Promotional Jus Cogens: A Critical Appraisal of Jus Cogens' Legal Effects' (2008) 77 Nordic Journal of International Law 440 cited in Costelloe (n 4) 15.

12 According to Kelsen, the operation of the principle of *ex iniuria ius non oritur* is dependent on the level of the legal order's procedural development. H Kelsen, *Principles of International Law* (Holt Rinehart and Winston 1966) 425. "[S]o long as the international legal order remains in its present condition of decentralization, so long as it lacks the effective collective procedures characteristic of the state, substantial scope will be afforded to the principle of effectiveness and, in consequence, to the operation of the principle *ex injuria jus oritur*." ibid 433.

13 Covenant of the League of Nations (signed 28 June 1919, entered into force 10 January 1920) 225 CTS 195, art 10 and arts 12–16.

14 General Treaty for Renunciation of War as an Instrument of National Policy (signed 27 August 1928, entered into force 25 July 1929) 94 LNTS 57, art I. See also treaty developments in Latin America at the time. Anti-War Treaty of Non-Aggression and Conciliation (signed 10 October 1933, entered into force 13 November 1935) 163 LNTS 393, art II ("Saavedra Lamas Treaty"). Convention on Rights and Duties of States (signed 26 December 1933, entered into force 26 December 1934) 165 LNTS 19, art 11.

15 R Hofmann, 'Annexation' in MPEPIL (online edn, OUP 2013) para 10.

and should not be recognised.[16] Derived from the principle of *ex iniuria ius non oritur*,[17] this latter position also found its expression in the formulation of the US policy, later known as the Stimson doctrine, towards a puppet State Manchukuo installed as a result of a Japanese military invasion in Manchuria.[18] In 1932, the US Secretary of State Henry L Stimson declared the US would not "recognize an situation, treaty, or agreement which may be brought about by means contrary to the covenants and obligations of the Pact of Paris of August 27, 1928."[19] Later, the Assembly of the League of Nations adopted the resolution in the same sense.[20] Ultimately, the Assembly recognised Chinese sovereignty over Manchuria and found Japanese recognition of Manchukuo illegal.[21]

Considering an overall inter-War practice and *opinio iuris* and developments during WWII, it is difficult to establish that outside of the above treaty provisions, these normative developments unequivocally achieved the status of a general international law before 1945.[22] However, even at this early stage, the proposition already applied to purported State-creations.

---

16 For the early elements of this practice, see I Brownlie, *International Law and the Use of Force by States* (Clarendon Press 2002) 410–413. On the distinction between conquest and annexation, see MG Kohen, 'Conquest' in MPEPIL (online edn, OUP 2015) para 8.

17 See more *infra*.

18 D Turns, 'The Stimson Doctrine of Non-Recognition: Its Historical Genesis and Influence on Contemporary International Law' (2003) 2 Chinese Journal of International Law 105, 109–110.

19 'Identic Note by the United States to China and Japan' (7 January 1932) reproduced in Q Wright, 'The Stimson Note of January 7, 1932' (1932) 26 AJIL 342, 342.

20 On 11 March 1932, the Assembly of the League of Nations adopted Resolution according to which "[t]he Assembly … declares that it is incumbent upon the members of the League of Nations not to recognize any situation, treaty, or agreement which may be brought about by means contrary to the Covenant of the League of Nations or to the Pact of Paris." 'Resolution of the Assembly of the League of Nations' (11 March 1932) reproduced in Q Wright, 'The Stimson Note of January 7, 1932' (n 19) 343. Before that the Council of the League of Nations adopted a Note in which it was stated that "no infringement of the territorial integrity and no change in the political independence of any member of the League brought about in disregard of this article ought to be recognised as valid and effectual by the members of the League of Nations." 'Note by members of the Council of the League of Nations other than China and Japan (16 January 1932) reproduced in ibid. On the other hand, according Lauterpacht, non-recognition of Manchukuo was not due to illegality of the Japanese invasion, but due to Manchukuo's lack of actual independence. Lauterpacht, *Recognition in International Law* (n 3) 420.

21 M Fabry, *Recognizing States: International Society and the Establishment of New States since 1776* (OUP 2010) 135.

22 Hofmann (n 12) para 12; Lagerwall (n 9) 39–40 and 148; See also Grant, 'Doctrines (Monroe, Hallstein, Brezhnev, Stimson)' (n 9) para 10. Christakis points out that certain States continued their policy of non-recognition, and legal fictions concerning the continuity of previously annexed States were used in the Peace Treaties following WWII. T Christakis,

2.1.2 Post-1945 Practice and *Opinio Iuris*

2.1.2.1 *Unlawful Territorial Acquisitions*

The United Nations Charter (UN Charter) outlawed the threat or use of force; today, this prohibition has attained a peremptory character.[23] As its corollary, territorial acquisitions resulting from the threat or use of force are denied legal effects and recognition.[24] The same effects apply to territorial acquisitions

---

'L'obligation de non-reconnaissance des situations créées par le recours illiite à la force ou d'autres actes enfreignant des règles fondamentales' in C Tomuschat and JM Thouvenin (eds), *The Fundamental Rules of the International Legal Order. Jus Cogens and Obligations Erga Omnes* (M Nijjhof Publishers 2006) 138. See also Brownlie, *International Law and the Use of Force by States* (n 16) 413–418; Fabry (n 21) 136–138; Costelloe (n 4) 193–197.

23 ILC, Draft Articles on the Responsibility of States for Internationally Wrongful Acts, with Commentaries in 'Report of the International Law Commission on the Work of its Fifty-Third Session (23 April 1 June and 2 July-10 August 2001)' UN Doc A/56/10, commentary to art 40, para 4 ("ARSIWA"). O Dörr, 'Use of Force, Prohibition Of' in MPEPIL (online edn, OUP 2015) para 32. For the opposite view, see U Linderfalk, 'The Effect of Jus Cogens Norms: Whoever Opened Pandora's Box, Did You Ever Think About the Consequences?' (2007) 18 European Journal of International Law 853, 859 et seq.

24 The practice is unequivocal in this regard. "The territory of a State is inviolable; it may not be the object, even temporarily, of military occupation or of other measures of force taken by another State, directly or indirectly, on any grounds whatever. No territorial acquisitions or special advantages obtained either by force or by other means of coercion shall be recognized." Charter of the Organization of American States (signed 30 April 1948, entered into force 13 December 1951) 119 UNTS 3, art 21; See also Annex to the Draft Declaration on Rights and Duties of States, UNGA Res 375 (IV) (6 December 1949) UN Doc A/RES/375(IV), art 11 in connection with art 9; African Union Non-Aggression and Common Defence Pact (adopted 1 January 2005, entered into force 18 December 2009) 2656 UNTS 285, art 4(c). "The territory of a State shall not be the object of acquisition by another State resulting from the threat or use of force. No territorial acquisition resulting from the threat or use of force shall be recognized as legal." Declaration on Principles of International Law concerning Friendly Relations and Co-operation among States in accordance with the Charter of the United Nations, UNGA Res 2625 (XXV) (24 October 1970) UN Doc A/RES/2625(XXV) ("Friendly Relations Declaration"); "No territorial acquisition or special advantage resulting from aggression is or shall be recognized as lawful." Definition of Aggression, UNGA Res 3314 (XXIX) (14 December 1974) UN Doc A/RES/3314(XXIX), Annex, art 5(3); Declaration on the Strengthening of International Security, UNGA Res 2734 (XXV) para 5; Final Act of the Conference on the Security and Cooperation in Europe (adopted 1 August 1975) principle VI reprinted in ILM 14 (1975) 1293–1298; Declaration on the Enhancement of the Effectiveness of the Principle of Refraining from the Threat or Use of Force in International Relations, UNGA Res 42/22 (18 November 1987) UN Doc A/RES/42/22, Annex, para 10. With respect to Iraq's annexation of Kuwait, the UNSC adopted Resolution 662 (1990), in which it unanimously decided that "annexation of Kuwait by Iraq under any form and whatever pretext has no legal validity, and is considered null and void," and called upon States "not to recognize that annexation, and to refrain from any action or dealing that might be interpreted as an indirect recognition of the annexation." UNSC Res 662 (9 August 1990) UN Doc S/RES/662, paras 1 and 2; *Legal Consequences of the*

violating the right to self-determination.[25] Due to a *prima facie* analogy between the rejection of unlawful territorial acquisitions and State-creation via secession in the similar context, the practice and and *opinio iuris* about the former offer relevant normative guidelines for the latter.

2.1.2.2 *Treaties and Codification Works on State Succession*

Treaties and codification works on State succession support the claim on the relevance of international law to secession. Since the inclusion of Article 6 of the Vienna Convention on Succession of States in Respect of Treaties (VCST),[26] according to which the Convention "applies only to the effects of a succession of States occurring in conformity with international law and, in particular, the principles of international law embodied in the Charter of the United Nations", all major treaties and codification works on this topic have contained the provision to the same effect.[27] The drafting history of Article 6 VCST shows that

---

Construction of a Wall in the Occupied Palestinian Territory (Advisory Opinion) [2004] ICJ Rep 136, para 87 ("*Wall*"). For a detailed overview of the relevant practice see MG Kohen, *Possession contestée et souveraineté territoriale* (PUF 1997) 390–393; Hofmann (n 12) paras 16–20; Lagerwall (n 9) 37–48 and 141–159; Christakis, 'L'obligation de non-reconnaissance' (n 22) 135–142. For a rather critical view that denies that the duty of non-recognition would follow "by necessary implication" from art 2(3) and (4) of the UN Charter or customary law at the time, see H Kelsen, *Principles of International Law* (n 12) 430–432.

25 *Legal Consequences for States of the Continued Presence of South Africa in Namibia (South West Africa) notwithstanding Security Council Resolution 276* (Advisory Opinion) [1971] ICJ Rep 16 ("*Namibia*"); See also the Court of Justice of the European Union's judgments concerning Western Sahara Case C-104/16 P *Council v Front Polisario* [2016] ECLI:EU:C:2016:973, para 92; Case C-266/16 *Western Sahara Campaign UK v Commissioner for Her Majersty's Revenue and Customs, Secretary of State for Environment, Food and Rural Affairs* [2018] ECLI:EU:C:2018:118, para 63.

26 Vienna Convention on Succession of States in Respect of Treaties (adopted 23 August 1978, entered into force 6 November 1996) 1946 UNTS 3 ("VCST").

27 ibid art 6. "The present Convention applies only to the effects of a succession of States occurring in conformity with international law and, in particular, with the principles of international law embodied in the Charter of the United Nations." Vienna Convention on Succession of States in Respect of State Property, Archives and Debts (adopted 23 August 1978, not yet entered into force), art 3; "The present draft articles apply only to the effects of a succession of States occurring in conformity with international law and, in particular, with the principles of international law embodied in the Charter of the United Nations." ILC, Draft Articles on Nationality of Natural Persons in Relation to the Succession of States with Commentaries' contained in 'Report of the International Law Commission on the Work of its Fifty-First Session' (3 May-23 July 1999) UN Doc A/54/10, art 3; "The present Resolution applies only to the effects of a succession of States occurring in conformity with international law and, in particular, the principles of international law embodied in the Charter of the United Nations." Institut de droit international, 'Resolution on Succession of States in Matters of International Responsibility' (28 August

its origins date back to 1972 when some members of the International Law Commission (ILC) suggested clarifying that the provision on the transfer of territory only applied to lawful transfers.[28] Ultimately, the clause to that effect was included into general provisions because it was feared that including the caveat of legality only with respect of one mode of State succession would create the impression that the Convention covered illegal situations in other situations.[29]

First, the practice has been remarkably consistent and constant for almost 50 years. Even though each document has dealt with the succession in its own field, they all intersected in limiting their scope only to the effects of successions occurring in conformity with international law. Thus, at a minimum, it follows that international law, and "in particular, the principles of international law embodied in the Charter of the United Nations"[30] *can be* applied in these contexts.

Second, these provisions drew a clear line between the spheres of legality and illegality. "The principles of State succession do not, it seems, apply to cases involving the violation of the Charter, and in particular of Article 2 paragraph 4."[31] These documents reject the notion that both situations are of the same legal quality and that they are both allowed to profit from the codification of State succession.[32] These provisions preclude "illegal situations from claiming the benefit of rights emerging from the rules of State succession."[33]

2015) (Tallin Session) (Rapporteur: Marcelo Kohen), art 2(2). "[A]ll situations leading to a succession of States should take place in full conformity with public international law, and in particular with humanitarian law and human rights." Institut de droit international, 'Resolution on State Succession in Matters of Property and Debts' (26 August 2001) (Vancouver Session) (Rapporteur: Georg Ress), preamble.

28 ILC, 'Second Report on Succession of States In Respect of State Responsibility, by Pavel Šturma, Special Rapporteur' (6 April 2018) A/CN.4/719, para 25 ("Second Report"); G Gaggioli, 'Article 6' in G Distefano, G Gaggioli and A Hêche (eds), *La Convention de Vienne de 1978 sur la succession d'Etats en matière de traités: commentaire article par article et études thématiques* (Bruylant 2016) 184.

29 Second Report (n 28) para 25; Gaggioli (n 28) 184–185.

30 VCST (n 26) art 6.

31 J Crawford, *The Creation of States in International Law* (n 1) 131–132.

32 In this context, it is difficult to agree with the proposition that "[l]a dichotomie succession légale *versus* succession illégale n'existerait donc pas en droit coutumier en ce qui concerne la succession d'États en matière de traités." Even Gaggioli seems to underline "[d]ans la majorité des cas cependant, tout dépandra de la réaction des États (et de la Communauté internationale dans son ensemble) face à la succession illégale en question." Gaggioli (n 28) 219–221.

33 Institut de droit international, Travaux préparatoires of the Tallin Session 'Succession of States in Matters of International Responsibility' (2015) Fourteenth Commission

Nevertheless, they do not exclude the applicability of international law to unlawful situations as such; however, to ascertain its scope requires a separate and delicate analysis.[34] Moreover, these provisions do not offer conclusions as to the consequences of unlawfulness. Their main objective is to delineate the scope *ratione materiae*. Opinions on the issue of consequences vary. On the one hand, according to some scholars, in the case of unlawfulness, there would be no State succession at all. "An illegal situation, such as one of conquest, there is no State succession precisely because of its illegal character."[35] "Illegal entities claiming to be a State, as was the case of Southern Rhodesia, for example, are not cases of State succession, since the entity concerned cannot claim to be a State."[36] Nothing in the wording of these documents undermines such a proposition. On the other hand, other scholars claim that the wording of Article 6 VCST referring to "the effects of a succession of States" confirms that even an unlawful succession can occur and produce effects.[37] Nevertheless, Gaggioli stated that the wording of Article 6 VCST was modelled on Article 1 VCST, according to which "[t]he present Convention applies to the effects of a succession of States in respect of treaties between States."[38] Thus, Article 6 VCST only aims to delimit the scope of the Convention in line with Article 1 VCST[39] and should not be taken as conclusive concerning the consequences of illegality.

In summary, State succession codifications confirm the applicability of international law in the context of State-creation and draw the line between the spheres of legality and illegality. Nevertheless, they do not provide conclusive evidence on the issue of the legal consequences of unlawfulness.

(Rapporteur: Marcelo Kohen) in Institut de droit international, (2015) 76 Annuaire de l'Institut de droit international (2015) 523 ("Travaux préparatoires").

34 Any such analysis requires a preliminary question as to the illegality of situations from which it would be possible to infer rules. Indeed, this is partly the objective of Section 2.

35 Travaux préparatoires (n 33) 523. Also cited in the Second Report (n 28) para 36.

36 ibid 522 (*footnote omitted*). Also cited in the Second Report (n 28) para 36.

37 Tancredi infers from these provisions that law cannot cancel the State's existence as a social person even if succession occurs not in compliance with international law. "At best, it might influence the legal consequences arising from that event." A Tancredi, 'Neither Authorized Nor Prohibited? Secession and International Law After Kosovo, South Ossetia And Abkhazia' (2008) 18 The Italian Yearbook of International Law Online 37, 53, ftn 100. See *infra* for the discussion of this strand of doctrine.

38 Gaggioli (n 28) 196.

39 Gaggioli (n 28) 196.

2.1.2.3 *Other Relevant Practice and Opinio Iuris of a General Character*

While *Kosovo* advisory opinion is detailed below, it needs to be already underlined at this stage that the ICJ confirmed in this opinion that declarations of independence may be illegal but not because of their unilateral nature *per se* but because "they were, or would have been, connected with the unlawful use of force or other egregious violations of norms of general international law, in particular those of a peremptory character (*jus cogens*)".[40]

The US Restatement of the Foreign Relations Law also supports the proposition on the relevance of peremptory norms to secession. It corroborates the conclusion that the violation of the prohibition of the use of force precludes the emergence of a new State because it refers to "an entity" rather than "the State" even in situations when the entity acquires the qualifications of statehood.[41] Moreover, the Restatement mentions that the obligation of non-recognition is an autonomous obligation, independent from the UNSC determinations[42] and clarifies,

> [a] state has an obligation not to recognize or treat as a state an entity that has attained the qualifications for statehood as a result of a threat or use of armed force in violation of the United Nations Charter.[43]

40 *Kosovo* (n 10) para 81. See *infra* on the positions of States before the ICJ in these proceedings.

41 "An entity might acquire the characteristics of statehood (§ 201) unlawfully, if its territory is detached from that of another state and its independence is achieved as a result of the use of force by other states in violation of Article 2(4) of the United Nations Charter." Restatement (Third) of the Foreign Relations Law of the United States (1987), § 202, reporters' note 5 ("Restatement").

42 "International law forbids treating as a state an entity that was created by threat or use of force by one state upon another in violation of the United Nations Charter. See Articles 2(4) and 51. The United Nations Security Council, acting within its mandatory authority, may impose upon member states an obligation not to treat an entity as a state, as it did in respect of Rhodesia under the Smith regime (1965–1980) before the establishment of the state of Zimbabwe ... In the absence of such an authoritative determination by the Security Council, states are guided by their own determinations as to whether the Charter has been violated and, in time, are more likely to accept a *fait accompli*." Restatement (n 41) § 202, comment (e).

43 ibid § 202 (2).

2.1.2.4 *Practice and Opinio Iuris in Specific Cases*

2.1.2.4.1 Southern Rhodesia

Southern Rhodesia had the status of a *sui generis* British colony when negotiations were held over its future independence during the early 1960s.[44] However, "opinions differed on the notion of majority rule, with the Southern Rhodesian government objecting to the British government's demand that more Blacks be allowed to participate in the electoral process", which ultimately led to the breakdown of the negotiations, issuance of the unilateral DoI by Ian Smith's government of Southern Rhodesia on 11 November 1965 and the declaration of a republic in 1970.[45]

Even before the DoI, the United Nations General Assembly (UNGA) issued a resolution in which it condemned "any attempt on the part of the Rhodesian authorities to seize independence by illegal means in order to perpetuate minority rule in Southern Rhodesia" and declared "the perpetuation of such minority rule would be incompatible with the principle of equal rights and self-determination of peoples."[46] After the issuance of the DoI, the United Nations Security Council (UNSC) adopted Resolution 216 (1965) in which it condemned the DoI by a racist minority regime and decided to call upon "all States not to recognize this illegal racist minority regime."[47] Importantly, the UNSC Resolution 217 (1965) not only called upon "all States not to recognize this illegal authority", but also regarded "the declaration of independence by it as having no legal validity."[48] As analysed below, *Kosovo* referred to UNSC Resolutions 216 and 217 (1965) when discussing the illegality attached to declarations of independence.[49]

Later, the UNSC Resolution 288 (1970) reaffirmed "its condemnation of the illegal declaration of independence in Southern Rhodesia."[50] The UN Secretary-General rejected the claim that Southern Rhodesia could participate

---

44 Ronen (n 8) 27–28.

45 ibid 28.

46 UNGA Res 2012 (XX) (12 October 1965) UN Doc A/RES/2012(XX) paras 1 and 2; See also UNGA Res 2022 (XX) (5 November 1965) UN Doc A/RES/2022(XX), especially paras 2 and 4. After the issuance of the declaration of independence, the UNGA issued other resolutions that *inter alia* condemned "the unilateral declaration of independence made by the racialist minority in Southern Rhodesia." UNGA Res 2024 (XX) (11 November 1965) UN Doc A/RES/2024(XX) para 1. See for more *infra*.

47 UNSC Res 216 (12 November 1965) UN Doc S/RES/216, paras 1 and 2.

48 UNSC Res 217 (20 November 1965) UN Doc S/RES/217, paras 3 and 6.

49 *Kosovo* (n 10) para 81. See *infra*.

50 UNSC Res 288 (17 November 1970) UN Doc S/RES/288, para 1. A number of the UNSC resolutions, some even adopted under Chapter VII of the UN Charter, as well as the UNGA resolutions followed and *inter alia*, imposed mandatory economic sanctions against the illegal regime in Southern Rhodesia. For example, the UNSC resolutions adopted under the

in the UNSC debates as a State under Article 32 of the UN Charter; instead, he held that Southern Rhodesia had a legal status of a non-self-governing territory.[51] In addition, the Organization of African Unity (OAU) called upon other States and international organisations not to recognise the racist regime.[52]

From this practice followed that despite Southern Rhodesia fulfilling the traditional criteria of statehood,[53] the relevant UNSC and UNGA resolutions never referred to it as a "State" or an "illegal State", but merely as an "illegal regime" or "illegal authorities".[54] Furthermore, from the wording of the UNGA and UNSC resolutions followed that the illegality stemmed from the violation of self-determination[55] and the prohibition of racial

---

Chapter VII of the UN Charter include UNSC Res 232 (16 December 1966) UN Doc S/RES/232; UNSC Res 277 (18 March 1970) UN Doc S/RES/277. For more see Ronen (n 8) 30–31.

51 The Southern Rhodesian regime sent telegrams to the UN Secretary-General requesting its participation in the UNSC debates on Rhodesia under Article 32 of the UN Charter, which allows for the participation of a State that is not a member of the UN in debates concerning disputes to which this State is a party. The Secretary-General informed the UNSC that the legal status of Southern Rhodesia was that of a Non-Self-Governing Territory under UNGA 1747 (XVI) and thus Article 32 of the UN Charter did not apply. Moreover, he informed the UNSC that he had decided not to respond to the requests of the South Rhodesian authorities, in line with the policy of not entering into communication with illegal regimes. There was no objection against such conclusions or the approach of the UN Secretary-General. SCOR, 1280th meeting (18 May 1966), paras 7 and 8. See also J Crawford, *The Creation of States in International Law* (n 1) 129, ftn 116.

52 OAU (Council of Ministers) Resolution on Southern Rhodesia CM/Res 75 (VI), para 1 contained in 'Resolutions of the Sixth Ordinary Session of the Council of Ministers Held in Addis Ababa, Ethiopia from 28 February to 6 March 1966.' See for more Ronen (n 8) 31.

53 J Crawford, *The Creation of States in International Law* (n 1) 129; JE Fawcett, 'Security Council Resolutions on Rhodesia' (1965) 41 BYBIL 103, 110.

54 J Dugard, *Recognition and the United Nations* (Grotius 1987) 93–94. Dugard underlined that this terminology confirms that the UNSC viewed Southern Rhodesia as a British colony and not as an independent State. This is further confirmed by the wording of UNSC Resolution 277 (1970), as it called on the Member States to preclude Southern Rhodesia's membership in international organizations. ibid 94. See also Ronen (n 8) 34.

55 See UNGA Res 2012 (XX) (12 October 1965) UN Doc A/RES/2012(XX), paras 1 and 2; See also UNGA Res 2022 (XX) (5 November 1965) UN Doc A/RES/2022(XX), especially paras 2 and 4. The UNGA called upon "the States not to recognize any form of independence in Southern Rhodesia without the prior establishment of a government based on majority rule in accordance with General Assembly resolution 1514 (XV)." UNGA Res 2379 (XXIII) (25 October 1968), para 2. Later, the UNGA reaffirmed "the inalienable right of the people of Zimbabwe to self-determination, freedom and independence and the legitimacy or their struggle to secure by all means at their disposal the enjoyment of that right as set of forth in the Charter of the United Nations and in conformity with the objectives of General Assembly resolution 1514 (XV)" and "the principle that there should be no independence before majority rule in Zimbabwe." UNGA Res 3115 (XXVIII) (12 December 1973) UN Doc A/RES/3115(XXVIII) paras 1 and 2 and see also UNGA Res 2508 (XXIV) (21 November 1969) UN

discrimination.[56] The UNSC regarded the DoI as "illegal" and as "having no legal validity" and no State ever recognised it as an independent State.[57]

2.1.2.4.2 Katanga

The issue of an external military intervention came to the forefront with Katanga's attempted secession from the Republic of Congo 11 days after the latter acquired independence from Belgium on 30 June 1960. The UNSC Resolution 146 (1960) called upon the Government of Belgium to withdraw its troops from the province.[58] Although the Belgian army departed, military instructors and mercenaries remained present.[59]

UNSC Resolution 169 (1961) deplored the secessionist actions with the help of external resources and foreign mercenaries and completely rejected the claim that Katanga was "a sovereign independent nation"[60] and even declared "that all secessionist activities against the Republic of Congo are contrary to the *Loi fondamentale* and Security Council decisions."[61]

Doc A/RES/2508(XXIV) para 1. Moreover, Ronen points out, UNSC resolutions including the UNSC Res 217 (20 November 1965) UN Doc S/RES/217, para 2, UNSC Res 253 (29 May 1968) UN Doc S/RES/253, para 2 and UNSC Res 318 (28 July 1972) UN Doc S/RES/318, para 2 directly referred to the UNGA Res 1514 (XV). Ronen (n 8) 31–32. According to Ronen the OAU resolutions had not directly offered explanation as to the ground for illegality. Self-determination appeared only later on, in 1972, but indirect references can be seen also in resolutions of 1968. See OAU (Council of Ministers) Resolution on Rhodesia CM/Res 135 (X), paras 6 and 7 contained in 'Resolutions Adopted by the Tenth Ordinary Session of the Council of Ministers Held in Addis Ababa, Ethiopia from 20 February to 24 February 1968;' OAU (Council of Ministers) Zimbabwe CM/Res 267 (XIX), preambular paras 7 and 9 and paras 2 and 5 contained in 'Resolutions and Statements of the Nineteenth Ordinary Session of the Council of Ministers Held in Rabat, Morocco from 5 to 12 June 1972;' OAU (Council of Ministers) Resolution on Zimbabwe CM/Res 550 (XXIX), preambular para 5 contained in 'Resolutions Adopted by the Twenty-Ninth Ordinary Session of the Council of Ministers Held in Libreville, Gabon from 23 June to 3 July 1977.' See *infra* on the doctrinal account of this practice.

56 Ronen (n 8) 32–33.

57 Ronen (n 8) 30; J Crawford, *The Creation of States in International Law* (n 1) 129.

58 UNSC Res 146 (9 August 1960) UN Doc S/RES/146, para 2.

59 F Baetens, 'Decolonisation: Belgian Territories' in MPEPIL (online edn, OUP 2017) para 9.

60 "Deploring all armed action in opposition to the authority of the Government of the Republic of the Congo, specifically secessionist activities and armed action now being carried on by the provincial administration of Katanga with the aid of external resources and foreign mercenaries, and *completely rejecting* the claim that Katanga is 'a sovereign independent nation.'" UNSC Res 169 (24 November 1961) UN Doc S/RES/169, preambular para 5 (*emphasis in original*).

61 UNSC Res 169 (24 November 1961) UN Doc S/RES/169, para 8.

Thus, according to the UNSC, the secessionist activities were themselves capable of violating the UNSC resolutions. Crawford observed that despite the fact that during the secessionist conflict the external involvement rendered the secessionist government more stable than a central government and despite its claim for self-determination, no State ever recognised Katanga as an independent State.[62] In 1963, the secession was ultimately terminated.[63]

2.1.2.4.3 Biafra

Biafra declared independence from Nigeria on 30 May 1967 and the so-called Republic of Biafra lasted until 15 January 1970.[64] Compared to Katanga, foreign intervention was less substantial.[65] While the UN remained silent during the secessionist war, the OAU strongly supported Nigerian territorial integrity.[66] Five States recognised the secessionist republic.[67] Ultimately, the question of an external intervention did not play a substantial role because Biafra had never fulfilled the criteria of statehood anyway[68] and was ultimately defeated.

2.1.2.4.4 Bangladesh

After the Pakistani military rejected the results of elections, which brought victory to the Awami League that called for the autonomy of East Pakistan, Bangladesh declared independence on 26 March 1971.[69] Civil war ensued; India intervened on 4 December 1971 and Pakistani forces were defeated on 16 December 1971.[70] Pakistan ultimately recognised Bangladesh in February 1974; the latter was admitted to the UN in September 1974, but even before that it

62 J Crawford, *The Creation of States in International Law* (n 1) 404–405.

63 Baetens, 'Decolonisation: Belgian Territories' (n 59) para 12.

64 H Lahman, 'Biafra Conflict' in MPEPIL (online edn, OUP 2009) para 1.

65 Crawford, *The Creation of States in International Law* (n 1) 406. See ibid para 17.

66 OAU (Assembly of Heads of State and Government) Resolution AHG/Res 51 (IV), preambular paras 1–3 contained in 'Resolutions and Declarations Adopted by the Fourth Ordinary Session of the Assembly of Heads of State and Government Held in Kinshasa, Congo, From 11 to 14 September 1967;' OAU (Assembly of Heads of State and Government) Resolution on Nigeria AHG/Res 54 (V), para 3 contained in 'Resolutions and Declarations Adopted by the Fifth Ordinary Session of the Assembly of Heads of State and Government Held in Algiers, Congo, From 13 to 16 September 1968.' Lahman (n 64) para 10.

67 Lahman (n 64) para 18. DA Ijalaye, 'Was "Biafra" at Any Time a State in International Law?' (1971) 65 American Journal of International Law 551, 555.

68 Lahman (n 64) paras 28; Ijalaye (n 67) 559.

69 L-A Thio, 'International Law and Secession in the Asia and Pacific Regions' in MG Kohen (ed), *Secession: International Law Perspectives* (CUP 2006) 305.

70 ibid.

had been recognised by a large number of States and even became a member of the Commonwealth.[71]

Even though the Pakistani army attacked India first,[72] many scholars claim Bangladesh's secession was facilitated by India's military intervention into civil war in East Pakistan.[73] Other authors suggest that India's intervention was not a decisive factor[74]or that intervention was justified because Bangladesh was a self-determination unit[75] or had the right of remedial secession.[76] Ultimately, a whole set of reasons singled out the secession of post-colonial Bangladesh as "more a unique, rather than precedent-setting case."[77] However, even if admitting that Bangladesh's secession successfully occurred in violation of the principle of *ex iniuria ius non oritur*, the fact that it would be a single case in more than 70 years would not undermine the proposition of the relevance of peremptory norms to secession.[78]

2.1.2.4.5 Bantustans

Although the situation in Bantustans does not concern secession *per se*, because it involved the consent of South Africa as the 'parent' State, it relates to the issue of State-creation in the context of the violation of peremptory norms. South Africa 'granted independence' to Transkei in 1976, Bophuthatswana in 1977, Venda in 1979 and Ciskei in 1981 based on the respective Status Acts adopted by the South African Parliament pretending to respond to the requests of the population.[79] However, South Africa controlled this process;[80] in reality, it sought to use these entitles for furthering the policy of apartheid.[81]

---

71 ibid 306, ftn 57. See also *infra* Chapter 5.

72 MG Kohen, 'Introduction' in MG Kohen (ed), *Secession: International Law Perspectives* (CUP 2006) 11. However, it is doubtful that the requirements of necessity and proportionality would ever legally justify a full-scale military intervention by India in East Pakistan.

73 Thio (n 69) 304; Crawford, *The Creation of States in International Law* (n 1) 141 and see also 393 and 386.

74 Kohen, 'Introduction' (n 72) 11–12.

75 Crawford, *The Creation of States in International Law* (n 1) 142 and see also 393.

76 See *infra* Chapter 3.

77 Thio (n 69) 306–308.

78 See also Chapter 5 for a general overview of the practice of unilateral secessionist attempts.

79 Ronen (n 8) 48; J Dugard, 'Collective Non-Recognition: The Failure of South Africa's Bantustan States' in J Dugard, *International Law: A South African perspective* (3rd edn, Juta 2004) 448–449.

80 Ronen (n 8) 48. See also MF Witkin, 'Transkei: An Analysis of the Practice of Recognition–Political or Legal' (1977) 18 Harvard International Law Journal 605, 613–615.

81 Dugard, 'Collective Non-Recognition' (n 79) 448.

Following the granting of independence of Transkei, the UNGA adopted Resolution 31/6A (1976)[82] in which it rejected "the declaration of 'independence' of the Transkei", declared it "invalid", called upon governments to "deny any form of recognition to the so-called independent Transkei" and requested States to adopt further restrictive measures vis-à-vis Transkei.[83] Later on, the UNGA also adopted similar resolutions concerning other Bantustans.[84] The UNSC unanimously endorsed the UNGA Resolution 31/6A (1976) and the UNSC's president made statements on behalf of the UNSC in which he declared the proclamation of Venda and Ciskei "totally invalid" and called upon the States to deny their recognition.[85]

According to the UNGA, the establishment of Bantustans was "designed to consolidate the inhuman policy of apartheid", "perpetuate white minority domination and to deprive the African people of the South Africa of their inalienable rights."[86] According to Dugard, although not explicit, this latter reason implied the violation of the right to self-determination because the people of South Africa as a whole were denied the possibility to "freely determine their political status" under UNGA Res 1514 (XV).[87] Moreover, the question arises whether the Bantustans fulfilled the criterion of an independent

82 The resolution was adopted by 130 votes to none, with the USA abstaining. See Dugard, 'Collective Non-Recognition' (n 79) 448.

83 UNGA Res 31/6A (26 October 1976) UN Doc A/RES/31/6A, paras 2–4.

84 "[The UNGA] [*d*]*enounces* the declaration of the so-called 'independence' of the Transkei and that of Bophuthatswana and any other bantustans which may be created by the racist régime of South Africa, and declares them totally invalid." UNGA Res 32/105/N (14 December 1977) UN Doc A/RES/32/105/N, para 2. This resolution was passed by 140 votes to none. Dugard, 'Collective Non-Recognition' (n 79) 449, ftn 15. See also UNGA Res 34/93/G (12 December 1979) UN Doc A/RES/34/93/G, para 2; UNGA Res 37/69/A (9 December 1982) UN Doc A/RES/37/69/A, para 14.

85 UNSC Res 402 (22 December 1976) UN Doc S/RES/402, para 1; UNSC Res 407 (25 May 1977) UN Doc S/RES/407, preambular para 6; Note by the President of the UNSC No S/13549 (1979), paras 3 and 4; Note by the President of the UNSC No S/14794 (1981), paras 3 and 4.

86 UNGA Res 31/6A (26 October 1976) UN Doc A/RES/31/6A, para 1; UNGA Res 32/105/N (14 December 1977) UN Doc A/RES/32/105/N, para 1; UNGA Res 34/93/G (12 December 1979) UN Doc A/RES/34/93/G, paras 1 and 3.

87 Dugard also points out other grounds mentioned in the UNGA resolutions, including the violation of the territorial integrity of the country viewed as a self-determination unit, as well as the summary deprivation of millions of Africans of South African citizenship as a result of the creation of Bantustans. Dugard, 'Collective Non-Recognition' (n 79) 450–453. See also Ronen (n 8) 50.

government.[88] The Bantustans were only recognised by each other and South Africa.[89] The UN bodies never designated them as States.

2.1.2.4.6 Turkish Republic of Northern Cyprus (TRNC)

Cyprus gained independence from the United Kingdom in 1960 with the constitution providing for a delicate distribution of powers between the Greek and Turkish Cypriots and upon the guarantees stemming from international agreements between Cyprus and the United Kingdom, Greece and Turkey.[90] However, this arrangement proved unworkable and following an unsuccessful coup aimed at uniting Cyprus and Greece in July 1974, Turkey invaded the island pretending to be acting under the terms of the Treaty of Guarantee.[91] At first, the Turkish Cypriots proclaimed the creation of an autonomous entity; later on, in 1975 they declared creation of a federative State and ultimately on 15 November 1983 they issued the DoI of the Turkish Northern Republic of Cyprus.[92]

Following the 1974 Turkish invasion of Cyprus, the UNGA adopted Resolution 3212 (XXIX), later endorsed by the UNSC Resolution 365 (1974), in which the UNGA unanimously called on all States "to respect the sovereignty, independence, territorial integrity" of the Republic of Cyprus.[93] Later, before the issuance of the DoI, the UNGA adopted Resolution 37/253 (1983) in which it *inter alia* demanded "the immediate withdrawal of all occupation forces from the Republic of Cyprus", considered that "the *de facto* situation created by the force of arms should not be allowed to influence" the resolution of the Cyprus problem and called upon "the parties concerned to refrain from any unilateral action which might adversely affect the prospects of a just and lasting solution"

---

88 "Their governments, although economically dependent and politically accountable to the government of South Africa, were in effective control." Dugard, 'Collective Non-Recognition' (n 79) 456. With respect to Transkei, Witkin (n 80) 615.

89 Ronen (n 8) 50.

90 Dugard, *Recognition and the United Nations* (n 54) 108; J Crawford, *The Creation of States in International Law* (n 1) 143. Treaty of Guarantee (signed 16 August 1960, entered into force 16 August 1960) 382 UNTS 3; Treaty Concerning the Establishment of the Republic of Cyprus (signed 16 August 1960, entered into force 16 August 1960) 382 UNTS 8.

91 Ronen (n 8) 62.

92 ibid 62–63.

93 It also called on States "to refrain from all acts and interventions directed against it" and urged "the withdrawal of all foreign armed forces and foreign military presence" and "the cessation of all foreign interference in its affairs." UNGA Res 3212 (XXIX) (1 November 1974) UN Doc A/RES/3212(XXIX), paras 1–2. UNSC Res 365 (13 December 1974) UN Doc S/RES/365, para 1. See also UNSC Res 367 (12 March 1975) UN Doc S/RES/367, para 2 where the UNSC regretted the declaration of a federative State by the Turkish Cypriots.

and from "any action, which violates or is designed to violate the independence, unity, sovereignty and territorial integrity of the Republic of Cyprus."[94]

After the DoI, the UNSC adopted Resolution 541 (1983), in which it deplored the declaration and considered it "legally invalid", called upon all States to "respect the sovereignty, independence, territorial integrity" of the Republic of Cyprus and "not to recognize any Cypriot State other than the Republic of Cyprus."[95] The UNSC Resolution 550 (1984) reaffirmed Resolution 541 (1983) and reiterated its call for the non-recognition of the TRNC, which it also designated as a "legally invalid."[96] Moreover, as will be discussed below, *Kosovo* referred to UNSC Resolution 541 (1983) in the context of illegality attached to declarations of independence.[97]

As for the grounds of the invalidity of the DoI, Resolution 541 (1983) did not explicitly mention the unlawful use of force, but its preamble stated that the declaration was "incompatible" with the 1960 Treaty of Guarantee and 1960 Treaty Concerning the Establishment of the Republic of Cyprus and, therefore, "the attempt to create" the TRNC "is invalid."[98] Since these agreements only bound their parties, this mention can be seen in a broader picture of the violation of Turkey's obligations to uphold the territorial integrity of the Republic of Cyprus by supporting the secessionists via the unlawful use of force and occupation.[99] Moreover, during the debate at the UNSC preceding the

94 UNGA Res 37/253 (13 May 1983) UN Doc A/RES/37/253, paras 8 and 12–14.

95 UNSC Res 541 (18 November 1983) UN Doc S/RES/541, paras 1–2 and 6–7.

96 UNSC Res 550 (11 May 1984) UN Doc S/RES/550, preambular para 6 and paras 1–3.

97 *Kosovo* (n 10) para 81. See *infra.*

98 UNSC Res 541 (18 November 1983) UN Doc S/RES/541, preambular paras 3–4 and para 2.

99 Similarly, Ronen points out that neither the violation of *inter se* agreements, nor secession as such could give rise to a universal obligation of non-recognition. "[W]hat is significant is that the TRNC was established following the use of force in Turkey in 1974." Ronen (n 8) 66. "[T]he obligation not to recognise a situation created by a serious breach of international law follows just the same from customary international law, which has been breached by the military occupation of parts of the Republic of Cyprus by Turkey. Notwithstanding the fact that the incompatibility of the declaration of independence with existing treaties has been declared the crucial reason for non-recognition, Resolution 541(1983) can be considered declaratory and binding in light of customary international law, at least with regard to the legal necessity not to recognise the TRNC." D Richter, 'Illegal States?' in W Czapliński and A Kleczkowska (eds), *Unrecognised Subjects in International Law* (SCHOLAR Publishing House 2019) 36 (*footnotes omitted*). H Dipla, 'Les résolutions du Conseil de sécurité imposant des mesures coercitives et leur mise en oeuvre: quelques réflexions concernant la responsabilité des États' in H Ruiz-Fabri, L-A Sicilanos and J-M Sorel, *L'effectivité des organisations internationales: méchanismes de suivi et de contrôle* (Pedone 2000) 42–43. See also Dugard, *Recognition and the United Nations* (n 54) 110–111; J Crawford, *The Creation of States in International Law* (n 1) 146–147. According to the UK, as the drafter of Resolution 541 (1983), "[t]he Turkish Cypriot action is incompatible with the

vote,[100] some States explicitly linked the DoI and Turkey's use of force,[101] whereas others pointed out that it violated previous UNSC and UNGA resolutions,[102] the territorial integrity of Cyprus and presented a serious obstacle to a peaceful solution of the conflict.[103]

Moreover, the Council of Europe deplored the TRNC's DoI, considered it "legally invalid"[104] and referred to Turkish illegal occupation of part of Cyprus.[105] The European Communities and the Commonwealth issued statements to the same effect.[106]

In addition, the European Court of Human Rights (ECtHR) while referring to international practice and the UNSC resolutions, held in *Loizidou* that "it is evident that the international community does not regard the "TRNC" as a *State under international law* and that the Republic of Cyprus has remained the sole legitimate Government of Cyprus."[107] Moreover, quite significantly,

---

state of affairs brought about by the treaties governing the establishment of the Republic of Cyprus." SCOR, 2500th Meeting (18 November 1983) S/PV.2500, para 85.

100 "The interpretation of Security Council resolutions may require the Court to analyse statements by representatives of members of the Security Council made at the time of their adoption, other resolutions of the Security Council on the same issue, as well as the subsequent practice of relevant United Nations organs and of States affected by those given resolutions." *Kosovo* (n 10) para 94.

101 According to the representative from Guyana, "[t]he action of 15 November is an attempt to consolidate and give legitimacy to a situation created by invasion and occupation." SCOR, 2500th Meeting (18 November 1983) S/PV.2500, para 5; "In no circumstances, however, can we support a solution dictated by the use of force, much less by a policy of secession." SCOR, 2500th Meeting (18 November 1983) S/PV.2500, para 43 (Zaire). "The decision to declare an independent Turkish Cypriot State is unacceptable and from all standpoints wrong, since it shatters, through the use of force, the unity, independence, sovereignty and territorial integrity of a Member State of our Organization and member of the Non-Aligned Movement. That decision must not have any international legal effect whatsoever. This Council must declare it null and void." SCOR, 2498th Meeting (17 November 1983) S/PV.2498, 51 (Nicaragua).

102 SCOR, 2500th Meeting (18 November 1983) S/PV.2500, para 24 (Poland), para 48 (Yemen), para 76 (France).

103 See eg SCOR, 2500th Meeting (18 November 1983) S/PV.2500.

104 CoE (Committee of Ministers) Res (83) 13 (24 November 1983), paras 1 and 2.

105 CoE (PACE) Recommendation 974 (23 November 1983), para 12 (c).

106 See *Loizidou v Turkey* ECHR 1996-VI 2216, paras 22 and 23 ("*Loizidou*"). See also Case C-432/92 *R v Minister of Agriculture, Fisheries and Food, ex parte SP Anastasiou (Pissouri) Ltd and Others (Anastasiou I)* [1994] ECR I-3116 ("*Anastasiou I*"), Opinion of AG Gulmann, para 13.

107 *Loizidou* (n 106), para 44 and see also para 56 (*emphasis added*). Similarly, see *Cyprus v Turkey* ECHR 2001-IV 1, para 90 ("*Cyprus v Turkey*") where the ECtHR declares that it does not put into any doubt "either the view adopted by the international community regarding the establishment of the "TRNC" ... or the fact that the government of the Republic of Cyprus remains the sole legitimate government of Cyprus." Similarly, *Demopoulos and*

in *Cyprus v Turkey* the ECtHR referred to "the illegality of the 'TRNC' under international law."[108] As for the European Union (EU) case law, the Court of Justice of the European Union (CJEU)[109] never referred to the TRNC as a State either.[110] Ultimately, until today, no State, except for Turkey, has ever recognised the TRNC as an independent State.[111]

2.1.2.4.7 Republika Srpska

In the *Genocide* case, Bosnia and Herzegovina claimed that the purported creation of the statehood of the Republika Srpska "came about as the result of the unlawful use of force by the Federal Republic of Yugoslavia (Serbia and Montenegro), and of the genocidal practice of ethnic cleansing."[112] Bosnia and Herzegovina argued that statehood's purported creation in violation of *jus cogens* norms "cannot have legal consequences."[113] Ultimately, the ICJ did not

---

Others v Turkey ECHR 2010-I 365, para 96; *Foka v Turkey* App no 28940/95 (ECtHR, 24 June 2008), para 84; *Protopapa v Turkey* App no 16084/90 (ECtHR, 24 February 2009), para 60; *Manitaras and Others v Turkey* App no 54591/00 (ECtHR, 3 June 2008), para 43; *Asproftas v Turkey* App no 16079/90 (ECtHR, 27 May 2010), para 72; *Petrakidou v Turkey* App no 16081/90 (ECtHR, 27 May 2010), para 71.

108 *Cyprus v Turkey* (n 107) para 236 in connection with paras 82–102. Recapitulating the European Commission of Human Rights' views, the ECtHR said "those courts functioned on the basis of the domestic law of the "TRNC" notwithstanding the unlawfulness under international law of the "TRNC"'s claim to statehood." ibid, para 231. "The Commission accepts that this is indeed the function of the remedies in question despite the fact that the framework within which they have been created and operate is illegal from the point of view of international law." *Cyprus v Turkey* (n 107), Report of the European Commission of Human Rights (4 June 1999), para 124. "The Commission does not consider that a requirement for victims of alleged violations to exhaust available 'TRNC' remedies amounts to indirect legitimisation of a regime, which is unlawful under international law." ibid para 127.

109 This book uses the abbreviation 'CJEU' also to cover previous iterations of the highest court of the European Union.

110 In *Anastasiou I*, the CJEU labelled it "an entity ... established in the northern part of Cyprus, which is recognized neither by the Community nor by the Member States" and as "the entity, which is not recognised." *Anastasiou I* (n 106) para. 63. In *Apostolides v Orams*, the CJEU used the terms "the northern area" to refer to "those areas of the Republic of Cyprus in which the Government of that Member State does not exercise effective control." Case C-420/07 *Meletis Apostolides v David Charles Orams, Linda Elizabeth Orams* [2009] ECR I-3571, para 12.

111 Ronen (n 8) 64.

112 *Case Concerning Application of the Convention on the Prevention and Punishment of the Crime of Genocide* (*Bosnia and Herzegovina v Serbia and Montenegro*) Memorial of the Government of the Republic of Bosnia and Herzegovina (15 April 1994), 264, para 6.3.2.8.

113 "In this particular case, purported creation of statehood came about as the result of the unlawful use of force by the Federal Republic of Yugoslavia (Serbia and Montenegro), and

deal with the unlawful origins of the Republika Srpska, but acknowledged that "[t]he Republika Srpska never attained international recognition as a sovereign State, but it had *de facto* control of substantial territory, and the loyalty of large numbers of Bosnian Serbs."[114] The Court also found that the Federal Republic of Yugoslavia (FRY) made "its considerable military and financial support available to the Republika Srpska" and "had it withdrawn that support, this would have greatly constrained the options" available to it.[115] As will be discussed below, the ICJ in *Kosovo* also referred to the UNSC Resolution 787 (1992) concerning the Republika Srpska.[116]

2.1.3 Iterim Conclusions

From this overview of practice and *opinio iuris* follows, the international community has not developed a centralised mechanism or a unified procedure in these situations. Even though the UNSC and UNGA have been the most prominent fora, other regional or judicial bodies have also been instrumental either instead of or alongside the UNSC or the UNGA and the States themselves.

Substantively, it follows from the abundant practice and *opinio iuris* that peremptory norms are relevant to the process of State-creation via secession. In particular, the peremptory norms of the prohibition of the use of force, the right to self-determination and the prohibition of apartheid and racial discrimination have underlain this practice. Moreover, the UNSC, the UNGA and other bodies have directly addressed these entities themselves, particularly in terms of the non-use of force and on certain occasions also the territorial integrity of the parent State.[117]

---

of the genocidal practice of ethnic cleansing. As the United Nations Security Council has made clear in numerous other cases, the creation or maintenance of an entity purporting to be a state in violation of the prohibition of the use of force, or all other rules of jus cogens, such as the prohibition of apartheid, and it is submitted, the obligation not to perpetrate genocide, cannot have legal consequences. Therefore, even as the so-called Serb Republic were to exercise some sort of effective authority, this would not endow it with international legal status. It remains a surrogate of the Federal Republic of Yugoslavia (Serbia and Montenegro)." ibid. See also *Arbitral Award in Arbitration for the Brcko Area* (*The Republika Srpska v The Federation of Bosnia and Herzegovina*) (1997) 36 ILM 399, 422, para 77.

114 *Case Concerning Application of the Convention on the Prevention and Punishment of the Crime of Genocide* (*Bosnia and Herzegovina v Serbia and Montenegro*) (Merits) [2007] ICJ Rep 43, para 235.

115 ibid para 241.

116 *Kosovo* (n 10) para 81. For the resolution's analysis, see *infra*.

117 See *infra* in detail on the scope of applicable law.

In addition, the wording of these documents shows that international bodies did not consider secessionist entities created in the context of the violation of peremptory norms as States, rather they referred to them as 'illegal regimes', 'authorities' or similar denominations. The States and international organizations (IOs) have also been frequently called upon not to recognise these entities. IOs and regional organs have also deemed the declarations of independence in these contexts as 'legally invalid.' Almost universally, the States have not recognised these entities as States.

2.2 *Doctrine*

2.2.1 Preclusion of the Emergence of Statehood Despite the Effectiveness of the Entity: A Legalist Position

Deriving from the above practice and *opinio iuris*, after 1945 a major doctrinal strand has gradually formed, claiming "when peremptory norms are violated in the process of State-creation, then, an entity otherwise effective is prevented from being regarded as a State, since *ex iniuria ius non oritur.*"[118] Tancredi called the authors of this group the legalists.[119] This approach dates back to Fawcett's account of the practice relating to the situation in Southern Rhodesia.[120]

> It would follow then that the illegality of the rebellion was not an obstacle to the establishment of Rhodesia as an independent State, but that the political basis and objectives of the regime were, and that the declaration of independence was without international effect.[121]

Later, Fawcett explicitly referred to the violation of the right to self-determination.[122] In 1976, Crawford, elaborated this approach further,

118 Tancredi, 'Neither Authorized Nor Prohibited?' (n 37) 37.

119 ibid. D'Aspremont divides the doctrine "between the *facticists* and the *legalists*, that is, between those arguing that statehood is a fact and those arguing that statehood is a legal construction" J D'Aspremont, 'The International Law of Statehood: Craftmanship for the Elucidation and Regulation of Births and Deaths in the International Society' (2013) 29 Connecticut Journal of International Law 204 (*emphasis in original*).

120 Cf S Talmon, *La non-reconnaissance collective des états illégaux* (A Pedone 2007) 21.

121 JE Fawcett, 'Security Council Resolutions on Rhodesia' (n 53) 113. "[T]o the traditional criteria for the recognition of a regime as a new State must now be added the requirement that it shall not be based upon a systematic denial in its territory of certain civil and political rights, including in particular the right of every citizen to participate in the government of his country, directly or through representatives elected by regular, equal and secret suffrage." ibid 112.

122 According to Fawcett, "it is arguable that state practice has developed a common policy in the international community that new régimes constitutionally based on the denial

suggesting the existence of "a fundamental criterion of legality regulating the creation of States" regardless of the effectiveness of the entity in question.[123] Based on the evolving practice and *opinio iuris*, he pointed to self-determination, illegal use of force and prohibition of apartheid in the context of *jus cogens*.[124] Similarly, in 2006, Crawford stated,

> [A]an entity may not claim statehood if its creation is in violation of an applicable right to self-determination ... [W]here a State illegally intervenes in and foments the secession of part of a metropolitan State other States are under the same duty of non-recognition as in the case of illegal annexation of territory. An entity created in violation of the rules relating to the use of force in such circumstance will not be regarded as a State.[125]

---

of the right of self-determination shall not be recognised as states." JE Fawcett, 'Note in Reply to Devine' (1971) 34 Modern Law Review 417, 417. See also Fawcett's earlier position: "The criterion of organized government is that here must be a central government having effective control over the national territory, for the purpose of making and executing all those decisions that good government entails. Here we may bring in the idea of self-determination. If there is a systemic denial to a substantial minority, and still more to a majority of the people, of a place and a say in the government, the criterion of organized government is not met. The massive condemnation of the unilateral declaration of independence in Rhodesia suggests that a new state cannot now claim recognition if it fails to meet this criterion. By 107 votes to 2 the U.N. General Assembly refused recognition, and this was the mark of a new conception of the state; if Rhodesia survives, it will survive as a fossil." JE Fawcett, *The Law of Nations: An Introduction to International Law* (Allen Lane the Penguin Press 1968) 38–39. "Southern Rhodesia was not a State because the minority government's declaration of independence was and remained internationally a nullity, as a violation of the principle of self-determination." Crawford, *The Creation of States in International Law* (n 1) 130. "The United Nations and its Members have decided, through authorized procedures, not to recognize the regime in Rhodesia as a state until it accommodates itself to the internal and external demands for a genuine sharing of power, majority rule, and conformity to the basic human rights principles of international law." MS McDougal and WM Reisman, 'Rhodesia and the United Nations: The Lawfulness of International Concern' (1968) 62 American Journal of International Law 1, 17. See V Gowlland-Debbas, *Collective Responses to Illegal Acts in International Law: United Nations Action in the Question of Southern Rhodesia* (M Nijhoff 1990). An example of an opposite view was presented by Devine, "the requirement is superfluous if one is prepared to apply the constitutive theory of recognition consistently." DJ Devine, 'The Requirements of Statehood Re-Examined' (1971) 34 Modern Law Review 410, 416.

123 Crawford, 'The Criteria for Statehood in International Law' (1976–77) 48 British Yearbook of International Law 93, 179–180 and footnotes provided therein. Cf Talmon, *La non-reconnaissance collective des états illégaux* (n 120) 22.

124 Crawford, 'The Criteria for Statehood in International Law' (n 123) 179–180 and footnotes provided therein and 144–148.

125 Crawford, *The Creation of States in International Law* (n 1) 131 and 148 (*footnote omitted*).

Since then, numerous authors have held a similar view including Christakis,[126] Raič,[127] and others.[128] According to Professor Kohen "the principle of legality, i.e., the conformity of a fact with the legal order, has become a significant 'constitutive element' in the creation of new States."[129]

Thus, according to this view, the non-fulfilment of the legality criterion leads to "*non-existence* rather than the *nullity* of such entity."[130] "An entity does not come into existence as a State under international law when it is created in violation of *jus cogens*, notwithstanding its effective existence."[131] From this perspective, compliance with peremptory norms would be a *sine qua non* condition for unilateral secession.[132] Therefore, it is inappropriate to speak about

---

126 Christakis, *Le droit à l'autodétermination en dehors des situations de décolonisation* (n 2) 261–283. "[L]es entités sécessionistes constituées à la suite d'une violation des règles fondamentales du droit international (plus précisement, de celle concernant l'interdiction du recours à la force et de celle concernant le droit à l'autodétermination) ne doivent pas être traités comme des Etats, quelle que soit leur effectivité." T Christakis, 'The State as "Primary Fact": Some Thoughts on the Principle of Effectiveness' in MG Kohen (ed), *Secession: International Law Perspectives* (CUP 2006) 165.

127 "[O]n the basis of the practice of explicit non-recognition of claims to statehood it must be concluded, that for the emergence of a State in the sense of, and thus under, international law, additional and new criteria for statehood must be met which are not based on effectiveness, and which can be grouped under the broader heading of the obligation to respect fundamental rules of international law (that is, at least *jus cogens*) during entity's creation." D Raič, *Statehood and the Law of Self-Determination* (Kluwer Law International 2002) 156.

128 "The best approach is to accept the development of self-determination as an additional criterion of statehood, denial of which would obviate statehood." MN Shaw, *International Law* (5th edn, CUP 2013) 185. "The exceptions are entities that come into being in violation of *jus cogens* rules. These are 'non-states', even if fully effective, by virtue of the offence against core rules of the international system that brought them into being (use of force, genocide, ethnic cleansing, apartheid, etc.)." M Weller, 'Modesty Can Be a Virtue: Judicial Economy in the ICJ Kosovo Opinion?' (2011) 24 Leiden Journal of International Law 127, 135; A Peters, 'Membership in the Global Constitutional Community' in J Klabbers, A Peters and G Ulfstein, *The Constitutionalization of International Law* (OUP 2009) 180; G Anderson, 'Unilateral Non-Colonial Secession and the Criteria for Statehood in International Law' (2015) 41 Brooklyn Journal of International Law 1, 71–72 and 88–89; JF Escudero Espinosa, 'The Principle of Non-Recognition of States Arising from Serious Breaches of Peremptory Norms of International Law' (2022) 21 Chinese JIL 79, 114.

129 Kohen, 'Introduction' (n 72) 20. MG Kohen, "Secession: a Legal Approach" in W Kälin and others (eds), *International Law, Conflict and Development: the Emergence of a Holistic Approach in International Affairs: Liber Amicorum for Joseph Voyame* (Martinus Nijhoff Publishers 2010) 17; MG Kohen, 'Création d'Etats en droit international contemporain' in (2002) VI *Cours euro-méditerranéens Bancaja de droit international* 629–630.

130 Dugard, *Recognition and the United Nations* (n 54) 131 (*emphasis added*).

131 Raič (n 127) 156–157.

132 See Anderson, 'Unilateral Non-Colonial Secession' (n 128) 67.

the nullity of the State, but rather about its inexistence due to a lack of one of the essential requirements.

2.2.2 Nullity of the State Due to Illegality of Its Creation

Dugard's position sets him apart from legalists. In his view, the UN Security Council or General Assembly resolutions

> condemn the non-recognized 'States' as 'null and void', 'invalid' and 'illegal', which strongly suggests that they are without legal effect as States, not because they fail to meet the essential requirements of statehood but because their existence violates a peremptory rule of international law.[133]

"The traditional criteria of statehood remain unchanged, and thus … the relevant territorial entities created in violation of international law *do* constitute *States*, but … these States, although existing in fact, are without legal effect."[134] Thus, Dugard focused on the nullifying effects of peremptory norms, rather than on the legality as a new criterion of statehood, the non-fulfilment of which would cause the entity's legal non-existence rather than nullity.

2.2.3 Illegality Without Drawing Any Consequences on the Status of the Entity

Several authors, particularly in the aftermath of *Kosovo*, accepted that the violation of *ius cogens* leads to the illegality of the DoI or the entity in question, but usually did not draw conclusions as to the existence of the statehood.[135]

2.2.4 Non-recognition of Illegal States or Their Social Isolation

Some scholars believe that despite an original illegality connected to secession, a new State would nevertheless emerge *ipso facto* by meeting the constitutive

---

133 Dugard, *Recognition and the United Nations* (n 54) 131 and see also 130, ftn 28 for references to other scholars with similar views. "An act in violation of a norm having the character of *jus cogens* is illegal and is therefore null and void. This applies to the creation of states and to the acquisition of territory. States are under a duty not to recognize such acts under customary international law and in accordance with the general principles of law." Dugard, 'Collective Non-Recognition' (n 79) 449, ftn 461.

134 Summary of Dugard's position by Raič (n 127) 153.

135 An in-depth overview of these positions will be provided in the following sections. "Hence military intervention by other states into intra-state conflicts or military support by other states to secessionist movements renders their 'independence' unlawful." R Värk, 'The Advisory Opinion on Kosovo's Declaration of Independence: Hopes, Disappointments and Its Relevance to Crimea' (2014) Polish Yearbook of International Law 115, 122.

criteria of statehood. Ensuing limitations, if any, towards such a State would be primarily linked to the duty of non-recognition.[136]

For instance, Talmon rejected the idea that the legality criteria would become the additional requirements of statehood; instead, he referred to them as "les critères de la reconnaissance."[137] According to Talmon, any entity fulfilling the criteria of statehood would become a State, notwithstanding illegality of its origin because "les États continuent à se référer exclusivement aux trois critères d'États classique – une population, un territoire et un gouvernement qui exerce le pouvoir effectif."[138] Talmon completely rejected the idea of applicability of the principle of *ex iniuria ius non oritur* and *ius cogens* to the State-creation.[139] "Si le droit international ne veut pas être exposé au reproche de faire abstractions de la réalité, il ne peut pas complétement nier des Etats qui existent de fait."[140]

Non-recognition of an illegal State would then either function as a countermeasure against the grave violation of international law breaching fundamental interests of international community or stem from binding UNSC resolutions resulting in the deprivation of its "droits impératifs" but not of its "engagements facultatifs", which would be legal at any time.[141] Talmon's

136 From his constitutivist stance, Hillgruber adopts a specific position – he does not conceptualize the non-recognition in this context as a duty, but approximates it to the confirmation of the traditional "standard of the ability and willingness of the new State to carry out at least the major international obligations." C Hillgruber, 'The Admission of New States to the International Community' 9 (1998) EJIL 491, 506.

137 "Il est dès lors probable que les critères juridiques ne constituent pas des critères de l'État, mais des critères de la reconnaissance ou des raisons pour la non-reconnaissance d'États existants." Talmon, *La non-reconnaissance collective des états illégaux* (n 120) 25.

138 Talmon, *La non-reconnaissance collective des états illégaux* (n 120) 24.

139 "Ni le principe *ex injuria jus non oritur* ni le concept de *jus cogens* ne s'appliquent à l'Etat dont l'existence est effective; une règle de droit international coutumier prévoyant la nullité d'un Etat dont la formation est intervenue au moyen d'une action illicite ne peut pas non plus être démontrée." ibid 39 and see also 27–28 and 32.

140 ibid 33.

141 Talmon speaks about 'l'effet négateur' of non-recognition. ibid 72. "La privation du statut juridique d'Etat ne veut pas dire que l'Etat qui s'est vu refuser la reconnaissance doit être traité comme un Etat inexistant. Les droits, les privilèges et les compétences doivent lui être refusés seulement dans la mesure où ils expriment une revendication de son statut d'Etat." ibid 42. See also S Talmon, 'The Duty Not "To Recognize as Lawful" a Situation Created by the Illegal Use of Force or Other Serious Breaches of a Jus Cogens Obligation: An Obligation without Real Substance?' in C Tomuschat and JM Thouvenin (eds), *The Fundamental Rules of the International Legal Order. Jus Cogens and Obligations Erga Omnes* (M Nijjhof Publishers 2006) 118–119, where he distinguishes between "the rights inherent in statehood" and "the optional relations between States." In a similar vein, "il n'est plus possible de mettre en doute l'existence actuelle d'un devoir de ne pas

position can be best summarised in the following sentence. “Même si les Etats non reconnus constituent des ‘Etats illégaux’, ils n’en restent pas moins les Etats.”[142]

Another author, Tancredi, describes his own position as “intermediate.”[143] While acknowledging that the State is a factual reality, Tancredi also noted that in the context of the State-creation, certain norms of due process[144] should be respected.[145]

> Their violation, however, does not automatically transform the ‘illegitimately born’ entity into a legally non-existent non-State. At most, it creates a situation of social isolation which gives rise to a factual limitation of its legal sphere.[146]

This would result in “a material condition of non-sociability.”[147] Cassese adopted a similar position when he acknowledged that certain extreme, anomalous situations when facts are not consistent with the “general values of the present world community” may give rise to almost unanimous non-recognition of the entity, but pointed out that the principle of effectiveness

reconnaître un État nouveau, ou toute autre situation, provenant d’un usage illicite de la force … Il est trop tôt par contre affirmer que le droit positif consacre une obligation générale de non-reconnaissance lorsque l’illicéité du nouveau régime est due a une autre cause que le recours à la force.” P Daillier and others, *Droit international public: formation du droit, sujets, relations diplomatiques et consulaires, responsabilité, règlement des différends, maintien de la paix, espaces internationaux, relations économiques, environnement* (8th edn, LGDJ 2009) 627.

142 Talmon, *La non-reconnaissance collective des états illégaux* (n 120) 24 (*footnote omitted*).

143 Tancredi, ‘Neither Authorized Nor Prohibited?’ (n 37) 54.

144 According to Tancredi, norms of due process include the following requirements: State creation takes place without the direct or indirect military intervention of third States; consent is expressed through the local referenda and *uti possidetis*. A Tancredi, ‘A Normative “Due Process”’ in MG Kohen, Secession: International Law Perspectives (CUP 2006) 189–193.

145 Tancredi, ‘Neither Authorized Nor Prohibited?’ (n 37) 54.

146 ibid.

147 ibid. “Non-recognition of unlawfully created States is a measure which is certainly the object of a customary duty – and this is the properly juridical aspect – whose implementation does not determine either the inexistence, or the absolute or partial loss of personality to the detriment of the unlawful entity, but a condition of social isolation which results in the material impossibility of acting.” Tancredi, ‘A Normative “Due Process”’ (n 144) 206 (*footnotes omitted*).

had not-yet been displaced by these values and, therefore, such entity would still be a State even though it was "deprived of international intercourse."[148]

2.2.5 Classical Factualist Doctrine

To complement this overview, today's version of a classical factualist position only refers to the constitutive criteria of statehood, without ever mentioning the influence of the violation of peremptory norms.[149] Kassoti[150] and Verhoeven[151] are exceptions in the sense that they explicitly rejected the influence of peremptory norms on secession.

2.2.6 Interim Conclusions

This section outlined five contemporary doctrinal strands offering perspectives on the effects of the violations of peremptory norms on the State-creation via secession. On balance, the majority of authors acknowledged one of the above consequences of violation of *ius cogens* in the context of secession; today the authors of a classical factualist doctrine are in minority.

As already outlined, the practice generally avoids referring to secessionist entities as 'States,' 'invalid States,' or calling for non-recognition of 'unlawful States,' which runs counter to the thesis of Dugard, Talmon, Tancredi, Cassese and that of classical factualists.[152] Moreover, numerous resolutions of the UN bodies mentioned invalidity, but contrary to Dugard's reading, they mostly referred to the invalidity of the declarations of independence, rather than to the invalidity of the States. From this follows that the legalist position, according to which the emergence of statehood is precluded when the secessionist

---

148 Particularly, he refers to Southern Rhodesia and points out that despite almost universal non-recognition (except for South Africa), "it did, nonetheless, possess autonomous rights and duties, although it was unable to make use of them." A Cassese, *International Law* (2nd edn, OUP 2005) 76.

149 Tancredi calls this group "realists." Tancredi, 'Neither Authorized Nor Prohibited?' (n 37) 37. See *supra* Chapter 1.

150 E Kassoti, 'The Sound of One Hand Clapping: Unilateral Declarations of Independence in International Law' (2016) 17 German Law Journal 215, 230–233.

151 "C'est simplement que l'on n'aperçoit pas quelle peut être l'incidence de la violation du *jus cogens* sur l'existence d'une personnalité étatique. L'État naît en effet de la seule conjonction de trois éléments «objectifs» – une population, un territoire et un gouvernement indépendant – à un moment donné." J Verhoeven, 'Sur les "bons" et les "mauvais" emplois du jus cogens' (2008) 5 Annuario brasileiro de direito internacional 133, 152.

152 Similarly, Raič (n 127) 155–156 and see Anderson, 'Unilateral Non-Colonial Secession' (n 128) 69–70.

attempt results from a violation of peremptory norms, corresponds to the outline practice and *opinio iuris* most adequately.[153]

3 Role of DoI in Secession

One of the most striking issues that follow from the above practice and *opinio iuris* is how frequently the documents refer to the declarations of independence and even declare them illegal, invalid, without legal effect, or call for their

153 Admittedly, the examples of practice in this regard, *alongside other instances of practice*, include the acts of non-recognition of these entities as States, ie amount to inaction, abstention or negative practice. "The very term *non-recognition* implies not positive action but abstention from acts signifying recognition." *Namibia* (n 25), Separate Opinion, Judge Petrén, 134. International Law Commission (ILC) held that practice for the purposes of identification of customary international law "may, under certain circumstances, include inaction." ILC, Draft Conclusions on Identification of Customary International Law, with Commentaries in 'Report of the International Law Commission of its Seventieth Session (2018)' UN Doc A/73/10, draft conclusion 6(1). In its Third Report, Special Rapporteur, Woods, stated that "[e]ven more than other forms of practice, inaction may at times be difficult to identify and qualify; in any event, as with other forms of practice, 'bare proof of … omissions allegedly constituting State practice does not remove the need to interpret such … omissions' in an attempt to verify whether, indeed, they are accepted as law." ILC, 'Third Report on Identification of Customary International Law' (27 March 2015) UN Doc A/CN.4/682, para 20 (*footnotes omitted*). Similarly, regarding the customary obligation of abstention from the threat or use of force, in *Nicaragua*, the ICJ held that it "has however to be satisfied that there exists in customary international law an *opinio juris* as to the binding character of such abstention." *Case Concerning Military and Paramilitary Activities in and against Nicaragua (Nicaragua v United States of America)* [1986] ICJ Rep 14, para 188 ("*Nicaragua*"). Analogously, it has been claimed that "[i]n the area of international humanitarian law, where many rules require abstention from certain conduct, omissions pose a particular problem in the assessment of *opinio juris* because it has to be proved that the abstention is not a coincidence but based on a legitimate expectation. When such a requirement of abstention is indicated in statements and documents, the existence of a legal requirement to abstain from the conduct in question can usually be proved." J-M Henckaerts and L Doswald-Beck, *Customary International Humanitarian Law, Volume I: Rules* (CUP 2005) xlvii. See, for example, the approach of the ICJ in *Nicaragua* (n 153) paras 188–190. See more generally, MH Mendelson, 'The Formation of Customary International law' (1998) 272 RCADI 207–209 and 273–274; GP Buzzini, 'Les comportements passifs des états et leur incidence sur la réglementation de l'emploi de la force en droit international général' in E Cannizzaro and P Palchetti (eds), *Customary International Law on the Use of Force* (Brill 2005) 81–84. In light of these observations, the above account presents an exhaustive examination of an *opinio iuris* underlying the practice of non-recognition on this issue. See also below the practice and *opinio iuris* regarding the technical aspects of this proposition and its legal consequences.

non-recognition. It is hardly conceivable that so much practice would occur concerning internationally immaterial documents.

However, from a classical perspective, the DoI does not have any role to play in secession. The constitutive criteria – territory, population and government – are the sole requirements of secession. International law textbooks never list the DoI among these criteria. There are few detailed scholarly analyses of this subject and those that exist are hardly reconcilable.[154] In addition, the States themselves presented radically different views in *Kosovo*.[155] Some States claimed that secession could even occur without issuing any DoI at all.[156] Even more astonishingly, the ICJ completely avoided this question; as Pertile stated, despite that *Kosovo* focused on the DoI, the ICJ never directly tackled the issue of its legal nature under international law.[157]

How to reconcile such an apparent paradox? Are the declarations of independence simply political documents or statements of aspiration or do they fulfil any legal function? Must the DoI accompany every secessionist attempt?

The following section argues that the DoI is an inseparable and inherent part of any secessionist attempt. It bases this argument on three partial claims including inferences from legal theory, an analogy with the law of acquisition of territorial sovereignty and the example of Taiwan. The section then outlines the implications of this conclusion for the legal nature of secession and the links between secession and the DoI.

---

154 Referring specifically to Kosovo's Declaration of Independence, Milano views this declaration as an international legal act whose validity can be assessed under international law. E Milano, 'Declarations of Independence and Territorial Integrity in General International Law: Some Reflections in Light of the Court's Advisory Opinion' in M Arcari and L Balmond (eds), *Questions de droit international autour de l'avis consultatif de la Cour internationale de Justice sur le Kosovo* (Giuffrè 2011) 64–69. Pertile's view is that a declaration of independence is "a mere fact" not regulated by international law. M Pertile, 'Self-Determination Reduced to Silence: Some Critical Remarks on the ICJ's Advisory Opinion on Kosovo' in M Arcari and L Balmond (eds), *Questions de droit international autour de l'avis consultatif de la Cour internationale de Justice sur le Kosovo* (Giuffrè 2011) 100, ftn 30. See also J Vidmar, 'Conceptualizing Declarations of Independence in International Law' (2012) 32 Oxford Journal of Legal Studies 153, 169–176 where author discusses the possibility of the illegality of declaration of independence as such. See also Kassoti (n 150) 215 where the author rejects the possibility that a declaration of independence could be an international legal act and instead sees it only as a political document in line with the factualist understanding of statehood.

155 See *infra*.

156 "An entity wishing to secede may very well become a State under international law without making a declaration of independence at all." *Kosovo* (n 10), Written Statement of Switzerland (25 May 2009), para 27.

157 Pertile (n 154) 99. See also Kassoti (n 150) 220.

3.1 *Inherent Part of a Secessionist Attempt*

3.1.1 An Intentional Act to Secede

The DoI is usually a formal and solemn act that *inter alia* declares the establishment of a new State on a particular territory.[158] Its wording usually indicates constitutive effects regarding the creation of a new State – the question that is discussed below. However, at this stage, regardless of any particular wording, its most fundamental element is the unequivocal expression of *will* of a certain population group of an existing State to secede.

Even though secession is traditionally perceived as establishing constitutive criteria – territory, population and an independent government – it is not a natural, but rather a human-driven factual phenomenon.[159] Despite a traditional 'pure fact' approach, facts do not occur randomly, but are unified into one concept of 'secession' or the 'secessionist attempt.' The unifying element in this regard is indeed the *will* to secede, which is encapsulated and expressed in the act of declaring independence.[160]

The *will* to secede and establish a new State is inherently assumed in all the factual criteria. There can be other territorial situations resembling secession or secessionist attempts including military occupation or annexation via the indirect use of force, territorial banditry[161] or gang-held territories outside the control of the central government. However, a criterion, which distinguishes

158 According to Gowlland-Debbas the declaration of independence of Southern Rhodesia represented "a claim to personality and to a new territorial status as well as a request for recognition, but in itself it could not create an international personality for Rhodesia." Gowlland-Debbas (n 122) 205. According to Crawford, the unilateral declaration of independence is a "unilateral act by which a group declares that it is seceding and forming a new State." J Crawford, 'State Practice and International Law in Relation to Secession' (1999) 69 BYBIL 85, 86.

159 "Par *fait juridique* on entend des événements naturels ou humains auxquels le droit attache une conséquence juridique." Kohen, *Possession contestée et souveraineté territoriale* (n 24) 131 (*emphasis in original*).

160 "The factual criteria for statehood are a defined territory, a permanent population, an effective government, and a capacity to enter into international relations. An important component is the desire to be regarded as a State, often expressed through a declaration of independence or other act signifying a move toward statehood, one that may occur before, as, or after the 'Montevideo' criteria are satisfied. The reactions of other States through the process of 'recognition' are an important part of this process of State formation." *Kosovo* (n 10), Written Contribution of the Authors of the Unilateral Declaration of Independence (April 2009), para 8.09 (*footnotes omitted*). "The unifying element which ties all varieties of secession together is an endogenously motivated withdrawal." Anderson, 'Unilateral Non-Colonial Secession' (n 128) 7.

161 See S Wheatley, 'The Emergence of New States in International Law: The Insights from Complexity Theory' (2016) 15 Chinese Journal of International Law 579, 593.

these other scenarios, is the attempt at 'secession',[162] which presupposes the intentional conduct of seeking the establishment of a new State. 'The factual side' of secession never exists on its own; it is an intentional human-driven phenomenon. Without the will to secede and establish a new State, there would be no secession. Rather, it would be a different territorial situation.

Therefore, the question as to whether secession can occur without the DoI is not a question of substance, but rather a question of form. Naturally, a written, formal and solemn DoI is the most frequent option, but nothing undermines the idea that the expression of will to secede, 'act of declaring independence', could also take the form of an oral or unwritten act or even a series of acts on the condition that the intent to secede could be inferred from them.[163] In practice, this would hardly pose radical problems because it is difficult to imagine, for example, the establishment of the units of government of a new State on the parent State's territory without any written or at least oral statement indicating their association with a new State.

3.1.2 Analogy with the Law of Acquisition of Titles of Territorial Sovereignty

The law of acquisition of titles of territorial sovereignty also offers a relevant guidance. Traditional international law does not include the creation of States among the modes of acquisition of titles of territorial sovereignty.[164] "The scheme is based upon the civil law modes for the transfer of property *inter vivos*; it does not provide, therefore, for the situation where a new State comes into existence."[165]

Even though the rules on the succession and the principle of *uti possidetis iuris* offer important directions,[166] they do not concern the State's emergence as such and are only triggered as soon as a new State is born.[167] For example,

162 Secession is defined in this book as "the creation of a new independent State through the separation of part of the territory and population of an existing State, without the consent of the latter." See *supra*, Chapter 1.

163 For the process of devolution of Canada, Australia and South Africa (even if it is not directly covered by this book), see Crawford, *The Creation of States in International Law* (n 1) 358–366 and 371–372.

164 RY Jennings, *The Acquisition of Territory in International Law* (Manchester University Press 2017) 20.

165 Jennings (n 164) 20 (*footnote omitted*). See Kohen, *Possession contestée et souveraineté territoriale* (n 24) 127 et seq.;.

166 MG Kohen and M Hébié, 'Territory, Acquisition' in MPEPIL (online edn, OUP 2011), para 12.

167 See *infra* Chapter 4 for details of temporal aspects of the application of *uti possidetis* and the principle of the stability of frontiers.

the law of succession "tends to accept the change of territorial sovereignty as *datum*, and very little if anything seems to hinge on the method by which the change was brought about."[168] Jennings offered a poignant explanation, "where a new State arises the law has looked chiefly to the emergence of a new subject rather than incidental transfer of territory; it has looked to the sovereign, rather than the territorial, element of territorial sovereignty."[169]

Ultimately, under traditional international law, the question is resolved either by the recourse to the constitutive theory, according to which international law does not regulate the question of the factual formation of State[170] or by accepting that the title of territorial sovereignty arises "simply from the fact of the emergence of a new State",[171] which is seen outside of the scope of international law.[172] "There is thus a primary regime associated with statehood, which logically and in practice takes priority over the rules relating to transfer of territory between existing States."[173]

Nevertheless, since "the creation of a new State entails the establishment of a new sovereignty over its territory"[174] it is justified to create an analogy between the State's emergence and the classical modes of the acquisition of titles of territorial sovereignty.[175] In particular, an analogy can be made between the constitutive criteria of statehood and the constitutive elements of *effectivités* under the law of acquisition of titles of territorial sovereignty.[176]

Undoubtedly, it is important to take into consideration differences between these two situations. First, *effectivités* must be attributable to a State,[177] while

---

168 Jennings (n 164) 21.
169 ibid 22.
170 See *supra*, Chapter 1. Jennings subscribed to this view; see ibid 22–23.
171 ibid 22.
172 For other doctrinal approaches to the origins of title of territorial sovereignty in the case of the emergence of a State, see A Beaudouin A, *Uti possidets et sécession* (Éditions Dalloz 2011) 64–79.
173 Crawford, *The Creation of States in International Law* (n 1) 665. See also Beaudouin (n 172) 79–82.
174 Kohen and Hébié, (n 166) para 12.
175 The objective of the following analogy is not to dwell on the specifics of the relationship between the law of statehood and the law of acquisition of territorial sovereignty. A reference can be made to Crawford's conclusion: "If it is necessary to categorize acquisition of territory by new States as a distinct 'mode' of acquisition, still the rules applicable are those relating to acquisition of statehood." Crawford, *The Creation of States in International Law* (n 1) 665 (*footnote omitted*).
176 The French term *effectivités* refers "to acts undertaken in the exercise of State authority through which a State manifests its intention to act as the sovereign over a territory." Kohen and Hébié, (n 166) para 25.
177 Kohen and Hébié, (n 166) para 26.

in the case of a new State's emergence the establishment of constitutive criteria is by definition performed by secessionist non-State actors. Second, the threshold required for both situations might be different – while the threshold of *effectivités* depends on the existence of the competing claim of sovereignty, a relatively high threshold of the constitutive elements of statehood stems from the presence of the parent State's opposing claim.[178] Nevertheless, these divergences cannot undermine the fundamental analogy between two situations, which is based on the fact that both a new State's emergence and *effectivités* require the control and display of authority over a certain territory.

Thus, it is notorious that based on a private law and Roman law inspired tradition,[179] for the possession under the law of acquisition of title of territorial sovereignty to exist, both *corpus possessionis* and *animus possidendi* must be fulfilled.[180] While *corpus* as a material element refers to acts attributable to a State, which constitute "manifestations of the exercise of State sovereignty",[181] *animus* as a subjective element represents an intent to act as a sovereign over certain territory.[182] Only when both these elements are present is possession complete and, when accompanied by other conditions, can lead to the title of territorial sovereignty.[183]

Therefore, based on this analogy, it is submitted that the establishment of the constitutive criteria of statehood also involves material and subjective elements. Specifically, territory, population and government can be seen as *corpus* in the State's emergence and an act of declaring independence can be

178 For the understanding of the constitutive criteria of statehood, see Chapter 1. Regarding the conditions of possession, see Kohen, *Possession contestée et souveraineté territoriale* (n 24) 205–225; Kohen and Hébié, (n 166) paras 25–32. *Western Sahara* (Advisory Opinion) [1975] ICJ Rep 12, para 92 ("Western Sahara"). With respect to the elements of effective occupation, see I Brownlie, *Principles of Public International Law* (7th edn, Oxford University Press 2008) 133–138; G Distefano, *L'ordre international entre légalité et effectivité: le titre juridique dans le contentieux territorial* (Pedone 2002) 267–27; SP Sharma, *Territorial Acquisition, Disputes and International Law* (Martinus Nijhoff 1997) 63–107.

179 See H Lauterpacht, *Private Law Sources and Analogies of International Law: With Special Reference to International Arbitration* (Longmans Green 1927) 99–104.

180 Kohen, *Possession contestée et souveraineté territoriale* (n 24) 205. See also *Legal Status of Eastern Greenland* (Denmark v Norway) [1933] PCIJ Rep Series A/B No 53, 45–46; *The Minquiers and Ecrehos Case* (France/United Kingdom) [1953] ICJ Rep 47, 71; *Western Sahara* (n 178) para 92.

181 Kohen and Hébié, (n 166) para 31; MG Kohen, *Possession contestée et souveraineté territoriale* 206–223.

182 See Kohen, *Possession contestée et souveraineté territoriale* (n 24) 223.

183 Kohen and Hébié, (n 166) paras 33–38.

considered the expression of *animus* to establish a new State.[184] Indeed, even Jennings held that every mode of acquisition of titles of territorial sovereignty "requires the presence of *corpus* as well as *animus*."[185]

The means of evidence of *corpus* and *animus* are not strictly separated. "Comme pour les deux éléments de la coutume, un seul et même acte, ou ensemble des faits, peut témoigner simultanément de la réalisation de l'une et de l'autre condition."[186] Apart from acts simultaneously demonstrating the existence of *corpus* and *animus*, other acts can only reflect the intention to act as a sovereign without being the evidence of *corpus*.[187] Thus, *per* analogy where appropriate the constitutive criteria of statehood assume intent to act as a new sovereign, their establishment could be seen as simultaneous evidence of *corpus* and *animus*, while the DoI is the document solely expressing intent (*animus*) to establish a new State.

3.1.3 Relevance of the Taiwan Example

Taiwan "appears to comply in all respects with the criteria for statehood based on effectiveness but is universally agreed not to be a separate State and is recognized by no other State as such."[188] Indeed, the government in Taiwan claims to be the government of the State – the Republic of China (ROC) – encompassing also the mainland territory not under its control; it is even recognised as such by several States.[189] However, Taiwan's characterisation as a *separate*

184 During the *Kosovo* proceedings, Finland offered a similar perspective. "A declaration of independence involves a claim about the exercise of sovereignty in a territory. In accordance with the well-known formula in the *Island of Palmas* case (1928) sovereignty 'in the relations between States signifies independence. Independence in regard to a portion of the globe is the right to exercise therein, to the exclusion of any other State, the functions of a State.' The possession of sovereignty (and hence statehood) has been understood to require the presence of an 'animus' and a 'corpus'– that is to say, 'intention and will to act as a sovereign and some actual exercise or display of such authority.' As stated in Opinion No. 1 of the Arbitration Commission of the Conference on Yugoslavia, the existence of a State (i.e. the presence of 'animus' and 'corpus') is 'a question of fact.'" *Kosovo* (n 10), Statement of Finland (16 April 2009), 2–3.

185 Jennings (n 164) 17.

186 Kohen, *Possession contestée et souveraineté territoriale* (n 24) 206.

187 ibid 223–4.

188 Crawford, *The Creation of States in International Law* (n 1) 198.

189 Currently, 15 States recognise the ROC; these diplomatic relations "do not constitute an international acceptance of Taiwan as a state, but rather represent a recognition of the ROC government as the representative of China." TC Heller and AD Soafer, 'Sovereignty: The Practitioners' Perspective' in SD Krasner (ed), *Problematic Sovereignty: Contested Rules and Political Possibilities* (Columbia University Press 2001) 28 ftn 8. 'Diplomatic Allies' <https://www.mofa.gov.tw/en/AlliesIndex.aspx?n=DF6F8F246049F8D6&sms=A76B7230ADF29736> accessed 20 April 2020.

State distinct from the mainland is precluded due to the lack of its own will to declare such a separate State on the territory under the ROC government's control.[190] Crawford offered a detailed analysis of Taiwanese internal legislation, judicial decisions and its foreign policy and concluded that even though a certain trend towards a formal claim can be detected,[191] the relevant acts and statements are extremely ambiguous and cannot be interpreted as the DoI of a separate State.[192]

Thus, undoubtedly, this matter is complicated due to the competing claims of the Peoples' Republic of China and the ROC to be the government of the whole of China,[193] but the example is nevertheless relevant for the present purposes as it highlights that a mere presence of the constitutive criteria of statehood is insufficient for the State's emergence; these criteria must be accompanied by a corresponding claim to statehood. Since Taiwan has not unambiguously claimed a separate legal status as a State, it cannot be regarded as such.[194] "Statehood is a claim of right. Claims to statehood are not to be inferred from statements or actions short of explicit declaration."[195] "An entity

---

190 See Crawford, *The Creation of States in International Law* (n 1) 219.

191 "Since the 1990s, the official territorial claim to the mainland was relaxed." B Chang, *Place, Identity, and National Imagination in Post-war Taiwan* (Routledge 2015) 58. However, according to Ahl, although Taiwan "lost effective control of the Chinese mainland, it continued to claim sovereignty over all of China until the beginning of the 1990s." B Ahl, 'Taiwan' in MPEPIL (online edn, OUP 2008), para 5. Nevertheless, he also notes that "[t]he territory of mainland China is not treated as 'foreign' territory and, according to the Constitution, the State of China has a 'free area' and a 'mainland area.'" ibid, para 19.

192 See Crawford, *The Creation of States in International Law* (n 1) 212–219.

193 Crawford analysed the competing claims of the ROC and the PRC, and with respect to the legal status of Taiwan came to the conclusion that "in the apparent absence of any claim to secede the status of Taiwan can only be that of a part of the State of China under separate administration." Crawford, *The Creation of States in International Law* (n 1) 211. The PRC's claim of sovereignty over the territory of the island of Taiwan "has been recognized by most states in the world." Heller and Soafer (n 189) 28, ftn 8. The notion of the 'secession' of Taiwan is possible only if one accepts that Taiwan is part of the PRC. As mentioned above 15 States recognise the ROC.

194 Ahl (n 191) para 1.

195 Crawford, *The Creation of States in International Law* (n 1) 211 and 218–219. "No claim of separate statehood for Taiwan has been made and in such a case it is difficult to maintain that such an unsought status exists." MN Shaw, *International Law* (6th edn, CUP 2008) 234. Similarly see E T-L Huang, 'The Modern Concept of Sovereignty, Statehood and Recognition: A Case Study of Taiwan' (2003) 16 New York International Law Review 99, 115–116 and ftns 98 and 99 for references therein. *Contra:* Roth disputes Crawford's analysis on the non-existence of the unequivocal declaration of independence of Taiwan, but without offering conclusive evidence; the author also adopts the constitutive theory of recognition and refers to tacit recognition of Taiwan. Roth BR, 'The Entity That Dare Not Speak Its Name: Unrecognized Taiwan as a Right-Bearer in the International Legal Order'

which does not claim to be a State in international law will not be recognized as such."[196]

Ultimately, the three above arguments demonstrate the importance of the expression of will to secede and act as a new sovereign in secession. Even in the case of an undoubted presence of the so-called constitutive criteria of statehood, a new State is not born unless joined by a corresponding and unequivocal expression of will to secede. "Statehood does not flow automatically from the establishment of an independent and sovereign entity, but it requires the affirmation of relevant claim, entailing a transfer of sovereignty from the predecessor State."[197]

Thus, it follows that regardless of its form, an act of declaring independence, including a formal declaration as the expression of the will to establish a new State, is an inherent, inseparable and necessary element of any process leading to secession.[198] Therefore, to adequately ascertain the phenomenon of secession, both the presence of the constitutive criteria of statehood (*corpus*) and the intent to act as a new sovereign (*animus*) must be present.

This conclusion raises certain problems of legal classification. The literature on the acquisition of titles of territorial sovereignty has alluded to similar

(2009) 4 East-Asia Review 91, 102–103 and 108–109. The US Restatement of Law claims, "while the traditional definition does not formally require it, an entity is not a state if it does not claim to be a state. For example, Taiwan might satisfy the elements of the definition in this section, but its authorities have not claimed it to be a state, but rather part of the state of China." Restatement (n 41) § 201, comment (f). (*emphasis added*). Reporters Note 8 claims "[S]ince the authorities on Taiwan do not claim that Taiwan is a state of which they are the government, the issue of its statehood has not arisen ... If Taiwan should claim statehood, it would in effect be purporting to secede from China." See also TD Grant, 'Defining Statehood: The Montevideo Convention and Its Discontents' (1998) 37 Columbia Journal of Transnational Law 403, 439–441, on the claim of statehood as one of the potential criteria of statehood additional to the Montevideo criteria. Grant points to the example of Taiwan and the US Restatement of Law.

196 Crawford, 'State Practice and International Law in Relation to Secession' (n 158) 86, ftn 3. "This has hitherto been a justification for the non-recognition of a separate State of Taiwan." ibid.

197 This refers to the case of Taiwan as well. Milano, 'Declarations of Independence and Territorial Integrity in General International Law' (n 154) 65 (*footnote omitted*).

198 Obviously, such a conclusion seems to be rather in opposition to the approach of the ICJ in *Kosovo*, when the Court completely separated the question of the declaration of independence from the legal issues related to secession and the question of the creation of a new State. See, in particular, *Kosovo* (n 10) para 83. Similarly, according to Milano, "unilateral declarations of independence are acts that cannot be taken in isolation, but have to be considered within the processes of State formation they aim at sanctioning." Milano, 'Declarations of Independence and Territorial Integrity in General International Law' (n 154) 75.

issues. Kohen pointed to problems with the legal characterisation of *uti possidetis* and State succession[199] and effective occupation[200] as legal acts – titles of territorial sovereignty or legal facts – and sources of territorial sovereignty, ultimately classifying them as legal acts "titres juridiques."[201] According to Distefano, effective occupation is "'fait attributive' de titre juridique" composed of "trois exigences-éléments constitutifs du fait juridique",[202] whereas "le défaut" of one these elements would constitute the cause of nullity of this "fait juridique complexe."[203]

199 See Kohen, *Possession contestée et souveraineté territoriale* (n 24) 131. "L'uti possidetis doit être rangé parmi les titres juridiques car, bien que le transfert de souveraineté ne s'opère pas par un accord entre l'Etat prédécesseur et l'Etat successeur, le nouvel Etat, *de par sa volonté de devenir tel,* assume l'exercice des compétences étatiques sur un territoire donné au moment même de son arrivée à la vie d'Etat indépendant. ... Il en va de même pour les cas de succession d'Etats dans lesquels aucun accord n'intervient entre Etat prédécesseur et Etat successeur. ... On pourrait certainement reprocher à cette manière de voir que la décolonisation, l'éclatement d'Etats fédéraux ou les diverses hypothèses de succession d'Etats en général sont autant de faits juridiques auxquels le droit attache une conséquence juridique, à savoir un changement de souveraineté sur le territoire de la division administrative ou de l'Etat auquel le nouveau titulaire succède. En fait, l'uti possidetis et la succession d'Etats se substituent au titres proprement dits, à tel point que l'on peut même faire la distinction entre le negotium et l'instrumentum, celui-ci étant parfois constitué de toutes les preuves administratives à propos de l'assiette territoriale du nouvel Etat dans la période précédant son indépendance." Kohen, *Possession contestée et souveraineté territoriale* (n 24) 149–150.

200 "L'occupation effective soulève quelques difficultés de classement. S'il s'agit indéniablement d'un ensemble de faits auxquels le droit des gens attribue comme conséquence l'établissement de la souveraineté territoriale sur une *terra nullius*, il n'en demeure pas moins que la volonté de l'occupant joue un rôle primordial, et ce dans un double sens. Premièrement, quant à l'existence du mode lui-même, qui requiert chez l'occupant la présence de l'*animus*. Deuxièmement, l'occupation est indépendante de toute autre volonté et, doublée des conditions matérielles nécessaires, elle permet l'établissement de la souveraineté sur un territoire donné. Le premier aspect rattache l'occupation aux faits juridiques, le second aux actes ou titre juridiques ... L'attitude des autres sujets a l'égard de l'occupation de ceux-ci et de la volonté manifestée par l'occupant de déployer sa souveraineté sur ces territoires ne peut avoir aucun effet si les conditions exigées par le droit international pour que l'occupation soit valable sont remplies." Kohen, *Possession contestée et souveraineté territoriale* (n 24) 152 (*footnotes omitted*). Similarly, see also J-P Jacqué, *Eléments pour une théorie de l'acte juridique en droit international public* (LGDJ 1972) 214 and 219–220.

201 Kohen, *Possession contestée et souveraineté territoriale* (n 24) 500 where *uti possidetis* and effective occupation are classified as 'titres juridiques.'

202 Distefano (178) 277.

203 ibid 277. It should be highlighted that nullity is only possible with respect to legal acts.

Thus, despite secession being traditionally seen as the matter of a simple fact, it has been demonstrated that the voluntary element, even if coming from a non-State actor, must be added to the picture. Therefore, it is more precise to define secession as a subjective legal fact ("fait juridique humain"),[204] as the sum of factual and voluntary elements attributive of the status of statehood as well as of the title of territorial sovereignty.

3.2 *Links between the DoI and Secession*

There is an inherent paradox between the wording of a formal DoI usually suggesting that a new State is created simply by virtue of its issuance and a traditional factualist view of secession. To tackle this apparent ambiguity, it is important to outline the various scenarios of legal and temporal links between the DoI and secession based on the premise of the factualist statehood. In particular, it is especially important to establish whether and if so, under which conditions, the day of issuance of a formal DoI can also be considered the day of a new State's creation. As mentioned above, the form of the DoI, whether solemn, written or oral act or unwritten act or series of acts, does not play a decisive role. Yet, since a formal DoI is the most frequent option, the following analysis will primarily focus on this scenario, while attempting to accommodate other possibilities.

It is also important to come back to the terms used in this book. 'Secession' is defined here as the creation of a new independent State through the separation of part of the territory and population of an existing State, without the consent of the latter.[205] Thus, it is a finalised completion of the emergence of a new State; the mode of succession of States. On the other hand, for this book, a process leading to such a final outcome is understood to be a 'secessionist attempt'; this by definition occurs in a pre-State context.[206] "[T]he process ends and the outcome begins when the seceding territory completes the transformation to a new State."[207]

204 "Ainsi, à l'origine de tout fait juridique humain se trouve une activité volontaire." Jacqué (n 200) 193.

205 Deriving from the definition in Kohen, 'Introduction' (n 72) 3.

206 "Secession is not an instant fact. It always implies a complex series of claims and decisions, negotiations and/or struggle, which may – or may not – lead to the creation of a new State." Kohen, 'Introduction' (n 72) 14. Here the distinction is made between secession as a final outcome and a secessionist attempt leading to secession.

207 G Anderson, 'Secession in International Law and Relations: What Are We Talking About?' (2013) 35 Loyola of Los Angeles International and Comparative Law Review 343, 355.

Thus, several scenarios of temporal links between the issuance of a formal DoI, secessionist attempt and secession can be outlined.[208] First, such a document can be issued at the beginning of or during the course of the secessionist attempt.[209] In fact, the DoI can trigger such a factual process. Nevertheless, a new State would emerge upon the establishment of the constitutive criteria, which might or might not follow the issuance of the DoI.[210] Thus, a formal DoI would have neither declaratory nor constitutive effects with respect to the emergence of a new State.

Second, the issuance of a formal DoI can coincide with the end of the factual process of a secessionist attempt.[211] In this scenario, if the factual criteria are met, the issuance of the DoI could coincide with the emergence of a new State.[212] It is probably the only scenario when a formal DoI can have a

---

208 "For example, the question as to whether and at what moment entity becomes a State under international law is very different to the question as to whether and at what point in time independence was declared. An entity wishing to secede may very well become a State under international law without making a declaration of independence at all. Conversely, a declaration of independence by an entity wishing to secede does not necessarily lead to the birth of a State under international law." *Kosovo* (n 10), Written Statement of Switzerland, para 27.

209 See Proclamation of the Republic of Biafra (30 May 1967) (1967) 6 ILM 665 et seq.; Declaration of Independence of Transnistrian Moldovan Republic (25 August 1991) <https://novostipmr.com/ru/news/21-08-25/deklaraciya-o-nezavisimosti> accessed 20 October 2023 (*in Russian*); Congress of Representatives of Territorial Communities, Political Parties and Public Organizations, 'Act on Declaration State Independence of the Luhansk People's Republic' (27 April 2014) <https://lugansk-lg-ua.livejournal.com/177285.html> accessed 7 February 2019 (*in Russian*). Anderson refers to the situation when the declaration of independence antedates the outcome of secession. Anderson, 'Secession in International Law and Relations' (n 207) 379–380.

210 In a similar vein: "but sometimes a declaration of independence will not instantly create a new State or even lead to a state creation at all." J Vidmar, 'Unilateral Declarations of Independence in International Law' in D French (ed), *Statehood and Self-determination: Reconciling Tradition and Modernity in International Law* (CUP 2013) 64. Similarly, MG Kohen: 'Le problème des frontières en cas de dissolution et de séparation d'États: quelles alternatives?' in O Corten, B Delcourt, P Klein and N Levrat (eds), *Démembrements d'États et délimitations territoriales: l'uti possidetis en question(s)* (Bruylant 1999) 394–395.

211 See Rhodesia: Proclamation of Independence: Proclamation by Prime Minister (11 November 1965) in (1966) 5 ILM 230 et seq.; Declaration of Independence by Turkish Cypriot Parliament (15 November 1983).

212 Similarly, Anderson refers to the situation when the declaration of independence coincides with the outcome of secession, pointing to fulfiment of the Montevideo criteria. Other similar situation can occur when the withdrawal takes place via consitutional or politically negotiated processes. Anderson, 'Secession in International Law and Relations' (n 207) 379–380.

declaratory effect on the emergence of a new State. Although as already indicated above, even in this scenario, the declaration would not have constitutive effect concerning the emergence of a new State.[213] The decisive element and legal basis would always be the effectiveness of the entity. Moreover, it would probably have been possible to infer intent to secede from other prior acts such as the establishment of the units of government.

In summary, the day of issuance of a formal DoI cannot be automatically considered the day of emergence of a new State, the effectiveness of the secessionist entity would be a primary threshold. Thus, even though the declaration can be considered a necessary and inseparable element of any secessionist attempt, it would not be sufficient on its own.[214] In the scenario of *unilateral* secession,[215] a formal DoI has never had constitutive effects concerning the creation of a new State.[216] "In international law, a unilateral declaration of independence that takes the form of an act of secession *prima facie* does not have the effect of calling into existence the international legal personality of that entity."[217] The DoI can have legal implications as "a basis for the achievement of international personality, other subjects of international law considering this situation opposable to them … [b]ut to actually attain the end result something additional was needed."[218] According to Gowlland-Debbas, if the declaratory theory of recognition was taken as prevalent, "the vital element is the objective existence of the criteria of independent statehood."[219]

Building on the above outline, it is possible to identify different periods concerning the secessionist attempt and secession. First, it is the duration of the secessionist attempt, which might or might not be initiated by the issuance of a formal DoI. Second, it is the period following an unsuccessful secessionist

213 "Under international law a declaration of independence is not a necessary element of statehood, nor is statehood a pre-condition for the enactment of a declaration of independence." Pertile (n 154) 99.

214 "[A] declaration of independence is a necessary, but not a sufficient, condition for unilateral secession." Crawford, 'State Practice and International Law in Relation to Secession' (n 158) 86. *Contra*: "[A]ltough a formal declaration of independence might be politically useful for secession, it is legally unnecessary." Anderson, 'Secession in International Law and Relations' (n 207) 380.

215 This entails situations outside the decolonisation context and without any pre-existing right to secede.

216 "It needs to be noted that while a declaration of independence does not create a state, it is indicative of an attempt at secession." See Vidmar, 'Conceptualizing Declarations of Independence in International Law' (n 154) 154, ftn 6.

217 Costelloe (n 4) 168.

218 Gowlland-Debbas (n 122) 205.

219 ibid.

attempt when the parent State asserts its control. Third, alternatively, it is the period following a successful secessionist attempt with a new State emerging; the end of such a factual process might or might not be marked by the issuance of a formal DoI. Finally, there could also be the situation of the parent State not asserting its control, but with no new State emerging. This last scenario is the subject of the analysis of Section 2.

3.3 *Conclusion*

This section established that the act of declaring independence as the expression of will or intent to secede and establish a new State, frequently formalised in the DoI, is an inseparable part of any secessionist attempt. Without this intentional element, also conceptualised as *animus* based on the analogy with the law of acquisition of territorial sovereignty, there would be no secession. It would be a different territorial situation. Based on this, the section also defined secession as a subjective legal fact, as the sum of factual and voluntary elements attributive of the status of statehood and the title of territorial sovereignty. Moreover, it also outlined links among the DoI, the secessionist attempt and secession, highlighting that outside of decolonisation and any pre-existing right to secede, the DoI never has constitutive effects of creating a new State.

4 DoI and Secessionist Attempt within the Purview of Peremptory Norms

Under a classical view, outside of decolonisation or any pre-existing legal right to secede and subject to the laws of armed conflict, the secessionist attempt is considered the internal matter of the parent State.[220] The piercing of the parent State's veil is not presumed.[221]

However, as follows from the above overview of practice and *opinio iuris* and specifically from *Kosovo* in which the ICJ referred to illegality attached to declarations of independence stemming from the connection "with the unlawful

220 See O Corten, 'Are There Gaps?' in MG Kohen (ed), *Secession: International Law Perspectives* (CUP 2006) 235–239.

221 This position seems to fit the ILC's approach in avoiding the issue of international legal personality of insurrectional movements and preferring to frame the issue in terms of attribution. SI Verhoeven, 'International Responsibility of Armed Opposition Groups: Lessons from State Responsibility for Actions of Armed Opposition Groups', in N Gal-Or, C Ryngaert and M Noortmann (eds), *Responsibilities of the Non-State Actor in Armed Conflict and the Market Place* (Brill Nijhoff 2015) 294.

use of force or other egregious violations of norms of general international law, in particular those of a peremptory character (*jus cogens*)",[222] this view must be redefined. A reverse analysis of this formulation – starting from the notion of illegality as a consequence of the violation of international law – *presupposes* at least a limited regulation of international law of the declarations of independence themselves.[223] In attaching illegality to the act of the DoI itself, the ICJ followed the views of numerous States.[224]

222 *Kosovo* (n 10) para 81. See *infra* on the details of the scope of applicable law in this respect.

223 See *infra* on scholars of the same and similar views.

224 Vidmar, 'Conceptualizing Declarations of Independence in International Law' (n 154) 170; Värk (n 135) 122, ftn 38. "In international practice, declarations of independence have only been held to violate *international* law if conjoined with some other violation. This has notably been the case when a declaration of independence has been brought about by the illegal use of force by another state or in violation of an international agreement. A case in point would be Security Council resolution 541 (1983) of 18 November 1983, in which the UN Security Council considered the -declaration of independence by the Turkish Cypriot authorities as 'legally invalid' and called 'for its withdrawal.'" *Kosovo* (n 10), Statement of the Federal Republic of Germany (15 April 2009) 29–30; "Although international law does not, on principle and generally, prohibit secession, it nonetheless contains certain rules of a prohibitory nature, and the violation of those rules in connection with a declaration of independence could result in that declaration being illegal." *Kosovo* (n 10), Written Statement by the French Republic (17 April 2009) 28, para 2.11; "For a start, seceding entities are subject to and must comply with *erga omnes* rules under international law. It would, for example, be theoretically possible for a declaration of independence to contain an incitement to genocide, thereby breaching one of the peremptory norms of international law (*jus cogens*)." *Kosovo* (n 10), Written Statement by the Swiss Confederation (25 May 2009) 8, para 29; "Ireland acknowledges that it is well-established that illegality may arise where secession is attempted in violation of peremptory norms of international law." *Kosovo* (n 10), Statement of the Government of Ireland (April 2009) 7, para 22; "Although declarations of independence do not by themselves violate international law, they are at times conjoined with other events or acts in combination with which they might be characterized as serious international law violations. This is an important distinction. For example, where a declaration of independence is adopted in conjunction with an effort to establish an apartheid regime-which would amount to a serious violation of a peremptory norm of international law-declarations of independence have been characterized as unlawful." *Kosovo* (n 10), Written Statement of the United States of America (17 April 2009) 56 (*footnote omitted*). "The DoI is not prohibited by international law, unless there were a violation of a peremptory norm." *Kosovo* (n 10), Reply of the Government of the Republic of Albania (July 2009) 22, para 35; "There is abundant regional and universal practice demonstrating that the creation of new States is governed by international law. Suffice to mention the examples of Katanga, Rhodesia, Biafra, the Bantustans, the so-called 'Turkish Republic of Northern Cyprus,' Anjouan, 'Somaliland,' the Serb entities within Croatia and Bosnia and Herzegovina, and the autonomous Republics within Georgia, among others." *Kosovo* (n 10), Written Comments of the Argentine Republic (July 2009) 8, para 12 (*footnote omitted*). See also *Kosovo* (n 10),

> The Court attaches illegality to the declarations of independence as such (and not any other activity related to them). This seems astonishing at the first sight. The Court's position can only be explained if neither declarations of independence nor their authors are generally outside the reach of international law.[225]

Importantly, as follows from the above, the DoI is an inseparable and necessary element of any secessionist attempt and, therefore, the secessionist attempt as a whole arguably also falls within the purview of peremptory norms.

Despite the ICJ's *Kosovo* formula having far-reaching ramifications, the ICJ left too many questions unanswered.[226] For example, what are the substantive and procedural requirements for triggering illegality attached to the DoI as acts of non-state actors? Who is capable of violating peremptory norms in this scenario? Is this possibility limited only to States or could non-State actors

---

Written Statement by the Republic of Cyprus (3 April 2009) 47–49, paras 184–192; *Kosovo* (n 10), Written Comments of the United Kingdom (17 July 2009) 17–18, paras 36–37.

225 C Walter, 'Post-Script: Self-Determination, Secession, and the Crimean Crisis 2014' in C Walter, A Von Ungern-Sternberg and K Abushov (eds), *Self-determination and Secession in International Law* (OUP 2014) 301–302. "It is important to note that here we are not dealing with the prohibition of recognition (an obligation erga omnes) of an effective situation created by a breach of *jus cogens* but rather with the interpretation that a declaration of independence may be, under certain circumstances, itself an illegal act under international law." J Vidmar, 'The Kosovo Advisory Opinion Scrutinized' (2011) 24 Leiden Journal of International Law 355, 370 (*footnotes omitted*). "Analysis of the practice of the Security Council showed that it is possible to assess the legality of declarations of independence in light of international law and even pronounce them illegal." Värk (n 135) 122.

226 "As a result, the exact scope of exclusion of declarations of independence from international law remains unclear. Apart from outright military intervention, the advisory opinion does not provide for criteria as to when the involvement of outside power in an internal struggle renders international law applicable also to internal non-state actors striving for independence." Walter (n 225) 311. "The Kosovo Opinion is not as narrow as it is sometimes believed to be. It is certainly not a non-opinion. And if scrutinised in light of international legal doctrine, its pronouncements can be both very controversial and very far-reaching. But not controversial and far-reaching enough to tell whether or not Kosovo is a state." J Vidmar, 'The Kosovo Opinion and General International Law: How Far-Reaching and Controversial Is the ICJ's Reasoning?' The Hague Justice Portal (2010) 5 <https://papers.ssrn.com/sol3/papers.cfm?abstract_id=2060605> accessed 20 March 2018. "The Kosovo Court said that the use of force is prohibited in secession processes, but did not say whether the international prohibition of the use of force is applicable *within* the territory of a not yet definitely dissolved state, and *to whom* this prohibition is addressed." A Peters, 'Does Kosovo Lie in the Lotus-Land of Freedom?' (2011) 24 Leiden Journal of International Law 95, 105.

violate peremptory norms too? Can violation of peremptory norms invalidate the DoI?

The key elements of para 81 of the *Kosovo* Advisory Opinion can be outlined as follows: (i) the originating acts of 'the unlawful use of force or other egregious violations of norms of general international law, in particular those of a peremptory character (*jus cogens*)', (ii) the criterion of 'connection with' and (iii) the consequences of 'illegality attached to declaration of independence.' By reference to these elements, the following section examines the scope of applicable peremptory norms, the criterion of connection with violation, the addressees of peremptory norms and legal consequences from their violation. Where appropriate, the analysis also refers to the effects of peremptory norms on unilateral acts of States and their adaptation to the secessionist context.

4.1 *General Observations*

An older scholarship outright rejected the applicability of peremptory norms to unilateral acts of States. This doctrinal position relied on the definition and legal consequences of peremptory norms in Article 53 of the Vienna Convention on the Law of Treaties (VCLT).[227] In particular, the difference between the violation of a norm[228] and derogation from a norm[229] was highlighted. According to Paul Weil, the extension of theory of *jus cogens* norms to unilateral acts "apparaît logiquement intenable."[230] "The only question with

227 "Whether, therefore, peremptory norms could have effects 'outside' the law of treaties was a question that could hardly arise, because to frame the question in this manner sounded like asking whether the law relating to the invalidity of contracts could find application 'outside' the law of contracts." Costelloe (n 4) 93.

228 "A norm is *violated* when a conduct of a subject (or, subjects) of law, which is at variance with that norm, is directed against another subject (or, other subjects) of law without his (or, their) consent." J Sztucki, *Jus Cogens and the Vienna Convention on the Law of Treaties: A Critical Appraisal* (Springer-Verlag 1974) 67–68 (*emphasis in original*).

229 "A norm is *derogated from* when a conduct of a subject (or subjects) of law, which is at variance with that norm, is intended to produce consequences only for the derogating subjects themselves, and without affecting any rights of others." Sztucki (n 228) 68 (*emphasis in original*).

230 "Alors que dans le cadre du droit des traités la question se pose de savoir si les Etats peuvent déroger à une règle de *jus cogens,* il n'est pas question de dérogation pour ce qui est d'un acte unilatéral: un tel acte ou bien respecte le droit international, ou bien il le viole; il n'y déroge pas. L'application de la théorie *du jus cogens* aux actes ou agissements unilatéraux est tout simplement une impossibilité logique." P Weil, 'Le droit international en quête de son identité: Cours général de droit international public' in (1992) 237 RCADI 281.

regard to unilateral acts was thus whether they were legal or illegal; *jus cogens* and the possible nullity attaching to its violation were irrelevant."[231]

Today, such a doctrinal position is largely overcome. Some authors tend to assimilate unilateral acts of States to treaties.[232] Other scholars frequently invoke *a fortiori* reasoning.[233] "For if a jus cogens rule cannot be derogated by

---

231 K Zemanek, 'The Metamorphosis of Jus Cogens: From an Institution of Treaty Law to the Bedrock of the International Legal Order?' in E Cannizzaro (ed), *Law of Treaties Beyond the Vienna Convention* (OUP 2011) 393 (*footnote omitted*). "En ce qui concerne, par contre, les actes unilatéraux, l'activité d'un seul Etat n'a nullement besoin de cette construction: comme un *seul* Etat ne peut jamais légiférer en droit international, aucune confusion ne peut avoir lieu au sujet d'une creation légitime ou illégitime de normes de sa part." K Marek, Contribution à l'étude du *jus cogens* en droit international' in *Receuil d'études de droit international en hommage à Paul Guggenheim* (Imprimerie de la Tribune de Genève 1968) 441 (*emphasis in original*).

232 "Unilateral acts or omissions can contribute to the establishment of a legal regime supplanting a preexisting one. To that extent, they can be assimilated to treaties. This is why an act or omission, which is contrary to a jus cogens rule is devoid of any legal effect. It cannot give place through recognition, acquiescence or prescription, to a new legal regime, as would violations of other rules of international law." G Abi-Saab, 'Introduction' in *The Concept of Jus Cogens in International Law, Papers and Proceedings: Conference on International Law, Lagonissi, Greece, 3–8 April 1966* (Carnegie Endowment for International Peace 1967) 10–11. Similarly, Suy also highlights that "[i]f the specific effect of the application of the jus cogens is to render null and void (even between the Contracting Parties) a treaty whose object is contrary to its absolutely binding rules the same must apply to any legal act or any action which might lead in fact, through recognition or tolerance, to a tacit agreement." E Suy, 'The Concept of *Jus Cogens* in Public International Law' in *The Concept of Jus Cogens in International Law, Papers and Proceedings: Conference on International Law, Lagonissi, Greece, 3–8 April 1966* (Carnegie Endowment for International Peace 1967) 75.

233 "La vaste majorité des auteurs qui admet l'application du *ius cogens* aux actes unilatéraux s'en tient à un simple raisonnement *a fortiori*. Si le *ius cogens* protège des valeurs fondamentales de la communauté internationale et s'oppose par conséquent à la validité d'un accord particulier contraire, à plus fort raison doit-il s'appliquer à un acte inférieur dans la hiérarchie normative tel qu'un acte unilatéral, afin de garantir l'intégrité des intérets suprêmes auxquels il se prépose." R Kolb, *Théorie du ius cogens international: essai de relecture du concept* (PUF 2001) 90 (*footnote omitted*); "If all treaties in conflict with a peremptory norm are prohibited and, consequently, all acts based on such treaties are unlawful, it seems evident that the outcome is the comprehensive prohibition of all acts contrary to peremptory norms." L Hannikainen, *Peremptory Norms (Jus Cogens) in International Law: Historical Development, Criteria, Present Status* (Lakimiesliiton Kustannus 1988) 6. "It is difficult to justify that jus cogens rules are sacrosanct in one context and freely derogable in another." Crawford, *The Creation of States in International Law* (n 1) 109; "Once peremptory norms are seen as the product of general international law rather than any specific instrument, it follows that there is no inherent limitation as to the types or categories of acts and transactions to which such norms may apply." A Orakhelashvili, *Peremptory Norms in International Law* (OUP 2006) 206. "In answer to

treaty, it cannot *a fortiori*, be violated by a unilateral act or omission."[234] An underlying objective of removing the origins of a potential violation of peremptory norm seems to apply to treaties and unilateral acts in the same way.[235] Therefore, "[o]ne should speak of rules which should not be *violated* (instead of *derogated*) whether by treaties or by unilateral acts or omissions."[236] Thus, *a fortiori* reasoning also underlines their applicability to the secessionist context.

4.2 *Applicable Law*

Under the *Kosovo* formula, the illegality attached to the declarations of independence stems from the fact that they "were, or would have been, connected with the unlawful use of force or other egregious violations of norms of general international law, in particular those of a peremptory character (*jus cogens*)."[237] The ICJ provided no further explanations, apart from clarifying that illegality would not stem from the unilateral character of the DoI *per se*.[238] The ICJ referred not only to peremptory norms, but also to the norms of *general* international law.[239]

The ICJ built on the UNSC practice. Generally, the UNSC has on a number of occasions directly addressed the secessionists.[240] The ICJ itself said it "has not been uncommon for the Security Council to make demands on actors other than UN Member States and intergovernmental organizations."[241] In particular,

those who argue that, unlike that of international crimes, only the category of rules of jus cogens has entered the realm of treaty law and that the concept, as worded in the Vienna Convention, cannot logically be extended outside a treaty context to unilateral acts, it has been pointed out that it is difficult to accept the view that a rule should be sacrosant in one context and not in another, and that if a jus cogens rule cannot be derogated from by treaty it cannot *a fortiori*, be violated by a unilateral act or omission without having the same legal effects." Gowlland-Debbas (n 122) 248 (*footnote omitted*).

234 Abi-Saab summarizing position of other partipants of the Lagonissi conference. Abi-Saab (n 232) 10.

235 G Gaja, 'Jus Cogens Beyond the Vienna Convention' in (1969) 172 RCADI 295.

236 Abi-Saab summarizing the position of other participants of the Lagonissi conference. Abi-Saab (n 232) 10.

237 *Kosovo* (n 10) para 81.

238 ibid.

239 While from a classical perspective the declarations of independence are completely outside of international law regulation, the ICJ seems to suggest that their illegality could be due to a mere connection with egregious violations of a *general* international law.

240 See *Kosovo* (n 10) para 116–119.

241 *Kosovo* (n 10) para 116.

with respect to declarations of independence, the UNSC has adopted two approaches.[242]

First, more frequently, the UNSC has condemned the act, qualified it as illegal or invalid and derived legal consequences from such a qualification.[243] Such a determination *presupposes* the applicability of international law to the acts and actions of secessionist groups. In *Kosovo*, the ICJ referred to the UNSC resolutions concerning Southern Rhodesia and the TRNC. The determinations in the UNSC Resolutions 216 and 217 (1965) regarding Southern Rhodesia was derived from a pre-existing obligation of the Smith regime to respect the right of self-determination and not to violate the prohibition of racial discrimination.[244] The qualification in the UNSC Resolution 541 (1983) was connected with Turkey's violation of the prohibition of the use of force.[245] The reference to these resolutions supports a concluding part of para 81 that explicitly refers to *ius cogens*.

Similarly, from the above practice follows that only a fairly limited number of norms – the prohibition of the use of force, the right to self-determination

242 In this context, it is also important to rebut Kassoti's argument that limits the relevance of the ICJ finding in para 81 by pointing out that the ICJ specifically said that the UNSC "was making a determination as regards *the concrete situation existing at the time* that those declarations of independence were made." Kassoti (n 150) 232 referring to para 81 of *Kosovo*. It is true that the ICJ limited the relevance of the UNSC practice, but its purpose was to underline that this practice cannot be sufficient to induce a general prohibition of unilateral declarations of independence. Nevertheless, according to the ICJ, the practice seems to support a specific prohibition when the violation of peremptory norms occurs.

243 According to Murphy, "the Council at times addresses its resolutions to non-state actors and the failure of those to abide by the resolution might be regarded as a violation of international law." Nevertheless, Murphy contends that "in situations involving a declaration of independence, the Council (or the General Assembly) typically does not demand that the relevant actor refrain from issuing a declaration or withdraw a declaration that has been issued, nor decide that the declaration as such violates international law. Rather, the Council condemns the issuance of a declaration and decides that it should not be given legal effect by the United Nations or Member States. In other words, the approach taken is not to impose an obligation on the non-state actor but, rather, to make a determination as to the legal effect of that actor's conduct." S Murphy, 'Reflections on the ICJ Advisory Opinion on Kosovo: Interpreting Security Council Resolution 1244 (1999)' in M Wood and M Milanović (eds), *The Law and Politics of the Kosovo Advisory Opinion* (OUP 2015) 161–162 (*footnote omitted*). However, it is argued that the determination of the legal effects of a non-State actor's conduct in itself presupposes that these acts fall within the regulatory framework of international law, possibly also including obligations on the side of a non-State actor.

244 See also *supra*. Similarly, Milano, 'Declarations of Independence and Territorial Integrity in General International Law' (n 154) 72–73.

245 See *supra*.

and the prohibition of apartheid and racial discrimination – have been invoked in this context. All these norms are referred to as peremptory and, as such, entail legal effects without any qualifier as to the seriousness of their violation.[246] Crawford also stated, "the question must be whether the illegality is so central to the existence … of the entity in question that international law may justifiably treat an effective entity as not a State."[247] Incidental violations would not have such an effect.[248]

Second, less frequently, the UNSC has directly called on all the concerned parties to respect non-peremptory obligations.[249] "[A]ccording to the ICJ, even non-state actors may be duty-bearers under the lex specialis regime of Security Council resolutions."[250]

This scenario is supported by the ICJ's reference to the UNSC Resolution 787 (1992) regarding the Republika Srpska not adopted under chapter VII UN Charter. The UNSC reaffirmed its own determination that "any taking of territory by force or any practice of 'ethnic cleansing' is unlawful and unacceptable" and "its call on all parties and others concerned to respect strictly the territorial integrity of the Republic of Bosnia and Herzegovina" affirming "that any entities unilaterally declared or arrangements imposed in contravention thereof will not be accepted."[251] Thus, the UNSC required *inter alia* secessionists to

---

246 See *infra* on why qualifying the duty of non-recognition as a "serious" violation does not seem to be compatible with the purpose of peremptory norms. Similar reasoning is also applicable to the qualifier "egregious" in *Kosovo*.

247 Crawford, *The Creation of States in International Law* (n 1) 105.

248 "[I]n the context of territorial status, incidental violations of peremptory norms-however deplorable as incidents-can hardly be held to preclude the statehood of an entity otherwise qualified, and thus to impair the representation at the international level of the people concerned. War crimes may be committed during a war of national liberation, for example: a treaty could not provide for impunity in respect of such crimes, but is the status of the emergent entity to be denied because of them?" Crawford, *The Creation of States in International Law* (n 1) 102. But according to Peters, "[a] constitutionalist approach suggests extending the scope of this requirement of international legality so as to cover other peremptory precepts as well. It is unpersuasive to demand the observance of self-determination, but not of human rights which are *jus cogens*, such as basic humanitarian law norms, which may be violated in the course of a secession war." A Peters, 'Membership in the Global Constitutional Community' in J Klabbers, A Peters and G Ulfstein, *The Constitutionalization of International Law* (OUP 2009) 181.

249 In *Kosovo*, "[t]he ICJ did not, as a matter of principle, exclude a binding effect of a decision for a non-State actor." A Peters, 'Article 25' in B Simma and others (eds), *The Charter of the United Nations: A Commentary* (OUP 2012) 803.

250 Vidmar, 'Conceptualizing Declarations of Independence in International Law' (n 154) 169.

251 UNSC Res 787 (16 November 1992) UN Doc S/RES/787, paras 2 and 3. Milano argues that the respect principle of territorial integrity is directly applicable to secessionists. Milano,

respect the territorial integrity of the parent State; the principle of territorial integrity does not have a peremptory character, and according to the ICJ, normally, it is not even directly applicable to secessionists.[252]

Would violation of such an obligation lead to the same consequences as the violation of peremptory norms? The above account suggests so, even outside chapter VII UN Charter.[253] This is rather paradoxical, considering the ICJ's approach to the analysis of the same question with respect to the UNSC Resolution 1244 (1999) and the DoI of Kosovo.[254] Thus, overall, para 81 of *Kosovo* could be also understood as referring to obligations stemming from *lex specialis* of the UNSC. It is unclear what the ICJ meant by reference to the norms of *general* international law; the practice to support such a claim is lacking.

4.3 *Criterion of Connection with Violation*

The ICJ held that illegality attached to the DoI stemmed from the fact that "they were, or would have been, connected with" violations of *ius cogens* norms.[255] Scholars adopted various positions on what exactly the criterion of 'connected with' entails. Milano suggested, 'connection' might imply a *direct link* between egregious violation of international law and DoI or aim at *consolidation* of a

---

'Declarations of Independence and Territorial Integrity in General International Law' (n 154) 72.

252 "[I]f the Security Council had wanted to preclude a declaration of independence, it would have done so in clear and unequivocal terms in the text of the resolution, as it did in resolution 787 (1992) concerning the Republika Srpska." *Kosovo* (n 10) para 112.

253 "Even if the so-called State 'constitutive elements' are effectively fulfilled by an entity, it will not constitute a State if it was created … against of what was established by a Security Council Resolution (such as the case of Kosovo), or if the forcible secessionist attempt is considered as a threat to international peace and security, leading the Security Council to invoke the principle of territorial integrity." Kohen, 'Secession: a Legal Approach' (n 129) 16. "One possible explanation could be that Security Council resolutions may 'internationalize' declarations of independence. Under such a reading, the respective passage in resolution 787(1992) would not reflect the general position of international law on territorial integrity, but merely follow from the decision of the Security Council to ban such a declaration in the Bosnian context." Walter (n 225) 302. However, according to Milano, declarations of independence can violate even dispositive rules of international law. Milano, 'Declarations of Independence and Territorial Integrity in General International Law' (n 154) 73.

254 MG Kohen and K Del Mar, 'The Kosovo Advisory Opinion and UNSCR 1244 (1999): A Declaration of "Independence from International Law"?' (2011) 24 Leiden Journal of International Law 109, 123–124.

255 *Kosovo* (n 10) para 81.

situation produced by a grave violation of international law.[256] According to Pippan, this entails situation when,

> such a declaration *results directly from* racial discrimination and the suppression of the right of peoples to self-determination (the Southern Rhodesia scenario), the use of inter-state force (the Northern Cyprus scenario), or 'ethnic cleansing' and other massive and systematic human rights violations (the Republika Srpska scenario).[257]

According to Schmalenbach, unilateral acts of states "conflict with ius cogens if they *directly profit from* and *perpetuate* the ius cogens violation."[258] According to Vidmar, a narrow interpretation would entail the declaration as a direct consequence of breach of *jus cogens* norm but, by including the terms 'in connection with', the ICJ opted for a broader approach covering "an attempt at consolidation of an effective situation created in violation of a certain fundamental norm of international law."[259] "In other words, UDI is issued in violation of international law where it attempts to *consolidate* an unlawful effective territorial situation."[260] For Costelloe,

> [a] declaration of independence intended to regularize the breach of an obligation under certain fundamental norms of general international law cannot, in any event, generate the desired legal effect of endowing such an entity with attributes of statehood and international legal personality, according to State and Security Council practice.[261]

256 Milano, 'Declarations of Independence and Territorial Integrity in General International Law' (n 154) 73 (*emphasis added*).

257 C Pippan, 'The International Court of Justice's Advisory Opinion on Kosovo's Declaration of Independence: An Exercise in the Art of Silence' (2010) 3–4 European Journal of Minority Studies, 145, 155–156 (*emphasis added*).

258 K Schmalenbach, 'Article 53: Treaties Conflicting with a Peremptory Norm of General International Law ("Jus Cogens")' in Dörr O and K Schmalenbach (eds), *Vienna Convention on the Law of Treaties: A Commentary* (Springer 2012) 931 (*emphasis added*).

259 Vidmar, 'Conceptualizing Declarations of Independence in International Law' (n 154) 170–171.

260 ibid 171.

261 Costelloe (n 4) 168–169. "In sum, in present international law a declaration expressing a claim to statehood produces no legal effect where the underlying claim arises out of an unlawful use of force in violation of Article 2(4) of the Charter, where it emanates from an oppressive racist minority regime, or where it is in conflict with any peremptory norm." ibid 170.

Thus, according to scholars, the DoI can be 'connected with' the violations of peremptory norms either when such an act *directly results* from the breach of peremptory norms or when it aims at *consolidation* or *regularisation* of the situation created in violation of peremptory norms. In both of these cases, the issuance of the DoI temporarily follows the violation of peremptory norms.

However, from a temporal perspective, the issuance of the DoI does not need to occur only at the end of the secessionist process potentially tainted by the violation of peremptory norms, but it can also precede such a violation or occur in its course. The DoI cannot be separated from the secessionist attempt. In essence, what is decisive is that all these material and intentional elements form one factual process, which is interfered or supported by the violation of peremptory norms.

Therefore, the criterion of 'the connection with' needs to be formulated broadly. Essentially, it should not only cover the situations when the DoI aims at the consolidation of violation of peremptory norms, but also the cases when the violation of peremptory norms aims at the consolidation of an existing secessionist attempt already expressed in the DoI. Moreover, "connection with" is broad enough to cover the situations when the terms of the DoI directly violate peremptory norms.[262] However, in any case, as follows, this criterion requires nexus between the violation of peremptory norms and the existence of entity and/or its declaration of independence. Mere incidental violations would not be enough.[263]

4.4 *Addressees*

Kosovo does not directly clarify who the addressees of the obligation not to violate peremptory norms are. The ICJ did not provide any explicit clarification and the doctrine is divided. Some scholars believe that according to *Kosovo*, the secessionists are directly obliged to conform to peremptory norms,[264]

---

262 For example, in a case where the declaration of independence itself would call for the establishment of a state whose main purpose would be to violate peremptory norms such as the prohibition of racial discrimination or the right to self-determination.

263 Crawford, *The Creation of States in International Law* (n 1) 102 and 105.

264 "In light of this reasoning, it is conceptually unclear why an independence-seeking entity, as a non-state actor, cannot offend against the territorial integrity of states but, at the same time, can be responsible for 'egregious violations of [certain] norms of international law, in particular those of a peremptory character.'" J Vidmar, 'The Kosovo Advisory Opinion Scrutinized' (n 225) 369–370. "While the Court, in paragraph 80 of the Opinion quoted Article 2(4) of the Charter and stated that 'the scope of the principle of territorial integrity is confined to the sphere of relations between states', it did not make that statement with regard to the principle of non-use of force. Although both principles (territorial integrity and non-use of force) are enshrined on one provision of the Charter,

whereas other authors see the operation of peremptory norms only via the third State.[265] The following account will explore both scenarios separately.

4.4.1 Involvement of the Third State in the Secessionist Attempt

The scenario of the third State's violating peremptory norms and interfering in the secessionist process is supported by the ICJ's reference to the UNSC resolution concerning the TRNC.[266] There is no doubt that all States are at all times under the obligation not to violate peremptory norms including the prohibition of the use of force. However, a legitimate question arises "[w]hy should a possible violation of the prohibition of the use of force by a third state affect the legality of a declaration of independence made by a secessionist group?"[267] Similarly, Kassoti showed a tenuous link between the violation of the rule by the third State and secessionist conduct to attribute liability to the latter.[268]

The first impulse concerning the relationship between the acts of non-State actors and third States is to refer to attribution rules:

> The argument is not very clear, yet it could suggest that an act by a non-state actor (a declaration of independence, referendum) connected with the unlawful use of force by a foreign state could be attributed to this state and, as such, could be qualified as unlawful.[269]

However, in para 81 of *Kosovo* the ICJ did not mention any known attribution rules.[270] The ICJ used the criterion of 'connection with', which does not correspond to the known attribution rules and is premised on a lower threshold

---

they are not identical in contents. Given the different substance and normative status of those two principles, their addressees might differ as well." Peters, 'Does Kosovo Lie in the Lotus-Land of Freedom?' (n 226) 106. According to Peters, paragraph 81 of *Kosovo* seems to suggest that Article 2(4) of the UN Charter binds secessionists themselves. ibid.

265 Tancredi doubts that paragraph 81 of *Kosovo* applies to insurgents. A Tancredi, 'Secession and Use of Force' in C Walter, A Von Ungern-Sternberg and K Abushov (eds), *Self-determination and Secession in International Law* (OUP 2014) 75–76.

266 *Kosovo* (n 10) para 81.

267 Walter (n 225) 302.

268 "This would attribute liability to an entity for a breach committed by another subject and would be at variance with the rules of attribution under the law of State responsibility." Kassoti (n 150) 232 (*footnote omitted*) and 231.

269 V Bílková, 'Territorial (Se)Cession in Light of Recent Events in Crimea' in E Milano, M Nicolini and F Palermo (eds), *Law, Territory and Conflict Resolution: Law as a Problem and Law as a Solution* (Brill Nijhoff 2016) 214, ftn 86.

270 See ARSIWA (n 23) arts 4–11.

than the criterion of 'direction or control' under Article 8 ARSIWA.[271] It is highly unlikely that in para 81 of *Kosovo* the Court sought to formulate a new attribution rule.

Thus, it is argued that under para 81 of *Kosovo*, illegality is *attached* to the act of secessionists because the peremptory violations by the third State and this act are inter-linked and form part of the same phenomenon. Therefore, although non-State actors are not direct violators of peremptory norms, their acts and actions are not allowed to escape the regulatory framework of peremptory norms. This explanation echoes the corollary to the prohibition of the use of force resulting in unlawfulness of territorial situations such as the acquisition of territory in breach of peremptory norms.[272] In addition, it would be in line with the commentary to Article 41(2) ASRIWA that refers to unlawfulness of "situations resulting directly from serious breaches in the sense of article 40."[273] However, as mentioned, the analogy between unlawful territorial transfers and secession involving the violation of peremptory norms by the third State is not straightforward. While the former situation involves the application of international law *inter vivos* and its unlawfulness taints the acts of the same subject that creates an ensuing unlawful situation, the latter situation is more complex because it involves multiple actors. Thus, if the establishment of the constitutive criteria of statehood and the issuance of the DoI directly results from or in the ICJ's words is 'connected with' violation peremptory norms by the third State, the entire secessionist process including the DoI is tainted by illegality deriving from such violation by the third State. This underscores rather pervasive effects of peremptory norms that extend into a non-State secessionist context due to its 'connection with' the original violation by another subject.

---

271 "Such conduct will be attributable to the State only if it directed or controlled the specific operation and the conduct complained of was an integral part of that operation. The principle does not extend to conduct which was only incidentally or peripherally associated with an operation and which escaped from the State's direction or control." ARSIWA commentary to art 8, para 3. See also *Nicaragua* (n 153), paras 109 and 115 ("*Nicaragua*").

272 See Crawford, *The Creation of States in International Law* (n 1) 96–174. See also *supra*.

273 See ARSIWA (n 23) commentary art 41(2), para 5. ARSIWA also provides examples of unlawful "situations," including *inter alia* the Manchurian crisis, the Iraqi invasion of Kuwait, the situation in Namibia, Rhodesia, and Bantustans and by implication also in the TRNC. ARSIWA (n 23) commentary to art 41(2), paras 5–10 and ftn 661 referring to the case law of the ECtHR on the TRNC. However, it is quite surprising to find reference to the situation of Southern Rhodesia here. Indeed, such a reference seems to be rather misplaced, in view of the fact that ARSIWA deals only with State responsibility; the Special Rapporteur's writings suggest that Southern Rhodesia was never a State due to the violation of the right to self-determination by this entity without interference of any other State.

4.4.2 Secessionist Group as a Direct Bearer of Peremptory Obligations

Arguably, under para 81 of *Kosovo*, the secessionist group itself could be understood as a direct bearer of pre-existing obligations not to violate the peremptory norms of international law.[274] This scenario would entail the limited international legal personality of the secessionist group. There is nothing in the wording of para 81 of *Kosovo* that would contradict such a possibility.[275] On the contrary, this follows on from the ICJ's reference to the UNSC resolutions concerning Southern Rhodesia[276] and to the UNSC resolution on Republika Srpska as far as the potential separate obligations under the UNSC resolutions are concerned. Such a conclusion would not run counter to the original purpose of these resolutions.[277]

> [T]he fact that the United Nations determined there had been a violation of international law did not automatically imply that responsibility had to be imputed to an independent State … [f]ar from this constituting a

274 Roucounas came to a similar conclusion with respect to the legal position of insurrectional movements in an intermediate situation that is neither forming a new government, nor creating a new State. "Considering that in any case the movement is bound by the rules of customary international humanitarian law, it also must abide at least by the *erga omnes* rules of the system." E Roucounas, 'Non-State Actors: Areas of International Responsibility in Need of Further Exploration' in M Ragazzi (ed), *International Responsibility Today* (Brill 2005) 395 and 398.

275 "Security Council decisions cannot internationally bind actors who do not enjoy a however limited international legal personality, because those actors are by definition not capable of incurring any international legal obligation. However, repeated decisions addressing non-State actors may be considered as an indication of the Security Council members' legal opinion that these actors can indeed be saddled with international legal obligations, and thus contribute themselves to the recognition of their international legal personality." Peters, 'Article 25' (n 249) 803.

276 "[E]ven collective non-recognition towards Southern Rhodesia was motivated by the breach of cogent norms (particularly the principle of self-determination), which the illegal regime was evidently deemed bound to respect." Tancredi, 'A Normative "Due Process"' (n 144) 199–200.

277 "It would be odd if the SC accepted that an entity had the prerequisite legal personality to be able to commit an internationally wrongful act when the aim of the resolutions was precisely to deny such entities the capacity to become subjects of international law." Kassoti (n 150) 226–227. *Contra*: Regarding the argument concerning "the undesirable legal vacuum created where international law withholds legal status from effective legal entities," Crawford points out that "this simply is not the case. Relevant international legal rules can apply to *de facto* situations here as elsewhere." Crawford, *The Creation of States in International Law* (n 1) 99.

> recognition of independence … it would on the contrary constituted its negation.[278]

Generally, there are no inherent features of international law that would preclude such a conclusion.

> [T]he fact that secessionist movements are nonstate actors in no way hinders their subjection to international legal rules, because international law is no pure interstate law. Several rules of international humanitarian law apply to armed groups, and further international legal obligations may be imposed on them.[279]

"[S]ubjects of international law for particular purposes are created as and when a norm of international law is applied to them or by means of collective recognition."[280] Moreover, the ILC itself acknowledged the possibility of the international responsibility of the insurrectional movements.[281] The doctrine

---

278 Gowlland-Debbas (n 122) 231–232. Referring specifically to the case of Southern Rhodesia, Gowlland-Debbas derived the collective responsibility also from the specific contours of the right to self-determination: "[T]he view that European minority régime could have been held to have collective responsibility aside from any recognition of belligerency, would tally with or be implicit in the right of self-determination as a norm of international law creating rights and duties and not merely as a principle to be respected and complied with by States. For if, … it is recognized that the right of self-determination carries with it the implicit affirmation of the international personality of a people entitled to exercise this right … as well as the extension of this right to their representative organs, namely the national liberation movements, then it could be argued surely that there is no reason to limit the entity against whom this right can be invoked to a State." ibid 235–236. She also admitted that the UN was not approaching this matter entirely consistently. For example, on the one hand, the UK was held responsible for the application of the Charter and UNGA Res 1514 (XV) notwithstanding the UK's having no effective control over the territory and, on the other hand, sanctions were not directed against it. ibid 236–237.

279 Q Qerimi, 'What the Kosovo Advisory Opinion Means for the Rest of the World' (2011) ASIL Proceedings 259, 267.

280 Gowlland-Debbas (n 122) 236.

281 "A further responsibility is that the insurrectional movement may itself be held responsible for its own conduct under international law, for example for a breach of international humanitarian law committed by its forces." ARSIWA (n 23) commentary to art 10, para 16. On this topic and on the question of attribution of conduct to armed opposition groups, see SI Verhoeven, 'International Responsibility of Armed Opposition Groups' (n 221) 294–303. For the position of national liberation movements, see H Atlam, 'National Liberation Movements and International Responsibility' in M Spinedi and B Simma (eds), *United Nations Codification of International Responsibility* (Oceana Publications 1987) 35–56. See also the ICJ discussing the responsibility of *contras* for violation of humanitarian law *Nicaragua* (n 153)) para 116.

on numerous occasions inferred a limited personality of armed opposition groups – parties to non-international armed conflict as bearers of obligations[282] under the law of armed conflicts,[283] human rights law,[284] peace and ceasefire agreements[285] and the UNSC resolutions.[286] Therefore, there is nothing that would *a priori* exclude the above practice's reading with respect to the applicability of peremptory norms vis-à-vis secessionist groups themselves.

A critical issue would be to conceptualise the criterion that would render international law applicable in such a manner. In short, when does a relevant secessionist attempt – process leading to secession – begin from the perspective of international law?[287] Some scholars believe that an already established effectiveness of entity declaring independence should be a guiding criterion. For example, Vidmar claimed,

> it is thus effectiveness that leads to the difference between declarations of independence that are, in terms of international law, merely ink on paper and declarations of independence that are capable of having legal effects; only the former but not the latter fall outside of regulation under international law.[288]

282 See generally SI Verhoeven, 'International Responsibility of Armed Opposition Groups' (n 221) 285, ftn 2–5.

283 L Zegveld, *Accountability of Armed Opposition Groups in International Law* (CUP 2002); A Cassese, 'The Status of Rebels Under The 1977 Geneva Protocol on Non-International Armed Conflicts' (1981) 41 ICLQ 416; S Sivakumaran, 'Binding Armed Opposition Groups' (2006) 55 International and Comparative Law Quarterly 369.

284 Zegveld (n 283).

285 See PH Kooijmans, 'The Security Council and Non-State Entities as Parties to Conflicts' in K Wellens (ed), *International Law: Theory and Practice: Essays in Honour of Eric Suy* (M Nijhof Publishers 1998) 338; Roucounas (n 274) 395–397.

286 See G Cahin, 'Responsibility of Other Entities: Armed Bands and Criminal Groups' in J Crawford and others (eds), *The Law of International Responsibility* (OUP 2010) 338–341; A Constantinides, 'Human Rights Obligations and Accountability of Armed Opposition Groups: The Practice of The UN Security Council' (2010) 4 Human Rights and International Legal Discourse 89.

287 An arbitral tribunal in the case concerning maritime delimitation between Guinea-Bissau and Senegal searched for the moment when a national liberation movement acquired "une portée internationale." *Case Concerning the Delimitation of Maritime Boundary between Guinea-Bissau and Senegal* (1989) XX RIAA 119, para 51 ("*Maritime Boundary between Guinea-Bissau and Senegal*").

288 Vidmar, 'Conceptualizing Declarations of Independence in International Law' (n 154) 159. Moreover, "one needs to differentiate between quasi-declarations of independence issued by random groups and declarations of independence properly so-called, which are issued by representative authorities of the effective entity in question and cannot conceptually fall outside the purview of international law." Vidmar, 'Unilateral Declarations of

However, this test does not fit the temporal structure of links among the DoI, the secessionist attempt and secession. First, it might bring about the risk of excluding the relevant developments from the ambit of international law. For example, the DoI can be and usually is issued before the entity acquires required effectiveness.[289] Second, the meeting of these constitutive criteria entails the emergence of a new State. International law would apply anyway.

Therefore, it is argued that the relevant criterion should be conceptualised differently. It should still focus on 'effectiveness'[290] but this would be dissociated from the notion of 'effectiveness' for the attainment of statehood. The threshold would also be lower than one for the characterisation of the movement as insurrectional for the attribution of conduct of the insurrectional movement to a new State, which refers to the law of armed conflicts.[291] On one side of the spectrum, nominal attempts or proclamations of random groups would be outside of such delimitation.[292] On the other side of the spectrum,

---

Independence in International Law' (n 210) 66; Similarly, Milano claims, "the factual existence of an entity presenting all the factual elements of a State is the prerequisite of a claim to statehood, not the consequence of it." Milano, 'Declarations of Independence and Territorial Integrity in General International Law' (n 154) 67 and see also 65.

289 "[I]t is arguable that, in order to be 'able' to violate norms of international law, armed opposition groups must be bound by those rules at the same time that the violations occurred." Zegveld (n 283) 157.

290 "[M]odern international law should be a '*ius inter potestates*' and therefore should encompass every political organization that acts as an effective factor in international relations." W Wengler cited in Kooijmans (n 285) 339.

291 See ARSIWA (n 23) commentary to art 10, para 9, which refers to art 1(1) and (2) AP II to the Geneva Conventions as a "guide" for the definition of insurrectional movement. "1. This Protocol ... shall apply to all armed conflicts which are not covered by*Article 1 of the Protocol Additional to the Geneva Conventions of 12 August 1949, and relating to the Protection of Victims of International Armed Conflicts* (*Protocol I*)and which take place in the territory of a High Contracting Party between its armed forces and dissident armed forces or other organized armed groups which, under responsible command, exercise such control over a part of its territory as to enable them to carry out sustained and concerted military operations and to implement this Protocol." "2. This Protocol shall not apply to situations of internal disturbances and tensions, such as riots, isolated and sporadic acts of violence and other acts of a similar nature, as not being armed conflicts." Protocol Additional to the Geneva Conventions of 12 August 1949, and relating to the Protection of Victims of Non-International Armed Conflicts (Protocol II) (signed 12 December 1977, entered into force 7 December 1978) 1125 UNTS 609, art 1(1) and (2). This is, however, a very high threshold, "which would seem to limit the envisaged situations to those of a large-scale civil war." G Cahin, 'Attribution of Conduct to the State: Insurrectionla Movements' in J Crawford and others (eds), *The Law of International Responsibility* (OUP 2010) 252.

292 Vidmar provides an example in his hypothetical declaration of independence of Scotland. See Vidmar, 'Conceptualizing Declarations of Independence in International Law' (n 154) 156.

the question can be asked whether effective control by the group of some territory *to the exclusion of the parent State* would be a necessary prerequisite.[293] With respect to the outlined temporal links, arguably, territorial control as defined would be too high standard.

Rather, the notion of a 'minimum threshold of effectiveness' entailing the territorial delimitation of the secessionist group and its internal hierarchy should be preferred.[294] For example, local parliaments or the representative assemblies of regions seeking independence would be presumed to fall within such a definition.[295] Therefore, the criterion would encompass a broader scope of situations even before or outside the eruption of a non-international armed conflict.[296] Such a wide delimitation is justified because its objective is not to

---

293 This builds on the questions that Zegveld asked with respect to the attributability of acts to armed opposition groups. See Zegveld (n 283) 154–155.

294 For a more nuanced position by Vidmar, see: "[T]hus, when it comes to declarations of independence, only those matter which are issued by the authorities *capable* of acting on behalf of the effective government of a (future) state." Vidmar, 'Unilateral Declarations of Independence in International Law' (n 210) 66 (*emphasis added*). "Only a declaration of independence issued by the representatives of an entity which meets, or is *capable* of meeting, the effectiveness standards presumed under the Montevideo criteria for statehood can have the legal relevance of a declaration of independence under international law." Vidmar, 'Conceptualizing Declarations of Independence in International Law' (n 154) 177 (*emphasis added*). But Kassoti strongly disagrees with such a conclusion. "[T]here is something intrinsically problematic in suggesting that a prohibition only applies to entities that 'meet or are likely to meet the Montevideo criteria.' How would we know that an entity has reached that threshold in the absence of a central and objective authority that would determine Statehood, recognition typically serves as evidence that an entity has fulfilled the Montevideo criteria. How would this be extrapolated to Vidmar's schema?" Kassoti (n 150) 231. However, the absence of a centralized authority in international law is not generally an obstacle to accepting that the development of factual situations can trigger international law's applicability.

295 For work outlining how secessionist movements essentially structure themselves according to lines of pre-existing administrative boundaries, see Beaudouin (n 172) 280–290. "La proclamation des indépendances par les organes des entités administratives est l'aboutissement logique du phénomène déjà évoqué selon lequel les mouvements indépendantistes se structurent au sein des entités administratives existantes." ibid 302.

296 An arbitral tribunal in the case concerning maritime delimitation between Guinea-Bissau and Senegal defined the moment a national liberation movement acquired "une portée internationale" as occurring when its activities "constituent dans la vie institutionelle de l'Etat territorial un événement anormal qui le force à prendre des mesures exceptionnelles, c'est-à-dire lorsque, pour dominer ou essayer de dominer les événements, il se voit amené à recourir à des moyens qui ne sont pas ceux qu'on emploie d'ordinaire pour faire face à des troubles occasionnels." *Maritime Boundary between Guinea-Bissau and Senegal* (n 287), para 51. According to Beaudouin, even though the tribunal's analysis of the case itself is similar to the definition from the law of armed conflicts, this definition seems to be broader, including, for example, the situation in which the declaration of

confer any rights on the non-State group or entity in question, but to ensure compliance with the peremptory norms by the entity aspiring to be a future State during the course of the *whole* secessionist attempt.

Lastly, the scope of the peremptory norms that are directly applicable to the secessionist groups raises questions. While the prohibition of violation of self-determination and racial discrimination is directly applicable to secessionist groups, the prohibition of the applicability of the use of force is controversial. In particular, the ICJ explicitly limited the principle of territorial integrity, which is closely linked to the prohibition of the use of force, to the inter-State paradigm.[297] Moreover, the prohibition of the use of force to secessionists would not only substantially transform the understanding of secession as the phenomenon that depends on the development on the ground between the parent State and secessionists, but would also signify reinterpretation of Article 2(4) UN Charter.[298] Thus, it is not appropriate at the moment to conclude that the prohibition of the use of force applies to secessionists. Nevertheless, this does not deny an undoubted trend of the UNSC calling on all concerned actors to terminate hostilities and respect the territorial integrity of the parent State or declaring forcible secessions the threat to international peace and security.[299]

4.5 *Legal Consequences*

Essentially, there are three key legal consequences that flow from the violation of peremptory norms as outlined above regarding the emergence of State. They include illegality of the DoI and secessionist attempt, invalidation of the DoI and triggering of the aggravated regime of international responsibility.

---

independence is issued by a federal state. "Les actes d'un mouvement sécessioniste peuvent donc revêtir une portée internationale sans qu'il existe de conflit armé." Beaudouin (n 172) 422.

297 A Tancredi, 'Secession and Use of Force' (n 265) 76. Similarly, according to Corten, the ICJ refused to denationalize or privatize Article 2(4) of the UN Charter, as it clearly upheld an inter-state character of the rule – it did not apply *jus contra bellum* against secessionists. He also points out that none of the States pleaded in favour of an extension of the prohibition of the use of force vis-à-vis secessionists. O Corten, 'Territorial Integrity Narrowly Interpreted: Reasserting the Classical Inter-State Paradigm of International Law' (2011) 24 Leiden Journal of International Law 87, 90–91.

298 A Randelzhorfer and O Dörr, 'Article 2(4)' in B Simma and others (eds), *The Charter of the United Nations: A Commentary* (OUP 2012) 213–214.

299 See Kohen, 'Introduction' (n 72) 20 and 7–8. See also Peters, 'Article 25' (n 249) 802; U Saxer, 'Self-Determination, Changes of Statehood and the Self-Organization of the International System' (2010) 214 Beiträge zum ausländischen öffentlichen Recht und Völkerrecht 993, 997, 999 and 1115.

4.5.1 Illegality of the Declaration of Independence and Secessionist Attempt

The ICJ stated that illegality was attached to the DoI and since the DoI is the inherent part of the secessionist attempt, it follows that illegality is also attached to the secessionist attempt as a whole. While the ICJ did not elaborate on the consequences of this illegality for the claim to statehood, the above-mentioned practice and *opinio iuris* firmly show that the violation of peremptory norms during the secessionist attempt precludes the emergence of a new State in line with a legalist doctrinal position.

Chapter 1 established that secession is the issue of *legal* fact. International law determines which facts are considered relevant to the creation of a new State via secession. Therefore, in line with the principle of *ex iniuria ius non oritur* and taking into account the outlined practice and *opinio iuris*, it is contended that these *legal* criteria presuppose their compliance with peremptory norms of international law. Thus, "effectiveness and legality are not simple opposites, because, as explained, effectiveness is itself a legal principle which performs normative functions."[300] "[T]here is no inherent conflict between maxims *ex factis jus oritur* and *ex injuria jus non oritur.*"[301] "[L]es critères de 'légalité' sont intégrés à l'exigence d'effectivité."[302]

Contemporary international law bars the peremptory illegality of each of the constitutive criteria of statehood. Thus, the entities created in the context of the violation of peremptory norms have not met the constitutive criteria of statehood. Therefore, they cannot emerge as the States because facts established contrary to peremptory norms cannot be attributive of the status of statehood.[303] Even though this conclusion deviates from the claim of

---

300 A Peters, 'Statehood after 1989: "Effectivités" between Legality and Virtuality' (2010) 3 Proceedings of the European Society of International Law 171, 182.

301 Orakhelashvili (n 233) 367. "Effectiveness in a system with a defined concept of legality may be legally accepted only in cases in which it does not conflict with the norms that serve as criteria of legality. Within the co-ordinates of the *de jure* order *effectiveness versus legality* is an incorrect approach, because to accept effectiveness as a rule 'would indeed be to apply a hatchet to the very roots of the law of nations and to cover with its spurious authority an infinitive series of international wrongs and disregard for international obligations.'" JHW Verzjil, *International Law in Historical Perspective, Vol 1* (AW Sijthoff 1968) 293 (*emphasis in original*) cited in *Case Concerning Application of the Convention on the Prevention and Punishment of the Crime of Genocide* (*Bosnia and Herzegovina v Yugoslavia*) (Preliminary Objections) [1996] ICJ Rep 595, Dissenting Opinion of Judge Kreca, 709.

302 Beaudouin (n 172) 616.

303 See also Raič (n 127) 50 and 55–56.

an additional legality criterion of statehood,[304] in the end both perspectives would bring about the same result – a new State's non-existence due to the non-fulfilment of conditions prescribed by international law.

4.5.2 Invalidity of the Declaration of Independence

Generally, the ICJ's approach in *Kosovo* was to answer the question only in terms of the legality of the DoI and not in terms of its validity.[305] Therefore, even when dealing with the specific prohibition concerning the violation of peremptory norms, the ICJ did not pursue its analysis further.

Peremptory norms have invalidating effects only regarding a unilateral act seeking to produce legal consequences, ie a unilateral *legal* act.[306] While

304 See *supra* on the doctrinal strand. See also Beaudouin (n 172) 622.

305 The ICJ explicitly said that answering the question posed to it by the GA only involves the analysis of the lawfulness of the declaration under general international law or the special regime of the UNSC Res 1244 (10 June 1999) UN Doc S/RES/1244, see *Kosovo* (n 10) para 78.

306 See *supra.* "[T]he unilateral act of a State 'as a legal act,' ie the expression of the will of the State to create certain legal effects including rights and obligations." K Kawasaki, 'A Brief Note on the Legal Effects of Jus Cogens in International Law' (2006) 34 Hitotsubashi Journal of Law and Politics 23, 32. "It is well recognized that declarations made by way of unilateral acts, concerning legal or factual situations, may have the effect of creating legal obligations. Declarations of this kind may be, and often are, very specific. When it is the intention of the State making the declaration that it should become bound according to its terms, that intention confers on the declaration the character of a legal undertaking, the State being thenceforth legally required to follow a course of conduct consistent with the declaration. An undertaking of this kind, if given publicly, and with an intent to be bound, even though not made within the context of international negotiations, is binding. In these circumstances, nothing in the nature of a *quid pro quo* nor any subsequent acceptance of the declaration, nor even any reply or reaction from other States, is required for the declaration to take effect, since such a requirement would be inconsistent with the strict.ly unilateral nature of the juridical act by which the pronouncement by the state was made." *Nuclear Tests* (*Australia v France*) (Judgment, Jurisdiction and Admissibility) [1974] ICJ Rep 253, para 43. "[F]or the purposes of the present articles, 'unilateral act of a State' means an unequivocal expression of will which is formulated by a State with the intention of producing legal effects in relation to one or more other States or international organizations, and which is known to that State or international organization." ILC, 'Fifth Report on Unilateral Acts of States, by Mr. Victor Rodríguez Cedeño, Special Rapporteur' (4 and 17 April 2002 and 10 May 2002) A/CN.4/525, para 81. In the final text of guiding principles, the scope has been narrowed down only to unilateral acts *stricto sensu* taking the form of a formal declaration. ILC, Guiding Principles Applicable to Unilateral Declarations of States Capable of Creating Legal Obligations in 'Report of the International Law Commission on the Work of its Fifty-Eighth Session (1 May-9 June and 3 July-11 August 2006)' UN Doc A/61/10, see preamble. According to the Commentary to Article 53 VCLT, legal effects produced by unilateral act can be divided into those that "cover the assumption of obligations (*e.g.* by promise, waiver) and the

material unilateral actions or legal facts[307] can only be looked at from the perspective of legality and international responsibility, unilateral *legal* acts can also be analysed from the perspective of a normative conflict and ensuing validity. Thus, the following account first highlights the invalidating effects of peremptory norms on unilateral acts of States, second examines the legal nature of the DoI as a unique legal act and, lastly, offers conclusions as to operation of the invalidation of the DoI in the context of the violation of peremptory norms.

4.5.2.1 *Invalidating Effects of Peremptory Norms on Unilateral Acts of States*

Since "[t]he scope and content of the notion of conflict assumes a decisive role" for the applicability of the normative sanction under Article 53 VCLT,[308] it is necessary to clarify this issue.[309] With respect to treaties, "the test of a jus cogens rule is the legality of establishing a contrary legal regime."[310] Specifically,

---

affirmation of rights and situations (*e.g.* by recognition)." Schmalenbach (n 258) 930–931. However, according to Orakhelashvili, nullity applies also to legal facts. See Orakhelashvili (n 233) 205–223.

307 See *supra*. "[A] unilateral State act 'as a legal fact,' ie actual conduct to be attributed to the State and to be evaluated in light of the relevant international law rules in the context of the law of State responsibility." Kawasaki (n 306) 32. "A treaty that conflicts with *jus cogens* is void, whereas act or action that breaches peremptory norm establishing an *erga omnes* obligation invokes a special responsibility of the State." E Suy, 'Article 53' in O Corten and P Klein, *The Vienna Conventions on the Law of Treaties: A Commentary* (OUP 2011) 1228. "In this context, assertions such as 'an act of aggression is contrary to jus cogens and accordingly null and void' is not tenable because the act of aggression is not so much a legal act, susceptible to nullification and voidance, as an [il]legal fact to be evaluated in terms of State responsibility." Kawasaki (n 306) 32, ftn 20. "Donc les caractères: l'acte de droit public interne et l'acte juridique international, l'acte valable et l'acte nul, l'acte délictueux et l'acte juridique simplement nul peuvent se rencontrer dans un seul et même acte d'Etat et il est quelquefois fort difficile d'en analyser correctement les éléments juridiques essentiels." JHW Verzijl, 'La validité et la nullité des actes juridiques internationaux' (1935) 9 Revue de droit international 284, 292.

308 E Cannizzaro, 'Higher Law for Treaties?' in E Cannizzaro (ed), *The Law of Treaties Beyond the Vienna Convention* (OUP 2011) 427.

309 "Undoubtedly, the notion of conflict is among the most obscure of the Vienna Convention. Not only does the Convention shed no light on the subject; one also finds that subsequent practice is scant, and, all in all, it is hardly sufficient to sustain a legal doctrine. Furthermore, an analogy with other possible notions of conflict of laws in international law could be misleading. It cannot be taken for granted that a notion of conflict between rules having the same rank is immediately transposable to situations of conflict between rules whose relation is determined by a hierarchical order." Cannizzaro, 'Higher Law for Treaties?' (n 308) 427 (*footnotes omitted*).

310 Abi-Saab (n 232) 10.

the treaty conflicts with the peremptory norm if such a treaty "allows a conduct proscribed by *ius cogens* or prohibits a conduct prescribed by *ius cogens*. The same is valid if parties agree in inter se relations that a specific peremptory rule is not applicable."[311] Thus, normative conflict under Article 53 VCLT only concerns the treaty's object.[312] The VCLT only concerns a *narrow*[313] conflict. Some authors call this conflict by derogation.[314]

Thus, one might wonder whether by analogy with the VCLT the conflict between unilateral *legal* acts of States and peremptory norms could occur and, if so, how it would be conceptualised. According to Schmalenbach, "[a] normative conflict between unilateral act that produces legal effects and *ius cogens* is not logically impossible, but exceptional."[315] According to Costelloe following his own definition of "conflict" under the VCLT, the conflict between a unilateral legal act and peremptory norms occurs,

> where the unilateral act created an obligation the compliance with which necessarily at the same time amounted to breach of an obligation under a peremptory norms, or where the unilateral act purported to create a power to dispense with an international legal obligation arising under a peremptory norms, or a permission to act in breach of it.[316]

311 Schmalenbach (n 258) 923. "'Conflict' can, upon a narrow understanding of the term, refer to the contemporaneous incompatibility of two obligations – in the context of Article 53, that would be a conflict between a provision of the treaty in question and an obligation under a peremptory norm." "'Incompatibility' under the present working definition refers to the position according to which the compliance with an obligation necessarily amounts to the breach of one or more other obligation(s)…[t]he term 'conflict' can, under a slightly broader conception, also refer to a power to dispense with an international legal obligation arising under a peremptory norm, or to a permission to act in breach of such an obligation." Costelloe (n 4) 68.

312 Sztucki recalls the drafting history of this particular feature of Article 53 VCLT. Sztucki (n 228) 123–125.

313 Costelloe (n 4) 69.

314 Cannizzaro, 'Higher Law for Treaties?' (n 308) 428; Costelloe points out that 'derogation' is a broader concept than 'conflict' since "arguably all conflicts *ipso facto* constitute derogations, but no all derogations lead to conflict." Costelloe (n 4) 67.

315 Schmalenbach (n 258) 931 (*footnotes omitted*). The author built the structure of such a normative conflict based on *Kosovo*, making no distinction between legal acts of States and non-State actors.

316 Costelloe (n 4) 154.

Treaties creating an inter se regime that conflict with the peremptory norms are devoid of any legal effects.[317] An objective illegality of the treaty's object is traditionally seen as one of the grounds for an absolute invalidity.[318] *A fortiori*, the same legal consequence also applies to unilateral legal acts conflicting with peremptory norms.[319] The doctrine supports such a conclusion.[320] "In case of a

317 "Le *ius cogens* neutralise l'opération du principe *lex specialis derogat legi generali*, et frappe de nullité l'accord contraire." Kolb (n 233) 96. Costelloe (n 4) 69. E Milano, *Unlawful Territorial Situations in International Law: Reconciling Effectiveness, Legality and Legitimacy* (Martinus Nijhoff 2006) 140; Verzijl (n 307) 317.

318 However, invalidity under Article 53 VCLT does not correspond to the notion of absolute nullity in municipal law. "So far, therefore, one can identify the types of invalidity under the Convention with the corresponding types of relative and absolute nullity under most of the major legal systems. But the resemblances do not extend beyond the almost identical ratio legis of the two distinctive grounds. The provisions on the procedure and the consequences of invalidity adjusted – sometimes successfully sometimes not – to the peculiarities of the international legal system, impart to the types of invalidity a completely different and independent character from their domestic counterparts." C Rozakis, 'The Law on Invalidity of Treaties' (1974) 16 Archiv des Völkerrechts 150, 177 and 165–177. See also Costelloe (n 4) 73–74.

319 Orakhelashvili (n 233) 208; Moreover, art 41(3) ARSIWA refers to other consequences that a serious breach of peremptory norms may entail under general international law. According to Cannizzaro, among these consequences "one can also reasonably group normative consequences." Cannizzaro, 'Higher Law for Treaties?' (n 308) 426. "La nullité de certains actes illicites … repose sur l'idée que la violation d'une régle de droit international peut, indépendamment de la sanction qu'elle comporte en vertu des principes relatifs à la responsabilité internationale, avoir la conséquence de ne pas pouvoir créer une situation juridique valable … Nullité n'a pas son fondement dans l'absence de certains éléments essentiels, mais dans la volonté des destinataires des normes du droit international qui refusent de reconnaître certains actes illicites, et les considèrent comme absolument nuls." P Guggenheim, 'La validité et la nullité des actes juridiques internationaux' in (1949) 74 RCADI 226.

320 "If an international jus cogens exists it must, indeed, make necessarily null and void any of those legal acts and actions of States whose object is unlawful. If an agreement which does not conform with the rules of the *jus cogens* is considered null and void the reason is that its effects are contrary to international public policy. In that case, it is inconceivable that this effect should not extend to any act or action having in the hierarchy of legal norms a lower rank than treaties." E Suy, 'The Concept of *Jus Cogens* in Public International Law' (n 232) 75. "In the light of the VCLT's provisions regarding peremptory norms, and the general acceptance of most of them as defining elements of jus cogens, it seems that in contemporary international law treaties and other instruments conflicting with a peremptory norm are void. The invalidity of such instruments cannot be cured in the course of time, for example by acquiescence." Hannikainen (n 233) 267 (*footnotes omitted*). By virtue of their primacy, peremptory norms "may invalidate not just treaties, but other inconsistent legal acts, as well as affecting the legal consequences which would otherwise flow from factual situations inconsistent with them." Crawford, *The Creation of States in International Law* (n 1) 102. "C'est uniquement sur le plan de la validité de

normative conflict, it is broadly agreed that the unilateral act is invalid ab initio and therefore cannot be invoked by either the declaring entity or by other States."[321] Moreover, according to the ILC's Guiding Principles Applicable to Unilateral Declarations of States "[a] unilateral declaration which is in conflict with a peremptory norm of general international law is void."[322] Similarly, the Restatement (Third) of the Foreign Relations Law of the United States with respect to peremptory norms says, "[t]hese rules prevail over and invalidate international agreements and *other rules of international law* in conflict with them."[323]

---

l'acte juridique unilatéral que le droit impératif peut intervenir dans la mesure ou l'acte unilatéral n'est pas qu'un acte matériel mais aussi une source de droits (nullité)." Kolb (n 233) 91. "Inflicting nullity on a unilateral legal act that violates a norm of *jus cogens* is only appropriate if that act has created an obligation vis-à-vis another state and consequently a right for the latter." Zemanek (n 231) 393–394. Costelloe seems to disagree with the application of the term validity to unilateral legal acts, but broadly agrees with the consequences consisting in the exclusion of the act's legal effects. "[T]he concept of 'validity' in international law generally is a feature of the law of treaties," and therefore it is more accurate to say, "the act is one capable of generating legal rights and obligations or one incapable of doing so … By itself, a unilateral act is not necessarily void, valid or invalid; most acts imply occur or do not occur." Costelloe (n 4) 153–154. See also Talmon, *La non-reconnaissance collective des états illégaux* (n 120) 31–32.

321 Schmalenbach (n 258) 931 (*footnotes omitted*).

322 ILC, Guiding Principles Applicable to Unilateral Declarations of States Capable of Creating Legal Obligations in 'Report of the International Law Commission on the Work of its Fifty-Eighth Session (1 May–9 June and 3 July–11 August 2006)' UN Doc A/61/10, guiding principle 8. Unilateral act would be void *ab initio*. ILC, 'Third Report on Unilateral Acts of States, by Mr. Victor Rodríguez Cedeño, Special Rapporteur' (17 February 2000) UN Doc A/CN.4/505, para 150. Nevertheless, Costelloe points out difficulties connected with an underlying assumption that the binding force of such a declaration is the principle of good faith. "It seems that the principle of good faith would require that, where there is room for doubt, a State must be presumed not to have intended to create an obligation if that obligation would be in conflict with a peremptory norm of general international law. Anything else would amount to a presumption of bad faith on the part of the declaring State. The above-quoted Principle 8 of the ILC's 2008 Guiding Principles with respect to peremptory norms will perhaps never be applied." Costelloe (n 4) 177.

323 Restatement (n 41) § 102, comment (k). (*emphasis added*). Similar views are also presented in an Advisory Opinion, *Juridical Condition and Rights of Undocumented Migrants*, where the IACtHR held that "[i]n its development and by its definition, *jus cogens* is not limited to treaty law. The sphere of *jus cogens* has expanded to encompass general international law, including all legal acts." *Juridical Condition and Rights of Undocumented Migrants*, Advisory Opinion, OC-18/03, Inter-American Court of Human Rights, Series A No 18 (17 September 2003), para 98. See also the Concurring opinion of judge Cançado Trindade, para 70: "[T]he *jus cogens* reveals its real, wide and profound dimension, encompassing all juridical acts (including the unilateral ones), and having an incidence (including beyond the domain of State responsibility) on the very *foundations* of an international law truly

By analogy with treaties, a normative conflict between a unilateral act of a State and peremptory norms would only concern unilateral *legal* act's object. Nevertheless, numerous scholars have shown the limited relevance of such a technical normative conflict. Simply, "[a]s a matter of fact, States do not conclude agreements to commit torture or genocide or enslave people."[324] *A fortiori*, States do not issue unilateral *legal* acts pledging to violate peremptory norms.

Cannizzaro showed that a more frequent situation involved the conclusion of treaties in the aftermath of an *ius cogens* breach with the view of regulating the situation.[325] Under a classical view, notwithstanding legal obligations concerning the duty of non-recognition flowing from the law of state responsibility, the treaty would nonetheless be valid and binding upon the parties.[326] By analogy, it is arguable that the same would apply to unilateral *legal* acts of States in similar context. Vidmar highlighted that the limit to the operation of peremptory norm is a "conflict with *effet utile* of peremptory norm rather than with the peremptory norm itself."[327]

> According to the very notion of hierarchy, higher values are offended not only by rules, which purport to violate them directly, but also by rules, which aim to produce effects inconsistent with their *effet utile*.[328]

---

universal." See also *Prosecutor v Anton Furundzija* (Judgment) IT-95-17/1-T (10 December 1998), para 155. In addition, according to the commentary to ARSIWA, "various tribunals, national and international, have affirmed the idea of peremptory norms in contexts not limited to the validity of treaties." ARSIWA (n 23) commentary to art 26, para 5 and see ftn 415 referring to the ICTY's Furundzija case, the House of Lords' Pinochet case and the ICJ's Legality of the Threat or Use of Nuclear Weapons advisory opinion.

324 T Meron, *Human Rights Law-Making in the United Nations: A Critique of Instruments and Process* (Clarendon Press 1986) 190.

325 Cannizzaro, 'Higher Law for Treaties?' (n 308) 426.

326 ibid. This question will also be analysed in Section 2.

327 J Vidmar, 'Norm Conflicts and Hierarchy in International Law: Towards a Vertical International Legal System?' in J Vidmar and E De Wet (eds), *Hierarchy in International Law: The Place of Human Rights* (OUP 2012) 33.

328 E Cannizzaro, 'On the Special Consequences of a Serious Breach of Obligations Arising Out of Peremptory Rules of International Law' in E Cannizzaro (ed), *The Present and Future of Jus Cogens* (Sapienza 2015) 142. "In a different perspective, one cannot exclude that treaties which purport to regulate a situation created by a *jus cogens* breach interfere with the proper application of higher law, and, therefore, can be assessed as to their validity against the primary *jus cogens* rule. This perspective tends thus to abandon the idea that the rules which establish secondary consequences of a *jus cogens* breach necessarily have *jus co-gens* value. Rather, it remains in the area of primary rules and tends to enlarge the notion of conflict under Articles 53 and 64 of the Vienna Convention on the Law of Treaties, so as to cover situations of indirect conflict or even of occasional collisions

However, according to Schmalenbach "*effet utile* interpretation of *ius cogens* so as to maximize its normative force and effectiveness is unknown to international law so far."[329]

4.5.2.2 *DoI as a Legal Act*

From the existing literature and positions of States in *Kosovo*, three views can be derived on the legal nature of a DoI.[330] First, a DoI is viewed as a political statement, "a mere fact" belonging to *domaine reservé* of either the parent State or a new State and, therefore, it is not regulated by international law.[331]

---

between a treaty and a *jus cogens* rule." ibid. "This methodological frame could conveniently accommodate the vexed issue of the derogability of the 'substantive' consequences of a breach of *jus cogens*." ibid.

329 Schmalenbach (n 258) 924. "While there is little practice on the meaning of conflict in the context of peremptory norms, the International Court has seemingly preferred the narrow approach in the context of State immunity." Costelloe (n 4) 69.

330 "[T]he theory of legal acts under international law stems from the same conception of legal acts as under domestic law: a legal act is an expression of will made by one or more legal subjects aimed at producing legal effects as provided for under the relevant legal order." Milano, 'Declarations of Independence and Territorial Integrity in General International Law' (n 154) 62; "[T]oute 'manifestation de volonté' d'un ou plusieurs sujets du droit international à laquelle une norme de ce droit rattache certaines conséquences correspondantes." EP Nicoloudis, *La nullité de 'jus cogens' et le développement contemporain du droit international public* (Ed Papazissi 1974) 18. International legal acts are "actes d'Etat auxquels l'ordre juridique international reconnaît le pouvoir de produire des effets juridiques conformes à l'intention de leurs auteurs." Verzijl (n 307) 302. More specifically with respect to unilateral legal acts, Jacqué states, "[l']acte unilatéral émane d'une seule manifestation de volonté, qui peut être celle d'un organe collectif, et crée une norme destinée à être appliquée à des sujets de droit qui n'ont pas participé à l'élaboration de l'acte." Jacqué (n 200) 329.

331 "Any declaration of independence is an expression of will of a people or merely of a group, and, as such, of a political nature. The declaration alone cannot violate international law; any possible violation would rather stem from actions relating to the realization or putting into practice of the declaration, such as the use of force." *Kosovo* (n 10), Written Statement of the Czech Republic (14 April 2009) 6; "First, it is noted that a declaration of independence is not, as such, the object of regulation by public international law. In so far as it is considered a factual event or a political fact, it has for instance been held that international law largely limits itself to drawing consequences from it should such a declaration result in the establishment of effective stable state authorities." *Kosovo* (n 10) Written Statement of the Kingdom of Norway (16 April 2009) para 10 (*footnote omitted*); "It is widely accepted that declarations of independence, standing alone, present matters of fact, which are neither authorized nor prohibited by international law ... [S]ecession-which frequently involves a declaration of independence as an early step-is a matter of fact, which occurs outside the regulatory context of international law ... A declaration of independence is an expression of a will or desire by an entity to be accepted as a state by the members of the international community." *Kosovo* (n 10),

From this perspective, it would be impossible to assess its international legality.[332] Second, a DoI is seen as a legal fact, as "an event that international law perceives and legally qualifies"[333] and whose legality can thus be also assessed under international law.[334]

Written Statement of the United States of America (17 April 2009) 50, ftn 202 and 51 (*footnotes omitted*); "The DoI as a domestic constitutional act is not regulated by international law." *Kosovo* (n 10), Written Statement of the Government of the Republic of Albania (14 April 2009) para 47; "Albania would like to reaffirm that international law does not contain any rules concerning a DoI." *Kosovo* (n 10), Written Statement of the Government of the Republic of Albania (14 April 2009) 39, para 73; "However, a declaration of independence itself is neither a requirement of Statehood, nor does it presuppose fulfillment of the above-mentioned requirements of Statehood beforehand. Thus, a declaration of independence is in itself a factual event and is not legally relevant under international law; nor does international law have any rule or principle which governs the effectiveness of the issuance of a declaration of independence." *Kosovo* (n 10), Written Statement of the Government of Japan (April 2009) 2–3; "State practice is long-standing and consistent in the matter of declarations of independence: States have long acted on the basis that a declaration of independence is a fact not governed by international law." *Kosovo* (n 10), Written Statement of the United Kingdom (17 July 2009) para 36 (*footnotes omitted*); "Sur ce point, le Burundi soutient d'abord qu'aucune question de validité internationale de la déclaration d'indépendance n'est posée à la Cour parce que la déclaration en question est un *fait* au regard du droit international. Il est vrai qu'une déclaration d'indépendance peut constituer un acte juridique et que, comme tout acte juridique, elle doit être conforme aux règles de l'ordre juridique où elle est censée produire ses effets. Il est toutefois important de souligner ici qu'une déclaration d'indépendance, à supposer qu'il s'agit d'un acte juridique, constitue un *acte juridique purement interne* et non pas un acte juridique international … Il lui suffit de constater qu'il ne s'agit pas d'un acte juridique de l'ordre juridique international. N'étant pas un acte juridique international mais un simple acte juridique interne, la déclaration d'indépendance ne constitue pas un acte juridique et constitue *au regard du droit international*, un fait." *Kosovo* (n 10), Public sitting, Friday (4 December 2009) CR 2009/28, 30–31 (*footnotes omitted*). "A declaration issued by persons within a State is a collection of words writ in water; it is the sound of one hand clapping. What matters is what is done subsequently, especially the reaction of the international community." *Kosovo* (n 10), Public sitting, Friday (10 December 2009) CR 2009/32, 47, para 6; "State practice is long-standing and consistent in the matter of declarations of independence: States have long acted on the basis that a declaration of independence is a fact not governed by international law." *Kosovo* (n 10), Written Comments of the United Kingdom (July 2009) 17, para 36.

332 Pertile (n 154) 99–100.

333 ibid 99.

334 "The declaration of independence by a State is a factual, unique event occurring at a precise, more or less important moment in history … It would however be going too far to claim that international law remains entirely silent on the subject of declarations of independence and that such declarations thus fall into a legal vacuum." *Kosovo* (n 10), Written Statement of Switzerland (25 May 2009) paras 26 and 28. "However, the issuance of a

Third, a DoI is conceptualised as a legal act intended to produce legal effects.[335]

The first view does not correspond to the above practice, *opinio iuris* and *Kosovo* from which it follows that international illegality can be attached to declarations of independence.[336] As to the second view, even though it follows from the above practice and *Kosovo* that declarations of independence are capable of being internationally (un)lawful, this does not resolve the question

declaration of independence is a factual event, which can take place and may lead to the creation of a state … Therefore, the declaration of independence could in international practice be considered unlawful where certain principles of international law have been disregarded." *Kosovo* (n 10), Written Statement of Estonia (13 April 2009) 4. See *supra* on the position of States to the illegality of declarations of independence in the context of *ius cogens* violations.

335 With respect to Kosovo's Declaration of Independence, see Milano, 'Declarations of Independence and Territorial Integrity in General International Law' (n 154) 65. "The UDI, being an act which in the view of its authors and those that have recognised a so-called new independent 'State' has produced legal effects, can and must be examined in the light of its conformity or not with international law." *Kosovo* (n 10), Written Comments of the Argentine Republic (July 2009) para 32; "The UDI is an act adopted with the intention to produce legal effects, among others the existence of a new State … Thus, in the view of the authors, the UDI is a unilateral act that has a binding effect (*quod non,* because of its lack of conformity with international law). Given this intention of the authors, the analysis of its compatibility with applicable rules of international law cannot be denied." *Kosovo* (n 10), Written Comments of the Government of Serbia (July 2009) paras 181 and 184 (*footnotes omitted*).

336 Paradoxically, even though, during *Kosovo*, numerous States contented that the declarations of independence were only political statements not regulated by international law, the same States in the same proceedings also claimed that the violation of peremptory norms would in fact result in prohibition of the declaration of independence. These two positions are hardly reconcilable. "Moreover, it is noted in passing that many States promoting the secession of Kosovo from Serbia and advancing the 'factual' or 'international legal neutrality' argument have themselves identified in their written statements situations where international law nevertheless intervenes and prevents the creation of a new State, even where the factual constitutive elements for this creation have been present. According to these States, this is the case when rules concerning the prohibition of the use of force, racial discrimination, self-determination, foreign intervention, respect for international agreements, and more generally, the violation of peremptory norms, are at stake." Written Comments of the Argentine Republic (July 2009) 9, para 13 (*footnote omitted*). Among the most glaring examples of such an inconsistency are included in the pleadings of the Republic of Albania. "The DoI as a domestic constitutional act is not regulated by international law … Albania would like to reaffirm that international law does not contain any rules concerning a DoI." *Kosovo* (n 10), Written Statement of the Government of the Republic of Albania (14 April 2009) para 47 and para 73. "The DoI is not prohibited by international law, unless there were a violation of a peremptory norm." *Kosovo* (n 10), Reply of the Government of the Republic of Albania (17 July 2009) 22, para 35.

of the legal nature because both legal acts and facts can be internationally unlawful. Therefore, the analysis has to be made as to the third view that the DoI is a legal act. According to Pertile,

> the legal qualification of the Declaration should start from the assumption that a subjective legal fact may be considered as an international legal act if two requirements are fulfilled. Firstly, there has to be a subject of the legal order to which the act may be attributed. Secondly, a legal rule must connect the expected effects to the respective expression of will.[337]

First, the subject issuing the DoI is usually a non-State actor.[338] Thus, the question arises whether a non-State actor can be considered an international law subject.[339] It follows from above that the limited legal personality of the secessionist group may be required. This personality would not signify an entitlement to secede, but would be only limited to obligations not to violate peremptory norms of international law during the secessionist attempt including that concerning the DoI. The criterion for the activation of these obligations would be the minimum threshold of effectiveness of the group. It is argued that the same criterion of the minimum effectiveness of the group should be relevant for the regulation by international law of the declarations of independence.

Second, it follows that on its own the DoI does not produce any effects when creating a new subject of international law.[340] However, the international legal

337 Pertile (n 154) 100, ftn 30.

338 Subject to situations when the declaration of independence is issued after the fulfilment of the so-called constitutive criteria. See *supra*.

339 Kassoti is very critical of the approach that seems to view declarations of independence as unilateral legal acts without taking into account that they are issued by a non-State actor. "By arbitrarily transposing the doctrine of unilateral juridical acts to the sphere of non-State entities, this proposition assumes that international law bestows on non-subject the ability to create international legal effects through acts of will. Despite this, there is no evidence that international law treats the intention of a non-state entity similarly to that of a sovereign State." Kassoti (n 150) 222–223.

340 Pertile dismisses the possibility of a declaration of independence being an international legal act by pointing to a traditional factualist perception of statehood. "A declaration of independence is not a manifestation of will to which 'achievement of independence' can be reasonably connected. For international law, independence (and statehood) are issues of fact, 'primary facts.'" Pertile (n 154) 100, ftn 30. Similarly, Kassoti severely criticizes the view that a declaration of independence would be an international legal act because "it would mean that the effects of the declaration – the creation of a State – would arise solely by means of the declaration. In other words, accepting declarations of independence as unilateral legal acts would necessarily lead to the conclusion that international law allows an entity to become a State, its subject *par excellence*, purely by means of an

significance of declarations of independence is that they are formalised unilateral expression of will to secede (*animus*) as a voluntary element of secession. Moreover, apart from the claim to statehood, secessionist groups also frequently unilaterally assume other international legal obligations in their declarations of independence.

Therefore, it is contended that a DoI is a unique legal act situated on the borderline between municipal and international law. It is a unilateral expression of will by a non-State secessionist group fulfilling a minimum threshold of effectiveness to secede and establish a new subject of international law. "A declaration issued by an organ, a plurality of organs, or simply a group of people can be legally analysed through the prism of its validity."[341]

4.5.2.3 *Invalidating Effects of Peremptory Norms on the DoI*

It follows that a unilateral *legal* act of *State* in conflict with peremptory norms is void. The DoI can be considered a unique legal act; therefore, there is nothing that would preclude an analogical reasoning concerning the declarations of independence. Moreover, this is is also supported by numerous resolutions of UNSC and other international and regional bodies that declared the declarations of independence invalid.[342]

In addition, the doctrine supports this view too. Concerning Southern Rhodesia Crawford pointed out, "it must be concluded that Southern Rhodesia was not a State because the minority government's declaration of independence was and remained internationally a nullity, as a violation of the principle of self-determination."[343] According to Schmalenbach, DoIs "conflict with ius cogens if they directly profit from and perpetuate the ius cogens violation."[344] In Richter's view, "it seems appropriate to infer that the UNSC might consider a declaration of independence legally invalid, if it were in conflict with essential

act of will." But, according to Kassoti, "Statehood is a fact" … "A declaration of independence may not confer Statehood to an entity that was not a State before the declaration." Kassoti (n 150) 223–224.

341 Kohen and Del Mar (n 254) 113. See Guggenheim (n 319) 205; Verzijl (n 307) 308. See also Gowlland-Debbas (n 122) 239.

342 According to Kassoti, the UNSC is a political organ; therefore, invalidity in these resolutions should not been seen as necessarily corresponding to the legal concept of invalidity. Kassoti (n 150) 227. Talmon, *La non-reconnaissance collective des états illégaux* (n 120) 38–39. Costelloe (n 4) 181. Contrary to this, Dipla points out that the ICJ in *Namibia* sanctioned the practice of the UNSC and considered the pronouncements of the UNSC of a declaratory nature. Dipla (n 99) 42.

343 Crawford, *The Creation of States in International Law* (n 1) 130.

344 Schmalenbach (n 258) 931 (*footnote omitted*).

principles of the United Nations."[345] Costelloe holds that "a declaration produces no legal effect where the underlying claim arises out of a serious breach of an obligation under a peremptory norm."[346]

A normative conflict in this hypothesis would include not only the declarations of independence whose object would directly conflict with peremptory norms, but also declarations of independence that would be connected to the violation of international law by the State. Such an understanding of normative conflict is a significant deviation from a classical narrative of effects of peremptory norms, as it allows for invalidation of an act interfering with *effet utile* of peremptory norms.

Ultimately, secession is not merely a question of the factual, material elements, but it also requires the claim for statehood usually expressed in the DoI. Its connection with the violation of peremptory norms whether by a secessionist group or the third State entails an invalid claim for statehood. "A unilateral declaration of independence could be said to have no legal effect where it is in conflict with a peremptory norm, even where the other, primarily factual conditions for statehood are met."[347] An invalid DoI could not be "invoked by either the declaring entity or State or by other States."[348] Therefore, an apparent meeting of constitutive criteria without a valid claim for statehood could not produce the effects of attributing the status of statehood to the entity in question.

4.5.3 Consequences in the Field of International Responsibility

Today, the violation of peremptory norms undoubtedly produces legal effects outside the treaty law, including in the sphere of international responsibility. Apart from legal consequences that normally follow general international law violation,[349] Article 41 ARSIWA identifies additional obligations triggered by "a serious breach by a State of an obligation arising under a peremptory norm of

345 Richter (n 99) 34. "[T]he declaration of independence becomes poisoned by the grave violations of international law which preceded it, and therefore can be qualified 'as having no legal validity' – with such a qualification sometimes even accompanied by a clear statement that it 'will not be accepted.'" ibid 22 (*footnotes omitted*).

346 Costelloe (n 4) 287.

347 "But in this case it is not so much the declaration that has no legal effect as the fact that the claim to statehood is unsuccessful for the same legal reasons, i.e., that I came about as a result of a serious breach." Costelloe (n 4) 167.

348 Schmalenbach (n 258) 931 (*footnote omitted*).

349 ARSIWA (n 23) commentary to art 41, para 13. "[A] serious breach in the sense of Article 40 entails the legal consequences stipulated for all breaches in chapters I and II of Part Two." ibid.

general international law",[350] i.e. obligation to cooperate to bring to an end an unlawful situation, obligation not to render aid or assistance and obligation of non-recognition, which together form the regime of the so-called "aggravated responsibility."[351] Moreover, the picture of the relevant consequences must also be complemented by "*powers, rights, or claims* of third States" flowing from the violation of *erga omnes* obligations.[352]

This section only explores one of the outlined consequences – the obligation of non-recognition – because it is related to the objective of this chapter, ie the emergence of the statehood in the context of the violation of peremptory norms. From the overview of practice follows that IOs have frequently called for the non-recognition of secessionist regimes in the context of violations of peremptory norms.[353] Thus, the question arises as to the role of this duty regarding the status of the secessionist entity. This section explores this duty's two aspects – first, its legal basis and nature and second, its interplay with other consequences flowing from the violation of peremptory norms. Section 2 focuses on other consequences and the scope, content and parameters of the duty of non-recognition.

4.5.3.1 *Legal Basis of the Duty of Non-recognition*

The above practice supports the view that the duty of non-recognition flows automatically from a general international law and is not dependent upon determination by UN. The majority of documents calling for non-recognition are either non-binding UNGA resolutions or UNSC resolutions adopted under chapter VI of the UN Charter where a binding nature under Article 25 UN Charter is not always clear.[354] Thus, "[t]he focus here is not so much on the

---

350 ARSIWA (n 23) arts 40 and 41.

351 "While this is meant to be a relative neutral term, it does express the idea that responsibility for breaches in the sense of Article 40 entails consequences which are more severe than those triggered by ordinary breaches." CJ Tams, 'Do Serious Breaches Give Rise to Any Specific Obligations of the Responsible State?' (2002) 13 EJIL 1161, 1162.

352 A Cassese, 'The Character of the Violated Obligation' in J Crawford and others (eds), *The Law of International Responsibility* (OUP 2010) 420. In particular, ARSIWA (n 23) arts 48(2) and 54.

353 For example, UNSC Res 216 (12 November 1965) UN Doc S/RES/216 and UNSC Res 217 (20 November 1965) UN Doc S/RES/217on the Southern Rhodesia.

354 M Dawidowicz, 'The Obligation of Non-Recognition of an Unlawful Situation' in J Crawford and others (eds), *The Law of International Responsibility* (OUP 2010) 683; Talmon, 'The Duty Not "To Recognize as Lawful"' (n 141) 121–122. For the ICJ's test of binding character of the UN resolutions under Article 25, see UN Charter *Namibia* (n 25) para 114.

binding character of the determination, but more on its authoritativeness."[355] Numerous authors assert that this duty is self-executory and customary in nature.[356]

Regarding the type of obligation, violation of which triggers the duty of non-recognition, Milano pointed out that there are at least three different formulations of the duty.[357] First, according to *Namibia*, the duty has its roots in the declaration of illegality of South Africa's presence in Namibia "opposable to all States in the sense of barring *erga omnes* the legality of a situation which is maintained in violation of international law."[358] In Milano's opinion, this formulation entails that *any* violation, regardless of peremptory or *erga omnes* character of the obligation breached, should be deprived of its effects via non-recognition.[359] Milano believes that this is "the most accurate exposition of the doctrine of non-recognition."[360]

---

355 E Milano, 'The Doctrine(s) of Non-Recognition: Theoretical Underpinnings and Policy Implications in Dealing with De-Facto Regimes' (Paper from the Conference 'The Power of International Law at Times of European Integration', Budapest, 26–28 September 2007) 5. But see, for example, early views of FA Mann: "[i]t cannot, in fact, be denied that a general duty of non-recognition arising wherever an international illegality and its consequence are in issue, would involve far too high a standard and would be impracticable. It would go far beyond the Stimson doctrine, which expressed a policy rather than duty, and even so could not be consistently applied. It would strain the powers and resources of international law as at present practised. It would, in short, be wholly unrealistic and, therefore, unsound." FA Mann, 'The Doctrine of Jus Cogens in International Law' in A *Further Studies in International Law* (Clarendon Press 2008) 101.

356 Dawidowicz (n 354) 683; Christakis, 'L'obligation de non-reconnaissance' (n 22) 142; Raič (n 127) 150; Costelloe (n 4) 203; *East Timor (Portugal v Australia)* [1995] ICJ Rep 90, Separate Opinion of Judge Skubiszewski, para 125. For a more cautious approach see Gattini (n 5) 1189. *Contra*: A Pert, 'The "Duty" of Non-Recognition in Contemporary International Law: Issues and Uncertainties' (2012) 30 Chinese (Taiwan) Yearbook of International Law and Affairs 48, 59–63.

357 Milano, 'The Doctrine(s) of Non-Recognition' (n 355) 1.

358 *Namibia* (n 25) para 126. Milano, 'The Doctrine(s) of Non-Recognition' (n 355) 2. Similarly, Gattini points out that in *Namibia*, the illegality of South Africa's presence in Namibia is not due to apartheid, but to a failure to "submit to supervision and to render reports to General Assembly … it is probably correct to infer that the ICJ did not consider the reason for the illegality to be the determining factor, but rather the institution from which the decision originated." Gattini (n 5) 1189.

359 Milano, 'The Doctrine(s) of Non-Recognition' (n 355) 5.

360 Ibid 5–6. "However, on close scrutiny these additional consequences do not amount to very much at all. In addition, arguably at least two of them (ie the obligation of non-recognition and that not to render aid and assistance) should apply regardless of the character of the breach." P Gaeta, 'The Character of the Breach' in J Crawford and others (eds), *The Law of International Responsibility* (OUP 2010) 426.

However, neither ILC, nor other scholars espouse this position. Ronen argued that obligation under Article 25 UN Charter could be in fact analogised to a peremptory norm owing to its normative superiority under the UN Charter.[361] Similarly, Ronen also showed that the commentary to ARSIWA refers to *Namibia* as an authoritative statement in the context of non-recognition following the violation of peremptory norms despite that *Namibia* only indirectly relied on a peremptory character of the obligation breached.[362] Moreover, Lagerwall's study on the principle of *ex iniuria ius non oritur* did not outline a generalised theory of the operation of this principle, but rather accentuated that the consequences were dependent on the gravity of the breach and causality between the breach and illegal facts.[363] According to Aust, "there is no obligation of non-recognition which generally prevents States from recognising the effects of wrongful conduct committed by other States."[364]

Despite Milano's claim, it is clear that the *erga omnes* nature of obligations and ensuing illegality must be presumed to be at stake.[365] Moreover, an injured State (and not the third State) is allowed to acquiesce to the violation of non-peremptory obligations and waive the claim resulting therefrom.[366] The situation is different with respect to violations of peremptory obligations. The duty

361 Ronen (n 8) 6.

362 Ibid.

363 "On doit plutôt assigner au principe une portée plus restreinte qui consisterait à sanctionner les faits illicites différemment selon leur gravité et à empêcher que de tels faits puissent générer des droits uniquement lorsque ces droits sont si intimement liés aux faits illicites en question que la reconnaissance de ces droits aurait immanquablement pour effet de consolider la situation créée illégalement, préservant ainsi les droits des sujets tiers à cette situation." Lagerwall (n 9) 517.

364 HP Aust, *Complicity and the Law of State Responsibility* (CUP 2011) 335.

365 Milano refers to rights *erga omnes*, such as the principle of territorial integrity and state immunity – "they translate into a number of rights and prerogatives of each State, which should be respected by all other States." Milano, 'The Doctrine(s) of Non-Recognition' (n 355) 6. It can be argued that rights *erga omnes* of States translate into obligations *erga omnes*, and therefore the distinction with the Milano's second exposition of the duty of non-recognition is not entirely clear.

366 ARSIWA (n 23) art 45 and see also art 20. "Of course, those States entitled to the protection ensured by these principles and rights may decide to waive them under certain circumstances, hence providing room for subsequent lawful recognition by third parties; however, that should not be confused with a general power of third States to recognize the illegal *status quo*." Milano, 'The Doctrine(s) of Non-Recognition' (n 355) 6. "[R]ecognition of an unlawful situation is not necessarily forbidden by international law. A State directly affected may waive its rights in a particular matter, or other States may waive any interest they may have in the observance of the rule in question." Crawford, *The Creation of States in International Law* (n 1) 158.

of non-recognition applies to all States including the responsible State and, while the possibility of waiver by the injured State is not completely excluded, it still requires a strong communitarian element.[367]

Most importantly for the present study, the practice confirms and Milano also acknowledges, "the obligation of non-recognition always arises in practice from violations of fundamental norms."[368] This is especially true for territorial situations involving attempted secessions.[369]

Second, according to Milano, another understanding of the duty of non-recognition is spelled out in *Wall* where the ICJ made the duty of non-recognition dependent upon the *erga omnes* character of the obligation breached.[370] Two judges criticised the ICJ's approach because of the "linkage between non-recognition and obligations *erga omnes*" and "instead alluded to the peremptory character of the norms as the direct trigger for the obligation of non-recognition."[371] Nevertheless, it is generally acknowledged that there is an overlap between two types of obligations.[372]

367 "[S]ince the breach by definition concerns the international community as a whole, waiver or recognition induced from the injured State by the responsible State cannot preclude the international community interest in ensuring a just and appropriate settlement." ARSIWA (n 23) commentary to art 41, para 9 and see also commentary to art 45, para 7. A more detailed analysis of this aspect of the duty of non-recognition will be offered in Section 2.

368 Milano, 'The Doctrine(s) of Non-Recognition' (n 355) 5. However, to support his argument on the irrelevance of the peremptory character of a violated obligation, he points to a widespread non-recognition of various secessionist entities created in violation of the principle of territorial integrity, including Transnistria, Abkhazia and Kosovo. Milano asks: "Is such practice only the result of a policy convenience not to enter into international disputes with the parent State or is it also the result of a widespread opinio juris that States are duty bound not to recognize such situation as they are the result of an illegal act?" ibid 6. However, to make his argument work, Milano assumes, firstly, that secessionists are bound by the principle of territorial integrity and, secondly, that these situations did not involve the violation of peremptory norms. This will be explored in detail in Part 2.

369 Crawford, *The Creation of States in International Law* (n 1) 102 and 105.

370 *Wall* (n 24) para 159; Milano, 'The Doctrine(s) of Non-Recognition' (n 355) 3.

371 Ronen (n 8) 7. Judge Higgins referred to the ILC's view expressed in the ARSIWA that "there are certain rights in which, by reason of their importance 'all states have a legal interests in their protection.'" *Wall* (n 24), Separate Opinion of Judge Higgins, para 37. Judge Koojimas based his arguments on the assumption of identical consequences of violation of *erga omnes* and peremptory obligations. *Wall* (n 24), Separate Opinion of Judge Kooijmans, para 41.

372 "Whether or not peremptory norms of general international law and obligations to the international community as a whole are aspects of a single basic idea, there is at the very least substantial overlap between them ... While peremptory norms of general international law focus on the scope and priority to be given to a certain number of fundamental

Third, according to the ILC, the duty of non-recognition is triggered by "a serious breach of obligations arising under a peremptory norm of general international law."[373] However, some authors question whether *all* peremptory norms are relevant in this context as the factual acts resulting from genocide, torture and slavery are doubted to produce legal effects that could be denied recognition.[374]

Although it is true that practice has been limited to the violation of the prohibition of the use of force, self-determination and apartheid,[375] it is possible to imagine an attempt to create a new State premised upon a genocidal intent.[376] Therefore, rather than focusing on an individual peremptory norm, the question should be whether "the unlawful situation flowing from the breach of such a norm gives rise to a *legal* claim to status or rights by the wrongdoing State which is capable of being denied by other States."[377] Crawford limits the scope of peremptory violations in the State-creation context from the perspective of illegality's centrality to the entity's existence.[378]

According to the ILC, the duty of non-recognition is only triggered regarding a situation created by a *serious* breach, ie a breach involving "a gross or systemic failure by the responsible State to fulfil the obligation."[379] Nevertheless, particularly in the context of secessionist attempts, the question arises whether the violation of peremptory norms, which results in the establishment of an

---

obligations, the focus of obligations to the international community as a whole is essentially on the legal interest of all States in their compliance." ARSIWA (n 23) 111–112, para 7. See also ILC 'Third Report on Peremptory Norms of General International Law (Jus Cogens) by Dire Tladi, Special Rapporteur' (12 February 2018) A/CN.4/714, paras 103–111. "On closer scrutiny it appears that in fact – from the point of view of State responsibility – the distinction between the two categories (*erga omnes* obligations deriving from customary international rules, and obligations deriving from peremptory norms) is without merit. As noted above, the two categories coincide, at least as far as customary international law is concerned ... Both the notion of *erga omnes* and that of *jus cogens* aim at the same result, that is, to prevent State from freely disposing of, and disregarding, values safeguarded by international customary rules. It would therefore seem that the distinction drawn by the ILC between the two categories of obligations at issue is not well founded and in addition is likely to cause confusion and legal uncertainty." Cassese (n 352) 418 (*footnote omitted*).

373 See ARSIWA (n 23) arts 40 and see 41(2); Milano, 'The Doctrine(s) of Non-Recognition' (n 355) 3.

374 Talmon, 'The Duty Not "To Recognize as Lawful"' (n 141) 117–118.

375 Dawidowicz (n 354) 683.

376 Cf Talmon, 'The Duty Not "To Recognize as Lawful"' (n 141) 117–118.

377 Dawidowicz (n 354) 683 (*emphasis in original*).

378 See *supra*.

379 ARSIWA (n 23) art 40(2) in connection with arts 40(1) and 41(2).

unlawful *situation,* is not always inherently *serious* and, therefore, whether the criterion of seriousness is not essentially redundant.[380] It is difficult to see how a situation under Article 41 ARSIWA could be created without an intentional, large-scale violation.[381] Such a question is of a real practical concern. For example, would the duty of non-recognition only apply to situations resulting from a direct use of force or would the employment of an indirect use of force also qualify?[382]

In this context, it is impossible not to agree with Gaeta that any such limitations "would be preposterous and inconsistent with the extraordinary importance of the interests protected by all rules of *jus cogens*."[383] Ultimately, even Crawford admits that both thresholds of gross and systemic are "to an extent, illusory"[384] because "peremptory norms are among the most serious prohibitions in international law, and the mere fact of breach is ordinarily sufficient to warrant the label of 'serious'."[385]

---

380 Cf Gaeta (n 360) 425–426. See *contra* for the threshold of the criterion of seriousness Costelloe (n 4) 187–190.

381 "The obligation applies to "situations" created by these breaches, such as, for example, attempted acquisition of sovereignty over territory through the denial of the right of self-determination of peoples." ARSIWA (n 23) commentary to art 41, para 5. Christakis points out that what distinguishes "situation" from a simple fact is that "la première est toujours susceptible d'évoluer, y compris en amenant à un rétablissement du *statu quo ante* ou, au moins, à la situation la plus proche de celle qui existait avant le fait illicite." Christakis, 'L'obligation de non-reconnaissance' (n 22) 128.

382 "Factors which may establish the seriousness of a violation would include the intent to violate the norm; the scope and number of individual violations; and the gravity of their consequences for the victims. It must also be borne in mind that some of the peremptory norms in question, most notably the prohibitions of aggression and genocide, by their very nature require an intentional violation on a large scale." ARSIWA (n 23) commentary to art 40, para 8. See also Gaeta (n 360) 425–426.

383 Gaeta (n 360) 426. Milano elaborates on the criterion of seriousness but focuses on its impact on the rules of territorial sovereignty. "To envisage a too high threshold of malicious conduct means to render difficult the distinction between standard violations of a state's territorial sovereignty and serious violations, at the same time making the rules of territorial sovereignty particularly loose and weak in terms of remedies available. That is inconsistent with the enormous legal, political and symbolic importance states attach to territorial sovereignty." Milano, *Unlawful Territorial Situations in International Law: Reconciling Effectiveness, Legality and Legitimacy* (n 317) 188.

384 Unless "systemic conduct is a constitutive element of the breach." J Crawford, *State Responsibility: The General Part* (CUP 2013) 381.

385 ibid.

4.5.3.2 *Interplay with Other Effects of Peremptory Norms*

One and the same conduct can be 'wrongful' and produce legal effects in the sphere of international responsibility including the duty of non-recognition while simultaneously provoking consequences in other areas of international law.[386] Thus, the question arises as how these different consequences interact in the secessionist context.

While legalists claim that the violation of peremptory norms in the State-creation precludes the emergence of the State, other authors argue that the State would emerge *ipso facto*; however, its material and legal capacity to act would be substantially reduced thanks to the duty of non-recognition. The authors of this latter group point out that non-recognition would be futile in case of the State's non-existence.[387] In fact, they argue, there would be nothing to recognise in the first place.[388]

Under the factualist view of secession and declaratory theory of recognition, the statehood's existence depends on the so-called constitutive criteria of statehood. It follows that non-recognition even in its most expansive scope would not preclude the statehood's emergence. Even if the legal capacity of a

---

386 This depends on the conceptualization of different areas of international law and in particular on the distinction between primary and secondary rules. "How, the distinction between the two areas of law [law of treaties and law of international responsibility] is in the specific case less clear. By concluding a treaty in conflict with a peremptory rule, a state adopts at the same time a conduct – which could be considered wrongful *per se* aside from a subsequent implementation of the treaty-and a normative act-which can be legally qualified as void. Also to oblige all states not to recognize as lawful the situation created by the treaty, because it represents a grave breach of a peremptory rule, would bring the reactions to the wrongful act to the level of legality of the act, a level which is proper to the law of treaties." A Gianelli, 'Absolute Invalidity of Treaties and Their Recognition by Third States' in E Cannizzaro (ed), *The Law of Treaties Beyond the Vienna Convention* (OUP 2011) 338. Gianelli comes to the conclusion that the duty of non-recognition should be conceived of as "part of the content of the primary peremptory rule." ibid. Crawford, *The Creation of States in International Law* (n 1) 158. See also J Verhoeven, 'The Law of Responsibility and the Law of Treaties' in J Crawford and others (eds), *The Law of International Responsibility* (OUP 2010) 110. For the artificiality of distinctions between primary and secondary obligations see E David, 'Primary and Secondary Rules' in J Crawford and others (eds), *The Law of International Responsibility* (OUP 2010) 29 et seq.

387 Talmon, *La non-reconnaissance collective des états illégaux* (n 120) 23–24 and 35–36. See also for the same point but through different perspective J Vidmar, 'International Organizations and Non-State Territorial Entities' in BC Harzl and R Petrov (eds), Unrecognized Entities: Perspectives in International, European and Constitutional Law (Brill 2022) 39; Saxer (n 299) 1013.

388 ibid 23–24 and 35–36.

'new State' would be severely undermined, its legal personality would emerge *ipso facto* notwithstanding an original peremptory illegality.

Indeed, one may argue that from a practical perspective, there is not much difference between an "illegal State" subjected to the collective duty of non-recognition and a non-recognised entity precluded from becoming a State. However, to the contrary, this distinction is essential.[389] To accept that a new subject of international law could transpire from the violation of international law would be fundamentally contrary to the very idea of the principle of *iniuria ius non oritur.*[390] In addition, this distinction might prove crucial for the scope of subsequent relations that will be discussed in Section 2.[391]

The lack of a legal status as a State does not make the applicability of the duty of non-recognition redundant, as the two positions are not exclusive, but complementary. Talmon asks, "[p]ourquoi appeler à la non-reconnaissance s'il n'y a pas d'État qui puisse être reconnu?"[392] States can decide to commit

---

389 In this context, it is interesting that Talmon also believes in the importance of this distinction regardless of the fact that he comes to the exact opposite conclusion. "Même si les deux conduisent au même résultat, il y a toutefois sur le plan dogmatique et logique une très grande différence entre le fait qu'un acte illégal, qui est en vigueur, soit *privé* de tous effets juridiques et le fait qu'un acte illégal ne puisse ex tunc *produire* d'effets juridiques." ibid 34.

390 From Lagerwall's study, it implicitly follows that *ex iniuria ius non oritur* is translated in both propositions, but the scope of these situations is different. While nullity/non-existence is more inward looking, precluding the transfer of territorial sovereignty or the emergence of statehood – and by implication also all the connected rights, statuses and privileges – the duty of non-recognition targets the rights that would have benefited States as a result of recognition of the lawfulness of the situation in question. "Dans la mesure où cette règle entend exclure l'existence ou la revendication d'un droit (le titre de souveraineté relatif à un territoire) qui découlerait d'un fait illicite (la violation de l'interdiction de l'emploi de la force ou du droit des peuples à disposer d'eux mêmes) et ce, en raison du caractère illicite de ce fait, elle paraît bien traduire l'objet du principe ex injuria jus non oritur." Lagerwall (n 9) 47. The following chapters will explore to what extent the scope of the duty of non-recognition and the chain of nullity in this context are overlapping. "On peut aborder cette obligation comme une expression du principe dans la mesure où elle a pour objet de nier l'existence d'un droit (les droits découlant de la reconnaissance de la licétité d'une situation) qui proviendrait d'un fait illicite (la violation grave d'une norme de *jus cogens*) et ce, en raison du caractère illicite de ce fait." Lagerwall (n 9) 154.

391 Talmon's proposition indicates the importance of this distinction. "La privation du status juridique d'État ne veut pas dire que l'État qui s'est vu refuser la reconnaissance doit être traité comme un État inexistant. Les droit, les privilèges et les compétences doivent lui être refusés seulement dans la mesure où ils expriment une revendication de son statut d'État." Talmon, *La non-reconnaissance collective des états illégaux* (n 120) 42. "Only if a State exists at all can it be considered an 'illegal State.'" Richter (n 99) 28–29.

392 Talmon, *La non-reconnaissance collective des états illégaux* (n 120) 24.

an international wrongful act and recognise as a State an entity without such legal status. Such an act would arguably be "unlawful erga omnes."[393] The duty of non-recognition accentuates the motivation of the international community to prevent such additional violations. It "reinforces the legal position, and helps to prevent the consolidation of unlawful situations."[394] It "is not as such either a method of enforcement or a sanction. It is a precondition for other enforcement action and a method of asserting the values protected by the relevant rules."[395] It is "a tool to assert the illegality of situations."[396]

It is also difficult to agree with authors who highlight the role of non-recognition as the tool for the consolidation of nullity or non-existence.[397] This position deviates from a general theory that is relevant to both municipal and international law, which sees nullity or non-existence as an internal sanction of legal order for not complying with the pre-existing criteria of this order and which functions by the operation of law (*de plein droit*).[398] Therefore, it can be agreed with Lauterpacht who pointed out instances of non-recognition

---

393 Crawford, *The Creation of States in International Law* (n 1) 158.

394 "But the 'object' of non-recognition here is not merely a state of affairs, a set of facts, but an asserted legal status arising from those acts. Illegality may preclude the attribution of that status initially: non-recognition is an attempt to prevent its consolidation. There is thus no logical difficulty." ibid 160, ftn 243.

395 Crawford, *The Creation of States in International Law* (n 1) 159–160. Talmon conceptualizes non-recognition as a countermeasure. See Talmon, *La non-reconnaissance collective des états illégaux* (n 120) 57–60. However, it is difficult to see how the duty of non-recognition stemming from general international law could be characterized as a countermeasure. For more on the relationship between the duty of non-recognition and sanctions, see Section 2.

396 Gianelli (n 386) 339.

397 "[N]on-recognition is a strategy deployed in the process leading towards nullity." MW Reisman and D Pulkowski, Nullity in International Law in MPEPIL (online edn, OUP 2006) para 29.

398 Tancredi has an opposite view. "[I]n these cases, absolute nullity does not work 'by operation of law (*de plein droit*)', and it is not automatic. The denial of effectiveness is, instead, the result of the concurrence of material conduct carried out by those subjects who do not recognise the effects of the wrongful act or event. Therefore, the *erga omnes* void character of an unlawful act does not precede collective non-recognition; on the contrary, it represents its consequence." Tancredi, 'A Normative "Due Process"' (n 144) 197. (*footnotes omitted*). The ILC's Drafting Committee on State Responsibility seems to have rather different view from Tancredi. "[O]ther States had an obligation not to recognize as 'lawful' the situation created by the breach and the commentary would explain that the question of recognition was closely connected with, but different from, that of 'validity.'" ILC, Yearbook of International Law Commission (2000), vol I, 393, para 45. "[O]bligation of non-recognition was based on extensive practice, and that such non-recognition in the legal context was more a reaction to the invalidity of an act, not only to its illegality." ILC,

> were not intended to have or could have the effect of invalidating any act, or the results thereof, which but for the declaration of non-recognition would have been legally valid. They constitute … the declaration of an already existing duty not to contribute by a positive act to rendering valid the results of an act which is in itself devoid of legal force.[399]

4.6 *Conclusion*

Starting from para 81 of *Kosovo*, this section focused on the operation of the effects of violation of peremptory norms in the context of State-creation via secession. It focused on the scope of applicable peremptory norms, the criterion of 'connection with', the addressees of the prohibition and legal consequences of its violation.

The section first highlighted that the scope of peremptory norms applicable in this context is limited. It also argued that the violation of non-peremptory obligations imposed by the UNSC to secessionists, in particular the obligation to respect the parent State's territorial integrity, arguably produces the same effects as violation of peremptory norms. Second, the section defined the criterion of 'connection with' the violation of peremptory norms rather broadly, including a situation when the former results from or consolidates the latter.

Third, the section outlined two addressees of peremptory norms. First, *ratione personae*, the State can violate peremptory norms. In this scenario, the DoI and other elements of secessionist attempt would be tainted by illegality due to their connection with such third State's violation. This echoes corollary to the prohibition of the use of force and the rejection of unlawful acquisitions of territory and confirms a regulatory expansion of peremptory norms even to the non-State secessionist process. Second, the section also argued that peremptory norms bind the secessionist groups themselves in a pre-State context. Thus, these groups can possess a limited legal personality. The section outlined a possible criterion of 'minimum threshold of effectiveness' and the scope of relevant applicable norms, which would not include the prohibition of the use of force.

Lastly, the section examined the legal consequences flowing from outlined violation of peremptory norms and their impact on the secessionist claim to

---

'Report of the International Law Commission on the Work of its Fifty-Second Session (1 May–9 June and 10 July–18 August 2000)' UN Doc A/55/10, 61, para 379.

399 Lauterpacht, *Recognition in International Law* (n 3) 420. "The function of collective non-recognition in international law has consisted in the refusal to validate under international law an illegal act and its consequences, or a situation, which are considered invalid or null." Gowlland-Debbas (n 122) 276.

statehood. In line with outlined practice and *opinio iuris*, it contended that international law presupposes that facts attributive of statehood are achieved in conformity with peremptory norms. It reiterated that illegality attached to DoI and secessionist attempt precludes the attribution of legal status of statehood and a new State's emergence. The section concluded that the statehood in such a context would also be denied due to an invalid DoI. This section argued that the DoI is a unique legal act that can be invalidated in connection with the violation of peremptory norms. Such a conclusion departs from a traditionally narrow normative conflict between legal acts and peremptory norms and moves towards a broader conflict with *effet utile* of peremptory norms.[400]

The section also explored the role of the duty of non-recognition concerning the emergence of statehood. Non-recognition is frequently called for at the UN level; however, the duty is of a customary and self-executory nature. The chapter also demonstrated that non-recognition does not influence the entity's status, it only functions as an additional tool in preventing the consolidation of illegality.

5 Conclusion

This chapter demonstrated that, when the secessionist attempt is connected with the violation of peremptory norms, the emergence of a new State is precluded. It overviewed the practice and *opinio iuris* that support the claim on the relevance of the peremptory norms to secession and various doctrinal positions on the matter. It concluded that the 'legalist' position according to which violation of peremptory norms in the context of the secessionist attempt results in the denial of statehood to the entity corresponds to the outlined practice and *opinio iuris* best.

The chapter then proceeded to examine the technical aspects of this position. It drew on practice and *opinio iuris* including para 81 of the *Kosovo* Advisory Opinion. The Advisory Opinion focuses on the DoI in isolation from

400 "It would be logically absurd if *jus cogens* had the effect of invalidating treaties which impose merely the obligation to derogate from *jus cogens*, even if this obligation is not put into effect, but did not invalidate treaties or other law rules which give full effect to, and bestow legal stability on, an actual violation of *jus cogens* norms." Cannizzaro, 'Higher Law for Treaties?' (n 308) 440. However, even Cannizzaro seems to admit that the precise scope of the notion of such broader normative conflict and "the conditions under which potential interference turns into actual conflict, are doomed to remain controversial." ibid.

the claim of secession; therefore, the chapter first established the role of the DoI in secession. It argued that the DoI is an inherent and inseparable part of the secessionist attempt and that secession, a subjective legal fact, is the sum of factual and voluntary elements attributive of the status of statehood and the title of territorial sovereignty.

The chapter then analysed separate elements flowing from para 81 of the *Kosovo* Advisory Opinion, in particular the scope of applicable peremptory norms, the criterion of 'connection with', addressees of the obligation not to violate peremptory norms and legal consequences flowing from its violation. It concluded that in the situation when the secessionist attempt is connected to violation of peremptory norms, the statehood is denied to the entity on two grounds.

First, it drew on the conclusions of Chapter 1 that secession is a *legal* fact. This chapter demonstrated that in line with the developments of practice and *opinio iuris* and the principle of *ex iniuria ius non oritur*, today, the constitutive criteria of statehood as *legal* criteria presuppose their compliance with peremptory norms of international law. Thus, the entities created in the context of the violation of peremptory norms are not considered to have met the constitutive criteria of statehood. Second, even though the DoI on its own does not bring about the creation of a new State, its connection with the violation of peremptory norms entails an invalid claim for statehood without which secession cannot take place. The chapter also demonstrated that non-recognition has no impact on the entity's status; it only functions as an additional tool in preventing the consolidation of illegality.

In conclusion, it is important to recall one author, who claimed,

> [t]he expansion of jus cogens beyond the sphere of treaties to that of unilateral acts or actions would mean, in consequence, the perfection of the international legal system which would thus recognise the existence of the objective illegality of certain acts or actions of its subjects.[401]

From this perspective, the fact that the effects of peremptory norms in a pre-State order go as far as to prevent the State's emergence bolsters the claim that "[a]t present, the principle of legality is overriding."[402] Thus, this

401 C Rozakis, *The Concept of Jus Cogens in the Law of Treaties* (North-Holland 1976) 19.

402 A Cassese, 'Legal Considerations on the International Status of Jerusalem' in A Cassese, P Gaeta and S Zappalà, *The Human Dimension of International Law: Selected Papers of Antonio Cassese* (OUP 2008) 286–287.

reflects more than just a mere technical variation in the operation of the peremptory norms, but instead, presumes a radically different nature of international law. To what extent this claim proves true even regarding a legal framework that is applicable to an illegal secessionist entity will be the object of Section 2.

CHAPTER 3

Existence of the Right to Secession

1 Introduction

At the bottom of the discussion about the right of self-determination in contemporary international law lies an inherent paradox. On the one hand, the secessionist movements frequently invoke this right as the entitlement to secede, whereas on the other hand, outside decolonisation, these claims have virtually no normative grounds.[1] "[S]ub-state groups that feel dissatisfied with the post-colonial and non-colonial states they find themselves in keep invoking the right and demand independence regardless of the actual international practice of that right."[2] "In the process, the principle has evolved into a manipulable, oft-employed slogan."[3] Ultimately, as opposed to the violation of the right to self-determination during a secessionist attempt,[4] the invocation of the right of self-determination as a supposed entitlement to secede proves much less consequential for the outcome of contemporary secessionist claims.

The outlined misperception derives from the normative evolution of this right. While the right of self-determination in a decolonisation context entailed *inter alia* the entitlement of colonies to independence,[5] based on the analysis of the relevant State practice, documents and case law, this chapter demonstrates that the same does not hold for the sub-State entities outside of decolonisation and foreign occupation. "Decolonization and its aftermath thus revealed a major paradox: as self-determination was authoritatively declared to be a universal right and an unprecedented number of states entered the

1 M Fabry, 'The Right to Self-Determination as a Claim to Independence in International Practice' (2015) 14 Ethnopolitics 498, 498.

2 ibid 501.

3 GJ Simpson, 'The Diffusion of Sovereignty: Self-Determination in the Post-Colonial Age' (1996) 32 Stanford Journal of International Law 255, 259.

4 See *supra* Chapter 2.

5 However, the gaining of independence through decolonisation cannot be classified as secession because the territory of a colony has "a status separate and distinct from the territory of the State administering it." Declaration on Principles of International Law concerning Friendly Relations and Co-operation among States in accordance with the Charter of the United Nations, UNGA Res 2625 (XXV) (24 October 1970) UN Doc A/RES/2625(XXV), principle 5 ("Friendly Relations Declaration"). See MG Kohen, 'Introduction' in MG Kohen (ed), *Secession: International Law Perspectives* (CUP 2006) 1.

society of states under its banner, the chances for future emergence of new states narrowed more than ever."[6]

The mismatch between a general perception of the right of self-determination outside decolonisation as the entitlement to secede and its real legal content has also affected a doctrinal analysis of contemporary secession. It would appear that to understand secession, the right of self-determination should be placed centre stage and, indeed, following this line, the scholarly literature focusing on this right is vast. However, as mentioned, a closer look at normative aspects of this right reveals that its relevance for secession is only marginal. Therefore, the present book only focuses on the key elements of this right, which are critical for the analysis of contemporary secessionist claims.

To do so, after a brief overview of the historical context, the chapter examines the concept of 'peoples' as the holders of the right of self-determination and the content of the right of self-determination outside of decolonisation. The chapter then focuses on the existence of the so-called remedial secession in contemporary international law. Next, it investigates whether the right to secede might be derived from other legal sources. Lastly, it offers some concluding remarks.

2 Right of Self-Determination Outside Decolonisation

2.1 *Brief Historical Outline*

Two points must be stressed when referring to the historical origins of the right to self-determination. First, even though Fabry infers from the practice of attainment of independence of Latin American colonies in the 19th century a "negative self-determination" meaning the right that "applied to any self-defined people and outsiders were required to do no more than to recognize the *de facto* attainment of what was presumed to be their will",[7] it is impossible to speak about any *right* to independence at that time. As mentioned in Chapter 1, the creation of States during the period in question was derived

6 M Fabry, *Recognizing States: International Society and the Establishment of New States since 1776* (OUP 2010) 150.

7 ibid 117. "The emergence of such a *de facto* polity was deemed to furnish the most convincing vindication of the right of people to determine their government and, as such, the source of the claim to foreign recognition as a new state." M Fabry, 'International Involvement in Secessionist Conflict: From the 16th Century to the Present' in A Pavaković and P Radan (eds), *The Ashgate Research Companion to Secession* (Routledge 2011) 253.

from independence on the ground in the context of a natural law tradition rather than based on any presumed right to self-determination.[8]

Second, self-determination, which underlays the creation of new States following the end of WWI and, to a certain extent, the American and French Revolutions,[9] must be distinguished from today's understanding of the notion.[10] A standard narrative in this regard refers to Vladimir Lenin and Woodrow Wilson as prominent proponents of self-determination at the beginning of 20th century.[11] However, as opposed to a post-Charter right of *peoples* to self-determination, Wilsonian self-determination entailed the so-called principle of *nationalities* and was conceived as an extension of the doctrine of the consent of the governed.[12] Crucially, it was a political rather than a legal principle.[13] "[L]e droit international n'avait jamais consacré un droit à chaque nation de constituer son propre Etat indépendant."[14] From this perspective, Fabry also demonstrated that regardless of lofty rhetoric of self-determination, only those communities were recognised as new States in the period following WWI who had already achieved *de facto* independence.[15] This observation is in line with the conclusions of the Chapter 1 based on which a prevailing paradigm of the State-creation at that time rested on the principle of effectiveness.[16]

---

8 See *supra* Chapter 1. See also J Crawford, *The Creation of States in International Law* (2nd edn, Clarendon Press 2006) 388.

9 The ideas underpinning the American and French Revolutions are distinguished from the notion of self-determination. D Raič, *Statehood and the Law of Self-Determination* (Kluwer Law International 2002) 175.

10 MG Kohen, 'Création d'Etats en droit international contemporain' (2002) VI Cours euro-méditerranéens Bancaja de droit international 583. Crawford (n 8) 108 and 115.

11 L Mälksoo, 'The Soviet Approach to the Right of Peoples to Self-Determination: Russia's Farewell to Jus Publicum Europaeum' (2017) 19 Journal of the History of International Law 200, 202. See also Raič (n 9) 177–188. See *infra* Part 2, Chapter 10 on the Marxist-Leninist approach to national question.

12 A Stilz, 'The Value of Self-Determination' in D Sobel, P Vallentyne and S Wall *Oxford Studies in Political Philosophy, Volume 2* (OUP 2016) 98. D Thürer and T Burri, 'Self-Determination' in MPEPIL (online edn, OUP 2008) para 2 (*emphasis added*). "National aspirations must be respected; peoples may now be dominated and governed only by their own consent." W Wilson, 'Address to Congress, Analyzing German and Austrian Peace Utterances' (Washington DC, 11 February 1918) <http://www.gwpda.org/1918/wilpeace.html> accessed 26 April 2020.

13 "It was not at that time accepted as a free-standing legal principle." MN Shaw, 'Peoples, Territorialism and Boundaries' (1997) 8 EJIL 478, 480.

14 Kohen, 'Création d'Etats en droit international contemporain' (n 10) 583.

15 Fabry, *Recognizing States* (n 6) 117–118. According to Liebich, for Wilson, self-determination entailed democracy, "[t]he actual units of self-government were of secondary concern to him." A Liebich, 'Must Nations Become States?' (2003) 31 Nationalities Papers 453, 461.

16 See *supra* Chapter 1.

After the adoption of the UN Charter, which included the principle of self-determination in its purposes and provision on the promotion of human rights and international economic and social cooperation[17] and, more specifically, after the adoption of the UNGA Resolution 1514,[18] "[s]elf-determination became the legal principle that fuelled the decolonization process."[19] The ICJ held in *Chagos* that "although resolution 1514 (XV) is formally a recommendation, it has a declaratory character with regard to the right to self-determination as a customary norm, in view of its content and the conditions of its adoption."[20]

Under the UNGA Resolution 1541, a non-self-governing territory could reach "a full measure of self-government by (a) [e]mergence as a sovereign independent State; (b) [f]ree association with an independent State; or (c) [i]ntegration with an independent State."[21] The ICJ in *Kosovo* confirmed that self-determination entailed "a right to independence for the peoples of non-self-governing territories and peoples subject to alien subjugation, domination and

17 Charter of the United Nations (adopted 26 June 1945, entered into force 24 October 1945) 1 UNTS XVI, arts 1(2) and 55.

18 Declaration on the Granting of Independence to Colonial Countries and Peoples, UNGA Res 1514 (XV) (14 December 1960) UN Doc A/RES/1514/(XV).

19 Shaw (n 13) 480. See also, for example, UNSC Res 183 (11 December 1963) UN Doc S/RES/183; UNSC 218 (23 November 1965) UN Doc S/RES/218; *Legal Consequences for States of the Continued Presence of South Africa in Namibia (South West Africa) notwithstanding Security Council Resolution 276 (1970)* (Advisory Opinion) [1971] ICJ Rep 16, para 52; *Western Sahara* (Advisory Opinion) [1975] ICJ Rep 12, paras 54–59 ("*Western Sahara*").

20 *Legal Consequences of the Separation of the Chagos Archipelago from Mauritius in 1965* (Advisory Opinion) [2019] ICJ GL No 169, para 152 ("*Chagos*").

21 UNGA Res 1541 (XV) (15 December 1960) UN Doc A/RES/1541(XV), Annex, Principle VI. See *Chagos* (n 20) para 156. "The establishment of a sovereign and independent State, the free association or integration with an independent State, or the emergence into any other political status freely determined by a people constitute modes of implementing the right of self-determination by that people." Friendly Relations Declaration (n 5) principle 5, para 4. The first three modes reflect the language of the UNGA Res 1541 (XV) (15 December 1960) UN Doc A/RES/1541(XV), Annex, Principle VI. K Del Mar, 'The Myth of Remedial Secession' in D French, *Statehood and Self-Determination: Reconciling Tradition and Modernity in International Law* (CUP 2013) 85. "The external aspect of self-determination implies that all peoples have the right to determine freely their political status and their place in the international community based on the principle of equal rights and exemplified by the liberation of peoples from colonialism and by the prohibition to subject peoples to alien subjugation, domination and exploitation." Committee on the Elimination of Racial Discrimination 'General Recommendation XXI on the Right to Self-Determination' (15 March 1996) contained in Compilation of General Comments and General Recommendations Adopted by Human Rights Treaty Bodies (27 May 2008) UN Doc HRI/GEN/1/Rev.9, para 4 ("General Recommendation XXI").

exploitation."[22] "Decolonization was a phenomenon without precedent: never before had non-sovereign groups reached independence as a matter of mere assertion of aspiration."[23]

Later, the right of peoples to self-determination was explicitly provided for in a plethora of international documents, especially in Article 1 of two international covenants and in principle 5 of the Friendly Relations Declaration.[24] These documents unequivocally confirmed the status of the right of peoples to self-determination as a legal and *universal* right, not limited to a specific context of decolonisation.[25] Today, it is undoubted that "it is one of the essential principles of contemporary international law",[26] has *erga omnes* character[27] and attained the status of a peremptory norm.[28]

However, outside of a decolonisation context, the specific contours of this right, in particular its holder and content have remained the matter of controversy. The following section examines both of these issues by drawing comparison and parallels from the decolonisation process.

2.2 *Meaning of 'Peoples'*

The definition of the peoples as the holder of the right to self-determination is a key neuralgic point of any discussion about the right to self-determination

22 *Accordance with International Law of the Unilateral Declaration of Independence in Respect of Kosovo* (Advisory Opinion) [2010] ICJ Rep 403, para 79 ("*Kosovo*").

23 Fabry, *Recognizing States* (n 6) 148–149. "Voilà la portée révolutionnaire de ce principe: pour la première fois dans l'histoire du droit des gens, il existe désormais un droit de certains communautés humaines à constituter un Etat." Kohen, 'Création d'Etats en droit international contemporain' (n 10) 585.

24 International Covenant on Civil and Political Rights (adopted 16 December 1966, entered into force 23 March 1976) 999 UNTS 171, art 1 ("ICCPR"); International Covenant on Economic, Social and Cultural Rights (adopted 16 December 1966, entered into force 3 January 1976) 993 UNTS 3, art 1 ("ICESCR"); Friendly Relations Declaration (n 5) principle 5; See also Final Act of the Conference on the Security and Cooperation in Europe (adopted 1 August 1975) chapter VIII reprinted in ILM 14 (1975) 1293–1298 ("Helsinki Final Act"); African Charter on Human and Peoples' Rights (signed 27 June 1981, entered into force 21 October 1986) 1520 UNTS 217, art 20.

25 P Radan, 'International Law and the Right of Unilateral Secession' in A Pavković and P Radan, *The Ashgate Research Companion to Secession* (Routledge 2011) 322.

26 *East Timor* (Portugal v Australia) [1995] ICJ Rep 90, para 29 ("*East Timor*").

27 ibid.

28 See for example ILC, Draft Articles on the Responsibility of States for Internationally Wrongful Acts, with Commentaries in 'Report of the International Law Commission on the Work of its Fifty-Third Session (23 April–1 June and 2 July–10 August 2001)' UN Doc A/56/10, commentary to art 40, para 5 ("ARSIWA"). Kohen, 'Création d'Etats en droit international contemporain' (n 10) 583.

outside of decolonisation. Even though it is rather difficult to separate the question of the right-holder from its content, the issue of peoplehood needs to be outlined at least in broad terms. Essentially, the doctrinal discussion oscillates between two opposing views. On the one hand, an ethnic-national definition of the peoples claims that there are certain objective and subjective criteria that are characteristic of peoplehood.[29] However, such a reading has been met with deep distrust as a potential trigger of unstoppable fragmentation endangering peace and stability.[30] On the other hand, according to a territorial delimitation of the peoples, the right of self-determination belongs to "the peoples of the State in their entirety."[31] This approach has been criticised as giving more credence to pre-existing boundaries than to the "congruence of cohesion in the communities that inhabit such territory."[32] No international treaty has provided for the definition and, therefore, the practice must be a guiding criterion.[33]

It is useful to point out that during the decolonisation process, the units of self-determination were always delimited by pre-existing colonial

29 JD Vyver Van Der, 'The Right to Self-Determination and its Enforcement' (2004) 10 ILSA Journal of International & Comparative Law 421, 425.

30 Robert Lansing, the US Secretary of State under Woodrow Wilson, declared the term self-determination as "simply loaded with dynamite. It will raise hopes, which can never be realized. It will, I fear, cost thousand of lives. In the end it is bound to be discredited, to be called the dream of an idealist who failed to realize the danger until too late to check those who attempt to put the principle in force. What a calamity that the phrase was ever uttered! What misery it will cause!" R Lansing, *The Peace Negotiations: A Personal Narrative* (Houghton Mifflin Company 1921) 97–98 <http://www.gutenberg.org/cache/epub/10444/pg10444-images.html> accessed 11 November 2018. "Self-determination of the peoples does not imply self-determination of a secession of the population of a particular member State." UN Secretary-General U Thant cited in G Welhengama and N Pillay, 'Minorities' Claim to Secession by Virtue of the Right to Self-Determination: Asian Perspectives with Special Reference to Kosovo and Sri Lanka' (2013) 82 Nordic Journal of International Law 249, 253. "If every ethic, religious or linguistic group claimed statehood, there would be no limit to fragmentation, and peace, security and economic well-being for all would become ever more difficult to achieve." UN Secretary-General, 'An Agenda for Peace: Preventive Diplomacy, Peacemaking and Peace-keeping' (17 June 1992) UN Doc A/47/277, para 17. See also T Christakis and A Constantinides, 'Territorial Dispute in the Context of Secessionist Conflicts,' in MG Kohen and M Hébié (eds), *Research Handbook on Territorial Disputes in International Law* (EE Elgar 2018) 343.

31 See R McCorquodale, 'Self-Determination: A Human Rights Approach' (1994) 43 International and Comparative Law Quarterly 857, 866.

32 J Costellino, 'International Law and Self-Determination: Peoples, Indigenous Peoples and Minorities' in C Walter, A Von Ungern-Sternberg and K Abushov, *Self-Determination and Secession in International Law* (OUP 2014) 33.

33 Fabry, 'The Right to Self-Determination' (n 1) 499.

boundaries,[34] thereby following the *uti possidetis iuris* principle.[35] "Unless and until there was agreement of all pertinent parties to do otherwise, trust and non-self-governing territories were to accede to independence in their colonial boundaries."[36] "[T]he principle of self-determination was territorially defined."[37] In such a way, "the so-called 'self-determination unit' was identified with the *demos* living in the territory subject to illegal domination, and not with an *ethnos*."[38]

The *Chagos* Advisory Opinion entrenched this view of a self-determination unit when the ICJ held that "the right to self-determination of the people concerned is defined by reference to the entirety of a non-self-governing territory" as stated in para 6 of the UNGA Resolution 1514 (XV).[39] According to the ICJ, "*the peoples of non-self-governing territories* are entitled to exercise their right to self-determination in relation to their territory as a whole, the integrity of which must be respected by the administering Power."[40] Thus, the ICJ referred to the holders of the right of self-determination exclusively as the peoples of the entire non-self-governing territory.

This territorial approach to peoplehood during the decolonisation process has implications for the context outside decolonisation. In particular, it is because the right to self-determination is an on-going right.

> Self-determination has never simply meant independence. It has meant the free choice of peoples … It is not only at the moment of independence from colonial rule that peoples are entitled to freely pursue their economic, social and cultural development. It is a constant entitlement.[41]

34 See Fabry, *Recognizing States* (n 6) 149–150. See also *Western Sahara* (n 19) para 70; *East Timor* (n 26) paras 31 and 37.

35 See *infra* Chapter 4.

36 Fabry, *Recognizing States* (n 6) 161. See also G Alfredsson, 'Peoples' in MPEPIL (online edn, OUP 2007), paras 3–11.

37 Shaw (n 13) 481.

38 A Tancredi, 'In Search of a Fair Balance between the Inviolability of Borders, Self-Determination and Secession' in E Milano, M Nicolini and F Palermo (eds), *Law, Territory and Conflict Resolution: Law as a Problem and Law as a Solution* (Brill Nijhoff 2016) 94.

39 *Chagos* (n 20) para 160.

40 ibid (*emphasis added*).

41 R Higgins, *Problems and Process: International Law and How We Use It* (Clarendon Press 1994) 119–120. "The right of peoples to self-determination has lasting force, does not lapse upon first having been exercised to secure political self-determination and extends to all fields, including of course economic, social and cultural affairs." 'The Right to Self-Determination: Implementation of United Nations Resolutions: Study Prepared by Héctor Gros Espiell, Special Rapporteur of the Sub-Commission on Prevention of Discrimination

It would be absurd to claim that the holder of the right changes once independence is achieved. From this perspective, a territorial rather than an ethnic approach to peoplehood applies to decolonisation as well as to a post-colonial context, ie to peoples of newly independent States as a whole. Consequently, the same rationale also applies to a non-colonial context.[42] In fact, "practice shows that the international legal definition of 'peoples' acknowledges the existence of only one people where there exists a State."[43]

> Unless there was a domestic agreement, sanctioned by the central authorities of a colony or an existing state, on who were the bearers of the right to self-determination, external actors defined the right-bearing 'people' to be the entire population of that colony or state.[44]

A territorial approach to peoplehood outside decolonisation also follows from the fact that "the very UN instruments that proclaimed the foundation of self-determination also clearly prohibited the partial or total disruption of the national unity and territorial integrity of existing independent states."[45] In addition, Opinion No 2 of the Badinter Commission, stated

---

and Protection of Minorities' (1980) E/CN.4/Sub.2/405/Rev.1, 8, para 47 and see 22, para 114 ("Study Prepared by Héctor Gros Espiell").

42 It will be shown below that while outside decolonisation this right does not entail the right to independence of sub-parts of population of existing States, it "allows choices as to political and economic systems within the existing boundaries of the state." Higgins (n 41) 123. See *infra*.

43 Kohen, 'Introduction' (n 5) 9. See also Kohen, 'Création d'Etats en droit international contemporain' (n 10) 584–586.

44 Fabry, 'The Right to Self-Determination' (n 1) 499–500. The Supreme Court of Canada held a contrary position. "To restrict the definition of the term to the population of existing states would render the granting of a right to self-determination largely duplicative, given the parallel emphasis within the majority of the source documents on the need to protect the territorial integrity of existing states, and would frustrate its remedial purpose." *Re Reference By the Governor in Council Concerning Certain Questions Relating to the Secession of Quebec from Canada* (Canada, Supreme Court) (1998) 115 ILR 536, para 124 ("*Reference Re Secession of Quebec*"). For a contrary doctrinal position see D Murswiek, 'The Issue of a Right of Secession – Reconsidered' in C Tomuschat (ed), *Modern Law of Self-Determination* (Martinus Nijhoff Publishers 1993) 37.

45 Shaw (n 13) 482. See for the documents *infra*.

> whatever circumstances, the right to self-determination must not involve changes to existing frontiers (*uti possidetis juris*) at the time of independence except where the states concerned agreed otherwise.[46]

The fact that all the relevant documents and state practice emphasise territorial integrity "means that 'peoples' is to be understood in the sense of *all* the peoples of a given territory."[47]

Furthermore, *travaux préparatoires* of Article 1 ICCPR demonstrates that the term "nations" originally included in this provision was deleted because the term "peoples" was seen as being more comprehensive.[48] "Modern international law has deliberately attributed the right to Peoples, and not to Nations and States."[49]

In addition, "[b]y definition, a minority cannot but be identified within a wider human community."[50] Thus, the term peoples "encompasses other inhabitants than the ethnic or religious majority population of country/territory concerned."[51] From this perspective, members of the distinct minority are part of the peoples within a State and thereby are also holders of the right of self-determination.[52] "But minorities *as such* do not have a right of self-determination."[53] This is despite that "both apply within a State, and neither concerns the secession of territory."[54]

Additionally, outside of this general territorial understanding of peoplehood, recognition by the international community of certain groups within existing States as peoples can also have constitutive effects.[55] For example, the ICJ observed in the *Wall* opinion that "the existence of a 'Palestinian people'

46 'Opinion No 2 of the Arbitration Commission of Peace Conference for Yugoslavia' reprinted in (1992) 31 ILM 1494, 1498.
47 Higgins (n 41) 123.
48 M Bossuyt, *Guide to the "Travaux Préparatoires" of the International Covenant on Civil and Political Rights* (M Nijhoff 1987) 35. McCorquodale (n 31) 867. According to Tomuschat, though, the "*travaux* are quite inconclusive." C Tomuschat, 'Secession and Self-Determination' in MG Kohen (ed), *Secession: International Law Perspectives* (CUP 2006) 26.
49 Study Prepared by Héctor Gros Espiell (n 41) 9, para 56.
50 Kohen, 'Introduction' (n 5) 9.
51 Alfredsson (n 36) para 13.
52 Higgins (n 41) 124.
53 ibid. See *infra* on the position of the Human Rights Committee distinguishing between the right of self-determination and the rights of minorities.
54 Del Mar (n 21) 88.
55 Kohen, 'Introduction' (n 5) 9–10. See also Kohen, 'Création d'Etats en droit international contemporain' (n 10) 587.

is no longer in issue" and referring to the UNGA resolutions it considered that the rights of the Palestinian people "include the right to self-determination."[56] In addition, the recognition of various groups as peoples entitled to self-determination including the right to secede can occur also as the part of a municipal, usually constitutional, arrangement.[57]

2.3 *No Right to Secession*

The delimitation of peoples by reference to the entire territory of the State is intertwined with the fact that outside decolonisation and the situation of "alien subjugation, domination and exploitation"[58] the right of peoples to self-determination does not entail the right to secede. "[L]orsqu'il existe un Etat indépendant, sa population est considérée comme un peuple, ce qui exclut d'emblée qu'une partie de cette population puisse faire sécession en invoquant le droit à l'auto-détermination."[59] The relevant international documents, case law, doctrine and the practice of State-creation confirm such a conclusion.

Even though the key international and regional documents including the UNGA resolutions provide for a universal right of self-determination,[60]

56 *Legal Consequences of the Construction of a Wall in the Occupied Palestinian Territory* (Advisory Opinion) [2004] ICJ Rep 136, para. 118. See also Thürer and Burri (n 12) paras 119–120.

57 Kohen, 'Introduction' (n 5) 9. See also Kohen, 'Création d'Etats en droit international contemporain' (n 10) 586–7. Del Mar (n 21) 87. See *infra*.

58 See Friendly Relations Declaration (n 5) principle 5, para 2. "The other clear case where a right to external self-determination accrues is where a people is subject to alien subjugation, domination or exploitation outside a colonial context." *Reference Re Secession of Quebec* (n 44) para 133. The instance of alien domination was meant to include South Africa under apartheid. The right to external self-determination also applies to peoples under foreign occupation. Higgins (n 41) 115–116; Del Mar (n 21) 86–87.

59 Kohen, 'Création d'Etats en droit international contemporain' (n 10) 587.

60 According to the Friendly Relations Declaration, "all peoples have the right freely to determine, without external interference, their political status and to pursue their economic, social and cultural development." Friendly Relations Declaration (n 5) principle 5, para 1 and see also para 4. Vienna Declaration and Programme of Action of the World Conference on Human Rights contained the same provision. See Vienna Declaration and Programme of Action of the World Conference on Human Rights (25 June 1993) <https://www.ohchr.org/EN/ProfessionalInterest/Pages/Vienna.aspx> accessed 11 November 2018 ("Vienna Declaration"). Declaration on the Occasion of the Fiftieth Anniversary of the United Nations reaffirmed "the right of self-determination of all peoples, taking into account the particular situation of peoples under colonial or other forms of alien domination or foreign occupation, and recognize the right of peoples to take legitimate action in accordance with the Charter of the United Nations to realize their inalienable right of self-determination." UNGA Res 50/6 (24 October 1995) UN Doc A/RES/50/6, para 1 ("Fiftieth Anniversary Declaration") "By virtue of the principle of equal rights and

they also include safeguard clauses that preclude the interpretation of this right as creating any entitlement to impair the territorial integrity of the existing States.[61] The UNGA declarations in particular "strengthened the original position of the UN Charter where 'the right to self-determination' did not provide a rationale for secession by minority groups. Self-determination and secession are two separate issues and were treated as separate issues."[62] In addition, the key international and European documents on the rights of persons belonging to minorities[63] and indigenous

---

self-determination of peoples, all peoples have the right, in full freedom, to determine, when and as they wish, their internal and external political status, without external interference, and to pursue as they wish their political, economic, social and cultural development." Helsinki Final Act (n 24) chapter VIII, para 2.

61 "Nothing in the foregoing paragraphs shall be construed as authorizing or encouraging any action which would dismember or impair, totally or in part, the territorial integrity or political unity of sovereign and independent States." Friendly Relations Declaration (n 5) principle 5, para 7. Similarly, see also Vienna Declaration (n 60), para 2 and Fiftieth Anniversary Declaration (n 60) para 1. "The participating States will respect the equal rights of peoples and their right to self-determination, acting at all times in conformity with the purposes and principles of the Charter of the United Nations and with the relevant norms of international law, including those relating to territorial integrity of States." Helsinki Final Act (n 24) chapter VIII, para 1. Similarly, the Charter of Paris reaffirmed "the equal rights of peoples and their right to self-determination in conformity with the Charter of the United Nations and with relevant norms of international law, including those relating to territorial integrity of States." CSCE (Meeting of the Heads of State or Government of the Participating States of the Conference on Security and Co-Operation in Europe) 'The Charter of Paris for a New Europe' (adopted 19–21 November 1990) <https://www.osce.org/mc/39516?download=true> accessed 12 November 2018.

62 Welhengama and Pillay (n 30) 257.

63 "Nothing in the present Declaration may be construed as permitting any activity contrary to the purposes and principles of the United Nations, including sovereign equality, territorial integrity and political independence of States." Declaration on the Rights of Persons Belonging to National or Ethnic, Religious and Linguistic Minorities, UNGA Resolution 47/135 (18 December 1992) UN Doc A/RES/47/135, art 8(4); "The enjoyment of the rights to which article 27 relates does not prejudice the sovereignty and territorial integrity of a State party." UN Human Rights Committee 'General Comment No 23: 'Article 27 (Rights of Minorities)' (8 April 1994) UN Doc CCPR/C/21/Rev.1/Add.5, para 3.2. ("General Comment No 23"). "None of these commitments may be interpreted as implying any right to engage in any activity or preform any action in contravention of the purposes and principles of the Charter of the United Nations, other obligations under international law or the provisions of the Final Act, including the principle of territorial integrity of States." 'Document of the Copenhagen Meeting of the Conference on the Human Dimension of the CSCE' (adopted 29 June 1990) <https://www.osce.org/odihr/elections/14304?download=true> accessed 12 November 2018. "Nothing in this Charter may be interpreted as implying any right to engage in any activity or perform any action in contravention of the purposes of the Charter of the United Nations or other obligations under international law, including

peoples[64] also contain safeguard clauses preventing the interpretation of these rights as creating any entitlement to impair territorial integrity of existing States.

Article 1(1) ICCPR and ICESCR establish that "[a]ll peoples have the right to self-determination."[65] As will be discussed below in detail, the Human Rights Committee in its General Comment No 12 referred to Article 1(1) ICCPR only in terms of constitutional and political processes and did not mention any right to secession.[66] In addition, the Committee on the Elimination of Racial Discrimination in its General Recommendation XXI explicitly stated, "international law has not recognized a general right of peoples unilaterally to declare secession from a State."[67] "The right to secession from an existing State Member of the United Nations does not exist as such in the instruments or in the practice followed by the Organization."[68]

In addition, the case law also confirms the non-existence of a general right to secede flowing from the right to self-determination. In *Reference Re Secession of Quebec*, the Supreme Court of Canada held that

> international law expects that the right to self-determination will be exercised by peoples within the framework of existing sovereign states and consistently with the maintenance of the territorial integrity of those states.[69]

---

the principle of the sovereignty and territorial integrity of States." European Charter for Regional or Minority Languages (adopted 5 November 1992, entered into force 1 March 1998) 2044 UNTS 575, art 5. See also Framework Convention for the Protection of National Minorities (adopted 1 February 1995, entered into force 1 February 1998) 2151 UNTS 243, art 21.

64 See United Nations Declaration on the Rights of Indigenous Peoples, UN GA Res 61/295 (13 September 2007) UN Doc A/RES/61/295, Annex, art 46(1).

65 ICCPR (n 24) art 1(1) and ICESR (n 24) art 1(1).

66 UN Human Rights Committee 'General Comment No 12: Article 1 (Right to Self-Determination)' (13 March 1984) contained in Compilation of General Comments and General Recommendations Adopted by Human Rights Treaty Bodies (27 May 2008) UN Doc HRI/GEN/1/Rev.9 ("General Comment No 12").

67 General Recommendation XXI (n 21) para 6.

68 Study Prepared by Héctor Gros Espiell (n 41) 14, para 90.

69 *Reference Re Secession of Quebec* (n 44), para 122 and see para 131. The Commission of Rapporteurs in *Aaland island* case held that "to concede to minorities ... the right of withdrawing from the community to which they belong, because it is their wish or their good pleasure, would be to uphold a theory incompatible with the very idea of the State as a territorial entity." Report Presented to the Council of the League of Nations by the Commission of Rapporteurs (1921) LN Council Doc B7 21/68/106, 318. However, this case is not directly relevant to a contemporary analysis, as it was issued in the pre-Charter era.

The ICJ in *Kosovo* did not entertain the analysis of the existence of the right to secede flowing from the right to self-determination outside of a colonial context as it considered such analysis falling out of the scope of the question asked.[70] The ICJ simply noted that "radically different views were expressed by those taking part in the proceedings" on this issue.[71] However, such a statement is not without value because the presence of radically different views normally precludes the formation of custom.

Furthermore, in terms of post-colonial and post-Cold War State-creation, there is not one single case of an uncontested statehood achieved because of a generally acknowledged right to secede flowing from the right to self-determination.[72]

Lastly, the doctrine also rejects the existence of right to secede flowing from the right to self-determination. "Whatever the right to self-determination meant outside the colonial context … it excluded the right to unilateral secession."[73] Overall, in the post-1945 practice, "the principle of self-determination is not recognized as giving rise to unilateral rights of secession by parts of independent States."[74]

---

70 "Debates regarding the extent of the right of self-determination and the existence of any right of 'remedial secession', however, concern the right to separate from a State. As the Court has already noted … and as almost all participants agreed, that issue is beyond the scope of the question posed by the General Assembly." *Kosovo* (n 22) para 83 and see also para 56.

71 *Kosovo* (n 22) para 82.

72 Fabry, 'The Right to Self-Determination' (n 1) 499–501. The cases frequently invoked to support the existence of remedial secession will be analysed below.

73 Fabry, 'International Involvement in Secessionist Conflict' (n 7) 258 and see also 264; Vyver Van Der (n 29) 427; Welhengama and Pillay (n 30) 252; Lanovoy V, 'Self-determination in International Law. A Democratic Phenomenon or an Abuse of Right?' (2015) 4 Cambridge Journal of International and Comparative Law 388, 392; Christakis and Constantinides (n 30) 360; U Saxer, 'Self-Determination, Changes of Statehood and the Self-Organization of the International System' (2010) 214 Beiträge zum ausländischen öffentlichen Recht und Völkerrecht 993, 996.

74 Crawford (n 8) 415. Similarly, see A Cassese, *International Law* (2nd edn, OUP 2005) 63; Higgins (n 41) 124; T Christakis, *Le droit à l'autodétermination en dehors des situations de décolonisation* (La documentation française 1999) 617; P Pazartzis, 'Secession and International Law: The European Dimension' in MG Kohen (ed), *Secession: International Law Perspectives* (CUP 2006) 361; T Franck, 'Postmodern Tribalism and the Right to Secession' in C Brölmann, R Lefeber and M Zieck (eds), *Peoples and Minorities in International Law* (Martinus Nijhoff Publishers 1993) 11; Tancredi, 'In Search of a Fair Balance between the Inviolability of Borders, Self-Determination and Secession' (n 38) 93.

2.4 *Outline of the Content of the Right of Self-Determination*

Although the right to self-determination outside decolonisation does not entail the right to secede, it is a universal right, which applies to *all peoples*, ie populations of existing States, who by its virtue "freely determine their political status and freely pursue their economic, social and cultural development."[75] According to Special Rapporteur Espiell, "the right of peoples to self-determination encompasses political, economic, social and cultural aspects."[76]

As for the political aspects, the Human Rights Committee established that the right to self-determination is "an essential condition for the effective guarantee and observance of individual human rights and for the promotion and strengthening of those rights."[77] As part of their reporting obligations, the States were urged to inform the Committee about "the constitutional and political processes, which in practice allow the exercise of this right."[78] Moreover, the Committee on the Elimination of the Racial Discrimination also stressed "the right of every citizen to take part in the conduct of public affairs at any level."[79] Broadly, the right to self-determination is considered an essential condition "because if peoples are being subjected to oppression they are not in a position to have any of their individual rights fully protected."[80]

Thus, the focus is on intra-State relations and on the internal aspects of the principle[81] "The 'internal' aspect of the right concerns the right of peoples within a State to choose their political status, the extent of their political participation and the form of their government, i.e. a State's 'internal' relations are affected."[82] However, self-determination does not prescribe a particular form of government.[83] Moreover, even though the right under Article

75 ICCPR (n 24) art 1(1) and ICESR (n 24) art 1(1).

76 Study Prepared by Héctor Gros Espiell (n 41) 9, para 56. Even though other aspects of the right to self-determination are not directly relevant to secession, it is worth noting that economic aspects entail the right of peoples to determine their economic system and are also manifested in the right to permanent sovereignty over natural resources. ibid 26, paras 135–136. See also ICCPR (n 24) art 1(2) and ICECSR (n 24) art 1(2).

77 General Comment No 12 (n 66) para 1.

78 ibid para 4.

79 General Recommendation XXI (n 21) para 4.

80 McCorquodale (n 31) 872.

81 Thürer and Burri (n 12) para 33.

82 See McCorquodale (n 31) 864, and see more about the implementation of internal self-determination ibid 863–865.

83 "The rights under article 25 are related to, but distinct from, the right of peoples to self-determination. By virtue of the rights covered by article 1 (1), peoples have the right to freely determine their political status and to enjoy the right to choose the form of their constitution or government. Article 25 deals with the right of individuals to participate

1(1) ICCPR and rights under Article 25 ICCPR are related, they are nonetheless distinct.[84]

Importantly, self-determination needs to be distinguished from minority rights. Even the Human Rights Committee confirmed such a distinction.[85] Accordingly, while the right to self-determination belongs to peoples and is not cognisable under the Optional Protocol, the minority rights are "personal rights conferred on individuals" cognisable under the Optional Protocol.[86] International documents also confirm that the rights of minorities shall be exercised in compliance with the principle of territorial integrity of States. Even though the State's failure to fulfil its obligations concerning minority rights can fuel the secessionist sentiments in part of the population "with a strong group consciousness",[87] from a legal perspective, this does not form a legal basis of the right to secession. Another issue concerns the fact that indigenous peoples "in exercising their right to self-determination, have right to autonomy or self-government relating to their internal and local matters."[88] Overall,

> the principle of self-determination acts as a legal mechanism to achieve a range of relevant human rights within the territorial framework of independent states, and not as a tool legally justifying the dismantling of such states.[89]

3 Remedial Secession

The existence of the right to remedial secession has been one of the more controversial issues in the context of contemporary secession, albeit mainly in a

---

in those processes which constitute the conduct of public affairs. Those rights, as individual rights, can give rise to claims under the first Optional Protocol." UN Human Rights Committee, 'General Comment No 25: Article 25 (Participation in Public Affairs and the Right to Vote), The Right to Participate in Public Affairs, Voting Rights and the Right of Equal Access to Public Service' (12 July 1996) UN Doc CCPR/C/21/Rev.1/Add.7, para 2. Lanovoy (n 73) 393–394; Higgins (n 41) 120–121.

84 This includes a democratic form of government. See Lanovoy (n 73) 393–399.

85 General Comment No 23 (n 63) para 3.1. *Contra*: S Joseph and M Castan, 'Right of Self-Determination – Article 1' in S Joseph and M Castan, *International Covenant on Civil and Political Rights: Cases, Materials, and Commentary* (3rd edn, OUP 2013)160.

86 General Comment No 23 (n 63) para 3.1.

87 Vyver Van Der (n 29) 426.

88 Declaration on the Rights of Indigenous Peoples, art 4. As mentioned above, this declaration also includes saveguard clause ibid art 46(1). Del Mar (n 21) 88.

89 Shaw (n 13) 484.

doctrinal sphere. It can be agreed with Tomuschat "the only major controversy which still rages among legal writers centres on this concept."[90] While there are scholars who support the claim on the existence of the right to remedial secession,[91] many authors oppose such a conclusion.[92] Other observers simply leave the existence of the right to remedial secession open.[93]

An alleged right to remedial secession does not rest on a substantive practice, but on *a contrario* reading of safeguard clause, para 7 of the Friendly Relations Declaration. The argument goes that only those States can rely on the protection of their territorial integrity that conduct

> themselves in compliance with the principle of equal rights and self-determination of peoples ... and thus possessed of a government representing the whole people belonging to the territory without distinction as to race, creed or colour.[94]

According to the proponents of remedial secession, the adoption of the Vienna Declaration and the Fiftieth Anniversary Declaration, which referred to "a Government representing the whole people belonging to the territory without distinction of any kind",[95] strengthened this position. The underlying rationale is that when a certain part of the population is deprived of internal self-determination, this situation can be remedied by the entitlement of such a group to create a new State by way of unilateral secession.

However, apart from the lack of practice supporting such a contention, which is discussed below, there are many issues relating to the drafting of the

---

90 Tomuschat (n 48) 35.

91 See for example, Radan, 'International Law and the Right of Unilateral Secession' (n 25) 324–327; Joseph and Castan (n 85) 161; A Pellet, '*Kosovo* – The Questions Not Asked: Self-Determination, Secession, and Recognition' in M Milanović and M Wood, *The Law and Politics of the Kosovo Advisory Opinion* (OUP 2015) 272; G Anderson, 'Unilateral Non-Colonial Secession in International Law and Declaratory General Assembly Resolutions: Textual Content and Legal Effects (2013) 41 Denver Journal of International Law and Policy 345, 355; Raič (n 9) 316–332; Christakis, *Le droit à l'autodétermination en dehors des situations de décolonisation* (n 74) 316; Murswiek (44) 42.

92 Fabry, *Recognizing States* (n 6) 165–168; M Milanović, 'Arguing the *Kosovo* Case' in M Milanović and M Wood, *The Law and Politics of the Kosovo Advisory Opinion* (OUP 2015) 34; Kohen, 'Introduction' (n 5) 10; Shaw (n 13) 482–483; O Corten, 'A propos d'un désormais « classique »: Le droit à l'autodétermination en dehors des situations de décolonisation, de Théodore Christakis' (1999) 1 RBDI 1 (1999) 329, 341; Del Mar (n 21) 79–108.

93 Thürer and Burri (n 12) paras 35–36.

94 Friendly Relations Declarations (n 5) principle 5, para 7.

95 Vienna Declaration (n 60) para 2 and Fiftieth Anniversary Declaration (n 60) para 1.

Friendly Relations Declaration and structural problems specifically related to its implementation. Crucially, it is very unlikely that the States would opt for *a contrario* reading of a penultimate paragraph of the Friendly Relations Declaration to allow for the establishment of the right to unilateral secession.[96] In addition, it follows from the drafting history of this provision that States did not intend to do so and, instead, reacted to the situation in South Africa and Rhodesia at the time.[97] "The drafting, in fact, reveals virtually no positive intention to establish any right for minorities to secede under any circumstances."[98]

Additionally, the required threshold of violation proves problematic. Since the majority of the proponents of the remedial secession suggest a very high threshold reaching "extreme oppression"[99] or situations of very serious crimes such as genocide and ethnic cleansing, perceiving the secession as *ultima ratio* remedy,[100] the references made to the violation of the so-called internal self-determination (a lower level of violation) do not seem to be justified.

Any such violations should temporarily precede the act of the DoI. In other words, the secessionist tendencies should not be the root-cause of the violence by the State. Otherwise, the remedial aspect of the alleged right would be compromised. Moreover, the question can also be raised as to the process of transformation of the oppressed minority into peoples who are entitled to external self-determination[101] and the absence of this type of remedy in the general rules of the law of international responsibility.[102]

In addition, "no international judicial body has ever upheld the remedial secession argument in relation to a specific attempt at unilateral secession."[103] The Commission of Rapporteurs held in the *Aaland island* case that the separation of minority could "be considered an altogether exceptional solution,

96 Shaw (n 13) 483.
97 Kohen, 'Introduction' (n 5) 10.
98 J Summers, 'The Right of Self-Determination and Nationalism in International Law' (2005) 12 International Journal on Minority and Group Rights 325, 335. See for a reading of *travaux préparatoires* favourable to the existence of remedial secession see Raič (n 9) 319–321.
99 Crawford (n 8) 119. Tomuschat refers to 'unbearable persecution.' Tomuschat (n 48) 35.
100 For the criticism that remedial secession by definition is the remedy that comes too late, see Del Mar (n 21) 103.
101 Kohen, 'Introduction' (n 5) 10–11. See also Del Mar (n 21) 99–101.
102 Del Mar (n 21) 79. *Contra*: "[Remedial secession] is then more in the nature of a consequence of the violation ('remedy') of the principle of the right of peoples to self-determination than a component of that right." Pellet (n 91) 272.
103 J Vidmar, 'Remedial Secession in International Law: Theory and (Lack of) Practice' (2010) 6 St Anthony's International Review 37, 50–51.

a last resort when the State lacks either will or the power to enact and apply just and effective guarantees",[104] but this case was rendered during a pre-Charter period, which cannot be considered directly relevant to contemporary self-determination debate.[105] In addition, it was not found applicable in that case either. Moreover, the African Commission on Human Rights implied that except for the situation when the right of Katangese peoples to the participation in the government under Article 13(1) of the African Charter of Human and Peoples' Rights is violated, "Katanga is obliged to exercise a variant of self-determination that is compatible with sovereignty and territorial integrity of Zaire."[106] This case *a contrario* accepts the possibility of remedial secession; however, remedial secession was not found applicable in this case either. As for the *Reference Re Secession of Quebec*, the Supreme Court of Canada held that "it remains unclear" whether the right to remedial secession "reflects an established international law standard" and it was not necessary to make such a determination in that case because the required threshold would not have been met.[107]

With respect to the *Kosovo* proceedings, the ICJ did not provide any conclusion as to the existence of the right to remedial secession and simply pointed out the "radically different views" presented during the proceedings.[108] In this context, regarding "remedial secession/self-determination, of the 43 states (excluding Kosovo) that appeared before the Court in three rounds of pleadings, 14 asserted that this right existed in principle, 14 denied its existence, and the remaining 25 were neutral."[109] In such circumstances, it can be agreed with

104 Report Presented to the Council of the League of Nations by the Commission of Rapporteurs (1921) LN Council Doc B7 21/68/106, 318.

105 Del Mar (n 21) 91–93.

106 *Katangese Peoples' Congress v Zaire*, Communication of the African Commission of Human and Peoples' Rights No 75/92 (1995), para 6.

107 *Reference Re Secession of Quebec* (n 44), para 135. For a reading of this case favourable to the existence of remedial secession, see Raič (n 9) 331–332. The recent judgment of the UK Supreme Court has heavily relied on the findings concerning international law on the matter in *Reference Re Secession of Quebec* and stated that none of the raised contexts for the possible right of self-determination applied to Scotland. See *Reference by the Lord Advocate of Devolution Issues under Paragraph 34 of Schedule 6 to the Scotland Act 1998* [2022] UKSC 31, paras 88–89.

108 *Kosovo* (n 22) para 82.

109 Milanović (n 92) 43. Milanović also points that as far as permanent members of the Security Council are concerned, "Russia endorsed remedial self-determination in principle (while rejecting its applicability to Kosovo), China opposed it, while France, the UK, and the US remained neutral." ibid. The position of the Russian Federation can be explained by reference to its own argumentation with respect to the recognition of South

Milanović who claims that if these views were taken as *opinio iuris* of the international community, "the question of the existence of the right to remedial secession would remain inconclusive."[110]

Critically, the argument on the existence of the right to remedial secession lacks support in terms of the State practice.[111] The creation of Bangladesh is frequently invoked as a potential example of the State-creation based on the right to remedial secession. However, as pointed out by Fabry, "neither individual states (including those that supported India) nor the UN bodies suggested that there was a right to secede from even extremely repressive government."[112]

Moreover, the States participating in the *Kosovo* proceedings were split on the issue of the existence of the right to remedial secession and those States that supported that argument used it only in a secondary manner. Furthermore, the right to remedial secession can hardly be inferred from other situations that could *prima facie* be seen as fulfilling its factual requirements.[113] Overall, even the proponents of the existence of the right to remedial secession admit, "there exists no clear and undisputable precedent."[114]

4 Right to Secede Derived from Other Sources

4.1 *Right to 'Secede' with the Consent of the Parent State*

As suggested above, there is exception to a territorial definition of peoples, ie the population of entire State, in a situation when the parent State itself designates in its constitution a certain group within its population as peoples entitled to self-determination.[115] Alternatively, the constitution can also grant the right of secession for the section of its territory without the link to the right

Ossetia and Abkhazia. Del Mar (n 21) 82. For more on Russia's position to remedial secession, see *infra*, Part 2.

110 Milanović (n 92) 43. See also Del Mar (n 21) 81–85.

111 See Vidmar, 'Remedial Secession in International Law' (n 103) 50.

112 Fabry, *Recognizing States* (n 6) 167 (*footnotes omitted*). For the arguments in favour of remedial secession in this case, see Crawford (n 8) 142 and 393.

113 For example, the Sri Lankan government was criticised for its response towards Tamil Elam's secessionist attempt, but this did not lead to questioning of its sovereignty over Tamil territories. Fabry, 'International Involvement in Secessionist Conflict' (n 7) 264.

114 Pellet (n 91) 272.

115 For example, see the Constitution of the Federal Democratic Republic of Ethiopia, the Moldovan Law on Special Legal Status of Gagauzia and the 2009 Act on Greenland Self-Government. See more in detail *infra* Chapter 5.

to self-determination.[116] In addition, the right to secession can also flow from an agreement between the State and the secessionists.[117]

On a municipal law plane, these devolutionary arrangements,[118] subject to fulfilment of the conditions therein, produce constitutional or conventional rights for designated sub-State entities or groups to secede. On an international law plane, as is discussed in Chapter 5, rather than accentuating some type of autonomous or an original right of secessionists to independence, it is appropriate to refer to them as the expression of the parent State's consent. From an international law standpoint, a key factor and legal basis is consent by the parent State.[119] As is shown in Chapter 5, as opposed to unilateral secessionist attempts, practice unquestionably favours consensual devolutionary arrangements.

Nevertheless, the opposability to and enforceability of such a parent State consent under international law remains controversial.[120] Would the violation by the State of the constitution or the peace accords providing for the right to secession authorise the secessionists to claim the right to secede under international law? Today, the answer to this question would seem to be negative.[121] However, undoubtedly, such a violation would have political repercussions benefiting the secessionist cause.[122] In any case, the secessionists would not be prohibited by international law from seeking independence through classical methods outside of the context of the right to secede.

4.2 *Independence Referenda in Secessionist Contexts*

Holding of independence referenda has become a frequent, albeit not always present, component of the State-creation processes. Secessionists frequently

---

116 For example, see the former Constitutional Charter of the State Union of Serbia and Montenegro, the Constitution of Saint Christopher and Nevis, the Constitution of the Principality of Liechtenstein, the Constitution of the Republic of Uzbekistan and Charter for the Kingdom of the Netherlands. See more in detail *infra* Chapter 5.

117 See more in detail *infra* Chapter 5.

118 See more on the distinction between secession and devolution, *infra* Chapter 5.

119 "[C]e fait singulier témoigne de l'acceptation par le sujet concerné de l'applicabilité de l'autodétermination à l'entité sécessioniste. Le droit international ne fera que prendre acte de cette qualification faite par l'intéressé." Kohen, 'Création d'Etats en droit international contemporain' (n 10) 594.

120 See Raič (n 9) 316, ftn 37. Kohen, 'Création d'Etats en droit international contemporain' (n 10) 611.

121 Possibly subject to the exception of the acknoweldgment of a certain group as peoples entitled to right to self-determination. Kohen, 'Création d'Etats en droit international contemporain' (n 10) 611 and 614.

122 ibid 614.

rely on the results of their unilaterally organised referenda to justify their independence demands. Therefore, the question must be asked to what extent a successful unilateral independence referendum provides a legal basis and entitlement to secession in contemporary international law and what requirements, if any, with respect to the organisation of such referenda stem from international law.

4.2.1 Unilateral Referendum Does Not Give Rise to the Right to Secede

At the outset, even though at first sight certain factual situations involving independence referenda might look similar, at a closer look, their legal context and ensuing legal consequences are very different. Several legal situations can be detected. First, many referenda have been held under the UN auspices in the context of decolonisation.[123] The ICJ held that "the application of the right to self-determination requires a free and genuine expression of the will of the peoples concerned."[124] However, the ICJ also held that

> [t]he validity of the principle of self-determination, defined as the need to pay regard to the freely expressed will of peoples, is not affected by the fact that in certain cases the General Assembly has dispensed with the requirement of consulting the inhabitants of a given territory. Those instances were based either on the consideration that a certain population did not constitute 'people' entitled to self-determination or on the conviction that a consultation was totally unnecessary, in view of special circumstances.[125]

Second, independence referenda have been held in the context of the dissolution of the States during the post-Cold War period.[126] However, it is necessary to agree with Radan "there is no rule of international law that requires a

123 See for more ibid 607–609.

124 *Western Sahara* (n 19) para 55.

125 ibid para 59. See also *Chagos* (n 20) para 158. Study Prepared by Héctor Gros Espiell (n 41) 10–11, para 65.

126 For example, it is worth noting that in its Opinion No 4, the Badinter Commission requested a referendum of all citizens, without distinction and under international supervision, as the condition for the recognition of Bosnia and Herzegovina by the members of the European Community. It also noted the referenda, which took place in Slovenia, Croatia and Macedonia, in its opinions No 5–7 on recognition of the respective States. See 'Opinions Nos 4–7 of the Arbitration Commission of Peace Conference for Yugoslavia' reprinted in (1992) 31 ILM 1494, 1501–1518. IG Şen, *Sovereignty Referendums in International and Constitutional Law* (Springer 2015) 87–88.

referendum before state creation of this kind can occur."[127] For example, the dissolution of Czechoslovakia, which occurred without holding any referendum on independence, confirms such a conclusion.[128]

Third, holding of referendum might nevertheless also become a legal obligation based on the constitutional provision or the peace or other type of agreement.[129] Even in these instances, the requirement of holding referendum would be mandated by these specific legal instruments and not be the rule of a general international law.

Lastly, regarding unilateral referenda held outside of the above contexts, "there is no recognition of a unilateral right to secede based merely on a majority vote of the population of a given sub-division or territory."[130] "[S]tate practice indicates that referenda are of no relevance whatsoever."[131] Popular support does not establish a legal right to secession.[132] Similarly, the Supreme Court of Canada, even though the analysis was limited only to the context of the Canadian constitution, held "a referendum, in itself and without more, has no direct legal effect, and could not in itself bring about unilateral secession."[133]

However, notwithstanding the fact that a majority vote on its own does not give rise to the right to independence, it can certainly have political ramifications.[134] For example, the Supreme Court of Canada held that the clear rejection of the people of Quebec of the existing constitution would confer legitimacy on their demands and place obligation on other actors to enter into negotiations seeking amendment to the constitution.[135] However, this obligation was derived by the Court from the Canadian Constitutional principles and

---

127 P Radan, 'Secessionist Referenda in International and Domestic Law' (2012) 18 Nationalism and Ethnic Politics 8, 12.

128 Kohen, 'Création d'Etats en droit international contemporain' (n 10) 603.

129 See *infra* Chapter 5 for more detailed discussion of these modes of State-creation taking place with the parent State's consent. Radan, 'Secessionist Referenda' (n 127) 12–13.

130 Crawford (n 8) 417.

131 Radan, 'Secessionist Referenda' (n 127) 12; J Vidmar, 'The Scottish Independence Referendum in an International Context' (2013) The Canadian Yearbook of International Law 259, 263.

132 A Tancredi, 'A Normative "Due Process" in the Creation of States through Secession' in MG Kohen (ed), *Secession: International Law Perspectives* (CUP 2006) 191. See J Vidmar, S McGibbon and L Raible, Introduction to the Research Handbook on Secession' in J Vidmar, S McGibbon and L Raible (eds), *Research Handbook on Secession* (Edward Elgar 2022) 6.

133 See Radan, 'Secessionist Referenda in International and Domestic Law' (n 127) 18.

134 *Reference Re Secession of Quebec* (n 44) para 87.

135 "The clear repudiation by the people of Quebec of the existing constitutional order would confer legitimacy on demands for secession, and place an obligation on the other provinces and the federal government to acknowledge and respect that expression of

was criticised by part of the doctrine as lacking sufficient justification.[136] No such obligation of negotiation flows from international law. Overall, considering the above-mentioned, it is possible to agree with the statement that

> l'expression de la volonté des populations concernées en faveur de la constitution d'un Etat indépendant, sous une forme ou une autre, est devenue une condition nécessaire pour la création des nouveaux Etats. Elle n'est pas cependant une condition suffisante, même pas pour établir l'existence d'un droit à un Etat indépendant.[137]

4.2.2 Independence Referenda Within the Purview of International Law

Successful results of a unilateral referendum do not produce the legal right of independence; however, the question can be asked whether the mere holding of a unilateral referendum on its own could be seen as a violation of international law. In this context, the ICJ in the *Kosovo* Advisory Opinion held that "general international law contains no applicable prohibitions of declarations of independence"[138] and therefore it can be inferred that the holding of a referendum as such is not illegal under international law, "no more so for that matter than a unilateral declaration of independence that might follow on from such a referendum."[139]

However, a number of further points must be made. First, unlawfulness of unilateral referenda under a domestic constitution is immaterial from the point of view of international law.[140] Second, regarding the procedural

democratic will by entering into negotiations and conducting them in accordance with the underlying constitutional principles already discussed." ibid para 88.

136 See P Dumberry, 'Secession and Self-Determination' in MG Kohen (ed), *Secession: International Law Perspectives* (CUP 2006) 424–431 and 450–451.

137 Kohen, 'Création d'Etats en droit international contemporain' (n 10) 603. However, Tancredi, for example, argues that "the secessionist attempt must be founded on the consent of a majority of the local population, democratically expressed through plebiscites or referenda" as part of his 'due process' requirements (also including compliance with peremptory norms and the *uti possidetis* principle). According to Tancredi, only when a secessionist attempt fulfils 'due process' requirements and ends successfully, "can it be considered to have occurred 'lawfully.'" Considering that his analysis focuses primarily on compliance with peremptory norms, however, it is not entirely clear what the consequences of not holding a referendum would be. See A Tancredi, 'A Normative 'Due Process in the Creation of States Through Secession' (n 132) 190–194.

138 *Kosovo* (n 22) para 84.

139 T Christakis, 'Self-Determination, Territorial Integrity and *Fait Accompli* in the Case of Crimea' (2015) 75 ZaöRV 75, 91.

140 See this argument applied to the case of Crimea ibid 92.

requirements, many commentators point to the importance of issues such as the identification of voters and the clarity of the question posed.[141] Additional factors have been pointed out too.[142] Peters argues that "[*i*]*f* a state decides to hold a referendum, then it must satisfy international standards. And when these standards are not respected, a territorial referendum cannot serve as a legal basis for a territorial change."[143]

However, it is doubtful whether these international standards have already attained the level of positive rules of international law violation of which would render referendum without legal effects.[144] Even the Venice Commission admitted that not all the criteria "derive from binding international standards" and referred to "good practice" and "open-textured international standards."[145] Peters' argument is limited only to the context of the parent State-sanctioned referendum, not to a unilateral one. A unilateral referendum, as such, does not produce legal effects; therefore, the question of following or not emerging procedural standards can only have impact in a political and not in a legal arena.

It is important to refer back to the conclusions of Chapter 2. Accordingly, it can be assumed that the unilateral independence referendum also forms part of the secessionist attempt and, as such, if connected to the violations of peremptory norms, can also be unlawful under international law.[146] Essentially, the observations of Chapter 2 applicable to the DoI would also be applicable to referendum *mutatis mutandis*.[147]

141 See, for example, J Vidmar, 'The Scottish Independence Referendum' (n 131) 264–277; J Summers, *Peoples and International Law* (2nd edn, Martinus Nijhoff Publishers 2014) 48–52.

142 Peters includes in this framework peacefulness; universal, equal, free and secret suffrage; freedom of media; neutrality of the authorities and international observation. A Peters, 'The Crimean Vote of March 2014 as an Abuse of the Institution of the Territorial Referendum' in C Callies (ed), *Staat und Mensch im Kontext des Völker- und Europarechts: Liber Amicorum für Torsten Stein* (Nomos Verlag 2015) 272–273.

143 ibid 273.

144 With respect to the independence referendum in Crimea, see T Christakis, 'Self-Determination, Territorial Integrity and *Fait Accompli* in the Case of Crimea' (n 139) 92.

145 CoE (Venice Commission), 'Opinion on the Compatibility of the Existing Legislation in Montenegro concerning the Organization of Referendums with Applicable International Standards (19 December 2005) CDL-AD(2005)041, paras 11 and 64.

146 See *supra* Chapter 2.

147 Şen (n 126) 74.

5 Conclusion

This chapter sought to clarify whether contemporary international law contains the right for sub-State parts of population to secede. Considering secessionist arguments that rely on the right of peoples to self-determination, the chapter examined the holder and content of the right to self-determination. It came to the conclusion that outside decolonisation and the situation of alien subjugation, domination and exploitation, the right of self-determination does not entail the right to secede for sub-State groups within the existing States. International law also does not contain the right to remedial secession. However, the right to secede can derive from domestic constitutional or conventional arrangements essentially expressing the parent State consent, going beyond a mere unilateral secession.

The chapter also concluded that a holding of referendum has become an increasingly important part of the State-creation. Nevertheless, a unilateral referendum, even though not prohibited by international law, does not produce an international right to secede either. The illegality of referendum under municipal law is immaterial from an international law perspective because the secessionists are in principle free to attain constitutive criteria of statehood in the context of municipal illegality. However, based on the conclusions of Chapter 2, holding of referendum can be seen as part of a secessionist attempt and, therefore, as falling within the purview of peremptory norms. Their violation in connection with such a secessionist attempt would also render referendum internationally illegal.

Overall, the analysis revealed that the right to self-determination has a limited relevance for the emergence of a new State in contemporary international law and underlined a radical rupture between a general perception of this issue and international legal effects.

CHAPTER 4

Territorial Integrity of the Parent State and Neutrality of International Law Regarding Secession

1 Introduction

Previous chapters established three findings that have significant implications for the following discussion. First, to become a State, an entity must fulfil three pre-existent legal criteria – territory, population and government – linked together by the act of declaring independence. Second, there is no self-standing right of secession under international law. Third, there is a specific prohibition of secession in situations when the secessionist attempt is connected to the violation of peremptory norms. In addition to these three conclusions, the ICJ in the *Kosovo* Advisory Opinion also ruled that "general international law contains no applicable prohibition of declarations of independence"[1] and "the scope of the principle of territorial integrity is confined to the sphere of relations between States."[2] These ICJ pronouncements taken together with the doctrinal analysis[3] signify that contemporary international law does not prohibit secession *per se*.

Thus, at first sight, these conclusions would appear to confirm a classical thesis that, outside the violation of peremptory norms, international law is *neutral* towards secession and simply registers the outcome of the secessionist struggle. According to this view, secession is generally neither prohibited nor authorised and, therefore, the question of secession is referred back to a classical factualist doctrine as outlined in Chapter 1. Thus, the tension between the territorial integrity of the parent State and the drive by the secessionist entity for effectiveness defines the secessionist attempt. Accordingly, when the secessionist entity gains effectiveness on the ground, the territorial integrity of the parent State is trumped and a new State emerges.

1 *Accordance with International Law of the Unilateral Declaration of Independence in Respect of Kosovo* (Advisory Opinion) [2010] ICJ Rep 403, para 84 in connection with para 81 ("*Kosovo*").

2 ibid para 80.

3 T Christakis and A Constantinides, 'Territorial Dispute in the Context of Secessionist Conflicts' in MG Kohen and M Hébié (eds), *Research Handbook on Territorial Disputes in International Law* (Edward Elgar 2018) 364–365.

DOI:10.1163/9789004702646_007

The following chapter seeks to challenge this classical formula of the neutrality of international law towards secession. While it is true that secession is generally neither prohibited nor authorised, the chapter demonstrates that international law favours the territorial integrity of the parent State and erects numerous legal obstacles for secessionists on their path to statehood.[4] To do so, it first focuses on legal principles relevant to the establishment of the State's boundaries, in particular the principle of stability of frontiers and *uti possidetis iuris*. Second, it examines the role of the principle of territorial integrity in international law. Third, the chapter highlights practice, *opinio iuris* and doctrine affirming an increasing prevalence of the territorial integrity of the parent State in a contemporary secessionist struggle.

2 Formation of the Borders of a New State

Temporally, the formation of the State's borders *follows* the State's emergence, but *precedes* the application of the principle of territorial integrity.[5] Analysis of the principles of international law relevant to the boundary formation is important for the delimitation of the scope of the territorial integrity of the parent State and for that of a new State. Two legal regimes apply.

2.1 *International Frontiers*

The principle of stability of frontiers as "an overreaching postulate of the international legal system"[6] is a guiding criterion concerning the transformation of the former international frontiers. It has its roots deep inside the international system composed of sovereign States as "territorial expression of individual political and legal orders."[7] "La stabilité et la permanence des frontières répond à une nécessité logique sécrétée par le système international lui-même."[8] Accordingly, "in a properly ordered society, territorial boundaries will

4 ibid 365 and 362–366. O Corten, 'Are There Gaps?' in MG Kohen (ed), Secession: International Law Perspectives (CUP 2006) 254.

5 MG Kohen, 'Le problème des frontières en cas de dissolution et de séparation d'États: quelles alternatives?' in O Corten, B Delcourt, P Klein and N Levrat (eds), *Démembrements d'États et délimitations territoriales: l'uti possidetis en question*(s) (Bruylant 1999) 375 and 379–380.

6 MN Shaw, 'The Heritage of States: The Principle of Uti Possidetis Iuris Today' (1996) 67 BYBIL 75, 81.

7 ibid 83.

8 MG Kohen, *Possession contestée et souveraineté territoriale* (PUF 1997) 162.

be among the most stable of all institutions."[9] However, this does not mean that change as such is not possible, but it must take place in "a clear, secure and regulated manner."[10]

In concreto, this principle translates in the boundaries' objectivisation.[11] International frontiers are usually established by the virtue of consent expressed "in international treaties, whether bilateral or multilateral, including peace treaties."[12] The ICJ confirmed that, once established, the boundary has "a life of its own" and "when a boundary has been the subject of agreement, the continued existence of that boundary is not dependent upon the continuing life of the treaty under which the boundary is agreed."[13] "[A]ny other approach would vitiate the fundamental principle of the stability of boundaries."[14] Following the same logic, the boundaries are also protected from the consequences of the principle of *rebus sic stantibus.*[15]

Crucially, such objectivisation of boundaries is also expressed in the law of State succession, in particular in Article 11(a) VCST.[16] The Special Rapporteur stated, "the weight of both the opinion and practice seems clearly to be in favour of the view that boundaries established by treaties remain untouched by mere fact of succession."[17] Later, the ICJ in *Frontier Dispute* and the Badinter Commission in its Opinion No 3 also upheld this rule.[18] Ultimately, upon the

---

9 RY Jennings, *The Acquisition of Territory in International Law* (Manchester University Press 2017) 70.

10 ibid.

11 Shaw (n 6) 87–92.

12 ibid 112.

13 *Territorial Dispute* (*Libyan Arab Jamahiriya/Chad*) (*Judgment*) [1994] ICJ Rep 6, paras 72 and 73 ("Territorial Dispute").

14 ibid para 72. In the same sense, *Continental Shelf* (*Tunisia/Libyan Arab Jamahiriya*) (*Judgment*) [1982] ICJ Rep 18, para 84.

15 Vienna Convention on the Law of Treaties (adopted 23 May 1969, entered into force 27 January 1980) 1155 UNTS 331, art 62(2)(a) ("VCLT").

16 "A succession of States does not as such affect: (a) a boundary established by a treaty." Vienna Convention on Succession of States in Respect of Treaties (adopted 23 August 1978, entered into force 6 November 1996) 1946 UNTS 3, art 11(a) ("VCST").

17 ILC, 'First Report on Succession of States and Governments in respect of Treaties, by Sir Humprey Waldock, Special Rapporteur' (1968) A/CN.4/202, 92–93.

18 "There is no doubt that the obligation to respect pre-existing international frontiers in the event of a State succession derives from a general rule of international law." *Frontier Dispute* (*Burkina Faso/Mali*) (*Judgment*) [1986] ICJ Rep 554, para 24 ("*Frontier Dispute*"). "All external frontiers must be respected in line with the principle stated in the United Nations Charter, in the Declaration on Principles of International Law concerning Friendly Relations among States in accordance with the Charter of the United Nations (General Assembly Resolution 2625 (XXV)) and in the Helsinki Final Act, a principle which also underlines Article 11 of the Vienna Convention of 23 August 1978 on Succession of States

accession to independence, the international frontiers of the parent State transform into the international frontiers of a new State.

2.2 *Principle of Uti Possidetis Iuris*

For the transformation of former administrative limits into international frontiers, the principle of *uti possidetis iuris* is relevant. "*Uti possidetis iuris* rule transforms the former administrative boundaries – whether of colonies or component parts of a state from which secession is sought – into international frontiers, unless otherwise agreed."[19]

2.1.1 Applicability beyond Decolonisation

Having originated during the accession of the Latin American colonies to independence in the 19th century and having been applied during Africa's decolonisation in the 20th century, the ICJ confirmed in the *Frontier Dispute* case,

> the principle is not a special rule which pertains solely to one specific system of international law. It is a general principle, which is logically connected with the phenomenon of the obtaining of independence, wherever it occurs.[20]

The Badinter Commission also upheld the applicability of this principle beyond decolonisation in its Opinion No 3 when it stated,

> [e]xcept where otherwise agreed, the former boundaries become frontiers protected by international law. This conclusion follows from the principle of respect for the territorial *status quo* and, in particular, from the principle of uti possidetis … which is today recognized as a general principle.[21]

Several scholars criticised the transposition of this principle from the decolonisation to contemporary secessionist struggles, pointing to an inadequate

---

in Respect of Treaties." 'Opinion No 3 of the Arbitration Commission of Peace Conference for Yugoslavia' reprinted in (1992) 31 ILM 1494, 1500.

19 A Tancredi, 'In Search of a Fair Balance between the Inviolability of Borders, Self-Determination and Secession' in E Milano, M Nicolini and F Palermo (eds), *Law, Territory and Conflict Resolution: Law as a Problem and Law as a Solution* (Brill Nijhoff 2016) 91.

20 *Frontier Dispute* (n 18) para 20.

21 The Badinter Commission goes on to cite the ICJ's *Frontier Dispute* case. See 'Opinion No 3 of the Arbitration Commission of Peace Conference for Yugoslavia' reprinted in (1992) 31 ILM 1494, 1500.

reading of the post-Cold War practice, which they said derived from consent rather than from any pre-existing rule.[22] Some authors also highlighted the differences between two contexts going as far as to preclude any analogy between them.[23] Other scholars criticised the Badinter Commission for selectively quoting the *Frontier Dispute* case and, thereby, unjustifiably extending the application of the principle.[24] However, it is impossible to agree with such a doctrinal critique for the following reasons.

First, apart from the pronouncements by the above international tribunals, the post-colonial and post-Cold War practices have unequivocally supported the existence of a customary rule of *uti possidetis iuris*. Kohen asserted that the post-Cold War practice in Eastern Europe confirmed the perfect application of this rule.[25] Whether it was the dissolution of the USSR,[26] the Socialist Federal Republic of Yugoslavia (SFRY) or the Czech and Slovak Federal Republic, all of these instances confirmed adherence to a transformation of the former administrative limits to international frontiers.[27] Indeed, the USSR's and the Czech and Slovak Federal Republic's dissolution occurred based on agreements without an explicit reference to *uti possidetis*.

Nevertheless, Peters pointed out that the documents concerning the USSR's dissolution referred to this principle implicitly by "insisting on territorial integrity and on the intangibility of borders."[28] Therefore, it is difficult not to induce from this practice *opinio iuris* about an obligatory respect for the administrative boundaries at the moment of independence.[29] "Les actes formels proclamant le respect des frontières existantes ont donc une valeur déclarative du

22 O Corten, 'Droit des peuples à disposer d'eux-mêmes et uti possidetis: deux faces d'une même médaille?' in O Corten, B Delcourt, P Klein and N Levrat (eds), *Démembrements d'États et délimitations territoriales: l'uti possidetis en question*(s) (Bruylant 1999) 428–432. For other authors of this doctrinal opinion, see A Peters, 'The Principle of Uti Possidetis Juris: How Relevant Is It for Issues of Secession?' in C Walter, A Von Ungern-Sternberg and K Abushov (eds), *Self-determination and Secession in International Law* (OUP 2014) 105, ftn 45.

23 O Corten, 'Droit des peuples à disposer d'eux-mêmes' (n 22) 420–428. For an overall criticism of the principle, including its use in the decolonisation context, see S Ratner, 'Drawing a Better Line: Uti Possidetis and the Borders of New States' (1996) 90 AJIL 590.

24 J Vidmar, 'Confining New International Borders in the Practice of Post-1990 State Creations' (2010) 70 ZaöRV 319, 324–327.

25 Kohen, 'Le problème des frontières' (n 5) 379.

26 See in detail *infra*.

27 Kohen, 'Le problème des frontières' (n 5) 377–379.

28 Peters (n 22) 105.

29 Kohen, 'Le problème des frontières' (n 5) 378. Similarly, Christakis and Constantinides (n 3) 381.

droit en vigueur, reconnaissant une règle existante."[30] "L'existence d'une *opinio juris* semble pourtant la seule explication plausible d'une pratique aussi uniforme et abondante."[31]

Second, a doctrinal claim about the difference between the decolonisation and contemporary secessionist struggles precluding *uti possidetis iuris*'s transposition to the latter does not work either.[32] Both contexts share a fundamental underlying rationale – the accession to independence.[33] From a legal policy perspective, the principle's very essence is to avoid a legal vacuum in the context of accession to independence as such.[34] Kohen demonstrated that none of the doctrinal alternatives, in particular the recourse to effectiveness in connection with the duty to negotiate, would fill an inevitable void resulting from *uti possidetis iuris*'s non-applicability.[35] In any case, as will be shown below, *uti possidetis iuris* is a dispositive rule that is applicable unless otherwise agreed by the relevant parties, which are free to decide on any other criteria for the delimitation of their boundaries. The deniers of the principle's applicability to contemporary secession also overlook that it originated during Latin American decolonisation, which also occurred outside of any legal right to independence.[36] "*L'uti possidetis* est ainsi né pour être appliqué à des cas de sécession."[37]

Third, to claim that the dictum in the *Frontier Dispute* case did not mean what it said, ie that the principle of *uti possidetis* "is not a special rule which pertains solely to one specific system of international law" and that "[i]t is a general principle"[38] is an exaggeration. Moreover, while Peters admits that the *Frontier Dispute* judgment was ambiguous, she also points out that the

---

30 Kohen, 'Le problème des frontières' (n 5) 378. See also G Nesi, 'L'uti possidetis hors du contexte de la décolonisation: le cas de l'Europe' (1998) 44 AFDI 1, 8 and 14; G Nesi, 'Uti Possidetis Doctrine' in MPEPIL (online edn, OUP 2018) para 9.

31 "[A]utant d'acteurs auraient agi de façon identique par agrément ou courtoisie dans un domaine aussi sensible et important que la détermination du territoire de nouveaux États? Ou bien encore, par un incroyable hasard, tous les opportunismes, tous les calculs politiques, auraient convergé vers la solution du maintien des anciennes limites administratives?" A Beaudouin, *Uti possidetis et sécession* (Éditions Dalloz 2011) 564.

32 For Peter's criticism of this line of a doctrinal thought, see Peters (n 22) 107–115.

33 ibid 114.

34 "Its obvious purpose is to prevent the independence and stability of new States being endangered by fratricidal struggles provoked by the challenging of frontiers following the withdrawal of the administering power." *Frontier Dispute* (n 18) para 20. Peters (n 22) 114.

35 Kohen, 'Le problème des frontières' (n 5) 381–393.

36 ibid 375–376. See also *supra* Chapters 1 and 3.

37 ibid 376. Peters (n 22) 114.

38 *Frontier Dispute* (n 18) para 20.

Badinter Commission later assessed the ICJ judgment in a way that it judged was the most appropriate and it did so in a way that supported the principle's general applicability.[39] In sum, it follows that the principle of *uti possidetis iuris* is a rule of customary international law of general applicability wherever independence occurs.

2.1.2 Technical Aspects

The principle of *uti possidetis* is neutral concerning the legal basis of the State's emergence. Kohen stated, "*l'uti possidetis* se borne à établir l'étendue de l'assiette territoriale des nouveaux Etats au moment de l'indépendance, sans s'occuper des raisons de l'indépendance elle-même."[40] Therefore, it is not a new State's legal basis or title of its territorial sovereignty. It "is indifferent to the (legal) grounds of statehood as such."[41] From this follows that temporarily, "[l]e problème des frontières se pose seulement une fois l'indépendance acquise."[42] *Uti possidetis* "does not come into issue during the process of secession."[43]

Moreover, the question arises as to the nature of the administrative limits to which the principle of *uti possidetis* applies. From the Badinter Commission Opinion No 3 and the outlined post-Cold War practice of the dissolution of the Eastern European federal States follows that *uti possidetis* applied only to the first-level administrative boundaries, ie to boundaries between the federal republics.[44] No second- or third-level boundaries were recognised as international frontiers.[45] Thus, it arguably follows that the application of *uti possidetis* is limited only to the first-level administrative boundaries during one process of the accession to independence at a time. The doctrine also supports the claim that the principle applies not only to federal boundaries, but also to administrative limits of unitary States.[46] Thus, once a new State emerges

---

39 Peters (n 22) 110–111.

40 Kohen, 'Le problème des frontières' (n 5) 375.

41 Peters (n 22) 101.

42 Kohen, 'Le problème des frontières' (n 5) 375. Peters (n 22) 101.

43 MG Kohen, 'Introduction' in MG Kohen (ed), *Secession: International Law Perspectives* (CUP 2006) 15. Peters (n 22) 125. *Contra:* A Tancredi, 'A Normative "Due Process" in the Creation of States through Secession' in MG Kohen (ed), *Secession: International Law Perspectives* (CUP 2006) 192. Beaudouin (n 31) 404–423.

44 Peters (n 22) 121. See *contra* for an argument that *uti possidetis* applies only to "those boundaries that have a strong historical pedigree of delimiting self-determination units." Vidmar, 'Confining New International Borders' (n 24) 355 and 327–355.

45 Peters (n 22) 121.

46 For clear support see Peters (n 22) 122. Beaudouin (n 31) 588–594. However, according to Shaw, "[w]here this was a Federal State, the presumption will clearly be that new States emerging out of it will bear the same boundaries as the federal units possessed. The more

via secession the principle could apply again to the first-level administrative boundaries of this new State, whether federal or unitary, if the secessionist movement emerges and is successful there.[47] However, there has been no practice to support such a statement.

Lastly, as far as the validity of administrative boundaries in municipal legal order is concerned, Kohen suggested that for the administrative boundaries to be opposable in international law, they should be in accordance with the municipal legal order.[48] This condition is said to follow from the adjective *iuris* in the principle's title.[49] Nevertheless, there has not been much practice to support such a compliance-check before the accession to independence.[50]

---

unitary a State, the less strong will become the presumption, for *uti possidetis* requires an accepted administrative line." Shaw (n 6) 153.

47 See Peters (n 22) 119–124, for similar argumentation, but for limitation to the first-level boundary at one time. "Generally speaking, older administrative lines stemming from the pre-independence era (eg Soviet era) cannot be opposed against the currently existing 'mother' states (eg CIS states) if they are not acknowledged in their domestic law as it stands, too." ibid 136.

48 Kohen, 'Le problème des frontières' (n 5) 394.

49 ibid.

50 Kohen points to an arbitral award concerning frontiers between Guatemala and Honduras where a tribunal held that "[w]here administrative control was exercised by the colonial entity with the will of the Spanish monarch, there can be no doubt that it was a juridical control, and the line drawn according to the limits of that control would be a juridical line. If, on the other hand, either colonial entity prior to independence had asserted administrative control contrary to the will of the Spanish Crown, that would have been mere usurpation, and as, *ex hypothese*, the colonial regime still existed and the only source of authority was the Crown … such usurpation could not confer any status of 'possession' as against the Crown's possession in fact and law." *Honduras Borders (Guatemala, Honduras)* (1933) 2 RIAA 1307, 1324. *In concreto*, the tribunal examined the existence of the Spanish Crown's will as expressed through a relevant royal decree rather than the decree's conformity with municipal law. Since the decree lacked the King's signature, it was not proven that it was actually made, and therefore was not taken into account. ibid 1334. Beaudouin (n 31) 274. See MG Kohen, 'Le problème des frontières en cas de dissolution et de séparation d'États: quelles alternatives?' (1998) 1 Revue belge de droit international 129, 154 and ftn 55. The ICJ in the *Frontier Delimitation* case (*Benin/Niger*) noted that "it is not disputed between the Parties that the competence to create or establish territorial entities included the power to determine their extent and to delimit them, although during the colonial period this was never made explicit in any regulative or administrative act." *Frontier Delimitation (Benin/Niger) (Judgment)* [2005] ICJ Rep 90, para 47. However, it also later added, "[i]t is not for the Chamber to substitute itself for a domestic court (in this case, the French administrative courts) by carrying out its own review of the legality of the instruments in question in light of the 1907 decree, nor to speculate on what the French courts might have decided had they been seised of the matter." ibid, para 140. Importantly, the question refers to the laws and acts establishing administrative limits as of the critical date, i.e. the date of independence. According to Peters, "it is difficult to find

In addition, scholars oppose this view by highlighting that internal law establishing administrative lines is perceived as mere fact in international law.[51] Moreover, the question arises as to what line would be opposable instead of an invalid one under municipal law. Relatedly, the question can be asked to what extent would such an approach be in line with the underlying objective of *uti possidetis* to avoid a legal vacuum in the context of the accession to independence.

2.1.3 Uti Possidetis Iuris vs Effectiveness

The applicability of the principle of *uti possidetis iuris* to a secessionist context also requires the assessment of its relationship with the principle of effectiveness needed for the emergence of a new State. The principle of *uti possidetis iuris* and the principle of effectiveness serve divergent functions in the secessionist process. The effectiveness operates as the legal basis of a new State. Concerning *uti possidetis*, Kohen argues,

> [l]a pratique internationale cependant montre que, du moment où l'on considère que l'ancienne entité administrative sécessionniste s'est érigée en Etat indépendant, celui-ci a la même assiette territoriale que la première et ce, sans regard au contrôle effectif qu'il exerce sur le territoire en cause.[52]

This practice includes not only the cases of dissolutions and successful unilateral secessions,[53] but also contested or unsuccessful secessions. Beaudouin demonstrated that in all of these instances the secessionist movements structured themselves and were conceptualised by other actors according

---

support (in practice or as a matter of legal reasoning) for the claim that prior 'illegality' precludes uti possidetis. It is exactly the function of uti possidetis to terminate arguments about prior territorial illegality." Peters (n 22) 123.

51 Beaudouin (n 31) 267–276. See *Frontier Dispute* (n 18) paras 30 and 69; *Frontier Delimitation* case (n 50) para 46. See for a contradiction in *Frontier Dispute* case Beaudouin (n 31) 271–272. According to Beaudouin, the question of validity of internal acts can be examined in order to establish their evidentiary value. "Toutefois, si les juges internationaux ne s'estiment pas tenus d'établir la validité des actes juridiques internes, cela ne signifie pas qu'ils s'en désintéressent: ils peuvent examiner cette validité afin d'évaluer la force probant des actes qui leur sont présentées … [l]e juge international détermine librement si et dans quelle mesure la force probante d'un acte juridique interne est liée à sa validité interne." ibid 273 and 275. Peters sees *uti possidetis* as the exception from the premise that internal law is considered a fact in international law. Peters (n 22) 121–122.

52 Kohen, 'Le problème des frontières' (n 5) 382–383.

53 See *infra* Chapter 5.

to pre-existing administrative lines.[54] This practice is so abundant that it is difficult to find the secessionist movements that would not follow the parent State's previous administrative divisions.[55] Second, such an understanding of the relationship between effectiveness and *uti possidetis* also confirms the *neutrality* of the latter because a new State's eventual territorial scope would always be limited to the existing boundaries without regard to the scope of the military control, which might either not reach or exceed the administrative boundary lines.[56] "L'effectivité jouera un rôle pour l'existence de l'Etat, mais non pour la détermination de son assiette territoriale."[57]

2.1.4 Dispositive Rule and Its Relationship with Self-Determination

The doctrine frequently focuses on an apparent contradiction between the principle of *uti possidetis iuris* and the right of peoples to self-determination.[58] However, the ICJ rejected a discordant reading of the relationship between *uti possidetis* and self-determination.[59] Several authors also pointed out the different functions of both rules and the different temporal scope. "Self-determination means a people's right to choose its political, economic, and social status (not inevitably linked to domination over territory). Uti possidetis refers to territorial boundaries of states."[60]

54 Beaudouin (n 31) 280–326. See also Kohen, 'Le problème des frontières' (n 5) 383–384.

55 Beaudouin refers to only one example in this context – Israel. See Beaudouin (n 31) 594 ff. For the exceptional character of not finding previous administrative lines, see Kohen, 'Le problème des frontières' (n 5) 383–384.

56 For the presentation of this issue, see Beaudouin (n 31) 132. Beaudouin ultimately comes to the conclusion that *uti possidetis* is neutral in this regard. ibid 323. Kohen, 'Le problème des frontières' (n 5) 383 and 399.

57 MG Kohen, 'Le problème des frontières' (n 50) 144 (*emphasis removed*).

58 Ratner (n 23) 590–624. See for these views Peters (n 22) 126.

59 "At first sight this principle [*uti possidetis*] conflicts outright with another one, the right of peoples to self-determination. In fact, however, the maintenance of the territorial status quo in Africa is often seen as the wisest course, to preserve what has been achieved by peoples who have struggled for their independence, and to avoid a disruption which would deprive the continent of the gains achieved by much sacrifice. The essential requirement of stability in order to survive, to develop and gradually to consolidate their independence in all fields, has induced African States judiciously to consent to the respecting of colonial frontiers, and to take account of it in the interpretation of the principle of self-determination of peoples." *Frontier Dispute* (n 18) para 25. See also 'Opinion No 2 of the Arbitration Commission of Peace Conference for Yugoslavia' reprinted in (1992) 31 ILM 1494, 1498.

60 Peters (n 22) 126.

> Le problème des frontières se pose seulement une fois l'indépendance acquise. Ainsi, si le droit à l'autodétermination se trouve en amont de l'indépendance, l'*uti possidetis* entre en scène en aval de celle-ci et ne vise pas à donner une justification quelconque à l'existence de l'Etat.[61]

In addition, in a non-colonial context, this apparent tension is even less pertinent because international law does not include a self-standing right to secession for the fractions of populations of the existing States.[62]

Because *uti possidetis* is a dispositive rule, the question can be asked why a consensual boundary changes have not been done more frequently.[63] Undoubtedly, the concern for the territorial *status quo* seeking the preservation of peaceful relations among States arises. "Especially with regard to territorial issues, stability tends to prevent war."[64] Additionally, "[a] major reason why this has never been suggested is almost certainly normative antagonism toward claims based on ethnic or racial exclusivity" dating back to the lessons of WWII and going "beyond the concerns for order and stability."[65] "La frontière ethnique porte en elle les germes de l'épuration ethnique ou aboutit à la consécration de celle-ci" and it is also "porteuse d'irrédentisme et de conflits sans fin."[66] Ultimately, it can be agreed with Peters that, in an ideal world, an apparent tension between *uti possidetis* and self-determination would not have any place because the well-functioning State respecting the minority rights and human rights would "not need a specific ethnic composition or a specific territory."[67]

3 Principle of Territorial Integrity

3.1 *Underlying Rationales and Scope*

Once the State exists within the boundaries formed in accordance with the principle of stability of frontiers and *uti possidetis iuris*, the principle of territorial integrity begins to apply.[68] There is no doubt, "the principle of territorial

61 Kohen, 'Le problème des frontières' (n 5) 375. See also Nesi, 'L'uti possidetis hors du contexte de la décolonisation' (n 30) 19–20; Nesi, 'Uti Possidetis Doctrine' (n 30) para 27.

62 See *supra* Chapter 3.

63 M Fabry, *Recognizing States: International Society and the Establishment of New States since 1776* (OUP 2010) 205.

64 Peters (n 22) 116.

65 Fabry, *Recognizing States* (n 63) 206.

66 Kohen, 'Le problème des frontières' (n 5) 389 (*emphasis omitted*). Peters (n 22) 117–119.

67 Peters (n 22) 118–119.

68 Kohen, 'Le problème des frontières' (n 5) 379–380.

integrity is an important part of the international legal order."[69] It is enshrined in the UN Charter[70] and other key international and regional instruments, even though this is usually by the way of a negative definition.[71] This principle serves a number of purposes,[72] including aiming "to provide a guarantee against any dismemberment of the territory", by protecting its integrity.[73] Essentially, "[t]erritorial integrity refers to the territorial 'oneness' or 'wholeness' of the State."[74]

This principle protects the States from *external* breaches "or in other words, threats against the territorial sovereignty coming from abroad."[75] It is closely linked with the prohibition of threat or use of force and the principle of non-intervention into internal affairs. However, even though the use of force is

69 *Kosovo* (n 1) para 80.

70 Charter of the United Nations (adopted 26 June 1945, entered into force 24 October 1945) 1 UNTS XVI, art 2(4).

71 See Declaration on the Granting of Independence to Colonial Countries and Peoples, UNGA Res 1514 (XV) (14 December 1960) UN Doc A/RES/1514/(XV), para 6; Declaration on the Inadmissibility of Intervention in the Domestic Affairs of States and the Protection of Their Independence and Sovereignty, UNGA Res 2131 (XX) (21 December 1965) UN Doc A/RES/2131(XX) preamble recital 2 and 3; Declaration on Principles of International Law concerning Friendly Relations and Co-operation among States in accordance with the Charter of the United Nations, UNGA Res 2625 (XXV) (24 October 1970) UN Doc A/RES/2625(XXV), Annex, first, fifth principles and see also sixth principle, (d) for an affirmative approach to territorial integrity "[t]he territorial integrity and political independence of the State are inviolable." ("Friendly Relations Declaration"); Definition of Aggression, UNGA Res 3341 (XXIX) (14 December 1974), Annex, preamble recital 6 and art I; The 2005 World Summit Outcome, UNGA Res 60/1 (16 September 2005), para 5; See also Final Act of the Conference on the Security and Cooperation in Europe (adopted 1 August 1975) chapters I, II, IV and VIII reprinted in (1975) 14 ILM 1293 ("Helsinki Final Act"); Charter of the Organization of African Unity (adopted 25 May 1963, entered into force 13 September 1963) 479 UNTS 39, art II and III(3); Constitutive Act of the African Union (adopted 11 July 2000, entered into force 26 May 2001) 2158 UNTS 3, art 3(b); African Union Non-Aggression and Common Defence Pact (adopted 1 January 2005, entered into force 18 December 2009), art 1(c) and art 5(b). For other regional instruments in which the principle of territorial integrity is enshrined, see SKN Blay, 'Territorial Integrity and Political Independence' in MPEPIL (online edn, OUP 2010), para 30.

72 In another way, territorial integrity requires other international law subjects to respect the spatial exercise of the State's sovereignty and its inviolability. Kohen, *Possession contestée et souveraineté territoriale* (n 8) 375–376. Already in the *Corfu Channel* case the ICJ held, "[b]etween independent States, respect for territorial sovereignty is an essential foundation of international relations." *Corfu Channel Case* (*United Kingdom of Great Britain and Northern Ireland v Albania*) [1949] ICJ Rep 4, 35.

73 Kohen, 'Introduction' (n 43) 6.

74 SKN Blay (n 71) para 1.

75 Kohen, 'Introduction' (n 43) 6.

not the only way that the territorial integrity of the State could be violated,[76] the latter would be violated not only in the case of a direct occupation of the State's territory, but also in the case of an indirect use of force, most notably by supporting the secessionists inside the parent State.[77]

The question also arises whether the principle of territorial integrity could also apply *internally*, ie vis-à-vis the secessionist movements.[78] This would entail the prohibition of unilateral secession *per se*. "[T]erritorial integrity would not only prevent the emergence of a right to secessionist self-determination, but would also pose a prohibition to that effect."[79]

However, as already mentioned, the ICJ unequivocally rejected this position. It held, "the scope of the principle of territorial integrity is confined to the sphere of relations between States."[80] However, despite this, the practice is listed below that confirms that even though the principle of territorial integrity cannot be interpreted as implying the prohibition of unilateral secession *per se*, it nevertheless influences the outcome of the secessionist struggle. Corten even asserted that a number of factors, especially the recent UNSC practice, "nous permet de poser l'hypothèse que le droit international connaît *une tendance naissante* à condamner, voir à interdire, les mouvements sécessionnistes."[81]

3.2 *Territorial Integrity of the Parent State in the Secessionist Struggle*

The practice and *opinio iuris* support the prevalence of the territorial integrity of the parent State regarding the outcome of the secessionist struggle. First, the so-called safeguard clauses precluding the interpretation of the right of peoples to self-determination or rights of persons belonging to minorities as authorising any action aimed at dismemberment of territorial integrity of States must be taken into account.[82] Corten argues that even though these clauses confirm

---

76 Kohen, *Possession contestée et souveraineté territoriale* (n 8) 377.

77 SKN Blay (n 71) para 8. See also Kohen, 'Introduction' (n 43) 6. See Friendly Relations Declaration, Annex, principle 1, paras 8–9 and *Case Concerning Military and Paramilitary Activities in and against Nicaragua* (*Nicaragua v United States of America*) [1986] ICJ Rep 14, para 228 ("*Nicaragua*"). For other ways the State's territorial integrity can be violated, see Kohen, *Possession contestée et souveraineté territorial* (n 8) 373–374.

78 Kohen, 'Introduction' (n 43) 6.

79 Tancredi, 'In Search of a Fair Balance between the Inviolability of Borders, Self-Determination and Secession' (n 19) 97.

80 *Kosovo* (n 1) para 80.

81 See O Corten, 'Are There Gaps?' (n 4) 249 (*emphasis added*). *Contra*: Tancredi, 'In Search of a Fair Balance between the Inviolability of Borders, Self-Determination and Secession' (n 19) 97.

82 See in detail *supra* Chapter 3.

that there is no right to secession, they do not explicitly prohibit it, "mais tout en paraissant implicitement impliquer une interdiction."[83] Thus, while these clauses aim at excluding the right to secession, which is a different matter from the prohibition of secession,[84] they could be taken altogether as evidence of a generalised presumption against secession in international law.[85]

Second, the UNSC resolutions adopted in the context of secessionist armed conflicts also play an important role. On numerous occasions, for example regarding the secessionist conflicts in Bosnia and Herzegovina, Georgia and Azerbaijan, the UNSC not only generally affirmed the territorial integrity of the parent State throughout the duration of the conflict,[86] but sometimes directly addressed secessionists, calling on them to explicitly respect the territorial integrity of the parent State.[87] The UNSC Resolution 787 (1992) concerning Bosnia and Herzegovina not adopted under chapter VII UN Charter is particularly important.[88] This resolution was specifically singled out in the *Kosovo* Advisory Opinion concerning illegality attached to unilateral declarations of independence.[89]

Tancredi downplayed the importance of this practice by pointing to the fact that all these situations involved third State intervention and, therefore, are compatible with a traditional inter-State framework.[90] He also highlighted a political necessity of such wordings.[91] However, in each secessionist struggle, these resolutions provided for the prohibition of secession operating vis-à-vis non-State secessionists. This is a remarkable development because the ICJ restricted the applicability of the principle of territorial integrity only to

83 O Corten, 'Are There Gaps?' (n 4) 248.

84 Tancredi, 'In Search of a Fair Balance between the Inviolability of Borders, Self-Determination and Secession' (n 19) 99. T Christakis T, *Le droit à l'autodétermination en dehors des situations de décolonisation* (La documentation française 1999) 190–193.

85 See Fabry, *Recognizing States* (n 63) 160. Christakis and Constantinides (n 3) 364. J Vidmar, S McGibbon and L Raible, 'Introduction to the Research Handbook on Secession' in J Vidmar, S McGibbon and L Raible (eds), *Research Handbook on Secession* (Edward Elgar 2022) 2.

86 See in detail *supra* Chapter 2. See also (n 71) paras 40–41.

87 See for example, UNSC Res 787 (16 November 1992) UN Doc S/RES/787, para 3 (Bosnia and Herzegovina); UNSC Res 971 (12 January 1995) UN Doc S/RES/971, preamble recital 7 (Georgia); UNSC Res 896 (31 January 1994) UN Doc S/RES/896, para 4 (Georgia); UNSC Res 906 (25 March 1994) UN Doc S/RES/906, para 2 (Georgia). See in detail *supra* Chapter 2.

88 See in detail *supra* Chapter 2.

89 *Kosovo* (n 1) para 80. See in detail, *supra* Chapter 2.

90 Tancredi, 'In Search of a Fair Balance between the Inviolability of Borders, Self-Determination and Secession' (n 19) 98.

91 ibid.

inter-State relations.[92] Thus, even though at this stage it would seem difficult to induce any general international law prohibition of secession from a *lex specialis* of the UNSC practice, it is nevertheless justified to agree that "[t]his practice reveals a trend to enlarge the scope of application of the principle of respect of territorial integrity to cases where secessionist movements resort to force."[93]

The third element that exemplifies the preference of the international law for the territorial integrity of the parent State is the classical view that, contrary to the third States' support for secessionists,[94] the parent State is entitled to invite the third States to intervene on its side into the secessionist conflict.[95]

Lastly, the following chapter demonstrates that since 1945 the practice has unequivocally favoured consensual modes of State-creation and disfavoured unilateral ones. The parent State's consent is an expression of its legal capacity as a *de iure* holder of the title of territorial sovereignty to make dispositions with its own territory in favour of secessionists and, thereby, agree with a consensual dismembering of its own territorial integrity.[96] According to Crawford,

> [s]ince 1945 the international community has been extremely reluctant to accept unilateral secession of parts of independent States if the secession is opposed by the government of that State. In such cases, the principle of territorial integrity has been a significant limitation.[97]

According to Fabry, "[t]here can be little doubt that in the post-Cold War period territorial integrity continued … to be protected normatively against non-consensual changes from inside as well as outside."[98] Vidmar goes even further by claiming that new States do not emerge "upon meeting the traditional or additional criteria, because an independence-seeking entity needs to

92 For unwanted consequences of this ICJ pronouncement, see Christakis and Constantinides (n 3) 363.

93 Kohen, 'Introduction' (n 43) 8. See *supra* Chapter 2 for the assertion that at this stage this has not yet transformed into a general prohibition of secessionists to use force against the parent State.

94 See *Nicaragua* (n 77) paras 209 and 246.

95 O Corten, 'Are There Gaps?' (n 4) 252–253. See *Nicaragua* (n 77) para 246.

96 Nevertheless, Chapter 3 underlined that the opposability under international law of such consent, or more specifically the right stemming from the constitutional or conventional arrangements with the secessionists, is controversial. See *supra* Chapter 3.

97 J Crawford, *The Creation of States in International Law* (2nd edn, Clarendon Press 2006) 390.

98 M Fabry, 'The Contemporary Practice of State Recognition: Kosovo, South Ossetia, Abkhazia, and their Aftermath' (2012) 40 Nationalities Papers 661, 665.

overcome the counterclaim to territorial integrity in order to become a State."[99] Accordingly, the emergence of a new State also seems very unlikely, "because the burden of shifting the territorial *status quo* falls upon the independence-seeking entity."[100]

4 Conclusion

This chapter sought to challenge the classical view that international law is neutral vis-à-vis secession. First, it analysed the principles concerning the formation of the new State's frontiers, especially the principle of stability of frontiers and *uti possidetis iuris*. Second, the chapter provided a general overview of the principle of territorial integrity in international law. Third, it examined the role of the territorial integrity of the parent State in a contemporary secessionist struggle. This chapter highlighted instances of practice and legal mechanisms that express the bias of international law in favour of the territorial integrity of the parent State. As underscored by contemporary doctrine, while this practice does not entail the prohibition of unilateral secession *per se*, it precludes the maintenance of the classical thesis of international law's *neutrality* towards secession; in a contemporary secessionist conflict, international law favours the territorial integrity of the parent State.[101]

---

99 Vidmar J, 'Territorial Integrity and the Law of Statehood' (2012) 44 George Washington International Law Review 101, 113.

100 ibid.

101 O Corten, 'Are There Gaps?' (n 4) 254. Christakis and Constantinides (n 3) 365.

CHAPTER 5

Limits to the Effectiveness Paradigm

1 Introduction

Chapter 1 challenged the classical doctrinal view of secession as a mere fact, demonstrating that the factual criteria of statehood are *legal* criteria predetermined by international law. Chapter 4 showed that despite international law not being neutral towards secession, it does not prohibit it *per se*. Thereby, it refers back to the constitutive criteria of statehood. This chapter seeks to test this effectiveness paradigm further by exposing its limits from the point of view of theory and State practice and *opinio iuris*. The objective is to establish to what extent a factualist view of secession corresponds to contemporary international law and offers an explanatory force behind a secessionist State-creation today.

First, the chapter investigates the underlying theoretical issues concerning the factualist view of secession and a declaratory theory of recognition, in particular the automaticity of the State's emergence and the objectivity of the State. It introduces the view that even though these questions are frequently presented as being unique to international law due to its structural limitations, the same issues persist in municipal law. The chapter highlights the fact that in both international and municipal laws these theoretical issues broadly reflect the debate between realism and idealism in philosophy.[1] It draws implications from this conclusion for the doctrine of factualist secession.

Second, the chapter maps the practice of unilateral secessions occurring after 1945. To do so, it isolates the cases of unilateral secession from the instances of State-creation based on a colonial right of self-determination, those connected to the violation of peremptory norms and those involving pre-existing or eventual consent of the parent State. The analysis focuses on entities, which declared independence unilaterally and achieved a stabilised effectiveness. The assessment of their legal status helps test the factualist view of secession's relevance in contemporary international law.

1 See more broadly M Koskenniemi, *From Apology to Utopia: The Structure of International Legal Argument* (CUP 2005) 519–520.

 | DOI:10.1163/9789004702646_008

2 Perplexity of Automaticity of the State's Emergence and Its Objectivity

2.1 *Reflection of a Fundamental Debate in Philosophy*

According to a declaratory theory of recognition, the State is said to emerge *automatically* upon the fulfilment of the predetermined criteria of statehood;[2] it is said to exist *objectively* without the need for the recognition by the third States. As established, a legal rule pre-exists and determines the factual criteria of statehood and, therefore, international law precedes the State. However, the issues of the *automaticity* of the State's emergence and its *objectivity* raise further questions.[3]

These questions derive from the doctrinal opposition to certain tenets of a declaratory theory, which are premised on philosophical realism. Thus, broadly, the rivalry between the declaratory and constitutive theory of recognition[4] is the reflection in international law of the tension between realism[5] and idealism in philosophy[6] or more precisely between the understanding of legal facts through the prism of a metaphysical objectivity or subjectivity.

2 For a discussion about the problem with the automaticity of a State's emergence, see J Vidmar, 'Territorial Integrity and the Law of Statehood' (2012) 44 George Washington International Law Review 101, 101–149.

3 As mentioned in Chapter 1, D'Aspremont divides the doctrine "between the *objectivists* and the *subjectivitsts*, that is, between those contending that statehood is objectively ascertained by international law and those arguing that international law accommodates intersubjectivity in the determination of statehood." J D'Aspremont, 'The International Law of Statehood: Craftmanship for the Elucidation and Regulation of Births and Deaths in the International Society' (2013) 29 Connecticut Journal of International Law 201, 204 (*emphasis in original*). According to D'Aspremont, compared to the debate between the facticists and legalists, the divide between the objectivists and subjectivists is "more irreconcilable." ibid 206. Building on D'Aspremont's classification, Wheatley divides the doctrine between the objectivists/facticists, objectivists/legalists, subjectivists/facticists, and subjectivists/legalists. S Wheatley, 'The Emergence of New States in International Law: The Insights from Complexity Theory' (2016) 15 Chinese Journal of International Law 579, 583–585.

4 Building on Wheatley, this investigation will only apply to objectivists/legalists and subjectivists/legalists. See Wheatley (n 3) 583–585.

5 "*Metaphysical realism* is the view that what there is – the world – is independent of human minds in two senses. First, the existence and character of the world is not simply the extension of human mind (metaphysical or constitutive independence). Second, the existence and character of the world does not depend on the evidentiary tools available to us for gaining access to it (epistemic evidence)." B Leiter and JL Coleman, 'Determinacy, Objectivity, Authority' (1993) 142 University of Pennsylvania Law Review 549, 602 (*emphasis in original*).

6 See more broadly Koskenniemi, *From Apology to Utopia* (n 1) 519–520.

The State does not have a proper physical existence, it is not a 'brute fact', but it is a legal fact, a humanly conditioned fact,[7] an ideal entity,[8] a legal concept, which appears "not to mirror social reality but constitute what can be seen in it."[9] "Boundaries are defined and States are created according to the law. For this reason, 'defined territory' cannot be purely objectively factual."[10] A historical overview in Chapter 1 demonstrated that the understanding of the State and the beginning of its legal personality has not had a static meaning over time. However, some authors emphasise that metaphysical objectivity cannot be denied even to socially or culturally constructed objects, even though they "cannot be conceived as ontologically independent of our knowledge and culture"[11] and thereby do not correspond to classical realist premises foreseeing the existence of an ontologically objective reality.[12]

Thus, at the core of the declaratory theory and the factualist statehood is the understanding of the objectivity as metaphysical objectivity or strong objectivity, which refers to the representation of "things as they really are."[13] From this perspective,

> [t]he question about metaphysical objectivity, then, is the question about the *status* of these facts, that is, about whether they hold independently of what a particular judge happens to think, or perhaps independently of what all lawyers and judges would think.[14]

This is the key premise of the declaratory theory – the disagreement of the States as to the fulfilment of the constitutive criteria or that the non-recognition

7 O Weinberger, 'Facts and Fact-Descriptions: A Logical and Methodological Reflection on a Basic Problem for the Social Sciences' in N MacCormick and O Weinberger (eds), *An Institutional Theory of Law: New Approaches to Legal Positivism* (Kluwer 1986) 82.

8 "[I]f it is a matter of thinking about ideal objects, then their real existence will be established through their being implicated with the sphere of material reality and through the fact that ideal entities come into being as integral elements of real processes, and as things existing in time." Weinberger (n 7) 86.

9 Koskenniemi, *From Apology to Utopia* (n 1) 526.

10 Vidmar (n 2) 106.

11 A Marmor, *Positive Law and Objective Values* (OUP 2001) 117–118 and 147. See also the discussion about metaphysical realism in the context of legal facts in Leiter and Coleman (n 5) 602 and Koskenniemi, referring to legal "realism": Koskenniemi, *From Apology to Utopia* (n 1) 519–520.

12 Marmor (n 11) 117.

13 R Rorty, *Philosophy and the Mirror of Nature* (Princeton University Press 1980) 334.

14 Leiter and Coleman (n 5) 559.

by all other States cannot undermine a new State's objective status. It emerges *automatically* upon the fulfilment of the constitutive criteria.

However, the main opposing view[15] can be traced back to a broader anti-realist stance that rejects an automatic translation and *self-evidence of facts*.[16]

> [I]n fact statehood is not a physical fact that would be able to disclose itself mechanically for all the world to see, or whose presence or absence can be determined by some 'automatic' test ... [it] is a conceptual construct which refers back to the presence (or absence) of a set of criteria for the attainment of the relevant status. What those criteria are and whether they are present depends on acts of human cognition. If that act of cognition is not there, i.e. if nobody recognizes an entity as a 'State,' then there is little point in insisting that the status still exists.[17]

Meeting of constitutive criteria of statehood is not self-evident, and the emergence of States is not a matter of natural fact.[18] "The test of whether this 'normative' constituent fact is present in the 'person' of the new state cannot be carried out by simple subsumption, but requires a 'value judgment.'"[19] Similarly, an objective legal status may not be of much relevance in situations when the

---

15 For example, Wheatley's starting point is to understand the State, from the point of view of systems theory, as "the joining of the law and politics systems under the constitution." He continues by acknowledging that "[t]he fact of observation is integral to the identification of complex systems, including the complex systems of law and politics." Later, Wheatley reflects that "when we conceptualize the 'sovereign and independent' State in terms of the joining of the law and politics systems under a constitution, State does not exist as an objective reality: it is observed by a third party trying to make sense of the patterns of law and politics communications against the background noise of world society. Given the inherent indeterminacy in the modelling of the complex systems of law and politics, we cannot be certain that we have correctly identified emergent and autonomous systems of law and politics. In other words, once we accept that law and politics are complex systems, *we must reject any argument that a State can have an objective reality*, either because it exists as a fact of the world, or as an objective category that all reasonable observers would recognize, given that different actors may come to different conclusions as to the statehood claims of emergent entities, depending on the meaning that they allocate to the patterns of law and politics communications they observe." Wheatley (n 3) 592–593 and 595.

16 Koskenniemi, *From Apology to Utopia* (n 1) 275.

17 M Koskenniemi, *The Gentle Civilizer of Nations: The Rise and Fall of International Law 1870–1960* (CUP 2001) 385.

18 Vidmar (n 2) 107.

19 Hillgruber C, 'The Admission of New States to the International Community' 9 (1998) EJIL 491, 503.

relevant community does not to acknowledge it.[20] "A State or a government whose existence is acknowledged by nobody cannot successfully claim to be treated as such. Its status has reality only within its own solipsist universe."[21]

In addition, numerous scholars pointed out the difficulties regarding the automaticity of the constitutive criteria of statehood's fulfilment.

> Yet, while the criterion of actual effectiveness seems to promise an objective ground on which to evaluate the success or failure of state creations and thus avoid the political dilemma of constitutive recognition, the identification of effective states is not as readily apparent as the declaratory position assumes. Effective control is a 'matter of degree.'[22]

Similarly, "it is difficult to see how the existence of criteria of statehood is calculable in the same way as someone's age is, and whether such conditions are present in a given circumstance is much more factually ambiguous."[23] In addition, Chapter 2 highlighted that even though the State's emergence requires constitutive criteria, their fulfilment and differentiation from other factual territorial situations requires conceptualisation via the prism of an intention to secede.

Additionally, not only do the facts not translate themselves automatically and require cognition, but based on the epistemology and some strands of natural sciences[24] cognition cannot lead to an *absolute or objective knowledge of facts or an outside reality*. In short, the perception of reality is essentially observer-dependent and, therefore, relative. Thus, even if the State existed

---

20 BR Roth, 'Secessions, Coups and the International Rule of Law: Assessing the Decline of the Effective Control Doctrine' (2010) 11 Melbourne Journal of International Law 393, 398.

21 Koskenniemi, *The Gentle Civilizer of Nations* (n 17) 385.

22 J Grzybowski, 'Ontological Predicament of State Creation in International Law' (2017) 28 EJIL 409, 415. See also M Craven, 'Statehood, Self-Determination, and Recognition' in MD Evans (ed), *International law* (4th edn, OUP 2014) 216–217.

23 P Capps, 'Lauterpacht's Method' (2012) 82 BYBIL 248, 254.

24 This applies particularly to the consequences and impact of quantum mechanics' collapse of wave function. At its most extreme, this problem has led some physicists to explain the collapse of wave function by rejecting the idea of a single objective reality shared by multiple observers, instead highlighting "single observer's subjective knowledge." See A Gefter, 'A Private View of Quantum Reality' (*Quanta Magazine*, 4 June 2015) <https://www.quantamagazine.org/quantum-bayesianism-explained-by-its-founder-20150604> accessed 1 August 2018. For insights from cognitive science, see A Gefter, 'The Case Against Reality' (*The Atlantic*, 25 April 2016) <https://www.theatlantic.com/science/archive/2016/04/the-illusion-of-reality/479559/> accessed 1 August 2018.

objectively,[25] it would be impossible to reach the knowledge about it in an undistorted or objective way. Conversely, realism foresees direct access to objective facts as they really are.[26]

2.2 *Brief Reference to Municipal Law and Constitutive Theory*

The question arises as to how municipal law generally deals with the questions concerning the *automaticity* and *objectivity* of facts. The problem of *automaticity* is seemingly disposed of because the judicial body is vested with any dispute resolution as to the 'objective truth' regarding the factual determination understood within the parameters of that particular legal order.[27] That is why according to Kelsen "for the technical development of the law, no other step was of such an importance as the establishment of courts."[28]

However, legal theorists show that, at a closer look, the questions regarding *objectivity* are present even in municipal law; they re-appear when questioning the judicial decision-making. Even though "some sort of metaphysical objectivity may be a theoretical or conceptual commitment of our discourse about law",[29] the scholarly opinions on this issue also include references to modest objectivity,[30] minimal objectivity[31] and subjectivity. These questions have

---

25 "One should, in other words, agree that the idea of some objective reality, existing as it is independent of any subjective perception of it, apparently makes sense even for one who holds little hope for any of us knowing that there is such a reality, or knowing anything objectively about such a reality." DH Mulder, 'Objectivity' (*Internet Encyclopaedia of Philosophy*, 20 September 2018) <https://www.iep.utm.edu/objectiv/> accessed 20 September 2018.

26 See also PK Moser, *Philosophy after Objectivity: Making Sense in Perspective* (OUP 1993) 26; Leiter and Coleman (n 5) 603.

27 A reference could be made here to epistemic and procedural objectivity. "[W]hat justifies the outcomes of legal disputes is the fact that judges reach them by following objective procedures ... Having decisions reached by objective procedures is the only way to forge compromise among individuals with conflicting interests and philosophical conceptions...[a]djudication is objective in the metaphysical sense when the outcome of the adjudication coincides with the relevant legal fact." Leiter and Coleman (n 5) 596–598.

28 H Kelsen, 'The Law as a Specific Social Technique' (1941) 9 The University of Chicago Law Review 75, 95.

29 Leiter and Coleman (n 5) 599.

30 "Legal facts are modestly objective when what is a legal fact is what judges under ideal epistemic conditions would take that fact to be." Leiter and Coleman (n 5) 629. For a critique see CR Rosati, 'Some Puzzles about the Objectivity of Law' (2004) 23 Law and Philosophy 313–322.

31 "According to minimal objectivity, legal facts are fixed by what the majority of judges take them to be. Thus, there is no problem of epistemic access." Leiter and Coleman (n 5) 616. For the critique see Rosati (n 30) 306–313.

remained the key perplexities of the liberal legal theory and are the prominent target of critical legal studies.[32]

Thus, the underlying issues in municipal law are not much different from those in international law. A key difference is the latter's lack of a centralised body, which "leads to the conceptual problem of identifying an 'objective fact' in the decentralized legal system of international law."[33] This element puts the questions about objectivity and the self-evidence of facts in international law into the spotlight. Moreover, even though these questions pertain to international law as a whole, the issue of subject identification attracts even more attention. "A lack of clarity concerning the subject-status can be a cause of fundamental coordination problems because it implies that, a matter of law, it is unclear who owes what to whom."[34] Thus, "the primary defect of declaratory theory is that it does not include a necessary institutional mechanism which is capable of resolving difficult cases."[35]

Constitutive theory would cure the deficiencies of declaratory theory. The issue of *automaticity* or the self-evidence of facts does not arise because the procedure for the status determination is vested with the States themselves.[36] "La perception « constitutiviste » est pourtant moins simpliste … car elle n'admet pas le caractère achevé du nouveau-né à la naissance."[37] In addition, the question of *objectivity* is not raised either because the constitutivist approach is subjectivist and relativist.[38] However, this raises various other problems.[39] The constitutive theory is not supported by practice.[40] Moreover, it does not

32 Leiter and Coleman (n 5) 549.

33 Vidmar (n 2) 106.

34 Capps (n 23) 253.

35 ibid 253.

36 Salmon claims "il n'y a pas, à proprement parler, une réalité Etat qui pourrait être constatée comme un fait. Le rôle de Etats tiers dans la qualification est donc essentiel, soit par le biais des reconnaissances individuelles, soit par l'intermédiaire de procédures qui jouent un rôle similaire au sein des organisations internationales." Salmon, J., 'La construction juridique du fait en droit international' 32 (1987) Archive de philosophie du droit 136, 146.

37 E Wyler, *Théorie et pratique de la reconnaissance d'Etat: une approche épistémologique du droit international* (Bruylant 2013) 227. "Même si leur erreur a consisté à faire de l'acte unilatéral de la Reconnaissance un « élément constitutif » de l'État en tant que tel, les constitutivistes avaient, en conservant les autres éléments de l'État, entrevu d'une certaine manière l'horizon qu'est le droit international général pour le droit international particulier." ibid 323.

38 See J Crawford, *The Creation of States in International Law* (2nd edn, Clarendon Press 2006) 21.

39 See *supra* Chapter 1.

40 See Crawford (n 38) 22.

foresee a legal procedure for the ascertainment of the facts, but simply leaves the issue for political decision-making and, therefore, remains inherently arbitrary.

Due to the rejection of the self-evidence of facts, in his later works, Kelsen abandoned the declaratory theory and fully embraced the relativity of the State's legal personality, referring to Einstein's theory of relativity.[41] For similar reasons, Lauterpacht developed his theory of the duty of recognition.[42] Neither doctrine[43] nor practice[44] has followed these approaches.

2.3 *International Law Presumes a Strong Objectivity of Legal Facts*

Therefore, owing to the constitutive theory being discarded, a declaratory theory comes back into the picture. Can the meeting of factual criteria create an objective status without any centralised procedure for their ascertainment? Does the State become opposable to all parts of the international legal system and its stakeholders once the constitutive criteria of statehood are met?[45]

Importantly, international law *as a whole* is premised on strong or metaphysical objectivity of legal facts.

41 See *supra* on Kelsen's abandonment of declaratory theory. In the same respect, Tucker says, "there are no self-evident facts from the juristic point of view; there are only facts determined by a competent agency in a manner prescribed by law." R Tucker, 'The Principle of Effectiveness in International Law,' 41.

42 H Lauterpacht, *Recognition in International Law* (University Press 1947) 48–51. In this respect, Lauterpacht's duty of recognition was designed to tackle the issue of the need of cognition based on the premise that as "personality cannot be automatic and that as its ascertainment requires the prior determination of difficult circumstances of fact and law, there must be *someone* to perform that task." ibid 55. Nevertheless, it is not clear why personality cannot be automatic, but the legal duty to recognise can be, even though the existence of such a duty would also need to be preceded by ascertainment of factual criteria. Moreover, even if one hypothetically accepted the existence of the duty to recognise, States could still violate such duty, which would leave entities fulfilling the necessary criteria without international legal personality. See in the same respect, Crawford (n 38) 21. See also Vidmar (n 2) 106–108.

43 Grzybowski (n 22) 419, ftn 74.

44 For Lauterpacht's method of progressive interpretation in this context, see Capps (n 23) 257–280.

45 D'Aspremont (n 3) 206. "It remains to be asked only whether the position adopted by states, collectively or aggregatively, can be said to govern the entity's entitlements, or whether, by contrast, the entitlements are so fully objective that where the bulk of the international community is seen to misapply the fixed legal criteria, states treating the entity in accordance with that collective misapplication can be said thereby to breach their legal obligations. Either view is conceptually possible, but as a practical matter, the latter view seems implausible." Roth (n 20) 398.

> From the viewpoint of a legal system, only one answer can be legally correct. It may sometimes be hard to obtain such answer in a domestic law system. It is even harder in the sphere of international law. That does not change the situation.[46]

This applies to all issues of international concern including the legality of certain situations, the validity of treaties, or the triggering of the application of humanitarian law.[47] Crawford points out that a need for a constitutive cognition by the States does not generally present in international law.[48]

> If individual States were free to determine the legal status or consequences of particular situations and to do so definitively, international law would be reduced to a form of imperfect communications, a system for registering the assent or dissent of individual States without any prospect of resolution.[49]

Thus, a declaratory theory and factualist secession are in accordance with "the general structure of international law in which bilateralism is being replaced by objective and universally binding rules."[50] The constitutivist position "negates all objectivity in international relations and reduces its structure to an arbitrarily knitted net between entities that at the same time are and are not states."[51]

Additionally, the concept of an objective international personality follows from the ICJ's pronouncement in the *Reparations* Advisory Opinion,

---

46 H Blix, 'Contemporary Aspects of Recognition' (1970) 130 RCADI 587, 608–609. "It is true that the present state of the law makes it possible that different States should act on different views of the application of the law to the same state of facts. This does not mean that their differing interpretations are all equally correct, but only that there exists at present no procedure for determining which are correct and which are not. The constitutive theory of recognition gains most of its plausibility from the lack of centralized institutions in the system, and it treats this lack not as an accident due to the stage of development, which the law has so far reached, but as an essential feature of the system. It is in fact one more relic of absolutist theories of State sovereignty." JL Brierly, *The Law of Nations* (6th edn edited by Waldock, Clarendon Press 1963) 139.

47 See other examples Crawford (n 38) 20–21. Vidmar (n 2) 106–107.

48 Crawford (n 38) 20.

49 ibid 20.

50 B Dold, 'Concepts and Practicalities of the Recognition of States' (2012) 22 Swiss Review of International and European Law 81, 85.

51 ibid 85.

> that fifty States, representing the vast majority of the members of the international community, had the power, in conformity with international law, to bring into being an entity possessing objective international personality, and not merely personality recognized by them alone, together with capacity to bring international claims.[52]

Dold highlights that "[i]f an entity made up of states can have an objective existence in the sense described, the only logical conclusions seems that its parts, i.e. the member states, can do so as well."[53]

Thus, ultimately, while in a municipal legal order there is a final arbiter of any dispute as to the *objectivity* of facts, international law lacks such a tool. Therefore, it relies on the test of *automaticity* and self-evidence of facts, but it fails to explain the operation of 'the automaticity test' outside of the cognition of the States.[54] At a deeper end, this reflects an inherent paradox surrounding realism in philosophy – seemingly lacking conclusive justifications, but at the same time impossible to be completely discarded in the favour of idealism.[55] This limitation does not undermine the general operability of international law and does not justify a return to the constitutive theory. Importantly, other approaches and normative developments have sought to mute or have neutralised this apparent theoretical puzzle concerning the State's emergence.

2.4 *Tools Neutralising the Weaknesses of a Declaratory Theory*

Some scholars have highlighted the difference between the act of cognition and recognition, thereby craving a theoretical middle ground between the declaratory and constitutive theory of recognition. Crawford underlines that the constitutive theory "incorrectly identifies that cognition with diplomatic recognition."[56] The key issue is the difference between cognition of facts – the

---

52 *Reparation for Injuries Suffered in the Service of the United Nations (Advisory Opinion)* [1949] ICJ 174, 185.

53 Dold (n 50) 86. However, this pronouncement of the ICJ is not directly relevant to the issue of a State's objectivity, since the emergence of the UN was not automatic but was done on the basis of an international treaty. In addition, it seems to speak indirectly in favour of inter-subjectivity, since the objective status in international law was established only by 50 states.

54 "Similarly, to compare facts with some criteria about them is possible only through the comparing person's conceptual matrix which, in this sense, has a constitutive effect on whether correspondence is perceived or not." Koskenniemi, *From Apology to Utopia* (n 1) 275.

55 Koskenniemi, *From Apology to Utopia* (n 1) 517–520.

56 Crawford (n 38) 5.

meeting of the constitutive criteria of statehood – and the recognition by a new State that may or may not occur for political, legal or other reasons.[57] "[The cognition] always precedes [recognition] in time and constitutes a separate stage in the process of recognition as a whole."[58] Cognition could be likened to a fact-finding inquiry on whether the constitutive criteria of statehood are met.[59] It can be *assumed* that the meeting of the constitutive criteria of statehood (territory, population and government) is automatically cognisable by and opposable to all the States.[60]

However, even though this assumption would partially remove the problem concerning the automaticity and self-evidence of facts, in reality it would not offer much practical benefit. The reasons why the States do not act upon their cognition – why they do not recognise an entity as the State – might vary. Koskenniemi points out that one such reason could be the State's disagreement as to the meeting of the constitutive criteria in a particular case.[61]

> It must be pointed out that the border between non-cognition caused by uncertainty as to the fulfilment of required legal criteria of State or government and non-recognition cause by other reasons is very hard to draw in practice.[62]

In the case of uncertainty, the States prefer to employ non-recognition as an optional act, rather than refer to the non-fulfilment of the legal criteria of statehood.[63] However, other normative developments of international law have contributed to a substantial neutralisation of the weaknesses of the declaratory theory. Roth highlights,

57 For a different doctrinal perspective that distinguishes between recognition as "cognition of fact" and recognition as "political act," see Koskenniemi, *From Apology to Utopia* (n 1) 280, ftn 201.

58 CH Alexandrowicz, 'The Quasi-Judicial Function in Recognition of States and Governments (1952)' in D Armitage and J Pitts, *The Law of Nations in Global History* (OUP 2017) 376.

59 ibid 378.

60 See *contra* Koskenniemi: "Secondly, the point really is that it seems impossible to oppose to a State a view about what it has or has not taken cognizance of. If the State simply denies the presence of the (objective) cognitive criteria, we seem unable to argue that such cognition *had* taken place though the State now denies it. By denying 'cognition', the State will achieve precisely the same effect as denying a recognition in a constitutive system." Koskenniemi, *From Apology to Utopia* (n 1) 280, ftn 201.

61 Koskenniemi, *From Apology to Utopia* (n 1) 280, ftn 201.

62 Blix (n 46) 630.

63 ibid 631.

> the facts on the ground can hardly be said to speak for themselves, and yet remarkable coordination has prevailed in this area of state practice, as evidenced by the paucity of genuine recognition controversies in contrast to the plethora of intense crises of local authority.[64]

Authors have noted that there are clear centralisation tendencies concerning the status determination at the UN.[65] The role of peremptory norms of international law in the State-creation via secession has also decreased the importance of the constitutive criteria as the only relevant guidance, and thus made the status determination clearer. As is shown below, even though the parent State's consent cannot be considered the obligatory element of the status determination, it is conclusive and, therefore, also relativises the importance of the effectiveness criteria.

3 State Practice Mapping

After 1945, the cases of State-creation can be broadly divided into the following groups. First, there have been State-creation instances based on the right to self-determination during decolonisation.[66] These instances are outside of the

64 Roth (n 20) 398.

65 See J Dugard, *Recognition and the United Nations* (Grotius 1987).

66 It is possible to include East Timor's accession to independence and a recent independence referendum in New Caledonia in this category. MG Kohen, 'Introduction' in MG Kohen (ed), *Secession: International Law Perspectives* (CUP 2006) 4. New Caledonia is included in the List of Non-Self-Governing Territories; see 'Non-Self-Governing Territories' available <https://www.un.org/dppa/decolonization/en/nsgt> accessed 5 October 2023 and The Question of New Caledonia, UNGA Res 71/119 (6 December 2016) A/RES/71/119. Two independence referenda, in which the majority of voters rejected independence, took place on 4 November 2018 and on 4 October 2020 in compliance with the terms of the 1998 Numéa Accords signed by the French Republic and local populations. One more referendum on this issue can be held before 2022. See Accord sur la Nouvelle-Calédonie signé à Nouméa (signed 5 May 1998) <https://www.legifrance.gouv.fr/affichTexte.do?cidTexte=JORFTEXT000000555817&dateTexte=&categorieL> accessed 5 November 2018. See also J Smyth and H Agnew, 'New Caledonia Votes to Remain Part of France' (*The Financial Times*, 4 November 2018) <https://www.ft.com/content/c26d60ae-e023-11e8-a6e5-792428919cee> accessed 5 October 2023. 'New Caledonia Referendum: South Pacific Territory Rejects Independence from France' (*BBC News*, 4 October 2020) <https://www.bbc.com/news/world-asia-54410059> accessed 15 December 2020. To some extent, Eritrea's birth could also be linked to this category. The UNGA Res placed Eritrea under Ethiopia's sovereignty on the condition that it preserve Eritrea's autonomy, which Ethiopia subsequently breached. Ultimately, after years of civil war, the UN mandated an independence referendum in 1993. MG Kohen, 'Introduction' in MG Kohen (ed), *Secession: International Law*

scope of this book. Second, there have been unilateral secessionist attempts connected to the violation of peremptory norms and, therefore, precluded from attaining statehood. Chapter 2 analysed these cases. Third, there have been cases of a consensual State-creation. Even though a consensual State-creation is not the subject of the present book, this chapter briefly focuses on it to better depict contemporary dynamics. Lastly, the chapter examines instances of unilateral secession isolated from all the above categories to establish whether the classical effectiveness paradigm holds up in a contemporary State-creation practice.

3.1 *Relevance of the Parent State's Consent*

The term 'secession' used in this book refers to *unilateral* secession. Crucially, such a definition severely limits the State practice that falls within the analysis of this book because it excludes instances of dissolution and especially devolution.[67] By radically limiting the State practice, this methodology seeks to outline the exact contours of unilateral secession in international law.

Nevertheless, despite a seemingly clear-cut legal classification, the relevance of the parent State's consent is far more intricate because unilateral secessionist tendencies have initiated many instances of dissolution and devolution.[68] The parent State frequently grants consent possibly after unilateral DoI or civil wars.[69] However, what distinguishes devolution from unilateral secession is that the former's legal basis is derived from the parent State's consent.[70] "It is clear that if the former sovereign recognizes as a State a local unit exercising

---

Perspectives (CUP 2006) 4–5, 7, 12, 19. See also UNGA Res 390 (V) (2 December 1950) UN Doc A/RES/390(V). "De la sorte, la violation de l'obligation internationale de garantir l'autonomie à l'intérieur de l'Etat n'ouvre pas automatiquement la voie à la secession. Elle permet toutefois à la communauté internationale de décider d'ouvrir cetter voie, quelle que soit la position de l'Etat en cause." MG Kohen, 'Création d'Etats en droit international contemporain' in (2002) VI Cours euro-méditerranéens Bancaja de droit international 593. However, see also *infra* for the role of Ethiopia's consent to Eritrea's independence.

67 "When a new State is formed from part of the territory of another State with its consent, it is a situation of 'devolution' rather than 'secession.'" Kohen, 'Introduction' (n 66) 3. See also P Radan, 'Secessionist Referenda in International and Domestic Law' (2012) 18 Nationalism and Ethnic Politics 8, 9; Anderson G, 'Secession in International Law and Relations: What Are We Talking About?' (2013) 35 Loyola of Los Angeles International and Comparative Law Review 343, 344–355.

68 Kohen, 'Introduction' (n 66) 2; Crawford (n 38) 375 and 390–391.

69 However, the constitutional right of secession can predate a concrete secessionist struggle, or it can result from a change in the constitution following a secessionist struggle.

70 "Dans le cas de la "devolution"... le consentement se produirait en amont de l'indépendance. Il vient en aval dans le cas de la reconnaissance." Kohen, 'Création d'Etats en droit international contemporain' (n 66) 604.

actual control over certain territory then that entity is, at least prima facie, a State."[71] Such assent is required, "at least unless and until the seceding entity has firmly established control beyond hope of recall."[72]

The parent State's consent in cases of devolution can be expressed either as a pre-existing constitutional right to secede usually upon a successful referendum on this matter as in the case of Montenegro in 2006[73] or through an agreement between the parent State and an independence-seeking entity in which the parent State usually pledges to recognise the result of the independence referendum as was the case of South Soudan's emergence in 2011 based on the

71 Crawford (n 38) 376.

72 ibid 391. Christakis T and Constantinides A, 'Territorial Dispute in the Context of Secessionist Conflicts' in MG Kohen and M Hébié (eds), *Research Handbook on Territorial Disputes in International Law* (Edward Elgar 2018) 368.

73 The independence referendum in Montenegro was held on the basis of Article 60 of the 2003 Constitutional Charter of the State Union of Serbia and Montenegro, and upon the meeting of conditions prescribed therein, Montenegro became a new State. See Constitutional Charter of the State Union of Serbia and Montenegro (entered into force 4 February 2003) <http://www.worldstatesmen.org/SerbMont_Const_2003.pdf> accessed 5 November 2018 and Radan (n 67) 16. St. Kitts and Nevis's Constitution also includes the right of the island of Nevis to secede. The referendum in 1998 on the basis of this constitutional right did not attain a required two-thirds majority. See B Perrin, 'Terrorism, Secession and Multinational Constitutions: The Challenge of Sri Lanka' (2004) 16 Sri Lanka Journal of International Law 175, 203–208. The other States whose Constitutions include the right to secession are Ethiopia (in particular, the right to self-determination, including the right to secession for any relevant nation, nationality and people), the Principality of Liechtenstein (for individual communes) and Uzbekistan (for the Republic of Karakalpakstan). Radan (n 67) 15–16 and Kohen, 'Introduction' (n 66) 16 and 20. In addition, under Article 1(4) of the Law on Special Legal Status of Gagauzia, in case Moldova's status as an independent State changes, the "people of Gagauzia have the right of external self-determination." See 'Law on Special Legal Status of Gagauzia No 344-XII' (23 December 1994) <https://www.mskgagauzia.md/wp-content/uploads/2020/02/Zakon-344-angl.pdf > accessed 11 October 2023. Moreover, the 2009 Act on Greenland Self-Government stipulates that if the people of Greenland decide in favour of independence, negotiations between the Danish and Greenlandic governments must commence, with the view of introducing independence for Greenland. An eventual agreement must be approved by the Danish and Greenlandic parliaments and endorsed in referendum in Greenland. See Act on Greenland Self-Government No 473 (12 June 2009) <https://english.stm.dk/media/10522/gl-selvstyrelov-uk.pdf> accessed 11 October 2023. Lastly, Article 58(1) of the Charter for the Kingdom of the Netherlands provides that "Aruba may declare by country ordinance that it wishes to terminate the constitutional order enshrined in the Charter in respect of Aruba." Articles 58–60 of the Charter specify further conditions that must be fulfilled in this regard. See Charter for the Kingdom of the Netherlands (1954) <https://faolex.fao.org/docs/pdf/sxm150050anx.pdf> accessed 11 October 2023.

2005 Comprehensive Peace Agreement[74] and the Scottish independence referendum in 2014 based on the 2012 Edinburg Agreement.[75] Similarly, Ethiopia's consent also facilitated Eritrea's independence.[76]

Regarding the consensual dissolutions, such as the end of the USSR and Czechoslovakia, the predecessor State ceases to exist upon agreement among its constituent parts.[77] Moreover, the ex-SFRY republics became new States despite the opposition from a rump Yugoslav government and Serbia and Montenegro. However, as Fabry noted, it was only after the Badinter Commission designated the situation in the SFRY as the case of dissolution, legally equivalent to a consensual dissolution of the USSR and Czechoslovakia, when the ex-SFRY republics became "eligible for recognition" by the international community.[78] "[E]n l'espèce, la reconnaissance ne se fait pas contre la volonté de l'Etat prédécesseur, tout simplement parce qu'il est considéré

74 See Comprehensive Peace Agreement between the Government of Sudan and the SPLM/SPLA (with Annexes) (signed 9 January 2005) <https://peacemaker.un.org/node/1369> accessed 5 November 2018. AJ Christopher, 'Secession and South Sudan: an African Precedent for the Future?' (2011) 93 South African Geographical Journal 125.

75 Agreement Between the United Kingdom Government and the Scottish Government on a Referendum on Independence for Scotland (signed 15 October 2012) <http://webarchive.nationalarchives.gov.uk/20130102230945/http:/www.number10.gov.uk/wp-content/uploads/2012/10/Agreement-final-for-signing.pdf> accessed 5 November 2018. B Levites, 'The Scottish Independence Referendum and the Principles of Democratic Secession' (2015) 41 Brooklyn Journal of International Law 373, 393, ftn 139. "Because parent States are the principal objectors to attempted secessions by independence referendums, the consent of the United Kingdom obviated the debate about the legality of Scotland's secession under international law and could have assisted Scotland in attaining international recognition." ibid 395. Similarly, a non-binding referendum on independence of Bougainville from Papua New Guinea was held in 2019 on the basis of the Kopoko Agreement of 26 January 2001. See Radan (n 67) 13. See K Lyons, 'Bougainville Referendum: Region Votes Overwhelmingly for Independence from Papua New Guinea' (*The Guardian*, 11 December 2019) <https://www.theguardian.com/world/2019/dec/11/bougainville-referendum-region-votes-overwhelmingly-for-independence-from-papua-new-guinea> accessed 14 January 2020.

76 "Ethiopia's recognition of the right of Eritrea to become independent also contributed to make this case non-controversial in the end." Kohen, 'Introduction' (n 66) 12. According to Crawford, Eritrea is an example of a combination of "[e]lements of forcible seizure and free grant of independence." Crawford (n 38) 375 and see also 402. Vidmar (n 2) 120–121. "Even a clear-cut military victory by secessionist forces does not seem, in practice, to yield an international acknowledgment of independence until the original state concedes the point." Roth (n 20) 401.

77 See Crawford (n 38) 395 and 402.

78 M Fabry, 'The Right to Self-Determination as a Claim to Independence in International Practice' (2015) 14 Ethnopolitics 498, 501.

comme n'existant plus."[79] Ultimately, a non-consensual dissolution entailed that "no one party is allowed to veto the process."[80]

On balance, the number of cases, which started as unilateral secessionist attempts and later transformed into dissolution or devolution is overwhelming.[81] Fabry even went so far as to claim "practice [of the end of the Cold War] effectively precluded secession without the consent of the sovereign government in question as a legitimate way of acquiring statehood."[82] Thus, the sheer scale of the practice requires reflection regarding what (if any) limits the parent State's consent poses to *unilateral* secession and the effectiveness paradigm in contemporary international law.[83]

3.2 *Practice of Unilateral Secession*

Following a brief mapping of the different categories of State-creation, the question arises how many instances of *unilateral* secession based on a classical effectiveness paradigm have occurred since 1945. The answer to this question should help clarify whether outside of peremptory norms violation, enough practice and *opinio iuris* exists to support the constitutive criteria of statehood as the overriding customary criteria on secession[84] and how the importance of the growing parent State's consent in State-creation has influenced the effectiveness paradigm.

First, there have been numerous failed post-colonial and non-colonial secessionist attempts, which have not reached or maintained adequate effectiveness.[85] On the one hand, this practice can be taken as evidence of the

---

79 Kohen, 'Création d'Etats en droit international contemporain' (n 66) 605–606.

80 J Crawford, *The Creation of States in International Law* (n 38) 391.

81 According to Crawford, while the period before 1919 witnessed a great number of unilateral secessions, since then, "new States have been more often created with the consent of the former sovereign, especially in the course of decolonisation." Crawford (n 38) 375.

82 Fabry M, 'The Contemporary Practice of State Recognition: Kosovo, South Ossetia, Abkhazia, and their Aftermath' (2012) 40 Nationalities Papers 661, 664. Similarly, G Wilson, 'Crimea: Some Observations on Secession and Intervention in Partial Response to Müllerson and Tolstykh' (2015) 14 Chinese Journal of International Law 217, 217–218.

83 Vidmar claims that "[n]ew States do not emerge as a matter of fact upon meeting the traditional or additional statehood criteria, because an independence-seeking entity needs to overcome the counterclaim to territorial integrity in order to become a State." Vidmar (n 2) 113. For an elaboration of this argument, see ibid 113–149.

84 "The question remains, however, whether the concept of the additional statehood criteria [concerning violation of peremptory norms] explains exhaustively how State emerge in contemporary international law." Vidmar (n 2) 108.

85 It is possible to include in this group the attempted secession of the Faroe Islands from Denmark, the Island of Anjouan from the Comoros, secessionist entities from ex-SFRY republics, Chechnya from the Russian Federation, Tamil Elam from Sri Lanka, Catalonia

importance of effectiveness in State-creation; however, it cannot be seen as conclusive for the answer as to whether the effectiveness is the only overriding criterion. On the other hand, this practice also supports the importance of the territorial integrity of the parent State. For example, regarding the secessionist entities within the SFRY's ex-republics, "the principal external actors went so far as to insist on interim international administration within their territories rather than to sanction separation of their respective secessionist entities."[86]

Second, the number of entities, which secured effectiveness against the parent State's wishes and are generally considered States, is extremely limited. Even in these contexts, the parent State's consent ultimately plays an important role. Crawford concluded that "[o]utside the colonial context, the United Nations is extremely reluctant to admit a seceding entity to membership against the wishes of the government of the State from which it has purported to secede"[87] and that "[t]here is no case since 1945 where it has done so."[88] However, contrary to dissolution and devolution, the parent State's consent only confirms an already existing effective and legal reality, rather than forming the legal basis of a new statehood.[89]

---

from Spain, and many other unsuccessful secessionist attempts. See Crawford (n 38) 403–415. See also, for example, S Saeed, 'How the World Reacted to Catalan Independence Declaration' (*Politico*, 27 October 2017) <https://www.politico.eu/article/how-the-world-reacted-to-catalan-independence-declaration/> accessed 11 November 2018 and Y Serhan, 'Catalonia's Self-Defeating Independence Declaration' (*The Atlantic*, 27 October 2017) <https://www.theatlantic.com/international/archive/2017/10/catalonias-self-defeating-independence-declaration/544205/> accessed 11 November 2018. A notable exception to failed secessions from ex-SFRY republics is the case of Kosovo. See *infra*. Even in the context of some of these defeated secessions, Fabry points out that the lack of the parent State's consent led to non-recognition by third States "which legally maintained them as part of the states they had broken away from, leaving them continuously liable to being re-absorbed by the central government, as indeed 'Tamil Eelam' was in 2009." Fabry M, 'International Involvement in Secessionist Conflict: From the 16th Century to the Present' in A Pavaković and P Radan (eds), *The Ashgate Research Companion to Secession* (Routledge 2011) 259. Another way of reading this is that the conflict was ongoing, or that stabilized effectiveness was never reached.

86 M Fabry, 'The Contemporary Practice of State Recognition (n 82) 665.

87 Crawford (n 38) 417.

88 ibid 417 and see also 390.

89 "Undoubtedly, recognition by the parent State paves the way for an established confirmation of the existence of the new entity, although this is not a *conditio sine qua non* for that existence." Kohen, 'Introduction' (n 66) 12. Kohen, 'Création d'Etats en droit international contemporain' (n 66) 604.

Since 1945, only Bangladesh has achieved statehood through unilateral secession.[90] Bangladesh's secession from Pakistan raises many specific issues including the potential applicability of remedial secession[91] and the influence of India's military involvement in the establishment of Bangladesh's effectiveness.[92] However, Thio summarised all the reasons why the success of Bangladesh's secession was "more a unique rather than precedent-setting case."[93]

Bangladesh was admitted to the UN only after its recognition by its parent State – Pakistan.[94] However, the reason for the postponement of Bangladesh's admission to the UN was the Chinese claim that Bangladesh had not fulfilled the condition of Article 4 of the UN Charter – in particular the ability and willingness to fulfil the obligations contained in the Charter – and not its status as a State or the lack of recognition by the parent State.[95] Thus, Bangladesh achieved statehood prior to Pakistan's recognition.[96]

As for the other effective entities, their statehood has remained contested. For years, outside any violation of peremptory norms, Somaliland has possessed an effectiveness that is unparalleled to that of its original parent State of Somalia; however, no State has recognised it, which accentuates the above-mentioned weaknesses of the declaratory theory concerning the self-evidence of the Montevideo criteria.[97] Outside any recognition by other States,

---

90 Crawford (n 38) 391; L-A Thio, 'International Law and Secession in the Asia and Pacific Regions' in MG Kohen (ed), *Secession: International Law Perspectives* (CUP 2006) 304. After the Pakistani military rejected the results of elections won by the Awami League, which demanded the autonomy for East Pakistan, Bangladesh declared independence on 26 March 1971. Civil war ensued. Following India's intervention on 4 December 1971, Pakistani forces were defeated on 16 December 1972. ibid, 304–306. See also *supra*, Chapter 2.

91 See *supra* Chapter 3.

92 See *supra* Chapter 2.

93 Thio (n 90) 306 and 306–308.

94 M Fabry, 'The Contemporary Practice of State Recognition (n 82) 664, ftn 6. Pakistan recognised Bangladesh on 2 February 1974, and Bangladesh was admitted to the UN on 17 September 1974. Thio (n 90) 306, ftn 57.

95 Kohen, 'Création d'Etats en droit international contemporain' (n 66) 605. See also SCOR, 1659th meeting (24 August 1972) 2. Many States had recognised Bangladesh before Pakistan did; it was even admitted to the Commonwealth. Thio (n 90) 306, ftn 57.

96 Kohen, 'Création d'Etats en droit international contemporain' (n 66) 605.

97 See Grzybowski (n 22) 416–417; AK Eggers, 'When is a State a State? The Case for Recognition of Somaliland' (2007) 30 Boston College International and Comparative Law Review 211. "It is thus safe to assume that Somaliland meets both the traditional and the additional statehood criteria, leaving unanswered the question of why it is not a State." Vidmar (n 2) 110.

Somaliland's statehood is more apparent than real – rather than support, it undermines the effectiveness paradigm. However, even Crawford points out that the parent State's opposition or inability to deal with this issue is an important factor to be considered when analysing this case.[98]

The international community has been notoriously divided as far as Kosovo's recognition is concerned. Among many legal issues raised by Kosovo's alleged statehood, the doubts can be specifically cast on the foundation of its effectiveness, enabled by the establishment of an international administration based on the UNSC Resolution 1244. Ultimately, it is likely that the uncertainty regarding Kosovo's legal status will only be removed upon an eventual Kosovo–Serbia agreement.[99] Thus, it is difficult to see how Kosovo's alleged secession from Serbia could support the effectiveness paradigm in international law.

Finally, the post-Soviet secessionist instances represent the largest portion of a non-colonial practice. With a sustained effectiveness, none or only a minimal recognition and no membership in the UN, the self-proclaimed post-Soviet entities have remained key examples of a contested statehood today. A detailed analysis conducted in Part 2 demonstrates that all post-Soviet entities are endowed with sustained effectiveness; however, they are undermined by a contested claim to statehood that is in one way or another connected to the violation of peremptory norms, in particular through external military intervention. Thus, rather than normatively supporting the effectiveness paradigm, the post-Soviet secessionist practice is an example of the operation of the legality principle resulting in the statehood's denial. The self-proclaimed post-Soviet republics are not States; they are illegal secessionist entities.[100]

3.3 *Key Takeaways from the Reading of the Practice*

From this mapping of the practice follows that to secure an uncontested statehood, rather than focusing on the fulfilment of the constitutive criteria, secessionists should seek to obtain the parent State's consent.[101] The gravitation

---

98 Crawford (n 38) 416–417. Similarly, Christakis and Constantinides (n 72) 368.

99 See T Barber, 'Serbian PM Remains Cautious on Kosovo Peace Settlement' (*The Financial Times*, 4 November 2018) <https://www.ft.com/content/cf1bc0da-deab-11e8-8f50-cbae5495d92b> accessed 4 November 2018.

100 See *infra* Part 2, Section 3.

101 On the interplay between the parent State's constent and effectiveness, see Christakis and Constantinides (n 72) 368. See U Saxer, 'Self-Determination, Changes of Statehood and the Self-Organization of the International System' (2010) 214 Beiträge zum ausländischen öffentlichen Recht und Völkerrecht 993, 1005; J Vidmar, S McGibbon and L Raible, 'Introduction to the Research Handbook on Secession' in J Vidmar, S McGibbon and L Raible (eds), *Research Handbook on Secession* (Edward Elgar 2022) 4.

towards the parent State's consent as the most effective guarantee of an uncontested statehood shows how deeply the principle of territorial integrity is entrenched in contemporary international law and the extent to which it poses obstacles to a classical factualist and neutral vision of secession.[102]

In addition, the State-creation is getting conceptually closer and closer to the classical modes of sovereignty transfer, in which the State's consent plays a key role. Concerning a consensual State-creation initiated by unilateral secessionist tendencies, a new State's sovereignty can be conceived as being transferred from the parent State in favour of the secessionist non-State actor.[103] Thus, this trend substantially undermines the classical view of a new State's sovereignty as being original and not derived from any pre-existing sources.[104] Lastly, by granting its consent, the parent State removes doubts as to the new State's legal standing.[105] Thereby, it also eliminates the risk of a premature recognition[106] and neutralises the weaknesses of the factualist statehood. Because of the accent on the parent State's consent, a contemporary period can be likened to that of a dynastic legitimism.[107]

However, to argue that to obtain the parent State's consent is *the only way* that secessionists can create a new statehood would essentially equate to a ban on *unilateral* secession as such.[108] However, the practice does not support such a conclusion.[109] The possibility of attaining statehood through the constitutive criteria of statehood without the parent State's consent has not been discarded yet. Indeed, any requirement of the parent State's approval would eliminate the key secessionist tool – the possibility to initiate a unilateral secessionist attempt and thereby put pressure on the central government to concede to the secession of the part of its territory. This would ultimately transform such a situation into devolution. Thus,

---

102 See Vidmar (n 2) 113–149.

103 In this regard, Craven speaks about the parent State "'delegating' sovereign authority to the nascent regime" and about "creating the necessary legal 'space' through its evacuation of its claim to sovereignty, in order for the new State to then assert its rights over the territory and population concerned." Craven (n 22) 216. See also Christakis and Constantinides (n 72) 368 and 374.

104 See Craven (n 22) 216.

105 Crawford (n 38) 376.

106 See G Anderson, 'Unilateral Non-Colonial Secession and the Criteria for Statehood in International Law' (2015) 41 Brooklyn Journal of International Law 60.

107 M Fabry, *Recognizing States: International Society and the Establishment of New States since 1776* (OUP 2010) 150.

108 Kohen, 'Introduction' (n 66) 20.

109 ibid; D Raič, *Statehood and the Law of Self-Determination* (Kluwer Law International 2002) 93–94. See also Chapter 4.

> même si une tendance en faveur d l'exigence de la reconnaissance par l'Etat prédécesseur semble se dessiner, celle-ci n'est pas suffisamment étayée comme pour affirmer déjà son existence en droit positif.[110]

From the above overview follows that over more than 70 years, which have witnessed a heightened number of newly created States, there has been only *one* case of unilateral secession based on the classical effectiveness paradigm – that of Bangladesh. It is shown that the post-Soviet secessionist attempts have been connected to violations of peremptory norms.[111] Kosovo's case is specific owing to the UNSC involvement in the establishment of its effectiveness.

Ultimately, Somaliland with sustained effectiveness and outside of the violation of peremptory norms exemplifies the key problems with the factualist statehood. Under a declaratory theory, it is a State, but outside of acknowledgement by the international community and other States, such legal status is essentially devoid of substance. Rather than support the effectiveness paradigm, Somaliland's case undermines it. Overall, the lack of practice confirms the "depreciation of the effectiveness criteria" in the State-creation.[112] Contemporary international law leaves only a minor, if not a virtual, space for the successful translation of unilateral secession based on the constitutive criteria into an uncontested statehood.

4 Conclusion

The present chapter focused on the limitations of the factualist vision of secession from the perspective of theory and practice. The chapter acknowledged the perplexity derived from the absence of a centralised body authorised to ascertain the fulfilment of the constitutive criteria. In essence, the problems surrounding the automaticity and self-evidence of facts reflects a classical debate in philosophy concerning the objectivity of facts.[113] As such, it is not unique to the State-creation or even to international law as such. The structural limitations of international law only make these issues more obvious, but not special. However, as these structural limitations do not undermine the general operability of international law, they do not justify the abandonment of a prevailing theoretical approach to State-creation. The fact that factualist

110 Kohen, 'Création d'Etats en droit international contemporain' (n 66) 606.

111 See *infra* part 2.

112 Fabry, *Recognizing States* (n 107) 225.

113 Koskenniemi, *From Apology to Utopia* (n 1) 517–520.

secession and declaratory theory have been prevailing theories of the State-creation demonstrates wider tendencies regarding international law, including a radical de-bilateralisation.

The chapter also showed that normative developments of international law have largely neutralised these weaknesses of factualist statehood and declaratory theory. These developments include implications of peremptory norms and preference for a consensual State-creation. The overview of the post-1945 practice in this chapter demonstrated the scarcity of uncontested instances of unilateral secession occurring based on effectiveness criteria. Consequently, the occurrence of factualist secession as outlined in Chapter 1 has become extremely unlikely, albeit not definitely excluded.

This normative framework reflects the dynamics of the current international system. Even though greatly disfavoured by the territorial integrity of the parent State, the secessionists are principally not prohibited from declaring statehood and attaining it via the establishment of effectiveness.[114] However, without external intervention prohibited by the norms of international law, the possibility of reaching sustained effectiveness against the parent State is rather unlikely.[115]

However, paradoxically, devolution might be possible because the attainment of statehood via effectiveness is not prohibited. The parent State might be willing to concede to the demands of secessionists, knowing that at least hypothetically secessionists could establish a new State based on the constitutive criteria. The parent State might, therefore, prefer to seek to avert the civil disruptions or even conflicts. However, eventual parent State's consent might not only come because of negotiations, but also at a high price of violence and war. Thus, consensual methods offer legal clarity and thereby stabilise international relations, but international law has yet to devise a purely peaceful and consensual method of State-creation.

114 Christakis and Constantinides (n 72) 345.

115 Fabry seems to make a similar argument, but in the context of favouring a *de facto* statehood. Fabry, *Recognizing States* (n 107) 225.

Conclusion to Section 1

Part 1, Section 1 of this book demonstrated the inadequacy of a classical doctrinal narrative concerning secession by proving that first international law cannot be considered as not regulating secession as the international customary rule provides for the constitutive criteria of statehood; second, by highlighting that even though international law does not provide a legal right to secede and generally does not prohibit secession *per se*, it cannot be considered neutral because it contains a specific prohibition when the violation of peremptory norms is concerned and also inhibits secession through a variety of other legal tools; and lastly, by showing that the role of the criterion of effectiveness as an overriding rationale concerning secession has been severely limited because of the lack of relevant practice of the emergence of States through unilateral secession since 1945. Overall, Section 1 provided a comprehensive international legal framework that applies to the question of the *status* of statehood of the secessionist entities today.

Notably, a defining feature of this legal framework underlying the question of attainment of statehood via secession is the tension between effectiveness and legality. However, as shown, the tension between the maxims of *ex factis ius oritur* and *ex iniuria ius non oritur* is only apparent since contemporary international law presupposes that the facts attributive of statehood are achieved in conformity with the peremptory norms of international law. If the effectiveness of a secessionist entity is achieved in violation of peremptory norms, the emergence of statehood is precluded. This outcome shows the pervasiveness of the effects of peremptory norms going as far as a pre-State context and preventing the emergence of States. It signals a more profound transformation of international law where the public order norms play an essential role in the context of State-creation.

 | DOI:10.1163/9789004702646_009

SECTION 2

Legal Consequences Applicable to the Illegal Secessionist Entity

Introduction to Section 2

Part 1, Chapter 2 of this book demonstrated that when a secessionist attempt is connected with the violation of peremptory norms, the emergence of new States is precluded. Therefore, even if a secessionist entity possesses apparent effectiveness vis-à-vis the parent State, it will not become a State under international law. Instead, it will *de iure* remain part of the parent State. This chapter identifies the entity, which is connected with an underlying violation of a peremptory norm and possesses *prima facie* effectiveness vis-à-vis the parent State as 'an illegal secessionist entity.' According to Crawford,

> [i]t may also be argued that, if international law withholds legal status from effective illegal entities, the result is a legal vacuum undesirable both in practice and principle. But this assumes that international law does not apply to *de facto* illegal entities; and this is simply not so. Relevant international legal rules can apply to de facto situations here as elsewhere.[1]

The main objective of this section is to identify the exact international legal rules that apply to the context of the illegal secessionist entity and outline their interaction.[2] This book uses the term illegal secessionist entity not as a specific legal status, but as a descriptive notion that helps elucidate the scope of international law that applies to these situations. It is an umbrella concept that allows for defining legal consequences attached to the entity's key features. While the book does not prejudice the possibility that the 'entity' itself may be the subject of international rules, and thus be endowed with some incremental subjectivity, it seeks to outline the legal framework applicable to these situations more broadly.

In essence, this section continues to follow an apparent conflict between the effectiveness and legality that was so determinative for the analysis of the status of the entity, in the context subsequent to the original violation of peremptory norms. To do so, it is necessary to explore each side of this outlined normative framework and their interaction. How pervasive are the consequences of peremptory territorial illegality with respect to *prima facie* effective relations of illegal secessionist entity? How much effectiveness is required for

1 Crawford J, 'The Criteria for Statehood in International Law' (1977) 48 BYBIL 93, 145.

2 Where appropriate, the section also examines legal frameworks applicable to illegal occupations/annexations.

 | DOI:10.1163/9789004702646_010

triggering certain legal consequences? How do legal consequences of peremptory territorial illegality and those triggered upon effectiveness interact?

This section proceeds as follows. At the outset, it defines the key features of the notion of 'an illegal secessionist entity' and contrasts it with other terms used in the literature. Then, it outlines the applicable legal framework. First, it explores the legal consequences of peremptory territorial illegality on the *prima facie* effective relations of the entity. Second, it examines legal consequences deriving from the change of effective territorial control in the area of human rights law, IHL and law of State responsibility. Lastly, it seeks to outline how legal consequences of peremptory territorial illegality and of change of effective territorial control interact *in abstracto*. Part 2 of this book uses this framework to analyse the *concrete* legal situations in post-Soviet illegal secessionist entities.

CHAPTER 6

Notion of an Illegal Secessionist Entity

For this book, the four following features characterise an umbrella notion of an 'illegal secessionist entity.' First, it is an underlying original illegality, which is due to the violation of peremptory norms either by the secessionist group itself or by the third State intervening in the secessionist attempt. Because of this illegality, the entity is denied statehood, the parent State remains sovereign and the consequences of peremptory illegality including the obligation of non-recognition are imposed on the third States.

Second, an illegal secessionist entity is defined by a *prima facie* change of effective territorial control from a *de iure* parent State. This subsumes two scenarios. First, it is a self-standing, independent entity, which established effectiveness vis-à-vis the parent State and is not under control by any third State.[1] Second, it is the entity whose effectiveness is only apparent as it is in fact under the effective control of the third State. Because the latter scenario is far more frequent and also subject of the analysis of Part 2 of this book, the following account will be focused only on it.

Third, an illegal secessionist entity persists in claiming to be a State under international law and *prima facie* possesses the outward attributes of statehood. Fourth, an illegal secessionist entity *ratione temporis* only refers to an on-going situation and does not concern the modalities of return to the *status quo ante* or transition from an illegal regime.

In broad terms, the legal framework applicable to an illegal secessionist entity can be divided into two groups – consequences of the peremptory territorial illegality and consequences of the change of effective territorial control. On the one hand, the peremptory illegality of an entity's origins provokes legal consequences in legal areas such as those of State succession, the validity of acts and international responsibility, including the obligation of third

1 Southern Rhodesia can be considered as the only example of an illegal secessionist entity over which no outside State exercised control. On the basis of this one example, it is impossible to adduce generalized conclusions. However, in principle, it is not precluded that such an entity would be an independent holder of some international rights and obligations. See MG Kohen, 'Création d'Etats en droit international contemporain' (2002) VI Cours euro-méditerranéens Bancaja de droit international 569. See also D Richter, 'Illegal States?' in W Czapliński and A Kleczkowska (eds), *Unrecognised Subjects in International Law* (SCHOLAR Publishing House 2019) 28.

States not to recognise or assist in maintaining illegal situations. On the other hand, an illegal secessionist entity remains a *de iure* part of the parent State. However, the lack of the parent State's effective territorial control limits the scope of its responsibility. Thus, the consequences of *prima facie* effectiveness of an entity and of a third State's control over the entity must also be taken into account. All these normative layers together offer a comprehensive legal framework applicable to these entities.[2]

It is imperative to differentiate the notion of an illegal secessionist entity from other similar terms used in the literature. It is the notion of a *de facto* regime, which is defined by the regime's exercise of territorial control and by a simultaneous lack of its recognition as a State.[3] Importantly, the reasons for non-recognition whether due to legal obligation or a simple political decision are not relevant. What matters is only the fact of non-recognition. Thus, this notion does not capture the tension between the effects of peremptory illegality and the change of effective control and by implication does not offer a comprehensive applicable legal framework. Consequently, *de facto* regimes whose non-recognition is not due to peremptory illegality will not be used as the instances of practice in this book.[4]

The doctrine also uses other seemingly related notions. For example, Ivanel refers to a rather political concept of a 'puppet state', which stresses the lack of an entity's self-sustainability and its dependence on the sponsor State.[5] Ivanel describes this situation as a "covert occupation",[6] which seems to be too narrow and limited to situations where control by the third State over an entity reaches a specific limit.[7] Similarly, Grant identifies the notion of a

---

2 This is without prejudice to, for example, a regime stemming from the *lex specialis* of cease-fire agreements. These are beyond this book's scope.

3 JA Frowein, 'De Facto Regime' in MPEPIL (online edn, OUP 2013), paras 1–3.

4 In this context, it is possible to completely agree with Christakis that "la pratique interne concernant les décisions nationales de non-reconnaissance fondées sur une "faculté" (ex. refus de reconnaître l'URSS, la RDA, la Chine, Taiwan, etc.) n'est que peu pertinente pour éclairer notre recherche sur le contenu précis de *l'obligation* de non-reconnaissance." T Christakis, 'L'obligation de non-reconnaissance des situations créées par le recours illicite à la force ou d'autres actes enfreignant des règles fondamentales' in C Tomuschat and JM Thouvenin (eds), *The Fundamental Rules of the International Legal Order. Jus Cogens and Obligations Erga Omnes* (M Nijhoff Publishers 2006), 145–146 (*emphasis in original*).

5 B Ivanel, 'Puppet States: A Growing Trend of Covert Occupation' in TD Gill (ed), *Yearbook of International Humanitarian Law Volume 18, 2015* (TMC Asser Press 2016) 46–48. Ivanel also distinguishes the puppet State from the notion of a *de facto* State, which fulfils the Montevideo criteria, but lacks recognition from the nascent State. ibid 46–47. It seems to be inappropriate to use the term 'State' in connection with an entity that does not fulfil statehood criteria.

6 ibid 44–48.

7 See *infra* Chapter 8 for tests relevant in these situations.

"frozen conflict" and its juridical features;[8] however, the concept is applicable in different situations. Moreover, even though there are obvious overlaps with the notion of an illegal secessionist entity, neither of these terms takes into account the consequences of peremptory illegality and, therefore, fails to identify the applicable framework in its entirety and normative complexity.[9]

Other authors have introduced notions that are conceptually closer to that of an illegal secessionist entity. For example, Milano uses the term "unlawful territorial situation", which implies that "the display of legal authority may not be complemented by a valid legal basis."[10] Ronen uses the term "illegal territorial regime".[11] Territorial regime is illegal "when its creation involves the violation of a peremptory norm of international law, principally the prohibition on the use of force or the obligation to respect the right of peoples to self-determination."[12] According to Ronen, there are different types of illegal territorial regimes, but she only focuses on the ones involving the claims of sovereignty – purported States and purported annexations.[13] Unlike these broader notions, the term illegal secessionist entity refers only to those entities that claim to be the States and excludes illegal annexations.

8 TD Grant, 'Frozen Conflicts and International Law' (2017) 50 Cornell International Law Journal 361, 377 and 390.

9 Another example is Cullen and Wheatley's position. When speaking about a *de facto* regime, Cullen and Wheatley acknowledge the relevance of peremptory norms violations precluding the birth of such regimes as States. However, in the following analysis they do not take peremptory illegality into account at all, instead referring to a *de facto* regime as a regime in *statu nascendi*. A Cullen and S Wheatley, 'The Human Rights of Individuals in De Facto Regimes under the European Convention on Human Rights' (2013) 13 Human Rights Law Review 691, 693–694 and 699–700.

10 E Milano, *Unlawful Territorial Situations in International Law: Reconciling Effectiveness, Legality and Legitimacy* (Martinus Nijhoff Publishers 2006) 8. "[W]e can define 'territorial situation' as a state of affairs where an international actor displays factual control *and* general legal authority over a certain territory." Ibid 6. "Thus, the definition of unlawfulness concerning territorial situations relates in principle to the right or the competence to rule over a certain territorial area, rather than the fact that such competence is exercised, or the way in which it is exercised." Ibid 8.

11 Ronen understands "territorial regime" as "an entity in which a functioning governing apparatus exercises control over a population in a territory, and makes a claim of sovereignty over that territory." Y Ronen, *Transition from Illegal Regimes under International Law* (CUP 2011) 1.

12 Ibid 1. This term is also used by Azarova, see V Azarova, 'An Illegal Territorial Regime? On the Occupation and Annexation of Crimea as a Matter of International Law' in S Sayapin and E Tsybulenko (eds), *The Use of Force Against Ukraine and International Law: Jus Ad Bellum, Jus in Bello, Just Post Bellum* (TMC Asser Press 2018) 43.

13 Ronen (n 11) 4.

Lastly, Richter uses the term of an "illegal *de facto* regime", but it is not entirely clear what a differentiating criterion is.[14] Crawford uses the notion "effective illegal entity" or "illegal de facto entity" to refer to situations similar to ones explored in this book,[15] but does not seek to identify the applicable law.

---

14 At the same time, it is not clear whether introducing a plethora of denominations is helpful. For example, Richter labels Transnistria as an "illegal regional administration," Nagorno-Karabakh as territory "de facto annexed by Armenia," South Ossetia as an "illegal entity short of statehood," Abkhazia as an "illegal State-like entity" and TRNC as an "illegal *de facto* regime." Ultimately, only Abkhazia and TRNC qualify as "illegal States," but this possibility is rejected. Richter instead refers to each as an "illegal *de facto* regime" or an "illegal entity." Richter (n 1) 28 and 55–56.

15 J Crawford, 'The Criteria for Statehood in International Law' (1977) 48 BYBIL 93, 145.

CHAPTER 7

Consequences of Peremptory Territorial Illegality

1 Introduction

Chapter 2 focused in detail on the effects of the violation of peremptory norms regarding the acquisition of a legal status of statehood.[1] It was established that a new State would not emerge due to illegality of its origins and invalidity of the DoI.[2] However, the consequences of this original violation are not limited to the issue of legal status, but spread further into other spheres of international law.[3] These effects form one side of normative context of an illegal secessionist entity.

This chapter examines these consequences in the area of the rules of State succession, invalidity and the aggravated regime of international responsibility vis-à-vis *prima facie* effective legal order and relations of such entity. Specifically, the chapter provides a general overview of the duty of cooperation, non-assistance and non-recognition. Next, it examines the implications of the duty of non-recognition in particular areas including relations of illegal secessionist entity at a purportedly inter-State level, economic and other dealings and the official laws and acts of an illegal secessionist entity. The chapter highlights policy and normative conflicts raised by the duty of non-recognition. Lastly, it assesses the outlined content of the duty of non-recognition against the criticism that this duty is without real substance.[4]

---

1 See *supra* Chapter 2.

2 See *supra* Chapter 2.

3 The following account will only discuss the consequences that are clearly linked to the violation of peremptory norms and are pertinent to the normative context of an illegal secessionist entity defined by the control of territory and exercise of government-like functions. It does not seek to provide a comprehensive overview of all the consequences triggered by violations of peremptory norms. Moreover, it will not examine third-State obligations under common Article 1 to Geneva Conventions.

4 S Talmon, 'The Duty Not "To Recognize as Lawful" a Situation Created by the Illegal Use of Force or Other Serious Breaches of a Jus Cogens Obligation: An Obligation without Real Substance?' in C Tomuschat and JM Thouvenin (eds), *The Fundamental Rules of the International Legal Order. Jus Cogens and Obligations Erga Omnes* (M Nijjhof Publishers 2006) 103–104; *Legal Consequences of the Construction of a Wall in the Occupied Palestinian Territory* (Advisory Opinion) [2004] ICJ Rep 136, Separate Opinion of Judge Kooijmans, para 44 ("*Wall*"). See also E Kassoti and A Duval, 'Setting the Scene: The Legality of Economic Activities in Occupied Territories' in A Duval and E Kassoti (eds), *Legality of*

© KONINKLIJKE BRILL BV, LEIDEN, 2024 | DOI:10.1163/9789004702646_012

2 Inapplicability of the Rules of State Succession

As mentioned in Chapter 2, all major codifications in the area of State succession, including Article 6 VCST, limit the scope *ratione materiae* of these documents "only to the effects of a succession of States occurring in conformity with international law and, in particular, the principles of international law embodied in the Charter of the United Nations."[5] As mentioned, this remarkably constant practice delineates the spheres of legality and illegality in the context of State succession, impeding "illegal situations from claiming the benefit of rights emerging from the rules of State succession."[6] This practice is also in line with two further conclusions reached in this book.

First, there is no new State emerging because of the secessionist attempt connected with the violation of peremptory norms; therefore, the rules of State succession simply cannot apply. For the rules of 'State' succession to be applicable, two States – the predecessor State and successor State – must exist. As demonstrated in Chapter 2, there will be no successor State in situations involving secession connected to the violation of peremptory norms.[7] Second, the applicability of rules of State succession could also be considered as giving "*legal effect* to a factual situation which is considered to be illegal under international law."[8] Therefore, it would also violate the obligation of non-recognition discussed below.[9]

Nevertheless, some authors argue that the rules of State succession particularly in the context of succession in respect of treaties would apply by virtue of customary international law.[10] It is argued here that such a position is flawed

---

Economic Activities, Occupied Territories: International, EU Law and Business and Human Rights Perspectives (Taylor & Francis Group, 2020) 6.

5 Vienna Convention on Succession of States in Respect of Treaties (adopted 23 August 1978, entered into force 6 November 1996) 1946 UNTS 3 ("VCST"). See *supra* Chapter 2.

6 Institut de droit international, Travaux préparatoires of the Tallin Session 'Succession of States in Matters of International Responsibility' (2015) Fourteenth Commission (Rapporteur: Marcelo Kohen) in Institut de droit international, (2015) 76 Annuaire de l'Institut de droit international (2015) 523. See *supra* Chapter 2.

7 As mentioned in Chapter 2, the wording of provisions in the codification works on State succession does not offer conclusions as to the consequences of unlawfulness in the emergence of a new State. Nevertheless, their inclusion strongly supports this book's conclusion. See *supra* chapter 2.

8 P Dumberry, *A Guide to State Succession in International Investment Law* (Edward Elgar Publishing 2018) 198. See *supra* chapter 2.

9 See *supra* Chapter 2. See ibid 214–215.

10 "However, the presence of this limitation clause in the VCST does not necessarily have a bearing on any equivalent customary status of the moving treaty-frontier rule reflected in Article 15 VCST and Article 29 VCLT. There could at least conceivably ... be room under

not only because the two above-mentioned reasons would equally apply to the customary rules of State succession,[11] but also because of the method of identification of customary law. To ascertain which customary rules apply to the illegal secessionist entity and what their content is, it is necessary to analyse the practice of illegal situations and not just simply transpose rules derived from lawful contexts to illegal ones. It is one of the objectives of this chapter to decipher the rules applicable to the latter.

3 Invalidity Deriving from Peremptory Illegality

Chapter 2 outlined the effects of the violation of peremptory norms on the unilateral act of the secessionist group – DoI – not only in terms of its unlawfulness, but also its invalidity.[12] However, such invalidity not only taints the declarations of independence, but also the other acts of an illegal secessionist entity. Indeed, "[t]he consequences of a violation of a peremptory norm is a legal nullity which operates *erga omnes*."[13]

> [O]nce the exercise of sovereign authority entails, or is consequential upon, a breach of a peremptory norm, the acts performed become subject to the overriding effect of jus cogens. Not only are they illegal – which would be the case for every wrongful act, but they are also void.[14]

---

general international law for a separate rule that allows a treaty's territorial application in unlawfully acquired territory." D Costelloe, 'Treaty Succession in Annexed Territory' (2016) 65 International & Comparative Law Quarterly 343, 350. "[A] treaty could arguably apply with respect to territory that a State controls and over which it claims sovereignty, even if unlawfully." ibid 358. "It is true that the rules of State succession that reflect customary law will continue to apply to situation of illegal annexation." Dumberry (n 8) 213–214 and see also 200.

11 Dumberry highlights that such an approach would be especially incompatible with a customary rule of non-recognition. See Dumberry (n 8) 214–215. Gaggioli points out the importance of reactions by other States and the international community to such an illegal secession. G Gaggioli, 'Article 6' in G Distefano, G Gaggioli and A Hêche (eds), *La Convention de Vienne de 1978 sur la succession d'Etats en matière de traités: commentaire article par article et études thématiques* (Bruylant 2016) 220.

12 See *supra* Chapter 2.

13 R Ronen, *Transition from Illegal Regimes under International Law* (CUP 2011) 4.

14 A Orakhelashvili, *Peremptory Norms in International Law* (OUP 2006) 216.

However, the question can be asked as to how far the chain of invalidity in the context of an illegal secessionist entity extends and how it overlaps with the duty of non-recognition.

3.1 *Chain of Invalidity in the Context of an Illegal Secessionist Entity*

Jennings referred "to a question of remoteness, ie how far it is useful to regard a nullity as being so to speak contagious, where what is in issue is the legal status of a chain of acts or consequences stemming from an original illegality."[15] In his opinion, there is a difference between "the original illegality which ought not to be regarded as a source of title for the wrongdoer, and remoter consequences precipitated by new situations, which may themselves, within certain limits, be creative of legal rights and obligations."[16]

In contemporary international law, it is useful to focus separately on the validity of acts purportedly carried out at an international level and internal acts. As for validity of purported treaty relations, the distinction between unlawful occupations/annexations and an illegal secessionist entity comes to the forefront. Indeed, the conclusion of treaties with illegal secessionist entities is much less frequent than the conclusion of treaties with an unlawful occupant extending to an occupied territory.[17] A treaty concluded with an illegal entity in which it would be accorded the status of a sovereign State may be considered *non-existent* under international law because of the lack of statehood of one of the parties. This lack of status would result from an original illegality and, therefore, could be part of the chain of invalidity. Nevertheless, this conclusion does not preclude the conclusion of agreements governed by international law including, for example, cease-fire agreements, in which these entities are not accorded the status of a sovereign State.

As for the conclusion of treaties with an unlawful occupant extending to an occupied territory, there are essentially two possible grounds of invalidity.[18] First, "[i]t is not uncommon for states to conclude treaties in the aftermath of a jus cogens breach with a view to regulating the factual situation created by the breach."[19] However, as mentioned in Chapter 2, the VCLT only foresees a

---

15 RY Jennings, 'Nullity and Effectiveness in International Law' in *Cambridge Essays in International Law: Essays in Honour of Lord McNair* (Stevens and Sons 1965) 75.

16 ibid 75.

17 Ronen, *Transition from Illegal Regimes under International Law* (n 13) 110.

18 ibid 111–112.

19 E Cannizzaro, 'Higher Law for Treaties?' in E Cannizzaro (ed), *The Law of Treaties Beyond the Vienna Convention* (OUP 2011) 426.

narrow normative conflict between the treaty terms and *ius cogens* and does not prescribe invalidity in the case of a broader *effet utile* conflict in situations where a treaty seeks to consolidate the violation of peremptory norms.[20] "Accordingly, the content of a treaty is the exclusive yardstick for its compatibility with peremptory norms."[21]

Some authors argue in favour of a broader conflict with peremptory norms.[22] Indeed, these treaties "tend to aggravate the misconduct by cooperating with the responsible state in relation to a situation created by the *jus cogens* breach."[23] However, at this stage of development of international law, it is not clear to what extent such treaties would be void on this ground only, even if their conclusion would be violation of the duty of non-recognition.[24] Nevertheless, the peremptory illegality also attaches to competence to conclude treaties. Thus, the lack of competence of one of the parties to dispose of the territory over which it does not possess the title may result in the invalidity of the treaty[25] and its

20 Portugal's request in East Timor "was based on the conceptual paradigm that *jus cogens* is breached not only by way of derogation, but also by a treaty which regulates a factual situation in a way that diverges from that which would have existed if *jus cogens* were duly complied with." Cannizzaro (n 19) 430. Ronen sees the Timor Gap Treaty's content as violating the right of Timorese people to dispose of their natural resources and their self-determination. "It should have been treated as invalid." Ronen, *Transition from Illegal Regimes under International Law* (n 13) 153. *East Timor* (*Portugal v Australia*) [1995] ICJ Rep 90, Dissenting Opinion of Judge Weeramantry 113 ("*East Timor*"). With respect to the Fisheries Partnership Agreement concluded between the EU and Morocco, Milano argues that its conflict with a *ius cogens* norm of self-determination does not make it invalid, because it "simply does not touch upon the issue and it would not touch upon it even if its practice was to extend to the waters of Western Sahara." E Milano, 'The New Fisheries Partnership Agreement Between the European Community and the Kingdom of Morocco: Fishing Too South?' (2006) 22 *Anuario español de derecho internacional* 413, 433–434. But Milano previously argued that "the occupying power, by entering into international commitments with regard to the territory will violate norms of *ius cogens* – e.g. the right of self-determination –, thus rendering those agreements a nullity under Article 53 of the VCLT." E Milano, *Unlawful Territorial Situations in International Law: Reconciling Effectiveness, Legality and Legitimacy* (Martinus Nijhoff 2006) 140.

21 Ronen, *Transition from Illegal Regimes under International Law* (n 13) 111.

22 Orakhelashvili, *Peremptory Norms in International Law* (n 14) 136–139.

23 Cannizzaro (n 19) 429.

24 A Pert, 'The "Duty" of Non-Recognition in Contemporary International Law: Issues and Uncertainties' (2012) 30 Chinese (Taiwan) Yearbook of International Law and Affairs 48, 68–69.

25 See, similarly, Milano's analysis of the validity of the Fisheries Partnership Agreement between the EU and Morocco, assuming that it covers the waters of Western Sahara. "[W]e must first analyse the position of Morocco with regard to Western Sahara and whether it is indeed in the position to create international legal rights and obligations with regard

non-opposability[26] with respect to the territory in question.

> General international law provides that the illegality of a certain territorial situation displays its effects in terms of 'invalidity', in the sense that the occupying power is in violation of another state's or people's territorial sovereignty; thus it does not have a legal competence to create rights and obligations concerning that territory.[27]

This would be because "the effective control of the regime over the territory, which enables it to enter into the treaty, is grounded in a violation of a peremptory norm."[28]

Second, while the internal acts of an illegal secessionist entity produce effects internally where they are shielded by its overwhelming effectiveness, their invalidity can be raised in proceedings at an international level[29] or at a domestic level in litigation involving the choice of law or recognition and enforcement of foreign judgments in civil matters or in public law procedures.[30]

---

to the Territory. The answer must be answered in the negative as Morocco does not have sovereignty over the Territory, it is not an administering Power, nor is its presence justified by other legal means, such as a consent expressed by the Saharawi people, by the former administering power Spain or a Ch. VII mandate by the Security Council." Milano, 'The New Fisheries Partnership Agreement' (n 20) 429. A key reason why the ICJ found itself without jurisdiction in the *East Timor* case had to do with questions around Indonesia's lack of treaty-making competence, as a presumed unlawful occupant, and related requirements concerning Indonesia's consent. "[T]he very subject-matter of the Court's decision would necessarily be a determination whether, having regard to the circumstances in which Indonesia entered and remained in East Timor, it could or could not have acquired the power to enter into treaties on behalf of East Timor relating to the resources of its continental shelf. The Court could not make such a determination in the absence of the consent of Indonesia." *East Timor* (n 20) para 28. See also Counter-Memorial of the Government of Australia (1 June 1992), para 187.

26 Apart from the Fisheries Partnership Agreements invalidity, Milano highlights that it may be considered non-opposable with regard to the Western Sahara. Milano, 'The New Fisheries Partnership Agreement' (n 20) 416 and see 434.

27 Milano, *Unlawful Territorial Situations in International Law* (n 20) 139. "Consequently, all international legal acts, such as treaties entered into by the occupying power, agreements or unilateral behaviours having international legal relevance are deprived of their legal effects." ibid 139–140.

28 Ronen, *Transition from Illegal Regimes under International Law* (n 13) 111.

29 For example, concerning the exhaustion of domestic remedies or grants of nationality within the context of diplomatic protection. Ronen, *Transition from Illegal Regimes under International Law* (n 13) 82. See also *infra*.

30 The public context may include the refugee status-determination procedure. See Ronen, *Transition from Illegal Regimes under International Law* (n 13) 82, ftn 33. See ILA, 'Second Interim Report on Recognition/Non-Recognition' (Washington Conference, March 2014).

In these fora, laws and acts of an illegal secessionist entity are considered null and void, ultimately expressing the principle of *ex iniuria ius non oritur*.[31] "[T]he rule on the invalidity of official internal acts of illegal regimes"[32] was pronounced by the ICJ in *Namibia*. The ICJ held that "official acts performed by the Government of South Africa on behalf of or concerning Namibia after the termination of the Mandate are illegal and invalid."[33] As is shown below, the practice of regional and domestic courts supports such a rule.[34] In particular, while it is shown below that the ECtHR gave effects to certain acts and laws for the TRNC based on the *Namibia* exception,[35] since the landmark *Loizidou* case, it has been constant in denying validity to provisions of the so-called constitution of the TRNC.[36]

However, the *Namibia* Advisory Opinion also encapsulates the rule on the validity of certain official internal acts, which rests on the divide between their benefit and detriment to the inhabitants of the territory.[37] This divide

---

31 In this context, Jennings already held that "there is a marginal group of cases where the normal considerations of comity, or of act of state doctrine are, or may be, displaced by the consideration that the foreign law or action in question is violative of a rule of public international law, and courts on occasions may accordingly refuse recognition to the foreign law on that ground; i.e., in a word that the foreign law in question is to be regarded as a nullity in the law of the forum, because it is, or is considered to be, repugnant to the principles of international law. The reasoning behind such decisions is clearly an application, within the confines of that municipal system, of the principle *ex injuria jus non oritur*." Jennings (n 15) 79. See also Orakhelashvili, *Peremptory Norms in International Law* (n 14) 217. GI Hernández, 'Territorial Change, Effects of' in MPEPIL (online edn, OUP 2010) para 22.

32 Ronen, *Transition from Illegal Regimes under International Law* (n 13) 82.

33 *Legal Consequences for States of the Continued Presence of South Africa in Namibia (South West Africa) notwithstanding Security Council Resolution 276 (1970) (Advisory Opinion)* [1971] ICJ Rep 16, para 125 ("*Namibia*"). "[N]o State which enters into relations with South Africa concerning Namibia may expect the United Nations or its Members to recognize the validity or effects of such relationship, or of the consequences thereof ... States Members of the United Nations are under obligation to recognize the illegality of South Africa's presence in Namibia and the invalidity of its acts on behalf of or concerning Namibia." ibid paras 126 and 133(2).

34 See *infra*.

35 See *infra* in detail.

36 In *Loizidou*, basing its conclusion on international practice and UNSC resolutions from which it was evident that "the international community does not regard the 'TRNC' as a State under international law and that the Republic of Cyprus has remained the sole legitimate Government of Cyprus," the ECtHR held that it "cannot attribute legal validity for purposes of the Convention to such provisions as Article 159" of the TRNC's Constitution. *Loizidou v Turkey* ECHR 1996-VI 2216, para 44 ("*Loizidou*"). See *infra* for more.

37 "[T]his invalidity cannot be extended to those acts, such as, for instance, the registration of births, deaths and marriages, the effects of which can be ignored only to the detriment

"is not endogenous to a legal act *per se*" and does not reflect a classical criterion of validity of acts.[38] Therefore, the validity of a particular act based on the *Namibia* exception arguably does not operate automatically, but must be declared in proceedings with possible effects *ex tunc*. A starting premise concerning all acts and laws of an illegal secessionist entity is their automatic invalidity.[39] Even though the *Namibia* exception suggests "[a] regime representing a non-state ... is not an absolute nullity",[40] it is argued that this contention is minimised and relativised in the context of the third State's control over an entity in situations when acts valid under the *Namibia* exception can be attributed to the third State.[41] The *Namibia* exception is discussed in detail below in the context of the duty of non-recognition.

3.2 *Relationship between Invalidity of Acts and the Duty of Non-recognition*

As already discussed in Chapter 2, the relationship between the duty of non-recognition and the invalidity of acts is rather complex. On the one hand, it is difficult to accept the proposition that due to the lack of a compulsory jurisdiction in international law, the non-recognition constitutes invalidity rather than

of the inhabitants of the Territory." *Namibia* (n 33) para 125. Milano, *Unlawful Territorial Situations in International Law* (n 20) 138.

38 Milano, *Unlawful Territorial Situations in International Law* (n 20) 138. For Milano, this differentiation is "part of political decision-making" and is "based on an extra-legal appreciation, an appreciation of the international legitimacy of the act involved." ibid.

39 Tancredi adopts the opposite position. "[T]he acts adopted by the unlawful regime will not be null and void, but only deprived of the possibility to display their effect in single case, remaining effective in different contexts before different authorities. In other words, the act will not be effective vis-à-vis the State which complies with the duty of non-recognition. However, the act will remain potentially effective (and therefore abstractly valid), where a national or international court upholds the doctrine of necessity, or where a government considers the protection of its national interests (for instance, where it has political, administrative or economic contacts with the unrecognised regime) as prevailing over its duty of non-recognition." A Tancredi, 'A Normative 'Due Process in the Creation of States Through Secession' in MG Kohen (ed), *Secession: International Law Perspectives* (CUP 2006) 204.

40 Restatement (Third) of the Foreign Relations Law of the United States (1987), § 205, Reporters' Notes, para 3 ("Restatement").

41 See *infra* for the ECtHR case law on the *Namibia* exception, where the Court arguably applies a lower threshold of attribution than one foreseen in ILC, Draft Articles on the Responsibility of States for Internationally Wrongful Acts, with Commentaries in 'Report of the International Law Commission on the Work of its Fifty-Third Session (23 April-1 June and 2 July-10 August 2001)' UN Doc A/56/10 ("ARSIWA").

the other way round.[42] According to these views, the role of an obligatory judge "may be replaced with the duty of third-party subjects to consider, diffusely, an unlawful act or situation deprived of its legal effects."[43] It is argued here,

> the absence of an organized procedure does not do away with nullities, and there is no warrant for the idea that there can be no nullity if there is no appropriate court to take cognizance of it.[44]

On the other hand, it must be also admitted that even though under Article 53 VCLT, "[a] treaty conflicting with *ius cogens* is void *ab initio*, *ie* has not come into legal existence on the international plane", the procedural requirements imposed by Articles 65 and 66 VCLT "challenge the idea of the *ex lege* absolute nullity of any treaty contrary to *ius cogens*."[45] "No light is shed on the issue of how third states may claim the invalidity of treaties considered absolutely void."[46] It is in this context where some scholars have stated the importance of the duty of non-recognition.[47]

---

42 Tancredi, 'A Normative "Due Process"' (n 39) 197. "[N]on-recognition is a strategy deployed in the process leading towards nullity." MW Reisman and D Pulkowski, 'Nullity in International Law' in MPEPIL (online edn, OUP 2006) para 29.

43 Tancredi, 'A Normative "Due Process"' (n 39) 197. "[I]n these cases, absolute nullity does not work 'by operation of law (*de plein droit*)', and it is not automatic. The denial of effectiveness is, instead, the result of the concurrence of material conduct carried out by those subjects who do not recognise the effects of the wrongful act or event. Therefore, the *erga omnes* void character of an unlawful act does not precede collective non-recognition; on the contrary, it represents its consequence." ibid. (*footnotes omitted*). See also A Tancredi, 'Some Remarks on the Relationship between Secession and General International Law in the Light of the ICJ's Kosovo Advisory Opinion' in P Hilpold, *Kosovo and International Law: The ICJ Advisory Opinion of 22 July 2010* (Brill 2012) 99–100.

44 *Effects of Awards of Compensation Made by the United Nations Administrative Tribunal (Advisory Opinion)* [1954] ICJ Rep 47, Individual Opinion of Judge Winiarski, 65. Similarly, T Christakis, 'L'obligation de non-reconnaissance des situations créées par le recours illicite à la force ou d'autres actes enfreignant des règles fondamentales' in Tomuschat C and Thouvenin JM (eds), *The Fundamental Rules of the International Legal Order. Jus Cogens and Obligations Erga Omnes* (M Nijhoff Publishers 2006) 130–131.

45 K Schmalenbach, 'Article 53' in O Dörr and K Schmalenbach (eds), *Vienna Convention on the Law of Treaties* (Springer 2012) 925–926. "To avoid any inconsistency of these rules and Art 53, the latter should be interpreted as proceeding from the apparent validity of a treaty, which needs to be eradicated through a declaratory procedure." ibid 926.

46 A Gianelli, 'Absolute Invalidity of Treaties and Their Recognition by Third States' in E Cannizzaro (ed), *The Law of Treaties Beyond the Vienna Convention* (OUP 2011) 335.

47 "Treaties are legal acts; their non-recognition can well express states' appreciation of their validity or invalidity according to the law of treaties." ibid 347. "If third states were obliged, following Article 41 of the state responsibility codification, not to recognize as lawful the situations arising from the treaty, it would indeed come very close to saying that the treaty

Still, non-recognition does not constitute invalidity,[48] but can be understood as the corollary to the invalidity.[49] According to Orakhelashvili, "[a]cts of non-recognition do not themselves make contested acts illegal and void. They assume the existence of obligations, according to which the acts in question would be anyway devoid of legal validity."[50] This is supported by the below-mentioned practice, which calls for the non-recognition of certain acts while simultaneously declaring their lack of legal effects.[51]

---

should be considered void by third parties." ibid 357. "By concluding a treaty in conflict with a peremptory rule, a state adopts at the same time a conduct – which could be considered wrongful per se aside from a subsequent implementation of the treaty – and a normative act – which can be legally qualified as void." ibid 338.

48 See J Crawford, *The Creation of States in International Law* (2nd edn, Clarendon Press 2006) 158; V Gowlland-Debbas V, *Collective Responses to Illegal Acts in International Law: United Nations Action in the Question of Southern Rhodesia* (M Nijhoff 1990) 276. Therefore, one can agree with Lauterpacht, who pointed out that instances of non-recognition "were not intended to have or could have the effect of invalidating any act, or the results thereof, which but for the declaration of non-recognition would have been legally valid. They constitute … the declaration of an already existing duty not to contribute by a positive act to rendering valid the results of an act which is in itself devoid of legal force." H Lauterpacht, *Recognition in International Law* (University Press 1947) 420.

49 Milano, *Unlawful Territorial Situations in International Law* (n 20) 140 and see also 184. The duty of non-recognition has a broader scope of application, as it affects the legal situation not only of a responsible State but also of all other States. SM Villalpando, *L'émergence de la communauté internationale dans la responsabilité des Etats* (PUF 2005) 387–388.

50 A Orakhelashvili, 'International Public Order and the International Court's Advisory Opinion on Legal Consequences of the Construction of a Wall in the Occupied Palestinian Territory' (2005) 43 Archiv des Völkerrechts 240, 250. The ILC's Drafting Committee also seems to have a view rather different from these authors. "[O]ther States had an obligation not to recognize as "lawful" the situation created by the breach and the commentary would explain that the question of recognition was closely connected with, but different from, that of 'validity.'" ILC, *Yearbook of International Law Commission* (2000), volume I, 393, para 45. "[O]bligation of non-recognition was based on extensive practice, and that such non-recognition in the legal context was more a reaction to the invalidity of an act, not only to its illegality." ILC, 'Report of the International Law Commission on the Work of its Fifty-Second Session (1 May-9 June and 10 July-18 August 2000)' UN Doc A/55/10, 61, para 379.

51 See also Gianelli (n 46) 340–347. However, Tancredi suggests that "a void character does not represent the automatic effect of the resolution which contains the declaration of invalidity and the demand for non-recognition, since there is no organ having compulsory jurisdiction, endowed with the power to annul wrongful acts or situations (and certainly the UN organs are not empowered to do so)." Tancredi, 'A Normative "Due Process"' (n 39) 200. *Contra*: V Gowlland-Debbas, 'Legal Significance of the Legitimizing Function of the United Nations: The Cases of Southern Rhodesia and Palestine' in *Le droit international au service de la paix, de la justice et du développement: mélanges Michel Virally* (Pedone 1991) 323 and 327.

4 Aggravated Regime of International Responsibility

According to ARSIWA, a serious breach of obligation arising under a peremptory norm of general international law provokes secondary obligations in the area of international responsibility including the duty of non-recognition, non-assistance and cooperation.[52] These obligations are the expression of public order effects of peremptory norms.[53] While Chapter 2 focused on the general aspects of the duty of non-recognition including its customary and self-executory character and its effect on a statehood's emergence,[54] this section focuses on the scope and content of obligations belonging to this group. It does so by offering general observations and then focusing on specific content for different categories of acts and actions.

4.1 *General Observations*

The duties of non-recognition and non-assistance *ratione personae* apply to all States, including the wrongdoer and the injured State.[55] "The very purpose of these obligations lies in the fact that they should always, whenever they arise, be owed to the international community as a whole."[56] Relatedly, "the

---

52 ARSIWA (n 41) art 41. "Article 41. Particular consequences of a serious breach of an obligation under this chapter 1. States shall cooperate to bring to an end through lawful means any serious breach within the meaning of article 40. 2. No State shall recognize as lawful a situation created by a serious breach within the meaning of article 40, nor render aid or assistance in maintaining that situation. 3. This article is without prejudice to the other consequences referred to in this Part and to such further consequences that a breach to which this chapter applies may entail under international law."

53 See Orakhelashvili, *Peremptory Norms in International Law* (n 14) 579. V Lanovoy, *Complicity and Its Limits in the Law of International Responsibility* (Bloomsbury Publishing 2016) 120.

54 See more *supra* Chapter 2.

55 See more *infra* on the responsibility of an injured State in this context. "This obligation applies to all States, including the responsible State … Similar considerations apply even to the injured State: since the breach by definition concerns the international community as a whole, waiver or recognition induced from the injured State by the responsible State cannot preclude the international community interest in ensuring a just and appropriate settlement." ARSIWA (n 41) commentary to art 41, para 9. Villalpando (n 49) 383. See Orakhelashvili, *Peremptory Norms in International Law* (n 14) 398–404 and 408–409. However, as for the responsibility of the State responsible for violating the obligation of non-recognition, some scholars see it as not relevant in comparison with the responsibility entailed by the serious breach itself. CJ Tams, 'Do Serious Breaches Give Rise to Any Specific Obligations of the Responsible State?' (2002) 13 EJIL 1161, 1162–1163. D Costelloe, *Legal Consequences of Peremptory Norms in International Law* (CUP 2017) 194.

56 Costelloe, *Legal Consequences of Peremptory Norms in International Law* (n 55) 187.

effect of the acts concluded in breach of collective non-recognition will not be opposable to third-party subjects."[57] The obligations of non-recognition, non-assistance and cooperation also apply to international organisations.[58]

A serious breach of peremptory norms provokes ordinary consequences for the responsible State such as the obligation of cessation of the wrongful act, the obligation to offer guarantees and assurances of non-repetition and the duty to make reparation.[59] Eventually, the picture of the relevant consequences must also be complemented by the set of "*powers, rights, or claims* of third States" flowing from the violation of *erga omnes* obligations.[60]

4.1.1 Duty of Cooperation

Under the duty of cooperation, "[w]hat is called for in the face of serious breaches is a joint and coordinated effort by all States to counteract the effects of these breaches."[61] The duty of cooperation "does not stipulate a duty of third States or the injured State to cooperate with the responsible State in bringing to an end the serious breach of a jus cogens obligation, but rather a duty to cooperate among third States."[62] Although the ILC held that "States are under a positive duty to cooperate in order to bring to an end serious breaches", it did not elaborate on the specific actions that States are obliged to take except for highlighting the possibility of both institutional and non-institutional

57 Tancredi, 'A Normative "Due Process"' (n 39) 201.

58 ILC, 'Draft Articles on the Responsibility of International Organizations' 'Report of the International Law Commission of its Sixty-Third Session (26 April-3 June and 4 July-12 August 2011)' UN Doc A/66/10, art 42 ("DARIO"). See Costelloe, *Legal Consequences of Peremptory Norms in International Law* (n 55) 228–240.

59 ARSIWA (n 41) commentary to art 41, para 13. "While the scale or the gravity of a breach may have implications for the compensation due to an injured State, these elements do not alter its essentially compensatory character as a remedy in international law." See further Villalpando (n 49) 380–381; Tams (n 55) 1163–1180; Costelloe, *Legal Consequences of Peremptory Norms in International Law* (n 55) 185–186. "The obligation to respect another state's territorial sovereignty being an obligation to abstain and being the violation a continuing one, the secondary obligation to cease the wrongful conduct overlaps with the continued duty of performance of the obligation breached ... the typical remedy is withdrawal from the occupied territory, which is both resulting from the continued duty of performance of the primary obligation and from the secondary obligation to cease the wrongful conduct." Milano, *Unlawful Territorial Situations in International Law* (n 20) 173–174.

60 A Cassese, 'The Character of the Violated Obligation' in J Crawford and others (eds), *The Law of International Responsibility* (OUP 2010) 420; SM Villalpando (n 49) 380–381. In particular, ARSIWA (n 41) art 48(2) and art 54.

61 ARSIWA (n 41) commentary to art 41, para 3.

62 Talmon, 'The Duty Not "To Recognize as Lawful"' (n 4) 124.

cooperation through lawful means.[63] It is clear that the duty does not require any individual action.[64] Costelloe suggests, "the exercise of this obligation to cooperate may take the form of acts of retorsion, treaty-based response mechanisms such as the suspension of reciprocal obligations, or extra-conventional measures including, possibly, third-party countermeasures."[65] "The obligation could nevertheless ensure that States support measures that fall short of being obligatory by a decision of the Security Council."[66] The ILC left open the issue of its customary character.[67]

4.1.2 Duty of Non-recognition

The duty of non-recognition is of a customary nature.[68] "In fact, no other legal consequence of a serious breach is so firmly established in practice as the non-recognition of entities' legal claims."[69] Together with the duty of non-assistance, they are "duties of abstention", and thus do not require a positive action.[70] It is neither a countermeasure nor a sanction.[71] By isolating the illegal

---

63 ARSIWA (n 41) commentary to art 41, paras 2 and 3.

64 J Crawford, 'Third Party Obligations with Respect to Israeli Settlements in the Occupied Palestinian Territories' <https://www.tuc.org.uk/sites/default/files/tucfiles/LegalOpinionIsraeliSettlements.pdf> accessed 18 March 2020, para 74 ("Opinion").

65 Costelloe, *Legal Consequences of Peremptory Norms in International Law* (n 55) 214. See on third party countermeasures ibid 215–219.

66 NHB Jorgensen, 'The Obligation of Cooperation' in Crawford J and others, *The Law of International Responsibility* (OUP 2010) 697; Costelloe, *Legal Consequences of Peremptory Norms in International Law* (n 55) 214; Crawford, Opinion (n 64) para 74.

67 The ILC stated that it "may reflect the progressive development of international law." ARSIWA (n 41) commentary to art 41, para 3. Villalpando (n 49) 384.

68 On the customary nature of the obligation, see *supra* Chapter 2. "Given the character and the importance of the rights and obligations involved, the Court is of the view that all States are under an obligation not to recognize the illegal situation resulting from the construction of the wall in the Occupied Palestinian Territory, including in and around East Jerusalem." *Wall* (n 4) para 159. The ICJ found the duty applicable in the context of violation of the right to self-determination. Yet it did not specifically refer to violation of *ius cogens* obligations, but to *erga omnes* obligations. On this aspect, see *supra* Chapter 2. See *infra* for details of practice. Christakis, 'L'obligation de non-reconnaissance' (n 44) 137–142. Talmon, 'The Duty Not "To Recognize as Lawful"' (n 4) 103–104 and 113. *Contra*: Pert (n 24) 59–60. According to the ILA Report, the States were generally reluctant to proclaim an obligation of non-recognition, but due to lack of data, it was not possible to formulate general claims about the state of international law. See ILA, 'Second Interim Report on Recognition/Non-Recognition' (Washington Conference, March 2014).

69 Costelloe, *Legal Consequences of Peremptory Norms in International Law* (n 55) 202.

70 HP Aust, *Complicity and the Law of State Responsibility* (CUP 2011) 331. ARSIWA (n 41) commentary to art 41, para 4.

71 Aust (n 70) 331. Crawford, *The Creation of States in International Law* (n 48) 173. Richter points out that the obligation of non-recognition cannot be a countermeasure because,

regime, its objective is to induce either the illegal situation's collapse or implosion and assure the return to the *status quo ante*.[72] Nevertheless, some authors doubt the obligation's efficacy[73] and others claim that it is not entirely clear what its content actually is.[74]

In contemporary international law, the scope of the duty of non-recognition goes beyond non-recognition of "'status'-related questions" reaching also "the effects of serious breaches of peremptory norms in general."[75] It does not only prohibit formal and explicit recognition, but also all actions, which may *imply recognition*.[76] Thus, the notion of 'implied recognition' is critical for delineating

---

firstly, it would entail that the "the denial of the rights inherent in statehood would constitute a violation of international law, which does not conform to current doctrine"; secondly, it would not be in line with the understanding that the obligation of non-recognition is mandatory under international law, and therefore does not require justification. D Richter, 'Illegal States?' in W Czapliński and A Kleczkowska (eds), *Unrecognised Subjects in International Law* (SCHOLAR Publishing House 2019) 27.

72 "The obligation applies to 'situations' created by these breaches, such as, for example, attempted acquisition of sovereignty over territory through the denial of the right of self-determination of peoples." ARSIWA (n 41) commentary to art 41, para 5. Christakis points out that what distinguishes "situation" from a simple fact is that "la première est toujours susceptible d'évoluer, y compris en amenant à un rétablissement du *statu quo ante* ou, au moins, à la situation la plus proche de celle qui existait avant le fait illicite." Christakis, 'L'obligation de non-reconnaissance' (n 44) 128.

73 According to Verhoeven, this obligation is "fantaisiste qui a fait 'faillite.'" J Verhoeven, *La reconnaissance international dans la pratique contemporaine* (Pedone 1975) 841. Verhoeven also referred to it as "illusoire formule magique." J Verhoeven, 'La reconnaissance internationale, déclin ou renouveau?' (1993) 39 AFDI 7, 39. It is possible to agree with Christakis that the efficacy of the rule should not justify its existence, and that even though to claim that the duty of non-recognition was the sole cause of the collapses of illegal regimes would not be correct, "il serait aussi fallacieux de ne pas admettre sa contribution importante dans un grand nombre de cas." Christakis, 'L'obligation de non-reconnaissance' (n 44) 133.

74 Talmon, 'The Duty Not "To Recognize as Lawful"' (n 4) 103–104; *Wall* (n 4) Separate Opinion of Judge Kooijmans, para 44. Kassoti and Duval (n 4) 7.

75 Aust (n 70) 327; ARSIWA (n 41), art 41(2). See *infra* for the instances of practice.

76 *Namibia* (n 33) para 121. "It not only refers to the formal recognition of these situations, but also prohibits acts which would imply such recognition." ARSIWA (n 41) commentary to art 41, para 5. A contrary opinion was presented by Petrén "[I]n the international law of today, non-recognition has obligatory negative effects in only a very limited sector of governmental acts of a somewhat symbolic nature." *Namibia* (n 33), Separate Opinion of Judge Petrén, 134. Talmon points to the drafting history of the term 'recognition as legal' in the Friendly Relations Declaration, and later in the Definition of Aggression, as limiting the scope of non-recognition to formal recognition only. Even Talmon admits that the subsequent practice shows a more expansive reading of this obligation than "the prohibition of a formal admission of legality." Talmon, 'The Duty Not "To Recognize as Lawful"' (n 4) 108–112.

the duty's scope.[77] The core idea is that "certain dealings with an illegal regime will condone its exercise of jurisdiction and will thus help to consolidate its title over a given territory."[78] However, this obligation is not absolute and allows for exceptions.[79] Crawford even refers to its "inherent flexibility."[80] According to the ICJ, there are acts that "may imply recognition"; thus, *a contrario* suggests that there are acts that do not imply such an outcome and, therefore, are permitted.[81] Moreover, even acts that would normally fall within the duty's scope will be exempted if the criteria outlined by the ICJ are met. In light of the existing State practice and *opinio iuris*, the section below outlines the content of the duty in more detail.

4.1.3 Duty of Non-assistance

The goal of the duty of non-assistance "is to ensure that a State does not benefit from outside help in maintaining the unlawful state of affairs."[82] The prohibition could have "significant trade-related or financial repercussions for the wrongdoing State."[83] "What amounts to aid or assistance will depend on legal, political, economic and other contexts"[84] and will be discussed below. The

---

77 See Talmon, 'The Duty Not "To Recognize as Lawful"' (n 4) 112.

78 Aust (n 70) 330.

79 According to Raič, the League of Nations' policy of absolute non-recognition of all acts by Manchukuo, without any leeway for the "occurrence of practical necessities requiring some form of cognition," was probably "one of the gravest mistakes the League made." D Raič, *Statehood and the Law of Self-Determination* (Kluwer Law International 2002) 159.

80 "In my opinion, the obligation has an inherent flexibility that will permit (or, at least, not expressly prohibit) the acceptance of acts which do not purport to secure or enhance territorial claims, but which as a result of their commercial, minor administrative or 'routine' character, or which are of immediate benefit to the population, should be regarded as 'untainted' by the illegality of the administration. The 'population' in this respect is the local Palestinian population, not the settlers. Examples of such 'untainted' acts could include the registration of a birth or the sale of milk from a local settlement store (whether to settlers or Palestinian persons)." Crawford, Opinion (n 64), para 51. Raič also points out that it is "tenable" that "specific forms of cooperation and the recognition of specific acts is allowed to the extent these cannot be dispensed with without severe humanitarian consequences for the inhabitants of the entity, and insofar as such cooperation or recognition cannot be interpreted to imply the recognition or validation of the original illegality." Raič (n 79) 164.

81 Talmon, 'The Duty Not "To Recognize as Lawful"' (n 4) 114.

82 Costelloe, *Legal Consequences of Peremptory Norms in International Law* (n 55) 207; Orakhelashvili, *Peremptory Norms in International Law* (n 14) 282–283.

83 Costelloe, *Legal Consequences of Peremptory Norms in International Law* (n 55) 212.

84 ibid 207. However, according to the ICJ, "recognizing the immunity of a foreign State in accordance with customary international law does not amount to recognizing as lawful a situation created by the breach of a jus cogens rule, or rendering aid and assistance in

ICJ found this duty applicable in the context of Israeli's violation of the right of self-determination and ensuing an illegal situation.[85] It is of a customary nature.[86] While in certain aspects the duty of non-assistance can overlap with the sanctions regime under Article 39 UN Charter,[87] the legal basis and scope of the sanctions regime and the duty of non-assistance are not identical.[88] Its relationship to a general regime of complicity is critical for the understanding of its connection to the duty of non-recognition.

4.1.3.1 *General and Special Regime of Complicity*

The duty of non-assistance in Article 41(2) ARSIWA and Article 16 ARSIWA "express a common principle."[89] However, first, both types of complicity require the breach of different types of obligation on the part of the assisted State. While a general regime applies to the commission of any international wrongful act, prohibition under Article 41(2) ARSIWA only follows after the serious breach of a peremptory norm.

Second, complicity under Article 41(2) ARSIWA refers to the situation "after the fact" and "extends beyond the commission of the serious breach itself to the maintenance of the situation created by that breach, and it applies whether or not the breach itself is a continuing one."[90] Article 41(2) ARSIWA is particularly relevant to the situation of an illegal secessionist entity.[91] Thus, in this

---

maintaining that situation, and so cannot contravene the principle in Article 41 of the International Law Commission's Articles on State Responsibility." According to the Court, "[t]he two sets of rules address different matters." *Jurisdictional Immunities of the State (Germany v Italy: Greece intervening)* (Merits) [2012] ICJ Rep 99, para 93.

85 *Wall* (n 4) para 159.

86 Villalpando (n 49) 389.

87 Costelloe, *Legal Consequences of Peremptory Norms in International Law* (n 55) 208.

88 ibid 208–212. On the one hand, collective sanctions are institutional; they need not be taken in response to a serious breach of peremptory norms and can cover a broad range of activities. ibid. On the other hand, the duty of non-assistance is mandatory under general international law and therefore can substitute for a potential lack of action on the side of the UNSC due to political blockage. ibid. Outside the UNSC resolution, if a State or international organisation does render aid or assistance that goes to maintaining a situation flowing from a breach of peremptory norms, it violates Article 41(2) ARSIWA itself. Lanovoy (n 53) 115. NHB Jorgensen, 'The Obligation of Non-Assistance to the Responsible State' in J Crawford and others, *The Law of International Responsibility* (OUP 2010) 692. "In this situation, the secondary norm may be de facto operating as if it were a primary one." Lanovoy (n 53) 115.

89 Aust (n 70) 336. See *infra*.

90 ARSIWA (n 41) commentary to art 41, para 11.

91 See also Milano, *Unlawful Territorial Situations in International Law* (n 20) 173–174.

context, both articles apply because the applicability of Article 16 ARSIWA "is not excluded by the fact that the aid or assistance is rendered continuously."[92]

Third, even though the ILC refers to Article 16 ARSIWA for the elements of "aid or assistance" under Article 41(2) ARSIWA, the two regimes are not identical.[93] Thus, it is necessary to briefly outline the key elements of aid or assistance under Article 16 ARSIWA. Specifically, Article 16 ARSIWA requires the fulfilment of the material element, subjective element and the opposability rule.[94]

Regarding the subjective element, Article 16 ARSIWA requires that the State aids or assists in the commission of an internationally wrongful act if it does so "with knowledge of the circumstances of the internationally wrongful act."[95] However, the commentary on this issue is rather confusing, referring also to a higher threshold of intent.[96] Concerning the complicity under

---

92 Aust (n 70) 338. See Crawford, Opinion (n 64) para 75.

93 ARSIWA (n 41) commentary to art 41, para 11.

94 "First, the relevant State organ or agency providing aid or assistance must be aware of the circumstances making the conduct of the assisted State internationally wrongful; secondly, the aid or assistance must be given with a view to facilitating the commission of that act, and must actually do so; and thirdly, the completed act must be such that it would have been wrongful had it been committed by the assisting State itself." ARSIWA (n 41) commentary to art 16, para 3. However, art 16 ARSIWA contains only two explicit conditions for triggering responsibility for complicity.

95 ARSIWA (n 41) art 16 (a).

96 "Commentaries are not of much assistance on these questions, mixing the standards of knowledge, intent, and the knowledge of intent." Lanovoy (n 53) 222. The ILC firstly states that "[i]f the assisting or aiding State is *unaware of the circumstances* in which its aid or assistance is intended to be used by the other State, it bears no international responsibility." ARSIWA (n 41) commentary to art 16, para 4 (*emphasis added*). But in the following text, the ILC states that art 16 ARSIWA requires "the aid or assistance must be given with a view to facilitating the commission of the wrongful act, and must actually do so … a State is not responsible for aid or assistance unless the relevant State organ *intended* by the aid or assistance given, to facilitate the occurrence of the wrongful conduct." ARSIWA (n 41) commentary to art 16, para 5 (*emphasis added*). However, "[t]he 'knowledge of the circumstances' requires a more flexible link as opposed to the standard of intent." Lanovoy (n 53) 227. In fact, the latter standard "is sufficient to eclipse entirely the requirement of knowledge, as an overt intention to assist presupposes knowledge of assistance." J Crawford, *State Responsibility: The General Part* (CUP 2013) 407. This incoherence in the text of the commentaries seems to reflect an internal division within the ILC during the codification process. See Lanovoy (n 53) 102–103; Aust (n 70) 232–235. On the one hand, according to Lanovoy, "the requirement of intent is unnecessary and overly restrictive in the general regime of responsibility for complicity." Lanovoy (n 53) 103 and 240. On the other hand, according to Aust, "[a] complicity provision without an intent requirement would arguably move the provision very close to responsibility for lawful behaviour." Aust (n 70) 239 and see 237–249. "[T]o be responsible by way of complicity, the State concerned must have intended, by the aid or assistance given, to facilitate the occurrence

Article 41(2) ARSIWA, the ILC explicitly dispensed with the requirement of "knowledge of the circumstances of the internationally wrongful act", "as it is hardly conceivable that a State would not have noticed of the commission of a serious breach by another State."[97] Even though the ILC did not specifically mention intent in this context, scholars agree that the ILC's statement referred to a complete dispensation with the requirement of a subjective element.[98]

Regarding the material element, under Article 16 ARSIWA "[t]here is no requirement that the aid or assistance should have been essential to the performance of the internationally wrongful act; it is sufficient if it *contributed significantly* to that act."[99] Nevertheless, the ILC "did not provide any examples as to what this 'contributed significantly' standard actually means"[100] and in another part of the commentaries, it rather confusingly referred to the fact that "the assistance may have been only an incidental factor in the commission of the primary act, and may have contributed only to a minor degree, if at all, to the injury suffered."[101] Various authors agree that some type of factual or causal connection between the aid and assistance and the wrongful conduct must be present, but they diverge in the precise delimitation of the relevant criterion.[102]

---

of the wrongful conduct." Crawford, Opinion (n 64) para 77. ibid (*footnotes omitted*). See *Case Concerning Application of the Convention on the Prevention and Punishment of the Crime of Genocide* (*Bosnia and Herzegovina v Serbia and Montenegro*) (Mertis) [2007] ICJ Rep 43, para 421.

97 ARSIWA (n 41) commentary to art 41, para 11. Aust (n 70) 341–342.

98 Lanovoy (n 53) 115–116; H Moynihan, *Aiding and Assisting: Challenges in Armed Conflict and Counterterrorism* (Chatham House 2016) 22. Crawford, in his Opinion on Israeli Settlements, held that it "is not sufficient that the US supplies Israel with bulldozers which are subsequently utilised in the unlawful destruction of private property during construction of the Wall – the US must *know* and *intend* that those bulldozers are to be used in such a way." Crawford, Opinion (n 64) para 77 (*footnotes omitted*) (*emphasis added*). But in the context of a breach of peremptory norm of self-determination, which is at stake with respect to the construction of the Wall, it is misplaced to require knowledge and intent. Such a high threshold would seem to go against the purpose of the aggravated regime of responsibility, as the duty of non-assistance would be inadequately narrowed down.

99 ARSIWA (n 41) commentary to art 16, para 5 and see para 10. (*emphasis added*). See Aust (n 70) 197.

100 Lanovoy (n 53) 97.

101 ARSIWA (n 41) commentary to art 16, para 10. See Aust (n 70) 197.

102 Aust claims that a material element in this context does not in fact require a "causal" connection in a technical sense, but the relevant consideration should be that "the support must have made some difference for the main actor in carrying out its deed." Aust (n 70) 215 and 340. "In order to find responsibility of a complicit State, its support should

Nevertheless, it would seem to be below the threshold of 'a significant contribution.'[103]

Transposition of these unclear rationales to the context of Article 41(2) ARSIWA[104] leads to the conclusion that the connection between aid or assistance and the maintenance of an illegal situation does not need to be particularly stringent. According to Aust, because a material element under Article 16 ARSIWA is not "too demanding," "it would be problematic to further loosen these ties" with respect to the obligation under Article 41(2) ARSIWA.[105] Lanovoy claims that the aid or assistance under Article 41(2) ARSIWA "need not significantly contribute to the maintenance of the situation flowing from the serious breach of a peremptory norm."[106]

4.1.3.2 *Interplay with the Duty of Non-recognition*

It can be agreed with Aust that because the duty of non-recognition is conceptualised as covering "a potentially unlimited range of measures which can imply recognition," it can be seen as similar or even in competition with the duty of non-assistance.[107] Some authors claim that recognition always constitutes

---

have changed the situation for the main actor. It must have made it 'substantially' easier to commit the internationally wrongful act." ibid 215. "[I]t appears that the test is not direct causation or a 'but for' test, but that some causative connection is required." Moynihan (n 98) 8. "[A] clear factual or causal link between complicity and the commission of the principal wrongful act is sufficient." Lanovoy (n 53) 218. Similarly, Crawford, *State Responsibility* (n 96) 402.

103 "[T]here is relatively little practice and opinio juris that would require the showing of a particularly stringent link between complicity and the principal wrongful act such as, for example, one of significantly contributing to the wrongful act." Lanovoy (n 53) 218. Aust (n 70) 340. Contra: Crawford, *State Responsibility* (n 96) 403 and 405. Moynihan argues in favour of the connection to a significant contribution. Moynihan (n 98) 7–8.

104 The ILC stipulated that "[a]s to the elements of 'aid or assistance', article 41 is to be read in connection with article 16." Unlike with respect to a subjective element, however, it did not provide any other direction. ARSIWA (n 41) commentary to art 41, para 11.

105 Aust (n 70) 340. "The requisite impact of the aid or assistance cannot be measured as to its effect upon the commission of the wrongful act, but with respect to its contribution to the maintenance of the situation brought about by the serious breach." ibid.

106 Lanovoy (n 53) 116–117. Lanovoy claims that this is justified since the duty of non-assistance under Article 41(2) ARSIWA refers "to the maintenance of the situation brought about by the serious breach rather than the circumstances of the wrongful act which is yet to be committed." ibid 117; A Boivin, 'Complicity and Beyond: International Law and the Transfer of Small Arms and Light Weapons' (2005) 87 International Review of the Red Cross 467, 493.

107 Aust (n 70) 332. "Does for example, the financing by foreign States of a web of new roads in the occupied Palestinian territory, made necessary by the construction of the wall and the Israeli settlements in the West Bank, imply recognition of the illegal situation resulting from the construction of the wall? Or does it simply aid and assist in maintaining the situation created by the wall?" Talmon, 'The Duty Not "To Recognize as Lawful"' (n 4) 106.

a form of assistance and, therefore, the latter subsumes the former.[108] Other scholars see non-assistance as a more specialised form of non-recognition when the former can be deduced from the latter.[109] The ILC regards the duty of non-assistance "as a logical extension of the duty of non-recognition."[110]

However, the duty of non-assistance under Article 41(2) ARSIWA entails "a certain factual and 'causal' connection between the support rendered and the maintenance of the situation brought about the serious breach."[111] Therefore, "the category of non-recognition is wider than that of complicity."[112] According to Costelloe, "the obligation of non-assistance can be more concrete than the obligation of collective non-recognition, which may take the shape of little more than a policy statement."[113]

Thus, a critical question arises as to which measures would not imply recognition,[114] but at the same time would still be prohibited under Article 41(2) ARSIWA. Despite some positive doctrinal views[115] and the ILC's statement that the duty of non-assistance "has a separate scope of application insofar as actions are concerned which would not imply recognition",[116] it is difficult to see separate space for the independent application of the duty of non-assistance. This is because in the area of economic and other forms of relationship or dealings recognition is implied when these dealings "may entrench" the authority of an illegal entity over the territory.[117] It is difficult to see to what extent the criterion of 'entrenchment' of an illegal entity's authority over the territory is different from any of above-mentioned criteria of the material element of aid or assistance under Article 41(2) ARSIWA. In conclusion, because of a rather broad understanding of the duty of non-recognition, the difference between the two duties is more apparent than real. For this reason, the following account primarily focuses on the duty of non-recognition.

---

108 AL Paulus, 'Jus Cogens in a Time of Hegemony and Fragmentation' 74 (2005) Nordic Journal of International Law 297, 315. See Aust (n 70) 334 and Lanovoy (n 53) 108–109.

109 Villalpando (n 49) 389. See Aust (n 70) 334–335.

110 ARSIWA (n 41) commentary to art 41, para 12.

111 Aust (n 70) 336.

112 ibid.

113 Costelloe, *Legal Consequences of Peremptory Norms in International Law* (n 55) 212. In agreement is Lanovoy (n 53) 109. Similarly, Aust (n 70) 337.

114 *Namibia* (n 33) para 124 and see *infra*.

115 "[S]ome measures of concrete support for the maintenance of the situation brought about by the serious breach will not be identifiable as recognition of a legal situation. Nonetheless, they have the potential to entrench the unlawful state of affairs." Aust (n 70) 337.

116 ARSIWA (n 41) commentary to art 41, para 12.

117 *Namibia* (n 33) para 124.

4.2 *Specific Content*

For the content of the duty of non-recognition, the reference point must be the *Namibia* Advisory Opinion, in which the ICJ held that it will

> confine itself to giving advice on those dealings with the Government of South Africa which, under the Charter of the United Nations and general international law, should be considered as inconsistent with the declaration of illegality and invalidity in paragraph 2 of resolution 276 (1970), because they may imply a recognition that South Africa's presence in Namibia is legal.[118]

The following account will follow the categorisation introduced therein.

4.2.1 Selected Relations at Purportedly Inter-State Level

4.2.1.1 *Treaty Relations*

According to several authors, "the impermissibility of treaty relations is one of the few non-controversial elements of the customary obligation of non-recognition."[119] Indeed, according to the PCIJ, "the right of entering into international engagements is an attribute of State sovereignty."[120] "In sum, there is an intimate link between treaty-making capacity and territorial sovereignty."[121] Because treaty relations are only limited to sovereign States, they are "inapplicable when the status of sovereignty is denied."[122] "Acquisition of territory usually entails the extension of the territorial scope of existing treaties for the

118 According to the ICJ, "[t]he precise determination of the acts permitted or allowed" is within the competence of the political organs of the United Nations. *Namibia* (n 33) para 120. However, the fact that some matter is within the competence of certain organs does not mean, as suggested by Pert, that "*only* the resolution of an organ such as the Security Council, or the ICJ when called upon, can provide the necessary detail of what the obligation practically entails in any given situation." Pert (n 24) 65. Similarly, Talmon points out that a previously cited passage in an advisory opinion "does not relate to the obligation of non-recognition but, generally, to the appropriate measures to be taken by the United Nations and its member States to bring the illegal situation to an end." Talmon, 'The Duty Not "To Recognize as Lawful"' (n 4) 113.

119 Ronen, *Transition from Illegal Regimes under International Law* (n 13) 73.

120 *Case of the SS "Wimbledon" (Britain et al v Germany)* (Merits) [1923] PCIJ Rep Series A No 1, 25.

121 M Dawidowicz, 'Trading Fish or Human Rights in Western Sahara? Self-Determination, Non-Recognition and the EC-Morocco Fisheries Agreement' in D French (ed), *Statehood and self-determination: reconciling tradition and modernity in international law* (CUP 2013) 267.

122 Ronen, *Transition from Illegal Regimes under International Law* (n 13) 73.

acquired territory. … [i]n the case of illegal acquisition of territory, these rights are to be denied."[123] Indeed, any claim of an illegal occupant to the treaty-making capacity concerning occupied territory must be seen as a legal claim to sovereignty and, therefore, "extending the territorial scope of an agreement to an unlawfully acquired territory would certainly amount to breach of a third party's … obligation of non-recognition."[124]

4.2.1.1.1 Conclusion of Treaties with Illegal Entities

Without any doubt, entering into bilateral or multilateral treaties with an illegal secessionist entity in which it would be accorded the status of State violates the duty of non-recognition because this step would imply the entity's recognition as a State. Such a treaty would also be non-existent under international law owing to the lack of statehood of one party.[125] Peters highlights "any contractual expression of will should be regarded as *ipso iure* null and without effect, because the entity unlawfully created is devoid of legal capacity."[126]

However, a limited practice regarding the conclusion of agreement-like documents with illegal secessionist entities can be ascertained. This typically includes the signing of documents such as protocols, memoranda and the like in the area of conflict resolution where the denomination of documents and its parties precludes any conclusion as to the implied recognition of the entity as a State. This area is also linked with certain limited functional cooperation, which is allowed under the duties of non-recognition and non-assistance and is discussed below. The conclusion of agreements governed by international law in which entities are not accorded the status of statehood, such as ceasefire agreements, would not contradict the duty of non-recognition.

4.2.1.1.2 Extension of Occupant's Treaties to Illegally Occupied and Annexed Territories

Under *Namibia,* entering into treaties with an unlawful occupant concerning an occupied territory would breach the duty of non-recognition.[127] Such

123 Talmon, 'The Duty Not "To Recognize as Lawful"' (n 4) 117.

124 E Kassoti, 'The EU's Duty of Non-Recognition and the Territorial Scope of Trade Agreements Covering Unlawfully Acquired Territories' (2019) Europe and the World: A Law Review 1, 6. Kassoti and Duval (n 4) 7.

125 See *supra*.

126 A Peters, 'Statehood after 1989: "Effectivités" between Legality and Virtuality' (2010) 3 Proceedings of the European Society of International Law 171, 176.

127 *Namibia* (n 33) para 122. "The European Union expresses its commitment to ensure that – in line with international law – all agreements between the State of Israel and the European Union must unequivocally and explicitly indicate their inapplicability to the

treaties would also be invalid due to the lack of a treaty-making capacity concerning the occupied territory.[128] The same prohibition applies to the invocation of the previously existing bilateral and multilateral treaties, subject to "certain general conventions such as those of a humanitarian character, the non-performance of which may adversely affect" the people of unlawfully occupied territory.[129] Not only the formal conclusion of treaties extending to illegally occupied territories, but also the actual application of treaties to these territories implies recognition, and thus violates the duty.[130]

Moreover, the duty of non-recognition in this respect overlaps with other areas of general international law. First, it fits with the law of occupation based on which the Occupying Power does not have a treaty-making capacity concerning the occupied territory.[131] In addition, it aligns with Article 6 VCST, which precludes the applicability of 'the moving treaty-frontiers rule' as reflected in Article 15 VCST[132] to illegal annexations.[133] Similarly, it matches a

territories occupied by Israel in 1967, namely the Golan Heights, the West Bank including East Jerusalem, and the Gaza Strip." Council of the European Union, '3209th Council Meeting Foreign Affairs Brussels' (10 December 2012) PR CO 72. It is notorious that the ICJ ruled that it had no jurisdiction in the *East Timor* case, as it would have required ruling on Indonesia's presence in East Timor, which it could not do without Indonesia's consent. In his dissenting opinion, judge Skubiszewski pointed out that, by entering into the Timor Gap Treaty, Australia violated the obligation of non-recognition, which could have been decided upon regardless of Indonesia's consent. However, the ICJ did not proceed in such a way. East Timor (n 20), Dissenting Opinion of Judge Skubiszewski, paras 122–133. Ronen, *Transition from Illegal Regimes under International Law* (n 13) 149–150.

128 See *supra*.

129 *Namibia* (n 33) para 122. Ronen pointed out that this exception might have been specifically motivated by the fact that, at the time of the *Namibia* advisory opinion, the application of human rights treaties was seen as territorially bound. On the other hand, humanitarian law, both customary and conventional, was applied extraterritorially. Ronen, *Transition from Illegal Regimes under International Law* (n 13) 74–77. See *infra* in detail.

130 See Milano, 'The New Fisheries Partnership Agreement' (n 20) 444.

131 T Ferraro, *Expert Meeting: Occupation and Other Forms of Administration of Foreign Territory* (ICRC 2012) 59–61. Regarding limitations on treaty-making capacity of administering power with respect to NSGT, see Milano, 'The New Fisheries Partnership Agreement' (n 20) 430–431 and 436.

132 According to art 15 VCST, which covers succession in respect to parts of a territory, from the date of succession, treaties of the predecessor State cease to be in force and treaties of the successor State are in force unless exceptions provided therein are applicable. VCST (n 5) art 15.

133 "This article, like the draft articles as a whole, has to be read in conjunction with article 6 which limits the present articles to lawful situations ... Article 14 is limited to normal changes in the sovereignty or in the responsibility for the international relations of a territory." ILC, Yearbook of International Law Commission (1974) vol II, part one, 209, para 3.

rule on the territorial application of the treaties in Article 29 VCLT according to which unless a different intention is established, a treaty is binding upon each party concerning its entire territory.[134]

All these provisions understand the term 'territory' as territory over which the State holds a legal title. According to the ILC's commentary to Article 14 VCST (now Article 15 VCST), the moving treaty-frontiers rule entails that "at any given time a State is bound by a treaty in respect of any territory of which it is *sovereign*."[135] Even though the VCLT does not contain limitation akin to Article 6 VCST, the ILC's commentary strongly implies that the applicability of Article 29 only extends to *de jure* territory.[136]

> It would be straining the text to an impermissible extent to read into this provision an exception to the otherwise only *de jure* character of 'territory,' since that term cannot by itself sustain a reading that includes annexed territory.[137]

In Dumberry's view since the VCLT is a fundamental multilateral treaty, the ordinary meaning of the term 'territory' used in its provision "should not be understood as including a territory under occupation which has been illegally annexed by the use of force."[138] Recently, in *Ukraine v Russia* (*re Crimea*), the European Court of Human Rights (ECtHR) – when assessing the scope of territorial jurisdiction under Article 1 of the European Convention on Human Rights (ECHR) – relied on Article 29 VCLT.[139] It follows from the ECtHR's approach to

134 "Unless a different intention appears from the treaty or is otherwise established, a treaty is binding upon each party in respect of its entire territory." Vienna Convention on the Law of Treaties (adopted 23 May 1969, entered into force 27 January 1980) 1155 UNTS 331, art 29 ("VCLT").

135 ILC, Yearbook of International Law Commission (1974) vol II, part one, 208, para 6 (*emphasis added*).

136 Costelloe, 'Treaty Succession in Annexed Territory' (n 10) 350. According to Waldock, "[t]he rule that a treaty is to be presumed to apply with respect to all the territories under the sovereignty of the contracting parties means that each State must make its intention plain, expressly or by implication, in any case where it does not intend to enter into the engagements of the treaty on behalf of and with respect to all its territory." ILC, Yearbook of International Law Commission (1964), vol II, 13, para 4.

137 Costelloe, 'Treaty Succession in Annexed Territory' (n 10) 358. See M Milanović, 'The Spatial Dimension: Treaties and Territory' in CJ Tams and AE Richford (eds), *Research Handbook on the Law of Treaties* (E Elgar 2014) 187.

138 Dumberry (n 8) 215.

139 *Russia v Ukraine* (*re Crimea*) App nos 20958/14 and 38334/18 (ECtHR, 16 December 2020) para 345.

this issue that it understood the notion of "entire territory" to entail the sovereign territory of State Parties to the ECHR.[140]

Even though these articles create a presumption in favour of territorial application, as a matter of principle, they do not exclude a treaty's extraterritorial application.[141] Today, it is accepted that human rights treaties apply extraterritorially to occupied and annexed territories.[142] However, this extraterritoriality is not due to the expansion of the meaning of the term of territory.[143] Human rights treaties are applied extraterritorially with reference to the notion of jurisdiction and their object and purpose.[144]

In this context, in prominent and rather well researched cases[145] of the European Communities-Israel Association Agreement[146] and the EU-Morocco

---

140 ibid para 348. See how the Court applied this understanding to determine the nature of Russia's jurisdiction under Article 1 ECHR over Crimea from 18 March 2014 as extraterritorial, ie the exercise of effective control beyond its borders. See *infra* Part 2, Chapter 17.

141 "In its [Commission's] view, the law regarding the extra-territorial application of treaties could not be stated simply in terms of the intention of parties or of a presumption as to their intention; and it considered that to attempt to deal with all the delicate problems of extra-territorial competence in the present Article would be inappropriate and inadvisable." ILC, Yearbook of International Law Commission (1966), vol II, 213–214, para 5. Costelloe, 'Treaty Succession in Annexed Territory' (n 10) 359; Milanović (n 137) 191.

142 Dumberry (n 8) 216.

143 Milanović (n 137) 189. Costelloe argues that it neither narrows nor broadens the territorial application of treaties compared to Articles 15 VCST and Article 29 VCLT. Costelloe, 'Treaty Succession in Annexed Territory' (n 10) 371.

144 See *infra* in detail, Chapter 8. Milanović (n 137) 189; Costelloe, 'Treaty Succession in Annexed Territory' (n 10) 359–363 and 367–373.

145 International scholarship has examined these issues extensively. C Ryngaert and R Fransen, 'EU Extraterritorial Obligations with Respect to Trade with Occupied Territories: Reflections after the Case of Front Polisario before EU Courts' (2018) 2 Europe and the World: A Law Review 1; E Kassoti, 'The Empire Strikes Back: The Council Decision Amending Protocols 1 and 4 to the EU-Morocco Association Agreement' (2019) 4 European Papers Insight 307; Kassoti, 'The EU's Duty of Non-Recognition' (n 124) 1; E Kassoti, *The Legality under International Law of the EU's Trade Agreements Covering Occupied Territories: A Comparative Study of Palestine and Western Sahara* (Asser Institute 2017) 22–55.

146 This agreement applies "to the territory of the State of Israel." Euro-Mediterranean Agreement Establishing an Association between the European Communities and their Member States, of the One Part, and the State of Israel, of the Other Part [2000] OJ L 147/3, art 83. For the development before the Brita judgment, see G Harpaz, 'The Dispute Over the Treatment of Products Exported to the European Union from the Golan Heights, East Jerusalem, the West Bank and the Gaza Strip – The Limits of Power and the Limits of the Law' (2004) 38 Journal of World Trade 1049.

agreements,[147] the CJEU ruled that these agreements did not apply to the Occupied Palestinian Territory (OPT)[148] and Western Sahara respectively.[149] It is certainly true that the CJEU never explicitly referred to the obligation of non-recognition in these judgments[150] and its selective determination of

147 The EU-Morocco Association Agreement applies to the "territory of the Kingdom of Morocco." Euro-Mediterranean Agreement Establishing an Association between the European Communities and their Member States, of the One Part, and the Kingdom of Morocco, of the Other Part [2000] OJ L 70/2, art 94 ("EU-Morocco Association Agreement"). The Agreement in the Form of an Exchange of Letters between the European Union and the Kingdom of Morocco Concerning Reciprocal Liberalisation Measures on Agricultural Products, Processed Agricultural Products, Fish and Fishery Products, the Replacement of Protocols No 1, 2 and 3 and their Annexes and Amendments to the Euro-Mediterranean Agreement Establishing an Association between the European Communities and Their Member States, of the One Part, and the Kingdom of Morocco, of the Other Part [2012] OJ L 241/4 ("EU-Morocco Liberalisation Agreement"). The FPA applies to the "territory of Morocco and to the waters under Moroccan jurisdiction." Fisheries Partnership Agreement between the European Community and the Kingdom of Morocco [2006] OJ L 141/4, art 11 ("FPA"). Protocol between the European Union and the Kingdom of Morocco Setting out the Fishing Opportunities and Financial Contribution Provided for in the Fisheries Partnership Agreement between the European Union and the Kingdom of Morocco [2013] OJ L 328/2. Euro-Mediterranean Aviation Agreement between the European Community and its Member States, of the One Part, and the Kingdom of Morocco, of the Other Part [2006] OJ L 386/57 ("Aviation Agreement"). However, apart from the practice of the EU, it is worth noting that, while the Morocco-Russia Fisheries agreement is interpreted as extending to the waters of Western Sahara, the Morocco-EFTA Liberalisation Agreement and the US-Morocco free trade agreement are interpreted as excluding Western Sahara from their scope. RF De Vries, 'EU Judicial Review of Trade Agreements Involving Disputed Territories: Lessons from the Front Polisario Judgments' (2018) 24 Columbia Journal of European Law 497, 521; Milano, 'The New Fisheries Partnership Agreement' (n 20) 445 ftn 112; E Kontorovich, Economic Dealings with Occupied Territories' (2014) 53 Columbia Journal of Transnational Law 584, 635–636.

148 Case C-386/08 *Brita v Hauptzollamt Hamburg-Hafen* [2010] ECR I-01289 ("Brita").

149 Case C-104/16 P *Council v Front Polisario Front populaire pour la libération de la saguia-el-hara et du rio de oro (Front Polisario)* [2016] ECLI:EU:C:2016:973 ("Front Polisario") concerned the scope of EU-Morocco Association Agreement and EU-Morocco Liberalisation Agreement; Case C-266/16 *The Queen, on the Application of Western Sahara Campaign UK v Commissioners for Her Majesty's Revenue and Customs, Secretary of State, Food and Rural Affairs* [2018] ECLI:EU:C:2018:118 ("Western Sahara Campaign") concerned the scope of the FPA and its 2013 Protocol; Case T-275/18 *Front populaire pour la libération de la saguia-el-hara et du rio de oro (Front Polisario) v Council of the European Union* [2018] ECLI:EU:T:2018:869 concerned the Order of the General Court on the scope of the Aviation Agreement.

150 However, Advocate General Wathelet opined that the inclusion of Western Sahara into the FPA violates the duty of non-recognition and non-assistance. Western Sahara Campaign (n 149), Opinion of Advocate General Wathelet (10 January 2018), paras 187–213. See also the opinion of the Advocate General in the *Front Polisario* case, where he

applicable international law,[151] its unorthodox approach to interpretation and

---

opined that the application of trade agreements to Western Sahara implies recognition. *Front Polisario* (n 149), Opinion of Advocate General Wathelet (13 September 2016), paras 83–86. P Wrange, 'Western Sahara, the European Commission and the Politics of International Legal Argument' (2019) <https://papers.ssrn.com/sol3/papers.cfm?abstract_id=3507037> accessed 3 February 2020, 16–17. Kontorovich, 'Economic Dealings with Occupied Territories' (n 147) 597.

151 With respect to the *Front Polisario* case, Ryngaert and Fransen criticize the EU courts for defining the applicable law only in terms of the right to self-determination and law applicable to NSGT. "In case of occupation and breaches of peremptory norms of international law, it does not suffice to rely on the right to self-determination only for purposes of treaty interpretation, or of determining the extraterritorial reach of EU fundamental rights. Rather, the EU and its courts should observe all rules of international law that are relevant to the situation at hand." Ryngaert and Fransen (n 145) 2. This approach originated in the so-called Correl letter, in which the UN Under-Secretary-General for Legal Affairs analysed agreements between Morocco and certain foreign companies for exploration of mineral resources in Western Sahara only by analogy with the law applicable to the NSGT, despite Morocco not having the legal status of administering power in Western Sahara. The Corell letter did not mention the law of occupation or the duty of non-recognition. 'Letter Dated 29 January 2002 from the Under-Secretary-General for Legal Affairs, the Legal Counsel, Addressed to the President of the Security Council' (12 February 2002) S/2002/161. See on this point, H Corell, 'The Legality of Exploring and Exploiting Natural Resources in Western Sahara' in (2008) Western Sahara Conference Proceedings 231, 238. The Legal Service of both the EU Parliament and the EU Council then used the same approach and defined Morocco's position as a de facto administering power. See European Parliament (Legal Service), 'Legal Opnion' (20 February 2006) SJ-0085/06, para 37; European Parliament (Legal Service), 'Legal Opnion' (4 November 2013) SJ-0665/13, paras 12 and paras 17–18; However, there is no such a legal status as a de facto administering power in international law. In this respect, one can agree with the Opinion of Advocate General Wathelet, according to which "that [Corell] letter cannot serve as a basis for the existence, in international law, of the concept of 'de facto administering power', in particular with respect to the question of the conclusion of international agreements which, unlike the signature of contracts with private companies, is 'an attribute of … sovereignty.'" Western Sahara Campaign (n 149) Opinion of Advocate General Wathelet (10 January 2018), para 232. See also Kassoti and Duval (n 4) 14–16. For scholarly analyses of Morocco's position as the Occupying Power, see E Kassoti, 'The ECJ and the Art of Treaty Interpretation: Western Sahara Campaign UK' (2019) Common Market Law Review 209, 212; B Saul, 'The Status of Western Sahara as Occupied Territory under International Humanitarian Law and the Exploitation of Natural Resources' (2015) 27 Global Change, Peace and Security 301, 305–316; See also *infra* section on trade. Even though, under occupation law, the rules of usufruct do apply, Milano argues that "they should be interpreted in light of other applicable rules, such as that of permanent sovereignty over natural resources in NSGTs, hence to prohibit any exploitation of natural resources which is not conducted for the benefit and is not in accordance with the wishes of the local population." Milano, 'The New Fisheries Partnership Agreement' (n 20) 449. Similarly, "[i]n the absence of consent from the people of Western Sahara, Morocco does not have treaty-making capacity and cannot exploit the natural resources of the territory." Dawidowicz (n 121) 273. According to another view,

its use of the principle of *pacta tertiis*[152] was at a minimum unconvincing,[153] but in their underlying assumptions and outcomes, these judgments fit well with the scope of the duty of non-recognition in the area of treaty relations and trade.[154]

However, commentators[155] have shown that it is especially the CJEU's selective approach and omission of the analysis of the duties of non-recognition and non-assistance that provided the EU with a legal ground to later amend its Association Agreement with Morocco to explicitly cover the products originating in Western Sahara upon the consent of the people of Western Sahara[156] and to adopt a new Sustainable Fisheries Partnership Agreement that explicitly

---

"limitations on the conduct of an occupying power in occupied territories that follow from the law of occupation are, however, not substantially different from the rules related to Non-Self-Governing Territories." M Brus, 'The Legality of Exploring and Exploiting Mineral Resources in Western Sahara' in K Arts and P Leite Pinto (eds), *International Law and the Question of Western Sahara* (IPJET 2006) 207. Wrange argues that the law governing the administration of the NSGTs and the law of occupation are converging in certain aspects. P Wrange, 'Self-Determination, Occupation and the Authority to Exploit Natural Resources: Trajectories from Four European Judgments on Western Sahara' (2019) 52 Israel Law Review 3.

152 For an excellent comment on the Western Sahara Campaign case, see Kassoti, 'The ECJ and the Art of Treaty Interpretation' (n 151) 220–236.

153 See E Kassoti, *Trading with Settlements: The International Obligations of the European Union with Regard to Economic Dealings with Occupied Territories* (Asser Institute 2017) 6; J Odermatt, 'Council of the European Union v Front Populaire de la Libération de la Saguia-El-Hamra et du Rio de Oro (Front Polisario). Case C-104/16P' (2017) 111 American Journal of International Law 731, 738. De Vries (n 147) 513; G Van der Loo, 'Law and Practice of the EU's Trade Agreements with "Disputed" Territories: A Consistent Approach?' in I Govaere and S Garben (eds), *The Interface Between EU and International Law: Contemporary Reflections* (Bloomsbury 2019) 257–258; G Harpaz and E Rubinson, 'The Interface between Trade, Law and Politics and the Erosion of Normative Power Europe: Comment on Brita' (2010) 35 European Law Review 551, 561 and 566.

154 Ryngaert and Fransen (n 145) 2. See *Brita* (n 148) para 64. In *Brita*, the Court "recognised in passing, that the appropriate legal status of the territories under international law is relevant to the solution of the dispute." Harpaz and Rubinson (n 153) 561.

155 Kassoti, 'The ECJ and the Art of Treaty Interpretation' (n 151) 234–235; Kassoti, 'The Empire Strikes Back' (n 145) 310; V Azarova and A Berkes, 'The Commission's Proposals to Correct EU-Morocco Relations and the EU's Obligation Not to Recognize as Lawful the "Illegal Situation" in Western Sahara' (*EJIL Talk!*, 13 July 2018) <https://www.ejiltalk.org/author/aberkes/> accessed 11 December 2019.

156 Agreement in the Form of an Exchange of Letters between the European Union and the Kingdom of Morocco on the Amendment of Protocols 1 and 4 to the Euro-Mediterranean Agreement Establishing an Association between the European Communities and their Member States, of the One Part, and the Kingdom of Morocco, of the Other Part [2019] OJ L 34/4.

applied to the waters adjacent to the territory of Western Sahara.[157] It was doubtful that the EU Commission acquired such consent from the people of Western Sahara.[158] However, if reached, it would have been the first case of this kind.[159] Ultimately, in 2021, in *Front Polisario II*, the General Court annulled the Council decision approving the EU agreements with Morocco, citing the fact that the consultations carried out by the Commission and the European External Actions Service (EEAS) did not amount to the consent of the people

157 Sustainable Fisheries Partnership Agreement between the European Union and the Kingdom of Morocco [2019] OJ L 77/8, art 1(h).

158 According to the CJEU in the *Front Polisario* case, "the people of Western Sahara must be regarded as a 'third party' within the meaning of the principle of the relative effect of treaties" and "implementation must receive the consent of such a third party." *Front Polisario* case (n 149), para 106. It seems that the European Commission and EEAS sought to fulfil this condition by conduct of "wide-ranging consultation with the people concerned in Western Sahara." However, there are methodological problems, including uncertainty about who the addressees of this consultation were, as well as doubt as to what extent "a majority view in favour of amending liberalisation agreement" can be considered "the consent of people of Western Sahara." When the Front Polisario expressed negative views, it led the Legal Services of the European Parliament to conclude that "it seems difficult to confirm with a high degree of certainty whether these steps meet the Court's requirement of a consent by the people of Western Sahara." See European Parliament (Legal Services), 'Opinion of the Legal Service' (13 September 2018) SJ-0506/18, para 26. See European Commission, 'Proposal for a Council Decision on the Conclusion of the Agreement in the Form of an Exchange of Letters between the European Union and the Kingdom of Morocco on the Amendment of Protocols 1 and 4 to the Euro-Mediterranean Agreement Establishing an Association between the European Communities and their Member States, of the one Part, and the Kingdom of Morocco, of the Other Part' (11.6.2018) COM(2018) 481 final, 4–8 ("European Commission's Explanatory Memorandum on Amendment to the EU-Morocco Association Agreement"). See also European Commission, 'Commission Staff Working Document' (11 June 2018) SWD(2018) 346 final. See Azarova and Berkes (n 155); Wrange, 'Western Sahara, the European Commission and the Politics of International Legal Argument' (n 150) 24–28.

159 The question of the interplay between the law of occupation (in light of the law applicable to the NSGT) and the duty of non-recognition has not yet been subject of an in-depth analysis. Nevertheless, it follows from ARSIWA that the recognition by the injured State is not excluded, but requires the preservation of a strong communitarian character. In this case, it is not certain if this rule also applies to national liberation movements by analogy. However, with regard to the legal basis of the requirement of consent, it is argued that the consent of the Front Polisario would have a sufficient communitarian element and therefore would permit recognition in this context. "[S]ince the breach by definition concerns the international community as a whole, waiver or recognition induced from the injured State by the responsible State cannot preclude the international community interest in ensuring a just and appropriate settlement." ARSIWA (n 41) commentary to art 41, para 9. See Azarova and Berkes (n 155).

of Western Sahara.[160] Thus, without such consent, by explicitly extending the scope of these agreements to Western Sahara, the EU arguably violated its duty of non-recognition.[161] The EU's approach was thus akin to "creeping recognition."[162]

4.2.1.1.3 *Namibia* Exception in the Context of Treaty Relations

Under the *Namibia* exception, non-recognition "should not result in depriving the people of Namibia of any advantages derived from international co-operation."[163] Ronen points out a *Namibia*-specific context of this provision.[164] Generally, even in the area of humanitarian necessities, the States would be obliged to limit their recognition to acts of a "humanitarian and non-sovereign nature."[165] By definition, treaty relations are of a sovereign nature.[166] Moreover, there is no practice supporting that the *Namibia* exception justifies the extension of the occupant's treaties to annexed territories or the conclusion of treaties with an illegal secessionist entity.

In this context, it is impossible to agree with Costelloe who argued that the policy considerations of the ICJ's and ECtHR's treatment of the *Namibia* exception "also speak in favour of accepting a limited 'succession' of certain treaties

---

160 Case T-279/19 *Front Polisario Front populaire pour la libération de la saguia-el- hara et du rio de oro (Front Polisario) v Council of the European Union* [2021] ECLI:EU:T:2021:639, para 391; Case T-344/19 and T-356/19 *Popular Front for the Liberation of Saguia el-Hamra and Rio de Oro (Front Polisario) v Council of the European Union* [2021] ECLI:EU:T:2021:640, paras 364–365. See further J Odermatt, 'International Law as Challenge to EU Acts: Front Polisario II' (2023) 60 Common Market Law Review 217, 227–234.

161 Kassoti, 'The Empire Strikes Back' (n 145) 311; Azarova and Berkes (n 155). It is quite interesting to note that following the Front Polisario judgment Van der Loo predicted that "[p]resumably, the EU will try to include a territorial application clause explicitly excluding the application to the Western Sahara, although this would be difficult for Morocco to accept." Van der Loo (n 153) 259.

162 Dawidowicz (n 121) 276.

163 *Namibia* (n 33) para 122 in connection to para 125.

164 According to Ronen, the ICJ's reference to the '*people* of Namibia,' the collective interest protected by this pronouncement "may have been the realization of the right to self-determination." Ronen, *Transition from Illegal Regimes under International Law* (n 13) 80–81 (*emphasis added*). Indeed, the ICJ highlighted that "the injured entity is a people which must look to the international community for assistance in its progress towards the goals for which the sacred trust was instituted." *Namibia* (n 33) para 127.

165 Raič (n 79) 164, ftn 330. "This seems to follow from the fact that if such recognition would validate the illegal claim by the wrongdoer, this could eventually lead to a situation which might be even more harmful to the inhabitants of the territory than when no recognition would have been granted at all." ibid.

166 However, see the above-mentioned exception with respect to certain general conventions, such as those of a humanitarian character. *Namibia* (n 33) para 122.

in annexed territories."[167] Even Costelloe accepted that "[t]his position remains largely untested in practice."[168] As is shown below, the ECtHR indeed referred to the *Namibia* exception to give legal effects to certain acts and laws of illegal secessionist entities; however, the applicability of the ECHR as a treaty was based on the respondent State's effective control.

It is even more difficult to agree with Ryngaert and Fransen who argued that the *Namibia* exception justified that the EU-Morocco Liberalisation Agreement "applies to the territory of Western Sahara, insofar as the importation of products derived from Morocco's natural resources exploitation in Western Sahara benefits local population."[169] It is demonstrated below that the *Namibia* exception has been interpreted rather restrictively and never purely in terms of economic benefit to the local population.[170] In any case, the application of the *Namibia* exception in this context would also be rendered problematic by the difficulty in distinguishing between the indigenous population and implanted settlers.[171]

4.2.1.1.4 Applicability of the Parent State's Treaties to an Illegal Entity

A remaining question concerns the extension of the existing or newly concluded treaties of the parent State concerning its territory, which *de iure* also includes the illegal secessionist entity. Thus, rather than violation of the duty of non-recognition, this issue concerns the effects of the change of effective territorial control on treaties.

---

167 Costelloe, 'Treaty Succession in Annexed Territory' (n 10) 376.

168 ibid 378.

169 Ryngaert and Fransen (n 145) 17. Similarly, E Benvenisti, *The International Law of Occupation* (OUP 2012) 85–86.

170 For a similar view, see Western Sahara Campaign (n 149), Opinion of Advocate General Wathelet (10 January 2018), paras 288–292. S Koury, 'The European Community and Member States' Duty of Non-Recognition under the EC-Morocco Association Agreement: State Responsibility and Customary International Law' in K Arts and P Leite Pinto (eds), *International Law and the Question of Western Sahara* (IPJET 2006) 190; Azarova and Berkes (n 155). See also N Kyriacou, 'The EU's Trade Relations with Northern Cyprus Obligations and Limits under Public International Law' in A Duval and E Kassoti (eds), *Legality of Economic Activities, Occupied Territories: International, EU Law and Business and Human Rights Perspectives* (Taylor & Francis Group, 2020) 107.

171 Milano, 'The New Fisheries Partnership Agreement' (n 20) 446–447; Azarova and Berkes (n 155). See also Wrange, 'Western Sahara, the European Commission and the Politics of International Legal Argument' (n 150) 22–23. See *infra* on the *Namibia* exception in the context of acts and laws of illegal secessionist entity.

As a matter of principle, the parent State maintains its status of a *de iure* sovereign;[172] therefore, "its treaties should continue to apply in the territory."[173] In *Kibris*, the UK's Court of Appeal dismissed the appellants' claims that the entitlement of the Republic of Cyprus to exercise its rights under the 1944 Chicago Convention concerning northern Cyprus was suspended because of the lack of effective control over that territory.[174]

In this context, such a continued operation of these treaties might not be much use for the prospective injured State because the breaches of international law in the area outside of the effective control might not be attributable to the parent State.[175] As far as the conclusion of new treaties after the parent State's loss of effective control, they might include a specific provision concerning this issue.[176] Even in the area of human rights law based on the ECtHR's jurisprudence, the parent State is still held responsible for the residual positive human rights obligations.[177]

There is only a minimal possibility that the loss of territorial control might justify the invocation of a general international law grounds for the suspension or termination of treaties because of *rebus sic stantibus* under Article 62 VCLT and the supervening impossibility of performance under Article 61 VCLT.[178]

---

172 As mentioned above, because of peremptory illegality, rules of State succession do not apply. Ronen also shows the reasons why illegal regimes do not generally invoke or apply prior bilateral treaties of the predecessor State under the rules of State succession. According to Ronen, the stance regarding prior treaties would not have a conclusive impact on the status of illegal regimes. On the one hand, the continued application of these treaties could either be taken as a sign of the application of rules of State succession or an indication that the territory is still part of the parent State. On the other hand, non-application of these prior treaties could also be seen as the expression of a clean-slate policy on the part of a new purported State. Ronen, *Transition from Illegal Regimes under International Law* (n 13) 75. See VCST (n 5) art 34, which foresees continued application of treaties of the predecessor State in respect to the entire territory, in the case of the separation of part of a State; and Article 16 with respect to newly independent States.

173 Costelloe, 'Treaty Succession in Annexed Territory' (n 10) 373.

174 *Regina (on the Application of Kibris Türk Hava Yollari and CTA Holidays Limited) v Secretary of Transport (Republic of Cyprus, Interested Party)* (England, Court of Appeal) (2010) 148 ILR 683, 719–737.

175 Costelloe, 'Treaty Succession in Annexed Territory' (n 10) 374.

176 "The application of the acquis shall be suspended in those areas of the Republic of Cyprus in which the Government of the Republic of Cyprus does not exercise effective control." Protocol No 10 on Cyprus of the Act of Accession 2003 [2003] OJ L 236/955, art 1(1) ("Protocol No 10 to the Act of Accession").

177 See *infra* Chapter 8.

178 Costelloe, 'Treaty Succession in Annexed Territory' (n 10) 375; Dumberry (n 8) 220–221.

These provisions are very narrow in scope[179] and suspension or termination thereunder is not automatic, but rather requires a notification procedure under the VCLT.

The change of the effective territorial control in this context can also overlap with the outbreak of hostilities.[180] In the Articles on the Effects of Armed Conflict on Treaties (AREAC), which sought to codify customary law on the matter, the ILC stipulated a general principle that treaties are not *ipso facto* terminated or suspended upon the existence of armed conflict.[181] It also provided for rules for the ascertainment of the susceptibility of treaties to termination, withdrawal or suspension of operation in the event of an armed conflict.[182] Under Article 15 AREAC, an aggressor State "shall not terminate or withdraw from a treaty or suspend its operation as a consequence of an armed conflict

179 Giegerich suggests that impossibility under art 61 VCLT "will ensue when the control of a certain territory is indispensable for the execution of a treaty," by pointing to the "example of a State, which after having concluded an agreement conceding the use of one of its ports by another State becomes landlocked as a result of the loss or cession of its maritime littoral." T Giegerich, 'Article 61' in O Dörr and K Schmalenbach (eds), *Vienna Convention on the Law of Treaties* (Springer 2012) 1056, ftn 35. See T Giegerich, 'Article 62' in O Dörr and K Schmalenbach (eds), *Vienna Convention on the Law of Treaties* (Springer 2012) 1067–1104. See also J Ostřanský, 'The Termination and Suspension of Bilateral Investment Treaties Due to an Armed Conflict' (2015) 6 Journal of International Dispute Settlement 136, 139–140. Gagliani calls for a reconceptualization of the supervening impossibility of performance. See G Gagliani, 'Supervening Impossibility of Performance and the Effect of Armed Conflict on Investment Treaties: Any Room for Manoeuvre?' in KF Gómez and others (eds), *International Investment Law and the Law of Armed Conflict, European Yearbook of International Economic Law* (Springer 2019) 360.

180 Neither the provisions of the VCLT nor of the VCST prejudge any question that may arise in regard to a treaty from the outbreak of hostilities between States. VCLT (n 134) art 73; VCST (n 5) art 39.

181 "The existence of an armed conflict does not *ipso facto* terminate or suspend the operation of treaties: (a) as between States parties to the conflict; (b) as between a State party to the conflict and a State that is not." ILC, 'Draft Articles on the Effects of Armed Conflict on Treaties' Treaties in 'Report of the International Law Commission of its Sixty-Third Session (26 April-3 June and 4 July-12 August 2011)' UN Doc A/66/10, art 3 ("AREAC"). Institut de droit international, 'Resolution on the Effects of Armed Conflicts on Treaties' (28 August 1985) (Helsinki Session) (Rapporteur: Bengt Broms), art 2. For historical antecedents of this principle, see A Pronto, 'The Effect of War on Law – What Happens to Their Treaties When States Go to War?' (2013) 2 Cambridge Journal of International and Comparative Law 227, 227–233; Gagliani (n 179) 350–353.

182 AREAC (n 181) arts 4–7. According to the commentary, "the greater the involvement of third States in a non-international armed conflict, the greater the possibility that treaties will be affected, and vice versa." ibid, commentary to art 6, para 4.

that results from the act of aggression if the effect would be to the benefit of that State."[183]

4.2.1.2 *Establishment of Diplomatic and Consular Relations*

Building on the *Namibia* Advisory Opinion,[184] sending diplomatic missions, special missions or consular agents to an illegal secessionist entity would violate the obligation of non-recognition. The key rationale is the same as that for treaty relations because the diplomatic and consular relations[185] are only "reserved to sovereign States."[186] As pointed out by Raič, the establishment or maintenance of diplomatic relations is an example of implied recognition *par excellence*.[187]

However, similar to the area of treaty relations, international practice tolerates a certain very informal practice of establishing informal centres and offices such as the Rhodesian Information Office and the TRNC Representative Office. However, as their establishment is governed by domestic private law and they do not possess any attributes of sovereignty, this practice underlines rather than undermines the prohibition of recognition in this area.[188]

4.2.2 Economic and Other Dealings with an Illegal Secessionist Entity

Under the *Namibia* Advisory Opinion, the duty of non-recognition requires States "to abstain from entering into economic and other forms of relationship or dealings with South Africa on behalf of or concerning Namibia which

183 AREAC (n 181) art 15.

184 *Namibia* (n 33) para 123. See also for the UNSC practice in this context UNSC Res 283 (29 July 1970) UN Doc S/RES/283, paras 1–3; UNSC Res 217 (20 November 1965) UN Doc S/RES/217, para 6; UNSC Res 277 (18 March 1970) UN Doc S/RES/277, para 9(a); UNSC Res 550 (11 May 1984) UN Doc S/RES/550, para 2. Christakis, 'L'obligation de non-reconnaissance' (n 44) 149–151.

185 It is worth noting that the League of Nations' non-recognition of Manchukuo did not cover consular relations with Manchukuo, but "consuls would be under an obligation to avoid any action which might be interpreted as express or implied recognition of Manchukuo as a State." Raič (n 79) 159. Christakis, 'L'obligation de non-reconnaissance' (n 44) 149–150. The practice seems to have transformed in this aspect. In particular, States withdrew their consuls from Salisbury after Southern Rhodesia declared independence, and they never sent any to the TRNC and Bantustans. ibid 150.

186 Ronen, *Transition from Illegal Regimes under International Law* (n 13) 77–78.

187 "…because this will be interpreted as validating or 'curing' either an illegal claim to statehood, or to a title to territory." Raič (n 79) 161–162.

188 Similarly, Christakis, 'L'obligation de non-reconnaissance' (n 44) 150–154.

may entrench its authority over the Territory."[189] This group of relationships does not fall within the category of international legal acts mentioned above or internal laws and acts discussed below.[190] When dealings *entrench* or consolidate an illegal regime's authority over the territory, this in turn implies recognition.[191] In this area, the duties of non-recognition and non-assistance conflate. For clarity, the following account does not differentiate between the duties of non-recognition and non-assistance. From the *Namibia* Advisory Opinion follows that prohibition is not absolute; those dealings that do not entrench the entity's authority are not prohibited. Moreover, the *Namibia* exception also applies.[192] However, the latter has not been interpreted as justifying dealings providing the local population with benefits of a purely economic nature; it is mainly limited to the humanitarian sphere.[193] This section analyses economic and other dealings separately.

4.2.2.1 *Economic Dealings with an Illegal Secessionist Entity*

The duties of non-recognition and non-assistance do not require a complete economic blockade of an illegal secessionist entity[194] for at least two reasons. First, the prohibition is not absolute and allows for a limited exception. Second, while these duties bind States, it is not entirely clear what, if anything, they require the States to do concerning private actors under their jurisdiction, especially importers and exporters of goods.[195]

---

189 *Namibia* (n 33) para 124. See for the UNSC practice UNSC Res 276 (30 January 1970) UN Doc S/RES/276, para 5; UNSC Res 283 (29 July 1970) UN Doc S/RES/283, paras 4–6. Christakis, 'L'obligation de non-reconnaissance' (n 44) 154–157.

190 Ronen, *Transition from Illegal Regimes under International Law* (n 13) 78.

191 Some of the dissenting and separate opinions argued that only those dealings that imply a formal recognition rather than entrench actual authority are prohibited. *Namibia* (n 33), Separate Opinion of Judge Onyema, 149; *Namibia* (n 33), Separate Opinion of Judge Petrén, 134 and 137. Ronen, *Transition from Illegal Regimes under International Law* (n 13) 78–80. However, as Ronen highlights, the fact that judges considered themselves dissenting seems to *a contrario* confirm that the majority interpreted the notion of 'dealings' more broadly, "possibly including any act that might entrench South Africa's effective control in Namibia, rather than merely formal authority." ibid 79.

192 *Namibia* (n 33) para 125. See T Moerenhout, 'The Obligation to Withhold from Trading in Order Not to Recognize and Assist Settlements and Their Economic Activity in Occupied Territories' (2012) 3 Journal of International Humanitarian Legal Studies 344, 351. See also Crawford, Opinion (n 64) paras 49, 84, 91, 136.

193 See *supra* the *Namibia* exception in the context of treaty relations.

194 See N Caspersen, 'Collective-Non-Recognition of States' in G Vizoka, J Doyle and E Newman (eds), *Routledge Handbook of State Recognition* (Routledge 2019) 233.

195 For the difference in language concerning State-owned companies and companies under State control, on the one hand, and companies not under a direct governmental control,

This uncertainty is reflected in scholarship where opinions range from a complete prohibition of all outgoing and incoming trade[196] to a fully permissive attitude to trade.[197] The majority of doctrine sees this issue as inconclusive.[198] To shed some light on this topic, the following account focuses on the direct economic relations of a State, exports from third States to an illegal secessionist entity and non-preferential and preferential imports from an illegal secessionist entity to third States.

4.2.2.1.1 Direct Economic Relations of Third States with an Illegal Entity

4.2.2.1.1.1 *Direct Trade*

Because the duties of non-recognition and non-assistance *ratione personae* bind States, direct economic and commercial dealings between third States and an illegal entity, which may entrench an illegal entity's authority over territory, would violate these duties.[199] Trade relations with an illegal secessionist entity, in which the third State acts as a direct party in the capacity of purchaser or seller whether through its State organs or based on attribution, would be prohibited if such relations entrenched the illegal entity's authority over territory. For example, even if this situation does not concern an illegal secessionist entity specifically, in the context of Israeli settlements, prohibited dealings would include "the purchase of agricultural produce from settlements."[200] It is very difficult to construe situations where direct economic dealings would not entrench an illegal entity's authority over territory as they by definition

---

on the other hand, see UNSC Res 283 (29 July 1970) UN Doc S/RES/283, paras 4–6 and para 7.

196 Moerenhout, 'The Obligation to Withhold from Trading' (n 192) 360–461.

197 "[S]tate practice supports a fully permissive approach to economic dealings with occupying authorities and their nationals by third-party states or nationals in territories under prolonged occupation or illegal annexation." Kontorovich, 'Economic Dealings with Occupied Territories' (n 147) 587.

198 Kassoti considers this to be open question. Kassoti, 'The EU's Duty of Non-Recognition' (n 124) 6. According to Ryngaert and Fransen, "[t]his line of reasoning is admittedly far from generally accepted." Ryngaert and Fransen (n 145) 17. "[T]he extent to which international norms on the responsibility of third states cover private dealings remains unclear." V Azarova, 'Business and Human Rights in Occupied Territory: The UN Database of Business Active in Israel's Settlements' (2018) 3 Business and Human Rights Journal 187, 200. See also Kassoti and Duval (n 4) 7–8.

199 See Crawford, Opinion (n 64) para 84 and see para 136. *Contra* mainly due to a different reading of EU case law, see Kontorovich, 'Economic Dealings with Occupied Territories' (n 147) 584–637.

200 Crawford, Opinion (n 64) para 85.

provide an economic lifeline to it. Moreover, the *Namibia* exception plays only a very limited role in the area of direct economic dealings.[201]

4.2.2.1.1.2 *Direct Provision of Aid*

Under the *Namibia* Advisory Opinion, direct investment, financing and the provision of aid by third States to an illegal entity consolidating its authority over territory are also prohibited.[202] From this follows that aid that does not entrench an illegal entity's authority over the territory is allowed. Presumably, this would include humanitarian aid or assistance. For example, concerning Israeli settlements, "the provision of financial or other assistance in the construction of settlements buildings or infrastructure" would be prohibited.[203] However, "the financing by a State of an organisation operating inside a settlement, which is in fact engaged in the provision of health services to the Palestinian population, would likely be considered an act 'untainted' by the illegality of the settlement regime."[204]

In this context, the EU's policies appear rather incoherent.[205] Concerning Israeli settlements, the EU adopted guidelines on the eligibility of Israeli entities working within Israeli settlements in Palestine for EU funding in 2013.[206] The EU explicitly linked the adoption of these guidelines with its obligation of non-recognition.[207] "The EU found itself obliged to exclude facts arising from Israel's unlawful acts in Palestinian territory from the scope of EU-Israel relations."[208]

---

201 See *supra* the *Namibia* exception in the context of treaty relations. Humanitarian aspects refer more to the area of provision of direct aid than to direct economic dealings.

202 *Namibia* (n 33) para 124; See also UNSC Res 232 (16 December 1966) UN Doc S/RES/232, para 5.

203 Crawford, Opinion (n 64) para 85.

204 ibid para 91.

205 See, for example, E Kontorovich, 'A Tale of Two Green Lines' (*The Chronicle of Higher Education Blogs: The Conversation*, 17 November 2014) <http://chronicle.com/blogs/conversation/2014/11/17/a-tale-of-two-green-lines/> accessed 12 March 2016.

206 'Guidelines on the Eligibility of Israeli Entities and their Activities in the Territories Occupied by Israel since June 1967 for Grants, Prizes and Financial Instruments Funded by the EU from 2014 Onwards' (2013) 2013/C 205/05 ("Guidelines").

207 "Their aim is to ensure the respect of EU positions and commitments in conformity with international law on the non-recognition by the EU of Israel's sovereignty over the territories occupied by Israel since June 1967." ibid para 1.

208 V Azarova, 'On the Regulatory Logics of UNSC Resolution 2334 (2016) on Israeli Settlements' (*Jurist*, 21 February 2017) <https://www.jurist.org/commentary/2017/02/valentina-azarova-resolution-2234/> accessed 12 November 2019; F Dubuisson, *The International Obligations of the European Union and Its Member States with Regard to Economic Relations with Israeli Settlements* (Centre de droit international de l'Université

Concerning the TRNC, the EU's approach was very different. The EU rendered direct aid to Turkey without any requirement to limit its use in the TRNC.[209] However, even more importantly, Article 3 to the Protocol No 10 states, "nothing in this Protocol shall preclude measures with a view to promoting the *economic* development of the area."[210] The Financial Aid Regulation was later adopted for these purposes.[211] According to the EC, between 2006 and 2023, "the EU allocated EUR 688 million to projects in support of the Turkish Cypriot community."[212]

While some of the objectives of this aid do not raise problems as to the duties of non-recognition and non-assistance,[213]others such as social and economic development and development of infrastructure are much more complicated and place a practical difficulty on distinguishing between the acts of humanitarian nature and those entrenching the regime to the forefront.[214] Moreover, while half of the TRNC population are EU citizens, the programme does not exclude the Turkish settlers from being its beneficiaries.[215] Thus, it is difficult to reconcile the duties of non-recognition and non-assistance with some of the aspects of this multi-million dollar aid package. Nevertheless, the fact that the Republic of Cyprus consented to the provision of this aid highlights the role of the parent State in shaping the response to peremptory illegality.[216]

As for Western Sahara, the EU and the USA have rendered direct aid to Morocco without any limitation as to its use in Western Sahara.[217] The Advocate General Wathelet considered the rendering of a financial contribution

---

libre de Bruxelles 2014) 35–38; Kontorovich, 'Economic Dealings with Occupied Territories' (n 147) 594–595.

209 Kontorovich, 'Economic Dealings with Occupied Territories' (n 147) 619.

210 Protocol No 10 to the Act of Accession (n 149) art 3 (*emphasis added*).

211 Council Regulation (EC) No 389/2006 of 27 February 2006 Establishing an Instrument of Financial Support for Encouraging the Economic Development of the Turkish Cypriot Community and Amending Council Regulation (EC) No 2667/2000 on the European Agency for Reconstruction [2006] OJ L 65/5 ("Financial Aid Regulation").

212 European Commission, 'Aid Programme for the Turkish Cypriot Community' <https://commission.europa.eu/funding-tenders/find-funding/eu-funding-programmes/support-turkish-cypriot-community/aid-programme-turkish-cypriot-community_en> accessed 31 October 2023.

213 For example, the preparation of legal texts aligned with acquis communautaire, the provision of scholarships, and information about the EU. Financial Aid Regulation (n 211) art 2.

214 Financial Aid Regulation (n 211) art 2. See Kyriacou (n 170) 104 and 110.

215 Kontorovich, 'Economic Dealings with Occupied Territories' (n 147) 621–622.

216 See *infra* and see also Caspersen (n 194) 235–236.

217 Kontorovich, 'Economic Dealings with Occupied Territories' (n 147) 607–608.

to Morocco under FPA and its 2013 Protocol as a violation of the duty of non-assistance.[218]

Overall, while Kontorovich derived from this incoherent practice that there was no prohibition regarding the provision of third State financial contribution to illegal entities, the EU practice explicitly following the duty of non-recognition in its dealings with Israeli settlements and a general rule pronounced by the ICJ rather points to the existence of such a prohibition and its possible violation in concrete instances of practice.

4.2.2.1.2 Private Economic Operators of Third States Exporting to an Illegal Entity

Another question is whether the duty of non-recognition mandates the third States to adopt a ban on trade with illegal entities that applies to non-State economic actors domiciled in their jurisdiction. As mentioned, the duties of non-recognition and non-assistance apply to the third States. "[S]ince corporations are not direct holders of international law obligations, the duties of non-recognition and non-assistance do not extend to their activities."[219] However, business activities undoubtedly help consolidate and entrench the illegal regime not only through activities directly upholding the purported sovereignty claims, but also through mundane transactions such as "the rental or purchase of property, or the sale, purchase or provision of services, products or financial capital."[220]

---

218 Western Sahara Campaign (n 149) Opinion of Advocate General Wathelet (10 January 2018), para 211.

219 E Kassoti, 'Doing Business Right? Private Actors and the International Legality of Economic Activities in Occupied Territories' (2016) 7 Cambridge International Law Journal 301, 302. The question whether and to what extent corporations are directly subject to international law falls outside the scope of this book. See ibid 314–319. See also Y Ronen, 'Responsibility of Businesses Involved in the Israeli Settlements in the West Bank' (Research paper No 02–15 2015) <https://papers.ssrn.com/sol3/papers.cfm?abstract_id=2594851> accessed 23 January 2020, 5 and with respect to Decree No 1 for the Protection of Natural Resources of Namibia see 10–11. M Pertile, 'The Changing Environment and Emerging Resource Conflicts' in M Weller (ed), *Oxford Handbook of the Use of Force under International Law* (OUP 2015) 1089. However, Dumberry argues that corporations have an international legal personality in the context of State contracts and are bound by the duty of non-recognition and non-assistance in this context. Yet Dumberry admits that he has "found no example in the past where a non-recognition obligation had been *directly* imposed on corporations." Dumberry (n 8) 203–212. Kassoti and Duval (n 4) 20–21.

220 See V Azarova, 'Business and Human Rights in Occupied Territory' (n 198) 196; Kassoti, 'Doing Business Right?' (n 219) 313–314. For examples of types of activities, see 'Report of the Independent International Fact-Finding Mission to Investigate the Implications of the Israeli Settlements on the Civil, Political, Economic, Social and Cultural Rights of

According to Crawford, the duty of non-assistance cannot be considered breached when State merely permits "corporations within its jurisdiction to trade commercially" with an unlawful occupant.[221]

> The corporation, by definition, is formally separate from the State; as such there must be specific direction in relation to the conduct which constitutes the breach which is complained of, or a specific delegation of powers characterized as governmental whoever preforms them.[222]

However, according to Moerenhout, the duty of non-recognition "includes a negative obligation to refrain from trading with an illegal actor."[223] Similarly, in an Open Letter, legal experts called on the EU "to withhold incoming as well as outgoing trade with settlements in compliance with the duty of non-recognition."[224] In the same vein, Dubuisson claimed that,

> [b]y allowing the trading and importation of goods from Israeli settlements, the member states of the European Union incontrovertibly contribute to their economic prosperity thereby undeniably providing 'aid' and 'assistance' in maintaining the illegal situation created by Israel's settlement policy.[225]

Azarova argued, "the state could find itself wrongfully extending recognition to the basis of rights and revenues gained by business via the business' home

---

the Palestinian People Throughout the Occupied Palestinian Territory, Including East Jerusalem' (7 February 2013) A/HRC/22/63, para 96 ("Fact-Finding Report").

221 Crawford only links this statement with art 16 ARSIWA, but it is believed the same rationale applies to the obligations flowing from art 41(2) ARSIWA. "For the purposes of Article 16, the link between the unlawful conduct of Israel and the conduct of the third State lacks a sufficient nexus in such a case." Crawford, Opinion (n 64) para 91 and see paras 92 and 136.

222 Crawford, Opinion (n 64) para 98. "[A] private sector entity or person does not bear any international legal responsibility for aiding or assisting the unlawful settlement program, nor for ensuring that the people of Palestine can exercise their right to self-determination, nor for ensuring that Israel complies with its obligations under international law." ibid, para 136.

223 Moerenhout, 'The Obligation to Withhold from Trading' (n 192) 360.

224 See 'European Legal Experts Call on EU to Stop Trading with Settlements' (*Mondoweiss*, 23 December 2015) <https://mondoweiss.net/2015/12/european-trading-settlements/> accessed 12 November 2019.

225 Dubuisson (n 208) 41.

state authorities in the course of the application of domestic law to their overseas operations."[226]

Even though there is the trend for home States to adopt measures aimed at discouraging trade of private actors in illegal entities, especially in connection with various soft-law instruments described below,[227] there is no generalised practice and *opinio iuris* that would support the view that the State is required by the duty of non-recognition or non-assistance to prohibit private economic actors under its jurisdiction from carrying out all outgoing trade with illegal entities.[228]

---

226 V Azarova, 'The Secret Life of Non-Recognition: EU-Israel Relations and the Obligation of Non-Recognition in International Law' (2018) 4 Global Affairs 23, 32.

227 See UNSC Res 283 (29 July 1970) UN Doc S/RES/283, paras 7 and 11. See Dubuisson (n 208) 41–43. Since 2013, 18 European governments have issued advisories alerting their businesses about reputational, economic and legal risk connected with conducting business in Israeli settlements in the OPT. However, these advisories "neither specify the potential regulatory consequences business may face in their domicile country for claiming to enjoy titles and rights that were wrongfully constituted or obtained, nor sets out the types of risks that business could expect to incur." V Azarova, 'Business and Human Rights in Occupied Territory' (n 198) 201. The Human Rights Council urged all States to provide information to individuals and businesses on the financial, reputational and legal risks of becoming involved in economic and financial activities in illegal settlements in the OPT. See UNHRC Res 25/28 (28 March 2014) UN Doc A/HRC/RES/25/28, para 11 (c); UNHRC Res 28/26 (27 March 2015) UN Doc A/HRC/RES/28/26, para 12 (c); UNHRC Res 31/36 (24 March 2016) UN Doc A/HRC/RES/31/36, para 12 (c); UNHRC Res 34/31 (24 March 2017) UN Doc A/HRC/RES/34/31, para 13 (c); UNHRC Res 37/36 (23 March 2018) UN Doc A/HRC/RES/37/36, para 12 (c); UNHRC Res 40/24 (22 March 2019) UN Doc A/HRC/RES/40/24, para 12 (c). See also UN Special Representative of the Secretary-General on the issue of human rights and transnational corporations and other business enterprises, 'Guiding Principles on Business and Human Rights' (21 March 2011) UN Doc A/HRC/17/31 ("UNGP"), Principle 7. See, for examples of States discouraging their economic operators from conducting business in illegally occupied territories, *Trading Away Peace: How Europe Helps Sustain Illegal Israeli Settlements* (Trócaire 2012) 28; Kassoti, 'Doing Business Right?' (n 219) 321–325. See further *infra*.

228 See, for example, United Nations High Commissioner for Human Rights, 'Database of All Business Enterprises Involved in the Activities Detailed in Paragraph 96 of the Report of the Independent International Fact-Finding Mission to Investigate the Implications of the Israeli Settlements on The Civil, Political, Economic, Social and Cultural Rights of the Palestinian People Throughout the Occupied Palestinian Territory, Including East Jerusalem' (1 February 2018) UN Doc A/HRC/37/39 ("Database"); Regarding the involvement of foreign companies in Israeli settlements, see Kassoti, 'Doing Business Right?' (n 219) 314. Azarova, 'The Secret Life of Non-Recognition: EU-Israel Relations and the Obligation of Non-Recognition in International Law' (n 226) 32. "The European Union apparently does not maintain that international law bars its corporations from conducting business in occupied territory, even when such activities assist an illegal annexation or otherwise maintain an illegal situation, as the implantation of settlers." Kontorovich,

However, despite this, the limitation on trading with illegal entities flows from other areas of law. First, trading or foreign investments in an illegal entity is limited by other aspects of the duty of non-recognition, in particular, non-recognition by the third States of public law acts of an illegal secessionist entity required for the conduct of business operations such as licenses and concessions.

> A third state whose domestic legal order gives effect to the illegal situation, including the rights, titles and entitlements that it purports to create would be liable for wrongfully recognizing as lawful the proceeds of a serious breach of a peremptory norm of international law.[229]

As is shown below, the recognition of these acts is not even justified based on the *Namibia* exception. Foreign economic actors bear substantial risks when operating with an illegal entity, in particular in terms of non-recognition by the third States of ownership transfers that derive from illegal expropriations. Moreover, private transactions might not be opposable in the context of transition from an illegal regime.[230]

Second, human rights law and soft-law human rights-based standards can play an important role. Because the host State's responsibility is negated by the overwhelming effectiveness of an illegal regime, two levels of responsibility remain available. Some authors claim that there is a trend of the home State of economic operators being responsible in the context of its nascent extraterritorial obligation "to act with due diligence to regulate the (horizontal) rights abuses of private actors."[231] Azarova argued that "the very idea of home

'Economic Dealings with Occupied Territories' (n 147) 598–599, with respect to business activities in the Western Sahara, see 603, and with respect to the TRNC 616–619. See, for instance, 'Doing Business in Cyprus: 2011 Country Commercial Guide for US Companies' <https://photos.state.gov/libraries/cyprus/788/pdfs/2011%20CCG.pdf> accessed 18 January 2020. However, for example, with respect to Bantustans, the UNGA requested States to "take effective measures to prohibit" all corporations under their jurisdiction from having dealings with Bantustans. UNGA Res 31/6A (26 October 1976) UN Doc A/RES/31/6A, para 4; UNGA Res 32/105/N (14 December 1977) UN Doc A/RES/32/105/N, para 6; UNGA Res A/34/93/G (12 December 1979) UN Doc A/RES/34/93/G, para 6.

229 Azarova, 'Business and Human Rights in Occupied Territory' (n 198) 199–200.

230 See *infra*.

231 Azarova, 'Business and Human Rights in Occupied Territory' (n 198) 198. "The numerous recommendations suggest that home States are required to adopt mainly regulatory measures: they are encouraged to appropriately regulate the investments and activities of their corporate nationals and to adapt their legislative framework (civil, criminal and administrative) to ensure the legal accountability of companies and their subsidiaries, operating in or managed from the States parties' territory, regarding abuses of human

state regulation supposes the creation of consequences for corporate nationals that would protect the domestic legal order and dis-incentivize certain transnational activities" and that "home states should ensure that domestic regulatory authorities are able to address restrictive measures to its corporate nationals."[232] This is in line with the home State's role as outlined in the United Nations Guiding Principles on Business and Human Rights (UNGP).[233]

Businesses are also themselves subjected to soft-law human rights standards such as those flowing from the UNGP.[234] The instruments such as the UNGP "show great potential in bringing about a change of corporate conduct towards

---

rights." A Berkes, 'Extraterritorial Responsibility of the Home States for MNCs Violations of Human Rights' in Y Radi (ed), *Research Handbook on Human Rights and Investment* (Edward Elgar 2018) 333. (*footnotes omitted*). Dubuisson (n 208) 60–68. "At present States are not generally required under international human rights law to regulate the extraterritorial activities of businesses domiciled in their territory and/or jurisdiction. Nor are they generally prohibited from doing so, provided there is a recognized jurisdictional basis. Within these parameters some human rights treaty bodies recommend that home States take steps to prevent abuse abroad by business enterprises within their jurisdiction." UNGP (n 227), Commentary to Principle 2. Database (n 228) para 34. See also Crawford, Opinion (n 64) paras 108–109. The Human Rights Council urged all States to implement the UNGP and to take measures to encourage businesses domiciled in their territory and/or under their jurisdiction "to refrain from committing or contributing to gross human rights abuses of Palestinians." See UNHRC Res 25/28 (11 April 2014) UN Doc A/HRC/RES/25/28, para 11 (b); UNHRC Res 28/26 (27 March 2015) UN Doc A/HRC/RES/28/26, para 12 (b); UNHRC Res 31/36 (24 March 2016) UN Doc A/HRC/RES/31/36, para 12 (b); UNHRC Res 34/31 (24 March 2017) UN Doc A/HRC/RES/34/31, para 13 (b); UNHRC Res 37/36 (23 March 2018) UN Doc A/HRC/RES/37/36, para 12 (b); UNHRC Res 40/24 (22 March 2019) UN Doc A/HRC/RES/4024, para 12 (b). See also Fact-Finding Report (n 220) para 117. See also OEIGWG Chairmanship, 'Revised Draft: Legally Binding Instrument to Regulate, in International Human Rights Law, the Activities of Transnational Corporations and Other Business Enterprises' (16 July 2019), arts 5–7 <https://www.ohchr.org/Documents/HRBodies/HRCouncil/WGTransCorp/OEIGWG_RevisedDraft_LBI.pdf> accessed 14 December 2019.

232 "This entails calibrating the application of laws related to taxation, financial regulation, procurement and consumer protection to these titles and rights in view of their invalidity as a matter of international law." V Azarova, 'Business and Human Rights in Occupied Territory' (n 198) 200.

233 Kassoti, 'Doing Business Right?' (n 219) 319–320. UNGP (n 227) Principles 1–10.

234 UNGP (n 227) Principles 11–15. The Human Rights Council directly called upon business enterprises to comply with the UNGP with respect to their activities in settlements and to avoid contributing to their "establishment, maintenance, development or consolidation." See UNHRC Res 40/24 (22 March 2019) UN Doc A/HRC/RES/40/24, para 13; UNHRC Res 37/36 (23 March 2018) A/HRC/RES/37/36, para 13; UNHRC Res 34/31 (24 March 2017) A/HRC/RES/34/31, para 14; UNHRC Res 31/36 (24 March 2016) A/HRC/RES/31/36, para 13; UNHRC Res 28/26 (27 March 2015) A/HRC/RES/28/26, para 13. See also Fact-Finding Report (n 220) para 117.

occupied territories."[235] Under the UNGP, businesses have a responsibility to conduct human rights due diligence and, in the context of the conflict-affected areas, "enhanced" due diligence.[236] Ultimately, considering "the severity of the human rights risks" and credible human rights assessments of operating in such an environment, the economic actor "may need to consider the termination of operations."[237]

In addition, corporate activities in illegally occupied or annexed territories or illegal entities can create the risk of individuals being criminally responsible in cases of the violation of International Humanitarian Law (IHL), particularly for the exploitation of natural resources.[238] States can also adopt the sanctions regime, which might extend the prohibition of commercial dealings with respect to corporations.[239] However, its legal basis would not be the duties of non-recognition and non-assistance of the general international law.[240]

235 Kassoti, 'Doing Business Right?' (n 219) 303.

236 UNGP (n 227) Principle 14; Working Group on the Issue of Human Rights and Transnational Corporations and Other Business Enterprises, 'Statement on the Implications of the Guiding Principles on Business and Human Rights in the Context of Israeli Settlements in the Occupied Palestinian Territory' (6 June 2014) 9–10 <https://www.ohchr.org/Documents/Issues/Business/OPTStatement6June2014.pdf> accessed 23 January 2020 ("Statement on the Implications of the UNGP on Business and Human Rights in Israeli Settlements"); Kassoti, 'Doing Business Right?' (n 219) 320–321.

237 Statement on the Implications of the UNGP on Business and Human Rights in Israeli Settlements, 10. The UNGP does not explicitly require companies to terminate their activities when involved in human rights abuses; they state that such companies need to be prepared to accept any consequences of such a link. Database (n 228) para 38 and paras 39–41. UNGP (n 227) Principles 17–19. See also Kassoti, 'Doing Business Right?' (n 219) 321; V Azarova, 'Business and Human Rights in Occupied Territory' (n 198) 195.

238 Saul (n 151) 316–319 and 321–322. Ruys T, 'The Role of State Immunity and Act of State in the NM Cherry Blossom Case and the Western Sahara Dispute' (2019) 68 International and Comparative Law Quarterly 67, 89. Crawford, Opinion (n 64) paras 100–102 and para 119.

239 Ruys (n 238) 89. See, for example, sanctions imposed on Southern Rhodesia, including calling for a break of economic relations with Southern Rhodesia UNSC Res 217 (20 November 1965) UN Doc S/RES/217, para 8; UNSC Res 277 (18 March 1970) UN Doc S/RES/277, para 9(a), UNSC Res 318 (1972) UN Doc S/RES/318, para 5 and for prevention of specific exports UNSC Res 232 (16 December 1966) UN Doc S/RES/232, para 2; UNSC Res 253 (29 May 1968) UN Doc S/RES/253, para 3 and see also para 12; UNSC Res 314 (28 February 1972) UN Doc S/RES/314, paras 3–4. See further UNSC Res 333 (22 May 1973) UN Doc S/RES/333, paras 3–8. Gowlland-Debbas, *Collective Responses to Illegal Acts in International Law* (n 48) 423–444.

240 See *supra* general observations.

4.2.2.1.3 Non-preferential Imports to the Third State

The extension of a preferential trade regime to products originating in an illegal entity is at the core of the trade aspects of the duties of non-recognition and non-assistance. As is shown below, preferential tariffs must not be applied to products originating in unlawfully occupied territories.[241] However, the issue of common imports from illegal entities to the third States irrespective of a preferential regime raise questions.[242] Even though some scholars and non-government organisations claim that all imports from illegal entities, including non-preferential ones, violate the duties of non-recognition and non-assistance,[243] the State practice does not support an all-out ban on non-preferential imports of products originating in illegal entities.[244]

---

241 With respect to Israeli settlements, see Talmon, 'The Duty Not "To Recognize as Lawful"' (n 4) 119–120. See Koury (n 170) 191 for what preferential access entails in terms of administrative cooperation between the occupant and the third State.

242 Ryngaert and Fransen (n 145) 16.

243 "[T]he fact that the EU allows trade with Moroccan and Israeli produce from occupied territories at all is a breach of its obligation of non-recognition." Moerenhout, 'The Obligation to Withhold from Trading' (n 192) 361. "[S]hort of a total ban on the import of settlement products, the EU is in breach of the obligation of non-recognition and non- assistance in maintaining an illegal situation created by a serious breach of a peremptory norm of international law to the extent that the import of these products facilitates the expansion and entrenchment of settlements in the occupied territories." Kassoti, *The Legality under International Law of the EU's Trade Agreements Covering Occupied Territories* (n 145) 33; Kassoti, *Trading with Settlements* (n 153) 8. *Trading Away Peace: How Europe Helps Sustain Illegal Israeli Settlements* (n 227) 41; A Tonutti, *Feasting on the Occupation: Illegality of Settlement Produce and the Responsibility of EU Member States under International Law* (Al-Haq 2013) 9–13 and 27–31. See for these opinions Kyriacou (n 170) 102.

244 "There is no limitation of exports to the European Union of products produced in the settlements. According to the Association Agreement, these products however do not benefit from exemptions from customs duties." EEAS, 'Frequently Asked Questions On: Guidelines on the Eligibility of Israeli Entities and Their Activities in the Territories Occupied by Israel since June 1967 for Grants, Prizes and Financial Instruments Funded by the EU from 2014 Onwards' <https://eeas.europa.eu/sites/eeas/files/20130719_faq_guidelines_eu_grants_en.pdf> accessed 14 December 2019. The report of the Special Rapporteur Falk claimed that steps "should" be taken with respect to the illegality of Israeli settlements in the OPT, "for example by ceasing trade with the settlements starting with a ban on imports of settlement produce." UNHRC, 'Report of the Special Rapporteur on the Situation of Human Rights in the Palestinian Territories Occupied since 1967, Richard Falk' (13 January 2014) UN Doc A/HRC/25/67, para 45. "The ruling of the Court in case C-104/16P did not impose any import ban on products originating in Western Sahara, but determined that at present the Association agreement contains no legal basis for granting tariff preferences to products coming from Western Sahara." European Parliament, 'Answer Given by Vice-President Mogherini on Behalf of the Commission' (22 March 2018) E-000150/2018. "Direct Trade from ports in the northern part of Cyprus to European Union Member States already exists today, although without EU trade preferences. However, given the policy of

As is shown, the non-existence of a ban on non-preferential imports is also confirmed by the fact that these imports are mostly seen in the context of correct labelling rather than a comprehensive trade ban.[245] Some authors view this approach as allowing the importation and commercialisation of goods in the EU markets and substantiating "a breach of the obligation not to provide assistance for maintaining an illegal situation."[246]

The question must be asked what differences exist between a preferential and non-preferential trade of products originating in illegal entities for the duties of non-recognition and non-assistance. First, in terms of factual consequences, the difference is not particularly astute. Even though tariff-free imports consolidate an illegal entity via the profits of its economic operators in a more clear-cut manner, even non-preferential imports help in doing so.[247] Second, preferential trade is undertaken based on international treaties and, therefore, the duty of non-recognition can be ascertained from a State-to-State bilateral perspective, rather than from the perspective of the activities of private economic operators or its factual contribution to the consolidation of an illegal regime.

Third, while the claim for a preferential tariff under a free trade agreement requires support by proof of origin, usually in the form of a certificate of origin issued by a competent authority of the exporting State,[248] thereby raising

---

non-recognition of the so-called 'Turkish Republic of Northern Cyprus' … trade is de facto impossible where the introduction of goods into the EU Customs territory requires the presentation of a document established by a recognised third-country authority; TRNC authority documents are not accepted by the EU Member States." European Parliament (Committee on Legal Affairs), 'Opinion on the Legal Basis of the Proposal for a Council Regulation on Special Conditions for Trade with Those Areas of the Republic of Cyprus in which the Government of the Republic of Cyprus Does not Exercise Effective Control' (20 October 2010) (COM(2004)0466 final – C7–0047/2010 – 2004/0148(COD)) ("Opinion of the EP's Committee on Legal Affairs") 3 (*footnotes omitted*). "[I]nternational law does not at present contain any requirement that States prohibit the import of goods originating in non-self-governing, occupied, or otherwise disputed territories." Ruys (n 238) 88. Similarly, Kyriacou (n 170) 102–103 and 108.

245 Kassoti, *Trading with Settlements* (n 153) 8.

246 Dubuisson (n 208) 55–56; Kassoti, *The Legality under International Law of the EU's Trade Agreements Covering Occupied Territories* (n 145) 29 and 33.

247 See Tonutti (n 243) 9–13.

248 World Customs Organization, *Guidelines on Certification of Origin* (World Customs Organization 2018) 6. "Rules of origin are relevant to territorial disputes because the origin of goods is commonly defined in international trade law on a territorial basis." M Hirsch, 'Rules of Origin as Trade or Foreign Policy Instruments–The European Union Policy on Products Manufactured in the Settlements in the West Bank and the Gaza Strip' (2002) 26 Fordham International Law Journal 572, 577. O Kanevskaia, 'EU Labelling Practices for

the issue of an implied recognition of public law acts of an illegal entity, the same does not apply to non-preferential imports.[249] "As a general rule, non-preferential proofs of origin should not be required for the importation of goods on which no specific trade policy measures are applicable."[250] Thus, admittedly, it can be agreed with Moerenhout,

> the custom authorities of a third party validate trade entries. Even if no preferential access is given, the act of importation remains a legal act, which requires the stamp of approval from the importing state, which holds a sovereign power over its trade policy.[251]

However, in non-preferential trade, the issue of the certification of origin does not directly arise as often as in preferential trade. Therefore, this can be one of the factors that influence a differentiated approach in this area.

In sum, the duties of non-recognition and non-assistance do not require third States and IOs to adopt an all-out non-preferential import ban on goods originating from illegal entities. However, the overview substantiates the weakness of the factual criterion of entrenching the illegality of the regime in the context of the duties of non-recognition and non-assistance. The trade aspects of the duties of non-recognition and non-assistance influence the conduct of the relevant actors only when formal issues such as implied recognition through the extension of bilateral treaties or the acceptance of certificates of origin are concerned.

4.2.2.1.4 Preferential Imports to the Third State

4.2.2.1.4.1 *Extension of a Preferential Trade to Illegally Occupied or Annexed Territories*

The EU's approach to the extension of preferential tariffs to goods originating from the illegally occupied territories and the issue of acceptance by the EU customs authorities of the certificates of origin issued by the occupant

---

Products Imported from Disputed Territories' (TILEC Discussion Paper 2019) <https://papers.ssrn.com/sol3/papers.cfm?abstract_id=3421419> accessed 20 January 2020, 4.

249 World Customs Organization (n 248) 15.

250 ibid, Guideline 14. However, if those certificates were required, this would entail "some form of acknowledgment of administrative capacity, albeit confined in the area of trade." Kyriacou (n 170) 109–110.

251 T Moerenhout, 'The Consequence of the UN Resolution on Israeli Settlements for the EU: Stop Trade with Settlements' (*EJIL: Talk!*, 4 April 2017) <https://www.ejiltalk.org/the-consequence-of-the-un-settlements-resolution-for-the-eu-stop-trade-with-settlements/> accessed 12 November 2019.

concerning goods originating in the occupied territory is particularly relevant. The EU courts denied the preferential tariff to goods originating in Israeli settlements in the OPT and Western Sahara not because of the factual effects of such preferential trade on the consolidation of illegal occupation, but due to the interpretation of trade agreements excluding their territorial application to occupied territories.[252]

While the EU requires a strict labelling policy concerning the importation of products from the Israeli settlements in the OPT based on its non-recognition of Israel's sovereignty over OPT,[253] which was upheld by the CJEU in the *Psagot* judgment,[254] the approach of the EU's political organs towards products from Western Sahara is very different.[255] Before the *Front Polisario* judgment, products originating in Western Sahara were preferentially imported to the EU.[256] Moreover, there has been no EU policy of differentiated labelling concerning products originating in Western Sahara.[257] After the *Front Polisario* judgment,

---

252 See *supra*.

253 "[L]abels stating the area where a good was produced communicate origin information directly to consumers," potentially influencing their decision to buy a certain product. Kanevskaia (n 248) 3–4. "Since the Golan Heights and the West Bank (including East Jerusalem) are not part of the Israeli territory according to international law, the indication 'product from Israel' is considered to be incorrect and misleading in the sense of the referenced legislation." European Commission, 'Interpretative Notice on Indication of Origin of Goods from the Territories Occupied by Israel since June 1967' (11 November 2015) C(2015) 7834 final, para 7 (*footnotes omitted*). "The aim is also to ensure the respect of Union positions and commitments in conformity with international law on the *non-recognition* by the Union of Israel's sovereignty over the territories occupied by Israel since June 1967." ibid, para 2 (*emphasis added*).

254 According to the CJEU, "foodstuffs originating in a territory occupied by the State of Israel must bear not only the indication of that territory but also, where those foodstuffs come from a locality or a group of localities constituting an Israeli settlement within that territory, the indication of that provenance." Case C-363/18 *Organisation juive européenne, Vignoble Psagot Ltd v Ministre de l'Économie et des Finances* [2019] ECLI:EU:C:2019:954 ("Psagot"), para 58. "[T]he fact that a foodstuff comes from a settlement established in breach of the rules of international humanitarian law may be the subject of ethical assessments capable of influencing consumers' purchasing decisions, particularly since some of those rules constitute fundamental rules of international law." ibid para 56.

255 Kontorovich, 'Economic Dealings with Occupied Territories' (n 147) 609–610.

256 Until the *Front Polisario* judgment, "the Customs authorities applied preferences on a de facto basis to products from Western Sahara certified to be of Moroccan origin." European Commission's Explanatory Memorandum on Amendment to the EU-Morocco Association Agreement (n 158) 2; Kassoti, *Trading with Settlements* (n 153) 9.

257 Kassoti, *The Legality under International Law of the EU's Trade Agreements Covering Occupied Territories* (n 145) 51–55. The EU Commission's rationale for a differentiated approach on the ground that Western Sahara is 'de facto' administered by the Kingdom of Morocco and the OPT are occupied by Israel, does not bear scrutiny, as there is no

the EU amended the Association Agreement (AA) to explicitly include the granting of a preferential regime to goods originating in Western Sahara. However, in *Front Polisario II*, the General Court annulled the decision amending the agreement because the consultations carried out by the Commission and the European External Actions Service (EEAS) did not amount to the consent of the people of Western Sahara.[258]

A number of observers pointed to a lack of uniformity or even double standards.[259] Nevertheless, at least at the level of the EU judicial bodies, the granting of preferential treatment to such products is prohibited. However, as mentioned above, this is due to the interpretation of preferential trade agreements and not by reference to the duty of non-recognition and its influence on the consolidation of an illegal regime.

4.2.2.1.4.2 *Extension of a Preferential Regime to an Illegal Secessionist Entity*

Another scenario concerns the extension of the parent State's preferential trade regime to an illegal secessionist entity. This situation involves legal consequences of the loss of effective control on the parent State's trade agreements, the question of implied recognition of the public law acts of an illegal secessionist entity and the compatibility of such trade with the duties of non-recognition and non-assistance owing to its effects on the entrenchment of an illegal secessionist entity's authority. A leading example is the EU's approach to trading with the TRNC.

Before Cyprus' membership in the EU, the 1972 Association Agreement provided for a legal basis of trade between the Community and Cyprus.[260] According to the 1977 Protocol to AA, the movement certificates EUR.1 issued by the customs authorities of the exporting State must have accompanied the

---

such term as a de facto administering power of a non-self-governing territory. Both of these territories are occupied in violation of the right of self-determination, and there is no such legal status as a de facto administering power in international law. See European Parliament, 'Joint Answer Given by Vice-President Mogherini on Behalf of the Commission' (4 February 2016) E-015222/2015, E-015472/2015. Kassoti, 'Doing Business Right?' (n 219) 304–312; Western Sahara Campaign (n 149) Opinion of Advocate General Wathelet (10 January 2018), para 232. See also *supra* in section on treaty relations.

258 See *supra*.

259 Hirsch (n 248) 588; Kassoti, *Trading with Settlements* (n 153) 10; Harpaz and Rubinson (n 153) 568; Van der Loo (n 153) 261–262. Kassoti and Duval (n 4) 11–12 and 16.

260 Agreement establishing an Association between the European Economic Community and the Republic of Cyprus [1973] OJ L 133/2 ("AA"). N Skoutaris, 'The Application of the *Acquis Communautaire* in the Areas not Under the Effective Control of the Republic of Cyprus: The Green Line Regulation' (2008) 45 Common Market Law Review 727, 740–741.

products imported to the EU.[261] In *Anastasiou I,* the issue was whether the importation to the UK of citrus products or potatoes produced in northern Cyprus with the movement and phytosanitary certificates issued by the TRNC could be justified given the special situation of Cyprus.[262]

The CJEU rejected this claim. It held that the system of acceptance of certificates by the customs authorities of the importing State reflects a mutual confidence in the system of checking the origin of products and that "[a] system of that kind cannot therefore function properly unless the procedures for administrative cooperation are strictly complied with" and

> such cooperation is excluded with the authorities of an entity such as that established in the northern part of Cyprus, which is recognized neither by the Community nor by the Member States; the only Cypriot State they recognize is the Republic of Cyprus.[263]

When the export to the community is involved, the only competent authorities to issue relevant certificates are those of the Republic of Cyprus.[264] Even

261 Council Regulation (EEC) No 2907/77 of 20 December 1977 on the Conclusion of the Additional Protocol to the Agreement Establishing an Association between the European Economic Community and the Republic of Cyprus [1977] OJ 339/1, Annex, art 6(1) and art 7(1).

262 Case C-432/92 *R v Minister of Agriculture, Fisheries and Food, ex parte S.P. Anastasiou (Pissouri) Ltd and Others* [1994] ECR I-3116 ("*Anastasiou I*"). In Anastasiou II, the CJEU decided that the Plan Health Directive allowed Member States to admit into their territory plants originating in a non-member country, accompanied by the phytosanitary certificates issued by a non-member country, if certain conditions are met. Case C-219/98 *R v Minister of Agriculture, Fisheries and Food, ex parte S.P. Anastasiou (Pissouri) Ltd and Others (Anastasiou II)* [2000] ECR I-5267 ("Anastasiou II"). However, upon modified Plant Health Directive, the Court held that in order to assure high level of phytosanitary protection, the certificates cannot be issued by a third country other than country of origin. Case C-140/02 *R v Minister of Agriculture, Fisheries and Food, ex parte S.P. Anastasiou (Pissouri) Ltd and Others (Anastasiou III)* [2003] ECR I-10657 ("*Anastasiou III*"). Skoutaris, 'The Application of the *Acquis Communautaire*' (n 260) 741–743; Kanevskaia (n 248) 16–17. See also Kyriacou (n 170) 90–96.

263 *Anastasiou I* (n 262) paras 39–40. According to the Court, the principle of non-discrimination "cannot in any event confer on the Community the right to interfere in the internal affairs of Cyprus. The problems resulting from the de facto partition of the island must be resolved exclusively by the Republic of Cyprus, which alone is internationally recognized." ibid, para 48.

264 *Anastasiou I* (n 262) para 54 and see paras 56–62. However, according to Skoutaris, *Anastasiou I* meant that "Turkish Cypriot goods could still be imported into the EC but were treated as goods from a country not associated with the EC, thus exposing them to

though the Court ruled exclusively by reference to community law,[265] its conclusions squarely fit the parameters of the duty of non-recognition of official acts as further discussed below.[266]

After the Annan Plan's rejection by the Greek-Cypriot Community, Cyprus acceded to the EU as a whole on 1 May 2004; however, the application of *acquis communautaire* was suspended in the areas that were not under the effective control of the Republic of Cyprus.[267] In April 2004, the General Affairs Council adopted conclusions in which it expressed its determination "to put an end to the isolation of the Turkish Cypriot community and to facilitate the reunification of Cyprus by encouraging the economic development of the Turkish Cypriot community."[268]

In this context, the Green Line Regulation[269] was adopted, under which goods originating in the TRNC cross the Green Line and are circulated not as third country goods, but as community goods.[270] It stipulated that these goods should be accompanied by a document issued by the Turkish Cypriot Chamber of Commerce, "duly authorised for that purpose by the Commission in agreement with the Government of the Republic of Cyprus, or by another

---

import duties ranging from 3 per cent to 32 per cent." Skoutaris, 'The Application of the *Acquis Communautaire*' (n 260) 741; S Talmon, 'The Cyprus Question before the European Court of Justice' (2001) 12 European Journal of International Law 727, 736–737. Kyriacou (n 170) 91 and 104–105. This seems to confirm the above-mentioned conclusions on non-preferential trade access.

265 SL Shaelou, 'The European Court of Justice and the Anastasiou Saga: Principles of Europeanisation through Economic Governance' (2007) 18 European Business Law Review 619, 626. The argument that certificates issued by the TRNC would be tantamount to violation of the UNSC resolutions was not addressed at all. See P Koutrakos, 'Legal Issues of EC-Trade Relations' (2003) 52 International and Comparative Law Quarterly 489, 492.

266 MG Kohen, 'Création d'Etats en droit international contemporain' (2002) VI Cours euro-méditerranéens Bancaja de droit international 569. See also Hirsch (n 248) 584. However, Talmon criticized the Court for misjudging the scope and consequences of non-recognition in international law. However, since the selected instances of practice that he relies upon are either non-applicable, as they do not involve violations of peremptory norms (Taiwan and GDR), or anachronistic (Manchukuo), overall outcome of the analysis does not seem to correspond to contemporary international law. Talmon, 'The Cyprus Question' (n 264) 742–750. See similarly for the criticism of Talmon Kohen (n 261) 568, ftn 48 and see also Kyriacou (n 170) 96.

267 Protocol No 10 to the Act of Accession (n 149) art 1(1).

268 Council of the European Union, '2576th Council Meeting – General Affairs' (26 April 2004) ST 8566 2004 INT, 9.

269 Council Regulation (EC) No 866/2004 of 29 April 2004 on a Regime under Article 2 of Protocol No 10 of the Act of Accession [2004] OJ L161/128 ("Green Line Regulation").

270 Skoutaris, 'The Application of the *Acquis Communautaire*' (n 260) 743.

body so authorised in agreement with the latter."[271] A critical factor of this arrangement was the consent by the Republic of Cyprus.[272] In practice, the scale of trade under the Green Line Regulation has been limited, with goods crossing the Green Line only rarely being subject to further intra-community transactions.[273]

The Commission also proposed the so-called Direct Trade Regulation,[274] which granted a preferential regime to products originating in northern Cyprus entering the EU Customs Territory and outlined the rules regarding the documents, which certified the origins of the goods. The Commission proposed that the Turkish Cypriot Chamber of Commerce or another duly authorised body would issue these documents.[275] While Cyprus' government opposed this proposal on the grounds that it would be tantamount to the TRNC's recognition, the Commission disagreed.[276] Because of these irreconcilable positions, the proposal for a Direct Trade Regulation "remains with the Council for

271 Green Line Regulation (n 269) art 4(5). If the documents are issued without fulfilling required conditions, "all duties and taxes due on the release for free circulation of the goods into the customs territory of the Community shall be due, at the rate applicable to third countries in the absence of any preferential treatment." Commission Regulation (EC) No 1480/2004 of 10 August 2004 Laying Down Specific Rules Concerning Goods Arriving from the Areas not Under the Effective Control of the Government of Cyprus in the Areas in which the Government Exercises Effective Control [2004] OJ L272/3, art 2(4).

272 The legal basis in the EU is art 2(1) of the Protocol No 10 to the Act of Accession, according to which "[t]he Council, acting unanimously on the basis of a proposal from the Commission, shall define the terms under which the provisions of EU law shall apply to the line between those areas referred to in Article 1 and the areas in which the Government of the Republic of Cyprus exercises effective control." Protocol No 10 to the Act of Accession (n 149), art 2(1).

273 Opinion of the EP's Committee on Legal Affairs (n 244) 2.

274 Commission of the European Communities, 'Proposal for a Council Regulation on Special Conditions for Trade with Those Areas of the Republic of Cyprus in which the Government of the Republic of Cyprus Does not Exercise Effective Control' (7 July 2004) COM(2004) 466 final ("Direct Trade Regulation"). Christakis, 'L'obligation de non-reconnaissance' (n 44) 155–157.

275 Skoutaris, 'The Application of the *Acquis Communautaire*' (n 260) 741.

276 European Parliament (Committee on International Trade), 'Working Document on the Commission Proposal for a Council Regulation on Special Conditions for Trade with Those Areas of the Republic of Cyprus in which the Government of the Republic of Cyprus Does not Exercise Effective Control' (13 March 2014) DT/1023171EN.doc, 3. The EP's Commission on Legal Affairs tackled the Commission's argument. "The difference between the position of Cyprus and that of territories such, for instance Ceuta and Melilla and Helgoland was that the latter were voluntarily placed outside the customs territory of the Union. Legally, Cyprus is part of the customs territory, factually part of Cyprus is not in that territory." Opinion of the EP's Committee on Legal Affairs (n 244) 8.

consideration."[277] The Opinion of the Legal Services of the Council in 2004[278] and the Opinion of the Legal Services of the European Parliament in 2010 examined the proposal.[279]

First, the key issue was the legal basis of this regulation.[280] Second, the Council's Legal Services concluded that a designation by the Commission of a body in northern Cyprus authorised to issue the certificates of origin without the Republic of Cyprus's consent "would constitute explicit recognition of another authority in the areas than the Government of the Republic of Cyprus, which would be contrary to both international law and EU primary law."[281] Accordingly, a key factor concerning the conferral of the functions of *ius imperii* on the body such as the Turkish Cypriot Chamber of Commerce was the consent of the Republic of Cyprus.[282]

From the overview of practice regarding the TRNC's imports to the EU follow three observations. First, the certificates of origin issued by the TRNC authorities were rejected by the CJEU and the proposal for authorising the Turkish Cypriot Chamber of Commerce to issue such certificates without the consent of the Republic of Cyprus was seen by the Council's Legal Services as incompatible with international law. This approach is in line with the duty of non-recognition of official acts of an illegal secessionist entity. Second, the consent of the Republic of Cyprus was critical for the application by the Green Line Regulation to products originating in the TRNC and the acceptance of proofs of origin issued by the Turkish Cypriot Chamber of Commerce. Thus, even though this arrangement might help factually consolidate an illegal entity, the alignment with the formal aspects of the duty through the parent State's

277 European Commission, 'Representation in Cyprus: Turkish Cypriot Community' <https://cyprus.representation.ec.europa.eu/about-us/turkish-cypriot-community_en> accessed 14 October 2023.

278 Council of the European Union, 'Opinion of the Legal Services of the Council of the European Union' (25 August 2004) 11874/04, 2–4 ("Opinion of the Legal Services of the Council of the European Union"). The Opinion of the Legal Services of the European Parliament is referred to in Opinion of the EP's Committee on Legal Affairs.

279 Opinion of the EP's Committee on Legal Affairs (n 244) 1–9.

280 The question was whether it was the EU treaty law concerning external trade or the Protocol No 10 to Act of Accession, as the latter would entail a partial withdrawal of the suspension of *acquis*, which would require the Council's unanimous decision. Opinion of the Legal Services of the Council of the European Union (n 278) 2–4. Both the Legal Services of the Council and EP concluded that the latter was a correct legal basis in this situation. ibid 8 and Opinion of the EP's Committee on Legal Affairs (n 244) 8.

281 Opinion of the Legal Services of the Council of the European Union (n 278) 7. See Kyriacou (n 170) 101.

282 ibid.

consent prevailed. Indeed, intra-communal trade is one of the aspects furthering possible reunification.[283] Thus, this aspect together with the parent State's consent could be considered in line communitarian interests.[284] Third, the analysis shows that the issue of the effects of this type of trade on the factual consolidation of the illegal regime's authority has not been considered at all.

4.2.2.2 *Other Dealings with Illegal Secessionist Entities*

Under the *Namibia* Advisory Opinion, other non-economic dealings are also prohibited under the duty of non-recognition if they entrench an illegal entity's authority over the territory. This is justified since the governments installed because of the violation of peremptory norms "are not to be treated as having the capacities of a government in international law."[285] The dealings below the threshold of entrenching an illegal entity's authority include certain limited types of functional contacts. For example, the UK's Special Commissioners held in *Caglar v Billingham* that "contacts which the Turkish Cypriot community in the north of Cyprus has with Her Majesty's government are not in the nature of government-to-government dealings but are functional contacts only."[286]

In practical terms, the duty of non-recognition would undeniably apply to a "joint military manoeuvre headed by chiefs of staff practising the defence of the disputed territory."[287] However, it would probably not apply to the "co-operation with health authorities of the illegal regime in order to avoid the spread of disease."[288] A similar rationale would apply to the payment of pensions benefiting the nationals of the third State residing in the illegal settlements.[289] In the same vein, cooperation in the sphere of fighting against epidemics, trafficking in narcotic drugs or organised crime would also not imply recognition.[290] Christakis in this regard referred to the "acts *jure gestionis,*

---

283 P Tani, 'The Turkish Republic of Northern Cyprus and International Trade Law' (2012) 12 Asper Review of International Business and Trade Law 115, 132–137.

284 See *infra* on the role of the parent State's consent in the context of consequences of the breach of peremptory norms.

285 Talmon, 'The Duty Not "To Recognize as Lawful"' (n 4) 119.

286 *Caglar v Billingham (Inspector of Taxes) and Related Appeals* (England, Special Commission) (1996) 108 ILR 510, 544 ("*Caglar*").

287 Ronen, *Transition from Illegal Regimes under International Law* (n 13) 101. Crawford mentions, as examples of prohibited dealings, purchases of agricultural products from illegal settlements and the provision of financial and other aid for the building of illegal settlements. Crawford, Opinion (n 64) para 85 and para 138.

288 Ronen, *Transition from Illegal Regimes under International Law* (n 13) 101.

289 Crawford, Opinion (n 64) para 85.

290 Christakis, 'L'obligation de non-reconnaissance' (n 44) 161. See also *Namibia* (n 33), Separate Opinion of Judge Dillard, 166–167.

which may be accepted in the interest of the local populations and acts *jure imperii,* ie acts which consolidate an unlawful title or authority, which must always be rejected."[291]

The ECtHR also examined the question where the line between two types of dealings rests in the context of human rights law. In *Güzelyurtlu and Others v Cyprus and Turkey*, which centred on the existence and scope of obligation to cooperate by Cyprus and Turkey under the procedural limb of Article 2 ECHR, the Court arguably implicitly drew the line between the scope of actions that implied recognition of the TRNC and the scope of the human rights obligations of Cyprus.[292] In particular, the case concerned multiple murders, which occurred in the Cyprus-controlled area and the suspected perpetrators, which were present in the TRNC-controlled territory.[293] Owing to the lack of diplomatic relations between Cyprus and Turkey, the communication occurred via the United Nations Peacekeeping Force in Cyprus (UNFICYP).[294] Ultimately, it resulted in a stalemate; while Cyprus refused to hand over evidence to the TRNC without the guarantee that suspects would be handed over to the Cypriot authorities, the TRNC rejected to do so; Turkey did not act upon Cyprus' extradition request.[295]

After the Court concluded that the Cyprus authorities used "all the means reasonably available to them to obtain the surrender/extradition of the suspects by Turkey",[296] a critical question remained as to whether Cyprus was required to supply the TRNC with evidence to fulfil its obligation under Article 2 ECHR. According to the Court, supplying an entire investigation file when the latter might be used for trial in the TRNC and without any guarantee for the suspects' surrender to Cyprus, "would go beyond mere cooperation between or prosecuting authorities."[297]

> It would amount in substance to a transfer of the criminal case by Cyprus to the 'TRNC' courts, and Cyprus would thereby be waiving its criminal jurisdiction over a murder committed in its controlled area in favour of the courts of an unrecognised entity set up within its territory.

291 Christakis, 'L'obligation de non-reconnaissance' (n 44) 166 and see also 162.

292 *Güzelyurtlu and Others v Cyprus and Turkey*, App no 36925/07 (ECtHR, 29 January 2019), para 221 ("*Güzelyurtlu*").

293 ibid paras 10–136.

294 See ibid paras 106–136.

295 See ibid paras 130–131 and paras 243–245.

296 ibid para 245.

297 ibid para 253.

> Indeed, the exercise of criminal jurisdiction is one of the main features of the sovereignty of a State. The Court therefore agrees with the Cypriot Government that in such a specific situation it was not unreasonable to refuse to waive its criminal jurisdiction in favour of the 'TRNC' courts.[298]

The Court had to distinguish this case from its previous case law. First, the Court differentiated this case from cases involving the *Namibia* exception.[299] Second, the Court referred to situations "in which a Contracting State other than Cyprus cooperates with those authorities."[300] Third, the Court differentiated this situation from "unofficial relations in judicial and security matters in the interest of crime prevention" such as information exchange and the summoning of witnesses, which due to their nature and limited character could not be considered support for the separatist regime.[301] This type of relations was examined in the *Ilaşcu* case in the context of Moldova's positive obligations and the Court held that this kind of cooperation could not be considered as support for the secessionist entity.[302] "On the contrary, they represent affirmation by Moldova of its desire to re-establish control over the region of Transdniestria."[303]

4.2.3 Official Acts of an Illegal Secessionist Entity

One of the aspects of the consequences of peremptory territorial illegality is that they do not stop at a purportedly inter-State level, but also affect the legality and validity of internal acts of an illegal secessionist entity.[304] As already

298 ibid, para 253. This is a sharp diversion from the Chamber's judgement, in which it held that it "does not accept that steps taken with the aim of cooperation in order to further the investigation in this case would amount to recognition, implied or otherwise of the 'TRNC' … Nor would it be tantamount to holding that Turkey wields internationally recognised sovereignty over northern Cyprus." *Güzelyurtlu and Others v Cyprus and Turkey*, App no 36925/07 (ECtHR, 4 April 2017), para 291.

299 "In all those cases the Court recognised the validity of those remedies and acts to the extent necessary for Turkey to be able to secure all the Convention rights in Northern Cyprus and to correct any wrongs imputable to it. The key consideration for the Court was to avoid a vacuum which would operate to the detriment of those who live under the occupation, or those who, living outside, may claim to have been victims of infringements of their rights." *Güzelyurtlu* (n 292) para 250.

300 ibid para 250.

301 ibid para 251.

302 *Ilaşcu and Others v Moldova and Russia* ECHR 2004-VII 179, paras 177–178 and para 345 ("*Ilaşcu*").

303 *Ilaşcu* (n 302) para 345.

304 See *supra* section concerning the validity of internal acts and laws of an illegal secessionist entity.

mentioned above, these acts are hardly challenged inside the illegal entity itself where they are shielded by the overwhelming effectiveness of illegality.[305] Internally, they produce legal effects up to the point of the reversal to the *status quo ante* and transition from an illegal regime.[306]

However, during the illegal entity's existence, the duty of non-recognition can play the role at an international[307] or domestic level in some public law proceedings[308] and most frequently in litigations involving the choice of law or recognition and enforcement of foreign judgments in civil matters. This challenges the traditional divide between public and private international law.[309] Similarly to the notion of a truly international public policy,[310] the expansion of the duty of non-recognition into the realm of private international law is one of the ways by which private international law gives effect to the substantive rules of public international law.[311]

305 See Y Ronen, 'Status of Settlers Implanted by Illegal Territorial Regimes' (2009) 79 British Yearbook of International Law 194, 231.

306 Cf Ronen, *Transition from Illegal Regimes under International Law* (n 13).

307 For example, as far as the exhaustion of domestic remedies or grants of nationality within the context of diplomatic protection are concerned. Ronen, *Transition from Illegal Regimes under International Law* (n 13) 82. See also *infra*.

308 The public context may include the refugee status-determination procedure. See Ronen, *Transition from Illegal Regimes under International Law* (n 13) 82, ftn 33. See also ILA, 'Second Interim Report on Recognition/Non-Recognition' (Washington Conference, March 2014).

309 See, for example, PS Berman, 'From International Law to Law and Globalization' (2004–2005) 43 Columbia Journal of Transnational Law, 518–523.

310 See *Kuwait Airways Corp v Iraqi Airways Co* (House of Lords) (2002) 125 ILR 602; A Mills, 'Mosul Four and Iran Six' in J Hohmann and D Joyce (eds), *International Law's Objects* (OUP 2018), 284–293; R O'Keefe, 'English Public Policy Internationalised-And Conversion Clarified Too' (2002) 61 Cambridge Law Journal 499; M Davies, 'Kuwait Airways Corp v Iraqi Airways Co: The Effect in Private International Law of a Breach of Public International Law by a State Actor' (2001) 2 Melbourne Journal of International Law 523. Orakhelashvili, 'International Public Order' (n 50) 241–245. See also *Application of the Convention of 1902 Governing the Guardianship of Infants (Netherlands v Sweden)* [1958] ICJ Rep 55, Separate Opinion of Judge Moreno Quintatna, 106–107.

311 "It may be suggested therefore that a state which breaches important norms of international law can no longer expect to benefit from the principles of sovereign equality and comity which underpin public and private international law." A Mills, 'Connecting Public and Private International Law' in V Ruiz Abou-Nigm, K McCall-Smith and D French (eds), *Linkages and Boundaries in Private and Public International Law* (Hart Publishing 2018) 26. *Per analogy*, the same applies in the context of an entity, which is not a State, due to violations of peremptory norms of international law in the process of its establishment.

4.2.3.1 *Starting Premise: Rule on Illegality and Invalidity of Official Acts*

Para 125 of *Namibia* is the expression of "the rule on the invalidity of official internal acts of illegal regimes."[312] According to the ICJ, "official acts" performed by an illegal entity are "illegal and invalid."[313] It is in this area where the scope of invalidity and the duty of non-recognition overlap.

The underlying rationale of this rule is that it is through the exercise of internal public functions, whether through judiciary or administrative apparatus, that the violation of peremptory norms is perpetuated and given effect on the ground.[314] The capacity of the administration to govern through these internal laws and measures depends on and derives from the original violation of peremptory norms.

However, the rule is not absolute. The ICJ also formulated the so-called *Namibia* exception according to which

> this invalidity cannot be extended to those acts, such as, for instance, the registration of births, deaths and marriages, the effects of which can be ignored only to the detriment of the inhabitants of the Territory.[315]

The exception's objective is twofold. First, it avoids the risk that non-recognition "would actually doubly victimize the population."[316] Second, it "is to safeguard the scope of sovereign authority that the rightful owner legally retains."[317] Thus, generally, to delineate the scope of the prohibition itself, it is necessary to define the scope of the exception.

---

312 Ronen, *Transition from Illegal Regimes under International Law* (n 13) 82.

313 *Namibia* (n 33) para 125. See, for example, UNSC 277 (18 March 1970) UN Doc S/RES/277, para 3. Christakis, 'L'obligation de non-reconnaissance' (n 44) 158–160.

314 "Internal acts constituted the bulk of activities carried out by South Africa with respect to Namibia, and were the means by which South Africa violated the Namibians' right to self-determination." Ronen, *Transition from Illegal Regimes under International Law* (n 13) 82. For example, with regard to the TRNC, the "TRNC is not recognized by any other jurisdiction as having a legal existence and no order made in a Court in TRNC can be enforced under any of the conventions, as it is not a party to any of them." *Trumann Investment Group Ltd v Societe Generale SA & Ors* [2004] EWHC 1769 (Ch), para 32.

315 *Namibia* (n 33) para 125.

316 A Mills, 'States, Failed and Non-Recognized' in J Basedow and others, *Encyclopaedia of Private International law* (Edward Elgar Publishing 2017) 1655.

317 A Orakhelashvili, 'The Dynamics of Statehood in the Practice of International and English Courts,' in C Chinkin and F Baetens (eds), *Sovereignty, Statehood and State Responsibility: Essays in Honour of James Crawford* (CUP 2015) 179.

Some studies have examined the consequences of non-recognition in the context of private international law in different jurisdictions.[318] However, these are not entirely relevant to the present inquiry as they focused on non-recognition without regard to its origin. For the same reasons, the case law, which is discussed below, is limited to selected US and UK cases that deal with illegal entities such as Southern Rhodesia, Bantustans and TRNC, excluding other cases that concern entities not recognised for political purposes.

Admittedly, foreign courts do not usually explicitly refer to the illegality of the entities as such, but rather accept the state of affairs of non-recognition whether deriving from the decision of the executive branch in case of 'one voice' policy or from the resolutions taken on an international plane. The conclusion on the illegality of the status of these entities undertaken in the first part of this book is the guiding criterion for the case law selection. For clarity and comparison, the examination is undertaken separately for the domestic and the ECtHR's case law.

4.2.3.2 *Namibia Exception in the Practice of Municipal Courts*

The following account begins by outlining the underlying tension concerning the scope of the *Namibia* exception. Then, it briefly examines its scope *ratione personae* and provides a comprehensive overview of its scope *ratione materiae*, which includes a basic outline of the exception's applicability, its operation in the context of trading and the transfers of ownership deriving from expropriation or similar operations.

4.2.3.2.1 Defining the Underlying Tension

The *Namibia* exception can be traced back to the US case law following the War of Secession.[319] The US Supreme Court elaborated the doctrine of necessity according to which the isolation to which the secessionist regime is subjected "must not endanger the day-to-day affairs of the people."[320] The distinction was made between the "acts necessary to peace and good order among citizens" and the "acts in furtherance or support of rebellion against the

318 ZM Nedjati, 'Acts of Unrecognised Governments' (1981) 30 International & Comparative Law Quarterly 388, 388–402; J Verhoeven, 'Rélations internationales de droit privé en l'absence de reconnaissance d'un état, d'un gouvernement ou d'une situation' (1985) 192 RCADI 9, 108–201.

319 See Ronen, *Transition from Illegal Regimes under International Law* (n 13) 84–87; Tancredi, 'A Normative "Due Process"' (n 39) 201–202.

320 Tancredi, 'A Normative "Due Process"' (n 39) 201.

United States"; with only the latter group being regarded as invalid and void.[321] The reference to the exception from non-recognition usually in the form of *obiter* or dissent has been gradually made in the UK case law, which originally treated all acts and laws of an unrecognised State as nullities.[322]

---

321 "It is not necessary to attempt any exact definitions, within which the acts of such a State government must be treated as valid, or invalid. It may be said, perhaps with sufficient accuracy, that acts necessary to peace and good order among citizens, such for example, as acts sanctioning and protecting marriage and the domestic relations, governing the course of descents, regulating the conveyance and transfer of property, real and personal, and providing remedies for injuries to person and estate, and other similar acts, which would be valid if emanating from a lawful government, must be regarded in general as valid when proceeding from an actual, though unlawful government; and that acts in furtherance or support of rebellion against the United States, or intended to defeat the just rights of citizens, and other acts of like nature, must, in general, be regarded as invalid and void." *Texas v White* (1868) 74 US 700, 733. "Laws made for the preservation of public order, and for the regulation of business transactions between man and man, and not to aid or promote the rebellion, though made by a mere de facto government not recognized by the United States, would be so far recognized as to sustain the transactions which have taken place under them. But laws made to promote and aid the rebellion can never be recognized by, or receive the sanction of, the courts of the United States as valid and binding laws." *Thomas v City of Richmond* (1871) 79 US 349, 357–358. "It would have been a cruel and oppressive judgment, if all the transactions of the many millions of people, composing the inhabitants of the insurrectionary States, for the several years of the war, had been held tainted with illegality, because of the use of this forced currency, when those transactions were not made with any reference to the insurrectionary government." *Hanauer v Woodruff* (1872) 82 US 439, 448. See also *Thorington v Smith* (1869) 75 US 1, 8; *Delmas v Merchants' Mutual Ins Co* (1871) 81 US 661, 669; *Planters' Bank v Union Bank* (1873), 83 US 483, 499; *Horn v Lockhart* (1873) 84 US 570, 580; *The Confederate Note Case* (1873) 86 US 548, 557; *Sprott v United States* (1874) 87 US 459, 461–465; *Williams v Bruffy* (1877) 96 US 176, 187–192; *Keith v Clark* (1878) 97 US 454, 476; *Ketchum v Buckley* (1878) 99 US 188, 191; *Baldy v Hunter* (1898) 171 US 388, 400–402. See Ronen, *Transition from Illegal Regimes under International Law* (n 13) 85–86.

322 See references to the exception from non-recognition in the UK's case law. "[N]on-recognition cannot be pressed to its ultimate logical limit, and that where private rights, or acts of everyday occurrence, or perfunctory acts of administration are concerned (the scope of these exceptions has never been precisely defined) the courts may, in the interests of justice and common sense, where no consideration of public policy to the contrary has to prevail, give recognition to the actual facts or realities found to exist in the territory in question … I should wish to regard it as an open question, in English law, in any future case whether and to what extent it can be invoked." *Carl Zeiss Stiftung v Rayner and Keeler Ltd (No. 2)* (House of Lords) (1966) 43 ILR 23, 66 (per Lord Wilberforce). ("*Carl Zeiss*"). See also references to the doctrine of necessity, *Madzimbamuto v Lardner-Burke* (Judicial Committee of the Privy Council) (1968) 39 ILR 61, 388–393 (per Lord Reid for majority), 393–405 (per Lord Pearce dissenting) ("*Madzimbamuto*"). "I would unhesitatingly hold that the courts of this country can recognise the laws or acts of a body which is in effective control of a territory even though it has not been recognised by Her Majesty's Government

Despite there being different interpretations of the criterion triggering the exception's applicability,[323] two approaches encapsulate the crux of the problem. On the one hand, exception is said to apply to the acts or laws of an illegal entity relating to private law affairs as opposed to the acts or laws that only regulate public law matters.[324] It needs to be clarified that the

de jure or de facto: at any rate, in regard to the laws which regulate the day to day affairs of the people, such as their marriages, their divorces, their leases, their occupations, and so forth." *Hesperides Hotels Ltd and Another v Aegean Turkish Holidays Ltd and Muftizade* (House of Lords) (1978) 73 ILR 9, 15 (per Lord Denning MR) ("*Hesperides Hotels*"). "I see great force in this reservation [Lord Wilberforce's reservation in Carl Zeiss Stiftung], since it is one thing to treat a state or government as being 'without the law,' but quite another to treat the inhabitants of its territory as 'outlaws' who cannot effectively marry, beget legitimate children, purchase goods on credit or undertake countless day-to-day activities having legal consequences. However, that is not this case." *Gur Corporation v Trust Bank of Africa Ltd* (England, Court of Appeal) (1986) 75 ILR 675, 694 (per Sir Donaldson MR) ("*Gur Corporation*"). "[T]he courts may acknowledge the existence of an unrecognised foreign government in the context of the enforcement of laws relating to commercial obligations or matters of private law between individuals or matters of routine administration such as the registration of births, marriages and deaths ... However, the courts will not acknowledge the existence of an unrecognized state if to do so would involve them in acting inconsistently with the foreign policy or diplomatic stance of this country." *Caglar* (n 286) 555–556. "I do think that in an appropriate case our courts will recognise the validity of judicial acts, even though they be the acts of a judge not lawfully appointed or derive their authority from an unlawful government." *In re James (An Insolvent)* (England, Court of Appeal) (1976) 72 ILR 29, 43 (Scarman LJ). See *infra* for case law directly applying the *Namibia* exception. For an overview of the UK case law, see Nedjati (n 318) 394–402; RD Leslie, 'Unrecognised Governments in the Conflict of Laws: Lord Denning's Contribution' (1981) 14 Comparative and International Law Journal of Southern Africa 165. See also P Athanassiou, 'The Orams Case, the Judgments Regulation and Public Policy: An English and European Law Perspective' (2009) 16 Maastricht Journal of European and Comparative Law 423, 433–435 and 438–442.

323 According to Tancredi, the *Namibia* exception entails that "[t]hird-party States, in particular, can recognize the effects of acts performed by the authorities of the illegal entity a) for humanitarian reasons; b) for agreements or transactions of a private or commercial nature; c) with regard to matters of routine administration." Tancredi, 'Some Remarks' (n 43) 103. Judge Dillard, in his Separate Opinion in the Namibia advisory opinion, offered a more extensive reading of the exception when he considered limitations to the prohibition of non-recognition in paras 122 and 125 of Namibia as too narrow. "The legal consequences flowing from a determination of the illegal occupation of Namibia do not necessarily entail the automatic application of a doctrine of nullity ... Were it otherwise the general interest in the security of transactions would be too greatly invaded and the cause of minimizing needless hardship and friction would be hindered rather than helped." *Namibia* (n 33), Separate Opinion of Judge Dillard, 155 and 136–137. See also Ronen, 'Status of Settlers Implanted by Illegal Territorial Regimes' (n 305) 233–234.

324 Raič (n 79) 162–163. "It would seem that the acts of the de facto authorities relating to the acts and rights of private persons should be regarded as valid (validity of entries in the

private legal transactions occurring in an illegal secessionist entity do not fall within the prohibition of recognition in the first place as the latter only covers 'official acts' of entity and, therefore, do not raise the issue of the *Namibia* exception.[325] The exception only comes into the picture for the laws and acts regulating these private affairs.[326] For example, according to the US Restatement of Laws, the US courts today give effect to the acts of unrecognised States "if those acts apply to territory under the control of that regime and relate to domestic matters only."[327] However, "[i]dentifying those private rights that form an exception to non-recognition involves a balancing act, and must be determined case-by-case."[328]

On the other hand, the *Namibia* Advisory Opinion referred to the act's detriment to the inhabitants of the territory,[329] rather than to a public-private divide.[330] More than the act's purpose or form, its consequences were decisive.[331] According to Ronen, this simultaneously allows for a wider and more flexible approach.[332]

In this context, Richter argued that if 'to the detriment' formula of the ICJ or the 'life goes on' formula of the ECtHR discussed below is interpreted in a wider sense,

---

civil registers and in the Land Registry, validity of marriages, validity of judgments of the civil courts, etc.). On the other hand, other States should not regard as valid any acts and transactions of the authorities in Namibia relating to public property, concessions, etc. States will thus not be able to exercise protection of their nationals with regard to any acquisitions of this kind." *Namibia* (n 33), Separate Opinion of Judge De Castro, 218–219.

325 *Namibia* (n 33) para 125. Benvenisti (n 169) 308.

326 "From this perspective, government is always in the background, creating and enforcing the rules of property, contract, tort, employment, and so on. These rules inevitably regulate social life by establishing and maintaining the type of 'private' relationships deemed appropriate or desirable." Berman (n 309) 520.

327 Restatement (n 40) § 205(3).

328 Costelloe, *Legal Consequences of Peremptory Norms in International Law* (n 55) 206.

329 *Namibia* (n 33) para 125. Ronen points out that the prohibition of recognition is seen by some authors as covering only acts that entail a formal authority, by some authors as covering only acts that directly contribute to the entrenchment of the regime, and by some authors as referring to all acts of the illegal entity, subject to the Namibia exception. Ronen, *Transition from Illegal Regimes under International Law* (n 13) 101.

330 Ronen, *Transition from Illegal Regimes under International Law* (n 13) 87.

331 ibid.

332 It is wider because it covers all acts of an illegal secessionist entity. At the same time, it is more flexible because it allows for recognition of any acts, "if circumstances require, even those that do entrench the illegal regime." ibid.

> the necessity of exception can be seen to extend not only to essential certificates on the civil status of persons (private-law relationships), but also to other acts regulating the interaction between the public and the law, where the latter must be considered indispensable in order to live a normal life and to enjoy plenitudes of human rights.[333]

However, "[t]he dilemma lies in the fact that an extension of the number of acts eligible for exemption can be helpful to the population of the illegal entity, while at the same time deepening and perpetuating illegal situation itself."[334] Thus, the tension surrounding the scope of the *Namibia* exception centres on the identification of the limit to the expansion of the exception's applicability from the acts and laws regulating private affairs to public law relationships. This risks trimming down the scope of the duty of non-recognition or even rendering the duty completely nugatory.[335]

4.2.3.2.2 Scope of the *Namibia* Exception *Ratione Personae*

The ICJ's reference to the "detriment of the *inhabitants* of the territory"[336] suggests a broader category of individuals than residents.[337] First, this group may include forced refugees, non-resident individuals affected by the illegal entity, for example "persons who own property which is subject to the actual control of the illegal regime."[338] Second, the group may also include settlers who move in after the establishment of the illegal secessionist entity.[339] Third, the group may also include the third country nationals conducting business in the illegal secessionist entity, in particular foreign investors.[340] However, as is shown below, the group of potential beneficiaries depends on the subject matter and other applicable criteria such as the requirement of good faith.

4.2.3.2.3 Namibia Exception's Scope *Ratione Materiae*

4.2.3.2.3.1 *Basic Outline*

On the one side of the spectrum, the States are obliged not to recognise acts and laws regarding public law matters including for example "the validity of an

333 Richter, 'Illegal States?' (n 71) 25.
334 ibid 25.
335 Orakhelashvili, 'The Dynamics of Statehood' (n 317) 178.
336 *Namibia* (n 33) para 125 (*emphasis added*).
337 Ronen, *Transition from Illegal Regimes under International Law* (n 13) 98.
338 ibid 99. *Demopoulos and Others v Turkey* ECHR 2010-I 365, para 96 ("*Demopoulos*").
339 ibid 99. For a complex issue of the status of settlers, see Ronen, 'Status of Settlers Implanted by Illegal Territorial Regimes' (n 305) 194–263.
340 Ronen, *Transition from Illegal Regimes under International Law* (n 13) 99.

internal law purporting to conscript residents of the disputed territory to serve in the illegal regime's military forces."[341] Similarly, the recognition of the passports of the illegal regime would also be prohibited.[342] For instance, the English Court held that the *Namibia* exception does not apply to the recognition of the TRNC nationality for immigration purposes.[343] Relatedly, standing to sue in domestic courts can also be raised as an issue. In the *Gur Corporation* case, one of the Bantustans was allowed to sue in the English courts based on rationales developed in *Carl Zeiss Stiftung*;[344] nevertheless, this approach was criticised by the doctrine as being incompatible with the purpose of non-recognition.[345]

341 ibid 101. According to the Opinion on Exhaustion of Local Remedies, "[t]he Namibia exception does not extend to: "(i) the making of laws or institutions that effect fundamental changes to the public order of that territory and which are designed to consolidate the control of the authorities over the area in which they apply; (ii) acts which are not clearly intended to benefit all of the inhabitants of the territory, and which can be denied legal effect without triggering humanitarian concerns; or to (iii) the judicial system established by the authority in unlawful occupation of the territory." Amersinghe R, Brownlie I and others, 'International Jurists Opinion on Exhaustion of Local Remedies' (4 December 2009), para 7 (*footnotes omitted*) <https://studylib.net/doc/7325624/experts--opinion-on-local-remedies#google_vignette> accessed 30 October 2023 ("International Jurists Opinion on Exhaustion of Local Remedies"). The Privy Council held that, since the UK retained its law-making capacity over Southern Rhodesia on the basis of the 1965 Southern Rhodesia Act and Order in Council 1965, the Emergency Powers Regulations made under a new Constitution by Smith's regime, had no legal validity, force or effect, and detention made under it was legally invalid. *Madzimbamuto* (n 322) 391–393.

342 The prohibition of recognition of passports already applied with respect to the situation of Manchukuo. Raič (n 79) 159.

343 *Dag v Home Secretary* (2001) 122 ILR 529, 538. Similarly, the question of recognition of TRNC citizenship laws was also at issue in *Caglar v Billingham*. "In our view the laws of citizenship are so related to the status of sovereign states in international law, and to their capability of offering diplomatic protection, that they could not be described as routine matters of administration in the same category as the registration of births, marriages and deaths. Neither are they commercial obligations nor matters of private law as between individuals. Accordingly, in our view they are not within the category of laws which the courts would recognise even when made by an unrecognised government." *Caglar* (n 286) 556.

344 In some situations, dealing with private matters in the context of an entity's non-recognition was carried out through the entity's consideration as a subordinate body of a recognised State. This reasoning was developed by the House of Lords in a case concerning the German Democratic Republic's being considered the USSR's subordinate body. See *Carl Zeiss* (n 322). However, as Mills points out, this argument is "both a stretch of legal logic and only available in a narrow set of factual circumstances, so cannot present an entirely satisfactory response to the potentially problematic consequences of non-recognition." Mills, 'States, Failed and Non-Recognized' (n 316) 1655–1656.

345 See the case concerning Ciskei being treated as a subordinate body of the South Africa *Gur Corporation* (n 322). "The aim of non-recognition is to ensure that the world presents

On the other side of the spectrum, "the registration of births, deaths and marriages" including divorce rendered by illegal secessionist entities should be recognised.[346] In addition, generally, "[t]ransactions between private individuals in which the involvement of the regime is limited to registration should therefore be given legal effect under the *Namibia* exception."[347] "This approach has been extended by statute in Australia and the United Kingdom to include recognition of the legal personality of foreign corporations established under non-recognized legal systems."[348] Moreover, in the area of inheritance law, the grant of administration by the South Rhodesia's public official was accepted by the New Zealand Court.[349] Furthermore, "an internal certification by the

---

a united front expressing its abhorrence for the system which spawned the 'independent' homelands; to allow one of these homelands to sue in the courts of a non-recognising country amounts to a significant chink in the armour." A Beck, 'A South African Homeland Appears in the English Courts: Legitimation of the Illegitimate?' (1987) 36 ICLQ 350, 358. For the criticism of this approach on other grounds, see FA Mann, 'The Judicial Recognition of an Unrecognised State' (1987) 36 ICLQ 348, 348–350.

346 *Namibia* (n 33) para 125. See *Emin v Yeldag* (England, High Court, Family Division) (2001) 148 ILR 663. It is worth noting that in this case the executive branch supported the recognition of the divorce despite the government's non-recognition of the TRNC. R Ronen, 'Recognition of Divorce without Recognition of Statehood' (2004) 63 Cambridge Law Journal 268, 270. The risk of injustice to a single mother of two children also played a role in the Court's consideration. Athanassiou, 'The Orams Case' (n 322) 441. In *B v B* the Court accepted the exception for acts concerning private affairs but distinguished the divorce without agreement from such cases. "If you fall out on a lease, you can go to litigation. When it comes to divorce, it cannot be handled without the blessing, the involvement of the State. Once you have had that involvement, you come up hard against the recognition point." *B v B (Divorce: Northern Cyprus)* [2000] 2 FLR 700, 715. See for the differentiation of these cases *Emin v Yeldag* (2001) 148 ILR 663, 677–678. See *Adams v Adams* (England, High Court) (1970) 52 ILR 45. For the US case law, see *supra*. "A marriage which is valid under the laws of the present government of Russia is quite universally regarded as valid in this country." *Banque de France v Equitable Trust Co. of New York* (1933) F.2d 202, 205.

347 Ronen, *Transition from Illegal Regimes under International Law* (n 13) 248. However, in an older US case, the court found it "troublesome" to establish whether the statutory or common-law requirements were met in respect to the authentication of birth records issued by the White Russian Soviet Socialistic Republic, Executive Committee of the County of Cherven, Province of Minsk. Additional evidence was needed. See *Claim of Werenjchik v Ulen Contracting Corp.* 255 NY 56, 58.

348 Mills, 'States, Failed and Non-Recognized' (n 316) 1657.

349 "The instant case, so it appears to me, does raise questions concerning the normal tasks which, of necessity, must be performed for the orderly protection of property in a civilised community." *Bilang v Rigg* (New Zealand, Supreme Court) (1971) 48 ILR 30, 33. For example, in *In re Luberg's Estate*, an estate proceeding, the US court recognized authentication by the Soviet officials of the power of attorney executed by persons residing in Estonia. The USA did not recognize the annexation of the Baltic Republics into the Soviet Union. "It is not every act of an official of an unrecognized government that is regarded as

illegal regime of the professional qualification of residents of that territory who trained as physiotherapist" would be exempted from the obligation of non-recognition.[350]

4.2.3.2.3.2 *Namibia Exception in the Context of Trading*

Private corporations are not prohibited by the duties of non-recognition and non-assistance from trading with or investing in an illegal secessionist entity. However, once these activities require a public law act by the latter, it follows from the case law that the recognition of such an act, notwithstanding any potential benefit that could arise for the population of the illegal entity, would violate such prohibition and would not be justified by the exception. As Raič claimed concerning the criteria of the *Namibia* exception, the harm to the well-being of the inhabitants should be evident and "not of an essentially economic character."[351]

In *Anastasiou*, the CJEU relied on the Opinion of the Advocate General, who found the recognition of the movement and phytosanitary certificates issued by the TRNC authorities for trading with the EU as not falling within the *Namibia* exception.[352] This situation would involve

> a question of the extent of the entitlement of the Member States of the Community ... to accept 'official acts' the purpose of which is to enable trade to take place with businesses from the area which is not to be recognized under the Security Council's resolutions.[353]

---

a nullity. The competence of the courts to give effect to such is only limited where the acts are political in character. If this were not so, many situations would become intolerable. It would be impossible to establish the elementary facts of birth, marriage, death or the like where the certification of the same was made by, or the official before whom proof was to be taken was an appointee of, the unrecognized regime." *In re Luberg's Estate* 243 NYS 2d 747, 750 (*references omitted*). "Even though the present government of Lithuania is not recognized by this country, since the powers of attorney relate to what has been determined to be solely a private, local and domestic matter, the inheritance rights of Lithuanian citizens, they will be given effect by the courts of this country." *Morkunas v Simutis* 481 F.Supp. 132, 134.

350 Ronen, *Transition from Illegal Regimes under International Law* (n 13) 101.

351 Raič (n 79) 163.

352 *Anastasiou I* (n 262) para 49. See also *Anastasiou I* (n 262), Opinion AG Gulmann, para 58. See also N Emiliou, 'Cypriot Import Certificates; Some Hot Potatoes' (1995) 20 European Law Review 202, 208–209.

353 *Anastasiou I* (n 262), Opinion AG Gulmann, para 58. Greenwood and Lowe argued that the Court erred in its application of the *Namibia* exception on the ground that the Court missed the point, "which is that a policy of non-recognition should not be applied to

> Presumably it would not be the case that property or energy concessions granted to a private corporation by a de facto authority in a territory unlawfully occupied must be recognized by a foreign court, because non-recognition of such a concession agreement would not, it seems, deprive an individual of the 'advantages of international co-operation.'[354]

Similarly, in *Kibris* the UK Court approved the decision by the Secretary of State for Transport to reject permission for a Turkish charter to fly from the UK to the TRNC,[355] which according to the Court of Appeal fell "well outside the ambit of the Namibia exception".[356]

> This case is not concerned with private rights, acts of everyday occurrence, routine acts of administration, day-to-day activities having legal consequences, or matters of that kind. The case involves public functions in the field of international civil aviation and the lawfulness of a public law decision.[357]

According to the Court, even though it was clear that opening up international flights to northern Cyprus would be "of great practical significance for persons resident in the territory," it "does not bring the case within the exception."[358] "The mere fact that the impugned public law decision has a knock-on effect on private lives cannot be sufficient for the purpose."[359]

---

the detriment of the population of the unrecognised entity." C Greenwood and V Lowe, 'Unrecognised States and European Court' (1995) 54 Cambridge Law Journal 4, 6.

354 Costelloe, *Legal Consequences of Peremptory Norms in International Law* (n 55) 206.

355 The case, as such, was decided on the basis of the 1944 Chicago Convention discussed above, but the Court also addressed the issue of the Namibia exception. *Regina* (*on the Application of Kibris Türk Hava Yollari and* CTA *Holidays Limited*) *v Secretary of Transport* (*Republic of Cyprus, Interested Party*) (England, Court of Appeal) (2010) 148 ILR 683 ("*Kibris*"). See for the analysis of this case, R O'Keefe, 'Decisions of British Courts During 2010 Involving Questions of Public or Private International Law' (2011) 81 BYBIL 339, 404–408; M Franklin, 'Sovereignty and the Chicago Convention: English Court of Appeal Rules on the Northern Cyprus Question' (2011) 36 Air and Space Law 109, 115–116; Chatzipanagiotis MP, 'Establishing Direct International Flights to and from Northern Cyprus' (2011) 60 ZLW 476.

356 Ibid 741.

357 ibid.

358 ibid.

359 ibid.

4.2.3.2.3.3 *Property Transfers Deriving from Expropriation*

At the outset, it was said above that transactions including property transfers between private individuals and entities do not raise the duty of non-recognition as the latter only applies to official acts and laws. However, an illegal secessionist entity may perform purported acts of confiscation, expropriation or nationalisation of property. Thus, the applicability of the *Namibia* exception can be raised in the context of private law transactions, if they are subsequent to such acts of confiscation, expropriation or nationalisation. In short, the issue would concern private law transactions involving items with a dubious legal title.[360] These transactions frequently involve implanted settlers and foreign investors.

The ECtHR's landmark case *Loizidou* is relevant as it concerned the question of the validity of expropriation of Greek-Cypriot immovable property in the TRNC by virtue of Article 159 of its constitution.[361] Referring to the UNSC resolutions declaring the proclamation of the TRNC legally invalid and calling for its non-recognition and in line with a systemic interpretation, the ECtHR concluded,

> international community does not regard the 'TRNC' as a State under international law and that the Republic of Cyprus has remained the sole legitimate Government of Cyprus.[362]

360 Ronen examines to what extent the acts of expropriation for public purposes could be recognised on the basis of the *Namibia* exception and comes to the conclusion that "[t]he scope of discretion allowed to illegal regimes should … be narrowly circumscribed." Ronen, *Transition from Illegal Regimes under International Law* (n 13) 249. Relatedly, the High Court of South Africa in the *Cherry Blossom* case decided that the ownership of a cargo of phosphate mined in Western Sahara was vested with the Sahrawi Arab Democratic Republic and not by the operating in Western Sahara and thus could not be sold by the latter to purchasers in the third country. *Sahrawi Arab Democratic Republic, the Polisario Front v NM Shipping SA and others* (Order) (South Africa, High Court) (23 February 2018) No 1487/2017 and see *Sahrawi Arab Democratic Republic, the Polisario Front v the Owner and the Charterers of the NM Cherry Blossom and others* (Judgment) (South Africa, High Court) (15 June 2017) No 1487/2017. For a critical comment on this case, especially due to a lack of restraint of this domestic court in cases having a foreign element, see Ruys (n 238) 67–90. See also '"Biggest Importer" of Phosphate Rock Is Pulling Out' (*Western Sahara Resource Watch*, 29 January 2019) <https://www.wsrw.org/a105x4051> accessed 6 December 2019.

361 *Loizidou* (n 36) paras 42–46.

362 ibid paras 42–44.

> Against this background the Court cannot attribute legal validity for the purposes of the Convention to such provisions as Article 159 of the fundamental law on which the Turkish Government rely.[363]

Even though the Court mentioned the *Namibia* exception in passing, it did not use it to validate the TRNC's expropriation.[364] The applicant was not deemed to have lost title to her property because of the provision of the TRNC constitution.[365] In one of its other cases, the Court called the TRNC's expropriation measures illegitimate because they were

> derived from the fact that the expropriation laws in question could not be attributed legal validity for the purposes of the Convention as they emanated from an entity which was not recognised in international law as a State and whose annexation and administration of the territory concerned had no basis in international law.[366]

In *Autocephalous Greek-Orthodox Church of Cyprus*, the US Court denied the validity of the confiscatory decrees passed by the Turkish Federated State of Cyprus.[367] The court denied that these decrees operated to divest the Church

---

363 ibid para 44.

364 *Loizidou* (n 36) para 45. See also E Katselli Proukaki, 'The Right of Displaced Persons to Property and to Return Home after Demopoulos' (2014) 14 Human Rights Law Review 701, 707. As will be shown below, the relevance of this judgment has been attenuated in later case law, which requires claimants firstly to exhaust local remedies before the TRNC Commission.

365 *Loizidou* (n 36) para 46. For *ratione temporis* aspects of the substantive finding of the Court that there was interference with the peaceful enjoyment of a possession rather than deprivation of a possession, see Z Douglas, *The International Law of Investment Claims* (CUP 2009) 334.

366 *Preussische Treuhand GmbH & Co KG aA v Poland* App no 47550/06 (ECtHR, 7 October 2008), para 61.

367 *Autocephalous Greek-Orthodox Church of Cyprus and the Republic of Cyprus v Goldberg and Feldman Fine Arts, Inc* (United States Court of Appeals, Seventh Circuit) (1990) 108 ILR 489, 504–505 ("*Autocephalous Greek-Orthodox Church of Cyprus*"). It needs to be added that, concerning the nationalization of property in Bolshevik Russia in 1917 that was later brought to the US, the US Court of Appeals of New York found itself having no jurisdiction to deny the validity of the nationalization decrees. "The mere fact that the United States has taken no step to recognize the existing government in Russia is of no importance so far as the internal affairs of that country are concerned." *Salimoff and Co. v Standard Oil Co.* (1933) 237 AD 686, 689. However, the Court in *Autocephalous Church of Cyprus* distinguished this case from other US case law on expropriation by the Bolsheviks. Apart from *Salimoff*, the US courts refused to give effect to these confiscatory decrees on different grounds including for being contrary to public policy, and

of the ownership of the mosaics, which were purchased by the defendants.[368] It *inter alia* relied on the fact that the TRNC had not supplanted the Republic of Cyprus or its officers, while the latter "remains the only recognized Cypriot government, the sovereign nation for the entire island."[369] The Court also pointed out that as far as the purchase of art work on the international market was concerned, the buyers "are not without means to protect themselves" and can and should take appropriate steps to verify the legal title of the purchaser.[370]

In *Hesperides Hotels*, the House of Lords found itself having no jurisdiction to entertain the question as to whether a legal title to hotels in northern Cyprus remained with pre-invasion or post-invasion owners.[371] In *Apostolides v Orams* the suit was filed by Mr Apostolides who claimed to own the land in northern Cyprus that he was forced to abandon after the Turkish invasion.[372]

---

highlighted that unlike the situation in Northern Cyprus, the US government recognized the Soviet government as a *de facto* government. *Autocephalous Greek-Orthodox Church of Cyprus and the Republic of Cyprus v Goldberg and Feldman Fine Arts, Inc* (United States Court of Appeals, Seventh Circuit) (1990) 108 ILR 489, 504–505. The British courts also recognised the Soviet nationalization decrees after receiving a certificate from the executive that the USSR was recognised as a *de facto* government. *Luther v Sagor* (England, High Court, King's Bench Division) (1921) 1 ILR 47. Similarly "[*a*] *fortiori*, the internal acts of the East German Government, insofar as they concern the parties here, should be given effect generally. At least, this is so in the absence of allegation that defendant's property was expropriated by wrongful governmental force, or that for other reasons the transaction in suit or that directly underlying it violates public or national policy." *Upright v Mercury Business Machines Co* (1961) 23 AD 2d 36, 40. "In a time in which governments with established control over territories may be denied recognition for many reasons, it does not mean that the denizens of such territories or the corporate creatures of such powers do not have the juridical capacity to trade, transfer title, or collect the price for the merchandise they sell to outsiders, even in the courts of nonrecognizing nations." ibid 41. However, neither of these cases involves an illegal secessionist entity *per se*. In this regard, the US's non-recognition of the Soviet annexation of the Baltic States is more analogous. In view of the non-recognition by the US government of the Soviet annexation of Latvia, the US court did not recognise the claim by a Soviet Latvian corporation to insurance proceeds for the sinking of three ships that had been in private ownership prior to nationalization decrees by the new government. See *Latvian State Cargo and Passenger S.S. Line v Clark* 80 F.Supp. 683.

368 *Autocephalous Greek-Orthodox Church of Cyprus* (n 367) 504–505.

369 ibid 505.

370 ibid 506.

371 "The consequence is that the appellants' action, as regards the hotels themselves, being land situate abroad, cannot be maintained. In view of this conclusion it is not necessary to enter upon the questions raised by the respondent's counsel as to the degree of notice (if any) which the courts should take of the situation in Cyprus and of 'laws' passed by the non-recognised Turkish Federated State of Cyprus." *Hesperides Hotels* (n 322) 30.

372 For the analysis of this case, see Athanassiou, 'The Orams Case' (n 322) 423–448; O'Keefe, 'Decisions of British Courts During 2010' (n 355) 341–345.

Orams, the defendants and the UK citizens, claimed to have purchased this immovable property in good faith from a third-party who had acquired it from the TRNC.[373] After obtaining favourable judgments from the Nicosia District Court, the plaintiff sought to enforce the judgment in the UK. During the appeals proceeding, the Cypriot Supreme Court *inter alia* held that due to the TRNC's illegality, any *bona fide* purchasers should be particularly vigilant and take appropriate steps regarding the verification of ownership of the land.[374]

Following the reference for a preliminary ruling, in which the CJEU held that the recognition and enforcement of judgments in civil and commercial matters under the EU regulation is not precluded "to a judgment, which is given by a Cypriot court sitting in the area of the island effectively controlled by the Cypriot government, but concerns land situated in areas not so controlled,"[375] the UK's Court of Appeal ultimately upheld the judgment of a lower court declaring enforceable the Cypriot judgments in the UK.[376] The Court of Appeal examined whether the recognition of these judgments would be contrary to international public policy and *inter alia* held that it would need to respect the UK's international obligations, which supported the enforcement of these judgments.[377]

---

373 Case C-420/07 *Meletis Apostolides v David Charles Orams, Linda Elizabeth Orams* [2009] ECR I-3571, paras. 18–19 ("Case C-420/07 *Meletis Apostolides v David Charles Orams*").

374 Ronen, *Transition from Illegal Regimes under International Law* (n 13) 305.

375 Case C-420/07 *Meletis Apostolides v David Charles Orams* (n 373) operative para. 1. "The fact that claimants might encounter difficulties in having judgments enforced in the northern area cannot deprive them of their enforceability and, therefore, does not prevent the courts of the Member State in which enforcement is sought from declaring such judgments enforceable." ibid, para 70. According to Grant, despite this judgment concerning the EU legal order, what can be distilled from it is that "the judicial system of a State continues to operate in respect of disputes over property in the State's territory, including property in territory unlawfully annexed by another State." TD Grant, *Aggression Against Ukraine: Territory, Responsibility, and International Law* (Palgrave Macmillan 2015) 93.

376 *Apostolides v Orams* (England, Court of Appeal) (2010) 154 ILR 443 ("*Orams*"). See for the excerpts of the Nicosia district court judgment "[l]e tribunal conclut donc que la procédure suivie pour l'acquisition du droit de propriété des défendeurs et la détention du patrimoine litigieux – du fait notamment que le titre de propriété leur a été cédé non pas par le titulaire légal, mais selon une procédure et des titres de propriété établis par une entité non reconnue en droit international – est illégale." *Reflets: Informations rapides sur les développements juridiques présentant un intérêt communautaire* 1 (2006) 15, 16.

377 "Security Council resolutions, while urging negotiations and settlement and stressing the importance and delicacy of property issues (as does the Government of the United Kingdom), have consistently required respect for the territorial integrity of the Republic of Cyprus under a single sovereignty. That must include respect for the courts as the judicial arm of the sovereign state." *Orams* (n 376) 517.

Regarding transactions after the expropriation of property, the question can be raised as to what extent good faith can play any role.[378] First, the hypothesis concerns the settlers implanted in the illegal entity. The ICJ in *Namibia* did not consider the good faith criterion when dealing with this issue.[379] The ECtHR considered the interest of the Turkish settlers when justifying exhaustion of local remedies in the TRNC based on the *Namibia* exception without dwelling on the good faith aspect.[380] However, Ronen presumably only *ex hypothesi*, as no precedent would support her claim, suggested the scenario when the recognition of grants of expropriated property to the settlers based on the *Namibia* exception should not be discarded.[381] This would entail situations when no alternative property would be available to the grantees and, therefore, they could not be considered to have made "a voluntary choice to collude with the regime."[382]

Second, it would be difficult to demonstrate good faith in legal transactions of foreign investors,[383] "particularly where the investors have the means of ascertaining the legal status of the property, or where such means are not available but the investors nonetheless pursue the transaction."[384] Foreigners "have no compelling need to purchase property" in illegal entities and when no possibility of verifying the legal titles is available, they should assume responsibility for what is later revealed.[385] It follows from the above case law that increased vigilance is required in this context on the side of purchasers. Indeed, Skoutaris claimed that the CJEU in *Apostolides* put an end to the notion of a *bona fide* purchaser of Greek-Cypriot dispossessed land in northern Cyprus.[386]

Overall, it follows that because the acts of expropriation by the illegal entity are invalid, the subsequent purported legal operations cannot divest a legal title of the original owners. Even the *Namibia* exception does not justify such

378 See Benvenisti (n 169) 313–314.

379 Ronen, *Transition from Illegal Regimes under International Law* (n 13) 99–100.

380 ibid 100. See *Demopoulos* (n 338) paras 84–85.

381 Ronen, *Transition from Illegal Regimes under International Law* (n 13) 249–250 and 100. See also Richter, 'Illegal States?' (n 71) 25.

382 Ronen, *Transition from Illegal Regimes under International Law* (n 13) 250.

383 Athanassiou, 'The Orams Case' (n 322) 444.

384 Ronen, *Transition from Illegal Regimes under International Law* (n 13) 250. However, Ronen also claimed that "[w]here foreign investors are not implicated in the illegality of the regime, there seems to be no reason to deny them legal protection." ibid 99.

385 Ronen, *Transition from Illegal Regimes under International Law* (n 13) 304.

386 N Skoutaris, 'Building Transitional Justice Mechanisms Without a Peace Settlement: A Critical Appraisal of Recent Case Law of the Strasbourg Court on the Cyprus Issue' (2010) 35 European Law Review 720, 731.

an outcome.[387] However, this does not prejudice the outcome of any post-transition talks. The issue of purported property transfers would certainly come to the forefront of any such negotiations and would involve a complex balancing of competing interests such as human rights and other relevant criteria including good faith.[388] Nevertheless, this type of process is a political one and is separate from the recognition of the validity of property transfers derived from expropriation during the existence of an illegal entity.[389]

4.2.3.3 *Namibia Exception in the ECtHR's Case Law*

Three key issues must be examined in the context of the *Namibia* exception in the ECtHR's case law compared to the ICJ's *Namibia* ruling – its scope, an implicit operationalisation of the attribution rule based on the effective control test and the risk of legitimation of peremptory illegality.

4.2.3.3.1 Different Uses of the Namibia Exception

The *Namibia* exception has been raised in the context of the requirement to exhaust local remedies.[390] According to the ECtHR, remedies offered in the TRNC can be considered 'domestic remedies' of the respondent State.[391] There are several problems with the Court's approach.

---

387 Recognising expropriatory effects of the TRNC Constitution "would be to, indirectly, recognize an unlawful de facto situation, which, from its inception the Crown has consistently refused to recognize." Athanassiou, 'The Orams Case' (n 322) 446.

388 See Ronen, *Transition from Illegal Regimes under International Law* (n 13) 250–251 and especially Y Ronen, 'The Dispossessed and the Distressed: Conflicts in Land-Related Rights in Transitions from Unlawful Territorial Regimes' in E Brems (ed), *Conflicts between Fundamental Rights* (Intersentia 2008) 546–547. Regarding the Israeli illegal settlements, Crawford highlighted that "[i]ndividual property rights or other commercial interests 'acquired' by corporations that stem from the unlawful regime are not likely to be opposable to an independent Palestinian State, in the absence of a specific agreement to this effect." Crawford, Opinion (n 64) para 110 and see para 138.

389 "The logical extension of the principle *ex injuria ius non oritur* is that when the unlawful regime is replaced by a lawful regime (the transition stage), reversion to the legal *status quo ante* should take place, to put facts in line with the law. This reversion is not, however, imperative or necessarily comprehensive. The extent of reversion reflects a political stance." Ronen, 'The Dispossessed and the Distressed' (n 388) 522.

390 *Cyprus v Turkey* ECHR 2001-IV 1, paras 82–102 ("*Cyprus v Turkey*").

391 ibid para 102. See also *Adali v Turkey*, App no 38187/97 (ECtHR, 31 March 2005), para 186 ("*Adali*"); *Kallis and Androulla Panayi v Turkey*, App no 45388/99 (ECtHR, 27 October 2009), para 32 ("*Kallis and Androulla Panayi*"); *Kyriacou Tsiakkourmas and Others v Turkey*, App no 13320/02 (ECtHR, 2 June 2015), para 157 ("*Kyriacou Tsiakkourmas*").

First, regarding the benefit of the TRNC remedies in the context of the violation of Article 1 of Protocol No 1 ECHR,[392] the Court *inter alia* relied on a misconstrued reading of the *Namibia* Advisory Opinion.[393] In particular, the Court referred to separate opinions, which interpreted the duty of non-recognition more restrictively than the Advisory Opinion itself.[394] Furthermore, the Court simply *assumed* the benefit of these remedies. In *Cyprus v Turkey*, the Court stated that

> [i]t appears *evident* to the Court … that the absence of such institutions would work to the detriment of the members of that [the Greek-Cypriot community in the northern Cyprus] community.[395]

The underlying motivation was the Court's effort to avoid an undesirable vacuum in human rights protection.[396] For the Court, "[l]ife goes on in the territory concerned for its inhabitants" and that "in the very interest of the inhabitants" the acts of TRNC "cannot simply be ignored by third States."[397] However,

---

392 *Cyprus v Turkey* (n 390) paras 86–88. "[W]here it can be shown that remedies exist to the advantage of individuals and offer them reasonable prospects of success in preventing violations of the Convention, use should be made of such remedies." ibid para 91.

393 See Katselli Proukaki (n 364) 716. The Court also referred to writings on the subject of *de facto* entities in international law and to judgments of domestic courts concerning the decisions of *de facto* authorities that went even further, by recognising acts related to public-law situations. *Cyprus v Turkey* (n 390) paras 94–97. However, the TRNC must be distinguished from *de facto* entities due to its underlying illegality. Therefore, this reference does not offer much support either.

394 *Cyprus v Turkey* (n 390) para 97. "The fact that the judges regarded themselves as dissenting on this issue from the majority opinion indicates that the majority interpreted the prohibition on 'dealings' more widely." Ronen, *Transition from Illegal Regimes under International Law* (n 13) 79. See also ibid.

395 *Cyprus v Turkey* (n 390) para 92 (*emphasis added*).

396 "[A]ny other finding would result in a regrettable vacuum in the system of human-rights protection in the territory in question by removing from individuals there the benefit of the Convention's fundamental safeguards and their right to call a High Contracting Party to account for violation of their rights in proceedings before the Court." *Cyprus v Turkey* (n 390) para 78 and para 91. *Demopoulos* (n 338) para 96.

397 "the obligation to disregard acts of de facto entities is far from absolute. Life goes on in the territory concerned for its inhabitants. That life must be made tolerable and be protected by the de facto authorities, including their courts; and in the very interest of the inhabitants, the acts of these authorities related thereto cannot simply be ignored by third States or by international institutions, especially courts, including this one." *Cyprus v Turkey* (n 390) para 96. "This reality, as well as the passage of time and the continuing evolution of the broader political dispute must inform the Court's interpretation and application of the Convention which cannot, if it is to be coherent and meaningful, be either static or blind to concrete factual circumstances." *Demopoulos* (n 338) para 85 and see also para 84.

such an assumption of benefit was ill-conceived as "the very illegality of the regime suggests a conflict of interests between the governing authority and the population."[398] "The obligation to *exhaust* remedies is not beneficial to the population. It is ... an obstacle to every individual seeking redress at the international level."[399] Moreover, the exhaustion of domestic remedies is linked to the protection of sovereignty, but "[w]here sovereignty is denied, there is no justification for such deference."[400]

Unlike the *Namibia*-specific criterion of the benefit to the population, the Court tests the Convention requirement of the effectiveness of remedies[401] in the specific circumstances where it arises.[402] In *Demopoulous v Turkey*, the ECtHR held for the first time that remedies offered by the TRNC's Immovable Property Commission were effective and, therefore, the application was found inadmissible.[403] As for the remedies against the violation of other rights in the

398 Ronen, *Transition from Illegal Regimes under International Law* (n 13) 91, 93–94 and 101–102.

399 ibid (n 13) 96; Y Ronen, 'Non-Recognition, Jurisdiction and the TRNC before the European Court of Human Rights' (2003) 62 Cambridge Law Journal 534, 537; *Cyprus v Turkey* (n 390) Partly Dissenting Opinion of Judge Palm, Joined by Judges Jungwiert, Levits, Pantiru, Kovler and Marcus-Helmons, 102. See the Court's counterarguments in *Demopoulos* (n 338) paras 97–98 and see also para 101. "The Court cannot subscribe to the position that it is somehow better for individuals to bring their cases directly before it than to make use of remedies available locally; this runs counter to the basic principle of exhaustion of domestic remedies." ibid, para 97; International Opinion on Exhaustion of Local Remedies (n 341) paras 13–14.

400 Ronen, *Transition from Illegal Regimes under International Law* (n 13) 96. Similarly, International Jurists Opinion on Exhaustion of Local Remedies (n 341) para 11. LG Loucaides, 'Is the European Court of Human Rights Still a Principled Court of Human Rights After the *Demopoulos* Case?' (2011) 24 Leiden Journal of International Law 435, 446–447.

401 *Cyprus v Turkey* (n 390) paras 98–99. "[T]he exhaustion rule is inapplicable where an administrative practice, namely a repetition of acts incompatible with the Convention and official tolerance by the State authorities, has been shown to exist and is of such a nature as to make proceedings futile or ineffective." ibid, para 99.

402 *Cyprus v Turkey* (n 390) para 102. See also *Adali* (n 391) para 186; *Kallis and Androulla Panayi* (n 391) para 32; *Kyriacou Tsiakkourmas* (n 391) para 157.

403 *Demopoulos* (n 338) para 103. Ronen argues that in the Court's decision in *Demopoulos* "on the obligation to approach the commission rather than the validity of any of its decisions, the court reaffirmed the shift ... of giving bread *ex ante* effect to norms of the TRNC rather than exceptional recognition *ex post facto* to specific acts based on these norms." Ronen, *Transition from Illegal Regimes under International Law* (n 13) 95. With respect to the IPC, "it is also the legislative, executive and judicial branches of the TRNC whose existence and efficacy have been recognized, at least indirectly, by the Court as it is the 'TRNC's 'Parliament,' its 'President' and its 'courts' that are involved in its establishment, in the appointment and dismissal of its members and in the hearing of appeals

TRNC or remedies in Transnistria, Nagorno-Karabakh and Abkhazia, the Court dismissed the objection of non-exhaustion of remedies namely due to their non-effectiveness.[404]

The ECtHR also applied *Namibia* exception-like considerations concerning substantive rights under the ECHR.[405] For example, regarding the right to a fair trial under Article 6 ECHR, the Court held in *Cyprus v Turkey* that

> notwithstanding the illegality of the 'TRNC' under international law, it cannot be excluded that applicants may be required to take their grievances before, *inter alia*, the local courts with the view to seeking redress.[406]

It also held that "there is a functioning court system in the 'TRNC' for the settlement of disputes relating to civil rights and obligations defined in 'domestic

---

against its awards." P Athanassiou, 'The Status of the "TRNC" through the Prism of Recent Legal Developments: Towards Furtive Recognition?' (2010) 22 The Cyprus Review 15, 34. According to Shaelou, it is questionable to what extent *Demopoulos* "is protective of fundamental rights in Europe as it appears to promote a piecemeal approach to Turkey's liability under the Convention and to weaken legal title to property ownership." SL Shaelou, 'Market Freedoms, Fundamental Rights, and the European Public Order: Views from Cyprus' (2011) 30 Yearbook of European Law 298, 340. For an in-depth analysis, see Loucaides (n 400) 435–465 and Katselli Proukaki (n 364) 701–732. See also RC Williams, 'Demopoulos v. Turkey (Eur. Ct. H.R.), Introductory Note' (2010) 49 ILM 816, 816–820.

404 For example, in the context of the TRNC, the Court did not find remedies before administrative courts concerning the refusal of permits at the 'green line' effective. See *Djavit An v Turkey*, App no 20652/92 (ECtHR, 20 February 2003), paras 28–37; *Adali* (n 391) para 191. Similarly, see *Kallis and Androulla Panayi* (n 391) para 32. See *Joannou v Turkey*, App no 53240/14 (ECtHR, 12 December 2017), paras 104–106. With respect to Transnistria, see, for example, *Vardanean v the Republic of Moldova and Russia*, App no 22200/10 (ECtHR, 30 May 2017), para 31 ("*Vardanean*"); *Sandu and Others v the Republic of Moldova and Russia*, App nos 21034/05 and 7 others (ECtHR 17 July 2018), para 46 ("*Sandu*"); *Draci and Others v the Republic of Moldova and Russia*, App no 5349/02 (ECtHR 17 October 2017), para 41 ("*Draci*"); *Iovcev and Others v the Republic of Moldova and Russia*, App no 40942/14 (ECtHR, 17 September 2019), para 53 ("*Iovcev*"); *Apcov v the Republic of Moldova and Russia*, App no 13463/02 (ECtHR, 30 May 2017), para 30 ("*Apcov*"); *Mangîr and Others v the Republic of Moldova and Russia*, App no 50157/06 (ECtHR, 17 July 2018), para 69 ("*Mangîr*"). With respect to Nagorno-Karabakh, see *Chiragov and Others v Armenia* ECHR 2015-III, para 118 ("*Chiragov*"). Regarding Abkhazia, see *Mamasakhlisi and Others v Georgia and Russia* App 29999/04 and 41424/04 (Merits) (ECtHR, 7 March 2023) paras 266–269.

405 *Foka v Turkey*, App no 28940/95 (ECtHR, 24 June 2008) paras 83–84 ("*Foka*"). See *Protopapa v Turkey*, App no 16084/90 (ECtHR, 24 February 2009) paras 60–64 and see also para 96 and paras 83–89 ("*Protopapa*"); *Cyprus v Turkey* (n 390) paras 231–240. See *infra* for further references.

406 *Cyprus v Turkey* (n 390) para 236.

law.'"[407] The ECtHR adopted a similar approach with respect to elements of 'lawful arrest or detention' in the TRNC under Article 5 ECHR.[408]

Ronen fiercely criticised the Court's approach in that the ECtHR presumed that "every act of the regime is in pursuit of respecting, securing or protecting the human rights of the population" even without analysis of the human rights consequences of specific acts of TRNC.[409] This was particularly visible in *Foka* and *Protopapa* where "[t]he detention and legal proceedings ... were carried out in order to enforce the TRNC's border control" and thus were directly furthering the TRNC's existence as separated from Cyprus.[410]

In *Ilaşcu,* in the context of alleged violation of Article 5 ECHR, the Court reiterated its position from the TRNC case law that

> a court belonging to the judicial system of an entity not recognised under international law may be regarded as a tribunal 'established by law' provided that it forms part of a judicial system operating on a 'constitutional and legal basis' reflecting judicial tradition compatible with the Convention.[411]

However, in contrast with its case law on TRNC, the Court specifically drew from the non-recognition of Transnistria and "its unlawful character under international law."[412] In particular, the Court held in the context of alleged violation of Articles 3 and 5 ECHR that the Supreme Court of Transnistria "was set up by an entity which is illegal under international law and has not

---

407 *Cyprus v Turkey* (n 390) para 237 and see paras 228–240. The ECtHR referred to the Commission's reference to Namibia advisory opinion. ibid, para 231. See also *Protopapa* (n 405) paras 83–89; *Asproftas v Turkey*, App no 16079/90 (ECtHR, 27 May 2010) paras 72–74; *Petrakidou v Turkey*, App no 16081/90 (ECtHR, 27 May 2010), paras 85–92 ("*Petrakidou*"). "The Court does not view the legal and judicial system operating in Northern Cyprus ... as devoid of lawful basis due to it being established by an unlawful regime." G Nuridzahanian, '(Non-)Recognition of De Facto Regimes in Case Law of the European Court of Human Rights: Implications for Cases Involving Crimea and Eastern Ukraine' (*EJIL: Talk!*, 9 October 2017) <https://www.ejiltalk.org/non-recognition-of-de-facto-regimes-in-case-law-of-the-european-court-of-human-rights-implications-for-cases-involving-crimea-and-eastern-ukraine/> accessed 28 November 2019.

408 *Foka* (n 405) paras 83–84; *Petrakidou* (n 407) paras 69–77.

409 Ronen, *Transition from Illegal Regimes under International Law* (n 13) 93.

410 ibid 94.

411 *Ilaşcu* (n 302) para 460; *Mozer v the Republic of Moldova and Russia*, App no 11138/10 (ECtHR, 23 February 2016) para 144 ("*Mozer*").

412 A Lagerwall, 'Is the Duty Not to Recognise 'States' Created Unlawfully Challenged by States' Practice and ECHR Case Law?' in W Czapliński and A Kleczkowska (eds), *Unrecognised Subjects in International Law* (SCHOLAR Publishing House 2019) 273.

been recognised by international community."[413] The Court rejected that the Transnistrian Supreme Court functions "on a constitutional and legal basis reflecting a judicial tradition compatible with the Convention" due to "patently arbitrary nature of the circumstances in which the applicants were tried and convicted."[414]

Nevertheless, in a more recent case *Mozer* the Court "no longer considered that the illegal nature of the de facto regime and its unrecognised status under international law in and of itself rendered the courts unlawful."[415] In the context of alleged violation of Article 5 ECHR, it stated that

> it cannot automatically regard as unlawful, for the limited purposes of the Convention, the decisions taken by the courts of an unrecognised entity purely because of the latter's unlawful nature and the fact that it is not internationally recognised.[416]

Nevertheless, focusing on the effectiveness of protection of rights under the Convention by reference to independence and the impartiality of Transnistrian courts, the Court concluded that the courts in Transnistria did not meet the test of forming "part of a judicial system operating on a 'constitutional and legal basis' … compatible with Convention."[417] The Court adopted the same approach when assessing the violations of Article 5(1)(a)(c) ECHR (regarding the issue of the lawfulness of arrest and detention) and 6(1) ECHR (the

413 *Ilaşcu* (n 302) para 436 and see also para 461.
414 ibid para 436.
415 Nuridzahanian (n 407).
416 *Mozer* (n 411) para 142.
417 *Mozer* (n 411) para 144. Firstly, the Court pointed out that it was for Russia, as the country having effective control over the unrecognised entity, to show that its courts fulfilled such a test, and Russia failed to do so. Secondly, unlike with respect to the TRNC, the Court pointed out that the Transnistrian judicial system is hardly compatible with the Convention, as it was never "part of a system reflecting a judicial tradition considered compatible with Convention principles before the split into separate judicial systems occurred in 1990." Thirdly, the Court also considered particular circumstances of the case, such as the order for the detention for an unspecified period time, the applicant's absence during the appeal against the decision to extend the detention, and media reports raising concerns about the independence and quality of Transnistrian courts. *Mozer* (n 411) paras 147–150. See also *Vardanean* (n 404) paras 38–39; *Soyma v the Republic of Moldova and Russia and Ukraine*, App no 1203/05 (ECtHR, 30 May 2017), paras 33–35; *Mangîr* (n 404) paras 36–38; *Braga v the Republic of Moldova and Russia*, App no 76957/01 (ECtHR, 17 October 2017), paras 57–58; *Draci* (n 404) paras 72–73; *Apcov* (n 404) paras 56–57; *Eriomenco v the Republic of Moldova and Russia*, App no 42223/11 (ECtHR, 9 May 2017), paras 71–73; *Iovcev* (n 404) paras 85–86.

existence of "tribunal established by law") by the *de facto* Abkhaz authorities in *Mamasakhlisi*.[418]

4.2.3.3.2 Attribution Test

The Court's jurisprudence on the *Namibia* exception reveals consequential information for the on-going scholarly debate on whether the effective control test employed by the ECtHR is only a jurisdiction-triggering test or the rule of attribution. Indeed, the Court's case law rests on the understanding that remedies provided by the TRNC are remedies offered by Turkey.[419] "[R]emedies available in the 'TRNC' may be regarded as 'domestic remedies' of the respondent State."[420] The Court explicitly held in *Demopoulos* that "[t]o the extent that any domestic remedy is made available by acts of the 'TRNC' authorities or institutions, it may be regarded as a 'domestic remedy' or 'national' remedy vis-à-vis Turkey."[421] Similar rationales were also upheld in *Foka v Turkey*[422] and

418 *Mamasakhlisi* (n 404) paras 419–428 and paras 437–440. Regarding the assessment of violation of Article 5(1) ECHR, the Court formulated the general principle in the following way: "[A]ssuming that the acts of the de facto Abkhaz authorities and courts were in compliance with the local laws in force within Abkhaz territory at the time of the facts complained of, those acts had in principle to be regarded as having a legal basis in domestic law for the purposes of the Convention." Ultimately, the Court did not have enough information about the legal system in Abkhazia and there was "no basis for assuming that there is a system reflecting a judicial tradition compatible with the Convention in the region, similar to the one in the rest of the Georgia." ibid, paras 425–426.

419 *Cyprus v Turkey* (n 390) para 101.

420 ibid para 102.

421 *Demopoulos* (n 338) para 89 and see para 98. Previously, in *Xenides-Arestis*, the Court pointed out that Turkey "must introduce a remedy which secures genuinely effective redress for the Convention violations," which concerned, in particular, violation of Article 1 of Protocol 1 to the ECHR. *Xenides-Arestis v Turkey*, App no 46347/99 (ECtHR, 22 December 2005), para 40. Following this judgment, the TRNC adopted the new compensation Law, under which the Immovable Property Commission (IPC) was established in the TRNC. This was then evaluated by the Court in *Demopoulos* (n 338) para 89 and see para 75.

422 The ECtHR held that in light of Turkey's accountability for the violation of human rights in the territory of TRNC on the basis of Turkey's overall control, it would not be consistent with Turkey's responsibility "if the adoption by the authorities of the 'TRNC' of civil, administrative or criminal law measures, or their application or enforcement within that territory, were to be denied any validity or regarded as having no "lawful" basis in terms of the Convention." *Foka* (n 405) para 83. "The Court, accordingly, considers that when as in the instant case an act of the 'TRNC' authorities is in compliance with laws in force within the territory of northern Cyprus, those acts should in principle be regarded as having a legal basis in domestic law for the purposes of the Convention." ibid, para 84.

Protopapa v Turkey.[423] In addition, this link flows from Russia's and Armenia's arguments in cases concerning Transnistria and Nagorno-Karabakh.[424]

From this follows that the ECtHR thereby operationalised the effective control test discussed below in detail as an implicit rule of attribution.[425] The Court understood the TRNC institutions as Turkish institutions, TRNC remedies as Turkish remedies and TRNC laws as Turkish domestic laws.[426] As Crawford pointed out, "the remedies available in the TRNC were 'domestic' remedies provided by Turkey."[427] The only factual link between the TRNC and Turkey mentioned in its case law is Turkey's effective control over the TRNC.[428]

4.2.3.3.3 Legitimation of Peremptory Illegality

The above partial conclusions must weigh in on the question of whether the ECtHR has unjustifiably legitimatised the peremptory illegality. First, as for the TRNC, the ECtHR held that

> [i]t appears indeed difficult to admit that a State is made responsible for the acts occurring in a territory unlawfully occupied and administered by it and to deny that State the opportunity to try to avoid such responsibility by correcting *the wrongs imputable to it in its courts.*[429]

The ECtHR disregarded the TRNC as a separate addressee of international responsibility under the ECHR and instead underlined Turkey's responsibility.

---

423 *Protopapa* (n 405) para 60 and see also paras 62 and 64.

424 Russia argued that the applicants should have exhausted domestic remedies against violations that occurred in Transnistria in the Russian Federation, but the Court emphasized the fact that Russia consistently rejected having jurisdiction over Transnistria and therefore dismissed these objections. *Vardanean* (n 404) para 28 and para 31; *Sandu* (n 404) paras 40–46; *Draci* (n 404) paras 40–41; *Iovcev* (n 404) paras 51–53; *Apcov* (n 404) para 30. Armenia adopted similar arguments with respect to violations committed in Nagorno-Karabakh. See *Chiragov* (n 404) para 119.

425 See *infra* Chapter 8.

426 In particular, this conclusion flows from the Court's pronouncement that it appears difficult "to deny that State [Turkey] the opportunity to try to avoid such responsibility by correcting the wrongs imputable to it in its courts." *Cyprus v Turkey* (n 390) para 101. A similar reading can be induced from the Court's statement that "it cannot be asserted, on the one hand, that there has been a violation of that Article because a State has not provided a remedy while asserting, on the other hand, that any such remedy, if provided, would be null and void." ibid, para 101. The only remedy available was the one available in the TRNC. See also *Foka* (n 405) paras 83–84; *Protopapa* (n 405) para 60.

427 Crawford, *State Responsibility* (n 96) 384.

428 See extensively *infra*.

429 *Cyprus v Turkey* (n 390) para 101 (*emphasis added*).

More broadly, the Court's disregard of the responsibility of the TRNC under the ECHR can be seen as flowing from its underlying illegality and hence from the lack of its status as State and a Contracting Party to the ECHR.

Bearing this mind, it is difficult to agree with Ronen[430] that the Court is increasingly willing "to recognize, under the Namibia exception, the authority of the illegal regime, rather than only the consequences of its acts. This authority accompanies the responsibility under international human rights law."[431] The Court's implicit use of attribution of TRNC's conduct to Turkey precludes any conclusion as to a direct TRNC's international responsibility.[432] The TRNC's understanding as Turkey's agent is more in line with a traditional State-oriented paradigm of human rights law.

Second, the assessment of the Court's approach to the underlying illegality of third State's presence in the context of secessionist entity must be made. This concerns especially the case law on the TRNC where the basic tenets of the Court's approach were laid down. While admittedly the ECtHR is not the Court of a general jurisdiction, through a systemic interpretation, the peremptory illegality should be accounted for especially when it is established at the level of the UNSC.[433] Indeed, the Court on numerous occasions referred to unlawfulness of Turkey's occupation under international law.[434] However, it does not seem that the Court took the illegality of Turkey's power, exercised through TRNC, into account when outlining the scope of the *Namibia* exception.[435] Even if accepted that the TRNC institutions were considered as Turkey's institutions, "the Court did not assess the validity of the 'TRNC' tribunals in the light of the unlawful character of their establishment."[436]

Drawing from its reading of *Namibia* exception, the Court held that "the mere fact that there is an illegal occupation does not deprive all administrative

---

430 Ronen, *Transition from Illegal Regimes under International Law* (n 13) 88–91.

431 ibid 88.

432 See Kohen (n 261) 567–568.

433 The Court itself highlighted the need for a systemic interpretation of the Convention in *Loizidou.* "Mindful of the Convention's special character as a human rights treaty, it must also take into account any relevant rules of international law." *Loizidou* (n 36) para 43.

434 See *Cyprus v Turkey* (n 390) para 101; *Demopoulos* (n 338) para 94 and para 114.

435 See International Jurists Opinion on Exhaustion of Local Remedies (n 341) paras 5–6. See on this point in detail Loucaides (n 400) 452–465. See *Namibia* (n 33) para 118.

436 Lagerwall (n 412) 272–273. Moreover, Lagerwall also points out that the Court used the argument on the need to avoid vacuum in human rights protection to justify some sort of recognition of the TRNC's judicial apparatus and also to justify Turkey's responsibility. "Quite interestingly, not to say paradoxically, the argument thus sustains two different approaches, which could be said to be irreconcilable." ibid 279.

or putative legal or judicial acts of any relevance under the Convention."[437] The Court also rejected the position "that institutions and procedures imposed by force by an occupying power cannot be treated as if they were established by the lawful government of the State."[438] Moreover, it derived conclusions from the longevity of the dispute and the passage of time.[439] Additionally, in the context of Turkey's illegal occupation, it also based its conclusions on a need to assure the fairness of the system towards the unlawful occupant.[440]

Indeed, the Court's reasoning is still grounded in the ICJ's Advisory Opinion, and thus showed "no intention to challenge it formally."[441] However, the outlined misbalance in the Court's reasoning leads to conclusion that the ECtHR's reading of the *Namibia* exception was too broad[442] and did not correspond to the ICJ's version of the exception. "[I]t seems that in substance the Court has departed from the ICJ's approach."[443]

This tends to *de facto* legitimatise Turkey's illegal occupation and by implication also indirectly the TRNC as Turkey's agent and "a local subordinate administration."[444] Even though the Court held "that allowing the respondent State to correct wrongs imputable to it does not amount to an indirect legitimisation of a regime unlawful under international law,"[445] it follows, the Court's

437 *Demopoulos* (n 338) para 94.

438 ibid para 100 in connection with para 94. See also *Cyprus v Turkey* (n 390) para 236; *Mozer* (n 411) para 143.

439 *Demopoulos* (n 338) paras 84–85. "The Court can only conclude that the attenuation over time of the link between the holding of title and the possession and use of the property in question must have consequences on the nature of the redress that can be regarded as fulfilling the requirements of Article 35 § 1 of the Convention." ibid, para 113. "The passage of time is therefore neither sufficient to take away the illegality of the act nor to remove the title concerned. Nor does it entitle the wrongdoing state to choose the form of remedy to be provided." *Katselli Proukaki* (n 364) 714 and see 719–729 for the issue of restitution in the ECtHR case law. See also Loucaides (n 400) 455–462.

440 See *Cyprus v Turkey* (n 390) para 101.

441 Lagerwall (n 412) 278.

442 "[T]he definition of what may be considered to be an internal and private law right capable of recognition has over time expanded, most notably in the case law of the European Court of Human Rights." Crawford, *State Responsibility* (n 96) 384; Ronen, *Transition from Illegal Regimes under International Law* (n 13) 88–98; Katselli Proukaki (n 364) 716. For Orakhelashvili, a narrow focus of adjudication and the Court's policy of admitting the exception only to the extent necessary to avoid stripping inhabitants of their rights, "is a possible countervailing factor that could constrain this exception within its proper limits." Orakhelashvili, 'The Dynamics of Statehood' (n 317) 178.

443 Nuridzahanian (n 407).

444 *Loizidou v Turkey* (Preliminary Objections) (1995) Series A no 310, para 62.

445 *Demopoulos* (n 338) para 96.

expansive reading of *Namibia* exception could be seen as contributing to such legitimation.[446] It cannot be agreed with the ECtHR that its approach does not "legitimise the 'TRNC' in any way."[447] Therefore, it can be agreed with Ronen,

> ECtHR effectively emptied the obligation of non-recognition of any meaning insofar as internal acts of the illegal regime are concerned. If this approach is followed, non-recognition can be implemented only at the inter-state level.[448]

4.3 *Policy and Normative Conflicts Raised by the Duty of Non-recognition*

The duties of non-recognition and non-assistance seek to preserve and protect of international public order. However, this cardinal objective can raise different types of conflicts, including clear-cut normative conflicts with other applicable legal regimes, conflicts with policy rationales influencing the application of these duties from outside or conflicts internal to the framework itself.

First, there is the broadest and most general conflict with the power of facticity itself. It concerns a classical rebuke of the principle of *ex iniuria ius non oritur* and duty of non-recognition raised even today. For example, Oeter rejected a rigid and strict application of the principle of *ex iniuria ius non oritur* requiring the exclusion of all the relations with an illegal entity including those below the threshold of formal recognition.[449] Oeter claims that

> [s]uch a complete disjuncture between legality and facticity would pose a risk of international law becoming isolated (or insulated) in a nice, but fictitious, niche of normative ideals, with any (presumably toxic) interface with the realities of international relations then being avoided.[450]

---

446 Similarly, see Y Ronen, 'Non-Recognition, Jurisdiction and the TRNC before the European Court of Human Rights' 537. *Cyprus v Turkey* (n 390) Partly Dissenting Opinion of Judge Palm, Joined by Judges Jungwiert, Levits, Pantiru, Kovler and Marcus-Helmons, 101.

447 *Cyprus v Turkey* (n 390) para 92. See also *Foka* (n 405) para 84; *Kallis and Androulla Panayi* (n 391) para 32; *Kyriacou Tsiakkourmas* (n 391) para 157. "[T]here is no direct, or automatic, correlation of the issue of recognition of the "TRNC" and its purported assumption of sovereignty over northern Cyprus on an international plane and the application of Article 35 § 1 of the Convention." *Demopoulos* (n 338) para 100 and see also para 96.

448 Ronen, *Transition from Illegal Regimes under International Law* (n 13) 95.

449 S Oeter, '*De facto* Regimes in International Law' in W Czapliński and A Kleczkowska (eds), *Unrecognised Subjects in International Law* (SCHOLAR Publishing House 2019) 73–74.

450 ibid 74. Oeter builds his approach on the pragmatism of introducing the notion of *de facto* regimes particularly with respect to non-recognition of the GDR. This allowed for the upholding of non-recognition of status, while at the same time conducting pragmatic

In this context, some authors also highlight the irrelevance of the duty of non-recognition in a long-term context.[451] "If it becomes clear ... that the aggressor has not been deterred and the illegal situation is in fact permanent, non-recognition loses its purpose and arguably its moral authority."[452] Or similarly, De Visscher claimed that "[u]ne tension trop prolongée entre le fait et le droit doit fatalement se dénouer, au cours du temps, au bénéfice de l'effectivité."[453]

However, these opinions do not correspond to the above practice and they are at odds with structural and systematic arguments that underlie peremptory norms. It is possible to agree with Orakhelashvili that "[i]f the rationale of the principle is accepted, it is unclear why that rationale is not relevant in the course of the practical operation of that principle."[454]

> When an illegal entity claims statehood, it claims not merely the formal status but also the practical ability to exercise, as a matter of real life, a variety of rights, powers and privileges which it considers as derived from its sovereignty, whether related to diplomatic intercourse, trade, valid issuance of documents and certificates, or administration in general.[455]

Thus, as a matter of principle in contemporary international law, these types of arguments are unfounded and rather anachronistic.

Second, the question can be asked what the return to the *status quo ante* as the key objective of the duty of non-recognition entails. The developments on the ground might call for attenuation of this objective. Should intransigence or flexibility prevail?[456] For example, in treaty relations, the question can be asked whether

---

relations with the entity. ibid 73–78. Nevertheless, the GDR did not originate as a result of a serious breach of peremptory norms.

451 When dealing with the issue of adequacy of redress in the context of holding title in the prolonged unlawful occupation of Northern Cyprus, the ECtHR concluded that "the attenuation over time of the link between the holding of title and the possession and use of the property in question must have consequences on the nature of the redress." *Demopoulos* (n 338) para 113 and see paras 110–112 and paras 114–119.

452 Pert (n 24) 66.

453 C De Visscher, *Les effectivités du droit international public* (Pedone 1967) 25.

454 Orakhelashvili, *Peremptory Norms in International Law* (n 14) 387.

455 ibid 388. If the duty of non-recognition did not encompass acts below the threshold of formality, "it would be a curious principle that would legitimize the hypocrisy of formal non-recognition accompanied by the cooperation with the non-recognized entity that enables that entity to effectively exercise what it claims as its sovereign powers." ibid.

456 Cannizzaro (n 19) 433.

> a treaty which aims at alleviating the violation of fundamental values of the international community, without bringing about a situation of full compatibility, is nonetheless in conflict with *jus cogens* and therefore invalid.[457]

The key task would then rest in finding a balance between the flexibility needed to achieve the broader objectives of the denial of peremptory illegality and a creeping subversion of the overall scheme.

Relatedly, it has been suggested that trading with an illegal entity should be accepted as it encourages negotiations with the view of conflict-settlement.[458] This might include treaties that would provide at least part of the profits from illegal exploitation and trade to the non-self-determined people.[459] "This argument rests ultimately on the consideration that a treaty reserving substantial advantages to the holder of the right to self-determination is to be preferred over the absence of any treaty."[460] However, it follows from above that purely economic rationale without other criteria never have justified attenuation of the duty of non-recognition.

Moreover, the position of the injured State or directly affected State in the context of the consequences of peremptory territorial illegality must be explored.[461] On the one hand, some authors claim that "[n]orms of jus cogens are thus not at the disposal of the injured State; it cannot unilaterally negotiate away the interests of the international community in ensuring a just and appropriate settlement."[462] On the other hand, the ILC did not completely

---

457 ibid. Cannizzaro ponders the compatibility of treaties that are objectively inconsistent with *ius cogens*, but "gradually promote compliance with *jus cogens* norms, on the ground that in doing so they act in the interests of the international community as a whole, which is the ultimate holder of the rights and duties deriving from a rule of *jus cogens*." ibid.

458 Moerenhout, 'The Obligation to Withhold from Trading' (n 192) 361.

459 Cannizzaro (n 19) 432.

460 ibid 433.

461 See ARSIWA (n 41) commentary to art 41, para 9. Orakhelashvili, *Peremptory Norms in International Law* (n 14) 398–404 and 408–409.

462 Talmon, 'The Duty Not "To Recognize as Lawful"' (n 4) 125 and 123–124. "La valeur ajoutée de l'art. 41, par. 2, est d'imposer une limitation à la discrétion de cet Etat [l'état victime], en ce sens que son choix ne pourra en tout cas pas impliquer la reconnaissance de la situation qui résulte de l'illicite; en d'autres termes, sa position de victime directe ne lui permet pas d'éluder les obligations qui lui incombent en tant que membre de la communauté internationale … Ainsi, par exemple, l'Etat victime d'un acte d'agression ne pourra pas reconnaître l'annexion d'une partie de son territoire par l'Etat envahisseur et les autres Etats pourront continuer de demander la cessation de l'illicite (perpétué par l'occupation) et s'abstenir de reconnaitre les effets de l'annexion." Villalpando (n 49) 389, ftn 1349.

discard the waiver or recognition by the injured State, but required that in doing so the interests of the international community must be preserved.

> [S]ince the breach by definition concerns the international community as a whole, waiver or recognition induced from the injured State by the responsible State cannot preclude the international community interest in ensuring a just and appropriate settlement.[463]

Arguably, these rationales should apply *a fortiori* if recognition is not induced by the responsible State. However, how these equivocal parameters translate in concrete cases is far from clear at this stage. Indeed, the above incremental practice shows that the injured State preserves a privileged position in shaping the response to the consequences of peremptory territorial illegality and to the question when the relevant communitarian interests are met.[464] The same rationale was suggested concerning non-self-determined people.

Lastly, a similar question can be raised as to how to reconcile efforts of conflict resolution with the peremptory illegal situation. In this context, Arcari suggested that the UNSC could not be precluded from "being called upon, sooner or later, to manage the temporal element inevitably accompanying the obligation vis-à-vis collective non-recognition."[465] This would entail that "the UNSC could be willing to reconsider the scope of the obligation of non-recognition, as well as its implications."[466] The UNSC in such a process would be critical for preserving the communitarian interests and the underlying duties flowing from the principle of ex *iniuria ius non oritur*. It would be also in line with the safeguard clause in the Friendly Relations Declaration according to which the

---

463 ARSIWA (n 41) commentary to art 40, para 9 and see also commentary to art 45, para 4.

464 "[S]ome parent states are willing to accept certain forms of engagement with their breakaway territories, including international links, if this is seen to further attempts to reach a negotiated settlement and reinforce their claim to territorial integrity." Caspersen (n 194) 235.

465 M Arcari, 'The UN SC, Unrecognised Subjects and the Obligation of Non-Recognition in International Law' in W Czapliński and A Kleczkowska (eds), *Unrecognised Subjects in International Law* (SCHOLAR Publishing House 2019) 239.

466 ibid 239. However, examples provided by Arcari refer mostly to situations of transition from illegal regimes involving a return to the *status quo ante*. Therefore the UNSC's address to members of illegal regimes to comply with proposed legal frameworks cannot in this context be seen as a modification of the application of the obligation of non-recognition or as incompatible with it. See ibid 239–240.

duty of non-recognition shall not affect "[t]he powers of the Security Council under the Charter."[467]

5 Conclusion

This chapter analysed the consequences of peremptory territorial illegality in the context of the outer boundaries of the facticity when directly confronted with the day-to-day administration and basic needs of a population living in an illegal secessionist entity. It highlighted such consequences as the inapplicability of rules of State succession and the invalidity of acts under general international law. However, it mainly focused on the content and operation of the duty of non-recognition.

Despite a frequent doctrinal criticism labelling this obligation as without substance, the above analysis demonstrated that it has an undeniable normative core.[468] It showed that once an entity is not recognised as a State under the duty of non-recognition, the latter is followed in the context of purportedly inter-State relations that raise the attributes of sovereignty such as treaty and diplomatic relations. It is also observed in the realm of government-to-government-like relations, which are completely denied subject to certain limited functional contacts that are beneficial to the local population. Moreover, the duty functions well in formal or law-application settings, where any type of recognition of public law acts of an illegal secessionist entity such as proofs of origin required for the grant of a preferential tariff, phytosanitary certificates or expropriation decisions in the context of ownership transfers concerning foreign investors is denied.

Admittedly, when the context is defined solely by a factual contribution to illegality or aid or assistance in maintaining illegal situation, such as in the area of direct aid or trade, it is more difficult to discern the line between prohibited and permitted actions. This is also linked with uncertainty as to what these duties require third States to do regarding the conduct of private economic operators. The analysis acknowledged this underlying paradox. While at this

467 Declaration on Principles of International Law concerning Friendly Relations and Co-operation among States in accordance with the Charter of the United Nations, UNGA Res 2625 (XXV) (24 October 1970) UN Doc A/RES/2625(XXV), principle 1, para 10(b). Similarly see Definition of Aggression, UNGA Res 3314 (XXIX) (14 December 1974) UN Doc A/RES/3314(XXIX), art 6; ARSIWA (n 41) art 59. See also *East Timor* (n 20), Separate Opinion of Judge Skubiszewski, para 132.

468 See also Caspersen (n 194) 231–240.

stage of development of international law, the duties of non-recognition and non-assistance do not require third States to ban private economic operators from conducting outgoing or incoming trade with illegal secessionist entities, this undeniably helps factually sustain the illegal entity's authority.

Nevertheless, it was also highlighted that this latter sphere is very frequently limited by other aspects of the duty, particularly in the context of non-extension of preferential trade treaties or non-recognition of public law acts required for carrying out business activities. In addition, the section also acknowledged that subject to the preservation of relevant communitarian interests, the consent of the parent State as an injured State might play a privileged position in the context of responses to peremptory illegality over the territory.

The above conclusions on a rather broad scope of the duty of non-recognition are also aligned with the fact that the municipal courts have interpreted the *Namibia* exception's scope in a restrained fashion,[469] generally following a public-private divide. Moreover, the benefit to the local population has not been interpreted as being only of purely economic nature. To the contrary, the application of the *Namibia* exception was rejected in the contexts, which would improve the economic position of the local inhabitants, but would require the recognition of public acts of the illegal secessionist entity. The ECtHR's jurisprudence on the *Namibia* exception was identified as posing risks to a limited scope of the exception introduced by the ICJ. Nevertheless, the ECtHR's approach cannot be taken as legitimising the illegal secessionist entity as a direct subject of international obligations, but only indirectly as an agent of the third State exercising the required level of control over it.

Thus, the analysis demonstrated that the effects of peremptory territorial illegality permeate purportedly inter-State relations and the internal legal sphere of the illegal secessionist entity in an extensive manner. Despite some uncertainties in the areas of a purely factual contribution to illegality, the duty of non-recognition proves to be a well-observed tool of decentralised responses to peremptory territorial illegality.

469 For example, in the UK case law, "Emin v Yeldag is the only precedent to date where an English court actually took cognizance of some of the TRNC's acts." Athanassiou, 'The Orams Case' (n 322) 438.

CHAPTER 8

Consequences of Change of Effective Territorial Control

1 Introduction

"[S]overeignty itself, with its retinue of legal rights and duties, is founded upon the fact of territory. Without territory a legal person cannot be a state."[1] "Indeed, the principle whereby a state is deemed to exercise exclusive power over *its* territory can be regarded as a fundamental axiom of classical international law."[2] Under general international law, "the jurisdictional competence of a State is primarily territorial."[3] In turn, what entails the State's territory is defined by reference to titles of territorial sovereignty.[4]

This picture presumes the alignment of these three foundational elements of international law – territory, sovereignty and jurisdiction.[5] However, what happens when they do not coincide as outlined? How does international law accommodate the entity's power over territory when it lacks titles of territorial sovereignty? What legal consequences does international law attach to the

1 MN Shaw, *International Law* (6th CUP 2008) 487. However, on the legal implications of climate change on the requirement of territory for the purposes of statehood, see D Wong, 'Sovereignty Sunk? The Position of "Sinking States" at International Law' (2013) 14 Melbourne Journal of International Law 1.

2 Shaw (n 1) 487–488 (*emphasis added*). "En effet, l'hypothèse la plus commune sera celle de l'exercice des compétences étatiques sur un territoire par celui qui en le titulaire. Les autres hypothèses sont plutôt exceptionnelles et peuvent encore se distinguer selon qu'elles sont établies conformément au droit international ou en violation de celui-ci". MG Kohen, *Possession contestée et souveraineté territorial* (PUF 1997) 77. See also A Orford, 'Jurisdiction without Territory: From the Holy Roman Empire to the Responsibility to Protect' (2009) 30 Michigan Journal of International Law 981.

3 *Banković v Belgium* ECHR 2001-XII 333, para 59 ("*Banković*"). "Jurisdiction is an aspect of sovereignty, it is coextensive with and, indeed, incidental to, but also limited by, the State's sovereignty". FA Mann, 'The Doctrine of Jurisdiction in International Law' in (1964) 111 RCADI, 1, 30 (*footnotes omitted*).

4 See Shaw (n 1) 489–492. See in detail Kohen, *Possession contestée et souveraineté territorial* (n 2) 127–154.

5 "Statehood is articulated by reference to a particular geographic territory; jurisdiction, in the sense of a sovereign's authority over persons or events, by reference to their location within that territory". HL Buxbaum, 'Territory, Territoriality, and the Resolution of Jurisdictional Conflict' (2009) 57 American Journal of Comparative Law 631, 632.

© KONINKLIJKE BRILL BV, LEIDEN, 2024 | DOI:10.1163/9789004702646_013

exercise of effective power outside of the State's own sovereign territory? And how does the context of illegal secessionist entity fit into this picture?

Indeed, the illegal secessionist entity's apparent effectiveness is undermined by a double paradox. Firstly, its effectiveness cannot produce the ordinary effects of State emergence as it is outweighed by a countervailing principle of legality. A previous chapter described the consequences of peremptory territorial illegality on the effective relations of such an entity subsequent to denial of statehood; they seek to protect the parent State's interests and fundamental values of public international order. Secondly, while such an entity *prima facie* displays powers and attributes of statehood, in reality, it frequently lacks independence vis-à-vis a third State, which exercises control over it.[6] As a result, the third State comes into the picture as the addressee of international norms triggered upon effectiveness. An underlying rationale is that only the entity, which *in fact* possesses effectiveness, should be held internationally responsible for violation of applicable international law.

This is in line with a ground-breaking *dictum* of the ICJ in *Namibia*, that "[p]hysical control of a territory, and not sovereignty or legitimacy of title, is the basis of State liability for acts affecting other States."[7] Under Article 2 ARSIWA, "[t]here is an internationally wrongful act of a State when conduct consisting of an action or omission: (a) is attributable to the State under international law; and (b) constitutes a breach of an international obligation of the State."[8] These two conditions of applicability of international legal rules and

6 See *supra* Chapter 6 for a detailed delimitation of the notion of an illegal secessionist entity, including the scenario of a self-standing entity outside of any State's control.

7 "The fact that South Africa no longer has any title to administer the Territory does not release it from its obligations and responsibilities under international law towards other States in respect of the exercise of its powers in relation to this Territory." *Legal Consequences for States of the Continued Presence of South Africa in Namibia (South West Africa) Notwithstanding Security Council Resolution 276 (1970) (Advisory Opinion)* [1971] ICJ Rep 16, para 118 ("*Namibia*"). MG Kohen, 'Création d'Etats en droit international contemporain' in (2002) VI *Cours euro-méditerranéens Bancaja de droit international* 568. As for the scope of law applicable extra-territorially in *Namibia*, it refers to "liability for acts affecting other States" and "obligations and responsibilities under international law towards other States". This advisory opinion was adopted before decisions by human rights bodies on the extra-territorial application of human rights treaties. R Wilde, 'Human Rights Beyond Borders at the World Court: The Significance of the International Court of Justice's Jurisprudence on the Extraterritorial Application of International Human Rights Law Treaties' (2013) 12 Chinese Journal of International Law 639, 662–663.

8 ILC, Draft Articles on the Responsibility of States for Internationally Wrongful Acts, with Commentaries in 'Report of the International Law Commission on the Work of its Fifty-Third Session (23 April -1 June and 2 July-10 August 2001)' UN Doc A/56/10, art 2 ("ARSIWA").

attributability of conduct to the State must be met even in an extra-territorial context.

The most prominent legal regimes applicable extra-territorially on the basis of effectiveness are humanitarian law, specifically, the law of occupation and human rights law. In particular, "[t]he trigger for the law of occupation, and one of the two triggers for the human rights law concept of 'jurisdiction' extra-territorially, are based on a *spatial* concept of territorial control."[9] As will be shown in more detail in the following chapter,[10] the reasons why these regimes have developed in such a way that they apply extra-territorially on the basis of effectiveness[11] could be seen in their underlying object and purpose, in particular the protection of the human dignity of individuals and humanitarian interests.[12]

This chapter specifically focuses on identifying levels of control over the territory required to trigger the applicability of humanitarian law and the extra-territorial applicability of human rights law and to establish State responsibility for their violation. It seeks to systematise conflicting practice, *opinio iuris* and contradictory doctrinal opinions to clarify the contours of contemporary international law in this area. While the chapter predominantly focuses on the

---

9 R Wilde, 'Triggering State Obligations Extraterritorially: The Spatial Test in Certain Human Rights Treaties' (2007) 40 Israel Law Review 503, 504.

10 See *infra* Chapter 9.

11 See *infra* for a detailed examination of the notion of jurisdiction.

12 Whether the State obtained control over a territory lawfully or not, its ability to affect and protect the human rights of its inhabitants is the same. Wilde, 'Triggering State Obligations Extraterritorially' (n 9) 508. On the difference of purpose between human rights law and general international law, and how it informs the notion of extraterritorial application of human rights treaties, see VP Tzevelekos, 'Reconstructing the Effective Control Criterion in Extraterritorial Human Rights Breaches: Direct Attribution of Wrongfulness, Due Diligence, and Concurrent Responsibility' (2014) 36 Michigan Journal of International Law 129, 130–131. See also M Milanović, *Extraterritorial Application of Human Rights Treaties: Law, Principles and Policy* (OUP 2011) 61. The justification for the human rights treaties' "extra-territorial application lies in the formulation of their general legal obligation." K Von Der Decken, 'Article 29: Territorial Scope of Treaties' in O Dörr and K Schmalenbach (eds), *Vienna Convention on the Law of Treaties* (2nd edn, Springer 2018) 534. "The doctrine of occupation serves as a useful device to fill the 'spatial problem' – the exercise of 'foreign state power in the territory of a continuing sovereign state.' The law of occupation operates as a gap-filler – in fact the only such gap filler – assigning authority to one state to act in the territory of another state ... Because occupation does not transfer sovereignty over the territory to the occupying power, international law must regulate the inter-relationships between the occupying force, the ousted government, and the local inhabitants for the duration of the occupation". E Benvenisti, *The Law of Occupation* (OUP 2012) 1 and 6.

issue of effective *territorial* control, due to interconnection, other levels of control, in particular over the *entity*, are also examined.

2 International Humanitarian Law

The exercise of control outside of a State's sovereign territory provokes specific consequences in the field of international humanitarian law (IHL). Firstly, there are situations when the State intervenes into a pre-existing secessionist non-international armed conflict (NIAC). Depending on the level of control over the armed group, the NIAC can become internationalised. Secondly, depending on the threshold of control over the territory and entity, the law of belligerent occupation can apply either alongside a NIAC or indirectly, through proxies.

2.1 *Extra-Territorial Intervention into a Non-international Armed Conflict*

According to the ICRC, there are two types of foreign intervention into a pre-existing NIAC. Firstly, a foreign State may intervene in support of the non-State party, but this support falls below the threshold of control.[13] In this case, the law of NIACs and IACs apply in parallel.[14] Secondly, the intervening State exercises overall control over the non-State party,[15] as a result of which the NIAC is internationalised.[16] In this situation, only the law of IACs applies, since "the only two parties remaining in the conflict are the intervening foreign power and the State party."[17] As a result, "there is an IAC, and so not only will that specific war crimes regime apply, but the Geneva Conventions should also create rights and obligations for the two states concerned."[18]

---

13 T Ferraro, 'The ICRC's Legal Position on the Notion of Armed Conflict Involving Foreign Intervention and on Determining the IHL Applicable to This Type of Conflict' (2015) 97 International Review of the Red Cross 1227,1245.

14 ibid 1245.

15 ibid 1249. See *infra* on the notion of overall control.

16 D Carron, 'When Is a Conflict International? Time for New Control Tests in IHL' (2016) 98 International Review of the Red Cross 1019, 1032.

17 Ferraro, 'The ICRC's Legal Position' (n 13) 1252.

18 A Clapham, 'The Concept of International Armed Conflict' in A Clapham and others (eds), *The 1949 Geneva Conventions: A Commentary* (1st edn, OUP 2015) 17; and see *infra* for more on due diligence obligations in this regard.

2.1.1 Internationalisation of NIAC: Parameters of Overall Control Test

After a substantial doctrinal and jurisprudential debate, the ICTY's overall control test seems to be generally accepted today as the relevant threshold for the purposes of internationalising a pre-existing NIAC.[19] Even the ICJ in *Bosnian Genocide* indirectly endorsed such a stance.[20] According to the ICTY, an overall control test requires the third State's role "in *organizing, coordinating or planning the military actions* of a military group, in addition to financing, training and equipping or providing operational support to the group".[21] In essence, it is a two-pronged test.

Firstly, "[t]he provision of economic, military or other assistance, in and of itself, is not sufficient to establish overall control."[22] Secondly, the third State's

19 See *Tadić case* (Judgment, Appeals Chamber) (IT-94-1-A) (15 July 1999), para 137 ("*Tadić*"). See also *Aleksovski case* (Judgment, Trial Chamber) (IT-95-14/1-T) (25 June 1999), Joint Opinion of the Majority, Judge Vohrah and Judge Nieto-Navia, para 27; *Aleksovski case* (Judgment, Appeals Chamber) (IT-95-14/1-A) (24 March 2000), para 134; *Delalić case* (Judgment, Appeals Chamber) (IT-96-21-A) (20 February 2001), para 26 ("*Delalić*"); *Prosecutor v Jadranko Prlić and others* (Judgment, Appeals Chamber) (IT-04-74-A) (29 November 2017), para 238 ("*Jadranko Prlić*"). For the ICC case law see *Prosecutor v Thomas Lubanga Dyilo* (Confirmation of Charges Decision) ICC-01/04-01/06, Pre-Trial Chamber (29 January 2007), para 210–211; *Prosecutor v Thomas Lubanga Dyilo* (Judgment) ICC-01/04-01/06, Trial Chamber (14 March 2012), para 541; *Prosecutor v Germain Katanga* (Judgment) ICC-01/04-01/07, Trial Chamber (7 March 2014), para 1178; *Prosecutor v Jean-Pierre Bemba Gombo* (Judgment) ICC-01/05-01/08, Trial Chamber (21 March 2016), para 130. The ICC did not explicitly indicate the legal source of the overall control test. For an opinion that references in ICC judgments indicate endorsement for the ICTY's position on the overall control test being the secondary rule of attribution, see R Jorritsma, 'Where General International Law Meets International Humanitarian Law: Attribution of Conduct and the Classification of Armed Conflicts' (2018) 23 Journal of Conflict and Security Law 405, 427–428. Similarly, the Office of the Prosecutor uses the overall control test in order to determine if the conflict in Eastern Ukraine has become internationalized. See *infra*. Ferraro, 'The ICRC's Legal Position' (n 13) 1237. However, Carron argues for a different control test, which would be general in its scope and strict in its intensity. Carron (n 16) 1034–1037.

20 "It should first be observed that logic does not require the same test to be adopted in resolving the two issues, which are very different in nature: the degree and nature of a State's involvement in an armed conflict on another State's territory which is required for the conflict to be characterized as international, can very well, and without logical inconsistency, differ from the degree and nature of involvement required to give rise to that State's responsibility for a specific act committed in the course of the conflict". *Case Concerning Application of the Convention on the Prevention and Punisment of the Crime of Genocide* (*Bosnia and Herzegovina v Serbia and Montenegro*) (Judgment) [2007] ICJ Rep 43, paras 404–5 ("*Bosnian Genocide*").

21 *Tadić* (n 19) para 137 (*emphasis in original*).

22 S Talmon, 'The Responsibility of Outside Powers for Acts of Secessionist Entities' (2009) 58 ICLQ 493, 506. See *Tadić* (n 19) para 145; *Delalić* (n 19) para 29. Simplifying the

role in organising, coordinating or planning the military actions of a military group needs to be also demonstrated, which can be rather intricate, as it requires evidence as to the internal workings between the State and an armed group. In fact, to prove the fulfilment of this second prong, the ICTY took into account several indicators, which can be divided into two groups – those that relate to personnel and those concerning decision-making.[23]

Firstly, the Court took into account the posting of the third State's army's officers into the units of armed groups,[24] the payment of salaries to members of the armed groups by the third State's government[25] and the identity of the structures and ranks of the armed groups and the armed forces of the third State.[26] Secondly, the Court assessed the pursuit of shared military objectives and strategy;[27] the reality of the third State's military command with respect to the armed groups, as opposed to ostensible structures and overt declaration;[28] and the joint direction of military operations.[29] In *Tadić*, the Court also took into account *ex post facto* the third State's wielding of general control over armed groups in the military and over the political sphere during negotiations and conclusion of the peace agreement.[30] The Court also held that if the third State is an adjacent State seeking territorial enlargement through the controlled armed groups, this threshold might also be easier to establish.[31]

However, "[u]nlike effective control, which materializes on the tactical level of specific military objectives, overall control … requires a more general, less-intrusive, level of direction and planning, done at the strategic and operational

---

acquisition of the intervening State's nationality was taken as one of the indicators of a strong connection between the secessionist entity and the third State. However, this strong connection was not sufficient to establish overall control. *Prosecutor v Naletilić and Martinović* (Judgment, Trial Chamber) (IT-98-34-T) (31 March 2003) para 198 ("*Naletilić and Martinović*").

23 N Quenivet, 'Trying to Classify the Conflict in Eastern Ukraine' (*INTLAWGRRLS*, 28 August 2014) <https://ilg2.org/2014/08/28/trying-to-classify-the-conflict-in-eastern-ukraine/> accessed 7 February 2019.

24 See *Tadić* (n 19) para 150; *Naletilić and Martinović* (n 22) para 201; *Prosecutor v Tihomir Blaškić* (Judgment, Trial Chamber) (IT-95-14-T) (15 July 1999), paras 112–119 ("*Tihomir Blaškić*"); *Jadranko Prlić* (n 19) para 283 and references therein.

25 See *Tadić* (n 19) para 150; *Naletilić and Martinović* (n 22) paras 199 and 201.

26 See *Tadić* (n 19) para 151; *Naletilić and Martinović* (n 22) para 199.

27 See *Tadić* (n 19) paras 150–153. In *Naletilić and Martinović*, the Trial Chamber established that the third State leadership issued orders to the armed groups to implement common goals. *Naletilić and Martinović* (n 22) para 201; *Tihomir Blaškić* (n 24) paras 108–111.

28 See *Tadić* (n 19) paras 151 and 154; *Tihomir Blaškić* (n 24) para 118.

29 *Jadranko Prlić* (n 19) para 283 and references therein.

30 See *Tadić* (n 19) paras 158–160; *Jadranko Prlić* (n 19) para 283 and references therein.

31 See *Tadić* (n 19) para 140.

level of military operations."[32] This test "can be fulfilled, even if the secessionist entity has autonomous choices of means and tactics while participating in a common strategy along with the outside power".[33] "In a Tadić-type IAC the 'overall-controlling' state directs neither the way the non-state armed group controls the territory nor its every operation."[34]

2.1.2 State Responsibility in the Context of Internationalised NIAC

A State is responsible for any violations of IHL committed by its own State organs, including its armed forces; violations committed by private actors attributable to it; and the State's own due diligence obligations.[35] A key contemporary controversy lies in the question of the relation of the overall control test to rules of attribution under general international law. Some authors call for this test to function both as the trigger for the internationalisation of a NIAC and for attribution of conduct in the context of State responsibility for violations during an internationalised NIAC.

In this regard, the overall control test is functionally equated to the attribution rules of general international law, in particular Article 8 ARSIWA, with respect to organised military groups, but not individuals or groups not organised into military structures.[36] As a result, not only a NIAC would become

32 Jorritsma, 'Where General International Law Meets International Humanitarian Law' (n 19) 410.

33 Talmon (n 22) 506.

34 T Gal, 'Unexplored Outcomes of Tadić: Applicability of the Law of Occupation to War by Proxy' (2014) 12 Journal of International Criminal Justice 59, 66–67. "Involvement must therefore go beyond mere logistical support, but that involvement does not imply that everything done by the group concerned is directed by the State taking part from a distance". S Vité, 'Typology of Armed Conflicts in International Humanitarian Law: Legal Concepts and Actual Situations' (2009) 91 International Review of the Red Cross 69, 71.

35 See ICRC, 'IHL Database of Customary IHL: Rule 149. Responsibility for Violations of International Humanitarian Law' (2005) <https://ihl-databases.icrc.org/customary-ihl/eng/docs/v1_rul_rule149> accessed 11 January 2020; ARSIWA (n 8) arts 4–11; *Case Concerning Armed Activities on the Territory of the Congo (Democratic Republic of the Congo v Uganda)* (Merits) ICJ Rep [2005] 168, paras 213–214 ("*Armed Activities*"); M Sassòli, 'State Responsibility for Violations of International Humanitarian Law' (2002) 84 Revue Internationale de la Croix-Rouge/International Review of the Red Cross 401, 404–412; M Longobardo, 'State Responsibility for International Humanitarian Law Violations by Private Actors in Occupied Territories and the Exploitation of Natural Resources' (2016) 63 Netherlands International Law Review 251, 256–257.

36 *Tadić* (n 19) para 132. Jorritsma, 'Where General International Law Meets International Humanitarian Law' (n 19) 410–412; Carron (n 16) 1024. However, Talmon points out that the overall control test was in fact intended to replace the strict control test rather than the effective control test. This was due to the ICTY's misreading of *Nicaragua*. Talmon (n 22) 506–507.

internationalised, but also any violation of IHL by armed groups acting as proxies on behalf of the third State or agents of the third State on the basis of the overall control would be attributable to that third State.[37] The ICTY[38] and ICRC[39] support this position. For the ICRC,

> the question of "attribution" plays a major role in defining an armed conflict as international since, by virtue of this operation, the actions of the armed group can be considered as actions of the intervening State and the relationship of subordination can be established.[40]

The main argument is that differentiation between two tests would result in an accountability vacuum due to the fact that the conduct of armed groups fighting on behalf of the third State would not be attributable to this State.[41] As a result, the controlling State would not bear international responsibility for the

---

37 Ferraro, 'The ICRC's Legal Position' (n 13) 1250.

38 "In order to attribute the acts of a military or paramilitary group to a State, it must be proved that the State wields overall control over the group, not only by equipping and financing the group, but also by coordinating or helping in the general planning of its military activity. Only then can the State be held internationally accountable for any misconduct of the group. However, it is not necessary that, in addition, the State should also issue, either to the head or to members of the group, instructions for the commission of specific acts contrary to international law." *Tadić* (n 19) para 131.

39 Ferraro, 'The ICRC's Legal Position' (n 13) 1235–1236.

40 ICRC, *Commentary on the First Geneva Convention: Convention (I) for the Amelioration of the Condition of the Wounded and Sick in Armed Forces in the Field* (2nd edn, 2016 CUP), para 268 (*footnote omitted*) ["The 2016 Commentary"]. "The Chamber first noted that it seemed logical to think that, for armed units fighting within a state to 'belong' to another state, it was necessary for this latter state wield some 'degree of authority or control' over those armed units (para. 97)". Since the IHL did not contain such a test, the ICTY used tests from the law of state responsibility. A Cassese, 'The Nicaragua and Tadić Tests Revisited in Light of the ICJ Judgment on Genocide in Bosnia' (2007) 18 European Journal of International Law 649, 656. According to Sassòli, "the law of State responsibility provides the only solution because international law does not contain any other general rules to determine what constitutes the conduct of a State and IHL contains no special rules to attribution necessarily human conduct to a State ... The rules on attribution of the law of State responsibility not only determine State responsibility; they are also used in international law to determine whether certain conduct is attributable to a State and therefore subject to rules of international law addressing States". M Sassòli, *International Humanitarian Law: Rules, Controversies and Solutions to Problems Arising in Warfare* (Edward Elgar 2019) 174.

41 Gal (n 34) 63; Sassòli, *International Humanitarian Law* (n 40) 175. According to ICRC, "the test that is used must avoid a situation where some acts are governed by the law of international armed conflict but cannot be attributed to a State." ICRC, The 2016 Commentary (n 40) para 271.

conduct performed on its behalf. Authors of this group claim that this position is untenable "due to the immutable connection that exists between belligerency in an IAC, and the responsibility that comes with it".[42] "It is simply inconceivable that a territorial State must apply IAC law in relation to OAGs fighting as proxies for a controlling third State, without being able to hold the third State responsible for the acts of the latter's agents."[43] There is also a minority group of authors who foresee the overall control test operating as a *lex specialis* rule of attribution in *ius in bello*.[44]

Conversely, the ICJ and ILC differentiate between two tests.[45] According to the ICJ, "the test for internationalizing a NIAC is found in the primary rules of IHL, without prejudice to the secondary attribution of State responsibility."[46] The rules of attribution under the rules of State responsibility, including a "complete dependency test" in the sense of Article 4 ARSIWA and an "effective control test" in the sense of Article 8 ARSIWA, remain much stricter and operate on the level of attribution of specific conduct.[47]

---

42 Jorritsma, 'Where General International Law Meets International Humanitarian Law' (n 19) 418 and see also 418–424. See also MJ Ventura, 'Two Controversies in the Lubanga Trial Judgment of the International Criminal Court: The Nature of Co-Perpetration's Common Plan and the Classification of the Armed Conflict' in *War Report* (Geneva Academy 2012) 11–18.

43 Jorritsma, 'Where General International Law Meets International Humanitarian Law' (n 19) 421.

44 ibid 406. Jorritsma takes a minority position that the overall control test creates a *lex specialis* rule of attribution within *ius in bello* applicable to acts of hostilities carried out by organized armed groups in the context of an armed conflict or possibly giving rise to an armed conflict. ibid 428–430. Akande outlines three approaches, including a *lex specialis* of international responsibility in IHL, either on the basis of a looser *de facto* relationship or on the basis of overall control. A third approach would rely on the use of force by the third State, on the basis of *ius ad bellum* rules. D Akande, 'Classification of Armed Conflicts: Relevant Legal Concepts' in Wilmshurst E, *International Law and Classification of Armed Conflicts* (OUP 2012) 61–62.

45 Jorritsma, 'Where General International Law Meets International Humanitarian Law' (n 19) 411–412. See also Milanović M, 'State Responsibility for Genocide' (2006) 17 European Journal of International Law 553, 582–583.

46 Jorritsma, 'Where General International Law Meets International Humanitarian Law' (n 19) 412.

47 *Military and Paramilitary Activities in and against Nicaragua* (Nicaragua v United States of America) (Merits) [1986] ICJ Rep 14, paras 110 and 115 ("*Nicaragua*"); *Armed Activities* (n 35) para 160; *Bosnian Genocide* (n 20) paras 393 and 400; ARSIWA (n 8) commentary to art 8, paras 3–5. See on the points of difference between the ICJ and ILC KE Boon, 'Are Control Tests Fit for the Future: The Slippage Problem in Attribution Doctrines' (2014) 15 Melbourne Journal of International Law 330, 342–345 and 346–348. See also M Milanović, 'State Responsibility for Acts of Non-State Actors: A Comment on Griebel and Plücken' (2009) 22 Leiden Journal of International Law 307, 308–319.

> This premise of *functional differentiation* … allowed the ICJ to reject the overall control test for the purposes of State responsibility, while not ruling out that this test applies to determine the existence of an IAC.[48]

Scholars on this side of the spectrum point out that

> the issue of the qualification of the legal nature of an armed conflict is solely one for international humanitarian law, and has nothing to do with the law of state responsibility, even though the factual patterns on which these branches of law operate might be very similar.[49]

Moreover, observers also highlight flaws of the ICTY's *Tadić* judgment, including misreading of the ICJ's *Nicaragua*,[50] as well as equating tests for the classification of individuals under IHL with tests for establishing international responsibility.[51] It is entirely possible that after the application of attribution rules of a general law of State responsibility, the actions of individuals fighting on behalf of a third State will not be attributable to it, even though such individuals could be held individually responsible.[52] In addition, a supposed accountability vacuum is always mitigated by the fact that the third State controlling the proxies can be held internationally responsible for violation of its own due diligence obligations.[53]

---

48 Jorritsma, 'Where General International Law Meets International Humanitarian Law' (n 19) 411.

49 Milanović, 'State Responsibility for Genocide' (n 45) 587. Similarly, "it would rather be worrying if, in order to apply the rules of IHL of international armed conflict to a particular individual, it was first necessary to establish that the actions of this individual could be attributed to a state which consequently incurred responsibility for his or her actions." K Del Mar, 'The Requirement of "Belonging" under International Humanitarian Law' (2010) 21 European Journal of International Law 105, 109. Similarly, see Carron (n 16) 1026–1028.

50 See Milanović, 'State Responsibility for Genocide' (n 45) 576–581.

51 Del Mar (n 49) 114–117. In addition, it was also observed that actions of combatant under Article 4A(2) GCIII are not *necessarily* attributable to the third State. ibid 118–119. Convention (III) Relative to the Treatment of Prisoners of War (singed 12 August 1949, entered into force 21 October 1950) 75 UNTS 135 ("GCIII").

52 Del Mar (n 49) 120. The situation is different when Additional Protocol I applies, as it includes a *lex specialis* rule of attribution. ibid 120–121. Protocol Additional to the Geneva Conventions of 12 August 1949, and Relating to the Protection of Victims of International Armed Conflicts (Protocol I) (signed 8 June 1977, entered into force 7 December 1978) 1125 UNTS 3, art 91 in connection with art 43(1) ("Additional Protocol I" or "API").

53 "Even where the acts of the fighters are not attributable to the state in question, due to there being no dependency or effective control, the state remains responsible for any failure to prevent violations of the Geneva Conventions which could reasonably have been prevented, as well as for ensuring respect for the Geneva Conventions through the

In any case, in contemporary international law, the same factual scenario can raise the applicability of separate tests.[54] "It is thus not only unproblematic, but expected, that the tests which have developed for different purposes are different."[55] Therefore, one might agree with the ICJ that two different tests may be used for the internationalisation of a NIAC and for the attribution of conduct for the purposes of international responsibility.[56]

This conclusion seems to be in line with the ECtHR's overt stance, according to which it uses different criteria for the purposes of the applicability of primary rules of the ECHR and for attribution in the context of international responsibility. Nevertheless, as will be argued below, in practice, the ECtHR seems to use one test for both purposes, thereby lowering the standard of attribution and creating a *lex specialis* rule of attribution in European human rights law. Thus, the above controversy seems to underlie an analogical development in the field of IHRL.

2.2 *Foreign Control in the Context of Occupation*

Two scenarios of foreign control can also be raised in the context of occupation. Firstly, there can be situations when foreign intervention in support of a non-State party may fall below the threshold of control over the group.[57] However, a belligerent occupation based on the State's exercise of effective territorial control can still exist alongside a NIAC.[58] Secondly, occupation by proxy, which is characterised by a State's exercise of control over the group and the group's control over the territory, can also come into the picture.

2.2.1 Effective Control Test in Belligerent Occupation

"The exercise of effective control by one state in a territory of another state without the other state's consent is subject to the law of occupation."[59] The

---

exercise of its overall control over the organized armed group." Clapham (n 18) 18 (*footnote omitted*). See also Del Mar (n 49) 121–123.

54 See Clapham (n 18) 19 for the summary of applicable tests under *ius in bello* and *ius ad bellum.*

55 Del Mar (n 49) 108.

56 M Milanović, 'The Applicability of the Conventions to "Transnational" and "Mixed" Conflicts' in Andrew Clapham and others (eds), *The 1949 Geneva Conventions: A Commentary* (1st edn, OUP 2015) 37.

57 Ferraro, 'The ICRC's Legal Position' (n 13) 1245.

58 ibid 1246.

59 E Benvenisti, 'Occupation and Territorial Administration' (2015) Global Trust Working Paper 11/2015, 1 <https://papers.ssrn.com/sol3/papers.cfm?abstract_id=2663115> accessed 30 October 2023.

authority of the occupant derives from a sheer facticity of its power.[60] It is a governance gap-filler extending until the return of the ousted government[61] and "quintessentially a temporary state of fact".[62]

Under Article 42 of the Hague Regulations,

> [t]erritory is considered occupied when it is actually placed under the authority of the hostile army. The occupation extends only to the territory where such authority has been established and can be exercised.[63]

The law of occupation applies even in situations of no armed resistance.[64] "[T]he determination of the existence of a state of occupation is a question of fact"[65] deriving from the interpretation given to Article 42 HR.[66] In particular, the existence of occupation is premised upon the core elements of the notion of effective control, especially "(1) foreign military presence, (2) the ability of the foreign forces to exert authority in the concerned territory in lieu of the local government, and (3) its non-consensual nature".[67]

Firstly, the presence of foreign forces "conforms to the principle of effectiveness underlying occupation law, according to which the Occupying Power must be capable of enforcing rights and duties under occupation law".[68] The

---

60 N Bhuta, 'The Antimonies of Transformative Occupation' (2005) 16 European Journal of International Law 721, 726.

61 Benvenisti, 'Occupation and Territorial Administration (n 59) 2.

62 Bhuta (n 60) 725.

63 Convention (IV) Respecting the Laws and Customs of War on Land and its Annex: Regulations Concerning the Laws and Customs of War on Land (signed 18 October 1907, entered into force 26 January 1910) ("HR" or "Hague Regulations"). See also *Legal Consequences of the Construction of a Wall in the Occupied Palestinian Territory* (Advisory Opinion) ICJ Rep [2004], paras 78 ("*Wall*"). According to the ICJ, "the provisions of the Hague Regulations have become part of customary law." ibid para 89. *Armed Activities* (n 35) para 172.

64 Under Common Article 2 to the Four Geneva Conventions, the Conventions "shall also apply to all cases of partial or total occupation of the territory of a High Contracting Party, even if the said occupation meets with no armed resistance." Convention (IV) Relative to the Protection of Civilian Persons in Time of War (singed 12 August 1949, entered into force 21 October 1950) 75 UNTS 287 ("Fourth Geneva Convention" or "GCIV").

65 *Naletilić and Martinović* (n 22) para 211.

66 P Spoerri, 'The Law of Occupation' in Clapham A and others (eds), *The 1949 Geneva Conventions: A Commentary* (1st edn, OUP 2015) 188.

67 ibid 188. See also the ICTY's occupation guidelines to help the factual determination if the authority of an occupying power has been proven. *Naletilić and Martinović* (n 22) para 217.

68 T Ferraro, 'Determining the Beginning and End of an Occupation under International Humanitarian Law' (2012) 94 International Review of the Red Cross 133, 147.

requirement of the presence of foreign forces or 'boots on the ground' is an important element of the criterion of effective control.[69] However, it will be shown below that proxies under the overall control of the Occupying Power may also exercise effective control.[70] Secondly, despite the ICJ's ruling in *Armed Activities*, it is asserted, in line with a doctrinal consensus, that rather than the exercise of *actual* authority by the foreign forces, only the *ability* of foreign forces to exert authority over an area is required.[71] In fact, the requirement of the ability to exert authority precludes the possibility that the Occupying Power would evade its duties "by installing government by proxy that would exercise governmental functions on its behalf".[72] Lastly, coercive character and the absence of consent are also defining features of an occupation.[73]

2.2.2 Occupation by Proxy: Underlying Rationales and Key Parameters

It is contended that occupation by proxy exists when the State exercises a certain amount of control over armed groups and these armed groups exercise effective control of territory based on the classic criteria of military occupation.[74] As a result, "a State would be considered an occupying power for the purposes of IHL."[75] On the one hand, the concept of occupation by proxy is motivated by the effort to prevent a legal vacuum resulting from the State's use of proxies.[76] On the other hand, the feasibility of imposing onerous obligations

69 Spoerri (n 66) 189; ibid 147; Benvenisti, *The Law of Occupation* (n 12) 43–54; Y Dinstein, *The International Law of Belligerent Occupation* (CUP 2009) 42–44. *Sargsyan v Azerbaijan* ECHR 2015-IV 1, para 94 ("*Sargsyan*").

70 See *infra*. Dinstein (n 69) 44.

71 *Armed Activities* (n 35) para 173. Ferraro, 'Determining the Beginning and End of an Occupation' (n 68) 147 and 150–151; Spoerri (n 66) 189; Benvenisti, *The Law of Occupation* (n 12) 43–51.

72 Ferraro, 'Determining the Beginning and End of an Occupation' (n 68) 151.

73 ibid 152.

74 ibid 158, ftn 77; Dinstein (n 69) 44. According to some authors, the fact that the occupation of territory can be carried out not only by regular armed forces, but by a proxy acting on behalf of a State finds its legal basis in art 29 GC IV. "The Party to the conflict in whose hands protected persons may be, is responsible for the treatment accorded to them by its *agents*, irrespective of any individual responsibility which may be incurred." GCIV (n 64) art 29 (*emphasis added*). See also Gal, 'Unexplored Outcomes of Tadić' (n 34) 65–66. See also V Koutroulis, *Le début et la fin de l'application du droit de l'occupation* (Pedone 2010) 29–31.

75 Ferraro, 'The ICRC's Legal Position' (n 13) 1250, ftn 55.

76 "[I]t prevents a legal vacuum arising as a result of a state making use of local surrogates to evade its responsibilities under occupation law." Ferraro, 'Determining the Beginning and End of an Occupation' (n 68) 160; Ferraro, 'The ICRC's Legal Position' (n 13) 1250, ftn 55. ICRC, The 2016 Commentary (n 40) para 332.

flowing from the occupation law must also be taken into account.[77] Moreover, there are different opinions on the exact level of the State's control over armed groups for these purposes.

Firstly, the majority of the doctrine and jurisprudence requires that the third State exercise *overall control* over "the local organized groups" and at the same time that these local organised groups are themselves in effective control over territory.[78] In other words, "overall control of the non-state actor by a state internationalises a NIAC and then the further effective control of territory by the non-state actor establishes an occupation by proxy."[79] The ICTY held already in *Tadić* that

> the relationship of de facto organs or agents to the foreign Power includes those circumstances in which the foreign Power "*occupies*" or operates in certain territory solely through the acts of local de facto organs or agents.[80]

In *Blaškić*, the ICTY's Trial Chamber found Croatia having the role of the occupying Power through its overall control over the Croatian Defence Council (HVO) – the Croatian organised armed group operating in Bosnia and Herzegovina.[81] Even though, later on in *Naletilić and Martinović*, the ICTY's

77 Gal (n 34) 69–70 and 72–75.

78 Ferraro, 'Determining the Beginning and End of an Occupation' (n 68) 158–160; Ferraro, 'The ICRC's Legal Position' (n 13) 1250; A Gilder, 'Bringing Occupation into the 21st Century: The Effective Implementation of Occupation by Proxy' (2017) 13 Utrecht Law Review 61, 61–70; Vité (n 34) 74; RULAC, 'Military Occupation of Azerbaijan by Armenia'<http://www.rulac.org/browse/conflicts/military-occupation-of-azerbaijan-by-armenia#collapse2accord> accessed 16 February 2019. Even though one expert disagreed with the notion of an indirect occupation, the ICRC expert meeting "eventually agreed that occupation could take the form of overall control exerted by a foreign State over local authorities who had effective control of a territory." ICRC, *Occupation and Other Forms of Administration of Foreign Territory: Expert Meeting* (ICRC 2012) 23.

79 Gilder (n 78) 66.

80 *Tadić case* (Opinion and Judgment, Trial Chamber) (IT-94-1-T) (7 May 1997), para 584 (*emphasis added*). See also *Prosecutor v Ivica Rajic* (Review of the Indictment Pursuant to Rule 61 of the Rules of Procedure and Evidence, Trial Chamber) (13 September 1996), paras 40–42.

81 "Croatia played the role of occupying Power through the overall control it exercised over the HVO, the support it lent it and the close ties it maintained with it. Thus, by using the same reasoning which applies to establish the international nature of the conflict, the overall control exercised by Croatia over the HVO means that at the time of its destruction, the property of the Bosnian Muslims was under the control of Croatia and was in occupied territory." *Tihomir Blaškić* (n 24) para 149.

Trial Chamber disputed the relevance of the overall control test, requiring a higher threshold for triggering the law of occupation,[82] the Appeals Chamber in *Prlić* relied on the overall control test over proxies that, in turn, exercised effective control over territory.[83]

Secondly, others favour more stringent control to be exercised over local insurgents in connection with more demanding obligations under the law of occupation.[84] Furthermore, the ICJ in *Armed Activities* accepted the possibility of occupation through a State's control of rebels in control over territory.[85] However, in the circumstances of the case, the Court did not find that Uganda

---

82 "The Chamber notes that the jurisprudence of the Tribunal relating to the legal test applicable is inconsistent. In this context, the Chamber respectfully disagrees with the finding in the Blaškić Trial Judgement argued by the Prosecution. The overall control test, submitted in the Blaškić Trial Judgement, is not applicable to the determination of the existence of an occupation. The Chamber is of the view that there is an essential distinction between the determination of a state of occupation and that of the existence of an international armed conflict. The application of the overall control test is applicable to the latter. A further degree of control is required to establish occupation. Occupation is defined as a transitional period following invasion and preceding the agreement on the cessation of the hostilities. This distinction imposes more onerous duties on an occupying power than on a party to an international armed conflict". *Naletilić and Martinović* (n 22) para 214. Ferraro convincingly argues that in Naletilić the ICTY confused "overall control over a territory with overall control over an entity that itself has effective control over the territory concerned." Ferraro, 'Determining the Beginning and End of an Occupation' (n 68) 158, ftn 78. Glider also agrees with Ferraro's reasoning Gilder (n 78) 64–65.

83 *Jadranko Prlić* (n 19) para 334. "Accordingly, the Chamber finds that if the Prosecution proves that the party to the armed conflict under the overall control of a foreign State fulfils the criteria for control of a territory as identified above, a state of occupation of that part of the territory is proven." *Prosecutor v Jadranko Prlić and others* (Judgment, vol 1, Trial Chamber) (IT-04-74-T) (29 March 2013), para 96.

84 In this context, Benvenisti argues, "further degree of control is required because the occupant is responsible not only for its own acts (and by extension of its proxies), but also for the acts of third parties that operate in the territory. At least for the latter type of responsibility, the general test of 'effective control' of the proxy seems more appropriate to establish the responsibility of occupant." Benvenisti, *The Law of Occupation* (n 12) 62 (*footnotes omitted*). Sassòli shares this view and points out, "the effective control test also applies to obligations to respect". M Sassòli, 'The Concept and the Beginning of Occupation' in A Clapham, P Gaeta and M Sassòli (eds), *The 1949 Geneva Conventions: A Commentary* (OUP 2015) 1399–1400, ftn 55; Sassòli, *International Humanitarian Law* (n 40) 309. Similarly, taking into account onerous obligations flowing from the law of occupation, Carron also argues in favour of a strict, but general test. Carron (n 16) 1040.

85 *Armed Activities* (n 35) para 177. Ferraro, 'Determining the Beginning and End of an Occupation' (n 68) 159.

exercised a sufficient level of control over the Congolese rebels; the ICJ relied on the test of effective control over the armed groups.[86]

2.2.3 State Responsibility in the Context of Occupation

A State is responsible for any violations of IHL committed by its own State organs, including its armed forces, and for violations committed by private actors attributable to it.[87] However, in the context of occupation, the State's due diligence obligation to prevent and punish violations of IHL by private actors in the occupied territory is particularly relevant.[88]

The issue of a relevant threshold of control for the attribution of private conduct to the State, for the purposes of State responsibility in the context of occupation by proxy, raises the same controversy, as does this issue in the context of an internationalised NIAC.[89] However, it is especially the Occupying Power's due diligence obligation that has led a number of scholars to require a higher threshold of effective control over the group in the context of occupation by proxy, than overall control.[90] In fact, the issue of responsibility for violation of the due diligence obligation and the threshold for the applicability of the law of occupation seem to be conflated in this context.

It is argued here that the State needs to exercise overall control over the armed group for the purposes of triggering the law of occupation and, by implication, the relevant due diligence obligation. Firstly, despite different

86 *Armed Activities* (n 35) para 177 in connection to para 160. Benvenisti, *The Law of Occupation* (n 12) 62. ICRC, The 2016 Commentary (n 40) para 330; Koutroulis (n 75) 31–32. However, Ferraro derives from the ICJ's reasoning a clear endorsement of the ICTY's test based on the overall control. See Ferraro, 'Determining the Beginning and End of an Occupation' (n 68) 159, ftn 79.

87 See ICRC, 'IHL Database' (n 35); ARSIWA (n 8) arts 4–11; *Armed Activities* (n 35) paras 213–214; Sassòli, 'State Responsibility' (n 35) 404–412; Longobardo (n 35) 256–257.

88 HR (n 63) art 43; *Armed Activities* (n 35) para 248 and 250; *Eritrea-Ethiopia Claims Commission – Partial Award: Central Front – Eritrea's Claims 2, 4, 6, 7, 8 and 22* (28 April 2004) XXVI RIAA 115, 138–139, para 67; Sassòli, 'State Responsibility' (n 35) 412 ftn 32; Longobardo (n 35) 262–269.

89 See *supra*. For example, for Ferraro the overall control derives from the rules of attribution under the law of international responsibility. Ferraro, 'Determining the Beginning and End of an Occupation' (n 68) 158, ftn 77 and 160, ftn 81. Thus, any violation of the law of occupation by proxies would be automatically attributable to the controlling State. It is said that any other approach would risk provoking an accountability vacuum. Gal (n 34) 64 and 77–80; Gilder (n 78) 79–80. It is the position of this book that similarly to the context of an internationalized NIAC, the attribution of conduct for the purposes of State responsibility should be carried out on the basis of the effective control test and other tests codified in ARSIWA.

90 See *supra*.

views, the majority of judicial decisions and doctrinal opinion seem to support the overall control test in this context. Moreover, if an effective control test required for the attribution of specific conduct were employed in this context, it would lead to a frequent change of classification, depending on the degree of control over specific acts.[91] Lastly, regarding the argument concerning too-onerous obligations flowing from the law of occupation, they do not seem to apply to State-like secessionist entities, which dispose of government-like structures and therefore can be presumed to be able to comply with obligations under the law of occupation.[92]

3 International Human Rights Law

The applicability of most human rights treaties is premised upon the notion of jurisdiction.[93] Due to the pertinence of the ECtHR's jurisprudence to case

91 Carron (n 16) 1034–1035. Sassòli uses this criticism as an argument against effective control as the criterion for the internationalization of NIAC but omits this problem with respect to effective control in the case of occupation by proxy. Sassòli, *International Humanitarian Law* (n 40) 175.

92 Gal argues in favour of a functional approach to the obligations and responsibilities of non-State armed groups under the law of occupation, depending on the amount of control they exert over the territory. However, according to Gal, state-like non-State armed groups "are most likely capable to comply with most (if not all) of the different provisions of Geneva Convention IV". Gal (n 34) 74.

93 The following international treaties' applicability is premised upon the notion of jurisdiction. European Convention for the Protection of Human Rights and Fundamental Freedoms (adopted 4 November 1950; entered into force 3 September 1953) 213 UNTS 221, art 1 ("ECHR"); American Convention on Human Rights (signed 22 November 1969; entered into force 18 July 1978) 1144 UNTS 123, art 1; Convention on the Rights of the Child (adopted 20 November 1989; entered into force 2 September 1990) 1577 UNTS 3, art 2 ("CRC"). See also *Wall* (n 63) para 113. The ICCPR's applicability functions in relation to those "within [the state's] territory and subject to its jurisdiction". International Covenant on Civil and Political Rights (adopted 19 December 1966; entered into force 23 March 1976) 999 UNTS 171, art 2 ("ICCPR"). The Human Rights Committee in fact defined "and" in this provision as disjunctive. See UN Human Rights Council 'General Comment No 31: Nature of the General Legal Obligations on State Parties of the Covenant' (26 May 2004) UN Doc CCPR/C/21/Rev./Add.13, paras 10–11 ("General Comment No 31"). The ICJ confirmed the ICCPR's extraterritorial applicability in *Wall* (n 63) paras 109–111 and in *Armed Activities* (n 35) paras 216–217. Convention Against Torture refers to "territory under its jurisdiction". Convention against Torture and Other Cruel, Inhuman or Degrading Treatment or Punishment (adopted 10 December 1984, entered into force 26 June 1987) 1465 UNTS 85, art 2 ("CAT"). ICESCR does not contain reference to the territorial scope of application. International Covenant on Economic, Social and Cultural Rights (adopted 19 December 1966; entered into force 3 January 1976) 993 UNTS 3. However, relying on the position of

studies analysed in Part 2 of this book, this section focuses on the ECHR-specific context, in particular, it seeks to outline the position of an illegal secessionist entity, a third State exercising effective control[94] over its territory, and the territorial State as three potential addressees of human rights obligations under the ECHR.

3.1 *Illegal Secessionist Entity*

At the outset, the Court has completely ignored illegal secessionist entities as direct holders of human rights obligations under the ECHR.[95] This is due to their non-recognition as States and by implication due to lack of their status as the Contracting Parties to the ECHR. Importantly, the Court's non-recognition of these entities as States has been based on the attitude of the international community. As outlined above, this attitude has been motivated by the questions of the legality under general international law.

In particular, in *Loizidou*, the Court discarded the TRNC as State by reference to a number of strongly worded resolutions of the UNSC, CoE and other IOs on the illegality and invalidity of the TRNC and its declaration of independence, leading the Court to conclude that the international community "refused to accept the legitimacy of the 'TRNC' as a State within the meaning of

---

the Committee on Economic, Social and Cultural Rights, the ICJ in Wall interpreted the Covenant in a way that it is applicable extraterritorially. *Wall* (n 63) para 112 and see also paras 109–111. In addition, the ICJ read the concept of jurisdiction into other treaties that did not contain such a reference, including the African Charter on Human and Peoples' Rights and Optional Protocol to the CRC. See *Armed Activities* (n 35) paras 216–217. A subset of obligations under CERD is premised upon jurisdiction. International Convention on the Elimination of All Forms of Racial Discrimination (adopted 21 December 1965; entered into force 4 January 1969) 660 UNTS 195, arts 3 and 6 ("CERD"). The ICJ inferred from the fact that CERD does not contain restrictions of a general nature relating to its territorial application, or specific restrictions in respect of particular provisions, that the relied upon provisions of CERD "generally appear to apply, like other provisions of instruments of that nature, to the actions of a State party when it acts beyond its territory." *Application of the International Convention on the Elimination of All Forms of Racial Discrimination* (*Georgia v Russian Federation*) (*Provisional Measures, Order*) [2008] ICJ Rep 353, para 109. See Wilde, 'Human Rights Beyond Borders at the World Court' (n 7) 662–668; Wilde, 'Triggering State Obligations Extraterritorially' (n 9) 505–508; R Raible, 'Title to Territory and Jurisdiction in International Human Rights Law: Three Models for a Fraught Relationship' (2018) 31 Leiden Journal of International Law 315, 316–318.

94 The book uses the notion of 'effective control test' to denote the test used by the ECtHR to establish jurisdiction, even though in its case law it also uses the notion of 'effective overall control' to describe the same situation. See *infra*.

95 See also above conclusions on the *Namibia* exception in the ECtHR's jurisprudence.

international law".[96] In *Cyprus v Turkey*, the Court reiterated that it is evident from international practice "that the international community does not recognise the 'TRNC' as a State *under international law*".[97] Even in situations where certain regard was given to the institutions of the TRNC, these were considered as institutions of Turkey, thereby underscoring the international responsibility of Turkey under the ECHR.[98]

In *Ilaşcu*, the Court generally highlighted non-recognition of Transnistria's statehood by the international community,[99] referred to it as an "illegal regime"[100] and held that Transnistria is "an entity, which is illegal under international law and has not been recognised by the international community".[101] In *Chiragov*, the Court highlighted the non-recognition of Nagorno-Karabakh's self-proclaimed independence by the international community.[102] The Court also used the term "*de facto* Abkhazia."[103] In *Georgia v Russia* (*II*), it stated that "[t]he terms 'Abkhazia' and 'South Ossetia' refer to the regions of Georgia which are currently outside the *de facto* control of the Georgian Government."[104] The Court also held that Russian recognition of Abkhazia and South Ossetia in August 2008 "was not followed by the international community."[105]

3.2 *Position of a Controlling Third State*

3.2.1 Extra-territorial Jurisdiction under ECHR: Effective Control

3.2.1.1 *Jurisdiction in International Human Rights Treaties and ECHR*

The notion of jurisdiction in human rights treaties requires some clarification. Firstly, "[i]t is a threshold criterion, which must be satisfied in order for the treaty obligations (at least some of them) to arise in the first place."[106]

96 *Loizidou v Turkey* 1996-VI 2216, para 56 in connection to paras 42–44, see also paras 19–23 ("*Loizidou* (Merits)").

97 *Cyprus v Turkey* ECHR 2001-IV 1, para 61 (*emphasis added*) ("*Cyprus v Turkey*").

98 See *supra* Chapter 7 in detail.

99 *Ilaşcu and others v Moldova and Russia* ECHR 2004-VII 1 para 30 ("*Ilaşcu*").

100 ibid paras 384–385.

101 ibid para 436.

102 *Chiragov and Others v Armenia* ECHR 2015-III 135, para 28 ("*Chiragov*").

103 *Mamasakhlisi and Others v Georgia and Russia* App 29999/04 and 41424/04 (Merits) (ECtHR, 7 March 2023) para 339.

104 *Georgia v Russia* (*II*) App no 38263/08 (Merits) (ECtHR, 21 January 2021) para 35, ftn 3. The same formulation is in *Georgia v Russia* (*IV*) App no 39611/18 (Decision as to Admissibility) (ECtHR, 20 April 2023) para 11, ftn 1.

105 ibid para 41.

106 Milanović, *Extraterritorial Application of Human Rights Treaties* (n 12) 19. See also R Jorritsma, 'Unravelling Attribution, Control and Jurisdiction: Some Reflections on the

Secondly, it "refers to the jurisdiction of a *state*, not to the jurisdiction of a court".[107]

Moreover, while jurisdiction in general international law concerns "rules prescribing the particular circumstances where a state is *legally* permitted to exercise its *legal* authority",[108] jurisdiction in human rights treaties essentially refers to "actual *power*, whether exercised lawfully or not".[109] For extraterritorial spatial jurisdiction, "[w]hether or not the state has title over the territory, and/or its presence there is or is not lawful, is irrelevant."[110] The extraterritorial applicability of human rights derives from the facticity of power.[111]

Referring to the context of the ECHR, under Article 1 ECHR, the Contracting Parties "shall secure everyone within their jurisdiction the rights and freedoms"

Case Law of the European Court of Human Rights' in H Ruiz Fabri (ed), *International Law and Litigation: A Look Into Procedure* (Nomos 2019) 670.

107 Milanović, *Extraterritorial Application of Human Rights Treaties* (n 12) 19 (*emphasis added*).

108 Wilde, 'Triggering State Obligations Extraterritorially' (n 9) 513 (*emphasis added*).

109 Milanović, *Extraterritorial Application of Human Rights Treaties* (n 12) 41 (*emphasis in original*).

110 Wilde, 'Triggering State Obligations Extraterritorially' (n 9) 508; A Buyse, 'Legal Minefield-The Territorial Scope of the European Convention' (2008) 1 Inter-American and European Human Rights Journal 269, 276–277. "Bearing in mind the object and purpose of the Convention, the responsibility of a Contracting Party may also arise when as a consequence of military action – whether lawful or unlawful – it exercises *effective control of an area outside its national territory*. The obligation to secure, in such an area, the rights and freedoms set out in the Convention derives from the fact of such control whether it be exercised directly, through its armed forces, or through a subordinate local administration." *Loizidou v Turkey* App no 15318/89 (Preliminary Objections) (ECtHR, 23 March 1995), para 62 (*emphasis added*) ("*Loizidou* (Preliminary Objections)") According to the UNHRC, the enjoyment of the rights under the ICCPR "also applies to those within the power or effective control of the forces of a State Party acting outside its territory, *regardless of the circumstances in which such power or effective control was obtained.*" General Comment No 31 (n 93) para 10 (*emphasis added*). However, it will be shown below that according to the ECtHR case law, title over territory remains relevant with respect to the jurisdiction of the State losing effective control.

111 Milanović, *Extraterritorial Application of Human Rights Treaties* (n 12) 60; Buyse (n 110) 276. O De Schutter, 'Globalization and Jurisdiction: Lessons from the European Convention on Human Rights' (2006) 6 Baltic Yearbook of International Law 185, 205–206 and 245. L Moor and AWB Simpson, 'Ghosts of Colonialism in the European Convention on Human Rights' (2006) 76 British Yearbook of International Law 121, 125. "The obligation to secure, in such an area, the rights and freedoms set out in the Convention derives from the *fact of such control* whether it be exercised directly, through its armed forces, or through a subordinate local administration." *Loizidou* (Preliminary Objections) (n 110) para 62 (*emphasis added*). See Raible (n 93) 332–333 and 326–333 for criticism of an overt approximation of jurisdiction in human rights treaties and title-inspired criteria.

provided for in the Convention.[112] According to the ECtHR, jurisdiction is "primarily territorial"; in particular, the Court held that

> [a]s to the "ordinary meaning" of the relevant term in Article 1 of the Convention, the Court is satisfied that, from the standpoint of public international law, the jurisdictional competence of a State is primarily territorial ... The Court is of the view, therefore, that Article 1 of the Convention must be considered to reflect this ordinary and essentially territorial notion of jurisdiction, other bases of jurisdiction being exceptional and requiring special justification in the particular circumstances of each case.[113]

Thus, the exercise of jurisdiction extraterritorially is only exceptional.[114] Exceptional cases include the establishment of jurisdiction "on the basis of power (or control) actually exercised over the *person* of the applicant (*ratione personae*)"[115] and "on the basis of control actually exercised over the foreign *territory* in question (*rationae loci*)".[116] Recently, the Court has also referred to "the criterion" of "a jurisdictional link" regarding the procedural obligation under Article 2 ECHR.[117] In *Georgia v Russia* (*II*), the ECtHR excluded "the active phase of hostilities in the context of an international armed conflict"

112 "The High Contracting Parties shall secure to everyone within their jurisdiction the rights and freedoms defined in Section I of this Convention." ECHR (n 93) art 1.

113 *Banković* (n 3) paras 59 and 61, see para 67; *Al-Skeini and Others v the United Kingdom* ECHR 2011-IV 99, para 131 ("*Al-Skeini*"); *Jaloud v the Netherlands* ECHR 2014-IV 229, para 139 ("*Jaloud*").

114 *Banković* (n 3) para 67; *Catan and Others v The Republic of Moldova and Russia* App nos 43370/04, 8252/05 and 18454/06 (ECtHR, 19 October 2012), para 104 ("*Catan*").

115 *Guide on Article 1 of the European Convention on Human Rights: Obligation to Respect Human Rights – Concepts of "Jurisdiction" and Imputability* (Council of Europe/European Court of Human Rights 2019) para 30 and see also paras 31–43 ("Guide on Article 1"). *Al-Skeini* (n 113) paras 138–140.

116 *Guide on Article 1* (n 115) para 30 and see also paras 43–67; *Al-Skeini* (n 113) paras 138–139. M Milanović, 'Jurisdiction and Responsibility: Trends in the Jurisprudence of the Strasbourg Court' in A Van Aaken and I Motoc (eds), *The European Convention on Human Rights and General International Law* (OUP 2018) 98. Tzevelekos criticises effective control as the basis for the extraterritorial applicability of human rights obligations. See Tzevelekos (n 12) 142–151.

117 *Ukraine and the Netherlands v Russia* App nos 8019/16, 43800/14 and 28525/20 (ECtHR, 25 January 2023) paras 559 and 573–575 ("*Ukraine and the Netherlands v Russia*"). *Güzelyurtlu and Others v Cyprus and Turkey* App no 36925/07 (ECtHR, 29 January 2019) paras 188–189; *Georgia v Russia* (*II*) (n 104) para 330.

from the extra-territorial jurisdiction; however, this exclusion was not absolute.[118] Due to the themes explored in this book, the chapter only discusses the spatial concept of jurisdiction as relevant to the existence of secessionist entities.[119] The key for spatial jurisdiction is the test of effective control, the parameters of which can be derived from the relevant case law, which is examined in chronological order next.

3.2.1.2 *Overview of the ECtHR Case Law*

A landmark case on the issue of spatial extraterritorial jurisdiction is *Loizidou*, in which the Court established that

> the responsibility of a Contracting Party may also arise when as a consequence of military action – whether lawful or unlawful – it exercises *effective control of an area outside its national territory*. The obligation to secure, in such an area, the rights and freedoms set out in the Convention derives from the fact of such control whether it be exercised directly, through its armed forces, or through a subordinate local administration.[120]

Similarly, in *Cyprus v Turkey*, the Court referred to "Turkish military and other support," but given the Court's reiteration of *Loizidou* "one can suppose that it is the military presence that mostly determined Turkey's effective control over

---

118 *Georgia v Russia* (*II*) (n 104) para 138. See *Ukraine and the Netherlands v Russia* (n 117) para 558 (referring to "the detention and treatment of civilians and prisoners of war even during the 'five-day war'"). Regarding the jurisdictional link and the case's 'special features' see *Georgia v Russia* (*II*) (n 104) paras 330–337. M Milanović, 'Georgia v. Russia No. 2: The European Court's Resurrection of Bankovic in the Contexts of Chaos' (*EJIL:Talk!*, 25 January 2021) <https://www.ejiltalk.org/georgia-v-russia-no-2-the-european-courts-resurrection-of-bankovic-in-the-contexts-of-chaos/> accessed 31 October 2023.

119 "[T]he trend at the ECtHR has been to apply the spatial jurisdiction test only to cases of prolonged occupation/*de facto* annexation." S Wallace and C Mallory, 'Applying the European Convention on Human Rights to the Conflict in Ukraine' (2018) 6 Russian Law Journal 8, 24. This is the focus of the present study. See on the concept of effective control beyond the secessionist entities. J Miklasová, 'Post-Ceasefire Nagorno-Karabakh: Limits to the ECtHR's Approach to Jurisdiction over Secessionist Entities under the ECHR' (2022) 82 ZaöRV 357, 372–374.

120 *Loizidou* (Preliminary Objections) (n 110) para 62 (*emphasis added*). Applied to the facts of this case, the ECtHR underlined that the applicant's loss of access to her property stemmed from the Turkish occupation of the northern part of Cyprus and the establishment of the TRNC there. ibid para 63. It was also not disputed that the Turkish troops themselves prevented the applicant from accessing her property there. ibid. See (n 122).

northern Cyprus."[121] Thus, a key factor for Turkey's effective control over TRNC was its military presence in the northern part of the island.[122] The question of the legality of such military presence was irrelevant to triggering the applicability of the Convention.[123]

In *Ilaşcu*, which concerned violations in Transnistria, the Court divided its analysis before and after Russia's ECHR's ratification. In the first period, the Court took into account several indicators, including the direct participation of the 14th ex-Soviet Army which "fought with and on behalf of the Transdniestrian separatist forces" in the secessionist war, voluntary transfers of the 14th ex-Soviet Army's weapons to the separatists and political declarations of support for the separatists.[124] The Court highlighted that Russia contributed militarily and politically to Transnistria's creation and continued to provide it with military, political and economic support,[125] "thus enabling it to survive by strengthening itself and by acquiring a certain amount of autonomy *vis-à-vis* Moldova".[126] Thus, "the Russian Federation's responsibility is *engaged* in respect of the unlawful acts committed by the Transdniestrian separatists".[127]

As for the second period, the ECtHR took note of the fact that "the number of Russian troops stationed in Transdniestria has in fact significantly fallen since 1992," but pointed out that their importance in the region and their "dissuasive influence persist" in light of the significant weapon stocks stationed there.[128] The Court also highlighted Russia's financial support to Transnistria.[129] Overall, the Court held that Transnistria, or the 'MRT',

121 A Berkes, 'The Nagorno-Karabakh Conflict Before the European Court of Human Rights: Pending Cases and Certain Forecasts on Jurisdiction and State Responsibility' (2013) 52 *Military Law and the Law of War Review* 379, 398–399. See *Cyprus v Turkey* (n 97) para 77.

122 *Loizidou* (Preliminary Objections) (n 110) para 64. *Loizidou* (Merits) (n 96) paras 16 and 56.

123 See *infra* Chapter 9 on the interplay between the consequences of peremptory territorial illegality and the human rights law.

124 See *Ilaşcu* (n 99) paras 380–381.

125 The relevant factors included, for example, the Russian military presence in Transnistria, including troops and weaponry; the participation of senior officers of the 14th Army in public life in Transnistria; public support of the Russian Duma for the separatist regime; the opening of the bank accounts for the Transnistrian Bank in the Russian Central Bank. See for more ibid paras 111–161.

126 ibid para 382.

127 ibid (*emphasis added*).

128 ibid para 387. The number of the Russian military personnel in Transnistria was 1500 troops. ibid para 131.

129 For example, by virtue of agreements with Transnistria on debt reduction and the provision of gas on advantageous terms. ibid para 390.

> vested with organs of power and its own administration, remains under the *effective authority*, or at the very least under the *decisive influence*, of the Russian Federation, and in any event … it survives by virtue of the military, economic, financial and political support given to it by the Russian Federation.[130]

Later on, in *Catan* and following case law, the Court established that "the MRT's high level of dependency on Russian support provides a strong indication that Russia exercised *effective control* and *decisive influence* over the 'MRT' administration during the period" in question.[131] The Court relied on Russia's military presence and its military and economic support.[132] Thus, compared to cases on the TRNC, the jurisprudence on Transnistria seemed to have lowered the test for the establishment of jurisdiction, since the number of Russia's troops in Transnistria was significantly smaller than Turkey's personnel in the TRNC.[133] Notwithstanding this, the Court established Russia's jurisdiction, taking into account the size of the Russian arsenal stored there, the relative importance of the Russian military presence in the region, as well as its military, political and financial support to Transnistria.[134]

---

130 ibid para 392 (*emphasis added*).

131 *Catan* (n 114) para 122 (*emphasis added*). *Mozer v the Republic of Moldova and Russia* App no 11138/10 (ECtHR, 23 February 2016) para 110 (*emphasis added*) ("*Mozer*"). See also *Turturica and Casian v the Republic of Moldova and Russia* Applications nos 28648/06 and 18832/07 (ECtHR, 30 August 2016), paras 30–31 and para 33 ("*Turturica*"); *Paduret v the Republic of Moldova and Russia* App no 26626/11 (ECtHR, 9 May 2017), paras 18 and 19 ("*Paduret*"); *Eriomenco v the Republic of Moldova and Russia* App no 42224/11 (ECtHR, 9 May 2017), paras 45–46 ("*Eriomenco*"); *Soyoma v the Republic of Moldova, Russia and Ukraine* App no 1203/05 (ECtHR, 30 May 2017), paras 22–23; *Vardanean v the Republic of Moldova and Russia* App no 22200/01 (ECtHR, 30 May 2017), paras 22 and 23 ("*Vardanean*"); *Apcov v the Republic of Moldova and Russia* App no 13463/07 (ECtHR, 30 May 2017), paras 23 and 24 ("*Apcov*"); *Braga v the Republic of Moldova and Russia* App no 76957/01 (ECtHR, 17 October 2017), paras 24–25 ("*Braga*"); *Case of Draci v the Republic of Moldova and Russia* App no 5349/02 (ECtHR, 17 October 2017), paras 28–29 ("*Draci*"); *Sandu and Others v the Republic of Moldova and Russia* App nos 21034/05 and 7 others (ECtHR, 17 July 2018), paras 36–37 ("*Sandu*"); *Case of Mangir and Others v the Republic of Moldova and Russia* App no 50157/06 (ECtHR, 17 July 2018), paras 28 and 29 ("*Mangir*").

132 This included the provision of a subsidized gas, pensions and financial assistance to schools, hospitals and prisons. *Catan* (n 114) paras 116–122.

133 Milanović, *Extraterritorial Application of Human Rights Treaties* (n 12) 138 and 140. Buyse (n 110) 289–290.

134 It is worth noting that in *Ilașcu* the Court determined that Transnistria was under Russia's "effective authority" or at the very least under its "decisive influence." In *Catan*, the Court returned to the term of "effective control." Berkes (n 121) 402–410.

In *Chiragov*, which concerned jurisdiction over the Nagorno-Karabakh (NKR) in the context before the outbreak of the 2020 war, the ECtHR held that, based on available evidence, it was not possible to conclusively rule on the composition of the forces participating in the secessionist conflict; however the Court also referred to evidence such as NGO reports,[135] and it held that "it is hardly conceivable" that the NKR was able to establish its control "without the substantial military support of Armenia".[136] The Court left open the issue of the *exact* number of Armenian soldiers present in the NKR.[137] But taking into account several indicators,[138] it ultimately found it

> established that the Republic of Armenia, through its military presence and the provision of military equipment and expertise, has been significantly involved in the Nagorno-Karabakh conflict from an early date. This military support has been – and continues to be – decisive for the conquest of and continued control over the territories in issue. [139]

The Court also held that "the evidence ... convincingly shows that the armed forces of Armenia and the 'NKR' are highly integrated."[140]

Moreover, the Court also highlighted integration between Armenia and the NKR in political, legislative, judicial and law-enforcement spheres[141] and the former's economic support for the latter.[142] The Court acknowledged the funding from other sources, in particular from the US and the Armenian diaspora, but held that Nagorno-Karabakh "would not be able to subsist economically without the substantial support stemming from Armenia".[143] Ultimately, the Court concluded that

---

135 In particular, to the conclusions of the Human Rights Watch Report and the statement of the former Armenian Minster of Defense. *Chiragov* (n 102) para 173.

136 ibid para 174.

137 ibid para 180.

138 Such as the 1994 Military Cooperation Agreement, based upon which Armenian conscripts could do their military service in the NKR; reports by IOs and NGOs and statements of high ranking officials confirming Armenia's participation in the conflict; and its military presence there. ibid paras 175–180.

139 ibid para 180.

140 ibid para 180.

141 ibid paras 181–182. For example, it took into account the interchange of prominent politicians between the two entities, the operation of Armenian law-enforcement agencies, and the extension of the Armenian courts' jurisdiction to Nagorno-Karabakh. ibid paras 181–182.

142 The Court noted that Armenia's loan provided to the NKR in 1993, while representing a significant portion of the NKR's public finances, has not yet been repaid. ibid para 183.

143 ibid paras 184–185.

> the "NKR" and its administration survives by virtue of the military, political, financial and other support given to it by Armenia which, consequently, exercises *effective control* over Nagorno-Karabakh and the surrounding territories, including the district of Lachin.[144]

Thus, in *Chiragov*, the Court lowered the threshold for the establishment of jurisdiction even further. Unlike in previous cases, where Turkey's and Russia's military presence in the breakaway regions was undisputed by the respondent governments,[145] in *Chiragov* it was not so.[146] Notwithstanding this, while leaving the issue of the exact number of Armenian troops in the NKR open, the Court nevertheless established Armenia's effective control over the NKR based on evidence of Armenia's military and non-military support[147] and its assertion that "it is hardly conceivable" that Nagorno-Karabakh would win over Azerbaijan without any outside help.[148] The Court not only lowered relevant factual parameters of the effective control test but also of evidentiary standards.[149]

In the *Ukraine v Russia (re Crimea)* admissibility decision, the ECtHR established Russia's jurisdiction over the peninsula in two periods.[150] First, concerning the period between the day of the seizure of the Crimea government

144 ibid para 186.

145 See *Loizidou* (Merits) (n 96) paras 16 and 56; *Ilașcu* (n 99) paras 70, 131, 354, 380, 387. See also *Catan* (n 114) paras 118–119. Although the Russian government refused to allow direct participation of its troops in the secessionist conflict, except for when they defended themselves against attacks. Ibid, paras 354 and 380. See also *Chiragov and Others v Armenia,* Dissenting Opinion of Judge Pinto de Albuquerque, para 25.

146 *Chiragov* (n 102) paras 158–164.

147 Frequently, the evidence included uncorroborated NGO reports M Milanović, 'The Nagorno-Karabakh Cases' (*EJIL Talk!*, 23 June 2015) <https://www.ejiltalk.org/the-nagorno-karabakh-cases/> accessed 23 January 2020.

148 Ibid.

149 Crawford and Keen point out that the Court conducted "a very limited analysis of the financial element" ignoring funding from other States, in particular from the USA, and that it did not analyse the "control structures" at all. J Crawford and A Keene, 'The Structure of State Responsibility under the European Convention on Human Rights' in A Van Aaken and I Motoc (eds), *The European Convention on Human Rights and General International Law* (OUP 2018) 195. Milanović characterizes the Court's approach to evaluation of evidence as "very relaxed." Milanović, 'Jurisdiction and Responsibility' (n 116) 99. For criticism of the Court's methodology for the analysis of evidence, see *Chiragov* (n 102), Dissenting Opinion of Judge Pinto de Albuquerque, paras 19–37. Milanović, 'The Nagorno-Karabakh Cases' (n 147).

150 *Ukraine v Russia (re Crimea)* App nos 20958/14 and 38334/18 (ECtHR, 16 December 2020) ("*Ukraine v Russia (re Crimea)*") para 335.

buildings on 27 February 2014 and the date of signature of the so-called admission treaty on 18 March 2014, relying heavily on adverse inferences,[151] the Court considered several factors to establish Russia's effective control. Specifically, it considered the actual size of the Russian forces present in Crimea at the relevant time, which "nearly doubled within a short space of time, namely between late January and mid-March 2014", amounting to around 20.000 Russian troops.[152] Notably, while the Court stated that the compliance of the Russian military presence with the applicable agreements between Russia and Ukraine "cannot be decisive" for the issue of effective control, it also made several observations in this regard.[153] The Court also took into account other elements, such as the superior military capacity of the Russian forces in comparison with the Ukrainian troops, their conduct, including immobilising, disarming and detaining Ukrainian troops and their active involvement in the transfer of power in Crimea.[154] The Court attached particular weight to two uncontested accounts by President Putin confirming the Russian servicemen's involvement in the takeover of Crimea.[155] Regarding the second period, Russian jurisdiction over the events taking place in Crimea after 18 March 2014 was uncontested. The Court nevertheless established the nature of such jurisdiction as extra-territorial and not territorial.[156]

In *Georgia v Russia (II)*, the Court established Russia's effective control over Abkhazia and South Ossetia in the period after the cessation of hostilities on 12 August 2008, relying on Russia's military presence, including the subsequent establishment of Russian military bases in these territories.[157] Moreover, the Court also considered Russia's political, military and economic support for the two entities.[158]

---

151 M Milanović, 'ECtHR Grand Chamber Declares Admissible the Case of Ukraine v. Russia re Crimea' (*EJIL:Talk!*, 15 January 2021) <https://www.ejiltalk.org/ecthr-grand-chamber-declares-admissible-the-case-of-ukraine-v-russia-re-crimea/> accessed 17 July 2023.

152 *Ukraine v Russia (re Crimea)* (n 150) para 321 in connection with paras 318–319.

153 ibid para 320 and 324–327. See *infra* Chapter 9 in detail on how peremptory territorial illegality plays out in the Court's case law, including in this case.

154 ibid paras 322, 328–329.

155 ibid paras 331–334.

156 See *infra* Chapter 9 in detail on the implications of this finding on Ukraine's sovereignty over Crimea.

157 According to Russia, in 2010, military base no 4 in South Ossetia "held 3,285 servicemen and had 305 items of military equipment," and military base no 7 in Abkhazia held "3,923 servicemen and 873 items of military equipment." *Georgia v Russia (II)* (n 104) para 165 in connection with paras 150–151. According to the ECtHR, in April 2023, Russian military bases hosted "up to 3,800 Russian soldiers in each of those two regions." *Georgia v Russia (IV)* (n 104) para 11.

158 *Georgia v Russia (II)* (n 104) paras 166–172.

Next, to establish Russia's effective control over the territories of the DPR and LPR in Eastern Ukraine in the period between 11 May 2014 and 26 January 2022, the Court analysed extensive evidence of Russia's military presence.[159] While it concluded that "there were Russian military personnel in an active capacity in Donbass," the ECtHR was unable to determine their exact number.[160] For the Court, it was not "established beyond reasonable doubt that the Russian Federation exercised effective control over the territory of the "DPR" and the "LPR" from April 2014 solely by virtue of the military presence of its own de jure soldiers."[161] It, therefore, considered other aspects of the effective control test. Notably, regarding Russia's military support of the separatists, it examined Russia's arming of separatists, its influence on their military strategy, their training (evidence was insufficient to establish such conclusion), and provision of artillery cover from Russia.[162] Notably, the Court also considered the deployment of the Russian troops in the border region, which – though not entailing any control over eastern Ukraine – "constitutes a further example of the military support offered to the separatists by the Russian Federation."[163]

The Court considered other factors, too. To establish political support for the secessionists, the Court examined Russia's role in appointing the leaders of the DPR, LPR, its stances in support of the separatists at the international level, its domestic legal acts and overseeing of separatist political mechanisms.[164] Regarding economic support, the Court considered various factors and ultimately established that "the Russian Federation has played an active role in the financing of the separatist entities."[165] Notably, the Court also considered the provision of humanitarian aid (in particular, 100 humanitarian convoys sent by Russia to the separatist territories between 2014 and 2020).[166] According to the Court, the aid alone is "not capable of establishing Article 1 jurisdiction."[167]

> But where the aid is extensive, as in the present case, it would be artificial to ignore the critical role that it may have played in the economic survival of the subordinate administration. The extent of the aid demonstrates

159 *Ukraine and the Netherlands v Russia* (n 117) para 695.
160 ibid para 611.
161 ibid.
162 ibid paras 613–654.
163 ibid para 662.
164 ibid paras 670–675.
165 ibid para 689.
166 ibid para 688.
167 ibid para 688.

> the degree to which the Russian Federation has invested in the economic future of the separatist entities in eastern Ukraine.[168]

In *Mamasakashvili*, which concerned, among others, Russia's extra-territorial jurisdiction over Abkhazia in the period before the 2008 Russia-Georgia War (from 2001 to 2007), the Court – facing a complex factual situation – arguably lowered the threshold of effective control even by comparison with *Chiragov*.[169] First, regarding Russia's intervention in the Abkhaz-Georgian conflict in the early 1990s, it held that the available material does not offer "conclusive evidence as to the composition of the armed forces that secured control over Abkhazia in September 1993."[170] While the Court held that the evidence did not allow for the conclusion as to the allegations of Russia's authorisation of the use of force and supply of weapons, it also held that "Russian military and Russian commanders stationed in Abkhazia actively supported the Abkhaz side" and that the Abkhaz victory in the conflict "would not have been possible without the involvement of at least certain forces and military equipment emanating from the territory of the Russian Federation."[171] The lack of engagement of the Court with the ARSIWA rules of attribution concerning the acts of State organs in excess of authority or in contravention of orders seems questionable.[172]

Moreover, at the relevant time, Russian peacekeepers, as part of the Commonwealth of Independent States Collective Peacekeeping Force (CIS CPF), were stationed in the region. The Court considered several factors concerning this peacekeeping mission – including a broader environment of the peace process as "left largely in the hands of Russia".[173] "The Court's analysis of this aspect is noteworthy since it is the first time that the presence of the peacekeeping forces (ie with a territorial State's original consent) featured so prominently in the assessment of extraterritorial spatial jurisdiction."[174] Considering

168 ibid para 688.

169 *Mamasakhlisi* (n 103) paras 325–327. J Miklasová, 'Mamasakhlisi and Others v. Georgia and Russia: Russia's Effective Control over Abkhazia Before the 2008 War: Peacekeepers, Passportisation and Other Hybrid Elements' (*Strasbourg Observers*, 13 June 2023) <https://strasbourgobservers.com/2023/06/13/mamasakhlisi-and-others-v-georgia-and-russia-russias-effective-control-over-abkhazia-before-the-2008-war-peacekeepers-passportisation-and-other-hybrid-elements/> accessed 19 October 2023.

170 *Mamasakhlisi* (n 103) para 223.

171 ibid.

172 See *infra* Part 2, Chapter 13 (n 210).

173 *Mamasakhlisi* (n 103) paras 325–327.

174 Miklasová, 'Mamasakhlisi' (n 169).

also "a strong signal of dissuasion against actions of the Georgian government to regain its control over Abkhazia" as well as subsequent events,[175] the Court concluded that "the Russian State wielded sufficient military influence over Abkhaz territory for it to be considered 'dissuasive' and as such decisive in practice."[176] Ultimately, considered together with other aspects of the political, economic and financial support by Russia, the Court concluded that "Russia exercised effective control and decisive influence over Abkhaz territory."[177]

3.2.1.3 *Summary of Key Parameters of Effective Control Test*

The Court summarised the general principles regarding the notion of effective control in *Al-Skeini*, highlighting two indicators guiding its assessment.[178] Firstly, "[i]n determining whether effective control exists, the Court will primarily have reference to the strength of the State's military presence in the area."[179] Secondly, "[o]ther indicators may also be relevant, such as the extent to which its military, economic and political support for the local subordinate administration provides it with influence and control over the region."[180] In *Ukraine and Netherlands v Russia*, the Court specifically held that if military presence "alone does not suffice to demonstrate effective control over the area, then it will be necessary to have regard to" other indicators.[181]

175 *Mamasakhlisi* (n 103) para 324.
176 ibid para 329.
177 ibid para 339 and see paras 330–337. See Miklasová, 'Mamasakhlisi' (n 169).
178 *Al-Skeini* (n 113) para 139.
179 *Al-Skeini* (n 113) para 139. See *Loizidou* (Merits) (n 96) paras 16 and 56; *Ilaşcu* (n 99) paras 387; *Chiragov* (n 102) paras 170–180.
180 *Al-Skeini* (n 113) para 139. See *Ilaşcu* (n 99) paras 388–394; *Chiragov* (n 102) paras 181–185. WA Schabas, 'Article 1. Obligation to Respect Human Rights' in WA Schabas, *The European Convention on Human Rights: Commentary* (OUP 2015) 103. However, PACE's Committee on Legal Affairs and Human Rights' Report states that the requirement of military strength and control through a subordinated local administration are *alternatives*. CoE (PACE), 'Report of the Committee on Legal Affairs and Human Rights: Legal Remedies to Human Rights Violations on the Ukrainian Territories Outside the Control of the Ukrainian Authorities' (26 September 2016) Doc 14139, para 56. In addition, the requirement of the exercise of all or some of the public powers spelled out in some cases on a extra-territorial jurisdiction (see *Banković* (n 3) para 71; *Al-Skeini* (n 113) para 135) does not seem to be required as part of the effective control test. Milanović, *Extraterritorial Application of Human Rights Treaties* (n 12) 140; Wilde, 'Triggering State Obligations Extraterritorially' (n 9) 516 et seq. *Contra* S Besson, 'The Extraterritoriality of the European Convention on Human Rights: Why Human Rights Depend on Jurisdiction and What Jurisdiction Amounts To' (2012) 25 Leiden Journal of International Law 857, 873–874.
181 *Ukraine and the Netherlands v Russia* (n 117) para 578.

Thus, the first and most critical factor is the third State's on-going military presence in the breakaway region. While the test seemingly requires a rather high threshold – "boots on the ground"[182] – it also covers a rather wide range of scenarios, including the presence of 30,000 Turkish troops in northern Cyprus; 1,500 Russian troops and a large stockpile of weapons in Transnistria;[183] 3,800 Russian troops in each of the regions of Abkhazia and South Ossetia;[184] around 20,000 Russian troops in Crimea during its takeover;[185] an undetermined number of Armenian troops in the Nagorno-Karabakh;[186] and ("[g]iven the covert nature of the involvement of members of the Russian military in eastern Ukraine") an unspecified number of Russian troops in the Donbas region in Eastern Ukraine.[187] As shown, the Court has considered the presence of Russian troops staffing the CIS CPF peacekeeping mission in Abkhazia before 2008 as part of the criterion of "military *involvement*."[188] The Court took several factors into account and concluded that "Russia's sustained military *connection* to the region … enables it to conclude that the Russian State wielded sufficient military *influence* over Abkhaz territory for it to be considered 'dissuasive' and as such decisive in practice."[189] This author argued elsewhere that this terminology "has not been used in the previous case law and arguably showcases a lower threshold of the military aspect of the jurisdictional test."[190]

Notably, while the indicator of "boots on the ground is important for establishing effective control, this is viewed in a larger context."[191] For example, it has been outlined above how the Court acknowledged that the number of Russian troops in Transnistria decreased, but in light of the weapons stocks, it nevertheless held that the Russian "military importance in the region and its dissuasive influence persist."[192]

---

182 Milanović, *Extraterritorial Application of Human Rights Treaties* (n 12) 141.

183 See *supra*. Milanović in this context refers to "the potential for control." "Russia could still be said to exercise effective overall control over Transdniestria, because if it wanted to it could easily make its power felt more overtly." Milanović, *Extraterritorial Application of Human Rights Treaties* (n 12) 140 and 141.

184 *Georgia v Russia (II)* (n 104) para 11; See also *Georgia v Russia (II)* (n 104) paras 150–151 in connection with para 165.

185 *Ukraine v Russia (re Crimea)* (n 150) para 321 in connection with paras 318–319.

186 *Chiragov* (n 102) paras 175–180.

187 *Ukraine and the Netherlands v Russia* (n 117) para 611.

188 *Mamasakhlisi* (n 103) para 325–327 (*emphasis added*).

189 ibid, para 329 (*emphasis added*).

190 "The Court seems to have adjusted the military aspect of the jurisdictional test, arguably lowering it even by comparison with Chiragov." Miklasová, 'Mamasakhlisi' (n 169).

191 Miklasová, 'Post-Ceasefire Nagorno-Karabakh' (n 119) 366.

192 *Ilaşcu* (n 99) para 384; ibid. See also *Chiragov* (n 102) paras 175–180; *Mamasakhlisi* (n 103) paras 323–328.

The second group of indicators include military, economic and political support for the local subordinate administration. In particular, in terms of military support, the Court considers the third State's direct participation in active hostilities on the separatists' side, the conclusion of military agreements, supply of weapons and equipment, influence on the military strategy of separatists, artillery cover, training, and other military support.[193] As for political support, the Court assesses the participation of the controlling State's nationals or the officers of its armed forces in the secessionist entity's political and public life, the public pronouncements of the controlling State's representatives in favour of the secessionist cause, the implications of passportisation and the controlling State's positions at the international scene favourable to secessionists.[194] In the economic sphere, the Court considers the provision of subsidised commodities, debt reduction, provision of aid or loans not repaid, and the proportion of such aid in respect to the overall budget of the entity in question, the cooperation agreements with different entities of controlling State, and the direct investments coming from the territorial State.[195] The author argued elsewhere that this "showcases the malleability of the effective control test (regarding economic and financial support), where the attribution rules do not seem decisive for certain factors to be taken into account."[196]

Generally, the effective control test does not require conclusion as to the third State's role in the coordination and planning of military operations, neither on a general basis nor in terms of specific conduct. This test also does not require a detailed examination of the third State's *control* of the actions and policies of the entity in question.[197] Rather, it focuses on the third State's control of the territory achieved via its military presence and/or via its *support* for the 'subordinate local administration'.

---

193 See for example *Ilașcu* (n 99) paras 380–382; *Chiragov* (n 102) paras 172–180; *Ukraine and the Netherlands v Russia* (n 117) paras 613–662; *Georgia v Russia (II)* (n 104) paras 166–173.

194 See for example *Ilașcu* (n 99) paras 381–382; *Chiragov* (n 102) para 181; *Mamasakhlisi* (n 103) paras 330–331; *Georgia v Russia (II)* (n 104) paras 166–173; *Ukraine and the Netherlands v Russia* (n 117) paras 670–675.

195 See for example *Ilașcu* (n 99) para 390; *Catan* (n 114) para 120; *Chiragov* (n 102) paras 183–185; *Mamasakhlisi* (n 103) paras 332–336; *Georgia v Russia (II)* (n 104) paras 166–173; *Ukraine and the Netherlands v Russia* (n 117) paras 684–689.

196 Miklasová, 'Mamasakhlisi' (n 169). Compare *Ukraine and the Netherlands v Russia* (n 117) para 551.

197 *Loizidou* (Merits) (n 96) para 56. See Crawford and Keene (n 149) 195. Even though in Chiragov, the Court concluded that "armed forces of Armenia and the 'NKT' are highly integrated." *Chiragov* (n 102) para 180.

3.2.2 Extra-territorial Responsibility under ECHR

The ECtHR frequently reiterates that

> the test for establishing the existence of "*jurisdiction*" under Article 1 of the Convention has never been equated with the test for establishing a State's *responsibility* for an internationally wrongful act under general international law.[198]

However, "overlapping terminology and a lack of clarity in the Court's reasoning has given rise to much academic debate and considerable confusion."[199] "In fact, it is the Court itself that has over the decades been the greatest culprit in conflating jurisdiction and state responsibility."[200] Upon closer inspection of the Court's case law, a clear-cut separation between these two concepts seems to be more apparent than real.

3.2.2.1 *Overview of the ECtHR Case Law*

In *Loizidou* the Court held that

> it is not necessary to determine whether ... Turkey actually exercises detailed control over the policies and actions of the authorities of the "TRNC". It is obvious from the large number of troops engaged in active duties in northern Cyprus ... that her army exercises *effective overall control over that part of the island.* Such control, according to the relevant test and in the circumstances of the case, *entails her responsibility* for the policies and actions of the "TRNC". [201]

---

198 *Catan* (n 114) para 115 (*emphasis added*). "A distinction must also be drawn between the issue of *jurisdiction*, within the meaning of Article 1 of the Convention, and that of the *imputability* of the alleged violation to the actions or omissions of the respondent State." *Guide on Article 1* (n 115) para 5 (*emphasis in the original*). It is claimed that the "questions whether the acts which form the basis of the applicant's complaints fall within the *jurisdiction* of the respondent State and whether that State is in fact *responsible* for those acts under the Convention are very different." ibid para 5 (*emphasis in the original*). The ECtHR has recently acknowledged that despite this distinction, "there may be some areas of overlap in so far as the Court is invited to examine whether any acts of the perpetrators are to be attributed to the State in the context of its jurisdiction assessment." *Ukraine and the Netherlands v Russia* (n 117) para 551.

199 Crawford and Keene (n 149) 190.

200 Milanović, 'Jurisdiction and Responsibility' (n 116) 103.

201 *Loizidou* (Merits) (n 96) para 56 (*emphasis added*).

The Court went on to say that the violation falls within Turkey's jurisdiction under Article 1 ECHR and "is thus *imputable* to Turkey".[202]

Firstly, the Court seems to have ignored ARSIWA rules on attribution and seemingly derived Turkey's responsibility from the fact that violations fell within its jurisdiction on the basis of effective control. "The error the Court made at the merits stage was to rely on its conclusion that there was State jurisdiction to conclude that Turkey was responsible for the particular conduct that gave rise to breach."[203] Extra-territorial jurisdiction and imputability seem "to derive the one from the other".[204] Other scholars also point to imprecise language such as "control … entails her [Turkey's] responsibility", which makes it difficult to establish

> whether the Court is holding Turkey directly responsible for the acts of the TRNC as a non-State actor or instead for its failure to exercise due diligence in preventing the infringement of human rights by the TRNC (i.e. indirect responsibility).[205]

Similarly, in *Cyprus v Turkey* the ECtHR held that Turkey's

> responsibility cannot be confined to the acts of its own soldiers or officials in northern Cyprus but *must also be engaged* by virtue of the acts of the local administration which survives by virtue of Turkish military and other support. It follows that, in terms of Article 1 of the Convention, Turkey's "jurisdiction" must be considered to extend to securing the entire range of substantive rights set out in the Convention and those

202 *Loizidou* (Merits) (n 96) para 57 and para 64. The Court also highlighted the importance of Turkey's acknowledgment that "the applicant's loss of control of her property stems from the occupation of the northern part of Cyprus by Turkish troops and the establishment there of the 'TRNC' … it has not been disputed that the applicant has on several occasions been prevented by Turkish troops from gaining access to her property." ibid para 54.

203 Crawford and Keene (n 149) 193. "In the process, it failed to apply the rules of State responsibility, which would instead have depended on the fact that it was Turkish troops who had denied the applicant access to her home." ibid. "[I]t appears as if the responsibility of Turkey for the acts of the TRNC *follows from* the existence of jurisdiction." Jorritsma, 'Unravelling Attribution' (n 106) 681. (*emphasis in the original*); JM Rooney, 'The Relationship between Jurisdiction and Attribution after Jaloud v. Netherlands' (2015) 62 Netherlands International Law Review 407, 416.

204 Talmon (n 22) 508.

205 Jorritsma, 'Unravelling Attribution' (n 106) 681–682. Milanović prefers the latter interpretation. Milanović, *Extraterritorial Application of Human Rights Treaties* (n 12) 41–51.

> additional Protocols which she has ratified, and that violations of those rights are *imputable* to Turkey.[206]

Thus, even though the Court uses vague language, such as responsibility "must be engaged" again, the reference to "imputability" seems to highlight Turkey's direct responsibility.[207]

In *Ilașcu*, in the first period, Russian soldiers were directly involved in violations. The Court held that

> all of the acts committed by Russian soldiers with regard to the applicants, including their transfer into the charge of the separatist regime, in the context of the Russian authorities' collaboration with that illegal regime, are *capable of engaging responsibility* for the acts of that regime.[208]

As for the second period, despite the fact that Russian soldiers did not directly participate in violations, according to the Court, "there is a continuous and uninterrupted link of responsibility on the part of the Russian Federation," since its support for Transnistria continued and it "made no attempt to put an end to the applicants' situation" and "did not act to prevent the violations allegedly committed after 5 May 1998".[209] Therefore, the applicants come within Russia's jurisdiction under Article 1 ECHR and Russia's "*responsibility is engaged* with regard to the acts complained of".[210] Thus, Russia's responsibility seems to have stemmed from the violation of its own negative and positive

206 *Cyprus v Turkey* (n 97) para 77 (*emphasis added*). The ECtHR also held, "the acquiescence or connivance of the authorities of a Contracting State in the acts of private individuals which violate the Convention rights of other individuals within its jurisdiction may engage that State's responsibility under the Convention. Any different conclusion would be at variance with the obligation contained in Article 1 of the Convention." ibid para 81.

207 Jorritsma, 'Unravelling Attribution' (n 106) 682. However, according to Jorritsma, the Court did not elucidate whether the relevant criterion in this regard was the effective control over the area or "the status of the TRNC as a local administration, or as surviving by virtue of crucial Turkish support." ibid.

208 *Ilașcu* (n 99) para 385 (*emphasis added*). The Court highlighted that the Russian soldiers "were fully aware that they were handing them [applicants] over to an illegal and unconstitutional regime" and "knew, or at least should have known the fate which awaited them." ibid, para 383.

209 ibid para 393. "Regard being had to the foregoing, it is of little consequence that since 5 May 1998 the agents of the Russian Federation have not participated directly in the events complained of in the present application." ibid.

210 ibid para 394 (*emphasis added*). See also *Case of Ivantoc and others v Moldova and Russia* App no 23687/05 (ECtHR, 15 November 2011), para 120 ("*Ivantoc*").

obligations, rather than from the attribution of the conduct of Transnistrian authorities to Russia.[211]

In *Catan*, the ECtHR explicitly rejected Russia's arguments that the Court could only find Russia in effective control in accordance with the ICJ's *Nicaragua* and *Bosnian Genocide* cases on the ground that it examined the issue of jurisdiction rather than attribution.[212] However, when dealing with Russia's responsibility for concrete violations, the ECtHR reiterated that since it established that Russia exercised effective control over Transnistria,

> it is not necessary to determine whether or not Russia exercised detailed control over the policies and actions of the subordinate local administration ... By virtue of its continued military, economic and political support for the "MRT", which could not otherwise survive, *Russia incurs responsibility* under the Convention.[213]

Thus, Russia incurred responsibility even though no Russian agents directly participated in the violation.[214] The Court's imprecise language could be read in two ways. Firstly, it could entail that the acts of the MRT are attributed to Russia on the basis of the effective test and secondly, it could refer to Russia's

211 Similarly see Talmon (n 22) 509. *Contra* and thus in favour of the interpretation that Transnistria's actions were attributed to Russia, Rooney (n 203) 418. See also Berkes (n 121) 402–418.

212 "The Court recalls that in the judgment relied upon by the Government of the Russian Federation, the International Court of Justice was concerned with determining when the conduct of a person or group of persons could be attributed to a State, so that the State could be held responsible under international law in respect of that conduct. In the instant case, however, the Court is concerned with a different question, namely whether facts complained of by an applicant fell within the jurisdiction of a respondent State within the meaning of Article 1 of the Convention. As the summary of the Court's case-law set out above demonstrates, the test for establishing the existence of 'jurisdiction' under Article 1 of the Convention has never been equated with the test for establishing a State's responsibility for an internationally wrongful act under international law." *Catan* (n 114) para 115.

213 *Catan* (n 114) para 150 (*emphasis added*). The same conclusion was also reached in *Moser*. "Russia's responsibility under the Convention is engaged." *Moser v the Republic of Moldova and Russia*, para 157. Similarly, "Russia's responsibility under the Convention will be *engaged* in an *automatic* manner as regards any violations of the applicants' rights which are found in the present case." *Turturica* (n 131) para 33 (*emphasis added*); *Paduret* (n 131) para 36; *Eriomenco* (n 131) para 64; *Soyma v the Republic of Moldova, Russia and Ukraine*, para 41; *Vardanean* (n 131) para 45; *Apcov* (n 131) para 48; *Braga* (n 131) para 48; *Draci* (n 131) para 62; *Sandu* (n 131) para 89; *Mangir* (n 131) para 43.

214 *Catan* (n 114) para 149; *Moser v the Republic of Moldova and Russia*, para 156.

responsibility for its own positive obligations to prevent violations in the territory under its effective control.[215]

In *Chiragov*, the ECtHR held that it needed to establish if Armenia "exercised and continues to exercise effective control over the mentioned territories and as a result may be held responsible for the alleged violations".[216] When assessing the concrete violations, it is not clear if the Court referred to the violation of positive obligations by Armenia or found it responsible on the basis of attribution.[217]

The Court continued using this rather vague language in *Georgia v Russia (II)*.[218] This is especially relevant as, for example, concerning "the killing of civilians and torching and looting of houses in Georgian villages in South Ossetia and the 'buffer zone,'" Russia argued that its forces "had not been in position to prevent every incident and in any case had not controlled the South Ossetians, who had often been criminals."[219] This statement points both to Russia's positive obligations and its non-control over the separatist force (the issue of attribution). The Court responded by referring to its previous case law and held that

> from the time when the Russian Federation exercised "effective control" over the territories of South Ossetia and the "buffer zone" after the active conduct of hostilities had ceased, it was also responsible for the actions of the South Ossetian forces in those territories, without it being necessary to provide proof of "detailed control" of each of those actions.[220]

This Court's pronouncement echoes the issue of attribution. However, later, the Court also referred to the fact that "on the ground the measures taken by the Russian authorities proved to be insufficient to prevent the alleged violations" – pointing to positive obligation of Russia.[221] Ultimately, the Court held

---

215 M Milanović and T Papić, 'The Applicability of the ECHR in Contested Territories' (2018) 67 ICLQ 779, 789. However, according to Rooney, the fact that the Court focused on Russia's support to entity rather than control of territory seems to favour attribution of conduct. Rooney (n 203) 418 and 420.

216 *Chiragov* (n 102) para 169.

217 See ibid paras 201, 207–8, 215. According to Crawford and Keene, *Chiragov* "deals only with positive obligations when it comes to the merits with little discussion of responsibility" and it "should have engaged with the secondary rules of attribution at its merits phase." Crawford and Keene (n 149) 196. Milanović, 'The Nagorno-Karabakh Cases' (n 147).

218 Milanović, 'Georgia v. Russia No. 2' (n 118).

219 *Georgia v Russia (II)* (n 104) para 213.

220 ibid para 214.

221 ibid para 218.

Russia responsible for violating several provisions of the Convention, but it is unclear whether it was based on failure to discharge its positive obligations or the conduct of South Ossetian forces attributed to it.[222]

In *Mamasakhlisi,* the Court established that there had been a violation of Article 3, Article 5(1)(a)(c) and Article 6(1) and (3)(c) of the Convention. These violations were committed by the *de facto* authorities of Abkhazia and not directly by the Russian State organs. The Court held that "it is not necessary to determine whether or not Russia exercised detailed control over the policies and actions of the subordinate local administration."[223] "By virtue of its continued military, economic and political support for Abkhazia during the relevant period, which could not have otherwise survived, Russia's responsibility under the Convention is *engaged* as regards the violation of both applicants' rights."[224]

In the *Ukraine and the Netherlands v Russia* admissibility decision, the Court was more explicit. When setting out the general principles applicable to jurisdiction and attribution, it essentially equated the acts of the local subordinate administration in the territory under extra-territorial jurisdiction of a State Party to the acts of its *de jure* State organs within its territorial jurisdiction.[225] This is rather problematic as under the jurisprudence of the ICJ, the non-State entity is treated as a *de facto* organ corresponding to a *de jure* State organ (within the meaning of Article 4 ARSIWA) only if the former is *completely dependent* on the latter based on the complete dependence test.[226] This then entails that *all* of its acts, when carried out in such a capacity (even when committed *ultra vires*), are attributable to that State and trigger that State's responsibility.[227] In short, this test requires a complete dependence of an *entity* on the

---

222 Milanović, 'Georgia v. Russia No. 2' (n 118). See also *Georgia v Russia (II)* (n 104) paras 248–249, paras 275–277; para 298 (the formulation reads as if both *de facto* authorities *and* Russia had positive obligations under Article 2, Protocol 4).

223 *Mamasakhlisi* (n 103) para 411. See also *supra* Chapter 7.

224 ibid (*emphasis added*).

225 *Ukraine and the Netherlands v Russia* (n 117) para 564. See M Milanović, 'The European Court's Admissibility Decision in Ukraine and the Netherlands v Russia: The Good, the Bad and the Ugly – Part II' (*EJIL:Talk!*, 26 January 2023) <https://www.ejiltalk.org/the-european-courts-admissibility-decision-in-ukraine-and-the-netherlands-v-russia-the-good-the-bad-and-the-ugly-part-ii/> accessed 31 October 2023.

226 *Nicaragua* (n 47) paras 109–110; *Bosnian Genocide* (n 20) paras 390–395; ARSIWA (n 8) commentary to art 4. Milanović, 'The European Court's Admissibility Decision' (n 225). Talmon (n 22) 498–502 and 511. A Berkes, *International Human Rights Law Beyond State Territorial Control* (CUP 2021) 211–216.

227 ibid.

State.[228] However, in *Ukraine and the Netherlands v Russia,* the Court proceeded based on its jurisdictional-triggering test of effective control over the foreign *territory*.[229] Later, it explicitly espoused this approach:

> The finding that the Russian Federation had effective control over the relevant parts of Donbass controlled by the subordinate separatist administrations or separatist armed groups means that the acts and omissions of the separatists are *attributable* to the Russian Federation in the same way as the acts and omissions of any subordinate administration engage the responsibility of the territorial State.[230]

Thus, the Court did not engage with the general rules of attribution as reflected in the ARSIWA and the case law of the ICJ – the point criticised by Milanović.[231] Instead, it seemingly confirmed the *lex specialis* test of attribution under the ECHR.[232]

3.2.2.2 *Effective Control as a Lex Specialis Attribution Test*

In cases concerning a spatial conception of jurisdiction, "where the jurisdiction-establishing conduct and the violation-establishing conduct are not identical", "a separate attribution analysis will also have to be carried out at the merits stage".[233] Nevertheless, as follows from the above overview, in many instances it is not clear if, once the spatial extra-territorial jurisdiction is established on the basis of effective control, the Court attributes the conduct of an illegal secessionist entity to the third State for the purposes of establishing responsibility

228 "[C]omplete dependence, according to the ICJ, means that the secessionist entity is 'lacking any real autonomy' and is 'merely an instrument' or 'agent' of the outside power." Talmon (n 22) 511. See *Bosnian Genocide* (n 20) paras 392–393. The test requires control "in all fields." *Nicaragua* (n 47) para 109.

229 See *infra* on the relationship between these tests.

230 *Ukraine and the Netherlands v Russia* (n 117) para 697 (*emphasis added*).

231 It can be agreed with Milanović that given the depth of evidence on which the Court based its conclusions in *Ukraine and the Netherlands v Russia*, this complete dependence test would have been likely met. The problematic part of the judgment is thus the lack of conceptual clarity and no reference or engagement with the rules of attribution of general international law. Milanović, 'The European Court's Admissibility Decision' (n 225).

232 See *infra*.

233 Crawford and Keene (n 149) 192. It is true that in a great majority of cases, the issue of attribution for the purposes of responsibility is raised neither by the Court nor by the parties, since the answer to this issue is usually obvious on the facts, but "the attribution inquiry is nonetheless still done *sub silentio*, since without it there can be no state responsibility for an internationally wrongful act." Milanović, 'Jurisdiction and Responsibility' (n 116) 105.

or finds it violating its own positive obligations.[234] Indeed, many formulations are open to both interpretations.[235] In any case, the reliance on positive obligations is problematic on its own as it seeks "to avoid engaging with the rules of State responsibility. Yet this has a detrimental result, as positive obligations restrict the extent of the State's responsibility".[236]

It is argued here that the above case law, together with the analysis of the ECtHR's dealing with the *Namibia* exception in the previous chapter,[237] and recent expliticit pronouncements in *Ukraine and the Netherlands v Russia*, demonstrate that the Court does not differentiate between the effective control test as a jurisdiction-establishing test and as an attribution test for the purposes of establishing responsibility.[238] Instead, it derives the latter from the former.[239] Several scholars seem to adopt the same assessment.[240] In fact, even

---

234 Milanović, *Extraterritorial Application of Human Rights Treaties* (n 12) 41–51 and in particular 49, ftn 126; Jorritsma, 'Unravelling Attribution' (n 106) 690–691; Berkes (n 121) 417–418. See *contra* position on the theory concerning the violation of positive obligations only Berkes, *International Human Rights Law* (n 226) 259.

235 The statements, such as "[t]he fact that the local administration survives as a result of the Contracting State's military and other support *entails* that State's responsibility for its policies and actions" do not offer much insight into this matter. *Guide on Article 1* (n 115) para 49 (*emphasis added*). See also Milanović, *Extraterritorial Application of Human Rights Treaties* (n 12) 49, ftn 126. M Milanović, 'Special Rules on Attribution of Conduct in International Law' (2020) 96 Int'L Stud 295, 354–355 (referring to the "survives by virtue of State support" formula).

236 Crawford and Keene (n 149) 196.

237 The Court considered the TRNC institutions as Turkish institutions, TRNC remedies as Turkish remedies and TRNC laws as Turkish domestic laws on the basis of an implicit rule of effective control without reference to any known attribution rules under ARSIWA. See *supra*, Chapter 7. Admittedly, the attribution of conduct in this context did not only refer to direct conduct breaching ECHR, but also to the fulfilment of admissibility criteria.

238 "It follows that, in terms of Article 1 of the Convention, Turkey's 'jurisdiction' must be considered to extend to securing the entire range of substantive rights set out in the Convention and those additional Protocols which she has ratified, and that violations of those rights are *imputable* to Turkey." *Cyprus v Turkey* (n 97) para 77 (*emphasis added*).

239 Talmon (n 22) 508.

240 "The Court has consistently applied the same legal consequence of the test, the automatic attribution of all conducts of the de facto regime to the outside State." Berkes, *International Human Rights Law* (n 226) 224. If the ICTY already stretched the connection between the organ and the State to a breaking point, "the ECtHR, by attributing all the acts of a secessionist entity to an outside power simply on the basis of the latter's effective overall control of the secessionist entity's territory, has gone one step beyond." Talmon (n 22) 511. "The European Court of Human Rights has not followed the general rules outlined by the International Court of Justice on the question of the responsibility of States parties to the ECHR: it does not require evidence of complete dependence and control." A Cullen and S Wheatley, 'The Human Rights of Individuals in De Facto Regimes under the European Convention on Human Rights,' 691, 705. S Zareba, 'Responsibility for

the ILC refers to *Loizidou* in the context of "the problem of the degree of State control necessary for the purposes of *attribution* of conduct to the State" under Article 8 ARSIWA.[241] Nevertheless, the test of attribution employed by the ECtHR is similar to the complete dependence test (akin to Article 4 ARSIWA) in that once it is met, all acts of non-State actor are attributable to the controlling State.[242]

On the one hand, such an approach might encroach upon "the fundamental principle governing the law of international responsibility, which provides that a State is responsible only for its own conduct".[243] Or more specifically, this would represent a substantial lowering of the threshold for attribution for the purposes of responsibility. Indeed, it is one thing to say that the State controls certain *geographical regions*, but another to say "that it controls *the non-state actor* that administers that region, and that hence whatever that actor does is attributable to" that State.[244]

On the other hand, it is arguable that a broadening of the attribution rule as a *lex specialis* to rules of attribution in general international law is justified on the basis of the ECHR's specific object and purpose.[245] This has, however, not ever been discussed by the ECtHR itself.[246] Thus, "it is regrettable that the Court shows such a reluctance to expressly apply, or reject without motivation, ARSIWA's attribution rules in establishing State responsibility."[247] The ECtHR did not outline to what extent these rules applied under the ECHR form a *lex specialis* to general international law.[248]

---

the Acts of Unrecognised States and Regimes' in W Czapliński and A Kleczkowska (eds), *Unrecognised Subjects in International Law* (SCHOLAR Publishing House 2019) 191; Rooney (n 203) 426.

241 ARSIWA (n 8) commentary to art 8, para 5, ftn 160 (*emphasis added*).

242 See *infra*. Berkes, *International Human Rights Law* (n 226) 239.

243 Talmon (n 22) 517.

244 Milanović, 'Jurisdiction and Responsibility' (n 116) 107; Talmon (n 22) 511. It seems to be problematic to derive responsibility of the State from "effective control" or "decisive influence" over the secessionist entities as *foreign territories*, instead of analysing the level of control over them as *persons* and *actors*, as required by the relevant provisions of ARSIWA. Jorritsma, 'Unravelling Attribution' (n 106) 691.

245 ARSIWA (n 8) art 55. See Berkes (n 121) 416–417; Rooney (n 203) 426; Milanović and Papić (n 215) 784, ftn 19; Berkes, *International Human Rights Law* (n 226) 226.

246 Talmon (n 22) 509–511. Milanović, 'The European Court's Admissibility Decision' (n 225).

247 Jorritsma, 'Unravelling Attribution' (n 106) 692.

248 ibid 124. Milanović, 'The European Court's Admissibility Decision' (n 225).

3.3 *Territorial State's Positive Obligations*

3.3.1 Overview of the ECtHR Case Law

The remaining question that needs to be addressed is what the legal consequences of the change of territorial control for the territorial State's jurisdiction and responsibility are. The starting point is the above-mentioned presumption that the jurisdiction under art 1 ECHR is "primarily territorial" and that it "is presumed to be exercised normally throughout the State's territory".[249] It followed from the earlier case law on the TRNC that this presumption was rebuttable in the case of the loss of territorial control.[250] "[T]he consequence of the rebuttal is lack of jurisdiction and therefore lack of any ECHR obligations."[251] There was no space for a reduced jurisdiction in line with *Banković*, where the Court held that positive obligations under Article 1 ECHR could not be "divided and tailored" according to the circumstances of the extra-territorial act in question.[252] The jurisdiction was an all-or-nothing concept; the presumption either stood or was rebutted.[253]

However, this approach changed in *Ilașcu*, when instead of referring to presumption's rebuttal, the Court introduced its *limitation* in exceptional circumstances

> where a State is prevented from exercising its authority in part of its territory ... as a result of military occupation by the armed forces of another State which effectively controls the territory concerned ... acts of war or

249 *Ilașcu* (n 99) para 312.

250 The Commission expressly stated that Cyprus does not exercise jurisdiction in the north of island due to the presence of Turkish armed forces. *Cyprus v Turkey* App no 8007/77 (Decision on the Admissibility) (ECmHR, 10 July 1978), paras 23–24. Moreover, one can agree with Milanović and Papić that the ECtHR's pronouncement in *Cyprus v Turkey*, that any other finding than Turkey's jurisdiction would allow for a "regrettable vacuum in the system of human rights protection," can be *a contrario* interpreted in a way that Cyprus did not exercise jurisdiction over Northern Cyprus. *Cyprus v Turkey* (n 97) para 78; Milanović and Papić (n 215) 785, ftns 21–22. In addition, the only case filed against Cyprus for violation of the ECHR in Northern Cyprus was found inadmissible. The Commission found *inter alia* that "the authority of the respondent Government is in fact still limited to the southern part of Cyprus. It follows that the Republic of Cyprus cannot be held responsible under Article 1 (Art. 1) of the Convention for the acts of Turkish Cypriot authorities in the north of Cyprus of which the present applicants complain." *An and Others v Cyprus*, App No 18270/91 (Decision as to the Admissibility) (ECmHR, 18 October 1991).

251 Milanović and Papić (n 215) 794.

252 *Banković* (n 3) para 75; ibid 788.

253 KM Larsen, 'Territorial Non-Application of the European Convention on Human Rights' (2009) 78 Nordic Journal of International Law 73, 86; Milanović and Papić (n 215) 788; De Schutter (n 111) 222.

> rebellion, or the acts of a foreign State supporting the installation of a separatist State within the territory of the State concerned.[254]

In concreto, the Court concluded that even though "the Moldovan Government, the only legitimate government of the Republic of Moldova under international law, does not exercise authority over part of its territory," it "still has a positive obligation under Article 1 of the Convention".[255]

Later on, the *Sargsyan* case filed again Azerbaijan concerned violations in Gulistan, situated in Azerbaijan's territory but on the line of contact established following the first Nagorno-Karabakh war.[256] Azerbaijan argued that the village was in nobody's effective control, mined, deserted and not accessible to any civilian.[257] However, the Court rejected the limitation of Azerbaijan's responsibility on the ground that, unlike in its previous case law, "it has not been established that Gulistan is occupied by the armed forces of another State or that it is under the control of a separatist regime."[258] Thus, the *Ilaşcu*-style limitation did not apply to "disputed areas" or "areas which are rendered inaccessible by the circumstances".[259] The Court saw this case more in line

254 *Ilaşcu* (n 99) para 312. Larsen doubts that the "acts of war or rebellion" would on their own, without the third State's involvement, be enough to reduce the territorial State's jurisdiction. Larsen points to the Chechen cases, in which Russia was automatically considered as exercising jurisdiction, without dwelling on the issue of reduction. Larsen (n 253) 82–83.

255 *Ilaşcu* (n 99) paras 330–331. These include "the diplomatic, economic, judicial or other measures that *it is in its power to take* and are in accordance with international law to secure to the applicants the rights guaranteed by the Convention." ibid, para 331 (*emphasis added*). The notion of positive obligations in this context seems to differ significantly from positive obligations developed in other case law, in that the latter is usually linked with the negative obligations and flows from the specific provisions of the ECHR. Larsen (n 253) 85–86; Milanović and Papić (n 215) 788. In the present context, positive obligations operate independently from negative ones and stem from jurisdiction under Article 1 ECHR. Larsen (n 253) 85–86; Milanović and Papić (n 215) 788; G Yudkivska, 'Territorial Jurisdiction and Positive Obligations of an Occupied State: Some Reflections on Evolving Issues under Article 1 of the Convention' in A Van Aaken and I Motoc (eds), *The European Convention on Human Rights and General International Law* (Oxford University Press 2018) 141.

256 *Sargsyan* (n 69).

257 ibid paras 46–49. While the Court did not have enough evidence to establish the military presence of Azerbaijan in Gulistan, it highlighted that the NKR did not have any troops or positions there in the period in question. ibid paras 132–138.

258 ibid paras 148. See Berkes (n 121) 427–430.

259 ibid paras 146 and 149. In this context, it is possible to agree with judge Yudkivska, who criticised the Court's lack of courage "to admit that we were dealing with a *sui generis* situation in which the absence of 'effective control' of any occupying power over Gulistan

with *Assanidze* than *Ilaşcu.*[260] The Court did not at all take into account the impact of the armed conflict – the element entirely absent in *Assanidze* – on the extent of Azerbaijan's control over Gulistan and its ability to secure a full range of rights there.[261] The effort to avoid a vacuum in the European legal order seems to have distinguished *Sargsyan* from previous case law where jurisdiction's limitation was "compensated by the finding that another Convention State exceptionally exercised jurisdiction outside its territory and thus had full responsibility under the Convention".[262]

These rationales were apparently outweighed in *Azemi*, in which the applicant alleged that Serbia violated the right to a fair trial due to non-execution of the municipal Court's judgment in Kosovo.[263] In this one case, the Court examined Serbia's position both from the perspective of exercise of effective control akin to Russia's position as an intervening third State in cases on Transnistria and from the perspective of positive obligations akin to Moldova's position as the territorial State in cases on Transnistria.[264]

Regarding the former, the Court held that there is no evidence that Serbia exercised any control over Kosovo's institutions or the UNIMK.[265] Regarding the latter, the Court highlighted that after Kosovo's declaration of independence,[266] it "is satisfied that there existed objective limitations which prevented Serbia from securing the rights and freedoms in Kosovo".[267] The Court "cannot point to any positive obligations that the respondent State had towards the applicant".[268] This seemingly allowed the Court to avoid ruling on the

does not inevitably mean that Azerbaijan exercises effective control over the disputed area." ibid, Concurring Opinion of Judge Yudkivska, 90.

260 ibid para 140 and 150. *Assanidze v Georgia* ECHR 2004-II 155 ("*Assanidze*").

261 See *Sargsyan* (n 69) Concurring Opinion of Judge Yudkivska, 85–93.

262 ibid paras 148; Milanović and Papić (n 215) 790. However, for example, Yudkivska highlights that the issue would not be to reject Azerbaijan's jurisdiction as such, but only to limit it in scope, for example, by pointing to the fact that it is a completely uninhabited area. ibid, Concurring Opinion of Judge Yudkivska, 90–93.

263 *Azemi v Serbia* App no 11209/09 (Decision as to the Admissibility) (ECtHR, 5 November 2013) ("*Azemi*"). Yudkivska (n 255) 147; Milanović and Papić (n 215)793.

264 *Azemi* (n 263) paras 45 and 47. Milanović and Papić (n 215) 792–793.

265 ibid para 45.

266 The Court also took into account that "[o]n 10 September 2012, apart from the exercise of certain 'residual responsibilities' by UNMIK, the end of 'supervised independence' was declared." ibid para 46.

267 ibid para 46.

268 ibid para 47. The Court also held that "the applicant has not been able to point to a particular action or inaction of the respondent State or substantiated any breach of the respondent State's duty to take all the appropriate measures with regard to his right which are still within its power to take." ibid para 47. See also K Istrefi, 'Azemi v Serbia in the

sovereignty issue because, even if Serbia was sovereign in Kosovo and therefore had positive obligations, "such obligations were not relevant or were discharged on the facts of the case".[269] However, this reasoning was at odds with the underlying principle that "residual positive obligations follow sovereign title over territory".[270] Ultimately, as Serbia was found not to have jurisdiction in Kosovo and the latter was not a party to the ECHR, Kosovo indeed seems to represent a vacuum in the European legal order.[271]

Recently, positive obligations of territorial States have been upheld and examined in *Mamasakhlisi* case filed against Russia and Georgia, but the Court ultimately found no violation by Georgia.[272]

3.3.2 Content and Responsibility for Violations of Positive Obligations

The Court in *Ilașcu* established that positive obligations included two sets of measures, those "needed to re-establish its control over Transdniestrian territory"[273] and those aimed at securing the applicants' rights.[274] The first category includes the obligation "to refrain from supporting the separatist regime" and to take "all the political, judicial and other measures to re-establish control" over secessionist territory.[275] The Court highlighted that it was not its responsibility to indicate the most appropriate measures or if they were sufficient; it only needed to verify the parent State's *will*, as expressed through specific acts and measures.[276] The Court in fact acknowledged that "there was little Moldova could do to re-establish its authority" over separatist territory vis-à-vis a regime supported by a power such as Russia.[277]

Concerning concrete measures, the Court is satisfied that the parent State discharges its obligation to re-establish control when it takes such measures as non-recognition of the secessionist entity,[278] diplomatic activities with a

---

European Court of Human Rights: (Dis)continuity of Serbia's De Jure Jurisdiction over Kosovo' (*EJIL Talk!*, 13 March 2014) <https://www.ejiltalk.org/azemi-v-serbia-in-the-european-court-of-human-rights-discontinuity-of-serbias-de-jure-jurisdiction-over-kosovo/> accessed 12 January 2020.

269 Milanović and Papić (n 215) 793.

270 ibid.

271 See ibid.

272 *Mamasakhlisi* (n 103) para 319.

273 *Ilașcu* (n 99) paras 339–340.

274 ibid para 339.

275 ibid para 340. See in detail Berkes, *International Human Rights Law* (n 226) 104–124.

276 ibid para 340 (*emphasis added*).

277 ibid para 341. According to Zareba, the Court is quite lenient with respect to the discharge of the obligation to re-establish control. Zareba (n 240) 177.

278 *Mamasakhlisi* (n 103) para 400.

view to settling conflict;[279] protests demanding the withdrawal of an intervening State's troops or protests against actions interfering with the territorial State's sovereignty and territorial integrity;[280] complaints before international bodies;[281] the opening of criminal proceedings against secessionist leaders;[282] and the prohibition of import and exports of goods from the entity.[283] According to the Court, the signature of economic cooperation agreements with Transnistria "cannot be regarded as support" for Transnistria, but it is "affirmation by Moldova of its desire to re-establish control" there.[284]

As for the obligation to ensure respect of an applicant's rights, the Court appreciated the seeking of assistance in international fora, from a controlling State, bilateral foreign partners or even the actors in the secessionist entity,[285] the opening of criminal investigation into the violation of rights in the secessionist entity or convicting the perpetrators by the legitimate courts,[286] the annulment of sentences rendered by the secessionist entity[287] and the awarding of financial assistance to the applicants or medication free of charge.[288] The Court also took into account contacts by way of letters between Moldova and Transnistria's political bodies, including the 'Ministry of Interior',[289] and even the provision of rent to Transnistria for relocated Latin-script schools.[290] On the other hand, the Court found Moldova's responsibility engaged for its lack of effort to reach agreement on guaranteeing the applicants' rights through negotiations with Transnistria and for not raising this issue of the applicants' release in bilateral talks with Russia.[291]

---

279 *Ilașcu* (n 99) para 344. *Mamasakhlisi* (n 103) para 400.
280 *Ivantoc* (n 210) paras 16, 29–30, 108. *Mamasakhlisi* (n 103) para 400.
281 *Ilașcu* (n 99) paras 341 and 343; *Mozer* (n 131) para 153.
282 *Ilașcu* (n 99) paras 342 and 344.
283 *Ivantoc* (n 210) para 19.
284 *Ilașcu* (n 99) para 345.
285 *Ilașcu* (n 99) para 347; *Vardanean* (n 131) paras 12 and 42; *Mamasakhlisi* (n 103) paras 402–3.
286 *Mozer* (n 131) para 153; *Draci* (n 131) paras 15 and 61, *Vardanean* (n 131) paras 12 and 42, *Eriomenco* (n 131) paras 32–33 and 60; *Paduret* (n 131) para 8; *Case of Mangir and Others v the Republic of Moldova and Russia,* para 16; *Mamasakhlisi* (n 103) para 404.
287 *Ilașcu* (n 99) para 346; *Mozer* (n 131) para 153; *Draci* (n 131) paras 16 and 61.
288 *Ilașcu* (n 99) paras 346 and 347; *Vardanean* (n 131) paras 13 and 42. *Mamasakhlisi* (n 103) para 405.
289 *Eriomenco* (n 131) paras 34–35 and para 60.
290 *Catan* (n 114) paras 49, 56, 61–62, 147.
291 *Ilașcu* (n 99) paras 348–352. This changed only when Moldova started raise this issue after 2004. *Ivantoc* (n 210) para 109.

3.3.3 Critical Assessment

The above overview requires several observations. Firstly, the territorial State is held responsible for violation of its *own* positive obligations; the matter does not concern the attribution of conduct by separatists. A reduced number of positive obligations derive from the fact that the parent State's jurisdiction is limited as a result of the loss of effective territorial control.[292] However, this approach seems to deviate from general international law, where a temporary loss of territorial control "does not affect the scope of its obligations or jurisdiction, doing nothing more than limiting the scope of its responsibility."[293]

Secondly, while jurisdiction under Article 1 ECHR in an extra-territorial context is understood as the actual power, in an intra-territorial context, the positive obligations are grounded in the sovereign title.[294] Authors point out that not only does such understanding undermine the main premise of the applicability of human rights, which is the factual power to affect human rights,[295] but these two ideas also cannot be coherently held at the same time.[296] "Jurisdiction in the sense of Article 1 is either the *right* to exercise a power, or the *actual exercise* of that power, whether lawfully or unlawfully; it cannot coherently be both".[297]

Thirdly, while the controlling State's extra-territorial obligations are derived from factual control and thus are divorced from the considerations of sovereignty, the applicability of positive obligations presumes an implicit assessment of this issue.[298]

Moreover, other scholars argue that the territorial State's jurisdiction is equally based on "the State's sovereign title and effectiveness."[299] In this context, the territorial State's jurisdiction may be viewed as functional – "adapted to the authority that the State *can* exercise towards the concerned individuals."[300]

---

292 As pointed out by Berkes, the focus on positive obligations "cannot exclude negative obligations which certainly continue to bind the territorial State." Berkes, *International Human Rights Law* (n 226) 79 and see 94–96.

293 Zareba (n 240) 176.

294 Larsen (n 253) 85–86; Milanović and Papić (n 215) 795.

295 Raible (n 93) 329–331.

296 Milanović and Papić (n 215) 795.

297 ibid (*emphasis added*).

298 Milanović and Papić (n 215) 796.

299 Berkes, *International Human Rights Law* (n 275) 81. According to the ECtHR, "Those obligations remain even where the exercise of the State's authority is limited in part of its territory, so that it has a duty to take all the appropriate measures which it is still within its power to take." *Ilaşcu* (n 99) para 313.

300 Berkes, *International Human Rights Law* (n 226) 82 (*emphasis added*). See S Wallace, *The Application of the European Convention on Human Rights to Military Operations* (CUP 2019) 35–41.

As this author expresses elsewhere, "[t]he Court is even cognisant of the limited capability of the State to secure its positive obligations."[301] The territorial State "has a duty to take all the appropriate measures which it is still within its power to take."[302] Berkes views the underlying principle of positive obligations in the due diligence standard.[303] In these situations, "applicants should specify the capacity that the State failed to use to prevent or mitigate the challenged human rights violation."[304]

Furthermore, the existence of positive obligations or their content had hardly been supported by the previous practice.[305] Moreover, in line with a high threshold for their violation, they do not seem to be of much practical significance either.[306] In addition, they also suffer from internal incoherence.[307] In fact, obligations to refrain from the separatist regime's support and obligations towards individuals seem to be mutually exclusive.[308] According to Zareba,

> the Court's clear insistence on at-least limited cooperation with a view to respect for the rights of applicants being secured ... appears both demanding, and hardly compatible with the obligation that control over the area under the authority of an unrecognised entity be re-established.[309]

Likewise, it will be shown below to what extent it is possible to reconcile these obligations with consequences of peremptory illegality, such as the duty of non-recognition.[310]

Overall, the above overview demonstrates that while the residual positive obligations are by now firmly rooted in the Court's case law, they also suffer from a number of structural problems, which raises questions about their conceptual coherence and overall utility.

---

301 Miklasová, 'Post-Ceasefire Nagorno-Karabakh' (n 119) 363.

302 *Ilașcu* (n 99) para 313. Compare *Mamasakhlisi* (n 103) para 401.

303 Berkes, *International Human Rights Law* (n 226) 96 et seq.

304 ibid 82–83.

305 See Yudkivska (n 255) 140–141. See also Berkes, *International Human Rights Law* (n 275) 79–81.

306 See Milanović and Papić (n 215) 795–796. See for a relatively high threshold for a violation and recognition that "in the specific circumstances of the present case", the opening of the judicial investigation would be "inconsequential and, at most, symbolic." *Mamasakhlisi* (n 103) para 407.

307 Yudkivska (n 255) 143 and see also 148.

308 ibid 143 and see also 148.

309 Zareba (n 240) 178.

310 See *infra*.

4 Overview of the Relevant Factual Tests

This chapter identified several factual tests, which under general international law or its special fields trigger certain legal consequences. Even though their fulfilment might derive from the same factual context, and therefore the determination of *facts* is relevant more broadly, they require different thresholds and thus the *legal* analysis of their fulfilment needs to be done separately.

Despite terminological overlap,[311] the effective control test, as a jurisdiction-triggering test and possible *lex specialis* rule of attribution under ECHR, must be distinguished from the effective control under Article 8 ARSIWA.[312] The effective control under ECHR test requires a considerably lower threshold of control.[313] Unlike the effective control test under ARSIWA, which requires the attribution of specific conduct, this test under ECHR is 'overall' in character and therefore does not require examination of the third State's control over specific conduct. "[I]f the state is in overall control of a territorial unit, everything within that unit falls within its 'jurisdiction', even if at lesser levels powers are exercised by other actors."[314]

Similarly, effective control over an area beyond State borders under ECHR is "less stringent" than a complete dependence test to establish a "de facto organ" corresponding to a State organ Article 4 ARSIWA.[315] "[T]here is simply a leap here from control over territory to the control over non-state entities operating

---

311 Undoubtedly, one of the key factors contributing to confusion in the ECtHR case law is to do with the different meanings of the notion of effective control, including the attribution test in international responsibility, the threshold for the beginning of belligerent occupation in IHL, and the relationship between superior and subordinate required for the command responsibility to be engaged in international criminal law. Milanović, *Extraterritorial Application of Human Rights Treaties* (n 12) 53. See also Milanović, 'Jurisdiction and Responsibility' (n 116) 104.

312 "The problem is that this 'effective control' test looks and sounds like an attribution analysis, but it actually concerns the question of what spatial control the State has over the territory in question for the purposes of determining jurisdiction." Crawford and Keene (n 149) 194. Berkes, *International Human Rights Law* (n 226) 239–240.

313 Milanović, 'Jurisdiction and Responsibility' (n 116) 99. With respect to cases concerning Nagorno-Karabakh, see Crawford and Keene (n 149) 195. According to Milanović, following a groundbreaking ruling in Al-Skeini, the ECtHR "has demonstrated a trend towards a clearer, more factual, and most importantly more expansive approach towards the question of the Convention's extraterritorial application and the interpretation of the jurisdiction clause in Article 1." Milanović, 'Jurisdiction and Responsibility' (n 116) 99. Zareba (n 240) 191.

314 Wilde, 'Triggering State Obligations Extraterritorially' (n 9) 524.

315 Talmon (n 22) 511. Berkes, *International Human Rights Law* (n 226) 225–226. See *Bosnian Genocide* (n 20) paras 392–393.

in that territory."[316] Nevertheless, both tests are similar in that once the test is met, all acts of non-State actor are attributable to the controlling State.[317]

Similarly, the effective control test in the jurisprudence of the ECtHR also differs from the ICTY's overall control test. Even though both tests are overall in character, the former concerns territorial control and the latter focuses on the control over entity. Firstly, the overall control test requires a cumulative fulfilment of the condition of military support and the third State's role in general organisation, coordination and planning of military operations. Secondly, even though the effective control test requires military presence and, possibly, the third State's direct participation in the secessionist conflict, it does not require the specific extent of control of the third State's armed forces over the secessionist entity's military operations.

Thus, *in abstracto*, the effective control or jurisdiction under ECHR does not automatically signify the existence of an internationalised NIAC, as the latter also requires analysis as to the internal inter-relation between the proxy and the controlling State, as far as military operations are concerned. While it is indisputable that the third State's direct participation in hostilities and its military presence in foreign territory, as elements of an effective control test, also trigger the applicability of an IAC, it might be possible that there could be an IAC and a NIAC applicable in parallel.[318]

Moreover, the fulfilment of effective control for the purposes of belligerent occupation could be taken *prima facie* as an indicator of the fulfilment of the effective control test for the purposes of jurisdiction and *vice versa*.[319] However,

316 Milanović, 'The European Court's Admissibility Decision' (n 225). Talmon (n 22) 511. However, according to Berkes, the control over territory and control over persons are "inherently related" Berkes, *International Human Rights Law* (n 226) 220.

317 See Berkes, *International Human Rights Law* (n 226) 239.

318 In this scenario, the IAC would apply as a result of the third State's direct participation in the hostilities or its own military presence; and the NIAC would apply because the level of control would fall below the threshold of the overall control test.

319 "[I]nternational human rights instruments are applicable 'in respect of acts done by a State in the exercise of its jurisdiction outside its own territory,' particularly in occupied territories." *Armed Activities* (n 35) para 216. See also *Wall*, paras 107–111. "In addition to the State territory proper, territorial jurisdiction extends to any area which, at the time of the alleged violation, is under the 'overall control' of the State concerned. Notably occupied territories." *Assanidze* (n 260) para 138. "[W]here the territory of one Convention State is occupied by the armed forces of another, the occupying State should in principle be held accountable under the Convention for breaches of human rights within the occupied territory." *Al-Skeini* (n 113) para 142. Milanović, *Extraterritorial Application of Human Rights Treaties* (n 12) 147. See also Wallace and Mallory (n 119) 23–24. *Georgia v Russia (II)* (n 104) para 196. In *Jaloud*, the Court noted that "the status of 'occupying power' within the meaning of Article 42 of the Hague Regulations, or lack of it, is not *per se* determinative."

bearing in mind the lowered threshold in *Ilaşcu and Mamasaklishi*, it might also be possible to establish jurisdiction without occupation.[320] In addition, previous consideration regarding the overall control tests are also relevant to the existence of occupation by proxy.

Lastly, the determination of facts relevant to a legal analysis of the fulfilment of the above tests also informs the constitutive criterion of independence for the purposes of the emergence of statehood as well as of the criterion of legality as developed in Chapter 2, Part 1.

5 Conclusion

This chapter examined the legal consequences of a change of effective territorial control in the context of the existence of an illegal secessionist entity. In particular, the chapter focused on humanitarian law and more specifically on the law of occupation, as well as human rights law under ECHR, as the most prominent legal regimes applicable extra-territorially on the basis of effectiveness alone.

It concluded that in the context of an illegal secessionist entity whose effectiveness is only apparent because of a third State's control over it, these regimes link the relevant consequences, including the triggering of their applicability and responsibility for their violation, only with the actual power and control of the third State. Thus, the illegal secessionist entity only acts as the third State's agent or proxy.

In the area of humanitarian law, deriving from the relevant case law, the chapter identified the factual parameters of the third State's overall control

Jaloud (n 113) para 142. It should be noted that this case involved the establishment of a personal jurisdiction. Similarly, in *Al-Skeini*, the Court also relied on personal jurisdiction rather than a spatial jurisdiction, even though the UK occupied the territory in question. *Al-Skeini* (n 113) para 149. However, both cases concerned the situation outside the territory of the Member States of the Council of Europe. "One possible explanation is that spatial jurisdiction is limited to existing contracting States, though the ECtHR has never acknowledged this to be the case." Wallace and Mallory (n 119) 27.

320 "[T]he term 'effective control' is broader and covers situations that do not necessarily amount to a situation of 'occupation' for the purposes of international humanitarian law." *Georgia v Russia (II)* (n 104) para 196. Milanović, *Extraterritorial Application of Human Rights Treaties* (n 12) 144, but see also 147. The Court did not directly pronounce itself on the issue of whether the situation in Transnistria was a military occupation, holding only "whether or not this is accompanied by military occupation by another State." *Ilaşcu* (n 99) para 333. See on the issue of occupation of Transnistria Berkes (n 121) 411–414. See *Mamasakhlisi* (n 103) para 339. See in detail Part 2, Chapter 16.

required for internationalisation of a NIAC and established that a more stringent test of effective control should be established in this context for the purposes of attribution in the area of State responsibility. Moreover, the chapter also examined the concept of occupation by proxy, which is particularly relevant to the context of illegal secessionist entities. Deriving from the relevant case law and scholarly opinions, it established that in order for the occupation by proxy to be established, the third State should exercise overall control over the armed group, which in turn exercises effective control over the territory in question.

As regards human rights law, due to its relevance to the case studies in this book, the chapter focused on the ECHR-specific context, in particular on a spatial concept of jurisdiction in the context involving an illegal secessionist entity. Firstly, the chapter showed that to discard the purported statehood of illegal secessionist entities the Court relied on the attitude of international community including the references to their unlawfulness. Then, from the relevant case law, the chapter derived factual parameters of the controlling State's effective control as the jurisdiction-triggering test. Next, it focused on the issue of attribution and responsibility of the controlling State. The chapter concluded – also in light of the recent admissibility decision in *Ukraine and the Netherlands v Russia*, which was explicit on the question of attribution – that at least in some cases, the Court in fact employed an effective control test as the test of attribution, implicitly creating a less stringent *lex specialis* rule of attribution in the ECHR-specific context. Based on the ECtHR's case law, the chapter also determined the content of the territorial State's positive obligations and concluded that, despite the fact that by now these obligations are firmly rooted in the Court's case law, this concept suffers from structural deficiencies.

Lastly, the chapter also outlined relationships and possible overlaps between various factual tests explored in the chapter, in particular effective control as an attribution test under ARSIWA, effective control as a jurisdiction-triggering and attribution test in the ECHR context, the effective control test for belligerent occupation and the overall control test for the internationalisation of NIAC.

Overall, despite overlapping terminology, conflicting case law and divergent doctrinal opinions, the chapter sought to clarify international law in this area by subscribing to the view that conceptual distinction should be maintained between the issue of extraterritorial applicability of legal regimes and the question of attribution for the purposes of establishing State responsibility.

CHAPTER 9

Overlap of Applicable Consequences

1 Introduction

A normative context for an illegal secessionist entity is defined by legal consequences flowing from peremptory territorial illegality and those stemming from the actual change of effective territorial control. Previous chapters focused on these consequences in isolation. But, how do they interact? What is the relationship between the legal consequences of effectiveness and illegality in the context of illegal secessionist entity subsequent to the denial of the status of statehood?

While the co-application of IHL and human rights law in the context of armed conflict is well researched, the analysis of the co-existence of consequences of peremptory illegality and these two legal regimes has received little doctrinal attention.[1] Instead, the relevant cases are analysed in isolation, either under one or another regime. Undoubtedly, the disinterest in this issue, particularly in the area of IHL and the law of occupation, is due to a sacrosanct separation between *ius ad bellum* and *ius in bello*.[2] Moreover, even if less dogmatic, a similar divide is also present in IHRL, where its extra-territorial

1 Except for A Orakhelashvili, 'Overlap and Convergence: The Interaction Between *Jus Ad Bellum* and *Jus in Bello*' 12 (2007) Journal of Conflict and Security Law 157; Y Ronen, 'Illegal Occupation and Its Consequences' (2008) 41 Israel Law Review 201. Azarova's work seeks to establish how the concurrent application of different regimes contributes to the interpretation, application and enforcement of the law of occupation and the regulation of illegal territorial regimes in international law. The law of occupation is thus a main point of reference as opposed to in this work. Azarova focuses on the illegality of occupation due to an excess of its normative parameters, as opposed to illegality flowing from the initial act of aggression and considers the duty of non-recognition as the enforcement mechanism of the law of occupation, which ultimately helps enhance its efficacy. V Azarova, 'Illegal Territoriality in International Law: The Interaction and Enforcement of the Law of Belligerent Occupation Through Other Territorial Regimes' (PhD Thesis, National University of Ireland, Galway 2015), 9; V Azarova, 'Towards a Counter-Hegemonic Law of Occupation: On the Regulation of Predatory Interstate Acts in Contemporary International Law' (2017) 20 Yearbook of International Humanitarian Law 113. Wrange analyses the overlap of the law of occupation, law governing the NSGT and the duty of non-recognition P Wrange, 'Self-Determination, Occupation and the Authority to Exploit Natural Resources: Trajectories from Four European Judgments on Western Sahara' (2019) 52 Israel Law Review 3. See *infra*.

2 See *infra*.

 | DOI:10.1163/9789004702646_014

application is triggered by the fact of a State's territorial control regardless of the legality of its establishment.[3]

However, taking into account peremptory rules, including the prohibition of the use of force, the question must be asked: to what extent does such isolation still hold true, or should it hold true, in contemporary international law?[4]

There are very good reasons why the triggering of the applicability of the two regimes, IHRL and the law of occupation, do not depend on legality or title. Indeed, IHRL and the law of occupation are different in that the former provides for the rights of individuals and the corresponding obligations of States, and the latter does not grant any 'right of occupation' to the Occupying Power, but simply establishes what it can do as long as this *de facto* situation lasts. Nevertheless, there is common ground in that their application is triggered upon effectiveness. This should be seen in the context of their underlying object and purpose.[5]

IHRL protects the interests of individual human beings. While the law of occupation originated as a vehicle to protect formal titles of ousted sovereigns and as a temporary governance gap-filler, today, increasing attention is paid to "the interests of the indigenous community under occupation".[6] Moreover, the consequences of peremptory illegality seek to uphold the interests of the injured State and international public order, with due account of the needs of the local population.

It is believed that only when *all* these interests and relations are simultaneously taken into account can the outcome reflect the values of contemporary international law in its entirety.[7] Otherwise, it is arguable that a restrictive

---

3 *Loizidou v Turkey* App no 15318/89 (Preliminary Objections) (ECtHR, 23 March 1995), para 62 ("*Loizidou* (Preliminary Objections)"). M Bothe, 'Current Status of Crimea: Russian Territory, Occupied Territory or What' (2014) 53 Military Law and Law of War Review 99, 105. See *Russia v Ukraine (re Crimea)* App nos 20958/14 and 38334/18 (ECtHR, 16 December 2020), paras 320–327 ("*Russia v Ukraine (re Crimea)*"). However, see UN Human Rights Committee, 'General Comment No 36' (3 September 2019) UN Doc CCPR/C/GC/36, para 70 ("States parties engaged in acts of aggression as defined in international law, resulting in deprivation of life, violate ipso facto article 6 of the Covenant").

4 Orakhelashvili, 'Overlap and Convergence' (n 1) 157–158.

5 For this question, see Chapter 8, Introduction.

6 E Benvenisti, 'Occupation and Territorial Administration' (2015) Global Trust Working Paper 11/2015, 2 and 3 <https://papers.ssrn.com/sol3/papers.cfm?abstract_id=2663115 > accessed 30 October 2023. E Benvenisti, *The International Law of Occupation* (2nd ed, OUP 2012) 1–7. H Cuyckens, *Revisiting the Law of Occupation* (Brill Nijhoff 2018) 103–108.

7 "[T]he application of occupation law in isolation from applicable lex generalis limits the reach of international law." Azarova, 'Illegal Territoriality in International Law' (n 1) 22. "The comprehensive and integrated application of multi-sourced international norms to situations of belligerent occupation provides additional incentive structures to comply with

vision of applicable law in these situations might result in incorrect conclusions of legal analysis.[8]

However, finding a method for outlining the interaction between these regimes can prove particularly daunting. On the one hand, it would seem that since the consequences of peremptory illegality derive from hierarchically superior peremptory norms, any potential regime conflict should be guided by the rule of *lex superior* broadly deriving from the principle of *ex iniuria ius non oritur*. However, this premise is not operational in this context. The same rationales that mandate that applicability of the law of occupation and the extraterritorial application of IHRL do not depend on legality or title continue to be relevant. On the other hand, it is argued that the rule of *lex specialis* also cannot apply straightforwardly, due to communitarian values protected by peremptory norms. Thus, instead, analysis should be built on the balancing of interests, depending on the context and protected values involved.

The objective of this chapter is thus to outline the broad lines of the interaction of these regimes, focusing on normative linkages and synergies, as well as their application in judicial practice. In case of divergences or even conflicts, on the basis of balancing the interests involved, the goal is to identify the limits to the co-operability of these regimes without frustrating their cardinal values. It needs to be highlighted that the chapter in no way seeks to undermine the fact that extra-territorial application of IHRL and IHL is triggered upon effectiveness, regardless of legality. Instead, it presumes such applicability and builds on the position that in the context of illegal secessionist entity, all these regimes apply simultaneously.

The account is neither exhaustive, nor detailed in terms of the examination of substantive provisions. Its purpose is to highlight the issues raised by the illegal secessionist entity's existence. Without any doubt, this chapter's key premise does not follow the position of the majority of doctrine and judicial bodies. Nevertheless, it is believed that shedding light on zones of interaction better reflects contemporary international law and responds to demands raised by the inherent complexity stemming from the illegal secessionist entity's existence.

---

such norms, and reinforces the normative power of the *lex specialis* of belligerent occupation." ibid.

8 Such as those reached by the CJEU in cases involving Western Sahara. See *supra*, Chapter 7.

2 Overlap of Effects of Peremptory Territorial Illegality and the Law of Occupation

2.1 *Key Premises*

2.1.1 Separation between *Ius in Bello* and *Ius ad Bellum*

The *ius in bello/ius ad bellum* divide is important in international law. It has been confirmed in case law,[9] reflected in the preamble of API[10] and almost unanimously accepted by scholars.[11] A number of reasons underlie this divide, the most fundamental among them being the objective to assure humanitarian protection, notwithstanding the question of the legality of the use of force.[12] Since, in practice, both sides in war claim to pursue a just cause, IHL "therefore only has a chance of being respected if it applies independently of the violation of *ius ad bellum* and if both sides apply the same rules".[13] Accordingly, some scholars claim that "the distinction between jus ad bellum and jus in bello constitutes a well-motivated exception to the general principle *ex iniura ius non oritur.*"[14]

---

9 *US v Wilhelm List et al* (*Hostage case*) (US Military Tribunal, Nuremberg, 19 February 1948) 15 ILR 632, 636–637. H Lauterpacht, 'The Limits of the Operation of the Law of War' (1953) 30 BYBIL, 206, 215–220. A Roberts, 'What Is a Military Occupation?' (1984) 55 BYBIL 249, 293–294. Even in *Armed Activities*, the ICJ found Uganda, as the occupying power, violating IHL and IHRL by taking certain measures, but it "did not consider their invalidity as stemming from the fact that the use of force leading to the occupation was itself unlawful." A Carcano, *The Transformation of Occupied Territory in International Law* (Brill 2015) 80.

10 Protocol Additional to the Geneva Conventions of 12 August 1949, and Relating to the Protection of Victims of International Armed Conflicts (Protocol I) (signed 8 June 1977, entered into force 7 December 1978) 1125 UNTS 3, preamble ("AP I").

11 See for a critical review of sources of the distinction R Giladi, 'The *Jus Ad Bellum/Jus In Bello* Distinction and the Law of Occupation' (2008) 41 Israel Law Review 246, 250–257. I Brownlie, *International Law and the Use of Force by States* (Clarendon Press 2002) 407.

12 M Sassòli, '*Ius ad Bellum* and *Ius in Bello* – The Separation between the Legality of the Use of Force and Humanitarian Rules to Be Respected in Warfare: Crucial or Outdated?' in M Schmitt and J Pejic (eds), *International Law and Armed Conflict: Exploring the Faultlines: Essays in Honour of Yoram Dinstein* (Martinus Nijhoff Publishers 2007) 245–246; Lauterpacht (n 9) 214.

13 Sassòli, '*Ius ad Bellum* and *Ius in Bello*' (n 12) 246. See also Giladi (n 11) 258–260. *Contra* arguments supporting this divide see Orakhelashvili, 'Overlap and Convergence' (n 1) 171–179.

14 Carcano (n 9) 80. Lauterpacht (n 9) 212. See also R Kolb and S Vité, *Le droit de l'occupation militaire: Perspectives historiques et enjeux juridiques actuels* (Bruylant 2009) 46–47. Other scholars, however, point out that IHL rather than conferring benefits to parties, seeks to protect individuals; therefore the principles of *ex iniuria ius non oritur* is not really relevant in this sphere. Giladi (n 11) 260. According to Orakhelashvili, "[t]he principle *ex injuria jus non oritur* is clearly applicable". Orakhelashvili, 'Overlap and Convergence' (n 1) 167.

Building on this divide, the concept of an illegal occupation is labelled as a "myth".[15] A traditional view is that "[t]he rights and obligations of an Occupying Power remain exactly the same, regardless of the chain of events in which the belligerent occupation was brought about (consisting of a war of aggression or a war of self-defence)".[16] "Even if the occupant is responsible for violating the jus ad bellum by invading the foreign country, this does not necessarily suggest that it is also responsible for violating the standard obligations under the law of occupation".[17]

2.1.2 Challenging the *Ius in Bello*/*Ius ad Bellum* Divide and Illegal Occupation

International bodies have referred to illegality in the context of occupation.[18] A minority of authors has challenged the rigidity of the *ius ad bellum*/*ius in bello* divide, specifically in the context of occupation.[19] Moreover, scholars have analysed the notion of an illegal occupation.[20] Rather than the expectation of

---

15 Y Dinstein, *The International Law of Belligerent Occupation* (CUP 2009) 2–3.

16 ibid 3.

17 Benvenisti, *The International Law of Occupation* (n 6) 198 and 16.

18 Ronen casts doubts on the use of *Namibia* in the context of illegal occupation; according to her it did not concern an "illegal occupant but an illegal claim to mandate status." Y Ronen, 'Illegal Occupation and Its Consequences' (2008) 41 Israel Law Review 201, 236. Nevertheless, it is argued that it does not preclude its use by analogy. "In substance, the Court has combined the duty of non-recognition with taking into account a *de facto* control." Bothe (n 3) 109. *Legal Consequences for States of the Continued Presence of South Africa in Namibia (South West Africa) notwithstanding Security Council Resolution 276 (1970) (Advisory Opinion)* [1971] ICJ Rep 16 ("*Namibia*"). See also the ECtHR's reference to "illegal occupation" of Northern Cyprus by Turkey. *Cyprus v Turkey* ECHR 2001-IV 1, para 101 ("*Cyprus v Turkey*"). *Demopoulos and Others v Turkey*, ECHR 2010-I 365, para 94 and para 114 ("*Demopoulos*"). On the practice of the UN referring to illegal occupation, see Ronen, 'Illegal Occupation' (n 18) 212–227. See also Roberts (n 9) 246–301; O Ben-Naftali, AM Gross and K Michaeli, 'Illegal Occupation: Framing the Occupied Palestinian Territory' (2005) 23 Berkeley Journal of International Law 551, 556–557.

19 Giladi (n 11) 246–301. See also Y Ka Lok, 'Exploiting Natural Resources in Occupied Territories – the Conjunction between *Jus in Bello, Jus Ad Bellum* and International Human Rights Law' in A Duval and E Kassoti (eds), *Legality of Economic Activities, Occupied Territories: International, EU Law and Business and Human Rights Perspectives* (Taylor & Francis Group, 2020) 30–40.

20 "[A]s any factual situation governed by international law, a situation of belligerent occupation may – depending, of course, on the circumstances – be legal or illegal (or may become illegal at some point, even if it were initially legal)." Carcano (n 9) 80–81. Ronen, 'Illegal Occupation' (n 18) 201–245. See J Dugard, 'Preface' in A Duval and E Kassoti (eds), *Legality of Economic Activities, Occupied Territories: International, EU Law and Business and Human Rights Perspectives* (Taylor & Francis Group, 2020) xi-xii.

reciprocity between armies, occupation involves hierarchical relationships.[21] Occupations also concern "control over territory and civilian populations and thus raise questions of governance, territorial sovereignty and world order".[22] Accordingly, Giladi claims, "[t]hese differences make at least some occupation norms less amenable to a strict application of the *jus ad bellum/jus in bello* divide."[23] Similarly, Azarova argues that a strict application of this divide "is at cross-purposes with the core values protected by the contemporary international legal system".[24]

Additionally, in contemporary practice, examples where the State accepts its position as the Occupying Power are rare.[25] Instead, Occupying Powers completely reject the occupation law's applicability, either by referring to purported new States in the occupied territory[26] or by an outright annexation of the occupied territory.[27] As a result, "law of occupation becomes practically irrelevant during the conflict and tends to resurface afterwards as law of individual and state responsibility."[28] Thus, this practice seems to render immaterial one of the key arguments for preserving a strict divide between *ius ad bellum* and *ius in bello*, namely an increase in the occupant's adherence to IHL.[29]

---

21 Giladi (n 11) 248.

22 ibid 248.

23 ibid 248 and 268.

24 Azarova, 'Towards a Counter-Hegemonic Law of Occupation (n 1) 131; Azarova, 'Illegal Territoriality in International Law' (n 1) 140–144. "The risk of allowing an occupying state to exploit the analytical distinction between its conduct in the context of an international armed conflict and the unlawful consequences of its acts under jus ad bellum, is that the occupier could then exempt itself from the legal consequences that arise from violations of either of these concurrently applicable international norms." ibid 165.

25 See R Kolb, 'Etude sur l'occupation et sur l'article 47 de la ivème Convention de Genève du 12 août 1949 relative à la protection des personnes civiles en temps de guerre: le degré d'intangibilité des droits en territoire occupé' (2003) 10 African Yearbook of International Law 267, 301.

26 See *infra*.

27 P Wrange, *Occupation/Annexation of a Territory: Respect for International Humanitarian and Human Rights and Consistent EU Policy* (European Union 2015) 22; Azarova, 'Towards a Counter-Hegemonic Law of Occupation (n 1) 117. For the dual origin and function of the rule against annexation, which suggests that separation between *ius in bello* and *ius ad bellum* is not as sharp as would seem at the first sight, see Giladi (n 11) 273–276; Benvenisti, *The International Law of Occupation* (n 6) 72–73.

28 M Pertile, 'The Changing Environment and Emerging Resource Conflicts' in M Weller (ed), *Oxford Handbook of the Use of Force under International Law* (OUP 2015) 1087.

29 Giladi (n 11) 278–280; Azarova, 'Towards a Counter-Hegemonic Law of Occupation (n 1) 132–133.

Occupation is not illegal in character because of breaches of the obligations of the Occupying Power under the law of occupation. For the purposes of this book, the notion of an illegal occupation also does not include the occupation that violates the normative premises of the law of occupation, such as its temporary character.[30] In this book, an illegal character of occupation *per se* derives specifically from the unlawfulness of the initial act of the use of force and from the violation of other peremptory norms of international law, such as the right to self-determination.[31]

A key question that must be asked is what legal consequences flow from the occupation's illegal character.[32] First and foremost, the Occupying Power should withdraw its forces and put an end to the occupation.[33] "[L]e moyen de mettre fin à cette situation illicite est le retrait des autorités et des forces d'occupation."[34] However, a critical question for the relevance of the *ius in bello/ius ad bellum* divide is whether peremptory illegality in any way alters the application of specific rules of occupation law under the Hague and Geneva law. This is dealt with below.

---

30 For authors who develop illegality of occupation *per se* on this ground, seeBen-Naftali, Gross and Michaeli (n 18) 554–555 and 559; Ronen, 'Illegal Occupation' (n 18) 209–210; Azarova, 'Towards a Counter-Hegemonic Law of Occupation (n 1) 117; Carcano (n 9) 81–82; Wrange, *Occupation/Annexation of a Territory: Respect for International Humanitarian and Human Rights and Consistent EU Policy* (n 27) 22. See also Benvenisti, *The International Law of Occupation* (n 6) 17. See also Dugard (n 20) xii. The question of the interaction of regimes as outlined in the introduction only applies to illegal occupation deriving from the violation of peremptory norms, and not to the violation of occupation's normative premises; the former provokes additional consequences that may interact with the rules of occupation.

31 See MG Kohen, 'L'administration actuelle de l'Irak: vers une nouvelle forme de protectorat?' in K Bannelier, O Corten, T Christakis and P Klein (eds), *L'intervention en Irak et le droit international* (Pedone 2004) 311; Carcano (n 9) 81; Ronen, 'Illegal Occupation' (n 18) 206–209; Wrange, *Occupation/Annexation of a Territory* (n 27) 22. *Namibia* (n 18) para 118.

32 Carcano (n 9) 82. Dugard argues in favour of a more severe regime "governed by more appropriate legal rules." Dugard (n 20) xii.

33 ibid; Azarova, 'Towards a Counter-Hegemonic Law of Occupation (n 1) 117 and 136–139; Ben-Naftali, Gross and Michaeli (n 18) 612; Ronen, 'Illegal Occupation' (n 18) 228. Dugard (n 20) xii.

34 Kohen, 'L'administration actuelle de l'Irak' (n 31) 311.

2.1.3 Illegal Occupation by Proxy

The context of the establishment of an illegal secessionist entity is complicated because it might involve the phenomenon of occupation by proxy.[35] The implications of peremptory illegality for the purposes of State responsibility in the context of occupation by proxy seem to be more difficult to outline, as different tests have been suggested in order to attribute acts of proxies to the controlling State.[36]

In this context, it also follows from the overview of the case law on the scope of the *Namibia* exception in Chapter 7, that in cases concerning giving legal effects to acts of illegal secessionist entities on expropriation and other property transfers, the municipal courts did not take into account the law of occupation as a relevant framework, and instead simply referred to non-recognition of these entities. Nevertheless, as is shown below, under both regimes, the outcomes would arguably be the same.

2.2 *Synergies*

For the most part, the law of occupation and the consequences of peremptory illegality are in a normative synergy. This is due to overlapping underlying postulates of primary norms of the law of occupation and of consequences of peremptory illegality.[37] A closer look at the function of these underlying postulates also helps to broadly delineate the zones of divergences.

---

35 See *supra*, Chapter 8. Benvenisti highlights the great extent to which the modern law on state sovereignty complicates the issue of the existence of occupation "by introducing normative criteria for analysis". Benvenisti, *The International Law of Occupation* (n 6) 199.

36 In the context of human rights adjudication, the acts of local subordinate administrations were attributed to the controlling State on the basis of the effective control test. In other situations, it seems the effective control test under Article 8 ARSIWA is preferred. See *supra*, Chapter 8. This question is different from Article 29 GCIV: "The Party to the conflict in whose hands protected persons may be, is responsible for the treatment accorded to them by its agents, irrespective of any individual responsibility which may be incurred." See Dinstein (n 15) 57.

37 According to Benvenisti, "secondary norms of international humanitarian law in general and the law of occupation in particular are much less clearly defined than primary norms." Benvenisti, *The International Law of Occupation* (n 6) 308. Even Benvenisti, who maintains a strict division between *ius ad bellum* and *ius in bello*, analyses the consequences of illegality in the context of human rights adjudication concerning occupation. ibid 307–317. "There is no doubt that recognizing the effects of illegal and invalid occupation measures diminishes the effectiveness of the law of occupation … But … there are normative, institutional, and pragmatic considerations weighing in the other direction, considerations which convinced governments and courts to adopt a balancing approach." ibid 317.

2.2.1 Non-transfer of Sovereignty

"Les opinions sont unanimes pour considérer que l'un des traits essentiels de l'occupation militaire est son caractère non translatif de souveraineté."[38] As mentioned, although a contemporary law of occupation is primarily focused on "the interests of the indigenous community under occupation", it originated as the vehicle to protect the formal titles of an ousted sovereign and therefore "is intimately related to the law of sovereignty".[39] Indeed, "[t]he law of occupation is not only a gap-filler but also a safeguard: it can be seen as indirectly defining the concept of sovereignty and protecting the sovereign's title."[40] "Occupation creates an exceptional situation in which the link between sovereignty and effective control is suspended."[41] The duty of non-recognition normatively overlaps with this principle.[42] Thus, as far as the non-transfer of sovereign titles, the two regimes undeniably overlap.

2.2.2 Non-alteration of Status Quo Ante

"The idea that occupation is a temporary situation, which may not generate permanent results, as illustrated by the non-transfer of sovereignty, is also at the basis of the conservationist principle underlying the law of occupation."[43] Thus, with the view of not altering the *status quo ante* during the course of the occupation, the Occupying Power is recognised as having only limited "temporary managerial powers",[44] and acts and measures adopted *ultra vires* are illegal or invalid.[45] Similarly, facilitating the preservation to *status quo ante*, consequences of violation of peremptory norms include invalidity of acts of

38 MG Kohen, *Possession contestée et souveraineté territorial* (PUF 1997) 102. On general principles governing military occupation, see A Cassese, 'Powers and Duties of an Occupant in Relation to Land and Natural Resources' in P Gaeta and Zappalà (eds), *The Human Dimension of International Law: Selected Papers* (OUP 2008) 251.

39 Benvenisti, 'Occupation and Territorial Administration' (n 6) 2. On the origins of the law of occupation introduced, as opposed to *debellatio* and annexation subject to a peace treaty, see N Bhuta, 'The Antimonies of Transformative Occupation' in (2005) 16 EJIL 721.

40 Benvenisti, *The International Law of Occupation* (n 6) 1–2.

41 Cuyckens (n 6) 71.

42 Ben-Naftali, Gross and Michaeli (n 18) 570. Orakhelashvili, 'Overlap and Convergence' (n 1) 180–182. According to Ronen, since occupation does not entail recognition of any legal claim of the occupant, there is no reason to apply non-recognition to this situation. Ronen, 'Illegal Occupation' (n 18) 233. However, this seems to also confirm a normative convergence of two sets of legal regimes.

43 Cuyckens (n 6) 73. Cuyckens mentions arts 43 and 55 HR and arts 47, 54 and 57 GCIV as examples of the conservationist principle. ibid 72–73, ftn 293.

44 Benvenisti, *The International Law of Occupation* (n 6) 6.

45 Cuyckens (n 6) 72–73. "[J]us ad bellum-based remedy for the predatory acts that underpin unlawfully prolonged occupation is its invalidation by operation of international

the illegal entity and prohibition of recognition of all acts and dealings that may imply its recognition.[46]

However, both of these key premises are qualified. In the law of occupation, the conservationist principle is not absolute; the exceptions form the occupant's limited managerial powers. The occupying power is bound to conduct itself "in the best interests of the people under occupation, subject only to the legitimate security requirements of the occupying military authority".[47] "The balancing act is further complicated by the fact that sometimes the interests of the local population will precisely push the occupying power to make changes."[48] However, this claim is also relative, as the survey of occupations demonstrates that the "social decisions taken and implemented in occupied territories were never incompatible with outcomes sought by occupants. Often these outcomes proved detrimental to the occupied territory."[49]

As shown in Chapter 7, the duty of non-recognition is also not absolute, as it allows for acts and functional contacts that do not imply recognition and provides for exceptions benefitting the local population. Thus, from this perspective, any divergences between the two regimes can foreseeably be located somewhere in the spheres of contact between these exceptions. It is where the balancing act between all relevant interests would need to be undertaken, specifically in light of the above conclusions on the fact that the *ius ad bellum*/*ius in bello* divide is less pertinent in the context of occupation than in other branches of IHL.

2.3 *Divergences*

2.3.1 General Observations

While the law of occupation contains rules that stipulate the standard of humane treatment of civilians in occupied territories, which parallel similar IHL rules, it also contains rules concerning governance and administration of territory, which are without parallel in other areas of IHL.[50] "Governance

law (ipso jure) of many of the acts of such *de facto* administrators." Azarova, 'Towards a Counter-Hegemonic Law of Occupation (n 1) 144.

46 See Azarova, 'Illegal Territoriality in International Law' (n 1) 266. See *supra* Chapter 7.

47 UNGA, 'Report of the Special Rapporteur on the Situation of Human Rights in the Palestinian Territories Occupied Since 1967' (23 October 2017) UN Doc A/72/556, para 34. A Gross, *The Writing on the Wall: Rethinking the International Law of Occupation* (CUP 2017) 27–29.

48 Cuyckens (n 6) 73.

49 Benvenisti, *The International Law of Occupation* (n 6) 79.

50 Giladi (n 11) 280–281.

norms, inescapably, are interpreted, applied or avoided in reference to the conflict's nature, origin and causes."[51]

While the authors in this context frequently refer to the *rights* of the occupant such as the right of administration, it needs to be highlighted that the law of occupation does not grant any rights to the occupying power, it only takes into account the factual situation and stipulates what the occupant can and cannot do, including providing for certain limited managerial powers. It is in the context of these limited powers that consistency with the third State's obligation to withhold recognition of certain acts of illegal regimes comes into the picture.

Orakhelashvili argues that "the possible conflict between ius ad bellum and ius in bello arises with regard to those provisions of the law of occupation that grant certain rights to the occupying power."[52] Moreover, according to Talmon, "[b]elligerent occupation of foreign territory gives rise to limited rights of administration of the occupying power under customary international law and treaties".[53] "It is arguable that, subject to humanitarian considerations and the interests of the civilian population in the occupied territory, these rights are to be denied to an aggressor."[54] According to Wrange, "[o]ne could certainly argue that even the quite limited rights of an occupying power should be denied to an aggressor."[55]

---

51 ibid 281.

52 Orakhelashvili, 'Overlap and Convergence' (n 1) 183. In this context, Orakhelashivili mentions Articles 48 and 49 HR, which allow the occupant to levy taxes and other payments to cover the needs of the occupation army; Article 52 HR on the requisitioning of property to meet the occupying army's needs; Article 53, allowing taking possession of state property; Article 51 GCIV, entitling the occupant to make the population of the occupied territory work for its army's needs and Article 53 GCIV, which prohibits the destruction of property "except where such destruction is rendered absolutely necessary by military operations." "If these clauses are applied indiscriminately to all belligerents, then the Hague and Geneva Conventions become tools to support the aggressor's war effort." ibid. According to Ronen, "[i]t is often proposed to interpret Namibia as denying the illegal actor the rights arising from its claimed status while maintaining the obligations arising from it." Ronen, 'Illegal Occupation' (n 18) 236.

53 S Talmon, 'The Duty Not "To Recognize as Lawful" a Situation Created by the Illegal Use of Force or Other Serious Breaches of a Jus Cogens Obligation: An Obligation without Real Substance?' in C Tomuschat and JM Thouvenin (eds), *The Fundamental Rules of the International Legal Order. Jus Cogens and Obligations Erga Omnes* (M Nijjhof Publishers 2006) 117.

54 ibid.

55 Wrange, 'Self-Determination, Occupation and the Authority to Exploit Natural Resources' (n 1) 25. According to Wrange, "[s]ince a state that has illegally annexed a piece of territory is an occupying power, it is bound by the law of occupation (in addition to international human rights law, of course). Since the authority of an OP is limited, third States

Similarly, Milano highlights potential incompatibility between certain aspects of the law of military occupation and consequences of territorial illegality.[56]

> In particular, it may be difficult to reconcile the duty of non-recognition of territorial situations established and maintained in serious violation of ius cogens principles, and the acceptance of certain legal powers and duties by the occupying power when its presence is blatantly illegal.[57]

According to Azarova, "invalidity may affect ... the scope of the occupying state's rights in ways that are significant but as yet under-determined."[58]

Nevertheless, both regimes converge in the area of humanitarian protection and the interests of local populations. This cardinal rationale finds its expression in Article 47 GCIV.[59] It was also accepted in the *Namibia* advisory opinion. If the test used in *Namibia* "is applied to belligerent occupation, it would

---

should treat legal acts carried out by the OP as null and void, unless they can be justified under IHL or international human rights law or under the 'Namibia exception.'" Wrange, *Occupation/Annexation of a Territory* (n 27) 23.

56 "The legal consequence flowing from the establishment of such military control is the recognition by international law of certain legal powers and legal obligation, regardless of the legality of the use of force in the first place and the territorial status of the occupied territories – i.e. regardless of the legality of the established military presence. This may appear to conflict with the affirmation of a series of principles of unlawfulness of territorial situations developed in the course of the 20th century." E Milano, *Unlawful Territorial Situations in International Law: Reconciling Effectiveness, Legality and Legitimacy* (Martinus Nijhoff Publishers 2006) 97.

57 ibid 97.

58 V Azarova, 'Towards a Counter-Hegemonic Law of Occupation: On the Regulation of Predatory Interstate Acts in Contemporary International Law,' 146. However, Azarova carries out her analysis only with respect to unlawfully prolonged occupation. Azarova highlights three sets of consequences flowing from the establishment of an illegal territorial regime in the occupied territory: denial of status, enforcement of responsibility for jus cogens violations and ongoing duty of the Occupying Power to provide welfare to civilians. Azarova, 'Illegal Territoriality in International Law' (n 1) 168.

59 According to the commentary, the provision of Article 47 GC IV aims to assure that acts of annexation "would have no effect on the rights of protected persons, who would, in spite of them, continue to be entitled to the benefits conferred by the Convention." J Pictet (ed), *Commentary on the Geneva Conventions of 12 August 1949: IV Geneva Convention Relative to the Protection of Civilian Persons in Time of War* (ICRC 1958) 276. Benvenisti, *The International Law of Occupation* (n 6) 73; See also Kolb (n 25) 315–316.

similarly explain that the occupant's acts performed purely in the interest of the inhabitants shall not be affected by nullity".[60]

Thus, based on these considerations, it can be argued that the duty of non-recognition can be relevant to and possibly alter *only* the occupant's limited powers and never obligations of a humanitarian character.[61] However, scholars also caution against simplified solutions deriving from this premise. Even governance norms are important from the perspective of collective and individual protection, therefore "recourse to jus ad bellum or a consequent differential application of some governance norms would only be justified for very compelling reasons of very specific types."[62]

Similarly, Orakhelashvili calls for "a functional distinction in defining which acts of the occupant are void and subject to the duty of non-recognition".[63] Ronen also highlights that "separating the powers from the responsibilities may not be conducive to the welfare of the occupation."[64] Bearing the above-mentioned considerations in mind, the following account highlights three

60 Orakhelashvili, 'Overlap and Convergence' (n 1) 184. On the acceptance of the validity of currency introduced by Japan in the occupied Phillipines, deriving from the Civil War rationales of the doctrine of necessity, which later developed into the *Namibia* exception, see *Aboitiz and Co v Price* (United States, District Court, Utah) (16 June 1951) 18 ILR 592, 593. Milano also suggest that the way to reconcile these two approaches is to focus on the operation of the so-called *Namibia* exception. Milano (n 56) 97.

61 "The following Articles shall be without prejudice to the effects which an illegal use of armed Forces may have in general international law upon the principle of non-discrimination in the application of non-humanitarian rules of armed conflict." Institut de droit international, 'Resolution on the Conditions of Application of Rules Other Than Humanitarian Rules, of Armed Conflict to Hostilities in which United Nations Forces May be Engaged' (13 August 1975) (Session of Wiesbaden) (Rapporteur: Edward Hambro), art 3(2).

62 Giladi (n 11) 296. "Furthermore, departures from the total separation paradigm will have to be justified on a balance: a minimal, if any, risk of lowering the threshold of protection versus compelling international public interest outweighing the risk to IHL efficacy." ibid.

63 Orakhelashvili, 'Overlap and Convergence' (n 1) 184. "The acts of an occupying power can be diverse in nature and have different purposes: to benefit the aggressor as such, necessary to administer the territory by providing law and order, or purely private in character and aimed at regulating ordinary transactions in private interest, such as marriages and births." ibid.

64 Ronen, 'Illegal Occupation' (n 18) 236. Building on the need to preserve *ius ad bellum/ius in bello* distinction, Ronen rejects the "operation of the obligation of non-recognition with respect to illegal occupation" and instead suggests that the answer comes from within the law of occupation itself, which would arguably preclude the idea that the illegal occupant relies on military necessity. ibid 237–238. According to Ronen, the removal of distinction would risk causing greater injury than benefit to the local population. ibid 244.

zones of interaction that might call for the alteration of the rules of occupation law concerning the occupant's powers.

2.3.2 Legislative Powers

The illegal occupant's limited legislative powers might interact with the consequences of peremptory illegality, which call for non-recognition of official laws and acts of an illegal entity. Under Article 43 HR, the Occupying Power "shall take all the measures in his power to restore, and ensure, as far as possible, public order and safety, while respecting, unless absolutely prevented, the laws in force in the country".[65]

Article 64 GCIV then defines what amounts to "a necessity to suspend the laws in force in an occupied territory or modify them".[66] This includes legislation *essential* to enabling it to fulfil its obligations under the GCIV[67] and allowing it to maintain an orderly government of the occupied territory and ensure its security.[68] The question of overlap in this area is largely unexplored in the

---

65 Convention (IV) Respecting the Laws and Customs of War on Land and its Annex: Regulations Concerning the Laws and Customs of War on Land (signed 18 October 1907, entered into force 26 January 1910), art 43 ("HR"); See Benvenisti, *The International Law of Occupation* (n 6) 89–95; Dinstein (n 15) 108–110. Benvenisti also claims that with the advent of 20th century, "the duty imposed on the occupant turned into a grant of authority to prescribe and create changes in a wide spectrum of affairs". Benvenisti, *The International Law of Occupation* (n 6) 78. "Indeed, the term "l'ordre et la vie publics," in an interesting historical twist, was soon invoked by the occupants to justify their extensive use of prescriptive powers." ibid.

66 Dinstein (n 15) 110. "The Occupying Power may, however, subject the population of the occupied territory to provisions which are essential to enable the Occupying Power to fulfil its obligations under the present Convention, to maintain the orderly government of the territory, and to ensure the security of the Occupying Power, of the members and property of the occupying forces or administration, and likewise of the establishments and lines of communication used by them." Convention (IV) Relative to the Protection of Civilian Persons in Time of War (singed 12 August 1949, entered into force 21 October 1950) 75 UNTS 287, art 64(2) ("GCIV"). See also Benvenisti, *The International Law of Occupation* (n 6) 96–102.

67 "The Geneva law of occupation imposes a variety of positive duties on the Occupying Power in addressing social and economic affairs, such as child welfare, labour, food, hygiene, and public health. The Occupying Power must modify and abrogate local laws that become incompatible with international humanitarian law (IHL) rules, or enact new laws to ensure effective guarantees of the rights of inhabitants under occupation." Y Arai-Takahashi, 'Law-Making and the Judicial Guarantees in Occupied Territories' in A Clapham and others (eds), *The 1949 Geneva Conventions: A Commentary* (1st edn, OUP 2015) 1423.

68 GCIV (n 66) art 64(2); Dinstein (n 15) 110–116. See also M Sassòli, 'Legislation and Maintenance of Public Order and Civil Life by Occupying Powers' (2005) 16 European Journal of International Law 661, 668–682.

literature, as it usually only comes up with respect to the extended powers of the occupant in the course of a prolonged occupation.[69]

However, from the outlined powers, it would seem that the majority of an illegal occupant's legislation would in fact overlap with the scope of the *Namibia* exception. The area of concern would probably be limited only to legislation essential to "ensure the security of the Occupying Power, of the members and property of the occupying forces or administration, and likewise of the establishments and lines of communication used by them".[70] However, as already mentioned, the line between the interests of an occupying power's security and those of a local population can be blurred, and therefore the relevant analysis would need to be made on a case-by-case basis. Nevertheless, taking all the interests into account, it can as a matter of principle be agreed with Talmon that "subject to humanitarian considerations and the interests of the civilian population in the occupied territory" States may "refuse to recognize and enforce laws enacted by the aggressor for the occupied territory".[71]

2.3.3 Property Transfers

The powers of an illegal occupant in the area of property transfers might interact with the consequences of peremptory illegality, which call for non-recognition of official acts of illegal entity. In this context, a major area of synergy between the two regimes lies in the fact that under the Hague Regulations, "private property cannot be confiscated".[72] Moreover, even though it is arguable

69 "[I]ndeed the very prolongation of the occupation provides a good basis for saying that occupiers must have wider powers to allow for the development of political and economic institutions." C Chinkin, 'Law of Occupation' in (2008) Western Sahara Conference Proceedings 196, 206. According to Orakhelashvili, "[t]he voidness of the forcible territorial acquisition also brings about the nullity of acts ensuing from the illegal exercise of sovereign powers claimed in the process of or after the forcible territorial acquisition. The typical case could be when the occupying power legislates with regard to the occupied territory in a way exceeding its powers under Articles 42–56 of the 1907 Hague Regulations." A Orakhelashvili, *Peremptory Norms in International Law* (OUP 2006) 221. Benvenisti, *The International Law of Occupation* (n 6) 78–79. The expert opinion on the issue of the Occupier's legislative powers dealt with the duty of non-recognition in the context of unlawful or extended powers, but did not assess its compatibility with the core powers of the unlawful occupant. T Boutruche and M Sassòli, 'Expert Opinion on the Occupier's Legislative Power over an Occupied Territory Under IHL in Light of Israel's On-Going Occupation' (2017) <https://www.nrc.no/globalassets/pdf/legal-opinions/sassoli.pdf> accessed 3 February 2020.

70 GCIV (n 66) art 64(2). Even this type of legislation may not provide for actions prohbitied by IHL rules. Sassòli, 'Legislation and Maintenance of Public Order' (n 68) 674.

71 Talmon (n 53) 117.

72 HR (n 65) art 46(2).

that private property can be expropriated, expropriation can only take place on the basis of legislation in force prior to the occupation and subject to other conditions.[73] As already suggested, because of this normative convergence, the conclusions of the case law of the ECtHR and of municipal courts on these issues, decided without reference to the occupation law, are nevertheless in line with it.[74]

However, under Article 53(2) HR, privately owned war materials can be seized,[75] and under Article 52 HR, private movable property may also be requisitioned subject to conditions stipulated in the Hague Regulations.[76] As for public movable property, it can be seized and "may be used for military operations".[77] A number of authors have pointed out an underlying incompatibility of these powers of the occupant with international invalidity of acts of illegal regimes and the duty of non-recognition thereof. According to Talmon, "subject to humanitarian considerations and the interests of the civilian population in the occupied territory", States "may deny recognition to title to property even if the acquisition of property was within the 1907 Hague Regulation on Land Warfare".[78] Brownlie similarly claimed that it is arguable that *ius cogens* "curtails various privileges",[79] pointing to an authority according to which "an

73 "The Occupying Power 'remains free to make use for its purposes of the expropriation legislation in force in the occupied enemy territory prior to the occupation', provided that this is done for reasons of public interest with adequate compensation." Dinstein (n 15) 225. "Private property may be expropriated in the public interest of the whole of the inhabitants of the occupied territory." Cassese (n 38) 252. Arai-Takahashi suggests further limitations flowing from art 43 HR and 64 GCIV. However, Arai-Takahashi also suggests that "the procedure for expropriation may exceptionally be the laws enacted by the occupation authorities." Y Arai-Takahashi, 'Protection of Private Property' in A Clapham and others (eds), *The 1949 Geneva Conventions: A Commentary* (1st edn, OUP 2015) 1527.

74 Dinstein in this regard points out to *Loizidou* judgment of the ECtHR. Dinstein (n 15) 225. See *supra* Chapter 7.

75 But these "must be restored and compensation fixed when peace is made." HR (n 65) art 53(2).

76 Requisitions can only be demanded "for the needs of the army of occupation" and "shall as far is possible be paid for in cash; if not, a receipt shall be given and the payment of the amount due shall be made as soon as possible." HR (n 65) art 52. Arai-Takahashi, 'Protection of Private Property' (n 73) 1522–1526.

77 HR (n 65) art 53(1).

78 Talmon (n 53) 117.

79 "[A]n aggressor would not benefit from the rule that belligerents are not responsible for damages caused to subjects of neutral States by military operation." I Brownlie, *Principles of International Law* (6th edn, OUP 2003) 490. Talmon (n 53) 117.

aggressor does not acquire title to property acquired even if the confiscation and requisition were within the Hague Regulations."[80]

2.3.4 Usufruct in the Context of Exploitation of Natural Resources

Under Article 55 HR, the Occupying Power is administrator and usufructuary of public immovable property. "It must safeguard the capital of these properties, and administer them in accordance with the rules of usufruct."[81] This provision is particularly pertinent to the regime of exploitation of natural resources. Even though Article 55 HR does not explicitly limit the purpose of the use of fruits, building on the evaluative and systemic interpretation of HR, Cassese convincingly demonstrated that the occupant is in fact not allowed to use them for any purposes whatsoever.[82] Instead, it can use such property only to "meet its own military or security needs", "to defray the expenses involved in the belligerent occupation" or to "protect the interests and the well-being of the inhabitants".[83] "An occupying power cannot use natural resources arbitrarily for its own purposes, only if that benefits the people of that territory or covers other legitimate costs of the occupation."[84] The use of

80 Brownlie, *Principles of International Law* (n 79) 490, ftn 37; Brownlie, *International Law and the Use of Force by States* (n 11) 406, ftn 3 with further references. J Crawford, *Brownlie's Principles of Public International Law* (8th edn, OUP 2012) 596. See also Roberts (n 9) 294 ftn 172 and references therein. Lauterpacht analysed this question and rejected such a stance, among others, taking into account the position of courts on this issue. Lauterpacht (n 9) 224–233. Similarly, according to art 3(1) of the Harvard Draft Convention on Rights and Duties of States in Case of Aggression "[t]itles to property are not affected by an aggressor's purported exercise of such rights." 'Draft Convention on Rights and Duties of States in Case of Aggression' (1939) 33 American Journal of International Law Supplement 819, 886.

81 HR (n 65) art 55. "[A]s is common in a usufruct, entitlements are limited to the rights of use (jus utendi) and consumption of fruits (jus fruendi)." Dinstein (n 15) 214. Benvenisti, *The International Law of Occupation* (n 6) 81–82.

82 Cassese (n 38) 257–260.

83 ibid 252–253. For the same conclusion see Pertile (n 28) 1086; T Moerenhout, 'The Obligation to Withhold from Trading in Order Not to Recognize and Assist Settlements and Their Economic Activity in Occupied Territories' (2012) 3 Journal of International Humanitarian Legal Studies 344, 350. For the conclusion without limitations, except for rules of usufruct, see Dinstein (n 15) 215–218; Azarova, 'Towards a Counter-Hegemonic Law of Occupation (n 1) 121.

84 P Wrange, 'Western Sahara, the European Commission and the Politics of International Legal Argument' (2019) 1, 9 <https://papers.ssrn.com/sol3/papers.cfm?abstract_id=3507037> accessed 3 February 2020. (*footnotes omitted*); A Van Engeland, 'Protection of Public Property' in A Clapham and others (eds), *The 1949 Geneva Conventions: A Commentary* (1st edn, OUP 2015) 1543. According to the Institut de droit international, "the occupying

natural resources cannot advance "the economic interests of the Occupying Power."[85]

Thus, the illegal occupant's position, in the context of the exploitation of natural resources in the occupied territory might interact with the consequences of peremptory illegality. These consequences include the duty of non-recognition, which prohibits economic dealings, which may entrench the illegal regime's authority over territory. On the one hand, referring to the consequences of peremptory illegality, Pertile highlights that "[s]tates shall not enter into any dealings concerning the natural resources of the territory with the *unlawful occupier*."[86] On the other hand, in line with rules applicable to public immovable property, Benvenisti recognises the occupant's power to conclude agreements concerning natural resources for the duration of the occupation.[87]

Balancing the occupant's interests with collective interests protected by the consequences of peremptory illegality, it would seem that the illegal occupant would be prohibited from any dealings concerning natural resources that would seek to sustain the costs of its own occupation or its own military needs, as they would certainly entrench the illegal regime's authority over territory. Whether the same applies with respect to dealings benefiting the population of the occupied territory needs to be analysed in detail.

Firstly, reference is frequently made in this regard to the *Namibia* exception. "It is also observed that this so-called Namibia exception is very similar to the occupying power's aforementioned right of usufruct to exploit the natural resources of an occupied territory to the benefit of the local population."[88]

power can only dispose of the resources of the occupied territory to the extent necessary for the current administration of the territory *and* to meet the essential needs of the population." Institut de droit international, 'Bruges Declaration on the Use of Force' (2 September 2003) 4. Similarly, Benvenisti, *The International Law of Occupation* (n 6) 82.

85 Van Engeland (n 84) 1543.

86 Pertile (n 28) 1088 (*emphasis added*). Pertile's claim on the *ius ad bellum*/*ius in bello* divide is quite symptomatic of the way doctrine treats these issues in isolation. "[I]t may well be the case that the activities of the occupying power, albeit in compliance with the law of occupation, constitute nonetheless a breach of the *jus ad bellum* as they take place in a war of aggression." "At the end of the conflict, the aggressor will have to provide reparations also for the exploitation or the depletion of natural resources carried out in compliance with the law of occupation." ibid 1086.

87 "Agreements between the occupant, as the administrator of the occupied country's natural resources, and neighboring countries – whether or not formally qualified as treaties under the Vienna law on treaties – will be therefore valid for the duration of the occupation, and expire automatically when occupation ends and a new regime comes to power." Benvenisti, *The International Law of Occupation* (n 6) 86 (*footnotes omitted*).

88 C Ryngaert and R Fransen, 'EU Extraterritorial Obligations with Respect to Trade with Occupied Territories: Reflections after the Case of Front Polisario before EU Courts' (2018)

However, as follows from the analysis of Chapter 7, the *Namibia* exception has not been used to justify merely economic benefits to local populations.

Secondly, the question can be asked whether economic dealings with natural resources solely benefiting the local population in the occupied territory would in fact entrench the illegal occupant's authority over that territory, and thus would be prohibited by the duty of non-recognition in the first place.[89] In this context, it seems that the concept of *benefit* to the population of an occupied territory in the context of the exploitation of natural resources by an illegal occupant needs to be further explored. Firstly, it is very difficult to ascertain what the benefit to a local population in the context of illegal occupation in fact is. As mentioned above, the issue of where the interests of occupant and local population overlap can prove rather relative. In fact, it is not clear why an illegal occupant should be providing benefit to a local population via its economic dealings concerning natural resources when the benefit from the natural resources would presumably be best achieved by the indigenous population itself after the withdrawal of the occupation forces. However, it can be presumed that the previous concerns can be offset in cases where the population of the occupied territory consents with such dealings. Nevertheless, as demonstrated by the difficulties experienced by the European Union in establishing the consent of the people of Western Sahara with respect to the EU-Morocco Sustainable Fisheries Agreement,[90] the idea of free consent in this context seems to be more a goal in theory than something that can be obtained in practice.

---

2 Europe and the World: A Law Review 1, 17. See for a completely opposite view: "There is no doubt that the usufruct referred to in article 55 of the Hague Regulation brings a profit that is made to the detriment of the occupied entity. By recognizing the prohibition to use force to occupy a territory, states also recognized the prohibition to exploit the territories' natural resources, every time this exploitation is carried out as a consequence of an illicit use of force." V Chapaux, 'The Question of the European Community-Morocco Fisheries Agreement' in K Arts and P Leite Pinto (eds), *International Law and the Question of Western Sahara* (IPJET 2006) 190.

89 Wrange highlights that the EU courts did not take into account the illegality of Morocco's control in Western Sahara and contends, "perhaps that is so because the authority of both an occupant and an administering power is now so circumscribed that there appears to be little need for a stricter governing regime for mala fide than for bona fide possessors." Wrange, 'Self-Determination, Occupation and the Authority to Exploit Natural Resources' (n 1) 26.

90 See *supra* Chapter 7.

3 Overlap of Effects of Peremptory Territorial Illegality and Human Rights Law

As already mentioned in the introduction, even though the separation between *ius ad bellum* and human rights law is not as dogmatic as the *ius in bello*/*ius ad bellum* divide, it is also present in the context of human rights law, in particular with respect to its extraterritorial application, which derives from the fact of the State's territorial control regardless of the legality of its establishment.[91] As mentioned, the objective of this account is not in any way to undermine such applicability – any other approach would create a vacuum in human rights protection. The objective is to explore the zones of interaction between the consequences of peremptory territorial illegality and IHRL in the context of their co-application. Firstly, the question arises as to a normative overlap between human rights law and the consequences of peremptory illegality, in particular with respect to the interests protected by the *Namibia* exception. Secondly, the question can be asked how, if at all, a judicial practice, in particular of the ECtHR, accommodates the peremptory illegality in the consideration and application of human rights law. The examined question is to what extent the actual application and interpretation of the ECHR by the Court take account of general international law consequences of peremptory territorial illegality.

3.1 *Synergies*

3.1.1 Namibia Exception and IHRL

The scope of the *Namibia* exception in the area of civil registration, which exempts official acts of illegal secessionist entity such as birth, death and marriage certificates from the duty of non-recognition,[92] overlaps with human rights law. In particular, it protects the same interests such as the right of everyone to recognition everywhere as a person before the law,[93] the right to birth registration[94] and the right to family and private life under Article 8

91 *Loizidou* (Preliminary Objections) (n 3) para 62. Bothe (n 3) 105.

92 See *supra* Chapter 7.

93 Universal Declaration of Human Rights, UNGA Res 217 (10 December 1948) UN Doc A/RES/217(III), art 6; International Covenant on Civil and Political Rights (signed 16 December 1966, entered into force 23 March 1976) 999 UNTS 171, art 16 ("ICCPR"); American Convention on Human Rights (adopted 22 November 1969, entered into force 18 July 1978) 1144 UNTS 123, art 3; African Charter on Human and Peoples' Rights (adopted 27 June 1981, entered into force 21 October 1986) 1520 UNTS 217, art 5. See also 'UN Guiding Principles on Internal Displacement' (11 February 1998) UN Doc E/CN.4/1998/53/Add. 2, principle 20(1)(2); CoE (Committee of Ministers) Recommendation Rec(2006)6, para 7.

94 ICCPR (n 93) art 24(2); The Convention on the Rights of the Child (signed 20 November 1989, entered into force 2 September 1990) 1577 UNTS 3, art 7(1); See also Report of the

ECHR.[95] In fact, the synergy between these two regimes is so complete that in practice they are rarely distinguished.[96]

3.1.2 ECtHR Accommodating the Effects of Peremptory Territorial Illegality

The case law of the ECtHR accommodates the consequences of peremptory territorial illegality, in particular the duty of non-recognition, in a number of ways. These aspects are predominantly explored in detail in different chapters of this book. Here, they are mostly briefly summarised. Firstly, in the area of non-recognition of status, the ECtHR rejected illegal secessionist entity as relevant bearer of human rights duties under the ECHR.[97] Instead of seeing it as State, the ECtHR referred to such an entity as an "illegal regime"[98] and "an entity, which is illegal under international law"[99] and frequently described its situation as "illegal occupation".[100]

Moreover, several aspects of the Court's case law indirectly confirm the continuous sovereignty of the parent States over the territories where the illegal secessionist entities are located. The Court's analysis of the territorial State's positive obligations is the most prominent.[101] Similarly, the Court's analysis in *Ukraine v Russia (re Crimea)* is relevant in several ways. The Court decided to determine the nature of jurisdiction over the Russia-annexed Crimea from the day of the conclusion of the purported treaty admitting Crimea and the city of Sevastopol to the Russian Federation on 18 March 2014 as "extra-territorial" (i.e. beyond Russia's *de iure* borders) and not territorial.[102] This arguably indirectly

---

Office of the United Nations High Commissioner for Human Rights: Birth Registration and the Right of Everyone to Recognition Everywhere as a Person Before the Law' (17 June 2014) UN Doc A/HRC/27/22.

95 European Convention for the Protection of Human Rights and Fundamental Freedoms (adopted 4 November 1950; entered into force 3 September 1953) 213 UNTS 221, art 8. See also *Guide on Article 8 of the European Convention on Human Rights: Right to Respect for Private and Family Life, Home and Correspondence* (Council of Europe/European Court of Human Rights 2019), paras 217–220 and paras 244–245.

96 See *infra* Part 2.

97 See *supra* Chapter 8, where the Court's non-recognition of these entities as States by the international community is *inter alia* referred to in the context of their unlawfulness.

98 *Ilaşcu and others v Moldova and Russia* ECHR 2004-VII 1, paras 384–385 ("*Ilaşcu*").

99 ibid para 436.

100 *Demopoulos* (n 18) para 94 and para 114; *Cyprus v Turkey* (n 18) para 101.

101 See *supra* Chapter 8. See *infra*.

102 *Russia v Ukraine (re Crimea)* (n 3), paras 338–349. See for the criticism of the Court's approach M Milanović, 'ECtHR Grand Chamber Declares Admissible the Case of Ukraine v. Russia re Crimea' (*EJIL:Talk!*, 15 January 2021) <https://www.ejiltalk.org/ecthr-grand-chamber-declares-admissible-the-case-of-ukraine-v-russia-re-crimea/> accessed 17 July 2023.

confirmed Ukraine's continuous sovereignty over the peninsula.[103] The Court noted that Russia has not "advanced a positive case that the sovereign territory of either party to the proceedings has been changed."[104] It also noted the fact that "a number of States and international bodies have refused to accept any change to the territorial integrity of Ukraine in respect of Crimea *within the meaning of international law*."[105] In this context, the Court held that UNGA resolution 68/262 on the territorial integrity of Ukraine, as reaffirmed in the subsequent resolutions, "cannot be disregarded".[106]

Furthermore, concerning Russia's extra-territorial jurisdiction in the period before Crimea's annexation (i.e. between 27 February 2014 and 18 March 2014), in line with its previous jurisprudence, the Court held that the compliance of the Russian military presence with the applicable agreements between Russia and Ukraine "cannot be decisive" for the issue of effective control.[107] However, it also made several observations, which arguably indirectly confirmed the illegality of such presence and the conduct of Russian troops under these agreements.[108]

Lastly, in the context of non-recognition of acts and laws of illegal secessionist entities, the ECtHR famously refused to "attribute legal validity for the purposes of the Convention" to an illegal secessionist entity's constitution.[109]

103 ibid.

104 *Russia v Ukraine* (*re Crimea*) (n 3) para 348.

105 ibid para 348 (*emphasis added*).

106 ibid para 348. The Court referred to its Loizidou case, where it established that "the international community … consistently refused to accept the legitimacy of the 'TRNC' as a State within the meaning of international law." *Loizidou* (n 109) para 56. Compare the position of the Arbitral Tribunal constituted under Annex VII to the 1982 United Nations Convention on the Law of the Sea, to which the ECtHR also made a direct reference. *PCA Case No 2017–06, Dispute Concerning Coastal State Rights in the Black Sea, Sea of Azov, and Kerch Strait* (*Ukraine v the Russian Federation*), Award Concerning the Preliminary Objections of The Russian Federation (21 February 2020) para 174. "Apart from the question of the legal effect of the UNGA resolutions, if the Arbitral Tribunal were to accept Ukraine's interpretation of those UNGA resolutions as correct, it would ipso facto imply that the Arbitral Tribunal finds that Crimea is part of Ukraine's territory. However, it has no jurisdiction to do so." ibid, para. 176.

107 *Russia v Ukraine* (*re Crimea*) (n 3) para 320.

108 ibid para 320 and 324–327. The Court held that Russia "did not refer to any evidence or any objective assessment, contemporaneous or otherwise, based on relevant material, that there had been any, let alone any real, threat to the Russian military forces stationed in Crimea at the time." ibid para 324.

109 *Loizidou v Turkey* ECHR 1996-VI 2216, para 44. See *supra* Chapter 7.

Moreover, the ECtHR has held that the obligation to cooperate under the procedural limb of Article 2 ECHR did not mandate a waiver of criminal jurisdiction as a feature of the State's sovereignty in favour of the authorities of the (illegal) secessionist entity.[110] Thereby, the Court implicitly gave effect to the prohibition of dealings that may imply recognition in the context of purported government-to-government interactions.

3.2 *Divergences*

3.2.1 Positive Obligations in Light of Effects of Peremptory Territorial Illegality

The territorial State's positive obligations can be seen from two perspectives. On the one hand,

> [t]he positive obligation drawn by the Court from the valid title justifying the sovereignty of a State over a specific territory pursues objectives that can be compared with those fulfilled by the obligation not to recognise any territorial situation established or maintained in contradiction with international law.[111]

On the other hand, as far as their substantive content is concerned, doubts can be raised as to the compatibility of some of these specific obligations with the duty of non-recognition and non-assistance.

In particular, a potential divergence can be outlined with respect to the group of obligations requiring the parent State to secure an applicant's rights. As outlined in Chapter 8, the Court in this context, for example, requires effort and negotiations to reach agreement on guaranteeing respect for the applicants' rights and other measures.[112] Moreover, in the context of the obligation

---

110 *Güzelyurtlu and Others v Cyprus and Turkey* App no 36925/07 (ECtHR, 29 January 2019), para 253 ("*Güzelyurtlu*"). See *supra* Chapter 7.

111 A Lagerwall, 'Is the Duty Not to Recognise 'States' Created Unlawfully Challenged by States' Practice and ECHR Case Law?' in W Czapliński and A Kleczkowska (eds), *Unrecognised Subjects in International Law* (SCHOLAR Publishing House 2019) 279; A Berkes, *International Human Rights Law Beyond State Territorial Control* (CUP 2021) 108–109.

112 This includes the effort and negotiations to reach agreement on guaranteeing respect for the applicants' rights; contact by way of letters between Moldova and Transnistria's political bodies, including the "Ministry of Interior"; or even the provision of rent to Transnistria for relocated Latin-script schools. See *Ilaşcu* (n 98) para 348; *Eriomenco v the Republic of Moldova and Russia* App no 42224/11 (ECtHR, 9 May 2017), paras 34–35 and para 60; *Catan and Others v The Republic of Moldova and Russia* App nos 43370/04, 8252/05 and 18454/06 (ECtHR, 19 October 2012), paras 49, 56, 61–62, 147.

to re-establish control and refrain from supporting the separatist regime, the Court indicated that such interactions as the conclusion of economic cooperation agreements with Transnistria, the establishment of relations between the Moldovan parliament and the Transnistrian parliament and cooperation in police and security matters[113] "cannot be regarded as support" for Transnistria, but they are "affirmation by Moldova of its desire to re-establish control" there.[114] Even though this book finds these contacts between Moldova and Transnistria compatible with the duty of non-recognition,[115] positive obligations, which as a matter of legal duty require contact between the parent State and the illegal secessionist entity, even if only in an informal setting, can be broadly seen as not aligned with the basic premise of the duty of non-recognition, ie the illegal entity's isolation.[116]

3.2.2 ECtHR Expanding the Namibia Exception's Scope

Chapter 7 analysed the ECtHR's jurisprudence building on or referring to the *Namibia* exception. Here this issue is only briefly summarized. For example, the Court held that remedies offered by an illegal secessionist entity could be considered "domestic remedies" of the respondent State.[117] It also found that, notwithstanding the illegality of the secessionist entity under international law, its courts could be considered "established by law" for the purposes of Article 6 ECHR.[118] The Court also applied similar premises to elements of "lawful arrest and detention" for the purposes of Article 5 ECHR.[119] It also generally

113 The Court differentiated the situation in *Güzelyurtlu*, which would entail a waiver of criminal jurisdiction in favour of the secessionist entity from these "unofficial relations in judicial and security matters in the interest of crime prevention," such as information exchange and the summoning of witnesses, which, due to their nature and limited character, could not be considered support for the separatist regime. *Güzelyurtlu* (n 110) para 251.

114 *Ilaşcu* (n 98) para 345.

115 See *infra*.

116 "While deciding on the conflict between the human rights of individuals in 'grey zones' and other international law obligations, such as the obligation of non-recognition, ne bis in idem or IHL, the territorial State should adopt the solution that both reconciles conflicting norms, using systemic integration under Article 31(3)(c) of the VCLT, and most favours the enjoyment of human rights." Berkes (n 111) 125.

117 *Cyprus v Turkey* (n 18) para 102.

118 ibid paras 236–237. The Court stated that "it cannot automatically regard as unlawful, for the limited purposes of the Convention, the decisions taken by the courts of an unrecognised entity purely because of the latter's unlawful nature and the fact that it is not internationally recognised." *Mozer v the Republic of Moldova and Russia* App no 11138/10 (ECtHR, 23 February 2016), para 142 ("*Mozer*").

119 *Foka v Turkey* App no 28940/95 (ECtHR, 24 June 2008), paras 83–84; *Petrakidou v Turkey* App no 16081/90 (ECtHR, 27 May 2010), paras 69–77.

rejected the position "that institutions and procedures imposed by force by an occupying power cannot be treated as if they were established by the lawful government of the State".[120]

It is true that these underlying premises were assessed and rejected on the facts in individual situations. For example, the Court did not consider remedies offered by Transnistria as effective[121] and did not find its courts meeting the test of forming "part of a judicial system operating on a 'constitutional and legal basis' … compatible with the Convention".[122] Questions as to the overall approach, however, persist.

The Court declared that its aim in adopting the above position was to avoid a vacuum in human rights protection, which would operate to the detriment of victims of human rights violations.[123] Moreover, the Court also referred to the need to allow the respondent State bearing human rights obligations on the basis of its effective territorial control to correct the wrongs imputable to it. By referring to the *Namibia* exception, the Court also sought to project normative harmony with the consequences of peremptory illegality.

However, it was demonstrated in Chapter 7 that the Court's reading of the *Namibia* exception was too broad, rendering almost irrelevant the duty of non-recognition with respect to acts and laws of illegal entities.[124] Concerning the exhaustion of domestic remedies, the Court simply assumed their benefit.[125] In other areas, the Court held that courts of illegal entity may be regarded as a tribunal 'established by law' subject to condition that its judicial and legal system operates on the bases compatible with the Convention.[126] Crucially, for the Court, international illegality of the respondent State's presence did not preclude such conclusions.

It might be possible to agree that a broader scope of the *Namibia* exception can be justified with the view of human rights law expansion since the ICJ's advisory opinion.[127] In any case, this analysis in no way undermines the responsibility of the respondent State for human rights violations in the territory over

120 *Demopoulos* (n 18) para 100 in connection with para 94. See also *Cyprus v Turkey* (n 18) para 236; *Mozer* (n 118) para 143.

121 For example *Vardanean v the Republic of Moldova and Russia* App no 22200/10 (ECtHR, 30 May 2017), para 31 and see *supra*.

122 *Mozer* (n 118) para 147. *Mamasakhlisi and Others v Georgia and Russia* App 29999/04 and 41424/04 (Merits) (ECtHR, 7 March 2023) paras 266–269, 419–428 and 437–440.

123 *Cyprus v Turkey* (n 18) para 78 and para 91. *Demopoulos* (n 18) para 96.

124 R Ronen, *Transition from Illegal Regimes under International Law* (CUP 2011) 92.

125 *Cyprus v Turkey* (n 18) para 92.

126 *Ilașcu* (n 98) 460.

127 Ronen, *Transition from Illegal Regimes under International Law* (n 124) 94.

which it exercises effective control. However, it is difficult to substantiate the Court's overly broad presumption of benefit of recognition of laws and institutions of illegal entity to victims of human rights violation.[128] "Since the regime does not enjoy the legitimacy of a sovereign state authority, its authority to discharge its human rights obligations should be recognised discriminatorily, so as to ensure that it does not abuse its powers."[129] It is suggested that a blind reliance on the *Namibia* exception could not only prove subversive with respect to values protected by communitarian norms, but in concrete instances, it could also be incompatible with the very individual interests that the Court seeks to protect.[130]

3.3 *Observations on the ECtHR's Approach to Peremptory Territorial Illegality*

As shown, in several aspects – especially concerning directly the issues of territorial status – the ECtHR took into account the general international law concerning peremptory territorial illegality. From these perspectives, its case law is in harmony with the consequences of peremptory territorial illegality, subject to serious limitations described above regarding a too broad scope of *Namibia* exception and legitimation of peremptory illegality.[131]

While, the ECtHR is admittedly not the Court of general jurisdiction, it is nevertheless part of an international legal system. "It is beyond doubt that the European Convention is not a treaty operating in a legal vacuum, but is governed by general international law and influenced by developments in that legal system including its public order elements."[132] Therefore, the Court's engagement with, among others, the UNGA and UNSC resolutions concerning the issues related to the (illegality) of secessionist attempts or unlawfulness of annexation is well justified.[133] It is also in line with the Court's formula,

128 See *contra* Benvenisti, *The International Law of Occupation* (n 6) 310–311.

129 Ronen, *Transition from Illegal Regimes under International Law* (n 124) 91 and see 94 and 101–102.

130 See similarly, Ronen, *Transition from Illegal Regimes under International Law* (n 124) 96 see 88–98.

131 Even the reference to *Namibia* exception and *Namibia* exception-like justifications concerning the substantive rights – even though interpreted and applied in a too broad fashion with the risks for the integrity of effects of peremptory norms outlined above – ultimately sought to project compliance with the general international law.

132 A Orakhelashvili, 'The European Convention on Human Rights and International Public Order' (2003) 5 Cambridge Yearbook of European Legal Studies 237, 269 and see 243.

133 *Loizidou* (n 109) para 56 in connection to paras 42–44, see also paras 19–23; *Cyprus v Turkey* (n 18) para 61; *Russia v Ukraine* (*re Crimea*) (n 3) para 348. See also on the Court's use of systemic integration O Dörr, 'Article 31: General Rule of Interpretation' in O Dörr

according to which "the principles underlying the Convention cannot be interpreted and applied in a vacuum. Mindful of the Convention's special character as a human rights treaty, it must also take into account any relevant rules of international law."[134]

The Court's consideration of general international law concerning peremptory territorial illegality in its human rights adjudication is not only of "symbolic value" or adding "little practical value."[135] On the contrary, the Court views the Convention as "a constitutional instrument of *European public order* (order public)."[136] From this perspective, the Court cannot disregard the broader questions of systemic peremptory territorial illegality (international public order).[137] The European human rights protection and the compliance with peremptory norms of international law are not two hermeneutically detached fields but exist along the same continuum as the underlying territorial illegality is the root cause of many human rights violations occurring within these territories.

Milanović, in this context, juxtaposes what he views as "the rights of states" (sovereignty) and "those of individuals".[138] However, it is argued that the present issue is better defined as the question of adherence to peremptory norms (international public order) in human rights litigation. Importantly, there is no opposition or juxtaposition. As Orakhelashvili claims,

> The object and purpose of the Convention overlaps with *jus cogens* of general international law in that it requires objective protection of the

and K Schmalenbach (eds), *Vienna Convention on the Law of Treaties* (2nd edn, Springer 2018) 606 *et seq*. See also Council of Europe (Committee of Ministers, Steering Committee for Human Rights (CDDH)) 'Report on the Place of the European Convention on Human Rights in the European and International Legal Order' (2020) CM(2020)2.

134 *Loizidou* (n 109) para 56.

135 M Milanović, 'Does the European Court of Human Rights Have to Decide on Sovereignty over Crimea? Part I: Jurisdiction in Article 1 ECHR' (*EJIL:Talk!*, 23 September 2019) <https://www.ejiltalk.org/does-the-european-court-of-human-rights-have-to-decide-on-sovereignty-over-crimea-part-i-jurisdiction-in-article-1-echr/> accessed 31 October 2023. See on a critical assessment of the Court's employment of the notion of the European public order K Dzehtsiarou, *Can the European Court of Human Rights Shape European Public Order?* (CUP 2021).

136 *Loizidou* (Preliminary Objections) (n 3) para 75 (*emphasis added*).

137 For a contrary view, see Milanovć (n 135). M Milanović, 'Does the European Court of Human Rights Have to Decide on Sovereignty over Crimea? Part II: Issues Lurking on the Merits' (*EJIL:Talk!*, 24 September 2019) <https://www.ejiltalk.org/does-the-european-court-of-human-rights-have-to-decide-on-sovereignty-over-crimea-part-ii-issues-lurking-on-the-merits/> accessed 31 October 2023.

138 Milanović (n 137).

> community interest rather than of individual State interests, and this requires respect for the consequences that the norms protecting community interest entail. The notion of the public order of Europe implies the application and interpretation of the Convention in accordance with the principles, trends and requirements of international public order.[139]

Therefore, a further alignment regarding the operation of other aspects of the duty of non-recognition (where the divergence was indicated above) would arguably also be the furtherance of broader principles underpinning the ECHR.[140]

4 Conclusion

This chapter outlined interactions between the consequences of peremptory illegality on the one hand and the law of occupation and IHRL on the other. In short, it followed the relationship between the legal consequences of effectiveness and illegality in the context of illegal secessionist entity subsequent to the denial of the status of statehood.

Firstly, the chapter's analysis was built on the premise that the *ius ad bellum/ius in bello* divide is less amenable in the context of the law of occupation than in other IHL rules. It concluded that consequences of peremptory illegality and the law of occupation are broadly normatively convergent, especially due to the synergy of key underlying principles, including the non-transfer of sovereignty and non-alteration of *status quo ante*. The *Namibia* exception, which seeks to uphold the interests of the local population, also overlaps with humanitarian rules of occupation law.

A key area of normative divergence lies in the scope of the occupant's powers under the law of occupation. The chapter focused on the occupant's legislative powers, powers in the area of property transfers and the occupant's position as usufructuary of natural resources. It balanced these powers with the values protected by consequence of peremptory illegality.

---

139 Orakhelashvili, 'The European Convention' (n 132) 244 and see 241. Orakhelashvili also points out that "[t]he very concept of bringing an inter-State case before the Court essentially overlaps with the action in public interest in international law, where States act not in pursuance of their interests, but as guardian of European (or international) public order." ibid, 254.

140 See *infra* Part 2, Chapter 19 for pending cases before the ECtHR concerning the post-Soviet secessionist attempts.

Secondly, the chapter highlighted the normative convergence between the scope of the *Namibia* exception in the area of civil registration and a number of human rights. It also briefly summarised the conclusions of different chapters with respect to areas in which the judicial practice of the ECtHR was convergent with the non-recognition of the status of statehood and official acts and laws of an illegal secessionist entity. However, the chapter also underlined the spheres of the ECtHR's practice diverging from the scope of duty of non-recognition, in particular in the context of the territorial State's positive obligations and most importantly in the context of an expansive interpretation of the *Namibia* exception, which was discussed in detail in Chapter 7. It offered general observations on the Court's approach to peremptory territorial illegality.

Overall, the chapter demonstrated a number of areas where the consequences of peremptory illegality converge with the law of occupation and the extraterritorial application of European human rights law. In the areas of divergence, the chapter cautioned against analysis carried out in isolation and outlined ways of balancing all relevant interests, including communitarian ones.

Conclusion to Section 2

Section 2 outlined the general international legal framework applicable to the context of an illegal secessionist entity, which is defined on the one hand by the legal consequences of peremptory territorial illegality and on the other hand by legal consequences flowing from the change of effective territorial control. In essence, it followed the cardinal dynamics between the principles of legality and effectiveness in the context of illegal secessionist entity subsequent to the denial of statehood.

Firstly, this section defined a descriptive notion of an illegal secessionist entity, which is characterised by four features. First, it is its peremptory territorial illegality deriving from the original violation of peremptory norms, either by the secessionist group or the third State intervening in the secessionist attempt. Second, illegal secessionist entity is characterised by the change of effective territorial control away from the parent State. This subsumes two scenarios. Firstly, it is either an independent effective entity not under the control of any other State or secondly, it is the entity, whose effectiveness is only apparent as it is in fact under the effective control of the third State. Due to the proliferation of these latter cases, this book only focuses on this latter possibility. Third, the illegal secessionist entity persists in claiming to be a State. Fourth, *ratione temporis*, it only refers to an on-going situation and does not concern the modalities of return to the *status quo ante* or transition from an illegal regime.

Secondly, this section examined legal consequences of peremptory territorial illegality on the effective relations and purported legal order of the illegal secessionist entity. It outlined consequences such as the inapplicability of rules of State succession, the invalidity of acts and the aggravated regime of international responsibility. However, it specifically examined the content and operation of the duty of non-recognition in the area of purported inter-State relations, economic and other dealings, and acts and laws of illegal secessionist entity. On the basis of the relevant State practice, *opinio iuris* and case law, it concluded that the duty of non-recognition has a rather expansive scope. This conclusion is also aligned with the fact that, unlike the ECtHR, the municipal courts have interpreted the *Namibia* exception in a restrictive fashion. Generally, this section demonstrated *vertical* effects of peremptory norms with respect to effective relations of illegal secessionist entity. The principle of legality protects the international public order by precluding production of legal effects deriving from a purported legal order of illegal secessionist entity subject to limited exceptions.

 | DOI:10.1163/9789004702646_015

Thirdly, the section outlined legal consequences of the change of effective territorial control, in particular the triggering of the law of occupation and applicability of the ECHR. The section built on a conceptual distinction between the issue of extraterritorial applicability of legal regimes and attribution of conduct for the purposes of establishing State responsibility. It determined the indicators of various factual tests, including effective control as an attribution test under ARSIWA, effective control as a jurisdiction-triggering and attribution test in the ECHR context, the effective control test for belligerent occupation and the overall control test for the internationalisation of a NIAC.

Fourthly, the section focused on the interaction between the legal consequences of peremptory territorial illegality and those stemming from the actual change of effective territorial control. While the section acknowledged that IHRL and the law of occupation are different in that the former provides for the rights of individuals and the latter does not grant any 'right of occupation' to the Occupying Power, but simply establishes what it can do as long as this *de facto* situation lasts, it also claimed that there is common ground in that their application is triggered upon effectiveness alone, regardless of legality or title. It argued that this is due to the underlying values that they seek to protect.

In fact, the section built on the premise of a simultaneous co-application of these two groups of consequences. It sought to outline their normative convergence and divergence as well as their application in judicial practice. Challenging the strict relevance of the *ius in bello/ius ad bellum* divide, particularly in the area of the law of occupation, the section argued that the rule of *lex superior* and *lex specialis* are not straightforwardly applicable. Instead, analysis should be built on the *horizontal* balancing of interests, depending on the context and protected values involved. Thereby, the outcome can reflect the values of contemporary international law in its entirety.

While the section concluded that consequences of peremptory illegality and the law of occupation are broadly normatively convergent, the area of normative divergence might be seen in the scope of the occupant's limited managerial powers under the law of occupation. In the area of human rights law, the section highlighted the normative convergence in the scope of the *Namibia* exception in the area of civil registration and number of human rights. It also highlighted areas of the ECtHR case law convergent with the duty of non-recognition. With respect to divergences, referring back to Chapter 7, the chapter specifically pointed to the ECtHR's expansive interpretation of the *Namibia* exception.

Overall, the section demonstrated that the effects of violation of peremptory norms in the context illegal secessionist entity continue to be relevant subsequent to the denial of statehood. These consequences operate in a *vertical* manner, with respect to effective relations and the purported legal order of illegal secessionist entity. Thereby, this book demonstrated that these effects are so extensive as to order effective relations of secessionist entities subsequent to the denial of statehood and expand even to the realm of private international law. The co-application of the consequences of peremptory territorial illegality and legal consequences of a change of effective territorial control requires *horizontal* balancing all the interests and values involved. This section cautioned against a restrictive vision of applicable legal framework and against the analysis carried out in isolation from all the relevant applicable regimes.

PART 2

Practice in the Post-Soviet Space

SECTION 3

Legal Analysis of the Status of Post-Soviet Secessionist Entities

Introduction to Section 3

The mapping of practice in Part 1, Chapter 5 identified that a critical number of contemporary secessionist attempts involving effective secessionist entities with a contested claim to statehood has taken place in the post-Soviet space. Therefore, an in-depth legal analysis of this practice can help clarify the understanding of secession in contemporary international law.

Even though the following chapters aim to map all the post-Soviet secessionist cases, they only provide an in-depth investigation of the secessionist attempts of entities that have remained outside their parent State's control until today – whether continuing claiming to be States or previously claiming to be States and now purportedly incorporated into another State, namely Transnistria, Abkhazia, South Ossetia, the Republic of Crimea, the Donetsk People's Republic (DPR), the Luhansk People's Republic (LPR), Kherson and Zaporizhzhia Regions. Given the long-term *prima facie* effectiveness of Nagorno-Karabakh before its recent recapture by Azerbaijan, the section also examines this case extensively. The section seeks to answer a key question. What is the status of these entities under international law? In order to do so, it applies a general legal framework from Part 1. It also assesses its conclusions on the status against the practice and positions of the existing States.

While the examination of each separate case is worthy for its own sake, the *collective* analysis of these situations might highlight certain patterns that would otherwise have been missed. Each chapter adopts an approximately similar structure, including a factual overview and legal analysis of the status. Taking such a methodological approach inevitably leads to a certain degree of repetition. Nevertheless, it is believed that rather than being to the detriment of the analysis, such an approach helps highlight the commonalities and key divergences among the cases under investigation. This might lead to a deeper understanding of a complex post-Soviet secessionist dynamics.

The section proceeds as follows. It firstly outlines fundamental tenets of Soviet federalism as a determining factor of post-Soviet secessionism. Next, it examines individual cases, starting from the secessionist attempts of Crimea, the DPR and LPR, Kherson and Zaporizhzhia Regions through Abkhazia and South Ossetia to that of Nagorno-Karabakh and ultimately Transnistria. The conclusion derives broader normative takeaways.

 | DOI:10.1163/9789004702646_016

CHAPTER 10

Soviet Federalism and the Dissolution of the Soviet Union

A full understanding of post-Soviet secessionist practice requires a brief preliminary inquiry into the Marxist-Leninist position on the national question and into the origins and theoretical underpinning of Soviet federalism. It is true that the Bolsheviks inherited a national problem "from the past, from imperial Russia",[1] but the way they approached this issue in the context of a federal architecture of the USSR determined the outcomes of the process when, almost 70 years later, the Soviet Union was brought to an end.

Generally, the predicates of classical Marxism are incompatible with national self-determination, which is inconsistent with the idea of a unified, borderless proletariat, as well as with federalism, which goes against the Marxist objective of a centralised government.[2] Nevertheless, in view of the situation on the ground and under the influence of strains of Marxist thought, Lenin and the Bolsheviks revised these premises.[3]

In fact, as early as 1903, the Second Congress of the Russian Social-Democratic Labour Party endorsed the principle of national self-determination for all nations comprising the State.[4] Nevertheless, around the same time, Lenin could write "undoubtedly the class antagonism has now pushed the national question far into the background."[5]

Later on, however, Lenin sharpened his position on this issue, in particular in the context of polemics with Rosa Luxemburg, who opposed the secession of

---

1 FJM Feldbrugge, *Russian Law: The End of the Soviet System and the Role of Law* (Martinus Nijhoff Publishers 1993) 40.

2 VV Aspaturian, 'The Theory and Practice of Soviet Federalism' (1950) 12 The Journal of Politics 20, 20. JA Armstrong, 'Federalism in the USSR: Ethnic and Territorial Aspects' (1977) 7 Federalism and Ethnicity 89, 90–91. For details on Marx and Engel's position on nationalism, including on the Polish and Irish Questions, see W Connor, *The National Question in Marxist-Leninist Theory and Strategy* (Princeton University Press 1984) 5–20.

3 See Connor (n 2) 28–38 on the development of Lenin's position on the nationality question.

4 'Examination of the Programme of the RSDLP at the Second Congress of the RSDLP in 1903' <http://www.agitclub.ru/center/comm/zin/1903project4.htm> accessed 10 May 2020 (*in Russian*). See also CC Herod, *The Nation in the History of Marxian Thought* (Springer Science+ Business Media 1976) 103–104.

5 VI Lenin, *Collected Works, Volume 6 (January 1902–August 1903)* (Progress Publishers 1964) 457–458.

© KONINKLIJKE BRILL BV, LEIDEN, 2024 | DOI:10.1163/9789004702646_017

Poland, which she considered to be the expression of bourgeois nationalism.[6] For Lenin, however, national self-determination was linked with the right to oppose oppression and as such overlapped with the interests of working classes in their struggle for liberation.[7] In any case, the right to self-determination was presented as "an *exception* to our general premise of centralisation".[8] According to Lenin, the freedom of self-determination did not seek the creation of small States, but, conversely, it ultimately sought the forging of large States and "even fusion of nations, only on a truly democratic, truly internationalist basis, which is *inconceivable* without the freedom to secede".[9] Moreover, the Bolsheviks also refined their position by opposing the premises of the Austro-Marxists, who, rather than territorial principle, favoured cultural-national autonomy on the basis of the personal principle as the solution to the nationality question in the multi-ethnic Austrian-Hungarian Empire.[10]

After the seizure of power, the Bolsheviks adopted the Declaration of the Rights of the Peoples of Russia, which formally proclaimed the "[r]ight of peoples of Russia to free self-determination, including secession and the formation of a separate state".[11] In the following period, until the end of 1918, "at least thirteen new states came into being within what was formerly the Russian Empire."[12]

Nevertheless, after their victory in the Civil War and consolidation of power, the Bolsheviks managed to return most of these regions to the Soviet control.[13]

---

6 HB Davis, 'Lenin and Nationalism: The Redirection of the Marxist Theory of Nationalism, 1903–1917' (1967) 31 Science and Society 164, 175.

7 ibid 175.

8 "This exception is absolutely essential in view of reactionary Great-Russian nationalism; and any rejection of this exception is opportunism (as in the case of Rosa Luxemburg); it means foolishly playing into the hands of reactionary Great-Russian nationalism. But exceptions *must not be* too broadly interpreted. In this case there is not, and *must not be* anything more than the *right to secede*." VI Lenin, *Collected Works, Volume 19 (March-December 1913)* (Foreign Languages Publishing House 1963) 501 (*emphasis in original*).

9 VI Lenin, *Collected Works, Volume 21 (August 1914-December 1915)* (Progress Publishers 1964) 413–414 (*emphasis in original*).

10 Armstrong (n 2) 94–95. Connor (n 2) 30. Stalin repudiated the idea of cultural-national autonomy, preferring regional autonomy. See JV Stalin, 'Marxism and National Question' (1913) <https://www.marxists.org/reference/archive/stalin/works/1913/03.htm> accessed 18 May 2020.

11 'Declaration of the Rights of the Peoples of Russia' (15 November 1917) <https://constitution.garant.ru/history/act1600-1918/5307/> accessed 18 May 2020 (*in Russian*).

12 Connor (n 2) 46; Feldbrugge (n 1) 41.

13 Connor (n 2) 51; Feldbrugge (n 1) 41.

> The advance of the Red Army and the consecutive extension of Soviet power in 1919–1921 had legally resulted not so much in annexation of new territories by the Russian Soviet Federative Socialist Republic (RSFSR), as in the creation of nominally independent republics.[14]

At first, these new Soviet republics recognised each other and together formed a community of seemingly independent States – satellites of Moscow bound together by diplomatic, treaty, "but also Party ties".[15] Nevertheless, in 1922, the Russian Soviet Federative Socialist Republic (RSFSR), Ukrainian Soviet Socialist Republic (Ukrainian SSR), Belarusian Soviet Socialist Republic (Belarusian SSR) and Transcaucasian Soviet Federative Socialist Republic joined to form the Union of Soviet Socialist Republics (USSR).[16] The treaty, with amendments and changes, was also incorporated in the 1924 Constitution of the USSR.[17] The process of setting up the USSR thus involved "the mix between confederal and federal influences".[18] This treaty-based federalism certainly corresponded to the needs of centralisation and assured coherence with the doctrinal tenets of Marxism-Leninism.[19]

Thus, federalism previously rejected by Marx and Lenin emerged in the post-revolutionary era; rather than being inconsistent with democratic centralism as previously argued by Lenin,[20] federalism was presented as "a transitional

14 E Forestier-Peyrat and S Dullin, 'Flexible Sovereignties of the Revolutionary State: Soviet Republics Enter World Politics' 19 (2017) Journal of the History of International Law 178, 181.

15 ibid 184 and see also 181. See also UW Saxer, 'The Transformation of the Soviet Union: From a Socialist Federation to a Commonwealth of Independent States' (1991) 14 Loyola of Los Angeles International and Comparative Law Journal 581, 611–612.

16 Treaty on the Creation of the USSR (signed 21 December 1922, entered into force 30 December 1922) <https://ru.wikisource.org/wiki/Договор_об_образовании_Союза_Советских_Социалистических_Республик> accessed 18 May 2020 (*in Russian*). Feldbrugge (n 1) 92–93.

17 'Constitution (Fundamental Law) of the USSR' (adopted 31 January 1924) <https://ru.wikisource.org/wiki/Конституция_СССР_(1924)_первоначальная_редакция> accessed 7 February 2019 (*in Russian*).

18 Forestier-Peyrat and Dullin (n 14) 185. See also Saxer (n 15) 611–615 and 713. Aspaturian (n 2) 27.

19 Saxer (n 15) 614. "Therefore, federalism in the Soviet Union was based on both a union treaty and a constitution founded upon that treaty." ibid.

20 "[W]hile, and insofar as, different nations constitute a single state, Marxists will never, under any circumstances, advocate either the federal principle or decentralisation. The great centralised state is a tremendous historical step forward from medieval disunity to the future socialist unity of the whole world, and only via such a state (inseparably connected with capitalism), can there be any road to socialism." VI Lenin, *Collected Works, Volume 20 (December 1913–August 1914)* (Progress Publishers 1964) 45–46.

form to the complete unity of the working people of different nations".[21] Importantly, it was also reconciled with national self-determination "as the latter was redefined within the framework of the former".[22] Throughout the existence of the Soviet Union, Soviet constitutions guaranteed Soviet republics the right to secede.[23] The 'latent sovereignty' of the Soviet republics was also expressed in the fact that some of them to a certain extent even participated in external relations.[24] Stalin, *a posteriori*, formulated three criteria that any Soviet republic had to fulfil: (i) an ethnic group or titular nation had to be the majority on its own territory; (ii) the republic needed to be located at the border of the USSR or at the open sea; (iii) its population had to be of a certain minimum size.[25]

The nationalities that did not fulfil these criteria were granted varying levels of autonomy within the Soviet republics, as autonomous republics, autonomous regions (*oblast*) and autonomous units (*okrug*).[26] Thus, for many decades, the distinction between the Soviet republics and other autonomous units was "sharp and significant".[27] Other autonomous units did not have such status and rights.[28] Most importantly, they did not possess the right to secede.

However, even though the Soviet Union's federal architecture was maintained throughout the whole Soviet era, in reality, it was only a façade

---

21 VI Lenin, *Collected Works, Volume 31 (April–December 1920)* (Progress Publishers 1966) 146.

22 Aspaturian (n 2) 25.

23 'Constitution (Fundamental Law) of the USSR' (adopted 31 January 1924), art 4 <https://ru.wikisource.org/wiki/Конституция_СССР_(1924)_первоначальная_редакция> accessed 7 February 2019 (*in Russian*); 'Constitution (Fundamental Law) of the USSR' (adopted 5 December 1936), art 17 <http://www.hrono.info/dokum/193_dok/cnst1936.php> accessed 7 February 2019 (*in Russian*); 'Constitution (Fundamental Law) of the Union of Soviet Socialist Republics' (adopted 7 October 1977, entered into force 7 October 1977), art 72 <https://www.departments.bucknell.edu/russian/const/77cons03.html> accessed 3 May 2019. In fact, prior to the adoption of the 1977 Constitution, there were drafts that abolished this right altogether, but it nevertheless reappeared in the final draft. Due to the fact that other provisions were formulated with the view of abolishing the right to secede, inconsistency was created in the text of the constitution. A Shtromas, 'The Legal Position of Soviet Nationalities and their Territorial Units According to the 1977 Constitution of the USSR' (1978) 37 The Russian Review 265, 267.

24 For an excellent account, see Forestier-Peyrat and Dullin (n 14) 189–198. The 1944 amendments to the 1936 Constitution especially granted republics the power to enter into relations with other States, conclude agreements and exchange diplomatic and consular representatives. Saxer (n 15) 617–618.

25 Feldbrugge (n 1) 122–123.

26 ibid 124–125.

27 ibid 94.

28 ibid 95 and 125. See *infra* the following chapters in detail.

preserved in the conditions of totalitarianism and absolute dominance by the Party – "behind the façade of a union of freely federated states arises an absolutely unitary state structure."[29] In particular, the exercise of a republic's right to secede would be considered as undermining the interests of the working people and thus would amount to a counterrevolution.[30] It was only after the introduction of *glasnost* and *perestroika* that this structure began to crumble.[31] Flexible sovereignty, which up until then had served the centre, now turned against it.[32] The above-mentioned features of the Soviet federalism re-emerged in the course leading to the dissolution of the Soviet Union.[33] The processes of the emancipation of the Soviet republics and the disintegration of the Soviet Union occurred simultaneously.[34]

After the period of contestation between the republics and the centre,[35] on 8 December 1991, Russia, Ukraine and Belarus signed the Minsk Agreement, in which they declared "that the Union of Soviet Socialist Republics as a subject of international law and a geopolitical reality no longer exists".[36] This act was contested because of the lack of capacity of only three republics to make such a decision.[37] On 21 December 1991, all the former Soviet Republics,

---

29 ibid 41 and see also 42 and 122.

30 ibid 127.

31 ibid 41–42 and 126–131.

32 Forestier-Peyrat and Dullin (n 14) 199.

33 "C'est seulement en identifiant l'URSS à un Etat confédéral – ce qui est tout à fait concevable-que l'on peut supposer que ses composantes avaient la capacité de la dissoudre." MG Kohen, 'Création d'Etats en droit international contemporain' in (2002) VI Cours euro-méditerranéens Bancaja de droit international 599. See also Saxer (n 15) 619, 675–676 and 713.

34 L Antonowicz, 'The Disintegration of the USSR from the Point of View of International Law' (1991–1992) 19 Polish Yearbook of International Law 7, 13.

35 See *infra* on the legal developments of this period as part of the analysis of each chapter.

36 Agreement Establishing the Commonwealth of Independent States (Republic of Belarus, the RSFSR and Ukraine) (signed 8 December 1991) reprinted in 31 (1992) ILM 143, 143–146 ("Minsk Agreement"). RSFSR ratified the Minsk Agreement on 12 December 1991 and on the same day it denounced the Treaty on the Creation of the USSR. See Supreme Soviet of the RSFSR, 'Resolution on Denouncement of the Treaty on the Creation of the USSR No 2015-I' (12 December 1991) <https://ru.wikisource.org/wiki/Постановление_ВС_РСФСР_от_12.12.1991_№_2015-I> accessed 20 May 2020 (*in Russian*).

37 On 11 December 1991, the Soviet Constitutional Oversight Committee adopted an opinion in which it held that the Soviet bodies could only cease their activity "after a constitutional decision has been made on the fate of the USSR and on the determination of successors to its rights and obligations." Moreover, the Committee also underlined that the first-time members of the USSR did not have any additional rights compared to republics that became members of the Soviet Union later. "Therefore, in deciding on the preservation, transformation or abolition of the Union of the Soviet Socialist Republics, its bodies

except for the Baltic States, which had restored their independence by that time, and Georgia, which was embroiled in civil war,[38] signed the Alma Ata Protocol, which formed an integral part of the Minsk agreement,[39] as well as the Alma Ata Declaration, in which they stated, "[w]ith the establishment of the Commonwealth of Independent States, the Union of Soviet Socialist Republics ceases to exist."[40]

Nevertheless, rump Soviet federal organs continued to exist even after these dates. Ultimately, on 25 December 1991, the president of the USSR resigned from his function.[41] On 26 December 1991, while the Soviet of the Union – the lower chamber of the Supreme Soviet of the USSR – already lacked quorum,[42] the Soviet of the Republics – the upper chamber of the Supreme Soviet of the USSR – adopted the declaration holding that, based on the will of the highest bodies of the mentioned republics,[43] "with the establishment of the Commonwealth of Independent States, the USSR as state and subject of international law ceases to exist."[44] Thus, the agreement of the constituent republics of the USSR on its dissolution was also upheld at the level of federal organs. Therefore, from the point of view of international law, the end of the USSR can be characterised as a voluntary dissolution.[45] The eleven participants in

---

and legislative acts, all republics that are currently members of the Union have the right to participate on an equal footing." Soviet Constitutional Oversight Committee, 'Opinion' (11 December 1991) <https://ru.wikisource.org/wiki/Заявление_Комитета_конституционного_надзора_СССР_от_11.12.1991> accessed 20 May 2020 (*in Russian*).

38 See *infra* in detail in the Chapter 13 on Abkhazia and South Ossetia.

39 Protocol to the Agreement Establishing the Commonwealth of Independent States Signed at into force on 8 December 1991 by the Republic of Belarus, the Russian Federation (RSFSR) and Ukraine (signed 21 December 1991, entry for each party upon ratification) reprinted in 31 (1992) ILM 147, 147.

40 Alma Ata Declaration (signed 21 December 1991) reprinted in 31 (1992) ILM 147, 148–149.

41 Feldbrugge (n 1) 135.

42 ibid 151.

43 These were signatories of the Minsk Agreement and the Alma Ata Protocol.

44 Soviet of the Republics of the Supreme Soviet of the USSR, 'Declaration in Connection with the Creation of the Commonwealth of Independent States No 142-H' (26 December 1991) <https://ru.wikisource.org/wiki/Декларация_Совета_Республик_ВС_СССР_от_26.12.1991_№_142-Н> accessed 20 May 2020 (*in Russian*).

45 Analogy can be made with the more orderly process of the dissolution of the Czech and Slovak Federative Republic on 31 December 1992. It took place after two governments of the federal republics had agreed on the dissolution of the State; then the Federal Assembly adopted a federal constitutional law on the dissolution of the federation, including the determination of a precise date of its termination. See for example 'The Emergence of the Independent Slovak Republic Was Preceded by the Adoption of a Constitutional Law' (*Teraz*, 28 December 2017) <https://www.teraz.sk/slovensko/vzniku-samostatnej-sr-predchadzalo-schva/299964-clanok.html> accessed 20 May 2020 (*in Slovak*). According

the meeting of the CIS on 30 December 1991 were undoubtedly independent States.[46] The former Soviet Republics emerged within their pre-existing boundaries.[47] The story of post-Soviet secessionist practice, in its early stages, is primarily the story of sub-republican autonomous units challenging this outcome.

---

to Kohen, "la situation de l'URSS peut être conçue comme un cas très particulier de dissolution dans lequel les Etats successeurs décident d'un commun accord que l'un d'entre eux assumera la condition d'Etat continuateur. C'est un cas de dissolution par accord des parties intéressées et avec l'assentiment des organs centraux de l'Etat qui cesse d'exister." MG Kohen, 'Création d'Etats en droit international contemporain' (2002) VI Cours euro-méditerranéens Bancaja de droit international 600.

46 Antonowicz (n 34) 13. Georgia did not participate in this meeting due to its embroilment in civil war. See *infra* in detail in the Chapter 13 on Abkhazia and South Ossetia.

47 See *infra*.

CHAPTER 11

Crimea

1 Outline of the Secessionist Attempt

Following the dissolution of the USSR, calls for the autonomy of Crimea in Ukraine, with its majority of Russian speakers and even its confederation with Ukraine, were backed by the Russian Parliament's resolution of May 1992 that declared the 1954 transfer of Crimea from the Russian Soviet Federative Socialist Republic (RSFSR) to the Ukrainian Soviet Socialist Republic (SSR) invalid.[1] However, a tense situation did not lead to an outbreak of violence, as it had in other parts of the post-Soviet space, and on the whole stabilised after the election of pro-Russian president Kuchma.[2] The 1994 Budapest Memorandum guaranteed Ukraine's territorial integrity and the inviolability of its borders,[3] the Ukrainian Constitution of 1996 granted Crimea broad autonomy, and the series of agreements between Russia and Ukraine partitioned the Black Sea Fleet in 1997.[4]

---

1 Supreme Council of the Russian Federation, 'Resolution on the Legal Evaluation of Decisions of the Highest Bodies of the RSFSR on the Change of the Status of Crimea Adopted in 1954 No 2809-I' (21 May 1992) <https://ru.wikisource.org/wiki/Постановление_ВС_РФ_от_21.05.1992_№_2809-I> accessed 7 February 2019 (*in Russian*); P Hilpold, 'Ukraine, Crimea and New International Law: Balancing International Law with Arguments Drawn from History' (2015) 14 Chinese Journal of International Law 237, 243. See *infra* in details.

2 Hilpold (n 1) 243.

3 Memorandum on Security Assurances in Connection with Ukraine's Accession to the Treaty on the Non-Proliferation of Nuclear Weapons (signed 5 December 1994, entered into force 5 December 1994) (Russian Federation, Ukraine, United Kingdom of Great Britain and Northern Ireland, United States of America) 3006 UNTS, arts 1 and 2 ("Budapest Memorandum"). For the assessment that the Budapest Memorandum contains legal commitments, see TD Grant, 'The Budapest Memorandum of 5 December 1994: Political Engagement or Legal Obligation' (2014) 34 Polish Yearbook of International Law 89. An important indication of the memorandum's legal character is its registration with the UN Secretariat on 2 October 2014 under No 52241.

4 Agreement between the Russian Federation and Ukraine on the Parameters of the Division of the Black Sea Fleet (signed 27 May 1997, entered into force 12 July 1999); Agreement between the Russian Federation and Ukraine on the Status and Conditions of the Presence of the Russian Federation Black Sea Fleet on the territory of Ukraine (signed 27 May 1997, entered into force 12 July 1999) ("the 1997 Status of Forces Agreement"); Agreement between the Government of the Russian Federation and the Government of Ukraine on Payments Associated with the Division of the Black Sea Fleet and Its Presence on the Territory of Ukraine (signed 27 May 1997, entered into force 12 July 1999) (together as "the Black Sea Fleet

However, the situation sharpened again in late 2013 and early 2014 in the context of the standoff between Ukraine's president, Viktor Yanukovych, who had refused to sign the Association Agreement with the EU and opted for closer ties with the Eurasian Customs Union, and protesters gathered in Maidan, the Central Square in Kyiv, who opposed Yanukovych's decision.[5] Following the violent and deadly turn of demonstrations, on 22 February 2014 Ukraine's *Verhovna Rada*, in violation of the Ukrainian Constitution, deposed president Yanukovych from his post.[6] Yanukovych had fled to Russia. On 23 February 2014, *Verkhovna Rada* nominated its speaker, Turchynov, as the Acting Head of State.[7]

Vladimir Putin, the president of the Russian Federation has admitted that, against the backdrop of these events, on the night of 22 to 23 February 2014, he told his colleagues "the situation in the Ukraine had developed in such a way that we had to start working on the return of the Crimea to Russia."[8] Putin

---

Partition Agreements"). These agreements provided for the partition of the Black Sea Fleet and for the conditions of the deployment of the Russian part (82%) in Crimea and the city of Sevastopol. Russia was allowed to maintain up to 25,000 troops in Crimea. V Bílková, 'The Use of Force by the Russian Federation in Crimea' (2015) 75 ZaöRV 27, 31–32. See regarding the conditions of the Russian military presence in Crimea under these treaties J Miklasová, 'Post-Soviet Secession: Crimea and Eastern Ukraine Under International Law' in K Gray (ed) *Global Encyclopedia of Territorial Rights* (Springer 2022) 2–3. Originally, the agreements were to expire in 2017, but in 2010 Ukraine and Russia signed another agreement extending their validity to 2042 in exchange for economic assistance. ibid 31. In March 2014, Russia unilaterally terminated these agreements citing Article 61 and 62 VCLT (supervening impossibility of performance and *rebus sic stantibus*). ibid. Hilpold (n 1) 243–244. See *infra*.

5 JF Escudero Espinosa, *Self-Determination and Humanitarian Secession in International Law of a Globalized World: Kosovo v. Crimea* (Springer 2018) 90.

6 S Perpetua, 'Parliament Votes to Dismiss Yanukovych' (*The New York Times*, 22 February 2014) <https://www.nytimes.com/video/world/europe/100000002728851/parliament-votes-to-dismiss-yanukovych.html> accessed 7 February 2019. According to the Ukrainian Constitution, three-quarters of the MPs, amounting to 338 votes, was required to remove the president from his post, along with a judgment by the Constitutional Court. However, only 328 MPs voted for Yanukovych's impeachment. Espinosa (n 5) 91, ftn 72.

7 'Ukraine: Speaker Oleksandr Turchynov Named Interim President' (*BBC News*, 23 February 2014) <https://www.bbc.com/news/world-europe-26312008> accessed 7 February 2019; C Urquhart, 'Ukraine MPs Appoint Interim President as Yanukovych Allies Dismissed – 23 February As It Happened' (*The Guardian*, 23 February 2014) <https://www.theguardian.com/world/2014/feb/23/ukraine-crisis-yanukovych-tymoshenko-live-updates> accessed 7 February 2019.

8 'The Boris Nemtsov Report in English: "Putin. The War," About the Involvement of Russia in the Eastern Ukraine Conflict and the Crimea' (2015) European Union Foreign Affairs Journal 5, 13–4 ("Nemtsov Report"); 'Putin Reveals Secrets of Russia's Crimea Takeover Plot' (*BBC News*, 9 March 2015) <https://www.bbc.com/news/world-europe-31796226> accessed 7 February 2019. See 'Crimea. The Way Home' (2015) <https://www.youtube.com/watch?v=nbGhKfWrfOQ> accessed 30 October 2023.

initially denied the affiliation of the so-called 'Little Green Men' – unidentified gunmen who appeared in Crimea and started to take over key installations there – with the Russian army,[9] but already on 17 April 2014, he admitted to it.[10] Today, the Russian army's involvement in the takeover of Crimea is no longer disputed.

On 27 February 2014, these Little Green Men, acting as a local self-defence militia, seized Crimean government buildings, including the Crimean Parliament, and raised the Russian flag there.[11] On the same day, the Crimean Parliament[12] voted no confidence in the existing government, installed pro-Russian Sergey Aksyonov as the new head of the Crimean government[13] and voted to hold a referendum on greater autonomy from Kyiv on 25 May 2014.[14]

---

9 Espinosa (n 5) 92–93.

10 "I did not hide the fact that our goal was to ensure proper conditions for the people of Crimea to be able to freely express their will. And so we had to take the necessary measures in order to prevent situation in Crimea unfolding the way it is now unfolding in southeastern Ukraine ... Of course, the Russian servicemen did back the Crimean self-defence forces. They acted in a civil but a decisive and professional manner, as I've already said." 'Direct Line with Vladimir Putin' (*President of Russia's Official Website*, 17 April 2014) <http://en.kremlin.ru/events/president/news/20796> accessed 7 February 2019. See also *Ukraine v Russia (re Crimea)* App nos 20958/14 and 38334/18 (ECtHR, 16 December 2020) ("*Ukraine v Russia (re Crimea)*") paras 331–334.

11 M-L Gumuchian, L Smith-Spark and I Formanek, 'Gunmen Seize Government Buildings in Ukraine's Crimea, Raise Russian Flag' (*CNN*, 27 February 2014) <https://edition.cnn.com/2014/02/27/world/europe/ukraine-politics/index.html> accessed 7 February 2019; H Salem, S Walker and L Harding, 'Crimean Parliament Seized by Unknown Pro-Russian Gunmen (*The Guardian*, 27 February 2014) <https://www.theguardian.com/world/2014/feb/27/crimean-parliament-seized-by-unknown-pro-russian-gunmen> accessed 7 February 2019.

12 Apart from the presence of gunmen in the Crimean Parliament building, the vote was also hampered by the procedural irregularities. Gumuchian, Smith-Spark and Formanek (n 11).

13 According to the Ukrainian Constitution, the prime minister of Crimea is nominated to his position by the Supreme Soviet with the consent of the president of the Ukraine. In this context, Aksyonov held that Vladimir Yanukovych had remained the legitimate president of Ukraine. At the same time, the Acting Head of Ukraine Turchynov decreed the nomination of Aksyonov as unconstitutional. See 'Aksyonov Nominated to the Position of the Prime Minster of Crimea in Violation of the Ukrainian and Crimean Constitution – Decree' (*Interfax Ukraine*, 1 March 2014) <https://interfax.com.ua/news/political/193644.html> accessed 7 February 2019 (*in Russian*).

14 Gumuchian, Smith-Spark and Formanek (n 11); S Ayres, 'Crimea Sets Date for Autonomy Vote Amid Gunmen, Anti-Kiev Protests' (*The Christian Science Monitor*, 27 February 2014) <https://www.csmonitor.com/World/Europe/2014/0227/Crimea-sets-date-for-autonomy-vote-amid-gunmen-anti-Kiev-protests> accessed 7 February 2019. See also 'Crimea. The Way Home' (2015) available <https://www.youtube.com/watch?v=nbGhKfWrfOQ> accessed 30 October 2023.

On 28 February 2014, Aksyonov appealed to Russia for "assistance in guaranteeing peace and calmness" in Crimea.[15] Similarly, the deposed President Yanukovych, who had found refuge in Russia, appealed to the Russian president "to use the armed forces of the Russian Federation to re-establish the rule of law, peace, order, stability and to protect the people of Ukraine".[16]

On 1 March 2014, the Upper House of the Russian Parliament approved the use of military force in Ukraine.[17] Meanwhile, the takeover of strategic installations in the peninsula continued, with no resistance from the Ukrainian army.[18] According to findings of the European Court of Human Rights (ECtHR), the presence of the Russian troops in Crimea "nearly doubled" between late January and mid-March 2014, amounting to approximately 20,000 forces.[19] The Court also took into account (relying on adverse inferences) the evidence provided by Ukraine that between the 27 February 2014 and 18 March 2014, Russian servicemen in Crimea, among others, actively carried out operations aimed at blocking, detaining and disarming Ukrainian troops, seizing Crimea's entry and exit points as well as actively participated in the transfer of power in Crimea.[20] Apparently, fears of a repetition of the 2008 Russia-Georgia War were taken into account by the heads of the Ukrainian national security apparatus when making a decision on how to react to this development.[21]

---

15 P Lewis, I Traynor and L Harding, 'Crimea Crisis: Pro-Russian Leader Appeals to Putin for Help' (*The Guardian*, 28 February 2014) <https://www.theguardian.com/world/2014/feb/28/barack-obama-vladimir-putin-ukraine-russia> accessed 7 February 2019.

16 Yanukovych's statement was presented during the UNSC session on 3 March 2014. See L Charbonneau, 'Russia: Yanukovich Asked Putin to Use Force to Save Ukraine' (*Reuters*, 4 March 2014) <https://www.reuters.com/article/us-ukraine-crisis-un/russia-yanukovich-asked-putin-to-use-force-to-save-ukraine-idUSBREA2224720140304> accessed 7 February 2019. However, a month later, Yanukovych claimed he had been wrong when inviting Russian troops to Crimea. See C Kriel and V Isachenkov, 'Ousted Ukrainian President Viktor Yanukovych: I Was Wrong to Invite Russia Into Crimea' (*The Sydney Morning Herald*, 3 April 2014) <https://www.smh.com.au/world/ousted-ukrainian-president-viktor-yanukovych-i-was-wrong-to-invite-russia-into-crimea-20140403-zqpxa.html> accessed 7 February 2019.

17 Espinosa (n 5) 93–94 and ftn 87.

18 M Kofman and others, *Lessons from Russia's Operations in Crimea and Eastern Ukraine* (RAND Corporation 2017) 9.

19 *Ukraine v Russia* (*re Crimea*) (n 10) para 321 in connection with paras 318–319.

20 ibid 328–329. See also Bílková, 'The Use of Force by the Russian Federation in Crimea' (n 4) 32.

21 See 'Transcript of the Secret Meeting of the National Security Council During the Annexation of Crimea. Full Text in Russian' (*Gordon*, 22 February 2016) <https://gordonua.com/publications/stenogramma-sekretnogo-zasedaniya-snbo-vo-vremya-anneksii-kryma-v-2014-godu-polnyy-tekst-na-russkom-yazyke-121122.html> accessed 31 October 2023 (*in Russian*).

On a political level, on 6 March 2014, the Crimean Parliament issued a resolution calling for a referendum to be held in Crimea on 16 March 2014 on the question of joining the Russian Federation or restoring the 1992 Crimean Constitution. The Ukrainian president suspended it the next day and the Ukrainian Constitutional Court found it unconstitutional on 14 March 2014.[22]

On 11 March 2014, the Crimean Parliament and the parliament of the city of Sevastopol issued the Declaration of Independence, subject to a positive result in the referendum.[23] Following the announcement of overwhelming votes in favour of Crimea's reunification with Russia,[24] the Crimean Parliament issued another declaration of independence on 17 March 2014.[25] On the very same day, the Russian Federation recognised the Republic of Crimea.[26] One day later, on 18 March 2014, the Russian president and the leaders of the purported Republic of Crimea signed the Agreement on the Accession of the Republic of Crimea to the Russian Federation.[27] On 21 March 2014, the Russian president

---

22 *Judgment in the Case on the Constitutional Petition of the Acting President of Ukraine, the Chairman of the Verkhovna Rada of Ukraine, the Ukrainian Parliament Commissioner for Human Rights Concerning the Compliance with the Constitution of Ukraine (Constitutionality) of the Resolution of the Verkhovna Rada of the Autonomous Republic of Crimea "On Holding of the All-Crimean Referendum No 1–13/2014"* (Ukraine, Constitutional Court of Ukraine) (14 March 2014) <https://zakon.rada.gov.ua/laws/show/v002p710-14#Text> accessed 31 October 2023 (*in Ukrainian*).

23 Supreme Council of the Autonomous Republic of Crimea, 'Declaration of Independence of the Autonomous Republic of Crimea and City of Sevastopol' (11 March 2014) <http://crimea.gov.ru/app/2988> accessed 17 July 2023 (*in Russian*) ("Declaration of Independence of Crimea"). Espinosa (n 5) 94.

24 According to officially published results, 83.10% of eligible voters took part in the referendum, of which 96.77% voted in favour of Crimea's reunification with Russia and 2.51% voted in favour of a restoration of the validity of the 1992 Constitution. See 'Results of the All-Crimean Referendum' <http://crimea.gov.ru/search?category=content-pages&q=+Результаты+общекрымского+референдума> accessed 30 October 2023 (*in Russian*). See also DM Herszenhorn, 'Crimea Votes to Secede from Ukraine as Russian Troops Watch' (*The New York Times*, 16 March 2014) <https://www.nytimes.com/2014/03/17/world/europe/crimea-ukraine-secession-vote-referendum.html> accessed 8 February 2019.

25 State Council of the Republic of Crimea, 'Resolution on the Independence of Crimea' (17 March 2014) <http://crimea.gov.ru/act/11748> accessed 31 October 2023 (*in Russian*) ("Resolution on the Independence of Crimea"). DM Herszenhorn and A Cowell, 'Lawmakers in Crimea Move Quickly to Split from Ukraine' (*The New York Times*, 17 March 2014) <https://www.nytimes.com/2014/03/18/world/europe/european-union-ukraine.html?hpw&rref=world&_r=1> accessed 8 February 2019.

26 'Executive Order of the President of the Russian Federation on Recognising Republic of Crimea' (17 March 2014) <http://en.kremlin.ru/acts/news/20596> accessed 7 February 2019.

27 Agreement between the Russian Federation and the Republic of Crimea on the Accession of the Republic of Crimea to the Russian Federation and on Forming New Constituent

signed the federal law ratifying the purported agreement and the Federal Constitutional Law on Admitting to the Russian Federation the Republic of Crimea and Establishing within the Russian Federation the New Constituent Entities of the Republic of Crimea and the City of Federal Importance Sevastopol.[28] Simultaneously, between 19 and 25 March 2014, Ukrainian troops and their families withdrew from Crimea.[29] On 27 March 2014, the UNGA adopted a resolution in which it affirmed its commitment *inter alia* to "territorial integrity of Ukraine within its internationally recognised borders", and the EU and the USA imposed sanctions on Russia.[30] According to Russian Prime Minister Medvedev, Crimea was fully integrated into the Russian Federation in July 2015.[31] Apart from Russia, until today, so far only seven UN Members have officially recognised Crimea as part of Russia.[32]

Entities of the Russian Federation (signed 18 March 2014, entered into force 1 April 2014, provisionally applied since the signature) <http://publication.pravo.gov.ru/Document/View/0001201403180024> accessed 7 February 2019 (*in Russian*) ("Russia-Crimea Agreement on Accession").

28 'Laws on Admitting Crimea and Sevastopol to the Russian Federation' (*President of Russia's Official Website*, 21 March 2014) <http://en.kremlin.ru/acts/news/20625> accessed 19 July 2023.

29 DM Herszenhorn and AE Kramer, 'Ukraine Plans to Withdraw Troops From Russia-Occupied Crimea' (*The New York Times*, 19 March 2014) <https://www.nytimes.com/2014/03/20/world/europe/crimea.html> accessed 7 February 2019; DM Herszenhorn, P Reevell and N Sneider, 'Russian Forces Take Over One of the Last Ukrainian Bases in Crimea' (*The New York Times*, 22 March 2014) <https://www.nytimes.com/2014/03/23/world/europe/ukraine.html?_r=0 > accessed 7 February 2019. Kofman (n 18) 11–12.

30 UNGA Res 68/262 (27 March 2014) UN Doc A/RES/68/262, para 1. See for more *infra*. O Corten, 'The Russian Intervention in the Ukrainian Crisis: Was *Jus Contra Bellum* "Confirmed Rather than Weakened"?' (2015) 2 Journal on the Use of Force and International Law 17, 18.

31 J McHugh, 'Putin Eliminates Ministry of Crimea, Region Fully Integrated Into Russia, Russian Leaders Say' (*International Business Times*, 15 July 2015) <https://www.ibtimes.com/putin-eliminates-ministry-crimea-region-fully-integrated-russia-russian-leaders-say-2009463> accessed 7 February 2019.

32 These States include Nicaragua, Cuba, Venezuela, Afghanistan, North Korea, Syria and Sudan. See 'Crimea is Yours: Who in the World Recognized the Peninsula as Part of Russia' (*Ria Novosti*, 20 February 2019) <https://crimea.ria.ru/politics/20181009/1115354765.html> accessed 16 June 2020 (*in Russian*). J Bender, 'These Are the 6 Countries on Board with Russia's Illegal Annexation of Crimea' (*Business Insider*, 31 May 2016). <https://www.businessinsider.com/six-countries-okay-with-russias-annexation-of-crimea-2016-5?r=US&IR=T> accessed 7 February 2019.

2 Legal Analysis of the Secessionist Attempt

The Russian Federation argues that incorporation of the Autonomous Republic of Crimea and the city of Sevastopol ("Crimea") in Russia was the expression of the consent of two sovereign States – the Russian Federation and the Republic of Crimea. Indeed, it is undeniable that any sovereign State is entitled to dispose of its own territory and decide about the termination of its existence, including its complete disappearance. If this argument on the existence of the Republic of Crimea were proved correct, it would preclude the possibility of arguing that Russia violated the fundamental rules of international law on the prohibition of forcible annexations and the inviolability of frontiers, and even its own treaty obligations to respect Ukraine's territorial integrity.[33]

However, for this argument to work, it needs to be demonstrated that Crimea indeed seceded from Ukraine and genuinely existed as a sovereign State. Thus, the following section examines key legal arguments raised in this context, including the right to self-determination, remedial secession and the consequences of the Russian military intervention. Prior to that, it also analyses the Crimean Parliament's official documents adopted during the secessionist crisis.

Before proceeding to legal analysis, it should be added that separatists in Crimea, in their declaration of independence, and President Putin, in his address on 18 March 2014, directly cited the passage from the *Kosovo* advisory opinion that "general international law contains no applicable prohibition of declarations of independence" as justification for the legality of Crimea's secession and an argument against the double-standard of the Western States with respect to secession.[34]

---

33 "[T]he realization of the right to self-determination in the form of secession is a natural and legitimate process that lawfully changes frontiers and territories of existing states and therefore can not qualify as a 'seizure' or 'usurpation.'" 'Legal Justifications of Russia's Position on Crimea and Ukraine' (27 October 2014) <https://germany.mid.ru/ru/press-centre/news/de_ru_2014_10_27_pravovye-obosnovaniya-pozicii-rossii/> accessed 31 October 2023 ("Legal Justifications of Russia's Position on Crimea and Ukraine"). See Corten (n 30) 20.

34 Putin also directly cited the Written Statement of the USA on the fact that municipal illegality of declarations of independence does not entail their international illegality. V Putin, 'Address by President of the Russian Federation' (The Kremlin, Moscow, 18 March 2014) <http://en.kremlin.ru/events/president/news/20603> accessed 7 February 2019 ("Putin's Address of 18 March 2014"); Legal Justifications of Russia's Position on Crimea and Ukraine (n 33); Declaration of Independence of Crimea (n 23) preamble. Moreover, as will be shown below, after Kosovo's declaration of independence, Russia's decade-long official policy towards South Ossetia and Abkhazia changed in 2008. Kosovo could be echoed in the U-turn in Russia's legal argumentation. It admitted the existence of the

Thus, the question arises about how to assess the relevance of Kosovo's declaration of independence and advisory opinion in this context. It should be admitted that by labelling Kosovo a *sui generis* case with no precedent-creating implications and by departing from (until then) a long-held trend in practice,[35] some of the Western States seemingly helped to destabilise law in this area, which allowed Russia and the secessionists to use this apparent uncertainty in their own legal justifications and actions.[36] Nevertheless, firstly, as is shown below, the legal context of Crimea (and other secessionist attempts in the post-Soviet space) and that of Kosovo are not identical, due to the third State's use of force to facilitate their secession.[37] Secondly, even if it were admitted that Western States violated international law in Kosovo, it clearly would not have justified Russia's or any other State's own violations – "two wrongs do not make a right."[38]

2.1 *Analysis of the Secessionist Documents and Actions*

In an official press release the Speaker of the Crimean Parliament issued on 26 February 2014, the question of Crimea's withdrawal from Ukraine was labelled a provocation.[39] However, only one day later, on 27 February 2014, after the seizure of the Parliament's building and the installation of a new pro-Russian government, the Crimean Parliament adopted a resolution in which it called for a local referendum on the question of Crimea's greater autonomy.[40] This

---

right to remedial secession when it recognised Abkhazia and South Ossetia in 2008, during the Kosovo proceedings and at the time of Crimea's incorporation into Russia. See *infra*.

35 See *supra* Part 1, Chapter 5.

36 See C Marxsen, 'The Crimea Crisis: An International Law Perspective' (2014) 74 ZaöRV 367, 387–389; T Christakis, 'Self-Determination, Territorial Integrity and Fait Accompli in the Case of Crimea' (2015) 75 ZaöRV 75, 76–80; MG Kohen, 'L'Ukraine et le respect du droit international' (*Le Temps*, 12 March 2014) <https://www.letemps.ch/opinions/lukraine-respect-droit-international> accessed 7 February 2019.

37 See *infra* in detail. The scholars consider the connection between NATO's illegal intervention in Kosovo in 1999 and Kosovo's 2008 declaration of independence as disrupted by virtue of the adoption of the Chapter VII UNSC resolution 1244 (1999), which authorized the presence of international forces in Kosovo. See R Geifs, 'Russia's Annexation of Crimea: The Mills of International Law Grind Slowly But They Do Grind' (2015) 91 International Law Studies Series. US Naval War College 425, 436–437.

38 Christakis (n 36) 78.

39 'Vladimir Konstantinov: "No Issue of the Withdrawal of Crimea from Ukraine in Crimean Parliament"' (*Press Centre of the Supreme Council of the ARC*, 26 February 2014) http://crimea.gov.ru/news/26_02_2014_1 accessed 30 October 2023 (*in Russian*).

40 Supreme Council of the Autonomous Republic of Crimea, 'Resolution on the Organization and Holding of Republic (Local) Referendum on Improvement of the Status and Powers

resolution did not break with the Ukrainian legal order, yet, as it included reference to compliance with the Ukrainian Constitution, it called for greater status and powers for Crimea within Ukraine and prescribed the date of referendum to 25 May 2014, which was also the date of the Ukrainian presidential elections.[41]

However, as the situation in the peninsula evolved, not only was the date of the referendum moved twice to an earlier date,[42] but its purpose significantly changed, too. In this context, the Crimean Parliament's resolution of 6 March 2014 seems to be crucial.[43] Firstly, this resolution called for the referendum on joining the Russian Federation or restoring Crimea's 1992 Constitution to be held on 16 March 2014, but it did so without any reference to the provisions of the Ukrainian Constitution, marking a clean break with the Ukrainian legal order. Secondly, neither of the referendum questions referred specifically to the creation of a separate Republic of Crimea.[44] In fact, nowhere in this document is it possible to find any mention of the creation of a separate sovereign Crimean Republic. Thirdly, in paragraph 1, the Crimean Parliament decides "to join the Russian Federation as a subject of the Russian Federation", and in paragraph 9 it addresses the Russian President and Parliament with the view of beginning the process of joining the Russian Federation.[45] Thus, already 10 days prior to the 16 March referendum, the Crimean Parliament officially decided to join the Russian Federation. The wording of the resolution implies that the joining of Russia was intended to take place without any specific mechanism of separate State creation.

This changed on 11 March 2014, when the Crimean Parliament adopted the Declaration of Independence.[46] In fact, it is difficult to see the purpose of this declaration being adopted before the referendum itself other than to supplant and clarify the previous resolution of 6 March 2014. Even the Venice

---

of the Autonomous Republic of Crimea' (27 February 2014) No 1630–6/14 <https://www.rada.crimea.ua/act/11610> accessed 7 February 2019 (*in Russian*).

41 See ibid.

42 A Novikova, 'Referendum on the Status of Crimea Was Changed to 30 March' (*Komsomolskaja Pravda*, 1 March 2014) <https://www.pskov.kp.ru/online/news/1674459/> accessed 7 February 2019 (*in Russian*). Ultimately, a referendum took place on 16 March 2014. See *infra*.

43 Supreme Council of the Autonomous Republic of Crimea, 'Resolution on the Holding of All-Crimean Referendum' (6 March 2014) No 1702–6/14 <http://crimea.gov.ru/act/11689> accessed 31 October 2023 (*in Russian*) ("Resolution on the Holding of All-Crimean Referendum").

44 ibid.

45 ibid.

46 Declaration of Independence of Crimea (n 23).

Commission commented on the implications of the unusual timing of this declaration.[47] In addition, after the referendum, one more declaration of independence – this time in the form of a Resolution of the Crimean Parliament – was adopted on 17 March 2014.[48] The need to issue two declarations of independence within the span of one week seems to be highly unusual.

Overall, it can be assumed that these documents reflect the evolution of the political thinking of the secessionists. At first, the idea of the withdrawal from Ukraine was seen as provocation. After the military seizure of the government building, joining Russia became a viable option. However, the latter was not officially linked in any way with the creation of an independent Crimean Republic until 11 March 2014, when the actual military takeover was well underway. This seems to imply that rather than reflecting a genuine intent to create a separate sovereign State, the mechanism of creating a new sovereign State of Crimea was added to the process of military seizure of the peninsula and *de facto* annexation. Indeed, the decision to join the RF was already made officially on 6 March 2014, before the holding of a referendum and before any mention of the creation of a separate Crimean Republic in an official document.

2.2 *History-Based Arguments*

Arguments referring to the unconstitutionality of the transfer of Crimea from the RSFSR to the Ukrainian SSR in 1954 were frequently invoked in the course of the secessionist crisis.[49] For example, according to President Putin, the 1954

---

47 CoE (Venice Commission), 'Opinion on 'Whether the Decision Taken by the Supreme Council of the Autonomous Republic of Crimea in Ukraine to Organise a Referendum on Becoming a Constituent Territory of the Russian Federation or Restoring Crimea's 1992 Constitution is Compatible with Constitutional Principles'' (21 March 2014) CDL-AD (2014)002, para 22 ("Venice Commission Opinion on Crimean Referendum").

48 Resolution on the Independence of Crimea (n 25).

49 The key documents concerning the transfer of Crimea from the RSFSR to the Ukrainian SSR included the resolution of the Presidium of the Supreme Soviet of the RSFSR of 5 February 1954, the resolution of the Presidium of the Supreme Soviet of the Ukrainian SSR of 13 February 1954 and the ordinance of the Presidium of the Supreme Soviet of the USSR of 19 February 1954. Under Article 16 of the Constitution of the RSFSR of 1937, the territory of the RSFSR could not have been changed without its consent. Based on Articles 19, 22 and 23 of this Constitution, it can be inferred that such consent was to be given by the Supreme Soviet of the RSFSR as a whole. The Constitution in Article 33 did not mention the power of the Presidium to adopt such a resolution. Taking into account Article 4 and 49 of the 1936 Constitution of the USSR, similar considerations also apply with respect to the lack of power of the Presidium of the Supreme Soviet of the USSR to adopt such ordinance. However, even if these decisions were considered unconstitutional as such, a broader context for their adoption should also be taken into account. Most importantly, Crimea's transfer was subsequently confirmed by the respective Soviet

decision was made in clear violation of the constitutional norms in place at that time and, in any case, was treated as a formality in the context of a totalitarian regime.[50] Russian scholars argue that the 1954 transfer did not have an international legal impact; "[i]t was merely a matter of administrative business."[51] "In people's hearts and minds, Crimea has always been an inseparable part of Russia."[52] These arguments seem to imply that, due to defects in the 1954 transfer, Crimea never validly became part of Ukraine.[53]

---

and Republican Laws and by the changes in the respective constitutions. Regarding the resolution of the Presidium of the Supreme Soviet of the RSFSR of 5 February 1954, "[t]he alleged exceeding of powers by the Presidium of the Supreme Council of the Russian SFSR could perhaps be considered legitimate had the territorial changes associated with the transfer of the Crimean Region not been fixed at the constitutional level twice during the Soviet era: on 2 June 1954, when the appropriate changes to the Constitution of the RSFSR of 1937 were made, and on 12 April 1978, with the adoption of the 'new' Constitution of the RSFSR." O Yarmish and A Cherviatsova, 'Transferring Crimea from Russia to Ukraine: Historical and Legal Analysis of Soviet Legislation' in E Milano, M Nicolini and F Palermo (eds), *Law, Territory and Conflict Resolution: Law as a Problem and Law as a Solution* (Brill Nijhoff 2016) 154 (*footnotes omitted*) and with respect to constitutionality of the acts of presidiums see 146–168. In addition, the modalities of the transfer reflected the constitutional practice of other territorial changes carried out by presidiums rather than whole supreme soviets. ibid 163. See G Sasse, *The Crimea Question: Identity, Transition and Conflict* (Harvard University Press 2007) 107–114 and p. 226. See Presidium of the Supreme Soviet of the RSFSR, 'Resolution on the Transfer of the Crimean District from the RSFSR to the Ukrainian SSR' (5 February 1954) <https://ru.wikisource.org/wiki/Постановление_Президиума_ВС_РСФСР_от_05.02.1954_О_передаче_Крымской_области_из_состава_РСФСР_в_состав_Украинской_ССР> accessed 7 February 2019 (*in Russian*); Presidium of the Supreme Soviet of the USSR, 'Resolution on the Transfer of the Crimean District from the RSFSR to the Ukrainian SSR' (19 February 1954) <https://ru.wikisource.org/wiki/Указ_Президиума_ВС_СССР_от_19.02.1954_о_передаче_Крымской_области_из_состава_РСФСР_в_состав_УССР> accessed 7 February 2019 (*in Russian*); 'Constitution (Fundamental Law) of the USSR' (adopted 5 December 1936) <http://www.hrono.info/dokum/193_dok/cnst1936.php> accessed 7 February 2019 (*in Russian*); 'Constitution (Fundamental Law) of the RSFSR (21 January 1937) <https://ru.wikisource.org/wiki/Конституция_РСФСР/1937/Редакция_02.06.1954> accessed 7 February 2019 (*in Russian*). See for the reference to the subsequent Soviet and Republican laws and constitutions concerning this matter Yarmisch and Cherviatsova (n 49) 147–148. See also Miklasová (n 4) 6–7. See also *infra* on the position of the Russian parliament and other bodies on the matter.

50 Putin's Address of 18 March 2014 (n 34).

51 AY Kapustin, 'Circular Letter to the Executive Council of the International Law Association' (6 June 2014) <https://mgimo.ru/about/news/departments/252984/> accessed 7 February 2019 ("Circular Letter").

52 Putin's Address of 18 March 2014 (n 34).

53 Geifs (n 37) 438.

Nevertheless, Ukraine, as a former Soviet Union Republic, emerged as a successor State to the Soviet Union within its pre-existing administrative boundaries, including Crimea, which followed from the respective Soviet and Republican laws and constitutions, by virtue of the principle of *uti possidetis iuris*.[54] Upon the accession to independence, the former federal boundaries of the Ukrainian SSR transformed into international frontiers of a new successor State of Ukraine.[55] A plethora of multi-lateral and bilateral documents has affirmed the applicability of the principle of *uti possidetis iuris* in the context of the dissolution of the USSR in general and the formation of a successor State of Ukraine in particular.

In Article 5 of the Minsk Agreement, Russia, Ukraine and Belarus "acknowledge and respect each other's territorial integrity and the inviolability of *existing* borders *within* the Commonwealth".[56] Similarly, in the Alma Ata Declaration, the former Union Republics declared that they recognise and respect "each other's territorial integrity and the inviolability of *existing* borders".[57] In addition, in Article 3 of the Charter of the CIS, the member States pledged to build their relations in accordance *inter alia* with the principle of "recognition of existing frontiers".[58] Similarly, the CIS declaration of 15 April 1994 provided for the provision on the respect for sovereignty, territorial integrity and inviolability of state borders.[59] References to "existing borders within Commonwealth" and "existing borders" or "existing frontiers" clearly cover former administrative boundaries of the republics,[60] including Crimea as part of Ukraine.

---

54 See *supra* Part 1 for more on the principle of *uti possidetis iuris*. See (n 49).

55 H Hamant, *Démembrement de l'URSS et problèmes de succession d'états* (Bruylant 2007) 172–177.

56 Agreement Establishing the Commonwealth of Independent States (Republic of Belarus, the RSFSR and Ukraine) (signed 8 December 1991), art 5 reprinted in 31 (1992) ILM 143, 143–146 ("Minsk Agreement") (*emphasis added*). See also Protocol to the Agreement Establishing the Commonwealth of Independent States Signed at into force on 8 December 1991 by the Republic of Belarus, the Russian Federation (RSFSR) and Ukraine (signed 21 December 1991, entry for each party upon ratification) reprinted in 31 (1992) ILM 147, 147 ("Alma Ata Protocol").

57 Alma Ata Declaration (signed 21 December 1991), preambular para 3 reprinted in 31 (1992) ILM 147, 148–149 ("Alma Ata Declaration").

58 Charter of the Commonwealth of Independent States (adopted 22 January 1993, entered into force 22 January 1994) 1819 UNTS 37, art 3 ("Charter of the CIS").

59 CIS, 'Declaration on Respect of Sovereignty, Territorial Integrity and Inviolability of Boundaries of the Member States of CIS' (15 April 1994) <http://docs.cntd.ru/document/1901148> accessed 9 May 2019 (*in Russian*).

60 MG Kohen, 'Le problème des frontières en cas de dissolution et de séparation d'États: quelles alternatives?' in O Corten, B Delcourt, P Klein and N Levrat (eds), *Démembrements d'États et délimitations territoriales: l'uti possidetis en question*(s) (Bruylant 1999) 377.

Moreover, in terms of bilateral Russian-Ukrainian relationships, it should be noted that even before the dissolution of the Soviet Union, in the 1990 treaty, the RSFSR and Ukrainian SSR recognised and respected each other's territorial integrity within existing boundaries within the USSR.[61] The 1990 treaty was concluded by the federal subjects of the USSR in the period following their declarations of sovereignty, but it remained in force until the adoption of the Ukraine-Russia Friendship Treaty of 1997, in which Ukraine and Russia again reaffirmed "the inviolability of the borders *existing* between them".[62] Russia, alongside the UK and USA, also reaffirmed its commitment to respect "the existing borders of Ukraine".[63] Ultimately, the technical issues relating to the Ukrainian-Russian border were settled in the 2003 Ukrainian-Russian State Border Treaty.[64]

Thus, all of the above-mentioned documents affirm the applicability of the principle of *uti possidetis iuris* with respect to former boundaries of the Ukrainian SSR. In none of the above instances was the course of the Ukrainian border in Crimea formally challenged by the RF.[65] In any case, as follows from

61 Treaty between the RSFSR and the Ukrainian SSR (signed 19 November 1990, entered into force 14 June 1991), art 6 <http://docs.cntd.ru/document/1900094> accessed 7 February 2019 (*in Russian*).

62 Treaty on Friendship, Cooperation and Partnership between Ukraine and the Russian Federation (signed 31 May 1997, entered into force 1 April 1999; expired 1 April 2019) 3006 UNTS, art 2 ("Ukraine-Russia Friendship Treaty") (*emphasis added*).

63 Budapest Memorandum (n 3) para 1.

64 See also the Treaty between Ukraine and the Russian Federation on the Ukrainian-Russian State Border (signed 28 January 2003, entered into force 23 April 2004) <http://kremlin.ru/supplement/1653> accessed 28 May 2019 (*in Russian*).

65 C Marxsen, 'Territorial Integrity in International Law – Its Concept and Implications for Crimea' (2015) 75 ZaöRV 7, 12. It should be noted that in May 1992 by almost a unanimous vote, the Russian Parliament adopted a resolution declaring the resolution on the transfer of Crimea in 1954 invalid. However, Russian president Yeltsin distanced himself from this parliamentary decision. In 1993, the Russian Parliament adopted another resolution by which it placed the city of Sevastopol under Russian jurisdiction. In reaction to this resolution, the UNSC President, on behalf of the UNSC members, including Russia, reaffirmed "its commitment to the territorial integrity of Ukraine" and declared the parliamentary resolution "incompatible with this commitment as well as with purposes and principles of the Charter of the United Nations, and without legal effect." Moreover, the Russian Federation sent a letter to the UNSC declaring the parliamentary resolution "emotional and declaratory" and departing "from the policy followed by the President and the Government of the Russian Federation." Supreme Council of the Russian Federation, 'Resolution on the Legal Evaluation of Decisions of the Highest Bodies of the RSFSR on the Change of the Status of Crimea Adopted in 1954' (21 May 1992) No 2809-I. <https://ru.wikisource.org/wiki/Постановление_ВС_РФ_от_21.05.1992_№_2809-I> accessed 7 February 2019 (*in Russian*); Supreme Council of the Russian Federation, 'Resolution on the Status of the City of Sevastopol' (9 July 1993) No 5359-I <https://ru.wikisource.org/wiki/Постановление_ВС_РФ_от_09.07.1993_№_5359-I> accessed 7 February 2019 (*in Russian*); UNSC,

the analysis in Part 1, and as confirmed by the above practice in the context of the dissolution of the USSR, the principle of *uti possidetis iuris* does not seem to require investigation as to the compliance of the establishment of pre-existing administrative boundaries with municipal law.[66] Therefore, the reference to the constitutionality of the 1954 transfer of Crimea from the RSFSR to the Ukrainian SSR has no legal relevance as a justification of Crimea's incorporation into Russia.[67] Russia was bound to respect pre-existing Ukrainian frontiers under treaty obligations and customary international law.[68] Ultimately, this was even admitted by President Putin during his address of 18 March 2014, when he stated that by agreeing to delimit border with Ukraine (based on the ex-Soviet borders) in the early 2000s, Russia "admitted de facto and de jure that Crimea was Ukrainian territory, thereby closing the issue."[69]

2.3 *Right to Self-Determination and Remedial Secession*

Russia seems to imply that the population of Crimea represents people entitled to self-determination by pointing to certain unique characteristics. Nevertheless, it is not exactly clear what the notion of the Crimean people entails.[70] In this context, even those authors who favour specific subjective

---

'Letter Dated 19 July 1993 from the Permanent Representative of the Russian Federation to the United Nations Addressed to the President of the Security Council' (19 July 1993) S/26109; Note by the President of the Security Council UNSC No S/26118 (1993); Sasse (n 49) 226–231. In 2015, the General Prosecution of the Russian Federation issued a letter in which it provided a legal analysis of the matter and found the 1954 resolution of the Presidium of the Supreme Soviet of the RSFSR on the transfer of Crimea unconstitutional and invalid from the moment of its adoption. See 'Letter of the General Prosecution of the Russian Federation Concerning Legality of the Transfer of Crimea to Ukraine in 1954' (18 May 2015) No OTV-22-4199-15 <https://ru.wikisource.org/wiki/Письмо_Генпрокуратуры_России_от_18.05.2015_по_поводу_законности_передачи_Крыма_Украине_в_1954_году> accessed 7 February 2019 (*in Russian*).

66 See *supra* Part 1, Chapter 4.

67 Marxsen, 'The Crimea Crisis' (n 36) 12. The same conclusion, but on different grounds, is reached by Christakis (n 36) 85.

68 CJ Borgen, 'Law, Rhetoric, Strategy: Russia and Self-Determination before and after Crimea' (2015) 91 International Law Studies US Naval War College 216, 255–261.

69 Putin's Address of 18 March 2014 (n 34).

70 "Crimea is a unique blend of different peoples' cultures and traditions. This makes it similar to Russia as a whole, where not a single ethnic group has been lost over the centuries. Russians and Ukrainians, Crimean Tatars and people of other ethnic groups have lived side by side in Crimea, retaining their own identity, traditions, languages and faith." Putin's Address of 18 March 2014 (n 34). "The Russian-speaking population of the south-eastern regions of Ukraine demands the respect for their rights, traditions, culture and language." Circular Letter (n 51).

and objective criteria of peoplehood, and therefore argue in favour of the possibility that certain fractions of the population of Crimea, such as Crimean Tatars or ethnic Russians, could be entitled to self-determination, admit that "it is debatable whether the population of Crimea *as a whole* constitutes a 'people' under international law" since it "is too diverse to meet the threshold of a 'people'".[71] In any case, it has been demonstrated in Part 1, Chapter 3 that the definition of peoplehood does not derive from ethno-national features, but follows a territorial conception.[72] Based on this conclusion, the people entitled to self-determination are the whole population of Ukraine, including the population of the Crimean peninsula. In any case, Part 1 showed that the right to self-determination does not entail a general right to secede, and therefore this argument does not prove relevant for establishing the legal right of Crimea to secede.[73]

Other arguments seem to imply the existence of factual circumstances justifying claim for remedial secession.[74] Even though, Part 1 established that there is no right to remedial secession in positive international law, the situation in Crimea fell short of the factual elements required by the doctrine. For example, following the ousting of President Yanukovych on 22 February 2014, *Verkhovna Rada* attempted to repeal the Law on the Principles of State Language Policy, thereby seeking to make Ukrainian the only State language at all levels.[75] This move was presented as an example of a hostile move against the Russian-speakers.[76] However, even when acknowledging the provocative nature of this step,[77] it must be pointed out that on 2 March 2014, the Acting Head of State did not accept *Verkhovna Rada*'s decision and instead proposed a new law in line with international standards.[78] Regardless, Putin claimed

71 SF Van den Driest, 'Crimea's Separation from Ukraine: An Analysis of the Right to Self-Determination and (Remedial) Secession in International Law' (2015) 62 Netherlands International Law Review 329, 350–351.

72 See *supra* Part 1, Chapter 3.

73 Van den Driest (n 71) 351.

74 See Borgen (n 68) 241–242 and 246.

75 OHCHR, 'Report on the Human Rights Situation in Ukraine' (15 April 2014) para 4; A Tancredi, 'The Russian Annexation of the Crimea: Questions Relating to the Use of Force' I (2014) QIL QDI 5, 12.

76 OHCHR, 'Report on the Human Rights Situation in Ukraine' (15 April 2014) para 4.

77 J Summers, 'The Crimea Crisis: A Case of Occupation, Annexation, Secession or Autonomy?' (*Lancaster University Law School*, 5 March 2014) <https://www.lancaster.ac.uk/law/blog-archive/research/the-crimea-crisis-a-case-of-occupation-annexation-secession-or-autonomy/> accessed 31 October 2023.

78 OHCHR, 'Report on the Human Rights Situation in Ukraine' (15 April 2014) para 4; Tancredi (n 75) 12–13.

that this law had only been set aside to be "reserved for the future".[79] As one scholar argues, this position would change the meaning of self-determination from an "extraordinary remedy for severely oppressed peoples to a potentially regular occurrence that could be applicable to almost any minority around the world".[80] It clearly fell short of doctrinal requirements of remedial secession.

Additionally, an argument for remedial secession seems to be implied in the claim that the people of Crimea failed to realise their right to self-determination within Ukraine and that this failure was further exacerbated by "the unlawful rise to power of those who do not represent the entire Ukrainian people".[81] Putin presented the protests in Kyiv as executed by "[n]ationalists, neo-Nazis, Russophobes and anti-Semites".[82] It needs to be recognised that extreme nationalists took part in the anti-Yanukovych demonstrations and even received seats in an interim government.[83] Nevertheless, this fact on its own does not fulfil the doctrinal standards for remedial secession or ones set by Russia itself.[84] Moreover, the claims of separatists or of Russia mostly referred to threats of persecution rather than actual persecution,[85] when only the latter

79 Putin's Address of 18 March 2014 (n 34).

80 WW Burke-White, 'Crimea and the International Legal Order' (2014) Faculty Scholarship Paper 1360 <https://scholarship.law.upenn.edu/faculty_scholarship/1360/> accessed 7 February 2019.

81 Legal Justifications of Russia's Position on Crimea and Ukraine (n 33). See also V Tolstykh, 'Reunification of Crimea with Russia: A Russian Perspective' (2014) 13 Chinese Journal of International Law 879.

82 Putin's Address of 18 March 2014 (n 34). See also Circular Letter (n 51).

83 D Stern, 'Ukraine's Revolution and the Far Right' (*BBC News*, 7 March 2014) <https://www.bbc.com/news/world-europe-26468720> accessed 7 February 2019; B Whelan, 'How the Far-Right Took Top Posts in Ukraine's Power Vacuum' (*Channel 4*, 5 March 2014) <https://www.channel4.com/news/svoboda-ministers-ukraine-new-government-far-right> accessed 7 February 2019; V Ischenko, 'Ukraine Has Ignored the Far Right for Too Long – It Must Wake Up to the Danger' (*The Guardian*, 13 November 2014) <https://www.theguardian.com/commentisfree/2014/nov/13/ukraine-far-right-fascism-mps> accessed 7 February 2019.

84 Russia's strict line on the conditions for remedial secession required "an outright armed attacked by the parent State, threatening the very existence of the people in question." *Accordance with International Law of the Unilateral Declaration of Independence in Respect of Kosovo* (Advisory Opinion) [2010] ICJ Rep 403, Written Statement of the Russian Federation (16 April 2009), para 88.

85 "Crimea has exhausted the possibilities to achieve a decent status as part of Ukraine. Our further stay in the political field of this state *threatens* the residents of Crimea not just with humiliation and discrimination on the basis of cultural and ethnic principles, but with the most literal physical extermination." V Konstantinov, 'Address of the Chairman of the Supreme Council of Autonomous Republic of Crimea to Residents of Crimea' (10 March 2014) <http://crimea.gov.ru/news/09_03_2014_1> accessed 31 October 2023 (*in*

is a precondition of remedial secession. In any case, the population of Crimea was neither threatened nor actually persecuted by the Ukrainian authorities at the time.[86] International organisations and observers also found "no evidence of violations or threats to the rights of Russian speakers".[87] Thus, overall, the population of Crimea or the Russian-speaking population of Crimea could not prevail upon any right to secede stemming from international law.

2.4 *Right to Secede under Municipal Ukrainian Law*

Part 1, Chapter 3 of this book established that the right to secede may be granted to the territorial sub-unit of the existing State on the basis of constitutional law or on the basis of devolutionary agreements between the parent State and the secessionists.[88] Under Article 2 of the Ukrainian Constitution, "Ukraine is a unitary State"; its territory within its present borders is "indivisible and inviolable".[89] Under Article 132, "the territorial structure of Ukraine is based on the principles of unity and indivisibility of the state territory, the combination of centralisation and decentralisation in the exercise of state power."[90] According to Article 134 of the Ukrainian Constitution, "[t]he Autonomous Republic of Crimea is an inseparable constituent part of Ukraine." From these provisions it follows that the Constitution of Ukraine does not grant any right to secede

Russian) (*emphasis added*). "Those who opposed the coup were immediately *threatened* with repression." Putin's Address of 18 March 2014 (n 34) (*emphasis added*).

86 "Despite unsubstantiated claims by Crimean politicians that the unconstitutional change of government in Kiev posed a threat to its people and that the Ukraine government was guilty of human rights violations, there is no plausible evidence to suggest that the people of Crimea, Donetsk and Luhansk were in any such danger." S Cavandoli, 'The Unresolved Dilemma of Self-Determination: Crimea, Donetsk and Luhansk' (2016) 20 The International Journal of Human Rights 875, 884. Hilpold (n 1) 265; Christakis (n 36) 90; Van den Driest (n 71) 351–352; J Vidmar, 'The Annexation of Crimea and the Boundaries of the Will of the People' (2015) 16 German Law Journal 365, 371–372; Geifs (n 37) 441; C Walter, 'Postcript: Self-Determination, Secession, and the Crimean Crisis 2014' in C Walter, A Von Ungern-Sternberg and K Abushov (eds), *Self-determination and Secession in International Law* (OUP 2014) 306–307.

87 'Developing Situation in Crimea Alarming, Says OSCE High Commissioner on National Minorities' (*OSCE Press Release*, 6 March 2014) <https://www.osce.org/hcnm/116180> accessed 7 February 2019. "It is widely assessed that Russian-speakers have not been subject to threats in Crimea." OHCHR, 'Report on the Human Rights Situation in Ukraine' (15 April 2014), para 89.

88 See *supra* Part 1, Chapter 3.

89 'Constitution of Ukraine' (adopted 28 June 1996, wording as of 13 March 2014) <https://www.refworld.org/docid/44a280124.html> accessed 7 February 2019 ("Constitution of Ukraine").

90 ibid.

to Crimea or to any sub-unit of Ukraine.[91] To the contrary, as underscored by the Venice Commission, "[a]ffirmation of *the indivisibility of the state* plainly implies outlawing secession."[92]

2.5 *Secessionist Referendum of 16 March 2014*

According to Russia, one of the key differences between the secessions of Crimea and Kosovo was the fact that the former took place on the basis of an affirmative vote expressed in referendum.[93] In addition, Russia's arguments seem to suggest that the will of people expressed in referendum alone is sufficient to attribute the status of statehood to these entities.[94] This argument is in fact in direct contradiction to the judgments of the Russian Constitutional Court in the Tatarstan case and Chechnya cases.[95]

---

91 See also Van den Driest (n 71) 349–350.

92 CoE (Venice Commission), 'Self-Determination and Secession in Constitutional Law' (12 January 2000) CDL-INF (2000) 2, 3 (emphasis in original).

93 Legal Justifications of Russia's Position on Crimea and Ukraine (n 33).

94 D Medvedev, 'Statement by President of Russia' (26 August 2008) <http://en.kremlin.ru/events/president/transcripts/1222> accessed 15 May 2019; Putin's Address of 18 March 2014 (n 34); Legal Justifications of Russia's Position on Crimea and Ukraine (n 33). See *supra* for details.

95 Tatarstan and Chechnya were the only two Russian autonomous republics that refused to sign the Federation Treaty in 1992. Tatarstan organised a unilateral referendum to support its 1990 declaration of sovereignty, in which 61.4% agreed that Tatarstan was a 'sovereign state.' Instead of declaring independence as did Chechnya, Tatarstan negotiated with Moscow and signed a treaty with a greater level of autonomy in 1994. However, the treaty was not extended in 2017. See S Shargorodsky, 'Russia Worried Over Tatarstan Referendum on Independence' (*AP*, 19 March 1992) <https://www.apnews.com/b980353468c8a8647b999f02e109d53c> accessed 15 June 2019; K Galeev, 'Fear and Loathing in Russia's Catalonia: Moscow's Fight Against Federalism' (*War on the Rocks*, 31 January 2018) <https://warontherocks.com/2018/01/moscows-fight-against-federalism-fear-and-loathing-in-russias-catalonia/> accessed 15 June 2019; L Smirnova, 'Tatarstan, the Last Region to Lose Its Special Status Under Putin' (*The Moscow Times*, 25 July 2017) <https://www.themoscowtimes.com/2017/07/25/tatarstan-special-status-expires-a58483> accessed 15 June 2019. As for Chechnya, it declared independence from the RSFSR in November 1991. Russia fought two wars to re-establish its control over the region. The first Chechen war, which lasted from 1994 to 1996, was terminated by the defeat of the Russian forces and the signature of the Khasavyurt ceasefire agreement, which foresaw *inter alia* the withdrawal of Russian forces and the reaching of an agreement on relations between the Russian Federation and the Chechen Republics by 31 December 2001. In 1997, the peace treaty was signed between the two presidents. No state recognised Chechnya as an independent State in that period. From 1999 Russia waged the second Chechen war, which finished in 2009 with Russia's victory. See 'Russia "Ends Chechnya Operation"' (*BBC News*, 16 April 2009) <http://news.bbc.co.uk/2/hi/europe/8001495.stm> accessed 16 June 2019; 'Khasavyurt Agreements' (*Kavkazskiy Uzel*, 31 August 2017) <https://www.kavkaz-uzel.eu/articles/295026/> accessed 16 June 2019 (*in Russian*); Peace Treaty and Principles of

Three further points should be made with respect to the referendum that took place in Crimea on 16 March 2014.[96] Firstly, as mentioned in Part 1, Chapter 3 independence referenda can be held under the provisions of municipal legislation.[97] It is true that the Resolution of the Crimean Parliament

---

Interrelation between the Russian Federation and the Chechen Republic Ichkeria (signed and entered into force 12 May 1997) <https://peacemaker.un.org/sites/peacemaker.un.org/files/RU_970512_PeaceTreatyRussiaChechenIchkeria.pdf> accessed 16 June 2019. In the case of Tatarstan, the Russian constitutional court held that "without negating the right of a People to self-determination exercised by means of the lawful expression of will, it is appropriate to proceed from the premise that international law restricts it by the observance of the requirements of the principle of territorial integrity and the principle of the observance of human rights. … The unilateral establishment by the Republic of Tatarstan of such a right [to secede] would mean recognition of the legitimacy of the complete or partial violation of the territorial unity of a sovereign federal state and the national unity of the peoples inhabiting it. Any actions aimed at violating this unity damage the constitutional system of the RSFSR and are incompatible with international norms on human rights and the peoples' rights. … The only lawful and fair means of solving this problem should be considered the law-based negotiation process, the participants of which should be all concerned subjects of the RSFSR." *Judgment on the Constitutionality of the Declaration of State Sovereignty by Tatarstan SSR of 30 August 1990, Law of Tatarstan SSR of 18 April 1991 on 'Changes and Amendments of Constitution (Basic Law) of Tatarstan SSR,' Law of Tatarstan SSR of 29 November 1991 on 'Referendum of Tatarstan SSR,' Decree of Supreme Soviet of Tatarstan Republic of 21 February 1992 on 'Holding of Referendum of Tatarstan Republic on State Status of Republic of Tatarstan'* (Russian Federation, Constitutional Court of the Russian Federation) (13 March 1992) <https://ru.wikisource.org/wiki/Постановление_Конституционного_Суда_РСФСР_от_13.03.1992_№_П-P3-I> accessed 31 October 2023 (*in Russian*). See J Summers, *Peoples and International Law: How Nationalism and Self-Determination Shape a Contemporary Law of Nations* (Martinus Nijhoff Publishers 2007) 275; GM Danilenko, 'The New Russian Constitution and International Law' (1994) 88 American Journal of International Law 451, 457–458 and 463–464. In the case of Chechnya, the Russian constitutional court held that "the constitutional goal of preserving the integrity of the Russian State accords with the universally recognised principles concerning the right of nations to self-determination." The Chechen case is cited in P Gaeta, 'The Armed Conflict in Chechnya before the Russian Constitutional Court' (1996) 7 European Journal of International Law 563, 565. The Court built its reasoning only on the first part of the saving clause in the Friendly Relations Declaration. ibid 565–566. See also M Bowker, 'Russia and Chechnya: The Issue of Secession' (2004) 10 Nations and Nationalism 461; D Draganova, 'Chechnya's Right of Secession under Russian Constitutional Law' (2004) 3 Chinese Journal of International Law 571. *Judgment on the Constitutionality of the Presidential Decrees and the Resolutions of the Federal Government Concerning the situation in Chechnya* (Russian Federation, Constitutional Court of the Russian Federation) (31 July 1995) <https://www.venice.coe.int/webforms/documents/default.aspx?pdffile=CDL-INF(1996)001-e> (*in English*) <http://doc.ksrf.ru/decision/KSRFDecision30248.pdf> (*in Russian*) accessed 16 June 2019.

96 Resolution on the Holding of All-Crimean Referendum (n 43).

97 See Borgen (n 68) 249–250. See *supra* Part 1, Chapter 3.

on the holding of the referendum referred to the provisions of the Crimean Constitution, which allowed for holding of local referenda.[98] However, under the Ukrainian Constitution, the Autonomous Republic of Crimea "decides on the issues ascribed to its competence within the limits of authority determined by the Constitution of Ukraine" and the normative acts of the Crimean parliament shall not contradict the Ukrainian Constitution.[99] According to the Venice Commission, the fact that one of the highest values of the Ukrainian Constitution is the indivisibility of territory "is an indication that a referendum on secession cannot be constitutional in Ukraine".[100] Moreover, Article 73 of the Ukrainian Constitution explicitly states that "[i]ssues of altering the territory of Ukraine are resolved exclusively by an All-Ukrainian referendum."[101] Thus, the holding of the referendum on 16 March was clearly unlawful under the Ukrainian Constitution.[102] Nevertheless, the referendum's constitutional illegality is irrelevant from the perspective of international law.[103]

Secondly, according to the Venice Commission, it appears "questionable whether the referendum of 16 March 2014 could be held in compliance with international standards".[104] In this context, a number of circumstances were mentioned, including the short period of time between the call for referendum and the referendum itself; doubts about the impartiality of authorities; the lack of neutrality in the question, which did not include the possibility to maintain the then *status quo*; ambiguity in the question regarding the return to the 1992 Constitution; and the lack of negotiations among relevant stakeholders.[105] In addition, the Venice Commission pointed out that the holding of an unconstitutional referendum "in any case contradicts European standards".[106]

98 Resolution on the Holding of All-Crimean Referendum (n 43).

99 Constitution of Ukraine (n 89) arts 134 and 135.

100 Venice Commission Opinion on Crimean Referendum (n 47) para 12.

101 Constitution of Ukraine (n 89) art 73.

102 See also the Judgment of the Ukrainian Constitutional Court on the Constitutionality of the All-Crimean Referendum (n 22). The secessionist referendum would thus require amendment of the Constitution, but under Article 157(1) the latter is prohibited in case the amendment is oriented towards a "violation of the territorial indivisibility of Ukraine." Constitution of Ukraine (n 89) art 157(1).

103 Christakis (n 36) 92; A Peters, 'The Crimean Vote of March 2014 as an Abuse of the Institution of the Territorial Referendum' in C Calliess (ed), *Staat und Mensch im Kontext des Völker- und Europarechts: Liber Amicorum für Torsten Stein* (Nomos Verlag 2015) 263.

104 Venice Commission Opinion on Crimean Referendum (n 47) para 22. Peters (n 103) 274–278.

105 Venice Commission Opinion on Crimean Referendum (n 47) paras 22–23 and 25–26.

106 ibid para 24.

According to the Venice Commission, "the massive public presence of (para) military forces is not conducive to democratic decision making."[107]

Thirdly, Part 1, Chapter 3 established that even though the holding of a unilateral referendum as such does not violate international law, a majority vote in favour of independence on its own does not give rise to the right to independence. Therefore, even though the referendum in Crimea on 16 March 2014 cannot be considered illegal under international law simply on the basis of its unilateral character,[108] it could not have conferred the right to secede on the population of Crimea, even if international and European standards discussed above were met. Nevertheless, it was also established in Part 1, Chapter 3 that referendum is illegal under international law if it is connected to violation of peremptory norms.[109] It is demonstrated below that by using force in Crimea, Russia violated the prohibition of the use of force.[110]

Overall, it follows that the unilateral independence referendum of 16 March 2014 did not confer any right to secede on the population of Crimea under municipal or international law; it was illegal under the Ukrainian Constitution and did not meet the relevant international and European standards.[111] In addition, it was illegal under international law due to the fact that it resulted from the violation of peremptory norms.[112]

The international community condemned this referendum as illegal, invalid and illegitimate and rejected its results. Nevertheless, different legal grounds have been invoked for such illegality in State practice. Importantly, the UNGA, in its Resolution on Territorial Integrity of Ukraine of 27 March 2014, noted in its preamble that the referendum of 16 March 2014 was not authorised by Ukraine, and in its operative part underscored that this referendum "having no validity, cannot form the basis for any alteration of the status of the Autonomous Republic of Crimea or of the city of Sevastopol"; and it called upon States, IOs and specialized agencies not to recognise alteration of the status of the Autonomous Republic of Crimea and the city of Sevastopol on the basis of this referendum and "to refrain from any action or dealing that might

107 ibid para 22.

108 Christakis (n 36) 91; Espinosa (n 5) 123. See for more *supra* Part 1, Chapter 3.

109 See *supra* Part 1, Chapter 3.

110 See *infra*.

111 The same conclusions: Espinosa (n 5) 117–123; Hilpold (n 1) 259–262. See Marxsen, 'The Crimea Crisis' (n 36) 382.

112 See Corten (n 30) 37–38; R Müllerson, 'Ukraine: Victim of Geopolitics' (2014) 13 Chinese Journal of International Law 133, 141; V Bílková, 'Territorial (Se)Cession in Light of Recent Events in Crimea' in E Milano, M Nicolini and F Palermo (eds), *Law, Territory and Conflict Resolution: Law as a Problem and Law as a Solution* (Brill Nijhoff 2016) 214.

be interpreted as recognizing any such altered status".[113] The adoption of this UNGA resolution was preceded by an attempt to adopt a resolution of similar wording in the UNSC, but the latter was thwarted by the veto of the Russian Federation.[114]

In this context, apart from pointing to the referendum's illegality under Ukrainian municipal law, some States, in debates in the UNSC and the UNGA, claimed the referendum was illegal, under international law, or illegitimate in the context of Russia's use of force in Crimea.[115] Referring to paragraph 5 of the UNGA resolution, Corten claimed "[s]ecession is not condemned as unconstitutional, but as lacking validity in international law."[116] He also underlined that in the process of the adoption of this resolution "no State has contested the customary status of rule prohibiting the recognition of a serious breach of a peremptory norm of international law."[117]

---

113 UNGA Res 68/262 (27 March 2014) UN Doc A/RES/68/262, preambular para 7 and paras 5–6. This resolution was adopted by 100 affirmative votes, 11 negative votes and 58 abstentions.

114 See UNSC Res S/2014/189 (15 March 2014). The resolution was supported by 13 votes; Russia voted against and China abstained. See 'Repertoire of the Practice of the Security Council' (19th Supplement, 2014–2015).

115 For example, France claimed, "the referendum that it [Russia] had instigated in Crimea was illegal and null and void under international law." UNSC, '7144th Meeting' (19 March 2014) S/PV.7144, 6. Liechtenstein stated that "[t]he annexation was preceded by an illegitimate declaration of independence based on a referendum held in violation of the Constitution of Ukraine and of basic tenets of international law, including paragraph 4 of Article 2 of the Charter of the United Nations." UNGA, '80th Plenary Meeting' (27 March 2014) A/68/PV.80, 7. Canada claimed, "Crimea's so-called referendum was not authorized by Ukraine. It was conducted while Crimea was under Russia's illegal military occupation. The referendum is therefore illegitimate and null and void. We do not and will not recognize its outcome." UNGA, '80th Plenary Meeting' (27 March 2014) A/68/PV.80, 9. For the position of Lithuania, see UNSC, '7134th Meeting' (13 March 2014) S/PV.7134, 19, UNSC, '7144th Meeting' (19 March 2014) S/PV.7144, 16; for the position of Australia, see UNSC, '7144th Meeting' (19 March 2014) S/PV.7144, p. 13; Ukraine UNSC, '7144th Meeting' (19 March 2014) S/PV.7144, 6; for the position of the United Kingdom, see UNSC, '7144th Meeting' (19 March 2014) S/PV.7144, 15; for the position of Turkey, see UNGA, '80th Plenary Meeting' (27 March 2014) A/68/PV.80, 11; for the position of Iceland, see UNGA, '80th Plenary Meeting' (27 March 2014) A/68/PV.80, 12. Corten (n 30) 37.

116 Corten (n 30) 26.

117 According to Corten, Russia never contested the rule itself, but only its application to this case, first by denying its military involvement, and later by denying the illegality of its involvement. Corten also points out that other States did not vote in favour of the resolution because it was unbalanced – as it did not condemn the Western States' interference in the change of government in Kyiv – not because of its opposition to the rule itself. Corten (n 30) 38. On the other hand, according to Douhan, the fact that the resolution was voted in the affirmative by only 51% of the UN Member States and 59% of the

Other regional and international bodies referred to the municipal illegality of the referendum. According to the EU, the decision by the Supreme Council of the Autonomous Republic of Crimea on holding the referendum was contrary to the Ukrainian Constitution and therefore illegal.[118] The OSCE PA also viewed the referendum of 16 March 2014 "as an illegitimate and illegal act, the results of which have no validity whosoever".[119]

2.6 *Russia's Use of Force in Crimea*

Russia undisputedly used force in Crimea by employing troops already stationed in Crimea on the basis of the 1997 Status of Forces Agreement and the so-called Little Green Men who were admitted by the Russian president to be servicemen of the Russian Army.[120] As mentioned in Part 1, the legality of this use of force by Russia could have a critical impact on Crimea's secessionist bid.

Despite the fact that no exceptions from the prohibition of the use of force under the UN Charter were applicable to Russia's use of force in Crimea,[121] Russia invoked two arguments to justify its intervention. Firstly, Russia claimed that its intervention was legal by pointing to the invitation by illegally deposed

---

States present at the voting signifies that it cannot be taken as an example of *opinio iuris*. AF Douhan, 'International Organizations and Settlement of the Conflict in Ukraine' 75 (2015) ZaöRV 195, 201. Similarly, Yuval Shany, 'Does International Law Grant the People of Crimea and Donetsk a Right to Secede?' (2014) 21 Brown Journal of World Affairs 233, 238–240. According to the PCA Award, the relevant UNGA resolutions were framed in "hortatory language" and not unanimously or by consensus, "but with many States abstaining or voting against them." PCA Case No 2017–06, *Dispute Concerning Coastal State Rights in the Black Sea, Sea of Azov, and Kerch Strait (Ukraine v the Russian Federation)*, Award Concerning the Preliminary Objections of The Russian Federation (21 February 2020) para 175.

118 Council of European Union, 'Statement of the Heads of State or Government on Ukraine' (6 March 2014), para 2; Council of European Union (Foreign Affairs), 'Council Conclusions on Ukraine' (17 March 2014), para 1.

119 OSCE (PA), 'Resolution on Clear, Gross and Uncorrected Violations of Helsinki Principles by the Russian Federation' (1 July 2014), para 15 and preamble referring to municipal illegality of the referendum; OSCE (PA), 'Resolution on the Continuation of Clear, Gross and Uncorrected Violations of OSCE Commitments and International Norms by the Russian Federation' (8 July 2015), para 22.

120 See Bílková, 'The Use of Force by the Russian Federation in Crimea' (n 4) 31–37. This admission entails that, rather than looking at the factual connection between these supposedly irregular troops and Russia in order to establish parameters of an indirect intervention, the issue only centres on the direct use of force by Russia. Tancredi (n 75) 9.

121 Charter of the United Nations (adopted 26 June 1945, entered into force 24 October 1945) 1 UNTS XVI ("UN Charter"). See Bílková, 'The Use of Force by the Russian Federation in Crimea' (n 4) 38–39.

president Viktor Yanukovych.[122] However, regardless of the municipal illegality of Yanukovych's ousting,[123] at the time of his request for assistance, president Yanukovych no longer had effective control of Ukraine as the president and therefore this "argument is not in conformity with classic international law, which requires a government to be both generally recognised and effective to be legally able to request an external intervention".[124] In addition, the argument of some scholars – that a government in exile, despite losing effectiveness, is entitled to invite foreign intervention based on its legitimacy or popular support – is not supported by practice.[125]

Moreover, under the Ukrainian Constitution, it is *Verkhovna Rada* that is authorised to approve decisions on inviting foreign troops onto the territory of Ukraine.[126] Therefore, President Yanukovych's request was not a valid consent under the relevant provision of ARSIWA.[127] In any case, it is difficult to accept

---

122 See *supra*. On the legality of the use of force if carried out on the basis of the consent of a territorial State, see O Dörr and A Randelzhofer, 'Article 2(4)' in B Simma and others (eds), *The Charter of the United Nations: A Commentary*, Volume I (3rd edn, OUP 2012), para 33.

123 See *supra*. "The international legal order is not a legal order of legal orders, but a legal order of sovereign political communities bearing the 'inalienable right' to choose their own political systems, and therefore to breach, alter, or overthrow their existing constitutions." BR Roth, 'The Virtues of Bright Lines: Self-Determination, Secession, and External Intervention' (2015) 16 German LJ 384, 388–389.

124 Corten (n 30) 33. Similarly, Bílková, 'The Use of Force by the Russian Federation in Crimea' (n 4) 42; JA Green, 'The Annexation of Crimea: Russia, Passportisation and the Protection of Nationals Revisited' (2014) 1 Journal on the Use of Force and International Law 3, 6–7; Roth (n 123) 389; Miklasová (n 4) 9–10.

125 The use of force in Kuwait and Haiti was carried out under the authorization of the UNSC. Tancredi (n 75) 16–17; Marxsen, 'The Crimea Crisis' (n 36) 377. In any case, authors also highlight that despite not fulfilling the constitutional requirements for impeachment, a rather clear vote in favour of his ousting proves that Yanukovych lacked legitimacy and popular support. G Wilson, 'Crimea: Some Observations on Secession and Intervention in Partial Response to Mullerson and Tolstykh' (2015) 14 Chinese Journal of International Law 217, 221; Marxsen, 'The Crimea Crisis' (n 36) 379.

126 Constitution of Ukraine (n 89) art 85(23).

127 Valid consent requires answering the question of whether "the agent or person who gave the consent was authorized to do so on behalf of the State (and if, whether the lack of that authority was known or ought to have been known to the acting State)." ILC, Draft Articles on the Responsibility of States for Internationally Wrongful Acts, with Commentaries in 'Report of the International Law Commission on the Work of its Fifty-Third Session (23 April–1 June and 2 July–10 August 2001)' UN Doc A/56/10 commentary to art 20, para 4 ("ARSIWA"). Mr Yanukovych was not authorized to invite foreign troops to Ukraine; this lack of authorization must have been known to Russia. Bílková, 'The Use of Force by the Russian Federation in Crimea' (n 4) 41–42; OHCHR, 'Report on the Human Rights Situation in Ukraine' (15 April 2014), para 4; Tancredi (n 75) 18.

that Yanukovych would have been authorised to invite foreign troops to undermine territorial integrity in Ukraine and to dissect part of its territory.[128]

After the declaration of independence, Russia started relying on the request from the Crimean authorities.[129] Under international law, the representatives of territorial sub-units are not authorised to request a valid military intervention.[130]

Secondly, Russia also claimed that its use of force was necessary to protect Russians in Crimea.[131] Firstly, it is difficult to accept that the justification of protection of nationals abroad, which is sometimes seen as the extension of the right to self-defence under Article 51 UN Charter,[132] and sometimes as a customary exception from the prohibition of the use of force under Article 2(4) UN Charter,[133] exists in positive international law.[134] Secondly, even though there were some reports of passportisation in Crimea,[135] it is difficult to assess

128 Bílková, 'The Use of Force by the Russian Federation in Crimea' (n 4) 42; Tancredi (n 75) 18; Marxsen, 'The Crimea Crisis' (n 36) 379.

129 See *supra*.

130 *Military and Paramilitary Activities in and against Nicaragua* (*Nicaragua v United States of America*) (Merits) [1986] ICJ Rep 14, para 246 ("*Nicaragua*"); Bílková, 'The Use of Force by the Russian Federation in Crimea' (n 4) 40–41; Green (n 124) 7; Wilson (n 125) 221.

131 The intervention was said to be justified because it prevented casualties. "Those who opposed the coup were immediately threatened with repression. Naturally, the first in line here was Crimea, the Russian-speaking Crimea … [I]f the Crimean local self-defence units had not taken the situation under control, there could have been casualties as well. Fortunately this did not happen." Putin's Address of 18 March 2014 (n 34).

132 Independent International Fact-Finding Mission on the Conflict in Georgia, *Report* (Vol II, IIFFMCG 2009) 287–288 ("Report").

133 ibid 285–287. Sometimes, the rescue of nationals abroad is justified as falling below the threshold of intensity required by Article 2(4) UN Charter. ibid 286.

134 For the same conclusion see Espinosa (n 5) 111; Report (n 132) 285–288. Intervention to protect nationals abroad "should not be used as a pretext for military intervention and should not have as a consequence the stationing of troops in order to ensure the continued protection of the citizens in question." CoE (Venice Commission), 'Opinion on the Federal Law on the Amendments to the Federal Law on Defence of the Russian Federation' (21 December 2010) CDL-AD (2010)052, para 46 and see paras 37–46.

135 E Sherwin, 'Caucasus History Almost Repeats Itself in Crimea' (*DW*, 8 March 2013) <https://www.dw.com/en/caucasus-history-almost-repeats-itself-in-crimea/a-17482549> accessed 22 June 2019; A Blomfield, 'Russia Distributing Passports in the Crimea' (*The Telegraph*, 17 August 2008) <https://www.telegraph.co.uk/news/worldnews/europe/ukraine/2575421/Russia-distributing-passports-in-the-Crimea.html> accessed 22 June 2019; K Stallard-Blanchetter, 'Russia Stands With Putin Over Ukraine Gamble' (*Sky News*, 2 March 2014) <https://news.sky.com/story/russia-stands-with-putin-over-ukraine-gamble-10415367> accessed 22 June 2019. Nevertheless, as will be shown below, the international illegality of this policy *per se* seems to be more arguable than would seem at the first sight. See *infra* the section on Abkhazia and South Ossetia.

the exact number of Russian nationals in Crimea (apart from the Russian soldiers already stationed there), especially since Ukrainian legislation bars dual nationality and Russian laws at the time did not provide a clear-cut basis for a large-scale grant of Russian citizenship to Russian-speaking, non-resident Ukrainian nationals.[136] The argument seems to have relied mostly on ethnic grounds and as such exceeded the contours of a traditional understanding of the doctrine, creating a dangerous precedent for intervention in countries with ethnic minorities.[137]

Thirdly, the conditions developed by the doctrine for the implementation of this doctrinal exception are extremely narrow and specific. The scholarship usually requires that the lives of nationals have to be genuinely in danger, that the territorial sovereign fails to protect them, that the intervening State does not pursue any other aims than the protection of nationals, and that the use of military force is proportionate to the purpose of the operation and thus its impact on the State's territory is minimal.[138] In the case of Russia's intervention in Crimea, the Russian minority was not in genuine danger[139] and Russia's intervention, resulting in Crimea's incorporation into to Russia, clearly

---

136 Under the Russian Citizenship Law at the time, non-residents of the Russian Federation could have obtained Russian citizenship through a simplified procedure if they lived in the components of the former USSR and remained stateless. This provision was the basis for the grant of Russian citizenship to populations in breakaway regions. See 'Federal Law on the Citizenship of Russian Federation No 62-F3 (31 May 2002) as amended, Article 14(1) <http://www.consultant.ru/document/cons_doc_LAW_36927/> accessed 22 June 2019 (*in Russian*) ("Russian Citizenship Law"). The amendment came into force on 20 April 2014; it made it easier for Russian-speakers to apply for Russian citizenship, but at the time Crimea had already been incorporated into to Russia (Article 14 (2.1)). Another amendment was passed in 2017 to make it easier specifically for Ukrainian nationals to renounce their Ukrainian nationality. A certified application, rather than a decision by Ukraine, is enough to prove the renunciation. (Article 14 (2.1)).

137 Walter (n 86) 308. See also Hilpold (n 1) 253–255; Marxsen, 'The Crimea Crisis' (n 36) 374; Espinosa (n 5) 112.

138 Dörr and Randelzhofer (n 122) para 61; CHM Waldock, 'The Regulation of the Use of Force by Individual States in International Law' in (1952) 81 RCADI 451, 467.

139 International organizations and observers came to the same conclusion. See 'Developing Situation in Crimea Alarming, Says OSCE High Commissioner on National Minorities' (*OSCE Press Release*, 6 March 2014) <https://www.osce.org/hcnm/116180> accessed 7 February 2019. OHCHR, 'Report on the Human Rights Situation in Ukraine' (15 April 2014), para 89. See Espinosa (n 5) 111–113; Bílková, 'The Use of Force by the Russian Federation in Crimea' (n 4) 47. Hilpold (n 1) 253; Tancredi (n 75) 12; Marxsen, 'The Crimea Crisis' (n 36) 374; Walter (n 86) 309. See also *supra* for the assessment of the applicability of remedial secession in Crimea.

went beyond a limited blitz-threshold foreseen by the doctrine.[140] In fact, the ECtHR established (in the context of determining Russia's effective control over Crimea) that "there was no concrete evidence to suggest that there had been any real threat to the Russian troops stationed in Crimea at the time."[141] Instead a real intent of the military operation followed directly from the statement of President Putin concerning his decision to "start working on the return of Crimea to the Russian Federation."[142] Therefore, overall, this argument also cannot justify Russia's use of force in Crimea.

Thus, by deploying its regular troops to Crimea, initially under the disguise of Little Green Men;[143] by using its troops stationed on the peninsula under the relevant treaties with Ukraine in contravention of the conditions provided therein;[144] and by military naval blockade,[145] Russia violated a peremptory prohibition of the use of force as contained in Article 2(4) UN Charter,[146]

140 Bílková, 'The Use of Force by the Russian Federation in Crimea' (n 4) 47; Tancredi (n 75) 13; Walter (n 86) 309.

141 *Ukraine v Russia (re Crimea)* (n 10) para 326 in connection with para 324.

142 ibid para 324.

143 Definition of Aggression, UNGA Res 3314 (XXIX) (14 December 1974) UN Doc A/RES/3314(XXIX), art 3(a) ("Definition of Aggression"). See Bílková, 'The Use of Force by the Russian Federation in Crimea' (n 4) 32–34; Tancredi (n 75) 20–21.

144 President Putin claimed that "Russia's Armed Forces never entered Crimea; they were there already in line with an international agreement. True, we did enhance our forces there; however … we did not exceed the personnel limit of our Armed Forces in Crimea, which is set at 25 000, because there was no need to do so." Putin's Address of 18 March 2014 (n 34). Notwithstanding, the actions of Russian armed forces in Crimea operating outside of their bases and supporting pro-Russian separatists seem to be in contravention of Article 6(1) of the 1997 Status of Forces Agreement, according to which military units operating in their place of deployment "respect the sovereignty of Ukraine, observe its legislation and do not allow interference into internal affairs of Ukraine" and with Article 15(5) according to which movements associated with the activities of military units outside their places of deployment, "are carried out after consultation with the competent authorities of Ukraine." Bílková, 'The Use of Force by the Russian Federation in Crimea' (n 4) 32–34. Indeed, the Definition of Aggression cites as an example of an act of aggression the use of force by armed of forces on the territory of one State with the agreement of that State in contravention of the conditions therein. Definition of Aggression (n 143) art 3(e). See also Tancredi (n 75) 19–20. While the ECtHR stated that the compliance of the Russian military presence with the applicable agreements between Russia and Ukraine "cannot be decisive" for the issue of effective control, it also made several observations, which indirectly confirm the illegality of such presence and the unlawfulness of the conduct of Russian troops in the period between 27 February and 18 March 2014. See *Ukraine v Russia (re Crimea)* para 320 and 324–327.

145 Definition of Aggression (n 143) art 3(c). Tancredi (n 75) 20.

146 UN Charter (n 121) art 2(4). For the peremptory character of prohibition, see ARSIWA (n 127) commentary to art 40, para 4. O Dörr, 'Prohibition of Use of Force' in MPEPIL (online

amounting to military aggression and an armed attack against Ukraine under Article 51 UN Charter.[147]

By using direct force against Ukraine, Russia also violated other fundamental principles of international law, including the prohibition of intervention into the internal affairs of Ukraine[148] and its territorial integrity.[149] Thereby, Russia also violated specific provisions of the Minsk Agreement, the Alma Ata Declaration, the Charter of CIS,[150] the Helsinki Final Pact,[151] as well as, specifically, the Ukraine-Russia Friendship Treaty in which Russia and Ukraine undertook to "honour each other's territorial integrity" and to "acknowledge the inviolability of the borders existing between them".[152] These actions also violated the Budapest Memorandum in which Russia, the UK and the US reaffirmed their commitment "to respect the independence and sovereignty and the existing borders of Ukraine" and "to refrain from the threat of use of force against the territorial integrity or political independence of Ukraine".[153]

The UNGA, in its Resolution on Territorial Integrity of Ukraine, affirmed "its commitment to the sovereignty, political independence, unity and territorial integrity of Ukraine within its internationally recognized borders",[154] and in its later resolution, it stressed that "the presence of Russian troops in Crimea is contrary to the national sovereignty, political independence and territorial

---

edn, OUP 2015) para 32. For the opposite view, see U Linderfalk, 'The Effect of Jus Cogens Norms: Whoever Opened Pandora's Box, Did You Ever Think About the Consequences?' (2007) 18 European Journal of International Law 853, 859 *et seq*. For the same conclusion, see Bílková, 'The Use of Force by the Russian Federation in Crimea' (n 4) 32. Hilpold (n 1) 247; Green (n 124) 6.

147 Definition of Aggression (n 143) art 3(a); UN Charter (n 121) art 51. See Tancredi (n 75) 29–34 for an extensive discussion. See also Bílková, 'The Use of Force by the Russian Federation in Crimea' (n 4) 32 and 36–37.

148 "[A]cts constituting a breach of the customary principle of non-intervention will also, if they directly or indirectly involve the use of force, constitute a breach of the principle of non-use of force in international relations." *Nicaragua* (n 130) para 209 and see also para 247.

149 UN Charter (n 121) art 2(4). See *supra* Part 1, Chapter 4 on the principle of territorial integrity.

150 See *supra*.

151 Final Act of the Conference on the Security and Cooperation in Europe (1 August 1975) reprinted in (1975) principles II, III and IV reprinted in 14 ILM 1293–1298 ("Helsinki Final Act").

152 Ukraine-Russia Friendship Treaty (n 62).

153 Budapest Memorandum (n 3) para 1 and 2.

154 UNGA Res 68/262 (27 March 2014) UN Doc A/RES/68/262, para 1. See also OSCE (PA), 'Resolution on the Restoration of the Sovereignty and Territorial Integrity of Ukraine' (9 July 2017), para 18.

integrity of Ukraine."[155] EU, NATO, PACE and the OSCE PA also condemned the violation of territorial integrity and the sovereignty of Ukraine by the Russian armed forces.[156]

The EU, the OSCE PA and PACE also characterised these acts of the Russian Federation as aggression.[157] According to PACE, the annexation of Crimea by the Russian Federation and its actions leading up to it constitute "grave violation of international law", including the UN Charter and the OSCE Helsinki Final Act,[158] and it urged the Russian Federation "to reverse the illegal annexation of Crimea".[159] PACE also referred to "the aggression started on 20 February 2014, which included the invasion, occupation and illegal annexation of Crimea by the Russian Federation."[160] The EU and G7 also reached the same conclusions.[161]

155 UNGA Res 73/194 (23 January 2019) UN Doc A/RES/73/194, para 1.

156 CoE (PACE) Res 1990 (10 April 2014), para 1; Council of European Union (Foreign Affairs), 'Council Conclusions on Ukraine' (3 March 2014), para 1; Council of European Union, 'Statement of the Heads of State or Government on Ukraine' (6 March 2014), para 2; NATO, 'Statement by the North Atlantic Council Following Meeting Atlantic Council Following Meeting Under Article 4 of the Washington Treaty' (4 March 2014) <https://www.nato.int/cps/en/natolive/news_107716.htm> accessed 7 February 2014; OSCE (PA), 'Resolution on Clear, Gross and Uncorrected Violations of Helsinki Principles by the Russian Federation' (1 July 2014), para 10.

157 Council of European Union (Foreign Affairs), 'Council Conclusions on Ukraine' (3 March 2014), para 1; European Parliament, 'Resolution on the Invasion of Ukraine by Russia' 2014/2627(RSP) (13 March 2014), para 1; European Parliament, 'Resolution on Ukraine' 2014/2717(RSP) (17 July 2014), para 7; CoE (PACE) Res 2067 (25 June 2015), para 2; OSCE (PA), 'Resolution on Ongoing Violations of Human Rights and Fundamental Freedoms in the Autonomous Republic of Crimea and the City of Sevastopol (Ukraine)' (11 July 2018), para 24. The 2017's OSCE resolution referred to "hybrid aggression." OSCE (PA), 'Resolution on the Restoration of the Sovereignty and Territorial Integrity of Ukraine' (9 July 2017), para 19; OSCE (PA), 'Resolution on Violations of Human Rights and Fundamental Freedoms in the Autonomous Republic of Crimea and the City of Sevastopol (Ukraine)' (4 July 2016), para 18.

158 The actions include, in particular, "the military occupation of the Ukrainian territory and the threat of the use of military force, the recognition of the results of the illegal so-called referendum." CoE (PACE) Res 1990 (10 April 2014), para 3; CoE (PACE) Res 2034 (28 January 2015), para 3. See for similar conclusions OSCE (PA), 'Resolution on Clear, Gross and Uncorrected Violations of Helsinki Principles by the Russian Federation' (1 July 2014), para 10; OSCE (PA), 'Resolution on the Continuation of Clear, Gross and Uncorrected Violations of OSCE Commitments and International Norms by the Russian Federation' (8 July 2015), para 19.

159 CoE (PACE) Res 2034 (28 January 2015), para 4.1; CoE (PACE) Res 2063 (24 June 2015), para 8.2.

160 CoE (PACE) Res 2482 (26 January 2023), para 1.

161 Council of European Union (Foreign Affairs), 'Council Conclusions on Ukraine' (3 March 2014), para 1; G7, 'Statement by G7 Leaders on Ukraine' (12 March 2014) <http://www.g8.utoronto.ca/summit/2014sochi/ukraine_140302.html> accessed 15 February 2019.

2.7 *Legal Status of Crimea*

From the above-mentioned, it follows that there was no legal ground on which the Republic of Crimea could secede from Ukraine. Moreover, Russia's illegal use of force was instrumental to this apparent secessionist claim. In fact, a military takeover of Crimea by Russian troops was already underway on 27 February 2014 when the change of the Crimean government took place, and well before the announcement of an independence referendum. As already mentioned, these secessionist plans were in fact added in the course of the military takeover.

Thus, the installation of a new government and the initiation and implementation of a secessionist bid, including the referendum, was a direct result of Russia's illegal use of force.[162] This conclusion compromises the independence of a purported new republic.[163] In addition, as follows from Part 1, Chapter 2 in cases where the secessionist attempt and declaration of independence result from the violation of peremptory norms, the emergence of a new State is precluded.[164] Thus, due to the peremptory illegality of Crimea's secessionist attempt and the illegal and invalid declaration of independence, the Republic of Crimea was precluded from becoming a new State.[165] For a brief period, the Republic of Crimea bore the characteristics of illegal secessionist entities, but its ostensible existence was only ephemeral. Consequently, since the Crimean Republic never emerged as a State, it could not have entered into the Russia-Crimea Agreement on Accession.[166] Therefore, this agreement is non-existent due to lack of one of its subjects.[167] Since the Republic of Crimea never seceded from Ukraine, its incorporation into Russia represents a prominent example of a forcible acquisition of territory – an illegal and invalid annexation.[168]

162 See Van den Driest (n 71) 359; Müllerson (n 112) 140.

163 Tancredi (n 75) 28. Walter also points out that the true purpose of the Crimean Republic was never to establish independent statehood, but to join Russia. In any case, in this short period, it is not possible to speak about an independent public power established in this supposed new republic. Walter (n 86) 303–304.

164 See *supra* Part 1, Chapter 2.

165 See Van den Driest (n 71) 359; Marxsen, 'The Crimea Crisis' (n 36) 384; Vidmar (n 86) 375–376; Geifs (n 37) 434–435. See also on illegality of Crimea's declaration of independence Walter (n 86) 301–303.

166 Marxsen, 'The Crimea Crisis' (n 36) 390. On the previous, ultimately abandoned, draft law of the Russian Federation that sought to dispense with the requirement of a bilateral treaty in the absence of an effective sovereign state government in a foreign state, Bílková, 'Territorial (Se)Cession in Light of Recent Events in Crimea' (n 112) 195–202.

167 Tancredi (n 75) 24.

168 See Geifs (n 37) 432–434; Peters (n 103) 257; MG Kohen, 'Conquest' in MPEPIL (online edn, OUP 2015), para 4.

"Consequently, no territorial change has occurred, Crimea remains Ukrainian territory. The presence of Russian State organs and, in particular, of Russian armed forces is presence on a foreign territory."[169] With respect to Crimea, "[a]t issue now is not the non-recognition of an aspirant State, but rather non-recognition of the territorial change of Russia."[170]

---

169 M Bothe, 'The Current Status of Crimea: Russian Territory, Occupied Territory or What' (2014) 53 Military Law and Law of War Review 99, 101. The same conclusion follows from the Ukrainian Law on Temporarily Occupied Territory of Ukraine adopted in April 2014, according to which "[t]he temporarily occupied territory of Ukraine ... is an integral part of the territory of Ukraine. The application of the Constitution and the laws of Ukraine shall extend to such territory." 'Law of Ukraine No 1207-VII On Securing the Rights and Freedoms of Citizens and the Legal Regime on the Temporarily Occupied Territory of Ukraine' (adopted 15 April 2014, entered into force 27 April 2014) art 1 <https://www.refworld.org/docid/5379ab8e4.html> accessed 10 January 2020 ("Law on Temporarily Occupied Territory of Ukraine").

170 Borgen (n 68) 254.

CHAPTER 12

Donetsk and Luhansk People's Republics, Kherson and Zaporizhzhia Regions

There was no distinct secessionist movement in Donbas with its majority of Russian speakers in the 1990s.[1] The secessionist crisis in Eastern Ukraine only began unfolding around the same time as Crimea's annexation in 2014. While legal arguments put forward by separatists in Eastern Ukraine did not essentially differ from those justifying Crimea's secession,[2] unlike in Crimea, the issue of Russia's direct or indirect involvement in the 2014–2022 conflict was highly contested.

Even though Russia's president Putin did not deny there were people carrying out certain military tasks in Eastern Ukraine, he maintained that Russia's regular troops never intervened in this conflict.[3] Formally, Russia denied being a party to the conflict. As a signatory, it claimed to be the guarantor of the Minsk agreements.[4] Nevertheless, a factual question about Russia's interference is of critical importance. It is decisive for the legal assessment

1 According to the last Soviet census in 1989, even though the majority of the population of this region identified as Ukrainians, the prevailing language was Russian. See 'Minorities at Risk Project: Chronology for Russians in Ukraine' (2004) <https://www.refworld.org/docid/469f38ed5.html> accessed 12 May 2020.

2 See *infra*.

3 "Finally, the question of whether Russian troops are present in Ukraine … I can tell you outright and unequivocally that there are no Russian troops in Ukraine." 'Direct Line with Vladimir Putin' (*President of Russia's Official Website*, 16 April 2015) <http://en.kremlin.ru/events/president/news/49261> accessed 7 February 2019. "'We never said there were not people there who carried out certain tasks including in the military sphere.' He insisted this was not the same as regular Russian troops." S Walker, 'Putin Admits Russian Military Presence in Ukraine For First Time' (*The Guardian*, 17 December 2015) <https://www.theguardian.com/world/2015/dec/17/vladimir-putin-admits-russian-military-presence-ukraine> accessed 7 February 2019.

4 Protocol on the Results of Consultations of the Trilateral Contact Group (signed 5 September 2014) <http://www.osce.org/home/123257> accessed 16 November 2016 (*in Russian*) ("Minsk I"); Memorandum Outlining the Parameters for the Implementation of Commitments of the Minsk Protocol of 5 September 2014 (signed 19 September 2014) <http://www.osce.org/home/123806> accessed 16 November 2016 (*in Russian*) ("Minsk Memorandum"); Package of Measures for the Implementation of the Minsk Agreements (signed 12 February 2015) <http://www.osce.org/ru/cio/140221?download=true> accessed 7 February 2019 (*in Russian*) ("Minsk II") (together as "Minsk agreements").

of the secessionist claim of the Donbas separatists, for the classification of the 2014–2022 conflict as non-international or international, for the applicability of various legal regimes and for matters of international responsibility. Therefore, the establishment of facts proving or disproving the issue of Russia's interference in the purported secessionist attempt and related conflict between 2014 and 2022 is the key focus of the analysis of the events of the corresponding period.

An all-out attack by the Russian Armed Forces against the Ukrainian territory, which started on 24 February 2022 and was preceded by Russia's recognition of the Donetsk People's Republic (DPR) and Luhansk People's Republic (LPR), radically transformed the existing *status quo*. The scale and the proclaimed objectives of the Russian offensive war ("demilitarise and denazify Ukraine")[5] are unprecedented by comparison with the 2014–2022 conflict and any other conflict examined in this monograph.

Nevertheless, given the legal justifications presented by the Russian Federation, in particular, the collective self-defense of the DPR and LPR, the question of the statehood of these two entities and the lawfulness of their recognition by Russia on the eve of the all-out attack are critical. The answer to these questions depends on the existence and legality of Russian interference in the secessionist attempts and conflict in the 2014–2022 period. Thus, even from the perspective of general international law governing secession, the two periods are interlinked and part of a larger dynamic.[6] Moreover, other ostensibly secessionist developments occurred in the course of a full-scale Russian attack against Ukraine – holding the referenda in the four regions of Ukraine in the areas under Russia's control, purported declarations of independence of the Kherson and Zaporizhzhia Regions, and the purported incorporation of four regions to Russia. They are also examined in the following pages.

5 V Putin, 'Address by President of the Russian Federation' (The Kremlin, Moscow, 24 February 2022) <http://en.kremlin.ru/events/president/transcripts/67843> accessed 13 August 2023 ("24 February 2022 Address").

6 See on the *ius ad bellum* and *ius in bello* A Kleczkowska, 'Acts of Aggression During an Ongoing Armed Conflict: How Can We View the Events of February 24?' (*Opinio Juris*, 14 March 2022) <http://opiniojuris.org/2022/03/14/acts-of-aggression-during-an-ongoing-armed-conflict-how-can-we-view-the-events-of-february-24/> accessed 13 August 2023.

1 Outline of the Secessionist Attempts

1.1 *DPR and LPR in the 2014–2022 Period*

Initially, a number of pro-Russian demonstrations calling *inter alia* for referendum on Ukraine's federalisation took place in cities of Eastern Ukraine around the time of Crimea's annexation.[7] In Donetsk and Kharkiv on 1 March 2014 and Luhansk on 9 March 2014, protesters seized government buildings.[8] But by 10 March 2014, the Ukrainian police had re-captured them.[9]

However, on 6 April 2014, the pro-Russian protesters re-seized regional administrative buildings in Donetsk and then declared the Donetsk People's Republic (DNR) on 7 April 2014.[10] The capture of administrative buildings in other Eastern Ukrainian cities followed.[11] According to the OHCHR, the seizure of buildings across the Donetsk and Luhansk regions was conducted "in a well-organized and coordinated fashion".[12] The Luhansk People's Republic (LPR) was declared on 27 April 2014.[13] The DPR and LPR organised secessionist referenda on 11 May 2014, which were said to bring overwhelming results in favour of independence.[14] Around this time, Russian citizens such as Igor

7 M Kofman and others, *Lessons from Russia's Operations in Crimea and Eastern Ukraine* (RAND Corporation 2017) 33–36.

8 ibid 34.

9 ibid, 37–38.

10 District Soviet of Donetsk District, 'Act on Declaration State Independence of the Donetsk People's Republic' (7 April 2014) <https://worldconstitutions.ru/?p=1060&attempt=1> accessed 7 February 2019 (*in Russian*). The declaration was to become valid upon its confirmation in an all-district referendum; Kofman (n 7) 39–40.

11 In this context, it is interesting to note that in Kharkiv, for example, pro-Russian separatists seized the building of the local opera and ballet thinking it was the city hall building. This seems to suggest that the separatist were not local residents. See 'Separatists in Kharkiv Confused the City Hall Building with the Opera and Ballet Theatre' (*Uralsk Week*, 7 April 2014) <https://www.uralskweek.kz/2014/04/07/separatisty-v-xarkove-pereputali-zdanie-merii-s-teatrom-opery-i-baleta/> accessed 31 October 2023 (*in Russian*).

12 OHCHR, 'Human Rights Violations and Abuses and International Humanitarian Law Violations Committed in the Context of the Ilovaisk Events in August 2014' (9 August 2018), para 4 ("Report on Ilovaisk Events").

13 Congress of Representatives of Territorial Communities, Political Parties and Public Organizations, 'Act on Declaration State Independence of the Luhansk People's Republic' (27 April 2014) <https://lugansk-lg-ua.livejournal.com/177285.html> accessed 7 February 2019 (*in Russian*). The declaration was to become valid upon its confirmation in all-district referendum.

14 It was claimed that turnout in the DPR was 74.87%, of which 89.7% voted for independence. In the LPR, the turnout was 75%, of which 96.2% voted for independence. The DPR's Prime Minister Pushilin also requested Russia to consider the DPR's joining the Russian Federation. See 'Luhansk and Donetsk Voted for Independence' (*RIA Novosti*, 12 May

Girkin (Strelkov), the so-called hero of the war in Transnistria and alleged Russian intelligence officer, became the leaders of the DPR.[15]

On 14 April 2014, Ukraine initiated anti-terrorist operations (ATO) to retake control of the territory in the East.[16] Initially, the Ukrainian military was underprepared to counter secessionists, and Ukrainian police either did not intervene or defected to the separatists.[17] On 30 April 2014, Ukraine's acting Head of State confirmed Ukraine had lost control of its eastern regions.[18] Around this time, it was reported that a large number of Russian volunteers, including the so-called Vostok Battalion formed of Russian and Chechen fighters, among others, had begun participating in the conflict.[19] However, it was not immediately evident whether Russian authorities coordinated their influx into Ukraine.[20] In late May 2014, the DPR and LPR announced the formation of the

---

2014) <https://ria.ru/20140512/1007522425.html> accessed 7 February 2019 (*in Russian*). See also 'Appeal of the Peoples of the Luhansk People's Republic' (12 May 2014) <https://lugansk-lg-ua.livejournal.com/177285.html> accessed 7 February 2019 (*in Russian*), in which the LPR asks the UN and other international organizations to recognise its statehood.

15 Strelkov claims to have persuaded the Russian president to start a war in Eastern Ukraine. See B Bidder, 'The Man Who Started the War in Ukraine' (*Spegiel International*, 18 March 2015) <http://www.spiegel.de/international/europe/the-ukraine-war-from-perspective-of-russian-nationalists-a-1023801.html> accessed 7 February 2019. Strelkov became the Minister of Defence of the DPR, while another Russian citizen, Aleksandr Borodai, became its Prime Minister. See T Balmforth, 'A Guide to the Separatists of Eastern Ukraine' (*RFE/RL*, 3 June 2014) <https://www.rferl.org/a/ukraine-separatists-whos-who/25408875.html> accessed 7 February 2019; Kofman (n 7) 38–40. For the view that the presence of these figures confirmed that Russia did not have control over these events at that time, see P Robinson, 'Russia's Role in the War in Donbass, and the Threat to European Security' (2016) 17 European Politics and Society 506, 512.

16 Report on Ilovaisk Events (n 12) para 4.

17 Kofman (n 7) 41.

18 L Harding, 'Ukraine's Government Has Lost Control of East, Says Acting President' (*The Guardian*, 30 April 2014) <https://www.theguardian.com/world/2014/apr/30/ukraine-government-lost-control-east-acting-president> accessed 7 February 2019.

19 C Bigg, 'Vostok Battalion, A Powerful New Player in Eastern Ukraine' (*RFE/RL*, 30 May 2014) <https://www.rferl.org/a/vostok-battalion-a-powerful-new-player-in-eastern-ukraine/25404785.html> accessed 7 February 2019.

20 A Luhn, 'Volunteers or Paid Fighters? The Vostok Battalion Looms Large in War With Kiev' (*The Guardian*, 6 June 2014) <https://www.theguardian.com/world/2014/jun/06/the-vostok-battalion-shaping-the-eastern-ukraine-conflict> accessed 7 February 2019; A Speri, 'Yes, There Are Chechen Fighters in Ukraine, and Nobody Knows Who Sent Them There' (*Vice News*, 28 May 2014) <https://news.vice.com/en_us/article/qvanpp/yes-there-are-chechen-fighters-in-ukraine-and-nobody-knows-who-sent-them-there> accessed 7 February 2019. See *infra* for further details.

Federal State of New Russia (Novo Rossyia), but the project was abandoned a year later.[21]

However, by August 2014, the Ukrainian army was close to the border and encircled the self-proclaimed republics.[22] In this context, according to numerous reports, on 24 August 2014, regular Russian troops intervened in the Battle of Ilovaisk, leading to the defeat of the Ukrainian army and its retreat.[23] As a result, the ceasefire agreement known as Minsk I was signed on 5 September 2014.[24] However, its terms were not followed, and in January 2015, the second offensive took place resulting in another Ukrainian defeat in the Battle of Debaltseve.[25] It was reported that armed Russian troops also took part in this offensive.[26] The Minsk II ceasefire agreement was signed on 12 February 2015.[27]

---

21 G Jasutis, 'The Conflict in Eastern Ukraine (Donbass): Dire Consequences and Zero Reconciliation' in A Bellal (ed), *The War Report: Armed Conflicts in 2018* (Geneva Academy 2019) 151.

22 Kofman (n 7) 44.

23 See *infra*.

24 Minsk I (n 4).

25 Kofman (n 7) 45.

26 See *infra*.

27 Minsk II (n 4). Minsk II contained conventional ceasefire agreement provisions. It provided for military clauses such as ceasefire, withdrawal of heavy weapons and foreign fighters from Ukraine, monitoring by the OSCE, reinstatement of the border between Russia and Ukraine, exchange of prisoners and amnesty for combatants; it also contained political provisions, which foresaw a dialogue on elections in eastern Ukraine, a law on the special status of the Donetsk and Luhansk regions and constitutional reform in Ukraine, including decentralisation. As foreseen by Minsk II, *Verhovna Rada* adopted 'Law of Ukraine on Interim Self-Government Order in Certain Areas of the Donetsk and Luhansk Regions 1680-VII' (adopted 16 September 2014, entered into force 18 October 2014) <https://zakon.rada.gov.ua/laws/show/1680-18#Text> accessed 31 October 2023 (*in Ukrainian*) ("Law on Special Status"). Even though this law became effective in October 2014, its main substantive provisions (articles 2–9) would come into force only after local elections are held in the Donetsk and Luhansk regions in compliance with international standards and under conditions of *inter alia* withdrawal of all illegal formations and fighters and mercenaries from Ukraine. ibid, art 10(4). In 2020, Ukraine extended the validity of the law by the end of 2022. The implementation of Minsk II stalled given different interpretations regarding the sequencing of obligations. While Ukraine insisted on the prioritisation of the fulfilment of military clauses as a precondition to political settlement, for Russia, local elections and special status were prerequisites to a military stabilisation. M Boulègue, *The Political and Military Implications of the Minsk 2 Agreements: Note nº 11/2016* (Fondation pour la recherche stratégique 2016) 4–5. Arguably, the biggest flaw of Minsk II stemmed from the fact that Russia was not acknowledged there as a party to the conflict. See further on the Ukrainian legislation pertaining to the legal regime of Donbas (including also the 2018 Reintegration of Donbas Law) M Rabinovych, 'The Interplay between Ukraine's Domestic Legislation on Conflict and Uncontrolled Territories and its

Over the years, violations of the Minsk agreements were observed on a daily basis,[28] including a major escalation in 2017.[29] In parallel, the governing structures of the DPR and LPR consolidated, reportedly thanks to the support of the Russian Federation.[30] No member of the UN, including the Russian Federation, had recognised the DPR and LPR as sovereign States until February 2022.

1.2 *Russia's Involvement in the 2014–2022 Conflict*

As has already been mentioned, the issue of Russia's involvement in the conflict is of critical importance. Fundamentally, the authoritative and detailed findings of fact of the European Court of Human Rights ("ECtHR" or "the Court") in the 2023 admissibility decision in *Ukraine and the Netherlands v Russia* are of primary relevance.[31] The ECtHR made these conclusions to ascertain the existence of Russia's effective control over the relevant parts of the Donetsk and Luhansk regions to establish jurisdiction under Article 1 European Convention on Human Rights ("ECHR").[32] However, these authoritative findings are also relevant for the present analysis under the *jus ad bellum* and international law relevant to secession. Beyond the factual findings of the ECtHR, the chapter outlines the domestic judgments and evidence from publicly available sources,

---

Strategic Use of "Lawfare" before Russia's 2022 Invasion of Ukraine – A Troubled Nexus?' (2022) 47 Review of Central and East European Law 268. See *infra* Chapter 16.

28 Office of the Prosecutor of the International Criminal Court, 'Report on Preliminary Examination Activities' (14 November 2016), para 167 ("Report on Preliminary Examination Activities").

29 The situation was described as 'slow burning.' B Jarábik and A Racz, 'Donbas Diplomacy: Ukraine Bides Its Time' (*Carnegie*, 16 March 2018) <https://carnegieendowment.org/posts/2018/04/donbas-diplomacy-ukraine-bides-its-time?lang=en> accessed 7 October 2023. See also UNSC Press Statement on the escalation of fighting 'Security Council Press Statement on Deterioration of Situation in Donetsk Region, Ukraine' (*UN Press Release*, 31 January 2017) <https://www.un.org/press/en/2017/sc12700.doc.htm> accessed 7 February 2019.

30 See *infra*.

31 *Ukraine and the Netherlands v Russia* App nos 8019/16, 43800/14 and 28525/20 (ECtHR, 25 January 2023) ("*Ukraine and the Netherlands v Russia*").

32 The ECtHR examined extensive evidence and drew inferences. "Where the respondent State alone has access to information capable of corroborating or refuting the applicant's allegations but fails to provide a satisfactory and convincing explanation in respect of events that lie wholly, or in large part, within the exclusive knowledge of the State's authorities, the Court can draw inferences that may be unfavourable for that Government. Before it can do so, however, there must be concordant elements supporting the applicant's allegations." *Ukraine and the Netherlands v Russia* (n 31) para 436 and see also para 459.

such as international monitoring bodies, open sources intelligence reports, investigative journalistic reports and think-tank reports.

Three different aspects of Russia's involvement in the conflict in Eastern Ukraine will be highlighted. First is the question of intervention by Russian regular troops and cross-border shelling. Second is the degree of Russia's military support of the DPR and LPR, including the question of arming and financing the separatist forces, the nature of the relationship between the Russian authorities and local separatist militia, the Russian 'volunteers' and other hybrid actors forming part of these armed groups. Third, Russia's support of the DPR and LPR in financial, economic and political spheres will also be examined.

1.2.1 Intervention of Russia's Regular Troops and Cross-Border Shelling

Based on the extensive evidence, including, among others, the OSCE Border Mission reports, OHCHR's reports, witness statements, intercept calls, reports of the NGOs, Bellingcat investigations, the ECtHR concluded that "there were Russian military personnel in an active capacity in Donbass."[33]

> Russian soldiers fought in the armed groups and senior members of the Russian military were present in command positions in the separatist armed groups and entities from the outset. From at the latest August 2014 in the context of the battle of Ilovaisk, there was a large-scale deployment of Russian troops.[34]

Indeed, a variety of sources reported the intervention of Russia's regular troops in the conflict in Eastern Ukraine,[35] specifically in decisive moments of the conflict in late August 2014[36] and in early

---

33 *Ukraine and the Netherlands v Russia* (n 31) para 611.

34 ibid para 611.

35 'Proofs of the Russian Aggression: InformNapalm Releases Extensive Database of Evidence' (*InformNapalm*, 4 December 2018) <https://informnapalm.org/en/proofs-of-the-russian-aggression-informnapalm-releases-extensive-database-of-evidence/> accessed 7 February 2019. See also other publications confirming a direct intervention of Russian troops in the conflict. M Czuperski and others, *Hiding in Plain Sight: Putin's War in Ukraine* (Atlantic Council 2015) 15–16 and 25–28; 'The Boris Nemtsov Report in English: "Putin. The War," About the Involvement of Russia in the Eastern Ukraine Conflict and the Crimea' (2015) European Union Foreign Affairs Journal 5, 14–23 ("Nemtsov Report"). V Peshkov, 'The Donbas: Back in the USSR' (*European Council on Foreign Relations*, 1 September 2016) <https://www.ecfr.eu/article/essay_the_donbas_back_in_the_ussr> accessed 7 February 2019.

36 'NATO Releases Satellite Imagery Showing Russian Combat Troops Inside Ukraine' (*Press Release*, 28 August 2014) <https://www.nato.int/cps/en/natohq/news_112193.htm?selectedLocale=en> accessed 7 February 2019. 'Russia's Path(s) to War' (*Bellingcat*, 21 September

2015.[37] Journalists reported the paths of individual Russian on-duty soldiers taking part in the hostilities in Eastern Ukraine,[38] secrecy surrounding the deaths of Russian soldiers who took part in the conflict in Eastern Ukraine[39] and on the awarding of medals for bravery in combat at a time when Russia officially had no combat operations.[40] Reports also confirmed

---

2015) <https://www.bellingcat.com/news/uk-and-europe/2015/09/21/bellingcat-investigation-russias-paths-to-war/> accessed 7 February 2019. See also S Walker, 'New Evidence Emerges of Russian Role in Ukraine Conflict' (*The Guardian*, 18 August 2019) <https://www.theguardian.com/world/2019/aug/18/new-video-evidence-of-russian-tanks-in-ukraine-european-court-human-rights> accessed 19 August 2019; M Fisher, 'Let's Be Clear About This: Russia is Invading Ukraine Right Now' (*Vox*, 27 August 2014) <https://www.vox.com/2014/8/27/6069415/lets-be-clear-about-this-russia-is-invading-ukraine-right-now> accessed 7 February 2019; Nemtsov Report (n 35) 14–16; Robinson (n 15) 512–514; Jasutis (n 21) 154. See *Ukraine and the Netherlands v Russia* (n 31) paras 605–607.

37 E Kostychenko, 'We All Knew What We Had to Do and What Could Happen' (*Novaya Gazeta*, 2 March 2015) <https://www.novayagazeta.ru/articles/2015/03/02/63264-171-my-vse-znali-na-chto-idem-i-chto-mozhet-byt-187> (*in Russian*) and <http://euromaidanpress.com/2015/03/02/the-story-of-a-russian-soldiers-war-in-ukraine-we-all-knew-what-we-had-to-do-and-what-could-happen/> (*in English*) accessed 7 February 2019; '5th Tank Brigade of the Russian Army in the Battle for Debaltseve' (*InformNapalm*, 4 March 2015) <https://informnapalm.org/en/5th-tank-brigade-russian-army-battle-debaltseve/> accessed 7 February 2019; T Parfitt, 'Separatist Fighter Admits Russian Tanks, Troops "Decisive in Eastern Ukraine Battles"' (*The Telegraph*, 31 March 2015) <https://www.telegraph.co.uk/news/worldnews/europe/russia/11506774/Separatist-fighter-admits-Russian-tanks-troops-decisive-in-eastern-Ukraine-battles.html> accessed 8 February 2019; Robinson (n 15) 514–515.

38 'Selfie Soldiers: Russia Check in to Ukraine' (*Vice News*, 16 June 2015) <https://www.youtube.com/watch?v=2zssIFN2mso&has_verified=1> accessed 7 February 2019.

39 T Parfitt, 'Secret Dead of Russia's Undeclared War' (*The Telegraph*, 27 December 2014)<https://www.telegraph.co.uk/news/worldnews/europe/russia/11314817/Secret-dead-of-Russias-undeclared-war.html> accessed 8 February 2019. See also A Pivovarchuk, 'Silent Deaths: The Price of a Russian Soldier's Life' (*The Moscow Times*, 27 October 2014) <https://themoscowtimes.com/articles/silent-deaths-the-price-of-a-russian-soldiers-life-40795> accessed 7 February 2019; 'Russian Reporters "Attacked at Secret Soldier Burials"' (*BBC News*, 27 August 2014) <https://www.bbc.com/news/world-europe-28949582> accessed 7 February 2019; Czuperski (n 35) 17.

40 PR Gregory, 'Russian Combat Medals Put Lie to Putin's Claim of No Russian Troops in Ukraine' (*Forbes*, 6 September 2016) <https://www.forbes.com/sites/paulroderickgregory/2016/09/06/russian-combat-medals-put-lie-to-putins-claim-of-no-russian-troops-in-ukraine/> accessed 7 February 2019; 'Russia's War in Ukraine: The Medals and Treacherous Numbers' (*Bellingcat*, 31 August 2016) <https://www.bellingcat.com/news/uk-and-europe/2016/08/31/russias-war-ukraine-medals-treacherous-numbers/> accessed 7 February 2019.

shelling of Ukrainian army in Eastern Ukraine from positions in the Russian Federation.[41]

According to the Report of the Office of the Prosecutor ("OTP") of the International Criminal Court ("ICC"), "[t]he increased intensity of fighting during these periods has been attributed to alleged corresponding influxes of troops, vehicles and weaponry from the Russian Federation to reinforce the positions of the armed groups."[42] According to the judgment of the first instance court of the Hague in the MH17 criminal case, "[f]rom the first half of July 2014 onwards, Russian soldiers would regularly move across the border and cross-border attacks would take place."[43]

Additionally, even though the OSCE's Special Monitoring Mission (SMM) was careful about drawing conclusions on Russia's interference, over the years it also reported the presence of specific types of weapons and tracks crossing the unsecured border with Russia and talked to soldiers captured by the Ukrainian army who claimed to be Russian soldiers fighting on rotation in Ukraine.[44] Similarly, the OHCHR reported the apprehension of active servicemen and officers of the Russian Armed Forces by the Ukrainian army.[45] PACE, in numerous resolutions, called upon Russia to "withdraw all its troops,

41 S Case and K Anders, *Putin's Undeclared War: Summer 2014: Russian Artillery Strikes* (Bellingcat 2015); 'Russian Artillery Attacks on Ukraine 2014' (*Bellingcat*, 22 December 2017) <https://bellingcatukraine.carto.com/builder/79a5c4ec-c29d-11e6-9676-0e05a8b3e3d7/embed> accessed 7 February 2019; M Fischer, 'These Satellite Photos Show Russia Committing an Act of Overt War Against Ukraine' (*Vox*, 28 July 2014) <https://www.vox.com/2014/7/28/5934095/did-russia-just-cross-a-line-with-ukraine> accessed 7 February 2019; Czuperski (n 35) 18–19 and 28–31.

42 Report on Preliminary Examination Activities (n 28) para 166. See also *Ukraine and the Netherlands v Russia* (n 31) para 652.

43 *Judgment Nos 09-748004/19, 09-748005/19, 09-748006/19, 09-748007/19* (The Netherlands, District Court of the Hague) (17 November 2022) 4.4.3.1.3 ("District Court of the Hague").

44 'OSCE's Hug on Russian Involvement in Donbas War: "Facts Speak for Themselves"' (*Unian Information Agency*, 26 October 2018) <https://www.unian.info/war/10314300-osce-s-hug-on-russian-involvement-in-donbas-war-facts-speak-for-themselves.html> accessed 7 February 2019; A Mackinnon, 'Counting the Dead in Europe's Forgotten War' (*Foreign Policy*, 25 October 2018) <https://foreignpolicy.com/2018/10/25/counting-the-dead-in-europes-forgotten-war-ukraine-conflict-donbass-osce/> accessed 7 February 2019; 'OSCE "Sees Russian Soldiers, Weapons in Ukraine for Two Years"' (*Kyiv Post*, 26 March 2016) <https://www.kyivpost.com/article/content/ukraine-politics/osce-sees-russian-soldiers-weapons-in-ukraine-for-two-years-410764.html?cn-reloaded=1> accessed 7 February 2019. See *Ukraine and the Netherlands v Russia* (n 31) paras 598–599.

45 OHCHR, 'Report on the Human Rights Situation in Ukraine' (16 May to 15 August 2015), paras 58–59; OHCHR, 'Report on the Human Rights Situation in Ukraine' (16 August to 15 November 2015), para 180 and ftn 128. See *Ukraine and the Netherlands v Russia* (n 31) para 603.

including covert forces, from Ukrainian territory".[46] It also urged *inter alia* the Russian Federation "to stop all military operations in the east of Ukraine".[47]

1.2.2 Russia's Military Support of the DPR and LPR

Several questions need to be examined in order to assess Russia's connection to and military support of the DPR and LPR's militias. Firstly, it is the issue of arming separatists. This point outlines the evidence of the presence of the Russia-originated weapons in the separatist conflict and seeks to accentuate its impact on boosting the capacity of separatists. In particular, numerous reports, including open-source intelligence reports, identified different types of weaponry and equipment used throughout the conflict in Eastern Ukraine as originating from the Russian Armed Forces and other law-enforcement agencies – and as not capable of simply being captured during hostilities.[48] Some of these weapons and equipment were highly sophisticated; their operation required special training.[49]

Furthermore, the Memorandum to Minsk I of 19 September 2014 includes a provision on the withdrawal of heavy military equipment, including, specifically, the Tornado-G, Tornado-U and Tornado-S.[50] Minsk II also refers to the withdrawal of the Tornado-S.[51] According to the Nemtsov Report, the multiple-launch rocket system Tornado "is designed in Russia and has not been delivered to any foreign country".[52] Thus, if this information were correct, the presence of Russia-made heavy weaponry in the conflict would have been confirmed directly by both ceasefire agreements.

---

46 CoE (PACE) Res 2034 (28 January 2015), paras 7.1 and 16; See also CoE (PACE) Res 2063 (24 June 2015) para 3.5.

47 CoE (PACE) Res 2112 (21 April 2016), paras 9 and 9.1.

48 See 'Proofs of the Russian Aggression: InformNapalm Releases Extensive Database of Evidence' (*InformNapalm*, 4 December 2018) <https://informnapalm.org/en/proofs-of-the-russian-aggression-informnapalm-releases-extensive-database-of-evidence/> accessed 7 February 2019. Czuperski (n 35) 8–13 and 21–23; See also E Volochine, 'The Russian Secret Behind Ukraine's Self-Declared "Donetsk Republic"' (*France 24*, 14 October 2016) <https://www.france24.com/en/20161014-video-reporters-donetsk-dependent-republic-russia-ukraine-weapons> accessed 7 February 2019.

49 'Database and Video Overview of the Russian Weaponry in the Donbas' (*InformNapalm*, 17 September 2016) <https://informnapalm.org/en/database-russian-weaponry-donbas/> accessed 7 February 2019.

50 See Memorandum of 19 September 2014 (n 4).

51 See Minsk II (n 4).

52 According to Nemtsov, Tornado S is presumably only a pilot project. Nemtsov Report (n 35) 33–34.

Moreover, international observers have systematically reported an increased presence of weapons, including heavy weapons, in the DPR and LPR since around June 2014,[53] while explicitly referring to the Russian origin of these weapons and to the nexus between their inflow and increased capacity of armed groups. For example, in the report of 17 August 2014, the OHCHR observed that "the armed groups are now professionally equipped and appear to benefit from a steady supply of sophisticated weapons and ammunition, enabling them to shoot down Ukrainian military aircraft."[54] In addition, around the time of the Battle of Debaltseve, the OHCHR stated that

> [c]redible reports indicate a continuing flow of heavy weaponry and foreign fighters ..., *including from the Russian Federation*, into areas of the Donetsk and Luhansk regions controlled by armed groups. This has sustained and enhanced the capacity of armed groups ... to resist the Government armed forces and to launch new offensives in some areas, including around the Donetsk airport, Mariupol and Debaltseve.[55]

The influx of arms continued even after the conclusion of Minsk II. According to the OHCHR, "[t]he inflow of ammunition, weaponry and fighters *from the Russian Federation* continues to fuel the conflict."[56] Over the years, the OHCHR has reported that "[t]he situation has been exacerbated since the beginning of the conflict by the presence of foreign fighters and the supply of ammunition and heavy weaponry reportedly from the Russian Federation."[57] Similarly,

53 OHCHR, 'Report on the Human Rights Situation in Ukraine' (15 June 2014) para 3; OHCHR, 'Report on the Human Rights Situation in Ukraine' (15 July 2014) para 8 ("Report of 15 July 2014"). See also *Ukraine and the Netherlands v Russia* (n 31) para 628.

54 OHCHR, 'Report on the Human Rights Situation in Ukraine' (17 August 2014), para 8.

55 OHCHR, 'Report on the Human Rights Situation in Ukraine' (1 December 2014 to 15 February 2015), para 3 and see also para 104 (*emphasis added*).

56 OHCHR, 'Report on the Human Rights Situation in Ukraine' (16 May to 15 August 2016), para 3 (*emphasis added*).

57 See OHCHR, 'Report on the Human Rights Situation in Ukraine' (16 August to 15 November 2017), para 3; OHCHR, 'Report on the Human Rights Situation in Ukraine' (16 May to 15 August 2017), para 3; OHCHR, 'Report on the Human Rights Situation in Ukraine' (16 February to 15 May 2017), para 3; OHCHR, 'Report on the Human Rights Situation in Ukraine' (16 November 2016 to 15 February 2017), para 3; OHCHR, 'Report on the Human Rights Situation in Ukraine' (16 February to 15 May 2016), para 2; OHCHR, 'Report on the Human Rights Situation in Ukraine' (16 August to 15 November 2015), paras 2, 22, 180, ftn 128; OHCHR, 'Report on the Human Rights Situation in Ukraine' (16 May to 15 August 2015), paras 2 and 58–59; OHCHR, 'Report on the Human Rights Situation in Ukraine' (16 February to 15 May 2015), paras 2 and 6. See also *Ukraine and the Netherlands v Russia* (n 31) paras 630–631.

the ECtHR was "persuaded by the evidence that the separatists relied on the Russian military to provide artillery cover and that it was provided."[58]

Moreover, according to the ECtHR, "[t]he evidence therefore demonstrates beyond reasonable doubt that the Buk-TELAR used to shoot down flight MH17 was provided by the Russian Federation in direct response to the separatists' call for anti-aircraft weaponry."[59] In 2018, the Netherlands and Australia officially held Russia internationally responsible for the downing of the MH17 aeroplane.[60] In 2022, the District Court of the Hague sentenced three individuals, including Igor (Strelkov) Girkin, a Russian national and a former so-called DPR Defence Minister, to life imprisonment for causing the MH17 flight to crash and for the murder of 298 people on board.[61]

Ultimately, the ECtHR found it

> established beyond any reasonable doubt that from the earliest days of the separatist administrations and over the ensuing months and years, the Russian Federation provided weapons and other military equipment to the separatists in eastern Ukraine on a significant scale.[62]

Secondly, there is no doubt about the presence of Russian foreign fighters in the conflict in Eastern Ukraine. The UN Working Group on the Use of Mercenaries confirmed "several levels of foreign engagement".[63] According to the Working Group, "[t]hese vary from volunteers to paid service men and women, and from independent militia members to professional military."[64] According to

58 *Ukraine and the Netherlands v Russia* (n 31) para 608.

59 *Ukraine and the Netherlands v Russia* (n 31) para 632. See District Court of the Hague (n 43) 6.2.2.6 and 6.2.4.4.

60 'MH17: The Netherlands and Australia Hold Russia Responsible' (*Government of the Netherlands*, 25 May 2018) <https://www.government.nl/topics/mh17-incident/news/2018/05/25/mh17-the-netherlands-and-australia-hold-russia-responsible> accessed 7 February 2019.

61 District Court of the Hague (n 43).

62 *Ukraine and the Netherlands v Russia* (n 31) para 639.

63 UN Working Group on the Use of Mercenaries, 'Preliminary Findings by the UN Working Group on the Use of Mercenaries on His Mission to Ukraine' (18 March 2016) <https://www.ohchr.org/en/statements/2016/03/preliminary-findings-un-working-group-use-mercenaries-his-mission-ukraine?LangID=E&NewsID=18492> accessed 31 October 2023.

64 ibid. According to these preliminary findings, Ukraine identified 176 foreign fighters serving in armed groups of the DPR and the LPR, which reportedly included "large numbers from the Russian Federation, Serbia, Belarus, France and Italy, among others." ibid. See on the participation of the Chechen fighters and the fighters from the Don Cossak community *Ukraine and the Netherlands v Russia* (n 31) paras 600–601.

the DPR's former prime minister, by September 2015, 30–60,000 Russian volunteers had joined the fight.[65]

These fighters have been frequently presented as Russian soldiers on leave. For example, according to the DPR's 'president', in the summer of 2014, around 3,000–4,000 Russian servicemen on leave were fighting alongside the separatists.[66] The OHCHR mentioned that foreign fighters in Eastern Ukraine included "servicemen from the Russian Federation".[67] According to the Nemtsov report, "the military personnel, serving under the contract in the Armed Forces of the Russian Federation, is expressly prohibited to be engaged in combat operations during holidays. A soldier on leave retains his status."[68] In this context, PACE expressed

> its dismay about the participation of large numbers of Russian 'volunteers' in the conflict in eastern Ukraine without any apparent action of the Russian authorities to stop this participation, despite it being in violation of the Criminal Code of the Russian Federation itself.[69]

PACE also called on Russia to "take credible measures to end the influx of Russian 'volunteers' into the conflict in eastern Ukraine".[70] The ECtHR found "unconvincing" Russia's explanation that "any Russian soldiers present in eastern Ukraine were on leave."[71]

> [I]t seems implausible that entire military units would have taken leave and travelled to Donbass simultaneously to fight there side by side, such as to be detected and identified as military units of the Russian armed forces by the relevant Ukrainian authorities, NGOs and even, on occasion, the SMM.[72]

---

65 International Crisis Group, *Russia and the Separatists in Eastern Ukraine* (ICG 2016) 10.

66 'Serving Russian Soldiers on Leave Fighting Ukrainian Troops Alongside Rebels, Pro-Russian Separatist Leader Says' (*The Telegraph*, 28 August 2014) <https://www.telegraph.co.uk/news/worldnews/europe/germany/angela-merkel/11060559/Serving-Russian-soldiers-on-leave-fighting-Ukrainian-troops-alongside-rebels-pro-Russian-separatist-leader-says.html> accessed 7 February 2019.

67 OHCHR, 'Report on the Human Rights Situation in Ukraine' (15 November 2014), para 241.

68 Nemtsov Report (n 35) 16. See also *Ukraine and the Netherlands v Russia* (n 31) para 609.

69 CoE (PACE) Res 2034 (28 January 2015), para 7.

70 ibid para 7.3.

71 *Ukraine and the Netherlands v Russia* (n 31) para 608.

72 ibid.

The role of these Russian 'volunteers' with respect to armed forces of the DPR and LPR needs to be examined. For example, in July 2014, the OHCHR reported that "[t]he professionalization of armed groups fighting in the east has become openly acknowledged and self-evident."[73] According to the OHCHR, leadership of these armed groups, which included many citizens of the Russian Federation, was instrumental to this change. "What was previously something of a rag tag of armed groups with different loyalties and agendas is now being brought together under the central command of these men."[74]

Thirdly, there are also some reports that the DPR's and LPR's 'armed forces' were *de facto* built up by the Russian army.[75] The International Crisis Group reported that secessionist militias were reorganised by Russian officers who operated as military *kurators* in local secessionist units.[76] "From the battalion level up, Russian officers now command the separatist units, with former local commanders sometimes acting as deputies."[77] In addition, "it seems likely that officers of the Russian Army took over many of the senior positions in the rebel armies."[78] The ECtHR confirmed this latter aspect in the recent judgment.[79]

Moreover, the ECtHR also inferred "from the material before it that the influence of the political hierarchy of the respondent Government [Russia] on the military strategy of the separatists was significant."[80] The Court stated that the intercept calls indicated that there existed the hierarchy between the leaders of the secessionist entities and the Russian officials – in case of the conflicting views, "the orders of 'Moscow' were to be obeyed."[81] The District Court of the Hague in the MH17 case established that in the summer of 2014 the key heads of the armed group of the DPR were under "the considerable influence" of the Russian authorities; the latter "were involved, at times directly, in coordinating and carrying out military activities even prior to the crash of flight MH17".[82]

Ultimately, in its resolutions, PACE called upon Russia to "withdraw all weapons" from Ukraine and "refrain from supplying weapons to the insurgent

73 Report of 15 July 2014 (n 53) para 8.
74 ibid para 8. See also *supra* on Vostok Batallion.
75 Volochine (n 48). Robinson (n 15) 515–517.
76 International Crisis Group (n 65) 8–9.
77 ICG based on the interviews. International Crisis Group (n 65) 8.
78 Robinson (n 15) 515 and 516. See also JR Schindler, 'Russia's "Secret Army" in Ukraine' (*The Interpreter*, 28 August 2015) <http://www.interpretermag.com/russias-secret-army-in-ukraine/> accessed 7 February 2019.
79 See *Ukraine and the Netherlands v Russia* (n 31) para 611.
80 ibid para 621.
81 ibid para 619 and see para 620.
82 District Court of the Hague (n 43) 4.4.3.1.3.

forces".[83] And the OSCE PA also called on Russia to "ensure the withdrawal of its armed formations, military equipment, and mercenaries from the territory of certain areas of the Donetsk and Luhansk regions of Ukraine".[84] Similarly, the European Parliament urged Russia "to immediately withdraw its presence in support of violent separatists",[85] and the Euronest Parliamentary Assembly called on Russia "to stop sending, supplying and financing mercenaries and supporting, training and arming irregular forces".[86]

1.2.3 Russia's Economic and Political Support of the DPR and LPR

It is estimated that the maximum sum of taxes that could have been collected from businesses operating in the self-proclaimed republics amounted only to 5% of their budgets.[87] Thus, according to several reports, Russia essentially subsidised the self-proclaimed republics' budgets, paying for pensions, salaries of public officials and social benefits.[88] Overall, it is estimated that Russia spent

---

83 CoE (PACE) Res 2112 (21 April 2016), para 9.1 and CoE (PACE) Res 2034 (28 January 2015), para 7.2, see para 7.3. See also CoE (PACE) Res 2063 (24 June 2015) para 3.5; CoE (PACE) Res 2198 (23 January 2018), para 10.1.

84 OSCE (PA), 'Resolution on Restoration of the Sovereignty and Territorial Integrity of Ukraine' (9 July 2017), para 28. The OSCE Parliamentary Assembly "calls on the Russian Federation to stop the supply and flow of heavy weaponry, ammunition, units of the Russian Armed Forces and mercenaries across the Russian border into eastern Ukraine, cease providing any military, financial or logistical aid to illegal armed groups in the Donetsk and Luhansk regions of Ukraine-– including by means of so-called 'humanitarian convoys,' and reverse the build-up of troops and military material along the Russian border with Ukraine." OSCE (PA), 'Resolution on the Continuation of Clear, Gross and Uncorrected Violations of OSCE Commitments and International Norms by the Russian Federation' (8 July 2015), para 25. See also OSCE (PA), 'Resolution on Restoration of the Sovereignty and Territorial Integrity of Ukraine' (9 July 2017), para 26.

85 European Parliament, 'Resolution on Russian Pressure on Eastern Partnership Countries and in Particular Destabilisation of Eastern Ukraine' (17 April 2014) PT_TA(2014)0457, para 2. See also European Parliament, 'Situation in Ukraine' (15 January 2015) 2016/C 300/6, para 5.

86 Euronest Parliamentary Assembly, 'Resolution on the Russian Military Aggression against Ukraine and the Urgent Need for a Peaceful Resolution to the Conflict' (23 September 2015) 2015/C 315/06, para 9.

87 Peshkov (n 35); J Röpke, 'How Russia Finances the Ukrainian Rebel Territories' (*Bild*, 16 January 2016) <https://www.bild.de/politik/ausland/ukraine-konflikt/russia-finances-donbass-44151166.bild.html> accessed 7 February 2019. See *Ukraine and the Netherlands v Russia* (n 31) para 685. In fact, private businesses in Donbas were usually subject to double taxation, both by Ukrainian authorities (if the business wanted to continue trading with Ukraine) and by the self-proclaimed republics. See more in the chapters *infra*.

88 According to estimates by the commander of the Vostok Batallion and the MP of the DPR's National Soviet, Aleksander Khodakovsky, Russia subsidized 70% of the DPR's budget and

1 billion EUR annually subsidising the self-proclaimed republics.[89] In fact, evidence before the ECtHR, supported the claim that Mr Surkov – a foreign affairs aide of President Putin – "was involved in arranging funds for the separatist entities and in overseeing their expenditure."[90] According to the Court, the material before it paints "a consistent picture of significant economic support from the Russian Federation."[91] The District Court of the Hague considered evidence that corroborated Russia's role in the financing of the DPR.[92]

In fact, in the second half of 2015, the Russian rouble was introduced as an official currency in both self-proclaimed republics.[93] However, due to the fact that at the time Russia did not officially recognise the DPR, money transfers were reportedly conducted through an elaborate scheme between the DPR's only bank and South Ossetia's and Abkhazia's banks, and from there to Russia, and the other way round.[94] Furthermore, according to other reports, this funding was also assured by large sums of Russian roubles in cash, carried physically by overnight special trains once a month from the Russian Federation.[95]

Russia also maintained a key influence on the political life of the DPR and LPR.[96] At first, as established by the ECtHR, Russian citizens including "members of the Russian military acting under Russian instruction" (and ties to Russian intelligence) became political leaders of the self-proclaimed republics in 2014.[97] However, these leaders left for Russia by the end of August

paid for pensions, public officials' salaries and welfare benefits. I Tumakova, 'Commander of the Vostok Batallion: Surkov – Patriot, Purgin – Putin's Apologist' (*Fontanka.ru*, 8 September 2015) <https://www.fontanka.ru/2015/09/07/163/> accessed 7 February 2019 (*in Russian*). See also M Bird, L Vdovii and Y Tkachenko, 'The Donbass Paradox' (*The Black Sea*, 9 December 2015) <https://theblacksea.eu/_old/pages/The%20Donbass%20Paradox.html> accessed 31 October 2023; International Crisis Group (n 65) 4–8.

89 Röpke, 'How Russia Finances the Ukrainian Rebel Territories' (n 87); International Crisis Group (n 65) 1 and 5. International Crisis Group, *Peace in Ukraine (III): The Costs of War in Donbas: Europe Report No 261* (ICG 2020) 20.

90 *Ukraine and the Netherlands v Russia* (n 31) para 686.

91 ibid para 689.

92 District Court of the Hague (n 43) 4.4.3.1.3.

93 Röpke, 'How Russia Finances the Ukrainian Rebel Territories' (n 87).

94 Volochine (n 48); J Röpke, 'How Russia Finances the Ukrainian Rebel Territories' (n 87).

95 Röpke, 'How Russia Finances the Ukrainian Rebel Territories' (n 87). Peshkov (n 35).

96 See S Pifer, 'Deepening Division in Donbas' (*Brookings*, 2 May 2017) <https://www.brookings.edu/blog/order-from-chaos/2017/05/02/deepening-division-in-donbas/> accessed 7 February 2019. According to the International Crisis Group, Russia controlled top leadership of the DPR and LPR especially on the issue of the Minsk Agreements and separatist militia, but left "domestic space – relations between separatist commanders, local political leaders, organized crime figures and corrupt officials on the other side of the separation line – unsupervised." International Crisis Group (n 65) 4, 7–8, 12–14.

97 *Ukraine and the Netherlands v Russia* (n 31) paras 670 and 590–594. See *supra*.

2014[98] and were replaced by local figures, later elected to their posts in self-organised 'elections' in November 2014.[99] Some experts argued that this exchange was due to upcoming negotiations in Minsk where local rebel leaders, instead of Russian citizens, represented the separatist republics.[100] Later on, after the DPR president's assassination in 2018, a Kremlin-backed candidate won another 'election' in November 2018.[101] Moreover, the ECtHR and the Hague District Court took into account evidence that indicated Russia's influence on appointments in the DPR.[102]

In addition, Moscow's political influence over the leaders of the DPR and LPR could also be inferred from Russia's positions at the international scene (including vetoing the plans of establishing international tribunal for prosecuting those responsible for MH17 downing)[103] and reports on the conclusion of Minsk II. Following its drafting in the Normandy format, including Russia, Ukraine, Germany and France, the document was presented to the representatives of the DPR and LPR. The separatists reportedly initially refused to sign

98 CJ Williams, 'Two More Top Separatist Leaders Abandon Eastern Ukraine Battle' (*The Los Angels Times*, 14 August 2014) <https://www.latimes.com/world/europe/la-fg-ukraine-russia-separatist-leaders-resign-20140814-story.html> accessed 7 February 2019.

99 S Walker, 'Russia Calls for Talks with Kiev after Separatist Elections' (*The Guardian*, 3 November 2014) <https://www.theguardian.com/world/2014/nov/03/germany-urges-russia-respect-unity-ukraine-donetsk-elections> accessed 7 February 2019; 'Russia Respects, But Not Necessarily Recognize Donetsk, Luhanks Elections: Kremlin' (*RIA Novosti*, 7 November 2014) <https://web.archive.org/web/20141108025039/http://en.ria.ru/politics/20141107/195255564/Russias-Respecting-Elections-in-Donetsk-Luhansk-Does-Not-Mean.html> accessed 7 February 2019.

100 Kofman (n 7) 56–57. See Robinson (n 15) 513 for the view that this change in leadership marked Russia's direct military intervention in the conflict.

101 A Luhn, 'Kremlin-Backed Candidate Elected Leader of Breakaway Donetsk Republic' (*The Telegraph*, 12 November 2018) <https://www.telegraph.co.uk/news/2018/11/12/kremlin-backed-candidate-elected-leader-breakaway-donetsk-republic/> accessed 7 February 2019; R Olearchyk, 'Breakaway Ukraine Republics Vote for New Leaders' (*The Financial Times*, 11 November 2018) <https://www.ft.com/content/a292087e-e43e-11e8-a6e5-792428919cee> accessed 7 February 2019. See also EU8 Statement, which described these elections as illegitimate, as they contravened commitments under Minsk Agreements, violated Ukrainian law and were incompatible with the sovereignty and territorial integrity of Ukraine. 'EU8 Members Joint Statement on Ukraine' (*Government Offices of Sweden*, 30 October 2018) <https://www.government.se/statements/2018/10/eu-members-joint-statement-on-ukraine/> accessed 7 February 2019.

102 *Ukraine and the Netherlands v Russia* (n 31) para 671. District Court of the Hague (n 43) 4.4.3.1.3.

103 *Ukraine and the Netherlands v Russia* (n 31) para 674.

the document.[104] Ms Merkel, the Chancellor of Germany, later noted that the Kremlin had to pressure the separatists so that they eventually did so.[105] Moreover, Minsk II was accompanied by the political declaration of the leaders of the Normandy format, in which they pledged to "use their influence on relevant parties to facilitate the implementation" of Minsk II.[106] Despite a generality of language, which applies to all the actors, this statement can be taken as the acknowledgment *inter alia* of Russia's influence over the DPR and LPR.[107] Russia was also said to influence the leaders of the DPR and LPR to postpone holding elections in 2016[108] and has generally controlled the decision-making in the DPR and LPR regarding the Minsk process.[109]

In 2017 the Russian president issued an executive order which temporarily recognised the validity of certain documents, including identity documents; diplomas; birth, marriage and death certificates; and vehicle registration certificates issued by bodies operating in the territories of certain areas of the Donetsk and Luhansk regions of Ukraine, and which established visa-free travel to Russia for permanent residents of these areas.[110]

---

104 'Source: The Leaders of the DPR and LPR Refused to Sign the Document Agreed Upon by the Quartet' (*TASS*, 12 February 2015) <https://tass.ru/mezhdunarodnaya-panorama/1762438> accessed 7 February 2019 (*in Russian*).

105 N MacFarquhar, 'Ukraine's Latest Peace Plan Inspires Hope and Doubts' (*The New York Times*, 12 February 2015) <https://www.nytimes.com/2015/02/13/world/europe/ukraine-talks-cease-fire.html> accessed 7 February 2019.

106 'Declaration of Minsk in Support of the "Package of Measures for the Implementation of the Minsk Agreements"' (*Press Release of the Federal Foreign Office*, 12 February 2015) <https://www.auswaertiges-amt.de/en/newsroom/news/150212-minsk-declaration/269274> accessed 31 October 2023 ("Political Declaration in Support of Minsk II").

107 See PR Gregory, 'Putin Comes Out on Top in New Minsk Agreement' (*Forbes*, 13 February 2015) <https://www.forbes.com/sites/paulroderickgregory/2015/02/13/putin-comes-out-on-top-in-new-minsk-agreement/#47dcc94e4ede> accessed 7 February 2019. See also the Council of the EU's Statement, which expected Russia to use its leverage on separatists to de-escalate the situation in Eastern Ukraine. Council of European Union, 'Statement of the Heads of State or Government on Ukraine' (27 May 2014), para 3.

108 'Ukraine Crisis: Pro-Russian Rebels 'Delay Disputed Elections'' (*BBC News*, 6 October 2015) <https://www.bbc.com/news/world-europe-34457317> accessed 7 February 2019.

109 International Crisis Group (n 65) 7.

110 See 'Executive Order of the President of the Russian Federation on Recognition in the Russian Federation of Documents and Registration Marks of Vehicles, Issued to Citizens of Ukraine and Stateless Persons Permanently Residing in the Territories of Certain Regions of the Donetsk and Luhansk Regions of Ukraine No 74' (18 February 2017) <http://kremlin.ru/events/president/news/53895> accessed 7 February 2019 (*in Russian*). For analysis see Section 4, Chapter 19.

In 2019, the Russian president issued another executive order facilitating the process[111] of obtaining Russian citizenship for permanent residents of certain areas of the Donetsk and Luhansk regions of Ukraine.[112] The grant of Russian citizenship to residents of Donbas was only justified by humanitarian purposes.[113] Ukraine considered this act to be 'null and void', not a basis for the alteration of Ukrainian citizenship of the residents of Donbas and "a blatant interference in Ukraine's internal affairs as well as Russia's creeping annexation of Ukraine's Donbas".[114] Ukrainian legislation does not recognise dual citizenship.[115]

The reports also suggested coordination between the Kremlin and separatists regarding governance and administration of Donbas.[116] Generally, Russia's

111 The simplified procedure allowed these permanent residents to obtain a Russian passport without living in Russia for five years, without the need to prove available means of subsistence, without proving knowledge of Russian and without the need to renounce citizenship of another State. 'A Simplified Procedure of Obtaining the Citizenship of the Russian Federation Introduced for the Residents of the DPR and LPR' (*Interfax*, 24 April 2019) <https://www.interfax.ru/russia/659197> accessed 7 May 2019 (*in Russian*).

112 See 'Executive Order of the President of the Russian Federation No 183 on the Determination of Categories of Persons Entitled to Apply for Citizenship of the Russian Federation under a Simplified Procedure for Humanitarian Purposes' (24 April 2019) <http://kremlin.ru/acts/news/60358> accessed 7 May 2019 (*in Russian*). See also 'Executive Order of the President of the Russian Federation No 187 on On Certain Categories of Foreign Citizens and Stateless Persons Entitled to Apply for Citizenship of the Russian Federation under a Simplified Procedure' (29 April 2019) <http://kremlin.ru/events/president/news/60429> accessed 7 May 2019 (*in Russian*).

113 'Executive Order of the President of the Russian Federation No 187 on On Certain Categories of Foreign Citizens and Stateless Persons Entitled to Apply for Citizenship of the Russian Federation under a Simplified Procedure.' The competence of the president to issue this type of executive order was only added to the Russian Citizenship Law in December 2018 (Article 14(8)). See 'Federal Law on the Citizenship of Russian Federation No 62-F3 (31 May 2002) as amended <http://www.consultant.ru/document/cons_doc_LAW_36927/> accessed 22 June 2019 (*in Russian*) ("Russian Citizenship Law"). See *infra* chapter on Abkhazia and South Ossetia for the analysis of Russia's passportisation policy.

114 See 'Statement of the Ministry of Foreign Affairs of Ukraine on the Provocative and Unlawful Decision by Kremlin to Issue Russian Passports to Ukrainian Citizens in Occupied Territories' (25 April 2019) <https://moldova.mfa.gov.ua/ru/news/10235-zayavlenie-mid-ukrainy-o-provokativnom-i-prestupnom-reshenii-kremlya-o-vydache-rossiyskikh-pasportov-grazhdanam-ukrainy-na-okkupirovannykh-territoriyakh> accessed 31 October 2023 (*in Russian*).

115 See *supra* section on Crimea.

116 'Breaking Down the Surkov Leaks' (*Digital Forensic Research Lab*, 25 October 2016) <https://medium.com/dfrlab/breaking-down-the-surkov-leaks-b2feec1423cb> accessed 7 February 2019. See also A Åslund, 'New Russian Management of the Donbas Signifies Putin May Be Ready to Negotiate' (*Atlantic Council*, 4 January 2016)

influence was reportedly wielded through the system of political *kurators*, among whom the highest was Vladislav Surkov, Putin's foreign affairs aide.[117] The ECtHR ultimately relied on evidence, including intercept calls and leaked emails, which showed "the extent to which the entire political mechanism of the separatist entities was overseen by Mr Surkov."[118] Among others, the separatist leaders referred to Mr Surkov as "our man in Kremlin" – the Russian government did not explain such a description.[119] According to the German newspaper Bild, the Russian Federation did not only support the DPR and LPR financially and materially, but in fact secretly governed these self-proclaimed republics through "the Inter-Ministerial Commission for the Provision of Humanitarian Aid for the Affected Areas in the Southeast of the Region of Donetsk and Luhansk".[120] According to documents obtained by Bild, this commission seemed to operate as a *de facto* government of Donbas coordinating the work of five Russian ministries and six working groups.[121] Separatists themselves were not members of this commission and were simply only informed about the conclusions of meetings.[122] There is no other evidence to corroborate this report.

1.3 *Post-February 2022 Developments*

This long-term *status quo* in Donbas changed when Russia recognised the DPR and LPR as independent States on 21 February 2022 amidst its military build-up at the borders with Ukraine.[123] It immediately signed the purported

<http://www.atlanticcouncil.org/blogs/new-atlanticist/new-russian-management-of-the-donbas-signifies-putin-may-be-ready-to-negotiate> accessed 7 February 2019. See also Volochine (n 48).

117 International Crisis Group (n 65) 12–14. See also 'Borodai: Surkov – Our Man in Kremlin' (*Aktualnye Kommentarii*, 16 June 2014) <http://actualcomment.ru/boroday_surkov_nash_chelovek_v_kremle.html> accessed 7 February 2019 (*in Russian*).

118 *Ukraine and the Netherlands v Russia* (n 31) para 673.

119 ibid para 672.

120 See the Government of the Russian Federation, 'Order No 2537' (15 December 2014) <http://static.government.ru/media/files/CPhV6tOcZNA.pdf> accessed 7 February 2019 (*in Russian*). J Röpke, 'Putin's Shadow Government for Donbass Exposed' (*Bild*, 29 March 2016) <https://www.bild.de/politik/ausland/ukraine-konflikt/donbass-shadow-government-45102202.bild.html> accessed 7 February 2019.

121 These working groups reportedly included Finance and Tax Law, Defining Wage Policies, as well as Residential and Public Service Matters, Restoration of Industry, Trade with Energy Sources, Establishment of a Market for Electricity, and Transportation Infrastructure. ibid.

122 ibid.

123 'Executive Order of the President of the Russian Federation No 71 on Recognition of the Donetsk People's Republic (adopted 21 February 2022; entered into force 21 February 2022) <http://publication.pravo.gov.ru/Document/View/0001202202220002> accessed 26 July 2023 (*in Russian*); 'Executive Order of the President of the Russian Federation No

agreements on friendship, cooperation and mutual assistance with the leaders of the DPR and LPR.[124] Among other things, these purported agreements stipulated that the parties “shall jointly take all available measures to eliminate the threat to peace, breach of the peace and counteract acts of aggression”, including through military assistance in exercise of the individual or collective right of self-defence under Article 51 of the UN Charter.[125] On 24 February 2022, claiming to act on the basis of the purported right of self-defence of these entities (among other reasons), the Russian Federation launched an all-out attack on Ukraine. The UNGA resolution ‘aggression against Ukraine’ adopted on 2 March 2022 deplored “in the strongest terms the aggression by the Russian Federation against Ukraine in violation of Article 2 (4) of the Charter.”[126] On 11 July 2022, after multiple previous modifications – the Russian President signed an executive order providing for a simplified procedure for all the citizens of Ukraine to obtain Russian citizenship.[127] Later in the year, North Korea and Syria recognised the independence of the DPR and LPR.[128]

---

72 on Recognition of the Luhansk People's Republic (adopted 21 February 2021; entered into force 21 February 2021) <http://publication.pravo.gov.ru/Document/View/0001202202220001> accessed 26 July 2023 (*in Russian*).

124 Agreement of Friendship, Cooperation and Mutual Assistance between the Russian Federation and the Donetsk People's Republic (signed 21 February 2022; entered into force 25 February 2022) <http://publication.pravo.gov.ru/Document/View/0001202202280001> accessed 26 July 2023 (*in Russian*); Agreement of Friendship, Cooperation and Mutual Assistance between the Russian Federation and the Luhansk People's Republic (signed 21 February 2022; entered into force 25 February 2022) <http://publication.pravo.gov.ru/Document/View/0001202202280002 > accessed 26 July 2023 (*in Russian*); See J Miklasová, ‘Russia's Recognition of the DPR and LPR as Illegal Acts under International Law’ (*Völkerrechtsblog*, 24 February 2022) <https://voelkerrechtsblog.org/russias-recognition-of-the-dpr-and-lpr-as-illegal-acts-under-international-law/> accessed 26 July 2023.

125 Agreement of Friendship, Cooperation and Mutual Assistance between the Russian Federation and the Donetsk People's Republic (n 124) art 4; Agreement of Friendship, Cooperation and Mutual Assistance between the Russian Federation and the Luhansk People's Republic (n 124) art 4.

126 UNGA Res ES-11/1 (2 March 2022) UN Doc A/RES/ES-11/1, para 2. See *infra*.

127 ‘Executive Order of the President of the Russian Federation No 440 ‘on Amending the Executive Order of the President of the Russian Federation No 183 of 24 April 2019, ‘On the Determination of Categories of Persons Entitled to Apply for Citizenship of the Russian Federation under a Simplified Procedure for Humanitarian Purposes’ and the Executive Order of the President of the Russian Federation No 187 of 29 April 2019 ‘On Certain Categories of Foreign Citizens and Stateless Persons Entitled to Apply for Citizenship of the Russian Federation under a Simplified Procedure” (11 July 2022) <http://static.kremlin.ru/media/events/files/ru/obTO6S1g5coRASXodOjRuI8wGLndsOzA.pdf> accessed 24 July 2023.

128 P Mesmer, ‘North Korea Recognizes Independence of Pro-Russian Territories in Eastern Ukraine’ (*Le Monde*, 19 July 2022) <https://www.lemonde.fr/en/international/article/2022/07/19/north-korea-recognizes-independence-of-pro-russian-territories-in-eastern-ukraine_5990644_4.html> accessed 13 August 2023; ‘Syria Recognizes Independence,

Several months of fighting followed. On 20 September 2022 – apparently preceded by calls from community chambers – the leaders of the DPR and LPR signed a law to hold referenda, between 23 and 27 September 2022, on joining the Russian Federation.[129] On the same day, apparently following similar calls, the heads of the military-civilian administrations of the Zaporizhzhia and Kherson Regions – installed by Russian forces – signed decrees on holding the referenda in the same period.[130] According to the Russian media, three questions were posed to the residents of the Zaporizhzhia and Kherson Regions; they concerned the exit of these regions from Ukraine, the creation of independent republics, and their accession to the Russian Federation.[131] Russia did not completely control any of the four regions at the time of referenda.[132] The announced results were presented as being overwhelmingly in support of the questions asked.[133]

On 28 September 2022, the leaders of the four regions appealed to Russian President Putin for their admission to the Russian Federation.[134] On 29 September 2022, Putin signed the executive orders recognising the

Sovereignty of Donetsk, Luhansk – State News Agency' (*Reuters*, 29 June 2022) <https://www.reuters.com/world/middle-east/syria-recognizes-independence-sovereignty-donetsk-luhansk-state-news-agency-2022-06-29/> accessed 13 August 2023.

129 'The History of the Admission of the Republics of Donbas, Zaporizhzhia and Kherson Regions into the Russian Federation' (*tass.ru*, 3 October 2022) <https://tass.ru/info/15941231> accessed 26 July 2022 (*in Russian*) ("History").

130 ibid. See *infra*.

131 History (n 129). The residents of the DPR and LPR were only asked about the exit of the secessionist entities from Ukraine and joining of the Russian Federation.

132 According to Ukrainian sources, around that time, "about 88% of Kherson oblast, 67% of Zaporizhzhia oblast, 57% of Donetsk oblast and 99% of Luhansk oblast were under occupation." M Menkiszak, M Domańska, P Żochowski, 'Russia Announces Annexation of Four Regions of Ukraine' (*OSW*, 3 October 2022) <https://www.osw.waw.pl/en/publikacje/analyses/2022-10-03/russia-announces-annexation-four-regions-ukraine> accessed 28 July 2023. See also below (n 137).

133 According to the announced results, 99,23% of the votes in the DPR favoured the joining of the DPR to the RF; 98,42% of the votes in the LPR favoured the joining of the LPR to the RF; 93,11% of the votes in the Zaporizhzhia Region were cast in support of the asked questions; 87,05% of the votes in the Kherson Region were cast in support of the asked questions. 'Results of the Referendums on Joining Russia: What Figures Were Announced by Elections Commissions' (*Kommersant*, 28 September 2022) <https://www.kommersant.ru/doc/5583018> accessed 23 July 2023.

134 History (n 129).

Zaporizhzhia and Kherson Regions as independent States.[135] On 30 September 2022, Putin and the four entities signed the purported agreements on the accession to the Russian Federation and the creation of new subjects of the Russian Federation.[136] The Russian Constitutional Court found the purported agreements to be in accordance with the constitution of the Russian Federation on 2 October 2022. On 4 October 2022, President Putin signed federal laws both ratifying the purported agreements and creating new constituent entities.

According to the purported agreements, the new subjects of the Russian Federation have the borders that existed on the day of their formation and admission into the RF and the formation of new subjects within the RF.[137] Based on the positions of Russian and occupation officials, this entailed boundaries

135 'Executive Order of the President of the Russian Federation No 685 on Recognition of the Zaporizhzhia Region (adopted 29 September 2022; entered into force 29 September 2022) <http://en.kremlin.ru/acts/news/69463> accessed 26 July 2023; 'Executive Order of the President of the Russian Federation No 686 on Recognition of the Kherson Region (adopted 29 September 2022; entered into force 29 September 2022) <http://en.kremlin.ru/acts/news/69464> accessed 26 July 2023.

136 Agreement between the Russian Federation and the Donetsk People's Republic on the Accession of the Donetsk People's Republic to the Russian Federation and the Establishment of a New Constituent Entity of the Russian Federation (signed 30 September 2022, entered into force 5 October 2022, provisionally applied since signature) <http://publication.pravo.gov.ru/Document/View/0001202210030001> accessed 26 July 2023 (*in Russian*); Agreement between the Russian Federation and the Luhansk People's Republic on the Accession of the Luhansk People's Republic to the Russian Federation and the Establishment of a New Constituent Entity of the Russian Federation (signed 30 September 2022, entered into force 5 October 2022, provisionally applied since signature) <http://publication.pravo.gov.ru/Document/View/0001202210030002> accessed 26 July 2023 (*in Russian*); Agreement between the Russian Federation and the Kherson Region on the Accession of the Kherson Region to the Russian Federation and the Establishment of a New Constituent Entity of the Russian Federation (signed 30 September 2022, entered into force 5 October 2022, provisionally applied since signature) <http://publication.pravo.gov.ru/Document/View/0001202210030003> accessed 26 July 2023 (*in Russian*); Agreement between the Russian Federation and the Zaporizhzhia Region on the Accession of the Zaporizhzhia Region to the Russian Federation and the Establishment of a New Constituent Entity of the Russian Federation (signed 30 September 2022, entered into force 5 October 2022, provisionally applied since signature) <http://publication.pravo.gov.ru/document/0001202210030004> accessed 26 July 2023 (*in Russian*) ("Zaporizhzhia Region Accession Agreement").

137 See eg Zaporizhzhia Region Accession Agreement (n 136) art 4(1). Despite its willingness to incorporate these entities in their administrative borders, Russia incorporated a small part of the Mykolaiv region into the Kherson region. Menkiszak, Domańska, Żochowski (n 132).

of the regions of Ukraine.[138] Residents of Ukraine (or the DPR/LPR) or stateless persons residing in these regions were considered Russian citizens upon the accession of these regions into the Russian Federation – except for those who, within one month, announced their wish to retain their other citizenship or remain stateless.[139] The agreements also foresee a transitional period, lasting until 1 January 2026, for the regions' integration into the Russian economic, financial, administrative and legal systems and its government framework.[140]

On 11 November 2022, Ukrainian forces re-captured the city of Kherson.[141] Although its own forces have retreated to the left bank of the Dnipro River, Russia maintains that it legally holds sovereignty over the whole Kherson Region.[142] So far, only Syria and North Korea have recognised the incorporation of these territories into Russia as legal.[143]

2 Legal Analysis of the Secessionist Attempts

2.1 *Period before 21 February 2022*

2.1.1 Legal Arguments of the Secessionists

From a legal perspective, the arguments initially used for secession by the self-proclaimed People's Republics in Eastern Ukraine were essentially similar to those in Crimea, in particular on the right to self-determination and the role of referenda. Since the legal context of the secessionist situation in Eastern Ukraine essentially did not differ from that of Crimea, the analysis is

138 K Tyshchenko, 'Borders Russian-Annexed Occupied Territories Announced' (*Ukrainska Pravda*, 2 October 2022) <https://www.pravda.com.ua/eng/news/2022/10/2/7370061/> accessed 28 August 2023.

139 See eg Zaporizhzhia Region Accession Agreement (n 136) art 5.

140 See eg ibid art 6.

141 C Maynes and A Westerman, 'Ukrainian Troops Enter Kherson City After Russia Retreats' (*NPR*, 11 November 2022) <https://www.npr.org/2022/11/11/1135995012/ukrainian-troops-enter-kherson-russia-withdrawal-ukraine> accessed 28 July 2023.

142 'Kremlin Says Kherson's Status as "Part of Russia" Unchanged Despite Retreat' (Reuters, 11 November 2022) <https://www.reuters.com/world/europe/kremlin-status-kherson-part-russia-unchanged-2022-11-11/> accessed 28 July 2023.

143 'North Korea Recognized Russia's Illegal Annexation of Ukrainian Territories per Sham Referendums' (*Ukrainian World Congress*, 4 October 2022) <https://www.ukrainianworldcongress.org/north-korea-recognized-russias-illegal-annexation-of-ukrainian-territories-per-sham-referendums/> accessed 24 August 2023; 'Syria's Assad Recognizes Territories Claimed by Russia in Ukraine as Russian' (*CNN*, 16 March 2023) <https://edition.cnn.com/europe/live-news/russia-ukraine-war-news-03-16-23/h_f05a96e19cb5caaf1c219c2d57704ba5> accessed 24 August 2023.

not exhaustively repeated here. Firstly, as follows from the general framework outlined in Part 1, Chapter 3 there is no general right to secede based on the right of self-determination outside of a decolonisation context, and therefore the population of the Donetsk or Luhansk People's Republics could not prevail upon it. As far as the invocation of the claim of remedial secession,[144] it was established in Part 1, Chapter 3 that this right is not part of positive international law. However, even if it were, as follows from the above factual overview of the 2014–2022 period, the requirements of extreme oppression justifying remedial secession were not present in Eastern Ukraine – in fact, the Ukrainian use of force occurred in reaction to acts of separatists.

Regarding independence referenda held in the DPR and LPR on 11 May 2014, it follows from Part 1, Chapter 3 that referendum on its own does not create a right to independence. In addition, compared to the Crimean referendum, these referenda fulfilled international standards even less.[145] For example, the OSCE Parliamentary Assembly President called for the cancellation of the "absurd" referenda in eastern Ukraine,[146] and the EU held that it would not recognise these referenda, "nor any future illegitimate and illegal 'referenda'".[147] In addition, since these referenda were connected to the violation of peremptory norms, they could be considered illegal under international law.[148]

144 See JJA Burke and S Panina-Burke, 'Eastern and Southern Ukraine's Right to Secede and Join the Russian Federation' (2015) 3 Russian Law Journal 33, 45–47 and 52–54 for the argument that residents of Eastern and Southern Ukraine constitute a 'people' on the grounds of their language, shared history with Russia and political preference to strengthen ties to Russia; and for the argument that since Ukraine abrogated its obligations both under the ICCPR and ICESR "by failing to ensure that 'self-determination' is handled internally without armed conflict," the separatists in East and South Ukraine who are a 'people' within the ordinary meaning of that term have a right to secede from Ukraine.

145 A Peters, 'The Crimean Vote of March 2014 as an Abuse of the Institution of the Territorial Referendum' in C Callies (ed), *Staat und Mensch im Kontext des Völker- und Europarechts: Liber Amicorum für Torsten Stein* (Nomos Verlag 2015) 258 in connection with ftn 3 and 280.

146 'OSCE PA President Calls for Cancellation of "Absurd" Referendums in Eastern Ukraine' (*OSCE Parliamentary Assembly Press Release*, 10 May 2014) <https://www.osce.org/pa/118469> accessed 7 February 2019.

147 Council of European Union (Foreign Affairs), '3312th Council Meeting' (12 May 2014) 9542/14, para 1.

148 See *supra* Part 1, Chapter 3.

2.1.2 Violation of the Prohibition of the Use of Force

Regarding the legal basis for Russia's use of force in Eastern Ukraine, Russia did not act under the UNSC resolution under Chapter VII UN Charter.[149] Its use of force also did not fulfil the requirements of self-defence under Article 51 UN Charter, as there had been no prior armed attack by Ukraine on Russia.[150] No other legal justification was invoked by Russia, since the latter flatly denied the use of military force in Eastern Ukraine in the 2014–2022 period. Therefore, without any applicable exceptions, it can be concluded that in the 2014–2022 period, Russia violated the peremptory prohibition of the use of force as contained in Article 2(4) UN Charter, both directly and indirectly.[151]

Firstly, Russia violated the prohibition of the use of force directly by deploying its regular troops, which intervened in the hostilities and through its cross-border shelling of Ukraine's territory.[152] The participation of soldiers of Russia's Army on leave could, arguably, be taken as additional evidence of a direct use of force by Russia, since members of the Russian Army on leave preserve their status as members of its armed forces and therefore could be considered State organs whose actions are attributable to Russia under Article 4 ARSIWA.[153]

149 Charter of the United Nations (adopted 26 June 1945, entered into force 24 October 1945) 1 UNTS XVI ("UN Charter").

150 ibid art 51.

151 ibid art 2(4). For the peremptory character of prohibition, see ILC, Draft Articles on the Responsibility of States for Internationally Wrongful Acts, with Commentaries in 'Report of the International Law Commission on the Work of its Fifty-Third Session (23 April -1 June and 2 July-10 August 2001)' UN Doc A/56/10 commentary to art 40, para 4 ("ARSIWA"). O Dörr, 'Use of Force, Prohibition Of' in MPEPIL (online edn, OUP 2015), para 32. For the opposite view see U Linderfalk, 'The Effect of Jus Cogens Norms: Whoever Opened Pandora's Box, Did You Ever Think About the Consequences?' 859 *et seq*.

152 These actions are also in violation of the Definition of Aggression, UNGA Res 3314 (XXIX) (14 December 1974) UN Doc A/RES/3314(XXIX), art 3(a)(b) ("Definition of Aggression"); Declaration on Principles of International Law concerning Friendly Relations and Co-operation among States in accordance with the Charter of the United Nations, UNGA Res 2625 (XXV) (24 October 1970) UN Doc A/RES/2625(XXV), principle 1 ("Friendly Relations Declaration").

153 See *supra*. ARSIWA (n 151) art 4. From the perspective of *ius in bello*, in *Naletilić and Martinović*, the ICTY assessed self-proclaimed volunteers to be members of the Croatian Army. Taken into account was evidence of Croatia's sending its regular troops to Bosnia and Herzegovina; of their concealing allegiance to its armed forces by replacing their uniforms or insignia for those of armed groups; and of their maintaining the right to their monthly salary. The ICTY assessed this as the example of a direct intervention. *Prosecutor v Naletilić and Martinović* (Judgment, Trial Chamber) (IT-98-34-T) (31 March 2003), para 195.

With respect to indirect intervention, based on available evidence, it is difficult to factually substantiate whether Russia sent the volunteers of Russian nationality to carry out acts of armed force against Ukraine or was substantially involved therein.[154] If, however, such allegations were proven correct, they would constitute a violation of the prohibition of the use of force.[155]

All of the above actions also arguably qualify as military aggression and armed attack against Ukraine under Article 51 UN Charter.[156] Accordingly, it is possible to agree with the OSCE Parliamentary Assembly that – already in the period before 24 February 2022 – the actions by the Russian Federation "in certain areas of the Donetsk and Luhansk regions of Ukraine, constitute acts of military aggression against Ukraine".[157]

Moreover, Russia also violated the prohibition of the use of force indirectly, by arming separatists.[158] However, compared to the above-mentioned acts,

---

154 Definition of Aggression (n 152) art 3(g).

155 According to the Definition of Aggression "[t]he sending by or on behalf of a State of armed bands, groups, irregulars or mercenaries, which carry out acts of armed force against another State of such gravity as to amount to the acts listed above, or its substantial involvement therein" qualify as acts of aggression. Definition of Aggression (n 152) art 3(g). The ICJ held that in this respect, this document reflects a customary international law. *Case Concerning Military and Paramilitary Activities in and against Nicaragua (Nicaragua v United States of America)* [1986] ICJ Rep 14, para 195 ("*Nicaragua*").

156 UN Charter (n 149) art 51; Definition of Aggression (n 152) art 3(a)(b)(g); *Nicaragua* (n 155) para 195; *Case Concerning Armed Activities on the Territory of the Congo (Democratic Republic of the Congo v Uganda)* (Merits) ICJ Rep [2005] 168, paras 146–147 ("*Armed Activities*"). See also G Nolte and A Randelzhofer, 'Article 51' in B Simma and others (eds), *The Charter of the United Nations: A Commentary*, Volume II (3rd edn, OUP 2012) paras 31–41.

157 OSCE (PA), 'Resolution on the Continuation of Clear, Gross and Uncorrected Violations of OSCE Commitments and International Norms by the Russian Federation' (8 July 2015), para 21. Later on, the OSCE Parliamentary Assembly reiterated its condemnation of "the ongoing Russian hybrid aggression against Ukraine in Donbas." OSCE (PA), 'Resolution on Restoration of the Sovereignty and Territorial Integrity of Ukraine' (9 July 2017), para 19. According to PACE, there is "the ongoing Russian war against Ukraine, which is taking place in certain areas of the Donetsk and Luhansk region." CoE (PACE) Res 2198 (23 January 2018), para 1. Similarly, the European Parliament condemned Russia's "waging an undeclared hybrid war against Ukraine, including … use of regular and irregular forces." European Parliament, 'Situation in Ukraine' (15 January 2015) 2016/C 300/6, para 5.

158 The Friendly Relations Declaration states "[e]very State has the duty to refrain from organizing, instigating, assisting or participating in acts of civil strife or terrorist acts in another State or acquiescing in organized activities within its territory directed towards the commission of such acts, when the acts referred to in the present paragraph involve a threat or use of force." Friendly Relations Declaration (n 152) principle 1, para 9. The ICJ claimed that in this regard the Friendly Relations Declaration indicates *opinio iuris* as to a customary international law. *Nicaragua* (n 155) para 191. See also *Armed Activities*

the provision of arms to separatists does not amount to an armed attack.[159] In addition, reports suggest Russia's role in financing the separatists. Based on the ICJ's holding in *Nicaragua,* this would not contravene the prohibition of the use of force but would violate the non-intervention principle.[160]

Thus, by using direct and indirect force against Ukraine, Russia also violated other fundamental principles of international law, including the prohibition of intervention into the internal affairs of Ukraine[161] and its territorial integrity.[162] Thereby, as in Crimea, Russia violated the Minsk Agreement, the Alma Ata Declaration, the Charter of CIS,[163] and did not respect the commitments in the Helsinki Final Pact.[164] It also specifically breached the Ukraine-Russia Friendship Treaty in which Russia and Ukraine undertook to "honour each other's territorial integrity" and to "acknowledge the inviolability of the borders existing between them".[165] These actions also violated the Budapest Memorandum, in which Russia, the UK and the USA reaffirmed their commitment "to respect the independence and sovereignty and the existing borders of Ukraine" and "to refrain from the threat of use of force against the territorial integrity or political independence of Ukraine"[166] and the Minsk I and II ceasefire agreements. By providing non-military assistance to separatists in

(n 156) para 162. Referring to the Friendly Relations Declaration, the ICJ held that the act of assistance amounts to the use of force when it involves "a threat or use of force" and that the arming of opposition groups in another State "can certainly be said to involve the threat or use of force." *Nicaragua* (n 155) para 228.

159 *Nicaragua* (n 155) para 247.

160 ibid para 228.

161 "[A]cts constituting a breach of the customary principle of non-intervention will also, if they directly or indirectly involve the use of force, constitute a breach of the principle of non-use of force in international relations." *Nicaragua* (n 155) para 209 and see also para 247.

162 UN Charter (n 149) art 2(4). See *supra* Part 1, Chapter 4 on the principle of territorial integrity.

163 See *supra.*

164 Final Act of the Conference on the Security and Cooperation in Europe (1 August 1975) principles II, III and IV reprinted in (1975) 14 ILM 1293–1298.

165 Treaty on Friendship, Cooperation and Partnership between Ukraine and the Russian Federation (signed 31 May 1997, entered into force 1 April 1999; expired 1 April 2019) 3006 UNTS, art 2 and 3. See also Treaty between Ukraine and the Russian Federation on the Ukrainian-Russian State Border (signed 28 January 2003, entered into force 23 April 2004) <http://kremlin.ru/supplement/1653> accessed 28 May 2019 (*in Russian*).

166 Memorandum on Security Assurances in Connection with Ukraine's Accession to the Treaty on the Non-Proliferation of Nuclear Weapons (signed 5 December 1994, entered into force 5 December 1994) (Russian Federation, Ukraine, United Kingdom of Great Britain and Northern Ireland, United States of America) 3006 UNTS, arts 1 and 2.

the DPR and LPR, Russia also violated the prohibition of non-intervention in Ukraine internal affairs.[167] Overall, one can agree with PACE, which described Russia's actions as "a gross violation of international law, including the Statute of the Council of Europe as well as of the Minsk Protocol to which Russia is a party".[168]

2.1.3 Independence of the DPR and LPR

The independence of the DPR and LPR, as a criterion for statehood, must also be assessed.[169] Even if an entity possesses the marks of formal independence, as is the case with the DPR and LPR,[170] if it lacks actual independence it could not be considered as fulfilling this criterion.[171] Firstly, the presumption against independence for an entity whose origin is in substantial illegality was relevant in this situation.[172] Secondly, the above evaluation of facts,[173] from which it follows that the DPR and LPR were dependent on Russia in military, political, financial and material spheres, must be taken into account.[174] Ultimately, based on extensive and granular examination of evidence, regarding the period between 11 May 2014 and 26 January 2022 the ECtHR concluded the following:

> The vast body of evidence above demonstrates beyond reasonable doubt that, as a result of Russia's military presence in eastern Ukraine and the decisive degree of influence and control it enjoyed over the areas under separatist control in eastern Ukraine as a result of its military, political

167 *Nicaragua* (n 155) para 205.
168 CoE (PACE) Res 2034 (28 January 2015), para 7.
169 See *supra* Part 1, Chapter 1.
170 "Formal independence exists where the powers of government of a territory (in internal and external affairs) are vested in the separate authorities of the putative State." J Crawford, *The Creation of States in International Law* (2nd edn, Clarendon Press 2006) 67. Formally, both the DPR and LPR have their own structures of government, constitution and municipal legal order.
171 Crawford (n 170) 88.
172 ibid 74–76, 80, 89. See *infra*.
173 Crawford includes into criteria that should be taken into account "that the entity concerned was established unlawfully, by the threat or use of external armed force; that it was imposed on, and rejected by the vast majority of the population it claimed to govern; that in important matters it was subject to foreign direction or control; that it was staffed, especially in more important positions, by nationals of the dominant State". ibid 80–81. In this context, even though the test for the independence of entity as the criterion of statehood is conceptually different from the factual tests developed in other areas of law, including human rights law and *ius in bello*, they rest on the same facts, and so their conclusions can be relevant for evaluating each other. ibid 81–83.
174 See *supra*.

> and economic support to the separatist entities, these areas were, from 11 May 2014 and subsequently, under the effective control of the Russian Federation.[175]

Therefore, in the period before Russia's recognition of the DPR and LPR on 21 February 2022, these entities did not fulfil the criterion of independence as required by the customary constitutive criteria of statehood.

2.1.4 Legal Status of the DPR and LPR in the 2014–2022 Period

Based on the above-mentioned factual account, it is indisputable that Russia's violation of a peremptory norm was instrumental to the victories of the armed groups of the DPR and LPR over Ukraine's government forces and their ability to establish effectiveness vis-à-vis the parent State.[176] The secessionist attempt was clearly connected to a violation of peremptory norms in that it profited from and was consolidated by Russia's illegal use of force. Indeed, the ECtHR established that "[t]he available evidence supports the conclusion that by the time of the 11 May 2014 'referendums', the separatist operation as a whole was being managed and coordinated by the Russian Federation."[177] Based on information explored in Part 1, Chapter 2 the violation of peremptory norms in the course of the secessionist attempt precludes the emergence of a new State. Facts deriving from illegality and an illegal and invalid declaration of independence cannot be attributive of statehood.

Therefore, under international law, the DPR and LPR were not States; they remained part of Ukraine.[178] These conclusions were also confirmed by the fact that until 21 February 2022 none of the members of the UN recognised them as sovereign States or referred to them as such. For example, the UNSC referred to the DPR as "Donetsk Oblast, Ukraine",[179] and to both the DPR and LPR as "eastern regions of Ukraine".[180] It also reaffirmed "full respect for the

175 *Ukraine and the Netherlands v Russia* (n 31) para 695. See also CoE (PACE), 'Report of the Committee on Legal Affairs and Human Rights: Legal Remedies to Human Rights Violations on the Ukrainian Territories Outside the Control of the Ukrainian Authorities' (26 September 2016) Doc 14139, para 56 ("PACE's Committee on Legal Affairs and Human Rights' Report").

176 PACE's Committee on Legal Affairs and Human Rights' Report (n 175) paras 54–55.

177 *Ukraine and the Netherlands v Russia* (n 31) para 693.

178 The same conclusion is reached by T Korotkyi and N Hendel, 'The Legal Status of the Donetsk and Luhansk "Peoples' Republics"' in S Sayapin and E Tsybulenko (eds), *The Use of Force Against Ukraine and International Law: Jus Ad Bellum, Jus in Bello, Jus Post Bellum* 148–149.

179 UNSC Res 2166 (21 July 2014) UN Doc S/RES/2166, para 1.

180 UNSC Res 2202 (17 February 2015) UN Doc S/RES/2202, preambular para 4.

sovereignty, independence and territorial integrity of Ukraine".[181] Similarly, PACE also referred to these entities simply as "the Donetsk and Luhansk regions".[182] PACE also held that "[t]he 'DPR' and 'LPR' – established, supported and effectively controlled by the Russian Federation – are not legitimate under Ukrainian or international law."[183]

However, despite being *de iure* part of Ukraine, the DPR and LPR *prima facie* exercised effective territorial control of Ukraine's territory. At the same time, they also lacked independence vis-à-vis Russia and persisted in claiming to be States. Their existence was due to violation of peremptory norms. Therefore, based on Part 1, Chapter 6 they can be characterised as illegal secessionist entities.

2.2 *Period after 21 February 2022*

2.2.1 Legal Arguments to Justify Russia's Recognition of the DPR and LPR

Russia recognised the purported statehood of the DPR and LPR on 21 February 2022 and concluded the purported agreements of friendship, cooperation and mutual assistance.[184] In his speech preceding the recognition, President Putin offered his narration of "[t]he collapse of the historical Russia known as the USSR."[185] However, despite the political relevance of these (pseudo-)historical claims, their legal significance was attenuated by Putin himself, who claimed that "Russia has done everything to preserve Ukraine's territorial integrity" and supported the implementation of the Minsk II agreements[186] (in which Donetsk and Luhansk were referred to as regions of Ukraine)[187] – acknowledging Ukraine's territorial scope and recognising it as including the DPR and LPR. In any case, as outlined in Part 2, Chapter 11, history-based arguments cannot justify the recognition of these separatist territories under international law, as Russia is bound to respect Ukraine's territorial integrity in its 1991 boundaries (including the Donetsk and Luhansk regions) as a matter of general international law and specific bilateral and multilateral commitments.[188]

---

181 ibid preambular para 1.

182 CoE (PACE) Res 2112 (21 April 2016), paras 9 and 9.1. The same denomination of the secessionist territories is also used in the CoE (PACE) Res 2067 (25 June 2015), para 6.

183 CoE (PACE) Res 2133 (12 October 2016), para 3.

184 See *supra*.

185 V Putin, 'Address by President of the Russian Federation' (The Kremlin, Moscow, 21 February 2022) <http://en.kremlin.ru/events/president/news/67828> accessed 30 July 2023 ("21 February 2022 Speech").

186 Miklasová, 'Russia's Recognition of the DPR and LPR' (n 124).

187 Minsk II (n 4), para 1.

188 See *supra* Part 2, Chapter 11. Miklasová, 'Russia's Recognition of the DPR and LPR (n 124).

To justify Russia's recognition of the DPR and LPR, President Putin also invoked a "genocide which almost 4 million people are facing" and claimed that "[n]ot a single day goes by without Donbass communities coming under shelling attacks."[189] These claims seem to echo the doctrine of remedial secession. However, as established in Part 1, Chapter 3, the right of remedial secession does not exist in positive international law. And in any case, factually, President Putin's statements were completely unfounded. Reports from international organizations and their observer teams, including those from the OSCE Special Monitoring Mission to Ukraine and the UN Human Rights Monitoring Mission in Ukraine (HRMMU), did not indicate any evidence supporting genocide claims.[190] Indeed, no evidence existed to support allegations that conduct by Ukraine amounted to genocide or "an intent to destroy in whole or in part any group in eastern Ukraine."[191] According to the ICJ's order on provisional measures, "the Court is not in possession of evidence substantiating the allegation of the Russian Federation that genocide has been committed on Ukrainian territory."[192] Ukraine, in fact, requested the Court to adjudicate that "contrary to what the Russian Federation claims, no acts of genocide, as defined by Article III of the Genocide Convention, have been committed in the Luhansk and Donetsk oblasts of Ukraine" and "recognition of the independence of the so-called 'Donetsk People's Republic' and 'Luhansk People's Republic' on 22 February 2022 is based on a false claim of genocide."[193] Notably, Russia did not institute any inter-State dispute-settlement mechanism against Ukraine alleging the commission of genocide.

Chronologically, the conflict of 2014–2022 occurred *in response to* the acts of separatists controlled by Russia; to the contrary, the doctrine of remedial secession is only triggered as a last resort remedy *in response to* the oppression perpetrated by the central government against part of the population of

189 21 February 2022 Speech (n 185).

190 See 'Daily and Spot Reports from the Special Monitoring Mission to Ukraine' <https://www.osce.org/ukraine-smm/reports> accessed 13 August 2023; 'UN Human Rights in Ukraine' <https://www.ohchr.org/en/countries/ukraine/our-presence> accessed 13 August 2023. JA Green, C Henderson and T Ruys, 'Russia's Attack on Ukraine and the Jus Ad Bellum' (2022) 9 Journal on the Use of Force and International Law 4, 26.

191 JB Bellinger III, 'How Russia's Invasion of Ukraine Violates International Law' (*CFR*, 28 February 2022) <https://www.cfr.org/article/how-russias-invasion-ukraine-violates-international-law> accessed 13 August 2023.

192 *Allegations of Genocide under the Convention on the Prevention and Punishment of the Crime of Genocide* (*Ukraine v Russian Federation*) (Order) [2022] ICJ Rep, General List No 182, para 59 ("Allegations of Genocide").

193 *Allegations of Genocide* (n 192) para 30.

the existing State. Overall, Ukraine *lawfully* attempted to regain part of its *de iure* territory by fighting the separatist militias and covert Russian troops.[194] Russia's claims thus have no basis in fact or law.

President Putin also invoked the supposed unwillingness of Ukraine to implement Minsk II.[195] It was unclear whether this point was presented as a separate argument or supporting the last resort nature of the doctrine of remedial secession.[196] In any case, the principle of peaceful settlement of disputes was applicable to both Ukraine and Russia.[197] Theoretically, even if Ukraine unilaterally denounced Minsk II (which it did not), this would not entitle Russia to act in an aggravating manner and recognise the secessionist entities in Donbas, and it would not provide the populations with the right of secession.[198] During his meeting with the UN Secretary-General, President Putin invoked Kosovo to justify Russia's recognition of the DPR and LPR.[199] But the legal context of the DPR and LPR differed from that of Kosovo; as is the case with Crimea, the DPR and LPR were created and sustained through Russia's previous unlawful use of force.[200]

Thus, from a legal standpoint, nothing had changed in the status of these entities before Russia's recognition. These were not States but Ukrainian territories outside its *de facto* control. They could be characterised as illegal secessionist entities. Russia's arguments offered no legal basis for its recognition. Ultimately, this act violated Ukraine's territorial integrity and sovereignty; it violated the principle of non-intervention and the duty of non-recognition; it violated Minsk II and specific treaties in which Russia undertook to respect Ukraine's territorial integrity.[201] The purported agreements on friendship, cooperation and mutual assistance signed between Russia and the DPR and

194 In any case, "indications are that they were very few civilian casualties in the weeks and months preceding the 2022 invasion." Green, Henderson and Ruys (n 190) 26, ftn 151 and see 19, ftn 98. See International Crisis Group, 'Conflict in Donbas: A Visual Explainer' <https://www.crisisgroup.org/content/conflict-ukraines-donbas-visual-explainer> accessed 11 August 2023. Between 2014 and 2021, this conflict cost life of over 3,000 civilians – out of total of 10,000 victims the majority of which were combatants. Green, Henderson and Ruys (n 190) 26, ftn 151 and 19, ftn 98. See *supra* Part 1, Chapter 3.

195 21 February 2022 Speech (n 185).

196 Miklasová, 'Russia's Recognition of the DPR and LPR' (n 124).

197 In further detail ibid.

198 ibid.

199 'Meeting with UN Secretary-General Antonio Guterres' (*Website of the President of Russia*, 26 April 2022) <http://en.kremlin.ru/events/president/news/68287> accessed 13 August 2023.

200 See *supra* Chapter 2.

201 Miklasová, 'Russia's Recognition of the DPR and LPR' (n 124).

LPR did not produce any effects under international law: in each case one of the parties was not a State.[202]

The UNGA deplored the 21 February 2021 recognition by the Russian Federation "as violation of the territorial integrity and sovereignty of Ukraine and inconsistent with the principles of the Charter" and demanded its unconditional reversal.[203] OSCE PA refused to recognise "the establishment through the use of force of any autonomous regions or independent entities within the internationally recognised borders of Ukraine."[204] PACE referred to "the illegal recognition" of the DPR and LPR.[205]

2.2.2 Russia's All-Out War of Aggression against Ukraine since February 2022

A large-scale all-out Russian invasion of Ukraine from multiple directions started on 24 February 2022. President Putin, in his speech preceding the attack, justified it on the basis of the right of self-defence under Article 51 of the UN Charter – both individual self-defence and collective self-defence.[206] These arguments flagrantly failed to satisfy the basic conditions of the lawfulness of self-defence, in particular, the existence of a prior armed attack and the necessity and proportionality of self-defence.[207] Importantly, the claim of collective self-defence was also flawed. In fact, "a request for assistance in collective self-defence must emanate from the government *of a state*."[208] However, the DPR and LPR – in whose name Russia claimed to have exercised self-defence – were not States, but illegal secessionist entities created through Russia's previous unlawful use of force and aggression.[209]

202 ibid.

203 UNGA Res ES-11/1 Aggression against Ukraine (2 March 2022) UN Doc A/RES/ES-11/1, paras and 6; UNGA Res ES-11/4 Territorial Integrity of Ukraine: Defending the Principles of the Charter of the United Nations (12 October 2022) UN Doc A/RES/ES-11/4, para 5.

204 OSCE (PA), 'Resolution on the Russian Federation's War of Aggression against Ukraine and Its People, and Its Threat to Security Across the OSCE Region' (6 July 2022) para 28.

205 CoE (PACE) Opinion 300 (15 March 2022) para 5.

206 24 February 2022 Address (n 5). Green, Henderson and Ruys (n 190) 8.

207 See in detail Green, Henderson and Ruys (n 190) 8–20. See also for other Russia's (potentially invoked) claims that do not justify the lawfulness of its attack. ibid 20–27. See also, for example, MN Schmitt, 'Russia's "Special Military Operation" and the (Claimed) Right of Self-Defense' (*Articles of War*, 28 February 2022) <https://lieber.westpoint.edu/russia-special-military-operation-claimed-right-self-defense/> accessed 13 August 2023.

208 Green, Henderson and Ruys (n 190) 18.

209 See *supra*. "It is patently absurd, however, to suggest that such ongoing intra-state hostilities could somehow be abruptly retrofitted into an 'armed attack' by one state against another, triggering the right of collective self-defence, through an act of recognition." Green, Henderson and Ruys (n 190) 19.

Ultimately, Russia's military offensive is a blatant violation of the prohibition of the threat or use of force amounting to an armed attack under Article 51 of the UN Charter. As Green, Henderson, and Ruys underline, Russia's attack "pretty much ticks every box" when it comes to aggressive acts in the Definition of Aggression.[210] This is confirmed by the UNGA resolution, which deplored "in the strongest terms the aggression by the Russian Federation against Ukraine in violation of Article 2 (4) of the Charter."[211] The UNGA also suspended Russia's membership in the UN Human Rights Council given "reports of gross and systemic violations and abuses of human rights and violations of international humanitarian law committed by the Russian Federation during its aggression against Ukraine."[212]

"Reaffirming that the aggression of the Russian Federation against Ukraine constitutes a serious violation by the Russian Federation of its obligations under Article 3 of the Statute of the Council of Europe," the Committee of Ministers of the CoE decided that Russia "ceases to be a member of the Council of Europe as from 16 March 2022."[213] The Opinion of PACE preceded this decision of the Committee of Ministers, stating (among other things) that Russia's armed attack against Ukraine "is in breach of the Charter of the United Nations" and amounts to aggression under the Definition of Aggression.[214] In this context, Russia also ceased to be the High Contracting Party to the European Convention on Human Rights on 16 September 2022.[215]

2.2.3 Legal Arguments to Justify the Purported Secessionist Attempt of the Kherson and Zaporizhzhia Regions

Russia's acts of recognition of the Kherson and Zaporizhzhia Regions of 29 September 2022 state that they are in accordance with "the principle of equal rights and self-determination of peoples enshrined in the Charter of the United Nations" and that they respect the will of the people of these regions as

210 ibid 6.

211 UNGA Res ES-11/1 Aggression against Ukraine (n 203) para 2. See also UNHRC Res 49/1 (4 March 2022) UN Doc A/HRC/RES/49/1.

212 UNGA Res ES-11/3 (7 April 2022) UN Doc AR/ES/ES-11/3, preambular para 2.

213 Coe (Committee of Ministers) CM/Res(2022)2.

214 CoE (PACE) Opinion 300 (n 205) para 3. See also CoE (PACE) Res 2482 (26 January 2023) para 4. OSCE (PA) (204) para 23.

215 ECtHR, Resolution of the European Court of Human Rights on the consequences of the cessation of membership of the Russian Federation to the Council of Europe in light of Article 58 of the European Convention on Human Rights (22 March 2022); Coe (Committee of Ministers) CM/Res(2022)3.

expressed in the referenda.[216] The Russian Foreign Ministry also issued a statement claiming that the referenda were the expression of the lawful right of self-determination of "the people of Donbas and south of Ukraine" in accordance with the UN Charter, the 1966 International Human Rights Covenants, the 1975 Helsinki Final Acts of the CSCE and the *Kosovo* advisory opinion. These assertions were made to demonstrate that the declarations of independence were not in violation of any international law norms.[217] The Chairman of the State Duma claimed that the accession of these entities to Russia was "the only way to save millions of people's lives from the criminal Kyiv regime. As well as to stop those attacks on civilian population, elderly people, women and children."[218]

To assess these arguments, one must first consider the claims to independent statehood made by the Kherson and Zaporizhzhia Regions. It is not clear that they even issued declarations of independence at all. The questions in a purported referendum reportedly included one concerning the creation of new States. The Russian president's official website mentions that the formal Declarations on the Independence and Sovereignty of the Kherson and Zaporizhzhia Regions were issued on 28 September 2022.[219]

However, it is difficult to find the texts of these documents, raising questions about whether they actually ever existed.[220] It is noteworthy that Russian media reported the following statement from Vladimir Saldo, the head of the

---

216 'Executive Order of the President of the Russian Federation No 685 on Recognition of the Zaporizhzhia Region (n 135); 'Executive Order of the President of the Russian Federation No 686 on Recognition of the Kherson Region (n 135). See V Putin, 'Signing of Treaties on Accession of Donetsk and Lugansk People's Republics and Zaporizhzhia and Kherson regions to Russia' (The Kremlin, Moscow, 30 September 2022) <http://en.kremlin.ru/events/president/transcripts/statements/69465/photos> accessed 13 August 2023.

217 'Statement of the Foreign Ministry in Connection with Holding Referenda in the DPR, LPR, Kherson and Zaporizhzhia Regions' (28 September 2022) <https://www.mid.ru/ru/foreign_policy/news/1831658/?TSPD_101_R...051af634b3f6083a0d6396104275ac082d71dc58a32c6a03caebabda1e42> accessed 27 July 2023 (*in Russian*).

218 'The State Duma Ratified Treaties and Adopted Laws on Accession of DPR, LPR, Zaporizhzhia and Kherson Regions to Russia' (*State Duma's Official Website*, 3 October 2022) <http://duma.gov.ru/en/news/55407/> accessed 28 July 2023.

219 See eg 'Federal Constitutional Law on the Accession of the Zaporizhzhia Region to the Russian Federation and the Establishment of a New Constituent Entity of the Russian Federation, the Zaporizhzhia Region' (*President of Russia's Official Website*, 5 October 2022) <http://en.kremlin.ru/acts/news/69515> accessed 27 July 2023.

220 "Any procedure for declaring independence of Zaporizhzhia and Kherson regions was not reported." 'Putin Recognised "Independence" of Kherson and Zaporizhzhia regions of Ukraine. It Is Formality for Their Annexation.' (*BBC News Russian Service*, 29 September 2022) <https://www.bbc.com/russian/news-63084494> accessed 27 July 2023 (*in Russian*).

military-civilian administration of the Kherson Region: "There will be sovereignty technically for some period of time, it just won't be declared on purpose. We have a slightly different situation than the Luhansk and Donetsk People's Republics, Kherson Region is immediately part of the Russian Federation."[221] Moreover, all the relevant documents issued by the supposed secessionist authorities of the Kherson and Zaporizhzhia Regions indicate an apparent willingness to join the Russian Federation; the notion of separate statehood is hardly mentioned. It is also relevant that the new 'States' (purportedly existing only from 28 to 30 September 2022) kept the designation "region" as their official (purported) name. This term is usually attached to a sub-state unit rather than indicating sovereignty. On balance, outside of the compromised referendum detailed below, the formal appearance of the secessionist acts and the claims to statehood by the Kherson and Zaporizhzhia Regions was only apparent.

Moreover, Russia's legal claims do not in any way justify the purported statehood of these entities. There was no ground for raising the doctrine of remedial secession – in the same way that it was irrelevant to recognising the DPR and LPR. Moreover, as shown in Part 1, Chapter 3, neither the right of peoples to self-determination nor a successful unilateral independence referendum equates to an entitlement under international law for populations of existing States to secede.

Additionally, apart from their unilateral character, the referenda held in the territories under Russian occupation could not offer any purportedly legal basis for the alteration of the status of the territories in question, as they did not genuinely reflect the will of the populations.[222] Apart from the glaring irregularities of their organization, which blatantly fell short of international standards, the voting *de facto* took place in regions under Russian occupation

---

221 'The Kherson Region Will Not Declare Independence' (*Info 24*, 27 September 2022) <https://info24.ru/news/hersonskaya-oblast-ne-budet-obyavlyat-o-nezavisimosti.html> 27 July 2023 (*in Russian*).

222 See also A Lieblich and Just Security, 'Q&A on Russia-Backed Referendums in Eastern Ukraine and International Law' (*Just Security*, 24 September 2022) <https://www.justsecurity.org/83221/qa-on-russia-backed-referendums-in-eastern-ukraine-and-international-law/> accessed 28 July 2023; K Parameswaran, 'The Sham "Referenda" at Gunpoint: Russia's Most Recent Violations of the International Law of Occupation in Ukraine' (*Völkerrechtsblog*, 20 October 2022) <https://voelkerrechtsblog.org/the-sham-referenda-at-gunpoint/> accessed 28 July 2023; L Mälksoo, 'Illegality of Russia's Annexations in Ukraine' (*Articles of War*, 3 October 2022) <https://lieber.westpoint.edu/illegality-russias-annexation-ukraine/> accessed 28 July 2023.

and during active military operations.[223] Moreover, according to reports, the regions were considerably emptied, with many residents having fled the fighting.[224] Several reports highlighted that 'voting' took place in the presence of armed men,[225] essentially precluding the expression of voters' free will.

A constitutive criterion of statehood requires not only formal but actual independence.[226] Significant parts of both Kherson and Zaporizhzhia were occupied by the Russian Federation at the time of the referenda or the declarations of independence (if they were issued at all).[227] The Russian occupying forces appointed the heads of the military-civilian administrations in both of these regions.[228] As argued by Crawford, "[a]n entity claiming statehood, but created during a period of foreign military occupation will be presumed not to be independent."[229] This presumption squarely applies to the Kherson and Zaporizhzhia Regions.

Cardinally, under modern international law, the purported referenda were only possible as a result of the illegal war of aggression by Russia against

223 'High Turnout in Empty Villages. How "Referendums" Are Held in the Captured Territories of Ukraine' (*BBC News Russian Service*, 27 September 2022) <https://www.bbc.com/russian/features-63040911> accessed 27 July 2022 (*in Russian*).

224 For example, reportedly, only 20% of the remaining residents of Melitopol took part in the vote, especially women and elderly men (as the men reportedly feared being drafted after the vote). 'High Turnout in Empty Villages. How "Referendums" Are Held in the Captured Territories of Ukraine' (n 223).

225 DL Stern and R Dixon, 'With Kalashnikov Rifles, Russia Drives the Staged Vote in Ukraine' (*The Washington Post*, 24 September 2022) <https://www.washingtonpost.com/world/2022/09/24/ukraine-putin-referendums/> accessed 27 July 2023; Y Gorbunova, 'Fictitious Annexation Follows "Voting" at Gunpoint' (*Human Rights Watch*, 30 September 2022) <https://www.hrw.org/news/2022/09/30/fictitious-annexation-follows-voting-gunpoint#:~:text=Vladimir%20Putin%20has%20just%20signed,in%20some%20cases%20at%20gunpoint> accessed 27 July 2023; 'High Turnout in Empty Villages. How "Referendums" Are Held in the Captured Territories of Ukraine' (n 223).

226 Crawford (n 170) 62–89.

227 See (n 132). According to Lieblich, the question of Russia's effective control over different territories of Ukraine "is a question that should be answered through a separate analysis ... if Russia is capable of administering so-called referendums in a given territory, then that territory must be under its control." Lieblich (n 222). For the evaluation of the referendums' compliance with IHL see Parameswaran (n 222).

228 'Russian-Occupied Kherson Names New Leadership Amid Pro-Ukraine Protests, Rocket Attacks' (*The Moscow Times*, 28 April 2022) <https://www.themoscowtimes.com/2022/04/28/russian-occupied-kherson-names-new-leadership-amid-pro-ukraine-protests-rocket-attacks-a77519> accessed 28 July 2023; 'What Is Known about the Acting Governor of the Zaporizhzhia Region Yevgeny Balitsky' (*TASS*, 4 October 2022) <https://tass.ru/info/15958133> accessed 28 July 2023 (*in Russian*).

229 Crawford (n 170) 148.

Ukraine. Given this violation of peremptory norms of international law, the referenda were tainted – together with the supposed declarations of independence – by peremptory illegality. In line with the principle of *ex iniuria ius non oritur*, these acts did not produce any legal effects under international law. No new States of the Kherson and Zaporizhzhia Region emerged; the duty of non-recognition applies to all States. Russia's recognitions of 29 September 2022 were thus separate unlawful acts violating the principle of non-intervention, territorial integrity, the duty of non-recognition, and specific bilateral and multilateral commitments respecting Ukraine's territorial integrity.

Many States and IOs have condemned these sham 'referenda'.[230] In particular, the UNGA resolution declared that "the illegal so-called referendums … have no validity under international law and do not form the basis for any alteration of the status of these regions of Ukraine."[231] It also demanded that the Russian Federation "immediately and unconditionally reverse" its recognition of the Kherson and Zaporizhzhia regions of Ukraine.[232] The UN Secretary-General said that "the so-called 'referenda' … cannot be called a genuine expression of the popular will."[233] The EU condemned "the illegal sham 'referenda'" and stated that "[t]heir outcome is null and void and cannot produce any legal effect whatsoever."[234] According to PACE, the referenda "are travesty, in contravention of international law and contrary to any substantive and procedural

230 However, Professor Snyder claimed, "[a] sham is shambolic but it does actually exist. What Russia is undertaking is nothing more than a media exercise designed to shape how people think about Russian-occupied Ukraine." T Snyder, 'Russia's Obscene "Referendums"' (22 September 2022) <https://snyder.substack.com/p/russias-obscene-referendums> accessed 28 July 2023.

231 UNGA Res ES-11/4 Territorial Integrity of Ukraine: Defending the Principles of the Charter of the United Nations (n 203) para 3.

232 ibid.

233 'Ukraine: UN Secretary-General Condemns Russia Annexation Plan' (*UN News*, 29 September 2022) <https://news.un.org/en/story/2022/09/1129047#:~:text=Ukraine%3A%20UN%20Secretary%2DGeneral%20condemns%20Russia%20annexation%20plan,-29%20September%202022&text=Russia%27s%20plan%20to%20annex%20four,in%20the%20seven%2Dmonth%20war.> accessed 28 July 2023.

234 'Ukraine: Declaration by the High Representative on Behalf of the European Union on the Illegal Sham "Referenda" by Russia in the Donetsk, Kherson, Luhansk and Zaporizhzhia Regions' (*Council of the EU Press Release*, 28 September 2022) <https://www.consilium.europa.eu/en/press/press-releases/2022/09/28/ukraine-declaration-by-the-high-representative-on-behalf-of-the-european-union-on-the-illegal-sham-referenda-by-russia-in-the-donetsk-kherson-luhansk-and-zaporizhzhia-regions/> accessed 28 July 2023.

standards for holding referendums. They must be considered null and void and with no legal or political effects."[235]

2.2.4 Legal Status of the DPR, LPR, Kherson and Zaporizhzhia Regions on 30 September 2022 and Thereafter

Neither the DPR, LPR, Kherson Region, nor Zaporizhzhia Region were States when the purported accession agreements were signed with the Russian Federation on 30 September 2022. The DPR and LPR have existed as illegal secessionist entities since 2014. For a brief period, Kherson and Zaporizhzhia Regions also bore the characteristics of illegal secessionist entities, but their ostensible existence was only ephemeral. Again, it is even doubtful that the Kherson and Zaporizhzhia Regions declared their independence, at least formally. As outlined, the purported so-called referenda of September 2022 offered no legal basis for altering the legal status of the four regions of Ukraine – whether that be new statehood for the Kherson and Zaporizhzhia Regions or accession to Russia for the four regions. The absence of statehood status in one of the parties renders each of these accession agreements non-existent under international law. There was, therefore, no legal basis for the transfer of sovereignty; no mode of State succession took place.

Lacking a legal basis or another contracting party, these purported accession agreements – provisionally applied since 30 September 2022 – thus express no more than the desire of the Russian Federation to unilaterally extend its sovereignty over the Ukrainian territories. These acts amount to an unlawful annexation of Ukrainian territory, violating fundamental principles of international law, according to which "[t]he territory of a State shall not be the object of acquisition by another State resulting from the threat or use of force" and "[n]o territorial acquisitions resulting from the threat or use of force shall be recognised as legal."[236]

The practice of international organisations overwhelmingly buttresses these conclusions. The UNGA resolution (adopted with 134 votes in favour; 5 votes against; 35 abstentions) declared that "attempted illegal annexations" of

235 CoE (PACE) Res 2463 (13 October 2022), para 2; See also CoE (PACE) Res 2482 (26 January 2023), para 1.

236 Friendly Relations Declaration (n 152), principle 1, para 9; Definition of Aggression (n 152) art 5(3). See also Mälksoo (n 222). See also PF Laval, 'Provinces ukrainiennes et « référendums d'annexion » – au-delà des limites imposées par le droit international' (*Le club des juristes*, 12 October 2022) <https://blog.leclubdesjuristes.com/provinces-ukrainiennes-et-referendums-dannexion-au-dela-des-limites-imposees-par-le-droit-international-par-p-f-laval/> accessed 28 July 2023.

the four regions "have no validity under international law and do not form the basis for any alteration of the status of these regions of Ukraine."[237] The UN Secretary-General stated that any decision to annex these four regions "would have no legal value."[238] PACE held that the "attempted annexation of the Ukrainian regions of Donetsk, Kherson, Luhansk and Zaporizhzhia … clearly violates the principle of international law according to which no territorial acquisition resulting from the use of force shall be recognised as legal."[239] The four regions remain part of Ukraine.

---

237 UNGA Res ES-11/4 Territorial Integrity of Ukraine: Defending the Principles of the Charter of the United Nations (n 203) para 3.

238 'Ukraine: UN Secretary-General Condemns Russia Annexation Plan' (n 233).

239 CoE (PACE) Res 2482 (26 January 2023), para 1.

CHAPTER 13

Abkhazia and South Ossetia

1 Outline of the Secessionist Attempts

1.1 *South Ossetia and Abkhazia Entering the USSR*

Following the tumultuous period of the 1917 revolutions, the formation of the Democratic Republic of Georgia, of which Abkhazia formed a part, and the ultimate victory of the Red Army in a civil war, the Georgian Soviet Socialist Republic (SSR) was proclaimed on 18 February 1921, and the Abkhazian SSR was declared on 4 March 1921.[1] On 16 December 1921, the Abkhazian SSR and the Georgian SSR concluded the Union Treaty, which established cooperation in a number of sectors but left foreign policy entirely in the control of the Georgian SSR.[2] Therefore, when the Transcaucasian Socialist Federative Soviet Republic (TSFSR) was formed on 13 December 1921, Abkhazia did not join it independently, but through Georgia.[3] Then, the TSFSR became one of the USSR's constituent republics. In the Soviet Union, the Abkhazian SSR was the only 'treaty' republic – declared equal with the Georgian SSR, but in practice subordinate to it.[4] Its status was ultimately downgraded to that of an autonomous republic within the Georgian SSR in 1931.[5]

As for South Ossetia, already during the Russian Empire, ethnic Ossetians lived in different administrative units, to the north and south of the Caucasus.[6] This division persisted after the 1917 revolutions, when South Ossetia became part of Democratic Georgia and North Ossetia joined the RSFSR.[7] Between 1918 and 1921, rebellion in support of Soviet Russia erupted in South Ossetia.[8]

---

1 A Nussberger, 'Abkhazia' in MPEPIL (online edn, OUP 2013) para 6.

2 ibid para 6.

3 ibid para 7.

4 "[T]he decision to grant Abkhazia a status of SSR was not part of any preconceived plan to generate leverage against either Georgia or Abkhazia. It appears that this decision was one of the many ad hoc solutions readily employed by the Bolsheviks to cater for their immediate political needs." A Saparov, *From Conflict to Autonomy in the Caucasus: The Soviet Union and the Making of Abkhazia, South Ossetia and Nagorno Karabakh* (Routledge 2015) 64 and 55 and for an excellent historical analysis see 42–64.

5 Nussberger, 'Abkhazia' (n 1) paras 7–8.

6 A Nussberger, 'South Ossetia' in MPEPIL (online edn, OUP 2013) para 3.

7 ibid para 4.

8 The rebels managed to take control of part of the territory, establish proto-autonomous organs there and demand unification with Bolshevik Russia. X Follebouckt, *Les conflits*

DOI:10.1163/9789004702646_020

However, Georgia suppressed it.[9] After the Bolshevik's ultimate takeover of Georgia in 1921, South Ossetia was granted the status of an autonomous region within the Georgian SSR.[10]

1.2 *Break-Up of the USSR, Independence Wars and Pre-2008 Period*

During the Soviet period, numerous policies helped exacerbate tensions between Abkhazia and South Ossetia on the one hand and Georgia on the other.[11] These tensions became more and more apparent with the gradual decline of Soviet power following the accession of Gorbachev and the introduction of the policies of *glasnost* and *perestroika.*[12] Georgia's move towards independence and growing nationalism in the late 1980s provoked reactions in its autonomous entities, which feared losing their status in the changing circumstances.[13]

Already on 10 November 1989, the South Ossetian parliament's demand for an upgrade of South Ossetia's status from autonomous region to autonomous republic was met with rejection by the Georgian Supreme Soviet.[14] Then, on 25 August 1990 and 20 September 1990, respectively, Abkhazia and South Ossetia declared their sovereignty from the Georgian SSR as separate republics within the USSR.[15] The Georgian SSR had itself declared sovereignty in March

gelés de l'espace postoviétique: genèse et enjeux (Presses universitaires de Louvain 2011) 55. See also Saparov (n 4) 66–87.

9 Nussberger, 'South Ossetia' (n 6) para 4. Today, this is seen by South Ossetians as genocide. See 'Declaration on Genocide of South Ossetians in 1989–1992' (26 April 2006) <http://cominf.org/node/1146047662> accessed 2 May 2019 (*in Russian*).

10 Nussberger, 'South Ossetia' (n 6) para 5. This solution did not satisfy anyone, since Ossetians wanted more autonomy and Georgians did not want any autonomy for this region. Folleboucktt (n 8) 55–56.

11 See Nussberger, 'South Ossetia' (n 6) paras 6–8; Nussberger, 'Abkhazia' (n 1) para 10. For example, during the Soviet period the proportion of Georgians living in Abkhazia grew from 33% in 1926 to 45% in 1989, while the proportion of Abkhaz declined from 28% in 1926 to 17.8% in 1989. Folleboucktt (n 8) 66.

12 See Folleboucktt (n 8) 71–72.

13 See ibid 86–92. In April 1989, mass protests against the discrimination of Georgians in Abkhazia transformed into a pro-independence demonstration. Soviet troops intervened and killed 19 people. ibid 89. In August 1989, the Georgian Supreme Soviet adopted the language law, which made the use of the Georgian language obligatory in the public sector in the whole republic; this provoked opposition in Abkhazia and South Ossetia. ibid 90.

14 J Summers, 'Russia and Competing Spheres of Influence: The Case of Georgia, Abkhazia and South Ossetia' in M Happold, *International Law in a Multipolar World* (Routledge 2012) 95–96.

15 This was preceded by Georgia's passing a law barring regional parties from participating in the elections in August 1990. ibid 96.

1990.[16] Georgia's Supreme Soviet, led by Zviad Gamsakhurdia, responded to South Ossetia's declaration of sovereignty by abolishing its autonomy and establishing a blockade in December 1990.[17] Subsequently, fighting broke out between Georgian and South Ossetian militias.[18]

On the one hand, in March 1991, Georgia – still part of the Soviet Union – refused to participate in the referendum on a new Union Treaty and instead organised its own independence referendum with overwhelmingly favourable results.[19] On the other hand, South Ossetia and Abkhazia took part in the Union referendum and approved a new Union Treaty by large margins.[20] Georgia declared its independence from the USSR on 9 April 1991, but at the time no State recognised it as an independent State.[21] In the meantime, fighting between South Ossetia and Georgia continued, with particularly dire consequences for civilian populations.[22] In April 1991, Soviet troops intervened in the conflict.[23]

After the USSR's break-up, Georgia was admitted to the UN on 31 July 1992 within the borders of the former Georgian SSR.[24] Previously, in January 1992, South Ossetia had held a referendum in which the majority favoured independence from Georgia and unification with Russia.[25] In May 1992, South Ossetia declared independence and appealed to join Russia, but the latter rejected the request.[26] "Russia acted ambivalently, emphasizing the territorial integrity of

16 Georgia declared the treaty on the formation of the USSR invalid for Georgia. Nussberger, 'South Ossetia' (n 6) para 10. Follebouckt (n 8) 89.

17 Summers (n 14) 96.

18 ibid. In January 1991, Gorbachev issued a decree ordering Georgian troops to withdraw from South Ossetia. ibid 97.

19 Follebouckt (n 8) 91.

20 ibid 91. South Ossetia never published its results. Summers (n 14) 96.

21 Summers (n 14) 96. Georgia, similarly to the Baltic States, declared the restoration of its pre-Soviet declaration of independence of 26 May 1918. See 'Act of Restoration of State Independence of Georgia' (9 April 1991) <https://matsne.gov.ge/en/document/view/32362?publication=0> accessed 1 May 2019.

22 In 1991, more than 100,000 Ossetians escaped to North Ossetia and 10,000 Georgians left the area too. Follebouckt (n 8) 94.

23 Summers (n 14) 96–97.

24 ibid 96. See UNGA Res 46/241 (31 July 1992) UN Doc A/RES/46/241.

25 Nussberger, 'South Ossetia' (n 6) para 11.

26 Summers (n 14) 97. 'Act of Declaration of Independence of the Republic of South Ossetia' (adopted 29 May 1992) <http://cominf.org/en/node/1127813812> accessed 2 May 2019 (*in Russian*). See also 'Declaration of Independence of Republic of South Ossetia (adopted 21 December 1991) <https://ru.wikisource.org/wiki/Декларация_о_независимости_Республики_Южная_Осетия> accessed 2 May 2019 (*in Russian*).

Georgia while lending sporadic support to the South Ossetian fighters."[27] In addition, South Ossetians also enjoyed the assistance of North Ossetians in terms of material support and an influx of volunteers.[28] As the fighting continued, voices started to be raised in Moscow about the need to end the war.[29] A number of sources confirm Russia's last-minute military engagement in the conflict.[30] Ultimately, on 24 June 1992, upon Yeltsin's personal intervention, the presidents of Russia and Georgia signed the so-called Sochi Agreement providing for a ceasefire and the deployment of a trilateral peacekeeping force composed of Russian, Georgian and Ossetian units.[31]

Later that year, on 23 July 1992, Abkhazia declared the 1978 Constitution of the Abkhazian ASSR terminated, restored the 1925 Constitution of the Abkhazian SSR, according to which Abkhazia was a Soviet republic, and demanded the conclusion of a new union treaty with Georgia.[32] These political

---

27 S Fischer, 'The Conflicts over Abkhazia and South Ossetia in Light of the Crisis over Ukraine' in S Fischer (ed), *Not Frozen! The Unresolved Conflicts over Transnistria, Abkhazia, South Ossetia and Nagorno-Karabakh in Light of the Crisis over Ukraine* (SWP 2016) 45. See also Summers (n 14) 97; A Nussberger, 'The War between Russia and Georgia – Consequences and Unresolved Questions' (2009) 1 GoJIL 341, 358.

28 Folleblouckt (n 8) 99.

29 ibid 95.

30 In June 1992, armoured units of the Russian army took positions around Tskhinvali; at the same time, Georgian forces were targeted by helicopter gunships. Folleblouckt (n 8) 95; SA Sotiriou, 'The Irreversibility of History: The Conflicts in South Ossetia and Abkhazia' (2019) 66 Problems of Post-Communism 172, 176; TW Waters, 'Plucky Little Russia: Misreading the Georgian War Through the Distorting Lens of Aggression' 49 (2013) Stanford Journal of International Law 176, 185. It is worth noting that Article 2 of the Sochi Ceasefire Agreement stipulates that "[i]n order to secure demilitarization of the conflict region and *to rule out the possibility of involvement of the Armed Forces of the Russian Federation in conflict*, the Russian Federation shall withdraw the Tskhinvali-district deployed 37th engineer-sapper Regiment and 292 separate fighting helicopter regiment within 20 days from the moment of cease-fire and separation of opposing parties." Agreement on Principles of Settlement of the Georgian-Ossetian Conflict (signed 24 June 1992, entered into force 24 June 1992) <https://peacemaker.un.org/georgia-sochi-agreement92> accessed 2 May 2019 ("Sochi Agreement") (*emphasis added*). Georgia's former president, Shevardnadze, discussed the context of the signing of the Sochi Agreement including the loss of Georgia and "the danger that Russian troops would interfere in the conflict." See 'Georgia: Shevardnadze Discusses 1992 South Ossetia Agreement' (*Radio Free Europe*, 23 February 2006) <https://www.rferl.org/a/1066081.html> accessed 2 May 2019.

31 Summers (n 14) 97. See Sochi Agreement (n 30).

32 Summers (n 14) 98. See Supreme Soviet of Abkhazia, 'Resolution on Termination of the Constitution of Abkhazian ASSR of 1978) (adopted 23 July 1992) <https://ru.wikisource.org/wiki/Постановление_ВС_Абхазской_АССР_от_23.07.1992> accessed 2 May 2019 (*in Russian*). This move was preceded by Georgia's restoration of the 1921 constitution

tensions[33] were followed by military conflict when Georgian troops entered Abkhazia on 14 August 1992.[34] The war was marked by a heavy toll on the civilian population, with more than 300,000 people fleeing their homes, including 250,000 Georgians, ultimately transforming the demographic structure of the region.[35] Numerous attempts to terminate the conflict included the establishment on 24 August 1993 of the United Nations Observer Mission in Georgia (UNOMIG) to verify the observance of a previous ceasefire.[36] Ultimately, the Russian-mediated ceasefire known as the Moscow Agreement of 14 May 1994 foresaw the deployment of a CIS peacekeeping force (CIS CPF) composed entirely of Russian troops.[37]

Even though the Russian president and other Russian officials publicly supported Georgia's territorial integrity and even delivered arms to Georgia itself,[38] the war in Abkhazia was also characterised by Russian intervention in support of the separatists. The latter became more and more apparent in the course of the conflict.[39] This must be seen in the context of Moscow's weakened control

---

of the Democratic Republic of Georgia, which was seen by Abkhazians as an attack on Abkhazia's autonomy. Follebouckt (n 8) 95–96.

33 On the political tensions preceding the break-up of the USSR, in particular the adoption of the Declaration of State Sovereignty of the Abkhazian SSR on 25 August 1990 and the participation of Abkhazia in the All-Union referendum in March 1991, see Independent International Fact-Finding Mission on the Conflict in Georgia, *Report* (Vol II, IIFFMCG 2009) 73–75 ("Report").

34 Summers (n 14) 98.

35 "Abkhaz victory in the war resulted in dramatic demographic change – by expelling Georgians the Abkhaz became the majority in Abkhazia for the first time since 1867." Saparov (n 4) 158. Summers (n 14) 98.

36 UNSC Res 858 (24 August 1993) UN Doc S/RES/858.

37 Summers (n 14) 99. The UNSC noted with satisfaction the beginning of the operation of the CIS peacekeeping operation. See UNSC Res 934 (30 June 1994) UN Doc S/RES/934, para 2. See Agreement on a Cease-fire and Separation of Forces, Signed in Moscow (14 May 1994), annex I to Letter from the Permanent Representative of Georgia to the United Nations Addressed to the President of the Security Council (17 May 1994) UN Doc S/1994/583 ("Moscow Agreement"). See *Mamasakhlisi and Others v Georgia and Russia* App 29999/04 and 41424/04 (Merits) (ECtHR, 7 March 2023) paras 325–327 ("*Mamasakhlisi*").

38 Follebouckt (n 8) 100–101. The deliveries of weapons took place on the basis of pre-existing bilateral agreements with Georgia. See Human Rights Watch, *Georgia/Abkhazia: Violations of the Laws of War and Russia's Role in the Conflict* (HRW 1995) 21.

39 "Here too, Russia played an ambiguous role, alternately supporting either side. As events progressed, however, Moscow stepped up its support for the Abkhaz separatists, placing the collapsing Georgian state under increasing military pressure." Fischer, 'The Conflicts over Abkhazia and South Ossetia' (n 27) 46. According to the Report, Russia's role in the War in Abkhazia "is still not easy to judge, but Russian support for the Abkhaz side at some crucial moments undoubtedly created a major obstacle to the establishment of friendly relations between Moscow and Tbilisi." Report (n 33) 80.

over Russian troops stationed abroad after the Soviet Union's break-up and the ensuing autonomous decision-making or disobedience of officials on the ground.[40] It was unclear whether Russian military involvement emanated from "local base commanders, senior levels of the Russian government, or one or another faction within the defense establishment".[41] Russia's growing involvement also reflected the change of Russian policy towards the so-called Near Abroad in the early years after the USSR's break up,[42] and it allowed Russia to put pressure on Georgia to join the CIS and preserve Russian military bases there.[43] While the ECtHR was unable, based on the evidence available to it, to rule on the composition of the armed forces that prevailed in the conflict, the type and level of external support and those who authorized it, it nevertheless held that

> the military victory of pro-Abkhaz fighters in their armed conflict with Georgian troops in the early 1990s would not have been possible without the involvement of at least certain forces and military equipment emanating from the territory of the Russian Federation.[44]

The Court held that "in the early 1990s Russian weapons found their way into Abkhaz hands;" a large number of among others ethnic Russians "fought on the Abkhaz side"; "Russian military and Russian commanders stationed in Abkhazia actively supported the Abkhaz side."[45] Other sources confirm that Russia armed Abkhazians with tanks, armoured vehicles, artillery pieces and rocket launchers.[46] "[T]here is little doubt that whatever weapons there were

40 Follebouckt (n 8) 100–101.

41 Human Rights Watch (n 38) 12. See also Report (n 33) 79–80.

42 According to Follebouckt, two phases can be distinguished with respect to Russia's policy towards the Near Abroad. From 1991 until 1992–1993, Russia's policy was characterized by certain restraint vis-à-vis this region and by the adherence to the principle of non-intervention in internal affairs. However, since the summer of 1992 and especially after the constitutional crisis of October 1993, Russia's approach to the Near Abroad has become more assertive and revisionist. Follebouckt (n 8) 125–127. This change corresponds to an increased Russian intervention in the war in Abkhazia. However, according to the Report, the political crisis in Moscow in October 1993 "ruled out any well-designed, balanced intervention by Russia at its southern border." Report (n 33) 79.

43 S Fischer, 'Russian Policy in the Unresolved Conflicts' in S Fischer (ed), *Not Frozen! The Unresolved Conflicts over Transnistria, Abkhazia, South Ossetia and Nagorno-Karabakh in Light of the Crisis over Ukraine* (SWP 2016) 12.

44 *Mamasakhlisi* (n 37) para 323. See *infra* on the rules of attribution at play in this context.

45 *Mamasakhlisi* (n 37) para 323.

46 Summers (n 14) 98–99; Follebouckt (n 8) 125–127.

came from Russian or Soviet sources."[47] According to Human Rights Watch, "at least some heavy weapons, transport and fuel were supplied by Russian forces."[48] Some sources also claim that the Russian troops intervened directly in the conflict too.[49] In fact, the Russian air force openly intervened in support of Abkhazians – for example, according to UN observers, in March 1993 a Russian major piloted a SU-27 that was shot down.[50] Moreover, Russian forces also provided support to Abkhaz operations, including sea attacks on Sukhumi in 1993.[51] Additional support for the Abkhazians came from the Confederation of Caucasian Mountain People, a paramilitary group composed of Chechens, other north Caucasian ethnic groups and Russians whose links to the Russian Federation were unclear.[52] According to Human Rights Watch, "Russian government officials in Moscow have sanctioned the sending of Russian fighters to Abkhazia as agents of the Russian Federation."[53] It is impossible to corroborate this report.

In late 1993, Georgia joined the CIS and signed a treaty with Russia on the legal status of the former Soviet military bases in Georgia.[54] However, this treaty never entered into force, and the issue of the withdrawal of the Russian forces remained one of the points of contention between the two countries.[55]

47 Human Rights Watch (n 38) 18. "[T]he sudden presence of armor, tanks, and heavy artillery among the previously lightly armed Abkhaz in the fighting between October and December 1992 realistically leaves little room for any conclusion except that some parties, within Russian forces, decided to supply the Abkhaz." ibid 32 and 38.

48 Human Rights Watch (n 38) 38.

49 Summers (n 14) 98–99.

50 Folleboucktt (n 8) 100; Summers (n 14) 98; Human Rights Watch (n 38) 38 and 53.

51 Human Rights Watch (n 38) 53.

52 See Summers (n 14) 98–99; Folleboucktt (n 8) 99–100.

53 Human Rights Watch (n 38) 53.

54 Folleboucktt (n 8) 161.

55 See Treaty between the Russian Federation and the Republic of Georgia on the Legal Status of Military Formations of the Russian Federation Temporarily Stationed on the Territory of the Republic of Georgia (signed 9 October 1993; never entered into force) <http://docs.cntd.ru/document/1900430> accessed 18 May 2019 (*in Russian*). Even if this agreement never entered into force, it was provisionally applied by the decision of both presidents. In 1995, a new treaty on the status of these troops was signed but never entered into force. See Treaty between the Russian Federation and the Republic of Georgia on the Military Bases of Russia on the Territory of Georgia (signed 15 September 1995; never entered into force) <https://dokipedia.ru/document/5191545> accessed 18 May 2019 (*in Russian*). See H Hamant, *Démembrement de l'URSS et problèmes de succession d'états* (Bruylant 2007) 382. Under the 1995 agreement, Russia could have retained four bases: at Viazani (near Tbilisi); Gudauta (in Abkhazia); Batumi (in Ajaria); and Akhalkalaki (near the Turkish border). See 'Russian Bases in Georgia' (2001) 7 Strategic Comments 1, 1–2. Ultimately, while Russia withdrew its troops and closed military bases in 2007, this did

After the war, in 1994, Abkhazia promulgated its new constitution and declared itself a sovereign republic; in 1999, after unilateral referendum, Abkhazia formally declared independence.[56] Following the end of hostilities, Abkhazia was cut off from the outside world. A key document establishing sanctions was the Decision by the Council of CIS Heads of State adopted in January 1996.[57] "[T]he importance of Russia in maintaining a blockade between 1994 and 1999, as well as in promoting CIS sanctions, has been established."[58] Between 1996–1999, Abkhazia's only foreign interaction was with Turkey – "without this trade outlet it is likely that Abkhazia would have ceased to function."[59] Coping strategies in Abkhazia in this period included a return to subsistence agriculture, depletive strategies and migration.[60]

---

not concern the base in Abkhazia. Georgia had doubts whether it had been closed and demanded international observers to check it. See M Antidze, 'Russia Closes Last Military Base in Georgia' (*Reuters*, 13 November 2007) <https://www.reuters.com/article/us-georgia-russia-bases/russia-closes-last-military-base-in-georgia-idUSL1387605220071113> accessed 2 May 2019. According to the ECtHR, "there was no internationally verified confirmation" of the base's closure and effectively its infrastructure "was transferred to the CIS CPF (in fact, Russian) peacekeeping force." *Mamasakhlisi* (n 37) paras 327. With Russia's recognition of Abkhazia and South Ossetia, Russia now operates the 7th Military Base in Gudauta, Abkhazia and the 4th Military Base in South Ossetia. See *infra*.

56 'Act of State Independence of the Republic of Abkhazia' (12 October 1999) <https://unpo.org/article/705> accessed 5 December 2020.

57 The document provided for a comprehensive set of measures in order to isolate the Abkhazian regime, including in economic and financial spheres, and declared Abkhazia "an internal part of Georgia." CIS Heads of State, 'Decision by the Council of CIS Heads of State on Measures to Settle the Conflict in Abkhazia, Georgia' (adopted 19 January 1996; entered into force 19 January 1996) <http://docs.cntd.ru/document/901818167> accessed 2 May 2019 (*in Russian*). See *Mamasakhlisi* (n 37) paras 35 and 332. On the issue of the isolation of Abkhazia, see N Akaba and I Gitsba, 'Abkhazia's Isolation/De-Isolation and the Transformation of the Georgian-Abkhaz Conflict: An Historical Political Analysis' in *The De-Isolation of Abkhazia* (International Alert 2011) 8–10.

58 G Prelz Oltramonti, 'The Political Economy of a de Facto State: The Importance of Local Stakeholders in the Case of Abkhazia' (2015) 3 Caucasus Survey 291, 293.

59 T Frear, 'The Foreign Policy Options of a Small Unrecognised State: The Case of Abkhazia,' (2014) 1 Caucasus Survey Online 1, 6 and 10–11. There is a considerable Abkhazian minority living in Turkey as a result of expulsions of Abkhazians in the 19th century after the Russian-Caucasian war and the Abkhazian rebellion. ibid, 11–12.

60 Prelz Oltramonti, 'The Political Economy of a de Facto State' (n 58) 293. Endemic corruption benefitted small-scale trade along the borders. ibid. In addition, in Abkhazia, "de facto authorities were able to maintain de facto independence only by fully embracing informality as a modus operandi." G Prelz Oltramonti, 'Trajectories of Illegality and Informality in Conflict Protraction: The Abkhaz-Georgian Case' (2017) 5 Caucasus Survey 85, 91. For example, Abkhaz authorities were unable to pay salaries to their employees and instead provided them with one loaf of bread per day. ibid.

Russia stopped observing these sanctions in 1999 and ultimately withdrew from them completely in March 2008.[61] The period between 1999 and 2008 was marked by growing Russian involvement. The ECtHR in *Mamasakhlisi* – when examining the period between 2001 and 2007 – concluded that

> combined aspects of Russia's sustained military connection to the region during the relevant period … and even before and after its end … enables it to conclude that the Russian State wielded sufficient military influence over Abkhaz territory for it to be considered 'dissuasive' and as such decisive in practice.[62]

Moreover, Russia supported Abkhazia through political backing,[63] economic aid, investment, payment of pensions and social benefits to Russian-passport holders.[64] In addition, Russian tourists have also been an important source of revenue for Abkhazia.[65] At the same time, some nominal political independence vis-à-vis Russia was preserved, for example, when the Russian-backed presidential candidate lost elections in 2004.[66]

As for South Ossetia, after the war, the border between Georgia and South Ossetia was quite permeable, tensions remained low and the conflict was regarded as being close to solution.[67] Criminal resources and smuggling of

61 Frear (n 59) 6.

62 *Mamasakhlisi* (n 37) para 329. To reach this conclusion, the Court considered several factors, including Russia's role in the Georgia-Abkhazia conflict in the 1990s (see *supra*), the element of Russian dissuasion against Georgia's attempt at retaking the territories and the role of the CIS CPF (but, *de facto* Russian) peacekeeping force. ibid, paras 323–329.

63 "[F]or instance, speaking at a rally in the Abkhaz capital Sokhumi on 30 September, Deputy Chairman of the Russian Duma Sergey Baburin called on the Georgian and Russian authorities to recognise the independence of Abkhazia." CoE (PACE), 'Report of the Monitoring Committee: Implementation of Resolution 1415 (2005) on the Honouring of Obligations and Commitments by Georgia' (5 January 2006) Doc 10779, para 47. *Mamasakhlisi* (n 37) paras 330–331.

64 Fischer, 'Russian Policy in the Unresolved Conflicts' (n 43) 17–18 and 22. *Mamasakhlisi* (n 37) paras 332–337.

65 NM Shanahan Cutts, 'Enemies Through the Gates: Russian Violations of International Law in Georgia/Abkhazia Conflict' 40 (2007) Case Western Reserve Journal of International Law 281, 293–294.

66 Frear (n 59) 7; A Achba, 'Abkhazia – Russia's Tight Embrace' (*ECFR*, 1 September 2016) <https://www.ecfr.eu/article/essay_abkhazia_russias_tight_embrace> accessed 2 May 2019.

67 P Kolstø and H Blakkisrud, 'Living with Non-Recognition: State- and Nation-Building in South Caucasian Quasi-States' (2008) 60 Europe-Asia Studies 483, 492.

goods helped maintain South Ossetia's economic survival in the 1990s.[68] Tensions escalated following the accession to the Georgian presidency of Saakashvili, who sought to reassert Georgia's authority over the region.[69] The closing of the Ergneti border-crossing market, a pillar of the local economy, was a particularly important element of this escalation.[70] The subsequent period was also marked by the growing influence of Russia.[71] Especially after 2004, "Russian officials had *de facto* control over South Ossetia's institutions."[72] In 2006, South Ossetia held an independence referendum accepted by a large margin of the population.[73] The Russian State Duma unanimously approved its results.[74]

Thus, generally, "the informal dependency of Abkhazia and South Ossetia [on Russia] grew continuously from the early 2000s to the Russo-Georgian War of 2008."[75] Even before 2008, Russia influenced these entities economically, militarily and politically.[76] In addition, in 2005, already 80% of Abkhazians and South Ossetians possessed Russian passports as a result of the policy of passportisation.[77] Before 2008, no UN Member State recognised South Ossetia and Abkhazia as independent States.[78]

---

68 T German, 'Russia and South Ossetia: Conferring Statehood or Creeping Annexation?' (2016) 16 Southeast European and Black Sea Studies 155, 161. See also CoE (PACE), 'Report of Political Affairs Committee: Situation in Georgia and the Consequences for the Stability of the Caucasus Region' (24 September 2002) Doc 9564, para 30.

69 Kolstø and Blakkisrud (n 67) 492.

70 ibid.

71 International Crisis Group, *South Ossetia: The Burden of Recognition: Europe Report N° 205* (ICG 2010) 1.

72 Nussberger, 'South Ossetia' (n 6) para 20. Report (n 33) 132–133. *Georgia v Russia (II)* App no 38263/08 (Merits) (ECtHR, 21 January 2021) para 170.

73 F Kochieva, 'The Ossetian Neverendum' (*ECFR*, 1 September 2016) <https://www.ecfr.eu/article/essay_the_ossetian_neverendum> accessed 2 May 2019.

74 'State Duma of the Russian Federation Unanimously Approved the Results of the Referendum in South Ossetia' (*news.ru*, 6 December 2006) <http://newsru.co.il/world/06dec2006/duma.html> accessed 2 May 2019 (*in Russian*).

75 Fischer, 'The Conflicts over Abkhazia and South Ossetia' (n 27) 47.

76 In addition to the mentioned examples of political influence, the former president of South Ossetia conducted visits to Moscow for 'consultations' and Russia openly acknowledged its preferred candidates in Abkhazia. Folleboukt (n 8) 169.

77 Folleboukt (n 8) 169. See *infra* on the process of passportisation. *Georgia v Russia (II)* (n 72) para 169. *Mamasakhlisi* (n 37) paras 324, 330, 335.

78 Nussberger, 'South Ossetia' (n 6) para 18; Nussberger, 'Abkhazia' (n 1) para 17.

1.3 *Post-2008 Developments*

Over the summer of 2008, the security situation in the region dramatically deteriorated ultimately culminating in the so-called 'five-day war.'[79] While the issue of who fired the first shot was the subject of intense controversy, the Independent International Fact-Finding Mission established that the outbreak of large-scale hostilities started with Georgian military operation against South Ossetia during the night of 7–8 August 2008.[80] Russia, supported by South Ossetian troops, counter-attacked and drove Georgia's units from South Ossetia, even occupying strategic parts of Georgia's territory.[81] "The Russian operation would progress to include large-scale military actions in central and western Georgia and Abkhazia as well as the occupation of a significant part of the undisputed territory of Georgia."[82] Ultimately, the Georgian and Russian presidents agreed on the EU-brokered Six-Point Ceasefire Agreement on 12 August 2008, which *inter alia* foresaw a cessation of hostilities, a return of the Georgian forces to their usual quarters and the withdrawal of Russian armed forces to positions held before the outbreak of hostilities.[83] Russian troops did not withdraw from Georgia proper until 10 October 2008.[84]

---

79 See Report (n 33) 200–209.

80 Report (n 33) 209. Summers (n 14) 103–104. See on this issue more broadly T de Waal, 'The Still-Topical Tagliavini Report' (*Carnegie Russia Eurasia*, 30 September 2015) <https://carnegiemoscow.org/posts/2015/09/the-still-topical-tagliavini-report?lang=en&center=russia-eurasia> accessed 3 October 2023. See on the deterioration of the security situation in the region preceding the large-scale hostilities Report (n 33) 204–209.

81 Summers (n 14) 104.

82 P Leach, 'South Ossetia' in E Wilmshurst (ed), *International Law and the Classification of Conflicts* (1st edn, OUP; The Royal Institute of International Affairs (Chatham House) 2012) 320. It was reported that Georgian troops began withdrawing to undisputed Georgian territory on 10 August 2008, but Russian forces continued their operations beyond that date. ibid 321. Russia also sent 9,000 troops to Abkhazia "to repel a planned Georgian assault on that region." K O'Reilly and N Higgins, 'The Use of Force, Wars of National Liberation and the Right to Self-Determination in the South Ossetian Conflict' (2009) 9 International Criminal Law Review 567, 572; Report (n 33) 230.

83 Six-Point Ceasefire Agreement <https://old.civil.ge/eng/article.php?id=19478> accessed 3 May 2019 ("Six-Point Agreement"). The Six-Point Agreement was proposed on 12 August 2008 and signed by Georgia and Russia on 15 and 16 August 2008 respectively. Leach (n 82) 321. See also Implementation of the Plan of 12 August 2008: Communiqué Issued by the Presidency of the Republic (9 September 2008) <https://peacemaker.un.org/georgia-implementation-plan2008> accessed 3 May 2019 ("Implementing Measures"). The UNSC welcomed and recalled arrangements entered into under both of these instruments. See UNSC Res 1866 (13 February 2009) UN Doc S/RES/1866, preambular para 3 and para 1.

84 Summers (n 14) 104. *Georgia v Russia (II)* (n 72) para 174.

Russia recognised both Abkhazia and South Ossetia as States on 26 August 2008.[85] Since then Nicaragua, Venezuela, Nauru, and Syria have also recognised these entities as States.[86] No other UN Member State has recognised them as independent States, and a number of international organisations, such as the EU, NATO, OSCE and the Council of Europe, condemned Russia's recognition of the breakaway entities as a violation of Georgia's territorial integrity.[87] Russia has concluded a large number of bilateral treaties with these entities, among them the most prominent being the 2008 friendship treaties, the 2014 Strategic Partnership Treaty with Abkhazia and the 2015 Integration Treaty with South Ossetia.[88] Russia claims that the recognition of both regions and the subsequent conclusion of bilateral agreements created a "new reality"

85 'Executive Order of the President of the Russian Federation No 1260 on Recognition of the Republic of Abkhazia' (adopted 26 August 2008; entered into force 26 August 2008) <http://kremlin.ru/acts/bank/27957> accessed 2 May 2019 (*in Russian*); 'Executive Order of the President of the Russian Federation No 1261 on Recognition of the Republic of South Ossetia (adopted 26 August 2008; entered into force 26 August 2008) <http://kremlin.ru/acts/bank/27957> accessed 2 May 2019 (*in Russian*).

86 Nussberger, 'Abkhazia' (n 1) para 20; Nussberger, 'South Ossetia' (n 6) para 31. See G Lomsadze, 'Syria Formally Recognizes Abkhazia and South Ossetia' (*eurasianet*, 29 May 2018) <https://eurasianet.org/syria-formally-recognizes-abkhazia-and-south-ossetia> accessed 2 May 2019. Apparently, Vanuatu has changed its mind on the issue of recognition. See Lomsadze G, 'Abkhazia: Vanuatu Changes Its Mind Again' (*eurasianet*, 18 March 2013) <https://eurasianet.org/abkhazia-vanuatu-changes-its-mind-again> accessed 2 May 2019. Similarly, see 'Tuvalu Retracts Recognition of Abkhazia, South Ossetia' (*Radio Free Europe*, 31 March 2014) <https://www.rferl.org/a/tuvalu-georgia-retracts-abkhazia-ossetia-recognition/25315720.html> accessed 22 October 2023.

87 See *infra*.

88 Treaty of Alliance and Strategic Partnership between Russia and Abkhazia (signed 24 November 2014; entered into force 5 March 2015) <http://kremlin.ru/supplement/4783> accessed 2 May 2019 (*in Russian*) ("Strategic Partnership Treaty"); Treaty of Alliance and Integration between Russia and South Ossetia (signed 18 March 2015; entered into force 30 July 2015) <http://kremlin.ru/supplement/4819> accessed 2 May 2019 (*in Russian*) ("Integration Treaty"); Treaty of Friendship, Cooperation and Mutual Assistance between the Russian Federation and the Republic of South Ossetia (signed 17 September 2008; entered into force 20 January 2009) <http://kremlin.ru/supplement/199> accessed 2 May 2019 (*in Russian*); Treaty of Friendship, Cooperation and Mutual Assistance between the Russian Federation and the Republic of Abkhazia (signed 17 September 2008; entered into force 23 December 2008) <http://www.kremlin.ru/supplement/200> accessed 2 May 2019 (*in Russian*). For an in detail analysis of 78 bilateral agreements signed between Abkhazia, South Ossetia and Russia between 2018 and 2015, see T Ambrosio and WA Lange, 'The Architecture of Annexation? Russia's Bilateral Agreements with South Ossetia and Abkhazia' (2016) 44 Nationalities Papers 673.

and took precedence over the ceasefire agreements.[89] In place of peacekeeping forces, Russia now maintains regular military bases there.[90]

Subsequently, in August 2008, Georgia withdrew from the CIS and denounced the Sochi and Moscow Ceasefire Agreements.[91] In October 2008, the CIS declared the mandate of its peacekeeping forces in Abkhazia terminated.[92] Russia vetoed the extension of the UNOMIG mandate.[93] In October 2008, Georgia passed the law on occupied territories of Georgia.[94] In September 2008, the EU established the Special Monitoring Mission (EUMM) to observe compliance with the Six-Point Ceasefire Agreement.[95] The EUMM has never been allowed to enter separatist territories.[96] Mandated by the Six-Point Ceasefire Agreement, the so-called Geneva International Discussions (GID) have taken place since 2008. However, this format co-chaired by the UN, EU and the OSCE with the participation of the representatives of Georgia, Russia, the US and the breakaway territories (in their individual capacities) has been "hamstrung by several unresolved ambiguities", especially as to "which conflict is being mediated" and "who the parties to the conflict are" (while Russia claims to be a 'facilitator' to the GID, Georgia sees Russia as an aggressor and the occupying power).[97]

89 International Crisis Group, *South Ossetia* (n 71) 9; International Crisis Group, *Abkhazia: Deepening Dependence: Europe Report No 202* (ICG 2010) 2.

90 Fischer, 'The Conflicts over Abkhazia and South Ossetia' (n 27) 49.

91 Nussberger, 'Abkhazia' (n 1) paras 21–22. See also 'Government Formally Scraps Russian Peacekeeping' (*civil.ge*, 29 August 2008) <https://civil.ge/archives/117309> accessed 2 May 2019. The denouncement was carried out on the basis of Article 60(1) VCLT.

92 Nussberger, 'Abkhazia' (n 1) para 22.

93 Ibid. 'Russia Vetoes Extension of UN Mission in Georgia' (*UN News*, 15 June 2009) <https://news.un.org/en/story/2009/06/303512-russia-vetoes-extension-un-mission-georgia> accessed 2 May 2019.

94 Nussberger, 'Abkhazia' (n 1) para 20; 'Law of Georgia No 431 on Occupied Territories as amended' (adopted 23 October 2008) <https://smr.gov.ge/uploads/prev/The_Law_of_928efod7.pdf> accessed 18 October 2016 ("Law on Occupied Territories"). This law as well as its later amendments were the subject of the opinions of the European Commission for Democracy through Law (Venice Commission). These opinions were generally rather critical of this law. See *infra* the following chapters.

95 Council of the European Union, 'Join Action on the European Union Monitoring Mission in Georgia, EUMM Georgia' (15 September 2008) 2008/736/CFSP.'

96 See EUMM, 'About Us' available <https://eumm.eu/en/about_eumm> accessed 4 May 2019.

97 'Geneva International Discussions' (Office of the State Minister of Georgia for Reconciliation and Civic Equality) <https://smr.gov.ge/en/page/26/geneva-international-discussions> accessed 21 October 2023. T Giuashvili and J Devdariani, 'Geneva International Discussions – Negotiating the Possible' (2016) 27 Security and Human Rights 381, 382. See *infra*.

Regarding Russia's post-2008 military presence in Abkhazia, according to Russian officials, there are around 5,000 Russian personnel there, including 3,500 military and 1,500 Russian Federal Security Service (FSB) officers and border guards.[98] In fact, Russia operates the 7th Russian Military Base in Gudauta.[99] According to the ECtHR, as of April 2023, this base hosts up to 3,800 Russian soldiers.[100] Russia also significantly invested in the upgrade of military infrastructure, including the largest military airport in the South Caucasus and a naval port in Ochamchire only 30 km from Georgian-controlled territory.[101] Other bilateral agreements foresee cooperation in the military sphere, and the Strategic Partnership Treaty provides for the creation of "common defense and security space."[102]

Regarding the political environment, a large majority of Abkhazians continue to favour independence.[103] The proportion of Russian nationals in important positions in Abkhazia was much smaller than in South Ossetia,[104] but at least in recent years, Russians without prior connection to the region have filled high-ranking posts in the region.[105] For example, a Russian officer was appointed to the position of the Chief of the General Staff of the Abkhazian Armed Forces in 2012.[106] Abkhazia also preserved a certain amount of (nominal) autonomy when negotiating the Strategic Partnership Treaty with Russia.[107] According to the International Crisis Group, "[a] big reduction in Russian support would have profound political and social consequences.

98 International Crisis Group, *Abkhazia: The Long Road to Reconciliation: Europe Report No 224* (ICG 2013) 3. See *Georgia v Russia (IV)* App no 39611/18 (Decision as to Admissibility) (ECtHR, 20 April 2023) para 12.

99 Agreement between the Russian Federation and the Republic of Abkhazia on the Joint Russian Military Base on the Territory of Abkhazia (signed 17 February 2010, entered into force 20 January 2012) <http://docs.cntd.ru/document/902216906> accessed 3 May 2019 (*in Russian*).

100 *Georgia v Russia (IV)* (n 98) para 11. See also *Georgia v Russia (II)* (n 72) para 165 in connection with para 151.

101 International Crisis Group, *Abkhazia: The Long Road to Reconciliation* (n 98) 4.

102 For further analysis of the Strategic Partnership Treaty see *infra*. See also Ambrosio and Lange (n 88) 680–681 for an overview of bilateral treaties in the military area.

103 Frear (n 59) 7.

104 International Crisis Group, *Abkhazia: Deepening Dependence* (n 89) 4–5.

105 AWM Gerrits and M Bader, 'Russian Patronage over Abkhazia and South Ossetia: Implications for Conflict Resolution' (2016) 32 East European Politics 297, 304. However, "[t]here are no Russians in parliament and all the key positions in the executive and legislative branches of government belong to Abkhazians." Achba (n 66).

106 Frear (n 59) 7. See regarding Russia's political support of Abkhazia *Georgia v Russia (II)* (n 72) paras 167–172.

107 See *infra*.

Abkhaz leaders have never made secret that their level of real independence is circumscribed by their reliance on Moscow."[108]

In terms of Abkhazia's public finances, since 2009, Russia has allocated about 1.9 billion roubles per year in direct budgetary support, which in 2012 accounted for 22% of Abkhazia's budget.[109] However, as in 2012, Russia also provided another 4.9 billion roubles as part of a comprehensive aid plan; the overall proportion of Russia's subsidy for Abkhazia's budget reportedly reached 70%.[110] Moreover, Russia is also said to pay for the pensions of Russian-passport holders.[111] This is coupled with Abkhazia's granting of offshore exploration rights to the Russian state-controlled Rosneft[112] and with Russia's railways controlling Abkhazia's rail network.[113] Abkhazia also adopted Russian technical and commercial standards, and even its electricity grid was united with the Russian one.[114] Russia itself acknowledged its economic and financial support to Abkhazia in this period.[115] The Programme of Formation of the Common Social and Economic Space between Russia and Abkhazia was adopted in 2020, foreseeing 45 targeted areas leading to a large-scale harmonisation of Abkhaz legislation with that of Russia (within three years), including in the field of dual citizenship, privatisation of the Abkhaz energy sector, custom, bank tax, digitalisation, and other areas.[116] Currently, the programme is the basis for the work of several working groups. The Abkhaz civil society has criticised the programme's adoption, seeing it as further circumventing Abkhaz self-rule and duplication of the Russian laws rather than harmonisation.[117]

---

108 International Crisis Group, *Abkhazia: Deepening Dependence* (n 89) 8; *Georgia v Russia (II)* (n 72) para 172 in connection with para 159. See *infra*.

109 International Crisis Group, *Abkhazia: The Long Road to Reconciliation* (n 98) 6.

110 ibid 6.

111 ibid.

112 Frear (n 59) 6.

113 Gerrits and Bader (n 105) 301.

114 ibid.

115 *Georgia v Russia (II)* (n 72) para 166 and see paras 167 and 172.

116 Programme of Formation of the Common Social and Economic Space between the Russian Federation and the Republic of Abkhazia on the Basis of Harmonization of Legislation of the Republic of Abkhazia with the Legislation of the Russian Federation (12 November 2020) <http://presidentofabkhazia.org/upload/iblock/dc5/programma-_1_.pdf> accessed 24 October 2023 (*in Russian*) ("Programme of Formation of the Common Social and Economic Space"). The programme even foresees a timeline for harmonization of Abkhaz laws on the example of Russian laws on non-commercial organisations and foreign agent law. ibid, para 37.

117 'Moscow Wins from the New Socio-Economic Deal with Sokhumi' (*civil.ge*, 26 April 2021) <https://civil.ge/archives/409826> accessed 24 October 2023; I Chania, 'Harmonization for the Benefit of Russian Business' (*Ekho Kavkaza*, 30 November

Recent years in Abkhazia have been marked by protests revolving, among others, around the issue of Russia's ownership of the lucrative real estate in Abkhazia and related perceived loss of sovereignty.[118] Unlike South Ossetia, Abkhazia did not formally send troops to fight on Russia's side in its war against Ukraine.[119] Even though more than 90% of its population holds Russian citizenship, it was not subjected to Russia's partial mobilization in 2022.[120] In the summer of 2023, former Russian President Medvedev published an opinion piece referring to the possibility of Abkhazia's and South Ossetia's incorporation into Russia in light of the popular support for such a step.[121] In response, the Secretary of Abkhazia's Security Council claimed that there were no political forces demanding Abkhazia's unification with Russia.[122]

Since 2009, Russia has operated the 4th Military Base with up to 4,000 troops in South Ossetia.[123] In 2010, a basing agreement was signed, providing for a 49-year lease that can be automatically renewed every 15 years.[124] As of April 2023, according to the ECtHR, there are 3,800 Russian soldiers in South Ossetia.[125] The presence of Russian troops in South Ossetia has strategic value

---

2023) <https://www.ekhokavkaza.com/a/30976783.html> accessed 24 October 2023 (*in Russian*). See also B Belkania, 'The "Common Social and Economic Space" Agreement between Abkhazia and Russia: A Path to Russia?' (2023) 11 Caucasus Survey 293; See *infra* (n 323 and 327).

118 'Abkhazia Faces Protests as Discontent Mounts' (*eurasianet*, 31 May 2023) <https://eurasianet.org/abkhazia-faces-protests-as-discontent-mounts> accessed 21 October 2023. See *infra* (n 327). Belkania (n 117) 300, footnote 5.

119 'Concerns over Conscription in Abkhazia as Russia Mobilizes' (*eurasianet*, 23 September 2022) <https://eurasianet.org/concerns-over-conscription-in-abkhazia-as-russia-mobilizes> accessed 21 October 2023.

120 G Menabde, 'Abkhazia Rejects Putin's Mobilization' (*Jamestown*, 23 October 2022) <https://jamestown.org/program/abkhazia-rejects-putins-mobilization/> accessed 21 October 2023.

121 D Medvedev, 'Lessons Not Learned: Dmitry Medvedev Analysed the Event of 2008' (*Argumenty i Fakty*, 23 August 2023) <https://aif.ru/politics/world/nevyuchennye_uroki_dmitriy_medvedev_proanaliziroval_sobytiya_2008_goda> accessed 21 October 2023 (*in Russian*).

122 'Abkhazia Says There Are No Political Forces Willing to Join the Russian Federation' (TASS, 23 August 2023) <https://tass.ru/mezhdunarodnaya-panorama/18568873> accessed 21 October 2023 (*in Russian*).

123 ibid 302.

124 Agreement between the Russian Federation and the Republic of South Ossetia on the Joint Russian Military Base on the Territory of South Ossetia (signed 10 April 2010, entered into force 7 November 2011) <http://docs.cntd.ru/document/902253381> accessed 3 May 2019 (*in Russian*).

125 *Georgia v Russia* (*IV*) (n 98) para 11. See also *Georgia v Russia* (*II*) (n 72) para 165 in connection with para 150.

due to its proximity to Tbilisi.[126] Other bilateral agreements foresee a deepening of military cooperation, and the Integration Treaty in fact stipulates that the Russian Federation assumes responsibility for the defence and security of South Ossetia and its borders.[127] South Ossetia's reliance on Russia's military strength has even led to a substantial downsizing of the personnel of its army and to a political controversy in South Ossetia concerning whether it should maintain its own army at all, which, for the moment, has been resolved in the affirmative.[128] In 2010, it was reported that five consecutive career Russian military officers have been appointed to the post of South Ossetia's Minister of Defence.[129]

In addition, it is estimated that there are around 900 Russian border guards in South Ossetia.[130] These guards in South and Abkhazia have taken part in a process called borderisation, which entails (i) the installation of infrastructure, including a fence along the administrative boundary line between South Ossetia/Abkhazia and Georgia; (ii) control and patrolling by Russian guards and the *de facto* actors; (iii) checks at the 'official' crossing points requiring specific documentation.[131] On a number of occasions the installation of the fence shifted this line further south into the territory of Georgia proper.[132] Georgia

---

126 International Crisis Group, *South Ossetia* (n 71) 8. It is estimated that the seizure of Georgia's East-West highway, which took place during the 2008 war, could be repeated in one hour today. ibid.

127 See *infra* for the analysis of the Integration Treaty. See, for other agreements in a military sphere 'Ministry of Defense of the Republic of South Ossetia: Agreements' <http://alania mil.org/voennoe-pravo/soglasheniya/> accessed 5 May 2019 (*in Russian*) and Ambrosio and Lange (n 88) 675–677.

128 J Kucera, 'South Ossetia Keeps Its Military, For Now' (*eurasianet*, 19 January 2017) <https: //eurasianet.org/south-ossetia-keeps-its-military-now> accessed 5 May 2019; L Fuller, 'South Ossetia's Leaders At Odds Over Military Accord With Russia' (*Radio Free Europe*, 5 March 2016) <https://www.rferl.org/a/south-ossetia-leaders-at-odds-over-military-acc ord-with-russia/27591004.html> accessed 6 May 2019.

129 'New South Ossetian Defense Chief Opposes Further Downsizing of Armed Forces' (*Radio Free Europe*, 5 August 2010) <https://www.rferl.org/a/New_South_Ossetian_Defense _Chief_Opposes_Further_Downsizing_Of_Armed_Forces/2119560.html> accessed 6 May 2019.

130 *Georgia v Russia (IV)* (n 98) para 12; International Crisis Group, *South Ossetia* (n 71) 8; See also German (n 68) 160–161.

131 *Georgia v Russia (IV)* (n 98) para 12; German (n 68) 162.

132 German (n 68) 162. See also P Salopek, 'Letter from the Caucasus: Vladimir Putin's Mysterious Moving Border' (*Politico*, 3 April 2016) <https://www.politico.com/magaz ine/story/2016/04/georgia-border-russia-vladimir-putin-213787> accessed 3 May 2019. Thereby, South Ossetia's *de facto* territory now includes a 1.6 km section of the BP-operated Baku-Supsa oil pipeline, which is only 0.5 km away from Georgia's principal transport corridor, the East-West highway. German (n 68) 162.

has lodged an inter-State application against Russia concerning the allegation of the administrative practice of human rights violations along this administrative boundary line; the case is pending at the ECtHR.[133]

As far as South Ossetian politics is concerned, Russian nationals have been appointed to high-ranking positions, even including three successive prime ministers.[134] It is true that in 2011 the Russian-backed candidate lost presidential elections and after a two-month-long standoff accepted the position of a Vice President.[135] Russian influence can also be inferred from the fact that, despite repeated public announcements of referendums on joining Russia, this is yet to take place.[136] "Ultimately, the decision about when the referendum takes place lies in Moscow, which finds that the precarious status quo suits it rather well."[137] Since the escalation of Russian aggression against Ukraine in 2022, South Ossetian troops have joined the fight on Russia's side.[138]

Since South Ossetia does not have any significant source of self-generated income, "almost the entire budget is made up of Russian financial aid."[139] For example, it was estimated that in 2010, 98.7% of South Ossetia's budget was made up of Russian aid.[140] According to the Russian Deputy Prime Minister, the volume of Russian financial aid to South Ossetia between 2008 and 2013

133 *Georgia v Russia (IV)* (n 98).

134 These include Yuri Morozov (2005–2008), Aslanbek Bulatsev (2008–2009) and Vadim Brovtsev (2008–2011). Gerrits and Bader (n 105) 304; Follebouckt (n 8) 167.

135 Gerrits and Bader (n 105) 308. See regarding Russia's political support of South Ossetia *Georgia v Russia (II)* (n 72) paras 167–172.

136 'President: South Ossetia Plans to Hold Referendum on Becoming Part of Russia Before August' (*TASS*, 11 April 2016) <https://tass.com/world/868630> accessed 5 May 2019; 'Expert: Any Talk About South Ossetia's Referendum on Joining Russia Is Pure Populism' (*TASS*, 20 October 2015) <https://tass.com/world/830285> accessed 5 May 2019; L Fuller, 'South Ossetia Referendum on Name Change Steers Clear of Thornier Unification Issue' (*Radio Free Europe*, 8 February 2017) <https://www.rferl.org/a/caucasus-report-south-ossetia-referendum-name-change/28298590.html> accessed 4 May 2019. J Kucera, 'Russia Praises South Ossetia's Decision to Drop Unification Referendum' (*eurasianet*, 1 June 2022) <https://eurasianet.org/russia-praises-south-ossetias-decision-to-drop-unification-referendum> accessed 21 October 2023.

137 Kochieva (n 73).

138 T Mandaria, 'South Ossetian Troops Fighting for Russia in Ukraine' (*eurasianet*, 29 March 2022) <https://eurasianet.org/south-ossetian-troops-fighting-for-russia-in-ukraine> accessed 21 October 2023.

139 Gerrits and Bader (n 105) 302. See regarding Russia's economic and financial support to South Ossetia *Georgia v Russia (II)* (n 72) para 166 and see paras 167 and 172.

140 International Crisis Group, *South Ossetia* (n 71) 4.

amounted to 34 billion roubles.[141] This figure did not include payments of pensions to Russian-passport holders in South Ossetia.[142] In 2016, Russian subsidies to South Ossetia amounted to 8 billion roubles.[143]

The 2023 Concept of the Foreign Policy of the Russian Federation formalised Russia's plans regarding both entities, according to which it will prioritise,

> comprehensively supporting the Republic of Abkhazia and the Republic of South Ossetia, promoting the voluntary choice, based on international law, of the peoples of these states in favor of a deeper integration with Russia.[144]

2 Legal Analysis of the Secessionist Attempts

From one perspective, the 2008 War and subsequent Russian recognition of Abkhazia and South Ossetia represented a watershed moment that transformed the existing *status quo* and allowed for the establishment of diametrically opposing lines of argumentation. While Russia considers Abkhazia and South Ossetia independent States, and consequently sees its military presence in the two regions as based on bilateral agreements fully in accordance with international law, Georgia perceives recognition of these regions as a violation of its territorial integrity and Russia's military presence there as illegal occupation of its territory.[145]

In order for Russia's argument to work, it would need to be proved that South Ossetia and Abkhazia were States at the moment of recognition and that since then no change of this determination has taken place. Thus, the analysis in this regard must be done with respect to the period before and after the summer of 2008.

141 'Khloponin: the Volume of Russian Financial Aid to South Ossetia since 2008 Amounted to 34 Billion Rubles' (*newsru.com*, 19 July 2013) <https://www.newsru.com/finance/19jul2013/sosetiarumoney.html> accessed 2 May 2019 (*in Russian*).

142 Gerrits and Bader (n 105) 303.

143 Kochieva (n 73).

144 'The Concept of the Foreign Policy of the Russian Federation' (31 March 2023) <https://mid.ru/en/foreign_policy/fundamental_documents/1860586/> accessed 21 October 2023.

145 See Nussberger, 'The War between Russia and Georgia' (n 27) 345–347.

2.1 *Pre-2008 Period*

2.1.1 History-Based Arguments

The claims for statehood based on historical arguments are primarily relevant to Abkhazia, as South Ossetia at no time prior to its declaration of independence possessed the status of statehood.[146]

Deriving from the Declaration of the Military Council of the Republic of Georgia of 23 February 1992, according to which Georgia recognised the supremacy of the Constitution of the Democratic Republic of Georgia of 21 February 1921, the Abkhaz Supreme Soviet on 23 July 1992 declared that this move entailed the emergence of a new Republic – the Georgian Democratic Republic – with which the Abkhazian ASSR had no relations, and that thereby an unacceptable legal vacuum was created between Abkhazia and Georgia.[147] On this ground, Abkhazia terminated the 1978 Constitution of the Abkhazian ASSR and restored its 1925 constitution under which it had the status of a Soviet republic "united on the basis of a Union Treaty with the Georgian SSR".[148]

However, upon reading the February 1992 Georgian Declaration, it is clear that no legal vacuum was created between Abkhazia and Georgia. In fact, Georgia declared the supremacy of the Constitution of the Democratic Republic of Georgia of 21 February 1921 "with due account of current realities" and explicitly stated that this measure did not change the current borders of the State, including "the territorial arrangement of the Republic of Georgia (with current status of Abkhazia and Ajaria)".[149]

Moreover, Abkhazia's self-upgrade to the level of a Soviet Republic should be seen in connection with the fact that, upon the dissolution of the USSR, only the Soviet Union republics were accepted as independent States. However, this step could not entail the same legal consequences for Abkhazia.

---

146 For South Ossetia's history-based arguments, see C Waters, 'South Ossetia' in Walter C and others (eds), *Self-Determination and Secession in International Law* (OUP 2014) 182.

147 'Declaration of the Military Council of the Republic of Georgia' (21 February 1992) <http://www.rrc.ge/law/dekl_1992_02_21_r.htm?lawid=1487&lng_3=ru> accessed 3 October 2023 ("Declaration of the Military Council of the Republic of Georgia") (*in Russian*); Supreme Soviet of the Abkhazia, 'Resolution on Termination of the 1978 Constitution of Abkhaz ASSR' (adopted on 23 July 1992) <https://ru.wikisource.org/wiki/Постановление_ВС_Абхазской_АССР_от_23.07.1992> accessed 8 May 2019 (*in Russian*) ("Resolution on Termination of the 1978 Constitution of Abkhaz ASSR").

148 Resolution on Termination of the 1978 Constitution of Abkhaz ASSR (n 147) Constitution of the Soviet Socialist Republic of Abkhazia (adopted on 1 April 1925) art 4 <https://abkhazworld.com/aw/reports-and-key-texts/589-constitution-ssr-abkhazia-1april1925> accessed 8 May 2019. See *supra*.

149 Declaration of the Military Council of the Republic of Georgia (n 147).

Firstly, it was established in Part 1, Chapter 4 that the principle of *uti possidetis* applies to the borders of newly emerged States as of the date of independence.[150] Thus, any unilateral alteration of the status of borders subsequent to the date of dissolution of the USSR would not have any legal relevance on the international plane. As shown below, Georgia emerged as a successor to the USSR within the borders of the former Georgian SSR, which included both Abkhazia and South Ossetia. Secondly, however, even if a return to its previous status would be accepted, hypothetically, this would not entail the emergence of the Abkhazian SSR as an independent State. Only full-fledged Union republics, constituent republics of the USSR, were seen as competent to dissolve the Union. As mentioned above, the legal status of the Abkhazian SSR was ambiguous – it was not identical to that of other Soviet Republics.[151]

2.1.2 Right to Secession under Municipal Law

From the above, it follows that the process of the dissolution of the USSR involved secessionist tendencies by Georgia, vis-à-vis the USSR, and Georgia's autonomous entities, vis-à-vis Georgia, accompanied by a number of actions, which could be assessed as legal or illegal depending on whether one takes Soviet or Georgian law as prevailing. Thus, in this context, it first needs to be assessed whether Abkhazia and South Ossetia had any right to independence under Soviet law.

Firstly, neither Abkhazia, as an autonomous republic within the Georgian SSR,[152] nor South Ossetia, as an autonomous region within the Georgian SSR,[153] had the right to secede under Soviet constitutional law; under Article 72 of the 1977 Soviet Constitution, the right to secede, even if nominal, only belonged to Union Republics, in particular the Georgian SSR.[154]

It is true that the Soviet Law on Secession from the USSR, adopted in April 1990, stipulated that the people of autonomous republics, autonomous regions and districts "retain the right to decide independently the question of remaining within the USSR or within the seceding Union republic, and also to raise

150 See *supra* Part 1, Chapter 4. Nussberger, 'Abkhazia' (n 1) para 28.

151 ibid para 28. See *supra*.

152 'Constitution (Fundamental Law) of the Union of Soviet Socialist Republics' (adopted 7 October 1977, entered into force 7 October 1977) art 85 <https://www.departments.bucknell.edu/russian/const/77cons03.html> accessed 3 May 2019 ("1977 Soviet Constitution").

153 ibid art 87.

154 ibid arts 72 and 71. See also Nussberger, 'The War between Russia and Georgia' (n 27) 356; Waters (n 146) 182–184; Report (n 33) 141–142.

the question of their own state-legal status".[155] Nevertheless, this law did not provide for an independent right to secede for these autonomous units, but only linked it with the Union Republic's secession from the USSR.[156] Ultimately, none of the Union Republics seceded from the USSR by observing the procedure prescribed by this law. The USSR dissolved upon the agreement of Union republics and, therefore, this law could not have served as a legal basis for the secession of Abkhazia and South Ossetia.

In addition, as mentioned above, it is true that while Georgia refused to participate in the March 1991 All-Union referendum on the preservation of the Soviet Union, South Ossetia and Abkhazia participated in it with results in favour of the Soviet Union's preservation.[157] This referendum took place in the period of extensive contestation between the federal centre and the republics. Indeed, the participation of Abkhazia and South Ossetia could be seen as legal under Soviet law, and the non-participation of Georgia could be assessed as illegal. Nevertheless, despite this, this referendum sought the preservation of the Soviet Union and did not concern itself as such with the secession of units of the Soviet republics. Therefore, it could not have provided legal entitlement for Abkhazia's and South Ossetia's separation from the Georgian SSR.

From a temporal perspective, an ultimate rupture, secessionist declaration of independence of both Abkhazia and South Ossetia from Georgia took place after the break-up of the Soviet Union.[158] Therefore, the provisions of the Georgian law must be assessed. In February 1992, Georgia restored its 1921 Constitution, which did not provide for any right to secession and in fact declared Georgia an indivisible State, with Abkhazia having autonomy in the

---

155 Law on Procedure for Resolving Questions Connected with a Union Republic's Secession from the USSR (3 April 1990) art 3(1) <http://soviethistory.msu.edu/1991-2/shevarnadze-resigns/shevarnadze-resigns-texts/law-on-secession-from-the-ussr/> accessed 9 May 2019 ("Law on Secession from the USSR").

156 "In a Union republic which includes within its structure autonomous republics, autonomous oblasts, or autonomous okrugs, the referendum is held separately for each autonomous formation." ibid art 3. According to the Resolution of the Supreme Soviet of the USSR, any action raising the issue of the secession of a Union Republic contrary to the Law on Secession from the USSR, taken before or after its entry into force has no legal consequences for the USSR and the Union Republics. Supreme Soviet of the USSR, Resolution on the Entry into Force of the Law of the USSR on Procedure for Resolving Questions Connected with a Union Republic's Secession from the USSR (3 April 1990) art 2, <http://www.consultant.ru/cons/cgi/online.cgi?req=doc&base=ESU&n=12#0760219549254760> accessed 9 May 2019 (*in Russian*).

157 Follebouckt (n 8) 91. South Ossetia never published its results. Summers (n 14) 96.

158 South Ossetia declared independence on 21 December 1991 and 29 May 1992, and Abkhazia declared independence on 23 July 1992. See *supra*.

administration of its affairs.[159] But in any case, as shown above, the February 1992 Declaration declared the preservation of Abkhazia's then current status.[160] Therefore, secession by Abkhazia and South Ossetia could not have been justified on the basis of the restored Georgian constitution either.

2.1.3 Right to Self-Determination and Remedial Secession

Both Abkhazia and South Ossetia justify their independence by reference to the right of peoples to self-determination.[161] In this context, some scholars claim that South Ossetians and Abkhazians are people entitled to self-determination, as they fulfil the relevant subjective and objective criteria.[162] Nevertheless, this book takes the position that for the purposes of the right to self-determination, peoples are defined territorially and, therefore, only the whole population of Georgia could be characterised as such.[163] In any case, even those authors who define South Ossetians and Abkhazians as holders of the right to self-determination admit that this right does not entail a right to independence or any other unilateral change of status[164] and, therefore, neither South Ossetia nor Abkhazia can justify its independence by reference to the right to self-determination.[165]

In addition, even though Part 1, Chapter 3 established that remedial secession does not form part of positive international law, the doctrinal parameters of its applicability must also be assessed. Thus, indeed, relations between Georgia and its autonomous entities were particularly strained at the time of

159 'Constitution of the Democratic Republic of Georgia' (adopted 21 February 1921, restored 21 February 1992) arts 1 and 107 <https://matiane.wordpress.com/2012/09/04/constitution-of-georgia-1921/> accessed 2 May 2019.

160 See *supra*.

161 Under the 1994 Abkhazian Constitution, the Republic of Abkhazia is "a sovereign, democratic state, established historically under the right of a people to free self-determination." Constitution of the Republic of Abkhazia (adopted 26 November 1994) <https://web.archive.org/web/20141029021227/http://apsnypress.info/en/constitution> accessed 5 May 2019. Constitution of the Republic of South Ossetia (adopted 15 October 2004) <https://web.archive.org/web/20081006092114/http://cominf.org/2004/10/15/1127818105.html> accessed 5 May 2019 (*in Russian*).

162 Nussberger, 'The War between Russia and Georgia' (n 27) 355; Nussberger, 'South Ossetia' (n 6) para 25; R McCorquoadale and K Hausler, 'The Application of the Right of Self-Determination' in JA Green and CPM Waters (eds), *Conflict in the Caucasus: Implications for International Legal Order* (Palgrave Macmillan 2010) 40; Report (n 33) 144 and 146. See also O'Reilly and Higgins (n 82) 580.

163 See *supra* Part 1, Chapter 3.

164 See *supra* Part 1, Chapter 3.

165 Nussberger, 'The War between Russia and Georgia' (n 27) 355; Nussberger, 'South Ossetia' (n 6) para 25; Nussberger, 'Abkhazia' (n 1) para 28.

the USSR's dissolution. "The outbreak of violence was fuelled by ideology, by what can be seen as an over reactive nationalism on both sides after the far-reaching suppression of national culture and heritage under Soviet rule."[166] In particular, some of Georgia's actions, such as the abolition of South Ossetia's autonomy and the imposition of an economic blockade towards it, could be seen as exacerbating secessionist tendencies.[167] But "[t]hese instances of political and cultural discrimination do not amount to the type of disastrous humanitarian transgression that have customarily been deemed necessary to legally justify" secession.[168] And in no case could the situation at the time have been described as "genocide".[169]

Furthermore, at the time of South Ossetia's and Abkhazia's final declaration of independence, the nationalist Gamsakhurdia had already been replaced by the more moderate Shevardnadze and therefore secession was not an *ultima ratio* tool – the potential for finding a political solution was higher in these new circumstances.[170] Moreover, it is true that during the war in Abkhazia "gross human rights violations had been committed by both sides."[171] "As this fact had not been interpreted as a reason for secession by the international community for almost two decades, it could not serve as a pretext for recognizing a right to secession after the [2008] war."[172] In addition, these violations occurred subsequently to attempts at separation, during the war that took place in reaction to them, and therefore could not be taken as meeting the criteria of remedial secession from a temporal perspective. Ultimately, the factual situation during the secessionist wars of the 1990s did not fulfil the doctrinal requirements for remedial secession.

2.1.4 Formation of a Successor State of Georgia

Apart from the war in South Ossetia, from late December 1991, Georgia also experienced a military coup and a civil war for central control against

166 Nussberger, 'The War between Russia and Georgia' (n 27) 357.

167 See ibid.

168 I Bleustein, 'Self-Determination, Secession, and Sovereignty: South Ossetia's Claim to Right of External Self-Determination and International Law' (2010) 12 Journal of International Relations 120, 126.

169 Nussberger, 'The War between Russia and Georgia' (n 27) 357. See 'Declaration on Genocide of South Ossetians in 1989-1992' (26 April 2006) <http://cominf.org/node/1146047662> accessed 2 May 2019 (*in Russian*).

170 Nussberger, 'The War between Russia and Georgia' (n 27) 358.

171 Nussberger, 'Abkhazia' (n 1) para 30. O'Reilly and Higgins (n 82) 581.

172 Nussberger, 'Abkhazia' (n 1) para 30.

authoritarian president Zviad Gamsakhurdia.[173] Due to these specific circumstances, Georgia was the only Soviet Union Republic not to sign the Alma Ata Protocol and Declaration on 21 December 1991 concerning the dissolution of the USSR,[174] and initially it did not become a member of the CIS.[175] However, the USSR dissolved not only because of the agreement of its constituent republics, but also upon the acts of Soviet federal bodies. In fact, the upper chamber of the Supreme Soviet of the USSR also formally accepted the dissolution of the USSR on 26 December 1991, upon which the USSR dissolved.[176] The fact that Georgia did not sign the Alma Ata Protocol and initially did not participate in the CIS does not have legal relevance on the fact that, together with other Soviet republics, it emerged as a successor State within the pre-existing borders of the Georgian SSR, including Abkhazia and South Ossetia.

Apart from the Russian Federation and the Baltic States, "[l]e problème du statut des autres anciennes républiques soviétiques ne s'est pas vraiment posé. Elles ont toutes été reconnues en tant qu'Etats nouveaux, successeurs de l'URSS."[177] Georgia was accepted as a successor State to the USSR.[178]

Moreover, even though a delicate situation in Georgia in the period immediately before and after the USSR's dissolution might have at least theoretically raised doubts about Georgia fulfilling the constitutive criteria of statehood, the international community did not entertain this question at all.[179] For example, the USA recognised Georgia as an independent State already on 25 December 1991.[180] It is true that the European Community recognised it later than other ex-Soviet republics, but this was motivated by the expectation of the fulfilment of the conditions for recognition and not by the doubts about the existence

---

173 JS Dixon and M Reid Sarkees, *A Guide to Intra-State Wars: An Examination of Civil, Regional, and Intercommunal Wars, 1816–2014* (CQ Press, 2015) 308–309.

174 See *supra* Chapter 10. Georgia only acceded to the Alma Ata Protocol, which is an integral part of the Minsk Agreement, on 9 December 1993. It also withdrew from it on 18 August 2009. See 'Protocol to the Agreement Establishing the Commonwealth of Independent States Signed at into force on 8 December 1991 by the Republic of Belarus, the Russian Federation (RSFSR) and Ukraine' (9 December 1993) <https://ir.rudn.ru/books/b1/p1/pp2.pdf> accessed 20 October 2023 (*in Russian*).

175 H Hamant, *Succession de l'URSS: Recueil de documents* (Bruylant 2010) 7.

176 See *supra* Chapter 10.

177 Hamant, *Succession de l'URSS: Receuil de documents* (n 175) 8.

178 Even though it originally sought to restore its 1918 independence, similarly to the Baltic States. ibid 5 and 8.

179 Hamant, *Démembrement de l'URSS et problèmes de succession d'états* (n 55) 181.

180 G Bush, 'Address of the President to the Nation: US Welcomes New Commonwealth of Independent States' (25 December 1991) reprinted in Hamant, *Succession de l'URSS: Receuil de documents* (n 175) 90–92.

of Georgia's statehood.[181] Importantly, the international community completely ignored South Ossetia's declaration of independence of May 1992 and Abkhazia's declaration of secession of 23 July 1992; these entities were considered to be integral parts of a newly emerged Georgia.[182]

Later on, the Council of the CIS Heads of State strongly denounced Abkhazian separatism,[183] and until 2008, UNSC resolutions consistently reaffirmed or called on parties to respect Georgia's territorial integrity.[184] For example, the UNSC resolution 1808 (2008), adopted in April 2008, reaffirmed the commitment to "territorial integrity of Georgia within its internationally recognised

181 "Si les Douze n'ont pas reconnu la Géorgie en même temps que les autres, c'était à cause de la guerre civile qui s'y déroulait." Hamant, *Démembrement de l'URSS et problèmes de succession d'états* (n 55) 182. See 'Déclaration de la Communauté européenne sur "les lignes directrices sur la reconnaissance de nouveaux Etats en Europe orientale et en Union soviétique"' (16 December 1991) reprinted in Hamant, *Succession de l'URSS: Receuil de documents* (n 175) 58–59; 'Déclaration de la Communauté européenne sur la reconnaissance d'anciennes républiques soviétiques' (31 December 1991) reprinted in ibid 62; 'Déclaration de la Communauté européenne sur la Géorgie' (adopted 8 January 1992) reprinted in ibid 63; 'Déclaration de la Communauté européenne sur la reconnaissance de la République de Géorgie' (adopted 23 March 1992) reprinted in ibid 65.

182 See Nussberger, 'Abkhazia' (n 1) para 12. See also F Mirzayev, 'Abkhazia' in C Walter, A Von Ungern-Sternberg and K Abushov (eds), *Self-determination and Secession in International Law* (OUP 2014) 199–204.

183 See CIS Heads of State, 'Decision by the Council of CIS Heads of State on Measures to Settle the Conflict in Abkhazia, Georgia' (adopted 19 January 1996; entered into force 19 January 1996) <http://docs.cntd.ru/document/901818167> accessed 2 May 2019 (*in Russian*).

184 UNSC Res 876 (19 October 1993) UN Doc S/RES/876, para 1; UNSC Res 896 (31 January 1994) UN Doc S/RES/896, para 4; UNSC Res 906 (25 March 1994) UN Doc S/RES/906, para 2; UNSC Res 937 (21 July 1994) UN Doc S/RES/937, preambular para 4; UNSC Res 971 (12 January 1995) UN Doc S/RES/971, preambular para 3; UNSC Res 993 (12 May 1995) UN Doc S/RES/993, preambular para 3; UNSC Res 1036 (12 January 1996) UN Doc S/RES/1036, preambular para 3; UNSC Res 1065 (12 July 1996) UN Doc S/RES/1065, para 3; UNSC Res 1096 (30 January 1997) UN Doc S/RES/1096, para 3; UNSC Res 1124 (31 July 1997) UN Doc S/RES/1124, para 3; UNSC Res 1150 (30 January 1998) UN Doc S/RES/1150, preambular para 3; UNSC Res 1187 (30 July 1998) UN Doc S/RES/1187, para 8; UNSC Res 1225 (28 January 1999) UN Doc S/RES/1225, para 3; UNSC Res 1255 (30 July 1999) UN Doc S/RES/1255, para 5; UNSC Res 1287 (31 January 2000) UN Doc S/RES/1287, para 4; UNSC Res 1462 (30 Janaury 2003) UN Doc S/RES/1462, para 2; UNSC Res 1494 (30 July 2003) UN Doc S/RES/1494, para 2; UNSC Res 1524 (30 January 2004) UN Doc S/RES/1524, para 2; UNSC Res 1554 (29 July 2004) UN Doc S/RES/1554, para 1; UNSC Res 1582 (28 January 2005) UN Doc S/RES/1582, para 1; UNSC Res 1615 (29 July 2005) UN Doc S/RES/1615, para 1; UNSC Res 1666 (31 March 2006) UN Doc S/RES/1666, para 1; UNSC Res 1716 (13 October 2006) UN Doc S/RES/1716, para 1; UNSC Res 1752 (13 April 2007) UN Doc S/RES/1752, para 1; UNSC Res 1781 (15 October 2007) UN Doc S/RES/1781, para 1; UNSC Res 1808 (15 April 2008) UN Doc S/RES/1808, para 1.

borders".[185] In addition, the UNSC consistently referred to "Abkhazia, Republic of Georgia" or "Abkhazia, Georgia".[186] Similarly, the UNGA has consistently referred to "Abkhazia, Georgia," "the Tskhinvali region/South Ossetia, Georgia" and to two regions being included in Georgia.[187]

Thus, Georgia's emergence within the pre-existing borders of the former Georgian SSR can be taken as a strong confirmation of the applicability of the

185 UNSC Res 1808 (15 April 2008) UN Doc S/RES/1808, para 1.

186 UNSC Res 849 (9 July 1993) UN Doc S/RES/849, preamble recital 2; UNSC Res 854 (6 August 1993) UN Doc S/RES/854, preamble recital 2; UNSC Res 876 (19 October 1993) UN Doc S/RES/876, preamble recital 2; UNSC Res 881 (4 November 1993) UN Doc S/RES/881, preamble recital 3; UNSC Res 892 (22 December 1993) UN Doc S/RES/892, preamble recital 3; UNSC Res 896 (31 January 1994) UN Doc S/RES/896, preamble recital 3 and para 8; UNSC Res 901 (4 March 1994) UN Doc S/RES/901, preamble recital 4; UNSC Res 937 (21 July 1994) UN Doc S/RES/937, paras 3 and 12; UNSC Res 971 (12 January 1995) UN Doc S/RES/971, para 3; UNSC Res 993 (12 May 1995) UN Doc S/RES/993, preamble recital 8; UNSC Res 1036 (12 January 1996) UN Doc S/RES/1036, para 2; UNSC Res 1065 (12 July 1996) UN Doc S/RES/1065, paras 2 and 6; UNSC Res 1096 (30 January 1997) UN Doc S/RES/1096, para 2; UNSC Res 1124 (31 July 1997) UN Doc S/RES/1124, para 2; UNSC Res 1150 (30 January 1998) UN Doc S/RES/1150, para 2; UNSC Res 1187 (30 July 1998) UN Doc S/RES/1187, paras 13 and 15; UNSC Res 1225 (28 January 1999) UN Doc S/RES/1225, preamble recital 7; UNSC Res 1255 (28 January 1999) UN Doc S/RES/1255, preamble recital 6 and para 6; UNSC Res 1311 (28 July 2000) UN Doc S/RES/1311, para 14; UNSC Res 1339 (31 January 2001) UN Doc S/RES/1339, para 16; UNSC Res 1364 (31 July 2001) UN Doc S/RES/1364, para 21; UNSC Res 1427 (29 July 2002) UN Doc S/RES/1427, preamble recital 6 and para 18; UNSC Res 1462 (30 January 2003) UN Doc S/RES/1462, para 21; UNSC Res 1494 (30 July 2003) UN Doc S/RES/1494, para 28; UNSC Res 1524 (30 January 2004) UN Doc S/RES/1524, preamble recital 3 and para 30; UNSC Res 1554 (29 July 2004) UN Doc S/RES/1554, preamble recital 3 and para 29; UNSC Res 1582 (28 January 2005) UN Doc S/RES/1582, preamble recital 3 and para 32; UNSC Res 1615 (29 July 2005) UN Doc S/RES/1615, preamble recital 3 and para 34; UNSC Res 1666 (31 March 2006) UN Doc S/RES/1666, para 12; UNSC Res 1716 (13 October 2006) UN Doc S/RES/1716, para 18; UNSC Res 1752 (13 April 2007) UN Doc S/RES/1752, para 14; UNSC Res 1781 (15 October 2007) UN Doc S/RES/1781, para 20; UNSC Res 1808 (15 April 2008) UN Doc S/RES/1808, para 17.

187 UNGA Res 62/249 (15 May 2008) UN Doc A/RES/62/249, paras 1–3; UNGA Res 63/307 (9 September 2009) UN Doc A/RES/63/307, para 1; UNGA Res 64/296 (7 September 2010) UN Doc A/RES/64/296, para 1; UNGA Res 65/287 (29 June 2011) UN Doc A/RES/65/287, para 1; UNGA Res 66/283 (3 July 2012) UN Doc A/RES/66/283, para 1; UNGA Res 67/268 (13 June 2013) UN Doc A/RES/67/268, para 1; UNGA Res 68/274 (10 June 2014) UN Doc A/RES/68/274, para 1; UNGA Res 69/286 (3 June 2015) UN Doc A/RES/69/286, para 1; UNGA Res 70/265 (7 June 2016) UN Doc A/RES/70/265, para 1; UNGA Res 71/290 (1 June 2017) UN Doc A/RES/71/290, para 1; UNGA Res 72/280 (12 June 2018) UN Doc A/RES/72/280, para 1; UNGA Res 73/298 (4 June 2019) UN Doc A/RES/73/298, para 1; UNGA Res 74/300 (3 September 2020) UN Doc A/RES/74/300, para 1; UNGA Res 75/285 (16 June 2021) UN Doc A/RES/75/285, para 1; UNGA Res 76/267 (8 June 2022) UN Doc A/RES/76/267, para 1; UNGA Res 77/293 (7 June 2023) UN Doc A/RES/77/293, para 1.

principle of *uti possidetis* to the borders of the Union republics in the context of the dissolution of the USSR.

2.1.5 Russian Intervention into the Secessionist Conflicts

Prior to an analysis of *ius ad bellum* rules applicable to the conflicts in Georgia, the legal status of ex-Soviet troops in the territory of Georgia needs to be examined.[188] Even before the break-up of the USSR, Georgia demanded the withdrawal of Soviet troops from its territory, and in September 1991 even declared their presence an "illegal military occupation".[189] The period immediately following the Soviet Union's dissolution was marked by the attempt to create the Joint Armed Forces of the CIS,[190] but Georgia was not even a member of the CIS at this stage.[191] Later, ex-Soviet republics started to form their own armies and the project of a supranational Joint Armed Forces of the CIS was gradually abandoned.[192] In particular, with the Executive Order of 16 March 1992, the Russian president created the Russian Ministry of Defence and started transferring military units of the former Soviet Union abroad under Russia's jurisdiction.[193]

With the Executive Order of 19 March 1992, the Russian president temporarily transferred the Transcaucasian Military District and the Caspian Flotilla of the Navy to the Russian Federation's jurisdiction and submitted it to the command of the Commander in Chief of the Joint Armed Forces of the CIS.[194] This order also foresaw negotiations with the republics on the legal status and

---

188 Hamant highlights that it is doubtful that Russia's claim to be the continuator of the USSR would be sufficient to justify its taking control of the ex-Soviet bases in the territory of newly emerged States. Their maintenance required consent of the latter. See Hamant, *Démembrement de l'URSS et problèmes de succession d'états* (n 55) 402–3.

189 ibid 381.

190 ibid 342–365.

191 See *supra.* Georgia's State Council adopted the resolution on the creation of its own armed forces on 11 April 1992. See 'CIS, Baltic States and Georgia: Military Service' (*Immigration and Refugee Board of Canada,* 1 June 1992) <https://www.refworld.org/docid/3ae6a80d10.html> accessed 5 June 2019.

192 See Hamant, *Démembrement de l'URSS et problèmes de succession d'états* (n 55) 399–403.

193 'Executive Order of the President of the Russian Federation No 252 on the Ministry of Defence of the Russian Federation and Armed Forces of the Russian Federation' (adopted 16 March 1992, entered into force 16 March 1992) <http://www.kremlin.ru/acts/bank/1029> accessed 10 May 2019 (*in Russian*). Hamant, *Démembrement de l'URSS et problèmes de succession d'états* (n 55) 366 *et seq.*

194 'Executive Order of the President of the Russian Federation No 260 on the Transfer of the Transcaucasian Military District and of the Caspian Flotilla of the Nay under the Jurisdiction of the Russian Federation' (adopted 19 March 1992, entered into force 19 March 1992), para 1 <http://kremlin.ru/acts/bank/1069> accessed 10 May 2019 (*in Russian*).

conditions of deployment of these formations in their territory.[195] It authorised the representative of the Russian Federation to adopt measures to suppress attempts to seize the weapons, military equipment and facilities of the district and the flotilla and the participation of the troops in inter-ethnic conflicts and to adopt measures to prevent their interference in internal affairs of independent States.[196] The order also established that until there was an agreement on co-funding, the military district and the flotilla would be funded from the Russian Federation's budget.[197] At the same time, the Russian Federation also took *de facto* control of military formations in Georgia.[198]

With the Executive Order of 7 May 1992, the Russian president created the Armed Forces of the Russian Federation.[199] Under this order, groups of troops and fleets stationed outside the Russian Federation but placed under its jurisdiction were integrated within the Armed Forces of the Russian Federation.[200] These formations unequivocally included ex-Soviet troops in Transcaucasia, as they had already been placed under Russia's jurisdiction.[201]

Thus, as of 19 March 1992, Russia unilaterally placed ex-Soviet troops in Georgia under its jurisdiction and after that took *de facto* control of them. It is true that at that time these formations were still formally submitted to the command of the Commander in Chief of the Joint Armed Forces of the CIS, as the Russian Armed Forces were yet to be formed.[202] However, with regard to Russia's effective control of these formations, their *de iure* submission under Russia's jurisdiction, their funding from Russia's budget and their submission to measures of the representative of the Russian Federation, they could be arguably considered organs of the Russian Federation under Article 4 ARSIWA. Since the creation of the Armed Forces of the Russian Federation on 7 May 1992, they were undoubtedly State organs under Article 4 ARSIWA. In addition, as mentioned above, in October 1993, Russia and Georgia signed a treaty on

195 ibid para 2.

196 ibid para 3.

197 ibid para 2.

198 Hamant, *Démembrement de l'URSS et problèmes de succession d'états* (n 55) 379.

199 'Executive Order of the President of the Russian Federation No 466 on the Creation of the Armed Forces of the Russian Federation' (adopted 7 May 1992, entered into force 7 May 1992) <http://kremlin.ru/acts/bank/1279> accessed 10 May 2019 (*in Russian*).

200 ibid.

201 Hamant, *Démembrement de l'URSS et problèmes de succession d'états* (n 55) 369.

202 See ibid 369. "Ce n'est pas de l'armée soviétique, mais des Forces armées unifiées qu' a héritées la Russie ... Pendant au moins les six mois qui ont suivi [signature of Minsk Agreement and Alma Ata Protocol], la Russie, du moins juridiquement n'avait pas d'armée." See ibid 402.

the legal status of Russia's military formations on Georgia's territory.[203] Even if it was not ratified, the treaty was provisionally applied and thus constituted Georgia's implicit recognition of Russia's extra-territorial jurisdiction over ex-Soviet troops on its soil.[204]

The extent of Russian intervention in the conflict in South Ossetia during the first half-year of the existence of the Russian Federation was ambiguous. Nevertheless, Russia, at least sporadically, provided material support to separatists, which according to *Nicaragua* constitutes a violation of the prohibition of the use of force.[205] Whether this happened on orders from Moscow, in contravention of such orders, or independently of Moscow is not clear, but under Articles 4 and 7 ARSIWA, the acts of the Armed Forces of the Russian Federation, as organs of the Russian Federation, were directly attributable to it, even in excess of authority or in contravention of instructions.[206] In addition, Russia's taking of military positions in the summer of 1992, allowing it to directly intervene in the conflict, as expressly reflected in Article 2 of the Sochi Ceasefire Agreement,[207] can be considered a threat of the use of force and therefore a violation of Article 2(4) UN Charter.[208]

During the conflict in Abkhazia, Russia provided weapons to separatists.[209] The above considerations of the ARSIWA attribution rules concerning acts of State organs on orders, in excess of authority and acts in contravention of instructions fully apply to this case, too.[210] Moreover, the UNSC Resolution 876

---

203 See *supra*.

204 Hamant, *Démembrement de l'URSS et problèmes de succession d'états* (n 55) 382. See *supra* on the evolution of the presence of ex-Soviet troops in Georgia.

205 See *supra*. *Case Concerning Military and Paramilitary Activities in and against Nicaragua* (*Nicaragua v United States of America*) [1986] ICJ Rep 14, para 228 ("*Nicaragua*").

206 ILC, Draft Articles on the Responsibility of States for Internationally Wrongful Acts, with Commentaries in 'Report of the International Law Commission on the Work of its Fifty-Third Session (23 April -1 June and 2 July-10 August 2001)' UN Doc A/56/10, arts 4 and 7 ("ARSIWA").

207 See *supra*.

208 Charter of the United Nations (adopted 26 June 1945, entered into force 24 October 1945) 1 UNTS XVI ("UN Charter").

209 See *supra*.

210 See *supra*. Notably, the ECtHR in *Mamasakhlisi* held that the Abkhaz victory in the conflict "would not have been possible without the involvement of at least certain forces and military equipment emanating from the territory of the Russian Federation." *Mamasakhlisi* (n 37) para 323. At the same time, the Court claimed that it did not find evidence "that it was the Russian government that authorised the use of such military force and supplied weapons during the 1990s." ibid. At the same time, it held that "Russian military and Russian commanders in Abkhazia actively supported the Abkhaz side" while pointing to sources confirming Russian solders' involvement in arming the Abkhaz fighters. ibid. Thus, given the ARSIWA rules on attribution (especially regarding State organs under

(1993) called on "all *States* to prevent the provision from their territories or by persons under their jurisdiction of all assistance ... to the Abkhaz side and in particular to prevent the supply of any weapons and munitions".[211] Taking into account the specific context, the target of the UNSC could only have been the Russian Federation. "Russia's provision of weapons to the Abkhaz was in violation of international law,"[212] in particular, the prohibition of the use of force.[213] However, these actions cannot be classified as armed attacks.[214] Russia also intervened in the conflict in Abkhazia directly via its air and sea attacks, which not only directly violated the prohibition of the use of force, but amounted to aggression and, depending on their scale and gravity, also to armed attack.[215] Furthermore, Russia's violation of the prohibition of the use of force also violated Georgia's territorial integrity and constituted an illegal intervention into Georgia's internal affairs.[216]

In both wars, different types of other actors, in particular volunteers from North Ossetia and the Confederation of Caucasian Mountain People, supported the separatists.[217] But since there is not enough evidence of their link

---

Article 4), the evidence of such governmental authorisation was arguably not required. In *Ilașcu,* in a similar context, the Court considered "the principle of States' responsibility for abuses of authority." *Ilașcu and others v Moldova and Russia* ECHR 2004-VII 1, para 380. J Miklasová, 'Mamasakhlisi and Others v. Georgia and Russia: Russia's Effective Control over Abkhazia Before the 2008 War: Peacekeepers, Passportisation and Other Hybrid Elements' (*Strasbourg Observers*, 13 June 2023) <https://strasbourgobservers.com/2023/06/13/mamasakhlisi-and-others-v-georgia-and-russia-russias-effective-control-over-abkhazia-before-the-2008-war-peacekeepers-passportisation-and-other-hybrid-elements/> accessed 19 October 2023.

211 UNSC Res 876 (19 October 1993) UN Doc S/RES/876, para 8.

212 Shanahan Cutts (n 65) 295–296.

213 *Nicaragua* (n 205) para 228 and see para 191. Declaration on Principles of International Law concerning Friendly Relations and Co-operation among States in accordance with the Charter of the United Nations, UNGA Res 2625 (XXV) (24 October 1970) UN Doc A/RES/2625(XXV), principle 1, para 9 ("Friendly Relations Declaration").

214 *Nicaragua* (n 205) para 247.

215 See *supra.* Definition of Aggression, UNGA Res 3314 (XXIX) (14 December 1974) UN Doc A/RES/3314(XXIX), art 3(a)(b) ("Definition of Aggression"). A decisive factor for the classification of these acts as armed attacks would be their intensity. See G Nolte and A Randelzhofer, 'Article 51' in B Simma and others (eds), *The Charter of the United Nations: A Commentary*, Volume II (3rd edn, OUP 2012) para 23.

216 "[A]cts constituting a breach of the customary principle of non-intervention will also, if they directly or indirectly involve the use of force, constitute a breach of the principle of non-use of force in international relations." *Nicaragua* (n 205) para 209 and see also para 247. UN Charter (n 208) art 2(4).

217 See *supra.*

to Russia, their actions are considered private and therefore outside the scope of this analysis.

2.1.6 Independence

Before 2008, both South Ossetia and Abkhazia fulfilled the constitutive criteria of territory and permanent population, and they even possessed formal signs of independence.[218] However, their actual independence must also be assessed. In this context, in the period immediately following the secessionist wars, Abkhazia and to a lesser extent South Ossetia were isolated both from Georgia and the Russian Federation. Nevertheless, the international community did not accept a *de facto* existence of these entities as attributive of statehood. This could be interpreted as attesting to a generalised aversion of States to accept a *de facto* outcome of the secessionist wars or to an extremely high threshold of effectiveness required in these situations, including abandonment by the parent State of the claim on the territory in question.[219] It might, however, reflect other normative prescriptions, too.[220]

Nevertheless, the factual situation changed around 2000, when Russian influence on these entities started to grow.[221] In its judgment in *Georgia v Russia (II)* the ECtHR considered the findings of the Independent International Fact-Finding Mission on the Conflict in Georgia concerning the pre-2008 period as "revealing as to the pre-existing relationship of sub-ordination between the separatist entities [Abkhazia and South Ossetia] and the Russian Federation", which lasted throughout and after the end of the 2008 conflict.[222] Factual dependence on Russia was confirmed by South Ossetia's president in June 2006 when he claimed, "South Ossetia is de facto an entity of the Russian Federation. We simply have to consolidate this legally."[223] In addition, a true commitment to statehood could be seen as being compromised by the fact that South Ossetia's ultimate goal was to unite with Russia rather than function as an independent State.[224] For these reasons, many scholars conclude, "South

218 See Report (n 33) 130–134.

219 See *supra* Part 1, Chapter 1 and Chapter 5.

220 See *infra* on legal consequences of Russia's intervention into secessionist wars.

221 The European Parliament called on Russia to withdraw support from separatist movements. See European Parliament, 'Resolution on the Situation in South Ossetia' (26 October 2006) C 313 E/430, para 4.

222 *Georgia v Russia (II)* (n 72) para 168.

223 E Kokoity, (*Yuzhnaya Osetiya*, 10 June 2006) cited in Leach (n 82) 337. See *supra* for the factual account.

224 Nussberger, 'South Ossetia' (n 6) para 21.

Ossetia cannot be qualified as a 'State' before the outbreak of the 2008 war."[225] The International Fact-Finding Mission classified South Ossetia as an "entity short of statehood", meaning an entity that did not even fulfil the constitutive criteria of statehood.[226]

As for Abkhazia, the International Fact-Finding Mission determined its status in the period between 2000 and 2008 as a "state-like entity", meaning it fulfilled the constitutive criteria of statehood but lacked international recognition.[227] To justify such conclusion, the Report highlighted both the wishes of the population and political elites to maintain an independent Abkhaz statehood and the electoral loss in 2004 of the Russian-backed candidate for president.[228] Nevertheless, even though these factors demonstrate a bigger sphere of independence and more advanced state-building than in South Ossetia, other factors, especially Russia's economic support for Abkhazia, should lead to the conclusion that even before 2008, Abkhazia's actual independence was compromised in favour of Russia.[229] This was confirmed by the ECtHR in *Mamasakhlisi* which established that

> *de facto* Abkhazia was only able to survive because of Russia's sustained and substantial political and economic support, and dissuasive military involvement. Abkhazia's high level of dependency on Russian support during the period in question [2001–2007] allows the Court to conclude that Russia exercised effective control and decisive influence over Abkhaz territory.[230]

Thus, before 2008, neither of these entities fulfilled the criterion of independence and on this ground alone could not be considered States. This is also supported by the presumption against the independence of an entity in a situation of substantial illegality of origin, which seems to be applicable in

225 ibid para 22.

226 Report (n 33) 134 in connection with 128–129.

227 ibid 134 in connection with 128–129 and 133–134. However, according to the mainstream declaratory theory of recognition outlined in Part 1, once an entity fulfils the constitutive criteria of statehood, it is a State regardless of the number of recognitions. However, the Report claims that Abkhazia should not be recognised, because its state-building was not legitimate as it did not possess the right to secession and did not fulfil basic requirements regarding human rights. Report (n 33) 135.

228 Report (n 33) 134 in connection with 128–129 and 133–134.

229 See *supra* for the factual account.

230 *Mamasakhlisi* (n 37) para 339.

these situations.[231] By providing non-military assistance to separatists in South Ossetia and Abkhazia, Russia violated the prohibition of non-intervention in Georgia's internal affairs.[232]

2.1.7 Legal Status

Violation of the prohibition of the use of force by Russia was a decisive element of the secessionist victories in the war against Georgia. According to Follebouckt, the Russian factor "est une composante centrale des victoires ossète et abkhaze".[233] According to Human Rights Watch, "Russian military aid to the Abkhaz was directly related to the conflict and intended to influence its course in favor of the Abkhaz."[234] Even if, immediately after the war, Russia interrupted links with separatists and even imposed sanctions on Abkhazia, its military intervention in the conflicts was at the core of the capacity of separatists to win against Georgia and establish effectiveness vis-à-vis Georgia; and it enabled Georgia's acceptance of the ceasefire framework legalising Russian military presence as peacekeepers. "Thus it was Russia's role as security guarantor that in fact created the external conditions for the establishment of state structures in the contested territories."[235]

Therefore, based on a normative framework developed in Part 1, Chapter 2 violation of peremptory norms during the secessionist attempt precludes the emergence of a new State. South Ossetia and Abkhazia did not become States, as their secessionist attempt was connected to and profited from a violation of peremptory norms.[236] Under international law, they remained part of Georgia.

Abkhazia and South Ossetia remained *de iure* part of Georgia and *prima facie* exercised effective territorial control of Georgia's territory, gradually lost their independence vis-à-vis Russia, persisted in claiming to be States and were created due to violation of peremptory norms. Thus, they can be characterised as illegal secessionist entities even before 2008.[237]

---

231 J Crawford, *The Creation of States in International Law* (2nd edn, Clarendon Press 2006) 74, 80, 89. See *infra*.

232 *Nicaragua* (n 205) para 205.

233 Follebouckt (n 8) 98 and 126.

234 Human Rights Watch (n 38) 53.

235 Fischer, 'Russian Policy in the Unresolved Conflicts' (n 43) 17.

236 Summers sees the origins of Abkhazia and South Ossetia occurring through the violation of humanitarian law and ethnic cleansing of the Georgian population, which is particularly acute when assessing Abkhazia's statehood "as its status as an Abkhaz-dominated self-governing entity is dependent on the continued displacement of the territory's ethnic Georgian population." Summers (n 14) 112.

237 See *supra* Part 1, Chapter 6.

2.2 *Post-2008 Period*

2.2.1 Legal Consequences of the 2008 War

The following account limits itself to highlighting key arguments on the use of force during the 2008 War, as this book's position is that legality or illegality of the use of force during this war does not have a decisive impact on the underlying question of statehood for the two entities.[238] Instead, the conclusions may corroborate previous findings. It also refers to the Report's conclusions.[239]

Firstly, the issue arose whether Georgia could have violated the prohibition of the use of force even if it used force within its internationally recognised territory.[240] Generally, the prohibition of the use of force is interpreted as not preventing the parent State's use of armed force against separatists in internal armed conflicts.[241] "The legal situation changes, however, when the rebels have succeeded in establishing a stabilized de facto regime."[242] Dörr and Randelzhofer claim, "it is almost generally accepted that de facto regimes exercising their authority in a stabilized manner are also bound and protected by Art. 2(4)."[243] The reading of the Friendly Relations Declaration seems to support this conclusion, too.[244] The same conclusion could also be reached *per analogy* with the possessory protection, which deriving from Article 2(4) UN Charter and supported by practice, entails that prohibition of threat or use of force applies to any actual territorial possession, regardless of legality or validity of title.[245] An underlying rationale is the limitation of territorial changes by

---

238 For an extensive analysis of *ius ad bellum* issues, see Report (n 33) 227–295.

239 It needs to be added that the Report's *ius ad bellum* analysis was met with scholarly criticism. See for example A Lott, 'The Tagliavini Report Revisited: Jus Ad Bellum and the Legality of the Russian Intervention in Georgia' (2012) 28 Utrecht Journal of International and European Law 4; C Henderson and JA Green, 'The Ius Ad Bellum and Entities Short of Statehood in the Report on the Conflict in Georgia' (2010) 59 ICLQ 129.

240 See TW Waters, 'Plucky Little Russia' (n 30) 209.

241 Report (n 33) 239. O Dörr and A Randelzhofer, 'Article 2(4)' in B Simma and others (eds), *The Charter of the United Nations: A Commentary*, Volume I (3rd edn, OUP 2012) para 32.

242 Dörr and Randelzhofer (n 241) para 32.

243 ibid para 29. Lott (n 239) 7–8.

244 "Every State likewise has the duty to refrain from the threat or use of force to violate international lines of demarcation, such as armistice lines, established by or pursuant to an international agreement to which it is a party or which it is otherwise bound to respect." Friendly Relations Declaration (n 213) principle 1, para 5. "This includes the borders of what are here called de facto regimes." JA Frowein, 'De Facto Regime' in MPEPIL (online edn, OUP 2013) para 5. Frowein also points to the explanatory note in the Definition of Aggression according to which the term State "[i]s used without prejudice to questions of recognition or to whether a State is a member of the United Nations." Ibid. Definition of Aggression (n 215) art 1.

245 MG Kohen, *Possession contestée et souveraineté territoriale* (PUF 1997) 403–405.

threat or use force without prejudging the issue of territorial sovereignty.[246] On the other hand, Corten and others reject the extension of regime of the use of force under the UN Charter to entities with disputed statehood.[247] The question arose also in the context of Azerbaijan's use of force to retake Nagorno-Karabakh in 2020 and 2023.[248] It must be underlined that the Report derived the extension of the prohibition of the use of force to South Ossetia from the interpretation of ceasefire agreements; yet these agreements do not seem to be generally relevant to this question.[249]

Secondly, it is one thing to claim that the prohibition of threat or use of force is extended to a *de facto* stabilised regime and illegal secessionist entity; it is another matter to derive from this conclusion the right of self-defence for such an entity. Indeed, such an approach would seem to directly contradict an original purpose of limiting the recourse to armed force. The Report inferred the right of self-defence for entity short of statehood simply from the fact that "otherwise the regime of use of force would not be coherent,"[250] without offering any analysis of practice or deeper insight.[251] Yet, later on, the Report itself made the regime of use of force incoherent when it claimed that such an entity was only entitled to an individual and not a collective right of self-defence.[252]

---

246 ibid 404.

247 O Corten, *The Law Against War: The Prohibition on the Use of Force in Contemporary International Law* (Hart 2010) 151–160. For the views rejecting the applicability of the prohibition of the use of force with respect to South Ossetia see JA Green, 'Passportisation, Peacekeepers and Proportionality: The Russian Claim of the Protection of Nationals Abroad in Self-Defence' in JA Green and CPM Waters (eds), *Conflict in the Caucasus: Implications for International Legal Order* (Palgrave Macmillan 2010) 70; Mirzayev (n 182) 196. According to PACE, taking into account the fact that the use of force took place within Georgia's territory, it was a violation of international humanitarian law and the commitment to resolve the conflict peacefully. CoE (PACE) Res 1633 (2 October 2008) para 5.

248 See *infra* Chapter 14 concerning Azerbaijan's use of force to retake Nagorno-Karabakh in 2020 and 2023.

249 Report (n 33) 239–242. "The various uses of force in the Caucasus by or against non-State entities may well breach the provisions of the agreements between them (and between them and State parties) that pledge to maintain peaceful relations, but this does not correspond to a breach of article 2(4)." Henderson and Green (n 239) 131–134.

250 Report (n 33) 242.

251 "If one accepts the applicability of article 2(4) to non-State entities, a corresponding application of article 51 of the UN Charter would make a degree of theoretical sense. Yet such a theoretical lap-however logical-is not a substitute for the identification of a positive legal basis for such an application of self-defense." Henderson and Green (n 239) 135.

252 Report (n 33) 280–283. Henderson and Green (n 239) 136–138.

Furthermore, the Report also established that an attack of sufficient scale and intensity emanating from a non-State actor could be considered an armed attack.[253] It suffices to say that this is an extremely controversial position – an in-depth analysis of which falls beyond the scope of the present analysis.[254]

The Report also established that Georgia's operations against Russia could not be justified as self-defence until Russian military action extended to Georgia and was conducted in breach of international law.[255] From this follows the issue of the legality of Russia's response to Georgia's operations. Since Georgia did not attack Russia's territory itself, Russia justified its use of force as self-defence against Georgia's attack against Russia's peacekeepers legally stationed in South Ossetia.[256]

The Report concluded that Russia's use of force could have been justified on this basis.[257] Nevertheless, questions were raised in the literature regarding the status of the Russian peacekeepers, as they operated under an internationalised regime of the Sochi Agreement and under an internationalised command, which challenged the Report's conclusion that peacekeepers resembled "state instrumentalities" of the Russian Federation.[258]

In any case, Russia's use of force would need to have complied with the conditions of necessity and proportionality, which it failed to do.[259] Any incursions of the Russian Federation beyond South Ossetia to Georgia proper "must be seen as an act of aggression rather than a justifiable or appropriate response to the initial Georgian mobilisation".[260] The bombing and occupation of Gori,

253 Report (n 33) 243–251.

254 See Lott (n 239) 8–10; Henderson and Green (n 239) 135–136.

255 Report (n 33) 252–262.

256 See 'Letter Dated 11 August 2018 from Permanent Representative of the Russian Federation to the United Nations Addressed to the President of the Security Council' (11 August 2008) UN Doc S/2008/545; TW Waters, 'Plucky Little Russia' (n 30) 210–211.

257 Report (n 33) 264–269.

258 Report (n 33) 268. "[I]t is important that the peacekeeping troops in South Ossetia were subjected to the JCC as well as the joint military command, and not to any one of the three allocating entities. The importance here is that, only the former can exercise command and control over the peacekeeping troops." Lott (n 239) 17–21.

259 Report (n 33) 269–275. O'Reilly and Higgins (n 82) 582. Petro holds the opposite view. "Clearly, if Russia had wanted to occupy the entire country, it could have done so with little difficulty after the collapse of the Georgian Army on August 11, 2008." NN Petro, 'Legal Case for Russian Intervention in Georgia' (2008) 32 Fordham International Law Journal 1524, 1532–33 and 1543–1544. See also CoE (PACE) Res 1633 (2 October 2008) para 6.

260 O'Reilly and Higgins (n 82) 583; JA Green, 'The Caucasus Conflict and the Role of Law' in JA Green and CPM Waters (eds), *Conflict in the Caucasus: Implications for International Legal Order* (Palgrave Macmillan 2010) 13. But "nothing in the laws of war limits a defender to the original territory, and operations there would fit comfortably in the broad discretion

the occupation of Poti and moves towards Tbilisi were "manifestly excessive in terms of scale when compared to the attacks on Russian nationals ... present in South Ossetia, to which Russia was ostensibly responding".[261] The defensive character of Russia's actions could therefore be doubted.[262] Therefore, Russia's intervention violated Article 2(4) UN Charter.[263]

Additionally, the Report discarded all of Russia's other arguments, including the invitation by South Ossetian authorities[264] and Russia's protection of its nationals in South Ossetia.[265] Apart from the fact that the latter justification does not seem to exist in positive international law,[266] the claim was also not substantiated factually.[267] There was no genocide in South Ossetia at the time of Russia's counter-attack.[268] This also applies to the claims on the existence of the right to remedial secession.[269] Moreover, many scholars also point to the

---

typically afforded to a defender to neutralize a military threat." TW Waters, 'Plucky Little Russia' (n 30) 221.

261 See also the analysis of Russia's operation in the Abkhazia, Report (n 33) 290–294. Green, 'Passportisation' (n 243) 69.

262 See Green, 'Passportisation' (n 243) 69.

263 ibid 70. "According to international law, the Russian military action taken as a whole was therefore neither necessary nor proportionate to protect Russian peacekeepers in South Ossetia." Report (n 33) 275.

264 Report (n 33) 275–284.

265 'Letter Dated 11 August 2018 from Permanent Representative of the Russian Federation to the United Nations Addressed to the President of the Security Council' (11 August 2008) UN Doc S/2008/545.

266 See *supra* chapters on Crimea and Easter Ukraine for details. See CoE (PACE) Res 1633 (2 October 2008), para 7. Report (n 33) 285–288.

267 Report (n 33) 288–289. "[T]he issue for the majority of states has been the *application* of the protection of nationals abroad justification, either on the basis that the response taken was disproportional, unnecessary, or that the attack or threat to nationals was not grave enough to constitute an armed attack." Green, 'Passportisation' (n 243) 63 (*emphasis in original*).

268 Nussberger, 'The War between Russia and Georgia' (n 27) 359–360; O'Reilly and Higgins (n 82) 582; Green, 'Passportisation' (n 243) 57. For the opposite view, see Petro (n 259) 1534–1537.

269 Similarly, President Medvedev's statement on the date of Russia's recognition of Abkhazia and South Ossetia, that Georgia's president Saakashvili "opted for genocide to accomplish his political objectives" on the night of 8 August 2008 has not been substantiated. D Medvedev, 'Statement by President of Russia' (26 August 2008) <http://en.kremlin.ru/events/president/transcripts/1222> accessed 15 May 2019. The tensions leading up to the war in 2008 should not be understood as "an exceptional circumstance of a last resort to enable a people to exercise their right of self-determination by external self-determination methods." McCorquoadale and Hausler (n 162) 42. See also Report (n 33) 144–145 and 146–147. Ultimately, neither during the secessionist wars of the 1990s nor in 2008, did the factual situation in Abkhazia and South Ossetia fulfil the doctrinal requirements for remedial secession.

fact that the process of passportisation undermined Russia's arguments in this regard, too.[270] Nevertheless, as will be shown below, international illegality of this policy *per se* seems to be arguable.

2.2.2 Passportisation

The term passportisation could be denoted as *en masse* conferral of Russian nationality on individuals residing in the territory of the former USSR but outside the Russian Federation, upon application by the persons concerned through a simplified procedure.[271] This practice needs to be distinguished from a collective, involuntary *ex lege* automatic conferral of nationality.[272] Despite certain unconfirmed allegations of coercion,[273] Russian nationality was granted in Abkhazia and South Ossetia with consent and upon the application of the persons concerned. Economic incentives, including access to Russian pensions, health care and social benefits are not considered to include elements of coercion.[274] Secondly, while passportisation is also characterised by a dramatic increase in naturalisations[275] – and therefore the qualifier 'en masse' seems to be justified, in connection with a previous point – the adjective "collective would not seem to be substantiated".[276]

The Russian policy of passportisation towards Abkhazia and South Ossetia began in 2002 and 2004, respectively,[277] and thus overlaps with Russia's

---

270 See *infra*.

271 Compare with the definition of naturalisation in O Dörr, 'Nationality' in MPEPIL (online edn, OUP 2006), para 18. "Legally speaking, the issuing of a passport and the conferral of nationality are two distinct legal acts. The possession of a passport does not convey or prove nationality." A Peters, 'Passportisation: Risks for International Law and Stability – Part I' (*EJIL Talk!*, 9 May 2019) <https://www.ejiltalk.org/passportisation-risks-for-international-law-and-stability-part-one/> accessed 21 June 2019 ("Passportisation I"). See *Georgia v Russia (II)* (n 72) para 169. *Mamasakhlisi* (n 37) paras 324, 330, 335.

272 According to the Report, this would be generally contrary to international law. Report (n 33) 161–163. The Report found that passportisation even if not collective in a formal sense could be equated to "collective (ex lege) naturalisation of foreign residents" and therefore is illegal. ibid 169–171.

273 See Green, 'Passportisation' (n 243) 66–67; Report (n 33) 148.

274 Peters, Passportisation I (n 271).

275 Since the grant of Russian citizenship to the population in Transnistria has been gradual over time, Nagashima does not consider it as such falling within the term of passportisation. See T Nagashima, 'Russia's Passportization Policy toward Unrecognized Republics Abkhazia, South Ossetia and Transnistria' (2019) 66 Problems of Post-Communism 186, 194–195.

276 *Contra* the Report points to large quantities of persons affected. Report (n 33) 170–171.

277 Even though a more favourable approach to these secessionist entities was visible when Russia unilaterally imposed a visa regime on Georgia, but exempted the residents of Abkhazia and South Ossetia. The European Parliament found this exception to be "*de facto*

increased support for secessionist entities and the corresponding deterioration of relations with Georgia described above.[278] This policy was connected with a change in Russian citizenship law in 2002 and increased administrative support that even preceded the change of this law.[279] As a result, the number of Russian citizens in Abkhazia and South Ossetia increased dramatically.[280]

Previously, the 1991 Russian Citizenship Law provided for an open-door citizenship policy; former Soviet citizens who wished to obtain Russian citizenship were only required to register within a specified period, ultimately extended to the year 2000.[281] In the new 2002 Citizenship Law, these privileges of former Soviet citizens were abolished, except for a loophole that allowed the populations of breakaway entities to apply for Russian citizenship in a simplified manner, in particular without the requirement of a 5-year residency.[282] Article 14(1) provided for a simplified citizenship procedure to individuals who "had Soviet citizenship, lived and live in countries that were components of the USSR, but have not obtained citizenship of these countries and remained stateless".[283] The population of Abkhazia and South Ossetia did not consider themselves to have Georgian citizenship, and since, at the time, these entities were not recognised by Russia, Russia could have considered them to be stateless.[284]

Many authors challenge this policy, mainly due to an apparent lack of a real or a genuine link between the Russian Federation and applicants for

annexation of these indisputably Georgian territories." European Parliament, 'Resolution on the Visa Regime Imposed by the Russian Federation on Georgia' (18 January 2001) C 262/259, para 1.

278 See *supra*. See Nagashima's detailed analysis of geopolitical factors that determined this policy's implementation in Abkhazia and South Ossetia. Nagashima (n 275) 190–194.

279 See ibid 188–190.

280 The change in law took effect in July 2002 and passportisation had begun already in June 2002 when the number of Russian citizens in Abkhazia rose from 20 to 70% in a single month. Before the war in 2008, virtually the whole population of South Ossetia was said to also have Russian citizenship. See ibid 188–190.

281 ibid 188. See also O Shevel, 'The Politics of Citizenship Policy in Post-Soviet Russia' (2012) 28 Post-Soviet Affairs 111, 120–127.

282 Nagashima (n 275) 189–190. It is worth noting that this clause was not originally included in the bill, but was only proposed by an opponent to the change of citizenship policy during the new law's adoption in the Duma. ibid 190. See also Shevel (n 281) 127–140.

283 'Federal Law on the Citizenship of Russian Federation No 62-F3 (31 May 2002) as amended, art 14(1) <http://www.consultant.ru/document/cons_doc_LAW_36927/> accessed 22 June 2019 (*in Russian*) ("Russian Citizenship Law"). English translation in Nagashima (n 275) 190.

284 See Report (n 33) 150–155 for a discussion on Georgian citizenship of populations of breakaway regions.

citizenship.[285] It is claimed that in order for nationality to be opposable at the international level, it needs to fulfil requirements of "real and effective" nationality.[286] In this regard, some authors claim that the grounds provided for by the Russian Citizenship Law do not constitute a sufficient factual link between individuals and the Russian Federation.[287] Therefore, naturalisations on this basis are exorbitant, invalid under international law and not opposable by third States.[288]

---

285 "A core question of passportisation is whether the conferral of a new nationality on persons living outside the naturalising state, and without having any other connection to that state, is *per se* illegal because of the lack of an appropriate factual connection and resulting arbitrariness." A Peters, 'Passportisation: Risks for International Law and Stability – Part II' (*EJIL Talk!*, 10 May 2019) available <https://www.ejiltalk.org/passportisation-risks-for-international-law-and-stability-part-two/> accessed 21 June 2019 ("Passportization II").

286 Green, 'Passportisation' (n 243) 67. See S Mantu, *Contingent Citizenship: The Law and Practice of Citizenship Deprivation in International, European and National Perspectives* (Brill 2015) 56.

287 "Former Soviet citizenship cannot be accepted as sufficient factual connection. Regardless of the qualification of the dissolution of the Soviet Union as a process of dismemberment or as a series of secessions, Russia is not identical with the Soviet Union as a state and as a subject of international law. Therefore the bond created by the Soviet citizenship between the citizens of the different Soviet Republics was irrevocably severed in 1991. On the basis of new laws on nationality, all former Soviet citizens redefined their status and determined to which of the CIS-States they wanted to belong. And even if the Russian nationality were considered to be the 'former nationality', it would only be accepted as a sufficient factual connection if the person again took residence in Russia." Report (n 33) 168 (*footnote omitted*). It is worth noting that the Report analysed this question on the basis of an incorrect provision – instead of art 14(1) of the Russian Citizenship Law, it focused on art 14(4). Nagashima (n 275) 190, ftn 4. "The conferral of Russian nationality to persons living outside the territory of the Russian Federation only because they had been citizens of the Soviet Union, have acquired a temporary residence permit, or on the basis of 'ethnicity,' does not fulfil the minimum requirement of a factual connection between the applicants and Russia." Peters, Passportization II (n 285). However, Peters generally claims that "today, habitual residence does not seem to be a necessary criterion for individual (as opposed to collective) naturalisations. Habitual residence may be supplanted by other types of factual connections." ibid. In addition, it needs to be added that the factual link analysed by Peters in her blogpost on passportization in Donbas only relates to South Ossetia and Abkhazia and not to Donbas, since the passportization there was only justified by 'humanitarian reasons.' For other authors, it is "unclear" whether such a factual test was met in 2008. Green, 'Passportisation' (n 243) 67. With respect to passportisation in Crimea, see JA Green, 'The Annexation of Crimea: Russia, Passportisation and the Protection of Nationals Revisited' (2014) 1 Journal on the Use of Force and International Law 3, 4.

288 Peters, Passportization II (n 285). Report (n 33) 179–183.

However, several inter-connected points need to be made. Firstly, the requirement of a genuine link is derived from the ICJ's famous holding in *Nottebohm*.[289] However, the ICJ itself suggested that its conclusion should only be limited to the circumstances of that particular case.[290] In addition, it is not clear to what extent the practice itself supports the requirement of a genuine link for naturalisations[291] or how intense this link should be.[292] Even Peters admits, "the factual relationship need not be very tight."[293] Thus, it is difficult to see how the conclusion on the lack of factual link could be reconciled with a general practice of naturalisations that, if at all, does not require a very tight factual link[294] and with a specific practice in the context of State successions.[295] In addition, it is not clear why the requirements of the Russian

---

289 *Nottebohm case* (*Liechtenstein v. Guatemala*) (Second Phase) [1955] ICJ Rep 4, 23 ("*Nottebohm*").

290 ibid 17. Even Peters claims, "[t]he better view is therefore that the genuine link requirement applies – if at all – only to the question of diplomatic protection (and possibly for resolving questions of dual nationality)." Peters, Passportization II (n 285). Report (n 33), 159–160. Similarly, E Fripp, 'Passportisation: Risks for International Law and Stability – Response to Anne Peters' (*EJIL Talk!*, 30 May 2019) <https://www.ejiltalk.org/passportisation-risks-for-international-law-and-stability-response-to-anne-peters/> accessed 21 June 2019 ("Response to Peters").

291 K Hailbronner, 'Nationality in Public International Law and European Law' in R Bauböck and others (eds), *Acquisition and Loss of Nationality: Policies and Trends in 15 European States* (Amsterdam University Press 2006) 60; Mantu (n 286) 56, ftn 115. For a rejection of the requirement of a genuine link in other contexts, see UNHCR 'Guidelines on Statelessness No 1' (20 February 2012) HCR/GS/12/01, para 47 and ftn 35; UNHCR, *Handbook on Protection of Stateless Persons Under the 1954 Convention Relating to the Status of Stateless Persons* (UNHCR 2014), para 54, ftn 38. In addition, even the ILC did not require the State of Nationality to prove an effective link between this State and its national for the purposes of the exercise of diplomatic protection, since according to the ILC, the *Nottebohm* case was limited to the facts of that case and did not intend to formulate a general rule. ILC 'Draft Articles on Diplomatic Protection with Commentaries' in 'Report of the International Law Commission on the Work of its Fifty-Eighth Session (1 May–9 June and 3 July–11 August 2006)' UN Doc A/61/10, commentary to art 4, para 5. According to Peters, international law "has never allowed a state to confer its nationality by naturalisation upon persons possessing the nationality of another state and to whom the conferring state has no factual connection at all." Peters, Passportization II (n 285); Report (n 33) 158–159.

292 Similarly, Response to Peters (n 290). CF Amerasinghe, *Diplomatic Protection* (OUP 2008) 93.

293 Peters, Passportization II (n 285).

294 Similarly, Response to Peters (n 290).

295 It would also entail that previous Russian citizenship laws that only required the registration of former Soviet citizens would also be incompatible with international law when it clearly was not considered as such.

Citizenship Law would fail to meet a supposed factual *Nottebohm* link in the first place.[296]

Authors also highlight that passportisation undermines the statehood of the parent State by diminishing one of its core elements, its people.[297] It is claimed that this would lead to the paradox that these territories would still be *de iure* part of the parent State, but their residents would be citizens of another State.[298] However, this outcome is also predetermined by the citizenship policy of these other States that bar double nationality in their legislation.[299] In any case, this argument does not seem to have direct relevance to legality and opposability of naturalisations on the international plane.

Moreover, it is true that PACE held that "the Russian Federation's en masse distribution of Russian passports to persons living outside the Russian Federation ("passportisation") is contrary to the Council of Europe's principles"[300] and in violation of the territorial integrity of the parent States.[301] Furthermore, some authors characterised this policy as violating the territorial sovereignty of other States and the principle of non-intervention.[302]

Nevertheless, these allegations do not seem to be firmly grounded in international law concerning naturalization. Indeed, it is true that "[t]he conferral of nationality is the *domaine réservé* whose scope is however contingent upon the existence of international rules."[303] But the key issue is that international law does not in fact contain specific limitations on the State's power of extra-territorial naturalisations.[304] Extraterritorial, voluntary individual

296 K Natoli, 'Weaponizing Nationality: An Analysis of Russia's Passport Policy in Georgia' (2010) 28 Boston University International Law Journal 389, 412–413.

297 Peters, Passportisation I (n 271). Peters also argues that the naturalising State thereby deprives the other State of its 'right of protection.' ibid.

298 "The extraterritorial conferrals of nationality thus extends Russia's legal sphere of influence, and might in the extreme case amount to a kind of 'personal' as opposed to territorial annexation." Peters, Passportisation I (n 271).

299 However, Peters argues that "[i]t remains the sovereign prerogative of states to determine in their internal law whether their nationals who acquire the nationality of another state retain their former nationality." Peters, Passportisation I (n 271).

300 CoE (PACE) Res 1989 (9 April 2014), para 6.

301 CoE (PACE) Res 1896 (2 October 2012), para 18.

302 Report (n 33) 171–175. Dörr (n 271) paras 5 and 20. See for overview, Natoli (n 290) 409–411. Moreover, the ECtHR in *Petropavlovskis* held that a State's discretion in choosing "the criteria for the purposes of naturalization procedure" may be limited by the principle of non-intervention *Petropavloskis v Latvia* ECHR 2015-I 111, para 80.

303 Peters, Passportisation I (n 271). See *Nationality Decrees Issued in Tunis and Morocco (Advisory Opinion)* [1923] PCIJ Rep Series B No 4, 24; *Nottebohm* (n 289) 20.

304 "[T]here is presently a marked absence of identified limits upon the rights of a State in relation to naturalisation." Response to Peters (n 290). "Thus, even the exhaustive and

naturalisations *per se* do not seem to violate international law.[305] Thus, "Russia cannot be held to have violated existing international *nationality* law."[306]

Nevertheless, this conclusion on its own does not entail the validity of *ius ad bellum* arguments on the protection of nationals abroad. Moreover, it can be agreed with some authors that if it were proven that the policy of passportisation was initiated in bad faith simply to advance arguments on military intervention, the doctrine of the abuse of rights would be applicable.[307] Lastly, it is arguable that changes of nationality under the conditions of illegal secessionist entity could fall within the scope of duty of non-recognition in the context of serious breach of peremptory norms.[308]

2.2.3 Independence

One of the criteria of statehood is independence, which could be analysed in terms of formal and actual independence. It is true that Abkhazians have opposed Russia's influence.[309] In both South Ossetia and Abkhazia, Russia-backed candidates lost elections.[310] Moreover, Abkhazia managed to garner concessions during the drafting of the Strategic Partnership Treaty.[311]

However, as follows from the above, Russian economic, financial, military and intergovernmental linkage with Abkhazia and South Ossetia has created a strong, one-sided dependence.[312] If Russia decided "to impose boycott, close a border crossing or raise tariffs, the regions would be heavily hit".[313] Without Russia's financial aid, the regions would be unable to pay public-sector wages,

---

impressive research undertaken by treatise writers in this field has been unable to identify, within the framework of international nationality law, an express, or even implied, prohibition on a state's power to confer its nationality extraterritorially." Natoli (n 290) 411. See Green, 'Passportisation' (n 243) 66–67. Therefore, based on this conclusion, even the passportisation policy regarding the residents of the Donbas, which is based only on "humanitarian grounds" would not *per se* seem to violate international law. See supra section on the DPR and LPR. *Contra*: Report (n 33) 150 and 155 *et seq*.

305 Report (n 33) 159–161.

306 Natoli (n 290) 413 and see 411–413 (*emphasis in original*).

307 See Green, 'Passportisation' (n 243) 67–68; Natoli (n 290) 413–416. The Report refers to this doctrine, but from a different angle. See Report (n 33) 176–178.

308 Response to Peters (n 290).

309 Gerrits and Bader (n 105) 308. See *supra*.

310 However, due to the fact that there is no alternative to Russia's influence, all political forces in these regions are aligned in terms of welcoming Russia's involvement. Gerrits and Bader (n 105) 308. Therefore, Russia does not need to micromanage the regions, since whoever wins elections will depend on Russian assistance. ibid.

311 See *supra*.

312 Gerrits and Bader (n 105) 306–307.

313 ibid 307.

maintain institutions or provide public services; and without Russia's military presence, it is unlikely that they would "hold back Georgian armed forces in a renewed conflict".[314] Having accounted for several factors, including Russia's military presence, and its political, economic and financial support of these entities, the ECtHR concluded that

> the Russian Federation exercised "effective control", within the meaning of the Court's case-law, over South Ossetia, Abkhazia and the "buffer zone" from 12 August to 10 October 2008, the date of the official withdrawal of the Russian troops. Even after that period, the strong Russian presence and the South Ossetian and Abkhazian authorities' dependency on the Russian Federation, on whom their survival depends, as is shown particularly by the cooperation and assistance agreements signed with the latter, indicate that there was continued "effective control" over South Ossetia and Abkhazia.[315]

In April 2023, the Court held that "this conclusion continues to be valid."[316] Thus, against this backdrop, it is clear that the requirement of actual independence was not fulfilled in Abkhazia and South Ossetia in the post-2008 period.[317]

In terms of formal independence, both Abkhazia and South Ossetia possess overt political landscapes, State structures and symbols of formal statehood. Nevertheless, with regard to the conclusion of the 2014 Strategic Partnership Treaty and the 2015 Integration Treaty, formal independence of these entities can also be challenged.[318] The aim of the following analysis is to provide a comprehensive view without prejudice to the validity of these agreements on the international plane.[319]

---

314 ibid. "Without Russian patronage, South Ossetia is not a viable state and would not survive, unable to function as a state entity." German (n 68) 158 and 164. Essentially, according to observers, the position of South Ossetia does not differ much from that of a republic in the Russian Federation – "Moscow sends money, protects the borders and handles international representation." International Crisis Group, *South Ossetia* (n 71) 23.

315 *Georgia v Russia (II)* (n 72) para 174.

316 *Georgia v Russia (IV)* (n 98) para 44.

317 J Socher, *Russia and the Right to Self-Determination in the Post-Soviet Space* (OUP 2021) 140 and 132.

318 See Ambrosio and Lange (n 88) 675–677 on the use of agreements as the means to manage mistrust and conflict-caused power imbalances between Russia and these entities.

319 See *infra* on the validity of these treaties under international law.

The two treaties are different in terms of form and substance in accommodating Abkhazia's aim to preserve its statehood.[320] For example, the title of the agreement with Abkhazia does not include the term 'integration' but instead contains just 'strategic partnership'.[321] The Strategic Partnership Treaty[322] is based on the principle of mutual respect of "state sovereignty and territorial integrity" and foresees the conduct of a "coordinated foreign policy", including Russia's obligation to increase the number of States recognising Abkhazia; the creation of a "common defense and security space" and a "common social and economic space" is also foreseen.[323] The parties should consult with each other on all the important matters affecting the security of each party and agree on a common position.[324] The treaty provides for a mutual defence pact and for the creation of a Joint Group of Forces to repel aggression in line with Article 51 UN Charter, which would, in the situation of aggression, be headed by a Russian commander and Abkhazian deputy.[325] This treaty also stipulates unification or harmonisation in other areas.[326] The provision on the acquisition of the citizenship is asymmetric, marking an important concession to Abkhazia.[327]

320 See 'Treaty on Partnership between Russia and Abkhazia: Modifications of the Abkhazian Side' (*Kavkazskiy Uzel*, 5 November 2014) <https://www.kavkaz-uzel.eu/articles/251796/> accessed 5 May 2019 (*in Russian*);'Drafts of the Treaty on Partnership between Russia and Abkhazia: Comparison' (*Kavkazskiy Uzel*, 24 November 2014) <https://www.kavkaz-uzel.eu/articles/252874/> accessed 5 May 2019 (*in Russian*).

321 While the Integration Treaty contains 15 provisions, is valid for 25 years and is automatically extended for a successive ten-year term, the Strategic Partnership Treaty includes 24 clauses, is valid for 10 years and is automatically renewed for a period of 5 years. German (n 68) 163–164.

322 For an in-depth analysis, see Ambrosio and Lange (n 88) 683–685.

323 Strategic Partnership Treaty (n 88) arts 1, 3 and 4. See Programme of Formation of the Common Social and Economic Space (n 116). According to Belkania, "[i]f all amendments are fully adopted and implemented, this will drastically reduce Abkhazia's level of internal autonomy, resulting in more Russia in Abkhazia and more Abkhazia in Russia." Belkania (n 117) 308.

324 ibid art 5.

325 ibid arts 5–7. See also Agreement between the Russian Federation and the Republic of Abkhazia on a Joint Group of Armed Forces of the Russian Federation and the Republic of Abkhazia (signed 21 November 2015; entered into force 3 December 2016) <https://docs.cntd.ru/document/420328062?section=text> accessed 3 October 2023 (*in Russian*).

326 The treaty also provides for the unification of military standards (art 8); joint protection and guarding of state borders (art 9); harmonization of customs legislation with that of the Eurasian Customs Union, adjustment of budget legislation as well as harmonization of healthcare and education legislation with that of the Russian Federation (arts 11, 17, 20). The Treaty also foresees the increase of public sector workers' average wages co-financed by the Russian Federation. (art 14).

327 Strategic Partnership Treaty (n 88) art 13. Russia accepted the Abkhazian amendment on the removal of the simplification of the procedure for acquiring Abkhazian citizenship for

The treaty can be denounced in the period of six months before its automatic renewal.[328]

The Integration Treaty[329] foresees conduct of an "agreed foreign policy" including Russia's obligation to increase the number of States recognising South Ossetia and the creation of a "single space of defense and security."[330] Under the treaty, the Russian Federation assumes responsibility for the defence and security of South Ossetia and its borders and to this end separate units of the South Ossetian Armed Forces and security bodies enter the Armed Forces and security bodies of the Russian Federation upon agreement of both parties.[331] The treaty also provides for a mutual defence pact.[332] Under this treaty, provisions of Russian legislation concerning Russian citizens with double nationality do not apply to Russian citizens with South Ossetian nationality.[333] The treaty can be denounced in the period of one year before its automatic renewal.[334]

Based on international law criteria for formal independence, it is difficult to conclude that the Strategic Partnership Treaty derogates from Abkhazia's formal independence.[335] A substantial delegation of competences, the creation

---

Russian nationals. This was due to fear on the Abkhazian side that this would lead to the purchase of real estate in Abkhazia. At the moment, only individuals with Abkhazian nationality can purchase real estate there. W Górecki, *Abkhazia's 'Creeping' Incorporation: The End of the Experiment of a Separatist Democracy: OSW Commentary No 164* (OSW 2015) 3. In September 2022, Russia and Abkhazia signed a dual citizenship agreement according to which the citizenship of either signatory can be acquired without giving up the current citizenship. 'Sokhumi, Moscow Sign Dual Citizenship Agreement' (*civil.ge*, 28 September 2022) <https://civil.ge/archives/509623?fbclid=IwAR0lMcKRTDUQa3pjPspa442CUzduM_qneIYX3fkQatHtMnsM3_yFRk2RFe4> accessed 21 October 2023.

328 Strategic Partnership Treaty (n 88) art 23.

329 Ambrosio and Lange (n 88) 685–687.

330 Integration Treaty (n 88) arts 1 and 2(1).

331 Integration Treaty (n 88) art 2(2). See Agreement between the Russian Federation and the Republic of South Ossetia on the Order of Entry of Individual Units of Armed Forces of the Republic of South Ossetia in the Armed Forces of the Russian Federation (signed 31 March 2017) <http://docs.cntd.ru/document/456059687> accessed 3 May 2019 (*in Russian*).

332 Integration Treaty (n 88) art 2(3). It also provides for free crossing of the Russian-South Ossetian border; the integration of customs bodies with those of the Russian Federation; an increase in the average wage of public sector workers, co-financed by the Russian Federation; and the adoption of education legislation corresponding to that of the Russian Federation (arts 3, 5, 7 and 10(2)).

333 Integration Treaty (n 88) art 6(2).

334 ibid art 15.

335 For instances when a formal independence is and is not derogated, see Crawford (n 231) 69–72.

of joint organs for certain purposes and a foreign military presence is carried out on the basis of treaty,[336] which defines delegated powers clearly and thereby formally precludes discretionary intervention into Abkhazia's internal affairs.[337] This treaty also foresees a "coordinated foreign policy" on the basis of mutual consideration of interests, which at least formally precludes the one-sided abdication of the conduct of foreign policy in favour of Russia as a critical point in the analysis of dependent status.[338]

The Integration Treaty, however, presents a more complex case, since South Ossetia's integration with Russia is much more extensive.[339] Even though it foresees "agreed foreign policy" on the basis of mutual consideration of interests, which at least formally precludes one-sided dominance by the Russian Federation in the conduct of South Ossetia's foreign policy, the fact that it delegates the responsibility for the defence and security of South Ossetia and its borders to the Russian Federation pushes the notion of a formal independence to its limits. It seems that, regardless of the fact that it is made on the basis of treaty, the delegation of competence in the sphere of defence and security is so broad and so closely related to fundamental aspects of sovereignty that it allows Russian discretionary interference in a key area of South Ossetia's internal affairs.[340]

Ultimately, it is true that both treaties provide for their denouncement and therefore allow for an ultimate tool of preservation of formal independence, but this is only a hypothetical scenario – with regard to the lack of actual independence of both entities, these provisions are clearly only nominal. None of

336 "[T]he right to enter into international engagements is an attribute of sovereignty." *Wimbledon* (*UK and others v Germany*) (Merits) [1923] PCIJ Rep Series A No 1, 25. "[T]he question is how extensive the loss of actual independence must be under a treaty of protection before the local entity can no longer be regarded as a State." Crawford (n 231) 288.

337 "As a general rule it may be said that the exercise of delegated powers pursuant to protectorate arrangements is not inconsistent with statehood if the derogations from independence are based on local consent, do not involve extensive powers of internal control and do not leave the local entity without some degree of influence over the exercise of foreign affairs." Crawford (n 231) 288.

338 ibid.

339 Other aspects of the treaty also underline differences with the Strategic Partnership Treaty. For example, rather than speaking about harmonizing legislation, the Integration Treaty provides for the adoption of legislation corresponding to that of the Russian Federation. Moreover, there is no provision on the mutual respect of sovereignty and territorial integrity.

340 See Crawford (n 231) 288–289. Even though, for the moment, South Ossetia at least formally preserves its own units of armed forces, which are not subsumed within Russian Armed Forces. See *supra*.

these entities are actually independent to the extent that would allow them to denounce these treaties. Overall, it is clear that neither Abkhazia nor South Ossetia meets the constitutive criterion of independence.

2.2.4 Legal Status

A key question of this legal analysis is whether the developments in the post-2008 period have in any way transformed previous conclusions on the legal status of these entities. As mentioned above, before 2008, these entities did not exist as States due to the illegality of their origins. Moreover, they also did not fulfil the criterion of independence.

Neither the armed conflict that took place in the summer of 2008 nor Russia's and other State's subsequent recognition changed this legal conclusion. Quite to the contrary – as mentioned above, since 2008 the dependence of these regions on Russia has grown. Moreover, Russia has also increased its military presence in the two regions, including the opening and operation of two military bases together totalling up to 7,600 troops. Since, based on the above analysis, neither Abkhazia nor South Ossetia was a State at the moment of Russia's recognition, their consent to the presence of military bases has no legal validity on the international plane.

Thus, the presence of Russian troops in these regions subsequent to the 2008 August War has been an unlawful use of force and has violated Georgia's territorial integrity.[341] Several international organisations have characterised Russian presence as unlawful (and its previous aggression) and demanded the withdrawal of Russian troops from Georgian territory.[342]

> Given the importance of Russian military support for the continued survival of Abkhazia and especially of South Ossetia, it may be legitimately

341 See AG Wills, 'The Crime of Aggression and the Resort to Force against Entities in Statu Nascendi' (2012) 10 Journal of International Criminal Justice 83, 92. See also Definition of Aggression (n 215) art 3(a). However, according to Nolte and Randelzhofer, the concept of permanent occupation "is not applicable to the notion of 'armed attack'" as it does not "necessarily involve the use of military force." Nolte and Randelzhofer (n 215) para 23. For the discussion concerning the extension of the regime of prohibition of the use of force under Article 2(4) UN Charter to 'stabilized de facto regimes' see *supra*.

342 OSCE (PA), 'Resolution on the Russian Federation's War of Aggression against Ukraine and Its People, and Its Threat to Security Across the OSCE Region' (6 July 2022), para 14; CoE (PACE) Res 2463 (13 October 2022), paras 15.3 and 16; EEAS, 'Georgia/Russia: Statement by the High Representative on the 15th anniversary of the Conflict between Russia and Georgia' (23 August 2023) <https://www.eeas.europa.eu/eeas/georgiarussia-statement-high-representative-15th-anniversary-conflict-between-russia-and-georgia_en> accessed 22 October 2023.

> asked whether, in consequence, Abkhazia's or South Ossetia's claim to statehood is invalid.[343]

Thus, apart from the fact that neither of these entities fulfils the criterion of independence, Russia's on-going illegal military presence in these entities is central to their continued existence. Russia's continued unlawful use of force after its 2008 recognition of these entities corroborates and substantiates their unlawful nature and thus further precludes their pre-2008 characterisation as States under international law. Their pre-2008 classification as illegal secessionist entities cannot be altered.

343 Wills (n 341) 92.

CHAPTER 14

Nagorno-Karabakh

1 Outline of the Secessionist Attempt

1.1 *Secessionist Tendencies and War (1992–1994)*

The secessionist attempt of Nagorno-Karabakh must be seen in the context of the complicated ethno-geographical conditions of the South Caucasus. Already, as part of the Russian Empire, "the Karabakh, with its Armenian majority in the highlands and Turkic population predominating in the plains, was one such region where the conflicting claims clashed."[1] In 1867, it became part of the Governorate Elisavetpol, predominantly in today's Azerbaijan, rather than the Governorate of Yerevan.[2] After the turbulent fall of tsarist Russia, the two revolutions of 1917 and the proclamation of independent Azerbaijan and Armenia, local Armenians and Armenia's government contested Azerbaijan's *de facto* control over the region.[3] Violent clashes followed.[4]

The situation only changed after the Bolshevik's takeover of Azerbaijan in 1920 and Armenia in 1921.[5] Although the Bolsheviks initially promised Nagorno-Karabakh to Armenia, and even adopted a decision to this end on 4 July 1921, the next day, 5 July 1921, that decision was revoked and the Karabakh was awarded to Azerbaijan.[6] The reasons behind this policy change were purely pragmatic.[7] To appease the Armenians, Nagorno-Karabakh

1 A Saparov, *From Conflict to Autonomy in the Caucasus: The Soviet Union and the Making of Abkhazia, South Ossetia and Nagorno Karabakh* (Routledge 2015) 91.

2 H Krüger, *The Nagorno-Karabakh Conflict: A Legal Analysis* (Springer 2010) 9. Despite a demographic majority of Armenians, the Karabakh's inclusion in the Elisavetpol governorate was favoured due to geographical conditions, which made access to the Karabakh easier from the East. Saparov (n 1) 91.

3 This period included short-term intervention by British forces, which placed Nagorno-Karabakh under Azerbaijan's rule. Saparov (n 1) 91–95. J Popjanevski, 'International Law and the Nagorno-Karabakh Conflict' in SE Cornell (ed) *The International Politics of the Armenian-Azerbaijani Conflict: The Original 'Frozen Conflict' and European Security* (palgrave macmillan 2017) 28.

4 Krüger (n 2) 13; X Follebouckt, *Les conflits gelés de l'espace postoviétique: genèse et enjeux* (Presses universitaires de Louvain 2011) 41.

5 Follebouckt (n 4) 41–42.

6 Saparov (n 1) 106–111.

7 The motives behind the initial decision to grant Nagorno-Karabakh to Armenia included the Bolshevik's aim to gain power in Armenia and especially to win over the rebellion in

was given the status of an autonomous region within the Azerbaijan SSR in 1923.[8]

During the Soviet period, Armenians sent appeals to Moscow demanding the joining of Nagorno-Karabakh with the Armenian SSR.[9] Thus, when Gorbachev introduced the policy of *glasnost* in the Soviet Union in the 1980s, Armenians were the first to openly voice their demands with respect to Nagorno-Karabakh.[10] On 20 February 1988, the Soviet of the Nagorno-Karabakh's autonomous region adopted a resolution demanding the joining of Nagorno-Karabakh with the Armenian SSR, which was ultimately rejected by the Azerbaijan SSR, the USSR's Supreme Soviet and the USSR's Communist Party.[11]

At the same time, the Armenian capital witnessed a mass mobilisation demanding the unification of Nagorno-Karabakh with Armenia.[12] In March 1988, the killing of two Azeris on the march to Stepanakert provoked a large anti-Armenian *pogrom* in the industrial town of Sumgait near Baku, leaving 32 people dead.[13] "The significance of the Sumgait *pogrom* was that it marked a point of no return in the conflict."[14] On 12 July 1988, Nagorno-Karabakh declared secession from the Azerbaijan SSR as the Armenian Autonomous Region of Artsakh.[15]

The Soviet authorities were unprepared to deal with the escalation, ultimately placing Nagorno-Karabakh under Moscow's direct rule in January 1989, and restoring Azerbaijan's control in November 1989.[16] As a response, on 1 December 1989, the Supreme Soviet of Armenian SSR and the National

---

Zangezur. When they reached these objectives, the reasons to grant Nagorno-Karabakh to Armenia disappeared. Economic ties and pressure from Azerbaijan's ally Turkey also spoke in favour of Azerbaijan's claims. Saparov (n 1) 111 and 123. Follebouckt (n 4) 57.

8 Follebouckt (n 4) 56.

9 Saparov (n 1) 123.

10 Already in 1987, a petition with 75,000 signatures demanding the transfer of Nagorno-Karabakh to the Armenian SSR was sent to Moscow, but it was ultimately rejected. Saparov (n 1) 123 and 165.

11 'Decision of the Special Session of the NKAO Council of Peoples' Deputies of XX Session on a Petition to the Supreme Councils of the Azerbaijani SSR and Armenian SSR on the NKAO's Secession from Soviet Azerbaijan and Its Transfer to Soviet Armenia' (adopted 20 February 1988) <https://karabakhfacts.com/nkao-decision-on-a-petition-to-the-supreme-councils-of-azerbaijani-ssr-and-armenian-ssr-on-the-nkaos-secession-from-soviet-azerbaijan-and-its-transfer-to-soviet-armenia/> accessed 29 May 2019; Krüger (n 2) 18.

12 Saparov (n 1) 166.

13 ibid.

14 ibid (*emphasis in original*).

15 Follebouckt (n 4) 78.

16 Saparov (n 1) 166–167.

Council of Nagorno-Karabakh adopted a joint decision on the unification of the region with the Armenian SSR.[17] The situation continued to deteriorate; low-scale warfare broke out.[18] After the August 1991 failed coup in Moscow, Azerbaijan declared its independence on 30 August 1991, and Armenia followed in September 1991.[19] On 2 September 1991, Nagorno-Karabakh, rather than pursuing the previous aim of unification with Armenia, formally declared its independence, to which Azerbaijan responded by revoking its autonomous status on 26 November 1991.[20] On 10 December 1991, a majority of Armenians in Nagorno-Karabakh voted in favour of independence in the referendum, which was, however, boycotted by Azeris still living in the region.[21] On 6 January 1992, Nagorno-Karabakh declared its national independence.[22]

After the USSR's break-up, the conflict transformed into a full-fledged inter-State war, which ceased only two years later in 1994 with the signing of the Bishkek Ceasefire Agreement.[23] The war ended with Azerbaijan's defeat and the loss of Nagorno-Karabakh and seven districts of Azerbaijan proper connecting Nagorno-Karabakh with Armenia, altogether totalling 14% of Azerbaijan's territory.[24] The war was particularly violent, claiming up to 30,000 casualties and was marked by mutual mass expulsions, including 750,000 Azeris leaving Nagorno-Karabakh and Armenia.[25] No peacekeeping forces were deployed to Nagorno-Karabakh.[26] No UN Member State, including Armenia, recognised Nagorno-Karabakh as an independent State.[27] The potential for the

17 Krüger (n 2) 18.

18 Saparov (n 1) 166–167; Krüger (n 2) 21.

19 'Declaration of the Supreme Soviet of the Republic of Azerbaijan about a Restoration of Independence of the Republic of Azerbaijan' (adopted 30 August 1991) <https://republic.preslib.az/ru_d1.html> accessed 29 May 2019 (*in Russian*); Follebouckt (n 4) 81.

20 'Proclamation of the Nagorno Karabakh Republic' (adopted 2 September 1991) <http://www.nkrusa.org/nk_conflict/declaration_independence.shtml> accessed 29 May 2019. Follebouckt (n 4) 81.

21 Krüger (n 2) 22.

22 'Declaration on State Independence of the Nagorno Karabakh Republic' (adopted 6 January 1992) <http://www.nkrusa.org/nk_conflict/declaration_independence.shtml> accessed 29 May 2019; Krüger (n 2) 22.

23 Bishkek Ceasefire Agreement (11 May 1994) <https://www.peaceagreements.org/viewmasterdocument/990> accessed 2 June 2019. A Saparov (n 1) 166–167.

24 Saparov (n 1) 167–168. The occupied territory outside the former Nagorno-Karabakh autonomous region was "close to double the territory of the former Soviet oblast." International Crisis Group, *Nagorno-Karabakh: Viewing the Conflict from the Ground: Europe Report No 166* (ICG 2005) 1.

25 Follebouckt (n 4) 83; Saparov (n 1) 167–168; Popjanevski (n 3) 23.

26 See Follebouckt (n 4) 118–119.

27 *Chiragov and Others v Armenia* ECHR 2015-III, para 28 ("*Chiragov*").

re-occurrence of hostilities in the region was high, as demonstrated by the so-called four-day war in April 2016, which resulted in a slight shift of the frontline in Azerbaijan's favour.[28]

1.2 *Armenia's Involvement in the Conflict (1992–1994) and Subsequent Links with Nagorno-Karabakh*

As follows from the above, even before the USSR dissolved, the Armenian SSR supported separatists in Nagorno-Karabakh.[29] Indeed, at that time there was no Armenian State and no Armenian army. Nevertheless, paramilitary groups started to form in Armenia, stealing or buying weapons from Soviet sources.[30] These irregular Armenian troops, rebels and partisans joined the conflict in Nagorno-Karabakh and took part in low-scale military operations.[31]

However, after the Soviet Union's break-up, the conflict turned into an inter-State war. After Azerbaijan's successful June 1992 offensive, Armenia's president and Defence Minster directly ordered the Armenian troops to intervene militarily.[32] Despite Armenia's public denials, its participation in the 1993 Kelbajar offensive was seen as likely[33] and its intervention in the conflict became apparent in the conflict's final phase, between October and May 1994.[34] "The Republic of Armenia has even sent members of its police force to perform police duties in occupied Azerbaijan."[35] Armenia's support included

28 See A Jarosiewicz and M Falkowski, 'The Four-Day War in Nagorno-Karabakh' (*OSW*, 6 April 2016) <https://www.osw.waw.pl/en/publikacje/analyses/2016-04-06/four-day-war-nagorno-karabakh> accessed 30 May 2019; A Mejlumyan, 'Armenia Begins Probe of 2016 War' (*eurasianet*, 14 June 2019) <https://eurasianet.org/armenia-begins-probe-of-2016-war> accessed 30 June 2019. See also CoE (PACE), 'Report of the Political Affairs and Democracy Committee: Escalation of Violence in Nagorno-Karabakh and the Other Occupied Territories of Azerbaijan' (11 December 2015) Doc 13930.

29 "It is clear that, from the beginning of the conflict, the Armenian SSR and the Republic of Armenia have strongly supported demands for Nagorno-Karabakh's incorporation into Armenia or, alternatively, its independence from Azerbaijan." *Chiragov* (n 27) para 172.

30 T De Waal, *Black Garden: Armenia and Azerbaijan Through Peace and War* (New York University Press 2004) 111–113; Human Rights Watch, *Azerbaijan: Seven Years of Conflict in Nagorno-Karabakh* (HRW 1994) 149. In this context, on 25 July 1990, Gorbachev issued a decree banning paramilitary formations. See President of the USSR, 'Decree on the Prohibition of the Creation of Armed Formations' (adopted 25 July 1990, entered into force 25 July 1990) <https://constitutions.ru/?p=3038> accessed 23 May 2019 (*in Russian*).

31 De Waal (n 30) 112–113.

32 Krüger (n 2) 101–102. De Waal (n 30) 210 and 212.

33 Human Rights Watch (n 30) 115.

34 Krüger (n 2) 102–103; Human Rights Watch (n 30) 117.

35 Human Rights Watch (n 30) 121.

sending its troops, including conscripts, to Nagorno-Karabakh and providing armaments and material support.[36]

Armenia's participation in the conflict can also be inferred from the UNSC resolutions. For example, UNSC Resolution 853 (1993) urged Armenia "to continue to exert its influence to achieve compliance by the Armenians of the Nagorno-Karabakh region of the Republic" with its previous resolution, and it urged "States to refrain from the supply of any weapons and munitions which might lead to an intensification of the conflict or the continued occupation of territory".[37] Even more directly, UNSC Resolution 874 (1993) urged "all States in the region to refrain from any hostile acts and from any interference or intervention which would lead to the widening of the conflict and undermine peace and security in the region".[38] Similar wording was also used in UNSC Resolution 884 (1993).[39] Taking into account the factual context, these resolutions could have only targeted Armenia.[40]

In addition, even though, during the Soviet period, Soviet soldiers in the region supported both Armenia and Azerbaijan, from 1992, Russia provided Armenia with more significant military support to preserve the balance between the two States at the time of Azerbaijan's offensive.[41] Today, both Russia and Armenia, but not Azerbaijan, are members of the Collective Security Treaty Organization, which is underpinned by the mutual defence clause.[42]

In the period subsequent to the end of the first Karabakh War in 1994, despite Armenia's claims to be merely a mediator, it in fact supported Nagorno-Karabakh militarily, institutionally, politically and economically.[43] Firstly, it was estimated that out of 20,000 soldiers present in Nagorno-Karabakh, the Armenian army directly provided half of the personnel.[44] This seems to

---

36 ibid 117–127. See the ECtHR's reference to the HRW's report *Chiragov* (n 27) para 60. See also Krüger (n 2) 102; De Waal (n 30) 235 *et seq*.

37 UNSC Res 853 (29 July 1993) UN Doc S/RES/853, paras 9 and 10.

38 UNSC Res 874 (14 October 1993) UN Doc S/RES/874, para 10.

39 UNSC Res 884 (12 November 1993) UN Doc S/RES/884, paras 2 and 6.

40 Krüger (n 2) 102.

41 Folleblouckt (n 4) 83 and 125–126. On the state of Russia's influence over the region, see A Petersen, 'Nagorno-Karabakh: Russia's Proxy War in the Caucasus' (*Fletcher Security Review*, 20 December 2013) <https://www.fletchersecurity.org/policy-w2014> accessed 4 June 2019.

42 See 'Collective Security Treaty Organization' <https://www.mfa.am/en/international-organisations/1> accessed 6 June 2019.

43 See Follebouckt (n 4) 154–160.

44 ibid 159; International Crisis Group (n 24) 1 and 9. "Today, Armenia has soldiers stationed in the Nagorno-Karabakh region and the surrounding districts." CoE (PACE), 'Report of the Political Affairs Committee: The Conflict Over the Nagorno-Karabakh Region Dealt With by the OSCE Minsk Conference' (29 November 2004) Doc 10364, para 6.

be confirmed by the fact that the resolution of the UNGA demanded "withdrawal of all Armenian forces from all the occupied territories of the Republic of Azerbaijan",[45] that the resolution of PACE and the European Parliament referred to the occupation by Armenian forces of the territory of Azerbaijan and that several proposals for the solution to the conflict within the OSCE Minsk Group demanded, "[t]he armed forces of Armenia will be withdrawn to within the borders of the Republic of Armenia."[46] There was obligatory military service in Armenia, and conscripts were sent directly to Nagorno-Karabakh.[47] This took place on the basis of the 1994 Agreement on Military Co-operation.[48] Armenia also provided Nagorno-Karabakh with equipment and weaponry, and its officers assisted with training.[49]

Moreover, Armenia and Nagorno-Karabakh were also interconnected through the political and military careers of individuals who served both in Armenia and in Nagorno-Karabakh, including the first president of Nagorno-Karabakh, Kocharyan, who later became Armenia's president, and others.[50] For example, the former Chief of Staff of the Armenian Armed Forces previously

---

45 UNGA Res 62/243 (14 March 2008) UN Doc A/RES/62/243, para 2.

46 *Chiragov* (n 27) para 61 and see paras 64, 69–70. CoE (PACE) Res 1416 (25 January 2005), para 1; European Parliament, 'Resolution on the Need for an EU Strategy for the South Caucasus' (20 May 2010) (2009/2216(INI)), para 8; European Parliament, 'Resolution Containing the European Parliament's Recommendations to the Council, the Commission and the European External Action Service on the Negotiations of the EU-Armenia Association Agreement' (18 April 2012) (2011/2315(INI)), para 1(b) ("European Parliament's Resolution on the Negotiations of the EU-Armenia Association Agreement"). See also *infra*.

47 Follebouckt (n 4) 159; De Waal (n 30) 247. The European Parliament called on "Armenia to stop sending regular army conscripts to serve in Nagorno-Karabakh." European Parliament's Resolution on the Negotiations of the EU-Armenia Association Agreement (n 46) para 1(r).

48 See Agreement on Military Co-operation between the Governments of the Republic of Armenia and the Republic of Nagorno-Karabakh in *Chiragov* (n 27) paras 74–75.

49 International Crisis Group (n 24) 10. PACE urged "all member states to refrain from the supply of any weapons and munitions which might lead to an intensification of the conflict or the continued occupation of the territory." CoE (PACE) Res 1416 (25 January 2005), para 3.

50 Follebouckt (n 4) 157–158; Krüger (n 2) 104. See *Chiragov* (n 27) para 78; CoE (PACE), 'Report of the Political Affairs Committee: The Conflict Over the Nagorno-Karabakh Region Dealt With by the OSCE Minsk Conference' (29 November 2004) Doc 10364, para 18; F Smolnik and U Halbach, 'The Nagorno-Karabakh Conflict in Light of the Crisis over Ukraine' in S Fischer (ed), *Not Frozen! The Unresolved Conflicts over Transnistria, Abkhazia, South Ossetia and Nagorno-Karabakh in Light of the Crisis over Ukraine* (SWP 2016) 68; 'Karabakh Defense Minister Gets Office in Capital Yerevan' (*news.am*, 15 June 2015) <https://news.am/eng/news/271978.html> accessed 2 June 2019.

occupied the post of Minister of Defence in Nagorno-Karabakh.[51] "[T]he military apparatuses of Armenia and Karabakh are already being synchronised through their leadership structures – by individuals who have strong roots in the governing command structure of Karabakh."[52] Institutional fusion was also visible from a number of agreements concluded between Armenia and Nagorno-Karabakh.[53] "The entire legislation of the NKR is adopted from Armenian laws."[54] The residents of Nagorno-Karabakh were entitled to Armenian passports for travel abroad.[55] In addition, on the international plane, "from 1998 Yerevan took over the responsibility of representing the interests of the de facto state in talks led by the Minsk Group, in which Nagorno-Karabakh itself was no longer involved."[56]

In the economic sphere, it was estimated that Nagorno-Karabakh's resources covered only between 20–25% of its budget.[57] Since 1993, Armenia provided Nagorno-Karabakh with an inter-State loan, which covered up to 50–70% of Nagorno-Karabakh's expenses.[58] In fact, it was a direct subsidy, as the loan was not repaid.[59] Exports from Nagorno-Karabakh were frequently labelled "made in Armenia".[60] The Armenian dram was the main currency.[61] Nagorno-Karabakh was also supported by USAID and the Armenian diaspora.[62]

1.3 *The 2020 War and Following Developments*

After the increased tensions in the summer, open hostilities erupted between Armenia and Azerbaijan on 27 September 2020.[63] The so-called 44-Day War

---

51 RULAC, 'Military Occupation of Azerbaijan by Armenia' <http://www.rulac.org/browse/conflicts/military-occupation-of-azerbaijan-by-armenia#collapse1accord> accessed 7 June 2019.
52 Krüger (n 2) 104.
53 Follebouckt (n 4) 157.
54 AY Melnyk, 'Nagorny-Karabakh' in MPEPIL (online edn, OUP 2013) para 8.
55 International Crisis Group (n 24) 5. See references to the ICG's Report by the ECtHR *Chiragov* (n 27) para 83. Krüger (n 2) 111.
56 Smolnik and Halbach (n 50) 67.
57 Follebouckt (n 4) 158.
58 ibid 158; Krüger (n 2) 111.
59 International Crisis Group (n 24) 12. See references to the ICG's Report by the ECtHR *Chiragov* (n 27) para 80. Follebouckt (n 4) 158.
60 International Crisis Group (n 24) 12; Follebouckt (n 4) 158.
61 International Crisis Group (n 24) 13; Follebouckt (n 4) 157.
62 "In 1998 Congress for the first time designated Nagorno-Karabakh a recipient of humanitarian aid distinct from Azerbaijan." International Crisis Group (n 24) 13; Follebouckt (n 4) 159.
63 For the issue of the legality of the use of force see T Ruys and F Rodríguez Silvestre, 'The Nagorno-Karabakh Conflict and the Exercise of "Self-Defense" to Recover Occupied

followed. The fighting ended upon the signature of the Russia-brokered ceasefire agreement signed on 9 November 2020 by the president of Azerbaijan, the prime minister of Armenia and the president of the Russian Federation.[64] Under the deal, Armenia and Azerbaijan were obliged to cease fire at midnight on 10 November 2020 and "stop in their current positions."[65] The war and the subsequent ceasefire agreement fundamentally transformed the *status quo* in the region.[66]

The agreement foresaw changes in territorial control. Firstly, Azerbaijan gained control of all seven districts surrounding Nagorno-Karabakh, which Armenia occupied since the end of the war in 1994.[67] Azerbaijan already controlled some of those territories as a result of the hostilities; the remaining districts were handed over to Azerbaijan by Armenia as per the timeline established in the ceasefire agreement.[68] Second, as a result of hostilities, Azerbaijan also acquired control of the parts of Nagorno-Karabakh itself, i.e. the part of the former Soviet autonomous region, including the strategically important city of Shusha.[69] Thus, the contact line ran through Nagorno-Karabakh itself.[70] Thirdly, the remnants of Nagorno-Karabakh including the capital city of Stepanakert continued to be under the control of the Armenia-backed separatists.[71] As a result, Nagorno-Karabakh was completely separated

---

Land' (*Just Security*, 10 November 2020) <https://www.justsecurity.org/73310/the-nagorno-karabakh-conflict-and-the-exercise-of-self-defense-to-recover-occupied-land/> accessed 5 December 2020; D Akande and A Tzanakopoulos, 'Use of Force in Self-Defence to Recover Occupied Territory: When Is It Permissible?' (*EJIL:Talk!*, 18 November 2020) <https://www.ejiltalk.org/use-of-force-in-self-defence-to-recover-occupied-territory-when-is-it-permissible/> accessed 5 December 2020; 'Le conflit au Haut-Karabakh et le droit international' (*Centre de droit international, Université Libre de Bruxelles*, 14 October 2020) <http://cdi.ulb.ac.be/conflit-haut-karabakh-droit-international-douze-questions/> accessed 5 December 2020.

64 'Statement by President of the Republic of Azerbaijan, Prime Minister of the Republic of Armenia and President of the Russian Federation' (9 November 2020) <http://en.kremlin.ru/events/president/news/64384> (in *English*) and <http://www.kremlin.ru/catalog/countries/AZ/events/64384/print> (in *Russian*) accessed 3 December 2020 ("Ceasefire Agreement").

65 ibid, art 1.

66 J Miklasová, 'The Recent Ceasefire in Nagorno-Karabakh: Territorial Control, Peacekeepers and Question of Status' (*EJIL:Talk!*, 4 December 2020) <https://www.ejiltalk.org/the-recent-ceasefire-in-nagorno-karabakh-territorial-control-peacekeepers-and-unanswered-question-of-status/> accessed 5 December 2020.

67 ibid.

68 ibid; Ceasefire Agreement (n 64), arts 2 and 6.

69 Miklasová (n 66).

70 ibid.

71 ibid.

from Armenia except for the so-called Lachin Corridor.[72] Under the deal, this was a 5-km wide corridor controlled by the Russian peacekeepers, which connected Nagorno-Karabakh and Armenia running through the Lachin District (since the hostilities under Azerbaijan's control).[73]

The ceasefire deal also provided for the deployment of the Russian peacekeeping forces amounting to "1,960 troops armed with firearms, 90 armoured vehicles and units of special equipment."[74] Under this agreement, the peacekeepers were deployed "along the contact line in Nagorno-Karabakh and along the Lachin Corridor."[75] The agreement also stipulated that Russian peacekeepers "shall be deployed concurrently with the withdrawal of the Armenian troops."[76] Their deployment to this conflict was unprecedented.[77]

Their mandate was foreseen for automatically renewable five-year terms "unless either Party notifies about its intention to terminate this clause six months before the expiration of the current term."[78] The ceasefire deal did not provide any specifications as to the Russian peacekeeping mission's status. While the deal did not specify any role to Turkey, after the signature of the agreement, it was announced Turkey would take part in the monitoring of the ceasefire.[79] The agreement also included clauses on the return of refugees and the IDPs, exchange of prisoners of war and detainees and on unblocking of economic and transport connections.[80]

Importantly, the deal contained no mention of Nagorno-Karabakh's final status or how to negotiate this issue.[81]

---

72 ibid. See also D Kuznets, 'Six-Week War in Nagorno-Karabakh: Results' (*Meduza*, 12 November 2020) <https://meduza.io/feature/2020/11/12/shestinedelnaya-voyna-v-nagornom-karabahe-itogi> accessed 5 December 2020 (*in Russian*).

73 ibid; Ceasefire Agreement (n 64), art 6.

74 Ceasefire Agreement (n 64), art 3.

75 ibid. See for the mission's geographical scope: 'Archive of Maps of the Situation in the Area of the Peacekeeping Operation' (*Website of the Russian Peace-making Mission in Nagorno-Karabakh*) <https://mil.ru/russian_peacekeeping_forces/infograf/archive.htm> accessed 5 October 2023 (*in Russian*).

76 Ceasefire Agreement (n 64), art 4.

77 Miklasová (n 66).

78 Ceasefire Agreement (n 64), art 4.

79 Miklasová (n 66). See 'Replies to Media Questions on Developments in Nagorno-Karabakh' (*Website of the President of Russia*, 17 November 2020) <http://en.kremlin.ru/events/president/news/64431> accessed 5 December 2020.

80 Ceasefire Agreement (n 64), arts 7–9. In particular, these connections include transport links between Azerbaijan's exclave Nakhichevan and Azerbaijan through the territory of Armenia. Miklasová (n 66); Kuznets (n 72).

81 Miklasová (n 66).

Neither was the OSCE Minsk Group mentioned in the agreement.[82]

In any case, after the 2020 ceasefire agreement, the secessionist entity of the Nagorno-Karabakh and its purported "army" and security forces, including the self-proclaimed Ministry of Defense and police, continued to operate in Nagorno-Karabakh.[83] However, several factors of Armenia's links to Nagorno-Karabakh in the post-ceasefire period must be underlined. The first factor concerns the direct military presence of the regular Armenian army. Under the deal, the Russian peacekeepers "shall be deployed concurrently with the withdrawal of the Armenian troops."[84] While there were contradictory positions regarding the interpretation of this clause as foreseeing the withdrawal of Armenian armed forces from Nagorno-Karabakh and regarding the question of the withdrawal itself,[85] several reports ultimately confirmed that the regular Armenian Army withdrew almost all its forces from Nagorno-Karabakh and stopped sending conscripts there.[86] "Armenia withdrew almost all its troops

82 ibid.

83 Kuznets (n 72); Miklasová (n 66).

84 Ceasefire Agreement (n 64), art 4 and see art 3.

85 Miklasová (n 66); International Crisis Group, 'Getting from Ceasefire to Peace in Nagorno-Karabakh' (*ICG*, 10 November 2020) <https://www.crisisgroup.org/europe-central-asia/caucasus/nagorno-karabakh-conflict/getting-ceasefire-peace-nagorno-karabakh> accessed 5 December 2020. While Azerbaijan claimed that the Armenian troops should have withdrawn from the whole of Nagorno-Karabakh in accordance with art 4 of the Ceasefire Agreement, Armenia relied on art 1 concerning the freezing of positions on the day of the ceasefire agreement. It claimed that art 4 only applied to territories surrounding Nagorno-Karabakh handed over to Azerbaijan by 1 December 2020. K Krivosheev and H Khalatyan, 'Armenia and Azerbaijan Unleashed the War of Interpretations' (*Kommersant* online, 15 December 2020) <https://www.kommersant.ru/doc/4615765> accessed 15 December 2020 (*in Russian*). However, it was clear that the withdrawal of Armenian troops was linked with the deployment of the Russian peacekeepers. Under the deal, the Russian peacekeepers were deployed to Nagorno-Karabakh. Ceasefire Agreement (n 64), art 4 and see art 3. It also should be noted that while the Russian version of the agreement contained the terms "the withdrawal of the Armenian armed forces", the English translation speaks about "the withdrawal of Armenian troops." The latter expression is more equivocal. See Ceasefire Agreement (n 64).

86 International Crisis Group, *Post-War Prospects for Nagorno-Karabakh War* (ICG 2021), 1, fn 4 and see 7. 'Bet on Contractors: Balasanyan on Recruits from Armenia in the Karabakh Defense Army' (*Sputnik Armenia*, 22 March 2021) <https://ru.armeniasputnik.am/20210322/Stavka-na-kontraktnikov-Balasanyan-o-prizyvnikakh-iz-Armenii-v-Armii-oborony-Karabakha--26888560.html> accessed 31 October 2023 (*in Russian*); '"Nobody Gives Any Guarantees": Parents of Conscripts in Karabakh Hold a Rally' (*Sputnik Armenia*, 8 January 2021) <https://ru.armeniasputnik.am/20210108/Nikto-ne-daet-nikakikh-garantiy-roditeli-sluzhaschikh-v-Artsakhe-srochnikov-provodyat-aktsiyu-26026928.html> accessed 31 October 2023 (*in Russian*); J Miklasová, 'Post-Ceasefire

and stopped sending weaponry to the conflict zone. The local troops were thus left to their own devices."[87] According to observers, the Russian peacekeeping mission was the key guarantor of security in Nagorno-Karabakh.[88]

Second, it was difficult to see how Armenia could continue to provide weapons, material and logistical support for the local separatist "army" since the only connection between Armenia and Nagorno-Karabakh was the Lachin Corridor, which was under the control of Russian peacekeepers.[89] According to the International Crisis Group (ICG), Armenia indeed stopped sending such support.[90] Despite this less intensive military support of Armenia in the post-ceasefire period, it is difficult to imagine that Nagorno-Karabakh could have continued to survive without Armenia fighting on the separatist side in the 44-Day War[91] and Armenia's continued essential political, economic and financial support for this entity.[92] Moreover, Armenia's prime minister (not the separatist leaders) signed the ceasefire agreement – the additional element of Armenia's control over the entity.

Nagorno-Karabakh: Limits to the ECtHR's Approach to Jurisdiction over Secessionist Entities under the ECHR' (2022) 82 ZaöRV 357, 366.

87 International Crisis Group (n 86) 1, fn 4. See *infra* on Ceasefire Agreement of 20 September 2023 (n 111), which foresaw the withdrawal of "remaining units and servicemen of the Armed Forces of the Republic of Armenia" from this region. According to the September 2023 Statement of the International Crisis Group, "[u]der the terms of a Russia-brokered ceasefire, Armenian troops agreed to leave the region." 'Responding to the Humanitarian Catastrophe in Nagorno-Karabakh' (*International Crisis Group*, 29 September 2023) <https://www.crisisgroup.org/europe-central-asia/caucasus/nagorno-karabakh-conflict/responding-humanitarian-catastrophe-nagorno#:~:text=In%20a%20move%20that%20seemed,who%20lay%20down%20their%20arms.> accessed 31 October 2023.

88 Kuznets (n 72). De Waal says, "Russia has become the security patron, not Armenia" and "de facto, it's now a Russian enclave." 'Interview: Thomas De Waal on What's Next For Nagorno-Karabakh, Armenian-Azerbaijani Relations' (*Radio Free Europe/Radio Liberty*, 7 December 2020) <https://www.rferl.org/a/interview-thomas-de-waal-on-what-s-next-for-nagorno-karabakh-armenian-azerbaijani-relations/30988513.html> accessed 10 December 2020.

89 Kuznets (n 72); Miklasová (n 66).

90 International Crisis Group (n 86) 1 and 7. Miklasová (n 86) 366. However, Azerbaijan claimed that Armenia still continued to use the corridor to send weapons to Nagorno-Karabakh. 'Tensions Rise After Azerbaijan Blocks Land Route from Armenia' (*Al Jazeera*, 23 April 2023) <https://www.aljazeera.com/news/2023/4/23/tensions-rise-after-azerbaijan-blocks-land-route-from-armenia> accessed 31 October 2023.

91 See in detail Miklasová (n 86) 366–367.

92 See ibid 367.

Two seemingly paradoxical developments dominated the post-ceasefire period.[93] On the one hand, Armenia and Azerbaijan embarked on negotiations to reach a comprehensive peace treaty. Several contentious points, however, slowed down the progress.[94] This included the delimitation and demarcation of the Armenia-Azerbaijan State border (which has not taken place since 1991), the creation of a transportation corridor linking Azerbaijan with its exclave Nakhichevan through Armenia, and the rights and security guarantees of the Nagorno-Karabakh Armenians.[95] Importantly, in April 2023, the Armenian prime minister publicly reaffirmed that Armenia recognises the territorial integrity of Azerbaijan (based on the borders of the former Union republic and thus including Nagorno-Karabakh), called on peace treaty in which both States would recognise each other's territorial integrity without "ambiguities and pitfalls" and sought to refocus the peace treaty negotiations on formalizing the guarantees of security and rights of the Nagorno-Karabakh Armenians.[96]

The negotiations also advanced slowly, given military clashes along the Armenia-Azerbaijan border that also took place in this period, with Azerbaijan making several military incursions into Armenia proper.[97] In particular, the mid-September 2022 fighting saw Azerbaijani troops crossing the border into the Armenian territory and taking positions there, which they have held until today.[98] "The presence of Azerbaijani troops inside Armenia adds a new issue

---

93 International Crisis Group, *Averting a New War between Armenia and Azerbaijan* (ICG 2023).

94 International Crisis Group (n 93) 4–7.

95 ibid.

96 "I now want to reaffirm that the Republic of Armenia fully recognizes the territorial integrity of Azerbaijan, and we expect that Azerbaijan will do the same by recognizing the entire territory of the Armenian SSR as the Republic of Armenia. I should also say that Azerbaijan's claims that during the peace treaty negotiations Armenia refused or refuses to fully recognize Azerbaijan's territorial integrity are untrue, and we can prove it. It was we who proposed that the maps of the Armenian and Azerbaijani SSRs, confirmed by the USSR, be attached to the treaty as a basis for the territorial integrity of the two countries." 'Prime Minister Nikol Pashinyan's Speech in the National Assembly when Presenting the Report on the Implementation Process and Results of the Government Action Plan 2021–2026 for the Year of 2022' (*The Prime Minister of the Republic of Armenia*, 18 April 2023) <https://www.primeminister.am/en/statements-and-messages/item/2023/04/18/Nikol-Pashinyan-Speech/> accessed 29 October 2023. See also K Krivosheev, 'Armenia Is Ready to Relinquish Nagorno-Karabakh: What Next?' (*Carnegie Russia Eurasia*, 28 April 2023) <https://carnegieendowment.org/politika/89635> accessed 29 October 2023.

97 International Crisis Group (n 93) 7. H Isayev, 'Armenia and Azerbaijani Leaders Meet for the Fifth Time in Brussels (*eurasianet*, 16 May 2023) <https://eurasianet.org/armenian-and-azerbaijani-leaders-meet-for-the-fifth-time-in-brussels> accessed 29 October 2023.

98 International Crisis Group (n 93) 1.

for peace negotiations to address and another flashpoint between the two sides."[99]

Since December 2022, pro-Azerbaijani activists (who were allegedly linked to the Azerbaijani government, but this connection was contested by Azerbaijan)[100] blockaded the Lachin Corridor (the only road linking Armenia and Nagorno-Karabakh after the Second Karabakh War), disrupting the supply of food, medicine and fuel to the region.[101] According to the 2020 ceasefire agreement, the corridor "shall remain under the control" of the Russian peacekeeping mission, and Azerbaijan "shall guarantee the security of persons, vehicles and cargo moving along the Lachin Corridor in both directions."[102] In April 2023, Azerbaijan set up a checkpoint on the Lachin Corridor, "effectively consolidating the blockade which had begun four months earlier."[103] Russian peacekeepers did not intervene.[104]

In February 2023, the ICJ indicated provisional measures to Azerbaijan "to take all measures at its disposal to ensure unimpeded movement of persons,

99 International Crisis Group (n 93) 1 and see 7–12.

100 While Armenia claimed that Azerbaijan was behind these protesters and the blockade, Azerbaijan held that the protests were genuine. 6–7. C Mills, 'What Is Happening in Nagorno-Karabakh?' (*House of Commons Library Research Briefing No 9862*, 28 September 2023) 6–7 <https://commonslibrary.parliament.uk/research-briefings/cbp-9862/> accessed 31 October 2023. According to the International Crisis Group, in December 2022, "Azerbaijan imposed what amounted to a blockade on the Lachin corridor." 'Responding to the Humanitarian Catastrophe in Nagorno-Karabakh' (n 87).

101 Mills (n 100) 6. "The Russian peacekeeping mission escorted supplies through the blockade, while the International Committee of the Red Cross (ICRC) delivered aid and facilitated the movement of people in need of urgent medical help." 'New Troubles in Nagorno-Karabakh: Understanding the Lachin Corridor Crisis' (*International Crisis Group*, 22 May 2023) <https://www.crisisgroup.org/europe-central-asia/caucasus/nagorno-karabakh-conflict/new-troubles-nagorno-karabakh-understanding-lachin-corridor-crisis> accessed 31 October 2023 ("New Troubles in Nagorno-Karabakh").

102 Ceasefire Agreement (n 64), art 6.

103 Mills (n 100) 7. In June 2023, Azerbaijan excluded "even ICRC and Russian access, causing severe shortages of food, fuel and medicine in the territory." L Boers, 'The Nagorno-Karabakh Wars Are Over, but Their Fallout Will be Lasting' (*WPR*, 25 October 2023) <https://www.worldpoliticsreview.com/armenia-azerbaijan-nagorno-karabakh/?loggedin=1> accessed 31 October 2023. See also L Shahveryan, 'Nagorno-Karabakh under Total Blockade' (*eurasianet*, 23 June 2023) <https://eurasianet.org/nagorno-karabakh-under-total-blockade> accessed 31 October 2023. New Troubles in Nagorno-Karabakh (n 101).

104 See L Boers, 'Russia Concedes Karabakh for State in New Regional Order' (*Chatham House*, 29 September 2023) <https://www.chathamhouse.org/2023/09/russia-concedes-karabakh-stake-new-regional-order> accessed 31 October 2023.

vehicles and cargo along the Lachin Corridor in both directions."[105] The ECtHR indicated similar interim measures.[106] In August 2023, the UN experts characterized the situation in the province as a "humanitarian emergency" and urged Azerbaijan "to immediately restore the free and secure movement of persons, vehicles and cargo" along the Lachin corridor in line with the ceasefire agreement.[107]

1.4 *Azerbaijan Retaking Control of Nagorno-Karabakh in 2023*

Against these developments, on 19 September 2023, Azerbaijan launched its "military operation" against Nagorno-Karabakh, which led to a mass exodus of Nagorno-Karabakh Armenians.[108] According to the International Crisis Group, Armenia "did not intervene in the conflict."[109] Azerbaijan's military operation

---

105 *Application of the International Convention on the Elimination of All Forms of Racial Discrimination* (*Armenia v Azerbaijan*) (*Provisional Measures, Order*) [2023] General List 180, para 67. This provisional measure was reaffirmed in the ICJ's subsequent order on the issue on 6 July 2023. *Application of the International Convention on the Elimination of All Forms of Racial Discrimination* (*Armenia v Azerbaijan*) (*Provisional Measures, Order*) [2023] General List 180, para 33.

106 The ECtHR indicated to Azerbaijan "to take all measures that are within their jurisdiction to ensure safe passage through the "Lachin Corridor" of seriously ill persons in need of medical treatment in Armenia and others who were stranded on the road without shelter or means of subsistence." 'European Court Decides to Indicate Interim Measures in the "Lachin Corridor"' (Press Release Issued by the Registrar of the Court, 21 December 2022) <https://hudoc.echr.coe.int/app/conversion/pdf/?library=ECHR&id=003-7528728-10337270&filename=Interim%20measures%20in%20the%20case%20Armenia%20v.%20Azerbaijan%20%28no.%204%29.pdf> accessed 31 October 2023. See also CoE (PACE) Res 2508 (22 June 2023).

107 'UN Experts Urge Azerbaijan to Lift Lachin Corridor Blockade and End Humanitarian Crisis in Nagorno-Karabakh' (*UN Press Release*, 7 August 2023) <https://www.ohchr.org/en/press-releases/2023/08/un-experts-urge-azerbaijan-lift-lachin-corridor-blockade-and-end#:~:text=The%20experts%20urged%20authorities%20in,ceasefire%20agreement%20of%20November%202020.> accessed 31 October 2023.

108 Boers highlights that Azerbaijan's actions took place against the backdrop of negotiations with the Karabakh Armenia, which "were pointing toward Azerbaijan's desired diplomatic outcomes." Boers (n 103).

109 'Responding to the Humanitarian Catastrophe in Nagorno-Karabakh' (*International Crisis Group*, 29 September 2023) <https://www.crisisgroup.org/europe-central-asia/caucasus/nagorno-karabakh-conflict/responding-humanitarian-catastrophe-nagorno#:~:text=In%20a%20move%20that%20seemed,who%20lay%20down%20their%20arms.> accessed 31 October 2023. Russian peacekeepers did not take any action. See M Young, 'Endgame in Nagorno-Karabakh' (*Carnegie Middle East*, 28 September 2023) <https://carnegieendowment.org/middle-east/diwan/2023/09/endgame-in-nagorno-karabakh?lang=en&center=middle-east> accessed 31 October 2023.

led to a collapse of the separatist forces within 24 hours.[110] On 20 September 2023, the local Karabakh troops accepted the Russian peacekeepers' ceasefire agreement proposal, according to which the armed units of the "Nagorno-Karabakh Defense Army" will be completely disarmed and disbanded.[111] The document foresaw the "withdrawal of the remaining units and servicemen of the Armed Forces of the Republic of Armenia from the area of deployment of the Russian peacekeeping contingent" (i.e. Nagorno-Karabakh) and "the withdrawal of heavy equipment and weapons."[112] Moreover, according to the agreement, the issues of reintegration and the rights and security of the Karabakh Armenians within the framework of Azerbaijan's constitution will be the object of the subsequent talks between the representatives of the local Armenian population and Azerbaijan's central authorities.[113] At the time of writing, these talks have not yet finished.[114]

On 28 September 2023, the Nagorno-Karabakh separatist leader publicly announced that until 1 January 2024, the *de facto* state structures of Nagorno-Karabakh would be dissolved.[115] This will mark the formal end of the existence of this secessionist entity, which for more than thirty years since it declared independence, secured no recognition. According to estimates, almost the

---

110 Boers (n 103).

111 NKR InfoCenter 'Announcement' (20 September 2023) <https://www.facebook.com/ArtsakhInformation/posts/pfbid022ZzupVTp3hfj3LxUY3fuFrGyRUaGaTYwushd6G7TGN1KAf6bDqT9HTfjBnxfXDpzl> accessed 31 October 2023 (*in Armenian and Russian*) ("Ceasefire Agreement of 20 September 2023").

112 Ceasefire Agreement of 20 September 2023 (n 111). The Armenian prime minister was cited as saying, "Armenia had not stationed any troops in the region." A Roth, S Jones and H Amos, 'Nagorno-Karabakh: Ceasefire Agreed After Dozens Killed in Military Offensive' (*The Guardian*, 20 September 2023) <https://www.theguardian.com/world/2023/sep/20/nagorno-karabakh-death-toll-azerbaijan-armenia-attack-conflict-russia-us> accessed 31 October 2023. See *supra* regarding the reported withdrawal of the Armenian regular army from Nagorno-Karabakh after the Second Karabakh War (n 87).

113 Ceasefire Agreement of 20 September 2023 (n 111).

114 See 'Responding to the Humanitarian Catastrophe in Nagorno-Karabakh' (n 87). K Krivosheev, 'What Dissolution of Nagorno-Karabakh Means for the South Caucasus' (*Carnegie Russia Eurasia*, 29 September 2023) <https://carnegieendowment.org/politika/90667> accessed 31 October 2023.

115 Decree of the President of the Republic of Artsakh on the Actions Arising from the Situation Created after 19 September 2023' (*Kavkazskiy Uzel*, 28 September 2023) <https://www.kavkaz-uzel.eu/articles/392937> accessed 31 October 2023 (*in Russian*); At the time of writing, it is unclear what the future of the Russian peacekeeping mission will be. P Ivanova, 'Azerbaijan's Victory over Armenian Enclave Raises Fears of Another War' (*The Financial Times*, 23 October 2023) <https://www.ft.com/content/0ccdf385-dab8-42f2-ba4a-b58c8cbbebe3> accessed 31 October 2023.

entire population of Nagorno-Karabakh (more than 100,000 people) has ultimately left the region for Armenia.[116]

At the time of writing, there are reports of the prospective conclusion of the comprehensive peace treaty between Armenia and Azerbaijan, formalising the contentious issues outlined above.[117] Other reports have, however, warned about the high risk of Azerbaijan's attack on Armenia proper to secure the connection to its exclave of Nakhichevan.[118]

2 Legal Analysis of the Secessionist Attempt

2.1 *Period before the 2020 War*

2.1.1 History-Based Arguments

In its declaration of independence, Nagorno-Karabakh justified its secession by reference to Azerbaijan's constitutional act declaring the restoration of the independence of the Azerbaijan Democratic Republic that existed from 1918 and 1920.[119] The argument goes that by "rejecting the legal heritage of the Azerbaijan SSR of 1920–1991, the Republic of Azerbaijan has lost all claims to the territories passed to Soviet Azerbaijan in July, 1921 – namely Nagorno-Karabakh – even if the latter's act of transfer was legitimate".[120] This claim does not work for several reasons.

Firstly, Azerbaijan's claim of restoration of its pre-Soviet independence only operated in the context of Azerbaijan's internal legal order. Internationally, upon the Soviet Union's dissolution, the Republic of Azerbaijan emerged as a successor State to the USSR within pre-existing borders, which included Nagorno-Karabakh.[121] As will be shown in detail below, the principle of *uti*

116 Boers (n 103).

117 G Gavin, 'Azerbaijan Says Peace with Armenia Is Within Reach' (*Politico*, 25 October 2023) <https://www.politico.eu/article/peace-armenia-reach-azerbaijan-foreign-minister-jeyhun-bayramov/> accessed 31 October 2023.

118 "[N]o 'rhetorical ceasefire' has followed Baku's military triumph, observers say, and no meaningful steps have been taken to reconcile two societies bitterly divided by decades of war." Ivanova (n 115). See 'Responding to the Humanitarian Catastrophe in Nagorno-Karabakh' (n 87).

119 See 'Proclamation of the Nagorno Karabakh Republic' (adopted 2 September 1991) <http://www.nkrusa.org/nk_conflict/declaration_independence.shtml> accessed 29 May 2019 and 'The Constitutional Act on the State Independence of the Republic of Azerbaijan' (adopted 18 October 1991) <http://azerbaijan.az/portal/History/HistDocs/Documents/en/09.pdf> accessed 5 June 2019 ("Constitutional Act").

120 S Avakian, *Nagorno Karabagh: Legal Aspects* (5th edn, MIA Publishers 2015) 21.

121 See *infra*.

possidetis transformed the previous administrative boundaries, including that of the Nagorno-Karabakh autonomous region, into the international borders of a newly independent Azerbaijan. In addition, Azerbaijan itself did not use this argument at the international level – "l'Azerbaïdjan n'a pas joué cette carte sur la scène internationale et les Etats tiers ne l'ont pas traité différemment des autres Etats post-soviétiques."[122]

Secondly, upon analysis of Azerbaijan's constitutional act, it is difficult to accept that its aim was to reject Soviet legal heritage and by implication Nagorno-Karabakh as part of Azerbaijan's territory.[123] It is true that this constitutional act declared the 1922 Treaty on the Establishment of the USSR in the sections concerning Azerbaijan invalid.[124] But it also contained an intertemporal provision on the validity of the 1978 Azerbaijan SSR's Constitution, insofar as it did not contradict the Constitutional Act.[125] It also provided for the validity of previous laws as long as they did not contradict "the sovereignty and territorial integrity of the Republic of Azerbaijan".[126]

Thirdly, even if, hypothetically, the claim on the rejection of the Soviet legal heritage were to be taken as correct and as producing legal effects internationally, which it does not, it would not entail the emergence of an independent Nagorno-Karabakh. This region "has never historically enjoyed independence",[127] and in the period before the Bolshevik's takeover it was the object of violent clashes between these two countries.[128] Even though Armenians have also invoked other history-based arguments – they referred to the situation before the decision of 5 July 1921, which assigned Nagorno-Karabakh to Azerbaijan and was later reflected in the Soviet constitutions – the present book would not deal with them.[129]

---

122 H Hamant, *Démembrement de l'URSS et problèmes de succession d'états* (Bruylant 2007) 179.

123 Krüger (n 2) 48–50.

124 Azerbaijan's Parliament was also to make the list of Soviet Laws that provisionally remained in force. Constitutional Act (n 119) art 3. This book does not develop further on the fact that the claim of invalidity could only have had internal and not international effects since, at the time of the Bolshevik's takeover of Azerbaijan and its incorporation into the Soviet Union, the prohibition of the use of force was yet to become part of positive international law. See Krüger (n 2) 3, 26 and 86–88.

125 Constitutional Act (n 119) art 4.

126 ibid. Krüger (n 2) 48–50.

127 Popjanevski (n 3) 28.

128 See *supra*.

129 But see Krüger (n 2) 44–47.

2.1.2 Right to Secede under Municipal Law

Similarly to the case of South Ossetia, Nagorno-Karabakh as an autonomous region[130] did not possess the right to secession under the Soviet Constitution; this right was only reserved to Union republics.[131] The Soviet Constitution did not provide any legal basis for the July 1988 and December 1989 decisions on Nagorno-Karabakh's unification with Armenia, since under the Soviet Constitution, any alteration of the Union Republic's territory required its consent, and the Azerbaijan SSR's consent was obviously lacking.[132] In addition, the alteration of boundaries between Union republics required mutual agreement by the respective republics and ratification by the USSR – such an agreement was never reached.[133] Moreover, even if Azerbaijan's revocation of Nagorno-Karabakh's status as an autonomous region could be considered illegal and invalid under the Soviet constitution, that would not have entailed Nagorno-Karabakh's right to secession.[134]

Nagorno-Karabakh's declaration of independence of 2 September 1991 made a direct reference to the Law on Secession from the USSR as a justification for secession.[135] Since this declaration was issued before the Soviet Union's dissolution, the applicability of this law must be assessed.[136]

As discussed with respect to Abkhazia and South Ossetia, even though this law stipulated that the people of autonomous republics, autonomous regions and districts "retain the right to decide independently the question of remaining within the USSR or within the seceding Union republic, and also to raise the question of their own state-legal status",[137] it could not have provided Nagorno-Karabakh with the right to secede from the Azerbaijan SSR. Firstly, many scholars challenge the constitutionality of this law.[138] Secondly,

130 'Constitution (Fundamental Law) of the Union of Soviet Socialist Republics' (adopted 7 October 1977, entered into force 7 October 1977), art 87 <https://www.departments.bucknell.edu/russian/const/77cons03.html> accessed 3 May 2019 ("1977 Soviet Constitution").

131 ibid art 72. Krüger (n 2) 28–29.

132 1977 Soviet Constitution (n 130) art 78 in connection with art 86. Krüger (n 2) 29.

133 1977 Soviet Constitution (n 130) art 78. Krüger (n 2) 29.

134 1977 Soviet Constitution (n 130) art 87. Krüger (n 2) 39.

135 'Proclamation of the Nagorno Karabakh Republic' (adopted 2 September 1991) <http://www.nkrusa.org/nk_conflict/declaration_independence.shtml> accessed 29 May 2019. *Chiragov* (n 27) para 13.

136 Krüger (n 2) 39.

137 Law on Procedure for Resolving Questions Connected with a Union Republic's Secession from the USSR (adopted 3 April 1990) art 3(1) <http://soviethistory.msu.edu/1991-2/shevarnadze-resigns/shevarnadze-resigns-texts/law-on-secession-from-the-ussr/> accessed 9 May 2019 ("Law on Secession from the USSR").

138 Popjanevski (n 3) 39; Krüger (n 2) 31–35.

regardless of the question of its constitutionality, the law provided for the right of secession of autonomous regions only in connection with the Union republic's secession from the USSR following the conditions prescribed therein.[139] None of the republics, including Azerbaijan, seceded on the basis of this law, and therefore the law "was arguably never valid for Nagorno-Karabakh".[140] It simply did not provide for an independent right of autonomous regions to secede.[141] Thirdly, in any case, Nagorno-Karabakh itself did not follow procedural conditions prescribed by this law.[142] Thus, overall, no municipal right to secession ever accrued for Nagorno-Karabakh.[143]

2.1.3 Right to Self-Determination and Remedial Secession

As in other post-Soviet secessionist attempts, the separatists invoked a people's right to self-determination as the justification for their secession. In particular, the declaration of independence of 6 January 1992 and the preamble of the Constitution of Nagorno-Karabakh made reference to the right of peoples to self-determination as well as to the will of the people expressed in the referendum of 10 December 1991.[144] Nevertheless, as follows from the analysis in Part 1, Chapter 3, it is questionable whether the Armenian population of Nagorno-Karabakh constitutes a people in terms of international law – "[r]ather it might be characterized as a national minority that could be entitled to some degree of internal self-determination or autonomy within Azerbaijan."[145] As follows from the above, the right of self-determination does not entail the right to secession.[146]

Moreover, separatists also referred to arguments that could be characterised as a claim of remedial secession. In particular, the declaration of independence of 2 September 1991 referred to "Azerbaijan's policies of apartheid and discrimination",[147] and the declaration of 6 January 1992 mentioned

139 Popjanevski (n 3) 39; Krüger (n 2) 36–37.
140 Popjanevski (n 3) 39; Krüger (n 2) 36–37.
141 Krüger (n 2) 36–37.
142 Popjanevski (n 3) 39; Krüger (n 2) 37–39.
143 Krüger (n 2) 40.
144 'Declaration on State Independence of the Nagorno Karabakh Republic' (adopted 6 January 1992) <http://www.nkrusa.org/nk_conflict/declaration_independence.shtml> accessed 29 May 2019; 'Constitution of the Republic of Artsakh' (adopted 20 February 2017) <https://www.worldstatesmen.org/Artsakh-Constitution-eng2017.pdf> accessed 29 October 2023.
145 Melnyk (n 54) para 14. See *supra* Part 1, Chapter 3. Krüger (n 2) 54–56.
146 See *supra* Part 1, Chapter 3.
147 'Proclamation of the Nagorno Karabakh Republic' (adopted 2 September 1991) <http://www.nkrusa.org/nk_conflict/declaration_independence.shtml> accessed 29 May 2019.

Nagorno-Karabakh's willingness to protect "the NKR population from aggression and threat of physical extermination".[148] It was claimed that the Azerbaijan SSR's discrimination could be inferred from the decrease of the Armenian population living in Nagorno-Karabakh between 1923 and 1989.[149] The abolishment of Nagorno-Karabakh's autonomy in December 1991 was also seen as a sign of Azerbaijan's discriminatory practices.[150]

However, even though Nagorno-Karabakh alleges discrimination in the pre-independence period, there is no available evidence to warrant such a conclusion.[151] The Azerbaijan SSR's discrimination cannot simply be inferred from the decrease of the Armenian population in Nagorno-Karabakh; other factors, especially the dynamics of the functioning of a totalitarian State should also be taken into account.[152]

Moreover, even though the conflict was marked by severe human rights violations and a number of civilian casualties and expulsions, "these humanitarian crimes have neither been one sided nor have they taken place exclusively in the territory of Nagorno-Karabakh; nor did they occur primarily *before* the territory sought to secede."[153] This also applies to the revocation of Nagorno-Karabakh's autonomy, which was taken only as a response to the declaration of independence.[154] In addition, Nagorno-Karabakh's secessionist path was not an *ultima ratio* in the political conflict with Baku.[155] Since the end of war in 1994, Azerbaijan lacked access to Nagorno-Karabakh, and therefore it was difficult to substantiate the claims that it persecuted the current population there.[156] Thus, overall, the establishment of Nagorno-Karabakh cannot be

148 'Declaration on State Independence of the Nagorno Karabakh Republic' (adopted 6 January 1992) <http://www.nkrusa.org/nk_conflict/declaration_independence.shtml> accessed 29 May 2019.

149 "Azerbaijan's discrimination towards Nagorno Karabagh had its impact on the welfare of its Armenian population and became a major migration factor ... while Armenians constituted 94,4 percent of the entire population of Nagorno Karabagh in 1923, their numbers dropped down to 76,9 percent of the population in 1989." Avakian (n 120) 26.

150 M De Hoon, 'Collateral Damage From Criminalizing Aggression – Lawfare Through Aggression Accusations in the Nagorno-Karabakh Conflict' (2012) 5 European Journal of Legal Studies 35, 53.

151 Popjanevski (n 3) 27; Krüger (n 2) 75–77.

152 Krüger (n 2) 75–77.

153 Popjanevski (n 3) 25 and see 25–27 (*emphasis in original*). Krüger (n 2) 77–80.

154 Krüger (n 2) 86.

155 ibid 81–82.

156 Popjanevski (n 3) 27.

justified by the reference to remedial secession.[157] In any case, it follows from Part 1, Chapter 3 that remedial secession is not part of positive international law.[158]

2.1.4 Formation of the Successor States of Azerbaijan and Armenia

Regardless of the secessionist claims of Nagorno-Karabakh, at the international level, upon the dissolution of the USSR, the international legal status of the Republic of Azerbaijan and Armenia did not raise particular legal problems – they emerged as successor States to the USSR within their pre-existing administrative boundaries, including Nagorno-Karabakh within Azerbaijan.[159] They were recognised as States, for example, by the European Community[160] and the USA.[161]

Documents on the USSR's dissolution, and those constituting the CIS and adopted by the CIS, confirmed the applicability of the principle of *uti possidetis* in the context of the Soviet Union's dissolution and the creation of new States.[162] In particular, in the Alma Ata Declaration, the former Union Republics declared that they recognised and respected "each other's territorial integrity and the inviolability of *existing* borders".[163] In Article 5 of the Minsk Agreement, they "acknowledge and respect each other's territorial integrity and the inviolability of *existing* borders *within* the Commonwealth".[164] In

157 Melnyk (n 54) para 14. For the opposite view, WR Slomanson, 'Nagorno-Karabakh: An Alternative Legal Approach to Its Quest for Legitimacy' (2012) 35 Thomas Jefferson Law Review 29, 43.

158 See *supra*. Krüger (n 2) 74.

159 See Krüger (n 2) 49; Hamant, *Démembrement de l'URSS et problèmes de succession d'états* (n 122) 180–182.

160 See 'Déclaration de la Communauté européenne sur "les lignes directrices sur la reconnaissance de nouveaux Etats en Europe orientale et en Union soviétique"' (16 December 1991) reprinted in H Hamant, *Succession de l'URSS: Recueil de documents* (Bruylant 2010) 58–59; 'Déclaration de la Communauté européenne sur la reconnaissance d'anciennes républiques soviétiques' (31 December 1991) reprinted in ibid 62.

161 G Bush, 'Address of the President to the Nation: US Welcomes New Commonwealth of Independent States' (25 December 1991) reprinted in ibid 90–92.

162 See Krüger (n 2) 44.

163 Alma Ata Declaration (signed 21 December 1991) preambular para 3 reprinted in 31 (1992) ILM 147, 148–149.

164 Agreement Establishing the Commonwealth of Independent States (Republic of Belarus, the RSFSR and Ukraine) (signed 8 December 1991), art 5 reprinted in 31 (1992) ILM 143, 143–146 ("Minsk Agreement") (*emphasis added*). See also Protocol to the Agreement Establishing the Commonwealth of Independent States Signed at into force on 8 December 1991 by the Republic of Belarus, the Russian Federation (RSFSR) and Ukraine (signed 21 December 1991, entry for each party upon ratification) reprinted in 31 (1992) ILM 147, 147 ("Alma Ata Protocol").

addition, in Article 3 of the Charter of the CIS, the member States pledged to build their relations in accordance *inter alia* with the principle of "recognition of existing frontiers".[165] Similarly, the CIS declaration of 15 April 1994 provided a provision on respect for sovereignty, territorial integrity and inviolability of state borders; however, this text was not signed by Armenia.[166] References to "existing borders within Commonwealth" and "existing borders" or "existing frontiers" clearly cover former administrative boundaries of the republics,[167] including Nagorno-Karabakh as part of Azerbaijan.

Furthermore, Azerbaijan's territorial integrity within its internationally recognised borders was consistently upheld at the international level. Already during the course of the war (1992–1994), the UNSC in its resolutions reaffirmed "the sovereignty and territorial integrity of the Azerbaijani Republic and of all other states in the region", "the inviolability of international borders and the inadmissibility of the use of force for the acquisition of territory".[168] These UNSC resolutions also referred to "the Nagorno-Karabakh region of the Azerbaijani Republic".[169]

Similarly, later on, the UNGA reaffirmed "continued respect and support for the sovereignty and territorial integrity of the Republic of Azerbaijan within its internationally recognized borders".[170] Moreover, the EU reiterated, "the importance it attaches to the territorial integrity and sovereignty of the Republic of Azerbaijan, in accordance with the principles of the CSCE".[171]

The OSCE Minsk Group Co-Chairs "support the territorial integrity of Azerbaijan and therefore do not recognize the independence of

---

165 Charter of the Commonwealth of Independent States (adopted 22 January 1993, entered into force 22 January 1994) 1819 UNTS 37, art 3 ("Charter of the CIS").

166 CIS, 'Declaration on Respect of Sovereignty, Territorial Integrity and Inviolability of Boundaries of the Member States of CIS' (adopted 15 April 1994) <http://docs.cntd.ru/document/1901148> accessed 9 May 2019 (*in Russian*).

167 MG Kohen, 'Le problème des frontières en cas de dissolution et de séparation d'États: quelles alternatives?' in O Corten, B Delcourt, P Klein and N Levrat (eds), *Démembrements d'États et délimitations territoriales: l'uti possidetis en question(s)* (Bruylant 1999) 377.

168 UNSC Res 853 (29 July 1993) UN Doc S/RES/853, preambular paras 8 and 9; UNSC Res 874 (14 October 1993) UN Doc S/RES/874, preambular paras 5 and 6. See also UNSC Res 822 (30 April 1993) UN Doc S/RES/822, preambular paras 7 and 8; UNSC Res 884 (12 November 1993) preambular paras 6 and 7.

169 See for example UNSC Res 853 (29 July 1993) UN Doc S/RES/853, para 9; UNSC Res 874 (14 October 1993) UN Doc S/RES/874, preambular para 3; UNSC Res 884 (12 November 1993) UN Doc S/RES/884, preambular para 4.

170 UNGA Res 62/243 (14 March 2008) UN Doc A/RES/62/243, para 1.

171 European Union, 'Statement on Nagorno-Karabakh' (*Press Release*, 9 November 1993) 93/448 contained in R Dehousee and others (eds), *European Political Cooperation Documentation Bulletin* (European University Institute 1993) 532.

Nagorno-Karabakh".[172] The OSCE PA called on parties to engage in negotiations "in full respect for the sovereignty, territorial integrity and inviolability of internationally recognized borders of … Azerbaijan".[173] The Organisation of Islamic Cooperation urged Armenia "to respect the sovereignty and territorial integrity of the Republic of Azerbaijan".[174] The Non-Aligned Movement encouraged the negotiated settlement of the conflict "within the territorial integrity, sovereignty and the internationally recognized borders of the Republic of Azerbaijan".[175]

2.1.5 Armenia's Use of Force in Nagorno-Karabakh

From an international law perspective, before the USSR's break-up, *ad bellum* rules were not relevant to the conflict in Nagorno-Karabakh. An armed conflict concerning secession from one federal unit to another or armed conflict between two federal units can be characterised as a civil war – the USSR's internal matter. However, the normative framework changed upon the Soviet Union's dissolution. The prohibition of the use of force in inter-State relations became applicable to the newly emerged Republics of Armenia and Azerbaijan.

An analysis of the applicability of these rules firstly requires an understanding of the process of creation of separate national armed forces. As mentioned in the section on Abkhazia and South Ossetia, the period following the USSR's break-up was marked by the attempt to create the Joint Armed Forces of the CIS.[176] Nevertheless, this project was gradually abandoned and former Soviet republics started to form their own national armies.[177] By the Executive Order of 19 March 1992, the Russian president temporarily transferred the Transcaucasian Military District and the Caspian Flotilla of the Navy to the Russian Federation's jurisdiction and submitted it to the command of

172 'OSCE Minsk Group Co-Chairs Issue Statement on Nagorno-Karabakh' (*Press Release*, 19 March 2008) <https://www.osce.org/mg/49570> accessed 2 June 2019.

173 OSCE (PA), 'Luxembourg Declaration' (8 July 2019), para 22.

174 See for example, OIC (Council of Foreign Ministers), 'Resolution on the Aggression of the Republic of Armenia against the Republic of Azerbaijan' (13–14 March 2008) 10/42-POL, para 4; OIC (Council of Foreign Ministers), 'Resolution on the Aggression of the Republic of Armenia against the Republic of Azerbaijan' (18–20 June 2008) 6/35-P, para 4; OIC (Islamic Summit Conference), 'Resolution on the Aggression of the Republic of Armenia against the Republic of Azerbaijan' (27–28 May 2015) 10/11-P(IS), para 4.

175 16th Summit of Heads of State or Government of the Non-Aligned Movement, 'Final Document' (26–31 August 2012) NAM 2012/Doc.1/Rev.2, para 391.

176 Hamant, *Démembrement de l'URSS et problèmes de succession d'états* (n 122) 342–365.

177 See ibid 399–403.

the commander-in-chief of the Joint Armed Forces of the CIS.[178] Nevertheless, Azerbaijan was one of the first Union republics to create its own army; on 17 December 1991, its president declared himself to be the commander-in-chief of all but strategic forces there.[179] As a result, regardless of the 19 March 1992 Executive Order, Russia was unable to take *de facto* control of former Soviet troops stationed in Azerbaijan.[180] On the other hand, Armenia was much more open to the creation of the Joint Armed Forces of the CIS, therefore it only started formally to create its own national army in the second semester of 1992.[181] Armenia agreed with Russia on the passage of former Soviet units stationed in Armenia under Russia's jurisdiction and on their legal status, and, later in 1995, it concluded an agreement on the preservation of military bases.[182] Thus, it follows that acts of the Armenian armed forces, in the second semester of 1992 at minimum, were undoubtedly attributable to the Republic of Armenia. This was also the period when Armenia's intervention in the conflict became apparent.[183]

On the one hand, Azerbaijan's use of force in seeking to reinstate its rule over the secessionist region was in accordance with rules on the prohibition of the use of force.[184] On the other hand, Armenia's direct and indirect military intervention in the conflict could be justified neither by exceptions from the prohibition under the UN Charter, nor by any other doctrinal justifications, and therefore it must be characterised as a violation of Article 2(4) UN Charter.[185]

---

178 'Executive Order of the President of the Russian Federation No 260 on the Transfer of the Transcaucasian Military District and of the Caspian Flotilla of the Nay under the Jurisdiction of the Russian Federation' (adopted 19 March 1992, entered into force 19 March 1992), para 1 <http://kremlin.ru/acts/bank/1069> accessed 10 May 2019 (*in Russian*). See Chapter 13 on Abkhazia and South Ossetia for further details.

179 Hamant, *Démembrement de l'URSS et problèmes de succession d'états* (n 122) 380–381. See 'CIS, Baltic States and Georgia: Military Service' (*Immigration and Refugee Board of Canada*, 1 June 1992) <https://www.refworld.org/docid/3ae6a80d10.html> accessed 5 June 2019.

180 Hamant, *Démembrement de l'URSS et problèmes de succession d'états* (n 122) 380–381.

181 ibid 391.

182 ibid 391. See also Treaty between the Russian Federation and Armenia on the Status of the Military Formations of the Russian Federation Stationed on the territory of Armenia (signed 21 August 1992) reprinted in Hamant, *Succession de l'URSS: Recueil de documents* (n 160) 172–182.

183 See *supra*.

184 O Dörr and A Randelzhofer, 'Article 2(4)' in B Simma and others (eds), *The Charter of the United Nations: A Commentary*, Volume I (3rd edn, OUP 2012), para 32.

185 Charter of the United Nations (adopted 26 June 1945, entered into force 24 October 1945) 1 UNTS XVI, art 2(4) ("UN Charter"); Krüger (n 2) 105–109.

Particularly by sending its troops to fight in the war, Armenia directly violated the prohibition of the use of force, and its actions could thus be characterised as aggression and armed attack under Article 51 UN Charter.[186] Moreover, Armenia's military presence in Nagorno-Karabakh after the end of hostilities in 1994, without Azerbaijan's consent, could also be characterised as a violation of the prohibition of the use of force.[187] The OIC characterised Armenia's actions as aggression.[188]

In addition, by providing separatists with arms and material assistance Armenia also indirectly violated the prohibition of the use of force.[189] However, these acts did not amount to armed attack.[190] If it were proven that the Armenian Army trained the so-called Nagorno-Karabakh army, this would also constitute a violation of the prohibition of the use of force.[191] Lastly, the violation of the prohibition of the use of force also violated Azerbaijan's territorial integrity and constituted an illegal intervention into Azerbaijan's internal affairs.[192] In this context, Armenia's non-military support of Nagorno-Karabakh could be characterised as a violation of the prohibition of intervention.[193]

---

186 Definition of Aggression, UNGA Res 3314 (XXIX) (14 December 1974) UN Doc A/RES/3314(XXIX), Article 3(a) ("Definition of Aggression"); UN Charter (n 185) art 51; G Nolte and A Randelzhofer, 'Article 51' in B Simma and others (eds), *The Charter of the United Nations: A Commentary*, Volume II (3rd edn, OUP 2012), para 23.

187 See also Definition of Aggression (n 186) art 3(a). However, according to Nolte and Randelzhofer, the concept of permanent occupation "is not applicable to the notion of 'armed attack'" as it does not "necessarily involve the use of military force." Nolte and Randelzhofer (n 186) para 23. For the discussion concerning the extension of the regime of prohibition of the use of force under Article 2(4) UN Charter to 'stabilized de facto regimes' see *supra* Chapter 13.

188 See for example, OIC (Council of Foreign Ministers), 'Resolution on the Aggression of the Republic of Armenia against the Republic of Azerbaijan' (13–14 March 2008) 10/42-POL, para 1; OIC (Council of Foreign Ministers), 'Resolution on the Aggression of the Republic of Armenia against the Republic of Azerbaijan' (18–20 June 2008) 6/35-P, para 1; OIC (Islamic Summit Conference), 'Resolution on the Aggression of the Republic of Armenia against the Republic of Azerbaijan' (27–28 May 2015) 10/11-P(IS), para 1.

189 *Case Concerning Military and Paramilitary Activities in and against Nicaragua (Nicaragua v United States of America)* [1986] ICJ Rep 14, para 228 and see para 191 ("*Nicaragua*"). See also Declaration on Principles of International Law concerning Friendly Relations and Co-operation among States in accordance with the Charter of the United Nations, UNGA Res 2625 (XXV) (24 October 1970) UN Doc A/RES/2625(XXV), principle 1, para 9.

190 *Nicaragua* (n 189) para 247.

191 ibid para 228.

192 "[A]cts constituting a breach of the customary principle of non-intervention will also, if they directly or indirectly involve the use of force, constitute a breach of the principle of non-use of force in international relations." ibid para 209 and see also para 247. UN Charter (n 185) art 2(4).

193 Krüger (n 2) 110. *Nicaragua* (n 189), para 205.

2.1.6 Nagorno-Karabakh's Independence

There are certain factors that need to be mentioned with respect to Nagorno-Karabakh's fulfilment of the criterion of independence in the period before the outbreak of the 2020 war. Firstly, the presumption that an entity lacks independence in the case of illegality in its origins seems to have been applicable here.[194] Similarly, the presumption against the fulfilment of the criterion of independence of entities under belligerent occupation seems to have been relevant in this context too.[195] Furthermore, Nagorno-Karabakh's claim of independent statehood could also be seen as compromised, since the original motivation of the movement was a wish to be joined with the Armenian SSR. Armenia's influence over Nagorno-Karabakh could be inferred from the UNSC resolutions, which urged the Armenian government to "continue to exert its influence to achieve compliance by the Armenians of the *Nagorno-Karabakh region of the Azerbaijani Republic*" with its resolutions and the Minsk Group proposals.[196] In *Chiragov*, the ECtHR established that

> the Republic of Armenia, from the early days of the Nagorno-Karabakh conflict, has had a significant and decisive influence over the 'NKR', that the two entities are highly integrated in virtually all important matters and that this situation persists to this day. In other words, the "NKR" and its administration survives by virtue of the military, political, financial and other support given to it by Armenia which, consequently, exercises effective control over Nagorno-Karabakh and the surrounding territories.[197]

Thus, taking these factors into account together with a factual overview demonstrating Nagorno-Karabakh's dependence on Armenia, Nagorno-Karabakh could not be considered as fulfilling the criterion of independence under international law conditions of statehood in the relevant period.[198]

---

194 J Crawford, *The Creation of States in International Law* (2nd edn, Clarendon Press 2006) 74, 80, 89.

195 ibid 74–76, 80, 89. Popjanevski (n 3) 29.

196 UNSC Res 853 (29 July 1993) UN Doc S/RES/853, para 9 (*emphasis added*). Similarly, UNSC Res 884 (12 November 1993) UN Doc S/RES/884, para 2.

197 *Chiragov* (n 27) para 186.

198 Popjanevski (n 3) 32; Krüger (n 2) 88; J Socher, *Russia and the Right to Self-Determination in the Post-Soviet Space* (OUP 2021) 111.

2.1.7 Legal Status of Nagorno-Karabakh

It follows that Armenia's illegal intervention was instrumental to Nagorno-Karabakh's victory over Azerbaijan's forces in the war in early 1990s. In fact, the first clearly documented case of Armenia's direct intervention took place as a response to Azerbaijan's offensive of June 1992, to avoid Azerbaijan's recapture of the region.[199] "Its focus was the success of the Armenian secession movement itself … [t]hat is why the situation must be considered as the war to finalize illegal secession."[200] Without Armenia's support, "[t]he region would therefore scarcely have been in a position to withstand a full-blown war of secession, force back the official Azerbaijani forces and establish an entity that exists to this day."[201] Thus, not only did Nagorno-Karabakh not fulfil the criterion of independence,[202] but its formation was also unlawful.[203] Therefore, based on the framework established in Part 1, Chapter 2 it was precluded from becoming a State and remained a *de iure* part of Azerbaijan.

PACE in this context reaffirmed that secession cannot take place "in the wake of an armed conflict leading to ethnic expulsion and the de facto annexation of such to another state".[204] In addition, according to the PACE Report, Nagorno-Karabakh was "not considered lawful".[205]

Since Nagorno-Karabakh remained *de iure* part of Azerbaijan, but at the same time *prima facie* exercised effective territorial control of Azerbaijan's territory, lacked independence vis-à-vis Armenia, persisted in claiming to be a State and was created due to violation of peremptory norms, in the period before the start of the 2020 war it could be characterised as an illegal secessionist entity.[206]

---

199 Krüger (n 2) 109.

200 ibid.

201 ibid 93.

202 Popjanevski argues that it does not fulfil any of the traditional constitutive criteria of statehood. Popjanevski (n 3) 28–32 and 40.

203 "Thus, if Armenia provides military assistance to the separatist authorities in Stepanakert, amounting to occupation of the region, the Stimson Doctrine should apply and the international community is obliged to refrain from recognition of the region's independence." Popjanevski (n 3) 32 and 40.

204 CoE (PACE) Res 1416 (25 January 2005), para 2.

205 CoE (PACE), 'Report of the Committee on Social Affairs, Health and Sustainable Development: Inhabitants of Frontier Regions of Azerbaijan Are Deliberately Deprived of Water' (12 December 2015) Doc 13931, para 41.

206 See *supra* Part 1, Chapter 6.

2.2 *Period After the Outbreak of the 2020 War*

As mentioned above, following the end of hostilities and the ceasefire agreement in November 2020, only part of Nagorno-Karabakh remained under separatist control. Armenia returned seven surrounding districts to Azerbaijan. Since these lands were *de iure* part of Azerbaijan's territory, there was no change in title, only change of control.[207] Pre-independence Soviet maps were used to facilitate the return of districts and the deployment of peacekeepers.[208] This seems to confirm the relevance of *uti possidetis iuris* to the determination of Armenia-Azerbaijan's boundaries.[209] The question can be asked whether any factual and legal developments since the outbreak of hostilities in 2020 impacted Nagorno-Karabakh's claim to statehood in the intervening period. The answer to this question must be negative for the following reasons.

Nagorno-Karabakh's dependence on Armenia for its security and defense was laid bare.[210] In fact, the conflict itself was seen as an international conflict between Armenia and Azerbaijan.[211] This entailed the fighting between the regular armies of Armenia and Azerbaijan and arguably Armenia's overall control over the armed groups of Nagorno-Karabakh. Moreover, Armenia's prime minister and not the separatists signed the ceasefire agreement.[212] As such, without Armenia's defense and military support, Nagorno-Karabakh would not have survived even in its circumscribed territory. Armenia's use of force in support of separatists in 2020 could thus be seen as the continuation of a violation of peremptory norms instrumental to Nagorno-Karabakh's existence and preservation. Thus, the unlawful origins of the entity and Armenia's

---

207 Miklasová (n 66).

208 Miklasová (n 66); Kuznets (n 72).

209 See in detail J Miklasová, 'Dissolution of the Soviet Union Thirty Years On: Re-Appraisal of the Relevance of the Principle of Uti Possidetis Iuris' in JE Viñuales, A Clapham, L Boisson de Chazournes and M Hébié (eds), *The International Legal Order in the XXIst Century / L'ordre juridique international au XXIeme siècle / El órden jurídico internacional en el siglo XXI: Essays in Honour of Professor Marcelo Gustavo Kohen / Ecrits en l'honneur du Professeur Marcelo Gustavo Kohen / Estudios en honor del Profesor Marcelo Gustavo Kohen* (Brill 2023).

210 Miklasová (n 66).

211 See for example M O'Brien, 'Nagorno-Karabakh Conflict: Shortage of Specifics Complicates Search for Solutions' (*Just Security*, 21 October 2020) <https://www.justsecurity.org/72974/nagorno-karabakh-conflict-shortage-of-specifics-complicates-search-for-solutions/> accessed 5 December 2020.

212 Miklasová (n 66); B Knoll-Tudor and D Mueller, 'At Daggers Drawn: International Legal Issues Surrounding the Conflict in and around Nagorno-Karabakh' (*EJIL:Talk!*, 17 November 2020) <https://www.ejiltalk.org/at-daggers-drawn-international-legal-issues-surrounding-the-conflict-in-and-around-nagorno-karabakh/> accessed 5 December 2020.

use of force critical to its *de facto* existence supported the characterization of Nagorno-Karabakh as an illegal secessionist entity in the wake of the 2020 War. It remained a *de iure* part of Azerbaijan's territory.

2.3 *Territorial Status Following Azerbaijan's Taking Control of Nagorno-Karabakh in 2023*

Following Azerbaijan's military operation between 19–20 September 2023, the defeat of the separatist 'army' and the conclusion of the ceasefire agreement between the Azerbaijani central authorities and the representatives of local Karabakh Armenians, Azerbaijan retook control of the secessionist entity, which was outside of its control since the war of 1992–1994. As shown above, Nagorno-Karabakh was never a State under international law, and therefore, Azerbaijan's military recapture of Nagorno-Karabakh did not involve the transfer of sovereignty. The latter remained vested with Azerbaijan ever since the dissolution of the Soviet Union in 1991. The announced dissolution of the self-proclaimed structures of this secessionist entity until 1 January 2024 will thus be a final step in the restoration of Azerbaijan's territorial integrity.[213]

Even though the legality of Azerbaijan's use of force to retake Nagorno-Karabakh is contested,[214] this question does not have an impact on the

213 Restoration of Azerbaijan's territorial integrity, however, does not settle many outstanding legal issues related to this conflict, in particular, those related to the status and property of the residents of Nagorno-Karabakh under IHL and IHRL. See *infra* Chapter 16 and 10 and supra Chapter 7.

214 Notably, the question first arose in relation to the 2020 conflict in Nagorno-Karabakh. The doctrine has reached completely opposed conclusions. On the one hand, Ruys and Rodríguez Silvestre argue that "the right of self-defence ceases to apply when a new territorial status quo is established, whereby the occupying state peacefully administers the territory concerned for a prolonged period." T Ruys and F Rodríguez Silvestre, 'Illegal: The Recourse to Force to Recover Occupied Territory and the Second Karabakh War' (2021) 32 EJIL 1287, 1289; T Ruys and F Rodríguez Silvestre, 'Military Action to Recover Occupied Land: Lawful Self-Defence or Prohibited Use of Force? The 2020 Nagorno-Karabakh Conflict' (2021) 97 Int L Studies 665; T Ruys and F Rodríguez Silvestre, 'The Nagorno-Karabakh Conflict and the Exercise of "Self-Defense" to Recover Occupied Land' (*Just Security*, 10 November 2020) <https://www.justsecurity.org/73310/the-nagorno-karabakh-conflict-and-the-exercise-of-self-defense-to-recover-occupied-land/> accessed 5 December 2020; In a similar direction, see VS Mariottini De Oliveira, 'On Ceasefire Agreements and (Counter)Offensives: Notes on the Armenia-Azerbaijan Conflict and a Word of Caution for Ukraine' (*Völkerrechtsblog*, 23 September 2023) <https://voelkerrechtsblog.org/on-ceasefire-agreements-and-counteroffensives/> accessed 31 October 2023. On the other hand, Akande and Tzanakopoulos argue that "in certain circumstances, it is legal for a state to use force in order to recover territory unlawfully occupied by another state as a result of an armed attack." D Akande and A Tzanakopoulos, 'Legal: Use of Force in Self-Defefence to Recover Occupied Territory' (2021) 32 EJIL 1299;

issue of the status of this territory as part of Azerbaijan. Nevertheless, it may have amounted to a separate wrongful act.[215] However, it is questionable to what extent the *jus ad bellum* framework applied to the context of the 2023 Azerbaijan's military operation at all, as Armenia did not intervene in the fighting directly, and it is doubtful that it exercised the relevant level of control over the Nagorno-Karabakh troops.[216]

D Akande and A Tzanakopoulos, 'Use of Force in Self-Defence to Recover Occupied Territory: When Is It Permissible?' (*EJIL:Talk!*, 18 November 2020) <https://www.ejiltalk.org/use-of-force-in-self-defence-to-recover-occupied-territory-when-is-it-permissible/> accessed 5 December 2020. In a similar direction, 'Le conflit au Haut-Karabakh et le droit international' (*Centre de droit international, Université Libre de Bruxelles*, 14 October 2020) <http://cdi.ulb.ac.be/conflit-haut-karabakh-droit-international-douze-questions/> accessed 5 December 2020. MN Schmitt and KS Coble, 'The Evolving Nagorno-Karabakh Conflict – An International Law Perspective – Part II' (*Articles of War*, 29 September 2023) <https://lieber.westpoint.edu/evolving-nagorno-karabakh-conflict-international-law-perspective-part-ii/> accessed 31 October 2023. See further in detail on this question *supra* Chapter 13.

215 Notably, the States have condemned Azerbaijan's use of force but did not expressly consider it unlawful under the UN Charter. See 'Latest Clash between Armenia, Azerbaijan Undermines Prospects of Peace, Speakers Warn Security Council, Calling for Genuine Dialogue to Settle Outstanding Issues' (*UN News*, 21 September 2023) <https://press.un.org/en/2023/sc15418.doc.htm> accessed 31 October 2023. PACE stated that it "strongly condemns the military operation launched by the Azerbaijani army in Nagorno-Karabakh on 19 September 2023. The Assembly recognises the territorial integrity of Azerbaijan. It underlines that this entails the responsibility of this country for the actions it takes within its internationally recognised borders." CoE (PACE) Res 2517 (12 October 2023) para 1. Armenia referred to "the large-scale military aggression of Azerbaijan against the peaceful population of Nagorno-Karabakh." 'Letter Dated 19 September 2023 from the Permanent Representative of Armenia to the United Nations Addressed to the President of the Security Council' (19 September 2023) UN Doc S/2023/687.

216 If this factual assessment was correct, Schmitt and Coble claim that "Azerbaijan would be engaged in a lawful law enforcement operation subject to its domestic law, international human rights law, and (perhaps) the law of non-international armed conflict, but not the *jus ad bellum*." Schmitt and Coble *supra* (n 214). However, Dörr and Randelzhofer highlight that the prohibition under Article 2(4) UN Charter also protects and binds "a stabilized de facto regime." O Dörr and A Randelzhofer, 'Article 2(4)' in B Simma and others (eds), *The Charter of the United Nations: A Commentary*, Volume I (3rd edn, OUP 2012) para 32. See *infra* Chapter 16. Notably, Azerbaijan used contradictory positions, defining its actions as "counter-terror measures" taking place within its sovereign territory and considering it "aligned with the sovereign right of Azerbaijan to self-defense enshrined in the UN Charter." 'Statement by Azerbaijani Foreign Minister at the UN Security Council Meeting' (*Apa*, 22 September 2023) <https://apa.az/en/foreign-policy/statement-by-azerbaijani-foreign-minister-at-the-un-security-council-meeting-full-text-412439> accessed 31 October 2023.

CHAPTER 15

Transnistria

A detailed legal analysis of the secessionist attempt aimed at determining Transnistria's legal status has been done elsewhere.[1] The following account will therefore briefly highlight the key elements of that analysis.

As in the case of Nagorno-Karabakh, Transnistria's secessionist attempt preceded the Soviet Union's dissolution. Transnistria declared independence from the Moldovan Soviet Socialist Republic (MSSR) on 2 September 1990 as a Soviet republic within the USSR,[2] and on 25 August 1991, it declared itself an independent State.[3] Referenda held in Transnistria in December 1991 and later in 2006 produced votes overwhelmingly in favour of independence.[4] The declaration of independence was followed by infighting and open conflict in 1992, which was terminated by the secessionist victory and the establishment of *de facto* independence.

As opposed to other secessionist cases in this section, Transnistria did not possess any autonomous or specific administrative-territorial status under Soviet law; the MSSR was a unitary republic.[5] Thus, no right to secession applied to Transnistria under Soviet constitutional law; it was only reserved for Union Republics.[6] Moreover, it is true that under Article 3(2) of the Law on Secession from the USSR, secession referendum results in localities with concentrations of ethnic groups constituting a majority there were to be recorded and considered separately.[7] However, the holding of a referendum and its separate record

---

1 J Miklasová, 'Secession in Contemporary International Law: The Case of Transnistria' (Master Thesis, Graduate Institute of International and Development Studies 2014). See also J Miklasová, 'Status of Transnistria Under International Law' in K Gray (ed) *Global Encyclopedia of Territorial Rights* (Springer 2022).

2 Miklasová, 'Secession' (n 1) 17.

3 'Declaration of Independence of Transnistrian Moldovan SSR' (25 August 1991) <https://ru.wikisource.org/wiki/Декларация_о_независимости_Приднестровской_Молдавской_ССР> accessed 8 October 2023 (*in Russian*). ibid. See in detail for the historical background and evolution of the conflict Miklasová, 'Status' (n 1) 1–5.

4 Miklasová, 'Secession' (n 1) 19, ftn 115.

5 ibid 36–38.

6 ibid. Miklasová, 'Status' (n 1) 5.

7 "In a Union republic on whose territory there are places densely populated by ethnic groups constituting a majority of the population of the locality in question, the results of the voting in these localities are recorded separately when the results of the referendum are being determined." Law on Procedure for Resolving Questions Connected with a Union Republic's Secession from the USSR (adopted 3 April 1990) art 3(2)

and consideration was related to the secession of the Union republic.[8] Since Moldova never seceded from the USSR under the conditions of this law, no auxiliary right to secede could have accrued for Transnistria.[9]

Furthermore, even though in its preamble Moldova's declaration of independence of 27 August 1991 referred to the fact that the Soviet Law of 2 August 1940 on the Creation of the MSSR[10] was without legal basis, this proclamation cannot be taken as producing legal effects of alteration of the MSSR's boundaries.[11] In particular, Moldova's declaration only operated with respect to its own internal legal order, and in any case, it could not be interpreted as an intentional renunciation of Transnistria or as consent to the dissolution of the MSSR.[12] On an international plane, Moldova's status did not raise any problems.

Upon the USSR's break-up, the Republic of Moldova emerged as a new State, a successor to the Soviet Union.[13] By virtue of the principle of *uti possidetis*, the MSSR's former administrative boundaries were transformed into new international frontiers.[14] Former Soviet Union republics declared respect for existing borders and territorial integrity in documents pertaining to the dissolution of the USSR and the creation of the CIS.[15] In addition, the Heads of State of the CIS adopted decisions specifically on the conflict in Transnistria, in which they

<http://soviethistory.msu.edu/1991-2/shevarnadze-resigns/shevarnadze-resigns-texts/law-on-secession-from-the-ussr/> accessed 9 May 2019 ("Law on Secession from the USSR").

8 Miklasová, 'Secession' (n 1) 38–39. Miklasová, 'Status' (n 1) 5.

9 Miklasová, 'Secession' (n 1) 38–39. Miklasová, 'Status' (n 1) 5.

10 This law merged into a new Soviet Republic the territory of Bessarabia, previously recaptured by Stalin from Romania, and districts today forming Transnistria, which were up until that point part of the Moldovan Autonomous Soviet Socialistic Republic – an autonomous unit within the Ukrainian SSR. Miklasová, 'Secession' (n 1) 13.

11 'Law on the Declaration of Independence of the Republic of Moldova No 691' (27 August 1991) ("Declaration of Independence") <http://lex.justice.md/index.php?action=view&view=doc&lang=2&id=313228> accessed 9 June 2019 (*in Russian*). See also Supreme Soviet of the Moldovan SSR 'Resolution on the Conclusions of the Commission of the Supreme Soviet of the Moldovan SSR on the Political and Legal Assessment of the Soviet-German Non-Aggression Pact and its Additional Secret Protocol of 23 August 1939 and their Consequences for Bessarabia and Northern Bukovina No 149' (23 June 1990) <http://lex.justice.md/index.php?action=view&view=doc&lang=2&id=308129> accessed 9 June 2019 (*in Russian*). Miklasová, 'Secession' (n 1) 29–31. Miklasová, 'Status' (n 1) 6.

12 In particular, the declaration itself referred to Transnistria as an "integral part of the historical and ethnic territory of our nation." See Moldova's Declaration of Independence. See Miklasová, 'Secession' (n 1) 29–31. Miklasová, 'Status' (n 1) 6.

13 See Miklasová, 'Secession' (n 1) 41–43; Miklasová, 'Status' (n 1) 5–6.

14 See Miklasová, 'Secession' (n 1) 46–47; Miklasová, 'Status' (n 1) 5–6.

15 See *supra*, for example, Chapter 14 on Nagorno-Karabakh. See Miklasová, 'Secession' (n 1) 45–47; Miklasová, 'Status' (n 1) 5–6.

considered “the preservation of territorial integrity of the Republic of Moldova a cornerstone of its policy in relations with this State”.[16] Moreover, even before the dissolution of the USSR, Ukraine specifically declared the former border with the MSSR its new international border.[17] This was later confirmed in the Border Treaty between Moldova and Ukraine.[18] Friendship treaties between Moldova and Ukraine and Moldova and Russia declared their parties’ adherence *inter alia* to the principle of inviolability of borders and territorial integrity.[19] Recently, the UNGA upheld Moldova’s territorial integrity.[20] The OSCE[21] and other international organisations adopted resolutions supporting Moldova’s territorial integrity.[22]

---

16 ‘Statement of the Heads of State – Members of the Commonwealth of Independent States on the Situation in the Left-Bank Region of Moldova’ (20 March 1992) <http://lawrussia.ru/texts/legal_185/doc185a655x748.htm> accessed 8 June 2019 (*in Russian*). See Miklasová, ‘Secession’ (n 1) 49.

17 “…[The] border between the Soviet Socialist Republic of Ukraine … and the Republic of Moldova as of 16 July 1990 constitutes international border of Ukraine.” ‘Law on Succession of Ukraine’ (adopted 12 September 1991, entered into force 5 October 1991) No 1543-XII, art 5 <https://zakon2.rada.gov.ua/laws/show/1543-12> accessed 8 June 2019 (*in Ukrainian*). See Miklasová, ‘Secession’ (n 1) 46–47.

18 Treaty between Ukraine and the Republic of Moldova on State Border (signed 18 August 1999, entered into force 18 November 2001) <https://zakon4.rada.gov.ua/laws/show/498_046> accessed 9 June 2019 (*in Ukrainian*).

19 Treaty of Neighbourhood, Friendship and Cooperation between Ukraine and Moldova (signed 23 October 1992; entered into force 5 January 1997), art 1 <https://zakon4.rada.gov.ua/laws/show/498_161> accessed 8 June 2019 (*in Ukrainian*); Treaty of Friendship and Cooperation between the Russian Federation and the Republic of Moldova (signed 19 November 2001, entered into force 13 May2002), art 1 <http://kremlin.ru/supplement/3400> accessed 8 June 2019 (*in Russian*). Miklasová, ‘Secession’ (n 1) 46–47.

20 According to the UNGA “the stationing of foreign military forces on the territory of the Republic of Moldova, without its consent, violates its sovereignty and territorial integrity.” UNGA Res 72/282 (22 June 2018) UN Doc A/RES/72/282, preambular para 6. Foreign military troops are stationed in Transnistria.

21 For example, OSCE (PA), ‘Luxembourg Declaration’ (adopted 8 July 2019), paras 12 and 22; OSCE (PA), ‘Minsk Declaration’ (9 July 2017), para 46; OSCE (PA), ‘Tbilisi Declaration’ (1 July 2016), para 54; OSCE (PA), ‘Resolution on Moldova’ (1 July 2016), para 9; OSCE (PA), ‘Resolution on the Continuation of Clear, Gross and Uncorrected Violations of OSCE Commitments and International Norms by the Russian Federation’ (8 July 2015), paras 39–40; OSCE (PA), ‘Resolution on Moldova’ (3 July 2012), para 11. For earlier OSCE documents supporting Moldova’s territorial integrity, see Miklasová, ‘Secession’ (n 1) 49–50, ftn 323–327.

22 CoE (PACE) Res 1572 (2 October 2007), para 15; European Parliament, ‘Resolution on Russian Pressure on Eastern Partnership Countries and in Particular Destabilisation of Eastern Ukraine’ (adopted 17 April 2014) PT_TA(2014)0457, para 33; European Parliament, ‘Resolution on Human Rights Violations in the Republic of Moldova’ (adopted 12 July 2007) P6_TA(2007)0358, para 6; European Parliament, ‘Resolution on Situation in

In any case, even if at first sight the process of the incorporations of Bessarabia and the Baltic States into the USSR could be seen as factually similar and therefore justifying invalidation of the creation of the MSSR, to which Moldova's declaration of independence alluded, there are in fact substantial legal differences. While the Baltic States were annexed to the Soviet Union in 1940 as independent States, Bessarabia was not an independent State during the inter-War period, but it was arguably occupied by Romania and then re-incorporated into the USSR as a result of the Soviet Union's threat of force.[23] Ultimately, in the 1947 Peace Treaty, Romania unequivocally recognised the Soviet Union's right to territorial sovereignty over Bessarabia.[24] Any return to *status quo ante* would thus require a challenge to this treaty, which has never taken place.[25]

Moreover, Transnistria's population is not ethnically homogeneous, but consists of portions of Russians, Ukrainians and Romanians, therefore questions can be raised with their characterization as peoples entitled to self-determination, even under the so-called objective criterion of ethnicity singled out by the part of the doctrine.[26] In any case, as follows from Part 1, Chapter 3

---

the Republic of Moldova' (adopted 7 May 2009) P6_TA(2009)0384, para 27; European Parliament, 'Resolution on Moldova (Transnistria)' (adopted 26 October 2006) P6_TA(2006)0455, paras 1–4; European Parliament, 'Resolution on Right to Education in the Transnistrian Region' (adopted 6 February 2014) P7_TA(2014)0108, para 9. NATO, 'Joint Press Point with NATO Secretary General Jens Stoltenberg and the Prime Minister of the Republic of Moldova, Pavel Filip' (*NATO Newsroom*, 29 November 2017) <https://www.nato.int/cps/en/natohq/opinions_149080.htm> accessed 12 June 2019. The OSCE Parliamentary Assembly supports the settlement process "based on the sovereignty and territorial integrity of the Republic of Moldova within its internationally recognized borders, with a special status for Transdniestria." OSCE (PA), 'Birmingham Declaration' (6 July 2022) para 27.

23 Miklasová, 'Secession' (n 1) 22–27. Miklasová, 'Status' (n 1) 6.

24 Miklasová, 'Secession' (n 1) 27–29. Treaty of Peace between Allied and Associated Powers and Romania (signed 10 February 1947, entered into force 15 September 1947) 42 UNTS 3, art 1. Miklasová, 'Status' (n 1) 6.

25 Miklasová, 'Secession' (n 1) 29–30. Miklasová, 'Status' (n 1) 6.

26 In 1989, the population of Transnistria was 39.3% Moldovans, 28.3% Ukrainians and 25.5% Russians. Miklasová, 'Secession' (n 1) 15, ftn 79. For the argument that the distinct character of the population of Transnistria qualifies it as 'peoples' entitled to self-determination through autonomy or a special status within Moldova, but not to external self-determination, see B Bowring, 'The Unexpected After-Life of the 'Soviet People'? The 'Pridnestraovskaya Moldavskaya Republika' as Political Fact and Legal Anomaly A Case Study' (2012), 9–12 <https://papers.ssrn.com/sol3/papers.cfm?abstract_id=1981954&download=yes> accessed 12 June 2019; B Bowring, 'Transnistria' in C Walter, A Von Ungern-Sternberg and K Abushov (eds), *Self-determination and Secession in International Law* (OUP 2014) 170–173. Miklasová, 'Status' (n 1) 5.

the right of self-determination does not entail the right to independence, and a unilaterally expressed will of a population in an unofficial referendum does translate into the right to independence for that section of the population.[27]

In addition, the claims of oppression and discrimination that would justify remedial secession could not have been substantiated either.[28] Historical research proves that during the Soviet period, Transnistria, as opposed to Bessarabia, was actually favoured by the Soviet centre.[29] It is true that violence and then open war took place between separatists and Kishinev, but only as a response to Transnistria's declaration of independence.[30] In any case, it follows from Part 1, Chapter 3 that the doctrine of remedial secession is not a part of positive international law.[31]

Crucially, the presence of the former 14th Army of the military district of Odessa of the Ministry of Defence of the USSR ("14th Army") in Transnistria, with large stockpiles of weapons and ammunition, played a key role in the secessionist victory in the war.[32] In particular, separatists stole or were given arms and ammunition from the former Soviet army.[33] In addition, in the key battle of Bender of June 1992, Russian soldiers stationed in Transnistria directly intervened and changed the course of the war in favour of separatists.[34] By that time, the Russian Federation had already placed former Soviet troops there under its jurisdiction and *de facto* control,[35] therefore their actions, which can be characterised as direct and indirect violations of the prohibition of the use of

---

27 See *supra* Part 1, Chapter 3.

28 Miklasová, 'Secession' (n 1) 55–56. Miklasová, 'Status' (n 1) 5.

29 See Miklasová, 'Secession' (n 1) 14–15. See C King, *The Moldovans: Romania, Russia, and the Politics of Culture* (Hoover Institution Press 2000) 183–184.

30 Miklasová, 'Secession' (n 1) 55–56.

31 See *supra*, Part 1, Chapter 3.

32 Miklasová, 'Secession' (n 1) 18; *Ilaşcu and others v Moldova and Russia* ECHR 2004-VII 1, para 32 ("*Ilaşcu*"). Miklasová, 'Status' (n 1) 7–8.

33 Miklasová, 'Secession' (n 1) 18. Miklasová, 'Status' (n 1) 7–8.

34 Miklasová, 'Secession' (n 1) . Miklasová, 'Status' (n 1) 7–8. Generally, the ECtHR held that "during the Moldovan conflict in 1991–1992 forces of the 14th Army ... stationed in Transdniestria, an integral part fo the territory of the Republic of Moldova, fought with and on behalf of the Transdniestrian separatist forces." *Ilaşcu* (n 32) para 380.

35 Miklasová, 'Secession' (n 1) 62–65. Miklasová, 'Status' (n 1) 7–8. 'Executive Order of the President of the Russian Federation No 320 on the Transfer of Military Units of the Armed Forces of the Former USSR Stationed on the Territory of the Republic of Moldova under the Jurisdiction of the Russian Federation' (adopted 1 April 1992) <http://kremlin.ru/acts/bank/1114> accessed 8 June 2019 (*in Russian*). See also H Hamant, *Démembrement de l'URSS et problèmes de succession d'états* (Bruylant, 2007) 379.

force, Moldova's territorial integrity and the prohibition of non-intervention,[36] were attributable to Russia by virtue of Article 4 ARSIWA.[37] The ceasefire was signed by the Russian and Moldovan presidents on 21 July 1992 and foresaw the establishment of a trilateral peacekeeping force subject to the tripartite Joint Control Commission.[38]

In the following period, Transnistria consolidated *de facto* independence with formal signs of statehood, but its survival has depended on Russia. Russia has maintained its troops, weapons and stockpiles of ammunition there despite persistent opposition from Moldova[39] and in violation of its own international commitments.[40] The troop presence has substantially decreased, currently amounting to 1.500 to 2.000 soldiers.[41] In 2018, the UNGA dealt with Russia's military presence in Transnistria for the first time and expressed deep

---

36 Miklasová, 'Secession' (n 1) 65–72. Miklasová, 'Status' (n 1) 7–8. The UNGA also recognised that "the stationing of foreign military forces on the territory of the Republic of Moldova, without its consent, violates its sovereignty and territorial integrity." UNGA Res 72/282 (22 June 2018) UN Doc A/RES/72/282, preambular para 6.

37 Miklasová, 'Secession' (n 1) 64–65. Miklasová, 'Status' (n 1) 7–8.

38 Agreement on Principles of a Peaceful Settlement of the Armed Conflict in the Transdniestrian Region of the Republic of Moldova (singed 21 July 1992, entered into force 21 July 1992) <https://peacemaker.un.org/moldova-peacefullsettlementdniestr92> accessed 8 October 2023. Miklasová, 'Secession' (n 1) 18. These troops, however, must be distinguished from the Operational Group of Russian Forces, which is stationed in Transnistria without Moldova's consent. The UNGA stressed "that the Operational Group of Russian Forces is not a part of the military component of the Joint Control Commission established under the 1992 ceasefire agreement, which also includes a rotating Russian contingent, and, as such, has not been entrusted with any peacekeeping or other legal mandate." UNGA Res 72/282 (22 June 2018) UN Doc A/RES/72/282, preambular para 12 (*footnotes omitted*).

39 See Parliament of the Republic of Moldova 'Resolution No 173 on Adoption of Declaration of the Parliament of the Republic of Moldova on Withdrawal of the Russian Armed Forces from its Territory' (adopted 21 July 2017) <http://lex.justice.md/viewdoc.php?action=view&view=doc&id=372283&lang=2> accessed 12 June 2019 (*in Russian*); A Tanas, 'Moldova Calls on Russia to Withdraw Troops from Breakaway Region' (*Reuters*, 21 July 2017) <https://www.reuters.com/article/us-moldova-russia-military/moldova-calls-on-russia-to-withdraw-troops-from-breakaway-region-idUSKBN1A61R0> accessed 12 June 2019; Miklasová, 'Secession' (n 1) 19–20.

40 During the 1999 OSCE Istanbul Summit, Russia committed itself to withdrawing its troops and ammunition from Moldova by 2002. See OSCE (Summit of Heads of State or Government), 'Istanbul Summit Declaration' (19 November 1999), 49–50, para 19.

41 M Nescutu, 'Russia Dismisses Compensating Moldova for "Occupying" Transnistria' (*BalkanInsight*, 24 January 2018) <https://balkaninsight.com/2018/01/24/russia-slams-moldova-s-demand-for-compensations-in-transnistria-01-24-2018/> accessed 12 June 2019. In 1995, the former 14th Army was downgraded to the Operational Group of Russian Forces (OGRF). Miklasová, 'Secession' (n 1) 19, ftn 113. Miklasová, 'Status' (n 1) 4.

concern “about the continued stationing of the Operational Group of Russian Forces and its armaments on the territory of the Republic of Moldova without the consent of that State Member of the United Nations” and urged the Russian Federation “to complete, unconditionally and without further delay, the orderly withdrawal of the Operational Group of Russian Forces and its armaments from the territory of the Republic of Moldova”.[42] Other international organisations have also called on Russia to withdraw its troops from Transnistria.[43] The on-going Russian military presence in Transnistria without Moldova’s consent is a continuous violation of the prohibition of the use of force.[44]

In addition, Russia supports Transnistria militarily, politically and economically.[45] It is estimated that Russia’s cost for supporting Transnistria, including free gas delivered through Gazprom, “over the last few years has reached an annual amount of almost one billion US dollars”.[46] However, several developments in late 2010s have had an impact on the economic situation there, including a reported reduction of Russia’s economic support for Transnistria

---

42 UNGA Res 72/282 (22 June 2018) UN Doc A/RES/72/282, para 1 and 2.

43 For example, CoE (PACE) Res 1896 (2 October 2012), para 25.34; CoE (PACE) Res 1955 (2 October 2013), para 27; OSCE (PA), ‘Luxembourg Declaration’ (8 July 2019), para 13; OSCE (PA), ‘Minsk Declaration’ (adopted 9 July 2017), para 46; OSCE (PA), ‘Tbilisi Declaration’ (1 July 2016), para 54; OSCE (PA), ‘Resolution on Moldova’ (1 July 2016), para 12; OSCE (PA), ‘Berlin Declaration’ (10 July 2018), para 40; OSCE (PA), ‘Berlin Declaration’ (adopted 10 July 2018), para 42; OSCE (PA), ‘Resolution on Moldova’ (3 July 2012), para 21; European Parliament, ‘Resolution on Human Rights Violations in the Republic of Moldova’ (adopted 12 July 2007) P6_TA(2007)0358, para 10; European Parliament, ‘Resolution on Human Rights Violations in Moldova and in Transnistria in Particular’ (adopted 16 March 2006) P6_TA(2006)0099, para 14; European Parliament, ‘Resolution on Right to Education in the Transnistrian Region’ (adopted 6 February 2014) P7_TA(2014)0108, para 14.

44 See also Definition of Aggression, UNGA Res 3314 (XXIX) (14 December 1974) UN Doc A/RES/3314(XXIX), art 3(a). However, according to Nolte and Randelzhofer, the concept of permanent occupation “is not applicable to the notion of ‘armed attack’” as it does not “necessarily involve the use of military force.” G Nolte and A Randelzhofer, ‘Article 51’ in B Simma and others (eds), *The Charter of the United Nations: A Commentary*, Volume II (3rd edn, OUP 2012), para 23. For the discussion concerning the extension of the regime of prohibition of the use of force under Article 2(4) UN Charter to ‘stabilized de facto regimes’ see *supra* Chapter 13.

45 Miklasová, ‘Secession’ (n 1) 20.

46 K Całus, ‘The Transnistrian Gambit’ (*Neweasterneurope*, 21 December 2017) available <http://neweasterneurope.eu/2017/12/21/the-transnistrian-gambit/> accessed 12 June 2019.

due to Western sanctions and increased expenses in other areas;[47] Ukraine's tighter control of the Moldova-Ukrainian border, aiming to curb smuggling through a *de facto* Transnistria's border;[48] and an extension to Transnistria of tariff-free access to the EU under the Deep and Comprehensive Free Trade Agreement between Moldova and the EU (DCFTA).[49] While direct and indirect funding from Russia is crucial for Transnistria's economic survival, two-thirds of 'real' exports, excluding those to Moldova, go to the EU, while only 16% go to the countries of the Eurasian Customs Union.[50] Despite these developments, Transnistria is dependent on Russia for its survival and therefore cannot be considered as fulfilling the criterion of independence for the purposes of statehood.[51] While the mid-2010s witnessed certain political momentum resulting in the signing of agreements between Moldova and separatists and the renewal of negotiations under the OSCE 5+2 format,[52] the all-out Russian aggression against Ukraine has destabilised the economic and political situation in the

47 ibid; T De Waal, 'An Eastern European Conflict the EU Got Right' (*Politico*, 16 February 2016) <https://www.politico.eu/article/transnistria-an-eastern-european-frozen-conflict-the-eu-got-right-moldova-russia-ukraine/> accessed 12 June 2019.

48 De Waal (n 47); R O'Connor, 'Transnistria Isn't the Smuggler's Paradise It Used to Be' (*Foreign Policy*, 5 June 2019) <https://foreignpolicy.com/2019/06/05/transnistria-isnt-the-smugglers-paradise-it-used-to-be-sheriff-moldova-ukraine-tiraspol/> accessed 12 June 2019. Ukraine also banned Russian military transports through its territory to Transnistria, which might cause supply problems for the Russian forces in Transnistria. K Büscher, 'The Transnistrian Conflict in Light of the Crisis over Ukraine' in S Fischer (ed), *Not Frozen! The Unresolved Conflicts over Transnistria, Abkhazia, South Ossetia and Nagorno-Karabakh in Light of the Crisis over Ukraine* (SWP 2016) 37.

49 Transnistria agreed to customs checks by Moldovan officials and registration in Moldova. R O'Connor, 'Transnistria Isn't the Smuggler's Paradise It Used to Be' (*Foreign Policy*, 5 June 2019) <https://foreignpolicy.com/2019/06/05/transnistria-isnt-the-smugglers-paradise-it-used-to-be-sheriff-moldova-ukraine-tiraspol/> accessed 12 June 2019. "Moscow has so far gone along with the deal because it knows its influence in Transnistria is largely unaffected." De Waal (n 47). The extension of DCFTA to Transnistria will be analysed in Section 4 in detail.

50 Büscher (n 48) 39–40.

51 Miklasová, 'Secession' (n 1) 76–80. Miklasová, 'Status' (n 1) 8. J Socher, *Russia and the Right to Self-Determination in the Post-Soviet Space* (OUP 2021) 119–120.

52 These agreements allowed Moldova to recognise diplomas from Transnistria's Shevchenko State University; improved the functioning of Moldova's schools; reinstalled direct communication services and allowed Moldovan farmers to get access to their lands under Transnistria's control. Całus (n 46). In 2018, the protocol decision was signed; vehicles in the Transnistrian region not performing commercial activities could be registered and get access to internationally recognised Moldovan neutral-design license plates to enable their participation in international road traffic. 'OSCE Mission to Moldova Welcomes Start of "Licence Plate" Agreement Implementation by the Sides' (*Press Release*, 1 September 2018) <https://www.osce.org/chairmanship/392231> accessed 12 June 2019.

region and impacted the conflict-settlement process.[53] "With two participants now openly at war with each other, the OSCE-facilitated 5+2 format … is now dysfunctional."[54] The process has mostly been limited to informal 1+1 talks.[55]

Most importantly, regarding the status determination of Transnistria, Russia's violation of the prohibition of the use of force was instrumental to a separatist victory, and its on-going illegal military presence, and other support, has been essential to its survival.[56] As follows from the analysis in Part 1, Chapter 2 a secessionist entity whose creation is connected to the violation of peremptory norms is precluded from becoming a State.[57] Therefore, Transnistria is not a State and remains *de iure* part of Moldova.[58] This is in line with ECtHR, which referred to Transnistria in its case law as an "illegal regime",[59] as an entity of an "unlawful nature"[60] and

53 See on the influx of Ukrainian refugees, the fragile economic and destabilization political situation after the beginning of the Russia-Ukraine War S Relitz and others, *Germany's Contributions to Civilian Conflict Management and Peacebuilding in the EU's Eastern Neighbourhood: Past Experience and Future Prospects* (Advisory Board to the Federal Government for Civilian Crisis Prevention and Peacebuilding 2023) 81.

54 N Douglas and S Wollf, 'Confidence Building in the Shadow of War: Moldova, Transdniestria and the Uncertain Future of the 5+2 Process' (2023) OSCE Insights 1, 3. Notably, the 5+2 process stalled before the Russian invasion of Ukraine, with the last official meeting taking place in 2019. ibid, 5.

55 ibid, 3. But, for example the 1+1 meeting in June 2023 was "attended by representatives of mediators and observers of the '5+2' format." 'Statement by the Special Representative of the OSCE Chairman-in-Office for the Transdniestrian Settlement Process' (*Press Release*, 21 June 2023) <https://www.osce.org/chairpersonship/546833> accessed 31 October 2023.

56 "[T]here was little Moldova could do to re-establish its authority over Transdniestrian territory. That was evidenced by the outcome of the military conflict, which showed that the Moldovan authorities did not have the means to gain the upper hand in Transdniestrian territory against the rebel forces supported by 14th Army personnel." *Ilașcu* (n 32) para 341. The 2022 Opinion of the Parliamentary Assembly of the Council of Europe refers to the Russian "act of military aggression against the Republic of Moldova." CoE (PACE) Opinion 300 (15 March 2022) para 5. Miklasová, 'Status' (n 1) 7–8.

57 See *supra* Part 1, Chapter 2.

58 Miklasová, 'Secession' (n 1) 75–76 and 82. Miklasová, 'Status' (n 1) 8.

59 "In the Court's opinion, all of the acts committed by Russian soldiers with regard to the applicants, including their transfer into the charge of the separatist regime, in the context of the Russian authorities' collaboration with that illegal regime, are capable of engaging responsibility for the acts of that regime." *Ilașcu* (n 32) para 385.

60 "Accordingly, it cannot automatically regard as unlawful, for the limited purposes of the Convention, the decisions taken by the courts of an unrecognised entity because of the latter's unlawful nature and the fact it is not internationally recognised." *Mozer v the Republic of Moldova and Russia* App no 11138/10 (ECtHR, 23 February 2016), para 142.

as a region "recognized *under public international law* as part of Moldova's territory".[61]

But since Transnistria *prima facie* exercises effective territorial control of Moldova's territory, lacks independence vis-à-vis Russia, persists in claiming to be a State and was created due to violation of peremptory norms, it can also be characterised as an illegal secessionist entity.[62]

61 *Turturica and Casian v the Republic of Moldova and Russia* Applications nos 28648/06 and 18832/07 (ECtHR, 30 August 2016), para 28 (*emphasis added*).

62 See *supra* Part 1, Chapter 6.

Conclusion to Section 3

This section provided an in-depth legal analysis of the secessionist attempts of Crimea, the DPR, the LPR, Kherson and Zaporizhzhia Regions, Abkhazia, South Ossetia, Nagorno-Karabakh and Transnistria. It concluded that none of these entities is or was a State under international law. All of these secessionist attempts, were in one way or another, connected to violations of the prohibition of the use of force, a peremptory norm of international law. In these cases, the third State's illegal intervention into secessionist conflict and unlawful use of force were instrumental to the purported victory of secessionists vis-à-vis the parent State.

Therefore, based on the legal framework established in Part 1, Chapter 2, they were precluded from becoming States. Abkhazia, South Ossetia, Transnistria, DPR and LPR (until September 2022), and Nagorno-Karabakh (until September 2023) can be characterised as illegal secessionist entities. They remain(ed) *de iure* a part of the parent State's territory; they exercise(ed) *prima facie* effective territorial control there; they lack(ed) independence vis-à-vis the third State; they persist(ed) in claiming to be States; and their existence is/was due to peremptory illegality. Crimea, Kherson and Zaporizhzhia Regions also bore the characteristics of illegal secessionist entities but their ostensible existence was only ephemeral. The notion of an illegal secessionist entity is nevertheless relevant to assessing the acts of annexation – purportedly inter-State treaties – and triggering the applicability of consequences of peremptory territorial illegality. Crimea, DPR, LPR, Kherson and Zaporizhzhia Regions are now illegally annexed to Russia. All five regions remain *de iure* part of Ukraine. The outlined practice of States and international organisations overwhelmingly bolsters these findings.

These conclusions also have significant broader consequences. Given that the post-Soviet secessionist practice represents the largest portion of the practice of a unilateral secession since 1945, the findings of this section underscore that, outside of violation of peremptory norms, the State-creation via secession that can be solely explained by reference to the Montevideo criteria is minimal. This section confirms the conclusion of Part 1, Chapter 5, that even though unilateral secession is not generally prohibited, since 1945, there has been only one example of State-creation via secession on the basis of effectiveness criteria alone.[1]

1 See Part 1, Chapter 5.

 | DOI:10.1163/9789004702646_023

Moreover, fundamentally, the *collective* analysis of the claims to statehood of the post-Soviet secessionist entities carried out in this section revealed an important normative pattern and demonstrated that the same legal basis – violation of peremptory norms – precluded the emergence of all these entities as States. This finding significantly contributes to the legal scholarship on post-Soviet secessionist practice.

Additionally, the applicability of inter-State prohibition of the use of force to newly emerged States that were former Soviet Union republics was predetermined by a strict adherence to the principle of *uti possidetis iuris* in the context of the dissolution of the Soviet Union. The above account of the practice and positions of the former Union republics and other States must be taken as significant confirmation of the adherence to this principle in a non-colonial context as outlined in Part 1, Chapter 4.[2] Moreover, the above analysis also demonstrated the limited relevance of the invocation of the right to self-determination and remedial secession for unilateral secessionist claims, as shown in Part 1, Chapter 3.

It is true that Russia changed its position on remedial secession and relied on it to support its recognition of Abkhazia, South Ossetia and Crimea and later DPR, LPR, Kherson and Zaporizhzhia Regions. But these instances cannot be taken as contradicting a general takeaway from the practice of States vis-à-vis the post-Soviet secessionist attempts. Despite a generalized invocation of this right by separatists, none of these entities was accepted as a State by the international community. Recognition of some of these entities by Russia and a very limited number of other States does not outweigh the overwhelming practice.

The collective analysis of the claims to statehood of the post-Soviet secessionist entities carried out in this section also reveals a pattern of schematic arguments in support of the secessionists and the ostensibility of the secessionist processes, especially since the purported declaration of independence of Crimea in 2014. In particular, a three-step-approach could be detected in several cases consisting of (i) holding of referenda in the prospective secessionist entity and declaration of independence; (ii) recognition by Russia; (iii) conclusion of the purported admission agreements with Russia and secessionist

2 See J Miklasová, 'Dissolution of the Soviet Union Thirty Years On: Re-Appraisal of the Relevance of the Principle of Uti Possidetis Iuris' in JE Viñuales, A Clapham, L Boisson de Chazournes and M Hébié (eds), *The International Legal Order in the XXIst Century / L'ordre juridique international au XXIeme siècle / El órden jurídico internacional en el siglo XXI: Essays in Honour of Professor Marcelo Gustavo Kohen / Ecrits en l'honneur du Professeur Marcelo Gustavo Kohen / Estudios en honor del Profesor Marcelo Gustavo Kohen* (Brill 2023).

entity.[3] This author argues elsewhere that Russia has misused the arguments based on the law of statehood with an ulterior motive of territorial expansion and unlawful annexation of territory.[4]

From a broader perspective, without a doubt, Russian interventions into the secessionist conflicts in the 1990s have raised difficult questions of fact and law. They must be seen in the context of the fallout from the Soviet Union's break-up, and in terms of Moscow's assertion of its power over former Soviet troops abroad. In fact, these early interventions exemplify the transitory character of that period.

On the one hand, from Moscow's perspective, what could have been seen before the break-up of the USSR as legitimate interventions by a federal centre in its federal units were after the Soviet Union's dissolution illegal interventions into internal matters of foreign States, and even illegal uses of force. From a newly emerged State's point of view, Russia's interventions and support for the separatists was seen as a direct assault aimed to subvert their newly achieved statehood and preserve dominance in the region.

Ultimately, international law rules were applicable as soon as the USSR dissolved and the former Soviet republics emerged as new States. *Ius ad bellum* rules and the law governing secession do not provide for any transitory period or for any attenuating circumstances for post-imperial fallout. [5] These rules have general applicability.

The *de facto* consolidation of these secessionist entities over time due to covert support from Russia, the emergence of new conflicts in 2014, and Russia's naked all-out aggression against Ukraine in 2022, accompanied by additional unlawful annexations covered in the language of the so-called declarations of independence underscores the importance and relevance of this underlying premise.

---

3 ibid 119.

4 J Miklasová, 'Russian Approaches to Post-Soviet Secessions: Bad Faith Argumentation and Its Limits' Baltic Yearbook of International Law (forthcoming 2024).

5 The case of Nagorno-Karabakh is different as it is independent of this underlying post-imperial context.

SECTION 4

Legal Consequences Applicable to Post-Soviet Illegal Secessionist Entities

Introduction to Section 4

It was established in Part 2, Section 3 of this book that Transnistria, Nagorno-Karabakh (until September 2023), DPR and LPR (until September 2022), Abkhazia, South Ossetia can be characterised not as States but as illegal secessionist entities. For a brief period, Crimea, Kherson and Zaporizhzhia Regions also bore the characteristics of illegal secessionist entities, but their ostensible existence was only ephemeral. None of the above entities has ever achieved statehood. Crimea, DPR, LPR, Kherson and Zaporizhzhia Regions are now illegally annexed by Russia. Section 4 draws legal consequences from the outcome of this status analysis as outlined in Section 3 and assesses them against the practice and positions of the existing States. As suggested above, an illegal secessionist entity is defined by the tension between effectiveness and legality, which is decisive not only for the issue of its status as State but also for its other relations.

The section, therefore, first generally outlines the consequences of peremptory territorial illegality and the consequences of a change of effective territorial control in the context of post-Soviet illegal secessionist entities. Secondly, the following chapters then analyse effective relations of these entities through the prism of international law.

This account does not provide an exhaustive list of all the possible relations that occur in the context of these post-Soviet illegal secessionist entities. Instead, it focuses on the most representative situations in the area of purported inter-State relations, economic dealings, and acts and laws of purported municipal law. The chapters primarily focus on the compatibility of these relations with the duty of non-recognition and non-assistance, and partially with other legal regimes deriving from effectiveness. In so doing, the objective is also to establish to what extent the practice and positions of States (including the parent States) align with the consequences of peremptory territorial illegality in this context. The amount of available practice is necessarily determined by the research possibilities and the extent of relations that each individual entity, in fact, undertakes.

 | DOI:10.1163/9789004702646_024

CHAPTER 16

General Outline of Applicable Legal Consequences

1 Consequences of Peremptory Territorial Illegality: Duty of Non-recognition of Claimed Territorial Statuses

Peremptory territorial illegality of secessionist entities of Abkhazia and South Ossetia, Nagorno-Karabakh, Transnistria, and Russia-annexed Crimea, DPR, LPR and Kherson and Zaporizhzhia Regions as established in the previous chapters, entails consequences in the area of law of State succession, validity of acts and State responsibility. In particular, the aggravated regime of international responsibility, including the duty of non-recognition, applies to all States. This duty requires non-recognition of the *status* of Crimea, DPR, LPR and Kherson and Zaporizhzhia Regions as part of Russia and of the *status* of statehood of other entities. In short, it mandates the prohibition of a formal recognition of these statuses.

The practice and positions of States regarding the non-recognition of these claimed statuses are in line with this duty. As detailed below, in many instances, international organisations have explicitly proclaimed the applicability of the duty of non-recognition and/or determined indicators of the underlying peremptory territorial illegality (triggering the duty of non-recognition). Even more so, the practice in this regard has been defined by the almost *universal* non-recognition of these statuses (save for very few exceptions) by the individual States.[1] Overall, this seems to attest to the adherence to the duty of non-recognition in these instances.

With respect to Crimea, only Russia and seven other UN Member States recognise it as part of Russia.[2] The UNGA resolutions have consistently reaffirmed the non-recognition of Crimea's annexation or any change of status.[3] The EU

1 Correspondingly, overwhelming explicit support by the States for the respective parent States' territorial integrity within internationally recognised borders (including the secessionist entities) was detailed in the previous chapters of Part 2.

2 See *supra* Chapter 11. See also *supra* Chapter 11 regarding the practice and positions of States and IOs on the illegality of Russia's use of force and overall underlying peremptory territorial illegality.

3 UNGA Res 68/262 (27 March 2014) UN Doc A/RES/68/262, para 6 (voting record: yes: 100, no: 11, abstention: 58). UNGA Res 71/205 (19 December 2016) UN Doc A/RES/71/205, preambular para 6; UNGA Res 72/190 (19 December 2017) UN Doc A/RES/72/190, preambular para 6; UNGA Res 73/194 (23 January 2019) UN Doc A/RES/73/194, preambular para 4; UNGA Res

© KONINKLIJKE BRILL BV, LEIDEN, 2024 | DOI:10.1163/9789004702646_025

strongly condemned "the illegal annexation of Crimea and Sevastopol by the Russian Federation" and reiterated it "will not recognise it".[4] In 2022, the EU also adopted the decision on the non-acceptance of travel documents of the Russian Federation "issued in or to persons in regions or territories in Ukraine, which are occupied by the Russian Federation", linking it explicitly with the non-recognition by the Member States of "illegal annexation" of Crimea and illegal occupation of Donetsk, Luhansk, Kherson and Zaporizhzhia regions of Ukraine.[5] PACE urged the Russian Federation "to reverse the illegal annexation of Crimea".[6] The OSCE PA called upon all participating States "to refuse to recognize the forced annexation of Crimea by the Russian Federation" and referred to "illegal occupation" in this context.[7] The position of States on the

---

74/168 (18 December 2019) UN Doc A/RES/74/168, preambular para 10 and operative para 3; UNGA Res 75/192 (16 December 2020) UN Doc A/RES/75/192, preambular para 11 and para 3; UNGA Res 76/179 (16 December 2021) UN Doc A/RES/76/179, preambular para 11 and para 3; UNGA Res 77/229 (15 December 2022) UN Doc A/RES/77/229, preambular para 12 and para 13. See also UNGA Res 73/263 (22 December 2018) UN Doc A/RES/73/263, para 3; UNGA Res 74/17 (9 December 2019) UN Doc A/RES/74/17, para 7; UNGA Res 75/29 (7 December 2020) UN Doc A/RES/75/29, para 9; UNGA Res 76/70 (9 December 2021) UN Doc A/RES/76/70, para 9; UNGA Res 77/229 (15 December 2022) UN Doc A/RES/77/229, preambular para 12. According to the PCA Award, "recognition of the existence of a dispute over the territorial status of Crimea in no way amounts to recognising any alteration of the status of Crimea from the territory of one Party to the other." PCA Case No 2017–06, *Dispute Concerning Coastal State Rights in the Black Sea, Sea of Azov, and Kerch Strait* (*Ukraine v the Russian Federation*), Award Concerning the Preliminary Objections of The Russian Federation (21 February 2020) para 178.

4 Council of European Union (Foreign Affairs), '3312th Council Meeting' (12 May 2014) 9542/14, para 10; Council of European Union, 'Statement of the Heads of State or Government on Ukraine' (27 May 2014), para 2; European Parliament, 'Resolution on Ukraine' (4 February 2016) 2016/2556(RSP), para 1. See also OSCE (PA), 'Resolution on Violations of Human Rights and Fundamental Freedoms in the Autonomous Republic of Crimea and the City of Sevastopol (Ukraine)' (4 July 2016), para 19.

5 Decision 2022/2512 of 14 December 2022 of the European Parliament and of the Council on the Non-Acceptance of Travel Documents of the Russian Federation Issued in Ukraine and Georgia [2022] OJ L326/1, art 1 and preambular para 7 ("EU Decision on Non-Acceptance of Travel Documents"). See further on invalidity of acts of post-Soviet illegal secessionist entities *infra* Chapter 19.

6 CoE (PACE) Res 2034 (28 January 2015), para 4.1; CoE (PACE) Res 2063 (24 June 2015), para 8.2.

7 OSCE (PA), 'Resolution on Clear, Gross and Uncorrected Violations of Helsinki Principles by the Russian Federation' (1 July 2014), para 16; OSCE (PA), 'Resolution on the Continuation of Clear, Gross and Uncorrected Violations of OSCE Commitments and International Norms by the Russian Federation' (8 July 2015), para 22; OSCE (PA), 'Resolution on Ongoing Violations of Human Rights and Fundamental Freedoms in the Autonomous Republic of Crimea and the City of Sevastopol (Ukraine)' (11 July 2018), para 28; OSCE (PA), 'Resolution on Violations of Human Rights and Fundamental Freedoms in the Autonomous Republic of Crimea and the City of Sevastopol (Ukraine)' (4 July 2016), para 20. See *infra* (n 35).

non-recognition of Crimea's referendum was already mentioned above.[8] Thus, it can be agreed with Corten that the case of Crimea confirms the general principle of *ex iniuria ius non oritur*, since no State really challenged its application, except for Russia and, presumably, other recognising States that refused its applicability *in casu*, claiming no violation of peremptory norms occurred.[9]

Similarly, only Russia, and then Syria and North Korea formally recognised the DPR and LPR as independent States after the full-scale Russian aggression against Ukraine.[10] The UNGA, and PACE deplored Russia's recognition of these entities as illegal acts and demanded their withdrawal.[11] OSCE PA refused to recognize "the establishment through the use of force of any autonomous regions or independent entities within the internationally recognized borders of Ukraine."[12] Later, regarding the 30 September 2022 annexation of the four regions of Ukraine, the UNGA stated that it

> [c]alls upon all States, international organizations and United Nations specialized agencies *not to recognize any alteration by the Russian Federation of the status of any or all* of the Donetsk, Kherson, Luhansk or

8 According to the Ukrainian Law on Temporarily Occupied Territory, the presence of foreign armed forces on the territory of Ukraine "is an occupation of a part of the territory of the sovereign state of Ukraine and an international unlawful act, subject to all consequences provided for by international law." 'Law of Ukraine No 1207-VII On Securing the Rights and Freedoms of Citizens and the Legal Regime on the Temporarily Occupied Territory of Ukraine' (adopted 15 April 2014, entered into force 27 April 2014) preamble <https://www.refworld.org/docid/5379ab8e4.html> accessed 10 January 2020 ("Law on Temporarily Occupied Territory of Ukraine").

9 O Corten, 'The Russian Intervention in the Ukrainian Crisis: Was *Jus Contra Bellum* "Confirmed Rather than Weakened"?' (2015) 2 Journal on the Use of Force and International Law 17, 39.

10 See *supra* Chapter 12. See also *supra* Chapter 12 regarding the practice and positions of States and IOs on the illegality of Russia's aggression and overall underlying peremptory territorial illegality.

11 For example, UNGA Res ES-11/1 Aggression against Ukraine (2 March 2022) UN Doc A/RES/ES-11/1, paras and 6; UNGA Res ES-11/4 Territorial Integrity of Ukraine: Defending the Principles of the Charter of the United Nations (12 October 2022) UN Doc A/RES/ES-11/4, para 5; CoE (PACE) Opinion 300 (15 March 2022) para 5. See further in detail *supra* Chapter 12. See also E Milano and N Zugliani, 'Meaning(s) of Illegality in Secession Processes' in J Vidmar, S McGibbon and L Raible (eds), *Research Handbook on Secession* (Edward Elgar 2022) 356–358.

12 OSCE (PA), 'Resolution on the Russian Federation's War of Aggression against Ukraine and Its People, and Its Threat to Security Across the OSCE Region' (6 July 2022) para 28.

> Zaporizhzhia regions of Ukraine, and to refrain from any action or dealing that might be interpreted as recognizing any such altered status.[13]

It also demanded that the Russian Federation "immediately and unconditionally reverse" its recognition of the Kherson and Zaporizhzhia regions of Ukraine.[14] Additional relevant practice and positions concerning the non-recognition of the results of the 'referenda' of September 2022 and attempted annexations are detailed in Chapter 12. The EU also decided not to accept travel documents of the Russian Federation issued in or for persons resident in occupied territories of Ukraine, specifically referring to the non-recognition by the Member States of "illegal occupation" of Donetsk, Luhansk, Kherson and Zaporizhzhia regions of Ukraine.[15] PACE also demanded non-recognition of the altered status of these territories.[16]

With respect to Abkhazia and South Ossetia, an overwhelming majority of the UN Member States, except for Russia and the four States mentioned above, do not recognise them as independent States.[17] PACE unequivocally condemned Russia's recognition of Abkhazia and South Ossetia and reaffirmed Georgia's territorial integrity; it also called on Russia to withdraw its recognitions and on the Member States not to recognise the independence of Abkhazia and South Ossetia.[18] The PACE resolutions also never referred to these entities as States and instead designated them as "break-away regions" and "de facto authorities".[19] OSCE PA reaffirmed Georgia's territorial integrity, called on Russia to withdraw its recognition of South Ossetia and Abkhazia; it also referred to "illegal occupation" of Abkhazia and South Ossetia.[20] The

---

13 UNGA Res ES-11/4 Territorial Integrity of Ukraine: Defending the Principles of the Charter of the United Nations (12 October 2022) UN Doc A/RES/ES-11/4, para 4 (*emphasis added*) (voting record: yes: 143, no: 5, abstentions: 35).

14 ibid para 3.

15 EU Decision on Non-Acceptance of Travel Documents (n 5) art 1 and preambular para 7. See further on invalidity of acts of post-Soviet illegal secessionist entities *infra* Chapter 19.

16 CoE (PACE) Res 2463 (13 October 2022), para 13.3. See also See also CoE (PACE) Res 2482 (26 January 2023), para 1.

17 See *supra* Chapter 13.

18 CoE (PACE) Res 1633 (2 October 2008), paras 9 and 24.1. Similarly, CoE (PACE) Res 1647 (28 January 2009), para 4. These two resolutions were reaffirmed by CoE (PACE) Res 1683 (29 September 2009), para 1 and CoE (PACE) Res 1896 (2 October 2012), para 25.3.

19 CoE (PACE) Res 1633 (2 October 2008) and CoE (PACE) Res 1647 (28 January 2009). See also CoE (PACE) Opinion 300 (15 March 2022) para 5.

20 OSCE (PA), 'Resolution on Ten Years After the August 2008 War in Georgia' (12 July 2008), paras 13 and 3; OSCE (PA), 'Resolution on the Security and Human Rights Situation in Abkhazia, Georgia, and the Tskhinvali Region/South Ossetia, Georgia' (8 July 2019), paras

EU extended its decision on non-acceptance of the Russian travel documents issued in Abkhazia and South Ossetia.[21] The European Parliament also deplored Russia's recognition of South Ossetia and Abkhazia "as contrary to international law".[22]

Moreover, *no* UN Member State (not even Russia and Armenia) recognised Transnistria and Nagorno-Karabakh as independent States. Indeed, non-recognition of these entities is not usually explicitly referred to in terms of their peremptory illegality. However, as follows from the above, Russia's and Armenia's violation of the prohibition of the use of force in this context is well documented. Moreover, the universal non-recognition of Transnistria and Nagorno-Karabakh must be viewed in the context of the explicit invocation and application of the duty of non-recognition in analogous cases characterised by the peremptory territorial illegality in this chapter.[23] Thus, the *universal* non-recognition of these entities may conceivably be seen as supporting the conclusions of this book as well.

As outlined in Part 1, Chapter 7, the legal consequences of peremptory illegality expand beyond the scope of this general aspect of the duty of non-recognition (concerning the abstention from a formal recognition of status), including the acts that may *imply* recognition. The operation of these further consequences, including the interplay with the consequences of a change of effective territorial control in the context of the post-Soviet secessionist entities, is detailed in the next chapters.

2 Consequences of Change of Effective Territorial Control: Applicability of IHL

As established in Part 1, Chapter 6, the legal framework applicable to illegal secessionist entities includes the consequences of a change of effective territorial control, namely the IHL (the law of occupation). Its applicability to the cases of illegal secessionist entities in the post-Soviet space is examined below.

5 and 16. See *infra* (n 85). See also *supra* Chapter 13 regarding the practice and positions of States and IOs on the illegality of Russia's presence in South Ossetia and Abkhazia.

21 EU Decision on Non-Acceptance of Travel Documents (n 5) art 1 and preambular para 7.

22 European Parliament, 'Resolution on the Need for an EU Strategy for the South Caucasus' (20 May 2010) 2009/2216(INI), para 14; European Parliament, 'Resolution on the Situation in Georgia' (3 September 2008) 2009/C 295 E/08, para 2.

23 See in detail *supra* Chapters 14 and 15. The 2022 Opinion of the Parliamentary Assembly of the Council of Europe refers to the Russian "act of military aggression against the Republic of Moldova." CoE (PACE) Opinion 300 (15 March 2022) para 5.

2.1 *Crimea*

Even though Russia's military takeover of Crimea occurred with minimal violence,[24] "the fact that it was coercive and non-consensual marks it as a belligerent occupation".[25] Under Article 2(2) common to four Geneva Conventions, occupation does not require armed resistance.[26] "Since the Russian Federation considers Crimea to form part of its own (sovereign) territory, it is *a fortiori* exercising direct, effective control over the territory in question and hence qualifies as the occupier of Crimea."[27] Russia has indisputably replaced the Ukrainian authority in Crimea through a military invasion.[28] Based on Putin's acknowledgement of Russia's involvement in the events, a strong case can be made for Russia "exercising direct, effective control over Crimea prior to the referendum in March 2014".[29] According to Ukrainian estimates, before the Russian all-out attack on Ukraine in 2022, the Russian military presence in Crimea amounted to over 30,000 troops.[30] Even if Russia does not recognise Crimea as occupied but as part of its territory, it is still bound to uphold its obligations as the Occupying Power alongside its human rights obligations.[31]

---

24 According to scholars, even the limited scale of violence in Crimea amounted to an international armed conflict followed by occupation under art 2. See M Bothe, 'The Current Status of Crimea: Russian Territory, Occupied Territory or What' (2014) 53 Military Law and Law of War Review 99, 103; R Heinsch, 'Conflict Classification in Ukraine: The Return of the "Proxy War"?' (2015) 91 International Law Studies 323, 354; LR Blank, 'Ukraine's Crisis Part 2: LOAC's Threshold for International Armed Conflict' (*Harvard Law School National Security Journal*, 25 May 2014) <https://harvardnsj.org/2014/05/ukraines-crisis-part-2-loacs-threshold-for-international-armed-conflict/> accessed 7 February 2019.

25 SR Reeves and D Wallace, 'The Combatant Status of the "Little Green Men" and Other Participants' (2015) 91 International Law Studies 361, 380.

26 Convention (IV) Relative to the Protection of Civilian Persons in Time of War (singed 12 August 1949, entered into force 21 October 1950) 75 UNTS 287, art 2(2) ("GCIV").

27 R Geifs, 'Russia's Annexation of Crimea: The Mills of International Law Grind Slowly But They Do Grind' (2015) 91 International Law Studies Series. US Naval War College 425, 443.

28 Reeves and Wallace (n 25) 380 and see 375. See also A Tancredi, 'The Russian Annexation of the Crimea: Questions Relating to the Use of Force' I (2014) QIL QDI 5, 24–27.

29 Geifs (n 27) 444.

30 'Already 31.500 Russian Troops Deployed in Occupied Crimea' (*Ukrinform*, 7 November 2019) <https://www.ukrinform.net/rubric-polytics/2813512-already-31500-russian-troops-deployed-in-occupied-crimea.html> accessed 15 January 2020. See also UNGA resolution expressing grave concern over the progressive militarization of Crimea by the Russian Federation. UNGA Res 73/194 (23 January 2019) UN Doc A/RES/73/194, para 2. See infra (n 140) para 321.

31 Geifs (n 27) 445. Both Russia and Ukraine are parties to the Convention (IV) Respecting the Laws and Customs of War on Land and its Annex: Regulations Concerning the Laws and Customs of War on Land (signed 18 October 1907, entered into force 26 January 1910) ("HR"); GCIV and Protocol Additional to the Geneva Conventions of 12 August 1949, and Relating to the Protection of Victims of International Armed Conflicts (Protocol I)

This conclusion also follows from the resolutions of IOs.[32] The UNGA Resolution 71/205 condemned the temporary occupation of a part of the territory of Ukraine, Crimea, and urged Russia "[t]o uphold all of its obligations under applicable international law as an occupying Power"[33] and "as the occupying Power, to withdraw its military forces from Crimea and to end its temporary occupation of Ukraine's territory without delay".[34] The OSCE PA also strongly condemned "the illegal occupation by the Russian Federation" of Crimea and the city of Sevastopol.[35] Ukraine itself has considered the Autonomous Republic of Crimea and the city of Sevastopol as temporarily occupied since 20 February 2014.[36] After the full-scale Russian aggression against Ukraine started on 24 February 2022, "the situation in Crimea is consumed by the larger armed

---

(signed 8 June 1977, entered into force 7 December 1978) 1125 UNTS 3 ("API"). Both Russia and Ukraine are bound by customary international humanitarian law.

32 In addition, under the Ukrainian Law on Temporarily Occupied Territory, the Autonomous Republic of Crimea and the city of Sevastopol are temporarily occupied, while the Russian Federation is referred to there as the occupying power. For a detailed definition of temporarily occupied territories, see Law on Temporarily Occupied Territory of Ukraine (n 8) art 3, and see also for example art 5(3).

33 UNGA Res 71/205 (19 December 2016) UN Doc A/RES/71/205, preambular para 7 and para 2; UNGA Res 72/190 (19 December 2017) UN Doc A/RES/72/190, preambular para 7 and para 3(a). See also UNGA Res 73/194 (23 January 2019) UN Doc A/RES/73/194, preambular para 4; UNGA Res 74/168 (18 December 2019) UN Doc A/RES/74/168, para 6(a); UNGA Res 75/192 (16 December 2020) UN Doc A/RES/75/192, para 6(a); UNGA Res 76/179 (16 December 2021) UN Doc A/RES/76/179, para 6(a). See also UNGA Res 77/229 (15 December 2022) UN Doc A/RES/77/229, para 2.

34 UNGA Res 73/194 (23 January 2019) UN Doc A/RES/73/194, para 8.

35 OSCE (PA), 'Resolution on Ongoing Violations of Human Rights and Fundamental Freedoms in the Autonomous Republic of Crimea and the City of Sevastopol (Ukraine)' (11 July 2018), para 23. See also OSCE (PA), 'Resolution on Clear, Gross and Uncorrected Violations of Helsinki Principles by the Russian Federation' (1 July 2014), para 11; OSCE (PA), 'Resolution on the Restoration of the Sovereignty and Territorial Integrity of Ukraine' (9 July 2017), para 19; OSCE (PA), 'Resolution on the Militarization by the Russian Federation of the Temporarily Occupied Autonomous Republic of Crimea and the City of Sevastopol, Ukraine, the Black Sea and the Sea of Azov' (9 July 2019), para 12; OSCE (PA), 'Resolution on the Destabilizing Military Build-Up by the Russian Federation near Ukraine, in the Temporary Occupied Autonomous Republic of Crimea and the City of Sevastopol, Ukraine, the Black Sea and the Sea of Azov' (20 July 2021), para 7; OSCE (PA), 'Resolution on the Russian Federation's War of Aggression against Ukraine and Its People, and Its Threat to Security Across the OSCE Region' (6 July 2022), para 28.

36 'Law of Ukraine No 1207-VII On Securing the Rights and Freedoms of Citizens and the Legal Regime on the Temporarily Occupied Territory of Ukraine' (adopted 15 April 2014; entered into force 27 April 2014) art 1(2) <https://zakon.rada.gov.ua/laws/show/1207-18#Text> accessed 31 October 2023 (*in Ukrainian*) ("Law on the Temporarily Occupied Territory of Ukraine").

conflict between Russia and Ukraine for the purpose of IHL, and Crimea is considered territory occupied by the belligerent power Russia".[37]

2.2 *DPR, LPR, Kherson and Zaporizhzhia Regions*

Regarding the applicability of IHL in Eastern and South-Eastern Ukraine, three periods should be distinguished. The first period started in 2014 and lasted until the all-out Russian invasion of Ukraine on 24 February 2022. The second period lasted until 30 September 2022 and the annexation of the Ukrainian regions by Russia. The third period concerned the applicability of IHL in the post-annexation period. Regarding the first period, according to the Office of the Prosecutor ("OTP") of the International Criminal Court ("ICC"), available evidence "would suggest the existence of an international armed conflict in the context of armed hostilities in eastern Ukraine from 14 July 2014 at the latest, in parallel to the non-international armed conflict".[38] Thus, the OTP established the existence of non-international armed conflict between separatists and Ukrainian government forces.[39] This statement also signified that

37 V Bílková, C Hellestveit and E Šteinterte, 'Report on Violation and Abuses of International Humanitarian Law and Human Rights Law, War Crimes and Crimes against Humanity, Related to the Forcible Transfer and/or Deportation of Ukrainian Children to the Russian Federation' (4 May 2023) 21 ("OSCE Moscow Mechanism Report").

38 Information such as reported shelling and detention of Russian soldiers and *vice versa* "points to direct military engagement between Russian armed forces and Ukrainian government forces that would suggest the existence of an international armed conflict in the context of armed hostilities in eastern Ukraine from 14 July 2014 at the latest, in parallel to the non-international armed conflict." Office of the Prosecutor of the International Criminal Court, 'Report on Preliminary Examination Activities' (14 November 2016) para 169 ("Report on Preliminary Examination Activities"). For the same conclusion see RULAC, 'International Armed Conflict in Ukraine' <http://www.rulac.org/browse/conflicts/%20international-armed-conflict-in-ukraine#collapse1accord> accessed 7 February 2019; A Szpak, 'Legal Classification of the Armed Conflict in Ukraine in Light of International Humanitarian Law' (2017) 58 Hungarian Journal of Legal Studies 261, 275–276; Human Rights Watch, 'Eastern Ukraine: Questions and Answers about the Laws of War' (*HRW*, 11 September 2014) <https://www.hrw.org/news/2014/09/11/eastern-ukraine-questions-and-answers-about-laws-war> accessed 7 February 2014. See also I Nuzov and A Quintin, 'The Case of Russia's Detention of Ukrainian Military Pilot Savchenko under IHL' (*EJIL Talk!*, 3 March 2015) <https://www.ejiltalk.org/the-case-of-russias-detention-of-ukrainian-military-pilot-savchenko-under-ihl/> accessed 7 February 2019.

39 In July 2014, ICRC characterized the conflict as non-international. ICRC, 'Ukraine: ICRC Calls on All Sides to Respect International Humanitarian Law' (*ICRC News Release*, 23 July 2014) <https://www.icrc.org/en/doc/resources/documents/news-release/2014/07-23-ukraine-kiev-call-respect-ihl-repatriate-bodies-malaysian-airlines.htm> accessed 7 February 2019. For the characterization of conflict as non-international, see Heinsch (n 24) 355–356; Reeves and Wallace (n 25) 382.

Russia's direct intervention in the conflict triggered the applicability of laws of international armed conflict.[40] The Hague District Court in the MH17 criminal case established that around the time of the downing of the MH17 flight, "the criteria for characterising the situation as a non-international armed conflict have been met."[41]

However, crucially, the question arose for the OTP and the Hague District Court whether there was, in fact, only one single internationalised armed conflict in Eastern Ukraine; that is, whether a non-international armed conflict was internationalised due to Russia's overall control over the separatist armed groups.[42]

Overall control requires the fulfilment of a two-pronged test. Firstly, regarding financing, training and equipping or providing operational support, there is sufficient evidence to conclude that the Russian Federation provided separatists, among others, with arms, weapons, ammunition and artillery cover.[43] The Hague District Court established that the DPR requested support from the Russian Federation "such as the manpower, military equipment and requisite training. This support was indeed provided."[44]

Secondly, the overall control test requires Russia's role in organising, coordinating or planning the military actions of the armed groups. The ECtHR (in the context of a jurisdictional decision) established that "senior members of the

40 Early assessments denied the existence of international armed conflict in Eastern Ukraine due to lack of evidence concerning Russia's direct intervention. N Quenivet, 'Trying to Classify the Conflict in Eastern Ukraine' (*INTLAWGRRLS*, 28 August 2014) <https://ilg2.org/2014/08/28/trying-to-classify-the-conflict-in-eastern-ukraine/> accessed 7 February 2019; Heinsch (n 24) 354–355, but see 356–357.

41 *Judgment Nos 09-748004/19, 09-748005/19, 09-748006/19, 09-748007/19* (The Netherlands, District Court of the Hague) (17 November 2022), 4.4.3.1.3 ("District Court of the Hague").

42 The Office of the Prosecutor examined information "that suggests that the Russian Federation may have exercised overall control over armed groups in eastern Ukraine for some or all of the armed conflict" Office of the Prosecutor of the International Criminal Court, Report on Preliminary Examination Activities (5 December 2019), para. 277. Report on Preliminary Examination Activities (n 38) para 170; see also Office of the Prosecutor of the International Criminal Court, Report on Preliminary Examination Activities (5 December 2018), para 73.

43 See *supra* Chapter 12. *Ukraine and the Netherlands v Russia* App nos 8019/16, 43800/14 and 28525/20 (ECtHR, 25 January 2023) paras 579–662. ("*Ukraine and the Netherlands v Russia*"). The evidence was, however, insufficient to establish whether Russia offered training to the separatists in eastern Ukraine. ibid, para 644.

44 District Court of the Hague (n 41) 4.4.3.1.3.

Russian military were present in command positions in the separatist armed groups and entities from the outset."[45]

Moreover, both Russia and the separatists broadly shared the same military objectives. The ECtHR concluded that "the influence of the political hierarchy of the respondent Government [Russia] on the military strategy of the separatists was significant".[46] In the case of conflicting positions of Moscow and the separatists, the former prevailed.[47] Regarding the question of whether "the Russian Federation assumed a coordinating role and issued instructions to the DPR", the Hague District Court established "that the case file contains abundant evidence for this".[48] Moreover, the ECtHR established Russia's support of the DPR and LPR in the political sphere, and other reports confirmed Russia's influence over the separatists in the context of the conclusion of Minsk II.[49]

The Hague District Court ultimately concluded that Russia "exercised overall control over the DPR from mid-May 2014, at least until the crash of flight MH17".[50] Therefore, the conflict was "internationalised and was therefore an international armed conflict".[51] In light of the relevant factual findings of the ECtHR (even if made in the context of human rights litigation), it is possible to conclude that Russia also continued to exercise overall control over the separatist armed groups in the subsequent period.[52]

45 *Ukraine and the Netherlands v Russia* (n 43) para 611. *Cf Tadić case* (Judgment, Appeals Chamber) (IT-94-1-A) (15 July 1999) para 150 ("*Tadić*"); *Prosecutor v Naletilić and Martinović* (Judgment, Trial Chamber) (IT-98-34-T) (31 March 2003) para 201 ("*Naletilić and Martinović*"); *Prosecutor v Tihomir Blaškić* (Judgment, Trial Chamber) (IT-95-14-T) (15 July 1999) paras 112–119 ("*Tihomir Blaškić*"); *Prosecutor v Jadranko Prlić and others* (Judgment, Appeals Chamber) (IT-04-74-A) (29 November 2017) para 283 and references therein ("*Jadranko Prlić*"). See also Part 1, Chapter 8.

46 *Ukraine and the Netherlands v Russia* (n 43) para 621. District Court of the Hague (n 41) 4.4.3.1.3. *Cf Tadić* (n 45) paras 150–153. In *Naletilić and Martinović*, the Trial Chamber established that to implement common goals, the third State leadership issued orders for the armed groups. *Naletilić and Martinović* (n 45) para 201; *Tihomir Blaškić* (n 45) paras 108–111.

47 *Ukraine and the Netherlands v Russia* (n 43) para 619.

48 District Court of the Hague (n 41) 4.4.3.1.3.

49 See *supra* Chapter 12. *Cf Tadić* (n 45) paras 158–160; *Jadranko Prlić* (n 45) para 283 and references therein.

50 District Court of the Hague (n 41) 4.4.3.1.3.

51 ibid.

52 Before the judgments of the ECtHR and the Hague District Court, the scholars pointed to the lack of evidence on planning of operations by Russia. See A Gilder, 'Bringing Occupation into the 21st Century: The Effective Implementation of Occupation by Proxy' (2017) 13 Utrecht Law Review 60, 71–72. Similarly, see Heinsch (n 24) 357–360; Reeves and Wallace (n 25) 382; Quenivet (n 40); Nuzov and Quintin (n 38).

Additionally, Ukraine itself has considered the separate parts of the Donetsk and Luhansk regions as temporarily occupied since 7 May 2014.[53] Since there is no conclusive available evidence of the exact number of Russian regular troops in Donbas in the period until 24 February 2022,[54] it may be concluded that Russia was the Occupying Power in Donbas through the proxies of the DPR and LPR. The relevant test for the occupation by proxy requires that the DPR and LPR exercised effective control for the purposes of belligerent occupation over the territory of Eastern Ukraine, and the Russian Federation exercised overall control over the DPR and LPR.[55] In view of the above, these criteria seemed to be fulfilled, as parts of the DPR and LPR (outside active battle zones) were under the effective control of the separatist militias.

The second phase of the applicability of IHL concerns the time between the all-out Russia's aggression against Ukraine on 24 February 2022 and 30 September 2022 – the day of the purported incorporation of the DPR, LPR, Zaporizhzhia and Kherson Regions into the Russian Federation. Already, on 21 February 2022, the Russian President ordered the Russian regular troops to enter the DPR and LPR on the basis of the purported treaties on friendship, cooperation and mutual assistance.[56] However, as shown in Part 2, Chapter 12,

53 See Verkhovna Rada of Ukraine, 'Resolution No 254-VIII on the Recognition of Individual Regions, Cities, Towns, and Villages of the Donetsk and Luhansk Regions as Temporarily Occupied Territories' (adopted 17 March 2015; entered into force17 March 2015) <https://zakon.rada.gov.ua/laws/show/254-19> accessed 10 January 2020 (*in Ukrainian*); Law of Ukraine on the Peculiarities of State Policy to Ensure the State Sovereignty of Ukraine over Temporarily Occupied Territories in the Donetsk and Luhansk Regions No 2268-VIII' (adopted 18 January 2018, entered into force 24 February 2018, repealed by Law of Ukraine No 2217-IX of 21 April 2022) art 2(1) <https://zakon.rada.gov.ua/laws/show/2268-19> accessed 31 October 2023 (*in Ukrainian*) ("Law on Reintegration of Donbas"). Since May 2022 the legal regime of the temporarily occupied territories of Ukraine is governed by Law on the Temporarily Occupied Territory of Ukraine (n 36).

54 *Ukraine and the Netherlands v Russia* (n 43) para 611.

55 See *supra* Part 1, Chapter 8.

56 'Executive Order of the President of the Russian Federation No 71 on Recognition of the Donetsk People's Republic (adopted 21 February 2022; entered into force 21 February 2022) <http://publication.pravo.gov.ru/Document/View/0001202202220002> accessed 26 July 2023 (*in Russian*); 'Executive Order of the President of the Russian Federation No 72 on Recognition of the Luhansk People's Republic (adopted 21 February 2021; entered into force 21 February 2021) <http://publication.pravo.gov.ru/Document/View/0001202202220001> accessed 26 July 2023 (*in Russian*); 'Russia-Ukraine Tensions: Putin Orders Troops to Separatist Regions and Recognizes their Independence' (*The New York Times*, 21 February 2022) <https://www.nytimes.com/live/2022/02/21/world/ukraine-russia-putin-biden#moscow-orders-troops-to-ukraines-breakaway-regions-for-peacekeeping-functions> accessed 24 August 2023.

these treaties failed to provide any legal basis for the presence of the Russian army on Ukrainian territory.[57] Thus, the subsequent full-scale attack on Ukraine on 24 February 2022 further extended the applicability of the laws of IAC.[58]

After 24 February 2022, the DPR and LPR "militaries" fought the Ukrainian army, at least nominally, alongside the Russian regular army. However, in light of the above previous links between Russia and the separatist forces of the DPR and LPR, Russia *a fortiori* exercised overall control over these forces during the full-scale assault against Ukraine.[59] Moreover, the newly captured parts of Ukraine's Donetsk and Luhansk regions were considered subject to the legal systems and administration of the DPR and LPR.[60] Given Russia's control over the separatist forces and Russia's open military presence in these regions, the territory of the DPR and LPR under the effective control of the separatists was occupied by Russia. In other regions of Ukraine coming under Russia's control, "Russia established 'Komendaturas', a type of civil administration by the occupying forces".[61] In light of the above, regardless of the claimed status of belonging to the DPR and LPR or not, Russia was the Occupying Power there.

The third phase of the applicability of IHL started on 30 September 2022 when the DPR, LPR, Kherson and Zaporizhzhia regions were annexed by the Russian Federation in their administrative boundaries.[62] From this date onwards, the parts of the Ukrainian regions controlled by Russia have been directly subjected to Russian laws and administration without the interposition of the purported separatist laws and acts. However, as the OSCE Moscow Mechanism report established,

> changes of formal status made by the occupying power to an occupied area does not influence applicability of the rules of IHL, and the benefit of 'protected persons' cannot be removed due to changes or agreements between the occupying power and the authorities of the occupied territory.[63]

---

57 See *supra* Part 2, Chapter 12.

58 OSCE Moscow Mechanism Report (n 37) 23.

59 See the same conclusion in the period just before the start of Russia's full-scale aggression. N Kalandarishvili-Mueller, 'Russia's "Occupation by Proxy" of Eastern Ukraine – Implications Under the Geneva Conventions' (*Just Security*, 22 February 2022) <https://www.justsecurity.org/80314/russias-occupation-by-proxy-of-eastern-ukraine-implications-under-the-geneva-conventions/> accessed 24 August 2023.

60 OSCE Moscow Mechanism Report (n 37) 26.

61 ibid.

62 *Supra* Chapter 12.

63 OSCE Moscow Mechanism Report (n 37) 26.

As shown in Part 2, Chapter 12, none of Russia's acts purportedly formalising incorporation of these regions were valid under international law; therefore, they cannot be seen as justifying Russian military presence there. These regions have remained occupied by Russia.

2.3 *Abkhazia and South Ossetia*

As follows from Part 2, Chapter 13, in the period before the 2008 Russia-Georgia war, Russia played an important role in terms of the economic, political and military support of Abkhazia and South Ossetia.[64] Russian troops were present in these regions as peacekeeping forces with the original consent of Georgia.[65]

However, the *status quo* changed in light of the Russia-Georgia War of 2008. There is no doubt that there was an international armed conflict between Georgia and the Russian Federation in August 2008, and neither of these States denies it.[66] The question arises whether the hostilities between Georgia and the secessionist forces constituted a parallel non-international armed conflict[67] or whether Russia exercised overall control over these forces in a way that there would be only one international armed conflict.[68]

To fulfil the exact conditions of an overall test as developed by *Tadić*, evidence of Russia's material support of the separatists and its role in organising, coordinating or planning the military actions of South Ossetian and Abkhazian forces in military actions would be required. The International Fact-Finding Mission did not provide a conclusive answer, limiting itself to pronouncing that the relationship between South Ossetia and Russia seems to

---

64 See *supra* Chapter 13.

65 See *infra* (n 152 and n 153). See on the complicated nature of a peacekeeping mission in Abkhazia *Mamasakhlisi and Others v Georgia and Russia* App 29999/04 and 41424/04 (Merits) (ECtHR, 7 March 2023) paras 325–326 ("*Mamasakhlisi*").

66 Independent International Fact-Finding Mission on the Conflict in Georgia, *Report* (Vol II, IIFFMCG 2009) 300 ("Report"); P Leach, 'South Ossetia' in E Wilmshurst (ed), *International Law and the Classification of Conflicts* (1st edn, OUP; The Royal Institute of International Affairs (Chatham House) 2012) 330 and 326–328; NM Shanahan Cutts, 'Enemies Through the Gates: Russian Violations of International Law in Georgia/ Abkhazia Conflict' 40 (2007) Case Western Reserve Journal of International Law 281, 297.

67 According to the Report, even Russia concluded that at the time of the conflicts, Abkhazia and South Ossetia were internationally recognized as part of Georgia. Report (n 66) 300. Thus, the conflict between Georgia and the South Ossetian and Abkhazian forces was a *prima facie* NIAC. Report (n 66) 300–301; M Milanović, 'The Applicability of the Conventions to "Transnational" and "Mixed" Conflicts' in Clapham A and others (eds), *The 1949 Geneva Conventions: a commentary* (1st edn, OUP 2015) para 66. On doubts about the nature of the South Ossetian forces, see Leach (n 66) 332–333.

68 Leach (n 66) 332; Milanović (n 67) para 66.

have been stronger than that between Abkhazia and Russia.[69] Other authors pointed to the lack of publicly available evidence, leading them to state that "it is correct to classify the hostilities as amounting to two concurrent conflicts, international and non-international".[70] However, a Pre-Trial Chamber I of the International Criminal Court, in its 2016 Decision on the Prosecutor's request for authorisation of an investigation stated,

> the Chamber considers, at this stage, that there is sufficient indication that the Russian Federation exercised overall control over the South Ossetian forces, meaning that also the period before the direct intervention of Russian forces may be seen as an international armed conflict.[71]

In addition, certain parts of Georgia, especially "the buffer zone", were occupied by the Russian Federation "until at least 10 October 2018".[72] Regarding South Ossetia and Abkhazia specifically, given the above conclusion of a Pre-Trial Chamber I and later factual developments,[73] it can be presumed that Russia *a fortiori* has exercised overall control over the separatist troops in the period subsequent to the active phase of hostilities.[74]

Moreover, in addition to an analysis of Russia's control over the proxy separatist militias, the question must also be asked whether, after the termination

69 Report (n 66) 301–304.

70 Leach (n 66) 339.

71 ICC (Pre-Trial Chamber I), 'Situation in Georgia: Decision on the Prosecutor's Request for Authorization of an Investigation' (27 January 2016) ICC-01/15, para 27 (*footnotes omitted*) ("Decision on the Prosecutor's Request for Authorization of an Investigation"). At the same time the Chamber considered this point "irrelevant at the present stage" since "the war crimes under consideration exist equally in international and non-international armed conflicts." ibid, para 28.

72 ibid, para 27. The ECtHR in its judgment *Georgia v Russia* (*II*) referred on several occasions to the "occupation phase" after the end of active hostilities (12 August 2008) and took the rules of the IHL relevant to occupation into account. See *Georgia v Russia* (*II*) App no 38263/08 (Merits) (ECtHR, 21 January 2021) paras 52, 145, 199, 234–237, 290–291 and 310–311. The existence of the state of occupation concerns different locations, with the Russian Armed Forces present in the aftermath of the 2008 War. For these locations, see Report (n 66) 306–309.

73 See *supra* Chapter 13.

74 Since the separatists exercise effective control in these entities, this would entail the fulfilment of the requirement of occupation by proxy. According to RULAC database Abkhazia and South Ossetia are under Russia's occupation by proxy. However, the test used in the analysis is the one developed by the ECtHR. See RULAC, 'Military Occupation of Georgia by Russia' <http://www.rulac.org/browse/conflicts/military-occupation-of-georgia-by-russia#collapse4accord> accessed 7 May 2019.

of hostilities in August 2008, the Russian Federation, through the continuing presence of its own troops in South Ossetia and Abkhazia, has directly exercised effective control in terms of Article 42 of the Hague Regulations. The threshold of effective control for the purposes of military occupation requires a foreign military presence, the ability to exert authority over the territory and the non-consensual nature of such a military presence.[75] Russia's military presence in each of these entities amounts to 3,800 troops.[76] Georgia has not agreed to the presence of these troops on its territory, and the purported treaties with these entities cannot provide a legal basis under international law.[77] Thus, it can be concluded that the presence of Russian Armed Forces in South Ossetia and Abkhazia amounts to an occupation.[78] This would take place in connection to Russia's occupation by proxy.[79] This conclusion seems justified by a complex factual situation on the ground. In any case, Russia is the Occupying Power in these territories.

Notably, according to the Office of the Prosecutor's application for arrest warrants, Russian troops "continue to occupy SO [South Ossetia] until this day".[80] The International Fact-Finding Mission,[81] Georgian Law on Occupied

---

75 See *supra* Part 1, Chapter 8.

76 See *supra* Chapter 13.

77 See *infra*. See also *supra* Chapter 13.

78 For a similar conclusion with respect to South Ossetia, see E Benvenisti, *The International Law of Occupation* (2nd ed, OUP 2012) 196. Regarding South Ossetia, see Leach (n 66) 353. See also N Kalandarishvili-Mueller, 'Guest Post: The Status of the Territory Unchanged: Russia's Treaties with Abkhazia and South Ossetia, Georgia' (*opiniojuris*, 20 March 2015) <http://opiniojuris.org/2015/04/20/guest-post-the-status-of-the-territory-unchanged-russias-treaties-with-abkhazia-and-south-ossetia-georgia/> accessed 7 May 2019; N Kalandarishvili-Mueller, 'On the Occasion of the Five-year Anniversary of the Russian-Georgian War: Is Georgia Occupied?' (*EJIL:Talk!*, 1 October 2013) <https://www.ejiltalk.org/on-the-occasion-of-the-five-year-anniversary-of-the-russian-georgian-war-is-georgia-occupied/> accessed 7 December 2020.

79 On this possibility in general, see Benvenisti (n 78) 62.

80 OTP, Public Redacted Version of "Prosecutor's Application pursuant to Article 58 for Warrants of Arrest against Mikhail Mindzaev, Gamlet Guchmazov and David Sanakoev" (10 March 2022) ICC-01/15-34-Conf-Exp, para 26. However, the Chamber responded that "[g]iven the standard of analysis, the Chamber need not consider, for the purposes fo the present decision, whether the situation in addition qualified as an occupation." ICC (Pre-Trial Chamber I), 'Situation in Georgia: Public Redacted Version of 'Corrected Version of the "Arrest Warrant for Mikhail Mayramovich Mindzaev"'' (24 June 2022) ICC-01/15, para 10.

81 "If, as asserted in the chapter of this report on the use of force, Russia's military intervention cannot be justified under international law, and if neither Abkhazia nor South Ossetia is a recognised independent state, IHL – and in particular the rules concerning

Territories,[82] NGOs,[83] and international organisations[84] also came to the same conclusion. The OSCE PA defined the situation as "illegal occupation" and "steps towards de facto annexation of Abkhazia, Georgia, and the Tskhinvali region/South Ossetia, Georgia".[85] Russia is thus bound to uphold its obligations as the Occupying Power in these territories.[86]

2.4 *Nagorno-Karabakh*

It follows from Part 2, Chapter 14 that due to Armenia's direct and indirect intervention in the conflict in Nagorno-Karabakh between 1992 and 1994, there was an international armed conflict between Armenia and Azerbaijan.[87] To

---

the protection of the civilian population mainly Geneva Convention IV) and occupation – was and may still be applicable." Report (n 66) 311.

82 'Law of Georgia No 431 on Occupied Territories as amended' (adopted 23 October 2008), art 2 <https://smr.gov.ge/uploads/prev/The_Law_of_928efod7.pdf> accessed 18 October 2016.

83 Human Rights Watch, *Up in Flames: Humanitarian Law Violations and Civilian Victims in the Conflict over South Ossetia* (HRW 2009) 123.

84 OSCE (PA), 'Resolution on the Situation in Georgia' (9 July 2012), paras 4 and 7; OSCE (PA), 'Enhancing Mutual Trust and Co-Operation for Peace and Prosperity in the OSCE Region' (9 July 2017), para 12; OSCE (PA), 'Resolution on the Conflict in Georgia' (5 July 2016), para 6; OSCE (PA), 'Resolution on Ten Years After the August 2008 War in Georgia' (12 July 2018), paras 4 and 7; see OSCE (PA), 'Birmingham Declaration' (6 July 2022), para 147; CoE (PACE) Res 1990 (1 April 2014), para 10. PACE also condemned "the Russian non-mandated military presence and the building of new military bases within the separatists regions of South Ossetia and Abkhazia." CoE (PACE) Res 1647 (28 January 2009) para 5.4. European Parliament, 'Resolution on an EU Strategy for the Black Sea' (20 January 2011) 2010/2087(INI), para 32; European Parliament, 'Resolution on the Strategic Military Situation in the Black Sea Basin Following the Illegal Annexation of Crimea by Russia' (11 June 2015) 2015/2036(INI), para K; European Parliament, 'Recommendation to the Council Concerning 72nd Session of the United Nations General Assembly' (5 July 2017) 2017/2041(INI), para 1 (a); European Parliament, 'Resolution on Association Agreements/Deep and Comprehensive Free Trade Areas with Georgia, Moldova and Ukraine' (21 January 2016) 2015/2032(RSP), para D; European Parliament, 'Resolution on Russian Pressure on Eastern Partnership Countries and in Particular Destabilisation of Eastern Ukraine' (17 April 2014) 2014/2699(RSP), para L.

85 OSCE (PA), 'Resolution on the Security and Human Rights Situation in Abkhazia, Georgia, and the Tskhinvali Region/South Ossetia, Georgia' (8 July 2019), paras 6 and 18. Similarly on "illegal occupation," see Euronest Parliamentary Assembly, 'Resolution on the Future of the Eastern Partnership – Combating Hybrid Challenges and Security Threats Together' 2018/C 99/03, paras G.

86 See OSCE (PA), 'Resolution on the Security and Human Rights Situation in Abkhazia, Georgia, and the Tskhinvali Region/South Ossetia, Georgia' (8 July 2019), para 6 and 18. Russia is party to the HR, GCIV and API. Georgia is party to GCIV and API. Both Russia and Georgia are bound by customary international humanitarian law.

87 See *supra* Chapter 14.

what extent the armed conflict between the Nagorno-Karabakh forces and Azerbaijan was internationalised depends on whether Armenia exercised overall control over the Nagorno-Karabakh forces. This would require information not only about Armenia's support for the separatist forces but also about Armenia's role in organising, coordinating or planning the military actions of the Nagorno-Karabakh forces.[88] However, it is difficult to assess that question from publicly available resources concerning that time period.

Nevertheless, evidence on the integration of Nagorno-Karabakh forces and the Armenian Army from the end of open hostilities in 1994 until the outbreak of the war in 2020 pointed in the direction of Armenia exercising overall control over the Nagorno-Karabakh forces.[89] In this context, joint military exercises suggested that "a joint defence of the captured territories is being coordinated".[90] For example, the planning of military activities seemed to have been coordinated, as followed from the Armenian Defence Minister's and other officials' participation in a meeting of Nagorno-Karabakh's Defence Army's Military Council summing up activities for 2014 and creating a 2015 action plan.[91]

"Moreover, the military body that is occupying Karabakh and the seven surrounding districts presents itself as one whole military body, consisting of troops from Armenia and Karabakh, even though details of existing command structures are not documented."[92] It also followed from the above that the same persons occupied the highest posts in the military sector both in Armenia and Nagorno-Karabakh.[93] Even the ECtHR concluded that the armed forces of both Armenia and Nagorno-Karabakh were "highly integrated".[94]

---

88 See *supra* Part 1, Chapter 8 for discussion of the overall control test.

89 "Armenia exercises its authority over Nagorno-Karabakh by equipping, financing or training and providing operational support to the self-proclaimed Nagorno-Karabakh Republic and its forces, but also in coordinating and helping the general planning of their military and paramilitary activities." RULAC, 'Military Occupation of Azerbaijan by Armenia' <http://www.rulac.org/browse/conflicts/military-occupation-of-azerbaijan-by-armenia#collapse1accord> accessed 7 June 2019.

90 H Krüger, *The Nagorno-Karabakh Conflict: A Legal Analysis* (Springer 2010) 105. See 'The Results of the 'Unity 2014' Military Exercise Have Been Summarized' (*mil.am*, 27 November 2014) <http://www.mil.am/en/news/3269> accessed 2 June 2019.

91 'Bako Sahakyan – We Will Give a Worthy Counter Back to Any Encroachment against Our Independence, Security and Dignity' (*Artsakh Press*, 16 January 2015) <https://artsakhpress.am/eng/news/10524/hamardzak-ev-arzhani-hakaharvats-ktanq-mer-ankakhutyan-dem-uxxvats-cankacats-otndzgutyan-bako-sahakyan.html> accessed 2 June 2019.

92 Krüger (n 90) 105 and 113.

93 See *supra* Chapter 14.

94 *Chiragov and Others v Armenia* ECHR 2015-III 135, para 180 ("*Chiragov*").

Armenia's role was not "restricted to mere logistic support but implies that it has a hand in the organisation, co-ordination and planning of the power established in Nagorno-Karabakh".[95] Thus, it followed that in the period between 1994 and 2020, Armenia most likely exercised overall control over the Nagorno-Karabakh forces; and since they exercised effective control over Nagorno-Karabakh and the seven surrounding districts, it would seem to have pointed to the fulfilment of requirements of occupation by proxy.[96]

However, the presence of regular Armenian troops on Azerbaijani territory[97] also seemed to point to the fulfilment of the requirements of effective control in connection to its occupation by proxy.[98] These considerations appeared to have been justified by a complex factual situation on the ground. In any case, it would consequently follow that in the relevant period Armenia, as the Occupying Power, was bound to comply with the treaty and with customary law of occupation in these territories.[99]

In this context, international organisations adopted a three-fold approach to characterising the situation. Firstly, some resolutions only referred to the occupation of districts surrounding Nagorno-Karabakh. For example, UNSC resolution 822 (1993) demanded the withdrawal "of all occupying forces from the Kelbadjar district and other recently occupied areas of Azerbaijan".[100]

95 S Vité, 'Typology of Armed Conflicts in International Humanitarian Law: Legal Concepts and Actual Situations' (2009) 91 International Review of the Red Cross 69, 75.

96 ibid 75; ICRC, *Occupation and Other Forms of Administration of Foreign Territory: Expert Meeting* (ICRC 2012) 23. According to RULAC, "[N]agorno-Karabakh and seven adjacent districts are under the effective control of the self-proclaimed Nagorno-Karabakh Republic (NKR), also known as the Republic of Artsakh. However, Armenia exercises overall control over the NKR." However, the test used in the analysis is the one developed by the ECtHR. RULAC, 'Military Occupation of Azerbaijan by Armenia' <http://www.rulac.org/browse/conflicts/military-occupation-of-azerbaijan-by-armenia#collapse1accord> accessed 7 June 2019. See *supra* Part 1, Chapter 8.

97 See *supra*. "[I]t is clear that official Armenian military forces are directly and indirectly involved in the military occupation of Nagorno-Karabakh." Krüger (n 90) 105.

98 The threshold of effective control for the purposes of military occupation requires a foreign military presence, the ability to exert authority over the territory and a non-consensual nature of the military presence. See *supra* Part 1, Chapter 8. J Popjanevski, 'International Law and the Nagorno-Karabakh Conflict' in SE Cornell (ed) *The International Politics of the Armenian-Azerbaijani Conflict: The Original 'Frozen Conflict' and European Security* (palgrave macmillan 2017) 40. "A key question, therefore, is not what level of influence Armenia exercises over the regional de facto authorities, but instead whether Yerevan exercises enough control in the region to replace Baku as the protector of human rights and humanitarian standards there." ibid 37.

99 See Krüger (n 90) 112. Armenia is party to the GCIV and API. Azerbaijan is party to GCIV. Both Armenia and Azerbaijan are bound by customary international humanitarian law.

100 UNSC Res 822 (30 April 1993) UN Doc S/RES/822, para 1.

Other UNSC resolutions had similar wording.[101] Secondly, UNGA resolutions, for example, referred to the occupied territories of Azerbaijan without further specification.[102] Thirdly, PACE referred to "the occupation by Armenia of Nagorno-Karabakh and other adjacent areas of Azerbaijan".[103] As follows from the above analysis, the third approach seems to be the most precise.

The Second Karabakh War, lasting between 27 September 2020 and 9 November 2020 and characterised as an international armed conflict between Azerbaijan and Armenia,[104] changed the existing *status quo*. The ceasefire agreement was signed on 9 November 2020. Regarding the presence of regular Armenian troops, it stated that the Russian peacekeepers "shall be deployed concurrently with the withdrawal of the Armenian troops".[105] Initially, there were conflicting reports on the withdrawal of regular troops of the Armenian Armed Forces, but ultimately, the International Crisis Group and other sources confirmed such retreat.[106]

---

101 UNSC Res 853 (29 July 1993) UN Doc S/RES/853, paras 1 and 3; UNSC Res 874 (14 October 1993) UN Doc S/RES/874, para 5; UNSC Res 884 (12 November 1993) UN Doc S/RES/884, para 4.

102 UNGA Res 60/285 (7 September 2006) UN Doc A/RES/60/285; UNGA Res 62/243 (14 March 2008) UN Doc A/RES/62/243. See also 'Report of the OSCE Fact-Finding Mission (FFM) to the Occupied Territories of Azerbaijan Surrounding Nagorno-Karabakh (NK)' annexed to 'Letter Dated 18 March 2005 from the Permanent Representative of Azerbaijan to the United Nations addressed to the Secretary-General' (21 March 2005) UN Doc A/59/747-S/2005/187.

103 CoE (PACE) Res 2085 (26 January 2016), para 4; PACE also referred to the fact that "[c]onsiderable parts of the territory of Azerbaijan are still occupied by Armenian forces, and separatists forces are still in control of the Nagorno-Karabakh region." PACE Res 1416 (25 January 2005), para 1. Similarly see for example OIC (Council of Foreign Ministers) 'Resolution on the Aggression of the Republic of Armenia against the Republic of Azerbaijan' (13–14 March 2008) 10/42-POL, para 4; OIC (Council of Foreign Ministers) 'Resolution on the Aggression of the Republic of Armenia against the Republic of Azerbaijan' (18–20 June 2008) 6/35-P, para 4; OIC (Islamic Summit Conference) 'Resolution on the Aggression of the Republic of Armenia against the Republic of Azerbaijan' (27–28 May 2015) 10/11-P(IS), para 4.

104 See for example M O'Brien, 'Nagorno-Karabakh Conflict: Shortage of Specifics Complicates Search for Solutions' (*Just Security*, 21 October 2020) <https://www.justsecurity.org/72974/nagorno-karabakh-conflict-shortage-of-specifics-complicates-search-for-solutions/> accessed 5 December 2020. See *supra* Chapter 14.

105 'Statement by President of the Republic of Azerbaijan, Prime Minister of the Republic of Armenia and President of the Russian Federation' (9 November 2020) <http://en.kremlin.ru/events/president/news/64384> (in *English*) and <http://www.kremlin.ru/catalog/countries/AZ/events/64384/print> (in *Russian*) accessed 3 December 2020, art 4 and see art 3 ("Ceasefire Agreement").

106 Azerbaijan continued to raise the issue of the presence of the Armenian regular army and the arming of the separatists. See in detail *supra* Chapter 14.

Secondly, after the withdrawal of Armenia's regular troops, the issue of continued occupation by proxy through Armenia's overall control over the armed groups in Nagorno-Karabakh had to be addressed. This required proof of Armenia's role in organising, coordinating or planning the military actions of separatist troops and its role in financing, training, equipping or providing operational support to them.[107] Since the ECtHR previously held that the Armenian armed forces and separatist armed forces were "highly integrated",[108] the first prong of the requirement was likely fulfilled. However, with respect to the second prong – the issue of support – the situation was more complex. In the period between November 2020 and September 2023, the only connection between Armenia and Nagorno-Karabakh was the Lachin Corridor, which was under the control of Russian peacekeepers until April 2023.[109] Therefore, as mentioned above, according to the report of the International Crisis Group (ICG), Armenia ceased sending military and material equipment to Nagorno-Karabakh upon the arrival of Russian peacekeepers.[110] Ultimately, the issue of until when Armenia continued to exert overall control over the local separatist troops and thereby occupy Nagorno-Karabakh by proxy in the period after the Second Karabakh War in 2020 requires more evidence and is fact- and time-dependent.[111] However, it may be estimated that the Armenian occupation of

107 See *supra* Part 1, Chapter 8 on parameters of overall control.

108 *Chiragov* (n 94), para 180.

109 See *supra* Chapter 14. See *infra* on the blockade of the Lachin Corridor.

110 International Crisis Group, *Post-War Prospects for Nagorno-Karabakh War* (ICG 2021) 1, footnote 4 and 7. According to the ICG, "[t]he troops manning the front line on the Armenian side are residents of Nagorno-Karabakh, with limited kit, under the command of the de facto government in Stepanakert. Yerevan, which had previously sent soldiers and armaments to the front lines, ceased doing so once Russian peacekeepers set up in the Lachin corridor." ibid, 7. "Stepanakert and Yerevan sustain regular contacts at the command level, primarily to transfer messages coming from the Russian peacekeepers or the Russian-Turkish observation centre." ibid, 1. See J Miklasová, 'The Recent Ceasefire in Nagorno-Karabakh: Territorial Control, Peacekeepers and Question of Status' (*EJIL:Talk!*, 4 December 2020) <https://www.ejiltalk.org/the-recent-ceasefire-in-nagorno-karabakh-territorial-control-peacekeepers-and-unanswered-question-of-status/> accessed 5 December 2020. However, Azerbaijan claimed that Armenia still continued to use the Lachin corridor to send weapons to Nagorno-Karabakh. 'Tensions Rise After Azerbaijan Blocks Land Route from Armenia' (*Al Jazeera*, 23 April 2023) <https://www.aljazeera.com/news/2023/4/23/tensions-rise-after-azerbaijan-blocks-land-route-from-armenia> accessed 31 October 2023. See also *supra* Chapter 14.

111 See for a contrary position MN Schmitt and KS Coble, 'The Evolving Nagorno-Karabakh Conflict – An International Law Perspective – Part II' (*Articles of War*, 29 September 2023) <https://lieber.westpoint.edu/evolving-nagorno-karabakh-conflict-international-law-perspective-part-ii/> accessed 31 October 2023.

Nagorno-Karabakh ended at some point between the stationing of the Russian peacekeepers following the signature of the November 2020 ceasefire and the beginning of the blockade of the Lachin Corridor in December 2022 at the latest.[112]

With Azerbaijan's military operation on 19–20 September 2023 taking control of Nagorno-Karabakh and the restoration of Azerbaijan's territorial integrity, the question of Armenia's occupation is no longer pertinent.[113]

2.5 *Transnistria*

Based on Part 2, Chapter 15, Russia intervened in the conflict in Transnistria in 1992, both directly and indirectly; therefore, there was an international armed conflict between Moldova and Russia. Based on publicly available sources, it is difficult to assess whether the non-international armed conflict between Moldova and Transnistrian separatists became internationalised by virtue of Russia's overall control over separatists. There is simply not enough evidence to substantiate a two-pronged test of overall control, particularly Russia's role in the organisation, coordination or planning of the military actions of separatists at that stage of the conflict.[114]

However, the question arises as to whether Russia's ongoing illegal military presence can be characterised as an occupation of Moldova. Of all the situations analysed in this chapter, the factual situation here seems to be the most complex. The first question is whether the presence of 1,500 Russian troops in the region not directly neighbouring Russia fulfils the criteria of effective control for the purposes of belligerent occupation.[115] In comparison, Russia's

---

112 See *infra* on the blockade of Lachin Corridor. It is argued *infra* that Armenia's effective control over Nagorno-Karabakh for the purposes of jurisdiction under ECHR continued even after the Second Karabakh War and arguably also after the blockade of the Lachin Corridor (in parallel to positive obligations of Azerbaijan).

113 However, arguably, the answer to the question of Armenia's overall control over the proxies in Nagorno-Karabakh has a bearing on the classification of the situation on 19–20 September 2023. Given previous conclusions, it is unlikely that this was an international armed conflict between Azerbaijan and Armenia. Notably, unlike the 2020 ceasefire agreement and the 1994 Bishkek ceasefire agreement, the ceasefire in 2023 did not involve the representatives of the Republic of Armenia but only the local Karabakh authorities. While Azerbaijan has portrayed its actions as an internal matter, an anti-terrorist operation, it can be agreed with Bagheri that the conflict has reached the threshold of NIAC. S Bagheri, 'Forced Movement of Civilians in Nagorno-Karabakh?' (*Opinio Juris*, 20 October 2023) <http://opiniojuris.org/2023/10/20/forced-movement-of-civilians-in-nagorno-karabakh/> accessed 31 October 2023.

114 See *supra* Part 1, Chapter 8 on parameters of overall control.

115 See *supra* Part 1, Chapter 8.

troop presence in South Ossetia, which has approximately the same territory as Transnistria, amounts to a higher number of around 4,000 troops.

However, Russia's regular troop presence cannot be analysed in isolation from the fulfilment of the criteria of occupation by proxy. Specifically, the question arises whether Russia exercises *Tadić*, overall control over Transnistrian separatists, who are in effective control of Transnistria's territory. Since the end of hostilities, Russia has supported Transnistria in military, political and economic spheres.[116] As far as its role in the organisation, coordination or planning of the military actions of Transnistrian separatists is concerned, for example, Russian troops in Transnistria conduct military exercises with the Transnistrian military.[117] This undeniably violates Article 4 of the 1992 Ceasefire Agreement.[118] The UNGA took note with concern of "the continuous illegal joint military exercises of the Operational Group of Russian Forces with paramilitaries of the separatist entity in the eastern part of the country".[119] According to the Euronest Parliamentary Assembly, Russia "has conducted joint military exercises with the military forces of the Transnistrian regime".[120] These exercises could be taken as evidence of shared military objectives and strategy.[121] Moreover, with respect to Russia subsidising Transnistria's budget, Russia can be considered as indirectly paying the salaries of Transnistrian soldiers.[122]

It is true that there is not enough publicly available evidence on other critical indicators of overall control, such as the direct participation of Russian officers in the Transnistrian army, the reality of its command structures, the direction of its military operations and the identification of its structures with

---

116 See *supra* Chapter 15.

117 M Necsutu, 'Russia Dismisses Compensating Moldova for "Occupying" Transnistria' (*BalkanInsight*, 24 January 2018) <https://balkaninsight.com/2018/01/24/russia-slams-moldova-s-demand-for-compensations-in-transnistria-01-24-2018/> accessed 12 June 2019.

118 1992 Ceasefire Agreement, art 4.

119 UNGA Res 72/282 (22 June 2018) UN Doc A/RES/72/282, preambular para 12.

120 Euronest Parliamentary Assembnly, 'Resolution on Security Challenges in the Eastern Partnership Countries and Enhancing Role of the EU in Addressing Them' (25 September 2018) 2018/C 343/01, para M.

121 The relevant case law also looks into the pursuit of such goals and strategies. *Cf Tadić* (n 45) paras 150–153. In *Naletilić and Martinović*, the Trial Chamber established that to implement common goals, the third State leadership issued orders for the armed groups. *Naletilić and Martinović* (n 45) para 201; *Tihomir Blaškić* (n 45) paras 108–111.

122 Even though the relevant case law seems to require a direct payment of salaries from the third State to the armed groups. *Cf Tadić* (n 45) para 150; *Naletilić and Martinović* (n 45) paras 199 and 201.

those of the Russian armed forces.[123] Nevertheless, with respect to the abovementioned factors and to Russia's direct military presence, it is potentially arguable that Moldova's region of Transnistria is under military occupation by the Russian Federation. As the Occupying Power, Russia would thus be bound to comply with the treaty and customary law of occupation.[124]

The complexity of the situation in Transnistria is also reflected in the inconsistent approach of IOs and doctrine. According to the 2017 judgement of Moldova's Constitutional Court, "the military occupation of a part of the territory of the Republic of Moldova" does not affect the validity of the constitutional provision on neutrality.[125] However, while, for example, the EU and OSCE have referred to the *occupation* of Abkhazia and South Ossetia, they have not employed the same language with respect to Russia's military presence in Transnistria.[126] They have simply urged Russia to withdraw its troops from the region.[127] However, the Euronest Parliamentary Assembly held that Russia maintains an illegal military presence "in the occupied territory and separatist region of Transnistria in the Republic of Moldova".[128] Similarly, the 2022 Opinion of the Parliamentary Assembly of the Council of Europe referred to Russian "military aggression" against Moldova and "occupation of its Transnistrian region".[129] The ECtHR did not draw any conclusion as to whether Transnistria is under the occupation of the Russian Federation.[130] In addition, for example, Georgia pleaded in *Georgia v Russia* that under *Ilașcu*,

123 See *supra* Part 1, Chapter 8 for indicators of overall control.

124 Russia is party to the HR, GCIV and API. Moldova is party to GCIV and API. Both Russia and Moldova are bound by customary international humanitarian law.

125 See *Judgment on the Interpretation of Article 11 of the Constitution* (Moldova, Constitutional Court) (2 May 2017) No 37b/2014, 31 <http://www.rulac.org/assets/downloads/Cst_Court_of_Moldova_Judgment_Neutrality.pdf> accessed 12 June 2019.

126 See for example European Parliament, 'Resolution on Association Agreements/Deep and Comprehensive Free Trade Areas with Georgia, Moldova and Ukraine' (21 January 2016) 2015/3032 (RSP)), para D. See *supra* section on Abkhazia and South Ossetia.

127 See *supra*.

128 Euronest Parliamentary Assembly, 'Resolution on Security Challenges in the Eastern Partnership Countries and Enhancing Role of the EU in Addressing Them' (25 September 2018) 2018/C 343/01, para M.

129 CoE (PACE) Opinion 300 (15 March 2022) para 5.

130 "The Court considers that where a Contracting State is prevented from exercising its authority over the whole of its territory by a constraining de facto situation, as such obtains when a separatist regime is set up, *whether or not this is accompanied by military occupation by another State.*" *Ilașcu and others v Moldova and Russia* ECHR 2004-VII 1, para 333 ("*Ilașcu*").

Russia exercised effective control in Transnistria "without military occupation".[131] Some scholars, including Popjanevski, Hannum and Grant, argue that Transnistria is occupied by Russia.[132] According to RULAC, Russia exercises overall control over Transnistrian authorities, which, in turn, exercises effective control over Transnistria as a *de facto* government.[133]

3 Consequences of Change of Effective Territorial Control: Applicability of Human Rights Law (ECHR)

The consequences of changing effective territorial control can also be detected in human rights law. This book only focuses on European human rights law, given its relevance to the cases under question. At the time of this book's finalisation, the ECtHR had rendered several consequential judgements regarding the applicability of the ECHR with respect to illegal secessionist entities in the post-Soviet space. The Court's approach in these cases is scrutinised prominently in Part 1, Chapter 8 and other chapters of this book. Therefore, the following text only provides a brief overview of the relevant conclusions, the pending cases and the implications of Russia's ceasing to be a party to the ECHR in September 2022. The chapter nevertheless provides an in-depth analysis of the applicability of ECHR with respect to the territories that have not been assessed in the case law yet, particularly Abkhazia and South Ossetia (before the outbreak of the 2008 Russia-Georgia War) and Nagorno-Karabakh (after the Second Karabakh War).

---

131 *Application of the International Convention on the Elimination of All Forms of Racial Discrimination (Georgia v Russian Federation)*, Provisional Measures, Oral Proceedings, Verbatim Record, Public Sitting (9 September 2008, 4:30pm) CR/2008/25, para 40.

132 Popjanevski (n 98) 29. H Hannum, 'Remarks' (2002) 96 American Society of International Law Proceedings 95, 99, ftn 12. TD Grant, *Aggression Against Ukraine: Territory, Responsibility, and International Law* (Palgrave Macmillan 2015) 83–84. See also A Berkes, 'The Nagorno-Karabakh Conflict Before the European Court of Human Rights: Pending Cases and Certain Forecasts on Jurisdiction and State Responsibility' (2013) 52 Military Law and the Law of War Review 379, 411–414.

133 RULAC, 'Military Occupation of Moldova by Russia' <http://www.rulac.org/browse/conflicts/military-occupation-of-moldova-by-russia#collapse4accord> accessed 12 June 2019. However, RULAC infers the fulfilment of the overall control test from the ECtHR case law.

3.1 *Case Law on the Applicability of the* ECHR *in the Post-Soviet Illegal Secessionist Entities*

By now, the extensive case law of the ECtHR established that Russia (and Armenia in Nagorno-Karabakh) exercised effective control over several post-Soviet illegal secessionist entities; thus, events occurring within these territories at a relevant time fell within its extra-territorial jurisdiction under Article 1 ECHR. In *Ilaşcu,* the ECtHR established that "the authorities of the Russian Federation contributed both militarily and politically to the creation of a separatist regime in the region of Transdniestria"[134] and ultimately held that Transnistria "remains under the *effective authority*, or at the very least under the *decisive influence*, of the Russian Federation".[135] The Court has consistently upheld this finding in the subsequent case law.[136] Regarding Nagorno-Karabakh, in *Chiragov,* the Court – in the context preceding the Second Karabakh War – concluded that "the 'NKR' and its administration survives by virtue of the military, political, financial and other support given to it by Armenia which, consequently, exercises *effective control* over Nagorno-Karabakh and the surrounding territories, including the district of Lachin".[137]

Concerning Russia's extra-territorial jurisdiction over Abkhazia and South Ossetia in the period after the 2008 Russia-Georgia War, the Court established in *Georgia v Russia (II)* that Russia exercised effective control over these

134 *Ilaşcu* (n 130) para 382. See *supra* Part 1, Chapter 8 on the factual elements that the Court took into account.

135 ibid para 392 (*emphasis added*).

136 *Mozer v the Republic of Moldova and Russia* App no 11138/10 (ECtHR, 23 February 2016) para 110 (*emphasis added*). See also *Case of Ivantoc and others v Moldova and Russia* App no 23687/05 (ECtHR, 15 November 2011), paras 118 and 120; *Catan and Others v The Republic of Moldova and Russia* App nos 43370/04, 8252/05 and 18454/06 (ECtHR, 19 October 2012), para 122; *Turturica and Casian v the Republic of Moldova and Russia,* paras 30–31 and para 33; *Paduret v the Republic of Moldova and Russia,* App no 26626/11 (ECtHR, 9 May 2017), paras 18 and 19; *Eriomenco v the Republic of Moldova and Russia,* App no 42224/11 (ECtHR, 9 May 2017), paras 45–46; *Soyoma v the Republic of Moldova, Russia and Ukraine,* App no 1203/05 (ECtHR, 30 May 2017), paras 22–23; *Vardanean v the Republic of Moldova and Russia* App no 22200/01 (ECtHR, 30 May 2017), paras 22 and 23; *Apcov v the Republic of Moldova and Russia* App no 13463/07 (ECtHR, 30 May 2017), paras 23 and 24; *Braga v the Republic of Moldova and Russia* App no 76957/01 (ECtHR, 17 October 2017), paras 24–25; *Case of Draci v the Republic of Moldova and Russia* App no 5349/02 (ECtHR, 17 October 2017), paras 28–29; *Sandu and Others v the Republic of Moldova and Russia* App nos 21034/05 and 7 others (ECtHR, 17 July 2018), paras 36–37; *Case of Mangir and Others v the Republic of Moldova and Russia* App no 50157/06 (ECtHR, 17 July 2018), paras 28 and 29.

137 *Chiragov* (n 94) para 186. KM Larsen, '"Territorial Non-Application" of the European Convention on Human Rights' (2009) 78 Nordic Journal of International Law 73, 92.

entities.[138] The ECtHR reached the same conclusion in April 2023 in *Georgia v Russia (IV)*.[139]

Moreover, the ECtHR established Russia's effective control over the Ukrainian Autonomous Republic of Crimea and the city of Sevastopol in *Ukraine v Russia (re Crimea)* in January 2021.[140] It did so in two steps. First, concerning the period between the day of the seizure of the Crimea government buildings on 27 February 2014 and the date of signature of the so-called admission treaty on 18 March 2014, the Court established that Russia exercised extra-territorial jurisdiction there (despite Russia rejecting that the events in Crimea at this time were within its jurisdiction). Second, Russian jurisdiction over the events taking place in Crimea after 18 March 2014 was uncontested. The Court nevertheless established the nature of such jurisdiction as extra-territorial rather than territorial.[141]

Ultimately, the ECtHR examined whether the Russian Federation "enjoyed at any point effective control over the relevant parts of the Donetsk and Luhansk regions" in its admissibility decision in *Ukraine and the Netherlands v Russia*.[142]

---

138 *Georgia v Russia (II)* (n 72) para 174; See F Mirzayev, 'Abkhazia' in C Walter, A Von Ungern-Sternberg and K Abushov (eds), *Self-determination and Secession in International Law* (OUP 2014) 208–209; R McCorquoadale and K Hausler, 'The Application of the Right of Self-Determination' in Green JA and Waters CPM (eds), *Conflict in the Caucasus: Implications for International Legal Order* (Palgrave Macmillan 2010) 44–46; Larsen (n 137) 90–91. See also *Application of the International Convention on the Elimination of All Forms of Racial Discrimination (Georgia v Russian Federation)*, Provisional Measures, Oral Proceedings, Verbatim Record, Public Sitting (8 September 2008, 10:00am) CR/2008/22, para 34. See also OSCE (PA) 'Resolution on Ten Years After the August 2008 War in Georgia' (12 July 2008), para 14; OSCE (PA) 'Resolution on the Security and Human Rights Situation in Abkhazia, Georgia, and the Tskhinvali Region/South Ossetia, Georgia' (8 July 2019), paras 10 and 18; CoE (PACE) Res 1633 (2 October 2008), paras 12 and 28; CoE (PACE) Res 1647 (28 January 2009), para 7; See also CoE (PACE) Res 1648 (28 January 2009), para 25.1; European Parliament, 'Resolution on Russian Pressure on Eastern Partnership Countries and in Particular Destabilisation of Eastern Ukraine' (17 April 2014) 2014/2699(RSP), para L; Euronest Parliamentary Assembly, 'Resolution on the Deterioration of the Human Rights Situation in the Regions of Transnistria, Abkhazia, Tskhinvali Region/South Ossetia, Crimea and parts of Donetsk and Luhansk Oblast' 2018/C 99/01, paras E, 7.

139 *Georgia v Russia (IV)* App no 39611/18 (Decision as to Admissibility) (ECtHR, 20 April 2023) para 44.

140 *Ukraine v Russia (re Crimea)* App nos 20958/14 and 38334/18 (ECtHR, 16 December 2020) ("*Ukraine v Russia (re Crimea)*") para 335.

141 *Ukraine v Russia (re Crimea)* (n 140) paras 338–349. See above Part 1, Chapter 8 and 9 for more details.

142 *Ukraine and the Netherlands v Russia* App nos 8019/16, 43800/14 and 28525/20 (ECtHR, 25 January 2023) para 578 ("*Ukraine and the Netherlands v Russia*"). See also CoE (PACE) Res 2133 (12 October 2016), paras 5–6; CoE (PACE), 'Report of the Committee on Legal Affairs and Human Rights: Legal Remedies to Human Rights Violations on the Ukrainian

The Court ultimately established that "as a result of its military, political and economic support to the separatist entities, these areas were, from 11 May 2014 and subsequently [i.e., until 26 January 2022], under the effective control of the Russian Federation".[143]

In line with the consistent case law of the ECtHR, the territorial State's jurisdiction in the situation of the loss of their effective control is reduced to positive obligations, which include two aspects: the need to "re-establish its control" over the territories and to secure concrete rights of applicants.[144] The ECtHR upheld such an approach in cases that were also filed against the territorial State, prominently in *Ilașcu* and *Mamasakhlisi*.[145]

Several cases concerning the post-Soviet secessionist entities are currently pending on merits, raising difficult questions concerning the interplay of the consequences of peremptory territorial illegality and the applicability of human rights law.[146] Moreover, numerous cases related to the post-Soviet illegal secessionist entities are pending at the admissibility stage, especially those concerning the human rights violations triggered by the all-out Russian invasion of Ukraine.[147] In this context, it needs to be underlined that Russia ceased to be party to the ECHR on 16 September 2022.[148] This has significant implications for the scope of the applicability of ECHR in Russia-annexed territories of Ukraine and Abkhazia, South Ossetia, and Transnistria. "After that date, Russia's effective control over these territories will no longer translate into

---

Territories Outside the Control of the Ukrainian Authorities' (26 September 2016) Doc 14139, para 56. Concluding Observations on the Seventh Periodic Report of the Russian Federation (28 April 2015) CCPR/C/RUS/CO/7, para 6. The Human Rights Committee called on the Russian Federation "to ensure the application of the Covenant in respect of acts perpetrated by armed groups and proclaimed authorities of the self-proclaimed 'Donetsk people's republic,' 'Luhansk people's republic' and 'South Ossetia,' to the extent that it already exercises influence over these groups and authorities which amounts to effective control over their activities."

143 *Ukraine and the Netherlands v Russia* (n 142) para 695.

144 See *Mamasakhlisi* (n 65) paras 317–319 and 399 *et seq*. *Cf Ilașcu* (n 130) paras 339–340. See *supra* Part 1, Chapter 8.

145 ibid.

146 See below Chapter 19.

147 See 'Questions and Answers on Inter-State Cases' (*Press Unit*, 18 July 2023) <https://www.echr.coe.int/web/echr/inter-state-applications> accessed 31 October 2023. See *infra* Chapter 19 for more details.

148 See ECtHR, Resolution on the Consequences of the Cessation of Membership of the Russian Federation to the Council of Europe in Light of Article 58 of the European Convention on Human Rights (22 March 2022) para. 1.

extra-territorial spatial jurisdiction under the ECHR."[149] In terms of the ECHR, these territories represent the long-feared vacuum in the *espace juridique* of the Convention "remedied only by the territorial State's positive obligations".[150]

3.2 *Abkhazia and South Ossetia (before the 2008 Russia-Georgia War)*

The applicability of ECHR with respect to Abkhazia and South Ossetia concerning the period until the Russia-Georgia War in August 2008 has not been entirely determined by the ECtHR. The most relevant cases on the issue are *Georgia v Russia (II)* and *Mamasakhlisi,* which concerned Abkhazia in the period between 2001 and 2007.[151]

Notably, in the period before 2008, the Russian military presence in South Ossetia formed two-thirds of a joint peacekeeping force (JPKF) under the command of the Joint Military Commission (JCC) under the 1992 Sochi Agreement.[152] In Abkhazia, it constituted the totality of the CIS peacekeeping force under the 1994 Moscow Agreement.[153] In *Mamasakhlisi,* the ECtHR concluded that given "Abkhazia's high level of dependency on Russian support ... Russia exercised effective control and decisive influence over Abkhaz territory".[154]

Georgia v Russia (II) also tangentially touched upon the question of Russia's control over the entities before 2008, referring to the conclusions of the Independent Fact-Finding Mission as to "the pre-existing relationship of subordination between the separatist entities and the Russian Federation"[155] and the Mission's reference to the notion of "creeping annexation" of these entities by Russia.[156]

There are other indicators of Russia's effective control in these areas before 2008, including Russia's direct participation and support of separatists in the

149 J Miklasová, 'Post-Ceasefire Nagorno-Karabakh: Limits to the ECtHR's Approach to Jurisdiction over Secessionist Entities under the ECHR' (2022) 82 ZaöRV 357, 376. See on the implications of this conclusion on jurisdiction of parent State. ibid, 376–377.

150 ibid 377.

151 *Mamasakhlisi* (n 65).

152 Agreement on Principles of Settlement of the Georgian-Ossetian Conflict (signed 24 June 1992, entered into force 24 June 1992) <https://peacemaker.un.org/georgia-sochi-agreement92> accessed 2 May 2019 "Sochi Agreement"); A Lott, 'The Tagliavini Report Revisited: Jus Ad Bellum and the Legality of the Russian Intervention in Georgia' (2012) 28 Utrecht Journal of International and European Law 4, 6–7.

153 See *supra* Chapter 13.

154 *Mamasakhlisi* (n 65) para 339. See Part 1, Chapter 8.

155 *Georgia v Russia (II)* (n 72) para 168.

156 ibid, paras 169–170.

secessionist conflicts;[157] the signature of the ceasefire agreements by Russia as a party;[158] the staffing with Russian nationals of the key political and security posts in the entities' apparatus;[159] the proclamations of Russian officials and bodies in favour of separatists;[160] the facilitation of passport procedures for the residents of these entities;[161] and the provision of pensions and social benefits and other economic and financial support and the proportion of this aid with respect to the entities' budgets.[162] However, Russia's influence over these entities only gradually increased in the period between 2000 and 2008. Therefore, the establishment of Russia's jurisdiction in this period would always have to be fact-specific and time-dependent.

3.3 *Nagorno-Karabakh (after the Second Karabakh War)*

The question of whether Armenia exercised effective control over the part of Nagorno-Karabakh under the separatist control under Article 1 ECHR, requires re-assessment in light of new factual circumstances in the period following the Ceasefire Agreement of 9 November 2020 after the Second Karabakh War.[163]

Firstly, to establish a third State's effective control over the area outside its borders, the Court primarily considers the strength of its military presence in the territory.[164] As mentioned above, in light of the ceasefire agreement, the ICG concluded that "Armenia withdrew almost all its troops and stopped sending weaponry to the conflict zone. The local troops were thus left to their own devices."[165] As outlined in Part 1, Chapter 8 of this book, the ECtHR has not yet

157 See *supra* Chapter 13. *Cf Ilașcu* (n 130) paras 380–381; *Catan* (n 136) para 118. See *Mamasakhlisi* (n 65) para 323.

158 See *supra* Chapter 13. *Cf Ilașcu* (n 130) para 381.

159 See *supra* Chapter 13. *Cf Chiragov* (n 94) paras 181–182; *Mamasakhlisi* (n 65) para 331; *Georgia v Russia (II)* (n 72) para 170.

160 See *supra* Chapter 13. *Cf Ilașcu* (n 130) para 381. *Mamasakhlisi* (n 65) paras 324 and 331.

161 See *supra* Chapter 13. *Cf Chiragov* (n 94) para 182. *Mamasakhlisi* (n 65) paras 324, 330, 335.

162 See *supra* Chapter 13. *Cf Ilașcu* (n 130) para 390. *Catan* (n 184) paras 116–122; *Chiragov* (n 94) para 183. *Mamasakhlisi* (n 65) paras 332–337.

163 During the hostilities, the ECtHR received several requests for interim measures. By decisions of 29 September 2020 and of 6 October 2020, the Court applied Rule 39 of the Rules of Court. See 'The Court Makes a Statement on Requests for Interim Measures Concerning the Conflict in and around Nagorno-Karabakh' (*Press Release Issued by the Registrar of the Court*, 4 November 2020) available <https://hudoc.echr.coe.int/app/conversion/pdf/?library=ECHR&id=003-6844996-9168687&filename=Statement%20on%20requests%20for%20interim%20measures%20concerning%20the%20conflict%20in%20and%20around%20Nagorno-Karabakh.pdf> accessed 17 October 2023.

164 See *supra* Part 1, Chapter 8 on parameters of effective control.

165 International Crisis Group (n 110) 1, fn 4. See *supra* Chapter 14. See also Miklasová (n 156) 366.

established a third State's effective control over the area outside its territory without any direct presence of regular troops.[166]

Secondly, the Court may also consider the extent to which the State provided military, political and economic support to the local subordinate administration.[167] As mentioned above, in the post-ceasefire period, Nagorno-Karabakh was territorially separated from Armenia, save for the Lachin Corridor (under the control of the Russian peacekeepers).[168] According to the ICG, Armenia ceased sending weapons and other military equipment upon the arrival of the Russian peacekeeping mission.[169] However, despite this diminished possibility of militarily supporting Armenia, Armenia's significant political, economic and financial support for Nagorno-Karabakh continued.[170] Indeed, it was only as a result of this essential support and the Armenian Army's fight on the side of separatists in the Second Karabakh War in 2020 that Nagorno-Karabakh was able to survive.[171] Therefore, the author argued elsewhere that this critical support by Armenia translated into its effective control over the region in the post-ceasefire period.[172]

However, an even more complex factual situation developed in the region between 12 December 2022 and 20 September 2023, raising questions about which State had jurisdiction under Article 1 ECHR over the events occurring inside Nagorno-Karabakh. December 2022 marked the beginning of the blockade of the Lachin Corridor by the Azerbaijani protesters, whose links to the Azerbaijani government were contested. The blockade, which "hindered Nagorno-Karabakh residents' access to basic necessities", is detailed in Chapter 14 above.[173] Importantly, on 23 April 2023, Azerbaijan established a checkpoint on the Lachin Corridor, changing "a status quo under which Russian peacekeeping forces regulated traffic along the Lachin corridor".[174] Azerbaijani officials saw the checkpoint as a "reclamation of sovereignty" and a tool to

166 See *supra* Part 1, Chapter 8. Miklasová (n 156) 367. *Mamasakhlisi* (n 65) paras 325–327.

167 See *supra* Part 1, Chapter 8 on parameters of effective control.

168 See *supra* Chapter 14.

169 International Crisis Group (n 110) 1, fn 4. Miklasová (n 156) 366–367. See *supra*.

170 Miklasová (n 156) 367.

171 ibid 367. See *supra* Chapter 14.

172 ibid 367–369.

173 'New Troubles in Nagorno-Karabakh: Understanding the Lachin Corridor Crisis' (*International Crisis Group*, 22 May 2023) 2 <https://www.crisisgroup.org/europe-central-asia/caucasus/nagorno-karabakh-conflict/new-troubles-nagorno-karabakh-understanding-lachin-corridor-crisis> accessed 31 October 2023 ("New Troubles in Nagorno-Karabakh"). See *supra* Chapter 14.

174 ibid, 3.

"observe, control and influence" the region.[175] The ICG also observed that the checkpoint did not "deliver the full measure of influence that Azerbaijan seeks over the enclave" but "[i]t is, however, a step in that direction".[176]

While Azerbaijan's obligations regarding the blockade stemmed from the 2020 ceasefire agreement and binding orders of the ICJ and ECtHR,[177] the question arose regarding the extent of Azerbaijan's jurisdiction over the region and corresponding obligations under ECHR in this context.[178] While it is doubtful that Azerbaijan could be seen as retaking full-fledged control over the territory, translating into a complete territorial jurisdiction in this period, it is undeniable that its control and influence over the region grew significantly. Notably, since establishing the checkpoint in April 2023, Azerbaijan controlled the entry and exit to and from the region and thereby, through its own State agents, exercised the element of influence and control over the developments inside Nagorno-Karabakh.

Even before the Second Karabakh War, Azerbaijan's jurisdiction continued to exist, albeit reduced to positive obligations, namely to two aspects: the need to re-establish control and respect for the rights of individual applicants.[179] As pointed out in Part 1, Chapter 8, some scholars argue that the territorial State's jurisdiction is equally based on "the State's sovereign title and effectiveness".[180] In this context, the territorial State's jurisdiction is functional – "adapted to the authority that the State *can* exercise towards the concerned individuals".[181]

Thus, given the growing degree of effectiveness of Azerbaijan's control over Nagorno-Karabakh in the period under question, it is argued that the positive obligations of Azerbaijan under ECHR should reflect such a development.[182]

---

175 Azerbaijani officials cited in ibid.

176 ibid.

177 See *supra* Chapter 14.

178 See, for example, J Andela and T Manucharyan, '130 Days and Counting: A Responsibility to End the Blockade of the Lachin Corridor' (*EJIL:Talk!*, 2 May 2023) <https://www.ejiltalk.org/130-days-and-counting-a-responsibility-to-end-the-blockade-of-the-lachin-corridor/> accessed 31 October 2023.

179 *Ilașcu* (n 130) para 339. *Mamasakhlisi* (n 65) paras 317–319 and 399 *et seq*. See *supra* Part 1, Chapter 8.

180 A Berkes, *International Human Rights Law Beyond State Territorial Control* (CUP 2021) 81. According to the ECtHR, "Those obligations remain even where the exercise of the State's authority is limited in part of its territory, so that it has a duty to take all the appropriate measures which it is still within its power to take." *Ilașcu* (n 130) para 313.

181 Berkes (n 180299) 82 (*emphasis added*). See S Wallace, *The Application of the European Convention on Human Rights to Military Operations* (CUP 2019) 35–41. See further Part 1, Chapter 8.

182 Compare the position of the Human Rights Committee in the context of Moldova's obligations vis-à-vis population in Transnistria: "[T]he State party's continuing obligation to

In light of the complexity of the factual set-up in Nagorno-Karabakh in this period, it is arguable that Azerbaijan's positive obligations under ECHR continued to exist in an extended fashion alongside those flowing from the extra-territorial jurisdiction of Armenia.[183]

It is undoubted that Azerbaijan's victory over the separatists in the conflict on 20 September 2023[184] and restoration of its territorial integrity translated into its full territorial jurisdiction over Nagorno-Karabakh. Azerbaijan is thus bound to secure everyone within its jurisdiction a full range of rights and freedoms under the ECHR.

4 Consequences of Change of Effective Territorial Control: Issue of International Responsibility

The Russian Federation is responsible for any violation of international obligations, negative or positive, the extra-territorial applicability of which is triggered by its exercise of a required level of control over the territory of Crimea, DPR and LPR, Kherson and Zaporizhzhia Regions, Abkhazia and South Ossetia, and Transnistria, as analysed above, and is committed by its State organs. The same rationale applies(d) to Armenia's responsibility with respect to Nagorno-Karabakh.

The annexation of Crimea (2014), DPR, LPR, Kherson and Zaporizhzhia Regions (2022) by Russia entails that there is no need to investigate the factual connection between the local authorities and Russia; they are the State organs under Article 4 ARSIWA, and their actions are directly attributable to Russia. The question of whether the acts of organs of illegal secessionist entities of Abkhazia and South Ossetia, Transnistria and Nagorno-Karabakh can be attributed to Russia and Armenia, respectively, should be analysed on a case-by-case basis by applying the rules of attribution as codified in ARSIWA or any

ensure respect for the rights recognised in the Covenant in relation to the population of Transdniestria within the limits of its effective power." UN Human Rights Committee, Concluding Observations: Republic of Moldova (4 November 2009) UN Doc CCPR/C/MDA/CO/2, para 5. See further Berkes (n 180) 83–84.

183 See in S Besson, 'Concurrent Responsibilities under the European Convention on Human Rights: The Concurrence of Human Rights Jurisdictions, Duties and Responsibilities' in A Van Aaken and I Motoc (eds), *The European Convention on Human Rights and General International Law* (OUP 2018) 162. Berkes (n 299) 89–92.

184 Almost the entire population of Nagorno-Karabakh has fled Nagorno-Karabakh for Armenia. See *supra* Chapter 14.

other applicable standards, including, for example, those found in European human rights law.[185]

5 Conclusion

This chapter broadly outlined the legal framework applicable to the illegal secessionist entities of Transnistria, Nagorno-Karabakh, Abkhazia, South Ossetia, Russia-annexed Crimea, DPR, LPR, Kherson and Zaporizhzhia Regions. Firstly, this framework includes the consequences of peremptory illegality, specifically the duty of non-recognition of the formal status of these entities. It was shown that a generalised non-recognition of these entities and the positions of international organisations explicitly proclaiming the duty of non-recognition or indicators of peremptory territorial illegality (triggering the duty of non-recognition) in many of these instances are in line with this obligation. Further consequences are analysed in the chapters below.

Secondly, the framework includes the consequences of the change of effective territorial control. The chapter specifically focused on the applicability of the law of occupation to the post-Soviet illegal secessionist entities based on the factual criteria developed in Part 1, Chapter 8. The chapter concluded that Crimea is occupied by Russia. Regarding the DPR and LPR, the chapter detailed the conclusions of the Hague District Court in connection with those of the ECtHR, which confirm that Russia exercised overall control over the Donbas separatist armed groups since the early stages of the conflict in 2014. Since the separatists exercised effective control over the areas of the DPR and LPR (beyond the ongoing conflict in the battle zones), the criteria of Russia's occupation by proxy seem to be met. The test of Russia's overall control over the separatists was thus *a fortiori* met since Russia's all-out invasion of Ukraine. Since Russia's annexation of the parts of Donetsk, Luhansk, Zaporizhzhia and Kherson regions, the parts of these territories under effective control of Russia are occupied.

While it was asserted that the pre-2008 situation in Abkhazia and South Ossetia requires a case-by-case analysis, post-2008 factual changes allow for a conclusion that Russia has exerted overall control over armed groups in Abkhazia and South Ossetia. However, the conclusion that these territories are under occupation by Russia is derived also from Russia's direct military

185 See *supra* Part 1, Chapter 8 in detail on the existence of an autonomous threshold for attribution in the case law of the ECtHR.

presence there. The agreements signed with the secessionist entities cannot serve as a legal basis for Russia's military presence as these entities still remain a *de jure* part of Georgia.

Moreover, with respect to the situation in Nagorno-Karabakh until the outbreak of hostilities in 2020, while the presence of the Armenian military in Nagorno-Karabakh led to the conclusion of Armenia's direct occupation, the chapter also highlighted a number of indicators that seem to support the conclusion that Armenia also exercised overall control over Nagorno-Karabakh's armed groups. Following the signature of the Ceasefire Agreement on 9 November 2020, credible sources confirmed that the Armenian Armed Forces withdrew from the region and ceased providing arms to the separatists. Thus, the question of the continued Armenian occupation of the region by proxy (ie, Armenia's overall control over the local Karabakh forces) arose. Given the practical difficulties (the Lachin Corridor being under the control of the Russian peacekeepers), the chapter estimated that the Armenian occupation may have ended at some point before the initiation of the blockade of the Lachin Corridor. Nevertheless, more evidence is necessary regarding the exact connection between Armenian and local forces in that period. The chapter argued that since the setting up of Azerbaijan's checkpoint on the Lachin Corridor in April 2023, Azerbaijan's influence and control over Nagorno-Karabakh grew significantly. Arguably, this was reflected in the extended scope of Azerbaijan's positive obligations in that period. As for Transnistria, Russia's ongoing military presence there, together with evidence of some, but not all, required elements of overall control over the armed groups, seems to allow for the conclusion that it can be characterised as occupied by Russia.

In the area of European human rights law, the chapter first overviewed the existing jurisprudence of the ECtHR, which established the applicability of ECHR (especially based on effective control of Russia and Armenia, but also through positive obligations of territorial States) in Transnistria, Nagorno-Karabakh before the war of 2020, Abkhazia and South Ossetia, Crimea and the DPR and LPR. It also outlined the implications of Russia ceasing to be a party to the ECHR in September 2022. Lastly, the chapter analysed more closely the question of the applicability of ECHR in Abkhazia and South Ossetia before the outbreak of the 2008 Russia-Ukraine War and in Nagorno-Karabakh in the period between the Second Karabakh War and Azerbaijan's takeover of the entity in September 2023, as these situations have not been exhaustively dealt with in the case law.

This generally outlined legal framework, consisting of two areas of legal consequences, determines the specific legal questions, that are further examined in the following chapters.

CHAPTER 17

Purported Inter-State Relations

1 Diplomatic and Consular Relations

1.1 *Diplomatic Relations*

Abkhazia and South Ossetia are recognised by several sovereign States, most importantly by the Russian Federation, but also by Nicaragua, Venezuela, Nauru and Syria.[1] Both Abkhazia and South Ossetia have their embassies in the Russian Federation and *vice versa*.[2] Abkhazia and South Ossetia also have embassies in Venezuela, which also covers relations with Nicaragua.[3] The ambassador of Venezuela to Russia is also accredited as ambassador to Abkhazia and South Ossetia.[4] Moreover, Abkhazia opened its embassy in Syria and South Ossetia plans to do the same.[5] Given the peremptory illegality of these entities, all of the above-mentioned States violated one of the core facets of the duty of non-recognition by establishing diplomatic relations with them and thereby committed a separate international wrongful act. Following Russia's recognition of the DPR and LPR in February 2022, these two entities

1 See *supra* previous chapters. This book will not analyse the mutual recognition and purported establishment of diplomatic and consular relations among post-Soviet illegal secessionist entities, as these relations are clearly non-existent from the perspective of international law.

2 'Embassy of the Republic of Abkhazia to the Russian Federation' <http://www.emb-abkhazia.ru> accessed 17 March 2020 (*in Russian*); 'Embassy of the Republic of South Ossetia to the Russian Federation' <http://www.osembassy.org> accessed 17 March 2020 (*in Russian*); 'Embassy of the Russian Federation in the Republic of Abkhazia' <https://abkhazia.mid.ru/ru/> accessed 17 March 2020 (*in Russian*); 'Embassy of the Russian Federation in the Republic of South Ossetia' <https://rfsosetia.mid.ru/ru/> accessed 17 October 2023 (*in Russian*).

3 See 'Embassy of the Republic of Abkhazia to the Bolivarian Republic of Venezuela' <https://emb-abjasia.com/embajada/acerca/> accessed 17 March 2020 (*in Russian*); 'Ambassador of South Ossetia in Venezuela and Nicaragua Awarded by the Order of Friendship' (*RES*, 28 February 2020) <http://cominf.org/node/1166528412> accessed 17 March 2020 (*in Russian*).

4 'Juan Vicente Paredes Torrealba is Appointed as an Ambassador of Venezuela to Abkhazia' (*Sputnik*, 3 September 2015) <https://sputnik-abkhazia.ru/Abkhazia/20150903/1015598375.html> accessed 17 March 2020 (*in Russian*).

5 'South Ossetia Is Getting Ready to Open Embassy in Syria' (*RIA*, 5 July 2019) <https://ria.ru/20190715/1556525831.html> accessed 17 March 2020 (*in Russian*); 'Opening of the Embassy of the Republic of Abkhazia in the Syrian Arab Republic Took Place in Damascus' (*Abkhazworld*, 6 October 2020) <https://abkhazworld.com/aw/current-affairs/1831-opening-of-the-embassy-of-abkhazia-in-the-syrian-arab-republic> accessed 31 October 2023.

opened their embassies in Russia in the summer of 2022 before their annexation later that year.[6] The Russian press reported that, according to DPR, a difficult military situation prevented the opening of the Russian embassy in DPR.[7]

1.2 *Consular Relations*

As established in Part 1, Chapter 7 while non-recognition of Manchukuo did not seem to be affected by the maintenance of consular relations, the post-1945 practice extended the duty of non-recognition also to this area of relations.[8] The ICJ in *Namibia* explicitly referred to the duty to abstain from establishing or maintaining consular relations.[9] The practice with respect to the post-Soviet illegal secessionist entities and annexed Crimea supports this conclusion.

Firstly, regarding the establishment of new consular relations, outside of Russia's and the other recognising States' relations with South Ossetia and Abkhazia,[10] no new consular relations were established between UN member States and the post-Soviet illegal secessionist entities. To the contrary, the reference to these territories is made in the context of consular relations of the respective parent States. This is usually done through a travel advisory with respect to the parent State, either because of the inability of the foreign State

6 'The Fate of the Embassies of the DPR and LPR after the Regions Became Part of Russia Has Been Revealed' (*Lenta.ru*, 6 October 2022) <https://lenta.ru/news/2022/10/06/posolstva/> accessed 31 October 2023 (*in Russian*). See also 'Syria Looking at Openining Embassies in DPR, LPR-Ambassador to Russia' (*TASS*, 4 July 2022) <https://tass.com/world/1475483?utm_source=google.com&utm_medium=organic&utm_campaign=google.com&utm_referrer=google.com> accessed 31 October 2023.

7 'The DPR Believes that the Difficult Military Situation Prevents the Opening of the Russian Embassy' (*TASS*, 8 September 2022) <https://tass.ru/mezhdunarodnaya-panorama/15695535> accessed 31 October 2023 (*in Russian*).

8 See *supra* Part 1, Chapter 7. See V Gowlland-Debbas, *Collective Responses to Illegal Acts in International Law: United Nations Action in the Question of Southern Rhodesia* (M Nijhoff 1990) 299.

9 The ICJ held that States are under obligation "to abstain from sending consular agents to Namibia, and to withdraw any such agents already there." States should also make clear that "the maintenance of diplomatic or consular relations with South Africa does not imply any recognition of its authority with regard to Namibia." *Legal Consequences for States of the Continued Presence of South Africa in Namibia (South West Africa) notwithstanding Security Council Resolution 276* (Advisory Opinion) [1971] ICJ Rep 16, para 123 ("*Namibia*").

10 Russian embassies in Abkhazia and South Ossetia contain consular divisions; see 'Embassy of the Russian Federation in the Republic of Abkhazia' <https://abkhazia.mid.ru/ru/> accessed 17 March 2020 (*in Russian*); 'Embassy of the Russian Federation in the Republic of South Ossetia' <https://rfsosetia.mid.ru/ru/> accessed 17 October 2023 (*in Russian*). Explicit information on consular services provided in Abkhazia and South Ossetia by other recognizing States is not directly available.

to provide consular assistance in these territories[11] or their severe limitation.[12] This approach can be taken as confirmation of the fact that these territories are still considered part of foreign State's consular districts in the parent State. The provision of consular assistance in these territories is limited or impossible due to factual circumstances, such as the inability of consular officers to travel to these areas, and not due to change of sovereignty there.

Secondly, as far as annexed Crimea is concerned, presumably apart from the seven States that recognise it as part of Russia,[13] consular districts of no other foreign State in Russia have been extended to cover the territory of Crimea. To the contrary, as in the previous case, the reference to Crimea is made in the context of consular relations with Ukraine, in the form of travel advisory warnings against travel to the territory of Crimea and the inability to receive consular assistance there.[14]

---

11 See, for example, the UK's travel advisory concerning Ukraine 'Foreign Travel Advice: Ukraine' <https://www.gov.uk/foreign-travel-advice/ukraine/safety-and-security> accessed 20 October 2023; The UK's travel advisory concerning Abkhazia and South Ossetia 'Foreign Travel Advice: Georgia' <https://www.gov.uk/foreign-travel-advice/georgia> accessed 16 October 2023; Germany's travel advisory concerning DPR, LPR, Zaporizhzhia, Kherson Regions 'Ukraine: Travel Warning/Request to Leave the Country' <https://www.auswaertiges-amt.de/de/ReiseUndSicherheit/ukrainesicherheit/201946> accessed 16 October 2023 (*in German*); US's travel advisory concerning Nagorno-Karabakh 'Azerbaijan Travel Advisory' <https://travel.state.gov/content/travel/en/traveladvisories/traveladvisories/azerbajian-travel-advisory.html> accessed 16 October 2023; The US's travel advisory concerning Abkhazia and South Ossetia 'Georgia Travel Advisory' <https://travel.state.gov/content/travel/en/traveladvisories/traveladvisories/georgia-travel-advisory.html> accessed 16 October 2023.

12 See, for example, the UK's travel advisory concerning Transnistria 'Foreign Travel Advice: Moldova' <https://www.gov.uk/foreign-travel-advice/moldova> accessed 16 October 2023; The UK's travel advisory concerning Nagorno-Karabakh 'Foreign Travel Advice: Azerbaijan' <https://www.gov.uk/foreign-travel-advice/azerbaijan> accessed 16 October 2023; Canada's travel advisory concerning Nagorno-Karabakh 'Official Global Travel Advisories: Azerbaijan' <https://travel.gc.ca/destinations/azerbaijan> accessed 16 October 2023; The US's travel advisory concerning Transnistria 'Moldova Travel Advisory' <https://travel.state.gov/content/travel/en/traveladvisories/traveladvisories/moldova-travel-advisory.html> accessed 16 October 2023.

13 There is no directly relevant information on the extension of the consular districts of these States in Russia. But due to recognition, they should also include Crimea.

14 See for example the UK's travel advisory concerning Ukraine 'Foreign Travel Advice: Ukraine' <https://www.gov.uk/foreign-travel-advice/ukraine/safety-and-security> accessed 16 October 2023; Germany's travel advisory concerning Crimea 'Ukraine: Travel Warning/ Request to Leave the Country' <https://www.auswaertiges-amt.de/de/ReiseUndSicherheit/ukrainesicherheit/201946> accessed 16 October 2023 (*in German*); Ireland's travel advisory concerning Ukraine 'Travel Advice: Ukraine' <https://www.dfa.ie/travel/travel-advice/a-z-list-of-countries/ukraine/> accessed 16 October 2023; France's travel

Lastly, a specific situation occurred with respect to the Consulate General of Poland in Sevastopol after the annexation of Crimea. This consulate continued its operation until September 2014, when, due to its effective inability to perform its mission in Crimea, its tasks were taken over by the Consulate General of Poland in Ukrainian Odesa.[15] The Ukrainian authorities agreed to the inclusion of the Sevastopol Consulate's consular district into the consular district of Odesa's Consulate General, which now has competence over the territory of Crimea.[16] The continued functioning of this consulate until September 2014, even after the annexation, clearly did not entail a violation of the duty of non-recognition, as consular functions were performed under the exequatur issued by Ukraine before the annexation.[17] Until September 2014, its consular district remained one of Poland's consular districts in Ukraine regardless of the annexation of Crimea by Russia.

1.3 *Diplomatic-Like and Consular-Like Relations of Other Post-Soviet Illegal Secessionist Entities*

DPR, LPR, Abkhazia, South Ossetia and Transnistria also sought to establish relations that simulated diplomatic or consular relations, especially by opening representative offices abroad. For example, the Representative Office of the Republic of South Ossetia was opened in Rome;[18] the DPR opened such offices in Turin and Verona in Italy,[19] in Greece,[20] in

advisory on Ukraine 'Ukraine' <https://www.diplomatie.gouv.fr/fr/conseils-aux-voyageurs/conseils-par-pays-destination/ukraine/#securite> accessed 16 October 2023. See also 'Latvia Issues Crimea Reminder' <https://eng.lsm.lv/article/politics/diplomacy/latvia-issues-crimea-reminder.a271618/> accessed 16 October 2023.

15 'Poland Evacuates Consulate in Crimea: Foreign Minister' (*Reuters*, 8 March 2014) <https://www.reuters.com/article/idUSBREA270E9/> accessed 16 June 2020.

16 ibid.

17 Gowlland-Debbas offers a similar analysis with respect to the maintenance of consular offices in Southern Rhodesia, which were performed under the exequaturs issued by the Queen before the declaration of independence and therefore were not accredited with Southern Rhodesia as a State. Calls for the withdrawal of such consular offices must be seen in the context of enforcement actions of the UNSC and not a general duty of non-recognition. Gowlland-Debbas (n 8) 300. See, for example, UNSC Res 277 (18 March 1970) UN Doc S/RES/277, para 10.

18 See *infra*.

19 'DPR to Open Second Representative Office in Italy on February 9 – Foreign Ministry' (*Donetsk News Agency*, 8 February 2019) <https://dan-news.ru/en/society/dpr-to-open-second-representative-office-in-italy-on-february-9-foreign-ministry/> accessed 17 March 2020.

20 'Representative Office of the DPR Opened in Greece' (*TASS*, 21 March 2017) <https://tass.ru/mezhdunarodnaya-panorama/4114028> accessed 17 March 2020 (*in Russian*).

Finland,[21] in Marseille in France[22] and in Ostrava in the Czech Republic.[23] The LPR also claimed to have opened an office in Vienna, Austria.[24] Moreover, despite the lack of Russia's recognition of Transnistria, the latter also opened its representative office in Moscow.[25]

These offices are opened under municipal private law of the 'host' States, usually as associations, non-profit organisations or non-governmental organisations.[26] The opening of these entities is frequently accompanied by a statement of the Ministry of Foreign Affairs of the respective 'host' State reiterating its position on non-recognition of the entity in question as a State, on its support for the parent State's territorial integrity and on the unofficial and non-diplomatic status of the office in question.[27] Given that none of the purported 'host' States consented to the establishment of diplomatic relations with these entities, it is difficult to find the existence of these offices incompatible with the duty of non-recognition.

---

21 'Representation of the DPR in Helsinki Will Not Have Legal Force' (*Ria Novosti*, 12 April 2017) <https://ria.ru/20171208/1510491372.html> accessed 17 March 2020 (*in Russian*). See 'Natalia Nikonorova Met with Guests from Foreign Countries' (*Website of the DPR's Ministry of Foreign Affairs*, 10 May 2019) <http://archive2018-2020.dnronline.su/2019/05/10/ministr-inostrannyh-del-dnr-natalya-nikonorova-vstretilas-s-zarubezhnymi-gostyami-video/> accessed 17 October 2023 (*in Russian*).

22 See *infra*.

23 See *infra*.

24 'Representation of the LPR Opens in Austria' (*Ria Novosti*, 8 September 2016) <https://ria.ru/20160908/1476416396.html> accessed 17 March 2020 (*in Russian*). See also '"Luhansk Peoples' Republic" Wants to Open Representation in Vienna' (*Die Presse*, 9 September 2016) <https://www.diepresse.com/5082882/luhansker-volksrepublik-will-vertretung-in-wien-eroffnen> accessed 17 March 2020 (*in German*).

25 'Representation Office of Transnistria Was Opened in Moscow, Russia' (*Moldova.org*, 26 January 2017) <https://www.moldova.org/en/representation-office-transnistria-opened-moscow-russia/> accessed 17 March 2020; M Nescutu, 'Breakaway Moldova Region to Open "Embassy" in Russia' (*BalkanInsight*, 14 January 2019) <https://balkaninsight.com/2019/01/14/russia-is-allowing-a-diplomatic-office-for-transnistria-01-14-2019/> accessed 17 March 2020.

26 See also A Myronuk, 'Inside the Donetsk People's Republic's Sisyphean Struggle for International Legitimacy' (*coda*, 2 October 2019) <https://www.codastory.com/disinformation/donetsk-international-legitimacy/> accessed 17 March 2020.

27 'Ministry of Foreign Affairs Press Release Regarding the Opening of the Self-Proclaimed Representative Office of the so-called "Republic of South Ossetia" in Rome' (*Press Release of the Ministry of Foreign Affairs and International Cooperation of the Italian Republic*, 4 January 2016) <https://www.esteri.it/mae/en/sala_stampa/archivionotizie/comunicati/2016/04/comunicato-della-farnesina-sull.html> accessed 17 March 2020; 'Foreign Ministry Spokesperson Stratos Efthymiou's Response to a Journalist's Question Regarding Reports of the Opening of a Self-Proclaimed "Official Delegation of the Donetsk People's Republic" in Greece' (*Press Release of the Ministry of Foreign Affairs of the Hellenic

In some situations, however, the national judiciary can find the objectives or the activities of these associations incompatible with municipal law or international law and dissolve them. For example, the district court in Ostrava in the Czech Republic ordered the dissolution of the DPR's Representative Office, pointing to the fact that the association rejected changing its name, while its head proclaimed herself to be the Donetsk People's Republic's honorary consul.[28] According to the Court, since the DPR was not recognised by any State, it could not have any honorary consul.[29] In similar proceedings, the French district court in Aix-en-Provence rejected the motion for the dissolution of the DPR's Representative Office in Marseille as it did not find established this association's "illegal character of its object or of pursued goal".[30] The Aix-en-Provence Court of Appeal reversed this first-instance judgment and ordered the dissolution of this representation.[31]

Republic, 21 March 2017) <https://www.mfa.gr/en/current-affairs/statements-speeches/foreign-ministry-spokesperson-stratos-efthymious-response-to-journalists-question-regarding-reports-of-the-opening-of-self-proclaimed-official-delegation-of-the-donetsk-peoples-republic-in-greece.html?fbclid=IwAR17BtAYdvAohkRKVsa9lPND_hBq_jeOTExID8mB-1t7G7nQAC2sd4ObWDw> accessed 17 March 2020.

28 See 'Court in Czech Republic Closes Ukrainian Separatist Mission in Ostrava' (*RFE/Radio Liberty*, 29 June 2017) <https://www.rferl.org/a/court-czech-republic-closes-ukrainian-separatist-mission-donetsk-peoples-republic-ostava-/28585123.html> accessed 17 March 2020.

29 The judgment was upheld on appeal. 'High Court Upheld the Dissolution of the Self-Proclaimed Donetsk Consulate in Ostrava' (*iDNES*, 26 April 2018) <https://www.idnes.cz/ostrava/zpravy/vrchni-soud-donecka-republika-konzulat-nela-liskova.A180426_110601_ostrava-zpravy_jog> accessed 17 March 2020 (*in Czech*).

30 'La justice rejette la dissolution d'une "représentation officielle" de la République du Donetsk' (*Franceinfo*, 6 September 2018) <https://france3-regions.francetvinfo.fr/provence-alpes-cote-d-azur/bouches-du-rhone/marseille/justice-rejette-dissolution-representation-officielle-republique-du-donetsk-1536736.html> accessed 17 March 2020; 'Marseille: la justice assigne la "représentation officielle" de Donetsk' (*Franceinfo*, 11 January 2018) <https://france3-regions.francetvinfo.fr/provence-alpes-cote-d-azur/bouches-du-rhone/marseille-justice-assigne-representation-officiellede-donetsk-1399485.html> accessed 17 March 2020.

31 T Rabino, 'La justice ordonne la dissolution d'une vraie-fausse représentation de "la République de Donetsk"' (*Marianne*, 23 March 2021) <https://www.marianne.net/monde/europe/la-justice-ordonne-la-dissolution-dune-vraie-fausse-representation-de-la-republique-de-donetsk> accessed 31 October 2023.

2 Treaty Relations

2.1 *Russia's Treaties with Post-Soviet Illegal Secessionist Entities*

Since Russia's recognition of Abkhazia and South Ossetia, numerous treaties have been signed between Russia and these two entities.[32] The most important among them were the 2008 Friendship Agreements, the 2014 Strategic Partnership Treaty with Abkhazia and the 2015 Integration Treaty with South Ossetia.[33] During the short-lived purported existence of the Crimean Republic, Russia and this self-proclaimed republic signed the Treaty on the Accession of the Republic of Crimea to the Russian Federation and on Forming New Constituent Entities of the Russian Federation on 18 March 2014.[34] The legal status of this treaty is of fundamental importance because, if valid, it would entail a valid succession of States. Similarly, in the wake of Russia's recognition of the DPR and LPR on 21 February 2022, Russia signed the purported agreements on friendship, cooperation and mutual assistance with the leaders of the DPR and LPR.[35] On 30 September 2022 – following Russia's recognition of the Kherson and Zaporizhzhia Regions – Putin and these four entities signed the purported agreements on the accession to the Russian Federation and the creation of new subjects of the Russian Federation.[36]

Abkhazia, South Ossetia the Crimean Republic, DPR, LPR, Zaporizhzhia and Kherson regions were characterised above as illegal secessionist entities, created in connection with the violation of a peremptory norm of international law. A number of legal consequences in the area of treaty relations follow. Firstly, these treaties can be considered as non-existent under international law, given the lack of statehood status of one of the parties and the consequent lack of competence of this entity to conclude treaties.[37] Secondly, by concluding these treaties, Russia undeniably violated the duty of non-recognition and thus committed a separate international wrongful act.

Regarding the purported treaties between Russia, Abkhazia and South Ossetia, the CoE's Committee of Ministers found that the Strategic Partnership Treaty and Integration Treaty violated "Georgia's sovereignty and territorial

---

32 Between 2008 and 2015 up to 78 bilateral agreements were signed between Russia and Abkhazia and South Ossetia. See *supra* Chapter 13.

33 See *supra* Chapter 13.

34 See *supra* Chapter 11.

35 See *supra* Chapter 12.

36 See *supra* Chapter 12.

37 See *supra* Part 1, Chapter 7. *Contra*: L Trigeaud, 'L'influence des reconnaisances d'Etat sur la formation des engagements conventionels' (2015) 119 RGDIP 571, 582–584.

integrity" and had "no legal validity".[38] NATO's Secretary-General and other international organisations have made similar statements.[39] The international community overwhelmingly rejected the purported treaties of 30 September 2022 between Russia and the DPR, LPR, Zaporizhzhia and Kherson Regions.[40] Most prominently, the UNGA resolution declared that "attempted illegal annexations" of the four regions "have no validity under international law and do not form the basis for any alteration of the status of these regions of Ukraine."[41]

2.2 *Armenia's Agreements with Nagorno-Karabakh*

Russia officially recognised Abkhazia, South Ossetia, the Crimean Republic, the DPR, LPR, Zaporizhzhia and Kherson Regions as sovereign States. In contrast, Armenia did not recognise the Nagorno-Karabakh Republic as such. However, this did not seem to preclude Armenia from concluding agreements with Nagorno-Karabakh in which they both acted as sovereign States. In particular, they concluded the Agreement on Military Co-operation between the Governments of the Republic of Armenia and the Republic of Nagorno-Karabakh on 25 June 1994, in which they foresaw multi-faceted co-operation in the military sphere.[42] Moreover, Armenia and Nagorno-Karabakh also signed the Agreement on the Organisation of the Passport System on 24 February 1999, according to which "the citizens of the Republic of Nagorno-Karabakh willing to leave the territory of either the Republic of Nagorno-Karabakh or

38 CoE (Committee of Ministers) CM/Res(2015)1227, para 2; CoE (Committee of Ministers) CM/Res(2017)1285, para 2; CoE (Committee of Ministers) CM/Res(2018)1315, para 2. See also CoE (Committee of Ministers) CM/Res(2016)1255, para 2; CoE (Committee of Ministers) CM/Res(2019)1345, para 2.

39 NATO, 'Statement by the NATO Secretary General on the So-called Treaty Between the Russian Federation and the South Ossetia Region of Georgia' (*NATO Press Release*, 18 March 2015) <https://www.nato.int/cps/en/natohq/news_118280.htm> accessed 15 May 2019. European Parliament, 'Resolution on the Strategic Military Situation in the Black Sea Basin Following the Illegal Annexation of Crimea by Russia' (11 June 2015) 2015/2036(INI), para J. EEAS, 'Statement by High Representative/Vice-President Frederica Mogherini on the Announced Signature of a "Treaty on Alliance and Integration" between the Russian Federation and Georgia's Breakaway Region of South Ossetia' (*Press Release*, 17 March 2015) <https://eeas.europa.eu/headquarters/headquarters-homepage/3300/statement-high-representativevice-president-federica-mogherini-announced-signature-treaty_en> accessed 16 May 2019.

40 See in detail *supra* Chapter 12.

41 UNGA Res ES-11/4 Territorial Integrity of Ukraine: Defending the Principles of the Charter of the United Nations (12 October 2022) UN Doc A/RES/ES-11/4, para 3.

42 Agreement on Military Co-operation between the Governments of the Republic of Armenia and the Republic of Nagorno-Karabakh (signed 25 June 1994) partially reprinted in *Chiragov and Others v Armenia* ECHR 2015-III 135, para 74 ("*Chiragov*").

the Republic of Armenia may apply and obtain a passport of the Republic of Armenia".[43] Similarly to the above-mentioned treaties between Russia and Abkhazia, South Ossetia, the Republic of Crimea the DPR, LPR, Zaporizhzhia and Kherson Regions, the agreements between Armenia and Nagorno-Karabakh can be considered non-existent under international law due to the lack of status of statehood of one of the parties and a consequent lack of competence in this entity to conclude treaties.[44] Moreover, Armenia thereby also flagrantly violated the duty of non-recognition and thus committed an additional international wrongful act.[45]

2.3 *Treaty-Like Relations of Other Post-Soviet Illegal Secessionist Entities*

Apart from Armenia's approach to Nagorno-Karabakh, other States and IOs that have not recognised the post-Soviet illegal secessionist entities as States do not have any treaty relations with these entities. For example, the EU notably ignored Transnistria's offer to conclude a separate bilateral trade agreement.[46] However, a limited practice of agreement-like documents with illegal secessionist entities can be observed. This includes ceasefire agreements,[47] documents signed in the framework of the conflict resolution and other documents adopted in the context of functional cooperation,[48] most notably between the entity and the parent State.

If the ceasefire agreements are considered governed by international law,[49] this confirms a certain limited international capacity of illegal secessionist

43 Agreement on the Organisation of the Passport System (signed 24 February 1999) partially reprinted in ibid para 83.

44 See *supra* Part 1, Chapter 7.

45 See *supra* Part 1, Chapter 7.

46 S Secrieru, 'Transnistria Zig-zagging towards a DCFTA' (*PISM*, 28 January 2020) <https://www.pism.pl/publications/PISM_Policy_Paper_no__4__145___Transnistria_Zig_zagging_towards_a_DCFTA> accessed 17 March 2020.

47 The analysis of ceasefire agreements, in particular Minsk II, was carried out *supra*. See also B Coppieters, 'Abkhazia, Transnistria and North Cyprus: Recognition and Non-Recognition in Ceasefire and Trade Agreements' (2019) Ideology and Politics 10, 18–26.

48 In the context of the MH17 crash, the DPR's leader and Malaysian officials signed the memorandum on the transfer of the black boxes. A Yuhas, 'Pro-Russian Rebels Hand Over MH17 Black Boxes to Malaysian Officials – As It Happened' (*The Guardian*, 21 July 2014) <https://www.theguardian.com/world/2014/jul/21/mh17-disaster-ukraine-obama-live-updates> accessed 17 March 2020.

49 Generally, ceasefire agreements are signed by leaders of non-State armed groups and frequently by third-party guarantors such as regional organisations as well. Article 3 VCLT makes clear that the non-applicability of the VCLT to international agreements between the States and other subjects of international law does not affect the legal force of such agreements or the applicability of VCLT rules by virtue of their customary character. As

entities to have rights and obligations within the specific framework of these ceasefire agreements. This practice, however, does not in any way imply recognition of their status as States.

Furthermore, the practice between Moldova and Transnistria is particularly relevant with respect to other types of documents. Firstly, the two sides have signed a number of agreements in the context of conflict resolution, foreseeing steps for a future reintegration.[50] Building on one of these agreements, the two sides even went as far as to sign an agreement of cooperation between the Moldovan Parliament and Transnistria's Supreme Soviet, in which they *inter alia* agreed to inform each other of their respective legislative plans.[51] Moreover, especially in the 1990s, a number of documents concerning functional cooperation were signed between Moldova and Transnistria, including in the area of economic cooperation,[52] internal affairs cooperation,[53] education,[54] prevention of infectious diseases,[55] statistics,[56] restoration of bridges across the

such, ceasefire agreements can arguably be considered as falling into the category of international agreements foreseen by Article 3 VCLT, with civil war factions seen as having international agreement-making capacity, "at least if they have achieved the *de facto* administration of a specific territory". Schmalenbach, 'Article 3: International Agreements not Within the Scope of the Present Convention' in O Dörr and K Schmalenbach (eds) *Vienna Convention on the Law of Treaties: A Commentary* (Springer 2012) 69–71. See C Bell, *On the Law of Peace: Peace Agreements and the Lex Pacificatoria* (OUP 2008) 127–128 and 130–132. Moreover, for example, the UNSC endorsed Minsk II, which can be seen as an additional layer of legalisation of its terms. See generally, ibid 155–156.

50 See for example, Memorandum on the Bases for Normalization of Relations between the Republic of Moldova and Transnistria (8 May 1997) available in NV Shtanski (ed), *Negotiation Process between Transnistrian Moldovan Republic and the Republic of Moldova in Documents* (MID TMR 2014) 57–58 (*in Russian*) and 302–303 (*in English*) ("Primakov Memorandum").

51 Agreement of Cooperation Between the Parliament of the Republic of Moldova and the Transnistrian Supreme Soviet (14 March 2000) available in Shtanski (n 50) 125–126 (*in Russian*) and 373–374 (*in English*).

52 See *infra*.

53 Agreement on the Basis of Cooperation between the Ministry of Interior of the Republic of Moldova and Internal Affairs Authorities of Transnistria (26 January 1996) available in Shtanski (n 50) 99–102 (*in Russian*) and 348–351 (*in English*).

54 Protocol Decision on the Solution of Problems Emerged in the Field of Restoration of Bridges across the Dniester (15 February 1995) available in Shtanski (n 50) 37 (*in Russian*) and 287 (*in English*).

55 Protocol Decision on the Prevention of the Spread of Infectious Diseases through Immunization of the Population (21 July 1998) available in Shtanski (n 50) 113 (*in Russian*) and 361 (*in English*).

56 Protocol Decision on Harmonization and Application of a Single System in Determination of Statistical Indexes and Exchange of Statistical Data between the Republic of Moldova

Dniester[57] and the like.[58]

These documents have been carefully worded and denominated. Apart from the term 'agreement', in some instances, titles such as 'memorandum', 'protocol decision', 'protocol of meeting' and other neutral-sounding titles have been frequently used. Moreover, labelling of the parties has also avoided explicit reference to an entity's statehood or to its self-proclaimed name. These documents have frequently simply referred to 'parties' or 'sides'. Moreover, titles of people signing the documents, such as 'president', 'minister' and the like, have also been avoided; the documents have simply referred to 'bodies' or to the name of a person signing 'on behalf' of Transnistria. Thus, these features preclude the conclusion as to an implied recognition of Transnistria as a State by way of these documents. In addition, the prevailing political climate has heavily determined the implementation of these documents. In many instances, the commitments thereunder simply have not been put in practice as originally foreseen.

2.4 *EU-Parent State Trade Agreements' Applicability to Post-Soviet Illegal Secessionist Entities*

2.4.1 Territorial Scope of the EU-Parent State Trade Agreements

In 2014, the EU signed a series of Association Agreements with Moldova, Georgia and Ukraine, integral parts of which were the Deep and Comprehensive Free Trade Agreements (DCFTA).[59] All three States currently have parts of their territory outside of their factual control. All three agreements stipulate that they "shall apply" to "the territory" of the respective State.[60]

---

and Transnistria (13 July 1999) available in Shtanski (n 50) 112 (*in Russian*) and 360 (*in English*).

57 Protocol Decision on the Solution of Problems Emerged in the Field of Restoration of Bridges across the Dniester (15 February 1995) available in Shtanski (n 50) 37 (*in Russian*) and 287 (*in English*).

58 See *Ilaşcu and others v Moldova and Russia* ECHR 2004-VII 1, para 345 ("*Ilaşcu*").

59 Association Agreement between the European Union and the European Atomic Energy Community and their Member States, of the One Part, and the Republic of Moldova, of the Other Part [2014] OJ L 260/4 ("EU-Moldova AA"); Association Agreement between the European Union and the European Atomic Energy Community and their Member States, of the One Part, and Ukraine, of the Other Part [2014] OJ L 161/3 ("EU-Ukraine AA"); Association Agreement between the European Union and the European Atomic Energy Community and their Member States, of the One Part, and Georgia, of the Other Part [2014] OJ L 261/4 ("EU-Georgia AA").

60 EU-Georgia AA (n 59) art 429(1); EU-Moldova AA (n 59) art 462(1); EU-Ukraine AA (n 59) art 483.

The EU-Georgia AA and the EU-Moldova AA also stipulate that the AA's or the DCFTA's application in relation to the regions over which the respective State "does not exercise effective control" shall commence once the respective State "ensures the full implementation and enforcement" of the AA or the DCFTA "on its entire territory".[61] The Association Council adopts the decision on when the full implementation and enforcement of these agreements is ensured on the respective State's entire territory.[62] Since the Association Council decides by consensus, the decision will require both the parent State and the EU to agree.[63] The EU-Georgia AA and the EU-Moldova AA also provide for the process of reconsideration of the continued application of these agreements in relation to the regions concerned[64] and preclude only partial application of the DCFTA.[65]

Regarding the EU-Ukraine AA, since it was initialised before Crimea's annexation, the issue of its application to Crimea was explicitly dealt with only in the Final Act upon its signature on 20 September 2014, which stipulated that the signatories agree that the AA

> shall apply to the entire territory of Ukraine as recognised under international law and shall engage in consultations with a view to determine the effects of the Agreement with regard to the illegally annexed territory of the Autonomous Republic of Crimea and the City of Sevastopol in which the Ukrainian Government currently does not exercise effective control.[66]

The EU had already imposed an import ban on goods originating in Crimea or Sevastopol with the exception of "goods originating in Crimea or Sevastopol which have been made available for examination to, and have been controlled

61 EU-Georgia AA (n 59) art 429(2); EU-Moldova AA (n 59) art 462(2).

62 EU-Georgia AA (n 59) art 429(3); EU-Moldova AA (n 59) art 462(3).

63 G Van der Loo, 'Law and Practice of the EU's Trade Agreements with "Disputed" Territories: A Consistent Approach?' in I Govaere and S Garben (eds), *The Interface Between EU and International Law: Contemporary Reflections* (Hart 2019) 262.

64 EU-Georgia AA (n 59) art 429(4); EU-Moldova AA (n 59) art 462(4).

65 EU-Georgia AA (n 59) art 429(5); EU-Moldova AA (n 59) art 462(5).

66 Final Act between the European Union and the European Atomic Energy Community and their Member States, of the One Part, and Ukraine, of the Other Part, as Regards the Association Agreement [2014] OJ L 278/4 ("Final Act"). See also Van der Loo (n 63) 264–265.

by the Ukrainian authorities and which have been granted a certificate of origin by the Government of Ukraine".[67]

Lastly, the 1996 Partnership and Cooperation Agreement between the EU and Azerbaijan provides for its application "to the territory of the Republic of Azerbaijan".[68] The relations between the EU and Armenia are governed by the 2017 Comprehensive and Enhanced Partnership Agreement, which also provides for its application "to the territory of the Republic of Armenia".[69]

All of the above-mentioned agreements provide for their application to "the territory" of the respective States.[70] Regardless of the equivocal wording discussed below, it is indisputable that the term 'territory' in these agreements covers the respective illegal secessionist entity. Firstly, the wording of other provisions of the EU-Moldova AA and the EU-Georgia AA, which refer to the solution of the secessionist conflicts while respecting the respective parent State's territorial sovereignty must be taken into account.[71] As for the EU-Ukraine AA, EU-Azerbaijan PCA and EU-Armenia CEPA, they contain specific provisions referring to the principles of the UN Charter and the Helsinki Final Pact of 1975.[72] Moreover, the EU-Georgia AA, the EU-Moldova AA and the Final

---

67 Council Decision 2014/386/CFSP of 23 June 2014 Concerning Restrictions on Goods Originating in Crimea or Sevastopol, in Response to the Illegal Annexation of Crimea and Sevastopol [2014] OJ L 183/70, arts 1 and 2.

68 Partnership and Cooperation Agreement between the European Communities and their Member States, of the One Part, and the Republic of Azerbaijan, of the Other Part [1999] OJ L 246/3, Article 101 ("EU-Azerbaijan PCA"). In February 2017, the EU started negotiations regarding a new comprehensive agreement to replace the actual one. Van der Loo (n 63) 265.

69 Comprehensive and Enhanced Partnership Agreement between the European Union and the European Atomic Energy Community and their Member States, of the One Part, and the Republic of Armenia, of the Other Part [2018] OJ L 23/4, art 383 ("EU-Armenia CEPA").

70 A Adarov and P Havlik, *Benefits and Costs of DCFTA: Evaluation of the Impact on Georgia, Moldova and Ukraine* (Vienna Institute for International Economic Studies and Bertelsmann Stiftung 2016) 68.

71 EU-Moldova AA (n 59) preamble, recital 15. "The Parties reiterate their commitment to a sustainable solution to the Transnistrian issue, in full respect of the sovereignty and territorial integrity of the Republic of Moldova, as well as to facilitating jointly post-conflict rehabilitation." ibid, art 8(2). "Recognising the importance of the commitment of Georgia to reconciliation and its efforts to restore its territorial integrity and full and effective control over Georgian regions of Abkhazia and the Tskhnivali region/South Ossetia." EU-Georgia AA (n 59) preamble, recital 16.

72 EU-Ukraine AA (n 59) art 9. "The Parties consider that it is essential for their future prosperity and stability that the newly independent States which have emerged from the dissolution of the Union of Soviet Socialist Republics, hereinafter called 'Independent States', should maintain and develop cooperation among themselves in compliance with the principles of the Helsinki Final Act and with international law and in the spirit of

Act upon signature of the EU-Ukraine AA contain specific provisions dealing with their application to the regions over which the respective State "does not exercise effective control".[73] This practice *a contrario* confirms that the term 'territory' in the territorial scope provisions also includes these regions. This seems to be in line with the conclusions established above that under general international law the term 'territory' is ordinarily understood as the State's sovereign territory regardless of whether it is outside the State's effective control.

In terms of EU practice, the above-mentioned treaties can be compared with the modalities of the Republic of Cyprus' accession to the EU, when it acceded to the EU as a whole, but the application of *acquis* was suspended in those areas in which it did not exercise effective control.[74] The Council, acting unanimously on the basis of a proposal from the Commission, has the right to decide on the withdrawal of such a suspension.[75]

Thus, it seems that a scheme analogical to that of the Republic of Cyprus has been replicated in the context of the above-mentioned AAs. However, the terminology used in these AAs, in particular that the treaties "shall apply" to the territory of the respective States and at the same time that their "application" in relation to regions outside of the parent State's effective control "shall commence" once the conditions are met, does not seem logical or technically correct. It is suggested that the reference to the "suspension" of the application

---

good neighbourly relations and will make every effort to encourage this process." EU-Azerbaijan PCA (n 68) art 3, see also art 2 and preamble, recitals 3 and 4. "Recognising the importance of the commitment of the Republic of Armenia to the peaceful and lasting settlement of the Nagorno-Karabakh conflict, and the need to achieve that settlement as early as possible, in the framework of the negotiations led by the OSCE Minsk Group co-chairs; also recognising the need to achieve that settlement on the basis of the purposes and principles enshrined in the UN Charter and the OSCE Helsinki Final Act, in particular those related to refraining from the threat or use of force, the territorial integrity of States, and the equal rights and self-determination of peoples and reflected in all declarations issued within the framework of the OSCE Minsk Group co-chairmanship since the 16th OSCE Ministerial Council of 2008; also noting the stated commitment of the European Union to support this settlement process." EU-Armenia CEPA (n 69) preamble, recital 11.

73 In particular, the EU-Georgia AA referred explicitly to "Georgia's regions of Abkhazia and Tskhinvali region/South Ossetia." EU-Georgia AA (n 59) art 429(2). The EU-Moldova AA referred to "those areas of the Republic of Moldova over which the Government of the Republic of Moldova does not exercise effective control." EU-Moldova AA (n 59) art 462(2). Final Act referred to "illegally annexed territory of the Autonomous Republic of Crimea and the City of Sevastopol." See *supra*.

74 Protocol No 10 on Cyprus of the Act of Accession 2003 [2003] OJ L 236/955, art 1(1) ("Protocol No 10 to the Act of Accession"). See *supra* Part 1, Chapter 7.

75 ibid art 1(2). See *supra* Part 1, Chapter 7.

of these agreements in relation to the regions outside of *de facto* control, as was the case with respect to northern Cyprus, would be more appropriate.

2.4.2 The EU-Moldova DCFTA's Application to Transnistria

Until today, the EU's DCFTA[76] is formally applied and implemented only in Transnistria. In fact, even prior to the signature of the EU-Moldova DCFTA, the exports of goods from Transnistria to the EU had been conducted on the basis of Moldova's certificates of origin.[77] Since 2008, when the EU granted Moldova asymmetric autonomous trade preferences (ATP), Transnistria's economic operators registered in Moldova also benefited from them.[78] However, the ATP regime, with respect to Transnistria alone, could not have been maintained simultaneously with the DCFTA, "since the EU cannot have one trading partner with two different trade regimes".[79] Upon Moldova's request, the ATP regulation was maintained until its expiry date on 31 December 2015.[80] However, after this date, without any arrangement regarding the DCFTA's applicability to Transnistria, the latter would lose preferential access to the EU.[81]

Ultimately, on 18 December 2015, the EU-Moldova Association Council adopted a decision according to which the DCFTA "shall apply to the entire territory of the Republic of Moldova from 1 January 2016".[82] This decision had been preceded by the technical deal between Moldova and Transnistria facilitated by the EU; though it was not officially made public, elements of it were nevertheless leaked.[83] Importantly, to be able to profit from free trade with

---

76 The EU-Moldova's DCFTA forms Title V of the EU-Moldova AA.

77 See *infra*.

78 Council Regulation (EC) No 55/2008 of 21 January 2008 Introducing Autonomous Trade Preferences for the Republic of Moldova and Amending Regulation (EC) No 980/2005 and Commission Decision 2005/924/EC [2008] OJ L20/1; Regulation (EU) No 1383/2014 of the European Parliament and of the Council of 18 December 2014 Amending Council Regulation (EC) No 55/2008 Introducing Autonomous Trade Preferences for the Republic of Moldova [2014] OJ L 372/1. See *infra*.

79 *The Impact of the EU-Moldova DCFTA on the Transnistrian Economy: Quantitative Assessment under Three Scenarios* (BE Berlin Economics GmbH 2013) iv.

80 European Parliament, 'Answer Given by Ms Malmström on Behalf of the Commission' (4 April 2016) E-001168/2016.

81 See *infra* Chapter 18.

82 Decision No 1/2015 of the EU-Republic of Moldova Association Council of 18 December 2015 on the Application of Title V of the Association Agreement between the European Union and the European Atomic Energy Community and their Member States, of the One Part, and the Republic of Moldova, of the Other Part, to the Entire Territory of the Republic of Moldova [2015/2445] [2015] OJ L 336/93, art 1.

83 European Parliament, 'Answer Given by Ms Malmström on Behalf of the Commission' (4 April 2016) E-001168/2016; Van der Loo (n 63) 263.

the EU, economic operators from Transnistria are required to obtain Moldova's certificate of origins; the Moldovan authorities should also be given access to conduct verification of the relevant standards in Transnistria.[84] On balance, the EU did not insist on the entire DCFTA's application to Transnistria, even though such an approach seems incompatible with the terms of the EU-Moldova AA itself.[85]

The extension of the EU-Moldova DCFTA to Transnistria on the basis of the decision of the Association Council is unprecedented under international law and even in terms of EU practice. Previously, the Green Line Regulation applied only to the line between government-controlled areas in Cyprus and the TRNC and had its explicit legal basis in the Accession Protocol.[86] Moreover, the Republic of Cyprus blocked the adoption of the Direct Trade Regulation, which would have been more analogical to the Moldova-Transnistria scenario, as it required the decision of the Council on the partial withdrawal of the suspension of the *acquis* in northern Cyprus.[87] Taking into account the fact that from a formal perspective the commencement of the application of the EU-Moldova DCFTA in Transnistria is in line with Transnistria being part of Moldova's sovereign territory, this decision cannot be considered incompatible with the duty of non-recognition. Its trade-related implications will be discussed below.

Additionally, regarding the AA or DCFTA's implementation in Abkhazia and South Ossetia, while it is unlikely to happen in the immediate future, taking into account current relations between Georgia and these illegal secessionist entities,[88] it will be shown below that some tentative proposals have already been suggested.

2.5 *Application of the Russia-Ukraine BIT to Russia-Annexed Crimea*

As of this writing, there have been ten known investor-State arbitrations[89]

---

84 K Całus, 'The DCFTA in Transnistria: Who Gains?' (*Neweasterneurope*, 15 January 2015) <http://neweasterneurope.eu/articles-and-commentary/1861-the-dcfta-in-transnistria-who-gains> accessed 30 October 2016. See in detail *infra*.

85 Van der Loo (n 63) 263.

86 Protocol No 10 to the Act of Accession (n 74) art 2(1). See *supra* Part 1, Chapter 7.

87 See *supra* Part 1, Chapter 7.

88 Van der Loo (n 63) 262. See *supra* Chapter 13.

89 (1) PCA Case No 2015–07, *Aeroport Belbek LLC and Mr. Igor Valerievich Kolomoisky v The Russian Federation* ("Belbek"); (2) PCA Case No 2015–21, *PJS CB PrivatBank v The Russian Federation*. (3) PCA Case No 2015–34, *PJSC Ukrnafta v The Russian Federation* ("Ukrnafta"); (4) PCA Case No 2015–35, *Stabil LLC and Others v The Russian Federation.* On 26 June 2017, the tribunal decided it had jurisdiction to hear cases. In both claims, Russia then moved to

under the Russia-Ukraine BIT[90] arising out of Russia's purported expropriations in Crimea. The pleadings remain confidential. From the available information, it follows that probably in all the known cases, Ukraine was allowed to make written submissions as a non-disputing party.[91] Initially, Russia did not participate in these cases,[92]

---

challenge the awards on jurisdiction before the Swiss Federal Tribunal as the supervising court of the seat of arbitration. On 16 October 2018, the Swiss court rejected the challenge and upheld the awards on jurisdiction. See *Judgment No 4A_398/2017* (Switzerland, Swiss Federal Tribunal) (16 October 2018) ("Swiss Federal Tribunal's Judgment on Jurisdiction"); *Judgment No 4A_396/2017* (Switzerland, Swiss Federal Tribunal) (16 October 2018) (*in German*). Later, on 12 April 2019, the tribunal issued awards upholding the claims and awarding $44.5 million to Ukrnafta and $34.5 million to Stabil, together with interests and costs. Russia challenged both awards before the Swiss Federal Tribunal. On 12 December 2019, the Swiss court rejected these challenges and upheld the awards. See *Judgment No 4A_246/2019* (Switzerland, Swiss Federal Tribunal) (12 December 2019); *Judgment No 4A_244/2019* (Switzerland, Swiss Federal Tribunal) (12 December 2019) (*in German*). (5) PCA Case No 2015–36, *Everest Estate LLC and Others v The Russian Federation* ("Everest"). The set-aside proceeding is ongoing. See *Judgment No 200.250.714/01* (The Netherlands, Hague Court of Appeal) (11 June 2019) (*in Dutch*). (6) PCA Case No 2015–29, *Lugzor LLC and Others v The Russian Federation* ("Lugzor"). (7) PCA Case No 2016–14, *Oschadbank v The Russian Federation* ("Oschadbank"). (8) PCA Case No 2017–16, *NJSC Naftogaz of Ukraine (Ukraine) and Others v The Russian Federation* ("Naftogaz"). (9) *PJSC DTEK Krymenergo v The Russian Federation* ("Krymenergo"). (10) *SE NPC Ukrenergo v The Russian Federation* ("Ukrenergo"). In 2022, the Hague Court of Appeal dismissed the set-aside applications regarding the arbitral awards in *Belbek*, *Everest* and *Privatbank*. The arbitral award in *Naftogaz* was annulled by the Hague Court of Appeal for the reasons of temporal jurisdiction. This reasoning was similar to the approach of the Paris Court of Appeal, which set aside the arbitral award in *Oschadbank* (but this was later reversed by the French Court de Cassation). Reportedly, so far, the Ukrainian claimants have been awarded 1,3 billion USD (without interest) against Russia and some have already initiated the enforcement of their awards. M Antonovych, 'Investment Arbitration Amidst War in Ukraine' (*Kluwer Arbitration Blog*, 17 February 2023) <https://arbitrationblog.kluwerarbitration.com/2023/02/17/2022-in-review-investment-arbitration-amidst-war-in-ukraine/> accessed 31 October 2023; T Ackermann and S Wuschka, 'The Applicability of Investment Treaties in the Context of Russia's Aggression against Ukraine' (2023) 38 ICSID Review 453, 460–461.

90 Agreement between the Government of the Russian Federation and the Cabinet of Ministers of Ukraine on the Encouragement and Mutual Protection of Investments (signed 27 November 1998; entered into force 27 January 2001) ("Russia-Ukraine BIT").

91 S Wuschka, 'Investment Claims and Annexation of Territory' in M Akbaba and G Capurro (eds), *International Challenges in Investment Arbitration* (Routledge 2018) 34.

92 Russia informed the PCA that the BIT "cannot serve as a basis for composing an arbitral tribunal to settle" the claims and that Russia "does not recognize the jurisdiction of an international arbitral tribunal at the [PCA] in settlement of the" claimants' claims. See for example, PCA, 'Arbitration between Aeroport Belbek LLC and Mr Igor Valerievich Kolomoisky as Claimants and the Russian Federation' (*Press Release*, 6 January 2016) <https://pcacases.com/web/sendAttach/1553> accessed 10 January 2020.

but in 2019 it changed its strategy and started taking part in the remaining proceedings.[93]

Russia's actions concerning Ukrainian or privately owned property situated in Crimea are analysed below in the framework of the purported validity of municipal legal acts.[94] In terms of the investor-State arbitrations under the Russia-Ukraine BIT, their jurisdictional phase is particularly relevant to the issues explored in this book. In all the cases reaching that stage, tribunals have reportedly upheld their jurisdiction.[95]

The key legal issues raised *inter alia* in the jurisdictional phase concerned firstly the jurisdiction *ratione loci*,[96] specifically the issue of a territorial scope of the Russia-Ukraine BIT, as the treaty applies to investments made by the investors of one party on the *territory* of the other party.[97] Under Article 1(4) of the Russia-Ukraine BIT "[t]erritory shall denote the territory of the Russian Federation or the territory of the Ukraine and also their respective exclusive economic zone and the continental shelf as defined in conformity with the international law."[98] Thus, in order for the treaty to apply to the substantive issues, ie the expropriation of Ukrainian assets in Crimea after Russia's annexation of Crimea, it must be established whether 'the territory of the Russian Federation' can be interpreted to include the territory of the Russia-annexed Crimea, ie the territory over which Russia only exercises *de facto* control.

The second key issue concerned the jurisdiction *ratione temporis*, ie whether investments made in Crimea by Ukrainian investors *before* Russia's assumption of *de facto* control there could be considered *investments* under this treaty; from the available reporting, it follows that tribunals in *Everest*, *Stabil* and *Ukrnafta* held that the conditions, that the claimant makes an investment and that investment is in the respondent state's territory, do not have to be satisfied simultaneously.[99]

93 S Perry, 'Russia Challenges Crimea Awards and Changes Strategy' (*Global Arbitration Review*, 6 June 2019) <https://globalarbitrationreview.com/article/1193767/russia-challenges-crimea-awards-and-changes-strategy> accessed 10 January 2020.

94 See *infra* Chapter 19.

95 See *supra* (n 89) for an overview of these cases. Ackermann and Wuschka (n 89) 460.

96 Or a geographical scope to the respondent state's consent to the arbitration of the investment dispute. See Z Douglas, *The International Law of Investment Claims* (CUP 2009) 151–152.

97 See Russia-Ukraine BIT (n 90) art 1(1).

98 Russia-Ukraine BIT (n 90) art 1(4).

99 The Swiss Federal Tribunal upheld this conclusion. Swiss Federal Tribunal's Judgment on Jurisdiction (n 89) paras 4.4.1.-4.4.7. See J Hepburn, 'INVESTIGATION: Full Jurisdictional Reasoning Comes to Light in Crimea-Related BIT Arbitration vs. Russia' (*IAReporter*, 9 November 2017) <https://www.iareporter.com/articles/full-jurisdictional-reasoning-comes-to-light-in-crimea-related-arbitration-everest-estate-v-russia/>

The following account will not analyse the latter issue but will focus on the former question as it pertains to themes of this book. It will firstly examine the tribunals' reasoning regarding the ordinary meaning of the term 'territory' by reference to the operation of the moving treaty frontiers (MTF) rule under general international law. Secondly, it will examine the treaty's teleological interpretation and arguments on analogy between investment and human rights treaties, and, thirdly, it will explore the relevance of Russia's conduct and Ukraine's consent.

None of the tribunals has reportedly engaged with the lawfulness of Crimea's transfer to Russia.[100] Nevertheless, the question will be asked: to what extent can the tribunals' reasoning be considered compatible with the consequences of the peremptory illegality of Crimea's incorporation into the Russian Federation under general international law? Since the awards have remained confidential, the analysis is mainly based on available reporting and the Swiss Federal Tribunal's reasoning in the *Stabil* and *Ukrnafta* cases.[101]

2.5.1 Operation of the Moving Treaty Frontiers Rule

Following the rules of interpretation in the VCLT, the arbitral tribunal in *Stabil* and *Ukrnafta* began its analysis by focusing on the ordinary meaning of the term 'territory'. It held that the ordinary meaning of this term was broad enough to encompass the entire territory under Russia's control.[102]

It reached this conclusion firstly by making references to English, Russian and Ukrainian legal dictionaries, which defined territory without reference to sovereignty.[103] Secondly, the tribunal held that the phrase "defined in

---

accessed 10 February 2020; J Hepburn and R Kabra, 'INVESTIGATION: Further Russia Investment Treaty Decisions Uncovered, Offering Broader Window into Arbitrators' Approaches to Crimea Controversy' (*IAReporter*, 17 November 2017) <https://www.iareporter.com/articles/investigation-further-russia-investment-treaty-decisions-uncovered-offering-broader-window-into-arbitrators-approaches-to-crimea-controversy//> accessed 10 February 2020.

100 L Rees-Evans, 'Litigating the Use of Force: Reflections on the Interaction between Investor-State Dispute Settlement and Other Forms of International Dispute Settlement in the Context of the Conflict in Ukraine' in KF Gómez, A Gourgourinis and C Titi (eds) *European Yearbook of International Economic Law* (Springer 2019) 186–187.

101 Some of the arbitral awards have recently been made public including *Stabil LLC and Others v The Russian Federation* (Award on Jurisdiction) PCA Case No 2015–35 (26 June 2017) ("*Stabil*"). *PJSC CB Privatbank and Finance Company Finilon v The Russian Federation* (Interim Award) PCA Case No 2015–35 (25 March 2017) ("*Privatbank*").

102 Hepburn and Kabra (n 99). *Stabil* (101) paras 138–148.

103 Hepburn and Kabra (n 99). *Stabil* (101) para 140.

accordance with international law" in Article 1(4) of the Russia-Ukraine BIT only applied to determine the extent of exclusive economic zones and continental shelves and did not qualify the term 'territory'.[104] Importantly, the tribunal also noted that "the entire territory" under Article 29 VCLT "was not limited to territory under a state's lawful occupation".[105] It seems that the latter argument was also accepted in the *Everest* and *Belbek* cases.[106]

During the proceedings before the Swiss Federal Tribunal on challenges to interim awards in *Stabil* and *Ukrnafta*, Russia argued that the Russia-Ukraine BIT's territorial scope only encompassed the territory of the two parties at the time of its conclusion in 1998.[107] "Since Crimea and Sevastopol were part of Ukraine at that time, the territorial scope of the BIT did not extend to Crimea as a Russian territory."[108] According to Russia, a special agreement should have been concluded regarding the BIT's application to Crimea.[109] Russia did not challenge that the treaty could also apply to territory that was effectively controlled by a contracting State.[110]

Limited by the scope of Russia's claims, the Swiss Federal Tribunal agreed with the arbitral tribunals in that the term 'territory' under Article 1(4) of the Russia-Ukraine BIT should not be interpreted restrictively as areas over which the contracting state has sovereignty in accordance with international law.[111] In particular, the Swiss court held that according to the general principles of international law concerning the spatial scope of international treaties, in particular the moving treaty frontiers rule expressed in Article 29 VLCT, in the event of territorial changes, the treaty continues to apply to the entire (ie now

104 The tribunal referred to the fact that this qualified phrase only appeared in Russia's investment treaties with States with which it had maritime boundaries. Moreover, the tribunal also noted that while the two states linked the definition of territory with sovereignty in other investment treaties, they had not decided to do so in this particular treaty. See Hepburn and Kabra (n 99). *Stabil* (101) paras 140–141 and 143. This conclusion is different from the award in the *Everest* case. See *infra*.

105 Hepburn and Kabra (n 99). See *Stabil* (101) paras 146–147.

106 ibid. It was reported that "[a]pplying the general principle in the Vienna Convention on the Law of Treaties, cited by the claimants, the tribunal found that the BIT applied to the entire Russian territory". Hepburn (n 99).

107 L Bohmer, 'In Now-Public Decisions, Swiss Federal Tribunal Clarifies Reasons for Dismissing Challenges to Two Crimea-Related Investment Treaty Awards Against Russia' (*IAReporter*, 16 November 2018) <https://www.iareporter.com/articles/in-now-public-decisions-swiss-federal-tribunal-clarifies-reasons-for-dismissing-challenges-to-two-crimea-related-investment-treaty-awards-against-russia/> accessed 10 February 2020.

108 ibid.

109 ibid.

110 Swiss Federal Tribunal's Judgment on Jurisdiction (n 89) para 4.3.2.

111 ibid para 4.3.2.

changed) territory.[112] According to the court, since Russia was not able to support her argument on the static application of the treaty's territorial scope, ie on the limitation of territorial scope only to the territory at the time of the treaty's conclusion, there was nothing against the tribunals' interpretation that the change of territory after the treaty's conclusion must be taken into account to determine the term 'territory' under Article 1(4) of the Russia-Ukraine BIT.[113]

There are several issues with the reasoning of the tribunals and the Swiss court with respect to the ordinary meaning of the term 'territory';[114] most important among them is the reasoning concerning the operation of the moving treaty frontiers (MTF) rule implicit in Article 29 VCLT. Because of the implications of this reasoning going beyond the strict confines of the interpretation of this treaty, the following account will pay specific attention to it.

According to Article 29 VCLT, "[u]nless a different intention appears from the treaty or is otherwise established, a treaty is binding upon each party in respect of its entire territory."[115] Firstly, it is true that Article 29 VCLT reflects an evolutive and not a static understanding of the territorial scope of treaties.[116]

---

112 ibid para 4.3.2.

113 ibid, para 4.3.2 in connection to para 4.3.1.

114 Regarding the arguments of the arbitral tribunal on the ordinary meaning of the notion 'territory', reference to three legal dictionaries seems to be insufficient to offset the abundance of legal scholarship to the contrary. Nevertheless, it is difficult to assess this issue without access to the tribunal's particular reasoning. Moreover, the tribunal's assessment of whether the expression "defined in accordance with international law" qualified and related to exclusive economic zones and continental shelves and not to the term 'territory' was disputed by the doctrine by pointing to relevant practices by Russia. MG Vaccaro-Incisa, 'Crimea Investment Disputes: Are Jurisdictional Hurdles Being Overcome Too Easily?' (*EJIL: Talk!*, 9 May 2018) <https://www.ejiltalk.org/crimea-investment-disputes-are-jurisdictional-hurdles-being-overcome-too-easily/> accessed 10 January 2020. It was also left open by another tribunal in the *Everest* case. See *infra*. P Dumberry, 'Requiem for Crimea: Why Tribunals Should Have Declined Jurisdiction over the Claims of Ukrainian Investors against Russian under the Ukraine–Russia BIT' (2018) 9 Journal of International Dispute Settlement 506, 523–524. See also D Costelloe, 'Treaty Succession in Annexed Territory' (2016) 65 International & Comparative Law Quarterly 343, 366.

115 Vienna Convention on the Law of Treaties (adopted 23 May 1969, entered into force 27 January 1980) 1155 UNTS 331, art 29 ("VCLT"). K Von Der Decken, 'Article 29: Territorial Scope of Treaties' in O Dörr and K Schmalenbach (eds), *Vienna Convention on the Law of Treaties* (2nd edn, Springer 2018) 531.

116 "In fact, if the 'moving treaty frontiers' rule was not included in Art 29, a treaty would only be binding upon each States Parties in respect of its territory at the time of the conclusion of the treaty. The intention of Art 29, however, is not to 'freeze' the territorial scope of a treaty at the time of its entry into force, but to provide for the application of the relevant treaty on the 'entire' territory of each States Parties." Von Der Decken (n 115) 531 (*footnotes omitted*).

"[T]he application of a state's treaties is automatically extended to newly acquired territory from the point of the acquisition onwards."[117] But this does not offer any support for the tribunals' and the Swiss court's conclusion that the 'evolution' also includes the transfer of *de facto* territorial control. To the contrary, a drafting history of Article 29 VCLT supports the understanding of the expression 'its entire territory' as the territory under the *sovereignty* of a State.[118] In the context of codification of the rules of State succession, H. Waldock presented the same understanding of the moving treaty frontiers rule as relating to territory "undergoing a change of *sovereignty*".[119]

Moreover, commentaries on Article 29 VCLT refer to five classic modes of territorial transfer and State succession as examples of territorial changes.[120] Irrespective of the actual existence of these modes in international law, all of them entail changes of *sovereignty*.[121] It is generally accepted that conquest is no longer accepted as a permissible mode of territorial change.[122] Acquisitive prescription is a controversial doctrine in international law. It is also a truism to say that occupation does not transfer territorial sovereignty[123] and therefore cannot be seen as a mode of territorial change foreseen by Article 29 VCLT.

---

117 R Happ and S Wuschka, 'Horror Vacui: Or Why Investment Treaties Should Apply to Illegally Annexed Territories' (2016) 33 Journal of International Arbitration 245, 257.

118 According to H. Waldock, "[t]he rule that a treaty is to be presumed to apply with respect to all the territories under the *sovereignty* of the contracting parties means that each State must make its intention plain, expressly or by implication, in any case where it does not intend to enter into the engagements of the treaty on behalf of and with respect to all its territory." ILC, 'Third Report on the Law of Treaties, by Sir Humphrey Waldock, Special Rapporteur' (1964) UN Doc A/CN.4/167, 13, para 4 (*emphasis added*). T Ackermann, 'Investments under Occupation: The Application of Investment Treaties to Occupied Territory' in KF Gómez, A Gourgourinis and C Titi (eds) *European Yearbook of International Economic Law* (Springer 2019) 81–82. Happ and Wuschka point to the fact that during the discussion by the ILC even the term "territory under the jurisdiction of State concerned" was discussed. Happ and Wuschka (n 117) 258. However, ultimately, this fact seems to confirm rather than weaken the conclusion that the notion of "territory" only refers to a State's *sovereign* territory.

119 ILC, 'Second Report on Succession in Respect of Treaties, by Sir Humphrey Waldock, Special Rapporteur' (1969) UN Doc A/CN.4/214, 52, para 2. According to the ILC's commentary to Article 14 VCST (now Article 15 VCST), the moving treaty-frontiers rule entails that "at any given time a State is bound by a treaty in respect of any territory of which it is *sovereign*." ILC, Yearbook of International Law Commission (1974) vol II, part One, 209, para 6 (*emphasis added*).

120 These modes include occupation of *terra nullius*, subjugation, accretion, prescription and cession. Von Der Decken (n 115) 532.

121 MG Kohen and M Hébié, 'Territory, Acquisition' in MPEPIL (online edn, OUP 2011), para 9.

122 ibid; MN Shaw, *International Law* (8th edn, CUP 2018) 371.

123 Kohen and Hébié (n 121) para 6.

In addition, the Swiss Federal Tribunal based its expansive understanding of the MTF rule by reference to two doctrinal sources.[124] Firstly, the court mentioned the sentence in Villiger's VCLT Commentary, according to which "[i]f there are territorial changes, the treaty continues, in principle, to apply to the entire territory".[125] However, this reference is unhelpful without context, as it does not explain what 'territorial changes' or 'territory' entail. In fact, one paragraph earlier, Villiger offers his definition of the term 'territory' under Article 29 VCLT, according to which territory "covers the area over which a party to the treaty *exercises sovereignty*".[126] Thus, based on such a definition, it is difficult to accept that territorial changes referred to by Villiger in the context of Article 29 VCLT would entail anything else than the changes of exercise of *sovereignty*.[127] Similarly, Von Der Drecken's commentary on Article 29 VCLT only explains the MTF rule by reference to five modes of territorial changes and State succession and, as mentioned above, these presuppose change of *sovereignty*.[128] Thus, doctrinal support offered by the court for its reading of this rule is rather slim, if not non-existent.[129] It seems inadequate in the context of a large number of

124 Swiss Federal Tribunal's Judgment on Jurisdiction (n 89) para 4.3.2.

125 ME Villiger, *Vienna Convention on the Law of Treaties* (Martinus Nijhoff Publishers 2009) 393.

126 ibid 392 (*emphasis added*).

127 According to Villiger, "[r]ecognition under international law of the State and its territory is not required." ibid 392. It is indeed true that the recognition of a State and its territory is not required for Article 29 VLCT to operate. In this context, Villiger refers to a journal article on South Africa's practice of extending its treaties to the territory of South West Africa (Namibia). ibid 392, ftn 26. There is nothing in this article that could be taken as supporting the conclusion that the term territory includes *de facto* changes of territory. In fact, the practice examined in this article supports a contrary conclusion, that the term "territory" is only limited to a State's *sovereign* territory. Moreover, the article also highlights a broader incompatibility of any extension of South Africa's treaties to Namibia with its obligations under general international law. "[I]t is questionable, especially in view of the 1971 Advisory Opinion of the International Court of Justice and the numerous United Nations resolutions describing South Africa's continued presence in the territory of South West Africa as illegal, whether the Republic will, in the future, be able to make a particular treaty applicable to South West Africa simply by utilizing one of the above formulae." RP Schaffer, 'The Extension of South African Treaties to the Territories of South West Africa and the Prince Edward Islands' (1978) 95 South African Law Journal 63, 70.

128 Von Der Decken (n 115) 532.

129 Outside of the court's judgment, the doctrinal support for the expansive reading of Article 29 can be found in Happ and Wuschka (n 117) 256–260. Happ and Wuschka cite Brownlie. Brownlie, however, only refers to the pragmatic approach of some national courts in not distinguishing between territory and jurisdiction and not directly to Article 29 VCLT in the context of international adjudication. In addition, practices highlighted by Happ and Wuschka do not offer much support, as the mentioned treaties do not only refer to "territory but also other terms such as 'authority.'" See ibid; DP Myers, 'Contemporary

resources that point to the operation of the MTF rule in Article 29 VCLT only in the context of transfers of *sovereignty*, ie lawful territorial changes.[130]

It needs to be added that concerning analogical question whether treaty terms "territory of the Kingdom of Morocco" in the EU-Morocco Association Agreement included the territory of Western Sahara, the CJEU in *Front Polisario* case held that it follows from Article 29 VCLT that

> a treaty is generally binding on a State in the ordinary meaning to be given to the term 'territory', combined with the possessive adjective 'its' preceding it, in respect of the geographical space over which that State exercises the fullness of the powers granted to sovereign entities by international law, to the exclusion of any other territory, such as a territory likely to be under the sole jurisdiction or the sole international responsibility of that State.[131]

Importantly, in *Ukraine v Russia (re Crimea)*, the ECtHR relied on Article 29 VCLT to define the scope of territorial jurisdiction under the European

---

Practice of the United States Relating to International Law' (1959) 53 American Journal of International Law 896, 899–901. The only directly relevant municipal case referred to by Happ and Wuschka supporting an expansive reading of 'territory' is *Schtranks*, which concerned an interpretation of the term in an extradition treaty between Israel and UK. According to the House of Lords, the 'territory' in the context of this agreement included "any area over which a contracting party exercised effective jurisdiction." See *Reg v Governor of Brixton Prison, Ex parte Schtranks* (House of Lords) (1962) 33 ILR 319, 332.

130 "It would be straining the text to an impermissible extent to read into these provision an exception to the otherwise only *de jure* character of 'territory,' since that term cannot by itself sustain a reading that includes annexed territory." Costelloe (n 114) 358. "The ordinary meaning of the term 'territory' found in a fundamental multilateral treaty such as the VCLT should not be understood as including a territory under occupation which has been illegally annexed by the use of force." P Dumberry, *A Guide to State Succession in International Investment Law* (Edward Elgar 2018) 215. See M Milanović, 'The Spatial Dimension: Treaties and Territory' in CJ Tams and AE Richford (eds), *Research Handbook on the Law of Treaties* (E Elgar 2014) 187. "Both, the moving treaty frontiers rule as well as the notion of territory in Article 29 VCLT, refer only to territory the State party has sovereignty over." Ackermann (n 118) 81. According to Rousseau, "il y a coïncidence exacte entre la sphère d'application spatiale du traité et l'étendue territoriale soumise à la souveraineté." C Rousseau cited in K Doehring, 'The Scope of the Territorial Application of Treaties: Comments on Art 25 of the ILC's 1966 Draft Articles on the Law of Treaties' (1967) 27 ZaöRV 483, 487. See also Vaccaro-Incisa (n 114).

131 Case C-104/16 P *Council v Front Polisario* [2016] ECLI:EU:C:2016:973, para 95 ("*Front Polisario*"). See also Case C-266/16 *Western Sahara Campaign UK v Commissioner for Her Majesty's Revenue and Customs, Secretary of State for Environment, Food and Rural Affairs* [2018] ECLI:EU:C:2018:118, para 62.

Convention on Human Rights (ECHR) since in the ECtHR's jurisprudence "a State's jurisdictional competence is primarily territorial."[132] It follows from its approach to this issue that the Court implicitly understood the notion of "entire territory" to entail "the sovereign territory" of State Parties to the ECHR.[133] The Court considered the lack of a positive case for the change of sovereign territory by Russia and the fact that "a number of States and international bodies have refused to accept any change to the territorial integrity of Ukraine in respect of Crimea within the meaning of international law."[134] It ultimately refused (albeit implicitly) to view Crimea's annexation as the change to a sovereign territory of either party and established that Russia's jurisdiction under Article 1 ECHR over the peninsula from 18 March 2014 onwards was of an extra-territorial nature (ie exercise by Russia of effective control *beyond* its *de iure* borders).[135]

Furthermore, the MTF rule implicit in Article 29 VCLT is explicitly provided for in provisions of VCST, especially Article 15 VCST.[136] However, the applicability of all the provisions of VCST is subjected to Article 6 VCST in that they apply "only to the effects of a succession of States occurring in conformity with international law and, in particular, the principles of international law embodied in the Charter of the United Nations".[137] The MTF rule is a "generally recognized principle of customary international law".[138] It is thus difficult to accept that iteration of the same general principle in one instrument – VCST – would be limited by the principle of legality,[139] but would not be so in another instrument – VCLT.[140] It is also difficult to accept that a customary rule of the MTF

132 *Russia v Ukraine* (*re Crimea*) App nos 20958/14 and 38334/18 (ECtHR, 16 December 2020) para 345.

133 ibid para 348.

134 ibid.

135 ibid paras 348–349.

136 Von Der Decken (n 115) 531.

137 Vienna Convention on Succession of States in Respect of Treaties (adopted 23 August 1978, entered into force 6 November 1996) 1946 UNTS 3, art 6 ("VCST"). "As a result, the MTF rule set out at Article 15 VCST does not apply to the annexation of Crimea." Dumberry (n 114) 514.

138 Von Der Decken (n 115) 531.

139 "This article, like the draft articles as a whole, has to be read in conjunction with article 6 which limits the present articles to lawful situations ... Article 14 is limited to normal changes in the sovereignty or in the responsibility for the international relations of a territory." ILC, Yearbook of International Law Commission (1974) vol II, part One, 209, para 3.

140 It was suggested that due precisely to the explicit limitation in art 6 VCST, "the moving treaty frontiers rule of Article 15 of the VCST did not figure in this case, even if this provision – like the moving treaty frontiers rule of Article 29 of the VCLT – reflected customary international law." O Ammann, 'Analysis of the Final Appeal Judgment, 4A_398/2017' in

rule on its own, detached from these instruments, would somehow apply to illegal transfers of *de facto* control.[141]

In addition, the reading of the MTF rule accepted by the arbitral tribunals and the Swiss court is difficult to reconcile with the duty of non-recognition under general international law.[142] In fact, the *Namibia* advisory opinion notably highlighted the States' obligation to limit the scope of their treaties with South Africa only to South Africa's territory excluding Namibia.[143] The practice shown in this book supports this aspect of the duty of non-recognition as customary and self-executory in character.[144] Moreover, as demonstrated above, the *Namibia* exception has not been used in order to solely advance economic interests.[145]

In this context, it is not by coincidence that Article 29 VCLT, Article 15 VCST, Article 6 VCST and Article 41 ARSIWA are perfectly aligned in underlying

---

A Nollkaemper and A Reinisch (eds), *Oxford Reports on International Law in Domestic Courts* (online edn, OUP 2019), A4.

141 See *supra* Part 1, Chapter 7.

142 It is a stretch too far to claim that the duty of non-recognition mandates the interpretation of the term 'territory' in an international treaty as including illegally annexed territory. It was demonstrated in Part 1, Chapter 7, that the duty of non-recognition prohibits not only formal acts of recognition but also those acts that imply recognition. *Contra* Ackermann and Wuschka (n 89) 462. While the interpretation of this specific BIT, harmonious with the general international law, would preclude its application at hand, other legal regimes' applicability (especially human rights law) is triggered by Russia's effective control over the peninsula, offering other layers of protection. See *infra* and S Lorenzmeier, 'Investment Disputes in Annexed Crimea from the Perspective of International Law' in BC Harzl and R Petrov (eds), *Unrecognized Entities: Perspectives in International, European and Constitutional Law* (Brill 2022) 98–102. *Contra* Ackermann and Wuschka (n 89) 462 (arguing that in case the tribunal declined jurisdiction, this "would allow Russia to escape obligations – including in relation to dispute settlement – it would have had if it had legally acquired the Crimean Peninsula"). Arguably, to deny obligations that would flow from sovereignty over a certain territory to an aggressor is consistent with the underlying purpose of the duty of non-recognition, which seeks to preclude the consolidation of territorial illegality/claim to sovereignty.

143 *Namibia* (n 9) para 122.

144 For more relevant practice, see *supra* Part 1, Chapter 7. "The EU has officially notified Russia that it considers bilateral agreements between the EU and the Russian Federation to be applicable only to the internationally recognised territory of Russia, and thus not to Crimea and Sevastopol." 'The EU Non-Recognition Policy for Crimea and Sevastopol: Fact Sheet' (12 December 2017) <https://eeas.europa.eu/headquarters/headquarters-Homepage/37464/eu-non-recognition-policy-crimea-and-sevastopol-fact-sheet_en> accessed 17 March 2020.

145 See *supra*. Lorenzmeier (n 142) 93–95. *Contra* Happ and Wuschka (n 117) 262–264 for deriving a policy rationale for an extensive interpretation of Article 29 VCLT from the *Namibia* exception.

assumptions and intended consequences. They are all different iterations of one and the same principle of general international law – the prohibition of alteration of territorial boundaries by force. By virtue of Article 31(3)(c) VCLT, even arbitral tribunals should take into account any relevant international law rules applicable in relations between the parties to inform the understanding of applicable rules.[146]

Thus, the reading of the arbitral tribunals and the Swiss court in fact renders this aspect of the duty of non-recognition nugatory. Some scholars argued that by considering Crimea as part of Russia's territory, understood as Russia's sovereign territory, the arbitral tribunal itself would have violated its duty of non-recognition.[147] Nevertheless, a peculiar interpretation of the operation of the MTF rule as pertaining also to the territory under *de facto* control, even if incorrect, was certainly designed to avoid such a conclusion.[148]

Regardless of motivations, an attempt to disturb this balance carries with it substantial risks. To justify the applicability of the Russia-Ukraine BIT to Ukrainian investments in the territory of Russia-annexed Crimea by reference to an incorrect interpretation of the customary rules of general international law could have broader subversive effects. In fact, there is value in keeping different notions of general international law distinguishable.[149] Ordinarily, as follows, there is a difference in meaning between the terms 'territory', 'jurisdiction' or 'control', as they broadly reflect the difference between the principle of legality and effectiveness. To render these lines blurred brings about the risk of undermining law by the effects of sheer power.

146 Dumberry (n 114) 527; Wuschka (n 91) 27. Rees-Evans (n 100) 185–186.

147 Dumberry (n 114) 528.

148 "[I]t is apparent in reading the Award on Jurisdiction that this Tribunal was – to smash two cliches together – bending over backwards to square the circle." C Miles, 'Lawfare in Crimea: Treaty, Territory, and Investor-State Dispute Settlement' (2022) 38 Arbitration International 135, 147.

149 For example, it is unhelpful to coin new expression such as a 'de facto sovereignty.' "The exercise of de facto sovereignty, accordingly, could be sufficient to establish 'territory' in cases where the de jure sovereign is completely deprived of the exercise of its rights." Happ and Wuschka (n 117) 264. In addition, since the tribunals interpreted the notion of 'territory' by reference to Article 29 VCLT, it is difficult to agree with the views of some authors that this interpretation was "self-contained" for the purposes of the BIT and "without further consequence." L Hill-Cawthorne, 'International Litigation And The Disaggregation of Disputes: Ukraine/Russia as a Case Study' (2019) 68 International and Comparative Law Quarterly 779, 799.

2.5.2 Interpretation of the Russia-Ukraine BIT in the Light of Its Object and Purpose

Following the rules of interpretation in Article 31 VCLT, the arbitral tribunals in *Stabil* and *Ukrnafta* also interpreted the term 'territory of the Russian Federation' under the Russia-Ukraine BIT in the light of its object and purpose. In this context, it is important to highlight that

> [t]he consideration of object and purpose finds its limits in the ordinary meaning of the text of the treaty. It may only be used to bring one of the possible ordinary meanings of the terms to prevail and cannot establish a reading that clearly cannot be expressed with the words used in the text.[150]

From this perspective, it was important that the arbitral tribunals in *Stabil* and *Ukrnafta* referred to a number of factors including their reading of the MTF rule and held that the ordinary meaning of the term 'territory' was broad enough to encompass the entire territory under Russia's control.[151]

Specifically, in *Ukrnafta* and *Stabil*, tribunals held that "it would be incompatible with the BIT's purpose to 'leave without protection foreign investments on a territory over which a State exercises exclusive control'."[152] Tribunals in *Belbek* and *Privatbank* focused on the effectiveness of Russia's occupation and "the consequent finding that Russia should be liable for protection of Ukrainian investors in that territory".[153] In *Everest* (for the purposes of *ratione temporis* jurisdiction) the tribunal held that the BIT's application was "more

---

150 O Dörr, 'Article 31: General Rule of Interpretation' in O Dörr and K Schmalenbach (eds), *Vienna Convention on the Law of Treaties* (2nd edn, Springer 2018) 586–587. Villiger adopts the same position. Villiger (n 125) 428. But other doctrinal approaches can be found, too. "In particular, even though the wording of most investment treaties and their reference to 'territory' could be read as a reference to sovereign territory only, the object and purpose of investment treaties mandates a different conclusion." Wuschka (n 91) 30.

151 Hepburn and Kabra (n 99).

152 Arbitral award cited in Hepburn and Kabra (n 99). See *Stabil* (101) para 158.

153 LE Peterson, 'In Jurisdiction Ruling, Arbitrators Rule That Russia Is Obliged under BIT to Protect Ukrainian Investors in Crimea Following Annexation' (*IAReporter*, 9 March 2017) <https://www.iareporter.com/articles/in-jurisdiction-ruling-arbitrators-rule-that-russia-is-obliged-under-bit-to-protect-ukrainian-investors-in-crimea-following-annexation/> accessed 10 February 2020. "[T]he Tribunal construes the term 'territory' for purposes of the Treaty to include territory over which a State exercises settled jurisdiction or control and on behalf of which it has assumed responsibility for international relations." *Privatbank* (101) para 185. The tribunal took "some guidance from the law on State succession" to develop this criterion. However, notably and inexplicably, the tribunal did not engage with another rule of the law on State succession as expressed in Article 6 VCST, ie the conformity with international law. It merely stated it left "aside any issue as might be

responsive to the purposes and objects of the BIT".[154] Thus, it seems that the factual control of the territory of Crimea by the Russian Federation and hence its position as the only State able to fulfil the object and purpose of the BIT, specifically, to protect foreign investments, weighed significantly in the reasoning of arbitral tribunals.

To justify such approach the claimants and many scholars have reasoned by analogy with human rights treaties. In *Everest*, claimants argued that the Russia-Ukraine BIT applied even to a *de facto* exercise of jurisdiction over the territory of Crimea, regardless of its international legality.[155] By analogy, between BITs and human rights treaties, the claimants argued that, according to the case law of the ICJ and ECtHR, treaties bind the Occupying Powers "if non-performance of treaty obligations would adversely affect the population of that territory".[156]

Some scholars claim that the investment treaties are analogical to human rights treaties, as they "serve to protect investors from arbitrary or discriminatory interferences with their investments", and therefore "title and sovereignty are not decisive factors for the territorial application of an investment treaty."[157] The teleological interpretation of the term 'territory' in investment treaties "indeed speaks in favour of the treaty's application to occupied territory."[158] They are also claimed to arguably confer rights on non-State actors, "and are thus, with due caution, in some respects comparable to human rights instruments".[159]

As far as the relevant test that would trigger the applicability of investment treaties, it seems that tribunals in *Ukrnafta* and *Stabil* referred to a State's 'exclusive control'.[160] Scholars suggest a very high level of effective control, which "must practically come close to (even though of course not *de jure*) sovereign territory".[161] The control must be "prolonged and relatively stable".[162]

---

engaged by the limitation expressed in Article 6 of the VCST." ibid, paras 171 and 174. The analysis, therefore, seems incomplete.

154 Hepburn (n 99).

155 Hepburn (n 99).

156 Hepburn (n 99).

157 Ackermann (n 118) 84.

158 ibid 84.

159 ibid 87.

160 Hepburn and Kabra (n 99). See *Stabil* (101) para 158. Additionally, the tribunal conducted a contextual interpretation according to which other provisions of the Russia-Ukraine BIT connected the meaning of territory with the State's ability to legislate in a particular area; at a decisive time, Russia was the only State with such ability. ibid. *Stabil* (101) paras 149–152.

161 Ackermann (n 118) 84.

162 ibid. Rees-Evans (n 100) 191–192.

As shown in Part 1, Chapters 8 and 9 the object and purpose of human rights treaties justify their applicability extra-territorially upon effective control, regardless of legality. However, as a preliminary step, the applicability of the majority of human rights treaties is premised upon the notion of jurisdiction, rather than of territory, which seems to exclude the straight-forward analogy with the Russia-Ukraine BIT.[163] In addition, it is true that based on its object and purpose, the ICJ found the ICESCR, which does not contain provision on the scope of its territorial application, applicable to the occupied territories.[164] However, it is one matter to establish extra-territorial application of the ICESCR in the light of its object and purpose, as it does not contain any provision on the scope of its territorial application, but it is another matter to interpret an explicit term 'territory' in the Russia-Ukraine BIT in the light of its object and purpose as including areas under State's *de facto* control. The latter approach seems to be too expansive.

Moreover, the analogy with human rights treaties generally is not entirely compelling. "[T]he promotion and protection of bilateral business is pursued for the benefit of economic growth, while the protection of fundamental rights and freedoms of persons is undertaken for the good of humankind."[165] A difference also rests in that "the most common investment treaty operates on the basis of *a quid pro quo* with *potential* third party beneficiaries."[166] While it is claimed by some authors that, because the interests of individuals are concerned, "title and sovereignty are not decisive factors for the territorial application of an investment treaty,"[167] "the majority of investment treaties operate to protect investments rather than putative investors".[168]

In addition, in this context, scholars refer to "[t]he individual's interest, protected by international investment law, to receive reparation for the harm suffered."[169] But this claim must be relativised, namely because of the fact that human rights law already applies to Crimea by virtue of Russia's effective

163 See *supra* Part 1, Chapter 8. "'Jurisdiction' is a wider concept than 'territory'. A State does not only have jurisdiction within its own territory; it may also have jurisdiction outside of it." Von Der Decken (n 115) 535.

164 See *supra* Part 1, Chapter 8. Ackermann (n 118) 83. *Legal Consequences of the Construction of a Wall in the Occupied Palestinian Territory* (Advisory Opinion) [2004] ICJ Rep 136, paras 107–112.

165 Vaccaro-Incisa (n 114).

166 Douglas (n 96) 135.

167 Ackermann (n 118) 84.

168 Douglas (n 96) 136.

169 This "conflicts with the international community's interest to sanction illegal acquisition of territory." Wuschka (n 91) 27.

control.[170] It is also true that due to an expansive reading of *Namibia* exception in the ECtHR case law, the Ukrainian investors would presumably be expected to exhaust local remedies in the Russian Federation, which seems to be inconceivable for the claimants.[171] In any case, the lack of dispute settlement forum to enforce rights is a different issue from assessing whether these treaties are analogical.[172] In sum, as shown above, the analogy between the present context and human rights treaties is not justified.[173] It is the position of this book that such an analogy risks normalising peremptory illegality and undermining communitarian interests involved. Nevertheless, other specific factors of this particular case mentioned below are of a fundamental importance for the interpretation of the term 'the territory of the Russian Federation' under the Russia-Ukraine BIT.

2.5.3 Relevance of Russia's Conduct and Ukraine's Consent

Tribunals in *Ukrnafta* and *Stabil* held that Russia cannot claim territorial control over Crimea and at the same time deny investment protection to Ukrainian investments there.[174] The tribunals relied on a good faith principle to prevent Russia from "blowing hot and cold" – from claiming Crimea as under Russia's territorial control and simultaneously denying BIT protection to Ukrainian investments there.[175] The tribunals stated that Russia's repeated unilateral public declarations on Crimea being part of Russia's territory "gave rise to legal obligations which could be relied upon by third parties".[176]

However, it is the position of this book that the practice of Russia concerning its position that Crimea is the part of its territory is limited by the consequences of peremptory territorial illegality including the duty of non-recognition. According to ARSIWA, the duty of non-recognition "applies to all States, including the responsible State."[177] A good faith interpretation presumes compliance with international law.

170 See *supra*. Dumberry (n 114) 518; Vaccaro-Incisa (n 114); Lorenzmeier (n 142) 98–99.

171 See *supra* Part 1, Chapter 7.

172 Happ and Wuschka (n 117) 267–268.

173 Lorenzmeier (n 142) 95. This position seems to be in line with the emphasis on extra-territoriality that has been a dominant feature of international law in recent years. S Karagiannis, 'The Territorial Application of Treaties' in DB Hollis (ed), *The Oxford Guide to* Treaties (OUP 2012) 327.

174 Hepburn and Kabra (n 99). *Stabil* (101) para 170.

175 Hepburn and Kabra (n 99). *Stabil* (101) para 166.

176 Hepburn and Kabra (n 99). See *Stabil* (101) paras 171–174.

177 ILC, Draft Articles on the Responsibility of States for Internationally Wrongful Acts, with Commentaries in 'Report of the International Law Commission on the Work of its Fifty-Third Session (23 April-1 June and 2 July-10 August 2001)' UN Doc A/56/10 commentary

The tribunal in *Everest* also reportedly noted that "Russia and Ukraine both agreed that the BIT applied to Crimea."[178] "Ukraine's submission maintained that Crimea remained Ukrainian territory, but that Russia's current occupation meant that, for the purposes of the BIT, Crimea was 'presently' part of Russian territory."[179] "Thus, for the tribunal, the territorial scope of the BIT was not in issue and had not changed; the treaty always applied, one way or another, to Crimea."[180] The position of Ukraine, that for the purposes of the Russia-Ukraine BIT Ukraine accepts that Crimea was 'presently' part of Russian territory, was also reportedly determinative for other decisions of the tribunals.[181]

Thus, the question arises as to the relevance of Ukraine's position in this context. At first, it would seem that Ukraine's position is equally limited by the consequences of peremptory territorial illegality including the duty of non-recognition.[182] However, even though this issue is rather underexplored in the literature, this book already highlighted the unique legal position of an injured State in shaping a response to the consequences of peremptory territorial illegality and the duty of non-recognition.[183] In fact, commentary to ARSIWA, despite not being very clear, provides for the special position of an injured State, subject to the preservation of communitarian interests.[184] Moreover, there is already some incremental practice to substantiate this claim. This practice concerns economic dealings with illegal entities on the basis of the parent

to art 41, para 9 ("ARSIWA"). For example, the CJEU did not hold as decisive, for the interpretation of the term "territory of the Kingdom of Morocco" in the EU-Morocco trade agreement, the fact that Morocco considers Western Sahara "an integral part of its territory." See, for the position of Morocco, *Front Polisario* (n 131) Opinion of Advocate General Wathelet (13 September 2016), para 66.

178 Hepburn (n 99). It is not entirely clear in what mode the tribunals took note of this fact with respect to the interpretation of the treaty term. It can be presumed that it was seen as a subsequent practice under art 31(3)(b) VCLT. Nevertheless, *stricto sensu*, it is not subsequent practice "in the application of treaty."

179 ibid.

180 Decisive for the tribunal was the issue of *ratione temporis* jurisdiction. ibid.

181 Rees-Evans (n 100) 186–187.

182 This is the position taken by Dumberry. "In my view, the position (apparently) adopted by Ukraine gives legal effect to the annexation of Crimea, a situation in violation of a jus cogens norm." Dumberry, *A Guide to State Succession* (n 130) 238.

183 See *supra* Part 1, Chapter 7.

184 "[S]ince the breach by definition concerns the international community as a whole, waiver or recognition induced from the injured State by the responsible State cannot preclude the international community's interest in ensuring a just and appropriate settlement." ARSIWA (n 177) commentary to art 41, para 9. On the communitarian interests of the duty of non-recognition, see Dumberry (n 114) 530–532. See also *supra* Part 1, Chapter 7.

State's certifications.[185] In addition, an analogy can be also made with the EU case law requiring the consent of the people of Western Sahara for the extension of the EU-Morocco trade agreement to the territory of Western Sahara under the *pacta tertiis* principle.[186] Arguably, this would *a fortiori* apply to the interpretation of the term of a bilateral treaty to which an injured State is itself a party.[187] Because of the confidentiality of awards it is not certain under what rationale tribunals paid regard to this issue. However, it is argued that the fact that the arbitral tribunals reportedly considered Ukraine's position that "for the purposes of the BIT, Crimea was 'presently' part of Russian territory"[188] as determinative would seem to go in the same direction as the outlined incremental practice.

2.5.4 Implications of Crimea-Focused Arbitrations for the DPR and LPR

Scholars have suggested that the existing Crimea-focused arbitral awards now show the way forward regarding the expropriations that have taken place in the territories of the DPR and LPR since 2014.[189] This practice of expropriation is detailed below in Chapter 19. However, without prejudice to the general criticism of the approach taken in these arbitral awards detailed above, at least two issues seem to complicate the picture further. First, Ackermann and Wuschka highlight that altough some tribunals referred to a *de facto* territorial control regarding the BIT's applicability, the critical date was, nevertheless, the formal unilateral act of Russia, ie the entry into force of the Russian law incorporating Crimea on 21 March 2014.[190] However, ultimately, a close reading of the awards reveals that neither has considered these formal statements of intent a "fixed criterion".[191]

185 See *supra* with respect to the extension of the EU-Moldova DCFTA to Transnistria and the Green Line regulation concerning trade with the TRNC.

186 See *supra* Part 1, Chapter 7. Similarly, Ackermann (n 118) 86.

187 See Ackermann (n 118) 86.

188 Hepburn (n 99). See for a different understanding of the relevance of Ukraine's position as a contribution to a "special meaning" under Article 31(4) VCLT. This understanding, however, does not deal with the consequences of peremptory illegality. Nevertheless, it complements the idea developed in this book. AF Papaefstratiou, 'Crimea as Russian Territory for the Purposes of the Russia-Ukraine BIT: Consent v. International Law?' (*Kluwer Arbitration Blog*, 5 February 2023) <https://arbitrationblog.kluwerarbitration.com/2023/02/05/crimea-as-russian-territory-for-the-purposes-of-the-russia-ukraine-bit-consent-v-international-law/> accessed 31 October 2023.

189 Ackermann and Wuschka (n 89) 464 *et seq*; Antonovych (n 89). Russia-Ukraine BIT "begins to look – without too much exaggeration – less like a BIT and more like the foundation of a de facto claims commission." Miles (n 148) 150.

190 Ackermann and Wuschka (n 89) 465.

191 Ibid, 466.

As Russia annexed the DPR and LPR on 30 September 2022, the tribunals would have to adopt a purely factual approach to interpreting the notion of "territory" in Russia-Ukraine BIT to cover the preceding period.[192] Scholars highlight recent judgments, most specifically the *Ukraine and the Netherlands v Russia* decision, where the ECtHR established that the separatist territories were under effective control of Russia since 11 May 2014.[193] It is argued in the literature that these conclusions would offer substantial support to investors seeking to demonstrate that Russia exercised *de facto* control over these territories for the purposes of the Russia-Ukraine BIT.[194]

Second, it was argued above that the position of Ukraine, holding that Crimea was 'presently' part of Russian territory, was of critical importance. It is difficult to imagine to what extent Ukraine would be willing to adopt such a controversial position in the current conditions, especially following the all-out Russia's aggression since February 2022.

3 Conclusion

In the area of purported inter-State relations, the present chapter demonstrated that, apart from States that officially recognised these entities as States and Crimea, DPR, LPR, Zaporizhzhia and Kherson Regions as part of Russia, the overwhelming majority of sovereign States scrupulously abide by the duty of non-recognition by not establishing direct diplomatic, consular and treaty relations with these entities. Similarly, the territorial scope of application of treaties concluded between the EU and the parent States also confirms the parent States' territorial sovereignty over illegal secessionist entities and consequent treaty-making capacity with respect to these territories.

The chapter also criticised the analysis of general international law principles on spatial application of treaties by arbitral tribunals in the proceedings involving expropriations of Ukrainian assets in the Russia-annexed Crimea under the Russia-Ukraine BIT. It demonstrated that tribunals' reasoning with

192 Ackermann and Wuschka (n 89) 467–468 (arguing in favour of the effective control test for the purposes of belligerent occupation).

193 *Ukraine and the Netherlands v Russia* App nos 8019/16, 43800/14 and 28525/20 (ECtHR, 25 January 2023) para 695.

194 Antonovych (n 89); 'Future Claims against Russia: Key Implications of the Ukraine and the Netherlands v Russia Decision' (*Shearman & Sterling Perspectives*, 1 February 2023) <https://www.shearman.com/en/perspectives/2023/02/future-claims-against-russia-key-implications-of-the-ukraine-and-the-netherlands-v-russia-decision> accessed 31 October 2023.

respect to the operation of the MTF rule and interpretation of the term 'its entire territory' under Article 29 VCLT as including not only changes of exercise of sovereignty, but also exercise of a *de facto* control was too expansive, incorrect and posing risk to established tenets of consequences of peremptory illegality under general international law. Moreover, despite acknowledging the importance of the interests of protection and promotion of investments, the chapter also concluded that in view of other communitarian interests involved, interpretation of the term 'territory of the Russian Federation' in the Russia-Ukraine BIT in the light of its object and purpose based on analogy with human rights treaties does not justify inclusion of illegally-annexed areas under State's *de facto* control. Lastly, the fact that the arbitral tribunals' reportedly saw Ukraine's position that "for the purposes of the BIT, Crimea was 'presently' part of Russian territory"[195] as determinative for the establishment of the territorial scope of the Russia-Ukraine BIT seems to go in the same direction as a previous incremental trend in practice that a *de iure* injured State has unique position in shaping the response to peremptory illegality within the framework of the duty of non-recognition.

195 Hepburn (n 99).

CHAPTER 18

Economic and Other Dealings

1 Parent States' Economic Dealings

1.1 *Ukraine's Approach to Crimea and the DPR and LPR Until 2022*

1.1.1 Local Trade between Mainland Ukraine and Russia-Annexed Crimea

Between 2014 and 2021, Ukraine's so-called Business in Crimea Act – adopted on the basis of the Law on Temporarily Occupied Territory of Ukraine – established a special legal regime – the free economic zone of Crimea (FEZ Crimea) for a period of 10 years in the territory of the Autonomous Republic of Crimea and the city of Sevastopol and prescribed a regulatory framework for legal relations concerning Crimea.[1] For example, according to this law, the FEZ Crimea was governed by a state-owned Managing Company; state taxes, but not local taxes were cancelled in the FEZ Crimea; legal entities and physical persons having a place of residence in the FEZ Crimea were non-residents for tax purposes.[2]

The FEZ Crimea encompassed a free customs zone of a commercial, service and industrial nature. Goods with Ukrainian custom status from other territories of Ukraine were supplied to the territory of FEZ Crimea according to a regime equivalent to an export customs regime; goods were supplied from the territory of FEZ into other territories of Ukraine for their free circulation according to an import custom regime.[3] "[G]oods released for free circulation

1 'Law of Ukraine No 1636-VII On Creation of "Crimea" Free Economic Zone and on Specifics of Economic Activity on Temporarily Occupied Territory of Ukraine' (adopted 12 August 2014; entered into force 26 September 2014, repealed by Law No 1618-IX of 1 July 2021) <https://zakon.rada.gov.ua/laws/show/1636-18> accessed 31 October 2023 (*in Ukrainian*) ("Business in Crimea Act"). The Business in Crimea Act was adopted on the basis of Article 13 of 'Law of Ukraine No 1207-VII On Securing the Rights and Freedoms of Citizens and the Legal Regime on the Temporarily Occupied Territory of Ukraine' (adopted 15 April 2014; entered into force 27 April 2014) <https://zakon.rada.gov.ua/laws/show/1207-18#Text> accessed 31 October 2023 ("Law on Temporarily Occupied Territory of Ukraine") (*in Ukrainian*).

2 Business in Crimea Act (n 1) arts 4 and 5.

3 ibid art 12. See 'New Crimea Law' (*NOBLES*, 29 September 2014) <http://media.wix.com/ugd/bbf62f_d5cc7051f68b4a9a8dda07dbe7577b75.pdf> accessed 17 March 2020; OM Denysenko, 'Cancellation of Free Economic Zone in Crimea: Implications for Business' (*Lexology*, 29 October 2015) <https://www.lexology.com/library/detail.aspx?g=7dbdda4f-7b27-43fb-b7ae-07bfb69e9115> accessed 17 March 2020.

 | DOI:10.1163/9789004702646_027

in the temporarily occupied territory of Ukraine are considered as goods originating from Ukraine and move freely to other territory of Ukraine without any duties upon presentation of a certificate of origin from Ukraine issued by Chambers of Commerce in other territory of Ukraine".[4] In December 2015, the Cabinet of Ministers of Ukraine adopted a resolution restricting the movement of goods exceeding certain amounts to and from Crimea, but the Kyiv Appellate Administrative Court found this resolution illegal and invalid in June 2017.[5]

Thus, in this period, Ukraine did not ban trade with annexed Crimea, but it established that crossing between mainland Ukraine and Crimea entails crossing the Ukrainian customs territory, with all its consequences.[6] The duty of non-recognition and non-assistance were not relevant in this context since, as established in Part 1, Chapter 7 these duties do not require States to extend the prohibition of economic dealings to private economic operators and their import/export transactions. Moreover, the adoption of this law, which regulated matters of local trade without recognising the change of sovereignty over the peninsula, demonstrated Ukraine's assertion of sovereignty there and the exercise of its legislative jurisdiction.

The Business in Crimea Act was ultimately repealed in 2021.[7] The press reported that the law was criticised by the civil society groups in Ukraine, among others, for simplifying business activities in the occupied territory – at the time under the sanctions regime.[8] At the same time, the Law on Temporarily Occupied Territory of Ukraine was amended to include a new provision according to which the movement of goods from the territory of Ukraine

---

4 Business in Crimea Act (n 1) art 6 (6.6).

5 Cabinet of Ministers of Ukraine, 'Resolution No 1035 on Restrictions for Supplying Certain Goods (Works, Services) from the Temporarily Occupied Territory of Ukraine to Another Territory of Ukraine and/or from Other Territory of Ukraine to Temporarily Occupied Territory' (adopted 16 December 2015) <https://zakon.rada.gov.ua/laws/show/1035-2015-п> accessed 17 March 2020 (*in Ukrainian*). See also European Commission, 'Information Note to EU Business on Operating and/or Investing in Crimea/Sevastopol' (25 January 2018) SWD(2018) 43 final, 5 ("Information Note").

6 Denysenko (n 3). According to Law on Temporarily Occupied Territory of Ukraine, the Autonomous Republic of Crimea and the City of Sevastopol are integral parts of the territory of Ukraine. See Law on Temporarily Occupied Territory of Ukraine (n 1) art 1 in connection to art 3.

7 'Law of Ukraine No 1618-IX' (adopted 1 July 2021; entered into force 21 November 2021) art I <https://zakon.rada.gov.ua/laws/card/en/1618-20> accessed 31 October 2023 (*in Ukrainian*).

8 'Zelensky Signed the Law on the Abolition of the Free Economic Zone "Crimea"' (*Radio Svoboda*, 19 August 2021) <https://www.radiosvoboda.org/a/news-krym-ekonomika-zona-skasuvannia/31418737.html> accessed 31 October 2023 (*in Ukrainian*).

to the occupied territory of Ukraine and *vice versa* by all means of transport was prohibited.[9] Such a complete ban on the movement of goods went beyond what is required under the duty of non-recognition. Nevertheless, Ukraine was not prohibited from imposing economic restrictions vis-à-vis its own territory (subject to its obligations and limitations flowing from other branches of international law, such as IHL and IHRL).[10]

1.1.2 From Trading to All-Out Trade Ban on the DPR and LPR

Until 2017, Ukraine had also allowed for trading with the coalmines and other large industrial enterprises situated in the DPR and LPR.[11] Despite being located in the separatist territories, these businesses were registered as Ukrainian entities and paid taxes in Ukraine.[12] The DPR's and LPR's secessionist authorities allowed for the uninterrupted operation of these industrial enterprises, which assured the stability of employment in the DPR and LPR.[13] For Ukraine, the supply of anthracite coal was essential for its energy sustainability, as its power plants run on this type of coal, but the mines are mostly located in the East.[14]

9 Law of Ukraine No 1618-IX (n 7), art II (2)(4). Law on Temporarily Occupied Territory of Ukraine (as amened) (n 1) art 13^{1}(1).

10 The law provided for the exception for "personal belongings in hand luggage and accompanied luggage" and the event of evacuation. See Law on Temporarily Occupied Territory of Ukraine (as amended) (n 1) art 13^{1}(2) and (4). A specific exception for humanitarian aid was inserted by the amendment after the Russian invasion of February 2022. See 'Law of Ukraine No 1618-IX' (adopted 1 July 2021; entered into force 21 November 2021) art I <https://zakon.rada.gov.ua/laws/card/en/1618-20> accessed 31 October 2023. Law on Temporarily Occupied Territory of Ukraine (as amended) (n 1) art 13^{1}(5). The law also prohibits the water supply to Crimea and Sevastopol. Ibid, art 13^{1}(6). On this issue, see further M Pertile and S Faccio, 'Access to Water in Donbass and Crimea: Attack against Water Infrastructures and the Blockade of the North Crimea Canal' (2020) 29 Review of European, Comparative and International Environmental Law 56.

11 M Bird, L Vdovii and Y Tkachenko, 'The Donbass Paradox' (*The Black Sea*, 9 December 2015) <https://theblacksea.eu/_old/mirror/theblacksea.eu/donbass/index.html> accessed 17 October 2016. See also International Crisis Group, *Peace in Ukraine (III): The Costs of War in Donbas: Europe Report No 261* (ICG 2020) 8.

12 I Burdyga, 'Nationalization under the Rules of "DPR" and "LPR"' (*DW*, 1 March 2017) <https://www.dw.com/ru/к-чему-приведет-внешнее-управление-предприятиями-в-донбассе/a-37771726> accessed 10 February 2020 (*in Russian*). International Crisis Group (n 11) 8.

13 These businesses provided jobs to nearly 200,000 people in the separatist regions. N Mirimanova, 'Donbas Businessmen: From Victims to Peace-Builders?' (*Carnegie Russia Eurasia Center*, 4 April 2018) <https://carnegieeurope.eu/posts/2018/04/donbas-businessmen-from-victims-to-peace-builders> accessed 31 October 2023. International Crisis Group (n 11) 8.

14 Bird, Vdovii and Tkachenko (n 11). R Cameron, 'Ukraine Paid $ 1.67 Billion to Russia for Coal Supplies' (*IEA Clean Coal Centre*, 13 December 2018) <https://www.iea-coal.org/ukraine-paid-1-67-billion-to-russia-for-coal-supplies/> accessed 10 February 2020. International Crisis Group (n 11) 8.

This trade was subject to an ambiguous legal regime in the context of the anti-terrorist operation (ATO) in the areas of the Donetsk and Luhansk regions.[15] Thus, some trading between government-controlled areas and the East had continued.[16]

However, in early 2017, Ukrainian veterans started an unauthorised blockade of the road and railway communications from the DPR and LPR to halt the trade, which they saw as sustaining the rebel-held entities.[17] Without the supply of raw materials, some of the plants in the DPR and LPR suspended their operations. The secessionist authorities at first gave an ultimatum to Kyiv to end the blockade by 1 March 2017, and then on 2 March 2017, they imposed an interim administration on companies previously under Ukrainian jurisdiction.[18]

On 1 March 2017, the Ukrainian government adopted its first-ever decree, which regulated trade between Ukraine-controlled and separatist-held territories.[19] Following the failed attempt at halting the unauthorised blockade, on 15 March 2017, the Ukrainian National Security and Defence Council legalised the blockade by issuing a decree formally banning all transfer of goods between the government-controlled areas and Donbas, subject to humanitarian

15 H Kostanyan and A Remizov, *The Donbas Blockade: Another Blow to the Minsk Peace Process* (CEPS 2017) 2. Mirimanova (n 13); N Mirimanova, *Business Opportunities Lost ... and Found* (Centre for Humanitarian Dialogue 2016) 2; NAKO, *Crossing the Line: How the Illegal Trade with Occupied Donbas Undermines Defence Integrity* (NAKO 2017) 11.

16 J Marson, 'Kiev Remains an Economic Lifeline for Separatist-Held East' (*The Wall Street Journal*, 9 December 2015) <http://www.wsj.com/articles/kiev-remains-an-economic-lifeline-for-separatist-held-east-1449714420> accessed 17 October 2016; Y Latynina, 'Expropriation or War' (*Novaya Gazeta*, 2 March 2017) <https://novayagazeta.ru/articles/2017/03/02/71660-ekspropriatsiya-ili-voyna> accessed 10 February 2020 (*in Russian*).

17 Y Zoria, 'Will the Makeshift Blockade in Donbas Hit the Russian-Backed Enclaves' Economy?' (*Euromaidanpress*, 9 February 2017) <http://euromaidanpress.com/2017/02/09/donbas-blockade-economy/> accessed 10 February 2020. International Crisis Group (n 11) 8–9.

18 'The DPR and LPR Imposed External Administration on Ukrainian Enterprises' (*RIA Novosti*, 1 March 2017) <https://ria.ru/20170301/1488981466.html> accessed 10 February 2020 (*in Russian*). See for more *infra*. International Crisis Group (n 11) 9.

19 "At least formally, it considerably restricted the possibilities of exploiting 'grey' zones, by limiting the list of goods permitted to cross the demarcation line, and also constraining their transport means, e.g. registered enterprises have to use the railways." Kostanyan and Remizov (n 15) 3. See Cabinet of Ministers of Ukraine, 'Resolution No 99 on Approval of the Procedure of Transfer of Goods To or From the Area of Anti-Terrorist Operation' (1 March 2017) <https://zakon.rada.gov.ua/laws/show/99-2017-п#Text> accessed 31 October 2023 (*in Ukrainian*); NAKO (n 15) 12.

exceptions.[20] Businesses in the DPR and LPR previously under Ukrainian jurisdiction reoriented their export routes and supply chains.[21] The export of coal has allegedly been conducted through Russia and the ports in Abkhazia to Turkey, or simply by way of re-labelling it as Russian and exporting it to third States, including the EU and even Ukraine.[22] In 2019, the Kyiv government took measures to ease the restrictions across contact line for small traders; these were not reciprocated by the *de facto* authorities.[23]

---

20 The blockade was declared temporary until the implementation of the Minsk agreements and the return of seized companies to Ukrainian jurisdiction. 'Decree of the President of Ukraine No 62/2017 on the Decision of the National Security and Defence Council of Ukraine of 15 March 2017 "On Urgent Additional Measures to Counter the Hybrid Threats to the National Security of Ukraine"' (15 March 2017) <https://www.rnbo.gov.ua/ua/Ukazy/441.html> accessed 10 February 2020 (*in Ukrainian*) ("Decree on Trade Embargo"). Kostanyan and Remizov (n 15) 3. See 'Ukraine Suspended Cargo Traffic with the Donbas' (*BBC Russian Service*, 15 March 2017) <https://www.bbc.com/russian/news-39278781> accessed 10 February 2020 (*in Russian*); NAKO (n 15) 12. The exception regarding humanitarian assistance is in line with para 7 of Minsk II. 'Package of Measures for the Implementation of the Minsk Agreements' (signed 12 February 2015) <http://www.osce.org/ru/cio/140221?download=true> accessed 7 February 2019 (*in Russian*) ("Minsk II").

21 Russia allegedly supplies these companies with raw materials. L Kushch, 'One Year after "Nationalization" in the "DPR:" What Is Going on There?' (*BBC News Ukraine*, 19 March 2018) <https://www.bbc.com/ukrainian/features-russian-43450664> accessed 10 February 2020 (*in Russian*). International Crisis Group (n 11) 23–25.

22 B Milakovsky, 'Cut Off: What Does the Economic Blockade of the Separatist Territories Mean for Ukraine?' (*Kennan Institute*, 9 January 2018) <https://www.wilsoncenter.org/blog-post/cut-what-does-the-economic-blockade-the-separatist-territories-mean-for-ukraine> accessed 10 February 2020; Kostanyan and Remizov (n 15) 11; A Melikishvili and A Kokcharov, 'Donbass-Abkhazia Coal Export Scheme' (*IHS Markit*, 1 March 2018) <https://ihsmarkit.com/research-analysis/Donbass-Abkhazia-coal-export-scheme.html> accessed 10 February 2020; M Potocki and K Baca-Pogorzelska, 'Anthracite FAQ. What's the Deal with the Donbas Coal?' (*gazeta prawna*, 19 November 2018) <https://serwisy.gazetaprawna.pl/energetyka/artykuly/1355739,anthracite-faq-what-s-the-deal-with-the-donbas-coal.html?utm_source=dlvr.it&utm_medium=twitter> accessed 10 February 2020. International Crisis Group (n 11) 23–24.

23 International Crisis Group, *Peace in Ukraine (III): The Costs of War in Donbas* (ICG 2020) 19. Since 2018, Ukraine extended the legal regime of occupation to the areas of the Donetsk and Luhansk regions. Accordingly, the Cabinet of Ministers shall elaborate rules on the transfer of goods across the contact line. 'Law of Ukraine on the Peculiarities of State Policy to Ensure the State Sovereignty of Ukraine over Temporarily Occupied Territories in the Donetsk and Luhansk Regions No 2268-VIII' (adopted 18 January 2018, entered into force 24 February 2018, repealed by Law of Ukraine No 2217-IX of 21 April 2022), art 12 <https://zakon.rada.gov.ua/laws/show/2268-19> accessed 31 October 2023 (*in Ukrainian*) ("Law on Reintegration of Donbas"). As the Law on Reintegration of Donbas was repealed after the all-out Russian invasion in February 2022, the legal regime of occupied territories is now governed by the 2014 Law on Temporarily Occupied Territory of Ukraine.

Regarding trade between the government-controlled areas and the DPR and LPR, despite a factual contribution to the consolidation of illegal regimes, the relevant economic actors in the DPR and LPR were still formally Ukrainian legal entities that were paying taxes to the Ukrainian budget. Thus, it is difficult to see to what extent the duty of non-assistance and non-recognition would be applicable to such a context. Moreover, these duties do not require States to prohibit economic operators under their jurisdiction from trading with economic operators in illegal entities. The 2017 complete ban on trade with the DPR and LPR would thus seem to go beyond the scope of the duty of non-recognition and non-assistance, as it banned all incoming and outgoing trade, subject to humanitarian exceptions. Nevertheless, Ukraine was not prohibited from imposing any type of economic restrictions with respect to secessionist entities considered part of its own territory (subject to limitations and its obligations flowing from other branches of international law, such as IHL and IHRL). However, it is worth noting that the majority of international actors criticised the imposition of these restrictions as not in line with the spirit of the Minsk agreements.[24] In any case, the duty of non-recognition and non-assistance were not raised in this context at all.

1.2 *Moldova's Approach to Transnistria*

1.2.1 Overview of Moldova's Trade Relations with Transnistria

The trade regime between Moldova and Transnistria has evolved significantly since the secessionist war in 1992. At first, and throughout the 1990s, trade was extremely flexible, as Moldova allowed Transnistrian authorities to use Moldovan custom stamps when conducting export of goods without being subjected to checks by the Moldovan authorities.[25] However, with Moldova's membership in the WTO in 2001, this practice could not continue.[26] Nevertheless, Ukraine started rejecting Transnistrian products with old Moldovan customs

24 Kostanyan and Remizov (n 15) 14–16.

25 This was done in the context of a dispute resolution process. See especially the Protocol Decision on Resolution of Problems Emerged in Activity of Customs Services of the Republic of Moldova and Transnistria (signed 7 February 1996) available in NV Shtanski (ed), *Negotiation Process between Transnistrian Moldovan Republic and the Republic of Moldova in Documents* (MID TMR 2014) 43–44 (*in Russian*) and 293–294 (*in English*). See G Balan, *Place of the Confidence Building Process in the Policy of Solving the Conflict in the Eastern Region of Moldova* (Black Sea Peacebuilding Network and IPP 2010) 4. N Popescu, *The EU in Moldova – Settling Conflicts in the Neighbourhood* (EU Institute for Security Studies 2005) 18.

26 Popescu (n 25) 18.

stamps and conducting stricter border controls only in 2006.[27] In this context, Moldova facilitated registration and access to Moldovan customs stamps for companies in Transnistria.[28] The Russian Duma described this move as Transnistria's economic blockade.[29]

In 2006, the EU also granted Moldova a generalised system of tariff preferences and, as mentioned above, since 2008 Moldova has benefited from the EU's autonomous trade preferences (ATP) regime.[30] Transnistrian companies registered with the Moldovan authorities also exported under these preferential tariffs;[31] as a result, Transnistrian exports to the EU significantly increased.[32]

---

27 This took place on the basis of the Moldovan and Ukrainian Prime Ministers' Joint Declaration on customs issues in December 2005. Upon the request of the Moldovan and Ukrainian presidents, the EU also established the European Union Border Assistance Mission, EUBAM, on the border between Moldova and Ukraine in late 2005 in order to enhance the capacities of Moldovan and Ukrainian services. Commission of the European Communities, 'Communication from the Commission to the Council and the European Parliament on Strengthening the European Neighbourhood Policy: ENP Progress Report: Moldova' (4 December 2006) COM(2006) 726 final, 5–6.

28 Commission of the European Communities, 'Communication from the Commission to the Council and the European Parliament on Strengthening the European Neighbourhood Policy: ENP Progress Report: Moldova' (4 December 2006) COM(2006) 726 final, 6.

29 'Statement of the State Duma on the Aggravation of the Situation around Transnistria in Connection with the Introduction by the Authorities of Ukraine and Moldova of a New Customs Regime on Transnistrian Section of the Ukrainian-Moldovan Border' (10 March 2006) <http://customs.gospmr.org/wp-content/uploads/2015/03/Zayavlenie-gosdumy-10.03.2006.pdf> accessed 17 March 2020 (*in Russian*). See also 'Declaration of the Presidency on behalf of the European Union on the Implementation of the Joint Declaration on Customs Issues of the Ukrainian and Moldovan Prime Ministers' P/06/45 (14 March 2006) <https://ec.europa.eu/commission/presscorner/detail/en/PESC_06_45> accessed 17 March 2020.

30 S Secrieru, 'Transnistria Zig-zagging towards a DCFTA' (*PISM*, 28 January 2020) <https://www.pism.pl/publications/PISM_Policy_Paper_no__4__145___Transnistria_Zig_zagging_towards_a_DCFTA> accessed 17 March 2020.

31 On the procedure of re-registering companies registered in Transnistria in the registration chamber of Moldova, see 'Registration of Transnistrian Enterprises in the Republic of Moldova' (*Chelyadnik & Partners Consulting*) <https://cipcons.com/registracija-pridnestrovskih-predprijatij-v-respublike-moldova/> accessed 17 March 2020 (*in Russian*). This procedure includes, for example, the submission of the extract from the register of legal entities in Transnistria.

32 Between 2005 and 2014, Transnistrian exports to the EU doubled. A Lupuşor, *DCFTA in the Transnistrian Region: Mission Possible?* (Expert-Group Independent Think-Tank 2015) 7. In September 2015, the EU's share in total volume of Transnistrian exports accounted for 30%, while that of the Russian Federation accounted for only 7.5%. I Groza, *Thematic Analysis: Preparing the Implementation of the Deep and Comprehensive Free Trade Area (DCFTA) in the Transnistrian Region of the Republic of Moldova* (Institute for European Policies and Reforms 2015) 4.

Some commentators even described this development as a "creeping economic integration of Transnistrian business into the Moldovan economy".[33]

However, as mentioned above, because of the EU-Moldova DCFTA and the related expiry of the ATPs by the end of 2015, it was necessary to find an arrangement with respect to the DCFTA's application to Transnistria.[34] Without such an agreement, higher MFN tariffs would have to be applied to Transnistrian exports, and a complete closure of the intra-Moldova-Transnistria 'border' and a strict separation of both economies would follow.[35] Transnistria could completely lose preferential access to the EU, which would have seriously damaged its economy.[36]

Ultimately, as shown above, the technical deal between Moldova and Transnistria was reached and, upon the Decisions of the EU-Moldova Association Council, the DCFTA has applied to the whole territory of Moldova, including Transnistria, since 1 January 2016.[37] On the one hand, Moldova agreed to continue to issue its certificates of origin to entities from Transnistria.[38] On the other hand, Transnistria's authorities agreed to give access to Moldova's customs officers to inspect deposits and production sites[39] and to verify compliance with sanitary and phytosanitary requirements; they also agreed to terminate import duties on EU goods in line with the EU-Moldova DCFTA, introduce a VAT in accordance with WTO rules and approximate legislation with EU standards.[40] As a result of the DCFTA's extension to Transnistria, the

33 N Popescu, *EU Foreign Policy and Post-Soviet Conflicts: Stealth Intervention* (Routledge 2011) 60.

34 See *supra*.

35 B Coppieters, 'Abkhazia, Transnistria and North Cyprus: Recognition and Non-Recognition in Ceasefire and Trade Agreements' (2019) Ideology and Politics 10, 28; Secrieru (n 30). W Konończuk and W Rodkiewicz, 'Could Transnistria Block Moldova's Integration with the EU?' (OSW, 23 October 2012) <https://www.osw.waw.pl/en/publikacje/osw-commentary/2012-10-23/could-transnistria-block-moldovas-integration-eu> accessed 17 March 2020.

36 Secrieru (n 30). See *infra*.

37 For the geopolitical determinants of this decision, see Secrieru (n 30).

38 G Van der Loo, 'Law and Practice of the EU's Trade Agreements with "Disputed" Territories: A Consistent Approach?' in I Govaere and S Garben (eds), *The Interface Between EU and International Law: Contemporary Reflections* (Bloomsbury 2019) 263.

39 Already under the ATP scheme, Moldovan customs officers were reportedly granted access to some companies in the region (although without the right to wear uniforms or possess arms), but this access was granted at the discretion of Transnistria's authorities. V Prohniţchi and A Lupuşor, *Transnistria and the Deep and Comprehensive Free Trade Agreement: A Little Stone that Overturns a Great Wain?* (Expert-Group 2013) 5; *The Impact of the EU-Moldova DCFTA on the Transnistrian Economy: Quantitative Assessment under Three Scenarios*, 10.

40 Van der Loo (n 38) 263; Secrieru (n 30).

proportion of Transnistrian goods exported to the EU has increased.[41] In 2019, 2.000 Transnistrian companies were registered in Moldova.[42] In practice, Transnistria has reportedly been slow in implementing these requirements.[43]

1.2.2 Assessment of Moldova-Transnistria Trade Relations under International Law

Moldova's approach to trading with Transnistria, as well as the commencement of the EU-Moldova DCFTA's application to Transnistria, raise the question of compliance with trade-related aspects of the duty of non-recognition and non-assistance. It is true that Moldova's practice of issuing certificates of origin to Transnistria's companies, which has allowed them to export their products, has been a vital element of the sustainment of Transnistria's economy since the very beginning of Transnistria's *de facto* separation from Moldova.

However, this mechanism is the expression of Moldova's sovereignty over Transnistria and upholds the duty of non-recognition. The implementation and enforcement of the EU-Moldova DCFTA in Transnistria is an important confirmation of Transnistria as part of Moldova's sovereign territory. In fact, Transnistria unwillingly accepted "a status of subordination to Moldova".[44] In particular, Transnistria's exports never entailed the recognition of public acts of illegal secessionist entity, as Moldova's Chamber of Commerce has been issuing the certificates of origin. Similarly, the conduct of checks of production sites by Moldova in Transnistria can be considered the exercise of Moldova's public powers and thereby a confirmation of its sovereignty over this region. Lastly, Moldova's consent with this arrangement seems to underline its specific position of the parent State as injured State, in the context of the duty of non-recognition and in the context of preservation of communitarian interests.

1.3 *Georgia's Approach to Abkhazia and South Ossetia*

In the 1990s, while South Ossetia maintained some economic contacts with Georgia itself, Georgia, Russia and other CIS Member States kept Abkhazia in complete isolation on the basis of the 1996 collective decision of the head of States of the CIS.[45] Nevertheless, the situation of both territories gradually

---

41 Coppieters, 'Abkhazia, Transnistria and North Cyprus' (n 35) 29.

42 ibid 27–28.

43 T De Waal, *Uncertain Ground: Engaging with Europe's De Facto States and Breakaway Territories* (Carnegie Europe 2018) 46.

44 Coppieters, 'Abkhazia, Transnistria and North Cyprus' (n 35) 29.

45 CIS Heads of State, 'Decision by the Council of CIS Heads of State on Measures to Settle the Conflict in Abkhazia, Georgia' (adopted 19 January 1996; entered into force 19 January 1996) para 6(a) <http://docs.cntd.ru/document/901818167> accessed 2 May

changed in the mid-2000s. On the one hand, Russia progressively relaxed its embargo towards Abkhazia, and in February 2008 lifted it completely.[46] On the other hand, Georgia severed its ties with South Ossetia and in 2004 even banned a key Ergneti market used for unofficial trade between Georgians and South Ossetians.[47] Following the 2008 War and Russia's recognition of South Ossetia and Abkhazia, the situation changed again. On the one hand, the two economies have been progressively integrated into the Russian economy.[48] On the other hand, Georgia has tightened the policy of economic isolation with respect to Abkhazia and South Ossetia and in connection with its adoption of the Law on Occupied Territories.[49] Other developments will be discussed separately.

1.3.1 Economic Isolation under the Law on Occupied Territories

The 2008 Law on Occupied Territories (Article 6(1)) prohibited economic activities with the two secessionist entities and stipulated the criminal punishment for its violation.[50] Moreover, the ban on economic activities extended not only to Georgian individuals and entities, "but also to international state and non-state organisations and economic actors"[51] and to related persons, "i.e. persons directly or indirectly participating in the capital and/or influencing decisions

---

2019 (*in Russian*). See also BG Punsmann and others, 'Review of Isolation Policies within and around the South Caucasus' (2016) Journal of Conflict Transformation: Caucasus Edition 1, 11.

46 S Fischer, 'Russian Policy in the Unresolved Conflicts' in S Fischer (ed), *Not Frozen! The Unresolved Conflicts over Transnistria, Abkhazia, South Ossetia and Nagorno-Karabakh in Light of the Crisis over Ukraine* (SWP 2016) 22.

47 Punsmann (n 45) 12.

48 See *supra*.

49 'Law of Georgia No 431 on Occupied Territories as amended' (adopted 23 October 2008) <https://smr.gov.ge/uploads/prev/The_Law_of_928ef0d7.pdf> accessed 18 October 2016 ("Law on Occupied Territories").

50 Prohibited activities include "[a]ny economic activity (entrepreneurial or non-entrepreneurial), regardless whether or not I is implemented for receiving profit, income or compensation," if under the Georgian laws "such activity requires a license, permit, authorization or registration or if, under the Georgian legislation, such activity requires an agreement but it has not been granted"; import and/or export of military products; international air and maritime traffic; railway traffic; international automobile transportation of cargo; use of natural resources; organization of cash transfer; financing of any of these activities. Law on Occupied Territories (n 49) art 6(1), and for criminal responsibility see art 6(3).

51 S Fischer, 'The Conflicts over Abkhazia and South Ossetia in Light of the Crisis over Ukraine' in S Fischer (ed), *Not Frozen! The Unresolved Conflicts over Transnistria, Abkhazia, South Ossetia and Nagorno-Karabakh in Light of the Crisis over Ukraine* (SWP 2016) 52.

of entities" involved in prohibited activities.[52] The only way to conduct economic activities in South Ossetia and Abkhazia was to obtain special permission from the Georgian government, which could be granted "if doing so serves the protection of the state interests of Georgia, promotion of peaceful conflict resolution, de-occupation, confidence building or humanitarian purposes".[53] The application of this prohibition was "extended to relations formed since 1990".[54]

Initially, the Law on Occupied Territories did not provide for the exception concerning the provision of humanitarian aid. The Venice Commission's Opinion highlighted this fact and pointed out that

> restriction and criminalisation of economic activities necessary for the survival of the population in occupied areas as well as a (potential) restriction and criminalisation of humanitarian aid is contrary to the rule of customary international law that the well-being of the population in occupied areas has to be a basic concern of those involved in a conflict.[55]

As a result, the law was amended to provide for the exception "to persons delivering immediate humanitarian assistance in the Occupied Territories in order to ensure the right to life of the population, in particular, by providing the population with food, medication and emergency supplies".[56]

---

52 Law on Occupied Territories (n 49) art 6(4) and 6(5).

53 ibid art 6(2). Between 2008 and 2016, the Georgian government issued 28 permits for economic activity in secessionist entities, the majority of which concerned the Enguri hydro-power plant, "the only joint enterprise of the Georgian and Abkhaz sides." International Crisis Group, *Abkhazia and South Ossetia: Time to Talk Trade: Europe Report No 249* (ICG 2018) 4, ftn 17. On the legal regulation of this power plant, see N Mirimanova, 'Abkhazia: Regulations for Trade with Disputed Statehood' 60 (2015) Politorbis 9, 10. CoE (Venice Commission), 'Information Note on the Law on Occupied Territories of Georgia Prepared by the Parliament of Georgia at the Request of the Rapporteurs' (5 March 2009) CDL-AD (2009)044, 6.

54 Law on Occupied Territories (n 49) art 11. In one of the amendments to the law, it was established that retroactive application did not apply to any provisions referring to criminal liability. See on this issue CoE (Venice Commission), 'Final Opinion on the Draft Amendments to the Law on Occupied Territories of Georgia' (14 December 2009) CDL-AD (2009)051, para 23.

55 CoE (Venice Commission), 'Opinion on the Law on Occupied Territories of Georgia' (17 March 2009) CDL-AD (2009)015, para 35 ("Venice Commission Opinion on the Law on Occupied Territories of Georgia"). See also E Benvenisti, *The International Law of Occupation* (OUP 2012) 105–106.

56 Law on Occupied Territories (n 49) art 6(6). Any such persons should notify the Georgian government prior to, or within a reasonable period of time after, the implementation of such activity. ibid, art 6(7). See also Government of Georgia, 'Regulation

Generally, the EU, as well as Georgia's Public Defender of Rights, encouraged the easing of trade relations and reviewing the law.[57] Nevertheless, despite these limitations, some incremental local trade between Georgia and the two entities,[58] as well as with external partners outside Russia,[59] has continued.

According to the Venice Commission, Article 6(1) of the Law on Occupied Territories could potentially cover any economic activity.[60] In light of this assessment, the scope of the prohibition exceeds the limits of the scope of the duty of non-recognition in two ways. The first is in subject matter, as the prohibition covers a very broad range of activities and not only those that help entrench the illegal regime's authority over territory. The second is the scope of *ratione personae*, as the prohibition extends to private economic actors, whether they are foreign or domestic. Nevertheless, the State is not prohibited from imposing economic restrictions with respect to an entity considered part of its own territory (subject to limitations from other branches of international law, such as IHL or IHRL). Moreover, the exception for the provision of humanitarian aid can be seen not only in the context of humanitarian law, as highlighted by the Venice Commission, but also as overlapping with the humanitarian aspects of the *Namibia* exception.

1.3.2 Russia-Georgia Trade Corridor through South Ossetia

The discussions were also held regarding formalising certain trade relations in the region. In particular, the Swiss-mediated 2011 Agreement between Russia and Georgia, adopted in the context of Russia's accession to the WTO, foresaw

No 320 on Approval Modalities for Engagement of Organizations Conducting Activities in the Occupied Territories of Georgia' (15 October 2010) <https://www.europarl.europa.eu/meetdocs/2009_2014/documents/dsca/dv/dsca_20110315_13/dsca_20110315_13en.pdf> accessed 18 November 2019.

57 'Association Agenda between the European Union and Georgia: 2017–2020' 26 <https://www.eeas.europa.eu/sites/default/files/annex_ii_-_eu-georgia_association_agenda_text.pdf> accessed 30 October 2023; 'EU-Georgia Association Agenda' (14 November 2014) EU-GE 4656/14, 13. 'Public Defender Calls for Revisiting Georgia's Law on Occupied Territories' (*Civil Georgia*, 11 February 2017) <https://old.civil.ge/eng/article.php?id=29850> accessed 18 November 2019.

58 International Crisis Group, *Abkhazia and South Ossetia: Time to Talk Trade* (n 53) 5–9; Mirimanova, 'Abkhazia' (n 53) 15.

59 Only a few countries that recognise Abkhazia and South Ossetia recognise their customs documents and product certificates. Usually, outgoing cargo is registered in Russia before continuing its journey westward. In Turkey, the Abkhaz diaspora helps conduct export/import-like operations with Abkhazia. International Crisis Group, *Abkhazia and South Ossetia: Time to Talk Trade* (n 53) 9–11.

60 Venice Commission Opinion on the Law on Occupied Territories of Georgia (n 55) paras 27–30.

the creation of three trade corridors, including one each going through South Ossetia and Abkhazia.[61] This Georgia-Russia Customs Agreement foresaw the establishment of a "Mechanism of customs administration and monitoring of all trade in goods that enter or exit predefined trade corridors".[62] The corridors through South Ossetia and Abkhazia were only mentioned in the annex to this agreement by their GPS indicators.[63] According to this agreement, the mechanism was composed of an Electronic Data Exchange System and an International Monitoring System.[64]

Under this agreement, both Russia and Georgia would sign a separate contract with a neutral private company, which would carry out some of the agreement's provisions, including risk management and auditing of data.[65] For years, negotiations were fruitless, but after the landslide in 2016, which completely blocked the Georgian military highway and caused substantial economic losses, the idea of a trade corridor through South Ossetia resurfaced.[66] Georgia and Russia signed the contracts with the Swiss private company SGS in December 2017 and May 2018, respectively.[67]

However, to make the corridor through South Ossetia operational, the issues of customs and passport control had to be resolved.[68] While Russia rejected Georgia's demand that all cargo passed through or at least was registered online with the Georgian customs, as it would undermine its recognition of

61 Agreement between the Government of Georgia and the Government of the Russian Federation on the Basic Principles for a Mechanism of Customs Administration and Monitoring of Trade in Goods (signed 9 November 2011; entered into force 22 August 2012) <http://iccn.ge/files/wto_mechanisms_eng.pdf> accessed 10 February 2020 ("Georgia-Russia Customs Agreement").

62 Ibid.

63 ibid annex I.

64 ibid.

65 ibid. "Based on the results of its risk management analysis, the neutral private company can recommend to the competent national customs officials to verity and check specific cargo at the terminals in the presence of a representative of the neutral private company as specified in Annex I." ibid.

66 International Crisis Group, *Abkhazia and South Ossetia: Time to Talk Trade* (n 53) 16–17.

67 Ibid 14. 'Press Release on the Signing of Russian-Swiss Documents' (*The Ministry of Foreign Affairs of the Russian Federation*, 19 May 2018) <https://www.mid.ru/tv/?id=1571871&lang=en > accessed 30 October 2023.

68 International Crisis Group, *Abkhazia and South Ossetia: Time to Talk Trade* (n 53) 15–19. According to the agreement's annex II, "[a]ll trade in goods that enters or exits the corridors shall be controlled and administered in accordance with the provisions of the respective national law by the national customs officials. The control and administration of this trade shall take place in customs terminals which are located at the exit/entry of the trade corridors." Georgia-Russia Customs Agreement (n 61) annex II.

South Ossetia's statehood, Georgia opposed customs control being conducted by secessionist officials, as it would strengthen their claim to statehood and their administrative capability.[69]

Two options were suggested as a solution to this issue. Firstly, Russia and Georgia could hire a private company to collect customs fees and provide security to freight convoys.[70] Such an agreement would also establish the proportion of custom revenue for South Ossetia.[71] The second option entailed transferring customs control fully to Russia on the basis of its status as the Occupying Power and integrating South Ossetian customs authorities to the Russian federal customs service.[72] In 2019, Georgia set up an *ad hoc* Commission to implement the contract with SGS,[73] and in February 2019, Switzerland announced that under the aegis of its good offices, the negotiations were concluded and all the conditions for the implementation of the Georgia-Russia Agreement were in place.[74] Further details (for example, regarding the arrangement concerning passport and customs control) have not been publicised. At the time of writing, it seems that the opening of corridor would only be possible in emergency situations.[75]

Thus, negotiations over the trade corridor through South Ossetia can be analysed from two aspects. Firstly, the Georgia-Russia Customs Agreement does not include a without-prejudice clause concerning the question of recognition

---

69 International Crisis Group, *Abkhazia and South Ossetia: Time to Talk Trade* (n 53) 15–16. See with respect to Abkhazia Mirimanova, 'Abkhazia' (n 53) 14.

70 International Crisis Group, *Abkhazia and South Ossetia: Time to Talk Trade* (n 53) 24.

71 Ibid.

72 ibid. See Agreement between the Republic of South Ossetia and the Russian Federation on the Integration of the Customs Authorities of the Republic of South Ossetia with the Customs Authorities of the Russian Federation (signed 25 April 2016) <http://docs.cntd.ru/document/420362962> accessed 10 February 2020 (*in Russian*).

73 G Lomsadze, 'Georgia Moves Closer to Transit Deal with Russia' (*eurasianet*, 23 January 2019) <https://eurasianet.org/georgia-moves-closer-to-transit-deal-with-russia> accessed 10 February 2020.

74 'Switzerland's Good Offices: All Conditions for Implementation of Russian-Georgian Customs Agreement are in Place' (*Press Release of the Swiss Government*, 5 February 2019) <https://www.admin.ch/gov/en/start/documentation/media-releases.msg-id-73896.html> accessed 10 February 2020.

75 N Kemoklidze and S Wolff, 'Trade as a Confidence-Building Measure in Protracted Conflicts: The Cases of Georgia and Moldova Compared (2020) 61 Eurasian Geography and Economics 305, 317. See also G Menabde, 'Abkhazia and South Ossetia "Block" Transit Agreement Between Russia and Georgia' (*Jamestown*, 22 February 2019) <https://jamestown.org/program/abkhazia-and-south-ossetia-block-transit-agreement-between-russia-and-georgia/> accessed 31 October 2023.

or status.[76] From this perspective, it can be agreed with Wolff that the Georgia-Russia Customs Agreement is not status-neutral.

> As neither region is a party to the agreement, the agreement is not simply status-neutral but confirms Georgia's competence to conclude treaties applicable to the whole of its internationally recognized territory and Russia's, at least implicit, recognition thereof.[77]

From this perspective, it is clearly in line with the treaty aspects of the duty of non-recognition. On the other hand, the fact that Russia itself is party to the agreement, which pertains to the customs administration and monitoring of trade in goods entering and exiting the corridor through South Ossetia, confirms not only Russia's factual dominance, but also its purported legal dominance over the secessionist entity, which ultimately undermines its claim of statehood. Secondly, regarding trade aspects of this regime, while it is unclear what the ultimate arrangement regarding customs and passport control entails, the proposal to transfer important functions to a private company, including possibly in the area of customs control and the provision of security to freight cargo, is extremely relevant. On the one hand, it would undermine South Ossetia's claim to statehood and exercise of jurisdiction in the area of trade; on the other hand, it would not preclude Georgia's claim to territorial sovereignty over South Ossetia's territory. Georgia's consent with this arrangement would be of critical importance. The fact that the secessionist entities would be given a portion of customs duties seems to be in line with the conclusion of this book that compliance with the formal aspects of the duty of non-recognition, even in the area of trade, seems to outweigh any implications of potential factual contribution to the sustainment of the secessionist economy. Regarding the other alternative, of Russia conducting customs control, such a position would be difficult to reconcile with South Ossetia's claim to statehood and Russia's recognition thereof.

---

76 Georgia-Russia Customs Agreement (n 61).

77 Professor Stefan Wolff, quoted in 'Russian-Georgian WTO Agreement and its Implications for Georgia-Russian Relations: Expert Comment' (*Georgian Institute of Politics*, 2019) <http://gip.ge/russian-georgian-wto-agreement-and-its-implications-for-georgian-russian-relations/> accessed 17 March 2020.

1.3.3 Modalities of the Extension of DCFTA's Preferential Regime to Abkhazia

Some officials and observers have also raised the tentative possibility of an extension of the EU-Georgia DCFTA to Abkhazia. In particular, with respect to a more challenging political context, given Russia's recognition of Abkhazia and Abkhazia's intransigence towards Georgia, the EU-Georgia DCFTA's application to Abkhazia would require an even less rigid approach to the question of issuance of certificates of origin, compared to the EU-Moldova DCFTA's application to Transnistria. The ideas on this issue include the issuance of status-neutral certificates of origin, the inspection and certification of standards by the Abkhaz Chamber of Commerce and the conduct of verification of procedures for issuance of certificates by the EU-certificated foreign company.[78] However, due to difficult political context, it is difficult to ascertain the likelihood of whether these discussions would ever transform into reality.[79]

On the one hand, the extension of the EU-Georgia DCFTA to Abkhazia, foreseeing the status-neutral certificates of origin, the inspection and certification by the Abkhaz Chamber of Commerce and the verification of procedures by the EU-certificated foreign company goes beyond any existing precedent. It seems that the closest analogy can be drawn from the proposal of Direct Trade Regulation, which foresaw the TRNC's Chamber of Commerce issuing the certificates of origin for goods originating in Northern Cyprus. However, negotiations over this proposal have been stalled due to the Republic of Cyprus's opposition. On the other hand, even though the parent State would not conduct the relevant procedures, they would still not be carried out by the separatist authorities and therefore would not condone their claim to statehood. Thus, it seems that a critical element of this proposal would be Georgia's consent with such an arrangement. Ultimately, its compatibility with the duty of non-recognition would need to be assessed against the arrangement's concrete wording.

78 International Crisis Group, *Abkhazia and South Ossetia: Time to Talk Trade* (n 53) 18.

79 Russia sees this development as unrealistic and Abkhazia seems to be more interested in imports than in exporting its products, due to low export potential. International Crisis Group, *Abkhazia and South Ossetia: Time to Talk Trade* (n 53) 26. See also P Gaprindashvili and others, *One Step Closer – Georgia, EU-Integration, and the Settlement of the Frozen Conflicts?* (GRASS Reformanda 2019) 15–21. Kemoklidze and Wolff (n 75) 323–324.

1.3.4 Trade Relations under "A Step to a Better Future Initiative"

In 2018, Georgia adopted the 'A Step to a Better Future' initiative seeking to facilitate trade.[80] In particular, it provided for simplified procedures for the identification of residents of Abkhazia and South Ossetia by assigning individual numbers.[81] The initiative established the possibility of local trade across the conflict line on the basis of accompanying documents issued in Abkhazia and South Ossetia and using status-neutral labelling.[82] It also set up special economic space in two villages near South Ossetia and Abkhazia with infrastructure allowing the Abkhaz and South Ossetian residents to obtain a legal registration address in Georgia, acquire Georgian certificates of origin and subject goods to inspection by the Georgian authorities in order to allow them to export the goods under the DCFTA.[83] The initiative specifically refers to the model of Moldova's relations with Transnistria.[84] It, however, does not change the regulation of economic relations in breakaway territories, including the requirement of a special permit from the Georgian government.[85] Both Abkhazia and South Ossetia have so far rejected this initiative.[86] In fact, "[t]here is resistance to any form of engagement that implies a hierarchical

80 '"A Step to a Better Future:" Peace Initiative: Facilitation of Trade Across Dividing Lines' (2018) <https://smr.gov.ge/uploads/prev/The_Law_of_928efod7.pdf> accessed 17 March 2020 ("A Step to a Better Future Initiative"); 'Georgia Unveils "Unprecedented" Peace Initiative for Abkhazia, South Ossetia' (*OC Media*, 4 April 2018) <https://oc-media.org/georgia-unveils-unprecedented-peace-initiative-for-abkhazia-south-ossetia/> accessed 17 March 2020. This initiative also has a component in the area of education. '"A Step to a Better Future:" Peace Initiative: Enhancing Educational Opportunities for the Residents of Abkhazia and Tskhinvali Region/South Ossetia' (2018) <https://smr.gov.ge/uploads/prev/Education__9dd0e9dc.pdf> accessed 17 March 2020. In 2010, Georgia published 'State Strategy on Occupied Territories. Engagement Through Cooperation' and 'Action Plan for Engagement' <http://gov.ge/index.php?lang_id=ENG&sec_id=225> accessed 17 March 2020. Georgia strongly promoted the idea of a neutral travel document that would allow Abkhaz to travel abroad, but the policy was unsuccessful – "almost no Abkhaz took up the identity papers." T De Waal, *Enhancing the EU's Engagement with Separatists Territories* (Carnegie Europe 2017) 3. See also 'Peace Fund for a Better Future' (*Office of the State Minister of Georgia for Reconciliation and Civic Equality*, 9 October 2019) <https://smr.gov.ge/en/news/read/1702/> accessed 31 October 2023.

81 A Step to a Better Future Initiative (n 80) 5.

82 ibid 14.

83 ibid 14 and 9.

84 ibid 9, ftn 4.

85 ibid 16, ftn 5.

86 International Crisis Group, *Abkhazia and South Ossetia: Time to Talk Trade* (n 53) 20 and 27–28; Coppieters, 'Abkhazia, Transnistria and North Cyprus' (n 35) 31.

relationship between Georgia and Abkhazia or gives the parent state control over activities in the de facto state."[87]

This initiative did not fundamentally change the prohibition of economic dealings with the secessionist entities, but it allowed for alleviation with respect to local trade. This seems to be in line with the scope of the duty of non-recognition, as this type of trade would not help entrench the illegal regime's authority. By allowing for the obtaining of a legal registration address in Georgia, the acquisition of Georgia's certificates of origin and the conduct of inspection of relevant goods by Georgia's authorities, this approach seeks to enforce Georgia's sovereign powers in the area of trade in the breakaway regions.

1.4 *Azerbaijan's Approach to Nagorno-Karabakh*

Azerbaijan did not have specific law on occupied territories[88] but considered Nagorno-Karabakh and the seven surrounding districts of Azerbaijan (before the 2020 war) outside of its control as part of its territory and thus subject to its legislation, including the regulatory framework for economic activities.[89] Notably, according to the International Crisis Group, since April 2016's escalation, Azerbaijan hardened its legal approach to the conflict, calling for a similar response by international bodies as to Russia's annexation of Crimea.[90] It also increased pressure on foreign investors not to pursue their activities in Nagorno-Karabakh.[91]

In this context, Azerbaijan's Foreign Ministry published an extensive report detailing economic dealings with Nagorno-Karabakh, including Armenian or Armenian-diaspora-funded projects or foreign investment, the provision of services or imports in Nagorno-Karabakh and exports – through the re-labelling of products originating in Nagorno-Karabakh as originating in the Republic of Armenia.[92] Moreover, the mining of natural resources, in particular gold and

87 N Caspersen, 'Recognition, Status Quo or Reintegration: Engagement with de Facto States' (2018) 17 Ethnopolitics 373, 383.

88 'MP on Legal Status of Occupied Territories Should Be Adopted in Azerbaijan' (*Azernews*, 13 March 2020) <https://www.azernews.az/nation/162875.html> accessed 17 March 2020.

89 *Illegal Economic and Other Activities in the Occupied Territories of Azerbaijan: Report by the Ministry of Foreign Affairs of the Republic of Azerbaijan* (Ministry of Foreign Affairs of the Republic of Azerbaijan 2016) 92 ("MFA Report"). This is seen in the context of Armenia's legal position as the Occupying Power.

90 International Crisis Group, *Nagorno-Karabakh's Gathering War Clouds: Europe Report No 244* (ICG 2017) 10–11.

91 ibid 11 and 16–17, ftn 89.

92 MFA Report (n 89) 43–55 and 81.

copper, carried out on the basis of licenses issued by the secessionist authorities, was also mentioned.[93]

If the status of Armenia as the Occupying Power in the relevant period were taken as correct,[94] Armenia could be considered in violation of its duties as administrator and usufructuary of natural resources.[95] Moreover, Armenia's re-labelling practice could also be considered as violating its duty of non-recognition and non-assistance. However, as suggested above, these duties do not extend to the activities of private economic operators.[96]

2 EU's Economic and Other Dealings

The EU's approach towards the claims of statehood of all the entities under investigation in this book is uniform; the EU does not recognise these entities as States. However, while the question of status is consistent, the EU's approach with respect to relations that fall below the threshold of the question of statehood and purported inter-State relations takes different forms.[97] Since this book has established that all these entities require the application of the duty of non-recognition and non-assistance, the following section will assess the compatibility of the EU's policies in its several facets with this general international law duty.

---

93 ibid 15 and 68–82; E Kontorovich, 'Economic Dealings with Occupied Territories' (2014) 53 Columbia Journal of Transnational Law 584, 624.

94 See *supra*.

95 Convention (IV) Respecting the Laws and Customs of War on Land and its Annex: Regulations Concerning the Laws and Customs of War on Land (signed 18 October 1907, entered into force 26 January 1910), art 55.

96 In this regard, the MFA Report stressed individual and corporate criminal responsibility. MFA Report (n 89) 102–103. See also 'Azerbaijani Prosecution Opens Probe Into Foreign Companies Operating in Karabakh' (*Sputnik*, 4 March 2017) <https://sputniknews.com/business/201703041051267859-foreign-companies-nagorno-karabakh/> accessed 17 March 2020.

97 Coppieters suggested that EU policy on these not-status-related matters depends on the characterization of the situation by EU bodies. B Coppieters, '"Statehood", "de Facto Authorities" and "Occupation": Contested Concepts and the EU's Engagement in Its European Neighbourhood' (2018) 17 Ethnopolitics 343.

2.1 *EU's Policy of Non-recognition of Annexation of Crimea and Sevastopol between 2014 and 2022*

The EU describes its response to the annexation of Crimea and Sevastopol as "the policy of non-recognition",[98] and therefore it is important to assess this policy with the duty of non-recognition under general international law. Firstly, the EU has imposed a travel ban and asset-freeze measures against natural persons "for being responsible for actions that undermine or threaten the territorial integrity, sovereignty and independence of Ukraine".[99] The EU measures also listed legal persons, including those who benefited from the transfer of ownership contrary to Ukrainian law.[100] The EU's restrictive measures include the prohibition of import into the European Union of goods originating in Crimea and Sevastopol, unless a certificate of origin issued by the Ukrainian authorities accompanies them.[101] This covers both preferential and non-preferential imports.[102] As of December 2014, these restrictive measures

---

98 See 'The EU Non-Recognition Policy for Crimea and Sevastopol: Fact Sheet' (12 December 2017) <https://eeas.europa.eu/headquarters/headquarters-Homepage/37464/eu-non-recognition-policy-crimea-and-sevastopol-fact-sheet_en> accessed 17 March 2020.

99 Council Regulation (EU) No 269/2014 of 17 March 2014 concerning restrictive measures in respect of actions undermining or threatening the territorial integrity, sovereignty and independence of Ukraine [2014] OJ L78/16 (as amended) art 2(1); Council Decision 2014/145/CFSP of 17 March 2014 concerning restrictive measures in respect of actions undermining or threatening the territorial integrity, sovereignty and independence of Ukraine [2014] OJ L78/16 (as amended), art 3(1). See also Council Decision 2014/119/CFSP of 5 March 2014 concerning restrictive measures directed against certain persons, entities and bodies in view of the situation in Ukraine [2014] OJ L66/20 (as amended); Regulation (EU) No 208/2014 of 5 March 2014 concerning restrictive measures directed against certain persons, entities and bodies in view of the situation in Ukraine [2014] OJ L66/1 (as amended).

100 For example, these measures included JSC Chernomorneftegaz and Fedosia. Council Decision 2014/265/CFSP of 12 May 2014 amending Decision 2014/145/CFSP concerning restrictive measures in respect of actions undermining or threatening the territorial integrity, sovereignty and independence of Ukraine [2014] OJ L137/16; Council Regulation (EU) No 811/2014 of 25 July 2014 amending Regulation (EU) No 269/2014 concerning restrictive measures in respect of actions undermining or threatening the territorial integrity, sovereignty and independence of Ukraine [2014] OJ L221/11.

101 Council Decision 2014/386/CFSP of 23 June 2014 concerning restrictions on goods originating in Crimea or Sevastopol, in response to the illegal annexation of Crimea and Sevastopol [2014] OJ L183/70; Council Regulation (EU) No 692/2014 of 23 June 2014 concerning restrictions on the import into the Union of goods originating in Crimea or Sevastopol, in response to the illegal annexation of Crimea and Sevastopol [2014] OJ L183/9.

102 Information Note (n 5) 7 and 11.

also include a full ban on investment in Crimea.[103] "Europeans and EU-based companies may no longer buy or participate in real estate or entities in Crimea and Sevastopol, finance companies from the Crimean peninsula, create joint ventures or provide investment services."[104] EU economic operators are also prohibited from offering tourism services in Crimea or Sevastopol.[105] The EU ban also extends to the export of certain goods and technology to companies in Crimea or for use in the Crimean peninsula.[106] Lastly, the package of measures also includes restrictions with regard to sectors of the Russian economy.[107]

The EU measures restricting economic relations undoubtedly exceed the scope of the duty of non-recognition and non-assistance in a number of ways. Firstly, the EU prohibition extends to the preferential import of goods, unless a certificate of origin issued by the Ukrainian authorities accompanies them. This approach is in line with previous EU practice,[108] as well as with the prohibition of recognition of official acts of an illegal regime and other trade aspects of the duty of non-recognition.[109] However, the EU measures also apply to

103 Council Decision 2014/933/CFSP of 18 December 2014 amending Decision 2014/386/CFSP concerning restrictive measures in response to the illegal annexation of Crimea and Sevastopol [2014] OJ L365/92; Council Regulation (EU) No 1351/2014 of 18 December 2014 amending Regulation (EU) No 692/2014 concerning restrictive measures in response to the illegal annexation of Crimea and Sevastopol [2014] OJ L365/46; Council Decision 2014/507/CFSP of 30 July 2014 amending Decision 2014/386/CFSP concerning restrictions on goods originating in Crimea or Sevastopol, in response to the illegal annexation of Crimea and Sevastopol [2014] OJ L226/20; Council Regulation (EU) No 825/2014 of 30 July 2014 amending Regulation (EU) No 692/2014 concerning restrictions on the import into the Union of goods originating in Crimea or Sevastopol, in response to the illegal annexation of Crimea and Sevastopol [2014] OJ L226/2.

104 Information Note (n 5) 3.

105 Council Regulation (EU) No 1351/2014 of 18 December 2014 amending Regulation (EU) No 692/2014 concerning restrictive measures in response to the illegal annexation of Crimea and Sevastopol [2014] OJ L365/46, art 1.

106 Council Regulation (EU) No 1351/2014 of 18 December 2014 amending Regulation (EU) No 692/2014 concerning restrictive measures in response to the illegal annexation of Crimea and Sevastopol [2014] OJ L365/46, art 1.

107 Council Decision 2014/512/CFSP of 31 July 2014 concerning restrictive measures in view of Russia's actions destabilising the situation in Ukraine [2014] OJ L 229/13; Council Regulation (EU) No 833/2014 of 31 July 2014 concerning restrictive measures in view of Russia's actions destabilising the situation in Ukraine [2014] OJ L229/1; Council Decision 2014/659/CFSP of 8 September 2014 amending Decision 2014/512/CFSP concerning restrictive measures in view of Russia's actions destabilising the situation in Ukraine [2014] OJ L271/54; Council Regulation (EU) No 960/2014 of 8 September 2014 amending Regulation (EU) No 833/2014 concerning restrictive measures in view of Russia's actions destabilising the situation in Ukraine [2014] OJ L271/3.

108 In line with *Anastasiou* judgment. See Van der Loo (n 38) 264.

109 See *supra* Part 1, Chapter 7.

non-preferential imports and constitute an all-out import ban, which goes beyond the scope of the duty of non-recognition.[110]

Moreover, the fact that the EU's restrictive measures also apply to any investment activity in Crimea and Sevastopol, including certain categories of exports and the purchase of real estate, went beyond the scope of the duty of non-recognition. The latter does not prohibit private economic operators from investing in or exporting to illegal secessionist entities, nor does it prohibit private actors from purchasing real estate there.[111] Thus, even though the EU labels its response following the annexation of Crimea and Sevastopol as a policy of non-recognition, it follows that it exceeds the scope of the duty of non-recognition under general international law and thus should be better qualified as sanction.[112]

2.2 *EU Restrictive Measures against Russia in the Context of Russian Aggression against Ukraine since 2022*

The EU has adopted further restrictive economic measures in the context of Russian aggression against Ukraine since February 2022. The overview of the far-reaching measures is beyond the scope of this chapter.[113] Nevertheless, notably, the EU adopted the packages of sanctions in response to Russia's actions analysed in this book, in particular its recognition of the DPR and LPR on 21 February 2022 and the annexation of DPR, LPR, Kherson and Zaporizhzhia regions on 30 September 2022.[114] As with the initial measures in response to

---

110 See *supra* Part 1, Chapter 7.

111 See *supra* Part 1, Chapter 7.

112 See N Kyriacou, 'The EU's Trade Relations with Northern Cyprus Obligations and Limits under Public International Law' in A Duval and E Kassoti (eds), *Legality of Economic Activities, Occupied Territories: International, EU Law and Business and Human Rights Perspectives* (Taylor & Francis Group, 2020) 108. Kontorovich draws a different conclusion. "This is what a robust non-recognition regime looks like, and it is conspicuously absent anywhere else in the world. Thus, while international law allows for such sanctions (assuming they are otherwise consistent with international trade law), it does not require them." Kontorovich (n 93) 629.

113 'Timeline – EU Restrictive Measures against Russia over Ukraine' <https://www.consilium.europa.eu/en/policies/sanctions/restrictive-measures-against-russia-over-ukraine/history-restrictive-measures-against-russia-over-ukraine/> accessed 31 October 2023.

114 'EU Adopts Package of Sanctions in Response to Russian Recognition of the Non-Government Controlled Areas of the Donetsk and Luhansk Oblasts of Ukraine and Sending of Troops Into the Region' (*Press Release*, 23 February 2022) <https://www.consilium.europa.eu/en/press/press-releases/2022/10/06/eu-adopts-its-latest-package-of-sanctions-against-russia-over-the-illegal-annexation-of-ukraine-s-donetsk-luhansk-zaporizhzhia-and-kherson-regions/> accessed 31 October 2023; 'EU Adopts its Latest Package of Sanctions against Russia over the Illegal Annexation of Ukraine's Donetsk,

the annexation of Crimea, these measures went well beyond what is required under the duty of non-recognition.

2.3 *EU-Parent State's Trade Agreements*

The practice of concluding the Association Agreements, including the DCFTA with Ukraine, Moldova, and Georgia, was analysed above and generally seems to support the parent States' treaty-making capacity with respect to their entire territory, including the illegal secessionist entity. It also allows for preferential trade on the basis of the documents issued by the parent State.[115] Thus, this practice seems to be in line with the duty of non-recognition under general international law.

2.4 *EU's Policy of Non-recognition and Engagement of Abkhazia and South Ossetia*

In 2009, the EU designed the policy of non-recognition and engagement (NREP) with respect to Abkhazia and South Ossetia with a view to helping "lift their isolation and enable greater political, economic and societal exchange".[116] A non-paper behind this policy was approved but never published, and thus the key document setting out the policy is Sabine Fischer's 2010 EUISS paper.[117] Even though the policy was presumed to operate also with respect to South Ossetia, due to the extent of Russia's influence over it, the policy has only been implemented with respect to Abkhazia.[118] Moreover, despite a similar factual and legal context, the policy has not been extended to other similar situations,

---

Luhansk, Zaporizhzhia and Kherson Regions' (*Press Release*, 6 October 2022) <https://www.consilium.europa.eu/en/press/press-releases/2022/10/06/eu-adopts-its-latest-package-of-sanctions-against-russia-over-the-illegal-annexation-of-ukraine-s-donetsk-luhansk-zaporizhzhia-and-kherson-regions/> accessed 31 October 2023. See further ibid.

115 See *supra*.

116 S Fischer, 'Conclusions and Recommendations: European Peace Policy in the Unresolved Conflicts' in S Fischer (ed), *Not Frozen! The Unresolved Conflicts over Transnistria, Abkhazia, South Ossetia and Nagorno-Karabakh in Light of the Crisis over Ukraine* (SWP 2016) 83. This policy is premised on the separation of the international legal dimensions of sovereignty from governance. For more, see A Cooley and LA Mitchell, 'Engagement without Recognition: A New Strategy toward Abkhazia and Eurasia's Unrecognized States' (2010) 33 The Washington Quarterly 59. On US practice, see E Berg and S Pegg, 'Scrutinizing a Policy of "Engagement Without Recognition": US Requests for Diplomatic Actions With *De Facto* States' (2016) 14 Foreign Policy Analysis 388.

117 De Waal, *Enhancing the EU's Engagement with Separatists Territories* (n 80) 2. S Fischer, *The EU's Non-Recognition and Engagement Policy Towards Abkhazia and South Ossetia* (European Institute for Security Studies 2010) 1–9.

118 Fischer, *The EU's Non-Recognition and Engagement Policy* (n 117) 1.

such as to Transnistria.[119] In addition, Coppieters points out that the policy of non-recognition and engagement, where non-recognition determines the forms of engagement, must be distinguished from the "policy of engagement without recognition", which is applied to situations where the EU takes a status-neutral stance.[120]

According to the 2010 EUISS paper, the NREP "focuses on de-isolation and transformation".[121] The policy foresaw several areas of engagement, including developing more systematic contact with civil society, populations at large[122] and *de facto* authorities within the framework of non-recognition; funding projects supporting private entrepreneurs; and reconstructing railway links in the South Caucasus.[123] In practice, since 2008 the EU has provided almost €40 million for projects in Abkhazia, including supporting NGOs, upgrading healthcare and education, repairing water facilities and buildings and supporting missing-person projects.[124] However, until today, none of the ambitious goals foreseen by the 2010 paper has been met.[125]

In this regard, Georgia has been suspicious about this policy, fearing "creeping recognition" of South Ossetia and Abkhazia by the EU.[126] De Waal points out that "[i]t is probably no coincidence that the EU has lowered its profile in Abkhazia as its bilateral relationship with Georgia, the success story of the Eastern Partnership, has burgeoned."[127] However, some observers call for the strengthening of the engagement aspect of this policy to raise the effectiveness of its programmes.[128]

---

119 B Coppieters, 'Engagement without Recognition' in G Visoka, J Doyle, and E Newman (eds), *Routledge Handbook of State Recognition* (1st edn, Routledge 2019) 243–244.

120 ibid 245 and 247–249.

121 Fischer, *The EU's Non-Recognition and Engagement Policy* (n 117) 1.

122 This would include, for example, granting visas to inhabitants of Abkhazia and South Ossetia, offering 80–100 scholarships, and opening an EU Information Office in Sukhumi. Fischer, *The EU's Non-Recognition and Engagement Policy* (n 117) 6–9.

123 ibid 26.

124 De Waal, *Enhancing the EU's Engagement with Separatists Territories* (n 80) 4–5.

125 ibid 6. De Waal, *Uncertain Ground* (n 43) 26.

126 Fischer, 'Conclusions and Recommendations' (n 116) 91. The implementation of the EU's policy was also complicated by Georgia's own Strategy on Occupied Territories: Engagement Through Cooperation, which was more limited than the EU's policy. De Waal, *Enhancing the EU's Engagement with Separatists Territories* (n 80) 3. Fischer, *The EU's Non-Recognition and Engagement Policy* (n 117) 4. Contrary to the views of some political scientists, who claim that "recognition, in a legal sense, does not creep," this book has demonstrated that the duty of non-recognition prohibits even acts and actions that might imply recognition. See Caspersen (n 87) 376. De Waal, *Uncertain Ground* (n 43) 11.

127 De Waal, *Uncertain Ground* (n 43) 27.

128 ibid 17 and 73–77.

So, the question can be asked to what extent the EU policy of non-recognition and engagement in its abstract form, as well in terms of its implementation in Abkhazia, is in line with the parameters of the duty of non-recognition. As outlined, the duty of non-recognition does not prohibit all dealings with illegal entities and allows for those dealings that do not entrench the illegal entity's authority over territory. From the overview of the projects implemented in Abkhazia, it would seem that they fall into the category of permitted acts, as they were either essentially of humanitarian character or sought to support healthcare or education.

On a general level, one can agree with the statement that policy should avoid so-called hard engagement, which "refers to links that build state capacity, i.e. that assist with the building of *de facto* state institutions" and only focus on soft engagement, which "refers to links not directly strengthening the de facto authorities such as educational exchanges".[129] Thus, the programmes aimed at strengthening *de facto* institutions, for example in the areas of legislative power, economic management or supporting democratic State reform, should be excluded.[130] However, it is possible to agree that engagement aimed at supporting democratisation efforts of civil society could be outside of the scope of the duty of non-recognition.[131] Nevertheless, a critical complexity rests in the fact that "[i]n practice, it is hard to draw the line between what is governmental and what is nongovernmental, especially in a small society where individuals move between the two sectors".[132] Therefore, any assessment of the compatibility of individual policy measures must be done on a case-by-case basis.

3 Conclusion

This chapter focused especially on the parent State's policies in the area of economic dealings. The practice is far from uniform. While Georgia and Ukraine imposed trade embargoes on Abkhazia and South Ossetia and the DPR and LPR, Crimea (since 2021) respectively, Moldova's approach to Transnistria and Ukraine's position to trading with annexed Crimea (until 2021) were more relaxed. On balance, an all-out economic embargo is not mandated by the duty of non-recognition, as it does not extend to private economic operators,

129 Caspersen (n 87) 377.
130 Coppieters, 'Engagement without Recognition' (n 119) 249. Coppieters, '"Statehood"' (n 97) 348.
131 Coppieters, 'Engagement without Recognition' (n 119) 249.
132 De Waal, *Uncertain Ground* (n 43) 17.

but the parent State is not prohibiteed under general international law from adopting any measures with respect to territories that seek to secede, subject to humanitarian exceptions.

Moreover, even the policy of States, which did not impose a trade embargo, such as Moldova, is in line with the parameters of the duty of non-recognition. To benefit from preferential export tariffs under the EU-Moldova DCFTA, Transnistrian companies are obliged to register in Moldova, obtain Moldovan certificate of origin and allow the Moldovan authorities to conduct necessary on-site inspections. Thus, the export of goods from Transnistria is formally and factually subjected to Moldova's legal order and therefore in line with the duty of non-recognition.

In addition, the proposals concerning the formalisation of trade with South Ossetia and Abkhazia seem to rest on an analogical rationale of preserving the nominal sovereign position of Georgia in the area of trade. However, some of the not-yet-accepted proposals go further than the previous precedents.

The chapter also analysed the EU's policy as the key third-party actor outside the Russian Federation. While at first sight its approach to relations with the post-Soviet illegal secessionist entities below the threshold of status and inter-State relations seems to be rather heterogeneous, a closer look reveals the compatibility with the basic tenets of the duty of non-recognition and non-assistance. The EU's policy of non-recognition of the annexation of Crimea and the city of Sevastopol and the restrictive measures adopted in the context of Russian aggression against Ukraine in 2022 undoubtedly exceed the scope of the duty of non-recognition because of their all-out ban on trade and investment and other measures, and thus would be better qualified as sanctions. The EU association agreements with the parent States demonstrate the parent States' treaty-making capacity with respect to illegal secessionist entities. The EU's policy of non-recognition and engagement of Abkhazia and South Ossetia can be broadly seen as compatible with the duty of non-recognition, as it concerns dealings that do not seem to entrench the illegal entity's authority over the territory. However, it is not excluded that the compatibility of individual policy tools may raise questions in the future.

CHAPTER 19

Purported Acts and Laws of Municipal Law

1 Selected Property Transfers

Numerous private and public legal operations take place under the laws of illegal secessionist entities. Among them, the most consequential are undoubtedly transfers of property, in particular real estate. Different scenarios can be outlined. It was established in Part 1, Chapter 7 that purely private transactions, carried out between private parties, are in principle outside the scope of the duty of non-recognition, which only pertains to official acts and laws of illegal secessionist entity.[1] However, the situation is different when the transfers concern an item of dubious legal title, especially if such title derives either from the expropriation of private assets by an illegal entity or the privatisation of purportedly entity-owned assets.[2] The validity of such a title can thus be compromised by virtue of illegality and invalidity of acts and laws of illegal secessionist entity. These subsequent transfers can involve either entities operating, or individuals living, in the territory of the entity, or foreign legal entities or individuals.[3] As a matter of representative example, the following account provides analysis of privatisation in Transnistria and Abkhazia and nationalisation in Crimea and the DPR and LPR before Russia's all-out aggression against Ukraine in 2022.

1.1 *Privatisation in Transnistria and Abkhazia*

1.1.1 Overview of the Privatisation Transactions

In Transnistria in the early 2000s, the secessionist authorities carried out privatisation of strategic industrial assets, including steel and cement plants, power plants and other assets, principally to Russian investors.[4] For example, non-transparent investors privatised the Moldova Steel Works (MMZ); before

1 See *supra* Part 1, Chapter 7.
2 See *supra* Part 1, Chapter 7.
3 See *supra* Part 1, Chapter 7.
4 R Chamberlain-Creanga and LK Allin, 'Acquiring Assets, Debts and Citizens: Russia and the Micro-Foundations of Transnistria's Stalemated Conflict' (2010) 18 *Demokratizatsiya: The Journal of Post-Soviet Democratization* 329, 333–335. See also CJ Borgen, 'Thawing a Frozen Conflict: Legal Aspects of the Separatist Crisis in Moldova: A Report from the Association of the Bar of the City of New York' (*Legal Paper Research Paper Series No 06-0045*, 2006) 66–68; A Gudim, 'Privatization in Transnistria: Risks and Profit' (*Center for Strategic Studies and Reforms*, 2004) <https://www.cisr-md.org/reports/cont-transn-dec04.html> accessed 10 January 2020; MM Balmaceda, 'Privatization and Elite Defection in de Facto States: The

DOI:10.1163/9789004702646_028

the financial crisis the latter accounted for more than half of Transnistria's industrial output and tax revenues; the controlling shareholder was a Russian Kremlin-linked and Gazprom-linked businessman named Alisher Usmanov.[5] "At its height in 2002, such sales contributed to nearly a third of state revenues."[6] Privatisation was carried out on the basis of Transnistrian Law on Denationalisation and Privatisation and other laws.[7] Reportedly, in order to increase protection of new owners, the practice of resale from a new owner to another supposed *bona fide* owner was approved in 2004 with respect to the two largest enterprises – MMZ and the Moldovan Hydroelectric Power Station.[8] In 2004, Moldova adopted its own law on privatisation in Transnistria, according to which any privatisation carried out in violation of this law and Moldova's legislation, was invalid from the moment of the conclusion of a privatisation agreement.[9]

A similar situation took place in Abkhazia, where in 1997 the Law on Privatisation was adopted, under which tourism and production facilities were privatised; rights to the exploitation of natural resources were given in concessions of 49 years.[10] Georgia also adopted its own law, which stipulated that

---

Case of Transnistria, 1991–2012' (2013) 46 Communist and Post-Communist Studies 445, 447–451.

5 Balmaceda (n 4) 449–451; Chamberlain-Creanga and Allin (n 4) 333–335.

6 Balmaceda (n 4) 448.

7 'Law on Denationalization and Privatisation No 233–3' (adopted 27 January 2000 as amended) <https://ulpmr.ru/ul/show/RspqiIeo4s5hSDkxeYPhrpf8WRxYKwgoh4ZQ=> accessed 10 October 2023 (*in Russian*). 'Law on "State Program on Denationalization and Privatisation in Transnistrian Moldovan Republic for the Years of 2001–2002 No 46-Z-III"' (adopted 10 September 2001) <https://www.ulpmr.ru/ul/show/6cO5COVghriRjSg4vYsX3wXfxcRBdsxcoB4c=> accessed 10 January 2020 (*in Russian*).

8 M Burla and others, *Transnistrian Market and its Impact on Policy and Economy of the Republic of Moldova* (Friedrich Ebert Foundation 2005) 9.

9 'Law on Privatization of Enterprises in the Settlements of the Left Bank of Dniester and the Municipality of Bender No LP338/2004 (adopted 14 October 2004; entered into force 1 January 2005), Article 12(1) (*in Russian*). It is worth noting that in 2001 both Moldova and Transnistria concluded the Protocol according to which "[th]e activities of foreign investors and entrepreneurs in the territory of Transnistria are guaranteed by the legislation of the Republic of Moldova, Transnistria and international law." See Protocol Decision on Guarantees of Attracting and Protecting Foreign Investment and Cooperation in the Field of Investment Activity (signed 16 May 2001) <https://mid.gospmr.org/ru/mrG> accessed 30 October 2023 (*in Russian*).

10 G Prelz Oltramonti, 'The Political Economy of a de Facto State: The Importance of Local Stakeholders in the Case of Abkhazia' (2015) 3 Caucasus Survey 291, 296. See 'Law of the Republic of Abkhazia on Privatization No 350-c-XIII' (adopted 14 July 1997, entered into force 1 November 1997) <https://abkhaz-project.ru/wp-content/uploads/2015/01/Закон-PA-O-приватизации.pdf> accessed 10 January 2020 (*in Russian*).

"[a]ll the civil-legal transactions, concluded from August 14, 1992 regarding the appropriation of state property and refugees and internally displaced persons' private property in Abkhazia must be considered unlawful."[11] In 2016, the Abkhaz People's Assembly adopted a new privatisation law.[12]

1.1.2 Assessment of the Privatisations under International Law

Under international law, the starting point of any assessment of the validity of these transactions must be that neither Transnistria nor Abkhazia ever emerged as a new State, due to their original illegality. Therefore, the rules on State succession in respect to State property did not apply in this context; Moldova and Georgia respectively remained holders of territorial sovereignty and also of the State-owned assets therein.[13] As a result, neither Transnistria nor Abkhazia ever became the owners of the state-owned assets located in their territory. On the basis of the *nemo dat quod non habet* principle, the secessionist authorities could thus not have transferred the ownership of property over which they did not have any title. Therefore, any such transfer would be null and void. This would also be in line with the invalidity of any privatisation legislation adopted by the illegal secessionist entity, as such legislation would derive from the entity's original peremptory illegality.[14]

Moreover, as follows from the case law overview in Part 1, Chapter 7 of this book, foreign municipal courts and international courts would not attribute legal validity to such legislation and, by implication, to property transfers thereunder.[15] Regarding the transfer of property with dubious title, foreign investors would be precluded from relying on the good faith principle, and the *Namibia* exception would not apply to such transactions either.[16] Therefore, investors would bear all the risks connected with privatisation transactions carried out

11 'Law on the Illegal Privatization of State property and the Private Property of Refugees and Forcibly Displaced Persons in Abkhazia No 1331-RS' (adopted 20 March 2002) <https://reliefweb.int/report/georgia/georgia-unlawful-misappropriation-state-property-and-refugees-and-internally> accessed 10 January 2020.

12 'Law of the Republic of Abkhazia on Privatization of the Republican and Municipal Property No 4219-c-V' (adopted 20 July 2016) <http://abkhazinform.com/dokumenty/item/4563-zakon-respubliki-abkhaziya-o-privatizatsii-respublikanskoj-i-munitsipalnoj-sobstvennosti> accessed 10 January 2020 (*in Russian*).

13 See Vienna Convention on Succession of States in Respect of State Property, Archives and Debts (adopted 8 April 1983; not yet in force), art 17 in connection with art 3; Borgen uses the law of occupation *per analogy* to examine these issues Borgen (n 4) 68–71.

14 See *supra* Part 1, Chapter 7.

15 See *supra* Part 1, Chapter 7.

16 See *supra* Part 1, Chapter 7.

in the context of illegal secessionist entities.[17] Nevertheless, the question of property rights could still be the subject of negotiations in the context of transition and a potential reunification.[18]

1.2 *Nationalisation in Crimea and DPR and LPR before 2022*

1.2.1 Overview of the Process of Nationalisation of Assets

Even before the independence referendum, the self-appointed authorities in Crimea announced their intention to nationalise the Ukrainian assets there.[19] The Declaration of Independence of the Republic of Crimea of 17 March 2014 declared that the State property of Ukraine located in the territory of Crimea on the day of its adoption was the State property of the Republic of Crimea and that institutions, enterprises and other organisations established by Ukraine or with its participation became the institutions, enterprises and other organisations established by the Republic of Crimea.[20] On the same day, 17 March 2014, the State Council of the Republic of Crimea also issued a resolution nationalising the seaports and transport infrastructure located in the territory of Crimea.[21] On the same day, the State Council of the Republic of Crimea also declared that all the property of the Ukrainian-owned oil and gas company, Chernomorneftogaz, located in the territory of Crimea, was the property of the Republic of Crimea, and it created the Crimean Republican Enterprise from these assets.[22] After the purported admission of the Republic of Crimea and the City of Sevastopol to the Russian Federation, the Crimean State Council continued issuing resolutions on nationalisation of Ukrainian State-owned

---

17 See *supra* Part 1, Chapter 7. Borgen (n 4) 71; Balmaceda (n 4) 448.

18 See *supra* Part 1, Chapter 7.

19 A Sambros, 'Imitating Chavez: A Year of Nationalization in Crimea' (*Carnegie Russia Eurasia Center*, 19 March 2015) <https://carnegiemoscow.org/posts/2015/02/imitating-chavez-a-year-of-nationalization-in-crimea?lang=en&center=russia-eurasia> accessed 10 October 2023.

20 State Council of the Republic of Crimea, 'Resolution on the Independence of Crimea' (17 March 2014), paras 5–7 <http://crimea.gov.ru/act/11748> accessed 7 October 2023 (*in Russian*).

21 See 'Resolution of the State Council of the Republic of Crimea on the Nationalization of Enterprises and Property of Sea Transport under Control of the Ministry of Infrastructure of Ukraine and the Ministry of Agrarian Policy and Food of Ukraine Located on the Territory of the Republic of Crimea and City of Sevastopol No 1757–6/14' (17 March 2014) <http://www.crimea.gov.ru/act/11761> accessed 10 February 2020 (*in Russian*).

22 This resolution also nationalised Ukrtransgaz, a division of Ukraine's Naftogaz and the Feodosiya Enterprise. See 'Resolution of the State Council of the Republic of Crimea on the Issue of the Energy Security of the Republic of Crimea No 1758–6/14' (17 March 2014) <http://www.crimea.gov.ru/act/11762> accessed 10 February 2020 (*in Russian*).

property, including among others, railways, public colleges, spas, mineral resources, fisheries and forestry and many others.[23] On 30 April 2014, the State Council of the Republic of Crimea adopted the resolution according to which "all State property (State of Ukraine) and ownerless property located on the territory of the Republic of Crimea is considered as property of the Republic of Crimea."[24]

Later on, even privately owned property was subjected to nationalisation by local Crimean authorities. However, the procedure was different, and the term 'nationalisation' was not used; the deprivation of ownership was carried out simply by the inclusion of the respective property in the list of republican property annexed to the regulation of 30 April 2014;[25] this practice was only retrospectively upheld by the amendment to the Crimean regional law.[26] For

---

23 A Zanina, A Rayskij, V Nikiforov, 'Tauris in its Own Juice: How Crimea Obtained Property of Ukraine and Ukrainians' (*Kommersant*, 4 March 2015) <https://www.kommersant.ru/doc/2679334> accessed 10 February 2020 (*in Russian*); E Fedunenko, 'What Was Nationalized in Crimea: History of the Issue' (*Kommersant*, 4 March 2015) <https://www.kommersant.ru/doc/2679403> accessed 10 February 2020 (*in Russian*). See also *Crimea Beyond Rules: Issue No 2: Right to Property* (RCHR, UHHRU 2018) 11.

24 See 'Resolution of the State Council of the Republic of Crimea on the Issues of Administration of Property of the Republic of Crimea No 2085–6/14' (30 April 2014 as amended) <https://docs.cntd.ru/document/413901094> accessed 30 October 2023 (*in Russian*) ("Resolution of 30 April 2014").

25 The resolution of 3 September 2014 amended the wording of the Resolution of 30 April 2014, adding "as well as property specified in the Annex to this Resolution" at the end of the previously cited provision. 'Resolution of the State Council of the Republic of Crimea No 2474–6/14 on the Amendment of the Resolution of the State Council of the Republic of Crimea of 30 April 2014 No 2085–6/14 on the Issues of Administration of Property of the Republic of Crimea' (3 September 2014) <http://www.crimea.gov.ru/act/12607> accessed 10 February 2020 (*in Russian*).

26 Only at the end of 2014 did the Crimean State Council amend its own regional law to provide legal basis for these lower acts. Art 2–1 was included in the Law on Peculiarities of Regulation of Property and Land Relations on the Territory of Crimea, according to which the right of property, including land plots and other real estate objects of previous ownership, terminates and arises for the Republic of Crimea on the day when such a property is included in the List of republican property approved by the Resolution of 30 April 2014. Art 2–1 also stipulated that the right to ownership by Ukraine of property in Crimea is considered terminated in connection with the declaration of independence of 17 March 2014. See 'Law of the Republic of Crimea on Peculiarities of Regulation of Property and Land Relations on the Territory of Crimea No 38-ZRK' (adopted 30 July 2014, entered into force 31 July 2014) <http://www.crimea.gov.ru/act/12456> accessed 10 February 2020 (*in Russian*); 'Law of the Republic of Crimea No 72-ZRK/2015 Amending "Law on Peculiarities of Regulation of Property and Land Relations on the Territory of Crimea No 38-ZRK"' (adopted 24 December 2014, entered into force 19 January 2015) <http://www.crimea.gov.ru/act/13228> accessed 10 February 2020 (*in Russian*). See, on this issue, Zanina, Rayskij, Nikiforov (n 23); A Pavlovskyi, 'How the Crimeans Are Seeking to Return Property Seized

example, on 3 September 2014, all the property of the former Dnipropetrovsk region's governor and oligarch, Igor Kolomoisky, including real estate of Privatbank, gas stations and other assets, were nationalised, as was the property of another Ukrainian oligarch – Dmitry Firtash.[27] Other privately owned property subjected to nationalisation included, for example, the property of the company Krymkhleb, owned by the Donetsk businessman Alexander Leshchinsky,[28] and the property of Rinat Akhmetov's company, DTEK Krymenergo, and many others.[29]

Until 1 March 2015, when the nationalisation process in Crimea was declared officially completed, the ownership of around 480 enterprises and institutions was transferred to the Republic of Crimea and the City of Sevastopol.[30] According to Russian legislation, nationalisation can only take place on the basis of law and with compensation;[31] none of the acts of nationalisation stipulated the payment of compensation to the previous holders.[32] The Russian

---

After 2014' (*Komsomolskaya Pravda*, 28 November 2017) <https://www.crimea.kp.ru/daily/26763/3794518/> accessed 10 February 2020 (*in Russian*); O Makarenko, 'Two Years After Russia's Takeover, No Crimean Spring' (*Euromaidan Press*, 16 March 2016) <http://euromaidanpress.com/2016/03/16/two-years-after-russias-occupation-is-life-for-civilians-possible-in-crimea/> accessed 10 February 2020.

27 'Resolution of the State Council of the Republic of Crimea No 2474–6/14 on the Amendment of the Resolution of the State Council of the Republic of Crimea of 30 April 2014 No 2085–6/14 on the Issues of Administration of Property of the Republic of Crimea' (3 September 2014) <http://www.crimea.gov.ru/act/12607> accessed 10 February 2020 (*in Russian*). See Fedunenko (n 23).

28 'Resolution of the State Council of the Republic of Crimea No 204–1/14 on the Amendment of the Resolution of the State Council of the Republic of Crimea of 30 April 2014 No 2085–6/14 on the Issues of Administration of Property of the Republic of Crimea' (12 November 2014) <http://www.crimea.gov.ru/act/12916> accessed 10 February 2020 (*in Russian*). Local Crimean authorities claimed that the profit from this company was used to finance anti-terrorist operations in eastern Ukraine. See Fedunenko (n 23).

29 'Resolution of the State Council of the Republic of Crimea No 416–1/15 on the Amendment of the Resolution of the State Council of the Republic of Crimea of 30 April 2014 No 2085–6/14 on the Issues of Administration of Property of the Republic of Crimea' (21 January 2015) <http://www.crimea.gov.ru/act/13225> accessed 10 February 2020 (*in Russian*). Fedunenko (n 23).

30 Zanina, Rayskij, Nikiforov (n 23). 'Crimea Completes Ukrainian Property Nationalization' (*TASS*, 27 February 2015) <https://tass.com/russia/780014> accessed 10 February 2020.

31 'Civil Code of the Russian Federation No 51-F3' (adopted 30 November 1994; entered into force 1 January 1995), art 235 and 306 <http://www.consultant.ru/document/cons_doc_LAW_5142/> accessed 10 February 2020 (*in Russian*).

32 "With respect to the Crimean nationalization, not a single act on the seizure of property and its transfer to the ownership of the republic does mention the payment of compensation to former owners." Zanina, Rayskij, Nikiforov (n 23). Only in 2016 did the Crimean State Council adopt laws on compensation with substantial exceptions covering the majority

Constitutional Court found the provisions of the abovementioned legal acts of the State Council of the Crimea in compliance with the Russian Constitution.[33]

Regarding the situation in the DPR and LPR, these entities initially only seized the assets of Ukrainian and foreign banks and other SMEs located in territory outside of Ukraine's control in a process not dissimilar to criminal banditry.[34] Generally, businesses were obliged to re-register with the separatist entities.[35] However, nationalisation of large oligarch-owned plants and mines did not initially take place; these plants remained registered as Ukrainian companies and paid taxes solely into the Ukrainian budget and continued to trade with Ukraine.[36]

The situation changed in connection with the trade blockade of the DPR and LPR in early 2017.[37] Following an ultimatum from the leaders of the DPR and LPR to Ukraine to end the blockade by 1 March 2017, the decision was taken to impose an interim State administration on around 40 large industrial

---

of Ukrainian oligarchs' property. See 'Law on Peculiarities of Regulation of Individual Property Relations in the Republic of Crimea No 345-ZRK' (adopted 28 December 2016, entered into force 30 December 2016) <http://www.crimea.gov.ru/act/15118> accessed 10 February 2020 (*in Russian*). No compensation has been granted until the end of 2017. Pavlovskyi (n 26). On 8 February 2018, the government of the City of Sevastopol adopted the Procedure for Making Decisions on the Reimbursement of the Value of Nationalized Property Previously Held in Private Ownership. See A Pokrovskyi, 'Nationalization in Sevastopol: Did the City's Authorities Decided to Pay for the Taken Businesses?' (*Radio Krym Realii*, 10 February 2018) <https://ru.krymr.com/a/29032072.html> accessed 10 February 2020 (*in Russian*).

33 However, individual decisions are subject to review by the courts. See Constitutional Court of the Russian Federation, 'Ruling of the Constitutional Court of the Russian Federation of 7 November 2017 N 26-P' <https://www.consultant.ru/document/cons_doc_LAW_282275/> accessed 10 October 2023 (*in Russian*). See also 'Constitutional Court Upheld Nationalization in Crimea' (fontanka.ru, 7 November 2017) <http://www.ksrf.ru/ru/News/Pages/ViewItem.aspx?ParamId=3362> accessed 10 February 2020 (*in Russian*); Pavlovskyi (n 26).

34 M Bird, L Vdovii and Y Tkachenko, 'The Donbass Paradox' (*The Black Sea*, 9 December 2015) <https://theblacksea.eu/_old/mirror/theblacksea.eu/donbass/index.html> accessed 17 October 2016; I Burdyga, 'Nationalization under the Rules of "DPR" and "LPR"' (*DW*, 1 March 2017) <https://www.dw.com/ru/к-чему-приведет-внешнее-управление-предприятиями-в-донбассе/a-37771726> accessed 10 February 2020 (*in Russian*).

35 Bird, Vdovii and Tkachenko (n 34).

36 See *supra* Chapter 18; on an initial hesitation to nationalise all Ukrainian assets in the territory of the DPR and LPR, see D Kirillov, 'Donbas Takes the Assets of Oligarchs' (*gazeta.ru*, 11 February 2017) <https://www.gazeta.ru/politics/2017/02/11_a_10520915.shtml> accessed 10 February 2020 (*in Russian*); 'Where Will the "External Administration" of Enterprises in the Donbas Lead?' (n 34); Bird, Vdovii and Tkachenko (n 34).

37 See *supra* Chapter 18.

enterprises under Ukrainian jurisdiction, a number of which were owned by the Ukrainian oligarch Akhmetov.[38] Even though the separatist leaders claimed that this process was not a nationalisation, as it did not entail the transfer of the ownership of the plants in question,[39] the decision resulted in the *de facto* loss of control over the companies by their owners.[40] Following this move, the plants and mines re-orientated their export schemes towards Russia.[41]

1.2.2 Assessment of the Nationalisations under International Law

Under international law, the nationalisation of assets in Crimea must be analysed in its consequent steps. First is the issue of succession of the Republic of Crimea to the property of Ukraine in the territory of Crimea. Since the Crimean Republic did not emerge as a new State and its declaration of independence was illegal and invalid under international law, the purported Crimean Republic never succeeded into the Ukrainian-owned State assets located in Crimea; they remained in the ownership of Ukraine. The provisions of its declarations of independence had no legal effect under international law; the acts and laws of the Republic of Crimea, including the resolutions on nationalisation on 17

---

38 Government of the DPR, 'The List of Enterprises and Institutions on Which the Interim Administration Is Imposed' (2 March 2017) <http://doc.dnronline.su/wp-content/uploads/2017/03/PerchenPrdpr_SovMin.pdf> accessed 15 October 2023 (*in Russian*) ("List of Enterprises"). See also 'Resolution of the Council of Ministers of the Donetsk People's Republic of 27 February 2017 No 2–1 On Amending the Resolution of the Council of Ministers of the Donetsk People's Republic of 26 September 2014 No 35–8 On the Procedure for Imposition of Interim Administration on Enterprises and Institutions' <http://npa.dnronline.su/2017-02-27/postanovlenie-soveta-ministrov-dnr-2-1-ot-27-02-2017-g-o-vnesenii-izmenenii-v-postanovlenie-soveta-ministrov-donetskoj-narodnoj-respubliki-ot-26-sentyabrya-2014-g-35-8-o-poryadke-vvedeniya-vremennyh.html> accessed 30 October 2023 (*in Russian*). See also '"DPR" Named 43 Enterprises It Plans to "Administer"' (*BBC Ukraine*, 3 March 2017) <https://www.bbc.com/ukrainian/news-russian-39153101> accessed 10 February 2020 (*in Russian*). International Crisis Group, *Peace in Ukraine (III): The Costs of War in Donbas: Europe Report No 261* (ICG 2020) 9.

39 'Details of the Imposition of External Administration: Interview with the Vice-Premier of the DPR A. Timofeev' (*DPR Live*, 7 March 2017) <http://dnr-live.ru/bolshoe-intervyu-a-timofeeva-o-vvedenii-vneshnego-upravleniya/> accessed 10 February 2020 (*in Russian*).

40 Various DPR ministries and a private company registered in the South Ossetia were named as interim administrators of these companies and institutions. See List of Enterprises (n 38). See L Kushch, 'One Year after "Nationalization" in the "DPR:" What Is Going on There?' (*BBC News Ukraine*, 19 March 2018) <https://www.bbc.com/ukrainian/features-russian-43450664> accessed 10 February 2020 (*in Russian*).

41 See *supra* Chapter 18. In 2019, the Ukrainian envoy in Minsk negotiations suggested that Kyiv would entertain the possibility of easing trade embargo only after the return of assets in the DPR and LPR to their owners. International Crisis Group, *Peace in Ukraine (III): The Costs of War in Donbas* (ICG 2020) 38–39.

March 2014, regardless of their similarity with the provisions of the declaration of independence, are illegal and invalid under international law, and third States and IOs are under obligation not to recognise them.

Secondly, since the Crimean Republic never existed as an independent State, the Treaty of Accession to the Russian Federation is invalid under international law. Thus, under international law, Crimea never became part of Russia, and the rules of State succession do not apply either.[42] As a consequence, Russia never acquired competence to legislate for the annexed Crimea under international law beyond the occupant's limited powers. The acts of nationalisation adopted by Crimea's State Council after Crimea's incorporation into the Russian Federation are thus null and void and fall within the scope of duty of non-recognition due to the fact that they stem from an original violation of the peremptory norm of prohibition of the use of force.

Thirdly, since Crimea can also be considered illegally occupied by the Russian Federation, the matter can also be analysed from the perspective of occupation law. As outlined in Part 1, Chapter 9 it is arguable that the powers of the illegal occupant with respect to the property transfers can be considered more limited in comparison with the position of the occupant-non-aggressor.[43] Nevertheless, even regardless of this proposition, it is clear that nationalisation of the State-owned and private property in Crimea fell outside the scope of the occupant's limited powers.

Firstly, under occupation law, the confiscation of private property is prohibited.[44] The expropriation of private property is arguably possible but would need to be carried out on the basis of Ukrainian legislation and conditions prescribed therein, including adequate compensation.[45] Secondly, the occupant is only usufructuary and administrator of the public immovable property, and thus any sweeping nationalisation of the public immovable assets in Crimea would not be compatible with such a position.[46] Thus, the nationalisation

42 See Vienna Convention on Succession of States in Respect of State Property, Archives and Debts (n 13) art 14 in connection with art 3.

43 See *supra* Part 1, Chapter 9.

44 Convention (IV) Respecting the Laws and Customs of War on Land and its Annex: Regulations Concerning the Laws and Customs of War on Land (signed 18 October 1907, entered into force 26 January 1910) art 46 ("HR").

45 See *supra* Part 1, Chapter 9. Any other interference with private property is only foreseen with respect to movable property; in any case, it would need to fall squarely within the conditions foreseen by the occupation law. See *supra* Part 1, Chapter 9.

46 HR (n 44) art 55. Any interference with public movable property would need to be justified by military necessity and would need to fall squarely within the conditions foreseen by the occupation law. See *supra*, general legal framework.

decrees clearly exceeded the scope of permitted powers of the Occupying Power and thus are null and void.

Fourthly, the nationalisation can also be assessed in terms of violation of Article 1 Protocol 1 ECHR by the Russian Federation, alleged by Ukraine in addition to other violations in its inter-State application before the ECtHR and in individual applications.[47] Lastly, as mentioned above, the Ukrainian investors deprived of their property in Crimea sought damages in several investor-State arbitrations against Russia under the relevant BIT.[48]

Additionally, in terms of nationalisation in the DPR and LPR, as follows from Chapter 12 above, neither of them ever emerged as a new State, due to their original illegality. As a consequence, these entities never acquired competence to legislate for the territories under their control. Moreover, any acts and laws, including any legislation providing the grounds for imposition of interim administration and any acts imposing such administration, are null and void, and third States and IOs are under obligation not to recognise such laws and acts. Thus, any purported legal operations deriving from such laws and acts would also be invalid and subject to non-recognition.

2 Namibia Exception

2.1 *Parent States' Practice*

Apart from foreign jurisdictions, the application of the *Namibia* exception can take place in the context of the parent State's interactions with an illegal secessionist entity. Such interactions are not held under the parent State's private international law rules, as it considers the secessionist entity to be part of its own territory and subject to its own legal order.

---

47 See *infra*. "It is alleged that property belonging to Ukrainian legal entities was subjected to unlawful control, namely by being taken by the self-proclaimed authorities of the Crimean Republic, which acts were later approved by Russian legislation." 'Grand Chamber to Examine Four Complaints by Ukraine against Russia over Crimea and Eastern Ukraine' (*Press Release Issued by the Registrar of the Court*, 9 May 2018) <https://hudoc.echr.coe.int/app/conversion/pdf/?library=ECHR&id=003-6081540-7832894&filename=Relinquishment%20to%20Grand%20Chamber%20of%20four%20interstate%20cases%20Ukraine%20v.%20Russia.pdf> accessed 17 October 2023. S Lorenzmeier, 'Investment Disputes in Annexed Crimea from the Perspective of International Law' in BC Harzl and R Petrov (eds), *Unrecognized Entities: Perspectives in International, European and Constitutional Law* (Brill 2022) 98–102.

48 See *supra* Chapter 17.

2.1.1 Ukraine's Practice

Initially, under the 2014 Law on Temporarily Occupied Territory of Ukraine applicable to Russia-occupied Crimea, any document or act issued by illegal entities or officials "is null and void, and shall give rise to no legal consequences".[49] No explicit exception was established for the documents of civil status issued by illegal authorities in Crimea.

During the early period after the annexation of Crimea and the purported declaration of independence of DPR, legal facts of birth and death occurring in these territories were not recognised in administrative procedure, but through judicial proceedings,[50] where the documents issued in Crimea or the DPR and LPR were evaluated as evidence.[51] Many observers pointed to an undue burden of judicial proceedings on the individuals concerned.[52] Since 2015,

---

49 'Law of Ukraine No 1207-VII On Securing the Rights and Freedoms of Citizens and the Legal Regime on the Temporarily Occupied Territory of Ukraine' (adopted 15 April 2014; entered into force 27 April 2014) art 9(3) in connection to art 9(2) <https://zakon.rada.gov.ua/laws/show/1207-18#Text> accessed 31 October 2023 ("Law on Temporarily Occupied Territory of Ukraine") (*in Ukrainian*).

50 'Universal Periodic Review: An Alternative Dimension: Third UPR Cycle, Ukraine' (2017) 166 <https://www.undp.org/sites/g/files/zskgke326/files/migration/ua/UPR_3rd-cycle_CSOs_en.pdf> accessed 10 January 2020. In 2016, the Ukrainian Code of Civil Procedure was amended to include Article 257–1, which stipulates peculiarities of procedure for the establishment of the fact of the birth or death of a person in the temporarily occupied territory of Ukraine, determined as such by Verhovna Rada. Crimea was determined as temporarily occupied by the 2014 Law on Temporarily Occupied Territory of Ukraine and areas of Donetsk and Luhansk regions were recognised as such by Verkhovna Rada of Ukraine, 'Resolution No 254-VIII on the Recognition of Individual Regions, Cities, Towns, and Villages of the Donetsk and Luhansk Regions as Temporarily Occupied Territories' (adopted 17 March 2015; entered into force17 March 2015) <https://zakon.rada.gov.ua/laws/show/254-19> accessed 10 January 2020 (*in Ukrainian*). V Matola, 'With or Without DPR: How Courts Handle Complaints by Residents of Occupied Territories' (*lv.ua*, 11 March 2017) <https://lb.ua/news/2017/05/11/366003_iz_dnr_chi_bez_yak_sudi_virishuyut.html> accessed 10 February 2020 (*in Ukrainian*).

51 I Kolisnyk, 'Ukrainian Courts in Dialogue on International Law' in A Wyrozumska (ed), *Transnational Judicial Dialogue on International Law in Central and Eastern Europe* (Lodz University Press 2017) 460. N Martsenko, 'Peculiarities of Recognition of Judgments and other Acts Issued by Unrecognized Authorities – The Example of the Autonomous Republic of Crimea, and Luhansk and Donetsk Oblasts ("LPR" and "DPR")' 65 (2019) OER Osteuropa Recht 223, 232–233. See also *Information Notice No 9 – 1129/0/4 – 16* (Ukraine, High Specialized Court of Ukraine for Civil and Criminal Cases) (15 April 2016) 3–5 <http://mv-mazur.at.ua/2016/docs/letter-2-15.04.2016.pdf> accessed 10 February 2020 (*in Ukrainian*). See also Matola (n 50); 'Namibia: Do You Recognise Occupation Papers?' (*precedent.ua*) <https://precedent.in.ua/2016/05/15/ukrayinska-namibiya-chy-vyznavaty-okup/> accessed 10 January 2020 (*in Ukrainian*).

52 OSCE, 'Thematic Report: Access to Justice and the Conflict in Ukraine' (2015) 14 available <https://www.osce.org/ukraine-smm/212311?download=true> accessed 10 January 2020.

the Ukrainian courts referred to the *Namibia* exception even in such cases.[53] Moreover, in 2019, the Ukrainian Supreme Cassation Court referred to the ICJ's *Namibia* exception and the ECtHR case law on the *Namibia* exception in order to justify the recognition of documents issued by the DPR's authorities certifying a number of working years for the purposes of establishing an individual's pension entitlement.[54]

The Law on Reintegration of Donbas adopted in early 2018 provided for an explicit exception from the invalidity of official acts of the DPR and LPR for documents confirming the fact of birth or death of a person in a temporarily occupied territory of the Donetsk and Luhansk regions.[55] This provision stated that such documents could be attached to the applications for registration of births and deaths and thus was seen as a way to potentially avoid judicial

---

Martsenko (n 51) 232–233. On the burden of such judicial proceedings and on the difference between the documents issued by the Russian Federation for facts taking place in Crimea and those issued by illegal authorities in the DPR and LPR, see M Popovych, 'Oleg Ilnitsky: A Person Does Not Make a Decision to Be Born or Die in Occupation' (*fraza.ua*, 21 February 2018) <https://fraza.com/interview/266897-oleg-ilnitskij-chelovek-ne-prinimaet-reshenie-rozhdatsja-ili-umirat-v-okkupatsii-> accessed 10 February 2020 (*in Russian*).

53 According to Stakhyra, between July 2015 and May 2019, 30, 718 judgments were adopted in which the courts referred to the *Namibia* exception. Between January 1991 and June 2015 no such judgment was adopted. H Stakhyra, 'Applicability of Private Law of De-facto Regimes' 65 (2019) OER Osteuropa Recht 207, 216 and 213. VF Nesterovych, 'Rule of Law and Provision of Human Rights in the Temporary Occupied Territories of Ukraine' in *Procedings. Volume 200, Law /National University of Kyiv-Mohyla Academy* (Naukma 2017) 90 (*in Ukrainian*). See for example *Judgment No 56177713* (Ukraine, Popasnyansky Regional Court) (24 February 2016) <http://mv-mazur.at.ua/publ/3-1-0-18> accessed 10 February 2020 (*in Ukrainian*). Other judicial decisions are cited and discussed in Kolisnyk (n 51) 458–462. See references to courts' decisions *Judgment No 56827104, Case No 423/1048/16-c* (Ukraine, Popasnyansky Regional Court) (31 March 2016) <https://court.gov.ua/fair/> accessed 10 February 2020 (*in Ukrainian*); *Judgment No 57379998, Case No 225/2173/16-c* (Ukraine, Dzerzhinsk City Court) (12 April 2016) <https://court.gov.ua/fair/> accessed 10 February 2020 (*in Ukrainian*); *Judgment in Case No 415/6977/15-c* (Ukraine, Lisichansky City Court) (3 December 2015) <https://court.gov.ua/fair/> accessed 10 February 2020 (*in Ukrainian*).

54 See A Tkacheva, 'Namibian Exceptions: Supreme Court Ruling Makes Life Easier for IDPs and Residents of ORDLO' (*Avdeevka City News*, 2 March 2019) <http://avdeevka.city/news/view/quotnamibijskie-isklyucheniya-quot-reshenie-verhovnogo-suda-oblegchit-zhizn-pereselentsam-i-zhitelyam-ordlo> accessed 10 February 2020 (*in Russian*).

55 'Law of Ukraine on the Peculiarities of State Policy to Ensure the State Sovereignty of Ukraine over Temporarily Occupied Territories in the Donetsk and Luhansk Regions No 2268-VIII' (adopted 18 January 2018, entered into force 24 February 2018, repealed by Law of Ukraine No 2217-IX of 21 April 2022), art 2 <https://zakon.rada.gov.ua/laws/show/2268-19> accessed 31 October 2023 (*in Ukrainian*) ("Law on Reintegration of Donbas").

procedure.[56] However, the adoption of regulations detailing such administrative procedure proved difficult.[57] At the same time, the administrative procedure (instead of a judicial one) for births, deaths and marriages in Crimea was not yet provided for.[58]

As the Law on Reintegration of Donbas was repealed after the all-out Russian invasion in February 2022, the legal regime of occupied territories is now governed by the 2014 Law on Temporarily Occupied Territory of Ukraine. This law was amended and provides for the general exception from the invalidity of documents issued by the occupying authorities for acts confirming births, death and marriages.[59] While the administrative registration procedure is foreseen, it is not yet available and the judicial procedure has been still widely used.[60]

2.1.2 Moldova's Practice

As for the Moldovan authorities' approach to recognising the documents on civil status issued by Transnistria, building on the 1997 Primakov Memorandum, Moldova and Transnistria signed the Protocol on Mutual Recognition of Validity on the Territory of Transnistria and the Republic of Moldova of the Documents Issued by Competent Bodies of the Parties in May 2001, which foresaw recognition of several rather broad categories of documents, including on civil status.[61] The protocol, however, has not been implemented on the

56 UNHCR, 'Briefing Note: Analysis of the Law of Ukraine "On Particular Aspects of Public Policy Aimed at Safeguarding State Sovereignty of Ukraine over the Temporarily Occupied Territory of Donetsk and Luhansk Regions"' (2018) 5–6 <https://reliefweb.int/report/ukraine/briefing-note-analysis-law-ukraine-particular-aspects-public-policy-aimed> accessed 10 January 2020.

57 United Nations Ukraine, 'Birth Registration: Briefing Note' (2020) <https://www.unhcr.org/ua/wp-content/uploads/sites/38/2020/03/Briefing-Note-Birth-registration_2020.pdf> accessed 31 October 2023; R Kuibida, L Moroz, R Smaliuk, 'Justice in the East of Ukraine During the Ongoing Armed Conflict' (2020) 11 International Journal for Court Administration 9, 18–19.

58 United Nations Ukraine (n 57).

59 Law on Temporarily Occupied Territory of Ukraine (n 49) Art 9(3) (as amended by Law of Ukraine No 2217-IX of 21 April 2022).

60 T Kurmanova, 'Ukraine: Births, Deaths and Pensions in Occupied Territory' (*Institute for War and Peace Reporting*, 13 September 2022) <https://iwpr.net/global-voices/ukraine-births-deaths-and-pensions-occupied-territory> accessed 31 October 2023.

61 These documents included certificates on civil registration, identification cards and passports, driver's licenses, certificates of education, documents certified by notary, certification on the registration of legal bodies, work record cards and others. Protocol on Mutual Recognition of Validity on the Territory of Pridnestrovie and the Republic of Moldova of the Documents Issued by Competent Bodies of the Parties (16 May 2001) available in NV Shtanski (ed), *Negotiation Process between Transnistrian Moldovan Republic and the*

ground.[62] Nevertheless, as will be shown below, this protocol has played an important role in the Russian approach concerning the recognition of acts and registrations carried out in Transnistria.

In 2017 Moldova amended its Law on Civil Status Acts.[63] According to this amendment, the facts of civil status recorded in Transnistria can be ascertained by way of the issuance of civil status documents by the Moldovan authorities if Transnistria's documents were registered in a manner analogical to that foreseen by Moldova's legislation.[64] An NGO advocating for this legislative change explicitly referred to the *Namibia* exception and ECtHR case law and highlighted the complexity of the legal situation of individuals before the amendment's adoption.[65]

Additionally, in 2018, in the framework of a negotiated process on the settlement of the Transnistrian issue, both sides signed a number of agreements, including an agreement on apostilisation of educational documents issued in Transnistria and the so-called 'licence plate' agreement stipulating the mechanism of participation of vehicles from Transnistria in international road traffic.[66] Prior to the adoption of these agreements, Moldovan experts and civil

---

Republic of Moldova in Documents (MID TMR 2014) 382–383 (*in Russian*) and 135–136 (*in English*) ("Protocol on Mutual Recognition").

62 'First Meeting in 2016 of Representatives on Political Issues of Pridnestrovie and Moldova in Kishinev' (*Ministry of Foreign Affairs of Pridnestrovian Moldovanian Republic*, 3 March 2016) <https://mid.gospmr.org/en/yTh> accessed 10 October 2023.

63 'Moldova Simplified Recognition of Civil Documents Issued in Transnistria' (*TASS*, 29 May 2019) <https://tass.ru/mezhdunarodnaya-panorama/6486478> accessed 10 January 2020 (*in Russian*).

64 'Law No 100 on Civil Status Acts' (26 April 2001), Article 13[1] <http://lex.justice.md/index.php?action=view&view=doc&lang=2&id=312727> accessed 10 January 2020 (*in Russian*). See also 'Government Resolution No HG286/2019 on Approval of the Instructions for Certifying the Facts of Civil Status that Took Place and Were Registered in the Settlements of the Left Bank of the Dniester and Bender Municipality' (29 May 2019) <https://www.legis.md/cautare/getResults?doc_id=114695&lang=ru> accessed 10 January 2020 (*in Russian*).

65 'Persons Represented by Promo-LEX Contributed to Modifying Legal Mechanism for Issuing Identity Documents to People Living on Left Bank of the Nistru' (*IPN Press Agency*, 3 August 2018) <https://www.ipn.md/en/dosar-transnistrean/92781> accessed 10 February 2020.

66 In 2018, a protocol decision was signed allowing vehicles not performing commercial activities in the Transnistrian region to be registered and get access to internationally recognized Moldovan neutral-design license plates to enable their participation in international road traffic. 'OSCE Mission to Moldova Welcomes Start of "Licence Plate" Agreement Implementation by the Sides' (*Press Release*, 1 September 2018) <https://www.osce.org/chairmanship/392231> accessed 12 June 2019. See also 'Protocol of the Official Meeting of the Permanent Conference for Political Questions in the Framework of the

society members published an Open Letter in which they drew attention of international partners that compelling unilateral concessions from Moldova "will not contribute in any case to the lasting resolution of the Transnistrian conflict, rather it will ensure the conservation of the conflict".[67]

2.1.3 Georgia's Practice

As mentioned in a previous chapter, Georgia adopted the Law on Occupied Territories in late 2008. According to the original wording of this law, an act issued by illegal authorities "shall be deemed invalid and shall not lead to anylegal consequences".[68] According to the Council of Europe's Commissioner for Human Rights, it was questionable whether this law, which did not provide for any exception concerning the recognition of civil acts, such as birth, death and marriage certificates, "can be considered to be in line with international human rights standards, notably the UN Convention on the Rights of the Child".[69] The UN Secretary-General's Representative on the Human Rights of IDPs offered a similar assessment.[70]

The Venice Commission held that, although there is no obligation to recognise acts of unrecognised entities, "this freedom ends where basic human rights would be violated. If Georgia refuses to accept e.g. basic status such as birth or death certificates, that would violate Article 8 of the ECHR."[71] Even though, according to Georgia's Information Note, its Law on Registration of

---

Negotiating Process of the Transdnestrian Settlement' (27–28 November 2017) <https://www.osce.org/chairmanship/359196?download=true> accessed 10 February 2020. See also *supra*.

67 'Declaration of the Civil Society regarding the Red Lines of Transnistrian Settlement' (21 August 2016) <https://promolex.md/2767-declaratia-societatii-civile-cu-privire-la-liniile-rosii-ale-reglementarii-transnistrene/?lang=en> accessed 17 March 2020; See also T De Waal, *Enhancing the EU's Engagement with Separatists Territories* (Carnegie Europe 2017) 5–6.

68 'Law of Georgia No 431 on Occupied Territories as amended' (adopted 23 October 2008) art 8(2) <https://smr.gov.ge/uploads/prev/The_Law_of_928efod7.pdf> accessed 18 October 2016 ("Law on Occupied Territories").

69 CoE, Commissioner for Human Rights, 'Special Follow-Up Mission to the Areas Affected by the South-Ossetia Conflict: Implementation of the Commissioner's Six Principles for Urgent Human Rights and Humanitarian Protection' (21 October 2008) CommDH(2008)33, para 81.

70 UNHRC, 'Report of the Representative of the Secretary-General on the Human Rights of Internally Displaced Persons, Walter Kälin, Addendum: Mission to Georgia' (13 February 2009) A/HRC/10/13/Add.2, para 56.

71 CoE (Venice Commission), 'Opinion on the Law on Occupied Territories of Georgia' (17 March 2009) CDL-AD (2009)015, para 43 and 50 ("Venice Commission Opinion on the Law on Occupied Territories of Georgia").

the Civil Acts provided for a simplified registration procedure for recognition of birth- and death-related facts,[72] the Venice Commission still called for a clarifying provision in the text of the law.[73] The amendments were introduced into the law, including the exception from invalidity for the purposes of issuing status-neutral ID and travel documents and a provision according to which the "[p]ossibility to establish facts of civil importance in the Occupied Territories is guaranteed under the law of Georgia 'On Procedure for Civil Acts Registration'."[74]

Ultimately, only in June 2018, in connection with Georgia's initiative "A Step to a Better Future", was the Law on Occupied Territories amended to provide for the exception from the invalidity of acts of illegal secessionist entities for the purposes of

> establishing the fact of and registering birth, marriage, divorce, decease or legitimate residence of a person in the Autonomous Republic of Abkhazia and Tskhinvali region (former Autonomous District of South Ossetia) according to the rule established under Georgian legislation.[75]

2.2 *Russia's Practice*

2.2.1 Russia's Practice Concerning the Illegal Secessionist Entities

Russia's position on the issue of the recognition of documents of unrecognised entities was outlined in the Ministry of Foreign Affairs' Letter to the Federal Notary Chamber of 2 July 2007.[76] In this letter, the Russian Foreign Ministry

---

72 CoE (Venice Commission), 'Information Note on the Law on Occupied Territories of Georgia Prepared by the Parliament of Georgia at the Request of the Rapporteurs' (5 March 2009) CDL-AD (2009)044, 3.

73 Venice Commission Opinion on the Law on Occupied Territories of Georgia (n 71) para 44.

74 Law on Occupied Territories (n 68) Article 8(2) and Article 8(3) as amended by the Law No 4994 of 1 July 2011 and the Law No 5576 of 20 December 2011. Even though the Venice Commission welcomed certain terminological changes in this provision, it also highlighted that it "does not have information concerning the details of the Georgian regulation." CoE (Venice Commission), 'Final Opinion on the Draft Amendments to the Law on Occupied Territories of Georgia' (14 December 2009) CDL-AD (2009)051, para 22.

75 Law on Occupied Territories of Georgia (n 68) art 8(2). See also 'A Step to a Better Future: Adopted Legislative Amendments' <https://smr.gov.ge/uploads/prev/Adopted_Le_b16e03ed.pdf> accessed 17 March 2020; N Ahmeteli, '10 Years After the War in Georgia: How the Law on Occupied Territories Work' (*BBC Russian Service*, 9 August 2018) <https://www.bbc.com/russian/features-45119933> accessed 10 February 2020 (*in Russian*).

76 Ministry of Foreign Affairs of the Russian Federation, 'Letter to the Federal Notary Chamber No 8349' (2 July 2007) ("Letter of the Ministry of Foreign Affairs").

declared, "international law does not prohibit States from recognizing the validity of certain legal acts of bodies exercising factual power over territories not under the control of official authority".[77] Referring explicitly to the *Namibia* advisory opinion and the ECtHR's *Loizidou* case, and pointing to the practice of municipal courts, the MFA concluded that "international law determines the criterion of legality and validity of acts of unrecognised entity and its compatibility with the rights and interests of its inhabitants, in particular rights guaranteed by international law."[78] The letter also specifically referred to the 2001 Protocol on Mutual Recognition signed by Moldova and Transnistria.[79]

Russia's practice concerning Transnistria is particularly relevant. For example, the 2014 Letter of the Russian Ministry of Justice confirms that the Russian Federation recognises the sovereignty and territorial integrity of the Republic of Moldova, and therefore the Russian Federation should not have any official contacts with Transnistria in the context of legal assistance.[80] However, exception is made for legal acts such as the registration of births, deaths and marriages where non-recognition could cause detriment to the inhabitants of these territories by pointing to the 2007 Ministry of Foreign Affairs Letters and references made therein.[81]

In a number of cases, the Russian courts recognised the legal personality of legal entities established in Transnistria and accepted their capacity to sue and be sued in Russian courts. In one instance, the Court based its conclusion on the status of legal entity by reference to the 2001 Protocol on Mutual Recognition signed between Moldova and Transnistria.[82] This reasoning does

77 ibid.

78 ibid.

79 ibid. See *supra*.

80 Ministry of Justice of the Russian Federation, 'Letter No 06/86999-MT on the Possibility of Recognition by the Russian Notaries for Preforming Notarial Acts of Documents Originating from State Entities Not Recognized by the Russian Federation as Independent Subjects of International Law' (26 September 2014) <https://ppt.ru/docs/pismo/minyust/n-06-86999-mt-56369> accessed 10 February 2020 (unofficial version) (*in Russian*) ("Letter of the Ministry of Justice").

81 ibid.

82 *Judgment in Case No A/40/7696-02* (Russian Federation, Federal Arbitration Court of the Moscow District) (20 November 2002) <https://www.lawmix.ru/fas-msk/106750> accessed 10 February 2020 (*in Russian*). In the first instance, the court concluded that the company did not have the status of a legal entity and terminated proceedings. A Antsiperova, 'Status of Legal Entity for the Period of Judicial Proceedings' (*Center Bereg*, 10 April 2018) <https://center-bereg.ru/b906.html> accessed 10 February 2020 (*in Russian*). See Stakhyra (n 53) 215 for the Ukrainian court's refusal to apply laws of Transnistria to assess the legal capability of appellants due to Transnistria's lack of statehood.

not seem to derive from the public international law character of the 2001 Protocol. Rather, it seems that the court applied Moldovan law as the law of the State of the establishment of the company to ascertain the entity's legal personality. In this instance, the Protocol on Mutual Recognition seemed to operate as part of Moldova's internal law, according to which Moldova recognised legal entities established in Transnistria. In other cases, the Court simply accepted the certificate of Transnistria's Registration Chamber as proper evidence confirming a company's legal status.[83] It is notable that in none of these cases, did the Russian courts directly refer to the *Namibia* exception.

The Russian court also recognised the period of service in the Transnistria Armed Forces for the purposes of an individual's pension entitlement in Russia.[84] The court highlighted that Transnistria is part of Moldova and not an independent subject of international law.[85] The Court then referred to the 2001 Protocol on Mutual Recognition signed by Moldova and Transnistria.[86] Nevertheless, it seems rather paradoxical for the court to base its decision on recognition of service in Transnistria's Armed Forces by reference to Transnistria being part of Moldova, since Transnistria's Armed Forces are one of the essential tools for maintaining a *de facto* separation. It is difficult to accept that the parties intended to give such an interpretation to the terms of the Protocol on Mutual Recognition. In any case, due to its undeniable link to

83 See *Judgment in Case No A/40/5612-05* (Russian Federation, Federal Arbitration Court of the Moscow District) (8 July 2005) <http://sudrf.kodeks.ru/rospravo/document/813310064> accessed 10 February 2020 (*in Russian*). See also *Decision in Case No A40-233514/2015* (Russian Federation, High Court of the Russian Federation) (17 April 2017) <https://legalacts.ru/sud/opredelenie-verkhovnogo-suda-rf-ot-17042017-n-305-es17-2834-po-delu-n-a40-2335142015/> accessed 10 February 2020 (*in Russian*). See references to other cases in which legal entities established in Transnistria were either petitioners or defendants before the Russian courts in V Yarkov and I Renz, 'Trans-border Aspects of Civil Procedure and Performance of Notarial Acts Using the Documents Originating in Territories of Unrecognized Entities' <https://www.eastlaw.uni-kiel.de/de/events/tagung-uber-die-rechtliche-stellung-nicht-anerkannter-staaten-des-postsowjetischen-raums-im-internationalen-handelsrecht-sowie-im-internationalen-privat-und-verfahrensrecht-2018> accessed 10 February 2020 (*in Russian*).

84 *Appeal Decision in Case No 33-1562/2013* (Russian Federation, Orlov Regional Court) (8 August 2013) <https://old.судебныерешения.рф/bsr/case/print/6052421> accessed 10 October 2023 (*in Russian*) ("*Appeal Decision in Case No 33-1562/2013*").

85 ibid. See Yarkov and Renz (n 83) for references to other cases of recognition of legal acts issued in Transnistria, in the context of the evidentiary phase of judicial proceedings in Russia.

86 *Appeal Decision in Case No 33-1562/2013* (n 84). For a critical analysis of this approach, see Antsiperova (n 82).

de facto public power of illegal entity, this instance would seem to fall out of the limited scope of the *Namibia* exception.

In another case, the court rejected enforcement in the territory of the Russian Federation of Transnistria's Tiraspol City Court's judgment for the recovery of alimony.[87] The judgment did not refer to Transnistria as being part of Moldova or to the 2001 Protocol on Mutual Recognition. Instead, it saw the matter from the perspective of public international law pointing to the lack of international treaty on mutual recognition of judicial decisions between the Russian Federation and Transnistria.[88]

Additionally, by reference to the conventions between Russia and Moldova, which dispense with the requirement of legalisation and recognition of high school certificates, and by reference to the 2001 Protocol on Mutual Recognition, the Russian education authorities also declared that for admission to Russian universities no recognition or legalisation of high school certificates issued in Transnistria is necessary.[89] This seems to be in line with the *Namibia* exception's scope.

2.2.2 Russia's Practice Concerning the DPR and LPR before 2022

With respect to the DPR and LPR, in early 2017, the Russian president issued an executive order that temporarily recognised the validity of certain documents, including identity documents, diplomas, birth, marriage and death certificates and vehicle registration certificates issued by bodies operating in the territories of certain areas of the Donetsk and Luhansk regions of Ukraine and established visa-free travel to Russia for permanent residents of these areas.[90]

---

87 *Appeal Decision in Case No 38-G09-7* (Russian Federation, High Court of the Russian Federation) (28 July 2009) <http://www.sudbiblioteka.ru/vs/text_big3/verhsud_big_42827.htm> accessed 10 February 2020 (*in Russian*).

88 ibid. See Yarkov and Renz (n 83) for references to other cases on recognition of judicial decisions issued by Transnistrian courts in judicial proceedings in Russia.

89 Federal Service for the Supervision of Education and Science, 'Letter No 90–21' (23 May 2016) <http://www.consultant.ru/cons/cgi/online.cgi?req=doc;base=ARB;n=105241#06444670505133041> accessed 10 February 2020 (*in Russian*).

90 See 'Executive Order of the President of the Russian Federation on Recognition in the Russian Federation of Documents and Registration Marks of Vehicles, Issued to Citizens of Ukraine and Stateless Persons Permanently Residing in the Territories of Certain Regions of the Donetsk and Luhansk Regions of Ukraine No 74' (18 February 2017) <http://kremlin.ru/events/president/news/53895> accessed 7 February 2019 (*in Russian*) ("Executive Order on Recognition of the Documents of the DPR and LPR").

The adoption of this document was met with criticism of the doctrine and international and regional bodies.[91] For example, the OSCE Parliamentary Assembly called on Russia "to revoke its decisions on the recognition of so-called 'documents' (passports, driving licences, birth certificates etc.) issued by illegal entities in certain areas of the Donetsk and Luhansk regions of Ukraine".[92] The Council of Europe's Parliamentary Assembly also urged Russia to "cease recognition of the passports and any other documents ... issued on the territories controlled by the illegal armed groups of the Donetsk and Luhansk regions".[93]

However, analysis of the compatibility of this executive order with international law calls for a more nuanced approach. On the one hand, recognition of the validity of the majority of the documents mentioned in this order can be substantiated under the *Namibia* exception.[94] Moreover, the executive order explicitly refers to the Donetsk and Luhansk regions as part of Ukraine and proclaims its validity until the political resolution of the issue.[95] On the other hand, recognition of passports of the DPR and LPR would seem to be outside the limited scope of the exception, as the passport is the expression and emanation of the State sovereignty.[96] Thus, from this perspective, the executive order seems to be excessive and not compatible with international law. To

91 In fact, the adoption of this executive order was mentioned as one of the reasons for the authorization of the trade blockade of the DPR and LPR. See 'Decree of the President of Ukraine No 62/2017 on the Decision of the National Security and Defence Council of Ukraine of 15 March 2017 "On Urgent Additional Measures to Counter the Hybrid Threats to the National Security of Ukraine"' (15 March 2017) preamble <https://www.rnbo.gov.ua/ua/Ukazy/441.html> accessed 10 February 2020 (*in Ukrainian*).

92 OSCE (PA), 'Resolution on Restoration of the Sovereignty and Territorial Integrity of Ukraine' (9 July 2017), para 27. See for reactions to this executive order. However, rather than calling the order a violation of international law, it was designated as incompatible with the spirit of the Minsk agreements. See T Korotkyi and N Hendel, 'The Legal Status of the Donetsk and Luhansk 'Peoples' Republics' in S Sayapin and E Tsybulenko (eds), *The Use of Force against Ukraine and International Law: Jus Ad Bellum, Jus in Bello, Jus Post Bellum* (Springer 2018) 155–158.

93 CoE (PACE) Res 2198 (23 January 2018), para 10.2.

94 See *supra* Part 1, Chapter 7. *Contra* "This decree includes a clear violation of the general principles of international law and Ukrainian legislation. Nothing in international humanitarian law, the reference to which is contained in the preamble to the decree, allows for accepting anything that is illegal from the point of view of international law." Korotkyi and Hendel (n 92) 155. On the broader context of the adoption of this executive order, see 'Why Does Moscow Recognize the Passports of the DPR and LPR and to Whom Is This a Signal?' (*BBC Russian Service*, 20 February 2017) <https://www.bbc.com/russian/features-39032141> accessed 15 February 2020 (*in Russian*).

95 Executive Order on Recognition of the Documents of the DPR and LPR (n 90).

96 On this aspect, see Martsenko (n 51) 230.

reject the executive order *en bloc* seems to be unjustified and not in line with the humanitarian and human rights predicates of the *Namibia* exception.

In this context, the Letter of the Federal Notary Chamber to the President of the Notary Chamber of the Stavropol Region regarding the possibility of recognition of documents such as powers of attorneys issued by the DPR's and LPR's notaries is also relevant.[97] Pointing to the above-mentioned 2007 Letter of the Ministry of Foreign Affairs and the Executive Order on Recognition of the Documents of the DPR and LPR, the Federal Notary Chamber concluded that "in order to ensure respect for rights and lawful interests of citizens, notaries can recognise documents verified by notaries of State entities not recognised by the Russian Federation as independent subjects of international law."[98] However, since the activity of notaries is the expression of public power within a particular territory, under the *Namibia* exception, it seems excessive to recognise all the documents verified in such a manner. Instead, recognition should be granted depending on the character of a particular document in question.

3 Purported Acts and Laws in the Cases Pending before the ECtHR

At the time of finalising this book, there are twelve inter-State cases and thousands of individual applications pending before the ECtHR related to the post-Soviet space and the events discussed in this book.[99] The criteria used by the

---

97 Federal Notary Chamber of the Russian Federation, 'Letter No 3056/06–13' (20 June 2018) <http://not-palata-sk.ru/wp-content/uploads/2018/08/O-priznanii-notarialnyh-dokumentov-DNR-i-LNR_20.06.18.pdf> accessed 15 February 2020 (*in Russian*).

98 The letter also suggests that any request for legal assistance by the notaries of the DPR and LPR must be conducted through judicial authorities. ibid.

99 *Georgia v Russia (IV)* App no 39611/18; *Ukraine v Russia (re Crimea)* App nos 20958/14 and 38334/18; *Ukraine and the Netherlands v Russia* App nos 8019/16, 43800/14, 28525/20 and 11055/22. In 2023, the Grand Chamber decided to join the applications relating to the conflict in Eastern Ukraine that started in 2014 and the downing of the MH17 flight with the inter-State application *Ukraine v Russia (X)* concerning the "allegations of mass and gross human-rights violations committed by the Russian Federation in its military operations on the territory of Ukraine since 24 February 2022." The admissibility and merits of *Ukraine v Russia (X)* will be analysed jointly with the merits of other applications in this case. 'European Court Joins Inter-State Case Concerning Russian Military Operations in Ukraine to Inter-State Case Concerning Eastern Ukraine and Downing of Flight MH17' (*Press Release Issued by the Registrar of the Court,* 20 February 2023) <https://www.echr.coe.int/w/four-inter-state-cases-joined> accessed 31 October 2023. Other inter-State applications include *Ukraine v Russia (VIII)* App no 55855/18 (concerning the events on the Kerch Strait in November 2018) *and Ukraine v Russia (IX)* App No 10691/21 (concerning Ukraine's allegation of targeted assassination by Russia in Russia and other States).

ECtHR in its previous case law will be further employed in these future cases concerning post-Soviet illegal secessionist entities.[100]

However, it is already clear at this time that three inter-Sate cases currently pending at the merits will require the analysis of the issues specific to this chapter, namely the issue of exception from the (implied) recognition of the acts of regulatory nature issued by the authorities of illegal secessionist entities (or annexed territories) in the context human rights litigation. Some of these cases will also relate to violations of human rights that – given their formulation – will require a pre-existing assessment of the territorial sovereignty.

In the *Ukraine v Russia* (*re Crimea*) admissibility decision, the Court itself already flagged out three such points when justifying why it was necessary to establish the nature of Russia's jurisdiction (ultimately as extra-territorial). It referred to Ukraine's complaint concerning the alleged existence of administrative practice in breach of Article 6 ECHR ("[u]nlawful requalification of Ukrainian judgments under Russian legislation in breach of Article 6 of the Convention"), the complaint under Article 2 of Protocol No 4 to the ECHR (the allegation of "restrictions of freedom of movement between Crimea and mainland Ukraine resulting from the *de facto* transformation by the respondent State of the administrative border line into a State border between the Russian Federation and Ukraine") and the complaint under Article 14 ECHR in connection with Article 2 of Protocol No 4 to the ECHR.[101] Among others, the complaint was raised also under Article 5 ECHR and Article 1 of Protocol 1 ECHR.[102]

Ukraine and the Netherlands v Russia (concerning the applications currently pending at the merits stage, ie those involving the DPR and LPR before the all-out Russian invasion in February 2022), among others, raise the complaint of

There are also seven inter-State applications mostly concerning the allegations of human rights violations in relation to the Second Karabakh War. See 'Questions and Answers on Inter-State Cases' (*Press Unit*, 18 July 2023) <https://www.echr.coe.int/web/echr/inter-state-applications> accessed 31 October 2023.

100 G Nuridzahanian, '(Non-)Recognition of De Facto Regimes in Case Law of the European Court of Human Rights: Implications for Cases Involving Crimea and Eastern Ukraine' (*EJIL: Talk!*, 9 October 2017) <https://www.ejiltalk.org/non-recognition-of-de-facto-regimes-in-case-law-of-the-european-court-of-human-rights-implications-for-cases-involving-crimea-and-eastern-ukraine/> accessed 28 November 2019. See also N Mustafayev, '"Sydney District" in Karabakh: Do Illegal Settlers Have Property Rights under the European Convention on Human Rights?' (*Opinio Juris*, 22 February 2023) <http://opiniojuris.org/2023/02/22/sydney-district-in-karabakh-do-illegal-settlers-have-property-rights-under-the-european-convention-on-human-rights/> accessed 31 October 2023.

101 *Ukraine v Russia* (*re Crimea*) (n 99) paras 342–343 and see also paras 424–428 and 500–503.

102 See ibid paras 414–419 and 484–487.

the alleged existence of administrative practice in violation of Article 5 ECHR and Article 1 of Protocol 1 ECHR.[103] *Georgia v Russia* (*IV*) comprises, among others, the complaints of the alleged administrative practice in violation of Article 5 ECHR and Article 2 of Protocol 4 to the ECHR (in connection with "restrictions on freedom of movement into and out of Abkhazia and South Ossetia resulting from the de facto transformation of the ABL into State borders").[104]

Regarding the complaints involving the acts of regulatory nature issued by the DPR and LPR and Abkhazia and South Ossetia, for example, under Articles 5 and 6 ECHR, it might be expected that, the factors guiding the Court's unfavourable assessment of judicial and legal systems in Transnistria and Abkhazia in the period before the 2008 Russia-Georgia War for the purposes of Articles 5 and 6 ECHR[105] will also determine similar conclusions with respect to judicial

---

103 *Ukraine and the Netherlands v Russia* (n 99) paras 843–847 and 865–867. The Ukrainian application reportedly submitted that "unlawfulness of the military operation launched by Russia, as well as the violation of its sovereignty and territorial integrity, prevents the interference with the rights protected by Articles 8, 9 ECHR and by Article 1 of Protocol No. 1 thereto from being in accordance with the law and, therefore, justified." Ukraine, Application, paras 249, 268 and 315 referred to in F Romani and G Gaggioli, 'Third-Party Intervention on Behalf of the Geneva Academy of International Humanitarian Law and Human Rights' (*Geneva Academy*, 30 May 2023) <https://www.geneva-academy.ch/news/detail/625-our-third-party-intervention-in-ukraine-and-the-netherland-v-russia> accessed 31 October 2023. The Geneva Academy's intervention focused on the implications of *jus ad bellum* violations relevant to the IHRL for IHL (specifically in the context of an active armed conflict and not precisely the situation analysed in this book). It submitted "that a State that commits an act of aggression can be automatically considered as responsible for a breach of the obligation to respect human rights under Article 1 of the Convention vis-à-vis all the other States partaking in the same human rights regime. But as for responsibility vis-à-vis individual victims, allegations of human rights violations would still need to be assessed on a case-by-case basis taking into account IHL, not ius ad bellum." ibid.

104 *Georgia v Russia* (*IV*) (n 99) para 70.

105 Unlike with respect to the TRNC, the Court pointed out that the Transnistrian judicial system is hardly compatible with the Convention, as it was never "part of a system reflecting a judicial tradition considered compatible with Convention principles before the split into separate judicial systems occurred in 1990." *Mozer v the Republic of Moldova and Russia* App no 11138/10 (ECtHR, 23 February 2016) paras 144–150. The Court also took into account the arbitrariness of trials and convictions. *Ilaşcu and others v Moldova and Russia* ECHR 2004-VII 1, para 436. *Mamasakhlisi and Others v Georgia and Russia* App 29999/04 and 41424/04 (Merits) (ECtHR, 7 March 2023) paras 419–428 and paras 437–440. See *supra* Part 1, Chapter 7. See on the so-called 'judicial system' in the DPR and LPR B Triebel, H Rank and D Dmytrenko, *The 'People's Republics' of Donetsk and Luhansk as Examples of Dispute Reoslution in Rebel Areas* (KAS 2022).

and legal systems of the DPR, LPR and Abkhazia and South Ossetia in these cases.[106]

However, the assessment with respect to events in the Russia-annexed Crimea can be expected to be different by reference to the principles of the ECtHR's case law on TRNC.[107] Since Crimea is completely incorporated into the Russian legal and judicial system, which can be seen as compatible with the Convention principles,[108] wide application of the *Namibia* exception can be foreseen. It is notable that the Court, already in its admissibility decision, stated that to determine the complaint under Article 6 ECHR,

> the Court would, in accordance with its consistent case-law, have to consider the provisions of 'domestic' law; it would, therefore, be necessary to determine what the applicable 'domestic' law was. It would be impossible for the Court to examine this complaint without first determining whether the relevant 'domestic law' by reference to which this complaint is to be assessed is that of Ukraine or that of the Russian Federation.[109]

At the same time, the Court reiterated "that the issue of the legality, as a matter of international law, of Crimea's admission into the Russian Federation and its consequent legal status thereafter, is outside the scope of the case."[110]

---

106 Nuridzahanian (n 100).

107 The ECtHR was willing to give effect to the legal and judicial system of the TRNC, since it was considered to be based on principles compatible with the Convention. ibid. See also *supra* Part 1, Chapter 7.

108 ibid.

109 *Ukraine v Russia (re Crimea)* (n 99) para 342. However, see the Court's approach to the issue of 'domestic law' in the analogous situation of TRNC: "As the Commission observed, the court system in its functioning and procedures reflects the judicial and common-law tradition of Cyprus (see paragraph 231 above). In its opinion, having regard to the fact that it is the 'TRNC domestic law' which defines the substance of those rights and obligations for the benefit of the population as a whole it must follow that the domestic courts, set up by the 'law' of the 'TRNC', are the fora for their enforcement. For the Court, and for the purposes of adjudicating on 'civil rights and obligations' the local courts can be considered to be 'established by law' with reference to the 'constitutional and legal basis' on which they operate. In the Court's opinion, any other conclusion would be to the detriment of the Greek-Cypriot community and would result in a denial of opportunity to individuals from that community to have an adjudication on a cause of action against a private or public body (see paragraph 96 above). It is to be noted in this connection that the evidence confirms that Greek Cypriots have taken successful court actions in defence of their civil rights … The Court would add that its conclusion on this matter in no way amounts to a recognition, implied or otherwise, of the 'TRNC''s claim to statehood." *Cyprus v Turkey* ECHR 2001-IV 1, paras 237–238.

110 *Ukraine v Russia (re Crimea)* (n 99) para 426.

To what extent an *a priori* position based on the pre-existing case law, with respect to acts and measures of the Russian authorities in annexed Crimea, would in fact be conducive to individual human rights protection, as well as to broader communitarian interests protected by peremptory norms, is discussed in Part 1, Chapters 7 and 9.[111] In any case, the undeniable peremptory illegality of Crimea's incorporation into Russia and its complete submersion within the structures of the Russian Federation will test the soundness of the Court's approach.

4 Conclusion

This chapter offered analysis of selected property transfers, including privatisation in Transnistria and Abkhazia and nationalisation in Crimea and the DPR and LPR. These purported ownership transfers carried out under the legislation of these entities do not have any validity under international law and would not be given recognition in potential foreign municipal or international proceedings. Foreign investors taking part in these purported transactions would be prevented from relying on the principle of good faith or the *Namibia* exception. They would be expected to bear the risks of participating in such transactions. However, it is not excluded that recognition of the validity of these transfers can be the subject of negotiations in the case of a future transition from illegal regime or potential reintegration.

In addition, despite the parent States' initial incoherent approach to the *Namibia* exception, today, at least at the level of statutory provisions, the exception from invalidity and illegality of acts of civil status such as the birth and death certificates issued by illegal authorities has been accepted. While the Ukrainian courts frequently refer to the *Namibia* exception, the birth and death certificates issued by illegal authorities are only evaluated in judicial proceedings as evidence. The administrative procedure is being developed. Similarly, Russian practice also supports the *Namibia* exception for the acts of civil status, as follows from the MFA's official position and the 2017 Executive Order on Recognition of Documents of the DPR and LPR. The latter, however, exceeded the narrow confines of the scope of the *Namibia* exception by including the respective self-proclaimed republics' passports. In areas of private relations concerning the illegal secessionist entities, the Russian courts' approach has been rather uneven.

111 Part 1, Chapter 7 with respect to the *Namibia* exception, and Chapter 9 more broadly.

Lastly, this chapter also overviewed the pending cases before the ECtHR concerning the post-Soviet illegal secessionist entities. Based on the analysis carried out in other parts of this book, it outlined the ways in which the Court can be expected to approach these cases.

Conclusion to Section 4

This section drew legal consequences from the conclusion of Section 3 that Transnistria, Nagorno-Karabakh (until September 2023), DPR and LPR (until September 2022), Abkhazia, South Ossetia can be characterised not as States, but as illegal secessionist entities. For a brief period, Crimea, Kherson and Zaporizhzhia Regions also bore the characteristics of illegal secessionist entities, but their ostensible existence was only ephemeral. None of the above entities has ever achieved statehood. Crimea, DPR, LPR, Kherson and Zaporizhzhia Regions are now illegally annexed by Russia. Firstly, the section broadly outlined the applicable legal framework, which is formed on the one hand by the consequences of peremptory territorial illegality and on the other hand by the consequences of a change of effective territorial control in the area of humanitarian law, human rights law and international responsibility.

The section highlighted that a generalised non-recognition of the formal status of statehood of these entities or their status as part of Russia supports the conclusions of Section 3. Importantly, in most cases, international organisations and bodies have explicitly proclaimed the duty of non-recognition or the peremptory territorial illegality with respect to these claimed statuses. Indeed, non-recognition in some instances (Nagorno-Karabakh and Transnistria) was not explicitly referred to in terms of their illegality. However, the violation of the prohibition of the use of force in these contexts is separately acknowledged and well-documented. Moreover, their universal non-recognition must be viewed in the context of the explicit invocation and application of the duty of non-recognition in analogous cases of this section. It thus can be conceivably viewed as supporting the conclusions of this book as well. Overall, the surveyed data is thus in line with the framework of general international law outlined in Part 1, Chapter 2, and can be taken as attesting to the adherence to the duty of non-recognition in these instances.

Moreover, based on criteria of effective control and criteria of occupation by proxy and recent case law, the section determined that Crimea, DPR, LPR, Abkhazia, South Ossetia and, arguably, Transnistria, have been occupied by Russia. Similarly, in the period before the outbreak of the 2020 War, Armenia occupied Nagorno-Karabakh. Furthermore, based on the relevant case law, Russia (Armenia in Nagorno-Karabakh) exercised effective control of these territories for the purposes of jurisdiction under Article 1 ECHR. It was also argued that Armenia continued to exercise effective control over Nagorno-Karabakh even after the Second Karabakh War. Based on the case law, the territorial States are also bound to discharge their positive obligations. It was

 | DOI:10.1163/9789004702646_029

argued that Azerbaijan possesed broader positive obligations at a minimum since April 2023, given the establishment of the checkpoint on the Lachin Corridor.

Secondly, the section also analysed effective relations of post-Soviet illegal secessionist entities and Russia's relations purportedly extending to its illegally annexed territories. By doing so, the above chapters traced the extent of the operation of the principle of legality in the context of concrete relations. From a certain perspective, the tension between legality and effectiveness is even more acute in these relations, as they are rooted in physical reality. The analysis of the practice and positions of States carried out in this section supports the conclusions of a general legal framework established in Part 1, Chapter 7.

On the one hand, certain types of effective relations persist without violating the duty of non-recognition. These relations include the establishment of contacts through the signing of documents that do not amount to treaty relations, with respect to the documents' wording, the parties' denotation and their character, as demonstrated by the practice in this area between Moldova and authorities in Transnistria. In addition, setting up representative offices abroad does not amount to diplomatic relations due to the lack of consent of the 'host' State and their establishment under local municipal law. For instance, the establishment of representative offices of the DPR in Italy, Greece and Finland falls into this category. Similarly, trading by private economic operators, funding of projects not contributing to the entrenchment of the illegal entity's authority, activities of a humanitarian nature and recognition of civil status documents on the basis of the *Namibia* exception are not prohibited. This was supported by the overview of the practice of the parent States' and EU's economic dealings as well as the practice concerning the *Namibia* exception.

On the other hand, the duty of non-recognition functions well and precludes relations of an official or formalised nature, as demonstrated by the lack of diplomatic relations and agreements that would accord the status of statehood to these entities. It is also supported by the practice of EU association agreements with the parent States that confirm the parent State's territorial sovereignty over territory of the illegal secessionist entities and consequent treaty-making capacity there. Moreover, the mechanism of issuance by Moldova of documents required for preferential exports of Transnistria's goods under the EU-Moldova DCFTA is also in line with Moldova's continued territorial sovereignty over Transnistria and therefore in line with the duty of non-recognition. The section also criticised the analysis of general international law principles on spatial application of treaties by arbitral tribunals in the proceedings involving expropriations of Ukrainian assets in the Russia-annexed Crimea under the

Russia-Ukraine BIT as too expansive and posing risk to established tenets of consequences of peremptory illegality under general international law.

More broadly, the above chapters primarily analysed the practice and positions of the parent States regarding the post-Soviet illegal secessionist entities. This examination supports incremental trend outlined in Part 1 of this book that the parent State, as an injured State, preserves a privileged position in shaping the response to peremptory illegality. This follows from its on-going competences with respect to territory of the illegal secessionist entity, which remains under its sovereignty but is outside of its control.

Overall, outside of a minimal number of States recognising the claimed status of these entities, the overview of the practice of States and their positions regarding legal relations concerning the illegal secessionist entities and Russia-annexed territories support the preservation of the parent State's sovereign powers. The section demonstrated that the principle of legality has continued to operate and protect the injured parent State's interests and communitarian values even in relations subsequent to the denial of claimed status. This confirms the prevalence of the principle of *ex iniuria ius non oritur*, even in the context of the post-Soviet illegal secessionist entities.

General Conclusion

1 Secession in Contemporary International Law

This book sought to establish a general international legal framework of contemporary secession. In this sense, the book followed up on the historical evolution of doctrinal thought and practice on secession. Part 1, Chapter 1 outlined this evolution from the period of dynastic legitimism, through a factualist period linked to a natural law tradition and a constitutive theory of recognition. It also provided the overview of a factualist theory of secession and a declaratory theory of recognition – a prevailing view of secession since the early 20th century. This book sought to challenge this latter view and thereby outline a contemporary legal paradigm of secession.

1.1 *Legal Analysis of the Status of the Secessionist Entity*

Based on the analysis of practice, *opinio iuris* and doctrine, Part 1, Chapter 4 of this book established that unilateral secession *per se* is not prohibited by contemporary international law; secessionists are not prohibited from initiating a secessionist attempt through the variety of means at their disposal.[1] A scenario of a new State emerging on the ground of its effectiveness alone has not been discarded yet. Nevertheless, while the book acknowledged that the principle of effectiveness and the constitutive criteria of statehood, which were in Part 1, Chapter 1 demonstrated to be *legal* criteria predetermined by a customary international rule, remain major reference points concerning contemporary secession, their actual impact on the resolution of the secessionist claims today has only been minor, if not virtual. As shown in Part 1, Chapter 4 short of the prohibition of unilateral secession, international law undoubtedly favours the parent State's territorial integrity.[2]

Normative developments have also substantially diminished the principle of effectiveness' role as the overriding criterion in the creation of States via secession. The mapping of the post-1945 practice and doctrine in Part 1, Chapter 5 showed that consensuality has been at the heart of State-creation outside decolonisation. Since 1945, potentially only Bangladesh has emerged through unilateral secession, meaning that it emerged as a State before the

1 MG Kohen, 'Introduction' in MG Kohen (ed), *Secession: International Law Perspectives* (CUP 2006) 20. For other authors reaching the same conclusion, see Part 1, Chapter 4.

2 O Corten, 'Are There Gaps?' in MG Kohen (ed), Secession: International Law Perspectives (CUP 2006) 254. For other authors reaching the same conclusion, see Part 1, Chapter 4.

 | DOI:10.1163/9789004702646_030

parent State's recognition.[3] The instance of Somaliland, short of any recognition by other States, exemplifies theoretical deficiencies of factualist statehood. Kosovo splits the international community and therefore cannot be taken as conclusive support for any of the approaches.

As demonstrated in Part 1, Chapter 5, in all other situations, unilateral secessionist tendencies have either faded away, were suppressed, or have forced the parent State to give its consent to the separation of a part of its territory.[4] This consent is a legal basis for a new State, ultimately transforming the secessionist process into a case of devolution. However, the preponderance of consensuality has not entailed a lack of intra-State violence; it has simply shown that practice favours consensually created international borders. Based on these observations, it seems that the lack of prohibition of secession mostly allows the secessionists to put pressure on the parent State to grant its consent, rather than to establish a new State against the wishes of the parent State on the basis of effectiveness alone.

Moreover, this book also demonstrated in Part 1, Chapter 3 that contemporary international law does not contain the right to secession by fractions of the populations of existing States, flowing from the right of peoples to self-determination outside decolonisation. In addition, despite significant doctrinal support, there is no practice to support the claim on the existence of remedial secession in positive international law. Lastly, the analysis also showed that the mere expression of the wishes of a fraction of a population expressed in unilateral referendum does not confer the right to secede on that population either. Thus, despite frequent reliance by the secessionists on the existence of the right to independence, the analysis did not demonstrate corresponding *legal* right in contemporary international law.[5]

Importantly, Part 1, Chapter 2 exhaustively analysed the relevance of violation of peremptory norms to the emergence of States via secession. It traced the evolution of the post-1945 practice and *opinio iuris* supporting the peremptory norms' relevance to secession and outlined doctrinal approaches on the effects of peremptory norms on secession.[6]

The book largely drew from the passage in *Kosovo* that pertained to the illegality attached to declarations of independence.[7] The book established that

3 J Crawford, *The Creation of States in International Law* (2nd edn, Clarendon Press 2006) 415–416.

4 See M Fabry, *Recognizing States: International Society and the Establishment of New States since 1776* (OUP 2010) 225. See further Part 1, Chapter 5.

5 See Crawford (n 3) 415. For other authors reaching the same conclusion, see Part 1, Chapter 3.

6 For an in-depth account of the doctrinal positions on this aspect, see Part 1, Chapter 2.

7 *Accordance with International Law of the Unilateral Declaration of Independence in Respect of Kosovo* (Advisory Opinion) [2010] ICJ Rep 403, para 81 ("*Kosovo*").

the act of declaring independence was an inherent and inseparable part of any secessionist attempt. Secession was then defined as a subjective legal fact, the sum of factual and voluntary elements attributive of the status of statehood and the title of territorial sovereignty. A finding on illegality attached to the declaration of independence can then be seen as relevant to the secessionist attempt as a whole.

More specifically, the book identified the scope of peremptory norms applicable in this context, in particular the right of self-determination, the prohibition of racial discrimination and apartheid and the prohibition of the use of force. Except for the latter, which applies only in the inter-State context, the book argued that these other norms are also directly applicable to the secessionist group as a non-State actor. Moreover, the book highlighted that even in cases where the non-State secessionist actors are not direct violators of peremptory norms, their acts and actions are not allowed to escape peremptory norms' regulatory framework. This confirms the rather expansive effects of peremptory norms that extend into a non-State secessionist context due to its 'connection with' the original violation committed by another actor – the third State.

The book then comprehensively analysed the legal consequences of violation of peremptory norms on the emergence of a State, including the illegality of the secessionist attempt and declaration of independence, the invalidity of the declaration of independence and the prohibition of recognition of the secessionist entity as a State. The analysis proved that the so-called legalist doctrinal approach according to which a connection of the secessionist attempt with violation of peremptory norms precludes the emergence of a new State fits the outlined practice and *opinio iuris* best. Moreover, the book built on the conclusions of Part 1, Chapter 1 that the criteria of statehood are *legal* criteria predetermined by a customary rule. The book demonstrated that in line with the developments of practice and *opinio iuris* and the principle of *ex iniuria ius non oritur*, these *legal* criteria presuppose their compliance with peremptory norms of international law. Thus, the entities created in the context of the violation of peremptory norms are not considered to have met the constitutive criteria of statehood. Secondly, violation of peremptory norms entails an invalid claim for statehood without which secession cannot take place. The duty of non-recognition as such does not influence the emergence of a new State; it functions as an additional layer, preventing the consolidation of illegality.

1.2 *Legal Consequences Applicable to the Illegal Secessionist Entity*

While scholarly works on secession limit themselves to analysis of the consequences of peremptory illegality on the emergence of statehood, the present book demonstrated that the denial of statehood is not the final word on the matter. It is just a starting point, as the principle of legality continues to order the subsequent relations concerning the effective entity following its denial of the status of statehood.

For the purposes of outlining the relevant effects, the book in Part 1, Chapter 6 defined the notion of an 'illegal secessionist entity'. Four features characterise this term: underlying illegality of origin, change of effective territorial control away from the parent State, persistent claims in being a State and temporal limitation to the on-going situation outside of the return to *status quo ante*. This notion covers both the scenario of an effective, independent entity outside of the third State's control and the scenario of an entity under the control of the third State – its effectiveness is thus only apparent. The book only examined the latter scenario. The book did not use the notion of an 'illegal secessionist entity' in terms of a specific status; it used it as a descriptive, 'umbrella' notion that helped outline international law applicable to these situations.

On the one hand, as showed in Part 1, Chapter 7, this international legal framework includes the consequences of peremptory territorial illegality, in particular the non-application of the rules of State succession; the invalidity of international and domestic acts of illegal secessionist entity; and the so-called aggravated regime of international responsibility. Above all, the book systematically analysed the scope and content of the duty of non-recognition. Despite frequent doctrinal criticism concerning the vagueness and imprecision of the duty's content, the book established that it has an undeniable normative core.

The duty of non-recognition is well observed in relations at a purportedly inter-State level, raising the attributes of sovereignty; in purportedly government-to-government relations subject to certain limited, functional cooperation beneficial to local populations; and in formal and law-application settings involving the acts and laws of illegal secessionist entity, such as certificates of origin and phytosanitary certificates. The book established that this duty does not require third States to ban their economic operators from trading with illegal secessionist entities and acknowledged uncertainty as to the operation of this duty in the context of factual contribution to illegality. However, on the basis of relevant *municipal* case law, the book established that the *Namibia* exception has been interpreted narrowly. It was rejected in situations that would have improved the economic position of local inhabitants but would have required the recognition of public law acts of illegal secessionist entity.

More broadly, it is true that the effects of violation of peremptory norms do not extend directly to effective relations within an internal order of the entity, where they are at least temporarily protected by the entity's overwhelming effectiveness. However, at the international or regional level, or in foreign jurisdictions, these relations, subject to the limited scope of the *Namibia* exception, are denied effect. This demonstrates the extensive and *vertical* effects of the violation of peremptory norms that find expression even in the realm of private international law and could be approximated to the concept of truly international public policy. Importantly, the book also demonstrated that subject of preservation of relevant communitarian interests the injured State has a privileged position in shaping the response to the peremptory territorial illegality.

On the other hand, as showed in Part 1, Chapter 8, the applicable international framework of illegal secessionist entity includes the legal consequences of change of effective territorial control. The book examined the applicability of the law of occupation and human rights law under ECHR and responsibility for violation of these regimes in the context of illegal secessionist entity when the latter is under control of a third State. These regimes link the relevant consequences only with the actual effectiveness of the controlling State. The entity is treated only as a proxy or agent of the controlling State.

The book provided an in-depth account of the factual tests used in this context, including effective control over a group for the attribution of responsibility under ARSIWA; effective territorial control and overall control over a group for the purposes of occupation by proxy; and effective control test over territory in the jurisprudence of the ECtHR. The book contended that apart from being a jurisdiction-triggering test, effective control test in fact operates as a *lex specialis* rule of attribution in the ECHR-specific context.[8] The book also provided a critical analysis of the residual positive obligations of the territorial State.

Lastly, in Part 1, Chapter 9, the book sought to outline the interaction between the consequences of peremptory illegality and human rights and the law of occupation. The book highlighted that this interaction does not correspond to a simple *vertical* effects between effectiveness and legality. The book suggested that regime interaction should be built on the *horizontal* balancing of interests, depending on the context and protected values involved.

Despite *ius in bello* and *ius ad bellum* divide, the book outlined of co-application between the duty of non-recognition and the law of occupation. The book highlighted that the two regimes are broadly normatively convergent as they are underpinned by the same principles of non-transfer of sovereignty

8 JM Rooney, 'The Relationship between Jurisdiction and Attribution after Jaloud v. Netherlands' (2015) 62 Netherlands International Law Review 407, 416. For similar doctrinal views, see Part 1, Chapter 8.

and the non-alteration to *status quo ante* and, and with respect to the *Namibia* exception, by humanitarian values. The book outlined normative divergences in the area of the occupant's limited managerial powers and suggested their limitation to better reflect communitarian interests involved.

Focusing specifically on the ECtHR's case law, the book also highlighted certain areas of convergence between the duty of non-recognition and judicial practice, particularly in the area of non-recognition of the status, the official acts and the laws of illegal secessionist entity. It was also argued that some aspects of the positive obligations of the territorial State can be seen as not aligned with the basic premise of the duty of non-recognition, ie the illegal entity's isolation. Importantly, the book underscored that it is difficult to substantiate the ECtHR's broad presumption of benefit of recognition of laws and institutions of illegal entity to victims of human rights violation under the *Namibia* exception. It was argued that an expansive reading of the *Namibia* exception by the ECtHR, as analysed in Part 1, Chapter 7, could prove subversive to communitarian interests and even to the individual interests involved.[9]

2 Practice in the Post-Soviet Space

2.1 *Legal Analysis of the Status of Post-Soviet Secessionist Entities*

Part 2, Section 3 used the general legal framework outlined in Part 1, Section 1 to analyse the claims to statehood and secessionist attempts in the post-Soviet space. The book acknowledged the complex factual and political context, particularly concerning the Soviet Union's disintegration, which formed the backdrop of the origins of some of the early secessionist attempts. Nevertheless, it submitted that these features and specificities did not justify the divergences or exceptions from general international law's regulation of secession.

Part 2, Chapters 11–15 carried out an extensive factual and legal analysis of the secessionist attempts of Crimea, the DPR, the LPR, Kherson and Zporizhzhia Regions, Abkhazia, South Ossetia, Nagorno-Karabakh and Transnistria including history-based claims, arguments relying on the provisions of Soviet law and the presence of ethnic or linguistic minorities. None of these claims provided a legal entitlement for secession of these entities under international or Soviet law.

The analysis showed an adherence to the principle of *uti possidetis iuris* by the former federal republics of the Soviet Union after the dissolution of the USSR.

9 R Ronen, *Transition from Illegal Regimes under International Law* (CUP 2011) 96 and see 88–98.

Importantly, the book demonstrated that none of the post-Soviet secessionist entities was a State under international law. In all cases, the third State's military intervention was decisive for the secessionist victory vis-à-vis the parent State. Thus, all these instances were in one way or another connected to violations of the prohibition of the use of force, a peremptory norm of international law. Thus, all these entities were precluded from becoming States. This outcome underscored the importance of the effects of peremptory norms and the principle of legality on the emergence of States in contemporary international law.

Importantly, the *collective* analysis of the claims to statehood of the post-Soviet secessionist entities demonstrated that the same legal basis – violation of peremptory norms – precluded the emergence of all these entities as States. Apart from Crimea, DPR, LPR, Zaporizhzhia and Kherson Regions, which are now directly annexed to Russia, all other *de facto* entities can now be characterised as illegal secessionist entities. This finding is a major contribution to the legal scholarship on the post-Soviet secessionist practice.

2.2 *Legal Consequences Applicable to Post-Soviet Illegal Secessionist Entities*

The book in Part 2, Chapter 16 outlined the general international legal framework applicable to these post-Soviet illegal secessionist entities. On the one hand, it included the consequences of peremptory territorial illegality, in particular, the duty of non-recognition of these entities as States. A generalised non-recognition of the formal status of statehood of these entities or their status as part of Russia supports the conclusions of this book on the applicability of the duty of non-recognition. Importantly, in most cases, international organisations and bodies have explicitly proclaimed the duty of non-recognition or the indicators of the peremptory territorial illegality with respect to these claimed statuses. Indeed, non-recognition in some instances was not explicitly referred to in terms of the duty of non-recognition, but violation of the use of force in these contexts was acknowledged and well-documented separately; it aligned with the invocation and application of the duty of non-recognition in analogous post-Soviet cases. Thus, their generalised non-recognition can thus conceivably be viewed as supporting the conclusion reached in Part 2, Section 3 as well.

Moreover, concerning the consequences of a change of effective control, based on the factual tests outlined in Part 1, Chapter 8 and the relevant case law of the ECtHR, the book determined that Russia's control over the DPR and LPR, Kherson and Zaporizhzhia Region, Crimea, Abkhazia and South Ossetia, Transnistria has reached the threshold of effective control in terms of the ECtHR's jurisprudence. Armenia exercised effective control over

Nagorno-Karabh before the Second-Karabakh War and arguably even in the period until Azerbaijan's recapture of the region in 2023. The territorial States are also bound to discharge their positive obligations. In addition, based on criteria of effective control for the purposes of belligerent occupation and criteria of occupation by proxy and recent case law, the book also determined that Crimea, the DPR and LPR, Kherson and Zaporizhzhia Region, Abkhazia, South Ossetia and, arguably, Transnistria are occupied by Russia. Similarly, before the 2020 war Armenia occupied Nagorno-Karabakh. It was argued that Armenia's occupation likely terminated at some point before Azerbaijan's recapture of the region in 2023.

Moreover, in Part 2, Chapters 17–19, the book focused on the operation of the duty of non-recognition with respect to effective relations of the post-Soviet illegal secessionist entities subsequent to the denial of claimed status. In line with the conclusions of Part 1, Chapter 7, the book demonstrated that the duty of non-recognition operates well in the context of official and formalised relations. Outside the minimal number of States that recognised these entities as States and Crimea, DPR, LPR, Zaporizhzhia and Kherson Regions as part of Russia, the overwhelming majority of sovereign States abide by the duty of non-recognition by not establishing direct treaty, diplomatic and consular relations with the entities claiming to be States. In addition, the analysis of agreements between the EU and the parent States supported the preservation of the parent State's treaty-making capacity with respect to illegal secessionist entities. Moreover, the mechanism of the extension of preferential tariffs to goods originating in Transnistria under the EU-Moldova DCFTA was formally and factually subjected to Moldova's legal order and therefore in line with the duty of non-recognition. The book also criticised the analysis of general international law principles on spatial application of treaties by arbitral tribunals in the proceedings involving expropriations of Ukrainian assets in the Russia-annexed Crimea under the Russia-Ukraine BIT as too expansive and posing risk to established tenets of consequences of peremptory illegality under general international law.

Since the duty of non-recognition does not extend to foreign private economic operators, the instances of all-out trade embargo, such as Georgia's trade embargo on Abkhazia and South Ossetia and Ukraine's approach towards the DPR and LPR (until 2021), are not required by the duty of non-recognition. Nevertheless, the parent State is not prohibited under general international law from adopting any trade measures with respect to its territories that seek to secede, subject to humanitarian exceptions. Similarly, the EU's policy of non-recognition of the annexation of Crimea and the city of Sevastopol since 2014 has exceeded the scope of the duty of non-recognition because of its all-out ban on trade and investment and other measures, and thus would be better qualified as sanction. The same conclusion applies to the EU restrictive measures adopted in the context of Russia's aggression against Ukraine since 2022.

Moreover, the practice of the parent States and Russia, at least at the level of internal statutory provisions, demonstrated the adherence to the recognition of civil status documents issued by illegal secessionist entities, which is in line with the content of the *Namibia* exception under general international law. Generally, the book focused on the analysis of the practice of the parent States with respect to the post-Soviet illegal secessionist entities This supported the incremental conclusions of Part 1 that, subject to the preservation of communitarian interests, they have a unique position in the context of the duty of non-recognition, determined by the preservation of their sovereignty vis-à-vis illegal secessionist entity.

3 Conclusion

Overall, based on doctrine, practice and *opinio iuris*, this book developed a contemporary general legal framework of secession, including legal consequences applicable to illegal secessionist entities. It was demonstrated that peremptory norms of international law have become fundamental component of this legal framework. This aspect does not simply signal a change in the technical operation of international law but harbingers a more profound transformation of its character. This book demonstrated that the effects of peremptory norms are so extensive as to apply to a pre-State secessionist context, preclude the emergence of a new State, and even order effective relations of secessionist entities subsequent to the denial of statehood. The analysis of the secessionist attempts in the post-Soviet space showed that they were connected to the violation of peremptory norms. Thus, these entities – even when *prima facie* effective – have never attained the status of statehood. The practice and positions of States vis-à-vis post-Soviet secessionism were demonstrated to be in line with the conclusions of this book regarding the denial of statehood to secessionist entities created through violation of peremptory norms and applicability of consequences of peremptory territorial illegality. Ultimately, the book showed that international public order expands to an area that has until recently been considered an apparent a-legal zone dominated by power politics. The book demonstrated that in contemporary international law, at least to the extent of peremptory norms of international law, this latter view no longer holds true.

Selected Bibliography

Monographs

Aust HP, *Complicity and the Law of State Responsibility* (CUP 2011).

Beaudouin A, *Uti possidetis et sécession* (Éditions Dalloz 2011).

Berkes A, *International Human Rights Law Beyond State Territorial Control* (CUP 2021).

Chen T-C, *The International Law of Recognition: With Special Reference to Practice in Great Britain and the United States* (Stevens 1951).

Christakis T, *Le droit à l'autodétermination en dehors des situations de décolonisation* (La documentation française 1999).

Corten O, *The Law Against War: The Prohibition on the Use of Force in Contemporary International Law* (Hart 2010).

Costelloe D, *Legal Consequences of Peremptory Norms in International Law* (CUP 2017).

Couveinhes-Matsumoto F, *L'effectivité en droit international* (Bruylant 2014).

Crawford J, *The Creation of States in International Law* (2nd edn, Clarendon Press 2006).

Crawford J, *State Responsibility: The General Part* (CUP 2013).

De Waal T, *Black Garden: Armenia and Azerbaijan Through Peace and War* (New York University Press 2004).

De Visscher C, *Théories et réalités en droit international public* (3rd edn, A Pedone 1960).

De Visscher C, *Les effectivités du droit international public* (Pedone 1967).

Distefano G, *L'ordre international entre légalité et effectivité: le titre juridique dans le contentieux territorial* (Pedone 2002).

Dubuisson F, *The International Obligations of the European Union and Its Member States with Regard to Economic Relations with Israeli Settlements* (Centre de droit international de l'Université libre de Bruxelles 2014).

Dugard J, *Recognition and the United Nations* (Grotius 1987).

Dumberry P, *A Guide to State Succession in International Investment Law* (Edward Elgar Publishing 2018).

Escudero Espinosa JF, *Self-Determination and Humanitarian Secession in International Law of a Globalized World: Kosovo v. Crimea* (Springer 2018).

Fabry M, *Recognizing States: International Society and the Establishment of New States since 1776* (OUP 2010).

Feldbrugge FJM, *Russian Law: The End of the Soviet System and the Role of Law* (Martinus Nijhoff Publishers 1993).

Ferraro T, *Expert Meeting: Occupation and Other Forms of Administration of Foreign Territory* (ICRC 2012).

Follebouckt X, *Les conflits gelés de l'espace postoviétique: genèse et enjeux* (Presses universitaires de Louvain 2011).

Gowlland-Debbas V, *Collective Responses to Illegal Acts in International Law: United Nations Action in the Question of Southern Rhodesia* (M Nijhoff 1990).

Grant TD, *The Recognition of States: Law and Practice in Debate and Evolution* (Praeger 1999).

Grant TD, *Aggression Against Ukraine: Territory, Responsibility, and International Law* (Palgrave Macmillan 2015).

Hamant H, *Démembrement de l'URSS et problèmes de succession d'états* (Bruylant 2007).

Hannikainen L, *Peremptory Norms (Jus Cogens) in International Law: Historical Development, Criteria, Present Status* (Lakimiesliiton Kustannus 1988).

ICRC, *Occupation and Other Forms of Administration of Foreign Territory: Expert Meeting* (ICRC 2012).

Jacqué J-P, *Eléments pour une théorie de l'acte juridique en droit international public* (LGDJ 1972).

Jellinek G, *L'État moderne et son droit* (Éd Panthéon-Assas 2005).

Jennings RY, *The Acquisition of Territory in International Law* (Manchester University Press 2017).

Kassoti E, *The Legality under International Law of the EU's Trade Agreements Covering Occupied Territories: A Comparative Study of Palestine and Western Sahara* (Asser Institute 2017).

Kassoti E, *Trading with Settlements: The International Obligations of the European Union with Regard to Economic Dealings with Occupied Territories* (Asser Institute 2017).

Kelsen H, *Principles of International Law* (2nd edn, Holt Rinehart and Winston 1966).

Kelsen H, *Pure Theory of Law* (Lawbook Exchange 2009).

King C, *The Moldovans: Romania, Russia, and the Politics of Culture* (Hoover Institution Press 2000).

Kohen MG, *Possession contestée et souveraineté territoriale* (PUF 1997).

Kolb R, *Théorie du ius cogens international: essai de relecture du concept* (PUF 2001).

Koutroulis V, *Le début et la fin de l'application du droit de l'occupation* (Pedone 2010).

Kreijen G, *State, Failure, Sovereignty and Effectiveness: Legal Lessons from the Decolonization of Sub-Saharan Africa* (M Nijhoff 2004).

Krüger H, *The Nagorno-Karabakh Conflict: A Legal Analysis* (Springer 2010).

Lagerwall A, *Le principe ex injuria jus non oritur en droit international* (Bruylant 2016).

Lanovoy V, *Complicity and Its Limits in the Law of International Responsibility* (Bloomsbury Publishing 2016).

Lauterpacht H, *Recognition in International Law* (University Press 1947).

Milano E, *Unlawful Territorial Situations in International Law: Reconciling Effectiveness, Legality and Legitimacy* (Martinus Nijhoff 2006).

Milanović M, *Extraterritorial Application of Human Rights Treaties: Law, Principles and Policy* (OUP 2011).

Nicoloudis EP, *La nullité de 'jus cogens' et le développement contemporain du droit international public* (Ed Papazissi 1974).

Orakhelashvili A, *Peremptory Norms in International Law* (OUP 2006).
Pasquier E, *De Genève À Nuremberg: Carl Schmitt, Hans Kelsen et le droit international* (Classiques Garnier 2012).
Raič D, *Statehood and the Law of Self-Determination* (Kluwer Law International 2002).
Ronen Y, *Transition from Illegal Regimes under International Law* (CUP 2011).
Rozakis C, *The Concept of Jus Cogens in the Law of Treaties* (North-Holland 1976).
Saparov A, *From Conflict to Autonomy in the Caucasus: The Soviet Union and the Making of Abkhazia, South Ossetia and Nagorno Karabakh* (Routledge 2015).
Sasse G, *The Crimea Question: Identity, Transition and Conflict* (Harvard University Press 2007).
Sassòli M, *International Humanitarian Law: Rules, Controversies and Solutions to Problems Arising in Warfare* (Edward Elgar 2019).
Socher J, *Russia and the Right to Self-Determination in the Post-Soviet Space* (OUP 2021).
Summers J, *Peoples and International Law* (2nd edn, Martinus Nijhoff Publishers 2014).
Sztucki J, *Jus Cogens and the Vienna Convention on the Law of Treaties: A Critical Appraisal* (Springer-Verlag 1974).
Tams CJ, *Enforcing Obligations Erga Omnes in International Law* (CUP 2010).
Talmon S, *La non-reconnaissance collective des états illégaux* (A Pedone 2007).
Villalpando SM, *L'émergence de la communauté internationale dans la responsabilité des etats* (PUF 2005).
Verhoeven J, *La reconnaissance international dans la pratique contemporaine* (Pedone 1975).
Wallace S, *The Application of the European Convention on Human Rights to Military Operations* (CUP 2019).
Wrange P, *Occupation/Annexation of a Territory: Respect for International Humanitarian and Human Rights and Consistent EU Policy* (European Union 2015).

Contributions to Collective Works

Ackermann T, 'Investments under Occupation: The Application of Investment Treaties to Occupied Territory' in KF Gómez, A Gourgourinis and C Titi (eds) *European Yearbook of International Economic Law* (Springer 2019).
Alexandrowicz C, 'The Quasi-Judicial Function in Recognition of States and Governments (1952)' in D Armitage and J Pitts, *The Law of Nations in Global History* (OUP 2017).
Alexandrowicz C, 'New and Original States: the Issue of Reversion to Sovereignty (1969)' in D Armitage and J Pitts, *The Law of Nations in Global History* (OUP 2017).
Arcari M, 'The UN SC, Unrecognised Subjects and the Obligation of Non-Recognition in International Law' in W Czapliński and A Kleczkowska (eds), *Unrecognised Subjects in International Law* (SCHOLAR Publishing House 2019).

Azarova V, 'An Illegal Territorial Regime? On the Occupation and Annexation of Crimea as a Matter of International Law' in S Sayapin and E Tsybulenko (eds), *The Use of Force Against Ukraine and International Law: Jus Ad Bellum, Jus in Bello, Just Post Bellum* (TMC Asser Press 2018).

Berkes A, 'Extraterritorial Responsibility of the Home States for MNCs Violations of Human Rights' in Y Radi (ed), *Research Handbook on Human Rights and Investment* (Edward Elgar 2018).

Bílková V, 'Territorial (Se)Cession in Light of Recent Events in Crimea' in E Milano, M Nicolini and F Palermo (eds), *Law, Territory and Conflict Resolution: Law as a Problem and Law as a Solution* (Brill Nijhoff 2016).

Bowring B, 'Transnistria' in C Walter, A Von Ungern-Sternberg and K Abushov (eds), *Self-determination and Secession in International Law* (OUP 2014).

Cannizzaro E, 'Higher Law for Treaties?' in E Cannizzaro (ed), *The Law of Treaties Beyond the Vienna Convention* (OUP 2011).

Cannizzaro E, 'On the Special Consequences of a Serious Breach of Obligations Arising Out of Peremptory Rules of International Law' in E Cannizzaro (ed), *The Present and Future of Jus Cogens* (Sapienza 2015).

Cassese A, 'Powers and Duties of an Occupant in Relation to Land and Natural Resources' in P Gaeta and Zappalà (eds), *The Human Dimension of International Law: Selected Papers* (OUP 2008).

Christakis T, 'The State as "Primary Fact": Some Thoughts on the Principle of Effectiveness' in MG Kohen (ed), *Secession: International Law Perspectives* (CUP 2006).

Christakis T, 'L'obligation de non-reconnaissance des situations créées par le recours illicite à la force ou d'autres actes enfreignant des règles fondamentales' in Tomuschat C and Thouvenin JM (eds), *The Fundamental Rules of the International Legal Order. Jus Cogens and Obligations Erga Omnes* (M Nijhoff Publishers 2006).

Christakis T and Constantinides A, 'Territorial Dispute in the Context of Secessionist Conflicts' in MG Kohen and M Hébié (eds), *Research Handbook on Territorial Disputes in International Law* (Edward Elgar 2018).

Corten O, 'Droit des peuples à disposer d'eux-mêmes et uti possidetis: deux faces d'une même médaille?' in O Corten, B Delcourt, P Klein and N Levrat (eds), *Démembrements d'États et délimitations territoriales: l'uti possidetis en question(s)* (Bruylant 1999).

Corten O, 'Are There Gaps?' in MG Kohen (ed), *Secession: International Law Perspectives* (CUP 2006).

Craven M, 'Statehood, Self-Determination, and Recognition' in MD Evans (ed), *International law* (4th edn, OUP 2014).

Crawford J and Keene A, 'The Structure of State Responsibility under the European Convention on Human Rights' in A Van Aaken and I Motoc (eds), *The European Convention on Human Rights and General International Law* (OUP 2018).

D'Aspremont J, 'The International Law of Statehood and Recognition: A Post-Colonial Invention' in T Garcia (ed), *La reconnaissance du status d'Etat à des entités contestées* (Pedone 2018).

Dawidowicz M, 'The Obligation of Non-Recognition of an Unlawful Situation' in J Crawford and others (eds), *The Law of International Responsibility* (OUP 2010).

Dawidowicz M, 'Trading Fish or Human Rights in Western Sahara? Self-Determination, Non-Recognition and the EC-Morocco Fisheries Agreement' in D French (ed), *Statehood and self-determination: reconciling tradition and modernity in international law* (CUP 2013).

Del Mar K, 'The Myth of Remedial Secession' in D French, *Statehood and Self-Determination: Reconciling Tradition and Modernity in International Law* (CUP 2013).

Dörr O and Randelzhofer A, 'Article 2(4)' in B Simma and others (eds), *The Charter of the United Nations: A Commentary*, Volume I (3rd edn, OUP 2012).

Dugard J, 'Collective Non -Recognition: The Failure of South Africa's Bantustan States' in J Dugard, *International Law: A South African perspective* (3rd edn, Juta 2004).

Fabry M, 'International Involvement in Secessionist Conflict: From the 16th Century to the Present' in A Pavaković and P Radan (eds), *The Ashgate Research Companion to Secession* (Routledge 2011).

Franck T, 'Postmodern Tribalism and the Right to Secession' in C Brölmann, R Lefeber and M Zieck (eds), *Peoples and Minorities in International Law* (Martinus Nijhoff Publishers 1993).

Frowein JA, 'De Facto Regime' in MPEPIL (online edn, OUP 2013).

Gaggioli G, 'Article 6' in G Distefano, G Gaggioli and A Hêche (eds), *La Convention de Vienne de 1978 sur la succession d'Etats en matière de traités: commentaire article par article et études thématiques* (Bruylant 2016).

Gaja G, 'Jus Cogens Beyond the Vienna Convention' (1969) 172 RCADI 271–316.

Gianelli A, 'Absolute Invalidity of Treaties and Their Recognition by Third States' in E Cannizzaro (ed), *The Law of Treaties Beyond the Vienna Convention* (OUP 2011).

Gowlland-Debbas V, 'Legal Significance of the Legitimizing Function of the United Nations: The Cases of Southern Rhodesia and Palestine' in *Le droit international au service de la paix, de la justice et du développement: mélanges Michel Virally* (Pedone 1991).

Green JA, 'The Caucasus Conflict and the Role of Law' in JA Green and CPM Waters (eds), *Conflict in the Caucasus: Implications for International Legal Order* (Palgrave Macmillan 2010).

Green JA, 'Passportisation, Peacekeepers and Proportionality: The Russian Claim of the Protection of Nationals Abroad in Self-Defence' in JA Green and CPM Waters (eds), *Conflict in the Caucasus: Implications for International Legal Order* (Palgrave Macmillan 2010).

Guggenheim P, 'La validité et la nullité des actes juridiques internationaux' (1949) 74 RCADI 191–268.

Ivanel B, 'Puppet States: A Growing Trend of Covert Occupation' in TD Gill (ed), *Yearbook of International Humanitarian Law Volume 18, 2015* (TMC Asser Press 2016).

Jasutis G, 'The Conflict in Eastern Ukraine (Donbass): Dire Consequences and Zero Reconciliation' in A Bellal (ed), *The War Report: Armed Conflicts in 2018* (Geneva Academy 2019).

Jennings RY, 'Nullity and Effectiveness in International Law' in *Cambridge Essays in International Law: Essays in Honour of Lord McNair* (Stevens and Sons 1965).

Jorgensen NHB, 'The Obligation of Cooperation' in Crawford J and others, *The Law of International Responsibility* (OUP 2010).

Jorgensen NHB, 'The Obligation of Non-Assistance to the Responsible State' in J Crawford and others, *The Law of International Responsibility* (OUP 2010).

Jorritsma R, 'Unravelling Attribution, Control and Jurisdiction: Some Reflections on the Case Law of the European Court of Human Rights' in H Ruiz Fabri (ed), *International Law and Litigation: A Look Into Procedure* (Nomos 2019).

Kalmo H, 'A Matter of Fact? The Many Faces of Sovereignty' in H Kalmo and Q Skinner (eds), *Sovereignty in Fragments: The Past, Present and Future of a Contested Concept* (CUP 2010).

Karagiannis S, 'The Territorial Application of Treaties' in Hollis DB (ed), *The Oxford Guide to Treaties* (OUP 2012).

Kassoti E and Duval A, 'Setting the Scene: The Legality of Economic Activities in Occupied Territories' in A Duval and E Kassoti (eds), *Legality of Economic Activities, Occupied Territories: International, EU Law and Business and Human Rights Perspectives* (Taylor & Francis Group, 2020).

Kelsen H, 'God and the State' in *Essays in Legal and Moral Philosophy* (D Reidel Publishing Company 1973).

Kelsen H, 'The Pure Theory of Law, "Labandism", and Neo-Kantianism. A Letter to Renato Treves' in SL Paulson (ed), *Normativity and Norms: Critical Perspectives on Kelsenian Themes* (OUP 1999).

Kohen MG, 'Le problème des frontières en cas de dissolution et de séparation d'États: quelles alternatives?' in O Corten, B Delcourt, P Klein and N Levrat (eds), *Démembrements d'États et délimitations territoriales: l'uti possidetis en question(s)* (Bruylant 1999).

Kohen MG, 'Création d'Etats en droit international contemporain' (2002) VI Cours euro-méditerranéens Bancaja de droit international.

Kohen MG, 'Introduction' in MG Kohen (ed), *Secession: International Law Perspectives* (CUP 2006).

Kohen MG, "Secession: a Legal Approach" in W Kälin and others (eds), *International Law, Conflict and Development: the Emergence of a Holistic Approach in International Affairs: Liber Amicorum for Joseph Voyame* (Martinus Nijhoff Publishers 2010).

Kolisnyk I, 'Ukrainian Courts in Dialogue on International Law' in A Wyrozumska (ed), *Transnational Judicial Dialogue on International Law in Central and Eastern Europe* (Lodz University Press 2017).

Korotkyi T and Hendel N, 'The Legal Status of the Donetsk and Luhansk "Peoples' Republics"' in Sayapin S and Tsybulenko E (eds), *The Use of Force Against Ukraine and International Law: Jus Ad Bellum, Jus in Bello, Jus Post Bellum.*

Koury S, 'The European Community and Member States' Duty of Non-Recognition under the EC-Morocco Association Agreement: State Responsibility and Customary International Law' in K Arts and P Leite Pinto (eds), *International Law and the Question of Western Sahara* (IPJET 2006).

Kyriacou N, 'The EU's Trade Relations with Northern Cyprus Obligations and Limits under Public International Law' in A Duval and E Kassoti (eds), *Legality of Economic Activities, Occupied Territories: International, EU Law and Business and Human Rights Perspectives* (Taylor & Francis Group, 2020).

Lagerwall A, 'Is the Duty Not to Recognise 'States' Created Unlawfully Challenged by States' Practice and ECHR Case Law?' in W Czapliński and A Kleczkowska (eds), *Unrecognised Subjects in International Law* (SCHOLAR Publishing House 2019).

Leach P, 'South Ossetia' in E Wilmshurst (ed), *International Law and the Classification of Conflicts* (1st edn, OUP; The Royal Institute of International Affairs (Chatham House) 2012).

Mann FA, 'The Doctrine of Jus Cogens in International Law' in A *Further Studies in International Law* (Clarendon Press 2008).

Marek K, Contribution à l'étude du *jus cogens* en droit international' in *Receuil d'études de droit international en hommage à Paul Guggenheim* (Imprimerie de la Tribune de Genève 1968).

Miklasová J, 'Post-Soviet Secession: Crimea and Eastern Ukraine Under International Law' in K Gray (ed) *Global Encyclopedia of Territorial Rights* (Springer 2022).

Miklasová J, 'Status of Transnistria Under International Law' in K Gray (ed) *Global Encyclopedia of Territorial Rights* (Springer 2022).

Miklasová J, 'Dissolution of the Soviet Union Thirty Years On: Re-Appraisal of the Relevance of the Principle of Uti Possidetis Iuris' in JE Viñuales, A Clapham, L Boisson de Chazournes and M Hébié (eds), *The International Legal Order in the XXIst Century / L'ordre juridique international au XXIeme siècle / El órden jurídico internacional en el siglo XXI: Essays in Honour of Professor Marcelo Gustavo Kohen / Ecrits en l'honneur du Professeur Marcelo Gustavo Kohen / Estudios en honor del Profesor Marcelo Gustavo Kohen* (Brill 2023).

Milano E, 'Declarations of Independence and Territorial Integrity in General International Law: Some Reflections in Light of the Court's Advisory Opinion' in M Arcari and L Balmond (eds), *Questions de droit international autour de l'avis consultatif de la Cour internationale de Justice sur le Kosovo* (Giuffrè 2011).

Milano E and Zugliani N, 'Meaning(s) of Illegality in Secession Processes' in J Vidmar, S McGibbon and L Raible (eds), *Research Handbook on Secession* (Edward Elgar 2022).

Milanović M, 'The Spatial Dimension: Treaties and Territory' in CJ Tams and AE Richford (eds), *Research Handbook on the Law of Treaties* (E Elgar 2014).

Milanović M, 'Arguing the *Kosovo* Case' in M Milanović and M Wood, *The Law and Politics of the Kosovo Advisory Opinion* (OUP 2015).

Milanović M, 'Jurisdiction and Responsibility: Trends in the Jurisprudence of the Strasbourg Court' in A Van Aaken and I Motoc (eds), *The European Convention on Human Rights and General International Law* (OUP 2018).

Mirzayev F, 'Abkhazia' in C Walter, A Von Ungern-Sternberg and K Abushov (eds), *Self-determination and Secession in International Law* (OUP 2014).

Murswiek D, 'The Issue of a Right of Secession – Reconsidered' in C Tomuschat (ed), *Modern Law of Self-Determination* (Martinus Nijhoff Publishers 1993).

Nesterovych VF, 'Rule of Law and Provision of Human Rights in the Temporary Occupied Territories of Ukraine' in *Procedings. Volume 200, Law /National University of Kyiv-Mohyla Academy* (Naukma 2017) (*in Ukrainian*).

Nolte G and Randelzhofer A, 'Article 51' in B Simma and others (eds), *The Charter of the United Nations: A Commentary*, Volume II (3rd edn, OUP 2012).

Nussberger A, 'Abkhazia' in MPEPIL (online edn, OUP 2013).

Nussberger A, 'South Ossetia' in MPEPIL (online edn, OUP 2013).

Oeter S, '*De facto* Regimes in International Law' in W Czapliński and A Kleczkowska (eds), *Unrecognised Subjects in International Law* (SCHOLAR Publishing House 2019).

Orakhelashvili A, 'The Dynamics of Statehood in the Practice of International and English Courts,' in C Chinkin and F Baetens (eds), *Sovereignty, Statehood and State Responsibility: Essays in Honour of James Crawford* (CUP 2015).

Pertile M, 'Self-Determination Reduced to Silence: Some Critical Remarks on the ICJ's Advisory Opinion on Kosovo' in M Arcari and L Balmond (eds), *Questions de droit international autour de l'avis consultatif de la Cour internationale de Justice sur le Kosovo* (Giuffrè 2011).

Peters A, 'The Principle of Uti Possidetis Juris: How Relevant Is It for Issues of Secession?' in C Walter, A Von Ungern-Sternberg and K Abushov (eds), *Self-determination and Secession in International Law* (OUP 2014).

Peters A, 'The Crimean Vote of March 2014 as an Abuse of the Institution of the Territorial Referendum' in C Callies (ed), *Staat und Mensch im Kontext des Völker- und Europarechts: Liber Amicorum für Torsten Stein* (Nomos Verlag 2015).

Popjanevski J, 'International Law and the Nagorno-Karabakh Conflict' in SE Cornell (ed) *The International Politics of the Armenian-Azerbaijani Conflict: The Original 'Frozen Conflict' and European Security* (palgrave macmillan 2017).

Randelzhorfer A and Dörr O, 'Article 2(4)' in B Simma and others (eds), *The Charter of the United Nations: A Commentary* (OUP 2012).

Rees-Evans L, 'Litigating the Use of Force: Reflections on the Interaction between Investor-State Dispute Settlement and Other Forms of International Dispute Settlement in the Context of the Conflict in Ukraine' in KF Gómez, A Gourgourinis and C Titi (eds) *European Yearbook of International Economic Law* (Springer 2019).

Richter D, 'Illegal States?' in W Czapliński and A Kleczkowska (eds), *Unrecognised Subjects in International Law* (SCHOLAR Publishing House 2019).

Ronen Y, 'The Dispossessed and the Distressed: Conflicts in Land-Related Rights in Transitions from Unlawful Territorial Regimes' in E Brems (ed), *Conflicts between Fundamental Rights* (Intersentia 2008).

Sassòli M, '*Ius ad Bellum* and *Ius in Bello* – The Separation between the Legality of the Use of Force and Humanitarian Rules to Be Respected in Warfare: Crucial or Outdated?' in M Schmitt and J Pejic (eds), *International Law and Armed Conflict: Exploring the Faultlines: Essays in Honour of Yoram Dinstein* (Martinus Nijhoff Publishers 2007).

Schmalenbach K, 'Article 53: Treaties Conflicting with a Peremptory Norm of General International Law ("Jus Cogens")' in Dörr O and K Schmalenbach (eds), *Vienna Convention on the Law of Treaties: A Commentary* (Springer 2012).

Summers J, 'Russia and Competing Spheres of Influence: The Case of Georgia, Abkhazia and South Ossetia' in Happold M, *International Law in a Multipolar World* (Routledge 2012).

Suy E, 'The Concept of *Jus Cogens* in Public International Law' in *The Concept of Jus Cogens in International Law, Papers and Proceedings: Conference on International Law, Lagonissi, Greece, 3–8 April 1966* (Carnegie Endowment for International Peace 1967).

Suy E, 'Article 53' in O Corten and P Klein, *The Vienna Conventions on the Law of Treaties: A Commentary* (OUP 2011).

Talmon S, 'The Duty Not "To Recognize as Lawful" a Situation Created by the Illegal Use of Force or Other Serious Breaches of a Jus Cogens Obligation: An Obligation without Real Substance?' in C Tomuschat and JM Thouvenin (eds), *The Fundamental Rules of the International Legal Order. Jus Cogens and Obligations Erga Omnes* (M Nijjhof Publishers 2006).

Tancredi A, 'A Normative "Due Process" in the Creation of States through Secession' in MG Kohen (ed), *Secession: International Law Perspectives* (CUP 2006).

Tancredi A, 'Some Remarks on the Relationship between Secession and General International Law in the Light of the ICJ's Kosovo Advisory Opinion' in P Hilpold, *Kosovo and International Law: The ICJ Advisory Opinion of 22 July 2010* (Brill 2012).

Tancredi A, 'Secession and Use of Force' in C Walter, A Von Ungern-Sternberg and K Abushov (eds), *Self-determination and Secession in International Law* (OUP 2014).

Tancredi A, 'In Search of a Fair Balance between the Inviolability of Borders, Self-Determination and Secession' in E Milano, M Nicolini and F Palermo (eds), *Law, Territory and Conflict Resolution: Law as a Problem and Law as a Solution* (Brill Nijhoff 2016).

Tomuschat C, 'Secession and Self-Determination' in MG Kohen (ed), *Secession: International Law Perspectives* (CUP 2006).

Tucker R, 'The Principle of Effectiveness in International Law' in GA Lipsky (ed), *Law and Politics in the World Community: Essays on Hans Kelsen's Pure Theory and Related Problems in International law*, (University of California Press 1953).

Van der Loo G, 'Law and Practice of the EU's Trade Agreements with "Disputed" Territories: A Consistent Approach?' in I Govaere and S Garben (eds), *The Interface Between EU and International Law: Contemporary Reflections* (Bloomsbury 2019).

Vidmar J, 'Norm Conflicts and Hierarchy in International Law: Towards a Vertical International Legal System?' in J Vidmar and E De Wet (eds), *Hierarchy in International Law: The Place of Human Rights* (OUP 2012).

Vidmar J, 'Unilateral Declarations of Independence in International Law' in D French (ed), *Statehood and Self-determination: Reconciling Tradition and Modernity in International Law* (CUP 2013).

Vidmar J, 'International Organizations and Non-State Territorial Entities' in BC Harzl and R Petrov (eds), *Unrecognized Entities: Perspectives in International, European and Constitutional Law* (Brill 2022).

Vidmar J, McGibbon S and Raible L, Introduction to the Research Handbook on Secession' in J Vidmar, S McGibbon and L Raible (eds), *Research Handbook on Secession* (Edward Elgar 2022).

Von Der Decken K, 'Article 29: Territorial Scope of Treaties' in O Dörr and K Schmalenbach (eds), *Vienna Convention on the Law of Treaties* (2nd edn, Springer 2018).

Walter C, 'Post-Cript: Self-Determination, Secession, and the Crimean Crisis 2014' in C Walter, A Von Ungern-Sternberg and K Abushov (eds), *Self-determination and Secession in International Law* (OUP 2014).

Waters C, 'South Ossetia' in C Walter, A Von Ungern-Sternberg and K Abushov (eds), *Self-determination and Secession in International Law* (OUP 2014).

Wuschka S, 'Investment Claims and Annexation of Territory' in M Akbaba and G Capurro (eds), *International Challenges in Investment Arbitration* (Routledge 2018).

Yarmish O and Cherviatsova A, 'Transferring Crimea from Russia to Ukraine: Historical and Legal Analysis of Soviet Legislation' in E Milano, M Nicolini and F Palermo (eds), *Law, Territory and Conflict Resolution: Law as a Problem and Law as a Solution* (Brill Nijhoff 2016).

Yudkivska G, 'Territorial Jurisdiction and Positive Obligations of an Occupied State: Some Reflections on Evolving Issues under Article 1 of the Convention' in A Van Aaken and I Motoc (eds), *The European Convention on Human Rights and General International Law* (Oxford University Press 2018).

Zareba S, 'Responsibility for the Acts of Unrecognised States and Regimes' in W Czapliński and A Kleczkowska (eds), *Unrecognised Subjects in International Law* (SCHOLAR Publishing House 2019).

Zemanek K, 'The Metamorphosis of Jus Cogens: From an Institution of Treaty Law to the Bedrock of the International Legal Order?' in E Cannizzaro (ed), *Law of Treaties Beyond the Vienna Convention* (OUP 2011).

Journal Articles

Ackermann T and Wuschka S, 'The Applicability of Investment Treaties in the Context of Russia's Aggression against Ukraine' (2023) 38 ICSID Review 453.

Akande D and Tzanakopoulos A, 'Legal: Use of Force in Self-Defefence to Recover Occupied Territory' (2021) 32 EJIL 1299.

Alexandrowicz CH, 'Theory of Recognition *In Fieri*' (1958) 34 BYBIL 176–198.

Anderson G, 'Secession in International Law and Relations: What Are We Talking About?' (2013) 35 Loyola of Los Angeles International and Comparative Law Review 343–388.

Anderson G, 'Unilateral Non-Colonial Secession in International Law and Declaratory General Assembly Resolutions: Textual Content and Legal Effects (2013) 41 Denver Journal of International Law and Policy 345–395.

Anderson G, 'Unilateral Non-Colonial Secession and the Criteria for Statehood in International Law' (2015) 41 Brooklyn Journal of International Law 1–98.

Antnonowicz L, 'The Disintegration of the USSR from the Point of View of International Law' (1991–1992) 19 Polish Yearbook of International Law 7–16.

Armstrong JA, 'Federalism in the USSR: Ethnic and Territorial Aspects' (1977) 7 Federalism and Ethnicity 89–105.

Athanassiou P, 'The Orams Case, the Judgments Regulation and Public Policy: An English and European Law Perspective' (2009) 16 Maastricht Journal of European and Comparative Law 423–448.

Athanassiou P, 'The Status of the "TRNC" through the Prism of Recent Legal Developments: Towards Furtive Recognition?' (2010) 22 The Cyprus Review 15–38.

Azarova V, 'Towards a Counter-Hegemonic Law of Occupation: On the Regulation of Predatory Interstate Acts in Contemporary International Law' (2017) 20 Yearbook of International Humanitarian Law 113–160.

Azarova V, 'Business and Human Rights in Occupied Territory: The UN Database of Business Active in Israel's Settlements' (2018) 3 Business and Human Rights Journal 187–209.

Azarova V, 'The Secret Life of Non-Recognition: EU-Israel Relations and the Obligation of Non-Recognition in International Law' (2018) 4 Global Affairs 23–37.

Beck A, 'A South African Homeland Appears in the English Courts: Legitimation of the Illegitimate?' (1987) 36 ICLQ 350.

Ben-Naftali O, Gross AM and Michaeli K, 'Illegal Occupation: Framing the Occupied Palestinian Territory' (2005) 23 Berkeley Journal of International Law 551–614.

Benvenisti E, 'Occupation and Territorial Administration' (2015) Global Trust Working Paper 11/2015, 1 <http://globaltrust.tau.ac.il/wps-2015-11-occupation-and-territorial-administration-2/> accessed 15 March 2020.

Berkes A, 'The Nagorno-Karabakh Conflict Before the European Court of Human Rights: Pending Cases and Certain Forecasts on Jurisdiction and State Responsibility' (2013) 52 Military Law and the Law of War Review 379–438.

Besson S, 'The Extraterritoriality of the European Convention on Human Rights: Why Human Rights Depend on Jurisdiction and What Jurisdiction Amounts To' (2012) 25 Leiden Journal of International Law 857–884.

Bílková V, 'The Use of Force by the Russian Federation in Crimea' (2015) 75 ZaöRV 27–50.

Borgen CJ, 'Law, Rhetoric, Strategy: Russia and Self-Determination before and after Crimea' (2015) 91 International Law Studies US Naval War College 216–280.

Borgen CJ, 'Thawing a Frozen Conflict: Legal Aspects of the Separatist Crisis in Moldova: A Report from the Association of the Bar of the City of New York' (*Legal Paper Research Paper Series No 06-0045*, 2006) 1–98.

Bothe M, 'The Current Status of Crimea: Russian Territory, Occupied Territory or What' (2014) 53 Military Law and Law of War Review 99–116.

Bowring B, 'The Unexpected After-Life of the 'Soviet People'? The 'Pridnestraovskaya Moldavskaya Republika' as Political Fact and Legal Anomaly A Case Study' (2012) <https://papers.ssrn.com/sol3/papers.cfm?abstract_id=1981954&download=ye> accessed 12 June 2019.

Burke JJA and Panina-Burke S, 'Eastern and Southern Ukraine's Right to Secede and Join the Russian Federation' (2015) 3 Russian Law Journal 33–57.

Buxbaum HL, 'Territory, Territoriality, and the Resolution of Jurisdictional Conflict' (2009) 57 American Journal of Comparative Law 631–675.

Buyse A, 'Legal Minefield-The Territorial Scope of the European Convention' (2008) 1 Inter-American and European Human Rights Journal 269–296.

Carron D, 'When Is a Conflict International? Time for New Control Tests in IHL' (2016) 98 International Review of the Red Cross 1019–1041.

Cassese A, 'The Nicaragua and Tadić Tests Revisited in Light of the ICJ Judgment on Genocide in Bosnia' (2007) 18 European Journal of International Law 649–668.

Cavandoli S, 'The Unresolved Dilemma of Self-Determination: Crimea, Donetsk and Luhansk' (2016) 20 The International Journal of Human Rights 875–892.

Chatzipanagiotis MP, 'Establishing Direct International Flights to and from Northern Cyprus' (2011) 60 ZLW 476–486.

Christakis T, 'Self-Determination, Territorial Integrity and *Fait Accompli* in the Case of Crimea' (2015) 75 ZaöRV 75–100.

Clark M, 'A Conceptual History of Recognition in British International Legal Thought' (2018) BYIL 18–97.

Cohen R, 'The Concept of Statehood in United Nations Practice' (1961) 109 University of Pennsylvania Law Review 1127–1171.

Corell H, 'The Legality of Exploring and Exploiting Natural Resources in Western Sahara' in (2008) Western Sahara Conference Proceedings 231–247.

Corten O, 'A propos d'un désormais «classique»: Le droit à l'autodétermination en dehors des situations de décolonisation, de Théodore Christakis' (1999) 1 RBDI 1 (1999) 329–349.

Corten O, 'Territorial Integrity Narrowly Interpreted: Reasserting the Classical Inter-State Paradigm of International Law' (2011) 24 Leiden Journal of International Law 87–94.

Costelloe D, 'Treaty Succession in Annexed Territory' (2016) 65 International & Comparative Law Quarterly 343–378.

Corten O, 'The Russian Intervention in the Ukrainian Crisis: Was *Jus Contra Bellum* "Confirmed Rather than Weakened"?' (2015) 2 Journal on the Use of Force and International Law 17–41.

Crawford J, 'The Criteria for Statehood in International Law' (1977) 48 BYBIL 93–182.

Crawford J, 'State Practice and International Law in Relation to Secession' (1999) 69 BYBIL 85–117.

Cullen A and Wheatley S, 'The Human Rights of Individuals in De Facto Regimes under the European Convention on Human Rights' (2013) 13 Human Rights Law Review 691–728.

D'Aspremont J, 'The International Law of Statehood: Craftmanship for the Elucidation and Regulation of Births and Deaths in the International Society' (2013) 29 Connecticut Journal of International Law 201–224.

Danilenko GM, 'The New Russian Constitution and International Law' (1994) 88 American Journal of International Law 451–470.

Davies M, 'Kuwait Airways Corp v Iraqi Airways Co: The Effect in Private International Law of a Breach of Public International Law by a State Actor' (2001) 2 Melbourne Journal of International Law 523–534.

De Hoon M, 'Collateral Damage From Criminalizing Aggression – Lawfare Through Aggression Accusations in the Nagorno-Karabakh Conflict' (2012) 5 European Journal of Legal Studies 35–59.

De Vries RF, 'EU Judicial Review of Trade Agreements Invovling Disputed Territories: Lessons from the Front Polisario Judgments' (2018) 24 Columbia Journal of European Law 497–524.

Devine DJ, 'The Requirements of Statehood Re-Examined' (1971) 34 Modern Law Review 410–417.

Dickinson ED, 'The Analogy Between Natural Persons and International Persons in the Law of Nations' (1917) 26 Yale Law Journal 564–591.

Douhan AF, 'International Organizations and Settlement of the Conflict in Ukraine' 75 (2015) ZaöRV 195–214.

Draganova D, 'Chechnya's Right of Secession under Russian Constitutional Law' (2004) 3 Chinese Journal of International Law 571–590.

Dumberry P, 'Requiem for Crimea: Why Tribunals Should Have Declined Jurisdiction over the Claims of Ukrainian Investors against Russian under the Ukraine–Russia BIT' (2018) 9 Journal of International Dispute Settlement 506–533.

Eggers AK, 'When is a State a State? The Case for Recognition of Somaliland' (2007) 30 Boston College International and Comparative Law Review 211–222.

Emiliou N, 'Cypriot Import Certificates; Some Hot Potatoes' (1995) 20 European Law Review 202–210.

Escudero Espinosa JF, 'The Principle of Non-Recognition of States Arising from Serious Breaches of Peremptory Norms of International Law' (2022) 21 Chinese JIL 79.

Fabry M, 'The Contemporary Practice of State Recognition: Kosovo, South Ossetia, Abkhazia, and their Aftermath' (2012) 40 Nationalities Papers 661–676.

Fabry M, 'The Right to Self-Determination as a Claim to Independence in International Practice' (2015) 14 Ethnopolitics 498–505.

Fawcett JE, 'Security Council Resolutions on Rhodesia' (1965) 41 BYBIL 103–121.

Fawcett JE, 'Note in Reply to Devine' (1971) 34 Modern Law Review 417–417.

Ferraro T, 'Determining the Beginning and End of an Occupation under International Humanitarian Law' (2012) 94 International Review of the Red Cross 133–163.

Ferraro T, 'The ICRC's Legal Position on the Notion of Armed Conflict Involving Foreign Intervention and on Determining the IHL Applicable to This Type of Conflict' (2015) 97 International Review of the Red Cross 1227–1252.

Forestier-Peyrat E and Dullin S, 'Flexible Sovereignties of the Revolutionary State: Soviet Republics Enter World Politics' 19 (2017) Journal of the History of International Law 178–199.

Franklin M, 'Sovereignty and the Chicago Convention: English Court of Appeal Rules on the Northern Cyprus Question' (2011) 36 Air and Space Law 109.

Frowein J, 'Transfer or Recognition of Sovereignty – Some Early Problems in Connection with Dependent Territories' (1971) 65 AJIL 568–671.

Gaeta P, 'The Armed Conflict in Chechnya before the Russian Constitutional Court' (1996) 7 European Journal of International Law 563–570.

Gal T, 'Unexplored Outcomes of Tadić: Applicability of the Law of Occupation to War by Proxy' (2014) 12 Journal of International Criminal Justice 59–80.

Geifs R, 'Russia's Annexation of Crimea: The Mills of International Law Grind Slowly But They Do Grind' (2015) 91 International Law Studies Series. US Naval War College 425–449.

Giladi R, 'The *Jus Ad Bellum/Jus In Bello* Distinction and the Law of Occupation' (2008) 41 Israel Law Review 246–301.

Gilder A, 'Bringing Occupation into the 21st Century: The Effective Implementation of Occupation by Proxy' (2017) 13 Utrecht Law Review 60–81.

Grant TD, 'Defining Statehood: The Montevideo Convention and Its Discontents' (1998) 37 Columbia Journal of Transnational Law 403–457.

Grant TD, 'The Budapest Memorandum of 5 December 1994: Political Engagement or Legal Obligation' (2014) 34 Polish Yearbook of International Law 89–114.

Grant TD, 'Frozen Conflicts and International Law' (2017) 50 Cornell International Law Journal 361–413.

Green JA, 'The Annexation of Crimea: Russia, Passportisation and the Protection of Nationals Revisited' (2014) 1 Journal on the Use of Force and International Law 3–10.

Green JA, Henderson C and Ruys T, 'Russia's Attack on Ukraine and the Jus Ad Bellum' (2022) 9 Journal on the Use of Force and International Law 4–30.

Greenwood C and Lowe V, 'Unrecognised States and European Court' (1995) 54 Cambridge Law Journal 4–6.

Grzybowski J, 'Ontological Predicament of State Creation in International Law' (2017) 28 EJIL 409–432.

Happ R and Wuschka S, 'Horror Vacui: Or Why Investment Treaties Should Apply to Illegally Annexed Territories' (2016) 33 Journal of International Arbitration 245–268.

Harpaz G, 'The Dispute Over the Treatment of Products Exported to the European Union from the Golan Heights, East Jerusalem, the West Bank and the Gaza Strip – The Limits of Power and the Limits of the Law' (2004) 38 Journal of World Trade 1049–1058.

Harpaz G and Rubinson E, 'The Interface between Trade, Law and Politics and the Erosion of Normative Power Europe: Comment on Brita' (2010) 35 European Law Review 551–570.

Heinsch R, 'Conflict Classification in Ukraine: The Return of the "Proxy War"?' (2015) 91 International Law Studies 323–360.

Henderson C and Green JA, 'The Ius Ad Bellum and Entities Short of Statehood in the Report on the Conflict in Georgia' (2010) 59 ICLQ 129–139.

Hillgruber C, 'The Admission of New States to the International Community' 9 (1998) EJIL 491–509.

Hilpold P, 'Ukraine, Crimea and New International Law: Balancing International Law with Arguments Drawn from History' (2015) 14 Chinese Journal of International Law 237–270.

Hirsch M, 'Rules of Origin as Trade or Foreign Policy Instruments-The European Union Policy on Products Manufactured in the Settlements in the West Bank and the Gaza Strip' (2002) 26 Fordham International Law Journal 572–594.

Ijalaye DA, 'Was "Biafra" at Any Time a State in International Law?' (1971) 65 American Journal of International Law 551–559.

Jorritsma R, 'Where General International Law Meets International Humanitarian Law: Attribution of Conduct and the Classification of Armed Conflicts' (2018) 23 Journal of Conflict and Security Law 405–431.

Kassoti E, 'The Sound of One Hand Clapping: Unilateral Declarations of Independence in International Law' (2016) 17 German Law Journal 215–236.

Kassoti E, 'The ECJ and the Art of Treaty Interpretation: Western Sahara Campaign UK' (2019) Common Market Law Review 209–236.

Kassoti E, 'The EU's Duty of Non-Recognition and the Territorial Scope of Trade Agreements Covering Unlawfully Acquired Territories' (2019) Europe and the World: A Law Review 1–18.

Kassoti E, 'The Empire Strikes Back: The Council Decision Amending Protocols 1 and 4 to the EU-Morocco Association Agreement' (2019) 4 European Papers Insight 307–317.

Kassoti E, 'The EU's Duty of Non-Recognition and the Territorial Scope of Trade Agreements Covering Unlawfully Acquired Territories' (2019) Europe and the World: A Law Review 1–18.

Kassoti E, 'Doing Business Right? Private Actors and the International Legality of Economic Activities in Occupied Territories' (2016) 7 Cambridge International Law Journal 301–326.

Katselli Proukaki E, 'The Right of Displaced Persons to Property and to Return Home after Demopoulos' (2014) 14 Human Rights Law Review 701–732.

Kawasaki K, 'A Brief Note on the Legal Effects of Jus Cogens in International Law' (2006) 34 Hitotsubashi Journal of Law and Politics 23–43.

Kelsen H, 'La naissace de l'État et la formation de sa nationalité: les principes; leur application au cas de la Tchécoslovaquie' (1929) 4 Revue de droit international 613–641.

Kelsen H, 'Recognition in International Law: Theoretical Observations' AJIL 35 (1941) 605–617.

Kelsen H, 'The Law as a Specific Social Technique' (1941) 9 The University of Chicago Law Review 75–97.

Kohen MG, 'Le problème des frontières en cas de dissolution et de séparation d'États: quelles alternatives?' (1998) 1 Revue belge de droit international 129–160.

Kohen MG and Del Mar K, 'The Kosovo Advisory Opinion and UNSCR 1244 (1999): A Declaration of "Independence from International Law"?' (2011) 24 Leiden Journal of International Law 109–126.

Kontorovich E, Economic Dealings with Occupied Territories' (2014) 53 Columbia Journal of Transnational Law 584–637.

Koutrakos P, 'Legal Issues of EC-Trade Relations' in (2003) 52 International and Comparative Law Quarterly 489–498.

Kuibida R, Moroz L, Smaliuk R, 'Justice in the East of Ukraine During the Ongoing Armed Conflict' (2020) 11 International Journal for Court Administration 9.

Lanovoy V, 'Self-determination in International Law. A Democratic Phenomenon or an Abuse of Right?' (2015) 4 Cambridge Journal of International and Comparative Law 388–404.

Larsen KM, '"Territorial Non-Application" of the European Convention on Human Rights' (2009) 78 Nordic Journal of International Law 73–93.

Leslie RD, 'Unrecognised Governments in the Conflict of Laws: Lord Denning's Contribution' (1981) 14 Comparative and International Law Journal of Southern Africa 165–178.

Lott A, 'The Tagliavini Report Revisited: Jus Ad Bellum and the Legality of the Russian Intervention in Georgia' (2012) 28 Utrecht Journal of International and European Law 4–21.

Loucaides LG, 'Is the European Court of Human Rights Still a Principled Court of Human Rights After the *Demopoulos* Case?' (2011) 24 Leiden Journal of International Law 435–465.

Mälksoo L, 'The Soviet Approach to the Right of Peoples to Self-Determination: Russia's Farewell to Jus Publicum Europaeum' (2017) 19 Journal of the History of International Law 200–218.

Mann FA, 'The Judicial Recognition of an Unrecognised State' (1987) 36 International & Comparative Law Quarterly 348–350.

Martsenko N, 'Peculiarities of Recognition of Judgments and other Acts Issued by Unrecognized Authorities – The Example of the Autonomous Republic of Crimea, and Luhansk and Donetsk Oblasts ("LPR" and "DPR")' 65 (2019) OER Osteuropa Recht 223–237.

Marxsen C, 'The Crimea Crisis: An International Law Perspective' (2014) 74 ZaöRV 367–391.

McCorquodale R, 'Self-Determination: A Human Rights Approach' (1994) 43 International and Comparative Law Quarterly 857–885.

McCorquoadale R and Hausler K, 'The Application of the Right of Self-Determination' in Green JA and Waters CPM (eds), *Conflict in the Caucasus: Implications for International Legal Order* (Palgrave Macmillan 2010).

McDougal MS and Reisman WM, 'Rhodesia and the United Nations: The Lawfulness of International Concern' (1968) 62 American Journal of International Law 1–19.

Miklasová J, 'Post-Ceasefire Nagorno-Karabakh: Limits to the ECtHR's Approach to Jurisdiction over Secessionist Entities under the ECHR' (2022) 82 ZaöRV 357–378.

Miklasová J, 'Russian Approaches to Post-Soviet Secessions: Bad Faith Argumentation and Its Limits' Baltic Yearbook of International Law (forthcoming 2024).

Milano E, 'The New Fisheries Partnership Agreement Between the European Community and the Kingdom of Morocco: Fishing Too South?' (2006) 22 *Anuario español de derecho internacional* 413–457.

Milanović M, 'State Responsibility for Genocide' (2006) 17 European Journal of International Law 553–604.

Milanović M, 'State Responsibility for Acts of Non-State Actors: A Comment on Griebel and Plücken' (2009) 22 Leiden Journal of International Law 307–324.

Milanović M, 'Special Rules on Attribution of Conduct in International Law' (2020) 96 Int'L Stud 295.

Milanović M and Papić T, 'The Applicability of the ECHR in Contested Territories' (2018) 67 ICLQ 779–800.

Miles C, 'Lawfare in Crimea: Treaty, Territory, and Investor-State Dispute Settlement' (2022) 38 Arbitration International 135.

Moerenhout T, 'The Obligation to Withhold from Trading in Order Not to Recognize and Assist Settlements and Their Economic Activity in Occupied Territories' (2012) 3 Journal of International Humanitarian Legal Studies 344–385.

Natoli K, 'Weaponizing Nationality: An Analysis of Russia's Passport Policy in Georgia' (2010) 28 Boston University International Law Journal 389–417.

Nedjati ZM, 'Acts of Unrecognised Governments' (1981) 30 International & Comparative Law Quarterly 388–415.

Nesi G, 'L'uti possidetis hors du contexte de la décolonisation: le cas de l'Europe' (1998) 44 AFDI 1–23.

Nussberger A, 'The War between Russia and Georgia – Consequences and Unresolved Questions' (2009) 1 GoJIL 341–364.

O'Keefe R, 'English Public Policy Internationalised-And Conversion Clarified Too' (2002) 61 Cambridge Law Journal 499–504.

O'Keefe R, 'Decisions of British Courts During 2010 Involving Questions of Public or Private International Law' (2011) 81 BYBIL 339–410.

O'Reilly K and Higgins N, 'The Use of Force, Wars of National Liberation and the Right to Self-Determination in the South Ossetian Conflict' (2009) 9 International Criminal Law Review 567–583.

Odermatt J, 'Council of the European Union v Front Populaire de la Libération de la Saguia-El-Hamra et du Rio de Oro (Front Polisario). Case C-104/16P' (2017) 111 American Journal of International Law 731–738.

Odermatt J, 'International Law as Challenge to EU Acts: Front Polisario II' (2023) 60 Common Market Law Review 217.

Orakhelashvili A, 'The European Convention on Human Rights and International Public Order' (2003) 5 Cambridge Yearbook of European Legal Studies 237.

Orakhelashvili A, 'Overlap and Convergence: The Interaction Between *Jus Ad Bellum* and *Jus in Bello*' 12 (2007) Journal of Conflict and Security Law 157–196.

Paulus AL, 'Jus Cogens in a Time of Hegemony and Fragmentation' 74 (2005) Nordic Journal of International Law 297–334.

Pert A, 'The "Duty" of Non-Recognition in Contemporary International Law: Issues and Uncertainties' (2012) 30 Chinese (Taiwan) Yearbook of International Law and Affairs 48–71.

Peters A, 'Statehood after 1989: "Effectivités" between Legality and Virtuality' (2010) 3 Proceedings of the European Society of International Law 171–183.

Peters A, 'Does Kosovo Lie in the Lotus-Land of Freedom?' (2011) 24 Leiden Journal of International Law 95–108.

Petro NN, 'Legal Case for Russian Intervention in Georgia' (2008) 32 Fordham International Law Journal 1524–1549.

Pippan C, 'The International Court of Justice's Advisory Opinion on Kosovo's Declaration of Independence: An Exercise in the Art of Silence' (2010) 3–4 European Journal of Minority Studies 145–166.

Pronto A, 'The Effect of War on Law – What Happens to Their Treaties When States Go to War?' (2013) 2 Cambridge Journal of International and Comparative Law 227–241.

Qerimi Q, 'What the Kosovo Advisory Opinion Means for the Rest of the World' (2011) ASIL Proceedings 259–274.

Rabinovych M, 'The Interplay between Ukraine's Domestic Legislation on Conflict and Uncontrolled Territories and its Strategic Use of "Lawfare" before Russia's 2022 Invasion of Ukraine – A Troubled Nexus?' (2022) 47 Review of Central and East European Law 268.

Raible R, 'Title to Territory and Jurisdiction in International Human Rights Law: Three Models for a Fraught Relationship' (2018) 31 Leiden Journal of International Law 315–334.

Ratner S, 'Drawing a Better Line: Uti Possidetis and the Borders of New States' (1996) 90 AJIL 590–624.

Reeves SR and Wallace D, 'The Combatant Status of the "Little Green Men" and Other Participants' (2015) 91 International Law Studies 361–401.

Ronen Y, 'Non-Recognition, Jurisdiction and the TRNC before the European Court of Human Rights' (2003) 62 Cambridge Law Journal 534–537.

Ronen Y, 'Recognition of Divorce without Recognition of Statehood' (2004) 63 Cambridge Law Journal 268–271.

Ronen Y, 'Illegal Occupation and Its Consequences' (2008) 41 Israel Law Review 201–245.

Ronen Y, 'Status of Settlers Implanted by Illegal Territorial Regimes' (2009) 79 British Yearbook of International Law 194–263.

Ronen Y, 'Responsibility of Businesses Involved in the Israeli Settlements in the West Bank' (Research paper No 02-15 2015) <https://papers.ssrn.com/sol3/papers.cfm?abstract_id=2594851> accessed 23 January 2020.

Rooney JM, 'The Relationship between Jurisdiction and Attribution after Jaloud v. Netherlands' (2015) 62 Netherlands International Law Review 407–428.

Roth BR, 'The Entity That Dare Not Speak Its Name: Unrecognized Taiwan as a Right-Bearer in the International Legal Order' (2009) 4 East-Asia Review 91–124.

Roth BR, 'Secessions, Coups and the International Rule of Law: Assessing the Decline of the Effective Control Doctrine' (2010) 11 Melbourne Journal of International Law 393–440.

Roth BR, 'The Virtues of Bright Lines: Self-Determination, Secession, and External Intervention' (2015) 16 German LJ 384–415.

Rosati CR, 'Some Puzzles about the Objectivity of Law' (2004) 23 Law and Philosophy 273–323.

Rozakis C, 'The Law on Invalidity of Treaties' (1974) 16 Archiv des Völkerrechts 150–193.

Ruys T and Rodríguez Silvestre F, 'Illegal: The Recourse to Force to Recover Occupied Territory and the Second Karabakh War' (2021) 32 EJIL 1287.

Ruys T and Rodríguez Silvestre F, 'Military Action to Recover Occupied Land: Lawful Self-Defence or Prohibited Use of Force? The 2020 Nagorno-Karabakh Conflict' (2021) 97 Int L Studies 665.

Ryngaert C and Fransen R, 'EU Extraterritorial Obligations with Respect to Trade with Occupied Territories: Reflections after the Case of Front Polisario before EU Courts' (2018) 2 Europe and the World: A Law Review 1–20.

Salmon, J., 'La construction juridique du fait en droit international' 32 (1987) Archive de philosophie du droit 136–151.

Saul B, 'The Status of Western Sahara as Occupied Territory under International Humanitarian Law and the Exploitation of Natural Resources' (2015) 27 Global Change, Peace and Security 301–322.

Saxer UW, 'The Transformation of the Soviet Union: From a Socialist Federation to a Commonwealth of Independent States' (1991) 14 Loyola of Los Angeles International and Comparative Law Journal 581–715.

Saxer U, 'Self-Determination, Changes of Statehood and the Self-Organization of the International System' (2010) 214 Beiträge zum ausländischen öffentlichen Recht und Völkerrecht 993.

Schaffer RP, 'The Extension of South African Treaties to the Territories of South West Africa and the Prince Edward Islands' (1978) 95 South African Law Journal 63–70.

Shaelou SL, 'The European Court of Justice and the Anastasiou Saga: Principles of Europeanisation through Economic Governance' (2007) 18 European Business Law Review 619–639.

Shanahan Cutts NM, 'Enemies Through the Gates: Russian Violations of International Law in Georgia/Abkhazia Conflict' 40 (2007) Case Western Reserve Journal of International Law 281–310.

Shany Y, 'Does International Law Grant the People of Crimea and Donetsk a Right to Secede?' (2014) 21 Brown Journal of World Affairs 233–243.

Shaw MN, 'The Heritage of States: The Principle of Uti Possidetis Iuris Today' (1996) 67 BYBIL 75–154.

Shaw MN, 'Peoples, Territorialism and Boundaries' (1997) 8 EJIL 478–507.

Shtromas A, 'The Legal Position of Soviet Nationalities and their Territorial Units According to the 1977 Constitution of the USSR' (1978) 37 The Russian Review 265–272.

Skinner Q, 'A Genealogy of the Modern State' (2009) 162 Proceedings of the British Academy 325–370.

Skoutaris N, 'The Application of the *Acquis Communautaire* in the Areas not Under the Effective Control of the Republic of Cyprus: The Green Line Regulation' (2008) 45 Common Market Law Review 727–755.

Skoutaris N, 'Building Transitional Justice Mechanisms Without a Peace Settlement: A Critical Appraisal of Recent Case Law of the Strasbourg Court on the Cyprus Issue' (2010) 35 European Law Review 720–755.

Stakhyra H, 'Applicability of Private Law of De-facto Regimes' 65 (2019) OER Osteuropa Recht 207–222.

Summers J, 'The Right of Self-Determination and Nationalism in International Law' (2005) 12 International Journal on Minority and Group Rights 325–354.

Talmon S, 'The Cyprus Question before the European Court of Justice' (2001) 12 European Journal of International Law 727–750.

Talmon S, 'The Constitutive Versus the Declaratory Theory of Recognition: Tertium Non Datur?' (2005) 75 BYBIL 101–181.

Talmon S, 'The Responsibility of Outside Powers for Acts of Secessionist Entities' (2009) 58 ICLQ 493–517.

Tams CJ, 'Do Serious Breaches Give Rise to Any Specific Obligations of the Responsible State?' (2002) 13 EJIL 1161–1180.

Tancredi A, 'Neither Authorized Nor Prohibited? Secession and International Law After Kosovo, South Ossetia And Abkhazia' (2008) 18 The Italian Yearbook of International Law Online 37–62.

Tancredi A, 'The Russian Annexation of the Crimea: Questions Relating to the Use of Force' 1 (2014) QIL QDI 5–34.

Tani P, 'The Turkish Republic of Northern Cyprus and International Trade Law' (2012) 12 Asper Review of International Business and Trade Law 115–137.

Tolstykh V, 'Reunification of Crimea with Russia: A Russian Perspective' (2014) 13 Chinese Journal of International Law 879–886.

Trigeaud L, 'L'influence des reconnaisances d'Etat sur la formation des engagements conventionels' (2015) 119 RGDIP 571–604.

Turns D, 'The Stimson Doctrine of Non-Recognition: Its Historical Genesis and Influence on Contemporary International Law' (2003) 2 Chinese Journal of International Law 105–143.

Tzevelekos VP, 'Reconstructing the Effective Control Criterion in Extraterritorial Human Rights Breaches: Direct Attribution of Wrongfulness, Due Diligence, and Concurrent Responsibility' (2014) 36 Michigan Journal of International Law 129–177.

Van den Driest SF, 'Crimea's Separation from Ukraine: An Analysis of the Right to Self-Determination and (Remedial) Secession in International Law' (2015) 62 Netherlands International Law Review 329–363.

Värk R, 'The Advisory Opinion on Kosovo's Declaration of Independence: Hopes, Disappointments and Its Relevance to Crimea' (2014) Polish Yearbook of International Law 115–131.

Verhoeven J, 'L'Etat et l'ordre juridique international – remarques' (1978) 82 RGDIP 749.

Verhoeven J, 'La reconnaissance internationale, déclin ou renouveau?' 39 (1993) AFDI 7.

Verhoeven J, 'Sur les "bons" et les "mauvais" emplois du jus cogens' (2008) 5 Annuario brasileiro de direito internacional 133–160.

Verzijl JHW, 'La validité et la nullité des actes juridiques internationaux' (1935) 9 Revue de droit international 284–339.

Vidmar J, 'Confining New International Borders in the Practice of Post-1990 State Creations' (2010) 70 ZaöRV 319–356.

Vidmar J, 'Remedial Secession in International Law: Theory and (Lack of) Practice' (2010) 6 St Anthony's International Review 37–56.

Vidmar J, 'The Kosovo Advisory Opinion Scrutinized' (2011) 24 Leiden Journal of International Law 355–383.

Vidmar J, 'Territorial Integrity and the Law of Statehood' (2012) 44 George Washington International Law Review 101–149.

Vidmar J, 'Conceptualizing Declarations of Independence in International Law' (2012) 32 Oxford Journal of Legal Studies 153–177.

Vidmar J, 'The Scottish Independence Referendum in an International Context' (2013) The Canadian Yearbook of International Law 259–288.

Vidmar J, 'The Annexation of Crimea and the Boundaries of the Will of the People' (2015) 16 German Law Journal 365–383.

Vité S, 'Typology of Armed Conflicts in International Humanitarian Law: Legal Concepts and Actual Situations' (2009) 91 International Review of the Red Cross 69–94.

Waters TW, 'Plucky Little Russia: Misreading the Georgian War Through the Distorting Lens of Aggression' 49 (2013) Stanford Journal of International Law 176–238.

Wallace S and Mallory C, 'Applying the European Convention on Human Rights to the Conflict in Ukraine' (2018) 6 Russian Law Journal 8–77.

Wills AG, 'The Crime of Aggression and the Resort to Force against Entities in Statu Nascendi' (2012) 10 Journal of International Criminal Justice 83–110.

Wilson G, 'Crimea: Some Observations on Secession and Intervention in Partial Response to Mullerson and Tolstykh' (2015) 14 Chinese Journal of International Law 217–223.

Wildeman J, 'The Philosophical Background of Effectiveness' (1977) 24 Netherlands International Law Review 335–351.

Williams RC, 'Demopoulos v. Turkey (Eur. Ct. H.R.), Introductory Note' (2010) 49 ILM 816–849.

Wilson G, 'Crimea: Some Observations on Secession and Intervention in Partial Response to Müllerson and Tolstykh' (2015) 14 Chinese Journal of International Law 217–223.

Witkin MF, 'Transkei: An Analysis of the Practice of Recognition–Political or Legal' (1977) 18 Harvard International Law Journal 605–627.

Wrange P, 'Western Sahara, the European Commission and the Politics of International Legal Argument' (2019) <https://papers.ssrn.com/sol3/papers.cfm?abstract_id=3507037> accessed 3 February 2020.

Wrange P, 'Self-Determination, Occupation and the Authority to Exploit Natural Resources: Trajectories from Four European Judgments on Western Sahara' (2019) 52 Israel Law Review 3–29.

Wrange P, 'Western Sahara, the European Commission and the Politics of International Legal Argument' (2019) <https://papers.ssrn.com/sol3/papers.cfm?abstract_id=3507037> accessed 3 February 2020.

Law Blogs

Akande D and Tzanakopoulos A, 'Use of Force in Self-Defence to Recover Occupied Territory: When Is It Permissible?' (*EJIL:Talk!*, 18 November 2020) <https://www.ejiltalk.org/use-of-force-in-self-defence-to-recover-occupied-territory-when-is-it-permissible/> accessed 5 December 2020.

Fripp E, 'Passportisation: Risks for International Law and Stability – Response to Anne Peters' (*EJIL Talk!*, 30 May 2019) <https://www.ejiltalk.org/passportisation-risks-for-international-law-and-stability-response-to-anne-peters/> accessed 21 June 2019.

Kalandarishvili-Mueller N, 'On the Occasion of the Five-year Anniversary of the Russian-Georgian War: Is Georgia Occupied?' (*EJIL:Talk!*, 1 October 2013) <https://www.ejiltalk.org/on-the-occasion-of-the-five-year-anniversary-of-the-russian-georgian-war-is-georgia-occupied/> accessed 7 December 2020.

Kalandarishvili-Mueller N, 'Guest Post: The Status of the Territory Unchanged: Russia's Treaties with Abkhazia and South Ossetia, Georgia' (*opiniojuris*, 20 March 2015) <http://opiniojuris.org/2015/04/20/guest-post-the-status-of-the-territory-unchanged-russias-treaties-with-abkhazia-and-south-ossetia-georgia/> accessed 7 May 2019.

Kalandarishvili-Mueller N, 'Russia's "Occupation by Proxy" of Eastern Ukraine – Implications Under the Geneva Conventions' (*Just Security*, 22 February 2022) <https://www.justsecurity.org/80314/russias-occupation-by-proxy-of-eastern-ukraine-implications-under-the-geneva-conventions/> accessed 24 August 2023.

Mälksoo L, 'Illegality of Russia's Annexations in Ukraine' (*Articles of War*, 3 October 2022) <https://lieber.westpoint.edu/illegality-russias-annexation-ukraine/> accessed 28 July 2023.

Miklasová J, 'The Recent Ceasefire in Nagorno-Karabakh: Territorial Control, Peacekeepers and Question of Status' (*EJIL:Talk!*, 4 December 2020) <https://www.ejiltalk.org/the-recent-ceasefire-in-nagorno-karabakh-territorial-control-peacekeepers-and-unanswered-question-of-status/> accessed 5 December 2020.

Miklasová J, 'Russia's Recognition of the DPR and LPR as Illegal Acts under International Law' (*Völkerrechtsblog*, 24 February 2022) <https://voelkerrechtsblog.org/russias-recognition-of-the-dpr-and-lpr-as-illegal-acts-under-international-law/> accessed 26 July 2023.

Miklasová J, 'Mamasakhlisi and Others v. Georgia and Russia: Russia's Effective Control over Abkhazia Before the 2008 War: Peacekeepers, Passportisation and Other Hybrid Elements' (*Strasbourg Observers*, 13 June 2023) <https://strasbourgobservers.com/2023/06/13/mamasakhlisi-and-others-v-georgia-and-russia-russias-effective-control-over-abkhazia-before-the-2008-war-peacekeepers-passportisation-and-other-hybrid-elements/> accessed 19 October 2023.

Milanović M, 'Does the European Court of Human Rights Have to Decide on Sovereignty over Crimea? Part I: Jurisdiction in Article 1 ECHR' (*EJIL:Talk!*, 23 September 2019) <https://www.ejiltalk.org/does-the-european-court-of-human-rights-have-to-decide-on-sovereignty-over-crimea-part-i-jurisdiction-in-article-1-echr/> accessed 31 October 2023.

Milanović M, 'ECtHR Grand Chamber Declares Admissible the Case of Ukraine v. Russia re Crimea' (*EJIL:Talk!*, 15 January 2021) <https://www.ejiltalk.org/ecthr-grand-chamber-declares-admissible-the-case-of-ukraine-v-russia-re-crimea/> accessed 17 July 2023.

Milanović M, 'Georgia v. Russia No. 2: The European Court's Resurrection of Bankovic in the Contexts of Chaos' (*EJIL:Talk!*, 25 January 2021) <https://www.ejiltalk.org/georgia-v-russia-no-2-the-european-courts-resurrection-of-bankovic-in-the-contexts-of-chaos/> accessed 31 October 2023.

Milanović M, 'The European Court's Admissibility Decision in Ukraine and the Netherlands v Russia: The Good, the Bad and the Ugly – Part II' (*EJIL:Talk!*, 26 January 2023) <https://www.ejiltalk.org/the-european-courts-admissibility-decision-in-ukraine-and-the-netherlands-v-russia-the-good-the-bad-and-the-ugly-part-ii/> accessed 31 October 2023.

Nuridzahanian G, '(Non-)Recognition of De Facto Regimes in Case Law of the European Court of Human Rights: Implications for Cases Involving Crimea and Eastern Ukraine' (*EJIL: Talk!*, 9 October 2017) <https://www.ejiltalk.org/non-recognition-of-de-facto-regimes-in-case-law-of-the-european-court-of-human-rights-implications-for-cases-involving-crimea-and-eastern-ukraine/> accessed 28 November 2019.

Peters A, 'Passporisation: Risks for International Law and Stability – Part I' (*EJIL Talk!*, 9 May 2019) <https://www.ejiltalk.org/passportisation-risks-for-international-law-and-stability-part-one/> accessed 21 June 2019.

Ruys T and Rodríguez Silvestre F, 'The Nagorno-Karabakh Conflict and the Exercise of "Self-Defense" to Recover Occupied Land' (*Just Security*, 10 November "2020)

<https://www.justsecurity.org/73310/the-nagorno-karabakh-conflict-and-the-exercise-of-self-defense-to-recover-occupied-land/> accessed 5 December 2020.

Schmitt MN and Coble KS, 'The Evolving Nagorno-Karabakh Conflict – An International Law Perspective – Part II' (*Articles of War*, 29 September 2023) <https://lieber.westpoint.edu/evolving-nagorno-karabakh-conflict-international-law-perspective-part-ii/> accessed 31 October 2023.

Index

www.ingramcontent.com/pod-product-compliance
Lightning Source LLC
LaVergne TN
LVHW010636300926
849161LV00005B/961